THE BIBLICAL PERIOD

EGYPT	SYRIA	PALESTINE	CULTURAL ACHIEVEMENTS
Ptolemaic rule			Canonization of Prophets section of Bible
	Seleucid rule	Ptolemaic rule	
		Seleucid rule	mid-3rd cent. Translation of Pentateuch into Greek (Septuagint)
		169-7 Antiochus IV outlaws Judaism	c.170 Book of Ben Sira (Ecclesiasticus)
		Profanation of the Temple	
		Beginning of Hasmonean revolt	
		164 Maccabean rule	134 First Book of the Maccabees written
		Rededication of the Temple	
	ROME	63 Romans under Pompey capture Jerusalem	
	44 Julius Caesar assassinated		
	27 BC-AD 14 Augustus	37-4 Herod the Great	
		c.4 BC Birth of Jesus	
		4BC-AD34 Herod Philip	
		4BC-AD39 Herod Antipas	
		26-36 Pontius Pilate	
		c.26 Baptism of Jesus	
		c.30 Crucifixion of Jesus	
		c.31 Stoning of Stephen	
		c.35 Conversion of Paul	
		47-48 Paul's 1st Missionary Journey	Letters of Paul
		c.48 Jerusalem Council	
		49-52 Paul's 2nd Missionary Journey	
	54-68 Nero	52-56 Paul's 3rd Missionary Journey	
		66 Beginning of revolt against Rome	
		70 Siege of Jerusalem	Gospels written
	93-96 Christians persecuted by Domitian		

The Archeological Periods in Palestine

Paleolithic (Old Stone Age)	700 000-15 000 BC	Iron Age IIB	900-800	Israelite III
Epipaleolithic (Middle Stone Age)	15 000-8300	Iron Age IIC	800-586	
Neolithic (New Stone Age)	8300-4500			
Chalcolithic	4500-3100	*Babylonian and Persian Periods*	586-332	
Bronze Age		*Hellenistic Period*		
Early Bronze Age I	3150-2850	Hellenistic I	332-152	
Early Bronze Age II	2850-2650	Hellenistic II (Hasmonean)	152-37	
Early Bronze Age III	2650-2350	*(Early Canaanite)*		
Early Bronze Age IV	2350-2200	*Roman Period*		
Middle Bronze Age I	2200-2000	Early Roman	37BC-AD 70	
Middle Bronze Age II	2000-1750	Middle Roman	70-180	
Middle Bronze Age III	1750-1550	*(Middle Canaanite)* Late Roman	180-324	
Late Bronze Age I	1550-1400			
Late Bronze Age II	1400-1300	*Byzantine Period*		
Late Bronze Age III	1300-1200	*(Late Canaanite)* Byzantine I	324-451	
		Byzantine II	451-640	
Iron Age				
Iron Age IA	1200-1150	*Early Arab Period*	640-1099	
Iron age IB	1150-1000	*(Israelite I)*		
Iron Age IIA	1000-900	*(Israelite II)* *Crusader Period*	1099-1291	

Illustrated Dictionary & Concordance of the

Bible

G.G. THE JERUSALEM PUBLISHING HOUSE LTD.

JERUSALEM

Published by The Reader's Digest Association, Inc., with permission of G.G. The Jerusalem Publishing House Ltd.

Planned and produced by G.G. The Jerusalem Publishing House Ltd.

ISBN 0-89577-407-0
Previously ISBN 0-02-916380-3

Printed in the United States of America

Reader's Digest Fund for the Blind is publisher of the Large-Type Edition of *Reader's Digest*. For subscription information about this magazine, please contact Reader's Digest Fund for the Blind, Inc., Dept. 250, Pleasantville, N.Y. 10570.

GENERAL EDITOR:
GEOFFREY WIGODER

EDITORS:
SHALOM M. PAUL
Old Testament

BENEDICT T. VIVIANO, O.P.
New Testament

EPHRAIM STERN
Biblical Archeology

CONCEPT AND DESIGN:
Shlomo S. (Yosh) Gafni

COORDINATOR:
Georgette Corcos

EDITORIAL SECRETARY:
Frances Gertler

LAYOUT ASSISTANT:
A. A. M. van der Heyden

PRODUCTION MANAGER:
Rachel Gilon

PRODUCTION ASSISTANT:
Yael Gafni

CONTRIBUTORS

Reuben Ahroni
Associate Professor, Ohio State University

Dan Barag
Professor of Classical Archaeology, Tel Aviv University

Athalya Brenner
Lecturer, Department of Biblical Studies, University of Haifa

James H. Charlesworth
George L. Collord Professor of New Testament Language and Literature, Princeton Theological Seminary

Harold R. (Chaim) Cohen
Senior Lecturer, Department of Bible and Ancient Near Eastern Studies, Ben Gurion University, Beersheba and Overseas Students' Division, Tel-Aviv University

James L. Crenshaw
Professor of Old Testament, Vanderbilt University, Nashville

Richard J. Dillon
Chairman of the Department of Theology and Associate Professor of New Testament, Fordham University, New York

David Noel Freedman
Professor of Biblical Studies, Director, Program on Studies in Religion, Arthur F. Thurnau Professor of Biblical Studies, University of Michigan

Theodore Friedman
Rabbi Emeritus of Congregation Beth El, South Orange; Dean, Jerusalem branch of Seminario Rabinico of Latin America

Shulamit Geva
Researcher, Van Leer Institute, Jerusalem

Maurice Gilbert S.J.
Professor of Old Testament Wisdom Literature and Rector of the Pontifical Biblical Institute, Jerusalem

Rivka Gonen
Senior Lecturer in Archaeology and Ancient Cultures, Bezalel Academy of Art and Design, Jerusalem

Mayer I. Gruber
Senior Lecturer, Department of Bible and Ancient Near East, Ben-Gurion University of the Negev, Beersheba and Visiting Professor of Bible, Spertus College of Judaica

Delbert R. Hillers
W.W. Spence Professor of Semitic Languages, Johns Hopkins University, Baltimore

Victor (Avigdor) Hurowitz
Instructor of Assyriology, Hebrew University, Jerusalem and Instructor of Bible, Ben Gurion University of the Negev, Beersheba

William Klassen
Dean, Interfaith Academy of Peace, Ecumenical Institute, Tantur, Jerusalem

Frederic Manns, O.F.M.
Professor of New Testament and Rabbinic Literature, Studium Biblicum Franciscanum, Jerusalem

Yaakov Meshorer
Associate Professor of Classical Archaeology, Hebrew University, Curator, Israel Museum, Jerusalem

Jacob Milgrom
Professor of Biblical Studies, University of California, Berkeley

Jerome Murphy-O'Connor, O.P.
Professor of New Testament Exegesis, Ecole Biblique et Archaéologique Française, Jerusalem

Avraham Negev
Professor of Classical Archaeology, Institute of Archaeology, Geography and Classical History, Hebrew University, Jerusalem

Shalom M. Paul
Chairman of the Department of Bible and Professor of Bible, Hebrew University.

Chaim Pearl
Rabbi Emeritus, Conservative Synagogue, Adath Israel of Riverdale, New York

Frank Polak
Junior Lecturer, Bible Department, Tel Aviv University

Ray Pritz
Executive Secretary of the Bible Society in Israel, Jerusalem

Donald Senior, C.P.
Professor of New Testament, Catholic Theological Union, Chicago

Yigal Shiloh
Associate Professor of Biblical Archaeology, Director of Institute of Archaeology, Hebrew University, Jerusalem

John R. Spencer
Associate Professor, Department of Religious Studies, John Carroll University, University Heights, Ohio

Ephraim Stern
Lauterman Professor of Biblical Archaeology, Hebrew University, Jerusalem

August Strobel
Director of the German Archaeological Institute, Jerusalem

Shemaryahu Talmon
J.L. Magnes Professor, Department of Bible Studies, Hebrew University, Jerusalem

Jeffrey H. Tigay
Abraham M. Ellis Associate Professor of Hebrew and Semitic Languages and Literatures, Department of Oriental Studies, University of Pennsylvania.

Emmanuel Tov
Professor of Bible, Bible Department, Hebrew University, Jerusalem

Benedict T. Viviano, O.P.
Professor of New Testament, Ecole Biblique et Archaéologique Francaise, Jerusalem

Elaine Wainwright, R.S.M.
Professor of New Testament, Archediocesan Seminary, Brisbane

Raymond Westbrook
Lecturer in Biblical Law (Bible Department) and Ancient Near Eastern Law (Law Faculty), Hebrew University, Jerusalem

Geoffrey Wigoder
Director of Oral History Department, Institute of Contemporary Jewry, Hebrew University of Jerusalem

James G. Williams
Professor of Religion, Syracuse University

Andrea Berlin, Jeff Black, Raphael Carse, Geula Cohen, Georgette Corcos, Edward Curtis, Luc Devillers, O.P., Shulamit Eisenstadt, The late Yohanan Eldad, Frances Gertler, Ayelet Gilboa, Lori Glasshofer, David Glatt, Raphael Greenberg, Isaac Kalimi, F. W. Knobloch, Jodi Magness, Ian C. Mann, Galen Marquis, Sasja Martel, Michelle Mazel, Leah Mazor, Elizabeth Miller, Scott Nikaido, Lucy Orkin-Plitmann, Lilach Peled, Claire Pfann, Stephen J. Pfann, Rony Reich, Baruch Schwartz, Oded Tammuz, David Tarler, Emmanuel White

ABBREVIATIONS

Acts	The Acts of the Apostles
Amos	The Book of Amos
Ant.	*The Antiquities of the Jews* (Josephus)
I Chr	The First Book of the Chronicles
II Chr	The Second Book of the Chronicles
Col	The Epistle of Paul the Apostle to the Colossians
I Cor	The First Epistle of Paul the Apostle to the Corinthians
II Cor	The Second Epistle of Paul the Apostle to the Corinthians
Dan	The Book of Daniel
Deut	The Fifth Book of Moses called Deuteronomy
Ecc	The Book of Ecclesiastes
Eccl	Ecclesiasticus
Eph	Ephesians
Est	The Book of Esther
Est Add	Additions to the Book of Esther
Ezek	The Book of Ezekiel
Ezra	The Book of Ezra
Ex	The Second Book of Moses Called Exodus
Gal	The Epistle of Paul the Apostle to the Galatians
Gen	The First Book of Moses Called Genesis
Hab	The Book of Habakkuk
Hag	The Book of Haggai
Heb	The Letter to the Hebrews
Hos	The Book of Hosea
Is	The Book of Isaiah
James	The Epistle of James
Jer	The Book of Jeremiah
Job	The Book of Job
Joel	The Book of Joel
John	The Gospel According to John
I John	The First Epistle of John
II John	The Second Epistle of John
III John	The Third Epistle of John
Jonah	The Book of Jonah
Josh	The Book of Joshua
Jude	The Epistle of Jude
Judg	The Book of Judges
I Kgs	The First Book of the Kings
II Kgs	The Second Book of the Kings

KJV	King James Version
Lam	The Book of Lamentations
Lev	The Third Book of Moses Called Leviticus
Luke	The Gospel According to Luke
Macc	Maccabees
Malachi	The Book of Malachi
Mark	The Gospel According to Mark
Matt	The Gospel According to Matthew
Mic	The Book of Micah
Nah	The Book of Nahum
Nat. Hist.	*Natural History* (Pliny)
Neh	The Book of Nehemiah
NKJV	The New King James Version
NT	New Testament
Num	The Fourth Book of Moses Called Numbers
Obad	The Book of Obadiah
Onom	*Onomasticon* (Eusebius)
OT	Old Testament
I Pet	The First Epistle of Peter
II Pet	The Second Epistle of Peter
Phil	The Epistle of Paul the Apostle to the Philippians
Philem	Philemon
Prov	The Book of Proverbs
Ps	The Book of Psalms
Rev	The Revelation of Jesus Christ
Rom	The Epistle of Paul the Apostle to the Romans
Ruth	The Book of Ruth
I Sam	The First Book of Samuel
II Sam	The Second Book of Samuel
Song	The Song of Solomon
I Thes	The First Epistle of Paul the Apostle to the Thessalonians
II Thes	The Second Epistle of Paul the Apostle to the Thessalonians
I Tim	The First Epistle of Paul the Apostle to Timothy
II Tim	The Second Epistle of Paul the Apostle to Timothy
Titus	The Epistle of Paul the Apostle to Titus
War.	*The Jewish War* (Josephus)
Zech	The Book of Zechariah
Zeph	The Book of Zephaniah

Moses reading from a scroll. Wall painting from the synagogue of Dura-Europos on the Euphrates River. 3rd century A.D.

INTRODUCTION

"Of making many books there is no end" says the Preacher, but even after all that has been written about the Bible, this volume presents an original and unique contribution. First it is a dictionary, in fact a one-volume encyclopedia of the Bible. Every place and person mentioned in the Old and New Testaments are given their own entry as are major religious concepts and general topics.

Second, it is a complete concordance with all references relating to each subject to be found in the margin next to the entry. (In a few key entries where the concordance is so extensive that it could not be accommodated in the margin, it appears in a special appendix at the end of the volume).

Third, it provides a wealth of illustrative material in color, portraying the world of the Bible, both in the Holy Land and in other parts of the Middle East connected with the Bible Story. In addition to pictures, the reader will find copious maps, constituting an atlas of the Bible. Another special feature is the attention paid to archeology and the light it throws on the Scriptures. Many of these entries have been written by the excavators themselves. Special attention has been paid to everyday life in Bible times.

The latest scholarship is reflected throughout the work which can serve as a ready reference work for laymen, students and scholars. Noted contributors have written the entries, all of them authorities in their field. Care has been taken to avoid technical information so that all the entries are clear and self-explanatory.

The English translation followed is the New King James Version (first published by Thomas Nelson Inc., 1979) which is also the basis of the spelling of proper names and of the concordance. Other translations have been consulted and cited where appropriate.

While the Apocrypha and the Apocryphal books are subjects of entries, the persons, places, etc. mentioned in these books do not form separate subject entries nor is the Apocrypha cited in the concordance.

As all proper names mentioned in the Bible are the subject of entries, it was not felt necessary to indicate cross-references whenever they are mentioned in other entries. The reader seeking further information can turn to the relevant entry. Limited cross-references in the body of an article or at its end refer readers to subjects whose entries contain essential supplementary material related to the heading being consulted.

A list of abbreviations (including the names of books of the Bible) is on pp. 8-9. The basic chronology used in this volume will be found in the endpapers. It is realized that scholars differ over chronology; one widely-accepted version was adopted and it was not possible to quote all the various theories concerning dates. The endpapers also list the main archeological periods and their approximate dating.

The Bible embraces an entire world — history, literature and, above all, inspiration. It is our hope that this volume will provide the reader with guideposts that will assist him in understanding and finding his way in all aspects of the Book of Books.

AARON Son of Jochebed and Amram of the tribe of Levi; brother of Moses and Miriam; forebear and founder of the Israelite priesthood. Because Moses suffered from a stammer, Aaron accompanied him to serve as his spokesman before both Pharaoh (Ex 5:1-5) and the Israelites (Ex 4:27-31). In many passages, Moses and Aaron are coupled to form, as it were, a team of leaders (Ex 5:4, 20; 7:8, 20). Aaron was empowered to wield the staff given by God to Moses and it was he who cast the staff to the ground where it turned into a serpent before Pharaoh's eyes (Ex 7:8-13). Several of the ten plagues (e.g. blood, frogs, lice) were instigated by Aaron wielding the staff (Ex 7:14-8:17). Aaron's role diminished during the actual Exodus. Together with Hur, he supported Moses' arms during the battle with the Amalekites (Ex 17:12).

Aaron pours oil into the seven-branched candelabrum of pure gold as described in Exodus 37:17-24. From an illuminated manuscript of Benjamin the Scribe, c. 1280 (possibly written in Troyes, France. (British Museum)

When Moses ascended Mount Sinai, Aaron and Hur were left behind in charge of the people (Ex 24:12). The Israelites, becoming anxious because of Moses' 40-day absence on the mountain, implored Aaron to make them a visible surrogate god for guidance and worship. Aaron collected gold from the people, melting it down to fashion a calf which the Israelites began to worship as an idol (Ex 32:1-7). When Moses came down from the mountain, the people were punished but Aaron was let off with a reprimand (Ex 32:20-30; Deut 9:20). When he joined Miriam in questioning Moses' authority, asserting that they too had been granted divine revelation, Aaron again escaped punishment, whereas Miriam was stricken with leprosy; she recovered after Aaron interceded with Moses on her behalf (Num 12:1-13).

Aaron's position was officially established when God ordered Moses to consecrate him and his sons as priests (Ex 28:1-29:37); they were anointed and consecrated by Moses (Lev chaps. 8-9). Thereafter, Aaron, assisted by his sons Eleazar and Ithamar, officiated at Moses' side. However, two other sons, Nadab and Abihu, likewise installed as priests, were killed by a divine fire for making an offering that had not been commanded, and "Aaron held his peace" (Lev 10:1-3). Indeed, Jewish tradition regards him as the personification of the pursuit of peace.

During the mutiny of Korah and his supporters, Aaron stood by Moses (Num 16:3, 20). After the rebels were destroyed by divine punishment, the people accused Moses and Aaron of killing the people of God. The pestilence, brought by God in retribution, was only stayed when Aaron offered incense to placate God (Num 16:46-47). Divine sanction of his election to the priesthood was demonstrated to all when his staff blossomed with almonds (Num 17:8).

Like Moses, Aaron was not allowed to enter the promised land, as punishment for Moses' transgression: having been ordered to speak to a rock to bring forth water for the thirsty people, Moses instead struck the rock with his staff (Num 20:1-13). Aaron died at Mount Hor, near the border of Edom, aged 123 (Num 20:22-29) and his priestly robes were transferred to his son Eleazar as a sign of succession (Num 20:28).

Outside the Pentateuch, Aaron is mentioned, along with Moses, as leader of the Exodus (I Sam 12:6, 8; Ps 77:20; 105:26; Mic 6:4) and as intercessor (Ps 99:6). In the NT he is seen as an imperfect priest when contrasted with the perfect priesthood of Jesus (Heb 5:4; 7:11).

AARONITES Priestly descendants of Aaron, the first high priest. See PRIESTS.

ABADDON ("place of destruction"). The word is used in the Hebrew Bible as a region of the dead, parallel to hell ("destruction" in Job 26:6; 28:22; 31:12; Ps 88:12; Prov 15:11) (See SHEOL). In the NT Abaddon is personified as "the angel of the bottomless pit", whose name in Hebrew is Abaddon, but in Greek has the name Apollyon "destroyer". He is said to reign over the locusts which rose from the bottomless pit at the sounding of the fifth trumpet, in the vision of the seven plagues of John the Apostle (Rev 9:11).

ABAGTHA One of the seven eunuchs at the palace of King Ahasuerus, attendants of the queen and the women of the royal court of Persia. During the seven-day festivities given by the king in honor of the princes of his provinces and the officials of the court at Shushan, Ahasuerus ordered the seven eunuchs, of whom Abagtha was one, to bring the queen, Vashti, "before the king wearing her royal crown, in order to show her beauty to the people and the officials" (Est 1:1-12).

ABANAH One of the two rivers of Damascus mentioned by Naaman, the commander of the Syrian army, when Elisha recommended that he bathe in the Jordan River as a cure for his leprosy (II Kgs 5:10-12).

ABARIM ("the borderland" or "regions beyond"). The mountainous region "before Nebo" in Moab, overlooking the Dead Sea and the Jordan Valley, where the Israelites camped before entering the promised land. From here Moses could catch a glimpse of the promised land, but he was not permitted to approach any nearer.

The mountainous region overlooking the Dead Sea "before Nebo", designated as Abarim in the Bible, where the Israelites encamped before entering Canaan (Num 33:47).

ABBA The transliteration of the Aramaic word for the vocative "father" or "my father". The term conveyed a sense of endearment (much as in its present-day use in Israel). It occurs three times in the NT, always accompanied by the Greek translation, i.e., "Abba, Father". Jesus' perception of God as his father was innovative, and his use of the term while praying in the Garden of Gethsemane before his arrest reflected his intimacy with, and dependence upon, the Father in his hour of greatest distress (Mark 14:36). Paul characterized the relationship of the believer with God as that of a child who can freely call upon his father (Rom 8:15) and declared that it is the spirit of Christ which enables the individual believer to do so (Gal 4:6). The privilege of the believer to address God as Abba, Father, reflects his promotion at salvation from the status of servant to that of full son (Rom 8:15-16).

ABBA
Mark 14:36.
Rom 8:15:
Gal 4:6

ABDA ("servant").

1. The father of Adoniram, who was the overseer of the forced labor during the reign of Solomon.

ABDA 1
I Kgs 4:6

2. The son of Shammua, a Levite, who returned to Jerusalem after the Babylonian Exile (Neh 11:17-18).

ABDA 2
Neh 11:17

ABDEEL ("servant of God"). Father of Shelemiah, one of the three men sent by King Jehoiakim to seize the prophet Jeremiah and his scribe Baruch.

ABDEEL
Jer 36:26

ABDI (probably a contraction of the name Abdiel, "servant of God").

1. The father of Kishi, a Levite of the house of Merari.

ABDI 1
I Chr 6:44

2. Also a Levite of the house of Merari, the father of Kish. Because of the similarity of their sons' names, some Bible scholars assume this Abdi to be identical with the one above.

ABDI 2
II Chr 29:12

3. One of the sons of Elam. He was among those who had married foreign wives but repudiated them in response to Ezra's exhortations (Ezra 10:10-12, 26).

ABDI 3
Ezra 10:26

ABDIEL ("servant of God"). A Gadite, the son of Guni and father of Ahi, who lived in the region of Gilead or Bashan at the time of Jotham, king of Judah, and Jeroboam, king of Israel (I Chr 5:11-17).

ABDIEL
I Chr 5:15

ABDON ("servile").

1. A town in the territory of Asher allotted to the Levites of the family of Gershon. It is identified with the site called Khirbet 'Abden, about 4 miles (6 km) east of Achzib.

ABDON 1
Josh 21:30.
I Chr 6:74

2. The son of Hillel from Pirathon in the territory of Ephraim. A

ABDON 2
Judg 12:13, 15

Coin bearing the name "Abdiel" struck in Judea or Samaria. 4th century B.C. (Israel Museum)

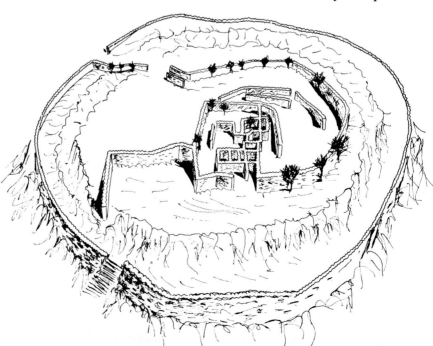

Plan of Abdon reconstructed by M. Prausnitz according to an air view of the site of the ancient fortress city. ("Eretz-Israel" vol.11, 1973, published by the Israel Exploration Society).

minor judge who ruled Israel for eight years, succeeding Elon the Zebulunite. He had 40 sons and 30 grandsons who rode on 70 young donkeys, which indicates that Abdon was a wealthy man. He was buried in his native town.

ABDON 3
I Chr 8:23

3. A Benjamite, son of Shashak, a head of family who lived in Jerusalem (I Chr 8:23-28).

ABDON 4
I Chr 8:30;
9:36

4. Another Benjamite, son of Jeiel and Maacah.

ABDON 5
II Chr 34:20

5. A son of Micah (or Michaiah), an official of King Josiah's court. See ACHBOR No.2.

ABED-NEGO
Dan 1:7; 2:49;
3:12-14, 16,
19-20, 22-23,
26, 28-30

ABED-NEGO ("servant of Nego", perhaps corruption of Chaldean god, Nebo). The Babylonian name was given to Azariah after he was taken, with Daniel, Hananiah and Mishael, to the court of Nebuchadnezzar, where they underwent a special three-year training course (Dan 1:6-7). The four young men, declining to eat of "the king's delicacies" which did not conform to their dietary laws, were given vegetables to eat instead (Dan 1:8-16). At the end of their training, the king found them ten times better than all the magicians and astrologers of his realm (Dan 1:19-20).

At Daniel's request, Abed-Nego (Azariah), Meshach and Shadrach (the Babylonian names given respectively to Mishael and Hananiah) were made administrators of the province of Babylon. The three young men were later accused of refusing to bow down to the king's golden image or worship the gods of Babylon (Dan 2:49; 3:1-12). Nebuchadnezzar had them thrown into a "burning fiery furnace", but they came out unharmed (Dan 3:19-25). Nebuchadnezzar, marveling at this miraculous deliverance, praised the God of Israel: "Blessed be the God of Shadrach, Meshach and Abed-Nego, who sent his Angel and delivered his servants who trusted in him, and they have frustrated the king's word, and yielded their bodies, that they should not serve nor worship any god except their own God!" (Dan 3:28).

ABEL ("breath/vapor/futility"?).

ABEL 1
Gen 4:2, 4, 8-
9, 25. Matt
23:35. Luke
11:51. Heb
11:4; 12:24

1. The second son of Adam and Eve, murdered by his brother Cain. Abel was a shepherd and Cain a "tiller of the ground". They both made an offering to the Lord from the fruits of their labor. The Lord expressed favor toward Abel's offering of the "firstlings of his flock and of their fat" but Cain's was rejected. In a fit of jealousy, Cain killed his brother (Gen 4:2-8).

Some farmers still use these ancient methods of plowing in the Holy Land.

In the NT Abel is called "righteous" (Matt 23:35) and is named by Jesus as a type of the innocent just man who suffers and is killed (Luke 11:51). Abel's sacrifice is judged greater than Cain's because of his faith and this faith speaks beyond the grave (Heb 11:4). His blood is compared to that of Jesus (Heb 12:24) and it is hinted that his blood also had atoning value.

2. Name appearing either on its own or with the addition of a further indicative place-name in the Bible (See below). **ABEL 2 I Sam 6:18**

In I Samuel 6:18, it is said that when the ark was returned to Israel by the Philistines it was set on the large stone of Abel. Some translators believe it should read simply "the large stone".

View of the Huleh Valley with Mount Hermon in the background, seen from the site of Abel Beth Maachah.

The region of Abel Keramim, south of Rabbath Ammon where Jephthah pursued the Ammonites.

ABEL BETH MAACHAH (ABEL OF BETH MAACHAH) (sometimes called Abel Maim, or simply Abel). A fortified city in the territory of Naphtali. David's men led by Joab besieged Abel to which the rebel Sheba, the son of Bichri, had fled (II Sam 20:1-2, 7, 13-15). **ABEL BETH MAACHAH II Sam 20:14-15, 18. I Kgs 15:20. II Kgs 15:29.**

Abel Beth Maachah was attacked by the Syrian king Ben-Hadad (I Kgs 15:20). Later, it was conquered by Tiglath-Pileser and its inhabitants were taken to Assyria (II Kgs 15:29).

The city has been identified with Abil al-Qamh at the site known as Tell Abil, a few miles north of the modern town of Kiryat Shemonah.

ABEL KERAMIM Place east of the Jordan, to which Jephthah pursued the Ammonites (Judg 11:29-33). It is believed to have been situated south of Rabbath Ammon. **ABEL KERAMIM Judg 11:33**

ABEL MAIM See ABEL BETH MAACHAH **ABEL MAIM II Chr 16:4**

ABEL MEHOLAH A city in the Jordan Valley. Gideon pursued the Midianites as far as Abel Meholah "by Tabbath" (Judg 7:22). It was in the fifth administrative district of the kingdom of Solomon (I Kgs 4:12) and was also the hometown of Elisha where Elijah found him plowing when he went to anoint him as his successor (I Kgs 19:16, 19). **ABEL MEHOLAH Judg 7:22. I Kgs 4:12; 19:6**

The site has not yet been identified, but it lay in the vicinity of Beth Shean.

ABEL MIZRAIM See ATAD **ABEL MIZRAIM Gen 50:11**

ABEL SHITTIM See SHITTIM

ABEZ (EBEZ). A town in the territory allocated to the tribe of Issachar. **ABEZ (EBEZ) Josh 19:20**

ABI See ABIJAH No.7 **ABI II Kgs 18:2**

ABI-ALBON A Benjamite, one of King David's "mighty men" (II Sam 23:31). His name is given as Abiel (I Chr 11:32), and in both references he is termed "the Arbathite", i.e., from Beth Arabah. **ABI-ALBON II Sam 23:31**

ABIASAPH ("the father has gathered", or "the father has added"). One of Korah the Levite's three sons (Ex 6:24).

ABIATHAR ("the father excels"). The last remaining son of the high priest Ahimelech of the priestly family of Eli of Shiloh. Abiathar was at Nob when King Saul ordered Doeg the Edomite to kill Abiathar's father and eighty-five other priests and other residents of the city because they had helped David. Abiathar was the only priest to escape. He then reported the massacre to David, himself a fugitive, and joined David's men at Adullam. He had brought with him an ephod (I Sam 23:6), which was used by the priests as an oracle. David asked Abiathar to use the ephod on two occasions (I Sam 23:9-13; 30:7-8). When David became king, Abiathar's line was established as the priestly line of the royal court together with that of Zadok (II Sam 8:17).

Abiathar was given the privilege, with the other priests, of bringing the ark from the house of Obed-Edom to Jerusalem (I Chr 15:11-12). He was one of King David's counselors (I Chr 27:33-34), and remained loyal to the king during Absalom's rebellion, reporting to him on the latter's actions (II Sam 15:24-36; 17:15; 19:11-14). Later, during another conspiracy for succession to the throne, when David was old, Abiathar supported Adonijah, while Zadok supported Solomon (I Kgs 1:1ff). When Solomon acceded, he banished Abiathar to Anathoth his hometown, and took away his privilege to act as high priest in Jerusalem (I Kgs 2:26-27), putting Zadok in his place (I Kgs 2:35).

In the NT it is said that when David was fleeing Saul, he went into the house of God "in the days of Abiathar the high priest and ate the showbread" (Mark 2:26).

ABIB The original name of the first month of the year falling at the beginning of spring. The Exodus from Egypt took place in Abib, which thus became the date for celebration of the Feast of Passover.

ABIDA, ABIDAH ("father of knowledge"). A son of Midian, and a grandson of Abraham by his wife Keturah. He had four brothers: Ephah, Epher, Hanoch and Eldaah (Gen 25:1-4).

ABIDAN ("my father judged"). The son of Gideoni. A leader of the tribe of Benjamin at the time of the census ordered by Moses in the Wilderness of Sinai (Num 1:1-11). He also represented his tribe at the inauguration of the tabernacle (Num 7:10, 60-65), and led the Benjamites in the march out of Sinai (Num 10:24).

ABIEL ("my father is God").

1. A Benjamite, the son of Zeror, father of Kish, and grandfather of Saul (I Sam 9:1) or the father of Ner, Saul's grandfather (I Sam 14:51).

2. One of David's thirty "mighty men"; called Abi-Albon in II Samuel 23:31.

ABIEZER ("my father is [my] help").

1. Abiezer son (or, according to I Chronicles 7:18, nephew) of Gilead, was the progenitor of the Abiezrites, one of the principal families of the tribe of Manasseh. The Abiezrites, prominent among whom was Gideon, played a crucial role in the battle against the Midianites (Judg 6:11, 34). When the Ephraimites complained that they had not originally been called to join in the battle, Gideon, alluding to their capture of two Midianite princes, declared "is not the gleaning of the grapes of Ephraim better than the vintage of Abiezer?" (Judg 8:2).

Several sites in the Jezreel Valley have been suggested as the location of Gideon's city Ophrah, and thus of the Abiezrites. The Samaria Ostraca, which mention Abiezer and other Manassite clans, show that in the early 8th century B.C. Abiezrites were living in the central Mount Ephraim area.

2. A warrior of Anathoth in Benjamin, and one of David's thirty

The ark of the covenant carried on a cart pulled by two oxen, depicted on one of the wall paintings of the synagogue of Dura Europos, a city on the Euphrates River, which was destroyed in the 3rd century A.D.

Abiathar was one of the priests chosen by David to accompany the ark to Jerusalem.

Carmel in the hilly region of Hebron, the hometown of Abigail, David's wife.

"mighty men" (II Sam 23:27; I Chr 11:28). According to the Chronicler, Abiezer had charge of the 24,000 servants of David whose turn of duty fell in the ninth month of the year (I Chr 27:12).

ABIEZRITE(S) See ABIEZER No.1

ABIGAIL

1. The wife of Nabal; later David's wife. Abigail's first husband, Nabal, was a wealthy man, but "harsh and evil in his doings". After the death of the prophet Samuel, David and his men moved into the area of Carmel in the Hebron mountains, where Nabal's flocks were pastured, and they protected Nabal's property. Hearing that Nabal was giving a sheepshearing feast, David requested that he and his men be invited. Following Nabal's refusal, David decided to use force. Abigail, hearing of this, took food supplies and rode out to meet David to convince him not to take vengeance and to prevent bloodshed. Returning home, Abigail waited for her husband to sober up from a drunken feast, and then informed him of her actions. "Nabal's heart died within him, and he became like a stone." He died ten days later. When this news reached David, he sent for Abigail and married her (I Sam chap. 25). Abigail accompanied David throughout his wanderings and was with him at Hebron when he became king (I Sam 27:3; 30:5). She bore him a son, Chileab, who is also called Daniel (II Sam 2:2; 3:3; I Chr 3:1).

2. David's sister or stepsister. In II Samuel 17:25 Abigail is said to be the daughter of Nahash and "sister of Zeruiah, Joab's mother" and mother of Amasa. Some commentators believe Nahash to be another name for Jesse (following the Septuagint), David and Zeruiah's father (I Chr 2:16).

ABIHAIL ("father of might"). Name borne by both men and women.

1. A Levite, the father of Zuriel; head of the family of Merari at the time of the Exodus.

2. The wife of Abishur of the tribe of Judah; she was the mother of Ahban and Molid.

3. A Gadite chief, son of Huri, who settled in Bashan.

4. The mother of Mahalath, King Rehoboam's wife.

5. The father of Queen Esther. He died when Esther was young.

ABIHU ("my father is he", or "He [God] is Father"). The second of Aaron's sons by his wife Elisheba, and the brother of Nadab, Eleazar and Ithamar (Ex 6:23; I Chr 6:3; 24:1). Abihu and Nadab were permitted to accompany Aaron and 70 of the elders of Israel as they approached Mount Sinai "and they saw the God of Israel" (Ex 24:1, 9-10). Abihu was appointed, together with his brothers, to serve as priest with his father (Ex 28:1, 40-43). On the eighth day of the ceremonies, Abihu and Nadab met an untimely and mysterious death during the consecration of the tabernacle, as they were assisting Aaron, "each took his censer and put fire in it, put incense on it, and offered profane fire before the Lord, which he had not commanded them. So fire went out from the Lord and devoured them, and they died before the Lord" (Lev 10:1-2). Abihu and Nadab had no children (Num 3:4), and thus their priestly line became extinct.

ABIHUD ("the father is majesty"). A descendant of Benjamin through his firstborn Bela.

ABIJAH ("Yah is my father"). Male and female name.

1. The second son of the prophet Samuel. Abijah and his elder brother Joel were appointed judges at Beersheba, but they were corrupt and perverted justice. This prompted the elders of Israel to urge the aging Samuel to designate a king (I Sam 8:1-5).

2. Hezron's wife, the mother of Ashur "the father of Tekoa" of the tribe of Judah.

3. A son of Becher. He was Benjamin's grandson and is listed seventh in the list of Becher's nine sons.

4. A descendant of Aaron and head of a family of priests. When King David divided the priesthood into twenty-four divisions, each to serve at the sanctuary for a one-week period every six months, Abijah was chosen by lot to head the eighth division (I Chr 24:1, 5, 10).

John the Baptist's father, the priest Zacharias, was "of the division of Abijah" (Luke 1:5).

5. King of Judah (911-908 B.C.) also called Abijam. He was the son of King Rehoboam and Maacah, the granddaughter of Absalom (I Kgs 14:31; 15:1-2). Rehoboam designated him "to be leader among his brothers; for he intended to make him king." (II Chr 11:20-22). Abijah succeeded his father and reigned for three years, following Rehoboam's sinful ways (I Kgs 15:3). However, he is shown as a pious king during the warfare with King Jeroboam of Israel, with whom he was in conflict throughout his reign. Abijah fought valiantly and wrested territory from the king of Israel, annexing Bethel, Jeshanah and Ephron (I Kgs 15:6-7; II Chr 13:1-19).

Abijah had 14 wives who bore him 22 sons and 16 daughters. When he died he was buried in the City of David, and was succeeded by his son Asa (II Chr 13:21-22; 14:1).

6. The son of King Jeroboam of Israel, who died in his youth as a punishment from the Lord because his father practiced idolatry. When Abijah became desperately sick, the king sent his wife in disguise to Shiloh, to consult the blind prophet Ahijah. But Ahijah, having recognized Jeroboam's wife, predicted that every male child of Jeroboam's would die, and none of his offspring would have a decent burial. Only Abijah would come to the grave "because in him there is found something good toward the Lord God of Israel in the house of Jeroboam" (I Kgs 14:1-18).

7. The daughter of a certain Zechariah (II Chr 29:1). She was the wife of King Ahaz of Judah and the mother of King Hezekiah (II Kgs 18:2 where her name is given in an abbreviated form as Abi).

8. A priest (perhaps identical with Abijah No.9) who returned to Jerusalem and was among those who sealed the covenant to "walk in God's Law", in the time of Nehemiah (Neh 10:1-8, 29).

9. One of the family heads of the Levites who returned to Jerusalem with Zerubbabel from Exile in Babylon (Neh 12:1, 4, 17, 26).

ABIJAM See ABIJAH No. 5

ABILENE A Roman district extending over the western slope of the Anti-Lebanon, north of Mount Hermon. It was named after its main city, Abila, situated in a gorge by the river Abanah (modern Barada), northwest of Damascus. Augustus assigned it to Herod the Great, and after the latter's death in 4 B.C. it was included in the province of Syria. At the time of Tiberius (emperor A.D. 14-37), it was governed by the tetrarch Lysanias (Luke 3:1).

ABIMAEL ("my father is God", or "God is father"). A descendant of Shem through Arphaxad. He was the son of Joktan (Gen 10:22-28; I Chr 1:17-22).

ABIMELECH ("the father is king" or "Melech is father").

1. King of Gerar. When Abraham and Sarah settled for a time in Gerar, Abimelech, mistaking the couple for brother and sister, took Sarah but did not touch her. Warned by the Lord in a dream that she was Abraham's wife, he restored Sarah to her husband (Gen 20:1-18). A similar incident is related in connection with Isaac and Rebekah (Gen 26:1-11). Later, Abimelech concluded covenants of peace with Abraham and with Isaac at Beersheba (Gen 21:27-32; 26:28-33).

Amethyst scaraboid seal found in Galilee. It bears the inscription "[Belonging] to Abiyau" (Abijah). 8th century B.C.

A coin struck in the 2nd century A.D. at Abila, the capital of the Roman district of Abilene.

The traditional site of Abraham's Well in Beersheba where the patriarch and Abimelech, the king of Gerar, made a covenant regarding the well dug by Abraham (Gen 21:29-34).

Possibly the reference is to two kings bearing the same name, although in both cases the king is accompanied by his military commander who is named as Phichol (Gen 21:22, 32; 26:26).

2. The son of Gideon born to his Shechemite concubine (Judg 8:30-31). After Gideon's death, Abimelech sought to make himself ruler of Shechem, although his father had 70 sons from his various wives. With the support of his mother's family and the local inhabitants Abimelech hired "worthless and reckless men". He then went to his father's house at Ophrah and murdered all but one of his half-brothers in order to eliminate any rival claim to power over Shechem. Jotham, the youngest, escaped the slaughter (Judg 9:1-5). After Abimelech had ruled for three years, "God sent a spirit of ill will between Abimelech and the men of Shechem". The latter conspired with Gaal the son of Ebed, but Abimelech set up an ambush for Gaal and his men outside the city and crushed the revolt. Abimelech took the city, killing its inhabitants, and devastating it; finally he "sowed it with salt" (Judg 9:22-45). He set fire to the temple of the god Berith, killing about a thousand men and women (Judg 9:46-49). He then attacked the nearby town of Thebez. From the city tower a woman hurled down a millstone on his head. Fatally wounded, Abimelech asked his armor-bearer to slay him lest it be said that he had been killed by a woman (Judg 9:53-54).

3. A Philistine king of Gath in David's time, mentioned in the title of Psalm 34. It has been suggested that this refers to Achish.

4. See AHIMELECH No.3 (given as Abimelech in I Chr 18:16).

ABINADAB ("my father is generous" or "noble").

1. An inhabitant of Kirjath Jearim in whose home the ark of the covenant was kept for 20 years. When the ark was brought from Beth Shemesh, being returned by the Philistines, it was taken to Abinadab's home where it remained until David transferred it to Jerusalem, Abinadab's son Eleazar being appointed to guard it (I Sam 7:1-2). As the ark was being conveyed to Jerusalem on a cart, Abinadab's sons Ahio and Uzzah walked alongside; when the oxen drawing the cart stumbled, Uzzah, while attempting to stop the ark from falling, touched it, arousing God's anger, and was struck dead (II Sam 6:1-7; I Chr 13:1-10).

2. One of David's brothers, the second son of Jesse, who went with Saul to fight the Philistines.

3. One of King Saul's sons who was killed by the Philistines on Mount Gilboa.

ABIMELECH 2
Judg 8:31; 9:1, 3-4, 6, 16, 18-25, 27-29, 31, 34-35, 38-42, 44-50, 52-53, 55-56; 10:1. II Sam 11:21

ABIMELECH 3
Ps 34:1

ABIMELECH 4
I Chr 18:16

ABINADAB 1
I Sam 7:1. II Sam 6:3-4. I Chr 13:7

ABINADAB 2
I Sam 16:8; 17:13. I Chr 2:13

ABINADAB 3
I Sam 31:2. I Chr 8:33; 9:39; 10:2

4. Father of the officer of one of King Solomon's 12 administrative districts. He came from Dor and was responsible for supplying food to the king's household one month out of the year. He married Solomon's daughter Tapath (I Kgs 4:7-11).

ABINOAM ("father of pleasantness"). The father of Barak, a descendant of the tribe of Naphtali and a native of Kedesh (Judg 4:6).

ABIRAM ("father of pride").

1. A Reubenite, the son of Eliab; he had two brothers, Dathan and Nemuel (Num 26:9). Abiram and his brother Dathan supported Korah in the rebellion against Moses and Aaron during the Exodus. Moses appealed to God for his judgment. While Korah and 250 of his supporters gathered at the entrance of the tabernacle, Dathan and Abiram stood at the entrance of their tents with their families. Moses ordered the rest of the people to withdraw from around the tents of the three ringleaders of the rebellion. God then manifested his displeasure by causing the ground to open up beneath the tents of these men, swallowing up Dathan and Abiram and their households. Korah and the rebels perished in the fire that erupted near the tabernacle (Num 16:1-36).

2. The firstborn son of Hiel of Bethel, who, during the reign of Ahab, rebuilt Jericho in spite of Joshua's curse after its destruction: "Cursed be the man before the Lord who rises up and builds this city Jericho; he shall lay its foundation with his firstborn" (Josh 6:26). Centuries later the curse was fulfilled: Hiel "laid its foundations with Abiram his first born...according to the word of the Lord, which he had spoken through Joshua the son of Nun" (I Kgs 16:34).

ABISHAG Beautiful young girl from Shunem who was brought to King David to minister to him in his old age (I Kgs 1:1-4). After David's death, his eldest son Adonijah sought to marry her and persuaded the queen-mother, Bathsheba, to convey his request to the new king, Solomon. However, Adonijah had already made one attempt to take the throne and Solomon, fearing that this request masked Adonijah's intention to renew his claim to the succession, had him executed (I Kgs 2:13-25).

ABISHAI The son of David's sister, Zeruiah, and brother to Joab and Asahel. Abishai was one of David's most loyal companions throughout his wanderings and after he became king. One of David's "mighty men" (II Sam 23:18-19; I Chr 2:16; 11:20), Abishai assisted his uncle in the latter's military campaigns. Abishai was impulsive and ruthless: when he and David stole into Saul's camp by night, he would have killed Saul had David not restrained him (I Sam 26:6-9). Abishai and his brothers defeated Saul's son Ishbosheth at Gibeon. After the battle they pursued Abner, the commander of Saul's army; during the pursuit, Abner killed Asahel (II Sam 2:18-24). Later, although Abner had meanwhile sided with David, Joab and Abishai avenged their brother's death by killing Abner (II Sam 3:30).

Abishai achieved renown by defeating the Edomites in the Valley of Salt, a battle in which 18,000 Edomites were killed (I Chr 18:12). Subsequently, he routed the Ammonites (II Sam 10:14; I Chr 19:11-15). Abishai helped crush the rebellion of Sheba, the son of Bichri (II Sam 20:1-7). During one of David's battles against the Philistines, Abishai saved the king's life from a Philistine giant "the weight of whose bronze spear was three hundred shekels" (II Sam 21:15-17). When Absalom rebelled against his father David, Abishai commanded one-third of the king's forces (II Sam 18:2). On two occasions David had to restrain Abishai from beheading Shimei, one of Absalom's supporters, who had cursed the king (II Sam 16:5-14; 19:21-23).

ABISHALOM See ABSALOM

ABISHUA ("my father is salvation"?).

1. The son of Phinehas and a great-grandson of Aaron. He was the father of Bukki (I Chr 6:4-5, 50), and an ancestor of Ezra (Ezra 7:5).

2. One of the sons of Bela, Benjamin's firstborn (I Chr 8:1-4).

ABISHUR ("my father is a wall"). A descendant of Judah through the family line of Jerahmeel. The son of Shammai and the father of Ahban and Molid by his wife Abihail (I Chr 2:25-29).

ABITAL ("my father is dew"). One of David's six wives by whom he had six sons during the time he ruled from Hebron. Abital was the mother of the fifth son, Shephatiah (II Sam 3:2-4; I Chr 3:1-3).

ABITUB ("my father of goodness"). A Benjamite, the son of Shaharaim and Hushim (I Chr 8:1, 8-11).

ABIUD The son of Zerubbabel and an ancestor of Joseph in the genealogy of Jesus given by Matthew (Matt 1:1, 13).

ABNER ("my father is Ner", or, "father of light"). The son of Ner of the tribe of Benjamin, and King Saul's uncle (I Sam 14:50-51). Abner commanded Saul's army which numbered up to 200,000 men (I Sam 14:50; 15:4). In Saul's court he occupied a place of honor, next to Jonathan, the king's son (I Sam 20:25).

Abner accompanied Saul in his pursuit of David; after entering Saul's camp at night unnoticed, David taunted Abner for failing to guard the king (I Sam 26:14-16). Following the death of Saul and three of his sons at the hands of the Philistines in the disastrous battle of Gilboa, Abner retreated across the Jordan to Mahanaim, taking with him Saul's son Ishbosheth, whom he proclaimed king, although David had been proclaimed king in Hebron by the tribe of Judah (II Sam 2:8-10). The armies of the two rival kings met at Gibeon. Abner proposed a contest between a dozen young warriors from each army, and this was followed by a fierce battle, in which Abner and his men were defeated. While fleeing, Abner was pursued by Asahel, Joab's brother. Abner pleaded with Asahel to call off his pursuit in order to avoid a deadly clash, but the stubborn Asahel would not listen, and Abner killed him in self-defense (II Sam 2:12-23). Abner begged Joab to stop the bloodshed, and returned to Mahanaim (II Sam 2:26-30).

Abner had fought for Ishbosheth and was "strengthening his hold on the house of Saul"; but his relations with Saul's concubine, Rizpah, probably reflecting his own ambitions to seize the throne, brought a rebuke from Ishbosheth. Stung by this reproach, Abner angrily switched his backing to the house of David "to set up the throne of David over Israel and over Judah, from Dan to Beersheba" (II Sam 3:6-10). The withdrawal of Abner's support left Ishbosheth helpless. Abner then rallied the elders of Judah and of Benjamin to offer the crown of a reunited kingdom to David (II Sam 3:11-19). Abner was well received by David at Hebron, and "he sent Abner away, and he went in peace". Joab was not present at the time, but upon returning to Hebron and hearing the news, he denounced Abner as a conniving spy. Without the king's knowledge, he tricked Abner into coming back to the city, where he stabbed him (II Sam 3:20-30), thereby combining vengeance for the death of his brother Asahel with the elimination of a potential rival. David, deeply shocked, cursed Joab and his house and lamented: "A prince and a great man has fallen this day in Israel" (II Sam 3:31-39). Many years later, on his deathbed, David remembered Abner's death and charged Solomon with avenging his treacherous murder (I Kgs 2:5, 32). Abner had a son named Jaasiel (I Chr 27:21).

ABRAHAM The first patriarch of Israel; son of Terah and brother of Nahor and Haran. At first his name was Abram (i.e. "the Father is

Structure marking the entrance to the cave below where the traditional grave of Abraham is to be found. It is in the main hall of the mosque built over the Cave of Machpelah in the center of Hebron.

exalted") but God changed it to Abraham (probably just a longer form of the name Abram, but explained in the Bible as "a father of many nations", Gen 17:5). His family originally lived near the southern Mesopotamian city Ur of the Chaldees, but Terah took him, along with Lot, the son of Haran, to the city of Haran in northwest Mesopotamia (Gen 11:31). This region was populated by seminomadic West Semitic (or Amorite) tribes unrelated to the indigenous peoples of Mesopotamia, and with their own language (apparently cognate with Hebrew and Aramaic), and political organization; evidence for their way of life has been detected in the archives of Mari, dating from the era of Hammurabi (18th century B.C.)

After the death of his father (Gen 11:32) the Lord commanded Abraham to leave his country and his kindred and to go to the land which would be shown to him; God also promised to make him into a great nation, a blessing for all the families of the earth (Gen 12:1-3). Accordingly, the 75-year old Abraham, accompanied by his wife Sarah and his nephew Lot, left for the land of Canaan. Upon his arrival he traversed the regions of Shechem and Bethel to the Negeb (Gen 12:4-9).

When a severe famine compelled him to travel to Egypt the Egyptian courtiers, entranced by the beauty of Sarah, brought her to the royal palace. Pharaoh was punished by God for taking her, but compensated Abraham with many gifts (Gen 12:10-20).

Upon their return to Canaan, Lot and Abraham separated because there was not sufficient grazing lands for their flocks. Abraham pitched his tents by the terebinths of Mamre near Hebron (Gen 13:1-18).

In these stories Abraham is described as a peaceful herdsman but the warlike aspects of his personality emerge in the chapter giving his exploits against four kings who had invaded Canaan to repress the rebellion of the local kings. The invaders were victorious and their captives included Lot (Gen 14:1-12). Abraham set out to rescue his nephew; with 318 retainers and his allies Aner, Eshcol and Mamre, he pursued the kings and defeated them near Hobah in the region of

A general view of Shechem, a short distance from Tell Balata, the site of the biblical town where Abraham built an altar to the Lord upon his arrival in Canaan (Gen 12:6).

Damascus, freeing all the captives including Lot (Gen 14:13-16). Upon his triumphant return, Abraham was greeted by Melchizedek, the king of Salem (probably another name for Jerusalem) and "priest of the God of the Most High", who blessed him and offered him a tenth of all his goods. Abraham magnanimously declined to accept the gift (Gen 14:21-24).

The main theme of the Abraham narrative is God's promise to multiply his descendants, who would inherit the land of Canaan (Gen 13:15-17). This promise contrasted with Sarah's hitherto childless state (Gen 11:30). The divine promise, however, is repeated and reinforced in the "Covenant between the pieces" (Gen 15:7-21). In answer to Abraham's demurral that he would die childless, God responded that he would have a son and heir (Gen 15:1-6).

Sarah tried to solve the problem by giving Abraham her maid, Hagar, as a wife. According to biblical chronology Abraham was 86 years old when Hagar gave birth to Ishmael (Gen 16:1-16). At the age of 99 Abraham experienced a further revelation predicting that Sarah would bear him a son although Ishmael would also benefit from God's blessing (Gen 17:14-22). In affirmation of his covenant with God, Abraham circumcised himself, his son Ishmael and all the males in his household (Gen 17:10-11, 23-27).

Abraham and Sarah were later visited by three angels who announced that within a year Sarah would give birth, notwithstanding her great age (Gen 18:1-15). The angels also heralded the divine purpose of destroying the wicked cities of Sodom and Gomorrah (Gen 18:16-22). Standing before the Lord Abraham boldly questioned the collective punishment of sinners and righteous together (Gen 18:23-25). God agreed to spare Sodom if as few as ten righteous men would be found in its midst (Gen 18:27-33), but Abraham failed to locate them. That night Sodom and Gomorrah were destroyed; only Abraham's nephew Lot was saved, together with his daughters (Gen 19:1-28). Abraham then traveled south, where he concluded a covenant with Abimelech, king of Gerar, by the wells of Beersheba (Gen 21:22-34). Eventually, when Abraham was 100 years old, Sarah gave birth to a son called Isaac (Gen 21:1-8). When the boy was growing up, Sarah urged Abraham to banish Hagar and Ishmael, to ensure that Isaac be his sole heir. As the Lord confirmed this demand and promised once again that Ishmael would also become a great nation, Abraham consented and sent them off to the desert where they were saved by an angel of God (Gen 21:9-21).

Afterwards the election of Isaac was reaffirmed in the divine testing of Abraham. The Lord commanded him to take his son Isaac and offer him as a burnt-offering on Mount Moriah (Gen 22:1-2). In full trust and obedience to the divine command Abraham took Isaac to Moriah and built an altar there. But as Abraham stretched out his hand to kill his son, an angel of God prevented the sacrifice. This incident of the Binding of Isaac became an important element in Jewish theology and a symbol of absolute trust and willingness to sacrifice.

The story may originally have been intended as a condemnation of human sacrifice. In Christian theology Abraham's submission to God's will was seen as a prefiguration of the death of Jesus.

Upon Sarah's death in Hebron, Abraham bought the cave of Machpelah for 400 shekels of silver from Ephron, one of the Hittites living in Hebron.

Approaching his own death, Abraham sent his servant back to his family in Mesopotamia, in order to procure a wife for Isaac from his own kindred. The servant returned to Isaac with Abraham's great-niece Rebekah (Gen 24:55-67). Abraham died at the age of 175 and was buried by Isaac and Ishmael in the cave of Machpelah (Gen 25:9-11).

11:22. Gal 3:6-9, 14, 16, 18, 22, 29. Heb 2:16; 6:13; 7:1-2, 4-6, 9; 11:8, 17. James 2:21, 23. I Pet 3:6

Abraham's call (Gen 12:1-3) is the origin and mainspring of Israel's election and religion (cf Josh 24:2-3; Is 51:2). The many altars he built were prototypes for Israel's worship (Gen 12:6-8; 13:18; 21:33), and the altar at Mount Moriah (Gen 22:9) became identified with the site of the Temple (II Chr 3:1).

Abraham is mentioned 72 times in the NT and was considered the father of all true believers, the first to receive God's promises. His story is summarized in Acts 7:2-8. All Christians are the children of Abraham whose righteousness was passed down to all believers in Jesus by virtue of Abraham's faith (Rom 4:13-25). Abraham's bosom (Luke 16:22) is the place of rest reserved for the righteous in the afterworld.

ABRAM See ABRAHAM

ABRONAH ("passage" or "place opposite"). A place where the Israelites camped on their way from Egypt to the Promised Land. It lay between Jotbathah and Ezion Geber (Num 33:1, 34-35).

ABSALOM, ABISHALOM ("father of peace"). The third of David's six sons, born in Hebron. His mother, Maacah, was the daughter of Talmai, the king of Geshur (II Sam 3:2-5). Absalom combined physical beauty with a smooth tongue and thus "stole the hearts of the men of Israel" (II Sam 14:25; 15:2-6). His sister Tamar and his daughter, likewise named Tamar, were also described as beautiful (II Sam 13:1; 14:25-27). His half-brother Amnon became infatuated with Tamar, Absalom's sister. Feigning illness, Amnon asked for Tamar to be sent to his quarters to cook for him, and thereupon violated her. His spent passion soon turned to hatred, and he sent her away. Absalom ordered Tamar to remain silent and took her into his home, biding his time to exact revenge for his sister's dishonor (II Sam 13:1-20). Two years later, during a sheepshearing feast, when Amnon "was merry with wine", Absalom ordered his servants to kill him. He then fled and sought refuge with Talmai, his grandfather, at Geshur (II Sam 13:23-39). After three years, Joab's good offices procured Absalom's return, but he was forbidden to appear before the king (II Sam 14:1-24). Absalom endured this for two years before again seeking Joab's help to appear before David. When Joab refused to visit him, Absalom used a stratagem to bring a response from Joab; the latter finally persuaded David to see his son and grant him full pardon (II Sam 14:28-33).

ABRAM
Gen 11:26-27, 29, 31; 12:1, 4-7, 9-10, 14, 16-18; 13:1-2, 4-5, 7-8, 12, 14, 18; 14:12-14, 19, 21-23; 15:1-3, 11-13, 18; 16:1-3, 5-6, 15-16; 17:1, 3, 5. I Chr 1:27. Neh 9:7

ABRONAH
Num 33:34-35

ABSALOM, ABISHALOM
II Sam 3:3; 13:1, 4, 20, 22-30, 32, 34, 37-39; 14:1, 21, 23-25, 27-29, 30-33; 15:1-4, 6-7, 10-14, 31, 34, 37; 16:8, 15-18, 20-23; 17:1, 4-7, 9, 14-15, 18, 20, 24-26; 18:5, 9-10, 12, 14-15, 17-18, 29, 32-33; 19:1, 4, 6, 9-10; 20:6. I Kgs 1:6; 2:7, 28. I Chr 3:2. II Chr 11:20-21. Ps 3:1

(left)
Monument in the Kidron Valley, known as the Pillar of Absalom. Although built in the 1st century B.C., nearly a thousand years later than the time of Absalom, it is held by popular tradition to be the site of Absalom's burial place.

The death of Absalom from a miniature in the San Isidoro Bible; Léon, Spain, 1162.

In spite of his affection for David, Absalom was ambitious and plotted against his father (II Sam 15:1-3). He organized a revolt from Hebron, with the support of Ahithophel, David's highly esteemed counselor (II Sam 15:7-12, 31). As the number of plotters grew, David fled Jerusalem to Transjordan with a group of faithful supporters, including the priests Abiathar and Zadok, whom he sent back to Jerusalem to serve as liaison agents. David also sent Hushai, his loyal friend to counteract Ahithophel's advice to Absalom. Absalom occupied the king's palace and, following Ahithophel's advice, took over his father's concubines (II Sam 16:15-23). Ahithophel urged Absalom to fight David immediately before the king could reorganize his forces (II Sam 17:1-4). Hushai, on the other hand, advised Absalom to wait until his troops gained strength and then to lead the attack himself. Hushai's advice was followed. All the while David was kept informed and he organized his forces from Mahanaim. The clash between the two armies took place in the woods of Ephraim where Absalom's newly-formed army was defeated. David had given strict orders that Absalom was not to be killed (II Sam 18:1-8), but while fleeing on horseback through the woods, Absalom was entrapped when his long hair became entangled in the branches of a terebinth; in spite of the king's instructions, Joab killed Absalom and had his body thrown in a pit (II Sam 18:9-17). David, grief-stricken, bitterly mourned the death of his son. His lament overshadowed his supporters' rejoicing at their victory. Joab reasoned with the king that he must face his responsibilities, pointing out that the tragic events they had all suffered were caused by Absalom (II Sam 18:19-32; 19:1-8).

Absalom had three sons (II Sam 14:27), but they must have died young as he had built a monument for himself during his lifetime saying "I have no son to keep my name in remembrance." He named the pillar after himself. "And to this day it is called Absalom's Monument" (II Sam 18:18).

ACACIA See PLANTS

ACACIA GROVE See SHITTIM

ACACIA GROVE
Num 25:1.
Josh 2:1; 3:1.
Mic 6:5

ACCAD A town in Shinar, or Mesopotamia, listed in the Table of Nations among the cities of the kingdom of Nimrod (Gen 10:10) and frequently mentioned in Babylonian inscriptions. It was probably north of the city of Babylon, near Sippar. From the time of Sargon I it was the first capital of the kings of the Accadian Dynasty, who ruled Babylon for about 200 years. In the days of the 3rd Dynasty of Ur (c. 2200-2100 B.C.) the name Accad was applied to the northern part of the kingdom of Babylon.

ACCAD
Gen 10:10

ACCO A Canaanite-Phoenician city referred to only once in the Bible: "Neither did Asher drive out the inhabitants of Acco...so the Asherites dwelt among the Canaanites, the inhabitants of the land: for they did not drive them out" (Judg 1:31-32). Acco is mentioned for the first time in the Egyptian Execration Texts of the 19th century B.C. and is also listed in the conquests of Thutmosis III (15th century B.C.), who conquered it in his first campaign. It often appears in the El Amarna Letters of the 14th century B.C. and its rulers, Suratu and Sutatna, bore non-Semitic names, apparently Indo-Iranian. At that time Acco was the most important harbor serving Galilee, and formed an important center for Egyptian rule. It was not conquered by the Israelites before the time of David, but Solomon presumably ceded it to Hiram king of Tyre (I Kgs 9:12-13; II Chr 8:1-2) and from then on it was a Phoenician city. Under the name of Akku it was conquered by Sennacherib in his campaign in 701 B.C. In the Persian period it was also an apparently autonomous Phoenician harbor. Cambyses probably assembled his

ACCO
Judg 1:31

Stele from Susa, Elam, of Naram-Sin, king of Accad c. 2250 B.C. The king stands facing a mountain; his headdress has horns to symbolize divine power.

A lead slingshot of the Hellenistic period found at Acco.

(left)
The modern harbor of Acco (Acre).

forces at Acco before his assault on Egypt, as did other Persian kings in the 4th century B.C. Classical sources mention Acco and its sandy plain in conjunction with the invention of glass blowing. In the Hellenistic period Acco was renamed Ptolemais and when Paul landed there after his third missionary journey, it was already the home of a Christian church (Acts 21:7). Ancient Acco is located at Tell el-Fukhar, 1 mile (1.6 km) east of Hellenistic, medieval and modern Acre. Extensive excavations on the site go back to the earliest settlement, from the transitional Chalcolithic period to Early Bronze Age I, when it was occupied by farmers. Part of the mound was submerged by the sea for a lengthy period of time, and was not resettled before Middle Bronze Age I, when the Canaanites began to urbanize the coast. By the Late Bronze Age, Acco was a well planned city. The rise of its rival, Tyre, apparently caused the decline of Acco in the Iron Age I-II (11th-9th centuries B.C.). The city revived in the 9th century and reached its zenith in the 8th and 7th centuries B.C. In this period Acco was a center of metal industry. In the Persian period, Acco turned into a cosmopolitan city, which retained its importance in the Hellenistic period.

View of the traditional site of Acel Dama at the eastern end of the Valley of Hinnom.

ACEL DAMA
Acts 1:19

ACEL DAMA (AKEL DAMA) ("field of blood", or, "field of sleeping"). The name given to a field outside the walls of Jerusalem, which was purchased by Judas Iscariot "with the wages of iniquity" paid to him for his betrayal of Jesus. Here Judas fell and "he burst open in the middle and all his entrails gushed out" (Acts 1:16-20). Hence also the name "field of blood". In the account in the Gospel According to Matthew (27:3-10), the field received its name because Judas, full of remorse following Jesus' condemnation, gave the money he had received in payment for his betrayal to the treasury of the Temple. Being the "price of blood" it was not acceptable for use by the Temple, so the priests used it to buy a plot belonging to a potter, to be used as a burial ground for foreigners. Acel Dama is also known by its former name as the "Potter's Field".

Since the 4th century the traditional site of Acel Dama has been on the south slope in the eastern end of the Valley of Hinnom where, up to the 17th century, deceased pilgrims were buried.

ACHAIA Region of Greece on the north coast of the Peloponnesus. Originally, the name referred to a small zone stretching across the Gulf of Corinth. Conquered by Rome in 146 B.C., it was administered as part of the Roman province of Macedonia. In 27 B.C. it became a separate province and the name "Achaia" was applied to all of the Peloponnesus and part of continental Greece. The province of Achaia came under senatorial administration and was ruled by a proconsul from its capital Corinth. Other towns in the province were Athens and Cenchrae. For some time Achaia and Macedonia were placed under imperial control and governed from the province of Moesia. In A.D. 44 Claudius restored it to the rank of a senatorial province. Achaia and Macedonia are often mentioned together in the NT when referring to all of Greece.

Gallio was the proconsul at the time of Paul's stay in Achaia. Paul was brought before him by the Jews of Corinth to be judged because he preached "to worship God contrary to the law" (Acts 18:12-16). In the Epistle to the Romans, Paul mentions the generosity of the Christians of the province who had helped their needy brothers in Jerusalem (Rom 15:26). The apostle spent much time there and expressed his love for the churches of Achaia (II Cor 11:10-11). Paul mentions Epaenetus and Stephanas whom he had baptized and who were "the firstfruits of Achaia" (Rom 16:5; I Cor 16:15).

ACHAIA
Acts 18:12, 27; 19:21. Rom 15:26; 16:5. I Cor 16:15. II Cor 1:1; 9:2; 11:10. I Thes 1:7-8

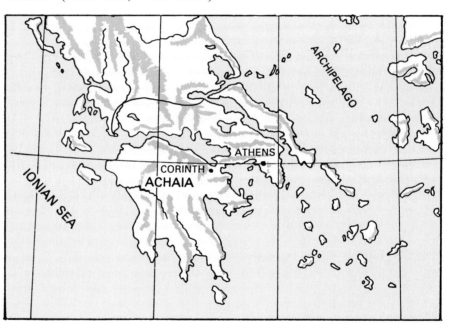

Achaia.

ACHAICUS A Christian of the Corinthian church who visited Paul and to whom he sent greetings in his first Epistle to the Corinthians (I Cor 16:16-18).

ACHAICUS
I Cor 16:17

ACHAN, ACHAR Son of Carmi of the tribe of Judah in the time of Joshua. When the Israelites crossed the Jordan and captured Jericho, Achan violated the ban placed on Jericho and took "a beautiful Babylonian garment, two hundred shekels of silver, and a wedge of gold weighing fifty shekels", burying them in the ground under his tent. Achan's sin brought retribution upon the Israelites, who were defeated in their attempts to take Ai. When lots were cast to determine the guilty party Achan was discovered. He then confessed his sin publicly before the Lord. Achan and his household were stoned in the Valley of Achor (Josh 7:10-25). In I Chronicles 2:7 Achan is called "Achar, the troubler of Israel".

ACHAN, ACHAR
Josh 7:1, 18-20, 24; 22:20. I Chr 2:7

ACHAR See ACHAN

ACHAR
I Chr 2:7

ACHBOR

1. The father of Baal-Hanan, king of Edom.

2. The son of Michaiah (or Micah), an official at King Josiah's court whom the king sent with four others to consult Huldah the prophetess regarding the book of the Law found by Hilkiah the high priest (II Kgs 22:12-14). This same Achbor is called Abdon the son of Micah in II Chronicles 34:20. His son Elnathan was an official at the court of King Jehoiakim (Jer 26:22; 36:12).

ACHIM The son of Zadok and father of Eliud, an ancestor of Joseph, husband of Mary, in the genealogy of Jesus given by Matthew (Matt 1:1, 14).

ACHISH

1. Son of Maoch, Philistine king of Gath, Achish reigned during the time of Saul and David. His realm included Ziklag and the environs (I Sam 27:2-6).

David, fleeing Saul, sought refuge in Achish's territory, but fell under suspicion of being an enemy; fearing for his life, David feigned madness to escape (I Sam 21:10-15). However, when he sought refuge a second time, with 600 men, Achish welcomed him and even gave him Ziklag where David remained for over a year, making Achish believe that he was raiding lands of the Geshurites, Girzites and Amalekites (I Sam 27:8-12). So convinced was Achish of David's loyalty that he even made him his bodyguard when organizing to attack King Saul. It was only at the insistence of the Philistine lords, who feared that David would side with his own people during the battle, that Achish sent him and his men back to the rear (I Sam 28:2; 29:1-11).

2. In the fourth year of Solomon's reign, a king of Gath also named Achish, is mentioned as the son of Maacah to whose territory two of Shimei's servants fled (I Kgs 2:39-40).

ACHMETHA The name of a place mentioned in Ezra 6:1, believed to refer to Ecbatane, the ancient capital of Media.

ACHOR, VALLEY OF ("valley of trouble"). Valley near Jericho, forming part of the territory of the tribe of Judah (Josh 15:7). Here Achan and his household were stoned to death for taking booty captured in Jericho which had been put in the treasury of the house of the Lord (Josh 7:1, 24-26).

(bottom of page)
The valley, northwest of Jericho, said to be the Valley of Achor.

Achamenian cuneiform inscriptions in three languages (Old Persian, Neo-Elamite and Neo-Babylonian) near Hamadan (Achmetha).

Figurines of Phoenician goddesses of the 8th/7th century B.C. found at Achzib.

ACHSAH ("anklet", "bangle"). The daughter of Caleb whom he promised in marriage to whoever would capture Debir. Othniel, the son of Caleb's younger brother Kenaz, took the city and married his cousin Achsah. When she left for her new home Achsah requested, and received from her father, water springs in addition to land in the South (Negeb) (Josh 15:15-19; Judg 1:12-15).

ACHSAH
Josh 15:16-17.
Judg 1:12-13.
I Chr 2:49

ACHSHAPH The seat of one of the Canaanite kings who, in response to the call of Jabin, king of Hazor, came together with their armies at the waters of Merom to fight the Israelites (Josh 11:1-5). The king of Achshaph was killed during the ensuing battle and his city was later included in the territory allotted to the tribe of Asher (Josh 19:24-25). Achshaph is believed to have been situated a short distance southeast of Acco, being located either at Tell Keisan or Tell el Harbaj (Tell Regev).

ACHSHAPH
Josh 11:1;
12:20; 19:25

ACHZIB

1. A town in the territory of Judah (Josh 15:44) whose destruction was foretold by Micah (Mic 1:13-15). It is believed to have been northeast of Mareshah.

ACHZIB 1
Josh 15:44.
Mic 1:14

2. A Canaanite city on the Mediterranean coast, in the territory of the tribe of Asher (Josh 19:29). Achzib not having been captured during the conquest by Joshua, its original inhabitants escaped expulsion and the Asherites settled among them (Judg 1:31-32).

ACHZIB 2
Josh 19:29.
Judg 1:31

View of Achzib, north of Acco, looking south.

Achzib is identified with ez-Zib 11 miles (18 km) north of Acco (Acre). Archeological excavations have brought to light the remains of fortifications and town walls, the earliest dating from 2000 B.C. Phoenician tombs were also discovered, containing pottery, figurines, ivories, seals and jewelry. To the east of the town another cemetery of the Phoenician and Persian periods was discovered.

ACTS OF THE APOSTLES The second part of a two-part history of the early church, traditionally by the author of the Gospel of Luke. Luke-Acts comprises the largest amount of material supplied by a single author in the NT.

Several indications point to the probability that Acts was in fact written by the same person who wrote Luke: (a) the prologues to both are addressed to one Theophilus, and Acts 1:1 indicates that it is a continuation of the previous work; (b) there is a marked unity of language and style; (c) numerous parallels in author's focus exist between the two books (for example, an emphasis on the work of the Holy Spirit or the role played by women). Scholars are almost universally agreed that the two books originally made up a literary unit.

The name of the author is not given in the text. From considerations of convenience and convention he may be called Luke, though the book was not associated with him before the latter part of the 2nd century

A.D. (Irenaeus, *Against Heresies* III 13, 3). The author was an eyewitness of and participant in some of the events described in the latter part of the book. These are the famous "we passages" (16:10-17; 20:5-15; 21:1-18; 27:1-28:16), in which events are described in the first person. Here the narrative reads as if it had been taken from a personal diary. These passages indicate that the author was closely associated with Paul, and this is borne out by the fact that the bulk of Acts deals with the evangelizing efforts of Paul.

The events described come to an abrupt end with Paul's arrival in Rome and subsequent two-year stay there, i.e., about A.D. 60. While this is a reasonably accurate starting point, estimates have varied widely as to the actual date of composition, ranging from Harnack's A.D. 63-64 to as late as A.D. 150 (when it was clearly used by Marcion). There are indications that Acts may have been known by Clement of Rome, and this would give us a latest date of 95. Attempts to narrow down the date of composition further are necessarily based on arguments of omission. So, for example, Acts does not mention a journey by Paul to Spain (cf Rom 15:24, 28) nor Nero's persecution and Paul's death c. 64. Considering that Acts was composed after Luke's gospel, the dating of the latter relative to the destruction of the Temple in 70 comes into the picture. If passages like Luke 19:41-44 and 21:20ff be taken as evidence of a post-70 composition of Luke, then Acts must also be later. Thus Acts is commonly dated between A.D. 80 and 90.

Although the place of writing cannot be determined from internal evidence (unless, of course, it was written soon after the last events described in Rome), one tradition assigns it to the capital of the Empire. Other sites mentioned are Achaia, Ephesus and Antioch.

Acts is a unique contemporary account of the history of the early church, and no similar narrative has survived. The book serves as a vital sequel to the story of the life of Jesus and a transition to the letters written by leaders of the movement he left behind. From these letters, especially those of Paul, it would have been possible to reconstruct some of that history, but it would have been a reconstruction lacking in broad areas of information. As it is, the narrowed focus of Luke leaves much that is unexplained. Nowhere does he tell us how the gospel was taken to

(left)
The Dome of the Church of the Ascension (foreground) built on the site believed to be the place where Jesus ascended to heaven.

The rock inside the Dome of the Ascension bearing what is said to be the footprint of Jesus.

Egypt or eastwards into Syria nor, for that matter, to Rome itself. Indeed, he gives us no report of the progress of the church in an area as close and important as Galilee. Luke's focus is exclusively on two individuals, Peter and Paul, and others (with the exception of Stephen in chapters 6 and 7) are mentioned only as they incidentally cross the paths of these two.

Acts may conveniently be broken down on the basis of its treatment of Peter and Paul. With the noted exception of Stephen's chapters, Peter figures prominently in the first 12 chapters. He is clearly the spokesman, the leader, and the dominant figure; this is consistent with Luke's earlier recorded words of Jesus (Luke 22:31-32) that he had selected Peter for just such a role. From chapter 13 on, the focus shifts entirely to Paul and Acts necessarily becomes a kind of travelogue as Paul embarks on a succession of "missionary journeys".

Another way of understanding the progression of the book is best set out in 1:8: "you shall be my witnesses in Jerusalem and in all Judea and Samaria and to the ends of the earth." Luke is relating the story of the spread of the gospel, starting from Jerusalem and finally arriving in Rome. It is a story of men bearing testimony. Chapters 1-7 take place in Jerusalem, chapter 8 in Samaria; chapter 9 moves momentarily to a community of believers in Syria and then tells of the gospel's spread in other parts of Judea. With the gospel being taken to the Gentiles in chapter 10, the stage is set for expansion into the surrounding countries in the remaining chapters.

At least two threads may be seen as running through the book in the preaching of the apostles. First and foremost is the message of Jesus' death and resurrection. According to Luke's account (seconded by Paul's letters) the apostolic preaching placed surprisingly little emphasis on the teachings of Jesus. The message of the church of Acts was straight and simple: "God anointed him...they put him to death...God raised him up" (10:38-40; cf 2:22-24; 3:15; 5:30; 13:23, 28-30; 17:3, 31). The second thread is the emphasis on the Holy Spirit as the motivating, guiding force in the young community. Until Paul's arrest in chapter 22, the Holy Spirit figures in no less than 16 chapters, and it is for this reason that some commentators have suggested that the book might be called "The Acts of the Holy Spirit".

(right)
Gamla in Golan, east of the Sea of Galilee. Paul probably passed this way en route to Damascus (Acts 9:1-3).

St Stephen's Gate, known also as Lions' Gate, one of the gates in the walls surrounding the Old City of Jerusalem. St Stephen is said to have been stoned to death nearby (Acts 7:57-60).

Finally, the book of Acts describes the onset of the process by which the fledgling church found itself increasingly separated from Judaism. It was a gradual development and certainly not an obviously necessary outcome from the beginning. The earliest church of Jewish Christians (variously called "the brethren", "the way", "the disciples", "Nazarenes") was in fact just one of several Jewish sects. As long as they refrained from proselytizing activities among members of other sects, they seem to have lived peacefully in Palestine among their Jewish brothers. The 27-year period of events in Palestine depicted in Acts records only five instances of conflicts between the church and their fellow Jews (4:1ff; 5:17ff; 6:9-8:3; 12:1ff; 21:27ff). Outside of the land, Paul's aggressive preaching met with opposition from some zealots (e.g., 13:45ff; 17:5, 13), and on these occasions Paul usually vowed to take his message to the Gentiles. But Luke faithfully records that wherever Paul went, he invariably chose the synagogue as the first place he preached. The book ends with Paul in the capital of the empire, preaching the gospel there.

Coin minted at Caesarea to mark the establishment of the city as a Roman colony (c. A.D. 200).

OUTLINE

An ancient street of Rome.

Hebrew seal impression inscribed "[Belonging] to Hilkia son of Adayah". 7th century B.C. (Israel Museum)

Adam depicted in relief on a 14th-century sarcophagus. (Grotte Vaticane, Rome)

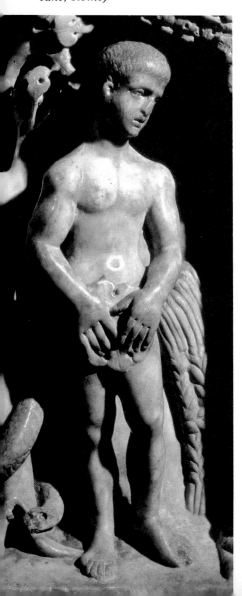

ADADAH See AROER

ADAH ("ornament").

1. The first of Lamech's two wives; mother of Jabal and Jubal. Lamech dedicated his song to both Adah and his other wife Zillah.

2. The daughter of Elon the Hittite and the wife of Esau. She was the mother of Eliphaz (Gen 36:1-16).

ADAIAH ("ornament of God").

1. A descendant of Levi's son Gershon, and an ancestor of Asaph (I Chr 6:39-43).

2. A Benjamite, son of Shimei (I Chr 8:1, 21).

3. The father of Maaseiah, one of the "captains of hundreds" who helped Jehoiada the priest to overthrow the wicked Queen Athaliah, and set Joash, King Ahaziah's son, on the throne of Judah.

4. A native of Bozkath in the territory of Judah (Josh 15:20, 39), the father of Jedidah who was the mother of King Josiah (II Kgs 22:1).

5. The son of Joiarib of the tribe of Judah who dwelt in Jerusalem at the time of Nehemiah (Neh 11:4-5).

6. A priest who dwelt in Jerusalem after the return from Babylonian Exile. He was the son of Jeroham (I Chr 9:10-12; Neh 11:12).

7. One of the sons of Bani who repudiated their alien wives after the Babylonian Exile (Ezra 10:29, 39, 44).

ADALIA One of Haman's ten sons, who, along with his brothers, was killed at Shushan.

ADAM ("man").

1. The progenitor of the human race. While the Hebrew word *adam* occurs only rarely as a name (Genesis 4:25; 5:1, 3-5; I Chr 1:1), it is used in over 500 cases (often with the definite article) to denote "man, mankind", though a few of these instances may in fact refer to "Adam" (Deut 32:8; Job 31:33; Hos 6:7). Genesis 2:7 suggests that *adam* is related to *adamah* "earth", but its etymology remains problematic.

The account of Genesis 1:1-2:4 describes the creation of man as male and female, in the image of God, on the sixth day. Man is told to multiply and subdue the earth. Genesis 2:4-4:25 tells how man was formed from the dust of the earth and placed in the Garden of Eden. He names the animals, but when he fails to find among them a fitting companion, God forms Eve from the man's rib. Adam and Eve eat of the fruit forbidden by God and are expelled from the garden and banished into a world where hardship and pain hold sway. Adam fathered Cain, Abel, and (at the age of 130) Seth; he died aged 930.

In the NT, Adam is juxtaposed with Christ: as Adam brought sin and death to his descendants, so Christ brings forgiveness and life to his. In Luke 3:38 the genealogy of Jesus is traced back to Adam. In I Timothy 2:11-15, Paul uses the story of Adam and Eve to argue for woman's subordination to man.

2. City "beside Zaretan" on the Jordan. It is identified today as Tell ed-Damiyeh. In the Book of Joshua (3:16) it is recorded that the waters here "failed and were cut off" allowing the Israelites to cross into Jericho.

ADAMAH Fortified city in the territory assigned to the tribe of Naphtali (Josh 19:32, 35-36).

ADAMI NEKEB A place in the southern part of the territory of the tribe of Naphtali, generally assumed to have been situated a few miles southwest of the Sea of Galilee (Josh 19:32-33).

ADAR

1. A town on the southern border of the territory assigned to the tribe of Judah (Josh 15:1-3) near Kadesh Barnea. It is given as Hazar Addar in Numbers 34:4.

2. The name given after the Babylonian Exile to the 12th month in the Hebrew calendar.

ADBEEL One of Ishmael's 12 sons. He was the head of a tribe bearing his name (Gen 25:12-16; I Chr 1:29).

ADDAN, ADDON Among the captives who returned to Jerusalem from Babylonian Exile, some, unable to identify their lineage from the records, were consequently excluded from the priesthood (Ezra 2:59, 62). Among these were families who came from Addan in Babylonia (Addon in Neh 7:61).

ADDAR, ARD A descendant of Benjamin through his first-born Bela (I Chr 8:3). His name is given as Ard in Numbers 26:40 and his descendants are designated as the Ardites. He is one of the 70 people of the house of Jacob that descended to Egypt.

ADDI The son of Cosam and father of Melchi in the genealogy of Jesus given by Luke.

ADDON See ADDAN

ADIEL ("an ornament is God").

1. The father of Azmaveth, whom King David appointed to take charge of the royal treasury.

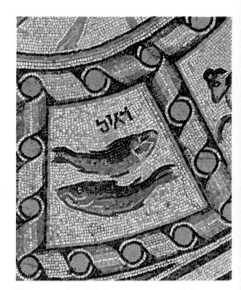

The month of Adar represented by the zodiac sign of Pisces on the mosaic pavement of an ancient synagogue at Tiberias.

Agate Moabite seal inscribed: "[Belonging] to Mesha [son of] Adiel". 6th century B.C. (Israel Museum)

Silver statuette of either a Mede or Persian dignitary from the court of Artaxerxes. (Staatliche Museen, East Berlin)

2. One of the family heads of the tribe of Simeon, who, during the reign of King Hezekiah, dispossessed the Meunites of their land (I Chr 4:36-41).

3. A priest whose father was Jahzerah. His son Maasai served at Jerusalem after the return from Babylonian Exile.

ADIN ("voluptuous"). The ancestor of a family which returned with Zerubbabel from Babylon, comprising 454 members according to Ezra 2:15 and 655 members according to the parallel list given in Nehemiah 7:20. They joined with Nehemiah in a covenant to dissociate themselves from the pagans (Neh 10:1-16). Another group of 51 members of the same family returned with Ezra (Ezra 8:6).

ADINA One of the "mighty men" who commanded David's troops. He was the son of Shiza, a chief of the Reubenites (I Chr 11:10, 42).

ADINO Called Adino the Eznite. He was the head of David's most outstanding "mighty men"; on one occasion, he killed 800 men. His real name was Josheb-Bashebeth the Tachmonite.

ADITHAIM City in the territory assigned to the tribe of Judah (Josh 15:20, 36).

ADLAI The father of Shaphat, who served as overseer of David's herds.

ADMAH A city in the Valley of Siddim inhabited by Canaanites (Gen 10:19). Shinab, the king of Admah, together with the kings of Sodom, Gomorrah, Zeboiim and Bela, were defeated by four kings from the east (Gen 14:8-11). Admah was later destroyed along with Sodom, Gomorrah and Zeboiim (Deut 29:23).

ADMATHA One of the seven princes of the provinces of King Ahasuerus "who ranked highest in the kingdom", whom the king consulted when Queen Vashti defied his command to appear before him wearing the royal crown (Est 1:12-14).

ADNA

1. A member of the family of Pahath-Moab, who returned with Ezra from Babylon. He agreed to repudiate his alien wife in response to Ezra's exhortations (Ezra 10:10, 30, 44).

ADNA 1
Ezra 10:30

2. A priest, descendant of Harim (or Rehum) in the days of the high priest Joiakim and Ezra and Nehemiah (Neh 12:12-15, 26).

ADNA 2
Neh 12:15

ADNAH

ADNAH 1
I Chr 12:20

1. A Manassite who deserted Saul's army and joined David's men on their way to Ziklag from the camp of the Philistines. He was a man of valor, captain of 1,000 men of his tribe, and fought at David's side against bands of raiders that ravaged the camp at Ziklag (I Chr 12:19-22).

2. A man of Judah who commanded 300,000 men in King Jehoshaphat's army stationed at Jerusalem (II Chr 17:12-14).

ADNAH 2
II Chr 17:14

ADONI-BEZEK ("lord of Bezek", or "lord of lightning"). A Canaanite ruler. After Joshua's death the combined forces of Judah and Simeon fought and defeated the Canaanites and the Perizzites at Bezek, killing 10,000 men. Adoni-Bezek fled but was caught, and his thumbs and big toes were cut off. Adoni-Bezek declared: "Seventy kings with their thumbs and big toes cut off used to gather their food under my table; as I have done, so God has repaid me." He was taken to Jerusalem where he died (Judg 1:1-7).

ADONI-BEZEK
Judg 1:5-7

ADONIJAH ("Yah is my Lord").

1. David's fourth son by Haggith. He was born while his father ruled from Hebron (II Sam 3:2, 4). Like Absalom, he was good-looking and ambitious (I Kgs 1:5-6). In David's old age — with the king's three eldest sons Amnon, Chileab and Absalom dead — Adonijah boasted that he would be Israel's next king. When David lay on his deathbed, Adonijah launched an attempt to seize power and forestall succession by Solomon. His coup was supported by Abiathar the priest and Joab, the commander of David's army. Adonijah gave a feast at En Rogel to which he invited all his followers and the princes with the exception of Solomon. Nathan the prophet and Bathsheba alerted David to the plot.

ADONIJAH 1
**II Sam 3:4.
I Kgs 1:5, 7-9,
11, 13, 18, 24-
25, 41-43, 49-
51; 2:13, 19,
21-24, 28.
I Chr 3:2**

En Rogel, southeast of Jerusalem, at the confluence of the Hinnom and Kidron valleys, where Adonijah gave a feast for his supporters.

The king immediately gave orders that Solomon be conducted on the royal mule to Gihon, to be anointed king of Israel and Judah. David's wishes were carried out by Nathan the prophet, and Benaiah the commander of the royal guard. Solomon was designated successor to the throne, to the joy of the people. When Adonijah and his supporters heard of this turn of events, they scattered in terror and Adonijah sought sanctuary by seizing hold of the horns of the altar. Solomon granted him pardon on condition that he prove himself worthy (I Kgs 1:1-53). After David's death, Adonijah persuaded Bathsheba to intercede with Solomon, to gain the king's consent for his marriage to Abishag who had been David's companion in his old age (I Kgs 2:13-18). This was regarded as a renewed attempt by Adonijah to seize the throne; Solomon accordingly ordered Benaiah to put him to death since he had violated the terms of his pardon (I Kgs 2:22-25).

ADONIJAH 2
II Chr 17:8

2. A Levite sent by King Jehoshaphat to teach the Law in the cities of Judah (II Chr 17:7-9).

ADONIJAH 3
Neh 10:16

3. See ADONIKAM

ADONIKAM
Ezra 2:13;
8:13. Neh 7:18

ADONIKAM ("the Lord is risen"). Head of a household at the time of the return from the Babylonian Exile. Six hundred and sixty-six (or six hundred and sixty-seven in another version) members of his family followed Zerubbabel back from Babylon (Ezra 2:13; Neh 7:18). The remainder of the family returned with Ezra (Ezra 8:1, 13). The name is given as Adonijah in Nehemiah 10:16 where he was among those who set their seal to the covenant of reforms.

ADONIRAM,
ADORAM,
HADORAM
II Sam 20:24.
I Kgs 4:6;
5:14; 12:18. II
Chr 10:18

ADONIRAM, ADORAM, HADORAM ("the Lord is exalted"). He was the son of Abda, and one of King David's high officials in charge of forced labor (II Sam 20:24). He continued in this capacity during the reign of Solomon (I Kgs 4:6) and was in charge of the labor force sent to Lebanon to bring timber and to cut stones to build the Temple (I Kgs 5:13-18). During the first year of the reign of Rehoboam, Adoniram, sent to Shechem to put the corvée in effect, was stoned to death by the inhabitants (I Kgs 12:18; II Chr 10:16-19).

ADONI-ZEDEK
Josh 10:1, 3

ADONI-ZEDEK ("Zedek is lord", or, "my lord is righteousness"). King of Jerusalem during the Israelite conquest of Canaan. He was at the head of a coalition, including four Amorite kings of Hebron, Jarmuth, Lachish and Eglon, formed to halt Joshua's conquest (Josh 10:1-3). The inhabitants of Gibeon having made peace with Joshua, the five kings responded by laying siege to Gibeon. Joshua went to the rescue of his new allies, and put the besiegers to flight. The five kings took refuge at Makkedah in a cave where they were trapped. Joshua killed Adoni-Zedek and his four allies, and had them hanged on trees. Their bodies were thrown into the cave in which they had hidden (Josh 10:1-27).

One of the caves in the region of Beth Gubrin in the southern Shephelah, thought to be in the vicinity of Makkedah.

ADOPTION It remains uncertain whether or not adoption was practiced in ancient Israel. Certain biblical passages relating to the patriarchal period, are interpreted by scholars as alluding to adoption e.g. Genesis 15:3; 16:2; 30:3. Jacob "adopted" his grandsons Ephraim and Manasseh granting them inheritance rights equal to those of his own sons, Reuben and Simeon (Gen 48:5). When the child Moses was brought to the daughter of Pharaoh, it is related that "he became her son"; the verse (Ex 2:10) is understood as the adoption of Moses. Ruth 4:16-17 is likewise interpreted as referring to adoption.

The assumption that adoption was practiced is probably influenced by the fact that adoption was widely diffused in ancient Mesopotamian culture. It would be strange, it is maintained, if an institution so widely practiced in ancient Mesopotamia were not to find some echo in the narratives of the patriarchal period, which is strongly influenced in its legal practices by those of ancient Mesopotamia.

In opposition to this view, other scholars maintain that (a) the verses cited may stand on their own without any allusion to legal adoption; (b) biblical legislation on the family, generally elaborate, makes no mention of adoption; and, (c) if legal adoption did exist in biblical times, it would certainly be part of the living legal tradition carried over into the rabbinic period, yet no trace of it is to be found in the Talmud. Even the two biblical verses (Est 2:7; Ps 2:7) that appear to refer explicitly to adoption can, on further consideration, be understood as implying guardianship rather than adoption. As for the verses in Genesis (16:2; 30:3-8) presumed to imply adoption, one must reckon with the fact that children by a maid or concubine were regarded as the legitimate offspring of their male progenitor (cf Judg 8:31). The institution of adoption did occupy a central place, however, in biblical theology. In the Bible the unique tie between God and the king is often expressed by means of a father-son imagery (II Sam 7:14; Ps 2:7-8) which can be traced back to the nomenclature of adoption known from Mesopotamian juridical documents. Similarly, on a national level, adoption terminology is employed to express the bond which exists between God and Israel. The nation, "adopted" by God, is called, "Israel, my firstborn" in Exodus 4:22; and in Jeremiah 31:9, God declares "I am a father to Israel, and Ephraim is my firstborn". Moreover, as a father bequeathes his inheritance to his son (i.e., eternal dynasty and gift of nations to the Davidic king), so God allots and validates his gift of the land of Israel to his "sons", the Children of Israel (Jer 3:19).

When the NT mentions adoption (Rom 8:23; Gal 4:5; Eph 1:5) it is in the theological sense of adoption as sons of God. Paul regarded adoption as a promise for the future yet to be realized: "And I will be his God and he shall be my son" (Rev 21:7).

ADORAIM A city of Judah, southwest of Hebron, located in the village of Dura. It was fortified by Rehoboam, who stationed troops there and established stores of food, oil and wine (II Chr 11:5-9, 11).

ADORAIM
II Chr 11:9

ADORAM See ADONIRAM

ADORAM
II Sam 20:24.
I Kgs 12:18

ADRAMMELECH Assyrian name.

1. An idol worshiped by the Sheparvites, one of the peoples brought from Babylon by the king of Assyria to settle in Samaria in place of the inhabitants whom he had deported to Babylon. The cult of Adrammelech and Anammelech, another Assyrian deity, was accompanied by human sacrifice (II Kgs 17:24-31).

ADRAMMELECH 1
II Kgs 17:31

2. The son of Sennacherib the king of Assyria. He and his brother Sharezer murdered their father in the temple of the god Nisroch at Nineveh, and then fled to the land of Ararat. The assassination ensued

ADRAMMELECH 2
II Kgs 19:37.
Is 37:38

View of the region of Adoraim, southwest of Hebron.

when Sennacherib "returned shamefaced to his land" after his failure to take Jerusalem during the reign of King Hezekiah (II Kgs 19:35-37; II Chr 32:20-22), as had been foretold by Isaiah (II Kgs 19:7; Is 37:37-38).

ADRAMYTTIUM
Acts 27:2

ADRAMYTTIUM A seaport on the Aegean Sea, situated in Mysia, at the northwest corner of Asia Minor, north of Pergamos. Paul, as a prisoner in the custody of the centurion Julius, embarked at Caesarea on a ship from Adramyttium sailing to various points on the Asia Minor coast (Acts 27:1-2).

ADRIATIC SEA
Acts 27:27

ADRIATIC SEA Paul, on his way to Rome, spent several turbulent days on this sea before being shipwrecked on the island of Malta (Acts 27:27). The Adriatic Sea (or the Sea of Adrias as it was known) is an arm of the Mediterranean Sea between Italy and the Balkan peninsula. The name referred initially to the part of the Gulf of Venice near the mouth of the river Po; later, it was applied more widely, and in the apostolic age referred to that part of the Mediterranean bounded by the coasts of Sicily, Italy, Greece and Africa.

The Adriatic Sea.

ADRIEL
I Sam 18:19.
II Sam 21:8

ADRIEL ("God is my help"). The son of Barzillai the Meholathite to whom Saul gave his daughter Merab in spite of having promised her to David (I Sam 18:17-19). Later, in expiation for Saul's attempted massacre of the Gibeonites, David handed over to them seven of Saul's descendants, including Adriel's five sons. They were all killed by the Gibeonites (II Sam 21:1-9).

ADULLAM, ADULLAMITE
Gen 38:1, 12, 20. Josh 12:15; 15:35. I Sam 22:1. II Sam 23:13. I Chr 11:15. II Chr 11:7. Neh 11:30. Mic 1:15

ADULLAM, ADULLAMITE An ancient city in the Shephelah mentioned as the home of Hirah the Adullamite. There Judah married the daughter of a Canaanite named Shua (Gen 38:1-2). Adullam was one of the 14 kingdoms defeated by Joshua during his conquest of Canaan (Josh 12:7, 15). The region was assigned to the tribe of Judah (Josh 15:20, 35). While David was a fugitive from Saul, he hid in one of the many caves of the region after escaping from Achish, the Philistine king of Gath. He was joined there by some 400 men (I Sam 22:1-5). Later, when he became king, David again used the cave as his headquarters while fighting the Philistines; three of his "mighty men" visited him there, bringing him water from the well of Bethlehem for which he had expressed a longing (II Sam 23:13-16; I Chr 11:15-18). Adullam was one of the chain of cities which, although fortified by King Rehoboam for the defense of Judah (II Chr 11:5-12), were taken by Sennacherib's troops during Hezekiah's rule (II Kgs 18:13). It was resettled by exiles returning from Babylonian captivity (Neh 11:30).

The region of Adullam.

ADUMMIM, ASCENT OF A steep pass between Jericho and Jerusalem, leading from the Jordan Valley to the Judean mountains. It marked the boundary between the territories of the tribes of Judah and Benjamin.

ADUMMIM, ASCENT OF
Josh 15:7;
18:17

The Ascent of Adummim.

AENEAS A man who was paralyzed and bedridden for eight years. He was cured by Peter at Lydda.

AENEAS
Acts 9:33-34

AENON A place on the River Jordan near Salim, where John baptized (John 3:23). According to Eusebius, Aenon was situated in the Beth Shean Valley, about 6 miles (10 km) south of Beth Shean. The Medaba map shows another Aenon, on the left bank of the river, opposite Beth Abara, where, according to a 6th-century Christian tradition, there was a cave known as Safsafas, in which Jesus dwelt while he was visiting John the Baptist.

AENON
John 3:23

AFTERLIFE Early biblical traditions assume that when people die they go to *Sheol* the "grave" (Gen 37:35), a vague designation which may denote the burial plot itself. In any case, no hint is given of an afterlife.

In late OT traditions, however, there are intimations of a resurrection, initially of a corporate nature embracing the entire people (Ezek chap. 37), and later perhaps even extending to individuals (Dan 12:2). Nevertheless, prior to the Babylonian captivity the belief in an afterlife as such probably did not exist.

Perhaps through Persian, or even Greek, influences, such a belief did gradually emerge. It included such features as a physical resurrection, which was accepted by the Pharisees, although not by the Sadducees (Mark 12:18). Some held that resurrection would be general, others that it would be confined to the righteous. Also included was a belief in the last judgment (Matt 25:31-46), a grand assize when the books of life would be opened for all to receive their just desserts, the good being rewarded with eternal bliss and the evil with eternal punishment.

Early Christians adopted a complete set of beliefs about the afterlife. They clearly accepted the last judgment, and a resurrection for all as well as a resurrection for the just. Jesus promises one malefactor that "Today you will be with me in paradise", (the word paradise is derived from the Persian for "garden" to designate the realm of the dead).

The NT places considerably more emphasis on the afterlife of the evil, who are destined to go to a place of torture, called Gehenna ("hell") (Matt

5:22-29; 10:28; 18:9; 23:33; Mark 9:43, 45, 47; Luke 12:5; James 3:6) in contrast to Hades which is a term for the realm of the dead (Matt 11:23; Luke 10:15; Rev 1:18; 6:8; 20:13-14). Indeed, the words found in Mark 9:48: "for their worm does not die and their fire is not quenched" come from Isaiah 66:24 and their application to the afterlife is found in an Aramaic translation prior to Jesus. Nevertheless the specific way in which NT sources depict the afterlife for the wicked ("The lake of fire" Rev 20:15) exceeds what is usually found in Judaism.

For Paul, the resurrection and the termination of history through a return of Christ, became major issues in the churches of Corinth (I Cor chap. 15) and Thessalonica (I Thes 4:13-5:28; II Thes chap. 2), thus giving support to the view that confusion and misunderstanding were bound to arise when Jewish apocalyptic notions were introduced into Greek soil. At the same time, early Christians like the author of the fourth gospel, the Epistle to the Hebrews, and I John, show little interest in the doctrine of the last things and even the later Paul when he says, "the Lord is at hand" (Phil 4:5) could very well be saying that the risen Christ is near spatially rather than that his physical return is temporally near. He seems to describe the afterlife simply as a state when he will be with the Lord (II Cor 5:8; Phil 1:23) while leaving aside any discussion of the shape of his body or the nature of his existence. There are, however, some distinctly Christian adaptations of certain doctrines. The last judgment, occasionally depicted as a moment when each person will receive his reward (Matt 8:11-12; II Cor 5:10; Rev 20:12), is also described as a time of surprises when individuals who have proclaimed their fidelity to Jesus will discover that in fact, they have no relation to him at all, while others who have made no claims for themselves will find their lives rewarded (Matt 7:21-23; Luke 13:25-30). Most strikingly, Paul makes the assertion that on the last day when all secrets of the heart will be revealed, God will render to each his praise (I Cor 4:5). Taken together, the last judgment references in the NT seem predominantly to offer a message of hope rather than threats of condemnation.

The contrast between Greek and Hebrew-Christian thought should be noted. The Greeks, as in some measure the Egyptians before them, were concerned with questions of the afterlife. For Jews, however, the here and now is the decisive issue, and Jewish interest in the afterlife was only evoked through influence from Persia, which gave rise to the belief that, beyond the earthly existence, there will be an eternal life in some form or other, and to some extent continuous with the earthly life. Rejecting the Greek notion of the immortality of the soul disembodied from the here and now, early Christians affirmed the resurrection of the body even when that caused them to be ridiculed by their Greek contemporaries (Acts 17:32). What they did affirm along with their Jewish coreligionists was that death could be overcome by God's power — it had lost its sting (Hos 13:14; I Cor 15:55). For Christians that conviction was grounded in the way in which Jesus faced his own death, but above all in their conviction that God had raised Jesus from the dead. The doctrine of the resurrection of Jesus dominated all other doctrines of the afterlife. This accounts for the fact that there was virtually no teaching about the type of existence found in the afterlife (I John 3:2). Even the Book of Revelation which describes the events of the end of time states that the martyrs will have their works following after them (Rev 14:13) and that eternity will be spent in praising and lauding the Almighty (Rev 22:3) or serving God. The new heaven and the new earth and the existence in the new Jerusalem will be characterized by an existence in which that which is considered of great value here (gold) will be so common that it will be used as paving blocks for streets (Rev 21:21) and where human obsessions with security on earth will be removed, for all the gates of the city will be open all the time (Rev 21:25).

The concept of reward and punishment, while present, acts mainly to preserve the doctrine of God's sovereignty. Vengeance serves simply to establish that sovereignty, and not to feed human desires. If God be truly just then the wrongs of this earthly existence must be righted eventually. But most early Christian writers are content to leave that matter with God's wrath and in the meantime they are instructed to remain faithful to the way of life shown them by Jesus (Rev 14:12). See also DEATH, RESURRECTION.

AGABUS A Christian prophet who went from Jerusalem to Antioch at the time that Paul was in the town. He predicted that a famine would take place in the reign of Claudius "throughout all the world" (Acts 11:27-28). Greek and Roman writers used the term "the world" to refer to the Greco-Roman world. Paul met Agabus again at Caesarea, and the prophet predicted Paul's future arrest by the Jews in Jerusalem (Acts 21:10-12).

AGABUS
Acts 11:28;
21:10

AGAG Possibly the title of the kings of Amalek or the name of two Amalekite kings:

1. Balaam, in his third prophecy, foretold that a king of Israel "shall be higher than Agag, and his kingdom shall be exalted" (Num 24:1-7).

AGAG 1
Num 24:7

2. Saul defeated the Amalekites in battle but spared their king Agag, together with the best of the spoil, although Samuel had declared that the Amalekites should be annihilated. This act of disobedience led to Saul's rejection by Samuel, who later personally cut Agag to pieces at Gilgal (I Sam chap. 15).

AGAG 2
I Sam 15:8-9,
20, 32-33

AGAGITE In the story of Esther, Haman is referred to as "the Agagite", thereby creating a link between the enemy of Persian Jews and the ancient enemies of Israel, the Amalekites.

AGAGITE
Est 3:1, 10;
8:3, 5; 9:24

AGEE The father of Shammah, one of David's "mighty men" (II Sam 23:8, 11).

AGEE
II Sam 23:11

AGRICULTURE The Hebrew patriarchs owned large flocks of sheep and goats, but they were not fully nomadic because they did sow seasonally, sometimes with success (Isaac at Gerar, Gen 26:6, 12). Genuine camel nomadism appears in the 13th-11th centuries B.C., with peoples such as the Midianites. From the clash between an agricultural urban society and immigrant semi-nomadic landless groups (15th-13th centuries B.C.), the Hebrews emerged as the dominant force. They were able to consolidate their hold on the hill country because they had already developed techniques for conserving water in plastered cisterns and for terrace cultivation. With improved security in the later royal period (9th-6th centuries B.C.) livestock were kept outside and the towns became the centers of agricultural industries. Settlement was within the framework of the tribe; later the kinship bore responsibility for keeping the family lots within the group. By the end of the 11th century iron had been introduced, probably by the Philistines, with consequent improved facilities for plowing and cultivation. A 10th century B.C. agricultural calendar found at Gezer regulated a mixed-farming pattern, composed of early and later-sown cereals, flax, olives, vines and undefined summer crops. Plant finds from Lachish in the Early Iron Age comprised olives, grapes, wheat, barley and other cereals and pulses.

Hebrew biblical agriculture was self-sufficient mixed farming based mainly on the small family unit. In the course of time it became highly diversified: the farmers of Transjordan brought cereals, lentils, butter, sheep and cattle to David. Later sources (Proverbs, Ecclesiastes) describe the large self-supporting household with orchards, vineyards and livestock, producing woollen, linen and leather goods for sale. Mishnaic references indicate manuring by the folding of stock or by farmyard manure. Unsown arable land was plowed three or four times, suggesting biennial fallow, but the Hebrew sabbatical (seventh) year fallow was also important to soil fertility. Some 30 lbs (13.5 kg) of seed were used to the half-acre (0.2 hectares), about half the quantity normally used today, possibly planted by dibbing. Summer crops, such as cumin and flax, were sown before barley and wheat. Irrigation was known, particularly in the Jordan Rift. Weeding was by hoe and harvesting by sickle, the stalk apparently being cut high. Grain was threshed by oxen, threshing sled or stone threshing roller. Legumes and

Seal depicting a man harvesting with a sickle. (Hecht Museum, University of Haifa)

barley were fed to stock, along with chopped straw and hay. While the vegetables recorded in the Bible are few — leeks, onions, garlic — a number of herbs and several plants (hyssop, myrtle, camphor, crocus, rose, etc.) were used for perfumes and incense as far back as the period of the United Monarchy. Among orchard and plantation produce were nuts, pomegranates, figs, dates, grapes, olives, the fruits of the sycamore and carob trees, *ethrogs* (a citrus fruit) and apples.

The foundation of the United Monarchy by David in 1020 B.C. led to the growth of larger estates held by the king and his nobles; the prophets provide evidence of land accumulation at the expense of the small peasant and the emergence of a royal tenantry. State control of production and systematic royal taxation began under David, who appointed stewards in charge of cattle rearing, vineyards, olive and sycamore groves and granaries. Stamped jar-handles and the ostraca found at Samaria attest the systematic taxation of oil and wine. Solomon's chariotry also implies a well-organized supply of grain and fodder; indeed Solomon also exported large quantities of wheat to Tyre annually, while the establishment of the Temple cult testifies to a well-developed animal husbandry, especially cattle. It seems that geese were fattened for the royal court, but other poultry do not appear before the 6th century B.C.

After the return from the Babylonian Exile, enslavement of small peasants for debt and land-grabbing by the aristocracy increased the number of large estates, though the process was checked by the efforts of Nehemiah. Judea remained a country of preponderantly peasant holdings until it fell within the Hellenistic orbit in 333 B.C. In western Samaria field-towers of the Hellenistic and earlier Roman periods, each representing a family holding, have been found to be connected with wine production, but were also associated with oil presses and threshing floors, the units varying from 1 to 6 acres (0.4 to 2.4 hectares). In southwest Samaria, four-roomed farmhouses from the Early Iron Age, each inhabited by 40 to 50 people, continued to be occupied into the Hellenistic age.

Hellenization accelerated technical progress and initiated gruelling taxation, only temporarily alleviated by the Hasmoneans. Ptolemaic control led to the expansion of state-owned lands worked by tied peasants. In the 3rd century B.C. the country was exporting summer wheat, olive oil, wine, meat and cheese. Some new introductions such as fenugreek (*Trigonella graecum*) probably preceded the arrival of the Greeks, who acclimatized Egyptian beans, lentils and gourds. Apricots,

Agricultural scenes depicted on a wall painting in the tomb of Menna, an Egyptian scribe. c. 1400 B.C.

peaches, cherries, oranges and lemons reached the area from Asia via Italy. Cotton and rice also entered the country in this period. Mishnaic and Talmudic sources list numerous plants first imported in the Hellenistic and Roman periods, including lupins, asparagus, marrows and turnips. The agriculture of the times was mixed and intensive, chiefly for home consumption and based primarily on grain, olives and vines. But it also included industrial crops (cotton, flax, hemp and perfume plants), fruit and market gardening. Oil production reached industrial proportions, perhaps associated with a cooperative system of distribution. Manuring was careful and intensive; this denotes a close relationship between cattle rearing and arable farming. Fallow was biennial, but summer crops must sometimes have resulted in a triennial rotation. The plow was a heavy beam plow to which mold-boards could be fitted. Iron plow-points were found from the early 1st millennium B.C. Irrigation machinery was also much elaborated, resulting in greatly increased grain yields. Farm units tended to shrink owing to population growth and Gentile pressure. Judea's prime exports were wine, dates and incense.

The Hellenistic and Roman periods saw the growth of the isolated farm as opposed to farming focused on village centers. Fields were customarily open in the lowlands and enclosed in the hills. Small square fields (possibly market gardens) have been noted near Ashkelon and in the northern Negeb. The earliest traces of arid zone run-off farming in the central Negeb date from the period of the Divided Monarchy (931 B.C. ff). Three successive phases, probably further developed by the Nabateans, may be noted, progressing from seasonal exploitation of wadi beds, through an expansion of the cultivated streambed areas to a year-round cultivation of enclosed summer and winter crops, combined with manuring, stock grazing and the benefits of a wider drainage area by means of canals.

Trial sections against ancient dams in the Negeb suggest a sharp rise in rainfall in the 9th century B.C. It is now thought that in the Middle East, between the 4th century B.C. and the end of Byzantine rule, a slow but steady decline towards increased aridity occurred.

Excavations at Heshbon have showed that sheep and goats were 75 percent of the bone finds from the Early Iron Age to the early Arab period. The domestic pig was most numerous in the Hellenistic period. Generally the number of livestock fell off in the Hellenistic and Roman periods. At Jericho cattle increased, but goats were more prominent.

AGRIPPA See HEROD AGRIPPA

AGUR The son of Jakeh, an otherwise unknown sage mentioned as the author of sayings in chapter 30 of the Book of Proverbs.

AHAB

1. The son of Omri, and the seventh king of Israel. Ahab reigned over the Israelite kingdom at Samaria for 22 years (c. 871-852 B.C.). He entered into a political marriage with Jezebel, daughter of Ethbaal, the king of the Sidonians (I Kgs 16:28-31). Under Jezebel's influence the cult of idols penetrated into Samaria where Ahab himself built a pagan temple (I Kgs 16:32-33). Some 450 priests of Baal and 400 prophets of the goddess Asherah enjoyed her royal protection (I Kgs 18:18-19). The altar of the Lord was destroyed (I Kgs 18:30) and Jezebel had Israel's prophets killed. It was only thanks to Obadiah — a court official and a devout worshiper of God — that 100 prophets were saved. Obadiah hid them in caves and fed them with bread and water (I Kgs 18:3-4, 13; 19:10). The prophet Elijah, who fought fiercely to preserve the monotheistic worship from the cult of Baal, warned Ahab that the

Carnelian Ammonite seal bearing the inscription "[Belonging] to Ahab [son of] YRMLK". (Israel Museum)

Remains of King Ahab's stables at Megiddo.

Ivory carvings from Ahab's palace in Samaria. 9th century B.C.

country would suffer a severe drought which would end at his bidding only. Elijah stayed out of reach until the due time (I Kgs 17:1-9; 18:1-10). The king blamed Elijah for the drought and resulting famine in Samaria, but Elijah refuted the accusation (I Kgs 18:18). He then challenged the pagan prophets on Mount Carmel and proved their inefficacy. The pagan priests were seized and executed (I Kgs 18:20-40), and the rains came. Ahab informed Jezebel of Elijah's victory and of the defeat of the priests of her cult, and the queen vowed to pursue him relentlessly (I Kgs 19:1-2).

Jezebel exerted an equally evil influence on the king in other matters: when Naboth the Jezreelite refused to sell or exchange his vineyard which Ahab desired, Jezebel had him falsely accused of "cursing God and King", and he was subsequently stoned to death (I Kgs 21:1-16). When Ahab went to take possession of the vineyard, he was confronted by Elijah who denounced him as a murderer. The prophet predicted that, as the dogs licked up Naboth's blood, so dogs would lick up Ahab and Jezebel's blood and "whoever belongs to Ahab" would be eaten by dogs. The execution of the punishment, however, was postponed because Ahab became deeply repentant (I Kgs 21:17-29).

During Ahab's reign the Kingdom of Israel played an important part in international affairs. Ahab continued the policies of his father Omri, maintaining peaceful relations with Phoenicia in the north and with Judah in the south. These were strengthened on the one hand by his marriage to Jezebel, and on the other by the marriage of his daughter, Athaliah, to Jehoram the son of Jehoshaphat, the king of Judah (II Kgs 8:18; II Chr 18:1).

Ahab was also very active in strengthening his kingdom internally. He completed the building of the city of Samaria begun by Omri, and fortified other cities, such as Jericho. Carved ivory plaques found at the site of Ahab's palace at Samaria confirm that here was "his ivory house" (I Kgs 22:39), and other finds also point to the wealth of the kingdom.

Ahab, however, was continually being harassed by Ben-Hadad the Aramean king of Damascus, who engaged Ahab in three wars. Ben-Hadad, together with 32 vassal rulers, succeeded in advancing as far as Samaria, and laid siege to the city. Ahab at first meekly accepted the enemy's demands, but Ben-Hadad's insulting and arrogant behavior roused Ahab's indignation, and brought the people to unite under his rule (I Kgs 20:3-6, 10, 13-21). The Syrians were routed. One year later Ben-Hadad reassembled his troops at Aphek, but was once more defeated. He then concluded a covenant with Ahab whereby Ben-Hadad was to return the Israelite cities which had previously fallen to the Syrians, as well as granting the Israelite merchants marketplaces in Damascus (I Kgs 20:22-34). At about this time (853) Ahab was one of the leaders of 12 kings who fought against the Assyrian king Shalmaneser III in the second battle of Karkar in Syria. He provided 10,000 infantry and 2,500 chariots. The battle, known from the inscriptions of the Assyrian king, probably ended in a stalemate, even though Shalmaneser claimed a total victory. Three years after the second battle with Ben-Hadad, the peace was broken; Ahab, in alliance with Jehoshaphat king of Judah, set out to liberate Ramoth Gilead from the Arameans. Ignoring the somber warning of the prophet Micaiah (I Kgs 22:1-28), Ahab stubbornly went to battle disguised as a soldier and was seriously wounded. In spite of his wound, he fought bravely all day propped up on his chariot, and died in the evening. The Israelite troops were forced to retreat and the dead king was brought back to Samaria where he was buried. "Then they washed the chariot at a pool in Samaria, and the dogs licked up his blood while the harlots bathed in it according to the word of the Lord which he had spoken." Ahab was succeeded by his son Ahaziah (I Kgs 22:29-40).

AHAB 2
Jer 29:21-22

2. Ahab the son of Kolaiah, a false prophet living among the Babylonian exiles. The prophet Jeremiah predicted that Ahab, and his associate Zedekiah the son of Maaseiah, would be burnt by Nebuchadnezzar, the king of Babylon, and their death would become an example which people would cite in curses.

AHARAH
I Chr 8:1

AHARAH The third son of Benjamin. (Probably identical with Ahiram, likewise mentioned as Benjamin's third son in Numbers 26:38).

AHARHEL
I Chr 4:8

AHARHEL Son of Harum of the tribe of Judah.

AHASBAI
II Sam 23:34

AHASBAI The father of Eliphelet, one of David's thirty "mighty men".

AHASUERUS Biblical name for Persian kings.

AHASUERUS 1
Dan 9:1

1. The father of Darius the Mede mentioned in the Book of Daniel.

King Darius I seated on his throne, behind him stands his son and successor Xerxes. Bas-relief from Persepolis.

He is generally identified by historians with Cyaxares, king of Media, who conquered Nineveh c. 612 B.C.

2. The Ahasuerus mentioned by Ezra (4:6) has been identified with Xerxes, the successor of Darius I, who reigned from 485 to 465 B.C. The same identification has been suggested for the Ahasuerus of the Book of Esther "who sat on the throne of his kingdom, which was in Shushan the citadel". After his accession Xerxes was confronted with revolts, first in Egypt and later in Babylon. After crushing the second revolt he attempted to subjugate Greece. His expedition was a disaster and his failure brought about a serious deterioration in Xerxes' character. He became involved in harem intrigues, and fell under the influence of courtiers, as reflected in the Book of Esther.

In the Bible Ahasuerus is said to have ruled over 127 provinces "from India to Ethiopia" (Est 1:1-2).

In the third year of his reign he gave a sumptuous banquet for the heads of his provinces and court officials and ordered his wife, the beautiful Queen Vashti, to present herself at the banquet. Upon her refusal to obey his order, he dismissed her as his wife (Est 1:3-8, 10-19), and chose Esther, a Jewess, to replace her (Est 2:1-4, 17). At the instigation of his chief minister Haman, a decree was issued for the annihilation of all the Jews living in the empire (Est 3:1-15). This scheme was thwarted by Esther and her cousin Mordecai. Haman was hanged and a new decree was issued by Ahasuerus allowing the Jews the right to kill their enemies (Est 8:3-14; 9:5-10, 13-14).

AHAVA A river or a place in Babylon. Ezra assembled a group of exiles there and held a fast before setting out to Jerusalem (Ezra 8:15, 21, 31).
AHAZ ("he held fast").

1. The father of Jehoaddah, or Jarah, mentioned in the family tree of King Saul. He was a son of Micah and great-grandson of Jonathan.

2. King of Judah (c. 733-727 B.C.). When Ahaz was 20, he succeeded his father Jotham and ruled for 16 years. He was one of the kings who "did not do what was right in the sight of the Lord his God" (II Kgs 15:38; 16:1-2; II Chr 28:1). He practiced idolatry, and engaged in pagan sacrifices, even burning his own son (II Kgs 16:3-4; II Chr 28:3).

Early in his reign, Rezin, king of Aram (Syria) and Pekah, king of Israel, concluded an anti-Assyrian alliance and attempted to persuade Ahaz to join them in a single front. When he refused, the Syro-Ephraimite war of 733 broke out and Judah was invaded (II Kgs 15:37; 16:5; II Chr 28:5-8). The coalition intended to place a certain "son of Tabeel" on the throne of Judah in order to secure an anti-Assyrian dynasty (Is 7:6). Many captives were taken to Damascus and to Samaria. It was only thanks to the intervention of the prophet Oded that the captives taken to Samaria were released (II Chr 28:5-15). At the same time the Edomites took Elath and the Philistines invaded the west and south of the kingdom. Ahaz lost control of Beth Shemesh, Aijalon, Gederoth, Sochoh, Timnah and Gimzo (II Kgs 16:6; II Chr 28:17-18). Ahaz was not strengthened by the prophet Isaiah's assurances that the Lord would not allow the Arameans and the Israelites to destroy Judah and place another king on the throne (Is 7:1-17). The helpless and terrified Ahaz turned to the king of Assyria Tiglath-Pileser III, and by despoiling the Temple treasury, bribed him to obtain his aid (II Kgs 16:7-8; II Chr 28:21). Tiglath-Pileser invaded Aram, captured its capital, Damascus, and killed Rezin. Ahaz, who is mentioned in one of Tiglath-Pileser's inscriptions, became his vassal and went to Damascus to render homage to the Assyrian king. While in Damascus he admired the pagan altar and sent a model of it to the priest Urijah in Jerusalem to have it copied, and later, upon his return, sacrificed upon this altar. He

AHASUERUS 2
Ezra 4:6. Est 1:1, 2, 9-10, 15-17, 19; 2:1, 12, 16, 21; 3:1, 6-8, 12; 6:2; 7:5; 8:1, 7, 10, 12; 9:2, 20, 30; 10:1, 3

AHAVA
Ezra 8:15, 21, 31

AHAZ 1
I Chr 8:35-36; 9:41-42

AHAZ 2
II Kgs 15:38; 16:1-2, 5, 7-8, 10-11, 15-17, 19-20; 17:1; 18:1; 20:11; 23:12. I Chr 3:13. II Chr 27:9; 28:1, 16, 19, 21-22, 24, 27; 29:19. Is 1:1; 7:1, 3, 10, 12; 14:28; 38:8. Hos 1:1. Mic 1:1. Matt 1:9

also had the ritual objects of the Temple removed "on account of the king of Assyria" (II Kgs 16:9-18), and installed a sundial in the Temple (II Kgs 20:11).

When Ahaz died he was buried in the City of David (II Kgs 17:20) "but they did not bring him into the tombs of the kings of Israel". He was succeeded by his son Hezekiah (II Chr 28:27).

Ahaz is listed in the genealogy of Jesus given in the Book of Matthew (Matt 1:1, 9).

AHAZIAH ("Yah holds firm"). The name of two kings, one of Israel, and one of Judah:

1. The son of Ahab and Jezebel, Ahaziah was the eighth king of Israel, and reigned for two years (c. 852-851 B.C.). Like his father, he worshiped the gods of his mother (I Kgs 22:40, 51-53). After Ahab's death in battle against the Arameans, Moab seized the opportunity to rebel against Israel, and its king Mesha refused to pay his yearly tribute (II Kgs 1:1; 3:1, 4, 5). Ahaziah made no effort to subjugate the Moabites — an omission possibly stemming from a serious injury he sustained during the second year of his reign, when he fell through a lattice in his palace at Samaria (II Kgs 1:2). Following his accident he sent messages to Ekron to inquire of the Philistine god Baal-Zebub as to his chances of recovery. On their way the messengers were intercepted by the prophet Elijah who predicted the king's death. Ahaziah sent a troop of 50 men to seize the prophet, but on approaching Elijah they were destroyed by fire. A second group suffered the same fate, and a third one was spared only after their leader pleaded with Elijah. Appearing before the king, the prophet confirmed his prediction that Ahaziah would die soon because he had consulted Baal-Zebub (II Kgs 1:2-16).

The only notable act of Ahaziah mentioned in the Bible is his attempt to draw Jehoshaphat the king of Judah into a maritime alliance for trading with Ophir. But this bid was foiled by Jehoshaphat's refusal and the wreckage of his ships before sailing from Ezion Geber (I Kgs 22:48-49; II Chr 20:35-37).

Ahaziah had no son and was succeeded by his brother Jehoram, the son of Ahab (II Kgs 1:17; 3:1).

2. The fifth king of Judah, Ahaziah reigned one year (843-842 B.C.). He was the son of Jehoram and Ahab's daughter Athaliah, and therefore nephew of Ahaziah No.1, above. On his accession, he was 22 years old (II Kgs 8:25-26) (according to II Chr 22:2, 42 years old). Ahaziah too was an idolator "like the house of Ahab" (II Chr 22:3-4). He allied himself with Jehoram — brother and successor of Ahaziah 1 — against Hazael, the king of Aram. The two kings were defeated at Ramoth-Gilead. Jehoram (sometimes written Joram in the Bible) was severely wounded in this battle. While Ahaziah was visiting him at Jezreel where he was recovering, a rebellion broke out in Israel, led by Jehu, an army commander and instigated by the prophet Elisha. As Jehu advanced towards the city, Ahaziah and Jehoram went out to confront him (II Chr 22:5-7). The king of Israel was killed and Ahaziah fled in his chariot. Jehu pursued him and wounded him at the ascent of Gur, but Ahaziah continued his flight as far as Megiddo where he died (II Kgs 9:14-29). He was taken to Jerusalem, to be buried in the City of David.

(Ahaziah is referred to as Azariah in II Chr 22:6 in some Bible versions. In II Chr 21:17 he is referred to as Jehoahaz, the only son of Jehoram who had not been killed by the raiding Philistines and Arabians during his father's reign).

AHBAN Son of Abishur and Abihai of the family of Jerahmeel (I Chr 2:25-29).

AHER A descendant of Benjamin (I Chr 7:6-12).

AHI ("my brother").

1. Son of Abdiel and a family head from the tribe of Gad (I Chr 5:11-15).

2. One of the sons of Shemer of the tribe of Asher (I Chr 7:30-34).

AHIAM The son of Sharar (or Sachar) the Hararite; he was one of King David's thirty "mighty men".

AHIAN The first son of Shemida of the tribe of Manasseh (I Chr 7:14, 19).

AHIEZER ("my brother is help").

1. The son of Ammishaddai. He represented the tribe of Dan in the census taken in the wilderness of Sinai (Num 1:1-3, 12), and made the offering on behalf of his tribe at the dedication of the tabernacle (Num 7:1-2, 10, 66-71). He also headed the army of his tribe which formed the rearguard of the marching line in the wilderness (Num 10:12, 25-28).

2. The chief of a group of bowmen from Saul's tribe who joined David while he was in hiding at Ziklag (I Chr 12:1-3).

AHIHUD

1. A leader of the tribe of Asher; the son of Shelomi (Num 34:27). He participated in the division of the land of Canaan among the ten tribes (Num 34:16-18, 27).

2. A Benjamite listed in King Saul's family tree. It is not clear whether he was the son of Heglam or Gera (I Chr 8:1, 7).

AHIJAH ("my brother is Yah", or, "the brother of Yah").

Bronze Hebrew seal inscribed: "Ahiyahu (Ahijah) [son of] Shem". 7th century B.C. (Israel Museum)

1. A priest of Shiloh in the time of Saul. He was the son of Ahitub, grandson of Phinehas, and great-grandson of Eli. He was with Saul at Michmash (I Sam 14:2-3). He wore the ephod, and was responsible for the ark of the covenant which followed the army (I Sam 14:18-19). His name may originally have been Ahimelech and he may be identical with Ahimelech No.1, the priest of Nob, likewise the son of Ahitub (I Sam 22:9, 11-12, 20).

2. The son of Shisha; one of Solomon's scribes (I Kgs 4:1-3).

3. Ahijah the Pelonite, one of David's "mighty men".

4. One of the sons of Jerahmeel; a member of the tribe of Judah.

5. A Levite appointed over the treasuries of the Temple in the time of David.

6. The father of Baasha, king of Israel; he was a member of the tribe of Issachar.

7. A family head in the tribe of Benjamin (I Chr 8:6-7); the son of Ehud.

He may be identical with the Ahoah of I Chronicles 8:4.

8. A prophet from Shiloh during the end of Solomon's reign, and the reign of Rehoboam and Jeroboam; he prophesied to Jeroboam that the kingdom of Israel would be divided and that he, Jeroboam, would

become king. To symbolize this Ahijah tore his (or Jeroboam's) new garment into 12 pieces and gave ten to Jeroboam saying: "Take for yourself ten pieces, for thus says the Lord, the God of Israel: 'Behold, I will tear the kingdom out of the hand of Solomon and will give ten tribes to you'" (I Kgs 11:26-39). Bearing out this prophecy, Jeroboam became the first king of the kingdom of Israel. He was regarded as a wicked king, who practiced idolatry, setting up golden calves at Bethel and Dan (I Kgs 12:25-33). When Ahijah was old and blind, Jeroboam sent his wife in disguise to consult the prophet about their son's illness. Ahijah recognized Jeroboam's wife and predicted the imminent death of the child and the doom of Jeroboam's house because of the sins of Jeroboam "who made Israel sin" (I Kgs 14:1-18; II Chr 9:29; 10:15).

AHIJAH 9
Neh 10:26

9. One of those who sealed Nehemiah's covenant "to walk in God's Law" (Neh 10:1, 26, 29).

AHIKAM
II Kgs 22:12, 14; 25:22.
II Chr 34:20.
Jer 26:24; 39:14; 40:5-7, 9, 11, 14, 16; 41:1-2, 6, 10, 16, 18; 43:6

AHIKAM ("my brother has risen"). The son of Shaphan, and the father of Gedaliah (II Kgs 22:12; 25:22). He was an official at the court of Josiah king of Judah, and a member of the deputation sent by the king to consult Huldah the prophetess concerning the Book of the Law found by Hilkiah the priest (II Kgs 22:8, 13, 14). During the reign of Jehoiakim, Ahikam took Jeremiah under his protection (Jer 26:22-24).

AHILUD
II Sam 8:16; 20:24. I Kgs 4:3, 12. I Chr 18:15

AHILUD ("a brother is born"). The father of Jehoshaphat, the official recorder under the reigns of Kings David (II Sam 8:16; 20:24) and Solomon (I Kgs 4:3). He was also the father of Baana, a district governor under Solomon (I Kgs 4:12).

AHIMAAZ

AHIMAAZ 1
I Sam 14:50

1. The father of King Saul's wife, Ahinoam.

AHIMAAZ 2
II Sam 15:27, 36; 17:17, 20; 18:19, 22-23, 27-29. I Chr 6:8-9, 53

2. One of the sons of Zadok, the high priest in David's reign (II Sam 15:27; I Chr 6:8, 53), and the father of Azariah (I Chr 6:9). He was one of the priests who carried the ark of the covenant out of Jerusalem when David fled the city at the time of Absalom's rebellion. King David ordered Zadok and Abiathar to return to the capital to await information from Hushai concerning Absalom's plans, and their sons Ahimaaz and Jonathan were stationed at En Rogel to serve as liaison; they relayed to the king the information brought to them by a maidservant (II Sam 15:24-37; 17:1-17). While there, they were detected, and hid in a well in a house in Bahurin. Absalom's men searched the place but a woman had camouflaged the mouth of the well; Ahimaaz and Jonathan escaped and joined David (II Sam 17:18-21).

After Absalom's defeat and death, Ahimaaz begged Joab to allow him to bring the news to David; but Joab refused, sending another messenger. Upon Ahimaaz' insistence, Joab finally gave way allowing Ahimaaz too to announce the victory to David. Ahimaaz arrived first, having outrun the other messenger, but he left it up to the latter to report the bad news of Absalom's death which he himself omitted (II Sam 18:19-33).

AHIMAAZ 3
I Kgs 4:15

3. A son-in-law of Solomon, married to the king's daughter Basemath (I Kgs 4:7, 15). He was one of the 12 officials appointed by Solomon to provide food for the king's household one month out of the year from the territory of Naphtali. (Some suggest that he may be identical with Ahimaaz No.2, the son of Zadok).

AHIMAN

AHIMAN 1
Num 13:22.
Josh 15:14.
Judg 1:10

1. One of the descendants of Anak who inhabited Hebron when Moses sent out spies to reconnoiter the land (Num 13:22, 28). Ahiman and his brothers, Sheshai and Talmai, were driven out by the Israelites (by Caleb, according to Joshua 15:14; by the men of Judah, according to Judges 1:10). Ahiman and his brothers were killed by Caleb (Josh 14:10-15; 15:14).

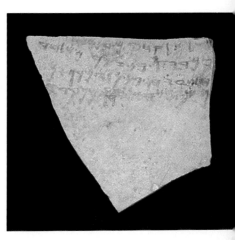

Ostracon of the 7th century B.C. found at the fortress of Ira in the Beersheba Valley, addressed to a person named Ahikam. (Tel Aviv University)

2. One of the Levites appointed as gatekeepers in Jerusalem after the return from Babylonian captivity. They were the descendants of gatekeepers previously appointed by David and Samuel "to this trusted office". They and their children were in charge of the gates of the house of the Lord, the house of the tabernacle (I Chr 9:17-27).

AHIMELECH ("brother of the king", or, "my brother is king").

1. The son of Ahitub; he was the high priest of Nob. Unaware that David was in flight from Saul, Ahimelech gave him the showbread to eat and the sword that had belonged to Goliath (I Sam 21:1-9). When informed of this by Doeg the Edomite, Saul ordered him to kill Ahimelech and his family and the other priests of Nob. Abiathar was the only son of Ahimelech to escape the massacre of the 85 priests of Nob (I Sam 22:7-23). In Psalm 52 (title), David recalls this wicked act of Doeg the Edomite.

2. A Hittite in the service of David whom David asked to accompany him on his clandestine infiltration of Saul's camp at night.

3. The son of Abiathar and grandson of Ahimelech (above), a priest in the days of King David (II Sam 8:17; I Chr 24:3, 6, 31).

AHIMOTH One of the sons of Elkanah; a Levite of the family of Kohath (I Chr 6:19-22, 25).

AHINADAB ("my brother is noble"). The son of Iddo; he was one of the twelve officials charged by Solomon with supplying provisions to the royal house for one month each year from the district of Mahanaim (I Kgs 4:7, 14).

AHINOAM ("my brother is joy").

1. The daughter of Ahimaaz No.1; she became Saul's wife.

2. Ahinoam the Jezreelitess whom David took to wife while already married to Abigail (I Sam 25:43; II Sam 2:2). Both wives accompanied him into his exile in Philistia. Taken captives by the Amalekites who raided Ziklag, they were swiftly rescued by David (I Sam 27:3; 30:1-5, 17-18). After Saul's death, Ahinoam returned to Hebron with David. She was the mother of his firstborn son Amnon (II Sam 2:1; 3:21).

AHIO ("his brother").

1. The son of Abinadab. Ahio and his brother Uzzah accompanied the cart carrying the ark from their father's house on its way to Jerusalem (II Sam 6:2-4).

2. The son of Beriah and grandson of Elpaal, a Benjamite from Aijalon.

3. One of the sons of Jeiel, a Benjamite (I Chr 8:31; 9:35-37).

AHIRA A leader of the tribe of Naphtali; the son of Enan (Num 1:15-16; 2:29). He was one of the tribal leaders who joined Moses in taking a census of the people, and represented his tribe in the inaugural ceremonies of the tabernacle (Num 7:1, 10-11, 78-83); he was also at the head of his tribe in the march out of the wilderness (Num 10:27-28).

AHIRAM, AHIRAMITES ("my brother is exalted"). Benjamin's third son and head of the family called the Ahiramites.

AHISAMACH ("my brother has supported"). The father of Aholiab of the tribe of Dan, a craftsman appointed, along with Bezalel, to make the tabernacle and its equipment (Ex 31:1-6; 35:34; 38:23).

AHISHAHAR ("brother of the dawn"). One of the sons of Bilhan of the tribe of Benjamin (I Chr 7:6, 10-11).

AHISHAR The chamberlain in Solomon's court.

AHITHOPHEL ("brother of folly"). A native of Giloh and highly esteemed adviser of King David: It was said that advice from Ahithophel was like an "oracle of God" (II Sam 16:23). He was the father of Eliam, one of David's "mighty men", and Bathsheba's grandfather (II Sam 11:3; 15:12; 16:23; 23:34). When Absalom rebelled

AHIMAN 2
I Chr 9:17

AHIMELECH 1
I Sam 21:1-2, 8; 22:9, 11, 14, 16, 20; 23:6; 30:7

AHIMELECH 2
I Sam 26:6

AHIMELECH 3
II Sam 8:17. I Chr 24:3, 6, 31

AHIMOTH
I Chr 6:25

AHINADAB
I Kgs 4:14

AHINOAM 1
I Sam 14:50

AHINOAM 2
I Sam 25:43; 27:3; 30:5. II Sam 2:2; 3:2. I Chr 3:1

AHIO 1
II Sam 6:3-4. I Chr 13:7

AHIO 2
I Chr 8:14

AHIO 3
I Chr 8:31; 9:37

AHIRA
Num 1:15; 2:29; 7:78, 83; 10:27

AHIRAM, AHIRAMITES
Num 26:38

AHISAMACH
Ex 31:6; 35:34; 38:23

AHISHAHAR
I Chr 7:10

AHISHAR
I Kgs 4:6

AHITHOPHEL
II Sam 15:12, 31, 34; 16:15, 20-21, 23;

against his father David, and was crowned in Hebron, Ahithophel joined the conspiracy against the king. After Absalom took Jerusalem, Ahithophel advised him to publicly violate David's concubines, who had been left in the palace, to show his followers that the breach with his father was complete and that he would now reign instead (II Sam 16:15, 20-22). Ahithophel then advised Absalom to lose no time in pursuing David, before he could reorganize his forces; he urged that David be killed to induce the people to accept Absalom as king (II Sam 17:1-4). But Ahithophel's advice was rejected when Hushai, David's spy, advocated the opposing view, advising Absalom to wait until all Israel could be mustered for battle (II Sam 17:5-14). Ahithophel subsequently left the capital, returned to his own house and committed suicide by hanging himself (II Sam 17:23).

AHITUB ("my brother is good").

1. The father of Ahimelech, or Ahijah, the priest (See AHIJAH No.1). He was the son of Phinehas, the son of Eli.

2. The father (or grandfather) of a priest named Zadok (II Sam 8:17; I Chr 6:8; 9:11).

AHLAB A Canaanite city in the territory of the tribe of Asher. The Asherites were unable to drive out its inhabitants at the time of the Israelite settlement. It has been identified with Khirbet el-Mahalib, a site about 4 miles (6.5 km) northeast of Tyre.

AHLAI

1. A daughter of Sheshan in the genealogical list of Jerahmeel (I Chr 2:25, 31, 35).

2. The father of Zabad, one of David's "mighty men".

AHOAH A son of Bela, Benjamin's son (I Chr 8:1-4); possibly identical with Ahijah (No.7) mentioned in I Chronicles 8:7.

AHOHITE Patronymic designation applied to persons of the family of Ahoah; or a geographic designation, as yet unidentified. It is used in reference to the valiant fighters in David's army: Dodo, Ilai and Zalmon (II Sam 23:8-9, 23; I Chr 11:11-12, 29; 27:4).

AHOLAH See OHOLAH

AHOLIAB One of the craftsmen appointed to assist Bezalel in making the tabernacle and its equipment. A Danite, the son of Ahisamach (Ex 31:1-7; 35:30-35), he was "an engraver and designer, a weaver in blue and purple and scarlet yarn, and fine linen thread" (Ex 38:23).

AHOLIBAMAH A male or female name.

1. One of the Canaanite wives of Esau; she was the daughter of Anah and granddaughter of Zibeon the Hivite. She bore Esau three sons: Jeush, Jaalan and Korah.

2. An Edomite chief (Gen 36:40-43).

AHUMAI The first-named son of Jahath in the genealogical list of Judah.

AHUZZAM The first-named son of Ashhur by his wife Naarah in the genealogical list of Judah (I Chr 4:1, 5-6).

AHUZZATH The "friend" — most likely the adviser — of Abimelech, king of Gerar, who accompanied him to Beersheba to make a covenant with Isaac (Gen 26:23-31).

AHZAI The son of Meshillemoth and ancestor of certain priests in Jerusalem after the return from Babylonian Exile (Neh 11:10, 13).

AI ("the ruin").

1. A Canaanite city east of Bethel. Abraham pitched his tent in the area shortly after arriving in Canaan, and revisited the place after his sojourn in Egypt (Gen 12:8; 13:3). During the Israelite conquest of Canaan after the fall of Jericho, Joshua, told by his spies that Ai was sparsely inhabited, despatched a small force to attack it. The Israelites

Clay incense stand found at Ai. Early Canaanite period. (Israel Dept. of Antiquities and Museums)

suffered an overwhelming defeat and were plunged into despair. Joshua appealed to God and was told that this setback was a punishment for Achan's sin (Josh 7:1-12). As soon as Achan was brought to justice (see ACHAN), Joshua attacked Ai a second time; the city was captured, burnt, and reduced to "a heap forever, a desolation to this day" (Josh 8:1-29).

Among the exiles returning from Babylon with Zerubbabel were men of Ai and Bethel (Ezra 2:1-2, 28; Neh 7:32).

Ai is identified by most scholars with et-Tell, 1 mile (1.6 km) southwest of the site of Bethel, to the north of Jerusalem. Excavations

14, 16-18, 20-21, 23-26, 28-29; 9:3; 10:1-2, 12:9. Ezra 2:28. Neh 7:32

Remains of a palace of the Early Canaanite period found at et-Tell (Ai).

have uncovered habitations of the Early Bronze Age, from c. 3000 B.C. The city was destroyed by the 24th century B.C. and remained in ruins until the 13th-12th century B.C. An Iron Age village on the site was probably the biblical Ai and the men of Ai defeated by Joshua were probably the first inhabitants of the renewed site.

2. A city mentioned with Heshbon in Jeremiah's prophecy against the Ammonites. The location is unknown (Jer 49:3).

AIAH ("falcon/hawk"). The father of Saul's concubine Rizpah (II Sam 3:7).

AIATH Another form of Ai. See AI No.1

AIJA Same as Ai No.1

AIJALON

1. The valley in which the city of the same name was situated. It was an important pass, northwest of Jerusalem, leading from the coastal plain up into the central mountainous region of Palestine. Joshua was in the Valley of Aijalon when he prayed for the sun and the moon to stand still over Gibeon while he was fighting the five Amorite kings who had attacked the Gibeonites (Josh 10:5-12). "And the sun stood still and the moon stopped, till the people had revenge upon their enemies" (Josh 10:13). At the end of the conquest of Canaan, Aijalon was assigned to the tribe of Dan (Josh 19:40-42), and later to the descendants of Kohath as a Levitical city (Josh 21:1, 20, 24). However the Danites had not succeeded in ousting the Amorites from Aijalon, but help came from the Ephraimites in the north, who subjugated the Amorites of Aijalon (Judg 1:34-35).

**AI 2
Jer 49:3**

**AIAH
II Sam 3:7;
21:8, 10-11**

**AIATH
Is 10:28**

**AIJA
Neh 11:31**

**AIJALON 1
Josh 10:12;
19:42; 21:24.
Judg 1:35.
I Sam 14:31.
I Chr 6:69;
8:13. II Chr
11:10; 28:18**

After Saul's first victory over the Philistines at Michmash, his son Jonathan pursued them as far as Aijalon (I Sam 14:31). In David's administrative reorganization, Aijalon became a city of refuge (I Chr 6:67-69). It was later included in the territory of Benjamin (I Chr 8:13), and was fortified by Rehoboam against invasions from the west or the north (II Chr 11:5-10). During the reign of Ahaz, it was taken by the Philistines (II Chr 28:18). The site of ancient Aijalon is identified with modern Yalu, east of Amwas (Emmaus). It was known in the Roman period as Jalo.

The Valley of Aijalon with the Judean Hills in the background.

AIJALON 2
Judg 12:12

2. A place in the territory of the tribe of Zebulun where the Zebulunite judge Elon was buried (Judg 12:12). Its site is not precisely known but it is believed to have been west of the Sea of Galilee.

AIN ("spring"). The name of two places. The word (often transliterated as "Ein" or "En") frequently appears in compounds such as En Rogel, En Gedi, En Rimmon.

AIN 1
Num 34:11

1. A place indicated by the Lord to Moses as the eastern boundary of "the land that shall fall to you as an inheritance — the land of Canaan to its boundaries" (Num 34:1-2, 10-11).

AIN 2
Josh 15:32;
19:7; 21:16.
I Chr 4:32

2. One of the southernmost cities assigned to the tribe of Judah (Josh 15:20, 32), later allotted to the tribe of Simeon "for the portion of the children of Judah was too much for them" (Josh 19:1, 7-9; I Chr 4:32), and given to the Levites (Josh 21:1-3, 9, 16).

AJAH
Gen 36:24.
I Chr 1:40

AJAH (another form of the name Aiah). The first son of Zibeon of the family of Seir the Horite, a chief in Edom (Gen 36:20, 24, 29: I Chr 1:38, 40).

AKAN
Gen 36:27

AKAN The son of Ezer of the family of Seir the Horite, a chief in Edom (Gen 36:27, 29). The name Akan is also given as Jaakan (I Chr 1:42).

AKEL DAMA
Acts 1:19

AKEL DAMA See ACEL DAMA

AKKAD See ACCAD

AKKUB 1
I Chr 3:24;
9:17

AKKUB

1. One of the seven sons of Elionenai of the family of Jeconiah, a remote descendant of David.

AKKUB 2
Ezra 2:42.
Neh 7:45,
11:19, 12:25

2. The head of a family of Levite gatekeepers who returned to Jerusalem from captivity in Babylon (Ezra 2:40, 42).

The Ascent of Akrabbim.

Khirbet Almit, identified with Almon-Alemeth.

3. The head of a family of Temple servants.

AKKUB 3
Ezra 2:45

4. One of the Levites who assisted Ezra in teaching the Law to the people (Neh 8:7-9).

AKKUB 4
Neh 8:7

AKRABBIM, ASCENT OF ("scorpion pass"). A pass between the south end of the Dead Sea and the Wilderness of Zin forming one of the landmarks on the southern boundary of Canaan (Num 34:1-4), and also

AKRABBIM
Num 34:4.
Josh 15:3.
Judg 1:36

of the territory assigned to the tribe of Judah (Josh 15:1-3; Judg 1:36).

ALAMMELECH A place in the territory of the tribe of Asher (Josh 19:24-26). The exact site has not been identified, but it is thought to be in the southern part of the Plain of Acco.

ALAMMELECH
Josh 19:26

ALAMOTH A word of uncertain meaning, used in connection with music, and thought to refer to a musical instrument or to the higher tones of the musical scale.

ALAMOTH
I Chr 15:20. Ps
46:1

ALEMETH

1. A son of Becher and grandson of Benjamin.

ALEMETH 1
I Chr 7:8

2. A son of Jehoaddah (or Jarah), and a direct descendant of Saul (I Chr 8:1, 36).

ALEMETH 2
I Chr 8:36;
9:42

3. A priestly city of Benjamin (I Chr 6:54, 60). It is identical with Almon (Josh 21:18).

ALEMETH 3
I Chr 6:60

ALEXANDER ("man's defender").

1. The son of Simon of Cyrene, and the brother of Rufus.

ALEXANDER 1
Mark 15:21

2. A relative of the high priest Annas. He was present at the trial of Peter and John (Acts 4:3, 6).

ALEXANDER 2
Acts 4:6

3. A Jew of Ephesus who tried to calm down the riot caused by Demetrius the silversmith. This happened when, in the course of his third missionary journey, Paul's success in making disciples for Christianity alarmed the smiths of the city who feared for their business. The Jews were unjustly blamed for undermining the goddess Diana (Artemis), the city's patron. Alexander tried to speak to the mob, but was shouted down (Acts 19:24-34).

ALEXANDER 3
Acts 19:33

4. A Christian of Ephesus mentioned by Paul together with Hymenaeus, among those who "concerning the faith have suffered shipwreck" (I Tim 1:18-20).

ALEXANDER 4
I Tim 1:20

5. A coppersmith whom Paul mentions as having done him much harm and opposed his mission (II Tim 4:14-15).

ALEXANDER 5
II Tim 4:14

ALEXANDRIA, ALEXANDRIAN(S) The capital city of Egypt throughout the Hellenistic and Roman periods. It was founded in 332 B.C. by Alexander the Great, after his conquest of Egypt. Under his successors, the town's population and wealth became enormous.

ALEXANDRIA
ALEXANDRIAN(S)
Acts 6:9;
18:24; 27:6;
28:11

The city is situated on the western arm of the Nile delta. The city proper was connected with the adjacent island of Pharos by a long mole, and in this way an excellent double harbor was formed. On the coast of the island of Pharos the world-famous lighthouse, one of the Seven Wonders of the World, was built in 297 B.C. The city itself consisted of five divisions and numerous suburbs. The most important building was the Museum, the greatest institution for study and research in antiquity which attracted outstanding scientists and scholars from many countries; the Library was the largest in the world. During the struggle between Caesar and Antony in 47 B.C., the great library was burnt down and its 900,000 volumes were lost. Antony rebuilt the library and brought books to it from Pergamon.

The city's prosperity came mainly from commerce. The economy was based on factories producing linen, papyrus, gold and silver objects and large potteries. The main source of income, however, was the Indian and Arab spice trade which reached Egypt via the Red Sea.

From the beginning Alexandria had a mixed population, including a very large Jewish community. The most outstanding work of the Alexandrian Jews was the translation of the Bible into Greek known as the Septuagint, made in the 3rd century B.C. The Jews of Alexandria were represented in Jerusalem by a sizeable community. There were Alexandrians among those who debated with Stephen, and accused him of blasphemy (Acts 6:9).

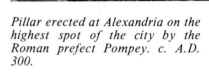

Pillar erected at Alexandria on the highest spot of the city by the Roman prefect Pompey. c. A.D. 300.

View of the harbor at Alexandria.

Apollos, who lived at Ephesus and was converted by Aquila and Priscilla, was a native of Alexandria (Acts 18:24-28).

During his stormy voyage to Rome, Paul sailed from Myria in Lycia to Italy on an Alexandrian ship (Acts 28:11-13).

ALGUM A valuable wood from Lebanon (II Chr 2:8) or from Ophir (II Chr 9:10-11). Probably an error for ALMUG.

ALIAH Another form of ALVAH (see below).

ALIAN Another form of ALVAN (see below).

ALLON ("oak"). A leader of the tribe of Simeon, the son of Jedaiah (I Chr 4:24, 37-38).

ALLON BACHUTH ("oak", or "terebinth of weeping"). Name given to terebinth (or oak) tree near Bethel under which Rebekah's nurse, Deborah, was buried.

ALMODAD ("God is a friend"). The first of Joktan's 13 sons whose descendants settled "from Mesha as you go toward Sephar", which is believed to be in Arabia (Gen 10:26, 30; I Chr 1:20).

ALGUM
II Chr 2:8;
9:10-11

ALIAH
I Chr 1:51

ALIAN
I Chr 1:40

ALLON
I Chr 4:37

ALLON BACHUTH
Gen 35:8

ALMODAD
Gen 10:26.
I Chr 1:20

ALMON A priestly city in the territory of Benjamin (Josh 21:18). In the parallel list of cities assigned to the priests in I Chronicles 6:60 it is mentioned as Alemeth.

ALMON
Josh 21:18

ALMOND See PLANTS

ALMON DIBLATHAIM One of the places where the Israelites stopped on their way to the promised land, following Dibon and preceding the mountains of Abarim (Num 33:46-47). It is believed to be identical with Beth Diblathaim.

ALMON
DIBLATHAIM
Num 33:46-47

ALMUG See PLANTS

ALOES See PLANTS

ALOTH A place in one of Solomon's 12 administrative districts governed by Baanah. It is located in the territory of Asher.

ALOTH
I Kgs 4:16

ALPHA AND OMEGA This conjunction of the first and last letters of the Greek alphabet is a symbolic divine name unique to the Book of Revelation. It is attributed to God (Rev 1:8; 21:6) and to Jesus (Rev 22:13), always used by the divine speaker in reference to himself. The meaning is made immediately clear in the context, by the words "the beginning and the ending", or in another form (Rev 1:17; 2:8), "the first and the last". This is a vision of the One who is Creator and Consummator, from whom and to whom all things come. The author of Revelation wrote in Greek, in the sphere of influence of Hellenistic thought. Near-contemporary gnostic sources use the Alpha-Omega conjunction in denoting the totality of existence, the Aeon. Thus, the application of this name to Jesus may seem to reflect an attribute of the gnostic Aeon.

ALPHA AND
OMEGA
**Rev 1:8, 11;
21:6; 22:13**

A more direct source, however, is in the Hebrew Scriptures, Isaiah 44:6 (cf also Is 41:4; 48:12): "Thus says the Lord... I am the first and I am the last, besides me there is no God".

ALPHAEUS
1. The father of James the Apostle.
2. The father of Levi the tax collector.

ALPHAEUS 1
**Matt 10:3.
Mark 3:18.
Luke 6:15.
Acts 1:13**

ALPHAEUS 2
Mark 2:14

ALTAR The primary purpose of the altar was to sacrifice animals to the Lord. Two types of altars were known in biblical times: the first, and more ancient, was the simple variety which could be used by all and needed no elaborate construction; the more complex were the altars of the second and later type, which were erected near, or outside, a temple, and where priests alone could officiate.

Though the primary function of the altars was the sacrifice of animals to the Lord, they also had secondary purposes e.g. as places of prayer and assembly or sanctuary (Ex 21:14; I Kgs 2:28ff). Excavations have discovered "horned altars" (Ex 27:2) (the person seeking sanctuary clung to the horns). Altars close to the temples were held to have a special sanctity, and as a rule only the best animals were offered there. It was to these altars that people came for the pilgrimage festivals, for the offering of the first fruits, and for the fulfillment of vows.

Simple altars were already built as far back as the times of the patriarchs; the first altar mentioned in the Scriptures is the one erected by Noah after the flood (Gen 8:20). The second was put up by Abraham after the Lord had promised his descendants the land of Canaan (Gen 12:7). The patriarchs constructed altars of stone or clay wherever they went or stayed. Altars were also erected to commemorate special events: the covenant between Jacob and Laban (Gen 31:44ff), Israel's victory over Amalek at Rephidim (Ex 17:14-15), Saul's victory over the Philistines (I Sam 14:35). Altars could be made of earth or clay, stone, bronze or gold: earth being used only for simple, popular altars, brass and gold solely for temple altars, and stone for either. On Mount Sinai, Moses was told "An altar of earth you shall make for me, and you shall

Alpha and Omega as they appear on the northeast tower in one of the buildings of the Russian Compound in Jerusalem.

sacrifice on it your burnt offerings and your peace offerings, your sheep and your oxen. In every place where I record my name I will come to you, and I will bless you; and if you make me an altar of stone, you shall not build it of hewn stone, for if you use your tool on it, you have profaned it" (Ex 20:24-25).

As altars of earth were easily destroyed, stone ones were preferred. These could be of natural stone: thus Manoah, the father of Samson "took the young goat and offered it upon the rock to the Lord" (Judg 13:19). The altar would sometimes consist of a single, large stone (I Sam 14:33, 35). Altars could also be made of smaller stones collected into a simple heap; as did Jacob in affirming his covenant with Laban (Gen 31:46). Another altar of stones was the one Moses ordered built on Mount Ebal (Deut 27:5-6).

Brass or bronze was used for the later ornate altars such as those in the temples, which were of large dimensions, with steps leading up to them and elaborate ornaments and decorations. (In earlier times, the use of steps had been forbidden, for fear of the officiant revealing his nakedness (Ex 20:26); however, the long garments worn by the priests obviated that risk). In the Temple there was another altar, smaller and covered with gold, used only for the burning of incense.

Early Christians substituted the Eucharist for actual sacrifices, and used tables similar to that of the Last Supper.

(top right and bottom)
Horned altars from Megiddo. 10th-9th centuries B.C.

(left)
Altar from the Judean sanctuary at Arad.

ALUSH A place between Dophkah and Rephidim where the Israelites camped on their journey through the wilderness.

ALVAH One of the 11 clan chiefs of the Edomites, descendants of Esau. The name is given as Aliah in I Chronicles 1:51 for the same person.

ALVAN Same as Alian. The first son of Shobal, a descendant of Seir the Horite (I Chr 1:40), given as Alvah in Genesis 36:40.

AMAD A town in the territory of the tribe of Asher.

AMAL The last named of Helem's sons listed in the family of Asher and described as "choice men, mighty men of valor, chief leaders" (I Chr 7:35, 40).

AMALEK, AMALEKITES Amalek was the son of Eliphaz, firstborn son of Esau by his concubine Timna (Gen 36:12, 16). He was one of the 14 leaders in the land of Edom. Amalek's name also designated the descendants of his tribe (Deut 25:17; Judg 7:12; I Sam 15:2).

The Amalekites, an ancient nomadic tribe who roamed the northern Sinai and the Negeb, were the first adversaries that the Israelites encountered after crossing the Red Sea; they were to remain enemies throughout biblical times. The Amalekites attacked the Israelites at Rephidim in the Sinai desert. Joshua led the battle against them under the inspiration of Moses supported by Aaron and Hur (Ex 17:8-13). After the Israelite victory God proclaimed that there would be war with Amalek "from generation to generation" (Ex 17:14-16; Deut 25:19).

ALUSH
Num 33:13-14

ALVAH
Gen 36:40

ALVAN
Gen 36:23

AMAD
Josh 19:26

AMAL
I Chr 7:35

AMALEK,
AMALEKITES
Gen 14:7; 36:12, 16. Ex 17:8-11, 13-14, 16. Num 13:29; 14:25, 43, 45; 24:20, 24. Deut 25:17, 19. Judg 3:13; 5:14; 6:3, 33; 7:12; 10:12; 12:15. I Sam 14:48; 15:2-3, 5-8, 15, 18, 20, 32; 27:8; 28:18; 30:1, 13, 18. II Sam 1:1, 8, 13; 8:12. I Chr 1:36; 4:43; 18:11. Ps 83:7

The oasis of Wadi Firan, identified with Rephidim, where Moses brought forth water from the rocks (Ex 17:1-6). Here the Children of Israel had to fight the Amalekites.

When the Israelites attempted to enter the promised land, they were defeated by the Amalekites and this is explained in the Bible as retribution for new sins against the Lord (Num 14:39-45). During the period of the Judges, the Amalekites again attacked the Israelite tribes, on at least two occasions in alliance with the Ammonites and Moab (Judg 3:12-13); and they also participated in battles in the Valley of Jezreel during the time of Gideon (Judg 6:33; 7:12). A major clash with the Amalekites took place during Saul's reign. The war commenced with a divine command conveyed by Samuel to Saul to attack Amalek and utterly destroy them (I Sam 15:1-3). Saul annihilated the Amalekite people but when he spared their king Agag, Samuel, angry over Saul's disobedience, personally "hacked Agag in pieces" (I Sam 15:10-33).

Before David became king, his forays out of Ziklag included Amalekite camps (I Sam 27:8-9); in retaliation, one day when David and his men were absent, the Amalekites attacked Ziklag, burning the city and capturing the women and children — including David's wives Ahinoam and Abigail (I Sam 30:1-5). David quickly rounded up a rescue expedition, recovered the persons and goods taken, and killed the Amalekites, with the exception of 400 of the men who escaped (I Sam 30:8-20). Subsequently, the Amalekites do not appear to have presented an active threat. In the reign of Hezekiah, the Simeonites defeated the Amalekites and settled their territory (I Chr 4:43). In rabbinical tradition, the Amalekites symbolize the enemies of the Jews and Haman "the Agagite" (Est 3:1) was regarded as a descendant of Agag.

Archeological surveys have shown that the kings of Judah strengthened their hold in the Negeb from the 10th century B.C. and this led to the decline and disappearance of the Amalekites.

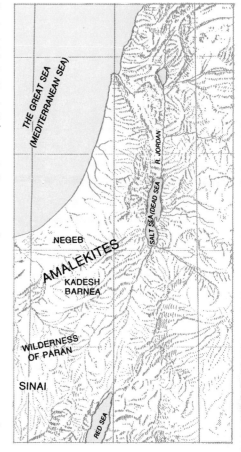

Territory of the Amalekites.

AMAM
Josh 15:26

AMAM A city at the southern border of the territory assigned to the tribe of Judah (Josh 15:20-21, 26).

AMANA
Song 4:8

AMANA Mountain in the Anti-Lebanon range, mentioned in the Song of Solomon together with the Senir and Hermon mountains. It has been identified with Jebel Zebedani (5,900 feet (1,800 m) high).

Amana is mentioned in Sumerian inscriptions as a source of marble or alabaster in the 3rd millennium B.C.

AMARIAH 1
I Chr 6:7, 52

AMARIAH 2
I Chr 6:11.
Ezra 7:3

AMARIAH

1. A descendant of Aaron's son Eleazar; the son of Meriaoth and the father of Ahitub (I Chr 6:1, 4, 7).

2. The name appears in successive generations of priests listed in the Chronicles. Thus another descendant of Aaron's son Eleazar was also Amariah, the son of Azariah (a high priest in Solomon's Temple), and the father of Ahitub.

AMARIAH 3
I Chr 23:19;
24:23

3. The second son of Hebron; a Levite allotted to the division of Kohath in David's organization of the priest and Levites for the Temple service (I Chr 23:3-4, 19; 24:23).

AMARIAH 4
II Chr 19:11

4. A chief priest during the reign of Jehoshaphat.

AMARIAH 5
II Chr 31:15

5. A Levite who assisted in the distribution of the offerings to the priests during the reign of Hezekiah (II Chr 31:14-15).

AMARIAH 6
Ezra 10:42

6. One of the sons of Bani who repudiated his alien wife at the behest of Ezra (Ezra 10:18, 34, 42).

AMARIAH 7
Neh 10:3;
12:2, 13

7. The name appears again several times in lists of priests in the Book of Nehemiah. It is difficult to ascertain whether the name applies to individuals or families: Amariah is mentioned as one of the priests who sealed the covenant "to walk in God's Law" (Neh 10:1, 3, 29); as a priest who returned with Zerubbabel from Babylon (Neh 12:1-2); among a group of priests in the time of Joiakim the high priest (Neh 12:10, 12-13, 26).

AMARIAH 8
Neh 11:4

8. The son of Shephatiah of the tribe of Judah and the ancestor of Athaiah who volunteered to reside in Jerusalem after the return from the Babylonian Exile (Neh 11:1, 4).

AMARIAH 9
Zeph 1:1

9. The son of Hezekiah father of Amariah and great-grandfather of Zephaniah.

AMARNA, TELL EL Place in Egypt. Pharaoh Amenophis IV built a new capital in the sixth year of his reign, naming it Akhetaton, "the horizon of the god Aton." About 160 miles (260 km) from the Nile Delta and 300 miles (480 km) north of Thebes, it is known today as El Amarna. The ancient city was a mile (1.6 km) wide and 4 miles (6.5 km) long and it was entirely consecrated to the worship of Aton. The king, the nobles, landowners and warriors occupied the acropolis, while the populace lived in the lower city and the surrounding villages; in a class of their own were the Habiru, nomads who wandered in the desert and the borderlands.

Two reliefs from Tell el Amarna depicting horses on one, and blind-folded musicians on the other. 14th century B.C. (Israel Museum)

In 1887 clay tablets began to come to light in this area. Now totaling 540, these have become known as the El Amarna Letters. They belong to the royal archives of Amenophis III and his son Amenophis IV and were written by the kings of Babylon, Assyria, Mittani, Arauwa, the Hittites, Cyprus and numerous petty kings of the city-states of Syria and Canaan. Most of them are written in Akkadian, the official diplomatic language of that time, in cuneiform script. The letters show that Canaan was inhabited by mixed elements of West Semites and Horites and divided into a large number of feudal states whose kings were subject to Egypt. In a period of slackening Egyptian authority there were constant quarrels between these petty kings.

The El Amarna Letters are a highly important source from which a great deal of knowledge has been gleaned concerning events in Canaan in the 15th and 14th centuries B.C. If the identification of the Habiru referred to in the letters with the Hebrews is correct, they provide the first evidence of the penetration of Hebrew tribes into the land of Canaan.

AMASA

1. Nephew of David, son of Jether the Ishmaelite (II Sam 17:25: Jithra the Israelite) and Abigail. Amasa may be identical with Amasai of I Chronicles 12:18.

AMASA 1
II Sam 17:25; 19:13; 20:4-5, 8-12. I Kgs 2:5, 32. I Chr 2:17

Absalom, when attempting his coup against his father David, appointed Amasa as commander of the army in place of another nephew of David, Joab, who remained loyal to the king. David's army defeated Amasa in the forest of Ephraim, and Absalom was killed by Joab, against David's orders. Thereafter, David urged the Judean elders to accept Amasa and offer him the command of his army in place of Joab. These offers accepted, David returned to Jerusalem; meanwhile, a rebellion of northern tribes had broken out. Amasa was instructed to muster the Judean army in three days, but he returned late, after the army had already set out, led by Abishai. Amasa joined them at Gibeon. There Joab, feigning a greeting, stabbed him to death. Years later Solomon avenged Amasa's death (I Kgs 2:5, 32).

2. An Ephraimite leader, son of Hadlai. He was among those who urged the release of Judeans whom Pekah had captured while fighting Ahaz.

AMASA 2
II Chr 28:12

AMASAI

1. The chief of the thirty "mighty men" from the tribes of Judah and Benjamin who joined David's men at Ziklag (I Chr 12:16-18).

AMASAI 1
I Chr 12:18

AMASAI 2
I Chr 6:25, 35

2. The son of Elkanah; a Levite of the family of Kohath. He appears also in the lists of musicians as the ancestor of Heman the singer in the time of David (I Chr 6:22, 25, 31, 33, 35).

AMASAI 3
I Chr 15:24

3. A priest in the time of David. He sounded the trumpet before the ark when David brought it to Jerusalem.

AMASAI 4
II Chr 29:12

4. A Levite of the family of Kohath whose son Mahath assisted in the cleansing of the Temple as ordered by King Hezekiah in the first year of his reign (II Chr 29:3-5, 12).

AMASHAI
Neh 11:13

AMASHAI The son of Azareel; a priest residing in Jerusalem in Nehemiah's time.

AMASIAH
II Chr 17:16

AMASIAH The son of Zichri, of the tribe of Judah. He was one of the commanders in King Jehoshaphat's army, and headed 200,000 men (II Chr 17:12, 16).

AMAZIAH 1
I Chr 6:45

AMAZIAH ("Yah is strong").

1. A Levite of the family of Merari. He was appointed by King David to "the service of the song" before the tabernacle (I Chr 6:31-32, 45).

AMAZIAH 2
I Chr 4:34

2. Father of Joshah of the tribe of Simeon (I Chr 4:24, 34).

View of the Valley of Salt where King Amaziah defeated the Edomites.

AMAZIAH 3
II Kgs 12:21;
13:12; 14:1, 8-
9, 11, 13, 15,
17-18, 21, 23;
15:1, 3. I Chr
3:12. II Chr
24:27; 25:1, 5,
9-11, 13-15,
17-18, 20-21,
23, 25-27;
26:1, 4

3. King of Judah (c. 798-769 B.C.). Amaziah succeeded his father Joash at the age of 25 and reigned for 29 years. His mother was Jehoaddin of Jerusalem, and his wife was Jecholiah (II Kgs 14:2). After consolidating his hold on the throne, he executed the men who had murdered his father but spared their children in accordance with the law of Moses (II Kgs 14:1-6; II Chr 25:1-4).

Amaziah assembled a force of 30,000 men from Judah and Benjamin to re-conquer Edom, which had gained its independence from Judah some 50 years earlier (II Kgs 8:20-22). Amaziah won a major victory in the Valley of Salt, capturing Sela, and killing 10,000 Edomites (II Kgs 14:7; II Chr 25:5, 11). Amaziah had also hired 100,000 men from Israel to participate in the battle, but gave up the idea in view of the opposition it aroused. He dismissed the men, although he had already paid for their recruitment. The discharged soldiers were displeased and on their way home they raided cities in Judah, indulging in plunder and murder (II Chr 25:6-10, 13). When Amaziah declared war on Joash, the king of Israel, Joash warned Amaziah that he would be defeated — comparing Judah to a thistle that confronts a cedar tree and is trampled by a passing wild beast. Amaziah did not heed the warning, and the confrontation took place at Beth Shemesh in Judah, where Amaziah's troops were routed and he himself was taken prisoner. Joash broke the walls of Jerusalem to enter the city and plunder it; a great amount of Temple treasure and hostages were carried off to Samaria (II Kgs 14:8-14; II Chr 25:17-24).

Amaziah worshiped the pagan gods of the Edomites. This led to a conspiracy against him and he was forced to flee to Lachish where he was killed (II Chr 25:14-15; II Kgs 14:17-19; 25-27). He was succeeded by his 16-year old son Azariah (Uzziah) (II Kgs 14:21; 15:1; II Chr 26:1).

4. A priest in Bethel during the reign of Jeroboam II. He tried to stop Amos from prophesying and told the king that the prophet was conspiring against him. But Amos refused to be intimidated by Amaziah, predicting that the priest's wife would become a harlot, his children would be slain, and Amaziah himself would die on unclean land (i.e., outside of Israel) (Amos 7:10-17).

AMAZIAH 4
Amos 7:10, 12, 14

AMEN A Hebrew word transliterated in Greek or sometimes translated "truly" (Jer 28:6, Septuagint), "let it happen," or "so be it" (Jer 11:5). In one text it is possible that God is called Amen or "God of Truth" (Is 65:16).

Amen is an exclamation by which listeners participate in a prayer, doxology, blessing or curse and declare their willingness to bear the results of this participation. By saying "Amen", the speaker promises to do as commanded by the king or God, and asks God to do what he has promised or what is requested in the prayer (I Kgs 1:36; Jer 11:5; 28:6).

Such a response can also be liturgical; e.g. when the wife accused of adultery responds to the curse of the priest with "Amen, so be it" (Num 5:22) and especially when the people respond to the curses of the Levites (Deut 27:15-26).

The doxological Amen is a special liturgical response with early roots going back at least to the Exile in Babylon (Ps 106:46-48). Although perhaps not used in the Herodian Temple, elsewhere the benediction "Blessed be the Lord", uttered by the leader or choir brought the congregation to respond with the word Amen (I Chr 16:36). The division of the books of Psalms was marked either with a single (Ps 106:48) or a double Amen (Ps 41:13; 72:19; 89:52).

The NT usage of Amen is mainly consistent with the above. It forms a response to a spoken prayer which all have understood (I Cor 14:16), to a doxology (Rev 1:6; 5:14), or to a promise of the heavenly Christ (Rev 22:20). Paul declares that the Christ proclaimed by him "was never a blend of Yes and No. With him it was and is, Yes. He is the Yes and Amen pronounced upon God's promises, every one of them." He argues further that this is the reason why, "when we give glory to God, it is through Christ Jesus that we say Amen" (II Cor 1:19-20, New English Bible). Three unique usages of the NT writers are reflected in this Pauline affirmation. "The Amen" becomes one of the titles of Christ as the faithful and the true witness (Rev 3:14). Paul also seems to be in touch with the solemn use of this formula by Jesus, reflected most strongly in the Johannine writings where it appears some 24 times in almost stereotypical fashion. The fact that the gospel tradition attributes it exclusively to the lips of Jesus, indicates something of the importance attached to it as a solemn statement having the force of an oath (Luke 23:43).

AMI The head of a family of exiles who returned from Babylon described as among "the sons of Solomon's servants" (Ezra 2:1, 55, 57). He is referred to as Amon in Nehemiah 7:59.

AMI
Ezra 2:57

AMITTAI ("true", "faithful"). Father of the prophet Jonah who was from Gath Hepher in the territory of Zebulun.

AMITTAI
II Kgs 14:25.
Jonah 1:1

AMMAH ("cubit"). A hill "before Giah" in Benjamin on the way from

AMMAH
II Sam 2:24

View of Ammah.

Gibeon toward the descent into the Jordan Valley. The exact site has not been identified. Abner, fighting for Saul's son Ishbosheth, was defeated by Joab's forces at Gibeon. After the battle he was pursued by Joab and Abishai. When Abner reached the hill of Ammah he asked for a truce and the troops returned to their respective camps (II Sam 2:24-30).

AMMIEL ("my kinsman is God").

1. One of the 12 men selected by Moses to spy out the land of Canaan. He was the son of Gemalli, and represented the tribe of Dan (Num 13:1-3, 12).

2. The father of Machir in whose house Mephibosheth, the son of Jonathan, was hidden at Lo Debar (II Sam 9:1-5). Later, when David fled Jerusalem because of Absalom's conspiracy, Ammiel was among those who aided him at Mahanaim (II Sam 17:27-29).

3. The father of Bathsheba, David's wife (Bathsheba is named as the daughter of Eliam in II Sam 11:3).

4. The sixth son of Obed-Edom; he was one of the gatekeepers in the Temple (I Chr 26:1, 4-5).

AMMIHUD ("my kinsman is splendor").

1. The father of Elishama, who was the leader of the tribe of Ephraim in the wilderness.

2. The father of Shemuel from the tribe of Simeon in the time of Moses.

3. The father of Pedahel from the tribe of Naphtali in the time of Moses.

4. The father of Talmai the king of Geshur to whom Absalom fled in fear of his father's anger after killing Amnon.

5. The son of Omri and a descendant of Perez of Judah. He was the father of Uthai and is listed among the first inhabitants to settle in Jerusalem after the return from Babylonian Exile.

AMMINADAB ("my kinsman is generous").

1. A son of Ram of the family of Hezron of the tribe of Judah and the father of Nahshon who was the leader of the tribe in the wilderness (I Chr 2:5, 9-10). His daughter Elisheba was the wife of Aaron (Ex 6:23). He was an ancestor of King David (Ruth 4:19-22), and of Jesus (Matt 1:4, 16; Luke 3:23, 33).

2. A son of Kohath and the father of Korah (I Chr 6:22) in the genealogy of the Levites (in verse 38 he is listed as Izhar, as well as in Ex 6:21).

3. A Levite, head of the family of the sons of Uzziel and among those chosen by David to carry the ark to Jerusalem (I Chr 15:10-12).

AMMISHADDAI The father of Ahiezer of the tribe of Dan who was the leader of his tribe in the wilderness (Num 1:1, 12; 2:25).

AMMIZABAD The son of Benaiah who was one of King David's thirty "mighty men".

AMMON, AMMONITES ("children of Ammon"). A people whose origin the Bible ascribes to the incestuous union of Lot with his younger daughter who bore him a son, Ben-Ammi, "the father of the people of Ammon to this day" (Gen 19:38). The land east of the River Jordan, on the north bank of the River Jabbok, was also called after the Ammonites who, according to archeological evidence, settled there at the beginning of the 13th century B.C., while the Moabites and the Edomites settled further south. The Ammonites may have originated from the Amorites (Num 21:25-31). Already in the time of Moses, the Ammonites — like the Moabites — were excluded from the Israelite community (Deut 23:3). There was continuous enmity between the Israelites and the semi-nomadic Ammonites who tried to encroach on the Israelite territory. Early in the period of the Judges, Jephthah

AMMIEL 1
Num 13:12

AMMIEL 2
II Sam 9:4-5;
17:27

AMMIEL 3
I Chr 3:5

AMMIEL 4
I Chr 26:5

AMMIHUD 1
Num 1:10;
2:18; 7:48, 53;
10:22. I Chr
7:26

AMMIHUD 2
Num 34:20

AMMIHUD 3
Num 34:28

AMMIHUD 4
II Sam 13:37

AMMIHUD 5
I Chr 9:4

AMMINADAB 1
Ex 6:23. Num
1:7; 2:3; 7:12,
17; 10:41.
Ruth 4:19-20.
I Chr 2:10.
Matt 1:4.
Luke 3:33

AMMINADAB 2
I Chr 6:22

AMMINADAB 3
I Chr 15:10-11

AMMISHADDAI
Num 1:12;
2:25; 7:66, 71;
10:25

AMMIZABAD
I Chr 27:6

AMMON,
AMMONITES
Gen 19:38.
Num 21:24.
Deut 2:19-20,
37; 3:11, 16;
23:3. Josh
12:2; 13:10,
25. Judg 3:13;
10:6-7, 9, 11,
17-18; 11:4-6,
8-9, 12-15, 27-
33, 36; 12:1-3.
I Sam 11:1-2,
11; 12:12;

Ammonite sculptures of deities found at Rabbat Ammon. 8th-7th centuries B.C. (The two top ones: M. Dayan Collection, Israel Museum; bottom: Archaeology Museum, Amman)

Limestone head of a woman, part of the balustrade of a window at the palace of the Ammonite kings at Rabbat Ammon. 8th-7th centuries B.C. (Archaeological Museum, Amman)

The territory of the Ammonites.

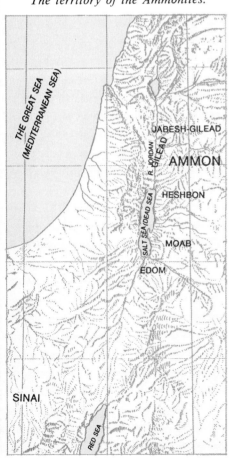

subdued the Ammonites (Judg 11:31-33). During the reign of Saul, the Ammonite king Nahash conquered Israelite territories and attempted to take Jabesh in Gilead. He besieged the city, proclaiming that its inhabitants could have peace on condition that he put out the right eyes of its menfolk. Hearing this, Saul rallied men from all the tribes of Israel and drove back the Ammonites (I Sam chap. 11). Nahash the Ammonite appears to have had good relations with David. At the beginning of the latter's reign, however, following the death of the Ammonite king, David sent men to comfort his son Hannun; the messengers were humiliated and this prompted a long war at the end of which Ammon was defeated (II Sam 11:1-6). The Ammonites sought military assistance from the Aramean states (II Sam 10:6; I Chr 19:6), but were repulsed. Subjugating Aram (II Sam 8:5-6; I Chr 18:5-6), David then proceeded to send another and stronger army against Ammon under the leadership of Joab who succeeded in taking their capital Rabbah (II Sam 11:1, 22-24; 12:26-29; I Chr 20:1).

During Solomon's reign peace was established and the ties became even stronger (I Kgs 14:21, 31; II Chr 12:13). Ammonite women were among Solomon's loves, and he married Naamah the Ammonitess. These women convinced him to build a sanctuary to their god Milcom, on the mountain opposite Jerusalem (I Kgs 11:7). The Ammonites were tributaries of Israel for almost a century before regaining their independence during the reign of Jehoshaphat. They joined the Moabites and the inhabitants of the mountainous region of Seir in fighting Judah, but the alliance suffered a crushing defeat (II Chr 10:1-4, 10-16). Jotham was faced with a rebellion of the Ammonites (II Chr 27:5), but succeeded in subduing them.

With the resurgence of Assyrian power under Tiglath-Pileser and his drive into Palestine (743-732 B.C.), all of Judah's vassal states were taken over. They retained their kings but had to pay tribute to the Assyrians in exchange for their protection. For most of the 7th century B.C. Ammon remained an Assyrian province. The transition from Assyrian to Babylonian rule at the end of this period did not bring any immediate change in its status. When Nebuchadnezzar attacked Ashkelon in c. 604 B.C. "all the kings of the land of Heth" paid tribute to him and this apparently included the king of Ammon. The Ammonites joined the Chaldeans in suppressing Jehoiakim's rebellion (II Kgs 24:1-2). The prophet Ezekiel describes the king of Babylon standing at crossroads, one leading to Rabbah, the other to Jerusalem (Ezek 21:19-22), and choosing to march on Jerusalem. When the Jews returned from Exile in Babylon, Nehemiah forbade them to marry Ammonites and Edomites (Neh 13:23). At that time Ammon was governed by Tobiah — possibly an appointee of the Persian rulers (Neh 2:19; 4:7; 6:14). By then many Jews had settled in this area. Under the Ptolemies it became a Jewish political entity, called Ammonitis. Its capital was Birta, or Tyros (today Araq el-Emir), the other important city being Rabbath Ammon renamed Philadelphia. At the end of the Seleucid period the whole region was known as Perea.

AMNON ("faithful").

1. The eldest son of King David, born in Hebron. His mother was Ahinoam the Jezreelitess (II Sam 3:2). Lusting after his half-sister Tamar, who was very beautiful, he lured her to his quarters by feigning illness and requesting her to prepare his food; he then raped her and cast her out (II Sam 13:1-14). When King David heard of this he was very angry but did not punish his son. However, Tamar's brother Absalom, enraged by Amnon's treatment of his sister, swore to avenge her (II Sam 13:15-22). Two years later Absalom invited Amnon and all the other

14:47. II Sam 8:12; 10:1-3, 6, 8, 10-11, 14, 19; 11:1; 12:9, 26, 31; 17:27; 23:37. I Kgs 11:1, 5, 7, 33; 14:21, 31. II Kgs 23:13; 24:2. I Chr 11:39; 18:11; 19:1-3, 6-7, 9, 11-12, 15, 19; 20:1, 3. II Chr 12:13; 20:1, 10, 22-23; 24:26; 26:8; 27:5. Ezra 9:1. Neh 2:10, 19; 4:3, 7; 13:1, 23. Ps 83:7. Is 11:14. Jer 9:26; 25:21; 27:3; 40:11, 14; 41:10, 15; 49:1-2, 6. Ezek 21:20, 28; 25:2-3, 5, 10. Dan 11:41. Amos 1:13. Zeph 2:8-9

AMNON I II Sam 3:2; 13:1-4, 6-10, 15, 20, 22, 26-29, 32-33, 39. I Chr 3:1

royal princes to a sheepshearing celebration at his estate at Baal Hazor. When Amnon's heart was merry with wine Absalom ordered his men to kill him (II Sam 13:23-33) and he then fled to Talmai, the son of the king of Geshur (II Sam 13:34-38).

2. Listed among the remote descendants of Judah. He was one of the sons of Shimon, together with Rinnah, Ben-Hanan and Tilon (I Chr 4:1, 20).

AMOK A priest who returned with Zerubbabel from captivity in Babylon (Neh 12:1, 7) and the ancestor of a priestly family represented later by his son Eber (Neh 12:12, 20).

AMON

1. The governor of Samaria during the reign of King Ahab. When the prophet Micaiah, the son of Imlah, predicted that Ahab would be unsuccessful in his attack against Ramoth Gilead, the king was angered, and imprisoned Micaiah under the custody of Amon (I Kgs 22:26-27).

2. King of Judah (c. 641-640 B.C.), the son and successor of King Manasseh. He ascended the throne at the age of 22, and reigned for two years. His mother was Meshullemeth the daughter of Haruz of Jotbah. Amon continued the worship of idols as in his father's reign. He was murdered in a court conspiracy by his servants. However, "the people of the land" subsequently executed all those who had conspired against him and placed his eight-year old son Josiah on the throne (II Kgs 21:1-26).

3. The family head of a group of exiles returning from Babylon, included in the list of "the children of Solomon's servants" (Neh 7:57-59) (he is referred to as Ami in Ezra 2:57).

4. A local Egyptian god of No (No-Amon, Thebes) who rose to the position of "king of the gods" under the name of Amon-Re (Amon-the sun) and whose high priest was head of all the Egyptian priesthood.

AMORITE(S) One of the peoples of northern Syria and Mesopotamia from about 3000 B.C., who also inhabited the land of Canaan before the Israelite conquest. The name derives from *Martu,* meaning "west" in Sumerian, and some believe that the *Martu* mentioned in Mesopotamian sources is the same as *Amu* in contemporary Egyptian sources, where the reference is to wanderers who overran Syria and Palestine and reached the borders of Egypt. Somewhat later they are referred to in the Akkadian documents as *Amurru,* which is very close to the biblical name. During the 2nd millennium B.C. the Amorites spread over large areas in Mesopotamia and east of the Jordan, pressing southwards and westwards. They reached their zenith in the middle of the same millennium, but declined rapidly and merged with the newly arriving elements, the Horites, Hittites, Canaanites, Hebrews, Arameans and other peoples.

From the 15th century B.C. onwards the name Amurru appears as a geographical designation and refers to the area of the Lebanon, central and southern Syria. This kingdom was sponsored by Egypt as a buffer state between the Egyptian-held territories in the south and the Hittite menace to the north. The Amorite kingdom was conquered from time to time by each of the struggling parties, until it was finally taken by the Hittites after the battle of Kedesh-on-the-Orontes in 1297 B.C. This state of affairs is well described in the El Amarna Letters. While the Hittites were pressing southwards the Amorite kingdom had to withstand growing pressure from the rising Assyrian kingdom. When contacts were established between them for the first time, in the days of the patriarchs, the Amorites possessed a culture that was influenced by that of Mesopotamia, with local Canaanite affinities.

Statue at Karnak of Pharaoh Amenophis III represented as the god Amon.

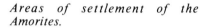

Areas of settlement of the Amorites.

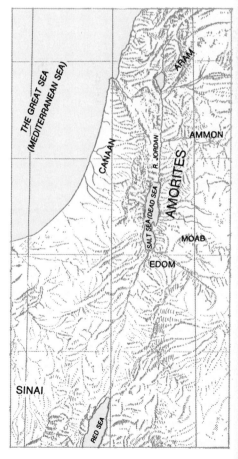

In the 18th-17th centuries B.C., the Amorites dwelt in several places in Palestine (Gen 14:7; 48:22), alongside the Hittites (Gen chap. 23). According to Deuteronomy (1:7, 20) the Amorites occupied the mountains. In the period of the Israelite conquest the kings of Jerusalem, Hebron, Jarmuth, Lachish and Eglon were Amorites (Josh chap. 10). The Gibeonites were the remnant of the Amorites (II Sam 21:2). The Amorites also dwelt far to the south, as far as Akrabbim (Judg 1:36), but paid tribute to the house of Joseph (Judg 1:35). To the east the realm of Sihon, king of the Amorites, extended from Arnon to the Jabbok (Num 21:21-31; Josh 12:2, etc.). Another Amorite kingdom, farther to the north, was that of Og, king of Bashan (Deut 3:8; 4:47), which was also conquered by the Israelites (Josh 12:4-5). In the period of the United Monarchy, when there was peace between Israel and the Amorites (I Sam 7:14), they paid tribute to Solomon (I Kgs 9:20 ff). There is no later mention of their history in the Bible.

II Chr 8:7. Ezra 9:1. Neh 9:8. Ps 135:11; 136:19. Ezek 16:3; 45. Amos 2:9-10

AMOS

1. A prophet who denounced King Jeroboam II and wealthy officials for oppressing the poor people of Israel. Amos was a Judean who pursued his prophetic activity in northern Israel, especially at Bethel.

AMOS 1 Amos 1:1; 7:8, 10-12, 14; 8:2

Jasper seal bearing the inscription "Amos the scribe" and two men beside an altar with their hands raised in prayer. 8th-7th centuries B.C. (Israel Musuem)

(right)
View from Tekoa, the birthplace of Amos, looking east.

His home was the small village of Tekoa, 10 miles (16 km) south of Jerusalem. According to Amos 7:14 prior to his being selected by God to prophecy, he worked as a herdsman, and was also a dresser of sycamore trees, slitting their fruit in order to accelerate the ripening process. Since sycamore figs did not grow in Tekoa, but thrived in lower altitudes, Amos must have traveled some distance from home in order to carry out his work. His call to prophesy occurred sometime during the middle of the 8th century B.C. during a period of prosperity and national expansion rivaled only by the era of Solomon. But the military victories, construction of elegant houses, and endless feasting was only one side of the picture. Amos saw the deeper implications of these circumstances: the poor who suffered at the hands of the land-grabbing rich, and the disparity between people who feasted and those who went hungry. He laid much of the blame on the wealthy minority. When he once went so far as to predict the death of King Jeroboam, Amaziah, the priest of Bethel transmitted the threat to the king (Amos 7:10-17).

Although Amaziah accused Amos of conspiracy, he nevertheless urged the seer to flee south of Judah and carry on his prophetic endeavor there. Bethel was effectively ruled "off limits" to him, for it was the royal sanctuary. Amos objected that he was not a professional prophet but that the Lord had taken him from his secular vocation and given him specific orders to prophesy against Israel (cf Amos 3:8). The prophet then announced an awful fate for Amaziah and his family: his wife would become a harlot, his sons and daughters slain, and Amaziah himself would die in an alien land, having seen his own property taken from him. (See AMOS, BOOK OF).

AMOS 2
Luke 3:25

2. Son of Nahum and father of Mattathiah, from the genealogy of Jesus.

AMOS, BOOK OF The third book in the twelve Minor Prophets according to the Hebrew order. Amos is the first of the classical literary prophets and he inaugurated a new epoch in Israelite thought and theology. By profession a herdsman and pincher of sycamore fruit (i.e. one who accelerates the ripening of the fruit to make it edible), he lived in Tekoa, some 10 miles (16 km) south of Jerusalem, until he was called by God to go and prophesy in northern Israel (1:1; 7:14). His oracles,

Fragment from the Book of Amos, found at Qumran. (Shrine of the Book, Jerusalem)

primarily devoted to the catastrophe about to befall Israel, were uttered in Bethel and probably also in Samaria. They preceded the westward expansion of the Assyrians under Tiglath-Pileser III in 745 B.C., since the enemy who would cause the downfall of the nation and send it into exile (5:5, 27; 6:7; 9:9 — a theme uttered for the first time by Amos) is never identified by name. Thus his prophetic pronouncements, dated during the reign of King Uzziah of Judah (769-733 B.C.) and Jeroboam II of Israel (784-748), all stem from the first half of the 8th century.

The book is arranged according to common literary genres. It commences with six stereotypically structured oracles against foreign nations: Arameans, Philistines, Phoenicians, Edomites, Ammonites and Moabites, followed by one against Judah, and culminating in the oracle against Israel (1:3-2:16). They are all introduced by the messenger formula, "Thus says the Lord", followed by the staircase numerical pattern, "for three sins and for four;" which leads to the pronouncement of the absolute irrevocability of the divine decision, "I will not turn away its punishment"; the specific heinous crimes are stated; and the corresponding punishment is announced. The oracles against the nations are also linked together in a concatenous pattern whose sequential ordering is determined by the mnemonic device of catchwords, phrases and ideas common to the two oracles contiguous to one another. There is no reason to doubt their authenticity, whether historical or literary. Whereas the other nations are condemned for historical acts of barbarity and inhumanity against one another, Judah is accused of religious transgressions, and Israel — the *raison d'être* for the entire literary unit — is taken to task for a series of moral and ethical crimes which include oppression of the poor by many different ways and means. Herein lies one of the major innovations of classical prophecy in general and Amos in particular: morality becomes the supreme value by which Israel is judged, and by which the destiny of the nation is ultimately determined. Israel was the one and only nation with whom the Lord conducted a covenant; hence she, and she alone, is held responsible for all social transgressions, no matter how insignificant (3:2), with minor infractions weighed as gravely as the barbaric atrocities of other nations.

The next series of oracles, chapters 3-5, are grouped together by their introductory words, "Hear this word" or "Hear" (3:1 ff, 13ff; 4:1 ff; 5:1 ff). These consist of moral reprimands and reproofs focusing on the sins committed by the affluent and opulent upper classes of Samaria. Within this section is the unique series of rhetorical questions characterized by analogies drawn from common experience and well-known empirical phenomena. By skillful logic, the prophet draws his audience into the flow of the inextricable sequence of cause and effect with relation to events and happenings in both the animal and human realms of existence. All this serves as justification and legitimization for his own prophetic commission. Forcefully and cogently, he argues that prophecy is not a self-generating act, but that the prophet is irresistibly compelled to deliver God's words: "A lion has roared! Who will not fear? The Lord God has spoken! Who can but prophesy?" (3:3-8).

In 4:6-12 there is a recitation of wasted opportunity. Successive calamities and chastisements having failed to induce Israel to repent, she is warned to prepare for the final climactic encounter with God.

Next come two woe-oracles, 5:18 ff; 6:1 ff. The first contains the "Day of the Lord" oracle, in which Amos reverses the popular concept prevalent in his day. Unlike the people's expectation of a time of light and salvation, the future appearance of the Lord will be one of darkness and disaster (5:18-20). The second gives a vivid description of the hedonistic life-style of the upper classes of the north, who spend their time sprawling on beds of ivory, wining and dining and anointing their bodies with the finest of oils. Their luxurious living habits coupled with their false sense of security have made them totally insensitive to the tragedy of their people (6:1-7). There then follows a group of five visions (7:1-3, 4-6, 7-9; 8:1-3; 9:1-4) interspersed with a biographical narrative (7:10-16) and a series of independent oracles (8:4-14; 9:7-10).

The visions escalate in severity from agricultural blights to the final destruction of the people. The first four have a common literary pattern, commencing with an identical introductory formula. In the first two — a swarm of locusts and a judgment by fire — Amos successfully intercedes, and the Lord withholds the punishment. The next two whose symbolic significance is not immediately understood by the prophet — the Lord standing by a wall with an instrument in his hand (not a plumbline as commonly assumed) and a basket of summer fruit — foreshadow the divine decision to execute judgment upon Israel. The final vision, which takes place by the altar in Bethel, represents the end of Israel. No place of escape will remain for them, not in Sheol, heaven, atop Mount Carmel, at the bottom of the ocean, or even in exile.

The biographical narrative recounts how Amaziah, the priest of Bethel, denounced Amos to King Jeroboam II, accusing him of sedition against the royal house, whereupon Amos was banished from the northern kingdom. Denying that he had chosen to be a prophet, Amos affirmed that he was summoned by the Lord from tending his flocks in order to deliver these oracles against the northern kingdom of Israel (7:14-16). His exact words are still the subject of two main interpretations: they are understood to be either, in the present tense, "I am no prophet...," which would be his public disavowal of any connection with the professional prophets; or in the past, "I was not a prophet...," which would be an assertion of the divine authority for his prophetic mission — "I was not a prophet..." until the Lord called me.

In 9:7-8, Amos declares that Israel cannot claim any precedence for divine favoritism. Just as the Lord brought them out of Egypt, so had he delivered the Philistines from Caphtor and the Syrians from Kir. And likewise the Lord who is the controller of history will punish any and every nation, including Israel, when they are found guilty.

The final literary unit contains an optimistic prophecy of comfort and consolation which describes the glorious future of the fallen "tabernacle of David" (9:11), a term which symbolizes the divided kingdom and not the end of the Davidic dynasty. Israel will be reunited as in the days of old (i.e., the Davidic-Solomonic period) and blessed with unfailing abundance and fertility; never again to be uprooted from its land. There is no reason to deny this concluding oracle to Amos himself.

Amos was a keen observer of urban life in Israel. He repeatedly denounced all acts of robbery, extortion, cheating, plunder, violence and miscarriage of justice. The rich, whether male or female (4:1, "cows of Bashan"), who prospered by exploiting the underprivileged classes, were leading Israel directly towards exile and destruction. Neither would strict observance of the cult save the people. In the bitter sarcasm of his attacks against the established legitimate cult (4:4-5; 5:4, 21-25), and cultic sites which were destined for destruction (3:14; 7:9; 9:1), Amos established the supremacy of morality over cultic observance. Only those who returned to the Lord and practiced righteousness would be saved (5:6, 14-15); they would be the surviving remnant (5:3, 15; 9:8). The Lord of Israel who is the judge of all nations (1:3-2:3; 9:7-8) is also praised in three doxologies and cosmic hymns (4:13; 5:8-9; 9:5-6).

Both in his polemics against popular beliefs and in his innovative ideas and distinctive literary style, Amos became the first of a series of major prophets who over the next 300 years shaped the existence of the nations of Israel and Judah.

OUTLINE

1:1-2:16	Oracles against foreign nations and against Israel
3:1-5:17	Reprimands and reproofs to Samaria
5:18-6:14	Prophecies of woe
7:1-9:6	Visions (locusts, judgment by fire, basket of fruit) forecasting doom
9:7-15	Hope and promise of restoration

AMOZ The father of the prophet Isaiah.

AMPHIPOLIS A city of Macedonia about 3 miles (5 km) from the Aegean Sea and about 30 miles (48 km) southwest of Philippi. In 167 B.C. when Macedonia was taken over by the Romans, it was divided into four districts. Amphipolis was chosen as the capital of the first district. Paul passed through here on his second missionary journey (Acts 17:1).

AMPLIAS (AMPLIATUS) A Christian in the congregation at Rome whom Paul greeted as "my beloved in the Lord" in his Epistle to the Romans.

AMRAM ("kinsman exalted").

1. The father of Moses, Aaron and Miriam, whose wife Jochebed was "his father's sister". Amram was the son of Kohath and Levi's grandson (Ex 6:18, 20; Num 26:59; I Chr 6:2-3; 23:12-13). He was the ancestor of the Levitical family who were designated as the Amramites (Num 3:19; 27; I Chr 26:23).

2. One of the sons of Bani, who, with others returning from Babylonian Exile, responded to the call to banish their pagan wives.

AMRAMITES The descendants of Amram, the grandson of Levi through Kohath. During the journey in the wilderness their camp was on the south of the tabernacle with all the families of the sons of Kohath, who were assigned duties in the sanctuary (Num 3:27-31).

AMRAPHEL King of Shinar in southern Mesopotamia, who, with Chedorlaomer king of Elam, and two other kings, attacked Sodom and other cities of the Valley of Siddim. Amraphel and his allies were later overtaken and routed by Abram who had come to the rescue of his nephew Lot (Gen 14:1-17).

AMZI ("my strength").

1. A Levite of the family of Merari, and ancestor of Ethan who was one of the Temple singers appointed by David (I Chr 6:31, 44, 46).

2. The son of Zechariah, and an ancestor of Adaiah, Amzi was listed as living in Jerusalem and doing service at the Temple in the time of Nehemiah.

ANAB A town in the southern part of Judah from which the Anakim were expelled by Joshua (Josh 11:21; 15:50). The site is identified with Anab, about 15 miles (24 km) south of Hebron.

AMOZ
II Kgs 19:2, 20; 20:1. II Chr 26:22; 32:20, 32. Is 1:1; 2:1; 13:1; 20:2; 37:2, 21; 38:1

AMPHIPOLIS
Acts 17:1

AMPLIAS
Rom 16:8

AMRAM 1
Ex 6:18, 20. Num 3:19; 26:58-59. I Chr 6:2-3, 18; 23:12-13; 24:20

AMRAM 2
Ezra 10:34

AMRAMITES
Num 3:27. I Chr 26:23

AMRAPHEL
Gen 14:1, 9

AMZI 1
I Chr 6:46

AMZI 2
Neh 11:12

ANAB
Josh 11:21; 15:50

Landscape in the vicinity of Anab.

ANAH A male and female name.

1. The daughter of Zibeon the Hivite and mother of Aholibamah (or Oholibamah), one of Esau's wives (Gen 36:2, 14, 18).

ANAH 1
Gen 36:2, 14, 18

2. A Horite clan chief; the fourth son of Seir "who found the water in the wilderness as he pastured the donkeys of his father Zibeon" (Gen 36:20, 24-25, 29).

ANAHARATH A town in the territory of the tribe of Issachar (Josh 19:18-19). It has been identified with modern en-Na'urah, a village in the Plain of Jezreel.

ANAIAH ("Yah has answered"). One of the men who stood at Ezra's side when he read the Law to the people and set his seal to the covenant (Neh 8:4-8).

ANAK, ANAKIM The son of Arba (Josh 15:13; 21:11), and a nation of giants who lived in Canaan before the Israelites. The city of Hebron owed its ancient name of Kirjath Arba to Arba "who was the greatest man among the Anakim" (Josh 14:15). The Anakim left a strong impression on the spies sent by Moses to explore the promised land, as reflected in their alarming report: "We were like grasshoppers in our own sight, and so we were in their sight." (Num 13:28, 32-33; Deut 2:21; 9:2). Most references to the Anakim in the Bible are connected with the southern part of the land of Israel, especially the Hebron region, which was then inhabited by Ahiman, Sheshai and Talmai, the descendants of

View in the neighborhood of Gaza, one of the places where the Anakim settled.

Anak (Num 13:22; Josh 15:14). They were driven out by Caleb (Josh 15:13-14), but in the summary of Joshua's conquest it is said that, although defeated, a remnant of the Anakim remained in Gaza, Gath and Ashdod (Josh 11:21-22).

ANAMIM A nation descended from Ham through his son Mizraim (Gen 10:6, 13; I Chr 1:11).

ANAMMELECH One of the deities worshiped by the Sheparvites, a people whom the king of Assyria brought to settle in Samaria (after 722 B.C.). The cult of Anammelech was said to involve child sacrifice.

ANAN One of those who signed Nehemiah's covenant to serve the Lord faithfully (Neh 10:1, 26).

ANANI ("cloudy"). The seventh son of Elionai, a descendant of Zerubbabel, listed among David's offspring (I Chr 3:1, 24).

ANANIAH

1. The father of Maaseiah, whose son Azariah helped to rebuild the walls of Jerusalem during the time of Nehemiah.

2. A village where members of the tribe of Benjamin settled after the return from Babylonian Exile (Neh 11:31-32).

It is believed to be the same as Bethany; today el-Azariyeh east of Jerusalem.

ANANIAS

1. A Christian of Jerusalem. He and his wife Sapphira were among those disciples who sold their property for the proceeds to be distributed among all the Christians in Jerusalem. But Ananias and Shapphira kept back a part of the money while pretending to give the full amount to the apostles. When Peter exposed his lie Ananias was struck dead. Sapphira appeared later before Peter and maintained the lie; she too was struck dead (Acts 4:32-37; 5:1-10).

ANANIAS 1
Acts 5:1, 3, 5

2. A Christian disciple living in Damascus when Paul arrived in that city after his conversion. Ananias had a vision in which he was instructed to go to Paul (Saul of Tarsus) to baptize him and give him back his sight. Ananias was at first hesitant as he knew the harm Paul had done to the Christians in Jerusalem. Finally he went boldly to Paul, explained Paul's vision on the road to Damascus, caused him to recover his sight and then Paul was baptized (Acts 9:10-19).

ANANIAS 2
Acts 9:10, 12-13, 17; 22:12

3. High priest who tried Paul when he was arrested in Jerusalem at the end of his third missionary journey (Acts 23:1-10). Later Ananias was among those who gave evidence against Paul in Caesarea when he was brought before the governor Felix (Acts 23:33-35; 24:1-9).

ANANIAS 3
Acts 23:2; 24:1

ANATH The father of Shamgar, the judge.

ANATH
Judg 3:31; 5:6

ANATHOTH, ANATHOTHITE

1. A priestly city in the territory of Benjamin (Josh 21:18; I Chr 6:54, 60). Two of David's "mighty men", Abiezer (II Sam 23:8, 27; I Chr 11:10, 28) and Jehu (I Chr 12:3), were Anathothites. Abiathar, the last chief priest descended from Eli, owned property in Anathoth and was banished there by Solomon (I Kgs 2:26). It was devastated by the Assyrian invading armies on their way to Jerusalem (Is 10:30). Jeremiah was from Anathoth and he first began to prophesy there, but his fellow citizens threatened his life and he predicted an ill fate to the city (Jer 1:1; 11:21-23). Jeremiah retained some ties with his native city, and was willing to redeem a field there from his cousin Hanameel (Jer 32:7-15). One hundred and twenty-eight men of Anathoth returned from Babylonian Exile with Zerubbabel (Ezra 2:2, 23). In the time of Nehemiah the city was settled by Benjamites (Neh 11:3, 32).

ANATHOTH,
ANATHOTHITE 1
Josh 21:18.
II Sam 23:27.
I Kgs 2:26.
I Chr 6:60;
11:28; 12:3;
27:12. Ezra
2:23. Neh
7:27; 10:19;
11:32. Is
10:30. Jer 1:1;
11:21, 23;
29:27; 32:7-9

Anathoth is probably a shortened form of Beth Anoth i.e., "the house of the goddess Anath". The name has been preserved in the modern Anata, a village 3 miles (5 km) north of Jerusalem. The original city was located about half a mile (1 km) to the southwest.

2. One of Becher's sons, a Benjamite.

ANATHOTH,
ANATHOTHITE 2
I Chr 7:8

Anata, north of Jerusalem, identified with Anathoth.

ANDREW
Matt 4:18;
10:2. Mark
1:16, 29; 3:18;
13:3. Luke
6:14. John
1:40, 44; 6:8;
12:22. Acts
1:13

ANDREW ("manly"). Son of Jonah (or John), and brother of Simon Peter; one of Jesus' first disciples (Matt 4:18-20). Jonah, or John, lived at Bethsaida on the northeast side of the Sea of Galilee (John 1:44). The two brothers had a fishing business in partnership with James and John (Matt 4:18; Mark 1:16; Luke 5:10). Andrew was a disciple of John the Baptist before he met Jesus. John the Baptist indicating Jesus said to Andrew and another unnamed person who had come to see him: "Behold the Lamb of God". The two then followed Jesus. Andrew became convinced that Jesus was the messiah and brought his brother Simon Peter to Jesus (John 1:35-41).

The two brothers returned to their fishing, but some time later, after John the Baptist had been arrested, Jesus saw Simon and Andrew by the Sea of Galilee and said to them: "Come after me, and I will make you become fishers of men" (Matt 4:18). He also called on James the son of Zebedee and his brother John, and they immediately followed Jesus (Mark 1:14-20). Simon and Andrew at this time lived at Capernaum (Mark 1:21, 29). Jesus always named Andrew among the first four apostles (Matt 10:2; Mark 3:14-18; Luke 6:13-14; Acts 1:13).

When the crowd that assembled near Tiberias to hear Jesus preach had to be fed, Andrew called attention to the boy who had loaves and fishes (John 6:5-9). At the time of the Passover festival celebration in Jerusalem, Andrew helped Philip to approach Jesus concerning some Greeks who wished to see him (John 12:20-22).

Andrew was one of the four apostles with Jesus on the Mount of Olives and inquired about the signs that would mark the End of the Age (Mark 13:3-4).

ANDRONICUS
Rom 16:7

ANDRONICUS A Christian of the congregation of Rome to whom Paul sent greetings along with Junia. Paul mentions them as "my kinsmen and my fellow prisoners" ("kinsmen" may simply mean "fellow-countrymen"). Like Paul, Andronicus had suffered imprisonment, and was now "of note among the apostles". He had become a Christian prior to Paul.

ANEM
I Chr 6:73

ANEM A city in the territory of Issachar given "with its suburbs" to the Gershonites.

ANER

ANER 1
I Chr 6:70

1. A city in the territory of Manasseh given "with its suburbs" to the Kohathites.

ANER 2
Gen 14:13, 24

2. One of the three Amorite chiefs of Hebron who were allies of Abraham and aided him in the pursuit of the four invading kings who had taken Lot captive (Gen 14:13). After the victory, Abraham refused to take any of the spoil but saw to it that his allies Aner and his brothers Eshcol and Mamre got their share (Gen 14:23).

ANGELS The biblical view of angels is that they are celestial beings, superior to mortal man, but always subordinate to the one God. Their primary function is that of messengers (the root of the Hebrew word for angel is "to send"). They are intermediaries between the celestial and terrestrial worlds, who also serve and praise God.

Since the angels sometimes appear in a human image, it is difficult at times to know whether a human or a celestial messenger is being described. Abraham was visited by "three men" (actually angels) who informed him that Sarah would have a son, despite her old age (Gen 18:2). So, too, Joshua, who saw an angel in the guise of a human being standing with a drawn sword (Josh 5:13-14). An angel of the Lord appeared to Balaam (Num 22:22), Manoah and his wife (Judg chap. 13), David (I Chr 21:16) and the shepherds in Bethlehem (Luke 2:9-15). In all these passages the angel delivers a message, performs an act, or sometimes does both. Instances of angels announcing the birth of a divine figure or an important personality are frequently found in the Scriptures, i.e., the birth of Isaac (Gen chap. 18), Samson (Judg chap. 13), John the Baptist (Luke 1:11), Jesus (Luke 1:26).

In several biblical narratives the speech of an angel of the Lord is interwoven with a reference to the presence of God. For example, in the Hagar stories the angel speaks to Hagar, but she acknowledges that it is God who speaks (Gen 16:7-13). In the revelation of God to Moses at Mount Horeb, the angel of the Lord and God himself are evident in the revelationary process. So too, the angel and God appear to Gideon (Judg 6:11 ff). Some scholars believe that the later editors of the narrative introduced the figure of the angel into the stories in order to detract from the obvious anthropomorphisms of God appearing and speaking. In that case the angel serves as the intermediary who appears and who speaks to the recipient of God's word.

Several categories can be distinguished among the angels. One is that of malevolent and benevolent angels. A malevolent angel, Satan, later also called Belial, is an instrument of God's punishment or may function as one who tests man, e.g. Job. Nevertheless Satan in the OT is entirely within God's power, and only in subsequent tradition did he become an independent evil demon. In post-OT literature there arose a belief in fallen angels who, because of their pride or in their attempt to usurp the position of God, were thrown out of heaven.

The majority of angels, on the other hand, are benevolent. Their primary function is to praise and minister to God. As functional extensions of God they sometimes intervene in human situations by rewarding or supporting the faithful or punishing the unjust.

The three faithful men, Shadrach, Meshach and Abed-Nego, though thrown in a fiery furnace by Nebuchadnezzar, king of Babylon, were not harmed at all, because they were protected by an angel (Dan 3:25-28); angels in general protect the righteous (Dan 10:13, 20; 11:1; 12:1). The first two angels identified by name are Gabriel and Michael (Dan 8:16; 9:21; 10:13, 21; 12:1). In the apocryphal book of Tobit, the angel Raphael is the constant companion of Tobias, Tobit's son, and reveals to him magic formulas to cure his father's blindness (Tob 5:4-11:19).

Another division is that of angels and archangels. Seven archangels head the world of angels: "the seven holy angels, which present the prayers of the saints, and which go in and out before the glory of the Holy One" (Tob 12:15). The seven archangels are Uriel, Michael, Jeremiel, Gabriel, Raphael, Raguel and Sariel. These angels are sent to carry out significant tasks or to deliver important messages (Luke 1:19, 26; Rev 8:2, 6). There are also cherubs and seraphs who praise the Lord of hosts (Is chap. 6), stand guard at the entrance of the Garden of Eden (Gen 3:24; cf Ezek 28:14, 16) and transport God through heaven (II Sam 22:11; Ps 18:10). Another name which is used collectively for angels is "hosts": the Lord is the God of the "host of heaven", a celestial army (I Kgs 22:19; II Chr 18:18).

In post-biblical times, Jewish and Christian tradition accepted the idea that righteous people after their death could be greater than angels. Moses was considered in such a way, and in the Epistle to the Hebrews Jesus is also glorified after his death, being made so much better than the angels (Heb 1:4 ff). In apocalyptic literature the descriptions of angels are all characterized by a kind of curiosity in penetrating hidden worlds like those of the angels.

The Pharisees, who represented the popular opinion, showed little interest in angels, while the Sadducees, who were more aristocratic in their thinking, completely denied their existence (Acts 23:8).

In the NT angels are prominent in the stories of the infancy of Jesus, the Resurrection and elsewhere. However, the role of the angel — as messenger or member of the heavenly host — is similar to that in the OT. Any worship of angels is condemned (Col 2:18). They are prominent in revelations but with their role unchanged from that of the earlier parts of the Bible.

ANIAM The fourth son of Shemida in the list of descendants of Manasseh (I Chr 7:14, 19).

ANIM A city in the mountains of southern Judah mentioned in the distribution of land in the days of Joshua (Josh 15:48, 50). It has been identified with Khirbet Ghuwein, about 11 miles (17.5 km) south of Hebron.

ANIMALS Given below in alphabetical order are the animals mentioned in the Bible. It is to be noted that translators differ as to the precise identification of some of them.

ANT A small insect noted in the Bible for its industrious traits.

ANTELOPE There is uncertainty as to the exact identification of the animal mentioned in Deuteronomy 14:5 which is translated "antelope" in certain versions. It could have been an antelope or deer. According to Isaiah 51:20 it is caught in a net.

The antelope has a slit hoof, is a cud-chewing animal and was consequently listed among the animals permitted to the Israelites as food (Deut 14:5).

APE See MONKEY below

ASP A name referring to several venomous snakes, especially the COBRA. It is used figuratively in the OT when speaking of violent men (Ps 140:1-3) and of the tongue of the unrighteous (Rom 3:13).

ASS See DONKEY below

BADGER The Hebrew word translated as badger in the KJV, is always mentioned in connection with its fur or pelt, which was used to cover the tabernacle in the Temple (Ex 25:5 etc.). However, since the skin of the badger is not suitable for that purpose, the word should be translated differently, but scholars are still not in agreement as to its identity. Some favor the dolphin. See also ROCK BADGER.

BAT A small flying mammal listed among the unclean birds unfit to be eaten (Lev 11:19; Deut 14:18). It is also mentioned once by Isaiah as a creature inhabiting dark caves (Is 2:20).

BEAR A large, four-footed mammal, covered with a thick coat of fur; the Syrian brown bear was indigenous to biblical Israel until the early 20th century. Although a known carnivore (I Sam 17:34), the bear subsists mostly on fruits, vegetables and insects. It is generally harmless to humans, but is known to become dangerous when it or its young are threatened or provoked (II Sam 17:8; Prov 17:12; Hos 13:8). Two female bears attacked the youths who mocked Elisha, mauling 42 of them (II Kgs 2:24). The bear also served as a symbol for Media in Daniel 7:5. Job twice refers to the stellar constellation known as "the Bear" (Job 9:9; 38:32).

BEE The bee is mentioned four times in the Bible, only once (Judg 14:8) in connection with the honey it produces. Other mentions of honey ("milk and honey") refer to that extracted from dates. Elsewhere, the enemies of Israel are likened to bees.

BITTERN A small bird, related to the heron, which lives in marshes. It is mentioned in Zephaniah in the description of the creatures which will inhabit desolate places. The identification of the Hebrew word for this bird is still problematic.

BOAR A wild pig, mentioned only once in the Bible: "the boar out of the woods" (Ps 80:13), which uproots a "vine out of Egypt" (Ps 80:8), alluding to Israel.

Addax (antelope)

Bees

Young boars

A bull depicted on a zodiac wheel on the mosaic floor at Beth Alpha.

Camel

Caterpillar

Chameleon

The same Hebrew word is also translated as "swine" in the lists of unclean animals in Leviticus 11:7 and Deuteronomy 14:8.

BULL Male cattle, used in the biblical world as a work animal (Deut 22:10; 25:4), but of primary importance to the Israelites for sacrificial purposes. As the largest sacrificial animal, the bull was offered for the most serious offenses: a sin of the high priest who brought guilt upon the entire nation (Lev 4:3), a sin committed by the people as a whole (Lev 4:13-14), as a priestly sin offering on the Day of Atonement (Lev 16:6). Bulls are also mentioned in the Bible as images of power and might (Deut 33:17; Is 34:7; Jer 50:27). The image of the bull is also used figuratively to describe the strength of Joseph (Deut 33:17) and the enemies of Israel (Ps 68:30; Is 34:7; Jer 50:27). There were 12 bronze bulls (oxen) supporting the bronze sea in the Temple of Jerusalem (Jer 52:20; cf I Kgs 7:25).

BUZZARD A bird of prey listed among the unclean birds unfit to be eaten. There is considerable doubt as to the bird's exact identification.

CALF See COW below

CAMEL The camel was part of daily life in biblical times and is frequently mentioned throughout the Scriptures. The single-humped Arabian camel was the standard mode of transportation in the ancient Near East. Even though the date of domestication of the camel is later than the patriarchal period, the earliest references list the patriarchs as owners of camels: Abraham sent his servant to Mesopotamia on camel-back, in search of a wife for Isaac (Gen 24:10); and Jacob presented his brother Esau with a gift of 30 milk camels and their young (Gen 32:15). These passages, however, (along with Gen 12:16; 30:43; 31:17), are considered by scholars to be anachronistic.

Camels were of vital importance to trade and commerce (Gen 37:25; I Kgs 10:2; Is 30:6). Long journeys would have been impossible without these sturdy animals, which are capable of several days of desert travel without stopping for water. They were also used by neighboring nations and warring tribes (Judg 6:3-5; I Sam 27:9; 30:17; I Chr 5:19-22). There were so many camels in the kingdom of David that a special overseer, Obil the Ishmaelite, was appointed (I Chr 27:30). On their way from Babylon the exiles used 435 camels and 6,720 donkeys (Neh 7:69). Isaiah foresees camels bringing the gifts of Midian and Ephah to Zion (Is 60:6) and the exiles returning to Jerusalem on camels (Is 66:20).

Jesus twice referred to camels in hyperbole: he told his disciples "it is easier for a camel to go through the eye of a needle than for a rich man to enter the kingdom of God" (Matt 19:24; Mark 10:25; Luke 18:25), and criticized the Pharisees and scribes, "who strain out a gnat and swallow a camel" (Matt 23:24). Elsewhere in the NT, it is mentioned that John the Baptist wore camel-hair garments (Matt 3:4; Mark 1:6).

Camels chew their cud, but do not possess split hooves; they are therefore considered unclean and unfit to eat (Lev 11:4; Deut 14:7).

CATERPILLAR An insect; the larval stage of a butterfly or moth which feeds upon leafy vegetation. The biblical references refer to its destructive effects.

CHAMELEON One of the eight creeping reptiles which are an abomination and may not be eaten (Lev 11:29-30); moreover "whoever touches them when they are dead shall be unclean until evening" (Lev 11:31). It occurs only once, in Leviticus 11:30 and not all scholars agree on its translation as chameleon, though it is a member of the lizard family.

COBRA A highly poisonous snake; the cobra mentioned in the Bible is thought to be the Egyptian cobra, rare in present-day Israel. According to Psalms 58:4-5, the wicked "are like the deaf cobra that stops its ear, which will not heed the voice of charmers, charming ever so skillfully". In the future, those who trust in the Lord "shall tread upon the lion and the cobra" (Ps 91:13), and "the nursing child shall play by the cobra's hole" (Is 11:8). See also SERPENT.

COLT The young of a horse, donkey or camel. Most references relate to the donkey's colt; Genesis 32:15 gives colt as the young of the camel. Drawing upon Zechariah 9:9, Jesus directed his disciples to bring him a colt, upon which he rode into Jerusalem (Matt 21:1-10; Mark 11:1-11; cf Luke 19:29-37; John 12:14-15). Both Matthew and John specify a donkey colt; Mark and Luke do not qualify it. See also DONKEY.

Sculptures of cow and calf. Israelite period.

COW, CALF, HEIFER The cow and its young calf were of great value in biblical Israel as sources of dairy products (I Sam 6:7, 10) meat (Gen 18:7-8; Luke 15:23), and as work animals. Their sacrificial importance is illustrated through the purification offering of the red heifer (Num chap. 19) and the sin offering of the calf (Lev 9:3-8). Calves played an important role in cultic worship throughout the Near East, which influenced Israelite worship. When Moses ascended Mount Sinai to receive the Law the Israelites persuaded Aaron to build a GOLDEN CALF (Ex chap. 32). King Jeroboam of Israel erected temples in Bethel and Dan, and placed a golden calf in each one (I Kgs 12:28-30; cf II Kgs 10:29). In Ezekiel's vision of the throne of God, the attending creatures possessed soles like calves' feet (Ezek 1:7). John's vision of the throne of God also featured a calf (Rev 4:6-7).

Figurative references to cows include Pharaoh's dream of seven fat cows devoured by seven thin ones (Gen chap. 41), the allusion to Israel as a "stubborn calf" (Hos 4:16) and the pampered elite women of Samaria who are called "cows of Bashan" after the name of the plush fertile lands of Bashan famous for its plump cows (Amos 4:1).

CRANE A large, long-legged bird; it originates in the north of Europe and migrates to the south during the winter. The crane is mentioned in Isaiah 38:14 although there is controversy as to which bird was in fact meant. The Hebrew word was long translated as "swallow".

Cranes

CRICKET An insect, listed along with the locust and grasshopper as permissible food, according to the dietary laws in Leviticus chapter 11.

DEER, DOE, FAWN, ROE, ROEBUCK Three species of the ruminant deer family — the red deer, the fallow deer and the roe deer — thrived in the Middle East in biblical times. It is thought that the OT writers were not precise in their naming of this animal and its relatives, and translations from the Hebrew reflect this imprecision. The fawn, a young deer, is mentioned in the Song of Solomon, where the author, describing his beloved, writes "Your two breasts are like two fawns" (Song 4:5; 7:3).

Persian fallow deer

DOE See DEER above

Dog

DOG A domestic member of the canine family. In ancient times, the dog was not kept as a pet and is depicted unfavorably by biblical authors as a scavenger and generally unattractive beast, which ate animal and human flesh (Ex 22:31; I Kgs 14:11; 16:4). A fool's repeated folly is likened to a dog that "returns to his own vomit" (Prov 26:11; cf II Pet 2:22). The prophets predicted that members of the houses of Kings Jeroboam, Baasha and Ahab would be eaten by packs of dogs (I Kgs 14:11; 16:4; 21:24) and indeed, dogs licked up the blood of Ahab and ate the flesh of his widow, Jezebel (I Kgs 22:38; II Kgs 9:35-36).

Contemptuous statements, indicating the lowly status of the dog were uttered by Goliath (I Sam 17:43) and by Mephibosheth the son of Jonathan (II Sam 9:8) to David. Abishai son of Zeruiah, referring to Shimei, son of Gera, said to King David "Why should this dead dog curse my lord the king?" (II Sam 16:9). When Elisha wept over the evil

Donkeys

Eagle depicted on a Tyrian shekel.

Falcon

he foresaw for Israel by the hand of Hazael, the latter asked "But what is your servant — a dog that he should do this gross thing?" (II Kgs 8:13). Here, "dog" is used figuratively for excessive humility. In Deuteronomy 23:18, it refers to a male prostitute. Paul also uses it as a term of insult (Phil 3:2), while the Book of Revelation classes dogs with sorcerers, murderers etc. who are excluded from the heavenly Jerusalem (Rev 22:15).

DONKEY, FOAL (ASS) An equine animal. The donkey was of prime importance in the ancient Near East as a work and transport animal. The numerous references to the beast indicate that it was common in the biblical world; there were specific laws governing its treatment (Ex 23:5; Deut 5:14; 22:10), and compensation to its owner upon its injury (Ex 21:33-34). Donkeys were ridden by all members of society (Ex 4:20; Judg 5:10; I Sam 25:42). Zechariah 9:9 states that the coming king of Zion would be mounted on a donkey. Jesus, drawing upon this verse, rode into Jerusalem on donkeyback (Matt 21:2-10; John 12:14-16).

One of the best known references to donkeys is the story of Balaam, who was sent by Balak king of the Moabites to curse the Israelites. Balaam's donkey turned aside when it saw God's angel, arousing Balaam's anger, but it talked when "the Lord opened the mouth of the donkey" (Num 22:22ff). The animal's popularity and value are highlighted by instances where the number of donkeys was recorded: the Israelites took 61,000 donkeys from the Midianites as plunder (Num 31:34); and the exiles of Judah returned from Babylon with 6,720 donkeys (Ezra 2:67; Neh 7:69).

DOVE See TURTLEDOVE below

DROMEDARY A swift riding camel of the one-humped Arabian species. While the dromedary is probably included in other biblical references to camels, it is specifically mentioned in Isaiah and Jeremiah. See also CAMEL.

EAGLE A large bird of prey (given as "osprey" in some versions), of which there are several varieties in the Near East. It is included among the unclean animals forbidden to be eaten (Lev 11:13; Deut 14:12). As the largest bird in the area, and as a creature possessing great speed and strength, the eagle is often alluded to in the Bible. God's deliverance of the Israelites from Egypt, and his protection through the wilderness is likened to a journey "on eagles' wings" (Ex 19:4) and to the bird's protection of its young (Deut 32:11). Impressed with the eagle's speed in flight, the prophets forewarned the people of the attacks of the enemy who shall fly "like an eagle" (Jer 48:40; 49:22; Hos 8:1); foreign rulers were also described as eagles (Ezek 17:3, 7; cf Dan 7:4). Other allusions to the eagle's swiftness are found in Deuteronomy 28:49, II Samuel 1:23 and Jeremiah 4:13. Ancient Near Eastern art and culture incorporated the eagle in images of deities and this influence is noted in prophetic visions of the throne of God and his attending creatures (Ezek 1:10; 10:14; Rev 4:7).

FALCON A medium-size bird of prey, considered unclean and therefore forbidden to the Israelites as a source of food (Lev 11:14; Deut 14:13). Job 28:7 makes note of the falcon's sharp vision.

FAWN See DEER above

FLEA A wingless parasitic insect. David, escaping from Saul, described himself as a flea, in an attempt to dissuade the king from wasting efforts on chasing such an insignificant person (I Sam 24:14; 26:20).

FLY Two Hebrew words are translated as "flies" — the first, *arov* ("swarms of flies" in Ex 8:21-31; Ps 78:45; 105:31), were stinging flies that descended upon Egypt as the fourth plague; the second *zevuv*, is thought to be the common housefly. Ecclesiastes 10:1 states that a dead fly in an ointment will spoil it like "a little folly to one respected for wisdom and honor", and Isaiah compared an invading Egyptian army to attacking flies (Is 7:18).

Baal Zebub ("the god of the fly") was worshiped in the Israelite town of Ekron (II Kgs chap. 1).

FOAL See DONKEY above

FOWL, CHICKS, HEN Any winged, feathered vertebrate; its modern definition is that of domestic poultry. Scholars are unsure as to when poultry was introduced into biblical Israel. The "fatted fowl" numbered among King Solomon's daily provisions (I Kgs 4:22-23), and the fowl prepared for Nehemiah (Neh 5:18) were probably some other type of bird or game. The quail provided by God to the Israelites after the Exodus (Num 11:31-32) are described in Psalms 78:27 as "feathered fowl like the sand of the seas". In the NT, Jesus laments over Jerusalem, wanting to protect the people "as a hen gathers her chicks under her wings" (Matt 23:37; cf Luke 13:34).

FOX A member of the dog family, with a long, bushy tail; known for its slyness and cunning (cf Luke 13:31-32), and its habit of prowling in ruins (Lam 5:18; Ezek 13:4 — the latter verse employs the image of foxes to describe false prophets). The fox lives in dens (Matt 8:20; Luke 9:58). Foxes and little foxes are used symbolically in Song of Solomon 2:15. The references to foxes in Judges and Nehemiah, may in fact denote the JACKAL.

FROG A tailless amphibian known for its agility in jumping and leaping. In the second plague visited upon Egypt, "Frogs came up and covered the land" (Ex 8:6). Frogs were among the creatures considered unclean to eat; this point is possibly reflected in Revelation 16:13, where "three unclean spirits like frogs" come forth.

GAZELLE A small antelope, renowned for its swiftness (II Sam 2:18; I Chr 12:8). The gazelle was one of the animals permitted to the Israelites as food (Deut 12:15, 22; 14:5; 15:22) and is listed among the provisions of King Solomon's palace (I Kgs 4:23). Both Asahel son of Zeruiah and brother of Joab, and David's mighty Gadite warriors were said to have been as swift as gazelles (II Sam 2:18; I Chr 12:8); the animal is also referred to figuratively in the Song of Solomon (4:5; 7:3).

GECKO A small, scaled lizard, listed among the "creeping things" that are forbidden to the Israelites as food.

GNAT A small two-winged insect; it is unknown exactly which variety is meant. Matthew 23:24 points to the scribes and Pharisees "who strain out a gnat and swallow a camel", i.e., they attach importance to minor issues while neglecting more serious religious practices and responsibilities.

GOAT, KID A horned, cud-chewing mammal, possessing a coat of long hair. As domesticated animals, goats and their young, kids, were gathered in herds (Gen 30:32; I Sam 25:2; I Chr 17:11). The goat met both secular and religious needs of the Israelites: as a dairy source (Deut 32:14; Prov 27:26-27), as permitted meat (Deut 14:4; Judg 6:19; Luke 15:29), as a source of fabric and leather (Ex 25:4; 26:7; I Sam 19:13, 16; Heb 11:37) and as a sacrificial offering of varying sorts (Lev 1:10; 3:12; 4:23).

In the religious realm, the goat stands out among all other sacrificial animals as the one that is sent out into the wilderness by the high priest on the Day of Atonement, as a scapegoat (see AZAZEL) for the sins of the nation (Lev 16:21-22). The prohibition against mixing meat and milk, a cornerstone of the post-biblical Jewish DIETARY LAWS, has its origins in the command, "you shall not boil a young goat in its mother's milk" (Ex 23:19; 34:26; Deut 14:21).

Desert fox

Frog

Geckoes

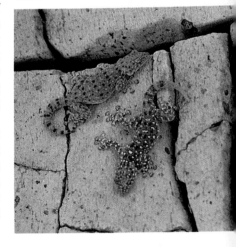

Hoopoe

Sculpture of a goat from Megiddo; wild goat on the right.

Young night heron

Hare

The small army of Israelites that fought against Ben-Hadad's Syrian forces were "like two little flocks of goats" (I Kgs 20:26-27). The goat was also used as an allusion for assorted foreign leaders and powers — Edom (Is 34:6-7), Greece (Dan 8:5-8), as well as the people of Israel (Ezek 34:17; Zech 10:3).

In his parable of the future judgment, Jesus uses the metaphor of separating the sheep from the goats (Matt 25:31-46).

GRASSHOPPER A leaping insect, often referred to interchangeably with the locust. The Israelites were permitted to eat this insect (Lev 11:22). Grasshoppers were known as destroyers of crops (Ecc 12:5; cf I Kgs 8:37; II Chr 6:28; Nah 3:15), and were used figuratively to depict insignificance (Num 13:33; Is 40:22), cowardice (Nah 3:17) and countless multitudes of people (Jer 46:23).

HARE A small mammal related to the rabbit, and considered unclean and unfit for Israelite consumption.

HAWK A small bird of prey, unfit for Israelite consumption (Lev 11:16; Deut 14:15). Other biblical references possibly point to the bird's migratory habits (Job 39:26; Is 34:15).

HEIFER See COW above

HEN See FOWL above

HERON One of a family of water birds with long legs and neck. It is forbidden as food for the Israelites.

HOOPOE A cinnamon-colored bird, about the size of a pigeon. The hoopoe has a head plume and long, slender bill. It is listed among the birds unclean and not fit for Israelite consumption.

HORNET A flying stinging insect; related to the wasp. God promised to send swarms of hornets to descend upon the Hivites, the Canaanites and the Hittites, as harbingers of the conquering Israelite tribes (Ex 23:28; cf Josh 24:12).

Clay horse from the Israelite period. (Israel Museum)

(left)
Horse and foal.

HORSE A four-legged mammal. The horse was primarily used in the biblical period for warfare and transportation. Most tribes in the ancient Near East employed horsepower for war, and warhorses were often hitched to chariots (Ex 14:9; Judg 5:22; II Sam 1:6; I Kgs 20:1; Is 5:28; Acts 23:23). As a means of transportation, horses were ridden by the wealthy and by nobility. Joseph was honored in Egypt by riding in one of the pharaoh's chariots (Gen 41:43), while in Persia, Mordecai was similarly honored (Est 6:7-11). David's son Absalom outfitted himself with chariots and horses (II Sam 5:1) and Elijah was carried up to heaven in a fiery chariot, drawn by "horses of fire" (II Kgs 2:11). King Solomon took an interest in accumulating and breeding horses (I Kgs 4:26); some of which he received as gifts from visiting foreigners (I Kgs 10:24-25; II Chr 9:28).

In the Song of Solomon, the beloved's beauty is compared with one of Pharaoh's horses ("filly" Song 1:9) and the Book of Job (39:19-25) contains a classic description of the warhorse. Man sins without regard to the consequences, "as the horse rushes into the battle" (Jer 8:6). Lust and idolatry are likened to horses in a sexual frenzy (Jer 5:8; Ezek 23:20). Habakkuk 3:8 envisions God's majestic steeds and "chariots of salvation".

In the NT, judgments upon the earth are symbolized by different colored horses: white as conquest; red as bloodshed; black as famine and pale as death (Rev 6:2-8). Jesus rides on a white horse (Rev 19:11).

HYENA A carrion-eating mammal, falling between the cat and the dog families; it is known for its disturbing howl (Is 13:22). The Hebrew, *tzeboa*, was incorporated into names of locations: the Valley of Zeboim (I Sam 13:18) and the town of Zeboim (Neh 11:34). Other possible references to the hyena are found in Isaiah 13:22; 34:14 and Jeremiah 50:39 where they occupy desolate places.

JACKAL A member of the canine family, resembling a wolf, but smaller and with a shorter tail. Common in biblical Israel, the jackal travels in packs and feeds on carrion as well as freshly killed animals. As a nocturnal animal, frequently inhabiting abandoned and desolate areas, the jackal is often referred to as a symbol of desolation and ruin (Is 34:13; 35:7; Jer 9:11; 10:22), and mention is made of its cry (Is 13:22; Mic 1:8). Babylon (Is 13:22; Jer 51:37), Edom (Is 34:13), the mountain of Esau (Mal 1:3), Jerusalem (Jer 9:11) and Mount Zion (Lam 5:18) are all listed as being, or fated to be, resorts of jackals. In the future, the haunts of jackals will sprout vegetation (Is 35:7), they, along with other wild animals, shall rejoice over the bounty of water in the wilderness (Is 43:20).

JACKDAW One of the birds listed among those forbidden as food to the Israelites.

KID See GOAT above

KITE A bird of prey and a scavenger, included among the unclean birds in the dietary laws of Leviticus and Deuteronomy.

LAMB See SHEEP below

LEECH A blood-sucking, slug-like animal, mentioned only once in the Bible, in Proverbs 30:15: "The leech has two daughters, crying 'give, give!'". The leech's daughter probably alludes to greed. Others, however, interpret this word as referring to the author of that section of proverbs.

LEOPARD A large member of the feline family; it was quite common in biblical Israel. Reference is made to its speed (Hab 1:8) and its predatory nature (Jer 5:6; Hos 13:7). Mention is also made of its spots (Jer 13:23), its peaceful cohabitation with a kid in the future period of peace (Is 11:6) and its abode in the mountains of Lebanon and Hermon (Song 4:8).

A four-headed, winged leopard in Daniel 7:6 symbolizes Persia; the beast from the sea in Revelation 13:2 symbolizing the Roman Empire, resembled a leopard.

LICE Small insects that breed on mammals. The Lord sent lice as the third plague upon the Egyptians. According to his instructions, "Aaron stretched out his hand with his rod and struck the dust of the earth, and it became lice on man and beast" (Ex 8:17). The plague is recalled in Psalm 105:31.

LION A large member of the feline family, mentioned numerous times in the Bible (there are seven Hebrew words for lion). The tribe of Judah was compared to a lion (Gen 49:9). Implicit in the variety of references is the strength and boldness of the lion (Prov 30:30). Its roar struck terror

Leopard

(right)
Two ivory lions from Samaria. 9th century B.C. (Israel Museum)

Mosaic of the Byzantine period from Beth Gubrin depicting a lion.

(Amos 3:8). Lions were encountered by shepherds and travelers (Judg 14:5-6; I Sam 17:34-35) and roamed the desert (Is 30:6). They were even set upon men as a death penalty (I Kgs 13:24-26; 20:36; Dan 6:16). The lion stands for courage (Num 23:24; I Chr 12:8; Prov 28:1) and wickedness (Ps 10:9; Prov 28:15; Ezek 22:25; I Pet 5:8) and represented divine justice and majesty (Ezek 1:10; 10:14; Rev 4:7). God himself is compared to a lion (Lam 3:10; Hos 5:14). Ornamental lions decorated Solomon's throne (I Kgs 10:19ff) and the Temple (I Kgs 7:27-29, 36; 10:19-20) and appeared in Ezekiel's vision (Ezek 41:18-19). In the messianic age the lion will lie down with the lamb (Is 11:6).

In the NT, Jesus is called "the lion of the tribe of Judah" (Rev 5:5).
LIZARD A small reptile of which numerous varieties are found in the Near East. It is listed among the unclean animals forbidden to the Israelites. Some have also seen a reference to a lizard in Proverbs 30:28.
LOCUST A leaping insect, related to the grasshopper. Locusts were sent upon Egypt as the eighth plague (Ex chap. 10). Swarms of locusts are capable of destroying entire crops, thus they were greatly feared in the biblical world (Deut 28:38, 42; II Chr 7:13). The image of destructive locust swarms was employed as a metaphor for attacking enemy armies (Judg 6:5; Jer 51:27; Joel 2:25; Nah 3:15), and as a harbinger of the Day of the Lord (Joel 2:1, 11). In order to remove the plague special ceremonies of fasting, praying and trumpet-blowing were proclaimed (Joel 2:12-17). The Israelites, according to Leviticus 11:22, were permitted to eat locusts, while in the wilderness of Judea, John the Baptist subsisted on locusts and wild honey (Matt 3:1, 4).
MAGGOT See WORM below
MOLE A small rodent that burrows in the ground. The biblical mole (Lev 11:29) is not identical to the true mole, which is not indigenous to the region. The latter eats insects, whereas the former, often referred to as a mole rat, feeds on plant roots and bulbs. The mole is one of the "creeping things" (Lev 11:29) considered unclean and not to be eaten.
MONKEY, APE Primates, unspecified as to type; they were brought back from Tarshish every three years on King Solomon's merchant ships, along with gold, silver and ivory.
MOTH An insect resembling a butterfly; the references in the Bible usually refer to the moth's damaging effects on clothes (Job 13:28; Is 50:9; 51:8; James 5:2). The moth's "house" in Job 27:18 is the cocoon created from cloth fibers by the insect in its caterpillar form. The reference to the delicate moth in Job 4:19 is a metaphor for the frailty of man before God.

Locusts

(top of page)
Locust depicted on a seal of the 8th century B.C. from Megiddo. (Israel Dept. of Antiquities and Museums)

(left)
Bronze monkey from Megiddo.

Sphinx-moth

MOUSE, RAT A small rodent, prohibited for Israelite consumption (Lev 11:29). It is also mentioned in Isaiah 66:17 where the prophet refers to a pagan cultic practice. A plague of mice visited the Philistines when they captured the ark of the covenant (I Sam 6:5), although the NKJV translates the Hebrew as "rats". When the Philistines returned the ark to the Israelites they include "five golden tumors and five golden rats" as a trespass offering (I Sam 6:3-4). The five golden rats represented the lords of the five Philistine cities, Ashdod, Gaza, Ashkelon, Gath and Ekron (I Sam 6:17-18).

MULE A hybrid offspring of a horse and an ass, the mule was probably introduced into biblical Israel by non-Israelites (cf Ezek 27:8, 14) as crossbreeding was prohibited, according to Leviticus 19:19. Mules were presented to Solomon as gifts from foreign visitors (I Kgs 10:24-25; II Chr 9:23-24), and 245 of them were brought to Israel with those returning from the Babylonian Exile (Ezra 2:66; Neh 7:68). Mules were ridden by the aristocracy (II Sam 13:29; 18:9; I Kgs 1:33, 38, 44) and were also used as burden-bearers (II Kgs 5:17; I Chr 12:40). Psalms 32:8-9 offers the guidance of God to man, so that he will "not be like the horse or the mule, which have no understanding which must be harnessed with bit and bridle".

ONAGER A wild donkey, now extinct, the Syrian variety was the only onager found in Israel in biblical times.

OSTRICH A flightless bird. The female lays her eggs in shallow pits, often leaving the nest during the day when the sun can warm them. At night, the male incubates the eggs. Most of the biblical references group the ostrich with the jackal and other wild animals, (e.g. Job 30:29; Lam 4:3). Job 39:13-18 relates several interesting characteristics of this bird. "She leaves her eggs on the ground and warms them in the dust... she treats her young harshly, as though they were not hers". According to Job, the ostrich is also stupid. The ostrich is prohibited for Israelite consumption (Lev 11:16; Deut 14:15).

OWL A nocturnal, small to medium size bird of prey renowned for its sharp night vision. Several species of owl are found in Israel and a number of different Hebrew words are translated as owl. Owls are among the unclean birds listed in the dietary laws in Leviticus chapter 11 and Deuteronomy chapter 14. Isaiah states that owls will dwell in the ruins of Babylon (Is 13:21) and Edom (Is 34:11).

OX A large mammal, member of the bovine family. Oxen were domesticated (Gen 12:16) and used as work animals (I Kgs 19:19; Job 1:14; Amos 6:12). Animal control laws covered both human injury caused by an ox and injury to an ox as a form of property (Ex 21:28-22:13). Oxen were rested on the Sabbath (Ex 23:12; Deut 14:4). The ox was permitted to the Israelites as food (Deut 14:4); and was a sacrificial victim for offerings (Num 7:88; II Sam 24:22; I Kgs 1:9; I Chr 21:23).

One of the faces of the four-faced creatures that attended God's throne in Ezekiel's vision was that of an ox (Ezek 1:10). The molten sea in the Temple was set upon 12 bronze oxen, three oxen facing each of the four directions (I Kgs 7:25; cf Jer 52:20), and oxen figures also decorated the panels of the ten bronze carts requisitioned by Solomon (I Kgs 7:29).

PARTRIDGE A small game bird. King Saul's continual pursuit of David was described by the latter as hunting "a partridge in the mountains" (I Sam 26:20), alluding to both the use of partridge as food and the bird's attempts to evade its hunters. "As a partridge that broods but does not hatch" (Jer 17:11) refers to the popular but mistaken belief that the partridge gathers the eggs of other birds.

PEACOCK The male of the peafowl bird, native to India. The peacock is offered as an alternative translation to three verses in the KJV edition of the Bible: for the reading "monkeys" in I Kings 10:22 and II Chronicles 9:21 and for "ostrich" in Job 39:13.

PELICAN A large, fish-eating bird, associated with ruin and desolation.

PIGEON A small game bird always listed with the turtledove in both the OT and NT. Most of the numerous references describe their ritual and sacrificial uses: as burnt and sin offerings (Lev 1:14; 5:7, 11); in ritual purification of a woman after childbirth (Lev 12:6, 8) and in similar rites for cured lepers (Lev 14:22, 30) and defiled Nazirites (Num 6:10). The pigeon and turtledove were often permitted as a sacrificial option for those too poor to afford sheep or lambs. Abraham included a young pigeon in his covenant with God in Genesis 15:9.

After the birth of Jesus, Mary made the customary purification sacrifice at the Temple (Luke 2:22-24). Pigeons were sold in Jerusalem for sacrificial purposes (cf Matt 21:12; Mark 11:15; John 2:14).

PORCUPINE A large member of the rodent family. Isaiah (34:11) refers to a porcupine in his image of the creature which will inhabit the desolate places of Edom. The translation is problematic.

QUAIL A small game bird, related to the partridge and the pheasant; quails served as supplementary food for the Israelites as they journeyed through the wilderness (Ex 16:13; Num 11:31-32). Quails are known to migrate in the spring from Africa to the Mediterranean area. After this exhausting flight they alight on the coast where they are easily caught.

RAM The adult male of the sheep. The ram was a source of meat (Ex 29:32) and was used as a sacrificial offering (Lev 1:10; 5:15; 6:6; 8:2, 18). The horns of the ram were used as a trumpet (Josh 6:4), and its skin was used with other materials as coverings for the tabernacle (Ex 26:14). At the last moment God provided Abraham with a ram in place of his son Isaac as a sacrifice (Gen 22:13). In judging between the good and evil of Israel, God will "judge between sheep and sheep, between rams and goats" (Ezek 34:17). In Daniel's vision of the rams, its horns were symbols of Media and Persia (Dan chap. 8). See SHEEP below.

RAT See MOUSE above

RAVEN A large black bird common in the Near East; it is mentioned in Genesis 8:7 as the first bird sent from the ark by Noah. The raven is included among the list of unclean birds in Leviticus 11:15 and Deuteronomy 14:14. Ravens delivered bread and meat to Elijah while he was in hiding (I Kgs 17:4, 6), and God's provision of food to young ravens (Job 38:41; Ps 147:9; Luke 12:24) serves as an example of his care for all of his creatures. Isaiah 34:11 lists the raven as one of the animals that would inhabit the ruins of Edom.

ROCK BADGER, HYRAX A small rabbit-like animal which lives in crags or rocks, hence its name. It was considered unclean and therefore not fit for Israelite consumption.

ROE, ROEBUCK See DEER above

ROOSTER (COCK) A male chicken, mentioned only in the NT. Jesus referred to "the crowing of the rooster" (Mark 13:35) as a specific time of day, that is, daybreak. The rooster's crowing is also an integral part of Jesus' prophecy: on the night before his death Jesus prophesies that Peter "even this night, before the rooster crows twice,... will deny me three times" (Mark 14:30; cf Matt 26:75; Luke 22:61; John 13:38). See FOWL above.

SCORPION A member of the arachnid family, the scorpion is nocturnal, and attacks its prey — insects and other arachnids — with an often painful, or even fatal, venom-releasing sting located at the end of its tail.

(left)
Asiatic wild asses (onagers)
(right)
Peacock on a mosaic of the Byzantine period in the Church of the Multiplication at Tabgha.

(left)
Ostriches.
(right)
Egyptian model of a man ploughing with a pair of oxen. c. 2000 B.C.

(left)
Barn owls
(right)
An owl depicted on a coin from Gaza, c.375

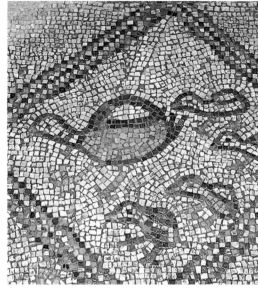

(left)
Partridge
(right)
Rock partridge and chicks depicted on a 6th-century mosaic floor of the synagogue at Beth Alpha.

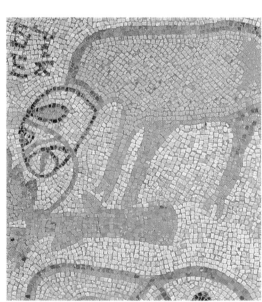

(left)
Porcupine
(right)
Ram caught in a bush depicted on the mosaic floor of the synagogue at Beth Alpha.

(left)
Raven with an Egyptian crown on a coin from Raphia. A.D. 117.
(right)
Hyrax (rock badger)

Scorpion

In Deuteronomy 8:15, the Lord is remembered for bringing the Children of Israel through the wilderness "in which were fiery serpents and scorpions". The desert habitat of the scorpion is reflected in the name given to the Ascent of Akrabbim, meaning scorpions, southwest of the Dead Sea (Num 34:4; Josh 15:3; Judg 1:36). King Rehoboam threatens Israel that he will place upon them a yoke much heavier than that of his father Solomon, it will be not only a whip, but a scorpion too (I Kgs 12:11; II Chr 10:11, 14). The prophet Ezekiel is encouraged by God not to fear the response of the people even though they are like briars, thorns and scorpions (Ezek 2:6).

In the NT, just as a father will not give his son a scorpion when he asks for an egg, but knows how to "give good gifts to your children", God the heavenly father will provide the holy spirit to those who ask (Luke 11:12-13). The scorpion's stinging tail and the torment it produces to man is recalled in Revelation 9:5, 10.

SEAGULL A bird that lives along seacoasts; it is one of the unclean birds listed in the dietary laws of Leviticus and Deuteronomy.

SERPENT, SNAKE A scaly reptile. Numerous varieties of serpents and snakes are found in the Near East; some pose little danger to man and animals, while others can inflict fatal injuries. Serpents plagued the Israelites as they journeyed to Canaan after the Exodus (Num 21:6), and their poisonous bites are recorded in other passages (Prov 23:32; Ecc 10:8, 11; Amos 5:19; cf Ps 58:4).

The serpent had great mythological and cultic significance in the ancient Near East; these influences are clearly seen in biblical accounts (cf Job 26:13; Is 27:1; Amos 9:3) Adam and Eve were expelled from the Garden of Eden, after being tempted by the sly and crafty serpent to partake of the fruit of the divinely forbidden tree of knowledge (Gen chap. 3). This "serpent of old" is called both "devil" and "Satan" in Revelation 12:9; 20:2. Moses and Aaron demonstrated their power

Poisonous viper

when Aaron's rod was cast to the ground, turned into a serpent and swallowed up the rods of Pharaoh's magicians who had done likewise with their rods (Ex 7:8-12). Numbers 21:6-9 relates that the Lord commanded Moses to make a copper (KJV: bronze) serpent for those bitten by snakes to look at for healing purposes. This serpent was later placed in the Temple and eventually destroyed by King Hezekiah as part of his reform measures (II Kgs 18:4).

The serpent is used figuratively to represent Assyrians (Is 14:29), Babylonians (Jer 8:17), the enemies of Israel (Deut 32:33), evil men in general (Ps 58:4), and Pharisees and Scribes (Matt 23:33). In Isaiah 27:1 the serpent is mentioned in a mythological-eschatological context, where "Leviathan the fleeing serpent" represents the enemies of the Lord who will be destroyed. Another reference to the serpent in the messianic age is in Isaiah 65:25, where it is stated that, along with the wolf and lamb feeding together, "dust shall be the serpent's food".

An indication of the mission of Jesus' disciples is that they have power over serpents (Luke 10:19). See NEHUSHTAN.

SHEEP, LAMB, EWE A four-legged mammal with fleece, domesticated and raised throughout the Near East. The adult male is the ram, the adult female is the ewe and the young sheep, both male and female, is the lamb. Sheep were tended in flocks by shepherds (Gen 29:9); the wealth of an individual could be measured by the size of his flocks (I Sam 25:2). Both dairy and meat products were available from sheep (II Sam 17:29; Ps 44:11; Is 7:21-22) as well as wool (Lev 13:47; Job 31:20), rough clothing (Heb 11:37) and covering for tents (Ex 26:14). Sheep were the principal sacrificial animal offered upon the altar for a range of sacrifices (Lev 1:10; 5:6, 15); a year-old male lamb or goat served as the Passover sacrifice in Egypt (Ex 12:1-5). The most common biblical metaphor involving sheep is that of the defenseless flock and the caring, guarding shepherd (Is 53:7; Jer 11:19; Mic 5:8; Matt 10:16; John

Sheep grazing

Wild sheep

Snails on a wooden post.

(bottom of page)
Swallows

Stork

10:3-4). Among the many OT images of Israel as the flock and of God and his assigned leaders as its shepherds, are Psalms 23:1; "The Lord is my shepherd; I shall not want", Isaiah 40:11: "He will feed his flock like a shepherd; he will gather the lambs with his arm"; Jeremiah 23:3-4: "I will gather the remnant of my flock out of the countries where I have driven them, I will set up shepherds over them who will feed them and they will fear no more" (see also Ezek 37:24ff). Two extended allegories of the shepherd and sheep appear in Ezekiel chapter 34 and John chapter 10.

The NT further develops the flock-shepherd metaphor with Jesus presented as the shepherd. When preaching to the multitudes, Jesus "was moved with compassion for them, because they were like sheep, not having a shepherd. So he began to teach them many things" (Mark 6:34). The Epistle to the Hebrews closes with a reference to Jesus as "that great shepherd of the sheep" (Heb 13:20). Jesus himself is mentioned as the LAMB OF GOD in the Book of Revelation.

SNAIL A small, slow-moving mollusk referred to only once in the Bible. According to Psalm 58:8, the wicked are cursed "like a snail which melts away as it goes". "Melts away" apparently refers to the slimy trail left by the snail.

SNAKE See SERPENT above

SOW See SWINE below

SPARROW Any small bird of the finch family found throughout Israel. The OT references are thought to be generic for any small bird. The sparrow nests in a variety of places including rooftops (Ps 102:7); in biblical times it must have also made its home within the Temple area (Ps 84:3). Sparrows were sold at a low price (Luke 12:6) in the market place. Jesus told his disciples that they were "of more value than many sparrows" (Matt 10:31). God is said to watch over every single sparrow (Luke 12:7).

SPIDER An arachnid, known for the delicate web it spins to entrap insects. The spider's web serves as an image of frailty and unreliability: in Job 8:14-15, the hypocrites' trust "is a spider's web. He leans on his house, but it does not stand", and sinners cannot adequately cover themselves with the spider's, "garments" (Is 59:5-6). The spider mentioned in Proverbs 30:28 is translated as "lizard" in some Bible editions.

STORK A large bird resembling a heron; it is among the unclean birds prohibited for Israelite consumption (Lev 11:19; Deut 14:18). The stork is know for its large wing-span (Zech 5:9) and its regular migrations (Jer 8:7). In one of his visions, the prophet Zechariah sees the woman, Wickedness, who possesses "the wings of a stork" (Zech 5:7-9).

SWALLOW A small bird possessing long wings, and known for its graceful flying. Swallows were said to have nested in the Temple area (Ps 84:3) and their flight is alluded to in Proverbs 26:2 and Jeremiah 8:7, while Isaiah 38:14 refers to their cry.

SWINE, SOW A pig, considered unclean as it does not meet the requirement of chewing the cud (Lev 11:7; Deut 14:8). Outside influences, however, must have swayed some Israelites to practice swine-sacrifice as implied in Isaiah 66:3: "He who offers a grain offering, as if he offers swine's blood" (cf Is 65:4; 66:17). For the Jewish people as a whole though, the swine took on a connotation of repulsion, filth and disgust, and biblical authors metaphorically employed the swine to convey this attitude. Proverbs 11:22 states: "As a ring of gold in a swine's snout, so is a lovely woman who lacks discretion."

As a reference to holiness, Jesus instructed his followers not to "cast your pearls before swine" (Matt 7:6). The NT tells how Jesus allowed exorcised demons to inhabit a herd of swine, which then rushed into the sea and drowned (Matt 8:30-32; Mark 5:11-13; Luke 8:32-33). In the parable of the lost son, the younger son, reduced to poverty, became a swineherd (Luke 15:15). A filthy swine, as an image of heresy, is found in II Peter 2:22.

TURTLEDOVE A small bird, often referring to a dove or a pigeon. The Latin designation *turtur*, like the Hebrew and Ugaritic *tor* and the Akkadian *turtu*, is thought to imitate the call of this bird. Brown with a bit of white at the tip of its tail, the turtledove is a migratory bird (Jer 8:7), whose arrival from Africa is one of the signs of the beginning of spring in Israel (Song 2:11-12). In August they return to Africa.

In Psalms 74:19 the turtledove represents a metaphor for the people of Israel. Elsewhere in the Bible the turtledove appears exclusively as a bird to be slaughtered in sacrificial worship. The turtledove is one of the species Abraham was required to sacrifice in concluding the "covenant between the pieces" (Gen 15:17). It can be presented as a voluntary burnt offering (Lev 1:14) or under certain circumstances, for a guilt offering (Lev 5:7). A woman who has recently given birth is required to present a young dove or a turtledove for a sin offering (Lev 12:6). If she is of limited means, she may substitute a young dove or turtledove for the burnt offering as well, instead of a lamb (Lev 12:8). Luke 2:24 suggests that the provision applied to Mary.

VIPER Any member of a family of poisonous snakes. In Jacob's last blessing, his son Dan is described as "a viper by the path, that bites the horse's heels" (Gen 49:17). The effects of wine are likened to the sting of a viper in Proverbs 23:32. Both Jesus and John the Baptist favored the expression "brood of vipers" as they castigated the Pharisees, the Sadducees and the scribes (Matt 3:7; 12:34; 23:33; Luke 3:7). When Paul was bitten by a viper the natives of Malta anticipated swelling, or even death (Acts 28:3-6).

VULTURE A large bird of prey, related to the eagle and the hawk. A carrion-eater, the vulture is listed among the unclean birds not fit for Israelite consumption (Lev 11:13; Deut 14:12). Abraham protected his sacrifice to the Lord from encroaching vultures (Gen 15:11). In Jeremiah 12:9, the prophet states that his people are acting towards him as a vulture, so he commands that the vultures should surround Israel as appropriate retribution.

WOLF The largest member of the canine family of mammals, and a carnivorous nocturnal hunter. The wolf was common in the Near East, yet most of the biblical references are illustrative and not literal. In Jacob's blessing, Benjamin is described as a "ravenous wolf", pointing to his fighting abilities (Gen 49:27). The ferocity and voracity of the wolf are applied to the princes of Israel (Ezek 22:27) and the judges of Jerusalem (Zeph 3:3). In the messianic age, "the wolf also shall dwell with the lamb" (Is 11:6; cf 65:25). In the NT, wolves symbolize false prophets and teachers (Matt 7:15; Acts 20:29), and Jesus sends his apostles to spread his word as sheep in the midst of wolves (Matt 10:16; Luke 10:3).

WORM, MAGGOT A crawling animal. Biblical references allude to the worm itself as well as to the maggot (larval) stages of insects. Worms and maggots are often used as images for the insignificance of man (Job 25:6). The psalmist claims "But I am a worm, and no man" (Ps 22:6); although the Lord promises to help his people, he nevertheless refers to them as "you worm Jacob" (Is 41:14). The biological roles of the worm are also noted: as a creature that feeds upon vegetation (Ex 16:20; Jonah 4:7) and upon corpses (Job 21:26; 24:20), especially those of the wicked (Is 51:8; 66:24; cf Mark 9:44-48).

Turtledove

(bottom of page)
Vultures

Carpet viper

ANISE (DILL) See PLANTS

ANNA ("favor; charm"; the Greek form of Hannah). A woman of 84, daughter of Phanuel; she spent her time in the Temple praying and fasting and witnessed Jesus' presentation at the Temple (Luke 2:36-38).

ANNA
Luke 2:36

The Presentation of Christ at the Temple, depicted on a stone relief of the 12th century, at the church of Moissac, France.

ANNAS (Greek abbreviation of the Hebrew "Hananiah"), high priest during the rule of Pontius Pilate as governor of Judea (Luke 3:2). After Jesus was arrested, he was first brought to Annas who sent him to his son-in-law Caiaphas (John 18:13, 24).

ANNAS
Luke 3:2. John 18:13, 24. Acts 4:6

John and Peter appeared later before Annas who sat with the Sanhedrin in Jerusalem (Acts 4:6).

In Luke, Annas and Caiaphas are both called high priests but in Acts Annas alone is mentioned as the high priest. It is believed by some scholars that Caiaphas was the high priest whereas Annas was the president of the Sanhedrin.

ANNUNCIATION The word "annunciation" arouses immediate associations with the scene recounted by Luke, and cherished by countless Christian artists, in which the angel Gabriel notified the Virgin Mary of the imminent birth of her child (Luke 1:26-38). In fact, that account is one of three birth-announcements similarly recounted in the gospels, the others being the announcement of Jesus' birth to Joseph in Matthew's gospel (Matt 1:20-21), and the announcement of the birth of John the Baptist adjoining that of Jesus' birth in Luke's first chapter (Luke 1:11-20). Modern biblical scholarship recognizes that these three NT birth-announcements share a common story-pattern which originated, not in Christian tradition, but in the historical books of the OT.

The announcement by messengers from heaven of the birth of an important individual was an established literary form in certain narrative traditions that antedated the OT writings. If one scans the annunciations of Abraham's offspring, Ishmael and Isaac (Gen 16:7-12; 17:15-19), and that of Samson's birth in the Book of Judges (13:3-14), it will be seen that these accounts always contain certain story-elements in more or less the same sequence. First comes the heavenly apparition,

God or his angel, usually accompanied by the familiar sequence of fear and reassurance to underscore the visitor's other-worldly provenance. Then the birth of a son is announced and his name is given. Finally, in more or less direct association with the etymology of its name, the

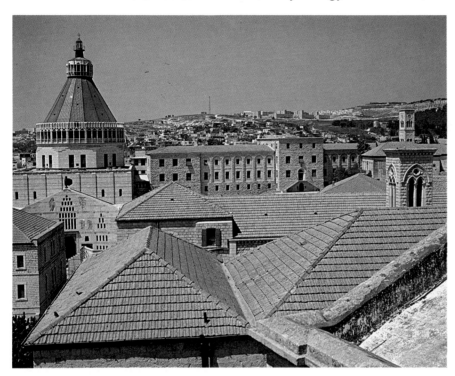

The Fountain of Mary, where, according to tradition, the Angel Gabriel appeared to Mary.

(left)
The Basilica of the Annunciation at Nazareth. It stands over the ruins of a church built in the 4th century on the site believed to be that of the Annunciation.

child's momentous future is revealed. The NT announcements adhere very closely to this pattern. The annunciation-form obviously impressed upon a listener familiar with the Bible that the child to be born would be a major contributor to the history of salvation inaugurated by the promise to Abraham.

The form-elements listed above do not account for the entire scope of Luke's annunciation, however. In each of them, the chosen parent expresses doubt or puzzlement as to the possibility of the birth, whereupon the angel gives further explanation and declares a sign which will give reassurance of the truth of the promise (Luke 1:18-20, 34-37). These further structural elements of the stories also conform to an OT model, but it is that of a different type of apparition, one that imparts a divine commission. Moses' commissioning before the burning bush (Ex 3:2-12), and Gideon's, in the Book of Judges (6:12-22), are the classic cases in point. In the standard sequence of apparition — commission, doubt, reassurance and ratifying sign — it is clearly the commission itself which is the center of interest, with doubt and reassurance serving to clarify the commission and to underscore the fact that it came from God and not from the man's own imagination or ambition.

It is thus clearly in the merger of corresponding elements from the annunciation and commission forms that Luke's announcement-stories gain their particular line of argument. In Jesus' annunciation, the definition of the child's future, belonging to the first form, and the divine commissioning of the second form, merge in the words of Gabriel that come before Mary's doubt (Luke 1:32-33). Those words can therefore be identified as the center and highpoint of the annunciation story, distinctly echoing the christological confession of the early Church, declaring the risen Christ to be God's Son and attributing to him the everlasting rule that had been promised to David's successor, the awaited messiah (II Sam 7:11-16; Ps 89:20-37; 132:11-12; Acts 1:3-4; Rom 1:3-4). The two titles which Easter faith applied to the risen Christ, "Son of God" and "messiah," (I Thes 1:10; Acts 2:36), are thus shown to have been divinely bestowed upon Jesus with his proper name before Mary conceived him. This assertion lies at the center of Luke's story and pinpoints the purpose of its telling.

Mary's doubt, with the angel's reassurance and the ratifying sign of Elizabeth's childbirth, bolsters the authenticity of Gabriel's promise and the exclusively divine causality of Mary's imminent conception. These elements complete a detailed parallelism which Luke's first chapter composition has drawn between the birth-announcements of the Baptist and Jesus. The meaning of the virgin birth is explained by its symmetry with Elizabeth's wondrous childbirth despite her barren state and advanced age: both births are humanly impossible, "for with God nothing is impossible" (Luke 1:37).

ANOINTING The practice of applying oil to the body, for cosmetic, therapeutic (Is 1:6) or sacral ("ceremonial") purposes, widespread throughout the cultures of the ancient Near East. Cosmetic anointing with oil is mentioned in the Bible especially after bathing (II Sam 12:20; Ruth 3:3; II Chr 28:15); however, there was a ban on anointing the body during times of fasting (II Sam 12:20) or mourning (II Sam 14:2; Dan 10:3). One of the verbs denoting the act *m-sh-h* (source of the word 'messiah', literally "the anointed one"), primarily indicates the anointing of humans or objects for sacred purposes, or as initiation for royal or prophetic office. Anointing of this kind was normally performed by pouring oil from a vessel onto the head (e.g., the high priest, Aaron, Ex 29:7; Lev 8:12, etc.; priests in general — Ex 28:41; 40:15, etc.; King Saul, I Sam 10:1; King David, II Sam 5:17, etc.).

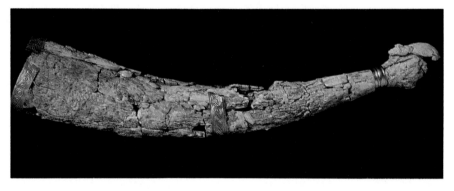

Horn of ivory with gold bands, made from a whole elephant's tusk, found at Megiddo. Late Bronze Age. This horn has its wide end sealed off, and the pointed end pierced with a hole. It was used for anointing as the oil dripped through the hole.

Objects (the altar, Ex 40:10; the laver, Ex 40:11; the entire tabernacle, Ex 40:10, etc.) were anointed to transmute them from the realm of the secular to that of the holy, i.e., "to sanctify" them. A special instance of anointing is the cleansing of the leper (Lev 14:10 ff), where the leper's oil is poured into the priest's hand and then sprinkled before the Lord, applied to the leper's ear and thumb, and finally his head. Anointing in this case has a special function of cleansing and purifying from the unclean state of leprosy.

The most frequently mentioned occasion for anointing, that of a king, signifies his dedication, qualification, and even endowment with charismatic qualities for the office and function of kingship. In this aspect the anointing of a king differs from that of a priest, the latter rite being analogous to the anointing of the tabernacle furniture and vessels — the priests are anointed as vessels for the divine service. Analogous to anointing for kingship is the anointing for prophetic service in the case of Elijah and Elisha (I Kgs 19:16; cf Ps 105:15), where some charismatic endowment is also implied. One of the Qumran texts refers to the messenger of the end-time as "the anointed with the Spirit". The general meaning of all these instances of anointing is God's presence with the anointed one, as in his dwelling in the anointed tabernacle.

Anointing *(aleiphō, chriō, myrizō)* in the NT has two main aspects: *aleiphō* is used of external, physical anointing, while *chriō* is employed in the higher sense of anointing by God. The former is used in Matthew 6:17 as a sign of joy, in Mark 6:13 and James 5:14 as a means of healing the sick, in Mark 16:1 as a service to the dead. In Luke 7:38 and chapter 46 it is an expression of a woman's love of Jesus and in John 11:2 and 12:3 the two functions of love and burial (12:7) are joined in Mary's anointing the feet of Jesus. The variant term *myrizō*, perfume, is used in Mark 14:8 in anticipation of Jesus' burial.

The more theological term *chrio* is the origin of the title Christ, which means Anointed One, a translation of the Hebrew *mashiah* or messiah, the title of God's agent in the time of his saving intervention. In Jesus' inaugural sermon (Luke 4:18) he cites Isaiah 61:1, "the Spirit of the Lord God is upon me, because the Lord has anointed me". In Hebrews 1:9 another OT text (Ps 45:7) is cited in relation to Jesus as God's Son. Acts 4:27 and 10:38 refer to the anointing of Jesus as messiah. In II Corinthians 1:21 Paul refers to the anointing (RSV: commissioning) of Christians in a baptismal context along with other effects of baptism (v. 22). Similarly I John 2:20, 27 uses the noun *chrisma* to speak of the anointing which Christians receive, understood as the gift of the Spirit.

The slab known as the Stone of Anointing in the Church of the Holy Sepulcher, Jerusalem, where Jesus is believed to have been laid after his body was taken down from the cross.

ANT See ANIMALS

ANTELOPE See ANIMALS

ANTICHRIST
I John 2:18,
22; 4:3.
II John v. 7

ANTICHRIST A term which can mean either "opposed to Christ" or "a substitute for Christ" or a blend of the two. It is used in the Johannine epistles to designate either individuals (II John 7) or the spiritual force (I John 4:3) which deny the Father and the son (I John 2:22) and that Jesus came in the flesh (I John 4:3; II John 7). The author of these epistles stressed that the present manifestation of the spirit of antichrist was a sign that the last hour had arrived (I John 2:18; 4:3). The term in the Johannine epistles is especially directed against docetism, an early form of Christian gnosticism, which denied that the man crucified was the Son of God. According to this view, the divine person had left his body before the crucifixion. Underlying John's use of the term is a dualistic cosmogony which anticipates a decisive spiritual battle in the last days between the forces of good and evil, Christ and Satan. The idea of a single human being opposed to Christ hearkens back to Daniel chapter 7 where a horned beast with one horn having "the eyes of a man" and boasting great things, is represented as standing over against the Son of man. The idea of many individuals opposing Christ appears in the apocalyptic discourse in Matthew's gospel in which Jesus predicted that in the last days many false christs and false prophets would arise and do such wonders as to deceive the very elect (Matt 24:4-5, 23-24).

No NT author other than John uses the term "antichrist", but a similar concept of a spiritual force opposed to Christ which will manifest itself in the last days in a specific human being is used by Paul in II Thessalonians 2:3-9 where he speaks of the "man of lawlessness". According to Paul, this individual, empowered by Satan and the embodiment of all that is opposed to God, will be defeated by Christ at his second coming (II Thes 2:8). Most interpreters link the man of lawlessness, the antichrist, with "the beast" of Revelation 11:7. Like the man of lawlessness, the beast is empowered by Satan (though he is not Satan) and will be defeated by Christ (Rev 19:19-20).

ANTIOCH

1. Antioch of Pisidia (sometimes referred to as Pisidian Antioch) in southwest Asia in the border zone between Pisidia and Phrygia. The ruins of ancient Antioch are located near Yalvaç in modern Turkey. The city was founded by Seleucus I c. 301 B.C. Under Roman rule it became a free city (188 B.C.), and was later incorporated into the Roman province of Galatia (c. 25 B.C.). It was on the trade route between Ephesus and Cilicia. Apart from the Greek-speaking inhabitants and Roman colonists, Antioch contained a large Jewish community.

Paul and Barnabas visited the city twice on their missionary journeys and Paul preached in the synagogue (Acts 13:14-44). The interest aroused angered the Jewish leaders who had them expelled from the city (Acts 13:45-52). In his Second Epistle to Timothy, Paul recalls his persecution at Antioch (II Tim 3:11).

ANTIOCH 1
Acts 13:14;
14:19, 21, 26.
II Tim 3:11

Remains of a frieze of a Greek temple at Antioch of Pisidia.

A statue of Tyche, goddess of Antioch, with the river Orontes at her feet, seated on a rock representing Mount Silpius on which the city was built. (Museum Vaticani)

2. Antioch on the Orontes in Syria, modern Antakya. The city was founded by Seleucus I in 300 B.C. and like Antioch of Pisidia, he named it after his father, Antiochus. It became the capital of the Seleucids who developed it lavishly. The city was about 16 miles (26 km) from the sea. Seleucia, at the mouth of the Orontes River, founded at the same time, was its port. The original population consisted of Macedonian and Athenian settlers. Josephus writes that the Seleucids encouraged Jews to settle in Antioch and gave them full citizen rights, thus establishing a sizeable Jewish population. Antioch's economy was based on its fertile hinterland and on commerce. It rose to be the third great city of the Roman empire after Rome and Alexandria. Pompey made it the capital of the new province of Syria in 64 B.C.

The first mention of Antioch in the Bible is in connection with a certain Nicolas of Antioch, a proselyte, who became a Christian and was at Jerusalem at the time of Stephen's martyrdom (Acts 6:5). Following Stephen's death and the persecution of Christians in

ANTIOCH 2
Acts 6:5;
11:19-20, 22,
26-27; 13:1;
15:22-23, 30,
35; 18:22. Gal
2:11

Jerusalem, some of the disciples were scattered as far as Phoenicia, Cyprus and Antioch, preaching to Jews (Acts 11:19). In Antioch, they also began preaching to "Hellenists" ("Greeks", i.e., most likely Gentiles interested in Judaism). When the Christian congregation in Jerusalem heard that many people were becoming believers of Christ in Antioch, they dispatched Barnabas, who seeing the great interest shown there, brought Paul from Tarsus to help. Paul and Barnabas stayed there a whole year, making many converts. The disciples were first called "Christians" in Antioch (Acts 11:21-26). When the congregation heard of the famine which occurred at the time of the emperor Claudius c. A.D. 46, as predicted by Agabus, they generously sent financial aid to their brethren in Jerusalem through Paul and Barnabas (Acts 11:27-30).

Paul's second missionary journey began from Antioch and ended there (Acts 18:22). Christianity made great progress in Antioch and the city rivaled Jerusalem as its center. Its great importance to Christianity comes from the fact that here the first Gentile church was founded.

ANTIPAS A martyr of the early church of Pergamum (Pergamos) (Rev 2:12-13).

ANTIPATRIS See APHEK No.1

ANTONIA A fortress (not mentioned by name: AV "castle", RSV "barracks") north of the Temple Mount in Jerusalem, which was fortified by Herod and renamed by him so honoring his friend Mark Antony. It incorporated a palace, courtyards, bath-houses and cisterns. The underground stairs and passages connecting the fortress with the Temple area were used by the Jews during the revolt against Rome (66-70). Some commentators identified it with Gabbatha (John 19:13) where Pilate sat in judgment on Jesus. At the entrance to the Antonia Paul addressed the Jerusalem multitude (Acts 21:37 ff). The remains of the fortress have been excavated in the grounds of the Sisters of Zion convent in the Via Dolorosa.

ANTIPAS
Rev 2:13

ANTIPATRIS
Acts 23:31

A coin of Antioch with a portrait of Elgabalus on one side and the city goddess seated near the Orontes River on the other. Minted in A.D. 220.

A model of the Antonia fortress. (Part of the model of Jerusalem in the Second Temple period, reconstructed by the late Professor Avi Yonah on the grounds of the Holy Land Hotel, Jerusalem).

Cuneiform clay tablet found at the site of the Late-Canaanite palace at Aphek (Dept. of Archaeology, Tel Aviv University)

ANTOTHIJAH (ANTHOTHIJAH) A son of Shashak of the tribe of Benjamin (I Chr 8:1, 24-25).

ANTOTHIJAH
I Chr 8:24

ANUB A son of Koz, and a descendant of Judah.

ANUB
I Chr 4:8

APE See ANIMALS

APELLES A Christian in the congregation of Rome to whom Paul sent greetings.

APELLES
Rom 16:10

APHARSATHCHITES A Persian official, one of the group associated with Rehum who sent a letter to the king of Persia Artaxerxes complaining about the rebuilding of Jerusalem by the returned exiles (Ezra 4:6-9).

APHARSATHCHITES
Ezra 4:9

APHEK

1. An important station on the ancient Via Maris, mentioned in the list of Pharaoh Thutmosis III. The king of Aphek was one of the 31 rulers of Canaan vanquished by Joshua (Josh 12:18). The Philistines gathered their armies there to go into battle against Israel (I Sam 4:1; 29:1).

APHEK 1
Josh 12:18.
I Sam 4:1;
29:1

Early in the Hellenistic period a fort on the border between the districts of Samaria and the Sharon was built at this place, then known as Pegai. John Hyrcanus I conquered it in about 132 B.C. At that period it was also known as Arethusa, both names implying that it was built near rich sources of water, as indeed it was. When Herod the Great ascended the throne he built a new city at Arethusa, renaming it Antipatris, after his father Antipater. This new city became the center of a district with many prosperous villages. When Paul was sent under escort from Jerusalem to Caesarea he spent a night there (Acts 23:31).

Aphek-Antipatris is identified with Tell Ras el-Ain, which is rich in springs and vegetation. The sizeable mound is now occupied by a large Turkish citadel, built on the remains of a Crusader castle. The site was extensively excavated, 1974-1984.

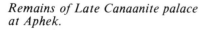

Remains of Late Canaanite palace at Aphek.

(right)
Aerial view of the fortress erected in the 17th century on the ruins of the Crusader castle at Antipatris (Aphek).

2. A site in the north of Canaan on the frontier with the Amorites; it was not conquered by Joshua but was regarded as part of Israel's inheritance (Josh 13:1-7).

APHEK 2
Josh 13:4

It is identified with modern Afka, some 15 miles (24 km) from ancient Byblos in Lebanon.

3. Canaanite Aphek, or Aphik as in Judges 1:31, a town in the territory of Asher, which was not conquered by the Israelites at the time of Joshua (Josh 19:24, 30), and whose inhabitants the tribe could not expel.

APHEK 3
I Kgs 20:26,
30. II Kgs
13:17

The site is identified with Tell Kurdaneh, southeast of Acre.

4. A town east of the Sea of Galilee, between Beth Shean and Damascus, where a great battle took place between the armies of Ben-Hadad, the king of Aram, and Ahab, king of Israel. The Arameans were defeated and those who were not killed fled to Aphek "into the city, then a wall fell on 27,000 men who were left. And Ben-Hadad fled and went into the city, into an inner chamber" (I Kgs 20:26-30). Here also, according to the prophecy of the dying prophet Elisha, King Jehoash of Israel would defeat the Arameans (II Kgs 13:17-19).

The biblical site is tentatively identified with Khirbet el-Apheq, near modern En Gev, on the eastern shore of the Sea of Galilee, where remains of an ancient Israelite town have been unearthed.

APHEKAH A city assigned to the tribe of Judah (Josh 15:20, 53). It was located in the Judean mountains at the site of Khirbet Canaan.

APHIAH A man of the tribe of Benjamin, an ancestor of King Saul (I Sam 9:1-2).

APHIK See APHEK No.3

A coin of Antipatris depicting Athena; 3rd century AD.

APOCRYPHA ("hidden"). Name given to a group of Jewish writings that date from approximately 300 B.C. to A.D. 70. Today the OT Apocrypha is a term denoting the 13 works contained in the oldest Greek codices of the OT but not in the Hebrew Bible. "Apocrypha" does not refer to "hidden" secrets, as in Daniel 12:9-10 and Ezra 14:44-48, but to extracanonical documents. Roman Catholics contend these works are "Deutero-canonical" and inspired; they are consequently to be found in the Catholic Bible. Protestants and Jews do not consider them canonical, even though some books, like Ecclesiasticus, are often acknowledged as authoritative and even inspired. All the books were written in a Semitic language and in Palestine, except for the Wisdom of Solomon and II Maccabees, composed in Greek, probably in Alexandria.

The Letter of Jeremiah was written long before 100 B.C. The original was composed sometime around 300 B.C. Containing only 72 or 73 verses, the work, influenced by Jeremiah 10:1-16, is an exhortation not to fear or worship idols.

Tobit was probably composed around 180 B.C. and is a romantic story teaching that God does indeed help those faithful to his laws.

Judith, composed about 150 B.C., is a story about how Judith beheaded the Assyrian general, Holofernes, and delivered her nation. The author intended to exhort Jews to be obedient to Torah and reject evil, especially as represented by an invading enemy.

I Esdras (also knows as III Esdras following the Septuagint where Ezra and Nehemiah are taken as I and II Esdras) was written sometime between 150-100 B.C.; it is a deliberate attempt to rewrite II Chronicles 35:1-36:23, Ezra, and Nehemiah 7:38-8:12. II Esdras 3:1-5:6 are independent of the OT. Notable features of the book are the elevation of Ezra as "high priest", the celebration of the Temple, and the preoccupation with Zerubbabel.

II Esdras (also known as IV Esdras or the Apocalypse of Ezra) is a Jewish apocalyptic work originally written in Hebrew or Aramaic (but known only in translation) not long after the destruction of the Second Temple. Facing the problem of Israel's suffering, it answers that while the world was created for Israel, Israel had sinned and must therefore pass through a period of purgation.

Prayer of Manasseh, a penitential psalm supplementing II Chronicles 33:11-13. Written in the 1st century B.C.

Additions to Esther are six expansions to the Book of Esther in its Greek form. The date for these additions is clearly pre-70 A.D., but may have been appended in different years between 167 to 114 B.C. or sometime in the 1st century B.C. The authors of these additions added color to the story, provided an apology for Judaism, and — most importantly — supplied the theological words and ideas conspicuously absent in Esther.

The Prayer of Azariah and the Song of the Three Young Men, Susanna and Bel and the Dragon are three additions to the Book of Daniel, dated between 165 and c. 100 B.C. *The Prayer of Azariah* turns the reader's attention to the Jews facing martyrdom and away from the wicked king; it stresses that there is only one God and that he is just. *Susanna* is a tale about a beautiful woman saved by Daniel when he cross-examined two elders and revealed that they were lying. *Bel and the Dragon* preserves two stories. One describes how Daniel proved that the food offered up to the idol Bel was in fact eaten by the priests; the other how Daniel destroyed an idol but was saved by Habakkuk with the aid of angels.

Baruch, which dates from the 1st or 2nd centuries B.C., is composite. It opens with an acknowledgement that Jerusalem was destroyed because of Israel's sins and with a plea for God's forgiveness, then moves through a poetic celebration of wisdom, to a description of how the lament from Jerusalem was heard.

Ecclesiasticus (Ben Sirach), probably composed around 180 B.C., by a conservative teacher in Jerusalem, is an apology for Judaism and a critique of Greek culture. Typical themes are the reverence of the Temple, the Torah and the belief in the one God who is just and merciful.

The Wisdom of Solomon, perhaps written in the 1st century B.C., is a blend of Israelite and Jewish wisdom traditions with Greek and Egyptian ideas. Wisdom is clearly personified.

I Maccabees, composed near the end of the 2nd century B.C., celebrates the military exploits of the Maccabees up to the rule of John Hyrcanus. The author is pro-Hasmonean, but does not articulate the importance or value of martyrdom. This document is a major source for studying the history of 2nd-century Palestine.

II Maccabees, written in the latter part of the 2nd century or the early decades of the 1st century B.C., is an epitome of a lost five-volume history by Jason of Cyrene. Much more theologically oriented than I Maccabees, II Maccabees stresses the resurrection of the body, the efficaciousness of martyrdom, and the revelatory dimension of miracles. It is anti-Hasmonean. Two letters introduce the epitome: the first, probably authentic, was composed around 124 B.C., in a Semitic language, and is an appeal to celebrate the festival of Hanukkah; the second letter, probably inauthentic, dates between 103 and 60 B.C. and may have been composed in Greek.

See also entries on the individual books.

APOLLONIA A city in Macedonia named after the sun-god Apollo, and to differentiate from other cities of the same name it was known as Apollonia Mygdonis from the name of the area in which it was situated. Paul and Silas passed though it on their way to Thessalonica.

APOLLONIA
Acts 17:1

APOLLOS A Jew of Alexandria, who was well versed in the Scriptures and was an eloquent speaker. He was a Christian who knew only the baptism of John until Aquila and Priscilla in Ephesus "explained to him the way of God more accurately". They gave him letters of recommendation for other congregations where he taught that Jesus was the messiah. He arrived in Corinth, where Paul had preceded him, and there he "watered" what Paul had "planted" (I Cor 3:5-10). It seems that when Paul wrote his First Epistles to the Corinthians there were divisions among the congregation (I Cor 1:10). Paul tried to change the views of the congregation where some saw Apollos as their

APOLLOS
Acts 18:24;
19:1. I Cor
1:12; 3:4-6,
22; 4:6; 16:12.
Titus 3:13

leader, while others favored Paul, and he pointed out the unimportance of individuals who are only men serving God and Christ: "For when one says, 'I am of Paul,' and another, 'I am of Apollos', are you not carnal? Who then is Paul, and who is Apollos, but ministers through whom you believed, as the Lord gave to each one?" (I Cor 3:4-5). Paul urged Apollos to visit Corinth but it seems that Apollos could not go at that time (I Cor 16:12). The last mention of Apollos is in Paul's Epistle to Titus where he asks Titus to help Apollos for some unmentioned trip (Titus 3:13).

APOLLYON
Rev 9:11

APOLLYON See ABADDON

APOSTLE Conventional Christian language tends to identify the term "apostle" with the twelve closest companions of Jesus during his public ministry, hence to fix the expression "the Twelve Apostles" (Matt 10:2; Luke 22:14) as a point of reference for the historic foundation of institutional Christianity. Luke's gospel offers the simplified rationale for this conventional usage in its report of the choice of "the Twelve": "And when it was day, he called his disciples to him, and from them he chose twelve, whom he also named apostles," (Luke 6:13; cf Acts 1:2). According to Luke's second book, the Acts of the Apostles, the eleven left after Judas' defection had to choose his replacement in the established circle of twelve from among the larger pool of those "who have accompanied us all the time that the Lord Jesus went in and out among us, beginning from the baptism of John..." (Acts 1:21-22). Luke thus paints the orderly picture of the origins of the Church which most people have: "apostles" were its founding authorities because they could vouch for its tradition about Jesus from comprehensive personal experience (Acts 13:31).

Yet even Luke, who seems to presume an equation of "the Twelve" and "the apostles", accords "apostle" status to the missionaries Barnabas and Paul in his account of the early Pauline missions in Asia Minor (Acts 14:4, 14). How could it be that Paul, who had no contact with Jesus during his earthly life, was classified as an "apostle" and even made vigorous claim to the title in his letters? (I Cor 9:1; 15:8-11; II Cor 12:11-12; Gal 1:1). His membership in the apostolic circle, even as "the least of the apostles" (I Cor 15:9), puts the prerequisite of companionship with the earthly Jesus in serious doubt.

Luke's prescription for Judas' successor did, however, include one feature which Paul could boast: namely the status of a witness of the resurrection (Acts 1:22). Paul's own list of resurrection witnesses, tailored to imply a closed series of which his experience was "the last of all" (I Cor 15:8), includes an appearance to "more than five hundred brethren at once" (I Cor 15:6) which effectively disqualifies "resurrection witness" as an adequately specific criterion for the apostle-status. Moreover, Paul's list further confuses the conventional picture by mentioning "the Twelve" and "all the apostles" separately in the appearance-series, clearly implying that, so far as he and his community knew, the two groups did not coincide after all (I Cor 15:5, 7). Correspondingly, the names which Paul mentions elsewhere in connection with the office of apostle — including "Andronicus and Junias" at Rome (Rom 16:7), "James, the Lord's brother in Jerusalem" (Gal 1:19; cf I Cor 15:7), perhaps even his own co-workers, Sylvanus and Timothy (I Thes 1:1) — range far beyond the lists of names of the Twelve given by the gospels and Acts, which, for that matter, are not consistent among themselves (Matt 10:2-4; Mark 3:16-19; Luke 6:14-16; Acts 1:13). All that can be concluded from Paul's evidence, therefore, is that although he knew the apostles as a closed circle to which he gained belated entrance as "last of all" (I Cor 15:8), he does not identify that circle with "the Twelve" of Jesus' ministry but includes several names associated with the development of the Gentile mission as well as those who were "apostles before me" at Jerusalem (Gal 1:17). Paul builds the argument for his own claim to apostolic status upon some fixed credentials of "apostle of Jesus Christ," but these were apparently so well known to his audiences that he never needed to list them (Rom 1:1-5; I Cor 9:1-6; 15:1-11; II Cor 11:5-15; 12:11-13; Gal 1:1-17). Consequently, his interpreter of today has to piece them together from mostly unspoken premises of his arguments, and the results of this are far from conclusive.

Research of the Greek word *apostolos* is not much more productive of decisive norms for the office. The noun's relation to the verb "send" *apostellein* is illustrated in the one use the fourth evangelist makes of the former (John 13:16). In Greek usage outside the Bible, this relationship is found mostly in reference to military and maritime expeditions, without the distinctive NT sense of an authorized "envoy". The Greek translation of the OT approaches that sense once, the only time it uses the noun (I Kgs 14:6). Only if we press our search beyond the precise word *apostolos* can we find a material parallel to the office of apostle, which heads the list of Church functions given twice in the Pauline letters (I Cor 12:28; Eph 4:11). The legal institution of the envoy-delegate, who carried the same authority and commanded the same respect as the person he represented, was legislated by the Talmud (cf *Mishnah Berakhot* 5:5) and comes close to the NT institution. But since the rabbinical provision was not confined to religious matters and is of uncertain origin, its influence on the NT cannot be demonstrated.

It looks finally as if "apostle" might be a language-innovation made by earliest Christianity, even though the usage was already fixed by the time of Paul's earliest writing. "Apostles of Jesus Christ" were fully authorized delegates of the risen Christ, dispatched by his personal revelation (Eph 2:20; 3:5) and, with the charismatic prophets, itinerant founders of the earliest Christian communities. By analogy, the authorized envoys of these communities in dealings with the rest of Christendom were sometimes called "messengers of the churches" (II Cor 8:23). There was, however, a unique apostolic charism of embodying the Lord's own person, and this accounts for the special play Paul gives to his personal embodiment of both the sufferings of Christ and the principle of salvation "by the grace of God" (I Cor 4:9-13; 15:9-10; II Cor 11:21-12:13; Gal 1:13-17; Phil 3:4-11). His theology of the cross applied to the apostolic mandate put a higher value on suffering for the mission than on the "signs and wonders and mighty deeds" (II Cor 12:12) which others relied on as the "signs of an apostle."

View of the Appian Way.

APPAIM ("nostrils"). A son of Nadab and descendant of Jerahmeel of the tribe of Judah (I Chr 2:25, 30-31).

APPHIA A Christian woman mentioned among the persons in the salutation of Paul's Letter to Philemon. It has sometimes been assumed that she was Philemon's wife or that she was the wife of Archippus whose name follows hers in the salutation.

APPII FORUM The Forum of Appius near Rome, through which Paul passed as a prisoner on his way from Puteoli on the Bay of Naples. A station on the famous Via Appia highway from Rome to the Bay of Naples, and located at the northern terminus of a canal that permitted boat travel through the Pontine Marshes, it was a marketplace and a busy trading center. It was here that the delegation of Christians from Rome came to greet Paul on his arrival (Acts 28:13-15).

APPLE See PLANTS

AQUILA A Jew, native of the province of Pontus in Asia Minor, whose

APPAIM
I Chr 2:30-31

APPHIA
Philem v. 2

APPII FORUM
Acts 28:15

AQUILA
Acts 18:2, 18, 26. Rom 16:3.
I Cor 16:19.
II Tim 4:19

wife Priscilla is always mentioned in association with him. They were banished from Rome by Emperor Claudius' decree against the Jews (in A.D. 50), and took up residence in Corinth. When Paul arrived on his first visit to Corinth he stayed with them, and a close friendship developed as they worked together in the same trade of tentmaking (Acts 18:1-3). When Paul left Corinth, about two years later, Priscilla and Aquila accompanied him as far as Ephesus where they remained (Acts 18:18-21). Whether they were Christian when Paul met them or became Christians in Corinth is not clear. At any rate they evangelized like Paul. In Ephesus they heard Apollos preach and "explained to him the way of God more accurately" (Acts 18:24-26).

The couple returned to Rome for some time, since, in his Epistles to the Romans, Paul sends greetings to Priscilla and Aquila, "my fellow workers in Christ Jesus, who risked their own necks for my life, to whom not only I give thanks, but also all the churches of the Gentiles. Likewise greet the church that is in their house" (Rom 16:3-5). Paul greeted them in his First Epistle to the Corinthians (I Cor 16:19), and in the Second Epistle to Timothy (II Tim 4:19).

(bottom)
Landscape in the Arabah.

View of Ar Moab.

AR (AR MOAB) A place or a region in Moab, located on the south bank of the Arnon River on the northern border of Moab (Num 21:15, 28). At times its name was used as a synonym for the land of Moab as a whole (Deut 2:9, 18, 29). In his prophecies of desolation against Moab, Isaiah foretold that Ar would be destroyed (Is 15:1).

ARA A son of Jether of the tribe of Asher.

ARAB A place in Judah, in the hill region of Hebron (Josh 15:48, 52), identified with modern el-Rabiyeh, about 8 miles (13 km) southwest of Hebron. Paarai the Arbite, one of David's "mighty men", was probably from Arab (II Sam 23:35).

ARABAH Region around the rift valley that stretches from both sides of the Jordan down to the Gulf of Akaba at the Red Sea (Deut 3:17; Josh 3:16). In the Bible it is also referred to as "plain" (Deut 11:30; II Sam 2:29; Jer 52:7), and in the AV as "the champaign" (Deut 11:30).

In the Bible Arabah is used to indicate any part of this long depression: the part south of the Dead Sea (Deut 2:8; this region being arid and sterile, the prophets used Arabah in the general sense of "desert" or "steppe"; Job 24:5; Ps 78:40; Is 34:14; Jer 17:6); the region east of the Jordan (Deut 4:49); west of the Jordan (Josh 11:16); or the entire Jordan Valley south of the Sea of Galilee (II Sam 4:7).

The Sea of the Arabah or Salt Sea is used sometimes in the Bible to indicate the Dead Sea (Deut 3:17; 4:49; II Kgs 4:25).

ARABIA, ARABIANS, ARABS A peninsula 2,000 miles (3,200 km) long and 600 miles (965 km) wide between Africa and Asia. Most of the central part is desert, with large scattered oases. The more fertile parts lie along its fringes, especially on the west, facing the Red Sea. The major trade routes connecting Arabia with the outside world led to Babylonia and Assyria, to Egypt and northwards along the coast to Palestine and Syria.

Arabia and the Arabs are mentioned frequently in the Bible. These Arabs were mostly the nomadic tent-dwellers who occupied the northwestern part of the peninsula, where they grazed their flocks (Is 13:20). Close relations were maintained between the Israelite kingdom and the Arabians, especially with the richer southern kingdoms, from the time of Solomon onwards. Gold and silver were brought from there (II Chr 9:14). Jehoshaphat received flocks of rams and goats as tribute from the nomads (II Chr 17:11), as did Tyre (Ezek 27:11), while spices, precious stones and gold were brought from Sheba and Raamah (Ezek 27:22). There is evidence that Arabs tried to settle in Judea after the destruction of the First Temple. It was these Arabs who attempted to prevent Nehemiah from rebuilding the fallen walls of Jerusalem (Neh 2:19). The NT mentions that Paul "went away to Arabia" (Gal 1:17).

ARABIA, ARABIANS, ARABS
I Kgs 10:15.
II Chr 9:14;
17:11; 21:16;
22:1; 26:7.
Neh 4:7. Is
13:20; 21:13.
Jer 3:2; 25:24.
Ezek 27:21.
Acts 2:11. Gal
1:17; 4:25

ARAD

1. One of the sons of Beriah of the tribe of Benjamin who at one time lived in Jerusalem (I Chr 8:1, 15-16, 28).

2. An important city in the eastern Negeb (South) which controlled the main road to Edom and Elath. The king of Arad attacked the Israelites as they approached Canaan, in the time of Moses. After his initial success, the Israelites counterattacked and destroyed the city, which they renamed Hormah, i.e., utter destruction (Num 21:1-3). The site was later occupied by the Kenites (Judg 1:16). The king of Hormah and the king of Arad are included in the list of the rulers vanquished by Joshua (Josh 12:14), where Arad is listed as Eder in the southern district of Judah (Josh 15:21).

During the period of the monarchy Arad was destroyed and burnt several times, but was rebuilt and served until the end of the First Temple Period as the royal, military and administrative center of the border area. Fortresses also stood here later, in the Persian, Hellenistic and Roman periods.

Excavations at the ancient site have revealed two different settlements: a large fortified city which existed there during the Chalcolithic and Early Bronze Age (c. 3000-2600 B.C.), and remains of a smaller Iron Age fortress.

ARAD 1
I Chr 8:15

ARAD 2
Num 21:1;
33:40. Josh
12:14. Judg
1:16

(top) Alabaster figurine from South Arabia. (Israel Museum)

(center left) South Arabian monumental inscription.

(center right) The Red Sea coast in the southwestern corner of the Arabian peninsula.

(bottom) A coin struck in Arabia, depicting "Arabia" holding two babies; 2nd century A.D.

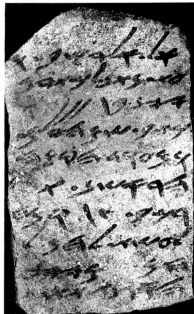

Model of the Israelite fortress at Arad looking north from the Early Canaanite town; the temple is at the top left-hand corner.

(top left)
View of the fortress at Arad.

(top right)
An ostracon from Arad of the early 6th century B.C.

The most remarkable discovery at Arad is the Iron Age temple. Its orientation, general plan and contents, especially the altars, are similar to the Temple of Solomon.

Among many Hebrew ostraca found in the temple are two which bear names of priestly families mentioned in the Bible, Meremoth and Pashhur. Other inscriptions belong to the archives of a man called Eliashib, son of Eshyahu, who was possibly the commander of the last citadel (c. 600 B.C.). In one there is a reference to the "House of Yahweh", probably the Temple at Jerusalem.

ARAH

1. One of the sons of Ulla of the tribe of Asher (I Chr 7:30, 39).

2. An ancestor of some of those who returned with Zerubbabel from the Babylonian Exile (Ezra 2:1-2, 5; Neh 7:6-7, 10).

ARAM

1. The fifth son of Shem; the father (or, see I Chr 1:17, the brother) of Uz, Hul, Gether and Mash — five of the seventy nations listed after the Flood (Gen 10:22-23). Their descendants were the Arameans.

2. The son of Kemuel and grandson of Nahor, Abraham's brother (Gen 22:21). The patriarchs had close family ties with the Arameans: Isaac married a granddaughter of Nahor, sister of Laban the Aramean (Gen 25:20), and Jacob married daughters of the same Laban (Gen 31:50-52). Jacob himself is even called the son of a Syrian (Aramean) (Deut 26:5).

3. One of the four sons of Shemer of the tribe of Asher.

ARAM, ARAMEANS A group of tribes spread over a wide area at the end of the 2nd millennium and in the first half of the 1st millennium B.C., from the Persian Gulf and Elam in the south and east and the Amanus mountains in the north to southern Syria and northern Transjordan in the west. Arameans are given as "Syrians" in English OT translations.

The origin of the Arameans is obscure. Some scholars claim they originated in the Syro-Arabian desert, while others believe that they may have arrived with some movement of the Horite tribes which migrated from the north. A city named Aram in the region of the upper Tigris (Hiddekel) is mentioned around 2000 B.C. According to the Bible, Aram was one of the descendants of Shem (Gen 10:22-23; I Chr

ARAH 1
I Chr 7:39

ARAH 2
Ezra 2:5. Neh 6:18; 7:10

ARAM 1
Gen 10:22-23.
I Chr 1:17

ARAM 2
Gen 22:21

ARAM 3
I Chr 7:34

ARAM, ARAMEANS (SYRIANS)
Gen 10:22-23; 22:21; 25:20; 28:5; 31:20, 24. Num 23:7. Deut 26:5. Judg 10:6 II Sam 8:5-6, 12-13; 10:6, 8-9, 11, 13-19; 15:8. I Kgs 10:29; 11:25;

Two Aramean dignitaries depicted on a relief from Sam'al. 9th-8th centuries B.C.

1:17). It is not until the end of the 2nd millennium that Aram is mentioned frequently in the Assyrian sources. In the documents of the 14th to 13th centuries they are referred to as invaders originating from the desert and penetrating the inhabited land. Tiglath-Pileser I of Assyria relates that in the fourth year of his reign (1112 B.C.) the Arameans came from the Arabian desert to invade the regions of Tadmor, Mount Lebanon and Babylon. At the same time they were already settling on the west bank of the Euphrates, where they founded cities. By the 11th century B.C. the Arameans had conquered the spacious plains of Mesopotamia and constituted a menace to Assyria. In the regions which they conquered they founded strong political units. By the 10th century B.C. their expansion to the west was checked by the kings of Israel, while in the east they were pushed back by the Assyrians. The frequent rebellions of the Arameans were cruelly put down by Sargon and Sennacherib, who deported many of the rebels to distant lands.

Aram Damascus, usually referred to simply as Aram, was the most important of the Aramean kingdoms in the 9th-8th centuries B.C. It was bordered by the Kingdom of Israel on the south, Hamath on the north and the Phoenician cities on the west. David defeated the Arameans of Damascus (II Sam 8:5; AV: Syrians of Damascus). In the days of the Divided Kingdom there was a constant state of war between Aram and Israel. Aided by Asa, king of Judah, the Arameans under Ben-Hadad I conquered the land of Naphtali (I Kgs 15:18-20). Omri, king of Israel, was forced to cede cities in Samaria to the Arameans (I Kgs 20:34), but Ahab succeeded in beating them back (I Kgs 20:1-34).

15:18; 19:15; 20:1, 20-23, 26-29; 22:1, 3, 11, 31, 35. II Kgs 5:1-2, 5, 20; 6:8-9, 11, 18, 23-24; 7:4-6, 10, 12, 14-16; 8:7, 9, 13, 28-29; 9:14-15; 12:17-18; 13:3-5, 7, 17, 19, 22, 24; 15:37; 16:5-7; 24:2. I Chr 2:23; 7:14; 18:5-6; 19:6, 10, 12, 14-19. II Chr 1:17; 16:2, 7; 18:10, 30, 34; 20:2; 22:5-6; 24:23-24; 28:5, 23. Is 7:1-2, 4-5, 8; 9:12; 17:3. Ezek 16:57; 27:16. Jer 35:11. Hos 12:12. Amos 1:5; 9:7

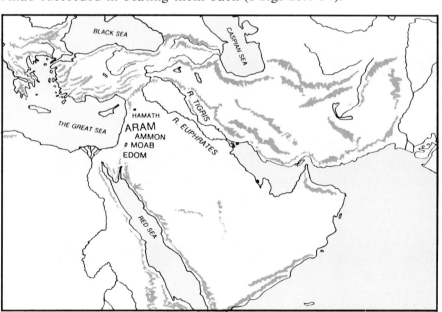

Aram

The rise of Assyria brought about a coalition between the kings of Syria and Israel. The great battle between Assyria and this coalition, in which thousands of chariots and myriads of infantry fought, took place in 853 B.C. near Karkar in the land of Hamath. Neither this battle nor those which followed could bring a final settlement. When Assyrian pressure diminished temporarily, Hazael, king of Damascus, conquered the whole of eastern Transjordan and penetrated into Israel, reaching the northern border of Judah (II Kgs 10:32-33; 12:18-19; 13:7). Renewed Assyrian pressure forced Ben-Hadad III to pay tribute to Assyria, while Jehoash and Jeroboam II freed the conquered parts of their kingdom and even captured Damascus (II Kgs 13:25; 14:25, 28). In

733-732 B.C. Tiglath-Pileser III conquered Damascus and put an end to the independence Damascus and Israel (722 B.C.), turning them into Assyrian satrapies and deporting many of their inhabitants. The Aramaic script and language survived the Arameans for many centuries (see ARAMAIC).

Aram Zobah was the largest and strongest of the Aramean kingdoms of Syria in the days of David. Its nucleus was in the Anti-Lebanon, from where it spread over the plain of Lebanon and Bashan, reaching eastwards as far as the Euphrates (II Sam 10:16). Enmity between Zobah and Israel started as early as the days of Saul (I Sam 14:47). By the time Hadadezer of Aram Zobah had subdued all the other kings (II Sam 10:19), he in turn was defeated by David in a series of battles, at the end of which David conquered Maachah, the land of Tob, and other regions (II Sam 8:3 ff; 10:6-14, 16-19). In 733 B.C. Zobah was conquered by the Assyrians and was turned into an Assyrian satrapy under the name of Subatu.

The Bible mentions several small Aramean kingdoms which sprang up to the north of the Kingdom of Israel. Among them were Aram Beth Rehov and Aram Maachah, the one being centered round the town of Beth Rehob, close to Dan (Judg 18:28), and the other in the upper Jordan Valley, round Abel Beth Maachah. Together with Aram Zobah and Aram Maachah, the Arameans of Beth Rehob participated in the war of the Ammonites against David (II Sam 10:6). After their defeat the two petty kingdoms came under Israelite rule. In later generations they were ruled either by the Israelites or by the Arameans of Damascus.

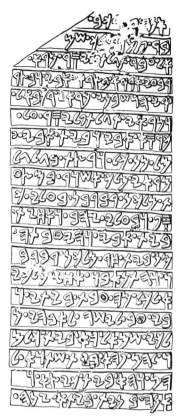

Aramaic monumental inscription of Bar-Rakib, king of Sam'al, late 8th century B.C.

(left)
Aramaic cursive letters, early 6th century B.C.

(left bottom)
Aramaic inscription in the Syrian Orthodox Church of St. Mark, Jerusalem.

(below)
Aramaic papyrus found at Saqqarah, Egypt, c. 600 B.C.

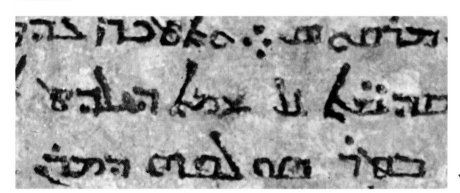

ARAMAIC
**II Kgs 18:26.
Ezra 4:7. Is
36:11. Dan 2:4**

ARAMAIC A North Semitic language, similar to Hebrew and written in the same square script. It emerged as the *lingua franca* of the countries along the commercial routes of the Fertile Crescent in about the 6th century B.C. Aramaic became the vernacular of Palestine and can be found in the OT (Ezra 4:8-6:18; 7:12-26; Jer 10:11; Dan 2:4-7:28 are written in Aramaic). It was still the spoken language in the days of Jesus and those of his utterances preserved in the original are in Aramaic (Matt 27:46; Mark 5:41). Many scholars maintain that the Greek gospels were composed on the basis of oral traditions originally in Aramaic.

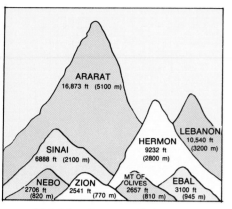

Heights of some of the most outstanding mountains mentioned in the Bible compared to that of Mount Ararat.

ARAN The second son of the Horite chief Dishan.

ARARAT The mountain on which Noah's ark came to rest (Gen 8:4). Mount Ararat is part of the Armenian ridge, in the easternmost part of Turkey, adjacent to the Armenian border. The mountain itself is the highest in the ridge, c. 16,000 feet (5,156 m) above sea level, and about 13,000 feet (4,000 m) higher than the neighboring peaks. The name Ararat has been applied to a wider area than the mountain itself. In Hittite and Assyrian records, from the 2nd millennium onwards, it referred to the earlier area surrounding Lake Van in eastern Anatolia.

During the 2nd and the beginning of the 1st millennia the area was divided between various small kingdoms ("Nairi lands"). It became a powerful kingdom in the 9th century, under the ruler Sarduri I, the founder of a new Urartian dynasty. From approximately this time and during most of the 9th and the 8th century Urartu is mentioned frequently in Assyrian inscriptions. The kingdom of Urartu reached its zenith in the days of Argishti I, who ascended the throne c. 786 B.C. and reigned until 764 B.C. Its slow decline commenced during the period of his son and successor, Sarduri II. This was completed by the Babylonian army which, together with the Medes, invaded the kingdom of Urartu and destroyed most of its main sites. In spite of frequent efforts to locate the exact site of Noah's ark, no serious evidence has ever been found in the mountains of Ararat, whose role in the Genesis story is therefore still a matter of legend. The mention of Ararat among the nations that would unite in coalition against Babylon (Jer 51:27) seems to have a more solid historical basis.

ARAN
Gen 36:28.
I Chr 1:42

ARARAT
Gen 8:4.
II Kgs 19:37.
Is 37:38. Jer 51:27

Mount Ararat in eastern Turkey.

ARAUNAH A Jebusite; owner of a threshing floor, traditionally located on Mount Moriah, where God restrained the angel from destroying Jerusalem as a judgment on David's sin of taking a census (II Sam 24:16; I Chr 21:15).

When David later offered to buy the threshing floor from Araunah as a fitting place for an altar, the latter was willing to give both his floor and oxen to the king, but David insisted on paying 50 shekels of silver for them (II Sam 24:24). In the parallel account of these events in the Chronicles, Araunah's name is given as Ornan (I Chr 21:15-18; II Chr 3:1).

ARBA ("four"). An inhabitant of Hebron, or Kirjath Arba, at the time

ARAUNAH
II Sam 24:16, 18, 20-24

ARBA
Josh 14:15; 15:13; 21:11

of the conquest of Canaan by Joshua (Josh 14:15). He was the "greatest man among the Anakim", or "race of giants", and seems to have been the founder of Kirjath Arba (Josh 15:13; 21:11).

ARBATHITE A resident of Beth Arabah, a city near Jericho (Josh 15:61; 18:21-22). One of David's "mighty men", Abi-Albon or Abiel was an Arbathite (II Sam 23:8, 31; I Chr 11:10, 32).

ARBITE A resident of Arab; Paarai the Arbite was one of David's "mighty men".

ARCHELAUS See HEROD ARCHELAUS

ARCHIPPUS A Christian living in or near Colossae, Asia Minor. In his Epistle to the Colossians Paul urges Archippus to fulfill his ministry (Col 4:17). He refers to him as "fellow soldier" (Philem v.2).

ARCHITE (S) A clan or family of the tribe of Benjamin established in the area of Ataroth, southwest of Bethel (Josh 16:2). Hushai, the counselor of David, and later of Absalom, was an Archite (II Sam 15:32; 16:16; 17:5, 14; I Chr 27:33).

ARD A son of Benjamin, and one of the 70 persons of the house of Jacob who went down to Egypt with him (Gen 46:21, 27). In Numbers 26:40 Ard is given as the son of Bela and grandson of Benjamin. In this case he is identical with Addar in I Chronicles 8:3.

ARDITES A Benjamite family descended from Ard, son of Bela.

ARDON One of the sons of Caleb the son of Hezron, of the tribe of Judah.

ARELI One of the sons of Gad; he was one of Jacob's family who went to Egypt (Gen 46:8, 16).

ARELITES A family descended from Areli who were included in the census in the wilderness shortly before entering the promised land.

AREOPAGITE A member of the court that met on the Areopagus in Athens (See below).

AREOPAGUS The "hill of Ares" (Mars Hill), situated west of the Athenian Acropolis, meeting-place of the ancient council or court of Athens, known as the "council of the Areopagus". Its functions varied from time to time; originally limited to cases of capital crime, and in mythology the Areopagus was a court of homicide even for the gods. Ares, the Greek god of war, would have been the first to be tried on the hill, for the slaying of Halirrhothius, Poseidon's son; and Orestes was later tried for the murder of his mother, Clytemnestra. At other times the court dealt with legal, political, educational and religious affairs. The Areopagus lost much of its power and influence with the development of the democracy in the 5th century B.C. Although its prestige declined, it survived until the late Roman Empire and still commanded honor and respect.

On one of Paul's visits to Athens, he was led to the Areopagus by Epicurean and Stoic philosophers (Acts 17:16-20). Paul addressed them but when he spoke of the Resurrection, they mocked him. However some believed, among them Dionysius the Areopagite and a woman named Damaris (Acts 17:22-34).

ARETAS The name borne by four Nabatean kings (See NABATEANS). The one mentioned in the NT is Aretas IV (9 B.C.-A.D. 40). His daughter married Herod Antipas, tetrarch of Galilee. She returned to her father, however, when Antipas married Herodias, the wife of his half-brother Herod Philip. Further aggravated by border disputes, Aretas attacked and defeated Herod Antipas.

At the time that Paul was in Damascus, Aretas IV controlled the city. Paul relates that the governor appointed by King Aretas had the gates of the city guarded in order to seize him but he was let down in a basket through a window in the city wall, and escaped (II Cor 11:32-33).

ARBATHITE
II Sam 23:31.
I Chr 11:32

ARBITE
II Sam 23:35

ARCHELAUS
Matt 2:22

ARCHIPPUS
Col 4:17.
Philem v. 2

ARCHITE(S)
Josh 16:2.
II Sam 15:32;
16:16; 17:5,
14. I Chr
27:33

ARD
Gen 46:21.
Num 26:40

ARDITES
Num 26:40

ARDON
I Chr 2:18

ARELI
Gen 46:16.
Num 26:17

ARELITES
Num 26:17

AREOPAGITE
Acts 17:34

AREOPAGUS
Acts 17:19, 22

ARETAS
II Cor 11:32

A coin of Aretas III, depicting the head of the king and the Tyche of Damascus. c. 75 B.C.

ARGOB

1. One of the men mentioned among those who were killed along with King Pekahiah of Israel, by Pekah in Samaria (II Kgs 15:23-25).

ARGOB 1
II Kgs 15:25

2. A part of the kingdom of Og, situated in Bashan north of Gilead and conquered by the Israelites before they crossed the Jordan. It is described as having 60 fortified cities besides many rural towns (Deut 3:3-6). Jair, son of Manasseh, who conquered this region, called it after himself, Havvoth Jair, i.e. "towns of Jair" (Deut 3:12-14). Under King Solomon the region of Argob and the towns of Jair were two separate districts and their governor resided at Ramoth Gilead (I Kgs 4:13).

ARGOB 2
Deut 3:4, 13-14.
I Kgs 4:13

ARIDAI One of Haman's ten sons who were killed at Shushan (Susa).

ARIDATHA One of Haman's ten sons who were killed at Shushan (Susa).

ARIDAI
Est 9:9

ARIDATHA
Est 9:8

ARIEH One of the men who participated in the assassination of King Pekahiah of Israel, under the leadership of Pekah.

ARIEH
II Kgs 15:25

ARIEL (possibly meaning "lion of God" or "hearth of God").

1. One of the chief men summoned by Ezra to bring "servants for the house of our God" before he departed from the river of Ahava to go to Jerusalem (Ezra 8:15-17, 31).

ARIEL 1
Ezra 8:16

2. A name applied to Jerusalem by Isaiah, or in Ezekiel 43:15-16 to a cultic object, probably an altar hearth.

ARIEL 2
Is 29:1-2, 7

ARIMATHEA The home of the rich disciple Joseph, who buried Jesus in his own new tomb (Matt 27:57; Mark 15:13; Luke 23:51; John 19:38). In the OT it was called Ramathaim Zophim, or Ramah, birthplace of Samuel (I Sam 1:1, 19).

ARIMATHEA
Matt 27:57.
Mark 15:43.
Luke 23:51.
John 19:38

ARIOCH

1. The king of Ellasar, who, in league with three kings including Chedorlaomer, waged war against five other kings and defeated them in the Valley of Siddim. After carrying off Lot and his household, they were overtaken and defeated by Abraham (Gen 14:1-16).

ARIOCH 1
Gen 14:1, 9

2. The captain of the guard of Nebuchadnezzar, the king of Babylon; he was ordered to kill all the wise men of Babylon after they failed to interpret the king's dream. When learning that Daniel could interpret the dream, he brought him to the king (Dan 2:12-25).

ARIOCH 2
Dan 2:14-15,
24-25

ARISAI One of the ten sons of Haman, who were killed at Shushan (Susa).

ARISAI
Est 9:9

ARISTARCHUS A Macedonian from Thessalonica; one of Paul's traveling companions. When Paul was in Ephesus Aristarchus was arrested with him when the devotees of Artemis rioted because of Paul's preaching of Jesus (Acts 19:29). The two were also together on Paul's voyage to Rome (Acts 27:1-2). Paul conveyed greetings from Aristarchus in the Epistle to the Colossians (Col 4:10) and in his letter to Philemon (Philem 24). Both the Acts and the Epistles show Aristarchus as a devoted and valued associate of Paul. Tradition has it that he was martyred in Rome in the time of the Emperor Nero.

ARISTARCHUS
Acts 19:29;
20:4; 27:2. Col
4:10. Philem
v. 24

ARISTOBULUS A Christian to whose family in Rome Paul sends greetings.

ARISTOBULUS
Rom 16:10

ARKITE(S) Descendants of Ham through Canaan. The name was probably taken from the city of Arkat near Tripoli in Phoenicia.

ARKITE(S)
Gen 10:17.
I Chr 1:15

ARK OF NOAH When God sent a flood to destroy his sinful creatures, he decided to spare the righteous Noah, ordering him to build an ark that would float on the water (Gen chaps. 6-8). The ark was to contain Noah, his wife, his three sons and their wives as well as specimens of all living creatures chosen to save God's creation from total extinction (Gen 6:14-21). Hence the huge dimensions of the ark: it was 300 cubits (450 feet or 140 m) long, 50 cubits (75 feet or 23 m) wide and 30 cubits (45 feet or 14 m) high. The deck space was approximately 100,000

ARK OF NOAH
Gen 6:14-16,
18-19; 7:1, 7,
9, 13, 15,
17-18, 23; 8:1,
4, 6, 9-10, 13,
16, 19; 9:10,
18. Matt
24:38. Luke

Noah building the ark. From the Sarajevo Haggadah, Spain, c. 1400. (Sarajevo National Museum)

17:27. Heb
11:7. I Pet
3:20

square feet (9,000 sq.m) and the vessel's volume was about 1,500,000 cubic feet (42,000 cubic m). The ark had windows in the roof (Gen 6:16) and a door in its side, and was three storeys high. It was constructed of gopher wood (quite possibly a kind of pine), covered inside and out with pitch (Gen 6:14). When the flood subsided, the ark settled atop one of the mountains of Ararat (i.e. Urartu — Armenia) (Gen 8:4). The Noah story is greatly influenced by Mesopotamian flood epics where the hero of the story (Ziusudra, Atrahasis, Utnapishtim) was saved by a boat. The difference, however, is telling: as the epic mentions a boat can be steered. In contrast an ark can only float aimlessly upon the waters. This highlights the main feature of the Noah story, where salvation of the righteous depends totally upon God. In the NT Peter cites Noah's ark as a type of baptism (I Pet 3:20-22).

ARK OF THE COVENANT (OF THE TESTIMONY, OF THE LORD)

ARK OF THE
COVENANT
(OF THE
TESTIMONY,
OF THE LORD)
Ex 25:10, 14-
16, 21-22;
26:33-34; 30:6,
26; 31:7;
35:12; 37:1, 5;
39:35; 40:3, 5,
20-21. Lev
16:2. Num
3:31; 4:5; 7:89;
10:33, 35;
14:44. Deut
10:1-3, 5, 8;
31:9, 25-26.
Josh 3:3, 6, 8,
11, 13-15, 17;
4:5, 7, 9-11,
16, 18; 6:4, 6-
9, 11-13; 7:6;
8:33. Judg
20:27. I Sam
3:3; 4:3-6, 11,
13, 17-19,
21-22; 5:1-4,
7-8, 10-11;
6:1-3, 8, 11, 13,
15, 18-19, 21;
7:1-2; 14:18

The Israelites' most holy cult-object: a wooden chest, built by Bezalel upon God's instruction to Moses at Mount Sinai (Ex 25:10-22; 37:1-9). Made of acacia wood and covered with gold, it was $2^1/_2$ cubits (c. $3^1/_2$ ft, 1.10 m) long; its breadth and height were $1^1/_2$ cubits (c. $2^1/_2$ ft, 70 cm) (Ex 25:10). Above it was a cover of pure gold, and at both sides, a cherub (Ex 25:17-20). Moses placed the tablets (the "testimony") of the law given to him by God on Mount Sinai (Ex 25:21; Deut 10:1-5) within the ark,

The holy ark on wheels, carved on a stone found in the synagogue at Capernaum dating from the late 3rd or 4th century A.D.

which was therefore called "ark of the testimony" (Ex 25:22), "ark of the covenant of the Lord" (Deut 10:8; Josh 3:3), the "ark of the Lord" (I Sam 4:6) and "the ark of God" (I Sam 4:11, 17-18, 21-22). From above the cover, between the cherubs, God spoke to Moses in order to give him his commandments (Ex 25:22). Thus the ark was a concrete sign of the divine presence in Israel (cf Ex 25:8).

The ark was placed in the tabernacle, in the Holy of Holies (Ex 40:20-21). Like the tabernacle and its contents, it was movable (Ex 25:12-14) and, during the wanderings of the Israelites, was carried by the Levite sons of Kohath (Num 4:5-6, 15). While marching or camping, the Israelites kept the tabernacle at their center (Num 2:1, 17), though according to another tradition it was carried in the vanguard (Num 10:33-36). The presence of the ark at the front of the people was a sign that the Lord went before them in battle (Deut 1:30-33): the walls of the city of Jericho fell down on the seventh day after Israel circumvallated the city with the ark (Josh 6:3-5, 12-16, 20). After the conquest of Canaan, the tabernacle with the ark in it was first set up in Shiloh (Josh 18:1, 10; 19:51). When the Israelites were defeated by the Philistines, and the latter captured the ark (I Sam 4:10-11), this event was perceived as a sign of divine displeasure, the ark's departure being described as the exiling of the glory from Israel (I Sam 4:21-22; Ps 78:60-61).

II Sam 6:2-4, 6-7, 9-13, 15-17; 7:2; 11:11; 15:24-25, 29. I Kgs 2:26; 3:15; 6:19; 8:1, 3-7, 9, 21. I Chr 6:31; 13:3, 5-7, 9-10, 12-14; 15:1-3, 12, 14-15, 23-29; 16:1, 4, 6, 37; 17:1; 22:19; 28:2, 18. II Chr 1:4; 5:2, 4-10; 6:11, 41; 8:11; 35:3. Ps 132:8. Jer 3:16. Heb 9:4. Rev 11:19

The holy ark represented on the mosaic floor of the synagogue at Beth Shean, built in the late 4th or early 5th century.

The Philistines carried the ark off to Ashdod, and placed it in the temple of Dagon near the statue of their god, whereupon the idol fell off its pedestal. On being raised, the idol fell a second time and broke to pieces (I Sam 5:1-5). Moreover, the people of Ashdod were afflicted with bubonic plague which spread to Gath and Ekron, after the ark was transferred to those towns (I Sam 5:6-12). Seven months later the Philistines were advised by their diviners to send the ark off with a guilt-offering (I Sam 6:1-7) and it was restored to Israel at Beth Shemesh. However, when the inhabitants of that town were also stricken by a plague, the ark was transferred to Kirjath Jearim, to the house of Abinadab (I Sam 6:13-7:1), where it remained throughout the Philistine domination of Israel and the entire reign of Saul. After David defeated the Philistines and conquered Jerusalem (II Sam 5:6-25), he decided to transfer the ark from the house of Abinadab (now living in Baale Judah (II Sam 6:2), or Baalah, according to I Chronicles 13:6) to his new capital (II Sam 6:1-5, also I Chr 13:1-8). The first attempt to convey the ark ended in disaster when Uzzah, son of Abinadab, touched it to prevent its falling: he died on the spot, whereupon David left the ark with Obed-Edom the Gittite (II Sam 6:7-11; I Chr 13:9-14). Only when Obed-Edom was blessed, did David venture to bring the ark to Jerusalem. Profuse offerings and a festive procession, led by David himself, accompanied the ark which was placed in a tent near the well of Gihon (II Sam 6:12-19; I Chr 15:1-16:3).

During David's reign no temple was built (II Sam 7:1-7) and the ark consequently remained in the tent, though it was taken out, carried by Zadok, Abiathar and the Levites, to accompany David's armies in times of war (II Sam 11:11; 15:23-24; cf I Kgs 2:26). The ark was still in the tent of Gihon when Solomon was anointed there (I Kgs 1:33-39, 43-45).

The situation changed when Solomon built the Temple. Now the ark was placed in the Holy of Holies under the cherubim (I Kgs 6:19, 23-28; 8:6-9), not unlike its place in the tabernacle built by Moses. Thus the ark took its place in the cult symbolism of the Temple and the chronicler called it "the footstool of our God" (I Chr 28:2). In Prophetic literature, including the cultic portions of the Book of Ezekiel, almost no mention is made of the ark. Jeremiah denounced the naive trust of the people in the ark, contrasting it with the ultimate certainty that Jerusalem itself is the "throne of the Lord" (Jer 3:16-17). The ark was not present in the Second Temple; it is not mentioned among the cult objects captured by Nebuzaradan (II Kgs 25:13-17) nor among those returned by Cyrus (Ezra 1:7-9; 5:14; 6:5). It is unknown whether the ark was destroyed in the fire which consumed the First Temple (II Kgs 25:9) or whether it had disappeared earlier. But according to II Chronicles 35:3, Josiah ordered the Levites to return the ark to its place in the sanctuary. The ark's absence in the period of the Second Temple was explained by its concealment (II Macc 2:1-8). In the NT it is mentioned as appearing in the heavenly temple (Heb 9:4; Rev 11:19).

ARMAGEDDON
Rev 16:16

ARMAGEDDON In the Book of Revelation, the place where the kings of the earth will assemble, led by demonic spirits (16:14-16), for the final

Aerial view of Megiddo.

battle between the forces of evil and the Word of God (19:11-21). The name is a direct transliteration from Hebrew, *Har* (i.e., "Mount") *Megiddon.* No mountain by that name is mentioned in the Hebrew Scriptures. The city of Megiddo (Josh 17:11 etc.), also called Megiddon (Zech 12:11), is in the Valley of Jezreel, strategically situated on the Via Maris, and was the scene of many battles (Judg 5:19; II Kgs 23:29; II Chr 35:22). In "Mount Megiddon", the author of Revelation may well have combined the strategic fame of Megiddo with the eschatological idea of a final conflict between Gog and Magog on the "mountains of Israel" (Ezek 38:8, 21).

ARMONI One of the two sons of King Saul by his concubine Rizpah. David delivered Armoni and his brother, Mephibosheth, to the Gibeonites to be hanged in order to expiate Saul's bloodguilt (II Sam 21:3-8).

ARMONI
II Sam 21:8

ARMY During the patriarchal age, the wandering in the desert and the conquest of Canaan, the tribes of Israel did not develop an independent military organization. Usually every adult was a trained warrior: "from twenty years old and above, all who were able to go to war" (Num 1:30), carrying his own arms day and night. At time of danger each family or clan had only to gather its men and be ready in a short time to meet the enemy. Such was the case with Abraham who "armed his three hundred and eighteen trained servants, born in his own house, and went in pursuit as far as Dan" (Gen 14:14).

The number of the "servants" mentioned is not common. Actually the size of the military units was completely dependent on the size of the clan or the tribe from which they were taken. For this we have an artificial fixed scheme: The largest unit or "division" mentioned in the Bible is the "ten thousand," which was derived from a coalition of a few

Warriors in formation trampling their enemies underfoot. From the Stele of the Vultures, Lagash, c.2500 B.C. (Louvre, Paris)

tribes. The smaller unit was the "thousand". This word is mentioned always as a term equivalent to the tribe (Num 1:16; Josh 22:14), but often to a clan or even a family (Judg 6:15; I Sam 10:19; 23:23). It seems therefore that the concept "thousand" in the Bible carries two meanings: the first and simple one stands for a regular military unit with a fixed number of warriors which might be divided into smaller units of hundreds or tens. The other appears as the equivalent term for a tribe or family (also in this case, always bound to their military duties); but in this case the number of soldiers cannot be fixed, and it changes according to the size of the particular tribe.

In war, the leadership among the Israelites was usually the same which governed them in time of peace: the elders of the tribe or the clan. Often, at a time of danger, new officers, who did not stem from this leadership but were able warriors, were elected. According to I Chronicles 12:24-38, it seems that each Israelite tribe had its own chosen weapon with which it specialized. When summoned, every warrior came with his own arms and supplies sufficient for a few days. If war lasted longer than that, supplies were sent to the individual soldiers by their families at home (cf I Sam 17:17-18).

Egyptian archer.

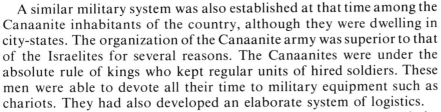

Assyrian warriors from a relief at Sennacherib's palace depicting the siege of Lachish.

Elamite soldier from the "Frieze of the Archers", Susa. 5th century B.C.

A similar military system was also established at that time among the Canaanite inhabitants of the country, although they were dwelling in city-states. The organization of the Canaanite army was superior to that of the Israelites for several reasons. The Canaanites were under the absolute rule of kings who kept regular units of hired soldiers. These men were able to devote all their time to military equipment such as chariots. They had also developed an elaborate system of logistics.

With the beginning of the period of Joshua's conquest and the Judges, conditions were changed. The wandering tribes found themselves inhabiting cities and villages which they had to defend, and the military problems were quite different. They were still divided into tribes but old institutions failed to unite the tribes in face of a common enemy, and this situation is clearly reflected in Deborah's song (Judg chap. 5). The sense of loyalty to the family or clan became stronger, and soon clashes between the tribes themselves ceased. In the course of time, people were more and more related to their places, cities and villages.

Soon it became obvious that against the Canaanites and Philistines with their developed military system and superiority of arms (iron), stronger military organization was badly needed. Consequently, and for a short period, the institution of the judge was born. These new military charismatic leaders who relieved the old one in time of distress, depended completely on personal courage and ability in battlefield, and solved the problem of a proper leadership. They were not able to change the general situation of the army, which, as in the previous period, was still in the state of a militia, and could be summoned only for a short period. Moreover, the judges were not able to unite all the forces of the tribes even in times of great danger, and usually they depended upon their own tribe or upon a few others who dwelt in the immediate neighborhood. Under the steady military pressure of the Philistines, it became clear that good military leadership alone without a proper army would not save the nation. The necessity for permanent and central rule, which alone would be able to build such an army, was recognized by all.

The transition period between the judges and the kings is symbolized by the leadership of Saul. Saul started his career as a typical charismatic judge by showing his military talent in the war against the Ammonites, but was later appointed king by Samuel. He soon turned to build a regular army corps. It was not until the days of David and Solomon, the period of the United Kingdom, that a standing army was created. David developed the first regular unit that he inherited from Saul and turned it into a well-organized and efficient tool, with which he gained a large territory for Israel and defeated all his enemies. Solomon completed the task by adding some new corps, such as units of war chariots.

David's army was composed of two different parts: the regular army and the militia. The regular army itself was built from two different groups, each of them derived from different ethnic elements. The first group was Israelite and developed from the band which gathered around David while he was wandering in the Judean border lands (cf I Sam 22:1-2). This band increased later to 600 people (I Sam 23:13; 27:2) headed by a little group numbering no more than thirty "mighty men"— the military elite. These men were later appointed to the highest posts in the regular army and in the militia as well (I Chr 11:10-12). Together they formed the military institution called the " Thirtieth" which probably served as the council of war.

The second group serving in the regular army was composed of hired non-Israelite mercenaries (Cherethites, Pelethites and Gittites). These people served as the king's bodyguard, and were mainly used in time of internal clashes against the king's personal enemies, since he could always depend on their loyalty (II Sam 15:18). David did not fail to recognize the second and bigger part of his army — the militia (I Chr chap. 27). Each unit composed of 24,000 men served one month every year. At times of danger it was comparatively easy to gather all of them, as their staff officers were regular army men who served the king during the whole year. When gathered, it should have been an enormous army for those days. The destruction of the main fighting power of the two kingdoms had driven the armies out of the open battlefield, where they used to meet their enemies in the previous period. The main military efforts were now concentrated in fortifying the walls of the cities to prepare them for long siege. Fine examples of this work were uncovered in the excavating of many Israeli and Judean cities.

Roman legionaries depicted on a fragment of frieze. 2nd century. (Museo di Antichita, Turino)

The other units of the armies of the two kingdoms were probably still organized as they were in the days of David and Solomon; each of them divided into little units of a regular army with some mercenaries and the militia.

In the post-exilic period, after the fall of Israel and Judah, the country was divided into many satrapies, ruled first by the Assyrians and later by the Babylonians and the Persians. There is no doubt that in this period the army units which were stationed there were part of the general military organization of these empires. The existence of Jewish troops did not end with the fall of their independent kingdom.

The revival of the Jewish army took place after the country regained its independence during the Hasmonean period. First it existed as scattered guerilla bands, and later — under John Hyrcanus — as paid soldiers, Jewish and Gentile alike.

In 63 B.C. Palestine was conquered by the Romans who brought with them their own army. For a short period they let their vassal kings,

Herod and his successors, keep their private little armies, in part composed of hired Thracians, Germans, Gauls and Greeks. This army ceased to exist after the first war against the Romans (A.D. 66-73). (See also WEAPONS)

ARNAN The son of Rephaiah and father of Obadiah, a descendant of Zerubbabel in the genealogy of David (I Chr 3:19, 21).

ARNON A stream in Transjordan, rising from the Syro-Arabian desert and flowing south to north, then turning west into the Dead Sea. In its 30-mile (48 km) course the river descends about 3,500 feet (1,000 m), the last part through a deep, narrow gorge. When the Israelites reached the eastern side of the Jordan in the period of the Exodus, the Arnon

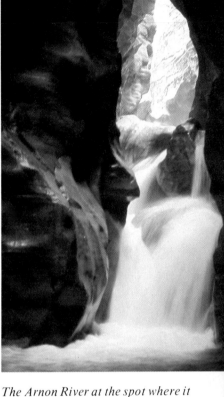

marked the boundary between Moab and the kingdom of Sihon, the Amorite (Num 22:36). The Israelites conquered the territory north of the Arnon up to the Jabbok from the Amorites. It was later allotted to the tribe of Reuben, becoming its border with Moab (Deut 3:8, 12, 16; Josh 12:1-2; 13:9, 16; Judg 11:18, 26). The northern part of the Arnon was conquered by Hazael of Syria, from Jehu, king of Israel (II Kgs 10:32-33). It figures in the prophecies directed against Moab (Is 16:2; Jer 48:20). The modern name of the Arnon River is Wadi el-Mujib.

The Arnon River at the spot where it falls into the Dead Sea.

(left)
The Arnon River.

AROD, ARODI, ARODITES A son of Gad and one of those whose family came into Egypt with Jacob (Gen 46:16). He became family head of the Arodites included in the census in the wilderness (Num 26:17).

AROER

1. A town on the bank of the Arnon, on the border of the Amorite kingdom (Deut 4:48; Josh 12:2). It was conquered by the Reubenites and formed part of their territory (Josh 13:16), but was fortified by the Gadites (Num 32:34). Aroer was the starting point of David's census (II Sam 24:5). It was conquered by Hazael, king of Aram (II Kgs 10:32-33) but by the time of Jeremiah was once more a Moabite town (Jer 48:19).

(left)
Edomite seal from Aroer in the Beersheba Valley inscribed with the name "Qosa". (Hebrew Union College, Jerusalem)

Fragment of Edomite pottery from Aroer. 7th-6th centuries B.C.

Aerial view of Aroer, in the Beersheba Valley.

A coin of Arvad (Aradus), depicting a head of Baal (?), and a galley. c. 400 B.C.

It has been identified with Ara'ir on the River Mujib (Arnon), where remains of Bronze Age and Iron Age settlements, and of a Nabatean settlement, have been found.

2. A town in Gilead on the border of the territory of Gad located near Rabbah of the Ammonites (Josh 13:25). This is possibly the city mentioned in the description of Jephthah's conquest of the Ammonites "from Aroer as far as Minnith" (Judg 11:33).

3. One of the 29 towns assigned to the tribe of Judah (called Adadah in Josh 15:22). After David's victory over the Amalekite raiders, it received a share of the spoil recovered (I Sam 30:26, 28).

The site has been identified with modern Ar'arah, about 12 miles (19 km) south of Beersheba, which, when excavated, revealed the remains of a Judean fortress dating to the 7th century B.C., as well as later settlements — Persian, Hellenistic and Roman.

AROERITE Hotham, the Aroerite, one of David's "mighty men", was a native of one of the three towns of Aroer mentioned above.

ARPAD An Aramaic city in northern Syria, today Tell Rif'at, about 20 miles (30 km) north of Aleppo. It is always mentioned with Hamath in the Bible, both being examples of cities destroyed by the Assyrians (II Kgs 18:34; 19:13; Is 36:19; 37:13; Jer 49:23). The inscriptions of its last ruler, Mati'el, have been found in the excavations.

ARPHAXAD (ARPACHSHAD) The third son of Shem (Gen 10:22) and the grandfather of Eber (Gen 10:24). Arphaxad was born two years after the Flood (Gen 11:10-13).

ARTAXERXES Name of three Persian kings one of whom authorized Ezra's mission to Jerusalem (Ezra 7:1-7, 11-26). It is believed that this was Artarxerxes I, known as Longimanus, the son of Xerxes I. He also allowed Nehemiah's two missions to Jerusalem (Neh 2:1, 7-8). He subdued revolts in Egypt, where unrest started in 460 B.C. and lasted until 454 B.C., and in other parts of the Persian Empire. During that time some of the Empire's possessions were lost. Ancient historians describe him as having a mild and generous character. It was probably during the troubled period of his reign that he caused the reconstruction of Jerusalem to be stopped temporarily (Ezra 4:7-23).

However, it is also possible that his grandson Artaxerxes II, son of Darius II, is the ruler referred to in the Books of Ezra and Nehemiah. Artaxerxes II, known as Mnemon, reigned from 404-359 B.C., and some scholars date Ezra's mission to the seventh year of his reign, 398/97 B.C. Artaxerxes II crushed the rebellion of his brother Cyrus and subdued revolts led by local satraps in the Empire. The palace he built at Susa is identified by some scholars with the palace described in the Book of Esther (1:5-6).

ARTEMAS An early Christian. Paul planned to send Artemas or Tychicus to Crete and then Titus, who was in Crete, could leave the island and join Paul in Nicopolis.

ARUBBOTH A town in the third of Solomon's 12 administrative districts. Ben-Hesed was responsible for the collection of provisions from the district, which included Sacho and Hefer.

Arubboth is believed to be located at modern 'Arabeh about 9 miles (14.5 km) north of Samaria.

ARUMAH The place where Abimelech the son of Jerubbaal resided after being driven out of Shechem (See ABIMELECH No.2). Arumah is thought to have been halfway between Shechem and Shiloh.

ARVAD, ARVADITES The people of Arvad, the Arvadites, are listed in the genealogy of Noah as sons of Canaan (Gen 10:1, 15, 18; I Chr 1, 13, 16). In Ezekiel 27:8, 11 the Arvadites are mentioned as skilled sailors and warriors who served in the navy and army of the city-state Tyre.

AROER 2
Josh 13:25.
Judg 11:26, 33

AROER 3
I Sam 30:28

AROERITE
I Chr 11:44

ARPAD
II Kgs 18:34;
19:13. Is 10:9;
36:19; 37:13.
Jer 49:23

ARPHAXAD
Gen 10:22, 24;
11:10-13.
I Chr 1:17-18,
24. Luke 3:36

ARTAXERXES
Ezra 4:7-8, 11,
23; 6:14; 7:1,
7, 11-12, 21;
8:1. Neh 2:1;
5:14; 13:6

ARTEMAS
Titus 3:12

ARUBBOTH
I Kgs 4:10

ARUMAH
Judg 9:41

ARVAD,
ARVADITES
Gen 10:18.
I Chr 1:16.
Ezek 27:8, 11

The ancient Phoenician city, Arvad, is located on the small island of Ruad off the coast of Syria.

ARZA Kgs 16:9

ARZA A steward in the household of King Elah of Israel in whose house at Tirzah, Elah was "drinking himself drunk" and was murdered by Zimri (I Kgs 16:8-10).

ASA

ASA 1
I Kgs 15:8-9, 11, 13-14, 16-18, 20, 22-25, 28, 32-33; 16:8, 10, 15, 23, 29; 22:41, 43, 46. I Chr 3:10. II Chr 14:1-2, 8, 10-13; 15:2, 8, 10, 16-17, 19; 16:1-2, 4, 6-7, 10-13; 17:2; 20:32; 21:12. Jer 41:9. Matt 1:7-8

1. The third king of Judah (reigned c. 908-867 B.C.); he was the son and successor of Abijah. His mother was Maachah (I Kgs 15:1-2). Asa was a loyal adherent of the worship of God and "did what was right in the eyes of the Lord". He instituted reforms to rid the land of heathen deities and practices. "He banished the perverted persons from the land, and removed all the idols that his father had made." (I Kgs 15:9-12). He also demoted Maachah from her position as queen mother "because she had made an obscene image of Asherah" (I Kgs 15:13-14). There were ten years of peace at the beginning of Asa's reign (II Chr 14:1), during which he fortified cities on his frontiers and raised an army of 580,000 men (II Chr 14:5-8). When Zerah the Ethiopian invaded Judah with an enormous army, Asa repulsed him at Maresha, taking much booty (II Chr 14:9-13). Asa was constantly engaged in border conflict with King Baasha of Israel. Baasha extended his domain as far as Ramah, some 5 miles (9 km) north of Jerusalem, and fortified it. Asa then turned for help to Ben-Hadad, the king of the Arameans, who attacked the Israelite cities of Ijon, Dan and Abel Beth Maachah (I Kgs 15:16-22).

In his old age Asa suffered from a disease which affected his feet; he was reproved by a prophet because he sought physicians rather than the Lord (II Chr 16:11). When he died he was buried in the City of David (I Kgs 15:24). Asa is mentioned in the genealogy of Jesus in Matthew.

ASA 2
I Chr 9:16

2. Asa, a Levite, the son of Elkanah, an ancestor of Obadiah; he lived in one of the villages of the Netophathites after the return from Babylon.

ASAHEL 1
II Sam 2:18-23, 30, 32; 3:27, 30; 23:24. I Chr 2:16; 11:26; 27:7

ASAHEL ("God has made").

1. A son of David's sister Zeruiah and brother of Joab and Abishai. Asahel was one of David's thirty "mighty men" (II Sam 23:24; I Chr 2:16; 11:26). After the defeat of Abner's troops at the battle at Gibeon, Asahel, "fleet footed as a wild gazelle", pursued the fleeing Abner. Abner, after having twice warned Asahel to stop chasing him, turned and killed him in self-defense (II Sam 2:17-23). Later, although David had made his peace with Abner, Joab avenged his brother by the treacherous murder of Abner at Hebron (II Sam 3:22-30).

ASAHEL 2
II Chr 17:8

2. One of the Levites designated to teach the people the Law of the Lord in the cities of Judah in the third year of the reign of King Jehoshaphat.

ASAHEL 3
II Chr 31:13

3. One of the overseers, under Cononiah and Shimei, who assisted in the collection of the contributions to the house of the Lord during the reign of Hezekiah.

ASAHEL 4
Ezra 10:15

4. The father of a certain Jonathan who opposed a proposal of Ezra regarding those men who had married foreign wives (Ezra 10:10-15).

ASAIAH

ASAIAH 1
II Kgs 22:12, 14. II Chr 34:20

1. "A servant of the king", who was among the delegation of five sent by King Josiah of Judah to the prophetess Huldah to enquire about the book of the Law discovered by Hilkiah the priest (II Kgs 22:8-14; II Chr 34:15-22).

ASAIAH 2
I Chr 4:36

2. A chieftain of the tribe of Simeon in the days of King Hezekiah. He was among those who took part in the conquest of the area in the vicinity of Gedor, "a land of good pasture", and dispossessed the Meunites who lived there previously (I Chr 4:24, 36, 41).

ASAIAH 3
I Chr 6:30; 15:6, 11

3. A descendant of Merari, Levi's third son; he was the son of

Haggiah and was among those who helped David bring the ark to Jerusalem (I Chr 6:29-30; 15:6, 11-12).

4. The firstborn of the Shilonites listed among those returning from Babylonian captivity (I Chr 9:1, 5).

ASAPH

1. The father of Joah, King Hezekiah's recorder (II Kgs 18:18, 37).

2. The son of Berechiah, a Levite, "appointed over the service of the song in the house of the Lord". During King David's reign Asaph, together with Heman and Ethan, was to accompany the singers when the ark was brought to Jerusalem (I Chr 6:31-44). Asaph and his sons seem to have had a prominent role in the group of singers and musicians in the Temple. They were among the Levitical singers when the ark was brought from the City of David into the Temple built by Solomon (II Chr 5:2, 12-13). In the time of King Jehoshaphat, Asaph's descendant Jahaziel, inspired by the divine Spirit offered up songs of praise to God to spur the men of Judah into victorious battle against the Edomites (II Chr 20:14-23). In the time of King Hezekiah Asaph's descendants participated in the purification of the Temple (II Chr 29:1-15); as Temple singers they took part in the celebration of the Passover in King Josiah's reign (II Chr 35:1, 15-16). Some of Asaph's descendants were also among those returning to Jerusalem from Babylonian Exile (I Chr 9:15; Neh 7:44; 11:17, 22). Twelve psalms are ascribed to Asaph (Pss 50 and 73 to 83).

3. A Levite, ancestor of a family of gatekeepers according to I Chronicles 26:1; however it has been suggested that the name should be emended to read Ebiasaph as in the parallel list in I Chronicles 9:19.

4. The "keeper of the royal forest" of Artarxerxes, the king of Persia, at the time of Nehemiah's return to Jerusalem.

ASAREL One of the four sons of Jehallelel of the tribe of Judah.

ASCENSION Ascension to heaven is an image originally associated with the rapture of divinely inspired persons, giving a kind of spatial expression to the privileged communion they enjoyed with God or his angels. The rapture could be temporary as in the case of prophets and apocalyptic visionaries (II Cor 12:1-4), the kind that Paul claims to have had early in his career; or it could be the definitive apotheosis that brought a holy life on earth to its fitting conclusion. Early traditions already attributed this second kind of heavenly journey to the prehistoric hero, Enoch (Gen 5:23-24). Better known is the ascension of the charismatic prophet Elijah, who was "taken up" in a fiery chariot before the eyes of his faithful disciple, Elisha (II Kgs 2:11; Eccl 48:9). This tradition accounts for the later belief that Elijah would return from his heavenly abode just prior to the end of the world (Mal 4:5-6; Matt 11:14; Mark 9:11-13; Luke 1:17). Some Jewish traditions also extended the privilege of definitive ascension to other revered prophets and visionaries, including Isaiah; and even Moses joined the ranks of the ascended in a few late and generally discredited voices (Deut 34:5-6), which have possible echoes in the NT (cf Mark 9:4; Rev 11:11-12). In this as in other respects, Judaism was sharing an expressive image with other religious cultures of antiquity, including Greek mythology and the Roman cult of emperors. Mainstream Judaism was nevertheless quite reticent about end-of life ascensions, reflecting its great reserve about any thought of creatures breaching the mighty barrier separating God's realm from the human world.

The bodily ascension of Jesus cannot be considered an early or a dominant conviction of NT writers. Only Luke and the late postscript of Mark's gospel narrate the event explicitly (Mark 16:19; Luke 24:50-53; Acts 1:9-11), though John's gospel anticipates it at one point, and a few

ASAIAH 4
I Chr 9:5

ASAPH 1
II Kgs 18:18, 37. Is 36:3, 22

ASAPH 2
I Chr 6:39; 9:15; 15:17, 19; 16:5, 7, 37; 25:1-2, 6, 9. II Chr 5:12; 20:14; 29:13, 30; 35: 15. Ezra 2:41; 3:10. Neh 7:44; 11:17, 22; 12:35, 46. Ps 50:73-83

ASAPH 3
I Chr 26:1

ASAPH 4
Neh 2:8

ASAREL
I Chr 4:16

Sartaba, a hill overlooking the Jordan River, which tradition holds to be the place from which Elijah was "taken up" in a fiery chariot (II Kgs 2:11).

other texts seem to specify it as a distinct moment of the Easter happening (John 20:17; Eph 4:8-10; I Tim 3:16). A point of departure for the idea's application to Christ was the *kerygma* of his exaltation, employing the Greek verb "lift high," as in "God also has highly exalted him" (Phil 2:9) or "(he was) exalted to the right hand of God" (Acts 2:33; 5:31; cf Rom 8:34). The source of this alternate expression for Jesus' resurrection is the OT refrain that God "lifts up", or vindicates, those whom earthly misfortune has brought low (I Sam 2:7-10; Ps 75:7, 10; 113:7; 149:4; cf Ezek 17:24) — a belief applied to the prophetic figure of the suffering "servant of God" in the famous poem of Deutero-Isaiah (Is 52:13; 53:10-12). According to Christian Easter faith, Jesus, the "humbled" servant, was "highly exalted" by the Father in his resurrection from the dead (Phil 2:8-9), bearing out an indomitable faith in a God who habitually lifts high the lowly (Luke 1:52; James 4:10) and "resists the proud" (I Pet 5:5). The additional influence of the OT's royal ideology, in which King David's descendants shared God's universal dominion as his viceroys (Ps 2:7-8; 89:20-29), can be seen in the phrase "at the right hand of God" (cf Ps 110:1) which sometimes accompanies the exaltation statements (Acts 2:33-35; 5:31; Rom 8:34).

Luke's explicit narration of Jesus' bodily ascension, appearing both at the end of the gospel (Luke 24:50-53) and at the beginning of Acts (Acts 1:9-11), is without parallel in the rest of the NT, and a decisive majority of scholars understand it to be the source of the postscriptor's addition to Mark's last chapter (Mark 16:19). Narratives of bodily ascension, both inside and outside the biblical tradition, share certain terminology ("taken up," "carried up") and standard features with Luke's accounts. In contrast to the temporary rapture of the visionary, the conclusive ascension is usually portrayed from an earthbound perspective: witnesses are on hand and are left behind, and the description does not follow the ascending personage beyond the reach of the earthly eye. In this way, the scene is identified as the ending of an earthly life, and the influence and heritage of the departing figure can be the major assertion of the narrator. Individual traits of the Lucan passages also contain standard features of the ascension genre: the mountain (Acts 1:12), the cloud (Acts 1:9), the adoration (Luke 24:52), the interpreting angels (Acts 1:11), and the witnesses' praise (Luke 24:53). Luke's narratives were composed with allusive (oblique) references to the OT accounts of Elijah's ascension (II Kgs 2:9-13; Eccl 48:9, 12), just as earlier passages in Luke's gospel contain echoes of

Tower of the Russian Church of the Ascension on the Mount of Olives, Jerusalem.

Philistine clay goddess of the 12th century B.C. found at Ashdod. The goddess is shown seated, her body merging into a four-legged throne.

comparable events in the ministry of Elijah (and Elisha) (Luke 7:11-17; 9:52-54). Luke may well be the transmitter of traditions which viewed Jesus' ministry as the conclusion of Israel's tradition of charismatic prophecy, of which Elijah and his pupil were founding figures (Acts 3:20-21; 9:36-43; 20:7-12). The bodily ascension would surely belong to any concluding expression of that tradition (I Kgs 17:17-24; II Kgs 1:10, 12; 4:8-37).

The different settings of Luke's ascensions, one ending the gospel and the other inaugurating the Acts, seem to account for the conflicting date given the event in the two narratives. The gospel has it at the conclusion of the single "third day" which began with the discovery of the empty tomb, and we are thus made to understand that the ascension belongs to the integral Easter event foretold in the Scriptures (Hos 6:2; Luke 18:31-33; 24:44-47). The Acts introduction, on the other hand, seems to place the ascension at the end of an extended period of instruction of his disciples by the risen Christ, to which the precise but obviously symbolic duration of "forty days" is assigned (Acts 1:3; cf Luke 4:1-2) In Acts, the ascension is part of the inauguration of the era of the Church, one of whose essential characteristics is the absence of Jesus' physical person, hence the need to express his vital presence and powerful activity through the ministry of his witnesses.

ASENATH The daughter of Potipherah the Egyptian priest of On whom Pharaoh gave to Joseph as his wife; she was the mother of Ephraim and Manasseh (Gen 41:45, 50-52; 46:20).

ASENATH
Gen 41:45, 50;
46:20

ASHAN ("smoke"). A city in the Shephelah or lowland region of Judah. It was originally assigned to Judah (Josh 15:42), and later given to Simeon "for the portion of the children of Judah was too much for them" (Josh 19:1, 7, 9; I Chr 4:32). From them it passed to the Levite family of the Kohathites (I Chr 6:54, 59). In the corresponding list of cities given to the Levites in Joshua 21:16, the city is called Ain. It is probably identical with Chorashan (or Borashan), one of the cities to which David sent spoils after his victory over the Amalekites (I Sam 30:30).

ASHAN
Josh 15:42;
19:7. I Chr
4:32; 6:59

The site is identified with Khirbet Ashan a short distance from Beersheba.

ASHARELAH A son of Asaph, musician and singer in the Temple in the time of David (I Chr 25:1-2), who prophesied under the direction of the king.

ASHARELAH
I Chr 25:2

In I Chronicles 25:14 his name is given as Jesharelah.

ASHBEA The house of Ashbea descended from Judah's son Shelah. The family won renown as fine linen workers.

ASHBEA
I Chr 4:21

ASHBEL, ASHBELITES A son of Benjamin; the ancestor of the family of the Ashbelites (I Num 26:38). He is mentioned as the third son of Benjamin in Genesis 46:21, and the second, in I Chronicles 8:1. He appears to be called Jediael in I Chronicles 7:6, 10.

ASHBEL,
ASHBELITES
Gen 46:21.
Num 26:38.
I Chr 8:1

ASHCHENAZ See ASHKENAZ

ASHCHENAZ
Jer 51:27

ASHDOD, ASHDODITES One of the five principal cities of the Philistines. Like the other Philistine city-states, it was originally inhabited by the Anakim ("giants") (Josh 11:22; 13:3). It lay inland, approximately 3 miles (5 km) from the coast in the southern coastal plain of Canaan.

ASHDOD,
ASHDODITES
Josh 11:22;
13:3; 15:46-47.
I Sam 5:1, 3,
5-7; 6:17.
II Chr 26:6.
Neh 4:7;
13:23-24. Is
20:1. Jer
25:20. Amos
1:8; 3:9. Zeph
2:4. Zech 9:6

At the time of the Israelite conquest it was assigned to the tribe of Judah (Josh 15:20, 46-47), but remained in the hands of the Philistines (Josh 13:1-3). Before the kingship of Saul, the Philistines defeated the Israelites at Ebenezer; they captured the ark of the covenant and brought it to Ashdod, placing it in the temple dedicated to their god Dagon. Following this, the stone image of the god Dagon fell on its face and broke, and the Ashdodites suffered a plague. The terrified Philistines decided that the ark could not remain with them and sent it back to Israel (I Sam 5:1-12). King Uzziah of Judah succeeded in capturing the city and built up the towns in the surrounding territory (II Chr 26:6). It was lost again by Ahaz (II Chr 28:18). In 734 B.C. Ashdod was taken by Tiglath-Pileser III of Assyria; in 712 B.C. Sargon II crushed a rebellion led by Ashdod (Is 20:1) and the city became the capital of an Assyrian province. Since Ashdod stood on the main road to Egypt, the war between Babylon and Egypt that followed the fall of the Assyrian empire left its mark upon the city. These events were alluded to by the prophets who mentioned Ashdod (Jer 25:20; Zeph 2:4; Zech 9:6). In the time of Nehemiah, "Ashdodite" was synonymous with "Philistine" and Nehemiah fought against its influence (Neh 4:1; 13:23-24).

During the Persian period it was the capital of the province and it remained an important Hellenistic city (known then as Azotus). It was taken and held by the Hasmoneans in 165 B.C. until its conquest by Pompey in 63 B.C. During the Roman period the city was rebuilt and prospered. It came under the control of Herod who gave it to his sister Salome. It had a mixed population of Jews and Gentiles. Philip the Evangelist passed through Ashdod (Azotus) in his preaching tour (Acts 8:40).

Excavations at Tell Isdud, the site of ancient Ashdod, have revealed 20 levels of occupation, beginning with the Middle Bronze Age (17th century B.C.) to the Byzantine period. Some of these strata represent the early Philistine period of occupation. From the later Iron Age other parts of the large town have been uncovered including the western city gate.

Earthenware figurine of a harp player found at Ashdod. Iron Age. (Israel Museum, Jerusalem)

(left)
Excavations of the gate area of ancient Ashdod.

The territory of Asher.

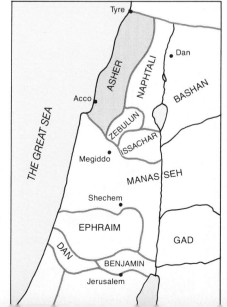

ASHER,
ASHERITES
Gen 30:13;
35:26; 46:17;
49:20. Ex 1:4.
Num 1:13,
40-41; 2:27;
7:72; 10:26;
13:13; 26:44,
46-47; 34:27.
Deut 27:13;
33:24. Josh
17:7, 10-11;
19:24, 34; 21:6,
30. Judg 1:31-32;
5:17; 6:35;
7:23. I Kgs
4:16. I Chr
2:2; 6:62;

ASHER, ASHERITES ("happy"). The name of a biblical figure and of a tribe descended from him.

The eighth son of Jacob and second of his two sons by Zilpah, Leah's maidservant (Gen 30:12-13, 35:26). His only full brother was Gad. Asher had four sons, Imman, Ishuah, Ishui, Beriah, and one daughter, Serah (Gen 46:17; I Chr 7:30). In Jacob's deathbed prophecy Asher was promised a life blessed with an abundance of food "bread from Asher shall be rich, and he shall yield royal dainties" (Gen 49:20).

In the second year of the Exodus from Egypt the tribe of Asher numbered 41,500 adult males (Num 1:41). Their number increased to 53,400 by the time of the second census taken by Moses, before entering the promised land (Num 26:47). In the camp of the Israelites, the tribe of Asher was encamped at the north side of the tabernacle, with the tribes of Dan and Naphtali (Num 2:25-30). Before entering Canaan Moses in his blessing again predicted the fertility of the territory of Asher (Deut 33:1, 24-25). The region allotted to Asher stretched along the Mediterranean coastal plains in the plain of Acco and in upper and lower West Galilee, as well as in the hinterland of the Phoenician Tyre and Sidon, and in part of the valley of Jezreel (Josh 17:7-11; 19:24-31). This territory contains some of the richest soil in all the country. The territories of Zebulun and Naphtali lay along Asher's east boundary, and Manasseh and Issachar to the south and southeast.

Asher did not succeed in driving out the inhabitants of certain Canaanite-Phoenician towns (Judg 1:27). Deborah reproached Asher for not taking part in the struggle against the coalition of the Canaanite kings (Judg 5:17). However the Asherites participated in the expulsion of the Midianites and Amalekites from the Plain of Jezreel by Gideon (Judg 6:1-2, 35; 7:23). Their territory is mentioned as one of the districts of Solomon (I Kgs 4:16). Solomon ceded to Hiram, king of Tyre, 20 cities in Asher as payment for timber and other materials supplied by him for the building of the Temple (I Kgs 9:11-13).

6:74; 7:30, 40; 12:36. II Chr 30:11. Ezek 48:2-3, 34. Luke 2:36. Rev 7:6

Bronze Astarte reproduced from a stone mold of the goddess, found at Naharya. c. 1900 B.C.

ASHERAH One of the principal female goddesses of the Canaanite pantheon, familiar equally from Canaanite mythology and from biblical references. Her name first appears at the time of the First Dynasty of Babylon as Ashratum, consort of Amurru. She is thus a goddess of the Semitic Amorites. In the Canaanite myths found in the city of Ugarit in northern Syria, Asherah appears in several roles. Most often she is known as the Lady of the Sea. As such she is consort of the chief god El and mother of the gods. She also plays the role of interceder in the myth of Baal and the Waters.

In her role as mother goddess, Asherah is often confused with another Canaanite goddess — Ashtoreth (Astarte), who seems to have replaced Asherah in the 1st millennium B.C. As goddess of fertility, Asherah takes the form of a tree, symbolizing the Tree of Life on which the animal kingdom feeds. Her sacred emblem in this role is a tree or a wooden post which is a stylized form of a Tree of Life. Such a post is called Asherah in the Bible.

The cult of Asherah as goddess of fertility connected with sacred trees was pervasive in ancient Israel. It was already practiced in the times of the Judges (Judg 6:25-28) together with the cult of Baal, and continued under the direction of some of the kings of Israel themselves (I Kgs 16:33; 18:19; II Kgs 12:6; 13:6; 17:10). During the religious reforms of Hezekiah and Josiah, kings of Judah, the trees of Asherah were cut down (II Kgs 18:4) including the one installed by King Manasseh inside the Temple (II Kgs 21:7; 23:6). The cult of Asherah probably had elements of divination and was quite promiscuous (Hos 4:12-13).

ASHERAH
Judg 3:7.
I Kgs 15:13;
18:19. II Kgs
21:7; 23:4.
II Chr 15:16.

Astarte figurine. Late Canaanite period. (Israel Museum)

ASHHUR Son of Hezron, Judah's grandson, and Abijah. He was born after his father's death and is said to be "the father of Tekoa" (I Chr 2:24), which may mean that he was the founder of the town by that name. He had seven sons by his wives Helah and Naarah (I Chr 4:5-7).

ASHHUR
I Chr 2:24; 4:5

ASHIMA A deity worshiped by the people from Hamath who were brought by the king of Assyria to settle in Samaria after he had taken the inhabitants into captivity (II Kgs 17:24-30).

ASHIMA
II Kgs 17:30

ASHKELON (ASKELON, ASCALON) One of the five principal cities of the Philistines in Canaan (Josh 13:3). The site of ancient Ashkelon is located 12 miles (19 km) north of Gaza and 10 miles (16 km) south of Ashdod. Ashkelon was one of the oldest and largest cities in the Holy Land. The earliest remains of human occupation date back to the Neolithic Period. Its earliest mention is found in the Egyptian Execration Texts of the 19th century B.C. Ashkelon was assigned to the tribe of Judah who captured it (Judg 1:18-19). However, in the times of the Judges, of Saul and of David, it was a Philistine city (Judg 14:19; I Sam 6:17). There is no mention in the Bible of the conquest of Ashkelon

ASHKELON
Josh 13:3.
Judg 1:18;
14:19. I Sam
6:17. II Sam
1:20. Jer
25:20; 47:5, 7.
Amos 1:8.
Zeph 2:4, 7.
Zech 9:5

by the Philistines, which may have taken place early in the 12th century B.C. Assyrian sources refer to Ashkelon as a kingdom whose area was reduced under Assyrian pressure in the 8th century B.C. A little later it was one of the states paying tribute to Tiglath-Pileser III (745-727 B.C.). Ashkelon revolted, was severely punished by the Assyrians in 732 B.C., rebelled again in the days of Sennacherib and was subjugated in 701 B.C., when its king Sidka was deported to Assyria. During the campaigns of Assurbanipal and Esarhaddon against Egypt, at the end of the 7th century and early 6th century B.C., the city was used as a base for their armies. During Nebuchadnezzar's campaigns many of the inhabitants of Ashkelon were deported. At the end of the Babylonian period, or early in the Persian period, it came under Tyrian control.

A coin of Ascalon depicting the god Poseidon and a bust of Marcus Aurelius. A.D. 59.

(left)
View of the coast at Ashkelon.

The prophets refer to the hardships which the city endured. Amos predicted punishment on the city (Amos 1:8). Jeremiah uttered two prophecies involving Ashkelon (Jer 25:17-20; 47:1-7), and Zephaniah foretold desolation (Zeph 2:4, 7). Zechariah predicted doom for the city in connection with that of Tyre (Zech 9:3-5).

After the conquest of Alexander the Great, Ashkelon was Hellenized and became a center of scholarship. It flourished throughout the Roman and Byzantine periods.

Archeological exploration at the site of ancient Ashkelon has brought to light remains of the Hellenistic and Roman periods.

ASHKENAZ, ASHCHENAZ The first named of the three sons of Gomer, the son of Japheth (Gen 10:3; I Chr 1:6), and a kingdom associated with Ararat and Minni (Jer 51:27). Many scholars have identified Ashkenaz with the group of tribes called Scythians of the Black Sea and Caspian Sea region.

ASHNAH

1. A town in the Shephelah. A tentative identification is the village of 'Aslin between Eshtaol and Zorah.

2. Another town in the Shephelah, identified with modern Idhna, about midway between Hebron and Lachish.

ASHPENAZ The chief eunuch in the palace of Nebuchadnezzar, the king of Babylon. He was ordered to bring handsome and intelligent Jewish youths to be trained for service in the royal court.

ASHKENAZ,
ASHCHENAZ
Gen 10:3.
I Chr 1:6. Jer
51:27

ASHNAH 1
Josh 15:33

ASHNAH 2
Josh 15:43

ASHPENAZ
Dan 1:3

ASHTAROTH (the plural form of "Ashtoreth", the name of the Canaanite fertility goddess). A Canaanite city; the capital of Og, the king of Bashan (Deut 1:4; Josh 12:4). After its conquest by the Israelites it was given to Machir, the son of Manasseh (Josh 13:31), and it later became a Levitical city (Josh 21:27 — where it is called Be-Eshterah). It was the home of Uzziah the Ashterathite, one of David's "mighty men" (I Chr 11:44).

ASHTAROTH
Deut 1:4. Josh 9:10; 12:4; 13:12, 31. I Chr 6:71

Conquest of Ashtaroth by the Assyrians. Relief from the palace of Tiglath-Pileser III. 8th century B.C.

It is identified with Tell Ashtareh, about 20 miles (32 km) east of the Sea of Galilee.

ASHTERATHITE A native or inhabitant of Ashtaroth.

ASHTERATHITE
I Chr 11:44

ASHTEROTH KARNAIM The site of the defeat of the Rephaim by Chedorlaomer, king of Elam.

It is thought to be located at Sheikh Su'ud a few miles from Ashtaroth. During the Assyrian period the whole region was called Qarnini after the city.

ASHTEROTH KARNAIM
Gen 14:5

ASHTORETH (ASTARTE) A goddess in the Canaanite pantheon, the Canaanite version of the Mesopotamian goddess Ishtar, goddess of war and love. Ashtoreth plays only a minor role in the Canaanite literature of Ugarit. In the myth of Baal and the Waters she is named consort of Baal, and in the other few references to her she is connected with this important god.

ASHTORETH
Judg 2:13; 10:6. I Sam 7:3-4; 12:10; 31:10. I Kgs 11:5, 33. II Kgs 23:13

Clay Astarte figurines. Israelite period. 8th-early 6th centuries B.C. (Israel Dept. of Antiquities)

Ashtoreth is better known from Egyptian references. Her cult, probably introduced by the Semitic Hyksos, became important in the New Kingdom. She had a joint temple with Baal in Memphis, where she seems to have been worshiped as a foreign goddess of war. She is closely associated with Anath, another Canaanite war goddess.

Her military aspects were appreciated by the Philistines, who hung Saul's armor in her temple (I Sam 31:10).

The cult of Astarte penetrated ancient Israel, although it does not seem to have figured very prominently. In the early days of the Judges she was worshiped alongside Baal (Judg 10:6; I Sam 7:3-4; 12:10). Somewhat later, after she became particularly closely connected with the town of Sidon, her cult was introduced into Jerusalem in the time of King Solomon under the influence of one of his wives (I Kgs 11:5, 33). The cult of this Ashtoreth of the Sidonites survived in Jerusalem for some 350 years until it was purged in Josiah's religious reforms (II Kgs 23:13).

Ashtoreth seems to have been the best represented Canaanite goddess. Hundreds of small clay plaques and many metal statuettes of the Late Bronze Age found in greater Canaan are referred to as Ashtoreth figurines. They depict her as a nude figure, emphasizing her qualities as a fertility goddess. Sometimes she stands on a horse or a lion, often brandishing a weapon in her right hand, a clear depiction of her warlike function. In the majority of plaques, however, she is standing holding flowers, especially lotus flowers, in her hands. The lotus, and the special coiffure of two thick locks curling down to the shoulders, are Egyptian elements connected with the goddess Hathor with whom Astarte is sometimes identified in Egypt. However, whenever Ashtoreth is identified in both representation and inscription she is modestly dressed, and her warlike rather than her fertility aspects are emphasized. This has led some scholars to reject the identification of the nude figure on the plaques and statuettes with Ashtoreth.

Pregnant Ashtoreth from Achzib; 5th century B.C.

ASHURITES A people who were subject to Ishbosheth, Saul's son. In II Samuel 2:9 the Ashurites are mentioned between Gilead and Jezreel. (Some Bible versions list here "Geshurites" instead of Ashurites.)

ASHVATH A man of the tribe of Asher, one of the sons of Japheth.

ASIA In the NT the name refers to the Roman province occupying the western part of what came to be known later as Asia Minor, together with the adjacent islands; some modifications took place in the course of time. When King Attalus III of Pergamum died in 133 B.C., he bequeathed his kingdom to Rome, and since the Romans knew the

ASHURITES
II Sam 2:9.
Ezek 27:6

ASHVATH
I Chr 7:33

ASIA
Acts 2:9; 6:9; 16:6; 19:10, 22, 26-27, 31: 20:4, 16, 18; 21:27; 24:18; 27:2. I Cor 16:19. II Cor 1:8. II Tim 1:15. I Pet 1:1. Rev 1:4, 11

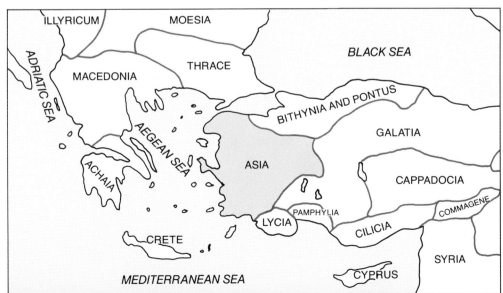

The Roman province of Asia.

Attalid kings as "kings of Asia", the new province was called Asia. It was organized in 129 B.C. and occupied the area between the Mediterranean to the west, Bithynia to the north, Cilicia and Galatia to the east. It incorporated Mysia, Caria, Lydia, part of Phrygia as well as coastal cities and islands in the Aegean Sea, including Rhodes and Patmos. Augustus made it a senatorial province ruled by a proconsul with Ephesus as its capital. Asia was regarded as one of the richest provinces of the Roman Empire and was famous for its wool weaving and dyeing factories. In the 1st century A.D. many Jews resided in the province and their synagogues were found in many cities.

Asia is listed along with the provinces of Cappadocia, Pontus, Phrygia and Pamphylia as the regions from which Jews came to Jerusalem for the Pentecost (Acts 2:9-10). There were also Jews from Asia in Jerusalem's Synagogue of the Freedmen, who disputed with Stephen (Acts 6:9). The province was the scene of much of Paul's missionary activity. On his second missionary journey, he and Timothy "were forbidden by the Holy Spirit to preach the word in Asia" (Acts 16:6). However, it seems that they did pass through the province and when they reached Troas, Paul had a vision (Acts 16:7-9). After completing his work in Macedonia and Achaia, Paul spent a short time at Ephesus (Acts 18:19-21). During his third journey he spent over two years in and around Ephesus, "so that all who dwelt in Asia heard the word of the Lord Jesus, both Jews and Greeks" (Acts 19:1, 10, 22). In his epistles, Paul mentions his hardships and his success in that province (Rom 16:5; I Cor 15:32; 16:8-9; II Cor 1:8). On his last journey to Jerusalem, Paul decided not to dally in Asia as he wanted to be back in time for the Pentecost (Acts 20:16).

In the Book of Revelation John addresses his messages to the seven churches in Asia: Ephesus, Smyrna, Pergamos, Thyatira, Sardis, Philadelphia and Laodicea (Rev 1:4, 11).

ASIEL ("made by God"). The ancestor of Jehu; he was one of the Simeonite chieftains in the time of Hezekiah (I Chr 4:24, 35, 41). | ASIEL I Chr 4:35

ASNAH The head of a family of Temple servants who returned with Zerubbabel from Babylonian Exile. | ASNAH Ezra 2:50

ASP See ANIMALS | ASPATHA Est 9:7

ASPATHA One of Haman's ten sons, who were killed at Shushan.

ASRIEL, ASRIELITES ("God has filled with joy"?). A descendant of Manasseh, the son of Gilead and founder of the family of the Asrielites mentioned in the second census taken by Moses (Num 26:2, 31; I Chr 7:14); they were allotted territory by Joshua (Josh 17:2). | ASRIEL, ASRIELITES Num 26:31. Josh 17:2. I Chr 7:14

ASS See ANIMALS

ASSHUR

1. One of the sons of Shem (Gen 10:22; I Chr 1:17), regarded as the forefather of the Assyrians. | ASSHUR I Gen 10:22. I Chr 1:17

2. In Hebrew, the same name applies both to Asshur, the son of Shem, and to Assyria, Assyrian. In Balaam's prophecy Asshur may refer either to the nation or to one of the principal cities of the Assyrians (See ASSYRIA). | ASSHUR 2 Num 24:22, 24

ASSHURIM Descendants of Dedan, a son of Jokshan, one of Abraham's sons by Keturah (Gen 25:1-3). The Asshurim, not to be confused with the Assyrians, are a North Arabian tribe. | ASSHURIM Gen 25:3

ASSIR ("prisoner" or "captive"). | ASSIR I Ex 6:24. I Chr 6:22

1. A Levite, son of Korah.

2. A son of Ebiasaph of the family of Korah. | ASSIR 2 I Chr 6:23, 37

3. A son of King Jeconiah, unless "the sons of Jeconiah were Assir" in I Chronicles 3:17 is interpreted as meaning "the sons of Jeconiah the captive". | ASSIR 3 I Chr 3:17

ASSOS A seaport of Mysia on the Gulf of Adramyttium on the northwest coast of Asia Minor. The city was located about half a mile (1 km) inland from the sea, on the terraced sides of a volcanic rock formation, and commanded a beautiful view.

On his third missionary journey, Paul heading back to Jerusalem, stopped at Troas. From here he sent Luke and his other companions by ship to Assos, while he himself went by foot — a distance of about 12 miles (19 km) — arriving in Assos in time to board the ship, which then sailed to Mitylene on the island of Lesbos (Acts 20:6, 13-14).

ASSYRIA, ASSYRIANS A country situated in the fertile alluvial plains created out of the Persian Gulf by the successive deltas of the Tigris and Euphrates Rivers. Wave after wave of semi-nomadic peoples of Sumerian and Semitic origin settled there over the centuries. This crucible gave rise to new types of writings, new languages, new civilizations. Assyria knew varying borders as its power waxed and waned, often in connection with its continual rivalry with its southern neighbor Babylon, the other mighty empire of Mesopotamia. The two warring empires had to withstand the constant pressure of neighboring nations: the hill people of Kurdistan to the north, Syrian kingdoms to the west, Aramean kingdoms to the south.

Detail of the bronze doors of Shalmaneser III's palace at Balawat showing a military expedition. 9th century B.C. (British Museum)

Though the successive empires of Assyria lasted from the 3rd millennium B.C. until the first half of the 1st millennium, it was only towards the end of that period that Assyrian history interacted closely with that of the Kingdoms of Israel and Judah.

The Bible gives few details about Assyria, its kings, its people and its customs. Assyrian sources, however, are of paramount importance in checking and dating biblical events. Available Assyrian chronicles list a detailed chronology of kings and kingdoms as well as of military expeditions. Constant references to lunar and solar eclipses have made it possible for contemporary scholars to date the corresponding chronology with a significant measure of accuracy.

The Hebrew word *Assur* is variously translated according to the context as (a) son of Shem and eponymous father of the Assyrians (Gen 10:22), (b) the primary god of the Assyrian people, to whom he gave his name: some representations show him as the tree of life; (c) the first capital of the Assyrian empire, sacred to the god Asshur; it was located on the western bank of the Tigris River. Though progressively losing its political importance, it remained to the end, the center of the cult of

Asshur. The city, which was destroyed in 614 B.C. by a Babylonian-led coalition has been identified with present-day Kalat Sharkat, 50 miles (80 km) south of Mosul; (d) the country or the empire of Assyria. This latter term sometimes includes Babylon.

Assyria is mentioned very early in the Scriptures, in the second chapter of Genesis: "Now a river went out of Eden to water the garden, and from there it parted and became four riverheads...the name of the third river is the Tigris, it is the one which goes towards the east of Assyria. The fourth river is the Euphrates" (Gen 2:10, 14).

According to the biblical account, Assyria was settled by Noah's great-grandson, Nimrod "a mighty hunter before the Lord" (Gen 10:9): "He went to Assyria and built Nineveh, Rehoboth Ir, Calah and Resen between Nineveh and Calah (that is the principal city)" (Gen 10:11).

Assyrians carrying cedar wood for the construction of the palace of Sargon II at Khorsabad. 8th-century bas-relief. (Louvre, Paris)

Nineveh was the second capital of Assyria, and its destruction in 612 B.C. marked the end of the neo-Assyrian empire. As to the city of Calah, mentioned frequently in the Assyrian chronicles, it has been identified with present-day Nimrud.

Between the Book of Genesis and the Second Book of Kings, there is only one other mention of Assyria (or Asshur): this is in the fourth prophecy of the seer Balaam (Num 24:22).

Only many centuries later did the Kingdoms of Israel and of Judah clash with the last great Assyrian empire, whose kings relentlessly pursued a policy of conquest to the south which was to lead them to the Mediterranean and to Egypt. According to the Bible the army of Tiglath-Pileser III invaded Samaria. To placate him King Menahem of Israel consented to be his vassal and assembled an enormous tribute. "So the king of Assyria turned back, and did not stay there in the land" (II Kgs 15:20) (738 B.C.). Possibly in consequence of non-payment of taxes, Tiglath-Pileser returned during the reign of Pekah the son of Remaliah. The Assyrian king devastated Israel and carried many of its people into captivity in Assyria (II Kgs 16:29) (732 B.C.). King Ahaz of Judah managed to seal an alliance with Tiglath-Pileser and thus saved his kingdom (II Kgs 16:7).

When Hoshea, the new king of Israel, conspired against Assyria, Shalmaneser V, the son of Tiglath-Pileser led a new campaign against the Kingdom of Israel, spelling its eclipse (722 B.C.) (II Kgs 17:3). The next Assyrian king, Sargon II, another son of Tiglath-Pileser and brother of Shalmaneser, resettled Samaria with people from all over his vast empire (II Kgs 17:24).

With Israel disposed of, the kings of Assyria turned to Judah. Towards the end of the 8th century, Sennacherib attempted the conquest of Judah and of Jerusalem (701 B.C.). In a vain bid to conciliate him, King Hezekiah stripped the Temple of its treasure to pay him tribute (II Kgs 18:15-16). This did not stop the armies of Sennacherib from laying siege to Jerusalem. According to the biblical record, the Assyrians were defeated through the intervention of the angel of the Lord and Sennacherib went back to his capital, Nineveh where he was killed by his sons Adrammelech and Sharezer (II Kgs 19:36, 37). Though the king's hasty retreat was probably due to the news

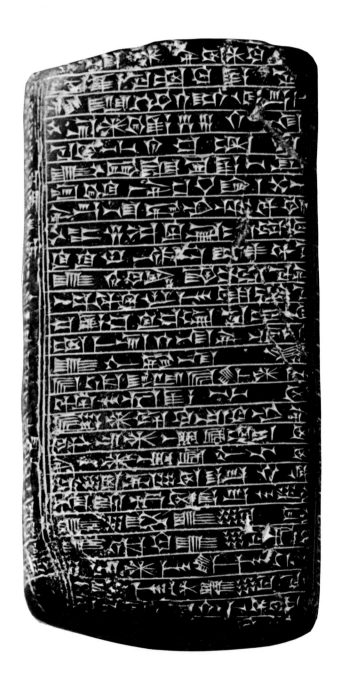

Assyrian cuneiform writing.

of a rebellion in Assyria, and the circumstances of his death are yet to be elucidated, this episode was to be the last time Assyria threatened Judah. Once again Mesopotamia was thrown into turmoil; Babylon was on the march and its armies, with their foreign allies, destroyed Nineveh in 612, and Haran in 610. The Assyrian empire did not rise again. However, the destruction of Israel by the Assyrians and their devastation of Judah were to be mentioned repeatedly by the prophets who interpreted these attacks as a sign of the Lord's anger against his nation. Nevertheless they continued to prophesy retribution: "And he will stretch his hand against the North, destroy Assyria and make Nineveh a desolation as dry as the wilderness" (Zeph 2:13). See also MESOPOTAMIA.

ASYNCRITUS A Christian in Rome to whom Paul sent greetings in his Epistle to the Romans.

ASYNCRITUS
Rom 16:14

ATAD See GOREN ATAD

ATAD

ATARAH ("crown", or, "wreath"). One of the wives of Jerahmeel of the tribe of Judah, and the mother of Onam.

Gen 50:10-11

ATARAH
I Chr 2:26

ATAROTH

1. One of the towns on the east side of the Jordan, conquered from the Amorites, which the Gadites and the Reubenites requested to be allotted to them because it was a good area for their livestock (Num 32:1-5). The site was rebuilt by the Gadites (Num 32:34).

ATAROTH 1
Num 32:3, 34

The king of Moab, Mesha, recounts in the inscriptions on the Stele of Mesha ("The Moabite Stone"), that the king of Israel had fortified Ataroth, but that he, Mesha, recaptured the city. The site has been identified with Khirbet-Atarus, about 10 miles (16 km) east of the Dead Sea, northwest of Dibon.

2. A town in the territory of Ephraim. The site has not been identified, but is thought to be identical with Ataroth Addar.

ATAROTH 2
Josh 16:2

3. A town on the northern boundary of the territory of Ephraim. The site is thought to be near the confluence of the Jordan and Jabbok Rivers.

ATAROTH 3
Josh 16:7

ATAROTH ADAR (ATAROTH ADDAR) A town in Ephraim whose exact location has not been identified, but in view of its position in Joshua 16:5 and 18:13 it may be identical with Ataroth No.2.

ATAROTH ADAR
Josh 16:5;
18:3

ATER The ancestor of a family that returned from Babylonian Exile (Ezra 2:16; Neh 7:21); among them were gatekeepers of the Temple (Ezra 2:42; Neh 7:45). A man named Ater was among those who sealed the new covenant after the Exile (Neh 10:17).

ATER
Ezra 2:16, 42.
Neh 7:21, 45;
10:17

ATHACH A place in Judah to which David sent part of the spoil taken from the Amalekites after their raid on Ziklag (I Sam 30:26, 30). Its exact location is unknown.

ATHACH
I Sam 30:30

ATHAIAH A descendant of Perez of the tribe of Judah, who resided in Jerusalem in Nehemiah's time (Neh 11:4, 7).

ATHAIAH
Neh 11:4

ATHALIAH

1. Queen of Judah (842-836 B.C.), the daughter of King Ahab of Israel and Jezebel, granddaughter of Omri (II Kgs 8:18, 26; II Chr 22:2-3), wife of Jehoram (Joram), king of Judah and the mother of King Ahaziah (II Kgs 8:26). She influenced her husband to do what was "wrong in the eyes of the Lord" during his eight-year reign (II Kgs 8:18; II Chr 21:4-6). She also introduced the worship of Baal, both during her husband's rule and her son's reign. Following Ahaziah's murder by Jehu, she seized power and killed all the members of the royal family who were possible rivals, with the exception of the infant son of Ahaziah, Joash, who was saved by his aunt Jehosheba, wife of the high priest Jehoiada (II Kgs 11:1-3; II Chr 22:10-12).

ATHALIAH 1
II Kgs 8:26;
11:1-3, 13-14,
20. II Chr
22:2, 10-12;
23:12-13, 21;
24:7

When Joash was seven years old, Jehoiada conspired to have the

Burial caves of the Hellenistic and Roman periods at Ataroth in Ephraim.

young boy crowned in the Temple as the legitimate king. Hearing this, Athaliah rushed to the Temple in an attempt to rally supporters and stop the ceremony, but Jehoiada had her seized and she was slain by his supporters (II Kgs 11:4-16; II Chr 23:12-15). The temple of Baal was destroyed and its priest Mattan was put to death (II Kgs 11:18; II Chr 23:17).

2. A Benjamite of the house of Jeroham who dwelt in Jerusalem (I Chr 8:1, 26).

3. The father of Jeshaiah of the family of Elam, who returned to Jerusalem with Ezra (Ezra 8:1, 7).

ATHARIM When journeying to the promised land, the Israelites led by Moses traveled "on the road to Atharim" in the Negeb, where they were attacked by the king of Arad.

ATHENS, ATHENIANS A city in southeast Achaia located 3 miles (5 km) inland from the Gulf of Agina, capital of the Greek district of Attica. In antiquity the city was composed of two sections, the lower city on the plain and the upper city on the acropolis. Athens, the center of the intellectual world in the 1st century A.D. was the most important of the three major cities of higher learning (Athens, Tarsus and Alexandria). It was famous as well for its statuary monuments and temples and the Athenians were noted for their religious curiosity and piety. Paul went to Athens from Beroea and Thessalonica on his second missionary journey and spoke daily in the synagogue and market place (Acts 17:15-17). While in the Areopagus, he spoke on the "unknown God" to whom the Athenians had dedicated an altar (Acts 17:22-23). Paul's sermon focused on the fact that the true God is invisible and will judge the world by the man whom he had raised from the dead. The concept of the resurrection of the dead drew a mixed response from the crowd and Paul departed to Corinth (Acts 18:1).

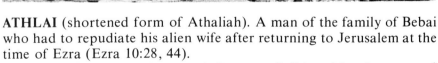

ATHLAI (shortened form of Athaliah). A man of the family of Bebai who had to repudiate his alien wife after returning to Jerusalem at the time of Ezra (Ezra 10:28, 44).

A coin of Athens, 5th century B.C., depicting Athena and an owl.

Remains of the Parthenon, the temple of Athena, on the Acropolis, Athens.

ATONEMENT The Hebrew verb "to atone" (*kipper*) has been traced back to two separate etymologies: from Arabic ("cover") and Akkadian ("wipe"). However, both meanings may go back to a common notion: "rub". Since a substance may either be "rubbed on" or "rubbed off", the derived meanings "wipe" and "cover" may be complementary and not contradictory.

In the OT the meaning "rub off" predominates in ritual texts. This is best illustrated by the blood of the purgation offering. Its use is restricted to the sanctuary, never on a person. This means that a person is never the object of the atonement rite but only its beneficiary. The blood of the purgation sacrifice serves, not to purge the worshiper of alleged sin, but to purge that to which it is applied, i.e. the sanctuary and its sanctums. Presumptuous sins and impurities, however, cannot be purged by the offender's own purgation sacrifice (Num 15:30-31), but must await the annual rite of purgation of the sanctuary and the nation. Expiatory sacrifices deal only with offenses committed against the deity; they do not redress wrongs against human beings.

The notion of "ransom" or "substitute" is clearly represented in the Bible in the instance of the scapegoat (See AZAZEL). The avowed goal is to siphon off the wrath of God from the entire community. The final stage in the evolution of the root *kipper* yields the abstract, figurative notion "expiate". Having begun as an action which eliminates dangerous impurity by absorbing it through direct contact (rubbing off) or indirectly (as a ransom/substitute), it eventuates into the process of expiation in general.

Whereas in ritual, the subject of "atonement" is invariably a priest and the direct object a contaminated thing, in the nonritual literature the subject is usually the deity and the direct object a sin (e.g. Ps 78:38; Jer 18:23; Ezek 16:63). Actually this represents no rupture with ritual atonement; on the contrary, it gives voice to its implicit meaning. As for the object; though the cult concentrates mainly on the purging of sanctuary impurity, it too recognizes that the source of the latter is human sin. The subject implies even less change: though the priest performs the rituals, it is only due to the grace of God that the ritual is efficacious. Thus, nonritual exhortations, requiring no priestly mediation, uncompromisingly turn to God, the sole dispenser of expiation.

The holiness of the sanctuary is complemented in the priestly source by the notion of the holiness of the land of Israel. Correspondingly, the land too is capable of defilement (e.g. Lev 18:25, 28, for sexual immorality; Num 35:33-34, for murder; cf also Ezek 36:17; Deut 21:23), and just as the sanctuary needs atonement, so does the land (Num 35:33). Furthermore, the implications are likewise identical: defilement of the land will result in the destruction of Israel just as it did for the previous inhabitants (Lev 18:28; 20:22), because God can no longer abide in it.

Another postulate of the biblical doctrine of atonement is that God will spare the community by virtue of the merit of the just people in it, e.g. Abraham's intervention on behalf of Sodom and Gomorrah (Gen 18:16-33). The atoning power of the righteous reaches out not only horizontally to the community but vertically to posterity. This principle undergirds all of God's covenants with Israel: with the patriarchs for offspring and soil (Gen chap. 15; 17:1-8; 22:17-18; 25:23; 35:9-12; Ex 32:13), with Phinehas for a priestly line (Num 25:11-13), and with David for a royal dynasty (II Sam 7:12-16). See DAY OF ATONEMENT.

In the NT the word atonement (or a close translation), appears infrequently (Rom 3:25; Heb 2:17; I John 2:2; 4:10). In each case it alludes to, or is taken from, an OT reference. In the OT it can be said that God atones (Is 53:10) and so on in the NT, God, through Christ, is reconciling the world unto himself (II Cor 5:19). Evidence for God's love is seen in the fact that he "sent his son to be the propitiation for our sins" (I John 4:10; cf I John 2:2). Paul used similar language when he spoke of Jesus as someone whom God put forth "a propitiation by his blood, through faith, to demonstrate his righteousness" for the remission of sins that have been committed (Rom 3:25). The imagery here is clearly from the Temple, or the mercy-seat in the ark. Just as the covering there had been the place where God's forgiving mercy was demonstrated, so God's saving mercy was manifested in the cross of Christ.

Consequently the NT writers spend little time debating who is the agent of atonement or who is being atoned. Rather they concentrate their attention on the conviction that, in Jesus, sin had been done away with, and that those who lived in faith under his lordship were able to share in his victory over sin. The *Christus Victor* model emerged as stronger than the model of Christ as paschal lamb who made atonement for all people's sins.

ATROTH BETH JOAB Mentioned with "the sons of Salma" in the genealogy of Judah. The name is thought to indicate the inhabitants of a place rather than a personal name.

ATROTH BETH
JOAB
I Chr 2:54

ATROTH SHOPHAN One of the cities taken by the Israelites from kings Og and Sihon in the Bashan and rebuilt by the tribe of Gad (Num 32:33-35). A suggested location is in the vicinity of Ataroth.

ATROTH SHOPHAN
Num 32:35

ATTAI ("timely").

1. A descendant of Jerahmeel of Judah; the son of Jahra, an Egyptian slave belonging to Sheshan and one of Sheshan's daughters (perhaps Ahlai). He was the father of Nathan (I Chr 2:25, 34-35).

ATTAI 1
I Chr 2:35-36

2. One of the "mighty men of valor" among the Gadites who crossed the Jordan to join David's troops at Ziklag (I Chr 12:8, 11-15).

ATTAI 2
I Chr 12:11

3. One of King Rehoboam's sons by his wife Maacah, the granddaughter of Absalom, whom he loved more than all his other wives (II Chr 11:18-21).

ATTAI 3
II Chr 11:20

ATTALIA A seaport of Pamphylia near Perga in Asia Minor. Towards the end of his first missionary tour, Paul embarked with Barnabas from Attalia on their way to Antioch in Syria (Acts 14:24-26). Founded c. 150 B.C. as the port for Perga, it soon displaced that city in importance. It is now known as Antalia.

ATTALIA
Acts 14:25

AUGUSTUS This title, implying divinity, was first given to Gaius Octavius (Octavian), the first Roman emperor, by the Senate in 27 B.C. Later Roman emperors assumed the title (Acts 25:21, 25 in AV), but by itself when used as a name it refers to Octavian. Born in 63 B.C., he was adopted by his uncle Julius Caesar, and became sole ruler of the Roman Empire in 44 B.C. Augustus was the architect of the *Pax Romana,* which for some years established peace and security in the Empire. He intervened little in local government of the provinces and simplified the procedure whereby the provincials could claim redress of abuses by the governors.

AUGUSTUS
Luke 2:1. Acts
25:21, 25

In Judea, Augustus was a patron of Herod the Great and added territories to his kingdom, supporting him in his efforts to fulfill his obligations as a loyal vassal to Rome and approving of his efforts to introduce Roman culture in Judea. Augustus reigned 44 years, and one month after his death in A.D. 14 he was deified.

For the purpose of tax collecting, Augustus ordered a census of the population. According to the NT "This census took place while Quirinius was governing Syria. So all went to be registered, everyone to his own city." As a result Joseph and Mary traveled from Nazareth in Galilee to Bethlehem to be registered, and Jesus was consequently born in Bethlehem (Luke 2:1-7).

AVA One of the towns from which colonists were brought to Samaria by the king of Assyria after capturing the city and deporting its inhabitants.

AVA
II Kgs 17:24

AVEN

1. In Ezekiel 30:17 Aven is generally believed to refer to ON, the city in

AVEN 1
Ezek 30:17

Egypt called Heliopolis by the Greeks. The Hebrew consonants for Aven (meaning "trouble, wickedness") are the same as for On but the vowel pointing differs. Some commentators suggest that the change in the vowel-point was a deliberate play on words to express contempt for the idolatrous city of On, the center of sun worship.

2. In Hosea 10:8 Aven is an abbreviation for BETH AVEN.

3. Amos 1:5 refers to the Valley of Aven. A place associated with Damascus in Amos' prophecy foretelling the exile of the people of Syria. Some scholars believe that this refers to the valley between the Lebanon and Anti-Lebanon mountains.

AVIM

1. The early Canaanite tribes in the region of Gaza who had been dispossessed by the Caphtorim (Philistines) (Deut 2:23). Shortly before Joshua's death, the Avim (or Avites) were still among the peoples that remained in Canaan (Josh 13:1-3).

2. A city in the territory of Benjamin, located between Bethel and Parah.

AVITES

1. The inhabitants of Ivah or Ava who were among the peoples brought by the Assyrians to settle in Samaria after the capture of the town and the deportation of its inhabitants (in 720 B.C.). Although taught "the fear of the Lord", the Avites continued to worship their own gods Nibhaz and Tartak (II Kgs 17:28-31). Later they and other peoples settled in Samaria came to be known as the Samaritans.

2. See AVIM No.1.

AVITH The capital city of Hadad, the fourth king of the Edomites who defeated the Midianites (Gen 36:31-35; I Chr 1:43-46).

AYYAH One of the towns in the domain of the tribe of Ephraim. It is believed by many to refer to Ai.

AZAL A place mentioned in Zechariah 14:5 as the point to which the valley would reach as a result of the cleavage of the Mount of Olives.

AZALIAH The father of Shaphan the scribe in the reign of Josiah.

AZANIAH ("Yah has heard"). Father of Jeshua, a Levite who was one of the witnesses of the covenant in the time of Ezra.

AZAREEL, AZAREL ("God has helped").

1. One of the "mighty men" who joined David at Ziklag (I Chr 12:1,6).

2. A musician of the family of Heman; he headed the 11th of the 24 divisions under David's rule (I Chr 25:1, 4, 18) (he is called Uzziel in verse 4).

3. The son of Jeroham; leader of the tribe of Dan under David's rule (I Chr 27:16, 22).

4. A descendant of Bani. He was among those who had married foreign wives, in the time of Ezra (Ezra 10:10, 34, 41).

5. The father of Amashai, a priest who dwelt in Jerusalem after the return from Babylonian Exile (Neh 11:1, 13).

6. A musician at the dedication of Jerusalem's rebuilt wall (Neh 12:31, 36) (Perhaps identical with Azareel No.2).

AZARIAH ("Yah has helped").

1. The son of Zadok the priest; one of the officers of King Solomon (I Kgs 4:2).

It is not clear from the text whether the attribute "the priest" refers to him or to Zadok. He may be identical with Azariah No. 5.

2. The son of Nathan; the superintendent of the 12 regional governors who "provided food for the king and his household" (I Kgs 4:7).

3. The son of Ethan; descended from Zerah of the tribe of Judah.

4. The son of Jehu, of the sons of Onam; descended from Jerahmeel, of the tribe of Judah. (I Chr 2:38-39).

AZARIAH 5
I Chr 6:9

5. A Levite descended from Aaron; the son of Ahimaaz and grandson of Zadok; the father of Johanan and grandfather of Azariah the priest (I Chr 6:10). He may be identified with Azariah No. 1.

AZARIAH 6
I Chr 6:10-11

6. A Levite descended from Aaron; the son of Johanan and father of Amariah. He served as priest in the Temple in the days of Solomon (I Chr 6:10). He is most probably identical with Azariah No. 5.

AZARIAH 7
I Chr 6:36

7. The son of Zephaniah and father of Joel; a Levite of the line of Kohath. An ancestor of the Levites who performed their musical duties in the Temple (I Chr 6:36). In I Chronicles 6:24, he is called Uzziah.

AZARIAH 8
I Chr 9:11

8. The son of Hilkiah. He is listed among the priests who lived in Jerusalem in the days of Nehemiah (I Chr 9:11). In the parallel list in Nehemiah 11:11, the name of the son of Hilkiah is Seraiah, which may be an interchanged name (See AZARIAH No. 21).

AZARIAH 9
II Chr 15:1

9. A prophet, the son of Oded. He encouraged King Asa of Judah to initiate a religious reform (II Chr 15:1).

AZARIAH 10
II Chr 23:1

10. The son of Jeroham; one of the officers who conspired to dethrone Athaliah (II Chr 23:1).

AZARIAH 11
II Chr 23:1

11. The son of Obed; one of the officers who conspired to dethrone Athaliah (II Chr 23:1). He is probably not to be identified with Azariah No.10 since they had different fathers.

AZARIAH 12
II Chr 21:2

12. The son of King Jehoshaphat of Judah. The name appears twice in the list of the six sons of Jehoshaphat (II Chr 21:2). It has been suggested that the second Azariah should read Uzziah; in Hebrew the second one is Azaryahu. He and his brothers were slain by their elder brother Jehoram, who succeeded their father as king of Judah (II Chr 21:1).

AZARIAH 13
II Chr 26:17, 20

13. The chief priest in the days of King Uzziah of Judah; he headed a group of priests who opposed the king's religious activities and defended the status of the house of Aaron (II Chr 26:17, 20).

AZARIAH 14
II Chr 28:12

14. The son of Johanan; one of the Ephraimite chiefs who persuaded the people of Israel to release the men of Judah whom they had captured during the war against Ahaz (II Chr 28:12).

AZARIAH 15
II Chr 29:12

15. A Kohathite Levite; his son, Joel, was among the Levites who cleansed the Temple in the days of King Hezekiah.

AZARIAH 16
II Chr 29:12

16. A Levite. The son of Jehalelel, one of the Merarites who cleansed the Temple at the time of King Hezekiah (II Chr 29:12).

AZARIAH 17
II Chr 31:10, 13

17. A priest of the house of Zadok; the "chief priest" in the time of King Hezekiah (II Chr 31:10). In II Chronicles 31:13, he is called "the ruler of the house of God". He may be identical with the son of Hilkiah named in the genealogical list of Aaron's descendants in I Chronicles 6:14; if so, he is identical with Azariah No.18. (II Chr 31:10, 13).

AZARIAH 18
I Chr 6:13-14.
Ezra 7:1

18. The son of Hilkiah and father of Seraiah (I Chr 6:13-14; Ezra 7:1). Some identify him with Azariah No.17.

19. The son of Meraioth and father of Amariah (Ezra 7:3).

AZARIAH 19
Ezra 7:3

20. The son of Maaseiah. He was among those who repaired the wall of Jerusalem in the days of Nehemiah (Neh 3:23-24).

AZARIAH 20
Neh 3:23-24

21. One of the leaders of the people who returned from the Exile with Zerubbabel (Neh 7:7). In the parallel list in Ezra 2:2, he is called or replaced by Seraiah.

AZARIAH 21
Neh 7:7

22. One of the Levites who stood beside Ezra and expounded the Law to the people (Neh 8:7).

AZARIAH 22
Neh 8:7

23. One of those who witnessed the sealing of the covenant. In Nehemiah 12:1, he is called Ezra.

AZARIAH 23
Neh 10:2

24. The son of Hoshaiah. One of the captains of the armed bands who, with Johanan son of Kareah and the remnant of Judah, ignored Jeremiah's counsel and left for Egypt (Jer 43:2). The Hebrew in Jeremiah 42:1 names him Jezaniah.

AZARIAH 24
Jer 43:2

25. One of the leading men of Judah who was appointed to take part in the dedication of the wall of Jerusalem (Neh 12:33).

26. King of Judah, better known as Uzziah (See UZZIAH).

27. An alternate name for King Ahaziah of Judah, given in some versions of the Bible. (See AHAZIAH No. 2).

28. The original name of one of David's companions. He was given the Babylonian name Abed-Nego when he was taken into captivity (Dan 1:6-7, 11, 19; 2:17).

AZARYAHU See AZARIAH No.12

AZAZ Father of Bela; listed in the genealogy of Reuben.

AZAZEL The word appears in Leviticus 16:8-10, 26 as the name of the place or the power to which one of the two he-goats in the Temple service was sent on the Day of Atonement. The ceremony commenced when the high priest cast lots over two goats: one was designated to the Lord and offered as a sin offering, while the other was "for/to Azazel". The high priest symbolically placed the iniquities and transgressions on the head of this goat which was banished into the wilderness, thereby removing the sins to a distant desolate place.

The above description provided alternative translations for the Hebrew word *Azazel*. The Greek translation interpreted it to mean "goat that departs", i.e. (e)scape-goat. The Talmud offers the view that Azazel was the name of a craggy cliff from which the goat was hurled to its death during Second Temple times. A few medieval commentators identify Azazel with the name of a demon in the wilderness, a view shared by some modern scholars. Related to this is the widespread opinion which identifies Azazel variously as the devil, a fallen angel or a wilderness satyr. However, it is unlikely that the Bible is describing a ritual sacrifice to a demon since this would run counter to the very strict prohibition of such practices in Leviticus 17:7. Leviticus 16:22 supports the view that Azazel is the name of a desolate wilderness.

AZAZIAH ("Yah is strong/strengthens").

1. A Levite harpist in the procession that brought the ark to Jerusalem in the reign of King David.

2. Father of Hoshea who was appointed officer over the tribe of Ephraim during David's reign.

3. An overseer under Cononiah and Shimei in King Hezekiah's time; he was responsible for the tithes and offerings brought for the Temple.

AZBUK Father of a certain Nehemiah who helped rebuild the wall of Jerusalem on the return from the Babylonian Exile.

AZEKAH A town in the northwest of Judah situated on one of the western passes leading from the coast to the Judean Hills. The

AZARIAH 25
Neh 12:33

AZARIAH 26
II Kgs 14:21;
15:1, 6-8, 17,
23, 27. I Chr
3:12

AZARIAH 27
II Chr 22:6

AZARIAH 28
Dan 1:6-7, 11,
19; 2:17

AZARYAHU
II Chr 21:2

AZAZ
I Chr 5:8

AZAZIAH 1
I Chr 15:21

AZAZIAH 2
I Chr 27:20

AZAZIAH 3
II Chr 31:13

AZBUK
Neh 3:16

AZEKAH
Josh 10:10-11;

Tell Zakariyeh, the site of Azekah.

15:35. I Sam
17:1. II Chr
11:9. Neh
11:30. Jer 34:7

Philistines gathered nearby to fight Israel in the days of Saul (I Sam 17:1). Among the cities fortified by Rehoboam for the defense of Judah (II Chr 11:5, 9), Azekah was one of the last two cities to withstand Nebuchadnezzar (Jer 34:7), the other being Lachish. Azekah is mentioned among the towns of Judah settled at the time of the return from the Babylonian Exile (Neh 11:30). It seems that Azekah should be identified with Tell Zakariyeh.

The site has been excavated. The town, probably built in the 10th century B.C. in the days of the United Monarchy, was one of a string of

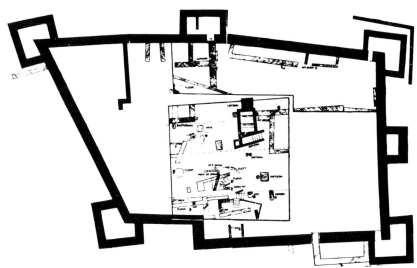

Plan of the Judean fortress at Azekah.

fortresses constructed along the boundaries of Judah to guard the major roads and other strategic points.

AZEL
I Chr 8:37-38;
9:43-44

AZEL Son of Eleasah and father of six sons; listed in the genealogy of King Saul.

AZGAD
Ezra 2:12;
8:12. Neh
7:17; 10:15

AZGAD The name of a family and of its ancestor. According to Nehemiah (7:17) 2,322 members of the family returned from Babylonian Exile with Zerubbabel. Among those who returned later with Ezra were 110 men of the family (Ezra 8:12). Its representative was among those who signed the covenant with Nehemiah (Neh 10:15).

AZIEL
I Chr 15:20

AZIEL A Levite at the time of King David; he was among the harp players when the ark was brought to Jerusalem. Aziel's full name (as it appears in verse 18 in the same chapter) was Jaaziel.

AZIZA
Ezra 10:27

AZIZA One of the sons of Zattu who was among those forced to divorce their foreign wives at the decree of Ezra.

AZMAVETH ("the god Mot is mighty"). Geographical and personal name related to the Benjamites.

1. A Benjamite from the city of Bahurim, one of David's thirty "mighty men".

AZMAVETH 1
II Sam 23:31.
I Chr 11:33

2. A son of Jehoaddah (I Chr 8:36; given as Jarah in I Chr 9:42), a descendant of King Saul.

AZMAVETH 2
I Chr 8:36;
9:42

3. The father of two brothers, Jeziel and Pelet, who joined David during his sojourn in Ziklag.

AZMAVETH 3
I Chr 12:3

4. A son of Adiel who was in charge of the royal treasures of David. Probably identical with No.2.

AZMAVETH 4
I Chr 27:25

5. A town in Benjamin, probably Ras Dukheir, 3 miles (5 km) northeast of Jerusalem and 6/10 mile (1 km) west of an Arab village named Hismeh which preserves the name, Beth Azmaveth. Forty-two people of this city were among those who returned with Zerubbabel after the Babylonian Exile (Ezra 2:24), and singers from Azmaveth took part in the dedication of the wall of Jerusalem (Neh 12:29).

AZMAVETH 5
Ezra 2:24.
Neh 12:29

AZMON A place between Hazar Addar and the Brook of Egypt. It lay along the southern border of Judah (Num 34:4-5). It is referred to as Heshmon in a list of border cities of the tribe of Judah (Josh 15:27). A possible location is at "Ain el-Qoseimeh" near Kadesh Barnea.

AZNOTH TABOR A village on the southern border of Naphtali. Present-day Umm Jebeil, 3 miles (5 km) north of Mount Tabor.

AZOR Son of Eliakim and father of Zadok, listed in the genealogy of Jesus.

AZOTUS The NT form of Ashdod; one of the cities where Philip preached on his way to Caesarea.

AZRIEL ("God is my help").

1. The father of Jeremoth, head of the tribe of Naphtali during the time of King David.

2. The father of Seraiah at the time of King Jehoiakim.

3. One of the heads of the families of the tribe of Manasseh.

AZRIKAM

1. Son of Neariah, a descendant of David through Zerubbabel.

2. One of the six sons of Azel; listed as a descendant of Saul and Jonathan in the genealogy of Benjamin.

3. Grandfather of Shemaiah who was part of the Levite family living in Jerusalem after the return from the Babylonian captivity.

4. The "officer over the house" of Ahaz, king of Judah, who was slain in battle by Zichri, "a mighty man", when Judah was defeated by Israel.

AZUBAH ("foresaken").

1. The mother of Jehoshaphat and daughter of Shilhi.

2. The wife of Caleb of Hezron. She had three sons: Jesher, Shobab and Ardon.

AZUR, AZZUR A prophet from Gibeon; father of the false prophet Hananiah.

AZZAN The father of Paltiel the chief (prince) of the tribe of Issachar, who helped in the division of the settlement of Canaan.

AZZUR

1. One of the people who sealed the covenant at the time of Ezra.

2. Father of Jaazaniah, one of the 25 men against whom Ezekiel was commanded to prophesy.

AZMON
Num 34:4-5.
Josh 15:4

AZNOTH TABOR
Josh 19:34

AZOR
Matt 1:13-14

AZOTUS
Acts 8:40

AZRIEL 1
I Chr 27:19

AZRIEL 2
Jer 36:26

AZRIEL 3
I Chr 5:24

AZRIKAM 1
I Chr 3:23

AZRIKAM 2
I Chr 8:38;
9:44

AZRIKAM 3
I Chr 9:14.
Neh 11:15

AZRIKAM 4
II Chr 28:7

AZUBAH 1
I Kgs 22:42.
II Chr 20:31

AZUBAH 2
I Chr 2:18-19

AZUR,
AZZUR
Jer 28:1

AZZAN
Num 34:26

AZZUR 1
Neh 10:17

AZZUR 2
Ezek 11:1

BAAL ("Lord").

1. A term for several Canaanite gods, and particularly for the storm-god, the head of the Canaanite pantheon and chief god of the Canaanites. The myth of his origin and rise to power is found in several epic texts discovered at Ugarit, written in the Canaanite language Ugaritic, a close relative of biblical Hebrew. His name is mentioned also in the El Amarna Letters and in Akkadian, Phoenician and Aramaic inscriptions. Baal was considered to be master of the wind and rain, and thus of fertility of the land, and so, by extension, of the earth itself. Some of his titles were borrowed as parallel epithets of the God of Israel in biblical poetry, e.g. he who "rides the heavens" (Deut 33:26) and "rides on the clouds" (Ps 68:4). There were several temples dedicated to Baal in Canaan and its vicinity, as indicated by the place names compounded with his name e.g. Baal Peor (Num 25:3, 5; Deut 4:3; Hos 9:10), Baal Hermon (Judg 3:3). Personal names compounded with Baal were also quite common among the Canaanites testifying to his popularity, and some of these are found in the Bible, (e.g. Ethbaal, Jerubbaal, etc.).

In the Bible, Baal in the plural is used as a general term for all the Canaanite gods, but Baal mostly refers to the popular Canaanite storm-weather-god. Baal-worship succeeded in enticing, at certain times, the Israelites from the pure worship of the God of Israel and resulted at times in a syncretistic mixture of Canaanite and Israelite worship. The ridding of such Canaanite influences thus becomes a mark of zeal and faithfulness towards God. So Gideon, at God's command, throws down the Baal altar of his father, an act which aroused the anger of the men of the city (Judg 6:25-32).

The most conspicuous period of Baal-worship in the Bible is in Ahab's time, due to the influence of his Canaanite wife Jezebel (cf I Kgs 16:32). It was then that the prophet Elijah staged his famous confrontation with the Baal-worshipers on Mount Carmel (I Kgs chap. 18). Baal worship, however, continued to find adherents among the nation, and the erection and subsequent destruction of Baal altars is a recurring motif in the history of the Kingdom of Judah (Athaliah builds — Joash destroys; Manasseh builds — Josiah destroys). Israel's prophets spoke out forcefully and frequently with great sarcasm and irony against the people's apparent proclivity to "adhere to" Baal-worship, up to the time of the destruction. Zechariah 12:11 refers to the heathen practice of mourning annually the death of Haddad Rimmon (Baal).

2. An ancestor of King Saul and the fourth son of Jeiel of Gibeon.

3. A Reubenite leader, father of Beerah and son of Reaiah; he was among those exiled to Assyria by Tiglath-Pileser.

(left)
Babylonian coin depicting Baal (?) seated, and a lion. c. 320 B.C.

Stele from Ugarit showing the Baal of Lightning. The Canaanite god brandishes a club in his left hand and holds a thunderbolt in his right hand; before him stands the king of Ugarit. 14th-13th centuries B.C.

BAALAH

1. Another name for Kirjath Jearim.

2. A city in the Negeb which fell to the lot of the tribe of Simeon when the land of Israel was divided among the tribes by Joshua. Its location is unknown (Josh 19:1, 3).

3. A mountain on the northern border of the territory of the tribe of Judah.

BAALATH

1. A city which fell to the lot of the tribe of Dan when the land of Israel was divided among the tribes by Joshua (Josh 19:40, 44).

2. One of the cities fortified by Solomon (I Kgs 9:17-18; II Chr 8:6). It is mentioned by Josephus Flavius as being west of Gezer.

View of Baalath in the region of Gezer.

BAALATH BEER A city in the southern part of the territory allotted to the tribe of Simeon (Josh 19:1, 8). Perhaps the same site as mentioned in I Chronicles 4:33.

BAAL-BERITH A deity whose sanctuary was located in Shechem (Judg 9:4). After the death of Gideon, the Israelites worshiped Baal-Berith (Judg 8:33) who is called "the god Berith" in Judges 9:46.

BAALE JUDAH Another name for Kirjath Jearim.

BAAL GAD A site on the northern border of the land of Canaan, the northernmost point of the conquests of Joshua (Josh 11:17) "in the valley of Lebanon under Mount Hermon". The name means "the house of Gad", the Canaanite god of good fortune, identical perhaps with Baal Hermon.

BAAL HAMON A place where Solomon had a vineyard (Song 8:11). It is mentioned only once in the Scriptures, nothing is known of its location, and scholars do not agree as to the exact meaning of the name.

BAAL-HANAN ("the Lord was compassionate").

1. The son of Achbor; he was the seventh king of Edom and ruled after Saul-of-Rehoboth-by-the-River; his successor was Hadad.

2. Baal Hanan the Gederite, a state official appointed by David, in charge of "the olive trees and the sycamores that were in the lowlands".

BAAL HAZOR A place in Ephraim (II Sam 13:23) which belonged to Absalom; there he had his brother Amnon killed (II Sam 13:28, 29) to avenge the rape of his sister Tamar (II Sam 13:22). Today identified with a mountain north of Bethel.

BAAL HERMON A mountain (Judg 3:3) or a city (I Chr 5:23) on the northern border of the land of Canaan. It is perhaps identical with Baal Gad.

BAALIS King of the Ammonites (Jer 40:14) who conspired to have the governor of Judah, Gedaliah, murdered (Jer 40:7, 14; 41:2). The murderer, Ishmael, then fled to the Ammonites (Jer 41:15). Scholars

BAALAH 1
Josh 15:9-10.
I Chr 13:6

BAALAH 2
Josh 19:3

BAALAH 3
Josh 15:11, 29

BAALATH 1
Josh 19:44

BAALATH 2
I Kgs 9:18.
II Chr 8:6

BAALATH BEER
Josh 19:8

BAAL-
BERITH
Judg 8:33; 9:4

BAALE JUDAH
II Sam 6:2

BAAL GAD
Josh 11:17;
12:7; 13:5

BAAL HAMON
Song 8:11

BAAL-HANAN 1
Gen 36:38-39.
I Chr 1:49-50

BAAL-HANAN 2
I Chr 27:28

BAAL HAZOR
II Sam 13:23

BAAL HERMON
Judg 3:3.
I Chr 5:23

BAALIS
Jer 40:14

explain this murder by the fact that the Ammonites, who had taken over the land of Gad (Jer 49:1), wanted to exert a greater influence on neighboring Judah. The name appears on a stamp found recently in Ammonite territory.

BAAL MEON A city in the land of Moab, believed to have been on the site of present-day Ma'in, a Christian village 4 miles (6 km) southwest of Medeba. Also called Beon (Num 32:3), Beth Meon (Jer 48:23) and Beth Baal Meon (Josh 13:17). The town, which belonged to the Moabites, was allotted by Moses to the tribe of Reuben (Num 32:3, 37-38). Their descendants lived there (I Chr 5:8) until Mesha king of Moab rebelled against the king of Israel and seized the whole area. In the monument he erected to commemorate his victory, the town is mentioned twice (lines 9 and 30).

BAAL MEON
Num 32:38.
Josh 13:17.
I Chr 5:8.
Ezek 25:9

BAAL-PEOR, BAAL OF PEOR One of the local Baals, worshiped on Mount Peor in Moab. While encamped at Shittim, on their journey through the wilderness, the Israelites participated in the worship of this particular idol and committed harlotry with the local Moabite women (Num 25:1-2). As punishment for being "joined to Baal of Peor" the Israelites were afflicted by a plague which swept through the camps, killing 24,000 people. The leaders of the Baal-worshiping incident were killed by the judges of the tribes (Num 25:3-5). See BAAL No.1, BETH PEOR, PEOR.

BAAL-PEOR, BAAL OF PEOR
Num 25:3, 5.
Deut 4:3. Ps 106:28. Hos 9:10

BAAL PERAZIM A hill south of Jerusalem where David defeated the Philistines (II Sam 5:20). The biblical text explains the name: "And David went to Baal Perazim, and David defeated them there and said, The Lord has broken through my enemies before me, like a breakthrough of water. Therefore he called the name of that place Baal Perazim" (from the Hebrew "to break forth, to breach"). Scholars have suggested this is a play on the original name of the place, where an altar of Baal used to stand.

BAAL PERAZIM
II Sam 5:20.
I Chr 14:11

BAAL SHALISHA A city from which barley and corn were brought to the prophet Elisha (II Kgs 4:42); probably the site of a temple of the Canaanite god Baal.

BAAL SHALISHA
II Kgs 4:42

BAAL TAMAR A city or a place near Gibeah in Benjamin (Judg 20:33), where the men of Israel regrouped before their last and victorious attack upon Gibeah (Judg 20:30-34, 40, 43). Its location is not clear.

BAAL TAMAR
Judg 20:33

BAAL-ZEBUB See BEELZEBUB

BAAL-ZEBUB
II Kgs 1:2-3, 6, 16

BAAL ZEPHON ("Lord of the North"). A place or city in Egypt, close to the last halt of the Children of Israel before the crossing of the Red Sea (Ex 14:2). According to the text, Baal Zephon was near Pi-hahiroth and Migdol; since nothing is known about the precise location of these localities, or about the exact spot where the Hebrews crossed the Red Sea, it is assumed that the place was somewhere in northwestern Egypt. Baal Zephon is a well known Canaanite god commonly associated with the sea and storms.

BAAL ZEPHON
Ex 14:2, 9.
Num 33:7

BAANA

1. Baana son of Ahilud; he was one of the 12 governors appointed by Solomon (I Kgs 4:7). His was the fifth district: Taanah, Megiddo and Beth Shean (I Kgs 4:12).

BAANA 1
I Kgs 4:12

2. Baana son of Hushai, likewise one of Solomon's 12 governors (I Kgs 4:7). His was the ninth district: Asher and Aloth (I Kgs 4:16).

BAANA 2
I Kgs 4:16

3. Baana father of Zadok (Neh 3:4); Zadok was among those who rebuilt the walls of Jerusalem at the time of Nehemiah (Neh 2:17). This Baana may be identical with Baanah No.4.

BAANA 3
Neh 3:4

BAANAH

1. Baanah the son of Rimon the Beerothite, from the tribe of Benjamin; he was captain of the troops of Ishbosheth son of Saul

BAANAH 1
II Sam 4:2, 5-6, 9

(II Sam 4:2) and together with his brother Rechab murdered his master (II Sam 4:7) to seek favor with David (II Sam 4:8). David, however, was angered and had them both slain (II Sam 4:12).

2. A man of Netophah who was the father of Heleb (II Sam 23:29), one of David's thirty "mighty men" (II Sam 23:8, 13).

3. Baanah, one of the exiles who returned from Babylon with Zerubbabel (Ezra 2:1-2).

4. Baanah, one of the leaders of the people who sealed the covenant made in the time of Nehemiah (Neh 10:1, 27). May be identical with Baana No.3 father of Zadok.

BAARA One of the two wives of Shaharaim (I Chr 8:8) in the genealogy of Benjamin (I Chr 8:1).

BAASEIAH Son of Malchijah and ancestor of Asaph; he was appointed by David as a Temple musician.

BAASHA Son of Ahijah of the tribe of Issachar; king of Israel, 906-883 B.C. He became king after assassinating King Nadab during the siege of Philistine-occupied Gibbethon (I Kgs 15:27-28). Baasha reigned for 24 years at Tirzah, the new capital of northern Israel. By massacring all the members of the house of Jeroboam I, he put an end to Ephraim's hegemony over the northern tribes. After concluding a treaty with King Ben-Hadad I of Aram-Damascus, Baasha undertook a military campaign against King Asa of Judah, and succeeded in capturing Ramah, north of Jerusalem (I Kgs 15:16, 32). However, Baasha capitulated when Ben-Hadad responded to Asa's bribe and invaded Israel's northern territory (I Kgs 15:17-20). According to the Bible, Baasha died a peaceful death (I Kgs 16:6).

BABEL, TOWER OF An edifice built after the Flood by the men of Shinar (Babylonia) to reach heaven. Their object was to make a name for themselves and to avoid dispersal over the earth. God punished their audacity by confounding their language — until then, all the world spoke a single language — to prevent them from communicating with one another and they were dispersed throughout the world (Gen 11:1-9). The name Babel (Babylon) derives from the Hebrew word "to confuse". The story was probably inspired by the high temple-towers (ziggurat) in Babylonia. The writer may have had in mind the great ziggurat of Marduk in Babylon which was six stories high, crowned with a golden shrine. He was familiar with building techniques of Mesopotamia as he specifically mentions the use of bricks and bitumen. Although the background of the narrative is Mesopotamian, no parallel story is known from that literature.

Reconstructed model of the ziggurat of Ur.

BABYLON (CITY OF) One of the most important cities of Mesopotamia, whose name originally meant "the gate of the gods". The Hebrews understood the name differently: "Therefore is the name of it called Babel; because there the Lord confused the language of all the earth" (Gen 11:9). See BABEL, TOWER OF. Babylon is the Greek form of the name. The greatness of Babylon began during its 1st Dynasty, especially in the reign of Hammurabi (c. 17th century B.C.), the sixth king of that line. During his reign and that of his son numerous temples were built there and irrigation channels were excavated but then the city suffered a rapid decline. It revived again in the 13th century B.C. but continued to suffer frequent onslaughts, resulting in destruction, at the hands of the rising Assyrian Empire. It was not until the downfall of Assyria that Babylon, in the time of Nebuchadnezzar II, rose again to the status of the most important city in Mesopotamia. Cyrus, king of Persia, conquered the city, which then became part of the Persian Empire. In 331 B.C. Babylon was conquered by Alexander the Great, who attempted to rebuild the venerated but decaying city. With his untimely death its long decline set in and in the Roman period it was no more than $3^1/_2$ square miles (9 sq. km). The whole area was surrounded explorer Pietro Della Valle brought back from Babylon the first cuneiform tablets. These soon attracted the attention of numerous scholars.

The ruins of Babylon form a vast triangle and extend over an area of more than $3^1/_2$ square miles (9 sq.km). The whole area was surrounded by walls, while on the west the city was defended by the Euphrates. Tell Babil, which has preserved the ancient name, rises in the northern part

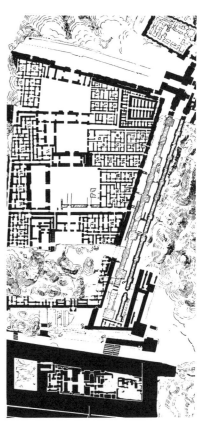

Part of a plan of Babylon showing the Procession Way leading to the Ishtar gate.

Reconstruction of the Gate of Ishtar in Babylon (with some of the original glazed bricks). 7th-6th centuries B.C.

of this triangle. Several additional mounds scattered over the area concealed some of the more important monuments. A huge bridge over the river connected old Babylon with the new city, built under Nebuchadnezzar II. In the excavations of Tell Babil extensive remains of his palace were discovered. It consisted of several large courts around which were grouped countless halls, rooms, stores and so on. The same palace was still further enlarged by subsequent rulers, especially Artaxerxes III Ochus. A monumental passageway led to the palace from the east, terminating in the third court, adjoining which was the magnificent throne hall. The walls of this vast hall were lined with bricks enameled in white, light blue, yellow and red, on a dark blue ground. Another huge palace was discovered in a mound in the northeastern quarter of the city. It consisted of a narrow passage, along which were grouped two lines of rooms, seven in each group. The excavators believed that these were the gardens of Queen Semiramis — the "Hanging Gardens of Babylon" famous in classical literature. Inscribed clay tablets were found here on which were written the portions of food allotted to foreign artisans and important captives, among them Jehoiakim, king of Judah.

Along the eastern side of the two palaces ran a ceremonial street connected with the inner city by the famous Ishtar Gate, decorated with enameled bricks on which wild oxen and legendary animals were depicted. The street led into the most sacred part of the city, where the most venerated shrines were situated. In the center of a huge court 1,200 feet by 1,500 feet (365 m by 460 m) stood the temple of Marduk, named E Sag Ila, and the "Tower of Babel". Owing to the rise in the level of the ground water the excavators were unable to penetrate the strata pertaining to the Babylon of Hammurabi but remains of the Persian, Hellenistic and Roman periods did come to light.

The story of the Tower of Babel is told in Genesis (11:1-9). This building is generally identified with the ziggurat, the tower which rises in the center of the court of the temple of Marduk. Isaiah referred to the glories of the city (13:19) and prophesied its downfall (13:20-22; 14:7-23). Babylon is referred to as the first city which was built by men and Jeremiah (51:7) describes it as "a golden cup in the Lord's hand."

In the NT, in I Peter 5:13 and in the Book of Revelation, Babylon is a code-word for Rome as the seat of the Roman Empire which claimed divine honors for the emperor (idolatry) and was oppressing the people of God. The Book of Revelation prophesies the fall of Babylon and its destruction and, referring to Babylon, says "For true and righteous are his judgments because he has judged the great harlot who corrupted the earth with her fornication; and he has avenged on her the blood of his servants shed by her" (Rev 19:2).

BABYLON, BABYLONIA, BABYLONIANS (Hebrew, *Babel*). Country and empire. (See also BABEL, TOWER OF).

It was because of the importance of its main city that the country came to be known as Babylon (See BABYLON, CITY OF); originally it was mentioned under several other names, the first of which was "the land of Shinar". (See SHINAR). Like neighboring Assyria Shinar was, according to the Bible, settled by Nimrod "And the beginning of his kingdom was Babel, Erech, Accad and Calneh in the land of Shinar" (Gen 10:10).

Another name commonly used in the Scriptures for this area is Chaldea. Abraham originated from "Ur of the Chaldeans." (Gen 11:31). The land so designated was in the fertile alluvial region of southern Mesopotamia, "between the two rivers" created out of the Persian Gulf by the successive deltas of the Tigris and Euphrates Rivers. Wave after wave of semi-nomadic peoples of Sumerian and Semitic

BABYLON, BABYLONIA, BABYLONIANS Josh 7:21. II Kgs 17:24, 30; 20:12, 14, 17-18; 24:1, 7, 10-12, 15-17, 20; 25:1, 6-8, 11, 13, 20-24, 27-28. I Chr 9:1. II Chr 32:31; 33:11; 36:6-7, 10, 18, 20. Ezra 1:11; 2:1; 4:9; 5:12-14, 17; 6:1, 5; 7:6, origin settled there over the centuries. Out of this crucible there emerged new types of writings, new languages, new civilizations. Two mighty empires fought for control over Mesopotamia: Assyria to the northwest and Babylon to the southwest. Babylon, with its access to the sea routes of the Persian Gulf and its better climate, had a distinct advantage over its rival.

It was in Babylon that the first great Mesopotamian empire, that of the first Babylonian dynasty, evolved and flourished. Its best-known ruler was Hammurabi, who set down the collection of laws bearing his name.

After the fall of the first Babylonian dynasty and the destruction of its capital Babylon (c. 1550 B.C.) a long period of Assyrian supremacy began which lasted until the 7th century B.C. Between the time of Abraham and the second Book of Kings, a period of over a thousand years, the Bible does not mention Babylon. Only when the Kingdom of Israel was destroyed by the Assyrians and its inhabitants taken into exile is there reference to people from Babylon (at the time a vassal of Assyria) who were among the settlers brought in by the new rulers (II Kgs 17:24). The rise of a powerful new kingdom in Babylon was at first greeted with relief in Jerusalem, since it meant the end of the pressure which had been exerted on the Kingdom of Judah by the rulers of Assyria over the previous decades. Indeed, according to the biblical record (which does not always coincide with the historical record) good relations between Babylon and Judah endured for a century, from the reign of King Hezekiah through those of Kings Manasseh, Amon, Josiah, Jehoahaz, Jehoiakim and Jehoiachin. At that point Nebuchadnezzar, the second king of the neo-Babylonian Empire captured Jerusalem for the first time and set up Zedekiah to reign there as his vassal (II Kgs 24:10, 12-13, 17-18). However, Zedekiah tried to rebel against Babylon whose armies then returned and took the city of Jerusalem a second time after a long, bitter siege: "Nebuzaradan the captain of the guard, a servant of the king of Babylon, came to Jerusalem; he burned the house of the Lord and the king's house; all the houses of Jerusalem, that is all the houses of the great men he burned with fire. And all the army of the Chaldeans who were with the captain of the guard broke down the walls of Jerusalem all around" (II Kgs 25:8-10).

Thus ended the First Temple period. A section of the population of Judah was taken in captivity to Babylon and this was the beginning of the BABYLONIAN EXILE. However, Babylon itself did not survive much longer than the Kingdom of Judah. Less than a quarter of a century later the armies of King Cyrus of Persia swept across Mesopotamia and ended the Babylonian Empire.

Limestone relief plaque with a representation of Hammurabi, dedicated to the goddess [Ash] ratum by a provincial governor. c. 1760 B.C.

Fragment of the Babylonian Epic of Gilgamesh found at Megiddo. 15th century B.C. (Israel Museum)

BABYLONIAN EXILE The exile of a section of the population of Judah to Babylonia in the 6th century B.C. Mass deportation of conquered populations was a common practice in both the Assyrian and Babylonian empires. After the fall of the Kingdom of Israel (722/1 B.C.), the population of the Northern Kingdom was carried away to Assyria (II Kgs 18:11-12) and over a century later a considerable section of the population of Judah was exiled to Babylonia in three successive waves. However, unlike the situation in the Northern Kingdom, no foreign population was transferred to Judah to replace its exiles. Nevertheless the Babylonian Exile, following the destruction of Jerusalem and the First Temple, was a deeply traumatic experience for the Jewish people. The first deportation in 598 B.C. followed the surrender of King Jehoiachin of Judah to the armies of Nebuchadnezzar who were besieging Jerusalem. The Babylonian king carried into captivity King Jehoiachin, his mother, his palace retinue, the Temple and palace treasures, along with 10,000 captives (II Kgs 24:12-16). The conquerors set up Zedekiah, Jehoiachin's uncle, as the new ruler of Jerusalem. However, Zedekiah also rebelled against Babylon. Once again Jerusalem was besieged; it fell and the Temple was destroyed in 587/6 B.C. The second deportation is described in II Kings 25:8-21; Jeremiah 39:8-10; 52:12-34. Shortly after the destruction of the Temple a new uprising against Gedaliah the governor appointed by the

Judean captives driven out of destroyed Lachish. From a relief from Nineveh.

Babylonians resulted in further deportations (582 B.C.). The exiles remained in Babylon until the edict of Cyrus which granted them permission to return in 538 (Ezra 1:1-4; II Chr 36:22-23). The historical books of the Scriptures come to an end with the beginning of the Babylonian Exile. There is no detailed chronicle of the Exile and the sparse information that exists is gleaned from the Prophetic books as well as from Ezra and Nehemiah. However, from these texts and available external sources such as Babylonian contract tablets it may be inferred that after an initial period of hardship the life of the exiles was eased. Most of them lived in small, agricultural communities (Ezek 1:1; 3:15) but some were engaged in trade (Neh 1:11; Is 55:1-2; Zech 6:9-11); some owned their own houses (Jer 29:5; Ezek 8:1); married (Jer 29:6; Ezek 24:18) and indeed, when Cyrus' edict made return to Zion possible, not all the exiles availed themselves of the opportunity. Many remained in Babylon where they were to form prosperous communities whose leaders were to compete for the leadership of the Jewish world with the sages of Jerusalem after the destruction of the Second Temple in A.D. 70. It was probably in the Babylonian Exile that the institution of the synagogue emerged — a meeting place where Jews could read their sacred literature and hear the expositions of their prophets.

The time of the Exile was one of great spiritual upheaval. Many believed the destruction of the Temple and the dispersion were divine retribution for the sinfulness of the people: this was the message of the prophets as exemplified, for instance, in the Book of Lamentations. But their message was also a message of hope: the Lord would forgive his erring children and restore Jerusalem and the Temple to their former glory (Is 44:26-28).

BACA
Ps 84:6

BACA A valley in the vicinity of Jerusalem (Ps 84:7); perhaps another name for the valley of Rephaim. The plural Becaim is used to designate a tree. While usually translated as "mulberry" (II Sam 5:23-24; I Chr 14:15), many scholars believe it referred to a species of poplar or perhaps balsam tree. See also Luke 17:6.

BACHRITES
Num 26:35

BACHRITES (BECHERITES) Belonging to the family line of Becher.

BADGER See ANIMALS

BAHARUMITE,
BARHUMITE
II Sam 23:31.
I Chr 11:33

BAHARUMITE, BARHUMITE A man from Bahurim. The site is mentioned twice, both times in connection with Azmaveth, one of David's thirty "mighty men".

BAHURIM
II Sam 3:16;
16:5; 17:18;
19:16. I Kgs
2:8

BAHURIM A city or village east of Jerusalem, on the way to Jericho; it is mentioned several times in connection with King David. There Paltiel son of Laish left his beloved wife Michal, daughter of Saul, who was being returned to her rightful husband David (II Sam 3:16). David, fleeing from his son Absalom, was cursed by Shimei as he went through the city (II Sam 16:5); later Jonathan and Ahimaaz hid in a well there (II Sam 17:18).

BAKBAKKAR
I Chr 9:15

BAKBAKKAR One of the Levites who settled in Jerusalem at the time of Nehemiah.

BAKBUK
Ezra 2:51.
Neh 7:53

BAKBUK A member of a family of Nethinim (Temple servants) who returned from the Exile in Babylon with Zerubbabel.

BAKBUKIAH 1
Neh 12:9

BAKBUKIAH The name of three Levites living in the time of Nehemiah:

1. One of the Levites who came to Jerusalem with Zerubbabel and is mentioned as helping his fellow priests in their duties (Neh 12:7-9); he may be identical with Bakbukiah No.2.

BAKBUKIAH 2
Neh 11:17

2. Bakbukiah "the second among his brethren" (Neh 11:17) a cantor, one of the Levites who settled in Jerusalem at the time of Nehemiah; perhaps identical with Bakbukiah No.1.

BAKBUKIAH 3
Neh 12:25

3. A "gatekeeper, keeping the watch at the storerooms of the gates", a Levite living in Jerusalem at the time of Nehemiah.

BALAAM
Num 22:5, 7-
10, 12-14, 16,
18, 20-23, 25,
27-30, 34-41;
23:1-5, 11, 16,
25-31; 24:1-3,
10, 12, 15, 25;
31:8, 16. Deut
23:4-5. Josh
13:22; 24:9-10.
Neh 13:2. Mic
6:5. II Pet
2:15. Jude v.
11. Rev 2:14

BALAAM A soothsayer from Pethor on the Euphrates (Num 22:5). Balak, king of Moab, sent him messengers with promises of great reward if he would come to curse the Israelites whom he feared were going to conquer his land. At first Balaam refused for he was told by God not to curse the Israelites "for they are blessed" (Num 22:12) but when a second delegation arrived, God allowed him to go on condition that he do only "the word which I speak to you." (Num 22:20). However, God was angry at his going and sent an angel "in the way as an adversary". The angel was discerned by his donkey but not by Balaam who beat the animal for its stubbornness. After this occurred three times, God enabled the animal to speak and ask why it was being beaten. God then opened Balaam's eyes to see the angel, who revealed that the donkey had saved his life by turning aside. Balaam confessed his sin and the angel reiterated God's word that he could proceed, but "only the word that I speak to you, that shall you speak" (Num 22:35). Arriving in Moab, God indeed spoke to Balaam but instead of a curse,

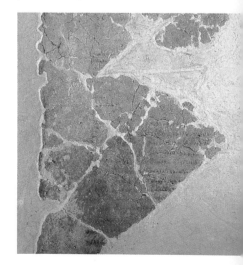

Inscriptions found at Deir Allah, Transjordan (Penuel in the OT), mentioning Bil'am (Balaam) son of Beor; end 8th century B.C. The text is believed to be of the kind generally found at cultic places where the story of their foundation was given. (Archaeological Museum, Amman)

he uttered a blessing saying "How shall I curse whom God has not cursed" (Num 23:8). Balak, perturbed, asked him to try again but now the words were more favorable to Israel and more threatening to Moab. Once more Balak pressed Balaam to speak. This time Balaam looked towards the wilderness and seeing the Israelite camp below gave voice to a poetic prophecy of the future triumph of Israel ("How lovely are your tents, O Jacob! your dwellings, O Israel!") (Num 24:3-9). This provoked Balak to anger but Balaam proceeded to predict the decline, defeat and destruction of Moab and the other nations of the region (the Edomites, Amalekites and Kenites). He thereupon left Balak and returned to his home. According to Numbers 31:8, 16 Balaam was subsequently slain by the Israelites because his counsel had led Israel astray and brought them to worship Baal at Peor (Josh 13:22).

Balaam is mentioned three times in the NT, with the OT references clearly in mind. In II Peter 2:15 he is presented as a paradigm of false teachers who like to be paid for their services ("the wages of unrighteousness", cf Deut 23:4; Neh 13:2). Jude 11 links Balaam with Cain and Korah as apostates, particularly as demonstrating the error of consciously teaching false doctrine for reward, and abusing certain gifts to lead God's people astray into idolatry. Revelation 2:14 similarly speaks of the doctrine of Balaam who taught to "eat things sacrificed to idols, and to commit sexual immorality." (a reference to Num chap.25) as one of the things wrong with the church in Pergamum.

BALADAN ("follower of Baal"). King of Babylon, father of Merodach-Baladan, the Chaldean king of Babylon who exchanged letters and presents with Hezekiah king of Judah.

BALADAN
II Kgs 20:12.
Is 39:1

BALAH A city in the Negeb which fell to the lot of the tribe of Simeon (Josh 19: 1, 3) when the land of Israel was divided among the tribes by Joshua (Josh 14:1). Its location is unknown.

BALAH
Josh 19:3

BALAK Son of Zippor, king of Moab (Num 22:2). He became concerned with the Israelites, who, having defeated the Amorites, advanced across the plains of Moab (Num 21:24-25; 22:1). Balak turned to Balaam (Num 22:5) asking him to curse the advancing armies (Num 22:6). When Balaam refused (Num 22:13) Balak insisted (Num 22:15) but to no avail.

BALAK
Num 22:2, 4, 7,
10, 13-16, 18,
35-41; 23:1-3,
5, 7, 11, 13, 15-
18, 25-30;
24:10, 12-13,
25. Josh 24:9.
Judg 11:25.
Mic 6:5. Rev
2:14

BALM See SPICES AND PERFUMES

BAMOTH One of the halts on the route of the Children of Israel from Egypt to the promised land, somewhere in the land of Moab on the eastern bank of the Jordan River. Some scholars identify this place with Bamoth Baal.

BAMOTH
Num 21:19-20

BAMOTH BAAL Place where Balak king of Moab took Balaam (Num 22:41) and at his request built seven altars on each of which he offered a bullock and a ram (Num 23:1-2). Later the place was included by Moses in the domain of the tribe of Reuben together with "Heshbon and all its cities that are in the plain" (Josh 13:17). Its location is not clear, but it is probably southwest of Mount Nebo.

BAMOTH BAAL
Josh 13:17

BANI ("build"). A number of biblical characters are called Bani; most of them were Levites and probably related. Most of them lived at the time of Ezra and Nehemiah. It is not always clear to which Bani some of the references relate. Some of the Bani listed separately below may well be identical.

1. Bani the Gadite, one of the thirty "mighty men" of David.

BANI 1
II Sam 23:36

2. A Merarite Levite, son of Shamer and father of Amzi, one of the ancestors of Ethan the singer, who lived during the time of David.

BANI 2
I Chr 6:46

3. A descendant of Perez the son of Judah; he was the father of Imri and the ancestor of Uthai who dwelled in Jerusalem after the return of the exiles from Babylon.

BANI 3
I Chr 9:4

BANI 4
Ezra 2:10

BANI 5
Neh 10:13

BANI 6
Ezra 10:29, 34, 38

BANI 7
Neh 8:7; 9:4-5; 10:14

BANI 8
Neh 9:4

BANI 9
Neh 3:17

BANI 10
Neh 11:22

4. The people of Bani, 642 in number, are listed among the captives who returned from Exile with Zerubbabel, though the parallel text in Nehemiah reads "the people of Binnui" (Neh 7:15).

5. A Levite who sealed the covenant at the time of Nehemiah.

6. No less than 33 sons of Bani, including one named Bani himself, are listed among the laymen who had taken pagan wives and were made to repudiate them by Ezra. They may have belonged to the Bani family (No.4).

7. A Levite, one of the men who helped the people understand the Law (Neh 8:7), who stood on the stairs of the Levites on the day of the great fast (Neh 9:4) and who sealed the covenant (Neh 10:14).

8. Another Levite who stood on the stairs of the Levites.

9. A Levite, father of Rehum who was in charge of the repairs in one section of the wall of Jerusalem at the time of Nehemiah.

10. A Levite, son of Hashabiah; his son Uzzi was overseer of the Levites in Jerusalem at the time of Nehemiah.

BAPTISM A Christian Greek word derived from a verb whose basic meaning is "to dip, to immerse, to wash". It is a NT institution though in Christian tradition typified in the OT by the crossing of the Red Sea (I Cor 10:1-2) and the flood of Noah (I Pet 3:20-21). Proselyte baptism of converts to Judaism may also have served as a historical antecedent. In Christian faith baptism has two aspects: an external washing or pouring with water and words in the name of Jesus, and an internal cleansing from sin (forgiveness of sins) and pouring in of the gift of the Holy Spirit. Being the commencement of Christian life, it is unrepeatable. Although the baptism into repentance given by John the Baptist was regarded as inadequate in the NT (Matt 3:11), the appearance of the Holy Spirit unto Jesus at his baptism by John in the Jordan (Matt 3:13-17; Mark 1:9-11; Luke 3:21-22) is taken as the model of Christian baptism which imparts the Spirit. In addition the baptism of Jesus was understood as his messianic anointing (Acts 10:38).

Paul presents a deeper theology of baptism (Rom 6:1-9; I Cor 12:13; Gal 3:27) as a sacramental dying and rising with Christ unto newness of life, a participation in his suffering and glory, and incorporation into his body, the church. Matthew 28:19 speaks of baptism in the name of Father, Son and Holy Spirit, the formula which has remained standard for this rite ever since. The baptized should find a new unity as summarized in Ephesians 4:5: "one Lord, one faith, one baptism." Baptism commits the believer to a new way of life, the pledge to God of an irreproachable conscience through the resurrection of Jesus Christ (I Pet 3:21). An additional aspect of baptism is a leave taking from the denial of God by a corrupt world, as the flood did for Noah and his family (I Pet 3:20-21).

(bottom of page)
The traditional site of Jesus' baptism in the Jordan River.

Part of a mosaic map of the 6th century, on the floor of St. George's church at Medeba, Transjordan. This section shows Aenon, on the left bank of the Jordan River, where John the Baptist baptized.

BARABBAS ("son of Abbas"). A prisoner released instead of Jesus. The evangelists called him a robber (John 18:40), a murderer (Luke 23:19), insurrectionist (Mark 15:7), and a notorious prisoner (Matt 27:16). Barabbas, a Jewish rioter, having participated in an act of terror in which a person was murdered, was caught by the Romans and imprisoned (Mark 15:7). He was released by Pontius Pilate on the choice of the multitude, persuaded by the chief priests and elders (Matt 27:20; Mark 15:11; Luke 23:18). Pilate did this in accordance with the custom "that I should release someone to you at the Passover" (John 18:39). Barabbas was due to be crucified together with two other prisoners, but as the impending Feast of Passover brought thousands of pilgrims to Jerusalem, the Roman authorities thought it circumspect to wait until after the Feast. Although the chief priests and elders were in favour of crucifying Barabbas, they knew that the multitudes admired him as a freedom fighter. Consequently Barabbas was released when Pilate heard the crowd shouting "Away with this man and release to us Barabbas" (Luke 23:18). Some scholars suppose that Barabbas belonged to the group of Zealots — patriots who fought against foreign rule. In some early versions his first name is given as Jesus.

BARACHEL ("whom God has blessed"). A Buzite, member of the Ram family and father of Elihu who was one of the three friends of Job.

BARAK ("lightning"). Israelite commander who led the armies of Deborah the prophetess to victory. Born in Kedesh-Naphtali to Abinoam of the tribe of Naphtali, he must have been already versed in the arts of war when Deborah asked him to lead her men and promised him victory in the name of the Lord (Judg 4:6-7). Barak insisted on her joining him as a condition of his acceptance (Judg 4:8). She agreed and together they defeated the armies of Jabin, king of Canaan, commanded by Sisera (Judg 4:15); Sisera managed to flee but was later killed by Jael (Judg 4:21).

BARBARIANS Common Greek name for foreigners (I Cor 14:11). In the NT the word is used to denote the inhabitants of Malta (Acts 28:4) who are described as friendly, and as a general designation for non-Greeks (Rom 1:14; Col 3:11)

BARHUMITE See BAHARUMITE

BARIAH ("fugitive"). One of the sons of Shemaiah in the enumeration of the line of David.

BAR-JESUS ("son of Jesus"). The patronymic of "a certain sorcerer, a false prophet" (Acts 13:6) who served the proconsul Sergius Paulus at Paphos on the island of Cyprus. Sergius Paulus "sought to hear the word of God" (Acts 13:7) from Barnabas and Paul. The sorcerer opposed them, trying to turn the proconsul away from the faith, and was struck blind temporarily when Paul pronounced divine judgment upon him (Acts 13:10ff). Bar-Jesus was also known by the title "Elymas" which means "sorcerer" (Acts 13:8). His personal name may well have been Hetoimos as attested by certain NT manuscripts.

BAR-JONAH ("son of Jonah"). Simon Peter's patronymic as it is found in Matthew's Gospel. John translates this Semitic patronymic literally as "son of John (Jonas)" (John 1:42) and "of John (Jonas)" (John 21:15-17).

BARKOS A family of Nethinim (Temple servants) who returned from Babylon with Zerubbabel.

BARLEY See PLANTS

BARNABAS An apostle (Acts 14:14) and colleague of Paul on his first missionary journey. He was a Levite from Cyprus, who having sold his property, gave all his money to the apostles. Barnabas was his surname, and his original name was Joses or Joseph (Acts 4:36-37).

46, 50; 14:12, 14, 20; 15:2, 12, 22, 25, 35-37, 39. I Cor 9:6. Gal 2:1, 9, 13. Col 4:10

Barnabas persuaded the Jerusalem community to accept Paul. The apostles were suspicious of Paul and did not believe that he was a disciple. Barnabas declared that Paul had seen the Lord and that he had preached at Damascus in the name of Jesus (Acts 9:26-27). The Jerusalem community sent Barnabas to Antioch to assist the rapidly growing group of believers (Acts 11:22ff) and he brought Paul from Tarsus to Antioch (Acts 11:25). The community in Antioch supported the Jerusalem church financially and gave their contribution to Barnabas and Paul (Acts 11:29-30), who took it to Jerusalem during the famine. On their return to Antioch, Paul and Barnabas were selected to visit cities to preach the Gospel (Acts 13:1ff). They went from Antioch to Selecuia and Cyprus, preaching in the synagogues (Acts 13:4-6). In Antioch of Pisidia they taught in the Jewish community, until some of the Jews became envious of their success and they were expelled (Acts 13:14-50). After they returned to Antioch, a controversy broke out concerning the obligations of exilic Christians to undergo circumcision and Paul and Barnabas were sent to Jerusalem to discuss the question with the council (Acts 15:1-2). On their journey, Barnabas refused to eat with the Gentiles (Gal 2:12) but at the Jerusalem discussion, Barnabas agreed that Jewish observances should not be imposed on Christians. When they returned to Antioch Paul prepared his second missionary journey but objected to taking Mark along on the grounds that he had already left them once on their first journey. As a result Paul and Barnabas separated, each going his own way. Paul chose Silas, while Barnabas took Mark and sailed to Cyprus (Acts 15:36-40).

BARSABBAS ("son of Sabba").

BARSABBAS 1
Acts 1:23

1. Joseph Barsabbas: One of the two disciples nominated to fill the vacancy among the twelve left by the death of Judas Iscariot (Acts 1:23). He accompanied the apostles during all the time that Jesus was among them "beginning from the baptism of John to that day when he was taken up" (Acts 1:21-22) and with the apostles he was a witness to the resurrection of Jesus. Lots were thrown to choose between Joseph Barsabbas and Matthias and the lot fell to Matthias. His eponym, "Justus" or "The Just", may indicate (as with James "the brother of the Lord") this disciple's strict adherence to the Law.

BARSABBAS 2
Acts 15:22

2. Judas Barsabbas: A member of the Jerusalem church. He and Silas, "leading men among the brethren", were chosen by the apostles and elders to accompany Paul and Barnabas to Antioch with the letter of injunction from the Apostolic Council to the Gentile believers (Acts 15:22-23). At Antioch, he and Silas ministered as prophets to the congregation and subsequently returned to Jerusalem (Acts 15:32). The fact that he and Joseph Barsabbas shared the same last name and were both from the Jerusalem church may indicate that they were members of the same family.

BARTHOLOMEW
Matt 10:3.
Mark 3:18.
Luke 6:14.
Acts 1:13

BARTHOLOMEW ("son of Talmai", "son of Ptolemy", or "inhabitant of Ptolemais"). An apostle who appears in the lists of the twelve in the synoptic gospels and Acts (Matt 10:3; Mark 3:18; Luke 6:14; Acts 1:13), usually paired with Philip. Bartholomew is a patronymic and thus not a person's familiar name. He does not appear in John's gospel and the association of Philip with an otherwise unknown Nathanael (John 1:45-51; 21:2) leads to the possibility that Nathanael was Bartholomew's personal name. This identification, i.e., "Nathanael Bar-Talmai" (cf "Simon Bar-Jonah"), although feasible, is by no means certain. Later traditions represent him as a missionary with Philip and Thomas. He is said to have preached the gospel in Armenia, India, Lycaonia, Mesopotamia, Persia and Phrygia, and Eusebius holds him personally responsible for bringing the Hebrew version of the Gospel of Matthew to India. Several apocryphal books have been attributed to him.

BARTIMAEUS ("son of Timai" or "son of value, honor"). A blind beggar in Mark's gospel (Mark 10:46-52) who remains unnamed in Luke's gospel (Luke 18:35-43). He was healed by Jesus at Jericho as Jesus was journeying to Jerusalem for the Passover. He is possibly one of two healed in Matthew's gospel (Matt 20:29-34). Bartimaeus' persistent faith in Jesus is exemplary for those who "have not seen and yet have believed" (John 20:29).

BARTIMAEUS
Mark 10:46

BARUCH ("blessed").

1. The son of Neriah, of a distinguished family in Judah; his brother Seraiah was a high ranking officer in the court of King Zedekiah (Jer 51:59). Baruch was confidant and secretary of the prophet Jeremiah. When the latter was under arrest, during Jehoiakim's reign, he sent Baruch as his messenger to the people. Jeremiah dictated to Baruch all the words spoken to him by God. Baruch read the scroll to the people of Judah (Jer 36:10), and the princes urged him and Jeremiah to go into hiding. The scroll was then read to the king by Jehudi son of Nethaniah, whereupon the king, despite the pleas of his courtiers, burnt it in the fireplace and ordered the arrest of Jeremiah and Baruch (Jer 36:21-26). The prophet then dictated the same scroll to Baruch with numerous additions (Jer 36:27-32).

BARUCH 1
Jer 32:12-13,
16; 36:4-5, 8, 10,
13-19, 26-27,
32; 43:3, 6;
45:1-2

Seal impression of Baruch the son of Neriah the scribe. (Israel Museum)

When Jeremiah bought property in his home town of Anathoth from Hanameel son of Shallum, he gave Baruch copies of the deed of purchase and instructed him to deposit them in an earthenware jar (Jer 32:12-14). An oracle of Jeremiah to Baruch is preserved in Jeremiah chapter 45. After the murder of Gedaliah the governor of Judah, Baruch accompanied the prophet and the remnant of Judah to Egypt. The leaders of the Judean remnant accused Baruch of inciting Jeremiah against them (Jer 43:2-7). An apocryphal book and several apocalypses were later attributed to him. See BARUCH, BOOK OF.

2. The son of Zabbai. He repaired the second section of the wall from the escarpment to the house of Eliashib, the high priest (Neh 3:20). He was among those who witnessed the sealing of the covenant in Nehemiah's time (Neh 10:6).

BARUCH 2
Neh 3:20;
10:6

3. A man of the tribe of Judah; the son of Col-Hozeh and the father of Maaseiah; a contemporary of Nehemiah.

BARUCH 3
Neh 11:5

BARUCH, BOOK OF An apocryphal book attributed to Baruch, the secretary of Jeremiah. In many manuscripts of the Septuagint, the Greek Bible, this work follows the Book of Jeremiah and it was often cited by Church Fathers as if it were either a part of the Book of Jeremiah or an appendix thereto. The date of writing is uncertain but seems to have been between the 4th century B.C. and the 2nd century A.D.

In the Eastern and Latin churches it is part of the biblical canon, and the text is extant in Greek, Syriac, Syro-Hexaplar, Latin, Armenian, Ethiopic, Coptic and Arabic, although it was probably written either in Hebrew or Greek.

The theme of the book's five chapters, Exile and Return, is to be found in all four parts of the book. The first part (1:1-14) describes how Baruch read his book in Babylonia to the Jewish leaders and others in the fifth year after the destruction of Jerusalem (c. 582 B.C.). The people wept, fasted, prayed and collected money which was sent to Jerusalem, asking the people there to pray for them and read the book. The second part is a penitential prayer (1:15-3:8), which the Jews wrote in Babylon and sent to Jerusalem. A poem on the Torah, the fountain of wisdom forsaken by the people of Israel, is the theme of the third part (3:9-4:4).

The last part consists of two poems of lamentation and comfort. A personified Jerusalem comforts the captives in Babylon by putting her hope in the "Everlasting, that he will save you" (4:22-29). The second poem is a comforting assurance to Jerusalem (4:30-5:9) that her children will be gathered and brought back to her (5:5-6). In the Latin Bible, the Vulgate, the Epistle of Jeremiah (Jeremy) is chapter 6 of the Book of Baruch, but this epistle should be considered as a separate apocryphal writing.

BARZILLAI

BARZILLAI 1
II Sam 21:8

1. A Meholathite whose son Adriel married one of the daughters of Saul (II Sam 21:8).

BARZILLAI 2
II Sam 17:27;
19:31-34, 39.
I Kgs 2:7. Ezra
2:61. Neh 7:63

2. Barzillai the Gileadite from Rogelim, an aged and very wealthy man (II Sam 19:33). At the time of Absalom's rebellion he was one of the three men loyal to David in Transjordan; they supplied the king and his men at Mahanaim (II Sam 17:27-29). After the rebellion was quashed, Barzillai conducted David over the Jordan. In reward for these services, David invited Barzillai to be part of his court in Jerusalem, but he declined in view of his old age, and sent his son Chimham instead. David took leave of Barzillai with a kiss and a blessing (II Sam 19:31-40). In I Kings 2:7 David's last will charged Solomon to "show kindness to the sons of Barzillai the Gileadite, and let them be among those who eat at your table", in reward for his succor and loyalty at Mahanaim. Ezra 2:61 and Nehemiah 7:63 may refer to the same Barzillai: "...the sons of Barzillai who took a wife of the daughters of Barzillai the Gileadites and was called by their name" who were disqualified from the priesthood because their priestly lineage could not be traced (Ezra 2:62).

BASEMATH 1
Gen 26:34;
36:3-4, 10, 13,
17

BASEMATH (BASHEMATH, BASMATH) ("perfume").

1. Daughter of Elon the Hittite (Gen 26:34) or of Ishmael (Gen 36:3) and wife of Esau; he married her when he was 40 years old (Gen 26:34) and she bore him one son, Reuel (Gen 36:4).

BASEMATH 2
I Kgs 4:15

2. A daughter of Solomon; she married Ahimaaz, governor of the eighth district of the kingdom of Solomon, that of Naphtali.

BASHAN
Num 21:33;
32:33. Deut
1:4; 3:1, 3-4,
10-11, 13-14;
4:43, 47; 29:7;
32:14; 33:22.
Josh 9:10;
12:4-5; 13:11-
12, 30-31;
17:1, 5; 20:8;
21:6, 27; 22:7.
I Kgs 4:13, 19.
II Kgs 10:33.
I Chr 5:11-12,
16, 23; 6:62,
71. Neh 9:22.
Ps 22:12;
68:15, 22;
135:11; 136:20.
Is 2:13; 33:9.
Jer 22:20; 50:19.
Ezek 27:6;
39:18. Amos
4:1. Mic 7:14.
Nah 1:4. Zech
11:2

BASHAN Region northeast of the River Jordan. Most of the area is a fertile plain, with an abundance of water. It borders on Mount Hermon to the north and Gilead to the south (Deut 3:8-10; Josh 12:1-5). The River Yarmuk forms the boundary between Bashan and Gilead. On the east Bashan extends as far as Salcah, on the slopes of Jebel ed-Druz (Deut 3:10), which was once covered by oak forests (Is 2:13; Ezek 27:6). It thus included the region later known as Trachonitis.

Landscape in Bashan.

The land of Bashan was renowned for its rich pasture, which supported large herds of cattle and sheep (Deut 32:14; Jer 50:19, etc.). Og was King of Bashan (Josh 9:10) until the Israelites defeated him at Edrei (Num 21:33-35). Then the region was allotted to the families of Jair (Deut 3:14) and Nobah of the sons of Manasseh, who received Kenath in Bashan (Num 32:42). After the division of the Kingdom of Judah Bashan became part of the Kingdom of Israel, but the kings of Syria soon conquered Ramoth Gilead (Mizpah) in Bashan (I Kgs 22:3 ff; II Kgs 8:28). The remaining part of Bashan fell to Syria in the days of Jehu (II Kgs 10:33) to be restored to Israel during the reigns of Jehoash and his son Jeroboam (II Kgs 13:25; 14:25, 28). In 732 B.C., Tiglath-Pileser III conquered it and deported many of its inhabitants (II Kgs 15:29, supplemented by the lists of Tiglath-Pileser).

In the Persian period a district named Karnaim was formed, which included Bashan and Golan. Judas Maccabee conquered part of the region (I Macc 15:17-45). In 63 B.C. Pompey annexed Bashan to the kingdom of the Itureans. When Herod the Great ascended the throne Bashan was given to him; after his death it was ruled by his son Philip. In A.D. 37 it formed part of Agrippa I's kingdom, and it belonged to the kingdom of Agrippa II until his death. It was then annexed to the Roman province of Syria.

BAT See ANIMALS

BATHING In the OT, bathing is mentioned primarily as a means of ritual purification (See PURITY). Various degrees of ritual impurity were removed by bathing, e.g. when a person had eaten carrion (Lev 17:15-16) or come into contact with a corpse (Num 19:19). Priests were particularly susceptible to impurity and a laver was placed in the tabernacle for them to wash their hands and feet on entering (Ex 30:18-21). On the Day of Atonement the high priest had to bathe himself frequently (Lev 16:24). The preparations for performing the priestly functions involved the washing of the hands and feet.

The most frequent form of ablution commanded in the OT involved the entire body: those requiring such immersion included the leper prior to eating holy flesh; a person suffering from an unclean issue; anyone who had touched a menstruating woman, as well as the menstruating woman herself; and the priest tending the red heifer. Naaman was instructed to bathe seven times in the Jordan as a symbol of his purification from his disease (II Kgs 5:9ff), while Jesus told the blind man to bathe in the Pool of Siloam (John 9:11). Visitors arriving after a long journey were furnished with water to bathe their feet (Gen 18:4; 19:2; 24:32). It is recorded that David bathed himself at the end of a period of mourning (II Sam 12:20). The Jewish custom was to wash the hands before meals but Jesus absolved his disciples from this requirement, for which he was criticized by the Pharisees; his response was to stress the cleanliness of the heart (Mark chap. 7).

(bottom right)
Bath at Herod's palace Masada. 1st century B.C.

(bottom left)
The floor of the hot room (calda-rium) *in the bathhouse at Masada was built on these small pillars and hot air was pumped into the space thus created.*

Phoenician clay figurine of a woman bathing. Achzib. 8th century B.C.

The normal dwelling rarely possessed bathing facilities and only the better houses had a special chamber with a tub used as a bath. A shallow clay bowl with a raised ridge in the middle was used for washing the feet.

Public baths were not built until the late Hellenistic and early Roman periods. The earliest baths in Palestine are those built by Herod at Masada and at Herodium, which were constructed on the regular Roman plan and comprised: the *apodyterium*, a room in which discarded clothes were kept in built-in cupboards; a *frigidarium*, a cold bath in which the bather was expected to cleanse himself before passing into the other parts of the bath; the *tepidarium*, a tepid bath, usually in the form of a shallow pool faced with water resistant plaster where the bather would warm himself before proceeding; the *caldarium*, a hot bath, which sometimes consisted of more than one room, one of which contained bathing tubs built of bricks and faced with plaster or marble, and another in which a steam-bath was taken.

The floors of the more luxurious bathhouses were paved with mosaics and the walls decorated with frescoes. The public bath became a social institution and baths built in this way have been found throughout Palestine, even in regions where water was scarce. Another kind of bath was built near or above hot springs thought to have medicinal properties, e.g. in Tiberias.

BATH RABBIM ("daughter of many"). A gate by "the pools of Heshbon" in the Song of Solomon.

BATH RABBIM
Song 7:4

BATHSHEBA King David's favorite wife and the mother of Solomon, the king's heir and successor. She is alternatively called Bathshua by a late biblical source (I Chr 3:5). Her father's name is given as Eliam in the earlier source (II Sam 11:3), but Ammiel in the later one (I Chr 3:5). She may have been of foreign stock. Her grandfather was Ahithophel the Gilonite (II Sam 23:34), David's wise counselor (II Sam 15:12). Originally she was the wife of Uriah the Hittite (II Sam 11:3), until David, seeing her bathing, coveted her. When he made her pregnant, Uriah was recalled from the battlefield to be with his wife, so that the child to be born would be considered his offspring. Uriah refused to go home, whereupon David ordered Joab, the commander of his army, to station Uriah in a position where he would be killed in battle (II Chr 11:15). After the death of Uriah, David married Bathsheba and a son was born. God sent the prophet Nathan to reprove David for his immoral behavior, invoking the classic parable of the poor man's sheep (II Sam chap. 12). The biblical account presents the episode as moral and historical justification for Absalom's subsequent public defilement of his father's concubines during his revolt (II Sam 12:9-12; 16:21-22), and for the troubles later attending the succession story as a whole (II Sam chaps. 11-20; I Kgs chaps. 1-2). The newly-born child died as a punishment for David's sin (II Sam 12:13-18), but Bathsheba eventually gave birth to another child, David's successor Solomon (II Sam 12:24).

BATHSHEBA
**II Sam 11:3;
12:24. I Kgs
1:11, 15-16,
28, 31; 2:13,
18-19**

In King David's old age, when the succession problem became acute, the court prophet Nathan — who had earlier opposed the union between Bathsheba and David on moral grounds — allied himself with Bathsheba. Together they reminded the old king that he had promised to make Solomon his heir, convincing him to effect the coronation before his own demise (I Kgs 1:13), and thereby thwarting the coalition supporting Solomon's half-brother Adonijah.

Once established, Solomon looked for an excuse to get rid of Adonijah. This was supplied by the latter's imprudent wish, conveyed by Bathsheba, to marry David's former concubine Abishag (I Kgs 2:13-25). Bathsheba interceded on Adonijah's behalf, but to no avail: although King Solomon paid his mother proper respect, such as seating her down beside his throne and listening to her request with apparent attentiveness (I Kgs 2:19-22), she apparently exerted little influence on her son. According to I Chronicles 3:5 Bathsheba had three more sons — Shimea, Shobab and Nathan. She is mentioned in the genealogy of Jesus as "the wife of Uriah" (Matt 1:6).

BATHSHUA ("daughter of Shua").

1. The daughter of a woman of Canaan named Shua. Judah son of Jacob met her at the house of Hirah the Adullamite (Gen 38:1-2). He married her and she bore him three sons: Er, Onan and Shelah (Gen 38:3-5).

2. An alternate form for Bathsheba.

BAVAI Bavai son of Henadad was ruler of "half of the district of Keilah", an administrative district at the time of Nehemiah; he was one of the Levites who helped repair the walls of Jerusalem (Neh 3:17-18).

BAZLITH, BAZLUTH Head of a family of Nethinim (Temple servants) who returned from Exile with Zerubbabel.

BEALIAH One of the men of the tribe of Benjamin who joined David at Ziklag (I Chr 12:1, 5). Like his fellows, Bealiah was equally proficient with his right and left hands in shooting the bow or hurling stones (I Chr 12:2).

BEALOTH

1. A city in the southern part of Judah near the border of Edom. Some scholars believe it to be another name of Baaloth Beer.

2. A town in the north of the country in the territory of Asher, the seat of one of Solomon's twelve administrative districts. In some translations the name appears as Aloth, the first two letters being taken for the Hebrew "in".

BEAN See PLANTS

BEAR See ANIMALS

BEATITUDES A beatitude is a literary form common in both the OT and NT which consists of a short cry of joy like "You happy man!" which can be expanded to include a reason for the person's good

BATHSHUA 1
Gen 38:2, 12.
I Chr 2:3

BATHSHUA 2
I Chr 3:5

BAVAI
Neh 3:18

BAZLITH,
BAZLUTH
Ezra 2:52.
Neh 7:54

BEALIAH
I Chr 12:5

BEALOTH 1
Josh 15:24

BEALOTH 2
I Kgs 4:16

The Church of Beatitudes overlooking the Sea of Galilee. It is octagonal in shape to commemorate the Eight Beatitudes.

fortune. The word beatitude comes from the Latin *beatus* meaning happy or blissful, an adjective representing the Hebrew *ashre* and the Greek *makarios*. These terms are to be distinguished from the passive participle *blessed*, often used in older English translations for the just mentioned set of terms as well as for Latin *benedictus*, Hebrew *baruch*, Greek *eulogetos*, thus leading to some confusion of blessing and beatitude. Properly the participle form is used only of God and is an invocation or wish. The adjective is used only of men and recognizes an existing state of happiness, represents an approving proclamation of fact, and contains an evaluative judgment. It is a proclamation of happiness, not merely a promise (though in the beatitudes of Jesus a promise is joined to it). It is a formula of congratulation or felicitation.

The preaching of Jesus begins as a cry of joy, as good news (Matt 5:3-11; Luke 6:20-22). This joy is based on the nearness of the Kingdom of God. The famous series of beatitudes at the beginning of Jesus' great discourse just referred to has, according to scholars, a complex evolution. Luke gives four of them, and the first three of these are short and based on Isaiah 61:1-4. These probably go back to Jesus himself and represent a kind of messianic manifesto of God's care for the poor, the hungry and those who weep (probably three adjectives for the same group of people). The fourth of Luke's list probably comes from the early Christian community and represents their first experiences of persecution. Matthew's much longer list of eight, nine or ten (scholars count them variously) adds some desirable qualities, justice, being pure of heart, merciful and peacemakers. He thereby makes the list into a program of Christian life, a series of virtues.

BEBAI

1. A family of exiles who returned from Babylon with Zerubbabel. It numbered 628 persons according to Nehemiah (Neh 7:16) and 623 according to Ezra (Ezra 2:11).

2. One of those who signed Nehemiah's covenant. Probably the head of the family.

BECHER ("a young camel").

1. The second son of Benjamin.

2. The second son of Ephraim and the father of the Bachrite line.

BECHORATH The son of Aphiah from the tribe of Benjamin and one of the forefathers of Saul (I Sam 9:1-2).

BEDAD Father of Hadad, king of Edom.

BEDAN

1. A man of Manasseh, son of Ulam by his Syrian concubine (I Chr 7:14, 17).

2. One of the men sent by the Lord together with Jerubbaal, Jephthah and Samuel, to deliver the people of Israel from the Philistines and the armies of Moab (I Sam 12:9).

BEDEIAH One of the three "sons of Bani" who had to repudiate his alien wife upon the decree of Ezra (Ezra 10:2, 11, 35).

BEE See ANIMALS

BEELIADA One of the sons David had by one of his wives in Jerusalem (I Chr 14:3, 7).

BEELZEBUB (BEELZEBUL) A name for the ruler of the demons, referring to the Philistine god of Ekron (II Kgs 1:2) Baal-Zebub, also called Baal-Zebul. The etymology of both names is still disputed. The Pharisees thought that Jesus used the ruler of demons to cast out demons, and thus expressed their strongest objection to him. Beelzebul was identified with Satan and Jesus answered them with a question: "And if Satan casts out Satan?" using the occasion to illustrate how the casting out of demons signifies the plundering of Satan's kingdom / house and releasing people to be brought into God's house. Jesus referred to the Pharisees' slander as "blasphemy against the Spirit" (Matt 12:22-32; Luke 11:14-23). See also SATAN.

BEER ("well").

1. A halt on the route of the Children of Israel from Egypt to the promised land. Upon the order of Moses, princes and nobles dug a well there (Num 21:16-18).

Most scholars believe the site to be north of the Arnon River, close to

BEBAI 1
Ezra 2:11;
8:11; 10:28.
Neh 7:16;
10:15

BEBAI 2
Neh 10:15

BECHER 1
Gen 46:21.
I Chr 7:6, 8

BECHER 2
Num 26:35

BECHORATH
I Sam 9:1

BEDAD
Gen 36:35.
I Chr 1:46

BEDAN 1
I Chr 7:17

BEDAN 2
I Sam 12:11

BEDEIAH
Ezra 10:35

BEELIADA
I Chr 14:7

BEELZEBUB
Matt 10:25;
12:24, 27.
Mark 3:22.
Luke 11:15,
18-19

BEER 1
Num 21:16

Wadi Tamed, where to this day water is to be found close to the surface.

2. The place to which Jotham son of Gideon fled for fear of his brother Abimelech. Believed to be 10 miles (16 km) northwest of Beth Shean.

BEER 2
Judg 9:21

BEERA ("well"). One of the sons of Zophah in the genealogy of Asher.

BEERA
I Chr 7:37

BEERAH ("well"). A leader or a prince of the tribe of Reuben who was taken into captivity to Babylon by Tiglath-Pileser III.

BEERAH
I Chr 5:6

BEER ELIM ("well of heroes"). A place in Moab mentioned by the prophet Isaiah; perhaps Beer No.2.

BEER ELIM
Is 15:8

BEERI ("well").

1. Beeri the Hittite, father of Judith, whom Esau married when he was 40 years old.

BEERI 1
Gen 26:34

2. The father of Hosea the prophet.

BEERI 2
Hos 1:1

BEER LAHAI ROI ("well of the Living One who sees me"). A well and oasis in the Negeb, between Kadesh and Bered, mentioned in the story of Hagar's flight from Sarai (Gen 16:14). It is also mentioned in Genesis 24:62 as the place near which Isaac saw Rebekah's camel train, and where he dwelt after Abraham's death (Gen 25:11).

BEER LAHAI ROI
**Gen 16:14;
24:62; 25:11**

A place in Negeb, between Kadesh and Bered, near which Isaac saw Rebekah's camel train.

BEEROTH ("wells"). One of the four cities of the Gibeonites (Josh 9:17) spared by Joshua (Josh 9:18) after the Israelites had been tricked into making a covenant with their inhabitants (Josh 9:3-6, 15). The town was later included in the territory of the tribe of Benjamin (II Sam 4:2).

Recent archeological finds tend to support the theory that Beeroth stood on the site of present-day El Bireh, 10 miles (16 km) north of Jerusalem.

BEEROTH
**Josh 9:17;
18:25. II Sam.
4:2. Ezra 2:25.
Neh 7:29**

A view in the neighborhood of Beeroth.

BEEROTH BENE JAAKAN ("the wells of the sons of Jaakan"). The place where Aaron died and was buried, near the border of Edom. See BENE JAAKAN. May be another name for Beeroth.

BEEROTHITE A native of Beeroth.

1. Rimon the Beerothite; he was the father of Baanah and Rechab (II Sam 4:2), who assassinated Ishbosheth.

2. Nahari the Beerothite "armorbearer to Joab the son of Zeruiah" one of David's "mighty men".

BEERSHEBA A town in the Negeb, prominent in the history of the patriarchs. The servants of Abimelech, king of Gerar, had seized a well which belonged to Abraham, but a covenant was made between the contestants on oath (*shebuah* in Hebrew), and from this the Bible derives the name Beersheba, "the Well of the Oath" (Gen 21:22-32). Beersheba could also mean "well of the seven (ewes)" (ibid.). Abraham planted a tamarisk (AV: "grove") there, called on the name of the Lord (Gen 21:33), and dwelt in Beersheba (Gen 22:19). Isaac went to live at Beersheba, concluded a covenant with Abimelech, and dug a well which he named Sheba (Gen 26:23-33). Later Jacob offered sacrifices at

(left)
Judean storerooms at Tell Es Seba.

(below, from top to bottom)
Ostrich egg from the Persian period found in a sanctuary at Tell Beersheba. (Tel Aviv University Dept. of Archaeology)
Krater from Tell Beersheba inscribed with the Hebrew letters KDS meaning "sacred". (Israel Museum)
Ivory figurines of the Chalcolithic period from Bir-es-Safadi south of Beersheba. (Israel Museum)

Beersheba (Gen 46:1-4). After its conquest by Joshua Beersheba was in the territory of Simeon within the territory of Judah (Josh 19:2). In the time of the Judges it was already a city, perhaps even the center of a district (I Sam 8:2). The saying "from Dan to Beersheba" reflects its religious and administrative importance (Judg 20:1; I Sam 3:20; II Sam 3:10, etc.).

Beersheba is also mentioned, together with Dan, Bethel and Gilgal, as a religious center in the later days of the Kingdom of Israel, when all four towns were reproached because of their rivalry with Jerusalem (Amos 5:5; 8:14). Josiah defiled all the high places from Geba to Beersheba (II Kgs 23:8). The town of Beersheba was resettled after the return from the Babylonian Exile (Neh 11:27). Later it was probably the southern limit of Idumea.

Biblical Beersheba is identified with Tell es-Seba 3 miles (5 km) to the east of modern Beersheba. Large scale excavations revealed the remains of six royal Israelite fortified towns dated from the 11th century B.C. up to the 7th century B.C. To these periods belong a number of Hebrew and Aramaic ostraca. Remains of a Roman Period fortress were also found. Iron Age tombs have been discovered within the limits of the modern city, which was built on the site of the Byzantine town.

BEESHTERAH A city east of the Jordan River which was given to the Levites of the family of Gershon (Josh 21:27) when Joshua divided the land among the Children of Israel (Josh 21:1-3).

Many believe it to be identical to Ashtaroth (I Chr 6:71).

BEL ("master, ruler"). Epithet of Marduk (Merodach in OT), the supreme god of the Babylonian pantheon. His degradation symbolizes the collapse of the kingdom of Babylon (Is 46:1-2; Jer 51:44). The name appears as synonymous with Merodach in Jeremiah 50:2.

BELA, BELAH

1. Bela the son of Beor; he was the first king of Edom. His capital was in Dinhabah (Gen 36:32).

2. The eldest son of Benjamin.

3. One of the descendants of Reuben, son of Azaz and grandson of Shema (I Chr 5:8) who dwelled "in Aroer, as far as Nebo and Baal Meon" and to the east "as far as the entrance of the wilderness this side of the River Euphrates" (I Chr 5:8-9) at the time of King Saul (I Chr 5:10).

4. Belah, a city, the seat of the fifth king in the coalition against Chedorlaomer king of Elam (Gen 14:2, 8); another name for Zoar.

Some scholars believe the name Belah here relates to the king and not to his city.

BELAITES The family of Bela No.2, in the line of Benjamin, as recorded in the census taken by Moses and Eleazar (Num 26:38).

BEL AND THE DRAGON Two stories preserved in the Apocrypha as Greek additions to the Book of Daniel. In the Greek Bible it is included at the end of the book; in the Latin Bible (the Vulgate), it constitutes chapter 14. The central message in both stories is the uniqueness of Daniel's God as the "living God". The narrative tells how Daniel showed up the fraud of the priests of the idol, Bel, by spreading ashes on the temple floor in order to catch the priests as they came at night with their women and children to eat the food which had been brought to Bel. When Daniel declared that the idol never ate or drank anything, but was just clay and brass, the king, Cyrus, challenged Daniel to prove his words. Entering into an ordeal that would have cost him his life had he failed (cf Dan 3:15-18), Daniel was vindicated and Bel was destroyed, as were the priests together with their wives and children.

But this sole proof did not convince the king to acknowledge the sovereignty of Daniel's God. The second story pits Daniel and his God against Cyrus and the dragon whom the Babylonians worshiped. Daniel caused the death of the dragon by feeding it a mixture of pitch, fat and hair. On hearing this, the Babylonians became very indignant and conspired against the king, demanding either the delivery of Daniel

BEESHTERAH
Josh 21:27

BEL
Is 46:1. Jer
50:2; 51:44

BELA, BELAH 1
Gen 36:32-33.
I Chr 1:43-44

BELA, BELAH 2
Gen 46:21.
I Chr 7:6-7;
8:1, 3. Num
26:38, 40

BELA, BELAH 3
I Chr 5:8

BELA, BELAH 4
Gen 14:2, 8

BELAITES
Num 26:38

Mythological scene showing a dragon spurting water. From a limestone relief from Ebla. 3rd millennium B.C. (Aleppo Museum)

or the king's death. Cast into a lion's den by the king, Daniel was miraculously protected from the lions and sustained with food brought to him by Habakkuk the prophet. After Daniel was delivered from the lions' den, the king acclaimed his God, and the Babylonian opponents were thrown to the lions.

One of the objects of these stories is the denunciation of idolatry as can be seen by the fact that the "living God" of Daniel is frequently mentioned. The stories' date and place of origin are uncertain. They may have originated in Babylonia in the 5th-4th century B.C. and could have originally been written in Aramaic.

BELIAL A Hebrew word referring to wicked persons and wickedness in general, and even to death and the underworld, personified in II Corinthians 6:15 as a name for Satan. He is utterly opposed to Jesus.

BELSHAZZAR ("O Bel [lit. 'lord', epithet of Marduk, the patron god of Babylon], protect the king"). Eldest son of Nabonidus, the last king of the Neo-Babylonian (also called Chaldean) Empire, who reigned 555-539 B.C. During Nabonidus' ten year stay in northwestern Arabia (552-542 B.C.), Belshazzar acted as ruler of Babylon in his stead. Since he served as co-regent with Nabonidus (to whom the Book of Daniel applies; legends elsewhere attributed to Nebuchadnezzar), Belshazzar appears (unhistorically) as the son of Nebuchadnezzar (Dan 5:18, 22), king of Babylon (Dan 7:1); king of the Chaldeans (Dan 5:30); or simply "the king" (Dan 5:1). According to Daniel chapter 5 the ominous handwriting on the wall came in response to Belshazzar's blasphemously serving wine at a state banquet from the golden vessels taken from the Temple of Jerusalem. That very night, after Daniel had interpreted the message contained in the handwriting on the wall and had been elevated to a triumvir, Belshazzar was slain, and Darius the Mede inherited his kingdom.

BELTESHAZZAR ("protect the life of the king"). The Babylonian name given to Daniel after he was taken in captivity (Dan 1:4, 7).

BEN ("son"). Listed in I Chronicles 15:18 as a Levite of the second rank, one of the gatekeepers of the ark at the time of David. Many scholars believe, however, that "Ben" is the first part of a name transcribed incorrectly.

BEN-ABINADAB See ABINADAB No.4.

BENAIAH ("God has built").

1. The son of Jehoiada of Kabziel, one of David's "mighty men". Three of his feats of prowess are mentioned in II Samuel 23:20-23 and I Chronicles 11:22-25: he slew two lion-like men of Moab, slew a lion in a pit in the time of snow, and killed a brawny Egyptian with his own spear (which is similar to David's killing of Goliath). By virtue of his bravery, he was placed at the head of the thirty "mighty men", though not numbered among the top three; David appointed him commander of his guard, perhaps the Cherethites and Pelethites (II Sam 8:18; 20:23; I Chr 18:17). Of David's 12 divisions of military service, Benaiah is named as the commander of those who served the third month (I Chr 27:5). He sided with Solomon (together with Zadok the priest and Nathan the prophet) to oppose Adonijah's attempt to seize the throne. When David ordered that Solomon be enthroned, Benaiah responded: "Amen! May the Lord God of my lord the king say so too. As the Lord has been with my lord the king, even so may he be with Solomon, and make his throne greater than the throne of my lord King David" (I Kgs 1:36-37). Benaiah carried out the several executions of those who rebelled against the establishment of Solomon's kingdom: Adonijah, Joab, and Shimei (I Kgs 2:25, 34, 46). As reward, he was appointed commander of the army in place of Joab (I Kgs 2:35).

Limestone Hebrew seal inscribed "[Belonging] to Benayahu [Benaiah] son of SBLY". 7th century B.C. (Israel Museum)

2. One of David's thirty "mighty men", from Pirathon (II Sam 23:30; I Chr 11:31); commander of the 11th division of David's militia (I Chr 27:14).

3. A priest in the time of David, one of those who blew the trumpets before the ark of the Lord when David brought it up to Jerusalem (I Chr 15:24 and later "regularly" 16:6).

4. One of the gatekeepers ("porters") appointed by David to make a joyful sound with musical instruments when the ark was brought up to Jerusalem; he played the "harp" (I Chr 15:18, 20). He is mentioned again as one of Asaph's companions who ministered with harps and psalteries before the ark (I Chr 16:5).

5. A Levite of the sons of Asaph, the grandfather of Jahaziel the prophet. Jahaziel offered words of encouragement to Jehoshaphat in his confrontation with the Ammonites and Moabites.

6. One of the overseers, appointed at Hezekiah's command, in one of the chambers of the Temple.

7. A prince of a Simeonite clan or family, perhaps from the days of Hezekiah (I Chr 4:36, 41).

8. Father of Pelatiah, one of the princes of the people, whose death was prophesied by Ezekiel.

9-12. Four men who married alien wives in the days of Ezra.

BEN-AMMI ("son of my kin"). The son of Lot from his youngest daughter; he was the forefather of the Ammonites. The derivation of his name indicating this inbred origin emphasized the incestuous origin of the Ammonites.

BEN-DEKER (BEN-DEKAR) ("son of Dekar"). A governor appointed by King Solomon; he was in charge of the second administrative district (I Kgs 4:7, 9) with Makaz as his seat.

BENE BERAK ("sons of lightning"). A city which fell to the lot of the tribe of Dan when Joshua divided the land of Israel among the tribes (Josh 18:10; 19:45). Today identified with a site near Tel Aviv.

BENE JAAKAN ("the sons of Jaakan"). One of the halts of the Children of Israel on their route from Egypt to the promised land, between Moseroth and Hor Hagidgad (Num 33:31-32). See BEEROTH BNEI JAAKAN.

BEN-GEBER ("son of Geber"). One of the governors appointed by King Solomon, in charge of the sixth administrative district; his seat was in Ramoth Gilead (I Kgs 4:13). May be identical with Geber the son of Uri mentioned in the same chapter (I Kgs 4:19) in connection with the same district.

BEN-HADAD The name of three kings of Aram.

1. Ben-Hadad I — son of Tabrimmon son of Hezion (I Kgs 15:18) was a contemporary of Kings Asa of Judah and Baasha of Israel. When war broke out between Israel and Judah, he ignored his treaty obligations to Baasha, responding to Asa's bribes by occupying and plundering Israel's territory in Transjordan and eastern Galilee (I Kgs 15:17-20); this forced Baasha to abandon further attempts at expansion. Ben-Hadad did not follow up his victory, due to the grave threat to his own northern border posed by the Assyrian king Adad-Nirari II's renewed campaigns. Perhaps this Ben-Hadad set up the votive stele dedicated to the Tyrian god Melqart (9th century B.C.) found near Aleppo, Syria.

2. Ben-Hadad II — (in Assyrian inscriptions Adad-Idri, probably Hadadezer) a contemporary of King Ahab of Israel, against whom he waged war three times. In the first battle he was accompanied by 32 vassals, but Ahab nevertheless succeeded in defeating him (I Kgs 20:2ff). He was defeated a second time at Aphek and taken prisoner (I Kgs

---

BENAIAH 2
**II Sam 23:30.
I Chr 11:31;
27:14**

BENAIAH 3
**I Chr 15:24;
16:6**

BENAIAH 4
**I Chr 15:18,
20; 16:5**

BENAIAH 5
II Chr 20:14

BENAIAH 6
II Chr 31:13

BENAIAH 7
I Chr 4:36

BENAIAH 8
Ezek 11:1, 13

BENAIAH 9-12
**Ezra 10:25, 30,
35, 43**

BEN-AMMI
Gen 19:38

BEN-DEKER
I Kgs 4:9

BENE BERAK
Josh 19:45

BENE JAAKAN
**Num 33:31-32.
Deut 10:6**

BEN-GEBER
I Kgs 4:13

BEN-HADAD 1
**I Kgs 15:18,
20. II Chr
16:2, 4**

BEN-HADAD 2
**I Kgs 20:1-2,
5, 9-10, 12,
16-17, 20, 26,
30, 32-34.
II Kgs 6:24;
8:7, 9**

20:26ff), but subsequently concluded a treaty of friendship with Ahab, returning territories occupied by him, and heading an alliance with the kings of Syria, Phoenicia and Israel in a war against King Shalmaneser III of Assyria, at Karkar in 853 B.C. But this coalition broke up three years later when Ahab, with the assistance of King Jehoshaphat of Judah, waged war against Aram at Ramoth Gilead, where Ahab met his death (I Kgs chap. 22). After Jehu's accession to the throne of Israel, Ben-Hadad II was assassinated by Hazael (II Kgs 8:15) who seized the throne of Aram (I Kgs 19:15; II Kgs 8:7-15).

BEN-HADAD 3
II Kgs 13:3,
24-25. Jer
49:27. Amos
1:4

3. Ben-Hadad III — son of Hazael, a contemporary of Kings Jehoahaz and Joash of Israel. During the early years of his reign, he occupied the greater part of the Kingdom of Israel (II Kgs 13:3-6) imposing conditions so repressive, that King Adad-Nirari III of Assyria was proclaimed "deliverer" when he renewed his war against Aram and broke Ben-Hadad's power in 802 B.C. (II Kgs 13:5).

BEN-HAIL
II Chr 17:7

BEN-HAIL A prince in the time of Jehoshaphat king of Judah; he was appointed by the king "to teach in the cities of Judah".

BEN-HANAN
I Chr 4:20

BEN-HANAN See AMNON No.2.

BEN-HESED
I Kgs 4:10

BEN-HESED A governor of the third administrative district in Solomon's time, who was responsible for providing provisions for the king and his household for one month each year. Arubboth, Sochoh and the region of Hepher were included in his district.

BEN-HUR
I Kgs 4:8

BEN-HUR ("the sons of Hur"). See HUR.

BENINU
Neh 10:13

BENINU ("our son"). A Levite; one of the men who sealed the covenant at the time of Ezra and Nehemiah.

BEN-JAHAZIEL
Ezra 8:5

BEN-JAHAZIEL See JAHAZIEL

BENJAMIN,
BENJAMITES 1
Gen 35:18, 24;
42:4, 36; 43:
14-16, 29, 34;
44:12; 45:12,
14, 22; 46:19,
21, 27. Ex 1:3.
Num 1:11,
36-37; 2:22;
7:60; 10:24;
13:9; 26:38,
41; 34:21.
Deut 27:12;
33:12. Josh
18:11, 20-21,
28; 21:4, 17.
Judg 1:21;
3:15; 5:14;
10:9; 19:14,
16; 20:3-4, 10,
12-18, 20-21,
23-25, 28, 30-
32, 34-36, 39,
40-44, 46, 48;
21:1, 6, 13-18,
20-21, 23.
I Sam 4:12;
9:1, 4, 16, 21;
10:2, 20-21;
13:2, 15-16;
14:16. II Sam
2:9, 15, 25,
31; 3:19; 4:2;
16:11; 19:16-17;
20:1; 21:14;
22:7; 23:29.

BENJAMIN, BENJAMITES ("son of my right hand" or "son of the south").

1. The youngest son of Jacob by Rachel; the head of the Benjamite tribe. The Book of Genesis relates his birth and his mother's death in childbirth (she called him "Ben-Oni", i.e. "son of my sorrow", Gen 35:18). Jacob sent his sons to Egypt for food in a time of famine, but kept Benjamin, his youngest son, at home. Benjamin's full brother Joseph, prime minister of Egypt at that time, insisted, however, that Benjamin be brought to him. On the brothers' return from Canaan with Benjamin, Joseph put them to the test by hiding his personal drinking cup in Benjamin's saddlepack and when it was discovered, declared that he would execute the thief. When the brothers refused to abandon Benjamin (as they had previously abandoned Joseph), Joseph realized that they finally had a change of heart and were now ready to risk their lives for their youngest brother. He dramatically revealed his identity to them, whereupon the entire family was joyously reunited. Benjamin thus functions as a narrative foil to highlight his brothers' repentance over selling Joseph (Gen chaps. 42-45).

Though the territory of the tribe of Benjamin was small (Benjamin being the youngest son) the tribe played an important role in the unification of the other tribes during the period of the Judges and the early years of the monarchy. Ehud, one of the first judges, was a Benjamite, as was Saul, the first king of Israel (Judg 3:15; I Sam 9:16-17). The territory of Benjamin extended from the hill-country of Ephraim to the north to the hilly area of Judah in the south, with the main north-south and east-west roads traversing it. Its strategic importance attracted attacks by the Moabites (Judg 3:12ff) and the Philistines (I Sam 10:5; 13:3) in particular. Saul the Benjamite gained his reputation as a deliverer from Philistine oppression (I Sam 9:16). Such prowess is reflected in Jacob's blessing to Benjamin in Genesis 49:27.

The episode of the concubine in Gibeah prompted the other tribes to

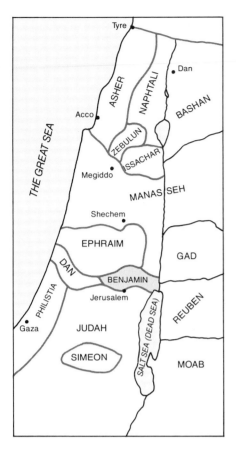

The territory of Benjamin.

(right)
Landscape in Samaria in the territory of Benjamin.

go to war against Benjamin. Benjamin was defeated and many of its inhabitants put to the sword. Only by abducting 600 married women from Jabesh-Gilead and Shiloh was the continuity of the tribe ensured (Judg chaps. 19-21). David's Kingdom of Judah did not originally include Benjamin, and Shimei son of Gera and Sheba son of Bichri gave expression to the Benjamites' resentment towards David whom they regarded as a usurper of Saul (II Sam 16:5-13; 20:1-2). After the division of the kingdom the territory of Benjamin served as a kind of buffer zone between the Kingdoms of Israel and Judah (I Kgs 15:22). Jeremiah came from the territory of Benjamin (Jer 1:1) and in the NT so did Paul (Rom 11:1; Phil 3:5).

2. The son of Bilhan, a Benjamite, and a great-grandson of Jacob.

3. One of Harim's sons who repudiated his foreign wife at the order of Ezra.

4. A priest who helped repair part of the walls of Jerusalem during the time of Nehemiah.

BEN-JOSIPHIAH ("son of Josiphiah"). A son of Shelomith; one of the men who returned from the Exile of Babylon with Ezra; he brought with him "one hundred and sixty males".

BENO ("his son"). The son of Jaaziah, a Levite at the time of David.

BEN-ONI ("son of my sorrow"). The name Rachel gave to the son whose birth caused her death: he was later renamed Benjamin by Jacob his father.

BEN SIRACH See ECCLESIASTICUS

BEN-ZOHETH ("son of Zoheth"). Son of Ishi in Judah's genealogy.

BEON A town disputed by the children of Gad and Reuben (Num 32:3); probably an alternate name for Baal Meon, Beth Baal Meon.

BEOR ("torch").

1. The father of Bela No.1 king of Edom.

2. The father of Balaam the prophet.

BERA King of Sodom in the time of Abraham; he was the ally of the kings of Gomorrah, Admah, Zeboiim and Bela (Gen 14:2). They were defeated by Chedorlaomer king of Elam at the battle of Siddim (Gen 14:1, 8-10).

BERACHAH ("blessing").

BERACHAH 1
I Chr 12:3

1. One of the soldiers who came to join David at Ziklag (I Chr 12:1, 3). He was from the tribe of Benjamin (I Chr 12:2) and was equally proficient in using right and left hand to shoot the bow or hurl stones (I Chr 12:2).

BERACHAH 2
II Chr 20:26

2. A valley in the wilderness of Judah (II Chr 20:26), where the armies of Jehoshaphat assembled on the fourth day after their victory over Ammon and Moab before returning to Jerusalem with their spoils (II Chr 20:22-28). Scholars believe it to be southeast of Tekoa.

The Valley of Berachah in the Judean Desert.

BERACHIAH
I Chr 6:39

BERACHIAH The father of Asaph; a Levite who sang before the ark in Jerusalem in the time of David. See BERECHIAH.

BERAIAH
I Chr 8:21

BERAIAH ("the Lord created"). The son of Shimei, one of the patriarchs of the tribe of Benjamin who settled in Jerusalem at the time of David.

BERECHIAH 1
I Chr 15:17

BERECHIAH ("God blessed").

BERECHIAH 2
I Chr 15:23

1. Son of Shimei and father of Asaph; a singer before the ark in Jerusalem in the time of David; perhaps identical with Berachiah.

BERECHIAH 3
II Chr 28:12

2. A Levite; one of the two gatekeepers of the ark when it was taken to Jerusalem by David.

BERECHIAH 4
I Chr 9:16

3. The son of Meshillemoth, one of the leaders of the tribe of Ephraim (II Chr 28:12) who rescued the captives of Judah taken by Pekah son of Remaliah and returned them to Jericho (II Chr 28:6, 8, 11-15).

BERECHIAH 5
I Chr 3:20

4. A Levite, son of Asa son of Elkanah, dwellers in the villages of the Netophatites.

BERECHIAH 6
Neh 3:4, 30;
6:18

5. A son of Zerubbabel, a descendant of David through Solomon.

6. The son of Meshezabeel and the father of Meshullam (who repaired the walls of Jerusalem in the time of Nehemiah).

BERECHIAH 7
Zech 1:1, 7.
Matt 23:35

7. The son of Iddo; the father of the prophet Zechariah.

BERED

BERED 1
Gen 16:14

1. A place near Beer Lahai Roi (where Hagar was delivered of her son Ishmael).

BERED 2
I Chr 7:20

2. The son of Shuthelah son of Ephraim and father of Tahath in the genealogy of Ephraim.

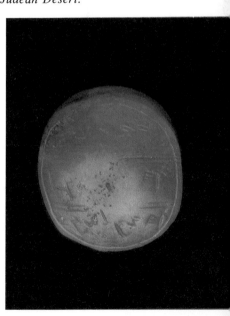

Agate Hebrew seal from Arad inscribed: "[Belonging] to Berechyahu Berechiah son of [...]hu son of Shelemyahu (Shelemiah)". 7th century B.C. (Israel Museum)

BERI The son of Zophah of the tribe of Asher.

BERIAH

1. The fourth son of Asher and ancestor of the Beriites. His family, including his two sons Heber and Malchiel, went to Egypt with Jacob.

2. A son of Ephraim: he was born after his brothers had been killed by the men of Gath. The popular etymology of his name reflects this misfortune: "because tragedy had come upon his house" (I Chr 7:23).

3. One of the sons of Elpaal. He was the head of a clan in Aijalon and helped to drive out the inhabitants of Gath. He had three sons, Michael, Ispah and Joha.

4. One of the sons of Shimei. He and his brother Jeush, having few sons, were assigned "as one father's house" at the time of the division of the Levites.

BERIITES Descendants of Beriah No.1, of the tribe of Asher.

BERITES An alternate spelling for Bichri. See also BECHER, BICHRI.

BERITH See BAAL-BERITH

BERNICE (BERENICE) Daughter of King Herod Agrippa I, sister of Agrippa II, and wife of her father's brother Herod of Chalcis. Together with her brother, who was king of southern Syria (Chalcis, Batanea and Trachonitis), she visited Governor Festus in Caesarea, where she listened to Paul's defense. According to Josephus (*Wars* II, 15) she intervened — in vain — with Governor Florus on behalf of Jews he had sentenced to death. She went to Rome with Titus who had fallen in love with her. She died after A.D. 79.

BERODACH-BALADAN An alternate name for Merodach-Baladan, son of Baladan king of Babylon.

BEROEA, BEREA A city in southern Macedonia, about 50 miles (80 km) southwest of Thessalonica, identified with modern Verria, to which Paul and Silas were sent by the Thessalonian believers after encountering opposition from the Jews of their city (Acts 17:10). In Beroea Paul and Silas preached in the synagogue and made many Jewish converts who devoted themselves to the study of the Scripture (Acts 17:11-12), as well as Greek converts from the noble classes. Paul was forced to flee from Beroea when the Thessalonian Jews stirred up the crowds there (Acts 17:13), but Silas and Timothy remained (Acts 17:14). It was the hometown of Sopater, the son of Pyrrhus, who accompanied Paul on a later visit to Macedonia (Acts 20:4).

BEROTHAH, BEROTHAI

1. A city on the northern border of Israel according to Ezekiel the prophet; maybe identical with No.2.

2. A city of Hadadezer, king of Zobah, by the Euphrates River. When David defeated the king, he took from the city "a large amount of bronze". Its present location is not known.

BEROTHITE, BEEROTHITE A native of the city of Beeroth.

BESAI A family of Nethinim (Temple servants) who returned from Babylon with Zerubbabel.

BESODEIAH ("in the secret of Yah"). Father of Meshullam (who rebuilt the walls of Jerusalem in the time of Nehemiah).

BESOR A brook near Ziklag in the extreme south of Judah (I Sam 30:9-10, 21) where David, pursuing the Amalekites, left those of his men too weary to go on (I Sam 30:21). Generally considered to be Wadi Azi, which has reverted to the name Nahal Besor on modern maps.

BETAH One of the cities of King Hadadezer conquered by David (II Sam 8:8) who took much brass (or bronze) from the place. Probably an alternate name for Tibhah (I Chr 18:8).

BETEN A city on the border of the territory of Asher believed to have been some miles southeast of Acco.

BERI
I Chr 7:36

BERIAH 1
Gen 46:17.
Num 26:44-45.
I Chr 7:30-31

BERIAH 2
I Chr 7:23

BERIAH 3
I Chr 8:13, 16

BERIAH 4
I Chr 23:10-11

BERIITES
Num 26:44

BERITES
II Sam 20:14

BERITH
Judg 9:46

BERNICE
Acts 25:13, 23;
26:30

BERODACH-
BALADAN
II Kgs 20:12

BEROEA, BEREA
Acts 17:10, 13;
20:4

BEROTHAH,
BEROTHAI 1
Ezek 47:16

BEROTHAH,
BEROTHAI 2
II Sam 8:8

BEROTHITE,
BEEROTHITE
I Chr 11:39

BESAI
Ezra 2:49.
Neh 7:52

BESODEIAH
Neh 3:6

BESOR
I Sam 30:9-10,
21

BETAH
II Sam 8:8

BETEN
Josh 19:25

View of the Nahal Besor region.

BETHABARA
John 1:28

BETHABARA A place "beyond the Jordan" where "John was baptizing" (John 1:28) and where Jesus came to him (John 1:29). Some scholars believe this place to be an alternate name for Betharabah.

BETH ACACIA
Judg 7:22

BETH ACACIA The place to which the Midianites fled after their defeat by Gideon. (It is given in Hebrew as Beth Shittah.) Identified with present-day Shatta a few miles west of Beth Shean.

Beth Acacia in the Beth Shean Valley.

BETH ANATH
Josh 19:38.
Judg 1:33

BETH ANATH A Canaanite city included in the territory of the tribe of Naphtali (Josh 18:10; 19:32, 38). The inhabitants were permitted to remain under the new rulers (Judg 1:33).

Several Canaanite cities may have borne the name Beth Anath before the advent of the Israelites; the name is mentioned in several Egyptian and Assyrian inscriptions. Anath was a Canaanite goddess.

BETH ANOTH
Josh 15:59

BETH ANOTH A city in the mountains of Judah which, with its villages, fell to the lot of the tribe of Judah (Josh 15:59) when the land of Canaan was divided by Joshua and Eleazar among the Children of Israel (Josh 14:1).

The name, a variation of Beth Anath, probably indicates that there was an altar of the Canaanite goddess Anath in the city.

BETHANY
Matt 21:17;
26:6. Mark
11:1, 11-12;
14:3. Luke
19:29; 24:50.
John 11:1, 18;
12:1

BETHANY A village about 1¾ miles (3 km) southeast of Jerusalem on the Mount of Olives and close to Bethphage. It was the home of the sisters Mary and Martha; here Jesus raised their brother Lazarus from the dead (John chap. 11). Jesus lodged in Bethany during his last week in Jerusalem and the palm procession set out from here (Luke 19:29). The anointing of Jesus two days before the Passover took place at the

A general view of Bethany, present-day al-Azariyya. On the right is the dome of the Church of St. Lazarus.

home of Simon the leper in Bethany. According to Luke 24:50, the ascension occurred in the vicinity. In Byzantine times, the village was named after Lazarus, hence its present Arabic name al-Azariyya.

BETH APHRAH (BETH-LE-APHRA). A term used by Micah the prophet in his mourning for Israel and Judah (Mic 1:10); it should probably be taken in the literal sense of "house of dust" and not as the name of an actual city or place.

BETH APHRAH
Mic 1:10

BETH ARABAH A place near the border of the territory allocated to Judah (Josh 15:1, 6) by Joshua and Eleazar (Josh 14:1). Lying somewhere in the wilderness of Judah (Josh 15:61) it marked the boundary with the territory of Benjamin (Josh 18:22).

In the Middle Ages many scholars identified this with the evangelical Bethabara where Jesus was baptized, because of the similarity in the names.

BETH ARABAH
Josh 15:6, 61; 18:22

BETH ARBEL Place conquered by Shalman, mentioned only once in the Bible. Identified with the mound of Irbid in Gilead.

BETH ARBEL
Hos 10:14

BETH AVEN ("house of iniquity").

1. A town near Ai, east of Bethel where Joshua sent men to spy out the land from Jericho (Josh 7:2). It served to indicate the boundary of Benjamin (Josh 18:12) and was the scene of a battle between Saul and the Philistines (I Sam 13:5; 14:23). Its exact location is uncertain but most likely it is to be identified with Tell Mariyam less than a mile (1 km) southwest of Michmash.

BETH AVEN 1
Josh 7:2; 18:12. I Sam 13:5; 14:23

2. A derogatory name for Bethel in Hosea's prophecies against the "calf of Beth Aven", referring to that set up at Bethel by Jeroboam (Hos 10:5; cf 4:15; 10:8).

BETH AVEN 2
Hos 4:15; 5:8; 10:5

The region of Beth Arabah in the Judean Desert.

Hizmeh, identified with Beth Azmaveth.

BETH AZMAVETH An alternate name for Azmaveth, a place in the vicinity of Jerusalem identified with the village of Hizmeh.

BETH BAAL MEON An alternate name for Baal Meon.

BETH BARAH A town or place seized by the men of Ephraim in the course of the war between Gideon and the Midianites (Judg 7:24). Its present location is unknown; it was probably in the mountains of Ephraim. During the Middle Ages some scholars sought there the place of crossing (Bethabarah) mentioned (John 1:28) as the site of the baptism of Jesus, because of the similarity in names.

BETH BIRI One of the cities of the tribe of Simeon, between Hazar Susim and Shaaraim. Its location is uncertain.

BETH CAR A place to which the Philistines fled when pursued by the armies of Samuel; its location is uncertain.

BETH DAGON

1. A city which fell to the lot of the children of Judah together with its surrounding villages (Josh 15:41) when Joshua divided the land of Canaan among the Children of Israel (Josh 14:1); situated between Gederoth and Naamah, near the present-day town bearing the same name, which indicates that it was the site of a shrine to the Canaanite god Dagon.

2. A city which fell to the lot of the tribe of Asher (Josh 19:24, 27) when Joshua divided the land of Canaan (Josh 14:1); it lay near the border with the territory of Zebulun (Josh 19:14). The site should be located in the modern village Jelame or nearby Tell el Par.

BETH DIBLATHAIM A city in Moab destined to suffer calamity together with the rest of that country according to Jeremiah. Perhaps an alternate name for Almon Diblathaim.

BETH EDEN A principal city in the Aramean kingdom identified with Bit-adini in the annals of Assyrian kings. In the prophecy against Damascus, Amos predicts the end of the ruler of Beth Eden (Amos 1:5). The place is also called Eden (Ezek 27:23) and according to II Kings 19:12 and Isaiah 37:12, the people of Eden were conquered by Assyria.

BETH EKED A place on the road from Jezreel to Samaria where Jehu had the kinsmen of Ahaziah king of Judah murdered in a pit (II Kgs 10:12-14).

BETHEL First mentioned during Abraham's wanderings in Canaan as one of the sites near which he built an altar and called on the name of the Lord (Gen 12:6-9). After going down to Egypt in a time of famine, Abraham returned to Bethel (Gen 13:1-4). It was here that Abraham's grandson, Jacob, had his dream of a ladder connecting heaven and earth, whereupon he called the place Bethel, that is, "house of God", "gate of heaven" (its former name was Luz). The stone which served as his pillow was anointed by Jacob with oil, to mark it as a holy place (Gen 28:1ff). Recalling the story of Abraham's wanderings in Canaan, Bethel again appears in connection with Jacob (Gen 35:1-15; cf 48:3-4), referring explicitly to the story of Genesis 28. Bethel is mentioned next in Joshua 7:2; 8:9, 12 as the site of the Israelites' ambush in the conquest of Ai; the reference employs almost exactly the same language as Genesis 12:8, apparently to recall the place's significance from Abraham's time. Judges 1:22-26 relates the conquest of Bethel and verse 23 refers to it by its former name of Luz, as in Genesis 35:6. The king of Bethel is listed with other defeated Canaanite kings in Joshua 12:16.

The Israelite temple at Bethel (cf Jacob's "pillar" there) was in existence for a long time: the tabernacle and the ark of the covenant were housed there in the period of the Judges (Judg 20:27), and the Israelites went there to inquire of the Urim and Thummim oracle and offer sacrifices (Judg 20:18, 26, 27; 21:2-4). Deborah judged Israel from

Beitin identified with Bethel.

the vicinity of Bethel (Judg 4:5) and Samuel visited Bethel on his yearly circuit (I Sam 7:16). A guild of prophets flourished there in Elijah's time (II Kgs 2:2ff). This indicates (cf also I Sam 10:3) that Bethel was a prominent tribal center, as well as being an important settlement, strategically located, where two-thirds of Saul's army camped (I Sam 13:2). Bethel's importance was diminished by the construction of Solomon's Temple in Jerusalem which overshadowed Bethel as the unique and central place of worship. With the division of the kingdom, however, Bethel was reestablished as one of the Northern Kingdom's centers of worship, where Jeroboam set up one of his golden calves in competition with the ark in Jerusalem. The short-lived capture of Bethel by Abijah, king of Judah, should be seen in this context (II Chr 13:19). The prophets Amos and Hosea railed against the shrine at Bethel, as did the anonymous prophet from Judah who predicted Jeroboam's downfall (I Kgs chap. 13). It was here that Amos encountered Amaziah the priest, who told him to go back to his native Judah (Amos 7:12-13). Hosea refers to the idolatry practiced at Bethel, calling it derogatively Beth Aven, "house of iniquity" (Hos 4:15; 10:5). Bethel finally fell, apparently in 721 B.C., when the Northern Kingdom was conquered by the Assyrians. Jeremiah saw this as deserved punishment (Jer 48:13). Nevertheless, the site still retained some sanctity (cf II Kgs 17:28) until Josiah's reform and unification of worship brought about the destruction and desecration of the "high place" at Bethel (II Kgs 23:15ff). Among the returnees from Babylonian Exile were 223 from Bethel and Ai (Ezra 2:28; Neh 7:32). Nehemiah 11:31 mentions Bethel and environs among the places where returning Benjamites settled.

Amos 3:14; 4:4; 5:5-6; 7:10, 13

Bethel is identified with modern Beitin, about 12 miles (19 km) north of Jerusalem. Excavations have determined a continuous occupation from 2000 B.C. to Christian times. It was apparently spared destruction at the time of the Assyrian conquest. It has an excellent water supply which made it a desirable location for settlement.

Bethel is recalled in the NT in John 1:51, where Jacob's dream is regarded as fulfilled with Christ as the ladder: in his humanity set up on earth and leading to heaven, and joining earth to heaven for the house of God (the church) for which the heavens are open.

BETH EMEK A city near Beth Dagon No.2 in the territory of Asher (Josh 19:27); probably Tell Mimas in the vicinity of present-day Acco;

BETH EMEK Josh 19:27

important archeological finds of that period were found there. The ancient name is preserved in the name of a nearby village, Amka.

BETHER The mountains of Bether mentioned in the Song of Solomon are considered to be a mythical place or perhaps should be translated as "the mountains of the morning", thus indicating a time and not a place.

BETHESDA (Bethzatha in RSV following some manuscripts) "A pool in Jerusalem where Jesus healed a sick man telling him to rise, pick up his bed and walk (John 5:2). Because this was the Sabbath day, the religious Jews told him it was not lawful for him to carry his bed; learning that it was Jesus who was healing people on the Sabbath, they persecuted him for this profanation (John 5:10-16).

Since the pool is located next to the Sheep Gate (John 5:2), it should be north of the city of Jerusalem and two pools with surrounding porticoes uncovered next to the church of St. Anne are identified as Bethesda.

BETH EZEL A city in Judah mentioned by Micah in his exhortations.

BETH GADER One of the main cities of Judah founded by Hareph, one of the sons of Caleb. Its location is unknown.

BETH GAMUL A city mentioned by Jeremiah in his judgment on Moab. Generally thought to be on the site of present-day Khirbet el-Jemeil, north of the Arnon River, in Jordan.

BETH HACCEREM, BETH HACCHEREM A town in the vicinity of Jerusalem where signal fires used to be set (Jer 6:1) and a district seat at the time of Nehemiah (Neh 3:14) ruled by Malchiah son of Rehab.

Of the three locations suggested by scholars, Ein Karem, Herodion and Ramat Rachel, none appears satisfactory.

The Pool of Bethesda in Jerusalem. Nearby stands the Crusader Church of St. Anne.

General view of the village of Ein Karem on the outskirts of Jerusalem, one of the places suggested as the site of ancient Beth Haccerem.

Landscape in the neighborhood of ancient Beth Hoglah.

BETH HAGGAN A town to which Ahaziah king of Judah fled when pursued by Jehu, not far from Ibleam and Megiddo.

Some scholars think that Beth Haggan is an alternate name for En Gannim, believed to be on the site of present-day Jenin.

BETH HARAM, BETH HARAN A town in the plains of Moab east of the Jordan River fortified by the Gadites (Num 32:36), who received it from Moses (Josh 13:27). Its location is uncertain. See ELON BETH HARAN.

BETH HOGLAH One of the cities which fell to the lot of the tribe of Benjamin (Josh 18:11) on the southern boundary where its territory adjoined that of Judah (Josh 15:6; 18:19) not far from where the Jordan enters the Dead Sea. The site was recently located near the spring of En Hoglah.

Margin references:
BETHER Song 2:17
BETHESDA John 5:2
BETH EZEL Mic 1:11
BETH GADER I Chr 2:51
BETH GAMUL Jer 48:23
BETH HACCEREM, BETH HACCHEREM Neh 3:14. Jer 6:1
BETH HAGGAN II Kgs 9:27
BETH HARAM, BETH HARAN Num 32:36. Josh 13:27
BETH HOGLAH Josh 15:6; 18:19, 21

BETH HORON A town in the territory of Ephraim, on the border of Benjamin (Josh 16:5; 18:13-14). There were in fact two places, adjacent to each other and distinguished by the description "upper" and "lower". The upper town was a key point on one of the main roads leading from the plain to the Judean Hills. After Joshua defeated the five kings of the Amorites he pursued them to upper Beth Horon (Josh 10:10; AV: "the way that goes up to Beth Horon"), and on the descent from there God cast down large stones from heaven on the fugitives (Josh 10:11). Beth Horon was given to the Levites of the family of Kohath (Josh 21:22) and one of the companies of the Philistines passed through it (I Sam 13:18).

BETH HORON
Josh 10:10-11; 16:3, 5; 18:13-14; 21:22. I Sam 13:18. I Kgs 9:17. I Chr 6:68; 7:24. II Chr 8:5; 25:13

(right)
Bet-Ur el-Foka and Bet-Ur el-Tahta, identified with Upper and Lower Beth Horon.

Partial view of Bethlehem with the mountains of Moab in the background.

Solomon built Upper Beth Horon (II Chr 8:5) and Lower Beth Horon (I Kgs 9:17). The place is mentioned in the list of conquests of Pharaoh Sheshonk. On the ascent of Beth Horon Judas Maccabee defeated the Syrian army (I Macc 3:16).

BETH JESHIMOTH, BETH JESIMOTH A halt of the Children of Israel on their route from Egypt to the promised land, east of the Jordan River (Num 33:49); a town in the plains of Moab taken from the Amorite king Sihon by the Children of Israel led by Moses (Josh 12:1,3). It was included in the domain of the tribe of Reuben (Josh 13:20) and mentioned by Ezekiel announcing the vengeance of the Lord upon the Ammonites (Ezek 25:9). Its location is unknown but should be northeast of the Dead Sea.

BETH JESHIMOTH, BETH JESIMOTH
Num 33:49. Josh 12:3; 13:20. Ezek 25:9

BETH-LE-APHRAH See BETH APHRA

BETH LEBAOTH A city which, with its villages, fell to the lot of the tribe of Simeon (Josh 19:1, 6) when Joshua divided the land of Canaan among the Children of Israel (Josh 14:1) in what had originally been the domain of Judah (Josh 19:9). Its location is unknown. Beth Lebaoth may be an alternate name for Lebaoth.

BETH LEBAOTH
Josh 19:6

BETHLEHEM, BETHLEHEMITE

1. A town in Judah, 5 miles (8 km) south of Jerusalem. Not far away, Rachel died and was buried (Gen 35:19; 48:7) and her traditional tomb

BETHLEHEM, BETHLEHEMITE 1
Gen 35:19; 48:7. Judg 17:7-9; 19:1-2, 18. Ruth 1:1-2, 19, 22; 2:4; 4:11. I

is venerated to this day. The Levite mentioned in the story of the concubine in Judges chapter 17 came from Bethlehem. It was the home of Elimelech, husband of Naomi and father-in-law of Ruth (Ruth 1:1) who later settled there. Her descendant, David, came from Bethlehem and there he was anointed by Samuel (I Sam 16:1-13). For a time, it was occupied by Philistines and three of David's "mighty men" penetrated the Philistine ranks to bring him water (II Sam 23:16). Asahel, Joab's brother, who was slain by Abner (II Sam 2:18-23), was buried in Bethlehem (II Sam 2:32). After the division of the kingdom, Rehoboam, son of Solomon, fortified Bethlehem with other cities of Judah (II Chr 11:6).

A general view of Bethlehem.

Interior of the Church of the Nativity in Bethlehem.

As the place of origin of David, Bethlehem was seen as the birthplace of the future descendant of David who will rule all Israel (Micah 5:2-5, a passage quoted in Matthew 2:6 and John 7:42, taking Jesus' birth in Bethlehem as the fulfillment of prophecy). The story of Jesus' birth in Bethlehem (Matt 2:1 ff; Luke 2:4 ff) is one of the best-loved sections of the NT. The birth in the manger, the arrival of the Wise Men from the east, and the flight to Egypt when Herod orders the massacre of all boys under the age of two in the town (Matt 2:13-18) are episodes of the story which have made Bethlehem one of the best-known places in Christendom. Since the 4th century the church built on the traditional site of the Nativity has been one of the great goals of Christian pilgrimage.

2. A town in the territory of Zebulun mentioned in a list in Joshua 19:15 and the home of the Judge Ibzan (Judg 12:8-10). Identified with Beit Lahm, 7 miles (11.5 km) nothwest of Nazareth.

BETH MAACHAH An alternate name for Abel Beth Maacah.
BETH MARCABOTH A city which fell to the lot of the tribe of Simeon (Josh 19:1, 5) when Joshua divided the land of Canaan among the Children of Israel (Josh 14:1; 18:10); the tribe of Simeon held it "until the reign of David" (I Chr 4:31). It is mentioned together with Ziklag and Hazar Sussa; its present location is unknown.

BETH MEON A city in Moab mentioned by Jeremiah; believed to be an alternate name for Baal Beth Meon and Beon.

BETH MEON
Jer 48:23

BETH MILLO An alternate name for Millo (cf), a suburb or part of the town of Shechem.

BETH MILLO
Judg 9:6, 20

BETH NIMRAH A city in the Jordan Valley, part of the domain allotted by Moses to the tribe of Gad (Josh 13:27) which fortified it (Num 32:36). The ancient name is probably preserved in Tell Nimmin some 8 miles (13 km) east of the Jordan River, one the road to A'salt.

BETH NIMRAH
Num 32:36.
Josh 13:27

BETH PAZZEZ A city which fell to the lot of the tribe of Issachar (Josh 19:17, 21) when Joshua divided the land of Canaan among the Children of Israel (Josh 14:1; 18:10); perhaps in the vicinity of Mount Tabor.

BETH PAZZEZ
Josh 19:21

BETH PELET A city on the southern border of the territory which fell to the lot of the tribe of Judah (Josh 15:20, 27) when Joshua divided the land of Canaan among the Children of Israel (Josh 14:1). Later some of the tribe of Judah settled there on returning from the Exile in Babylon (Neh 11:25-26). It was in the vicinity of Beersheba; its exact location is unknown.

BETH PELET
Josh 15:27.
Neh 11:26

BETH PEOR A city east of the Jordan River given to the tribe of Reuben by Moses (Josh 13:20); probably an alternate name for Baal Beth Peor, that is the sanctuary of the Canaanite god Peor. The Israelites camped there before defeating the Amorite king, Sihon (Deut 3:29; 4:46). Moses was buried not far from there "in a valley in the land of Moab, opposite Beth Peor, but no one knows his grave to this day" (Deut 34:6). The exact location of the place is unknown but it must have been a few miles east of Mount Nebo.

BETH PEOR
Deut 3:29;
4:46; 34:6.
Josh 13:20

BETHPHAGE ("house of figs"). A village east of the summit of the Mount of Olives and north of Bethany, near Jerusalem; it has been identified with the village of al-Tur. Coming here on his last journey from Jericho to Jerusalem, Jesus sent two of his disciples into the village where they found a she-ass and a colt (Matt 21:2; Mark 11:2 and Luke 19:30, only a colt). Jesus was to ride the colt into Jerusalem, in fulfillment of Zechariah 9:9 (Matt 21:5).

BETHPHAGE
Matt 21:1.
Mark 11:1.
Luke 19:29

BETH-RAPHA The name listed in the genealogy of Judah as that of the son of Eshton but is probably that of a whole clan; and the site would have been the place where the family lived.

BETH-RAPHA
I Chr 4:12

BETH REHOB See REHOB

BETH REHOB
Judg 18:28.
II Sam 10:6

BETHSAIDA Fishing village on the northeast shore of the Sea of Galilee near the mouth of the Jordan River. Jesus came here after feeding the five thousand (Mark 6:45; Luke 9:10) and later healed a blind man at the same place (Mark 8:22-26). The apostles Philip, Andrew and Peter came from Bethsaida (John 1:44; 12:21). Along with Chorazin and Capernaum, Bethsaida was reproached by Jesus for its stubbornness in not repenting and warned that its judgment would be worse than that of Sodom (Matt 11:20-24; Luke 10:13-15).

BETHSAIDA
Matt 11:21.
Mark 6:45;
8:22. Luke
9:10; 10:13.
John 1:44;
12:21

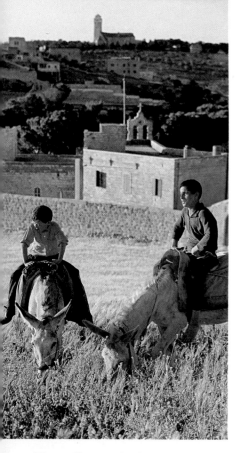

The village of al-Tur north of Bethany, identified as Bethphage.

The site of Bethsaida has never been identified precisely, but it was known as a fishermens' village along the shore of the Sea of Galilee.

BETH SHEAN,
BETH SHAN
Josh 17:11, 16.
Judg 1:27.
I Sam 31:10,
12. II Sam
21:12. I Kgs
4:12. I Chr
7:29

BETH SHEAN, BETH SHAN

A city at the eastern end of the Jezreel Valley. It occupied a highly strategic position at the junction of the Jezreel and Jordan Valleys.

In the Late Bronze Age it was an important stronghold of the Egyptian empire, especially in the period from Sethos I to Rameses III. It seems that the latter, after defeating the invading Sea Peoples (Philistines) early in the 12th century B.C., posted a garrison of mercenaries from among the vanquished armies in the city. In the biblical period it was one of the Canaanite towns that resisted the attack of the Israelites. After the defeat of the Israelites by the Philistines the bodies of Saul and his sons were displayed on the walls of Beth Shean (I Sam 31:10, 12). David conquered the city, with Megiddo and Taanach, during the expansion of his kingdom northwards and with these two cities it belonged to the fifth administrative district of Solomon, under Baana, one of the 12 officers of the Kingdom of Israel (I Kgs 4:12). In about 700 B.C. the site was deserted and was not reoccupied until the Hellenistic period, when it became known as Scythopolis, "city of the Scythians", a name which most probably originated from a unit of Scythian cavalry in the army of Ptolemy II. Under the Seleucids in the 2nd century B.C. the city received an additional name, Nysa, to commemorate the nurse of Dionysus who, according to legend, had been born there. Having been conquered by John Hyrcanus (135-104 B.C.), it was taken by Pompey in 63 B.C. and became the capital of the Decapolis. During that time it enjoyed great prosperity. Later it became a Christian city and the seat of a bishop. Its impressive mound has been extensively excavated and has revealed 18 levels of occupation dating back to the Chalcolithic Period.

A coin of Beth Shean (Nysa Scythopolis) showing Dionysos on one side and a portrait of Geta on the other. A.D. 207.

*(top left)
Tell Beth Shean.*

*(bottom left)
Remains of the Roman theater at Beth Shean.*

Inscribed stele of Pharaoh Seti I, found at Beth Shean, describing how the Egyptian army defeated the cities which were plotting against the king. End 14th century B.C.

BETH SHEMESH

1. Town in the Shephelah ("low hill country"), 12 miles (20 km) west of Jerusalem, situated on a main route from Philistia to Jerusalem. It probably derived its name (i.e. "house of the sun") from a sun cult pursued in the Canaanite city. In Joshua 19:41 it is called "Ir Shemesh" (i.e. "City of sun"). Not initially conquered by the Israelites, it remained a threat to the tribe of Dan (Judg 1:34-35 where Mount Heres may stand for Mountain of Sun). After its conquest, it belonged to the tribe of Judah (Josh 15:10) and was a Levitical city (Josh 21:16; I Chr 6:59). The ark of the covenant halted there on its way from Philistia to Kirjath Jearim (I Sam 6:12-21). Beth Shemesh is near the battlefield where the armies of Judah and Israel clashed (II Kgs 14:11-13) and King Amaziah of Judah was taken prisoner.

The town is identified with Tell Rumeilah near the Arab village of Ein Shams. Excavations have uncovered part of the Canaanite city — fortifications from Middle and Late Bronze periods, including the city gate. The destroyed Canaanite city was replaced by a Judean settlement which for a certain period of time in the 12th century B.C. was under Philistine influence and probably control (II Chr 28:18), as attested to by the large amounts of Philistine pottery found in these excavations. A planned and fortified city existing in the 10th century B.C. was probably destroyed by the Egyptian pharaoh Shishak (924 B.C.). King Rehoboam did not trouble to fortify Beth Shemesh unlike neighboring Zorah (II Chr 11:10). The city probably existed until the Babylonian destruction of Judah in 586 B.C.

2. Canaanite town allotted to the tribe of Naphtali but remaining unconquered by the Israelites.

3. Town in the territory of the tribe of Issachar. Some scholars believe it to be identical with Beth Shemesh No.2.

4. The city of Heliopolis (i.e. "city of the sun") in lower Egypt (today near Cairo); identical with On.

BETH SHITTAH See BETH ACACIA

BETH TAPPUAH A city in the district of Hebron included in the domain of the tribe of the children of Judah (Josh 14:1; 15:20, 53). See also TAPPUAH.

BETHUEL

1. The son of Milcah and of Abraham's brother Nahor, (Gen 24:15); the father of Rebekah and Laban. In Genesis 25:20 he is called a Syrian.

2. Part of the southern territory of Simeon and Judah when the land was divided among the tribes (I Chr 4:30). It is called Bethul in Joshua 19:4 and Chesil in Joshua 15:30. It may also be the town called Bethel to which David gave some of the Amalekite plunder (I Sam 30:27).

BETHUL See BETHUEL No.2

BETH ZUR Maon, of the clan of Caleb, was the "father" of a city which fell to the domain of the tribe of Judah (Josh 15:58; I Chr 2:45) when the

BETH SHEMESH 1
Josh 15:10;
21:16. Judg
1:33. I Sam
6:9, 12-15, 18-
20. I Kgs 4:9.
II Kgs 14:11,
13. I Chr 6:59.
II Chr 25:21,
23; 28:18

BETH SHEMESH 2
Josh 19:38.
Judg 1:33

BETH SHEMESH 3
Josh 19:22

BETH SHEMESH 4
Jer 43:13

BETH TAPPUAH
Josh 15:53

BETHUEL 1
Gen 22:22-23;
24:15, 24, 47,
50; 25:20;
28:2, 5

BETHUEL 2
I Chr 4:30

BETHUL
Josh 19:4

BETH ZUR
Josh 15:58.

Remains of a Byzantine period structure at the site of Tell Shams identified with Beth Shemesh.

Ancient ruins at the site of Beth Zur.

I Chr 2:45.
II Chr 11:7.
Neh 3:16

land of Canaan was divided by Joshua among the Children of Israel (Josh 14:1). King Rehoboam fortified it (II Chr 11:5, 7). In Nehemiah's time it was ruled jointly by a Nehemiah son of Azbuk (Neh 3:16) and another ruler whose name is not mentioned. Later the city played a key role in the wars of the Hasmoneans. It is identified with present-day Khirbet el Tubeiqa, 4 miles (6 km) north of Hebron where extensive excavations have uncovered large parts of the ancient town.

BETONIM
Josh 13:26

BETONIM A city included by Moses in the domain of the tribe of Gad (Josh 13:24, 26) believed to be on the site of present-day Khirbet Batneh, southwest of A'Salt, east of the Jordan River.

BEULAH
Is 62:4

BEULAH ("married"). A symbolic name for Israel, in referring to the restoration of Jerusalem, which will no longer be called "Forsaken" or "Desolate", but "Hephzibah" — "My delight is in her" and "Beulah" — "Married" (Is 62:4).

BEZAI

BEZAI 1
Ezra 2:17.
Neh 7:23

1. One of the families who returned from Exile with Zerubbabel. According to Ezra it numbered 323 persons (Ezra 2:17) and to Nehemiah 324 (Neh 7:23).

BEZAI 2
Neh 10:18

2. One of the Levites who sealed the covenant at the time of Nehemiah (Neh 10:1, 9, 18); he probably belonged to the Bezai family.

BEZALEL, BEZALEEL ("in God's shadow / protection") (cf Ps 91:1).

BEZALEL,
BEZALEEL 1
Ex 31:2; 35:30;
36:1-2; 37:1;
38:22. I Chr
2:20. II Chr
1:5

1. A Judahite, son of Uri son of Hur. Bezalel was the skilled artisan selected to be in charge of executing all the work of the tabernacle (Ex 31:2) and its vessels, including the ark, the priestly garments, the anointing oil and incense. The Bible relates that he was filled with the divine Spirit in wisdom and in all manner of skilled artistry in working metals, stone and wood. He was assisted by Aholiab son of Ahisamach, the Danite. Bezalel also executed the brass altar which, up until the time of David, stood before the Tent of Meeting at the great high-place in Gibeon, and upon which Solomon offered his sacrifices (I Kgs chap. 3).

BEZALEL,
BEZALEEL 2
Ezra 10:30

2. One of the eight sons of Pahath-Moab. He repudiated his alien wife at the behest of Ezra (Ezra 10:30).

BEZEK

BEZEK 1
Judg 1:4-5

1. A Canaanite city where Judah and Simeon defeated the Canaanites and the Perizzites led by Adoni-Bezek who managed to flee (Judg 1:3-5). Its location is unknown.

BEZEK 2
I Sam 11:8

2. The place where Saul mustered his men before going to the rescue of the men of Jabesh against Nahash the Ammonite (I Sam 11:3, 8).

Present-day Khirbet Ibzik, on the slopes of Mount Ras Ibzik, in the mountains of Ephraim, is considered to be the site of Bezek No.2.

BEZER

BEZER 1
Deut 4:43.
Josh 20:8;
21:36. I Chr
6:78

1. A city in the territory of Reuben belonging to the Merrari family, east of the Jordan River. Declared a place of refuge by Moses (Deut 4:43). See BOZRAH No.2.

BEZER 2
I Chr 7:37

2. The son of Zopha, of the tribe of Asher, listed in the genealogy of Asher.

BIBLE TRANSLATIONS, ANCIENT The most popular and widely printed book in the world, the Bible, has been translated very often, both in ancient and modern times. The translations constitute important cultural compositions in their respective languages in some of which they are the first written documents.

The nature of the translation differs from one version to another; similar differences are even visible within the same translation whose character varies from book to book. As in modern times, some ancient translators rendered their source more faithfully than others. Those who adhered closely to their source created "literal" translations reproducing all the characteristics of the source, including so-called

A' Salt, east of the Jordan River.

A view of the region in Ephraim where Saul mustered his men to go to the rescue of Nahash the Ammonite (I Sam 11:3).

Hebraisms. The 17th century King James Version, for example, employs the phrase "to find grace (favor) in the eyes of" which is the precise equivalent of the Hebrew expression, not found previously in the English language. Similar Hebraisms are found in all ancient versions.

By contrast, translators who did not aim at a literal representation of the Hebrew Bible incorporated differing quantities of exegesis at all levels. Words were rendered differently in accordance with the various contexts, and unusual translations also appeared. At the same time, details in the biblical texts were explained contextually in accordance with known exegetical traditions and the translator's imagination. Thus difficult expressions were clarified, and situations requiring explanation were elucidated in the translation. Some renderings contain more exegetical elements than others, and the more such elements are included, the freer the translations. Some ancient translations reflect such a large amount of contextual exegesis that the individual words of the Hebrew text can no longer be identified. In such cases one should speak of an ancient *midrash* or a paraphrase retelling of the biblical text. This, for example, is the case with the Greek and Aramaic translations of Esther which embellish the biblical story and add a religious background.

Page from the Codex Syriacus. (Library of Santa Caterina, Sinai)

Because of these added elements, most ancient translations are of great importance for our understanding of the interpretation of the Bible in antiquity. As such they are greatly studied by modern scholars.

A further reason for the importance of the ancient versions is that they date to an early period when the Hebrew text was not yet fixed. Hence some of the translations reflect an original which differs in major or minor details from the received Hebrew text (the so-called Masoretic Text). Much is now known about the Hebrew texts from which the ancient versions were made, especially because of the Hebrew scrolls found in Qumran (the "Dead Sea Scrolls") which resemble the Septuagint translation in many details. The Hebrew texts from which the ancient versions were rendered thus can often be reconstructed by retranslation into Hebrew, these reconstructed texts frequently differing from the received biblical text.

This is especially true of the Septuagint, the oldest written translation of the Bible. Written in Greek, the language of the Hellenistic world, the Septuagint was produced in Hellenistic Alexandria (Egypt) in the 3rd and 2nd centuries B.C. As with all ancient versions, the circumstances of its origin are disputed and obscure. As related in the "Letter of Aristeas", one of the extra-canonical biblical books, a Ptolemy (probably Ptolemy Philadelphus who reigned from 285 to 246 B.C.) summoned 72 elders (six from each tribe) from Jerusalem to translate the Jewish scriptures into Greek; in spite of working in separate cells, the divinely guided translators miraculously produced identical versions. The kernel of the story may be true since the Ptolemaic rulers were known to be interested in foreign cultures. At the same time, the Jewish community of Alexandria, being deficient in its knowledge of Hebrew, must have required a translation for its daily needs.

Early papyri of parts of the Septuagint have been found in various places in Egypt and Palestine, and there exist several early manuscripts of its complete text which provided the earliest attestations of the Bible until the recent discovery of the Hebrew scrolls near the Dead Sea.

Page from the Codex Sinaiticus. (British Museum)

Jewish in origin, the Septuagint was soon accepted as Holy Writ by the Greek-speaking Christian community, which was greatly influenced by its contents and terminology, as is evident from the NT. Even though internal evidence shows that it was produced by Jewish translators, the Septuagint became increasingly known as a document used by Christians, almost a Christian source, making it less attractive for the Jews who therefore abandoned it. Instead, they started to revise the Septuagint, making it acceptable to them by removing terms which had become "Christian" such as *christos*, the standard rendering for *mashiach* (anointed). These Jewish revisions are connected with the names of Aquila, Theodotion and Symmachus.

The Hebrew source of the Septuagint translation differed from the received Hebrew text, often in major details. Thus in the second part of Exodus, the sequence diverges from the received text, and the Greek Book of Jeremiah is much shorter than the Hebrew original. The Septuagint also contains several books which are not found in the collection of Hebrew sacred writings, such as the Books of Maccabees,

Judith and Baruch. Furthermore, the sequence of the books in the Greek Bible differs from the Hebrew counterpart. Thus the Book of Ruth is appended to Judges, and Lamentations (traditionally ascribed to the prophet Jeremiah) is appended to the Book of Jeremiah.

In antiquity the Septuagint was translated into various languages, among which was Latin . This "old Latin" translation introduced the contents and names of the books of the Septuagint into western cultures. In the Greek Orthodox Church, the Septuagint is still a sacred book.

Internal Jewish needs likewise prompted the translations into Aramaic, the major language of the Jews in the Babylonian Exile, which also progressively replaced Hebrew in Palestine. Several Aramaic translations were produced, first oral and afterwards written; they were named *targumim*, singular *targum* ("translation" or "paraphrase"). Of these, the best-known are the Targum Onkelos to the Pentateuch and Targum Jonathan to the prophets; both are of the "literal" type. The free and even paraphrastic type are represented by the so-called Targum Pseudo-Jonathan and Neophiti to the Pentateuch. All *targumim* were based on the Hebrew text, even though they reflect varying degrees of exegesis. Their dates of origin are not known. In the Jewish tradition the *targumim* were held in great esteem, as can be seen from the frequent quotations in the Talmud and medieval commentaries.

The Latin Vulgate (*vulgata*), produced by the Church father Jerome (A.D. 345-420) originated from Jerome's revision of the "Old Latin" translations (see above), but continued as a Latin translation of the Hebrew source itself. Produced in the years 390-405, it was a faithful, yet elegant, translation of the Hebrew, incorporating rabbinic exegesis; in due course it replaced the Septuagint as the sacred text of the Church.

In addition to these translations there is also a translation into Syriac, an Aramaic dialect. This translation (the Peshitta, the "straightforward one") is clearly based on Jewish exegesis, but little is known about its origin.

The cell in Bethlehem, where St. Jerome is believed to have translated the Bible into Latin.

BICHRI The father of Sheba, a man of Benjamin who rebelled against David (II Sam 20:1). Many scholars believe Bichri to be a family name, meaning from the clan or family of Becher.

BICHRI
II Sam 20:1-2, 6-7, 10, 13, 21-22

BIDKAR A captain of Jehu's troops. After Jehu killed Jehoram, the king of Israel (II Kgs 9:24), he ordered Bidkar to throw the body into the field of Naboth the Jezreelite (II Kgs 9:25).

BIDKAR
II Kgs 9:25

BIGTHA ("gift of God"). One of the seven eunuchs, chamberlains of King Ahasuerus, who were sent to bring Vashti the queen into the royal presence.

BIGTHA
Est 1:10

BIGTHAN, BIGTHANA ("gift of God"). One of the two eunuchs, chamberlains of King Ahasuerus, who conspired against Ahasuerus. Their plot was uncovered by Mordecai and they were hanged (Est 2:21-23).

BIGTHAN, BIGTHANA
Est 2:21; 6:2

BIGVAI One of the largest families among the exiles who returned from Babylon with Zerubbabel; according to Ezra it numbered 2,056 persons (Ezra 2:14) and to Nehemiah 2,067 (Neh 7:19). Bigvai himself is mentioned as one of the men who came with Zerubbabel (Ezra 2:2, Neh 7:7) and a Bigvai is among the Levites who sealed the covenant (Neh 10:16); two sons of Bigvai are listed among those who returned with Ezra (Ezra 8:14).

BIGVAI
Ezra 2:2, 14; 8:14. Neh 7:7, 19; 10:16

BILDAD Mentioned as the Shuhite and identified as one of the three friends of Job.

BILDAD
Job 2:11; 8:1; 18:1; 25:1; 42:9

BILEAM One of the cities of the Levites (I Chr 6:54, 70), from the territory of Ephraim (I Chr 6:66). Probably an alternate name for Ibleam.

BILEAM
I Chr 6:70

BILGAH

1. Bilgah, descendant of Aaron, was head of the 15th division of priests established by David (I Chr 24:5, 14).

2. One of the chiefs of the priests who returned from Exile with Zerubbabel.

3. The father of Shammua, a priest at the time of Zerubbabel; possibly identical with Bilgah No.2.

BILGAI One of the priests who sealed the covenant at the time of Nehemiah (Neh 10:1, 8), perhaps identical with Bilgah No.2.

BILHAH

1. A servant of Laban who gave her as a maid to his daughter Rachel when she married Jacob (Gen 29:29). Rachel, who was barren while her sister Leah was fruitful, sent her maid to Jacob her husband, so as to "have children by her" (Gen 30:3). Bilhah then bore two sons: Dan (Gen 30:5-6) and Naphtali (Gen 30:7-8). Later Reuben, Jacob's firstborn son by his wife Leah, "went and lay with Bilhah his father's concubine" (Gen 35:22).

2. A city belonging to the family of Shimei, from the tribe of Simeon; an alternate name for Baalah No.2.

BILHAN ("modest").

1. One of the children of Ezer, leader of the Horite clan at the time of Esau.

2. The only son of Jediael in the genealogy of Benjamin.

BILSHAN One of the leaders who returned from Babylon with Zerubbabel.

BIMHAL A son of Japhlet son of Heber, the head of one of the clans of the children of Asher in the genealogy of Asher.

BINEA The son of Moza and the father of Rephaiah in the line of Saul and Jonathan.

BINNUI The name of several biblical characters (some of them possibly identical) dating from the time of Ezra and Nehemiah.

1. Head of a family of exiles which returned with Zerubbabel (Neh 7:15) and numbered 648 members (this family may be identical with that of Bani No.4).

2. One of the Levites who returned with Zerubbabel (Neh 12:8), helped rebuild the wall of Jerusalem (Neh 3:24) and sealed the covenant (Neh 10:9). He may have belonged to the family of Binnui No.1.

3. A Levite, father of Noadiah, companion of Ezra.

4. A son of Pahath-Moab who took a foreign wife and had to repudiate her upon the decree of Ezra (Ezra 10:3, 30).

5. Another man who had taken an alien wife and had to repudiate her upon the decree of Ezra (Ezra 10:3, 38).

BIRSHA King of Gomorrah (Gen 14:2); one of the five kings who rebelled against King Chedorlaomer (Gen 14:1, 4) and were defeated in the Vale of Siddim (Gen 14:10).

BIRTH There are a number of indications that in biblical times, a woman gave birth either in a kneeling position (I Sam 4:19) or while sitting on a special birthstool (Ex 1:16). The baby was then placed on the knees of the person, either male or female, who claimed the newborn child as its own. Rachel told Jacob "Here is my maid Bilhah; go in to her and she will bear a child upon my knees" (Gen 30:3). Of the children of Machir, Joseph's grandson, we are told that they were born on Joseph's knees (Gen 50:23). Midwives were employed to assist at birth. Because of their special skill, they were held in high esteem (Ex 1:17-21).

The thrusting about of the twins, Jacob and Esau in the womb of Rebekah — a normal experience during the latter months of pregnancy — is interpreted as an omen of the future rivalry and struggle between the two brothers (Gen 25:22-23). When Tamar was giving birth to twin sons, Perez and Zerah, it is related that the latter put out his hand first but was then thrust aside by Perez, who emerged before him (Gen 38:28-30).

In antiquity, though not in the Bible, it was a prevalent, accepted practice to abandon unwanted children at birth, particularly female infants. Ezekiel referred to such practice when he compared the plight of Jerusalem to that of a newborn, abandoned child. From his description, we learn the normal procedure in caring for an infant at birth. "On the day you were born, your navel cord was not cut, nor were you washed in water to cleanse you; you were not rubbed with salt nor swathed in swaddling clothes" (Ezek 16:4). (The salt may have been intended, as in other instances, as a protection against the evil eye). Children were given their names at birth (Gen 29:32, 35; 30:6ff).

The pangs of childbirth are attributed to Eve, the prototype of all women. In the case of Eve, it is divine punishment for succumbing to the temptation by the serpent and eating of the fruit of the Tree of Knowledge. "I will greatly multiply your sorrow and your conception; in pain you shall bring forth children" (Gen 3:16). In the time to come, according to Isaiah 66:7 childbearing, like the restoration to Zion of her children, will be painless: "Before she travailed, she gave birth, before her pain came she delivered a male child". An instance of death in childbirth appears in the story of the death of Rachel (Gen 35:18; I Sam 4:19-20). After childbirth, a woman became impure for a period of time, whose length depended on whether the newborn child was a male or a female. (See PURITY, IMPURITY).

A woman who bears numerous children is deemed fortunate and happy (Gen 29:32-34; 30:20); whereas the barren woman is described as unfortunate and downcast (Gen 30:1; I Sam 1:11). "He grants the barren wife a home, like a joyful mother of children" (Ps 113:9). Child bearing by a hitherto barren woman is deemed a special act of divine favor. A number of such episodes are recounted (cf the births of Isaac, Gen 21:1-7; Samson, Judg chap. 11; Samuel, I Sam 1:1-2:10), the mother in each case being informed in advance, either by an angel or a prophet, that she is destined to bear a child. The prophet Elisha brought the glad tidings to the Shunammite woman (II Kgs 4:16). The prophet Isaiah foretells that his wife will bear a son, an event the prophet interprets as an omen of future events (Is 8:1-3).

In poetic language, birth pangs served as a metaphor for the painful evils that will befall Israel. "The sorrows of a woman in childbirth shall come upon him" (Hos 13:13). "...Pangs have seized you like a woman in labor. Be in pain and labor to bring forth, O daughter of Zion" (Mic 4:9-10). "...They shall be frightened; pangs and throes shall take hold of them; they shall be in pain like a woman in travail" (Is 13:8 and frequently thereafter).

The travail of childbirth served the prophet Isaiah (21:3) as a metaphor for the profound inner agitation that accompanies his receipt of a divine communication. Isaiah likewise described the forthcoming manifestation of God's power as that of a woman in labor. "I have been still and restrained myself, but now I will cry like a woman in labor, I will pant and gasp at once" (42:14). The future joy of Zion on the return of her exiled children is compared to that of a woman who gives birth after a long period of barrenness (54:1).

According to the NT, spiritually one may be born a second time, of the water and the Spirit, i.e. a new birth (John 3:3-7). See VIRGIN BIRTH.

BIRZAITH (BIRZAVITH) Person in the genealogy of Asher. Scholars believe that a village of that name belonging to one of the clans of Asher

BIRZAITH
I Chr 7:31

stood on the site of present-day Bir Zeit, 5 miles (8 km) north of Ramallah. Josephus names it as the site of Judas Maccabee's last battle with Bacchides.

BISHLAM (Ezra 4:7) One of the three men who wrote a letter to Artaxerxes complaining that the Jews were rebuilding the Temple. Many scholars believe however "Bishlam" stands for the salutation of the letter and not for the name of an actual person.

BITHIAH (I Chr 4:18) ("daughter of Yahweh"). Daughter of a pharaoh and wife of Mered son of Ezra in the genealogy of Judah.

BITHRON (II Sam 2:29) In his flight from the soldiers of David, Abner (who had Saul's son, Ishbosheth, crowned king of Israel) "crossed over the Jordan, and went through all Bithron" (II Sam 2:29). Scholars do not agree as to the meaning of Bithron. Some see it as a way through the mountains; for others it indicates a time, not a place.

BITHYNIA (Acts 16:7. I Pet 1:1) A Roman province since 74 B.C., it was located in northwest Asia Minor and was united with its eastern neighbor Pontus for administrative purposes. Paul planned to go there from Phrygia and Galatia but was prevented from doing so by the Spirit of Jesus (Acts 16:7). I Peter 1:1 is addressed to Bithynia (among other places) indicating the existence of Christians there in the 1st century A.D.

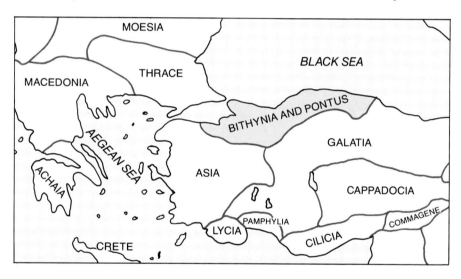

Bithynia in Asia Minor.

BIZJOTHJAH (BIZIOTHIAH) (Josh 15:28) A city on the southern border of the territory which fell to the lot of the tribe of Judah (Josh 15:20, 28) when Joshua divided the land of Canaan among the Children of Israel (Josh 14:1). It was in the district of Beersheba (Josh 15:28).

BIZTHA (Est 1:10) The second of the seven eunuchs sent by King Ahasuerus to bring Queen Vashti into the royal presence.

BLASTUS (Acts 12:20) A chamberlain of Herod Agrippa I who intervened on behalf of the people of Tyre and Sidon.

BLESSING AND CURSING Blessings and cursings are to be found throughout the Bible and are also well attested in ancient Near Eastern literature. They were pronounced ceremoniously over whole nations but also over individuals in situations of everyday life. In order to understand the significance of their widespread use in the cult, it is important first to examine their function in the framework of the covenant-treaty and the manner of their association with historical events.

The spoken declaration of good-to-come, or impending misfortune, derived its credibility from the belief in the deity's power to make the spoken word a reality. This may explain why the patriarchial blessing could not be revoked even if given to the wrong person (Gen 27:33-37; cf 48:13-20); nor could God's blessing be altered to a curse (Num chap. 24; Josh 24:9-10). The belief in the power of the spoken word was especially evident when it was uttered "before the presence of the Lord" (Num 5:16, 18, 21-22, 25, 30). A symbolic gesture may also accompany the blessing or curse (Gen 48:13; Num 5:16-30; Deut 25:9; Neh 5:12-13).

The records of ancient suzerainty treaties between the Hittite empire and its vassal states have been found to include blessings and cursings as a regular part of their format. The purpose of these treaties was to regulate in advance the obligations of the two parties entering into the agreement to which the gods of both nations were designated as witnesses, as well as natural forces represented by mountains, rivers, winds and clouds (cf Deut 32:1; Is 1:2). In the context of these treaties it is clear that the function of these blessings and cursings was to protect the terms of the covenant from future violations, i.e. to serve as a warning and incentive (cf Darius' warning in Ezra 6:12).

Scholars have pointed out that the covenant recorded in Deuteronomy between Israel and God contains all the elements of a suzerainty treaty. The blessings and cursings recorded (Deut chap. 28) were intended to serve as an incentive to Israel to abide by the agreement and to establish in advance the consequences of a breach. The striking difference is that this covenant-treaty was enacted, not between nations, but with God himself.

Blessings and cursings also played an important role in explaining historical experiences. The "prophetic" blessing-cursing of Noah (Gen 9:24-27), Isaac (Gen chap. 27) and Jacob (Gen chap. 49) concerning their sons were later interpreted in terms of particular events associated with the tribe or nation that bore that son's name (e.g. Gen 9:25 and I Kgs 9:20-21; Gen 49:5-6 and Josh 19:9; 21:1-42). It was God's blessing upon Abraham, Isaac and Jacob which destined them to become the patriarchs of the nation. Before Moses' death, he uttered a blessing over the twelve tribes foretelling their future in the land which the Lord was giving them (Deut chap. 33; cf Gen chap. 49). Even the etiological curses

Wall painting from the synagogue of Dura-Europos, depicting Jacob blessing his sons. On the left, Jacob is shown on his deathbed blessing his twelve sons, while on the right he is blessing Ephraim and Menasseh in the presence of Joseph. 3rd century A.D.

concerning the snake, the woman in childbirth and the man in his toil were pointed out as the factor responsible for the corresponding misfortunes (Gen 3:14, 17-19). During the partriarchal period therefore, the proclamation of blessings and cursings was viewed as being directly linked to the fortune and destiny of individuals and nations.

During the time of the confederacy of the twelve tribes, the curses seem to have functioned more in defining a basis for excommunication. After Joshua was deceived by the Gibeonites, he cursed them, condemning them to the status of slaves of the lowest class (Josh 9:22-23; cf Josh 6:26; Rom 9:3; Gal 1:8-9). In Judges 21:1, 18 a curse was proclaimed on anyone who gave a wife to the Benjamites. I Samuel 14:24ff records how Saul's curse almost resulted in the death of his son, Jonathan. The curses directed to the individual offender in Deuteronomy 27:12ff differ from those invoked upon the congregation (Deut 28:16ff) and may also serve for the purpose of defining deviant members.

The power to bless or curse was also shared by kings and priests. Both David and Solomon blessed the people (II Sam 6:18; I Kgs 8:14ff; 8:54ff; cf I Kgs 10:8-9, Queen of Sheba's blessing). David blessed Abigail for averting him from shedding innocent blood in anger (I Sam 25:33). The priests recited a blessing of prosperity over the people (Num 6:23-26; cf Gen 14:19-20, blessing of Melchizedek). Nehemiah also proclaimed a curse against the priests who defied the proclamations of reform (Neh 5:12-13).

In the daily life of the people blessings and curses were employed in a different fashion. Curses became "self-curses" which may be difficult to distinguish from an oath. The Hebrew word for "curse" is used interchangeably with "oath" in certain passages (e.g., Gen 24:8, 41). Blessings were used as salutations of greetings (Gen 24:31). In the Psalms the common expression "Blessed [or, Happy] is the man who..." appears many times (e.g., Ps 1:1; 32:1; 33:12; cf Jer 17:7ff). In Ezekiel 44:30 the people were instructed to set aside a special contribution for the priests "to cause a blessing to rest" on their houses. Both Job and Jeremiah expressed the distress of their circumstances by cursing the day of their birth (Job 3:1ff; Jer 20:14-18).

In the NT, the use of blessing is similar to the OT. Jesus blessed the food in the miracle of the multiplication of the loaves (Matt 14:19; Mark 6:41, etc.), the Eucharist (Matt 26:26) and the apostles at the ascension (Luke 24:50). The teaching to return a blessing for a curse (Luke 6:28) was reiterated by Paul (Rom 12:14). Mary was "blessed among women" (Luke 1:28, 42). Cursing was rare in the NT, but Paul cursed those who preached another gospel (Gal 1:8) and any man who did not love God (I Cor 16:22).

BLOOD In many respects, ancient Israel's attitude towards blood both as sacred and purifying (e.g., with respect to the Day of Atonement ritual), and as a major sign of ritual impurity (e.g., with respect to the monthly menstrual flow) was unique among the peoples of the ancient Near East. The Israelite conception of the sanctity of blood is expressed by the prohibition of its consumption, which occurs in the Bible in three forms: (a) the prohibition of blood consumption together with the positive ritual requirements of sprinkling upon the altar the blood of all slaughtered animals potentially valid for sacrifice (Lev 17:3-12; cf Lev 1:5; Is 1:11) and the covering up with dust of the blood of all game animals which are invalid for sacrifice (Lev 17:13-14); (b) the prohibition of blood consumption together with the specific Deuteronomic pronouncement that the blood of all animals slaughtered for non-sacrificial purposes should be poured out on the ground "like water" (Deut 12:16, 23; 15:23); (c) the prohibition "to eat upon or over blood" (Lev 19:26; I Sam 14:32-34; Ezek 33:25), a possible reference to pagan divination customs in which the blood absorbed by the earth is intended to satisfy thirsty deities or demons residing in the netherworld. The deities in return would reveal the future. The most persuasive evidence for this view is the context of Leviticus 19:26, which includes two other prohibitions against pagan divination customs. On the other hand, the idiom could also be translated "to eat together with the blood" giving a meaning similar to formulations 1 and 2 above. The eating of blood is forbidden because it is identified with life (Gen 9:4; Lev 17:10ff). The empirical observation concerning the association between blood and the lifeforce (Gen 9:4; Deut 12:23) was in all likelihood a result of the high visibility of blood from both the wounds of the living and the bodies of slain corpses from which it drained. Here also belongs the ritual impurity of the monthly menstrual flow (Lev 15:19, 25). The "spilling/shedding of blood" is a common phrase in the Bible; and the avenger of "spilt innocent blood" is called "the avenger of blood" (Num 35:27; Deut 19:6, 12; Josh 20:9; II Sam 14:11).

"Blood" appears together with "fat" as the two principal components of an animal, which must be offered to God when the animal is sacrificed (Num 18:17). The priestly techniques of offering the blood upon the altar were rendered in the following expressions: "sprinkle the blood all around on the altar" (Lev 3:2, 8, 13; II Chr 29:22); "drained out at the side of the altar" (Lev 1:15); "put it on the horns of the altar with your finger" (Ex 29:12; Lev 4:7, 18, 25, 30, 34), "drained out/poured out (at the base of the altar)" (Lev 5:9; 8:15; Deut 12:27). The fine distinctions between these four techniques are unknown today.

Blood-manipulation is most intensified in the Day of Atonement ritual (Lev chap. 16). Expiation is made by Aaron, the high priest, for the Shrine and the Tent of Meeting, by taking some of the blood of a slaughtered bull (on behalf of the priesthood) and that of a slaughtered he-goat (on behalf of all the Israelites) and sprinkling it seven times with his finger over the cover of the ark and in front of it. Then Aaron makes expiation for the altar by taking some of the remaining blood of the same two slaughtered animals (again on behalf of the priesthood and all Israelites respectively) and applying it to each of the four horns of the altar, and by taking the rest of the blood and sprinkling it with his finger seven times on the altar itself (Lev 16:14-19).

The use of the blood for expiation in Israelite ritual is quite intentional as is emphasized by Leviticus 17:11 and was also apotropaic. The blood of the Passover offering, which was smeared on the door posts of the homes of the Hebrews in Egypt during the eve of the first Passover, was intended to serve as a sign of Divine protection (see especially Ex 12:7, 13, 21-23).

The NT follows Judaism in using the term blood as equivalent to life or humanity. Thus the expression "flesh and blood" (Matt 16:17) means humanity and is generally used in contrast to Divine power and wisdom as in Galatians 1:16.

The term takes on special significance in the designation: "the blood of Christ" where it denotes his sacrificial death. Fundamental is the Pauline affirmation that now, independent of the law, God's way of righting wrong has been brought to light. It is effective in Christ through faith, now all are justified by God's free grace alone, through his act of liberation in the person of Christ Jesus "whom God set forth to be a propitiation by his blood, through faith" (Rom 3:25).

For the writer of Hebrews (chap. 9) the superiority of the new covenant consists in the fact that Jesus as high priest sacrificed his own blood (life) (Heb 9:12). Although reference is made to the blood of goats and calves he argues that if that was effective, how much more so is the blood of Christ effective to "purge your conscience from dead works to serve the living God?" (Heb 9:14). The Epistle to the Hebrew seeks to show that Christians have no inferior faith and that the blood of the new covenant is firmly related to the old covenant. Yet the new covenant provides a freedom of speech or boldness to enter the sanctuary and it is the blood of Jesus which provides this freedom (Heb 10:19-20). In this way the writer stresses the power of the death of Christ for the believer. One of the most serious things a Christian can do is to profane the blood of the covenant by trampling under foot the Son of God (Heb 10:29). Above all he is convinced that the sprinkled blood of Jesus "speaks better things than that of Abel" (Heb 12:24).

The Council of Jerusalem in the year 50 placed certain restrictions on the Gentile Christians and one of them was to "abstain from...blood" (Acts 15:20) out of respect for the Jews.

BLOODGUILT Bloodguilt is the inevitable liability caused by the shedding of human blood. Blood redeemer (or blood avenger) is the title given to the kinsman required by ancient law to avenge the blood shed.

According to the biblical concept, when human blood is shed by man it requires expiation: "whoever sheds man's blood, by man his blood shall be shed" (Gen 9:6). The importance of expiation is illustrated by such expressions as "The voice of your brother's blood cries out to me from the ground" (Gen 4:10) and in contrast to this, "his blood be upon his own head" (Josh 2:19; Ezek 33:4-5; cf Lev 20:9). If the incident goes unavenged, restitution falls upon the supreme avenger, God (Gen 9:5; Deut 32:43; II Kgs 9:7; Ezek 33:6).

However, the primary burden of revenge fell upon the blood redeemer or avenger, usually a close relative of the victim, who was lawfully authorized to slay one who murdered with malice aforethought (Num 35:20-25; Deut 19:11-13) or with a murderous instrument (Num 35:16-18). He thereby expiated the blood which was shed without himself acquiring bloodguilt (Num 35:27, 33). Several examples of blood redeemers are recorded in the Bible. These include Gideon (Judg 8:18-21); Joab (II Sam 3:27-30); the parable concerning Absalom (told by the Tekoite woman, II Sam 14:6-7); the Gibeonites (II Sam chap. 21); and Amaziah (II Kgs 14:5-6). However, uncontrolled blood-vengeance could lead to a blood feud, in which case counter-vengeance would continue until one kinship group was completely eradicated.

Blood redemption was not without limitations. According to the Mosaic ordinance six "cities of refuge" were to be set aside (Num 35:6, 12-13; Deut 4:41-43; Josh 20:4, 9) where an unintentional manslayer could seek refuge and be protected from the blood avenger. Haven was granted, on two conditions: that the killer was not found guilty of intentional murder, and that he remained within the boundaries of the city (Num 35:24-25; Deut 19:12; Josh 20:4-6). If he left the city of refuge, he was liable to be killed by the blood redeemer (Num 35:26-28).

In the case of an unknown killer, the bloodguilt fell upon the nearest city, probably on the assumption that the killer lived there (Deut 21:1-9). In this case, expiation was accomplished through the slaying of a heifer and a "confession" of innocence by the city's elders (Deut 3:3-7; cf the confession of Jehu, II Kgs 10:9). This communication of bloodguilt to a third party may also have been the basis for the release of the manslayer from the cities of refuge at the death of the high priest (Num 35:25-32).

A peculiar application of the principles of bloodguilt is seen in the laws governing the slaughter of sacrifices at illegitimate altars in Leviticus 17:4. Bloodguilt is also mentiuoned in connection with making a parapet for one's roof when building a new house so that no one would fall off the roof and thus bring bloodguilt upon the house owner (Deut 22:8), and the guarding of the city (Ezek 33:6; cf II Kgs 10:24).

The example of God's appointed blood avenger, Jehu, is instructive (I Kgs 19:16-17; II Kgs 9:7) in his excess of zeal, he was almost successful in eliminating both families of the rulers of Israel. According to Hosea 1:4-5 Jehu's cruelty brought upon the bloodguilt of Jezreel, therefore making Jehu bloodguilty himself. Bloodguilt was not incurred by homicide in self-defense (Ex 22:1), in war (I Kgs 2:5-6), or as a result of a court execution (Lev 20:9-16). However, bloodguilt may remain attached to both the manslayer and his family (II Sam 3:28ff) for generations (II Kgs 9:26). It even extends to his city (Jer 26:5), land (Deut 24:4) and nation (Deut 21:8).

BLOOD REDEEMER See BLOODGUILT

BOANERGES ("son of thunder"). A name bestowed on James and John because of their impetuousness (Mark 3:17). This is portrayed in Mark 9:38 when John tells Jesus that he and the disciples forbade someone who was casting out demons in Jesus' name to do so, because he "does not follow us". James and John are also named as those who sought to sit at Jesus' right and left hand in the Kingdom of God (Mark 10:35-40), an expression of their ambition.

BOANERGES
Mark 3:17

BOAR See ANIMALS

BOAZ A wealthy Bethlehemite landowner, related to Elimelech, husband of Naomi. After the death of Elimelech and his two sons in Moab, Naomi returned to Bethlehem with her widowed Moabite daughter-in-law Ruth. Ruth met Boaz in his field while exercising the right of the poor to gather the grain which falls to the ground during the harvest (cf Lev 19:9-10; 23:22). Boaz acted kindly toward Ruth and directed his servants to see that she took home barley beyond the amount of her legal entitlement (Ruth 2:15-16). When Ruth's brother-in-law refused to marry her (as required by law of levirate marriage cf Deut 25:5-10), Boaz agreed both to purchase the former landed estate of Elimelech and to marry Ruth so that the newly acquired field would remain in Elimelech's family. Ruth bore Boaz a son named Obed, who was to be grandfather of King David, and hence an ancestor of Jesus (Matt 1:5; Luke 3:32). See RUTH, BOOK OF.

BOAZ
Ruth 2:1, 3-5, 8, 11, 14-15, 19, 23; 3:2, 7; 4:1, 5, 8-9, 13, 21. I Kgs 7:21. I Chr 2:11-12. II Chr 3:17. Matt 1:5. Luke 3:32

BOCHERU ("firstborn"). The second of the six sons of Azel (I Chr 8:38), one of the descendants of Saul and Jonathan, in the genealogy of Benjamin.

BOCHERU
I Chr 8:38; 9:44

BOCHIM ("those who weep"). A place near Gilgal where the Angel of

BOCHIM
Judg 2:1, 5

Landscape in the Jordan Valley near Bochim.

the Lord rebuked the people (Judg 2:1) for failing to respect the covenant, following which the Children of Israel wept — hence the name of the place. It may have been close to present-day Bethel.

BOHAN ("thumb"). A boundary stone, "the stone of Bohan, the son of Reuben" (Josh 15:6; 18:17). It marked the border between the territories of Judah and Benjamin (Josh 15:5-7). Some scholars believe that there was no such person as Bohan son of Reuben and that the stone owed its name to its thumb shape.

BOOK OF LIFE, BOOK OF THE LIVING A heavenly record in which the names of the righteous are inscribed. The exact expression appears only once in the OT, in Psalms 69:28. Heavenly ledgers are referred or alluded to in many other passages of the OT (Is 65:6; Jer 17:13; 22:30; Mal 3:16; Ps 40:7; 87:6; 139:16; Job 13:26; Dan 7:10; 12:1; Neh 13:14), the Apocrypha and Pseudepigrapha (e.g. Jubilees 30:19-23; Enoch 47:3; 81:1ff; 97:6, 98ff; 103:2; 104:7; 108:3, 7; I Baruch 24:1), and the NT (e.g. Luke 10:20; Phil 4:3; Rev 22:19; Heb 12:23). In the NT inscription in the Book of Life comes to mean eternal salvation. The concept can be traced back to Mesopotamia where it was believed that the gods possessed tablets on which were recorded the deeds and destiny of men. One of these tablets is actually called the "Tablet of Life". Erasure from such a register is tantamount to death (cf Ex 32:32-33; Ps 69:29).

BOOK OF THE COVENANT The name, taken from Exodus 24:7, describes the earliest legal, moral and cultic corpus, found in Exodus 20:22-23:33. This literary complex can be divided into four major subdivisions: 20:22-26, cultic regulations; 21:2-22:17, legal prescriptions; 22:18-23:19, religious, moral and cultic instructions; and 23:20-33, epilogue. The legal section, 21:2-22:17 contains civil and criminal legislation on varied topics: male and female slaves, capital offenses, bodily injuries (including the laws of talion), goring ox, theft and burglary, grazing of animals and burning of fields, deposits and bailees, seduction. Many of the disparate individual prescriptions are linked together by the literary device of the association of key words and similar motifs.

Both in form and content, the legal portion of the Book of the Covenant shows great affinities to earlier cuneiform legal collections. As for content, analogues have been discerned relating to the thricefold maintenance requirement for a woman (Ex 21:10); to the equal division of assets and liabilities between two owners when one ox gores another to death (Ex 21:35-36; the laws of the goring ox in particular are paralleled in earlier Mesopotamian prescriptions); the laws of talion (Ex 21:23-25; first legislated in the legal collection of Hammurabi but restricted there to members of the upper class); the laws of assault and battery (Ex 21:18-19); the laws pertaining to injuries suffered by a pregnant woman which results either in a miscarriage or in her own death (Ex 21:22-23); and laws pertaining to the seduction of an unbetrothed girl (Ex 22:16-17).

Despite these affinities to earlier Near Eastern law, the Book of the Covenant is characterized by many distinguishing and unique features. The laws show great care and concern for the protection of the slave: his status is of a temporary state (Ex 21:2); his physical being is guarded against undue physical abuse and he is regarded as a human being in his own right (Ex 21:20, 26-27). Female slaves at times also share an equal rank with their male counterparts (Ex 21:20, 26-27, 32).

The laws relating to the goring ox also highlight major differences between the Bible value concepts and the philosophy of the cuneiform world. Whereas the latter's sole concern is economic, compensation for the victim's family, biblical law comprises an inherent religious evaluation. The ox itself is held liable; it is stoned, consumption of its flesh is prohibited, and its owner's execution is demanded. This unique prescription of the stoning of the ox and its taboo status presupposes the biblical concept of bloodguilt. An animal which takes a human life — endowed, according to the Bible, with the image of God — has committed a criminal act and is therefore objectively guilty and shall consequently be executed (Ex 21:29). Sacredness of human life is paramount in biblical corpora. Since life and property are incommensurable, and cannot be valued or interchanged, there is an absolute ban on composition (Ex 21:12). Vicarious talionic punishments found in the extra-biblical collection, are also prohibited (Ex 21:31).

The next section (Ex 22:18-23:19), consists of the following themes: laws against idolatrous customs, love and fellowship toward the indigent population; reverence toward God and the community's secular leader; prescriptions pertaining to the ritual; instructions applying to the practice of justice; and a cultic calendar. The concluding epilogue (Ex 23:20-33), contains the divine promise of protection during the future conquest of Canaan as long as Israel remains faithful to the entire corpus just presented to them.

An early date for this legislation is supported by its archaic vocabulary, its non-monarchic tribal polity; its reference to pastoral-agricultural (non-urban) society; the absence of all laws pertaining to commerce; the lack of any reference to courts and the fact that the civil and criminal laws are addressed to the injured party or the next of kin; the recognition of self-help; the absence of any reference to Israel as a body politic. All this points to an early pre-monarchial dating.

The "Book of the Covenant" found by King Josiah in II Kings chapter 23 is generally thought to have been the Book of Deuteronomy.

BOOK OF THE WARS OF THE LORD This lost book, which is mentioned only once in the OT (Num 21:14), was apparently a collection of war poems describing the victories of the Lord over the enemies of Israel. The poetic fragment found in verses 14-15 contains an obscure note which is very difficult to understand. The mention of the book confirms the fact that the older written documents (as well as oral traditions) were incorporated into Scripture. It is one of several literary works whose names are found in the Hebrew Bible but which have not been preserved.

BOOTHS, FEAST OF See TABERNACLES, FEAST OF

BOZEZ One of the two sharp rocks in the mountain pass traversed by Jonathan in order to slip into the garrison of the Philistines in Michmash. It was situated between Michmash and Gibeah (I Sam 14:2, 4-5).

BOZEZ
I Sam 14:4

BOZKATH (BOSCATH) The village of Jedidah wife of Amon and mother of Josiah king of Israel; probably the same town listed in the domain of the tribe of Judah (Josh 15:39), near Lachish.

BOZKATH
Josh 15:39.
II Kgs 22:1

BOZRAH

1. City of the kingdom of Edom, where Jobab the son of Zerah reigned (Gen 36:33); Amos predicted that the palaces of Bozrah would be destroyed by the fire sent by the Lord (Amos 1:12) to punish Edom. A similar fate is predicted by Isaiah (Is 34:6) and Jeremiah (Jer 49:13). Some scholars have suggested that the name Bozrah stands there for the whole of Edom because that town was one of the principal cities of the kingdom. It has been identified with Buseira, near Tafileh, east of the Jordan River. The site was recently excavated and large public buildings of the Iron Age were uncovered.

BOZRAH 1
Gen 36:33.
I Chr 1:44. Is 34:6; 63:1. Jer 49:13, 22.
Amos 1:12.

2. A city in Moab, perhaps an alternate name for Bezer No.1.

BOZRAH 2
Jer 48:24

General view of the excavations at the site of Bozrah in Edom.

Hebrew ostracon from Arad of the 10th-8th centuries B.C. in which a certain Eliashib is ordered to send flour.

BREAD AND BAKING The cultivation of corn in the ancient Near East dates back to Neolithic times. In the biblical period bread made of barley or wheat was a staple food. Wheaten bread was used in religious ceremonials (Ex 29:2) and at the king's court (cf I Kgs 4:22). Both barley (John 6:9, 13) and wheat were used in the preparation of bread in the Roman period. The shewbread was a bread offering placed in the sanctuary. On eating bread a special benediction was said (Matt 14:19, etc., and Jewish daily prayers). Bread was taken on long journeys (Mark 6:8; Luke 9:3) and was eaten at the Last Supper (Matt 26:26, etc.). Jesus called himself "the bread of life" (John 6:48-51).

The method of preparing and baking bread did not change much through the ages. The flour was mixed with water to make dough, which could be baked immediately after kneading to produce unleavened bread, or left for some time to rise with the addition of yeast. In biblical times loaves were baked by placing them on flat stones previously heated in an open fire, or in ovens made of clay. The ovens took the form of a truncated cone, with an opening at the bottom for stoking the fire. The prepared dough was stuck to the insides of the heated walls. Baking by either methods would result in very flat loaves, not more than an inch thick, which are frequently referred to in the Bible as cakes. Yet another method was the use of a flat bowl heated on an open fire. The flat loaves were placed on the upper (convex) side, which had small projections and cavities to facilitate their removal when ready. In the Hellenistic and Roman periods, as in more ancient times, bread was generally prepared by each housewife in the courtyard of her house.

Store pits at the bakery of the fortress of Masada. 1st century A.D.

Babylonian tablet inscribed with building instructions. 1800 B.C. (British Museum)

BROOM See PLANTS

BUILDING MATERIALS Palestine was a fairly heavily forested country (cf Josh 17:15; II Kgs 19:23, etc.). The ordinary people used the cheap local sycamore (I Kgs 10:27; Is 9:10), while palaces and the houses of the rich were built of timber brought from the Lebanon and Syria, areas rich in cedar and fir trees (I Kgs 5:8), or almug trees (a type of sandalwood, correctly called "algum") brought from Ophir (I Kgs 10:11). Timber was in fact relatively little used in Palestine.

As a great part of Palestine consists of rocky hills, stone was the most common building material. In Galilee basalt predominated, while on the coastal plain sandstone was much in use. Even a city as great and as important as Caesarea was built almost exclusively of this not very beautiful stone. In the hilly regions a harder limestone was available, of a quality which permitted the rough-hewn blocks to be polished and smoothed. Until the time of Solomon little ashlar was used; walls and houses, even temples and palaces, were built of rubble or roughly dressed stones.

The introduction of iron tools made stone-dressing easier. A good example of a wall built of dressed stones was found in Israelite Samaria. The stones were smoothed on three or four sides, leaving nicely polished margins and a projecting boss. At Israelite Megiddo a different system was employed. Ashlar pillars were incorporated at regular intervals in a rubble wall to give strength to the structure. The use of ashlar became more common from the Hellenistic period onwards.

In the Hellenistic period comparatively small stones were used for building, while in the early Roman period, especially in Herod's time,

Wall painting in the tomb of Rekhmire, Egypt, showing slaves making bricks and building a wall. 15th century B.C.

large blocks of up to 30 feet (9 m) in length were employed. The stones were highly polished along the edges, leaving either a very shallow boss or a projecting boss in the center.

With the invention of the arch in the early Roman period stone was also used in roofing. Granite and porphyry were imported from Egypt for columns and for facing floors and walls. It seems that marble was not imported into Palestine until the 2nd century A.D.

Brick was the most common and the cheapest building material. In the earliest periods mud was formed into irregularly shaped chunks, dried in the sun and used as bricks.

Bricks were produced by a simple method. A hole was dug in the ground and filled with water. The mud thus produced was then mixed with straw (cf Ex 5:7-13) and trodden until it became a thick pliable substance. At first this was shaped with the hands into bricks but later a a wooden mold was used, which gave greater uniformity. The newly made bricks were then laid out to dry in the sun. This quite primitive method was in use until the Roman period. The enormous building activity that began at that time necessitated a speedier method and the production of a much more durable brick suitable for the construction of bridges, aqueducts, large vaults and the like. It was then that the fired brick was invented, though it is possible that it was also known in the Iron Age. The Roman brick was considerably thinner than earlier ones and was square, rectangular, round or polygonal. Roof tiles were produced in the same manner, which made roofing cheaper.

Mortar, a mixture of lime, sand, ashes and water, was known in the Israelite period and was used for plastering cisterns and reservoirs to make them water-resistant. In the Roman period the quality of the mortar was greatly improved and it was used as a binding material in the construction of bridges, aqueducts, substructures of theaters, stadia, hippodromes, vaults, domes and so on. Plaster was also made much more durable and indeed reservoirs built and plastered in the Roman period still hold water today.

Philistine coffin lid shaped like a man, from Beth Shean.

BUKKI (a shortened form for Bukkiah).

BUKKI 1
Num 34:22

1. The prince of the tribe of the children of Dan, Bukki the son of Jogli (Num 34:22) was chosen to help Moses divide up the land of Canaan (Num 34:18).

BUKKI 2
I Chr 6:5, 51.
Ezra 7:4

2. The son of Abishua and the father of Uzzi in the priestly line of Aaron (I Chr 6:5, 51) and the forefather of Ezra (Ezra 7:4).

BUKKIAH
I Chr 25:4, 13

BUKKIAH A Levite, the first of Heman's 14 sons and the head of a division of singers in the time of David.

BUL
I Kgs 6:38

BUL The old Canaanite name of the eighth month of the year (I Kgs 6:38).

BULL See ANIMALS

BULLRUSH See PLANTS

BUNAH
I Chr 2:25

BUNAH Second son of Jerahmeel son of Hezron in the genealogy of Judah.

BUNNI

BUNNI 1
Neh 9:4

1. One of the Levites "who stood upon the stairs of the Levites" on the day of the great fast at the time of Ezra.

BUNNI 2
Neh 10:15

2. One of the leaders of the people who sealed the covenant at the time of Nehemiah.

BUNNI 3
Neh 11:15

3. The father of Hashabiah father of Azikram, a Levite listed among those who chose to dwell in Jerusalem in the time of Ezra (Neh 11:1, 15).

BURIAL The Bible is very explicit about the absolute necessity of proper burial. Among the severest forms of retribution is the lack of burial, and the prophets often curse sinful kings by predicting exposure of their bodies to wild animals (I Kgs 14:11; 16:4; 21:19, 24; II Kgs 9:10,

25-26, 33-37; Is 14:19-20; Jer 22:19). The proper mode of burial was in a family sepulcher; kings and common people hoped to be joined with their fathers in their grave. When a person died far from his domicile, bringing his body to interment in his family sepulcher was a most praiseworthy act (Gen 47:30; II Chr 25:28).

Despite the great importance of burial, the Bible supplies few details about the actual ceremony. In one case only is there a fairly detailed description: "And they buried him in his own tomb, which he had made for himself in the City of David... They made a very great burning for him" (II Chr 16:14). This description implies that the king's body was burned; the same custom is mentioned elsewhere (e.g. II Chr 21:19-20; Jer 34:5). It is not known whether this custom also prevailed among the common people.

Sarcophagus from Beth Shearim decorated with animal figures.

(right)
Façade of one of the catacombs in the necropolis at Beth Shearim, Galilee, dating from the 2nd to 4th centuries A.D.

According to the law of Moses, a corpse, a human bone and a grave are elements of ritual defilement, requiring purification rites for seven days (Num 19:14-16). Thus at no period did interment take place inside an Israelite settlement, with the exception of the burial sepulcher of the dynasty of David in Jerusalem. When a city expanded to include former extra-mural burial grounds, old burials were removed. This procedure was followed in Jerusalem in the 7th century B.C. and again in the Second Temple periods.

Archeological evidence on the whole bears out biblical testimony. The most common type of interment was a communal, apparently family, burial in a cave hewn out of rock. This often consisted of more than one chamber, each chamber encompassed with elevated rock benches upon which the deceased were temporarily placed. When this space was needed for fresh burials, the bones were collected and placed in a heap on the floor of the chamber or in a special pit or small chamber set aside for this purpose. Bone removal is a carry-over from Canaanite burial customs, as is the universally practiced custom of providing the dead with a rich collection of pottery vessels for food and drink, and various other objects such as pieces of jewelry, weapons and inscribed seals. Bone removal made it possible for a family sepulcher to house the remains of many successive generations. Nowhere is there evidence of cremation or fire in the numerous excavated burial caves of the First Temple period.

The custom of bench burial accompanied by bone removal continued with little modification after the return from the Babylonian Exile. A marked change in burial customs among Jewish families in Jerusalem and Judea occurred sometime during the Hasmonean period, around the year 100 B.C., when the bench burial caves were replaced by caves with loculi — long, narrow depressions in the walls. Each of these depressions (*kokhim* in Hebrew) was designed to house one body; it could be sealed with a well-fitting stone slab. A family sepulcher usually consisted of several chambers, each with several *kokhim* in its walls. The main entrance to the whole system of caves was closed by means of a large and heavy rolling stone. The sepulcher façade was often richly embellished with carved floral motifs, and looked out upon a spacious courtyard. This new type of burial cave, originating most probably in Alexandria in Egypt, eliminated the ungainly sight of decomposition. Here too the bones of each individual were collected after a period of one year, but instead of being placed in a communal pile, they were now stored in small individual stone boxes called ossuaries. These boxes were often decorated, and frequently carried the name of the deceased.

Numerous *kokhim* burial caves have been discovered, mainly around Jerusalem. The family sepulcher of Joseph of Arimathea, where Jesus was placed after the Crucifixion, must have been of this type (Matt 27:57-60).

BURNING BUSH A shrub in the desert from the midst of which God appeared to Moses (Ex 3:2-4). Although the bush was burning, miraculously it was not consumed. In Deuteronomy 33:16 God is referred to as the one "who dwelt in the bush". Early rabbinic and Christian traditions identify this bush with a type of thornbush or bramble, but this remains uncertain.

A trailing raspberry bush, which is believed to have grown from the original burning bush, in the courtyard of the Monastery of Santa Caterina in Sinai.

(left)
Mount Sinai with the Monastery of Santa Caterina in the foreground.

BUZ 1
Gen 22:21

BUZ 2
I Chr 5:14

BUZ 3
Jer 25:23

BUZI
Ezek 1:3

BUZITE
Job 32:2, 6

BUZ
1. The second son of Nahor, brother of Abraham, by his wife Milcah (Gen 22:20-21).
2. The head of a family or a clan of Gad dwelling in Bashan (I Chr 5:11, 14).
3. A place mentioned by Jeremiah together with Dedan and Tema.
BUZI Father of the prophet Ezekiel.
BUZITE A man of Buz; The father of Elihu was Barachel the Buzite.
BUZZARD See ANIMALS

C

CABBON A city included in the inheritance of the tribe of Judah (Josh 15:20, 40) when Joshua and Eleazar divided the land of Canaan among the Children of Israel (Josh 14:1). It was in the district of Lachish.

CABBON
Josh 15:40

CABUL Name of a city and a region located near the border of the land of Asher (Josh 19:27). The territory was given by King Solomon to King Hiram of Tyre (I Kgs 9:11-13) probably in payment for debts. It is identified with modern day Kabul, south of Acco. The site was recently excavated and proved to be an important Phoenician town.

CABUL
Josh 19:27.
I Kgs 9:13

Modern-day Kabul south of Acco, identified with biblical Cabul.

CAESAR The family name of the first Roman emperor Gaius Julius Caesar, which was retained by successive emperors as a title. The NT refers to the Roman emperors, Augustus, Tiberius and Claudius (Matt 22:17, 21; Mark 14:17; Luke 20:22-25).

CAESAR
Matt 22:17,
21. Mark
12:14, 17.
Luke 2:1; 3:1;
20:22, 25;
23:2. John
19:12, 15. Acts
11:28; 17:7;
25:8, 11-12,
21; 26:32;
27:24; 28:19

CAESAREA Ancient city on the Mediterranean coast of Palestine, capital of the Roman province of Judea for about 600 years. To distinguish it from other cities of the same name and founded at the same time, it was also called Caesarea Maritima, Caesarea Palaestina.

In the middle of the 3rd century B.C., the Phoenicians built a small fortified anchorage on the site which they called Strato's Tower (Straton being the Greek form of Abdashtart, the name of a Sidonian king). In 96 B.C. it was captured by the Hasmonean Alexander Janneus, and its first Jewish community was founded. After the Roman General Pompey conquered Palestine in 66 B.C. Strato's Tower became a non-Jewish city. Emperor Augustus returned it to Herod who built there an entirely new city in honor of the Emperor between 22 and 10 B.C. This became the seat of the Roman procurators of the province of Judea and also served as the headquarters of the Roman legions stationed in the province. Most of its inhabitants were Syrian Greeks but there was also

CAESAREA
Acts 8:40;
9:30; 10:1, 24;
11:11; 12:19;
18:22; 21:8,
16; 23:23;
25:1, 4, 6, 13

(right)
Aerial view of the Roman theater at Caesarea.

Capital of a column decorated with a menorah *(seven-branched candelabrum) from the synagogue at Caesarea.*

a considerable and economically strong Jewish community. Caesarea became the country's principal port and is mentioned in this connection in the Acts of the Apostles (9:30; 18:22; 21:8). It was reached by Philip the Evangelist and here Peter preached to Gentile listeners in the home of the centurion, Cornelius. Paul passed through Caesarea (Acts 18:22) and disciples from the city joined him on his journey to Jerusalem (Acts 21:16). As the residence of the Procurator, it was the scene of Paul's trial (Acts 23:23 ff). He was imprisoned there for two years (Acts 24:27), and from there he was taken in chains to Rome (Acts 27:1). Subsequently Caesarea was a famous church center and in the 3rd-4th centuries, the Church Fathers, Origen and Eusebius, taught in its school with its noted library. Out of this library came the edition of the Bible known as the *Hexapla.* Jerome says he saw the Hebrew original of Matthew's gospel there.

Roman statue found at Caesarea.

(left)
Roman columns in the sea at Caesarea.

Extensive excavations since the early 1950's have uncovered much of the ancient city. From Herodian times, the remains of the harbor have been examined, partly through underwater explorations. The finds from the Roman period include the temple of Augustus, a remarkably preserved theater (which has been restored and used for modern performances); the city wall, hippodrome and a paved square with impressive statues. Remains of a synagogue and churches have also been uncovered and the many inscriptions include the first known contemporary references to Pontius Pilate and to Nazareth.

CAESAREA
PHILIPPI
Matt 16:13.
Mark 8:27

CAESAREA PHILIPPI A city on the southern slope of the Hermon range, near one of the main sources of the River Jordan. The earliest mention of the city, under the name of Panion, is in Polybius, in his account of Antiochus III's victory over the Ptolemies (XVI, 18:2; XXVIII, 1:3). In the time of Zenodorus the region was called Panias. After his death Herod received the city from Augustus. His son Philip made it the capital of his tetrarchy and called it Caesarea, in honour either of Augustus or of Tiberius. To distinguish it from Caesarea Maritima and other cities, it is often called Caesarea Philippi. In Matthew (16:13) and Mark (8:27) it is mentioned as one of the cities visited by Jesus and his disciples. Here Peter confessed Jesus as the messiah (Mark 8:27-30).

Coin of Caesarea Philippi (Panias) with a portrait of Marcus Aurelius on one side and Pan on the other. A.D. 179

CAIAPHAS High priest from A.D. 18-36, son-in-law and successor of Annas. He belonged to the party of the Sadducees. John the Baptist's ministry took place under the priesthood of Annas and Caiaphas (Luke 3:2). It was at Caiaphas' palace that the priests and elders plotted to kill Jesus (Matt 26:3). At this meeting Caiaphas said that it was better for the Jews that one man die for the people, than that the whole nation be destroyed (John 11:50). According to Matthew (26:57), after his arrest Jesus was led to the house of Caiaphas, but according to John (18:12-24) he was first taken to Annas who sent him to Caiaphas. The latter, in turn, sent him to Pilate. Caiaphas presided over the Sanhedrin during the trial of Jesus.

CAIAPHAS
Matt 26:3, 57.
Luke 3:2. John
11:49; 18:13-
14, 24, 28.
Acts 4:6

Burial chamber under the Church of St. Peter in Gallicantu in Jerusalem, the traditional site of Caiaphas' palace. The chamber shown here is believed to have been the prison.

*(right)
Model of the house of Caiaphas, reconstructed on the basis of excavations conducted near Zion Gate in Jerusalem.*

Caiaphas was also a member of the court which called Peter and John to account for having cured a crippled man, and for preaching to the people in the Temple (Acts 4:6).

CAIN The eldest son of Adam and Eve, born after they were banished from the Garden of Eden. He was a tiller of the soil (Gen 4:2).

CAIN
Gen 4:1-3, 5-6,

Cain and Abel offering their sacrifices to God, as depicted on a 13th century stone relief, (Jacob's Chapel, Treasury of the Cathedral of Pistoia).

Cain and his brother Abel brought offerings to God; Cain of the first-fruits and Abel, a shepherd, of the firstlings of his flock (Gen 4:3-4). Without giving any reason, God accepted only the offering of Abel. Angered at this rejection, Cain killed his brother (Gen 4:8), for which he was subjected to a double curse: the ground would no longer yield to him its wealth (Gen 4:12), and he was condemned to be a "fugitive and a vagabond" on the earth for the rest of his life (Gen 4:12). The mark which God put on him (Gen 4:15) should not be understood as a punishment, but rather as a sign of protection.

Cain settled in the land of Nod (Gen 4:16), and married a woman who bore him a son named Enoch; Cain gave the same name to the city he built (Gen 4:17).

In the NT Cain is seen as the opponent of his righteous brother Abel, who brought a more excellent sacrifice (Heb 11:4); a symbol for an evil way of living (Jude v. 11) whose works were wicked (I John 3:12). As Abel was seen as a kind of prefiguration of Christ, some Church Fathers drew an analogy from the story of Cain and Abel, seeing them respectively as the Synagogue and the Church.

CAINAN

1. Son of Enosh who was Adam's grandson; he lived to age 910 and fathered several sons and daughters, including Mahalaleel.

2. Son of Arphaxad, and father of Shelah; he is listed in the genealogy of Jesus.

CALAH An Assyrian city. According to Genesis (10:11) it was built by Nimrod who also built Nineveh and the city of Rehoboth. Called Kalhu in Assyrian, the city was already in existence in the time of Hammurabi (second half of the 18th century B.C.). Ashurnasirpal attributes its "making" to Shalmaneser I (c. 1300 B.C.), which probably means that he rebuilt it and made it his capital. From that time onwards it served as one of the capitals of the kingdom along with the cities of Ashur and Nineveh.

Calah is situated at the junction of the river Great Zab and the river Tigris (Hiddekel) and is identified with Nimrud. The largest of the buildings was the ziggurat, which was built of bricks and lined with stone, and stood about 130 feet (40 m) high. Excavations at Nimrud uncovered the palaces of the Assyrian kings of the neo-Assyrian period. The palace walls were decorated with reliefs and paintings. The rooms

Ivory carving of the 8th century B.C. from Nimrud (Calah) representing a woman at the window.

contained many finds taken as spoil from Judah and Israel including a rich collection of ivories. Other important monuments found were the palace of Esarhaddon and the obelisk of Shalmaneser III. The city was surrounded by a wall strengthened with 108 towers, enclosing an area of more than 60 acres (24 ha).

CALAMUS See SPICES AND PERFUMES

CALCOL See CHALCOL

CALEB ("dog"; in Akkadian the cognate word is used as a metaphor for "loyal vassal of the king"). One of the 12 spies sent by Moses from Kadesh in the wilderness of Paran to scout the land of Canaan (Num 13:1-20). Caleb represented the tribe of Judah (Num 13:6). When the spies returned, Caleb advised an immediate conquest of Canaan (Num 13:30); his view was supported only by Joshua, the representative of the tribe of Ephraim (Num 14:6-8). The other ten spies argued, "We are not able to go up against the people, for they are stronger than we" (Num 13:31) and the Children of Israel determined that the best solution would be a return to Egypt (Num 14:4). As a result, it was decreed that all Israelites who at that time were aged 20 or more should be barred from entering the promised land, except for Caleb and Joshua (Num 14:29-30).

When Israel entered the land of Canaan 40 years later, Caleb requested and was granted by Joshua for himself and his descendants the city of Hebron as the reward for his faithfulness (Josh 14:6-14). Joshua 21:13 asserts, however, that Hebron was assigned as a Levitical city to the Kohathites. Joshua 21:9-12 and I Chronicles 6:54-56 resolve the contradiction by explaining that the city itself was given to the Kohathites while the surrounding villages were given to Caleb. Caleb dispossessed the giants — Sheshai, Ahiman, and Talmai — from Hebron (Josh 15:13-14). He promised the hand of his daughter Achsah in marriage to any Israelite who would conquer Debir, and Othniel son of Kenaz won the battle and the wife (Josh 15:17; Judg 1:12-13). Caleb gave the Negeb to Achsah (Josh 15:9; Judg 1:15) and a portion of that desert region was called the Negeb of Caleb (I Sam 30:14). In Numbers 32:12; Joshua 14:14 Caleb is called "the son of Jephunnah the Kenizzite" while according to Joshua 15:17; Judges 1:13 the brothers Caleb and Othniel are the sons of Kenaz. I Chronicles 2:18 lists Caleb as the son of Hezron the son of Perez, one of the twins born to Judah and Tamar (Gen 38:27-30; I Chr 2:4). According to I Chronicles 2:19 Caleb married Ephrath, who bore him a son named Hur. Hur appears also as a fourth name of the father of Caleb (I Chr 2:50). Caleb's concubines were Ephah (I Chr 2:46) and Maacah (I Chr 2:48).

CALEB EPHRATAH A place mentioned only once in the Bible as the scene of the death of Hezron, of the tribe of Judah (I Chr 2:24). The place has not been identified.

CALENDAR In the ancient world the Egyptians were alone in reckoning by solar time; the other nations of the ancient Near East all based their calendars on the cycles of the moon. At first the length of the month and of the year was fixed empirically, by the appearance of the new moon and its orbit during the month. To avoid the resultant irregularities months of a fixed length were ordained, with either 29 or 30 days each. The lunar year, with 354 days, lags behind the solar year, so that over a period the months shifted through all the seasons of the year. This system had a number of disadvantages which affected economic life as well as religious practice. In order to adjust the lunar to the solar year a system whereby an intercalary month was added was introduced in Babylonia in the 6th century B.C. On this basis there were three leap-years in a cycle of eight years. The Babylonian calendar was

Proto-Canaanite inscription bearing the name Caleb.

The Gezer Calendar, c. 950 B.C. An agricultural calendar found at Gezer, bearing the inscription reading: "Two months of ingathering. Two months of late sowing. A month of pulling flax. A month of barley harvest. A month when everything has been harvested. Two months of pruning [vines]. A month of summer fruit".

later adopted as the official calendar of the Persian empire and by the Jews in Palestine and Egypt.

In biblical times the Hebrew calendar was based on the lunar year and it may therefore be inferred that the Flood (cf Gen 7:11; 8:14) lasted 365 days (354+11). The Hebrew calendar, although based on the lunar year, was greatly influenced by the positions of the sun, as may be seen from the arrangement of the religious festivals. These fall on specific days of specific months of the lunar year, but they always fall in the same seasons of the solar year. The method by which this coordination between the lunar and the solar year was arrived at is still unknown. There is no direct reference in the Bible to a 13th (intercalary) month, the only possible hint of intercalation being the reference to a second Passover (Num 9:10ff). In fact it is not even known how the intercalation was effected in Babylon — whether by the addition of a fixed intercalary month or by the addition of days in a more haphazard way whenever the difference between the lunar and the solar years became too great. However, it seems that both in Babylon and in Palestine the adjustments were made quite arbitrarily. Intercalation was effected by the priests until after the destruction of the Second Temple, when it became the privilege of certain scholarly families such as that of Raban Gamaliel. Throughout the whole period of the Second Temple and in the centuries following its destruction the beginning of a new month was announced by beacons being lit on certain high mountains.

The year of the ancient Hebrews began in the fall. According to I Kings 12:32 it was celebrated in the Kingdom of Israel one month later than in the Kingdom of Judah. In Babylon, also, the civic New Year was

Sections of a Byzantine-period mosaic from Beth Shean, showing the months of the year and the agricultural activities with each season.

(right)
Two churches commemorating Jesus' first miracle at Cana. The one in the foreground is a Greek Orthodox church; the other is Franciscan.

General view of Cana, northeast of Nazareth.

celebrated in the fall, but alongside it was another, celebrated in the spring, which originated in Babylon and marked the beginning of the religious year. In Israel the religious calendar followed the cycle of the annual festivals, the first of the religious year being the Passover; the New Year therefore fell on the day of the new moon in the month of Nisan. It seems that a year which begins in the autumn is based on the needs of an agricultural society. Thus: "and the feast of Ingathering, which is at the end of the year, when you have gathered in the fruit of your labors from the field" (Ex 23:16). There is much evidence in the Bible to show that the Passover was considered to be the first feast in a cycle which terminated with the Feast of Tabernacles (cf Lev 23:5-36; Deut 16:1-16).

In the time of the Babylonian Exile the order of the months was fixed, Nisan, the month of spring, coming first, though the New Year was celebrated in Tishrei, the seventh month, in the fall.

In the Roman period the official reckoning of time in Judea followed the Julian calendar (devised in 47 B.C.). Caesar instituted a new solar calendar of 365¼ days, beginning on 1 January 47 B.C.

CALF See ANIMALS

CALNEH

1. A city in the kingdom of Nimrod the mighty hunter (Gen 10:9-10) in the "land of Shinar" (Gen 10:10). There is no mention of that city in any other text, and nothing is known about it. Some scholars believe it to be identical with Calneh No.2.

2. A city mentioned by Isaiah and Amos as a warning to the house of Israel (Is 10:9; Amos 6:2) not to be overconfident in the presence of the mighty kingdom of Assyria. From the biblical text it appears that this Calneh was in present-day northern Syria, in the vicinity of Arpad, but its present location is not known.

CALNO An alternate name for Calneh No.2.

CALVARY See GOLGOTHA

CAMEL See ANIMALS

CAMON The place where Jair, a man of Gilead who was judge over Israel for 22 years, died and was buried (Judg 10:3, 5). Located in northern Gilead but not yet identified.

CANA A village in Galilee 5 miles (8 km) south of Sepphoris. Scene of the first miracle of Jesus, the turning of water into wine in the course of the wedding at Cana (John 2:1, 11). It was also the site where Jesus

CALNEH 1
Gen 10:10

CALNEH 2
Amos 6:2.

CALNO
Is 10:9

CALVARY
Luke 23:33

CAMON
Judg 10:5

CANA
John 2:1, 11; 4:46; 21:2

healed a nobleman's sick son (John 4:46-54), and was the town of Nathanael (John 21:2). The place was little known but for the part it played in the early ministry of Jesus. In Byzantine and medieval times the place of the miracle was shown to pilgrims. Identified with Khirbet Qana.

CANAAN The ancient name for a region on the eastern coast of the Mediterranean Sea, strategically located between Egypt in the south and Mesopotamia in the north, and forming a land bridge connecting them. The term was used rather loosely, its geographical definition changing over various periods and its boundaries fluctuating according to the political situation at any given time.

In the earliest reference, in a 15th century B.C. written record from Mesopotamia, the name Canaan — Kinkha — refers to the Syrian coast, from the Gulf of Alexandretta in the north to the head of the Carmel Mountain range in the south. Other sources present different perceptions of the term, to include the city of Hazor in the upper Jordan Valley (Judg 4:2, 23-24); the coastal plain in general and the Jordan Valley (Num 13:29); or a much wider area including the entire coastal plain running south from Sidon to Gaza and from there eastwards to the southern part of the Dead Sea (Gen 10:19). The widest region falling

(left)
Canaan.

An early Proto-Canaanite inscription on a dagger found at Lachish.

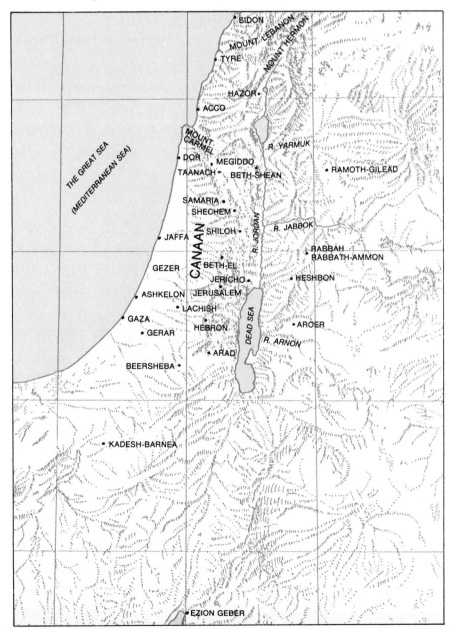

under the name Canaan is described in Numbers 34:2-13 and includes, in addition to the expanse between the Jordan River and the Mediterranean, parts of the Negeb and northern Sinai, areas east of the Sea of Galilee, as well as present-day Lebanon and southern and central Syria. It has been suggested that this area corresponds to the extent of Egyptian hegemony during the New Kingdom period. Egyptian written records of that time are likewise quite vague about the exact extent of Canaan, but they clearly specify what may be called southern Canaan with its capital city, referred to as "The Canaan" in Gaza.

The list of nations in Genesis chapter 10, in which Canaan appears as the youngest son of Ham, son of Noah, includes peoples known to have inhabited Canaan prior to the Israelite conquest, as well as names of cities in Phoenicia; the most important of the latter, Sidon, is referred to as Canaan's firstborn. This source thus expands the term Canaan to include both the Egyptian province of Canaan and the later Phoenician cities all the way up the Levantine coast.

After the Israelite conquest, the name Canaan was restricted to the coastal plain north of the Carmel range with the adjacent valleys (Josh 17:16). The coastal plain of Lebanon was not designated "Canaan", instead being named the Land of Sidon after its most important city. Nevertheless, up to the Hellenistic and Roman periods, the term "Canaan" was mentioned as the ancient name of the region, now called Phoenicia. Descendants of Phoenician settlers in North Africa referred to themselves as Canaanites up to the 2nd century A.D.

The name Canaan is related to the word Kinakhkhu — purple. The name Phoenicia, the Greek name for Canaan, likewise derives from the Greek word for purple — phonix.

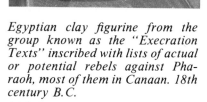

Egyptian clay figurine from the group known as the "Execration Texts" inscribed with lists of actual or potential rebels against Pharaoh, most of them in Canaan. 18th century B.C.

(right)
Canaanite jewelry.

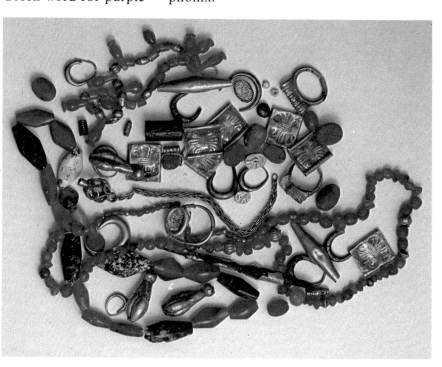

CANAANITES The inhabitants of the land of Canaan, who shared a common language, religion, material and culture; to some extent, they also experienced a common fate arising from their geographical position (See CANAAN, LAND OF). They never combined to form a political unity and were at all times fragmented into small political kingdoms, with changing frontiers as each sought to conquer land from the surrounding unit.

These internal struggles were enacted against a background of competition of the larger powers in the region, such as the conflict between the Babylonians and the Mitanni in the 15th-14th centuries and between Egypt and the Hittites in the 14th-13th centuries. Throughout Canaanite history, which spans the 3rd and 2nd millennia B.C., southern Canaan was strongly influenced by Egypt, while northern Canaan inclined more towards the influence of its northern neighbors, Mesopotamia in the first 1,500 years, the Hittite Empire from Anatolia in the latter three centuries. From early times, the Canaanite were a separate people — or rather, group of peoples — speaking a northwestern Semitic language. The strong Semitic character of their language emerges clearly in Egyptian texts from the 3rd Dynasty onwards, and in the rich collection of texts from Ebla in northern Syria.

The Canaanites included various Semitic peoples, such as the Phoenicians and the Amorites, as well as peoples of other origin, such as the Horites (Hurrians). They created a unique and mixed culture, manifested in both its spiritual and material aspects. They borrowed from their more powerful neighbors, but never succumbed to them, even when becoming part of their empires.

The whole region of the Canaanites was eventually shaken by political changes with the penetration of various Semitic tribes including the Edomites, Moabites, Ammonites, Philistines and Israelites (the last around 1200 B.C.). The Philistine and Israelite settlement effectively marks the conclusion of the Canaanite period although Canaanite culture remained in certain of the northern coastal cities such as Sidon and Tyre. The name Canaan came to be used only for the coastal strip of land, later called Phoenicia. Kings David and Solomon defeated the Canaanites, who soon lost their ethnic identity.

The early period of Israelite settlement was characterized by a tendency towards syncretism with the Canaanite religion to which the Israelites were attracted (e.g., Judg 2:2). The Bible frequently has to issue warnings against Canaanite worship and customs (Ex 23:23-24) and forbid relations with them (Deut 7:1ff). Their religion was characterized by numerous gods, loosely arranged in pairs.

The chief god El and his consort Asherah, parents of the gods, were replaced by the vigorous young god Baal who had no clearly specified wife. His sister Anath, although often referred to as a virgin, was also his wife. Baal was the god of storm and weather, and as such also cast his protection over vegetation and fertility. In practice the Canaanite religion was predominantly preoccupied with fertility, and its main myth centers around the kingship of Baal, initially wrested from the chaotic primeval water, and defended anew each year against drought and sterility. This myth, like others mentioning additional gods, has come to light mainly from the rich library discovered in the north Canaanite city of Ugarit (in Syria). This library also included other classes of text, such as legal and commercial documents, and heroic tales.

Knowledge of the Canaanites' material culture is largely confined to urban life. Their towns and cities were surrounded by defensive systems, at times free-standing walls built of stones or bricks, at others — in the first half of the 2nd millennium B.C. — massive earth ramparts which created an insurmountable slope around the settlement. The gates leading into the towns were particularly well protected with towers and guard rooms. These settlements lacked orderly planning and the inhabitants lived in poorly constructed houses. A few larger and better built houses have been found; presumably these were palaces of the local rulers. A necessary feature in every town seems to have been one or

Part of a wall painting depicting Canaanites paying tribute to Pharaoh Tutankhamon; 14th century B.C.

more temples; like the residences, they were rather crude in plan and mostly of poor construction.

The repertoire of household goods consisted to a large extent of typical pottery food vessels which served for storage, preparation, cooking and serving. The metal used by the Canaanites was initially copper, replaced later by bronze. Of the wooden furniture, the little that has survived indicates expertise in manufacture of low tables, stools and beds from wood and reeds. Glass came into use towards the end of the Canaanite period, and was considered a luxury material. Small glass objects were found mainly in temples and tombs.

The clothing adopted by the Canaanites is known mainly from Egyptian artistic representations. While the more nomadic classes, both men and women, wore multicolored wool dresses, the upper classes, mainly the merchants, enveloped themselves with a sari-like white cloth, often with colored fringes. Jewelry consisted of rings, earrings and bracelets, usually of bronze, but caches of very sophisticated gold jewelry with granulation and inlay have also been discovered.

Weapons too were forged of copper initially, and later, of bronze. Arrow heads, spear and javelin heads, daggers and swords of different shapes were most common. In the second half of the 2nd millennium the war chariot drawn by a pair of horses came into general use.

Ivory plaque from Megiddo depicting a victory celebration in the palace of a Canaanite king. 13th-12th century B.C. (Rockefeller Museum)

During some periods of their history, mainly in the second half of the 2nd millennium B.C., the Canaanites were actively involved in international trading with numerous parts of the eastern Mediterranean basin. They seem to have exported quantities of purple-dyed textiles, as their name indicates (See CANAAN); they also sold agricultural products such as cattle and oil. They imported metal and luxury goods, including numerous pottery vessels from Cyprus and Mycene which presumably contained some sought-after merchandise.

The Canaanites buried their dead communally in caves outside their settlements, supplying them with pottery vessels containing food and drink, and with other necessities such as furniture, weapons and jewelry. No attempt was made to preserve the body: on the contrary, the bones were scattered about the cave or heaped around the walls. In the first half of the 2nd millennium B.C. it became common to bury babies and young children in jars under floors of houses, a custom which reached its zenith in the 17th century B.C. before gradually declining. Individual burial of adults in pits outside settlements became general practice in the second half of the 2nd millennium B.C.

The Canaanites' greatest gift to the world is in the intellectual sphere — their invention of an alphabetic system of writing. The innovation occurred some time in the first half of the 2nd millennium B.C.; experiments in formalizing the shape of the characters went on for hundreds of years. Ugarit characters were based on the Mesopotamian cuneiform; in southern Canaan, letter shapes derived from Egyptian hieroglyphs. This south Canaanite script, succeeded by its immediate descendants — Hebrew, Phoenician and Aramaic — gave rise to all the alphabetic scripts used in the world today.

In prophetic and Wisdom literature, the word "Canaanite" is used to denote a merchant (e.g., Zephaniah 1:11 where the Hebrew "people of Canaan" is translated as "traders" in RSV) or as referring to Phoenicia (Is 8:10).

Panel from the chariot of Pharaoh Thutmosis IV depicting an Egyptian war against the Canaanites. End of the 15th century B.C.

CANDACE
Acts 8:27

CANDACE A title of the queen of Ethiopia (Acts 8:27). A eunuch of great authority under one of these candaces was baptized in the desert by the deacon Philip who was on his way back from Jerusalem to Gaza (Acts 8:26-38).

CANE See SPICES AND PERFUMES

CANNEH
Ezek 27:23

CANNEH A place mentioned by Ezekiel in his lamentation for Tyre (Ezek 27:2, 23). Its location is unknown and some scholars believe it to be an alternate name for Calneh No.2.

CANON The term canon refers to the authoritative collection of sacred writings acknowledged by a particular religious community.

The standard scholarly view of the history and question of the Jewish canon — of which there are various adaptations as well as numerous challenges — identifies the Torah or Pentateuch, i.e. the Five Books traditionally attributed to Moses (Genesis, Exodus, Leviticus, Numbers, Deuteronomy) as the first corpus to be accorded such authoritative status. In view of the stories about Ezra and the work attributed to him in the Books of Ezra and Nehemiah, the older consensus credited him with the promulgation of the Torah as the fundamental law and ultimate written authority of the Jewish community. The current view modifies that position slightly and specifies formal canonization of the Torah around 400 B.C.

The second grouping or section of the Hebrew Bible is called the Prophets and is divided into two formally equal parts of four books each: (a) Former Prophets: Joshua, Judges, (I and II) Samuel, (I and II) Kings; (b) Latter Prophets: Isaiah, Jeremiah, Ezekiel, and the Book of Twelve (Minor) Prophets.

The collection is rather artificially organized, since the Former Prophets are actually a continuation of the narrative begun in the Torah, while the Latter Prophets are a distinct literary grouping, containing primarily oracles and some biographical data about the prophets of the 8th to the 6th/5th centuries B.C. The process by which this collection of prophetic books was canonized is less clear and much debated, but a date around 200 B.C. is widely viewed as probable or at least plausible.

With regard to the remaining books of the Hebrew Bible, the Writings, it is widely believed that this end of the canon remained open well into the Greco-Roman period, the permanent boundaries or limits of the Hebrew canon not being firmly fixed until the rabbinical Council of Jamnia around A.D. 90. This collection included all the major poetical Books: Psalms, Proverbs and Job, as well as the five *megillot* or "rolls" (Ruth, Song of Songs, Ecclesiastes, Lamentations, and Esther), the Book of Daniel, and closing off the canon, the Books of Ezra-Nehemiah, followed in many codices by the Old Hebrew Book(s) of Chronicles.

In fixing the authoritative Palestinian canon, the rabbis ruled out books which had survived or were known only in Greek, and generally books of known or demonstrably late date. Thus books such as I and II Maccabees, Ecclesiasticus or Ben Sira, Judith and Tobit were excluded since the marks of late authorship were only too plain, whereas the

Book of Daniel, although roughly contemporary with some of the works mentioned, nevertheless was included and preserved in its Hebrew-Aramaic form because it was believed to be the work of a 6th-century B.C. prophet and therefore considered both authentically inspired and of early date.

The major differences between the Hebrew canon, and the Greek or so-called Alexandrian canon, involve the order of the books and their number. The Greek Bible (OT and Apocrypha only) is organized into four divisions rather than the three of the Hebrew Bible; in addition, a large number of books including some already mentioned and others (13 or 14 in all) were included in the Greek Bible though excluded from the Hebrew canon.

The divergence begins after the Torah. The Greek Bible follows with the historical books, including not only the books of the Former Prophets but others as well, such as Ruth (after Judges), the Chronicler's work (comprising, in addition to I and II Chronicles, a version of Ezra-Nehemiah and I and II Esdras), plus finally I and II Maccabees. These are followed by a collection of poetic and wisdom books, corresponding to the opening group of the writings in the Hebrew Bible, but including additional books such as Wisdom of Solomon, Ecclesiasticus, and others. The last section of the Greek Bible contains the books of the Latter Prophets and Daniel, the latter now promoted to equality with the rest of the prophetic literature.

The Greek Bible reflects the earlier canonical decisions made for the Hebrew Bible but clearly goes its own way both with regard to the order of the books and the limits of the canon. The Hebrew canon was clearly fixed not later than the end of the 1st century A.D., but in all likelihood the major components had already been in place for a long time. The Christian church, however, adopted the Greek canon, with its additional books and different order, and this has remained the official and canonical OT of the Catholic Church to the present-day, although the Apocrypha are often described as deutero-canonical to distinguish them from the books preserved in the original Hebrew (or Aramaic). The Protestant churches generally adopted the Hebrew canon for the OT, relegating the Apocrypha to secondary status and ultimately to no status at all.

While the actual process of canonization and its concluding decisions remain somewhat obscure, and the scholarly consensus survives only because nothing better has come along to explain and date the development, the formal decisions specify that canonical status is accorded to those books believed to bear the divine imprint. In practice this means that the authorship of the books was attributed by rabbinic tradition to authentic and attested prophets. Thus Moses, Israel's supreme lawgiver and prophet, as well as being the chief personality in Israel's formative period, was its historian and record-keeper as well. Other heroic and inspired figures contributed the books that bear their names, including Former and Latter Prophets. David and Solomon were credited with the major and some minor poetic and wisdom books, while Job was attributed to Moses. Ezra was credited with his own book, and in addition, with a major role in organizing the Chronicler's work as well as the rest of the Hebrew Bible. In terms of compilation, edition and publication, the Hebrew Bible was regarded as the work of the Great Assembly associated with Ezra in the latter part of the 5th century B.C.

It is generally accepted today that the books achieved their present form by a literary process, including prior and primary sources, the selections, arrangement, modification and adaptation of materials to create a literary work — a process involving persons and events over a period of time, until the point when the process effectively came to a stop, and a final form was imposed. Henceforth, one can speak of textual history as the book is copied and transmitted, the only changes being made by scribes. Canonicity refers to the point of transition from literary to textual history, when a certain version of the text is stamped with the imprimatur of an established authority and the book is given fixed and permanent status.

In looking at the finished literary product it is clear that neither arrangement of the books of the Bible adequately reflects the real connections and continuities present in the collection. Thus the largest single literary entity is the great narrative comprising the Torah and the Former Prophets of the Hebrew Bible. This work constitutes half of the Hebrew Bible and comprises the central, basic and core material — the main story on and around which everything else turns and depends. No one could claim this literary work to have been a single unified composition, but it has been edited to link each book to the next, to produce a narrative covering the people of Israel from the very beginning of time to the end of the dual Kingdom. This account records the demise of the Southern Kingdom (586 B.C.) and could neither have been written before the last recorded and dated event (c. 560 B.C., King Jehoiachin's release from prison in Babylon, II Kings 25:27-30), nor much beyond it. With the appearance of the Persian King Cyrus, his conquest of the moribund Babylonian empire, and the edict allowing and encouraging the Jewish captives to return home, a new chapter in the nation's annals could be written; this would require a revisionist approach to the antecedent history of the kingdom, as well as dramatic readjustments about the historical present and anticipated future of the people. The final editor of the Primary History must have compiled his account and completed his task in the years before the conquest of Babylon (560-540 B.C.). One can consequently speak of a major literary piece, the Primary History, as the first of the great canonical works contributing to the formation of the Hebrew Bible. Ezra, or a group of people from about that time, extracted the Torah books from this larger work thereby elevating the status of Torah to a level even higher than before and establishing Moses as the central figure of biblical religion. In laying the emphasis on Moses and his experience, this division also played down the monarchy and the traditions concerning David and his notable victories, which could have been a potentially dangerous theme for the Judean exiles in the post-exilic circumstances. This separation and shift in emphasis from David to Moses did not harm the status or prestige of either, but rather left the narrative both complete and intact, only divided in rank and importance.

It is essential to the argument that the text of the Primary History remained unchanged and intact even with the passage of time and the radical alterations in the experiences of the exilic community. For the sequel and aftermath of the events recorded in Kings, one must turn to an entirely different work, that of the Chronicler, a composite creation edited after the dramatic change in circumstances occasioned by the edict of Cyrus (539 B.C.). The power of canonicity was being affirmed even as questions arose about the scope of the canon. In Ezra at least the Torah was central and authoritative, mainly a codified law code, while the narrative emphasis of the Former Prophets (and e.g. in the Book of Genesis and elsewhere in the Pentateuch) was relegated to a secondary position.

The next unit of the Hebrew Bible, the Latter Prophets, revolves around the central themes of the decline and fall of the nation, and the imminent demise of Jerusalem and its Temple. In part this collection coincides with, and elaborates upon, the Primary History, especially the last few chapters of II Kings. Where the historical narrative is brief, laconic, and essentially a chronicle derived from chancellery archives, the prophetic literature is expansive, emotional and directly discursive. Jeremiah was the prophet on the scene when Jerusalem fell, while Ezekiel was in Babylon viewing the crisis from afar. These prophets offer eyewitness accounts of the central event and crowning tragedy of Israel's experience.

The remaining books of the prophetic corpus provide background and framework for this denouement, beginning with the terrible and terrifying events of the 8th century, which overshadowed the following 100 years or more and presaged the tragedy which was to come. In like manner, the prophets of the 8th century (Amos, Isaiah, Hosea and Micah) established the role and the message to kings, priests and commoners that could be echoed, amplified and adapted by the great prophets of the 7th and 6th centuries.

One can speak therefore of an original collection or canon of authoritative writings compiled and sponsored by the leaders of the Jewish community in the Babylonian Exile. This collection would have comprised the Primary History, Jeremiah, Ezekiel, and no doubt First Isaiah, ending with the account drawn from II Kings of the critical days of the siege of Jerusalem in the 14th year of Hezekiah's reign (701). Most of the Major Prophets would also have been included, with the clear exception of Haggai and Zechariah, and possibly others such as Malachi, and perhaps Jonah and Joel.

No doubt other materials, now found in the third part of the canon, were included as well, thus the tripartite division of the canon was established at an early stage. Much, if not most, of the Psalter would have been available; the same holds for Proverbs. Of other books, Ruth and Lamentations would have been extant, and Lamentations would have made a fitting adjunct and companion piece for the narrative account and the prophetic elaboration of the fall of Jerusalem.

In addition to all of this, however, the prophetic collection contained oracles of hope and restoration as well as the ominous messages of menace and doom which accompanied the earlier crises. This material, including the works of Haggai, Zechariah, II Isaiah, and others, extended the scope of the corpus past the limits of the Primary History into the Exile and beyond, to the moment of restoration and renewal, the return of the exiles and rebuilding of the Temple, into the reign of Darius I of the Persian empire.

This expanded picture is reflected in the Chronicler's work, which likewise reports the rebuilding and rededication of the Temple in post-exilic times. The fortunes, vicissitudes and destiny of Judah, Jerusalem, the Temple and the royal house, described in I and II Chronicles, come to a climax and happy conclusion with Ezra chapter 6. The Book of Ezra continues the story of II Chronicles down to the completion and consecration of the Temple in the sixth year of Darius (c. 516/15 B.C.), also being correlated with the books and reports of Haggai-Zechariah.

Beginning in 539 B.C. with the edict of Cyrus I permitting and encouraging the Jewish exiles to return to their homeland, and continuing until the rebuilding and rededication of the Temple, the new developments required acknowledgment and recognition, essentially a rewrite and revision of the whole story in the light of the great turn-around. This development, anticipated by the prophets, was now confirmed by events. New prophetic figures and utterances were added to the canonical collection, and a new account of Judah's history, parallel but distinctive, was provided as an alternative version of the basic narrative.

The next, penultimate, stage in the enhancement and extension of the canon, can be associated with the great coordinators and consolidators of the tradition, Ezra and Nehemiah. Ezra or Nehemiah or perhaps both can be credited in slightly different ways with the completion in its present form of the Chronicler's work, by the supplementation of personal memoirs of the overlapping and intersecting events which brings the biblical story to a climax, and at least temporary conclusion. Israel is back on its land, the city of Jerusalem has been rebuilt with walls and gates, and the people have the laws of God as a constitution by which to live. If it is not quite like the halcyon days of David and Solomon, at least the people are at peace, the Persian empire is firmly in control of the world and the future holds promise.

As for the canon of the Hebrew Bible, it would seem to be practically complete. We must credit Ezra with the separation of the Torah as the fundamental and ultimate law of the people of Judah and of Judaism from that time forth. The consolidation and completion of the prophetic corpus was also achieved by this time, with the incorporation of the historical books from Joshua to Kings, left over when the Pentateuch was identified. The latter prophets may already have been completed in the days of Haggai and Zechariah, but it is possible that Malachi, otherwise somewhat mystifying, and perhaps the final chapters of Zechariah (9-14), came later. The third section too would now be practically complete, including all the books previously mentioned and the present version of Chronicler-Ezra-Nehemiah. It is difficult to make decisions about marginal books such as Ecclesiastes and Esther, or even Job, but there is little or no reason to date any of them later than the Persian period. The only clear and certain exception is the Book of Daniel, which in its present form must come from the Greek period (165 B.C. in the opinion of most scholars). Since none of the other books deriving from this period, such as the Books of the Maccabees, the Esdras and Enoch literature, Ecclesiasticus and some other materials, is included in the Hebrew canon, evidently the latter at least was effectively fixed, although not closed. The Book of Daniel is a special case because it was presented and understood as a product of the Babylonian-Persian period just as its hero was a leading figure in the Babylonian Exile.

In the NT, canon referred to five times (II Cor 10:13, 15-16; Gal 6:16; Phil 3:16), denotes "sphere" or "rule" and could be rendered as "guideline." It was quite natural for the early church to apply this word to the consensus it reached about which books to be treated as authoritative and which discarded. That process began with the oral tradition and reached a decisive point at the Council of Carthage (397) when the present selection of NT books was largely agreed upon.

During the intervening centuries many forces were at work. The criteria that emerged in this selection process were: apostolicity, accordance with received teaching, and wide usage in the church. They did not include inspiration, at least not directly. The fundamental criterion was apostolicity — i.e. proximity to the apostolic age or to the Christ event so that a certain degree of authenticity could be posited. Sometimes it expressed itself in the question of authorship: when as in the case of the Epistle to the Hebrews, a work was attributed to an apostle, its way into the canonical collection was easier. On the other hand Luke-Acts, although not authored by an apostle, were considered apostolic and therefore never seriously questioned. Other works encountered objections because they struck a chord which ran counter to the ethos of the early church, e.g. Philemon had great difficulty, not only because the book advocated leniency for runaway slaves but also because it was written to one person and not to a whole congregation; as a personal letter, it could be disqualified, but in the end bore such clear marks of authenticity that the early church adopted it into its canon. A different set of criteria was invoked in the case of a work like the Book of Revelation. Only part of the church was attracted to apocalyptic genre of literature; others, perhaps seeing it as a remnant of Judaism which they might jettison, favored deleting it from the list, which they achieved by allowing it to fall into disuse. Finally, however, large sections of the church drew sustenance from apocalyptic literature and some form of the latter was included. In addition to the selection of entire books, sections of books were also subjected to canonical criticism. For example, the *pericope de adultera* (John 8:1-11), while not represented in the manuscript tradition of the fourth gospel before the fourth century, was found in other manuscripts and attributed to other gospel writers or regarded as a disembodied morsel of gospel tradition. Modern scholars are inclined to accept it as a genuine fragment while at the same time rejecting its connection with the Johannine community. Indeed it seems to have been accepted by communities which practiced leniency towards adulterers and rejected by those who took a hard line. Another factor in the selection process was, without doubt, the prestige of the community which backed it. Any document connected with Rome or Antioch, or supported by these two centers of influence, could be assured of a place in the canon: books like II Peter or Jude, though of relatively little intrinsic value, had connections sufficiently strong to gain a place in a collection of authoritative writings.

The earliest canonical list was the Canon Muratori, dated around A.D. 180, which has almost all of our present books. It was perhaps a response to the efforts of Marcion to establish a canon according to his highly idiosyncratic value system. He sought to excise all materials which were Jewish and thus to develop a uniquely Christian God separate from the God of Judaism. Important as his endeavors were in early Christian attempts to formulate a normative position, Marcion's approach was clearly rejected by the church, even though many of its writers and leaders had a limited appreciation of the relation between Judaism and Christianity. Though yet to formulate fully what they wanted to retain from Judaism or how the two sister religions related to each other, they were united in rejecting Marcion's solution.

The Gnostic approach was similar to Marcion, for Gnostics tended to develop their own literature to strengthen their interpretation of Christianity. Thus they constructed what they called a Gospel of Truth. Again the church as a whole decisively rejected more extreme Gnosticism and its vast body of literature, preferring the literature found in the received canonical corpus.

From the standpoint of the history of the nascent church an acquaintance with the canonical selection process is indispensable. Likewise the literature which hovered at the edges of the canonical process is of inestimable value in determining what the early Christians read for their entertainment and moral inspiration, and what in the last analysis the powers of the church rejected.

CANTICLES See SONG OF SOLOMON

CAPERNAUM A town on the western shore of the Sea of Galilee, on the highway from the Mediterranean coast to Damascus, with a small port for its population of fishermen. The town is known from the early Roman period onwards.

Capernaum is one of the places most frequently mentioned in the

CAPERNAUM
**Matt 4:13;
8:5; 11:23;
17:24. Mark
1:21; 2:1; 9:33.
Luke 4:23, 31;**

7:1; 10:15.
John 2:12;
4:46; 6:17, 24,
59

gospels. Jesus went there, to the borders of the territories of Zebulun and Naphtali, from Nazareth (Matt 4:13) and there found his first disciples, Peter, Andrew and the two sons of Zebedee (Matt 4:18-22). He taught there in the synagogue (John 6:24-59) and directed Peter to find a coin in the mouth of a fish with which to pay the tax-gatherers (Matt 17:24-27). He also lodged there in Peter's house, healing the sick and teaching (Mark 1:21, 29-34; 2:1-12; Luke 4:31, 38-41). Leaving Capernaum he condemned it along with other cities that had not heeded his calls to repentance (Matt 11:23; Luke 10:15).

In later Jewish sources Capernaum is referred to as a seat of *minim,* or sectarians, perhaps referring to the time of Jesus. In the 4th century A.D. the city had an almost exclusively Jewish population. The first Christian community gathered there c. A.D. 352 round the convert Joseph, and built a church on the site of Peter's house.

Excavations have uncovered the synagogue which is the most elaborate of the early type, found mostly in Galilee. The building is orientated north-south, stands on a podium and is built of nicely cut limestone, in contrast to the black basalt houses round about. Built to a height of two storeys, it is 65 feet (20 m) long and has an atrium on the east. Three doors lead into the synagogue proper, which is divided into a broad nave and two narrow aisles by rows of columns. Another row of columns facing the entrance connects the two longitudinal rows. Along the aisles are stone benches and there is no fixed position for the Torah shrine. The synagogue is distinguished for its richly carved stone ornamentation, which depicts stylized plants, fruits, geometric motifs, animals and even mythological figures. The style of architecture, the decoration and two dedicatory inscriptions in Aramaic and Greek point to a general dating between the end of the 2nd and the beginning of the 3rd century A.D.

Details of columns with Corinthian capitals from Capernaum synagogue.

(left)
Reconstructed synagogue at Capernaum.

Detail of carved stone ornamentation at Capernaum synagogue depicting a bunch of grapes and a five-pointed star.

To the Byzantine period belongs an octagonal church with a multicolored mosaic floor, supposedly standing on the site of Peter's house. Excavations beneath this church have revealed houses dating to the 1st century A.D. which were used as a cult place in the 2nd and 3rd centuries. The excavators believe that one of these houses was that of Peter, near which the first Jewish synagogue, mentioned in the gospels, was built.

Excavations at the village of the Roman and Byzantine periods, east of the synagogue at Capernaum.

(bottom right)
Wall painting of an acrobat or bull-fighter from Knossos, Crete.

Detail of a wall painting from Knossos, Crete, known as "The Prince". 1700-1400 B.C. (Heraklion Museum).

CAPHTOR, CAPHTORIM Place of origin of the Philistines (Jer 47:4; Amos 9:7). According to Genesis 10:4, the Caphtorim were the descendants of Ham, son of Noah, and they destroyed the Avim and lived in their place (Deut 2:23). There is clear evidence connecting the culture of Crete with that of the Philistines. Indeed in the Bible the Philistines are sometimes mentioned in conjunction with the Cherethites. Caphtor is also mentioned in the documents of Mari and Ugarit and many scholars tend for these reasons to identify Caphtor with Crete. Others prefer to identify it with the Keptiu of the Egyptian sources, a people who dwelt in Cilicia (Asia Minor).

CAPHTOR, CAPHTORIM
Gen 10:14.
Deut 2:23. I
Chr 1:12. Jer
47:4. Amos 9:7

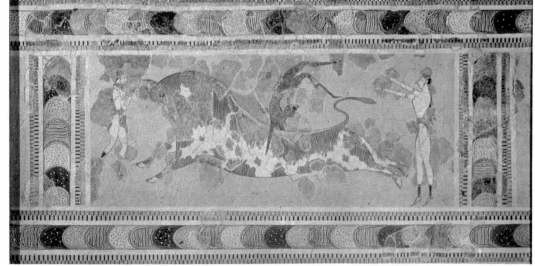

CAPPADOCIA
Acts 2:9.
I Pet 1:1

CAPPADOCIA A region in Asia Minor, which became a Roman province under Tiberius. The first epistle of the apostle Peter, addressed to the Christian communities of Cappadocia seems to have had its own language or dialect (Acts 2:8-9). A Jewish community lived there from the 2nd century B.C. (I Macc 15:22).

A coin of Caesarea-in-Cappadocia, depicting Mount Argaeus. 2nd century A.D.

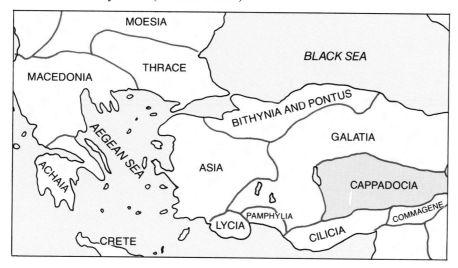

CARCAS
Est 1:10

CARCAS One of the seven eunuchs in attendance at the court of King Ahasuerus (See ABAGTHA).

CARCHEMISH
II Chr 35:20.
Is 10:9. Jer
46:2

CARCHEMISH An important Hittite city on the right bank of the Euphrates in northern Syria, identified with Jarablus. It is mentioned among the cities conquered by Thutmosis III. In the days of Rameses II it took part in the battle of Kadesh-on-the-Orontes. Tiglath-Pileser I devastated the city which was later conquered by Assur-Nasir-Pal II, who imposed a heavy tribute on it, as did Shalmaneser III. In the days of Sargon II the city attempted to free itself, but failed. Its citizens were deported and others were brought in to replace them (717 B.C.). Despite its subjection to Assyria, Carchemish was an important trading center. The Assyrians turned Carchemish into the capital of a province. In the days of Josiah, king of Judah, Pharaoh Necho came to Carchemish to help the Assyrians (II Chr 35:20ff), but four years later (605 B.C.) he was defeated by Nebuchadnezzar near the walls of the city (Jer 46:2), in a battle which decided the fate of western Asia.

CAREAH
II Kgs 25:23

CAREAH An alternate form of Kareah used in II Kings 25:23: "Johanan the son of Careah". (See JOHANAN; KAREAH).

CARMEL, MOUNT
Josh 12:22;
19:26. I Kgs
18:19-20, 42.
II Kgs 2:25;
4:25. II Chr
26:10. Song
7:5. Is 33:9;
35:2. Jer
46:18; 50:19.
Amos 1:2; 9:3.
Mic 7:14. Nah
1:4

CARMEL, MOUNT A mountain range, the northwestern continuation of the hills of Samaria, rising to 1,650 feet (500 m) above sea level. Carmel formed the southern limit of the territory of Asher (Josh 19:26) and the southwestern border of the Valley of Esdraelon (Jezreel) (I Kgs 18:42-46). The river Kishon flows at its foot (I Kgs 18:40). Falling steeply to the Mediterranean, it leaves only a narrow coastal plain (Jer 46:18) and its canyon-like cliffs are dotted with numerous caves, some of which served as dwellings in prehistoric times. Most of Carmel is covered with a thick deposit of good soil and abundant vegetation. It was noted as a symbol of beauty (Is 33:9; Song 7:5) and compared with Lebanon and Bashan (Is 29:17; 32:15; Jer 50:19). An altar to Baal was set up at the top of the mountain and it was here that Elijah confounded the prophets of Baal (I Kgs 18:17-46). Elisha dwelt there for some time (II Kgs 4:25).

The sanctity of Mount Carmel was still preserved in the Hellenistic period when a temple of Zeus stood on the mountain. There was also an altar and an oracle there, and a fragmentary inscription found on the mountain mentions a cult of Zeus Heiopolitanus. Christian tradition

Detail of a Hittite bas-relief from Carchemish depicting a trumpeter. 9th-8th centuries B.C. (Hittite Museum, Ankara)

(top left)
Cappadocia.

Cave on Mount Carmel.

(right)
View of Mount Carmel.

places the site of the altar of Baal at the southeastern extremity of the mountain.

CARMEL, CARMELITE, CARMELITESS A town in the hills of Judah (Josh 15:55) where Saul set up a monument after his victory over Amalek (I Sam 15:12). Nabal was shearing his sheep in Carmel when David's messengers arrived and his wife Abigail, a native of the town, went out from there to appease David (I Sam 25:2 ff; 27:3). It was also the birthplace of Hezro, one of David's "mighty men" (II Sam 23:35).

CARMEL,
CARMELITE,
CARMELITESS
Josh 15:55.
I Sam 15:12;
25:2, 5, 7, 40;
27:3; 30:5.
II Sam 2:2;
3:3; 23:35.
I Chr 3:1;
11:37

View of the remains of Carmel in the Judean Hills, south of Hebron.

CARMI
1. The fourth son of Reuben (Gen 46:9) who went with his father to Egypt (Gen 46:8) and was the ancestor of the Carmite family (Num 26:6) according to the census taken by Moses (Num 26:1-2).

2. One of the sons of Judah (I Chr 4:1) father of Achar or Achan, the "troubler of Israel" (I Chr 2:7). (See ACHAR, ACHAN).

CARMITES From the family of Carmi No.1.

CARPUS ("fruit"). An individual from Troas (Acts 16:8-11; 20:6-12) mentioned in II Timothy 4:13 with whom Paul had left a cloak, which he asked Timothy to bring to him.

CARSHENA One of the seven princes of provinces of Persia and Media "who ranked highest in the kingdom". Consulted by Ahasuerus when Queen Vashti defied the royal command to appear before him.

CARMI 1
Gen 46:9. Ex
6:14. Num
26:6. I Chr 5:3

CARMI 2
Josh 7:1, 18.
I Chr 2:7; 4:1

CARMITES
Num 26:6

CARPUS
II Tim 4:13

CARSHENA
Est 1:14

CASIPHIA One of the cities where the children of Judah dwelled in Babylonia. When Ezra sought Levites to be servants of the Temple (Ezra 8:15), he sent messengers to Iddo "the chief man at the place Casiphia", to ask for "servants for the house of our God" (Ezra 8:17). Its location is unknown, but it was probably in southern Mesopotamia.

CASLUHIM One of the sons of Mizraim (Egypt), son of Ham, the second of Noah's sons (Gen 10:1, 6, 14), who is considered the father of the Philistines (Gen 10:14). The name is obscure and there is no satisfactory identification with any of the known ancient peoples.

CASSIA See SPICES AND PERFUMES

CATERPILLAR See ANIMALS

CEDAR See PLANTS

CENCHREAE An Aegean port 7 miles (11 km) east of Corinth. Paul, journeying from Corinth to Ephesus, shaved his head at Cenchreae in observance of a vow (Acts 18:18). A deaconness, Phoebe (Rom 16:1), was from the church at Cenchreae.

CENSUS The counting or enrolling of people for the purpose of taxation or for conscription in preparation for war. The practice of census taking is documented in the Mari documents where periodic censuses are taken of the various tribes. The purpose was for military conscription, taxation and land distribution, and was accompanied by a purification ritual similar to the one recorded of the census of the Israelites in the wilderness.

Three times in the OT a major census is taken in order to ascertain the manpower available for war, and twice taxation is the basis for the census. A census is mentioned twice in the NT, both in Luke-Acts.

In Numbers God orders Moses to take a census of the people while they are in the wilderness of Sinai. The people are to be numbered by tribe and every male 20 years and older who is "able to go forth to war" is to be counted. The twelve tribes are numbered, yielding a total of 603,550 eligible males. This figure does not include the tribe of Levi which has been replaced by Manasseh in the list of twelve tribes and which is not to be numbered along with the twelve tribes in preparation for war (Num 1:47). Rather, members of the tribe of Levi a month and older are to be numbered separately (Num 3:15-16) and their war-time tasks include the carrying, defending and guarding of the tabernacle (Num 1:50-51, 54). When the Levites are finally numbered, they total 22,000 (Num 3:39) or 22,273 (Num 3:43) or 20,200 (based on a summation of figures for individual clans in Numbers chap. 3).

Again in Numbers chapter 26 all males "twenty years old and upward" are to be numbered. This counting is done in preparation for war (Num 26:2) and for the allotment of inheritance (Num 26:53). The males of the twelve tribes total 601,730 (Num 26:51), and the Levites number 23,000 (Num 26:62).

At the end of David's reign another census is taken (II Sam 24:1ff; I Chr 21:1-22). David instructs Joab and the commanders of the army to count "all the tribes of Israel from Dan to Beersheba." Joab warns David not to take the census (II Sam 24:3), but David refuses to listen. After the census is taken David realizes he has sinned (II Sam 24:10). He appeals to God who, responding through the prophet Gad, offers David three choices of punishment (II Sam 24:12-15). David opts for the pestilence which causes 70,000 deaths, but God "relented from the destruction" and spared Jerusalem (II Sam 24:16). David then buys a "threshing floor" from Araunah the Jebusite (II Sam 24:18-25) (Ornan; I Chr 21:18), builds an altar and offers sacrifice to God, and God responds by removing the plague (II Sam 24:25). There are three things to note about the account in II Samuel and its parallel in I Chronicles.

The first item is the precipitating cause of the census. In II Samuel 24:1 God is angry at David and causes David to take the census. In I Chronicles 21:1 it is Satan who causes David to take the census. This shift from the pre-exilic perspective of the Deuteronomic historian to the post-exilic writings of the Chronicler reflects the growing theological reluctance among the post-exilic community to accept the concept of God as causing evil — a semi-autonomous source of evil was needed. The second difficulty with this pair of passages is the reaction of Joab to the census. No reason is provided as to why Joab should object or why David should feel remorse for taking the census. The best explanation (suggested by Josephus), derives from Exodus 30:11-16, where it is said that each person must pay a shekel tax when counted in order to avoid the coming of a plague. David's omission of the tax would then be the reason for the plague. Another suggestion, based on Exodus 32:32-33, is that only God can record names. A third item to note about these two passages is the discrepancy in the numbers. In II Samuel a total of 1,300,000 men of arms are counted (II Sam 24:9). However in I Chronicles the number is 1,570,000 (I Chr 21:5). Many attempts have been made to reconcile this discrepancy, none of which is totally acceptable.

Exodus 30:11-16 is one of the passages where taxation seems to be the prominent motive for the census. One-half shekel is to go to the sanctuary and one-half as an offering to God. In Numbers 3:40-51 not only is a census taken and the people taxed, but in addition, the Levites are taken into the service of God instead of the offering of the firstborn of the people. The firstborn male children, more than one month old, total 22,273 (Num 3:43); and five shekels are to be paid for each firstborn over and above the number of male Levites. Thus a total of 1,365 shekels, measured by the standard of "shekels of the sanctuary" were paid to Aaron and his sons (Num 3:50-51).

In the NT the first reference to a census, and by far the most difficult and controversial one, is in Luke 2:1-3. For Luke, this census (or enrollment) accounts for Joseph and Mary's presence in Bethlehem at the time of Jesus' birth. According to Luke, this was in the time of Caesar Augustus (27 B.C.-A.D. 14) when Quirinius was governor of Syria. The problem lies in the date of the governorship of Quirinius and its affect on the date of Jesus' birth. According to Luke 1:5 (cf Matt 2:1) Jesus' conception was during the days of Herod, king of Judea (37-4 B.C.) — he was succeeded in Judea by his son Archelaus (4 B.C.-A.D. 6). However, it was not until A.D. 6 that Quirinius became governor of Syria, Archelaus was banished to Gaul, Judea became part of the province of Syria, and, according to Josephus, the census was taken. In addition, there is no record of "all the world" (Luke 2:1) being enrolled. Given this historical information it has been suggested that certain theological considerations were significantly more important to Luke than a sense of history with the modern expectation of precision.

The second reference to a census in the NT is in Acts 5:37. This census is placed after the revolt of Theudas and before the revolt of Judas the Galilean (Acts 5:36-37). Judas' revolt was in about A.D. 6, and, according to Josephus, Theudas' was later, not earlier, than Judas'. No particulars about the census are given, although it could well refer to the census of Quirinius in A.D. 6.

CEPHAS See PETER

CHALCOL, CALCOL One of the four wise men surpassed in wisdom by Solomon (I Kgs 4:31). They were all sons of Zerah (I Chr 2:6) son of Judah by his daughter in law Tamar (I Chr 2:4).

CHALDEA, CHALDEANS, CHALDEES The name of a nation

CEPHAS
John 1:42.
I Cor 1:12;
3:22; 9:5; 15:5.
Gal 2:9

CHALCOL,
CALCOL
I Kgs 4:31.
I Chr 2:6

(Is 23:13; Hab 1:6) and land (Is 23:13; Jer 24:5; 25:12; 50:1, 45; Acts 7:4) in southern Mesopotamia; synonymous with Babylon and the Babylonians (Ezek 1:3; 23:14-15 etc.), especially during the last Babylonian dynasty (625-539 B.C.).

According to the Bible, Chesed, the fourth son of Nahor (Gen 22:22) was the eponym of the Chaldeans. Described as desert marauders (Job 1:17), they — like other Aramean nomadic tribes — roamed along the Euphrates and the Tigris, between the Persian Gulf and the Arabian desert. Their connection to the nomadic tribes of Uz, Sheba, Shah and Teiman explains the infiltration of these elements into the southern cities of Babylon at the end of the 2nd millennium B.C. The combination of Ur "of the Chaldees" (Gen 11:28, 31; 15:7) could have developed at this period when the Chaldeans settled near Ur and established a population center of their own.

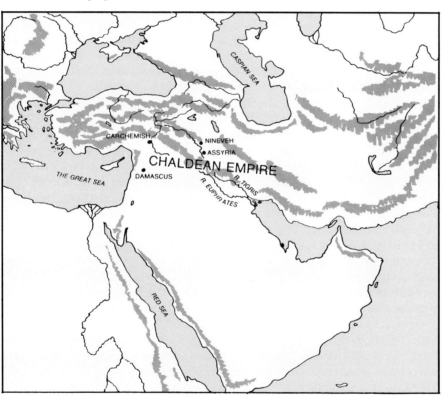

The Chaldean Empire.

Assyrian documents show that the Chaldean tribes were organized on patriarchal lines. As semi-nomads they lived in a loosely organized tribal society, loyal only to their clans,which were aligned in various "houses" (i.e., states). The Chaldeans adhered to Mesopotamian culture but enriched it with some special dimensions of their own. In their appearance and clothing, the prophet Ezekiel identified them with the Babylonians (Ezek 23:15). Scholars disagree as to whether their language was Aramaic or a local Akkadian dialect. Both the Bible and extrabiblical sources distinguish them from the Arameans (cf II Kgs 24:2) but they knew and spoke Aramaic (Dan 2:4) which was even the language of their magic spells. According to the Bible, they, like the Babylonians, worshiped the gods Bel and Nebo. But Assyrian documents describe certain unique religious customs; for example, when Merodach-Baladan fled from Sennacherib, he took with him his late father's bones. Astronomy and astrology were highly respected in Chaldean culture. The palace of Nebuchadnezzar housed a school where the Chaldean language and letters were taught (Dan 1:4), probably including the special language of astronomy and astrology. In the Book of Daniel the name "Chaldean" denotes astrologer (2:10; 4:4; 5:7, 11).

The Chaldeans were a constant threat to the Babylonian city dwellers. They are mentioned for the first time in the annals of Ashurnasirpal II (883-859 B.C.). Firmly opposing Assyrian efforts to subdue them, they developed their own political policy, aimed primarily at seizing the throne of Babylon. Tiglath-Pileser III succeeded in conquering the Chaldeans and, as was his policy, exiled many of them to Assyria. Merodach-Baladan II, who was head of the Chaldean state, seized the throne in Babylon (721-710 B.C.). He found allies among other states, and his messenger to King Hezekiah (II Kgs 20:12; Is 39:1) may have been trying to persuade the latter to join the rebellion against Assyria. The Chaldeans became an unsettling factor in Mesopotamia. Sennacherib exiled them from the main Babylonian cities — some to Nineveh and others to Israel (compare II Kgs 17:24). But many of them fled across the Tigris and settled near the mountains of Elam and the Persian Gulf. In the period of Esarhaddon and Ashurbanipal (7th century), the Chaldeans consolidated their position in the Babylonian cities. Nabopalassar (626-606 B.C.) became the ruler of Babylon. Under his rule and that of his son Nebuchadnezzar, Babylon was considered a Chaldean state, (the Neo-Babylonian-Chaldean empire). Judah was one of its vassal states, until conquered by Nebuchadnezzar (586 B.C.).

CHAMELEON See ANIMALS

CHEBAR, CHEBAR RIVER A main tributary of the Euphrates River, it ran through an area densely populated by exiles from Judah (Ezek 1:1). There Ezekiel had many of his visions (Ezek 1:4) and he often mentions the place (Ezek 3:15).

CHEBAR,
CHEBAR RIVER
Ezek 1:1, 3;
3:15, 23;
10:15, 20, 22;
43:3

Today called Chatt el Nil in its upper course and Chatt el Car in its lower, the Chebar River has been dry for generations; however, in ancient times it was filled with water which was used for irrigation and was mentioned many times in Babylonian documents.

CHEDORLAOMER Ruler of Elam who led a coalition of four kings against the kings of Sodom and Gomorrah and their allies. He was victorious and held his enemies vassals for 12 years (Gen 14:1, 4). They then rebelled against him (Gen 14:5), only to be defeated again (Gen 14:5-12) and the king and his allies took Lot captive. Abraham thereupon gathered his servants and pursued the allies almost to Damascus, defeating Chedorlaomer and his allies (Gen 14:14-17).

CHEDORLAOMER
Gen 14:1, 4-5,
9, 17

CHELAL One of the sons of Pahath-Moab who had taken alien wives at the time of Ezra (Ezra 10:18, 30) and had to repudiate them upon the decree of Ezra (Ezra 10:19).

CHELAL
Ezra 10:30

CHELUB

1. Brother of Shuhah and father of Mehir in the genealogy of Judah. It has been suggested that Chelub stands here for Caleb.

CHELUB 1
I Chr 4:11

2. Father of Ezri, a state official at the time of King David.

CHELUB 2
I Chr 27:26

CHELUBAI Son of Hezron, brother to Jerahmeel and Ram (I Chr 2:9) in the genealogy of the family of Judah (I Chr 2:3). It is widely thought that Chelubai is an alternate name for Caleb.

CHELUBAI
I Chr 2:9

CHELUH (CHELLUH) A son of Bani who had taken an alien wife and had to repudiate her upon the decree of Ezra.

CHELUH
Ezra 10:35

CHEMOSH The principal god of the Moabites who were also known as the "people of Chemosh" (Num 21:29). He may have been the god to whom Mesha king of Moab sacrificed his son (II Kgs 3:27). His name also appears in the Mesha Stele. Solomon tried to please his foreign wives by setting an altar to Chemosh "on the hill that is east of Jerusalem" (I Kgs 11:7), thus incurring the wrath of the Lord (I Kgs

CHEMOSH
Num 21:29.
Judg 11:24. I
Kgs 11:7, 33.
II Kgs 23:13.
Jer 48:7, 13, 46

11:33). King Josiah, some 400 years later, destroyed this altar together with the altars set up to other pagan gods (II Kgs 23:13). In his judgment on Moab (Jer chap. 48), Jeremiah the prophet says that "Chemosh shall go forth into captivity" (Jer 48:7) and that "Moab shall be ashamed of Chemosh" (Jer 48:13).

CHENAANAH ("man of Canaan"?).

1. Son of Bilhan son of Jediael (I Chr 7:10) in the genealogy of the family of Benjamin (I Chr 7:6).

2. Father of Zedekiah (I Kgs 22:11, 24) the false prophet at the time of Ahab king of Israel.

CHENANI ("man of Canaan"). One of the Levites who "stood on the stairs of the Levites and cried with a loud voice to the Lord their God" (Neh 9:4) at the time of the great fast in the time of Nehemiah (Neh 9:1).

CHENANIAH

1. A leader of the Levites at the time of King David; he "was instructor in charge of the music because he was skillful" (I Chr 15:22) and "wore a robe of fine linen" (I Chr 15:27).

2. An Izharite who together with his sons "performed duties as officials and judges over Israel outside Jerusalem" at the same period (I Chr 26:29).

CHEPHAR HAAMMONI One of the cities which fell to the lot of the tribe of Benjamin (Josh 18:11, 24) when Joshua divided the land of Israel (Josh 14:1). It has been suggested that this is the birthplace of Zelek the Ammonite, one of David's thirty "mighty men" (I Chr 11:39). Its present location is unknown.

CHEPHIRAH (HACHEPHIRAH) One of the four cities of the Hivites (Josh 9:17) spared by Joshua (Josh 9:15) because the Israelites had been tricked into making a covenant with their inhabitants (Josh 9:11-12, 15). It fell to the lot of the tribe of Benjamin (Josh 18:11, 26) when Joshua divided the land among the Children of Israel (Josh 14:1). The city lay northwest of Jerusalem and is usually thought to be on the site of present-day Khirbet Kefireh, north of ancient Kirjath Jearim. The exiles who returned from Babylon with Zerubbabel, included 743 people of "Kirjath Arim, Chephirah and Beeroth" (Ezra 2:25; Neh 7:29).

A view of Khirbet Kefireh believed to be on the site of ancient Chephirah.

CHERAN The fourth son of Dishon son of Seir the Horite, one of the chiefs of Edom in the genealogy of Esau.

CHERETHITES AND PELETHITES Foreign mercenaries who formed David's bodyguard. The Cherethites are first mentioned in I Samuel 30:14 which records the Amalekites' raid on Ziklag and the "south (Negeb, in Hebrew) of the Cherethites", an area also named the land of the Philistines (I Sam 30:16) implying that the Cherethites'

The valley of the Brook of Cherith thought to be where Elijah hid from Ahab and was fed by the ravens.

Seal from Jerusalem depicting a winged cherub with a crown. (Hecht Museum, University of Haifa)

territory constituted the southern part of Philistia. The Cherethite region may be identical with the Hazerim of Gaza (Deut 2:23), a territory of the Caphtorim of Caphtor.

After David's accession to the throne he established a military unit consisting of Cherethites and Pelethites under the command of Benaiah the son of Jehoiada (II Sam 8:18). The unit remained loyal to the king when Absalom revolted (II Sam 15:14, 18); it participated in the war against Sheba the son of Bichri (II Sam 20:7), and was present at Solomon's enthronement (I Kgs 1:38, 44). The Cherethites were still mentioned in the 6th century B.C. in Zephaniah's prophecy on the Philistines (Zeph 2:4-5), possibly indicating that the Philistines and the Cherethites were identical and that the Cherethites were named after Crete, their island of origin. It has also been suggested that the Cretans arrived before the Philistine invasion of the 12th century B.C. and that the two peoples merged. However, as the Cretan origin of the Cherethites is uncertain, the meaning of the name Cherethites and Pelethites still requires further research.

CHERITH, BROOK OF A brook "which flows unto the Jordan" (I Kgs 17:3). There Elijah went into hiding upon the command of the Lord (I Kgs 17:3) at the time of Ahab king of Israel. While in hiding Elijah drank from the brook (I Kgs 17:6) and was fed by ravens until the brook dried up "because there had been no rain in the land" (I Kgs 17:7).

The text does not indicate the exact position of the brook. Traditionally it is thought to be Wadi Kelt, on the west bank of the Jordan River, near Jericho.

CHERUB See ADDAN

CHERUB The English word, which is a transliteration from Hebrew, ultimately derives from the Akkadian language, in which it refers to an intercessor who brings the prayers of humans to the gods. In the Bible it denotes a winged celestial creature whose prototype is well-known from the art and iconography of the ancient Near East.

Cherubim appear in several different biblical contexts. They were stationed by God as guards at the entrance of the Garden of Eden after Adam and Eve's expulsion, in order to prevent the couple from reentering the Garden and gaining access to the tree of life (Gen 3:24). The tale of a cherub who once dwelt in Eden but was evicted as a result of his vaunting pride is related by the prophet Ezekiel in his parable about the downfall of the king of Tyre (Ezek 28:13ff).

God is often referred to as he "who dwells between the cherubim" (I Sam 4:4; II Kgs 19:15; Ps 80:1; 99:1; Is 37:16). Two wooden cherubim overlaid with gold, facing one another with outstretched wings, were constructed at the two ends of the mercy seat above the ark in the tabernacle, thereby serving as the throne of God (Ex 25:18-20; 37:7-9). Two cherubim were also found in the Holy of Holies in the Temple of Solomon (I Kgs 6:23ff). A cherub served, moreover, as God's chariot: "he rode upon a cherub and flew" (II Sam 22:11; Ps 18:10).

Cherubim were also employed as decorative figures for cultic purposes. They were embroidered on the curtains of the tabernacle (Ex 26:1; 36:8), as well as on the veil which separated the "holy" from the "most holy" (Ex 26:31; 36:35). In Solomon's Temple they were carved on all the inner and outer walls (I Kgs 6:29), the doors of the inner and outer sanctuary (I Kgs 6:32, 35) as well as on the panels (I Kgs 7:29, 36). They were also carved on the walls and doors of the Temple as seen in the vision of Ezekiel (Ezek 41:18-20, 25).

Several different descriptions of cherubim are given in the Bible. The two constructed in the tabernacle and in the Temple of Solomon each

15:18; 20:7, 23. I Kgs 1:38, 44. I Chr 18:17. Ezek 25:16. Zeph 2:5

CHERITH, BROOK OF
I Kgs 17:3, 5

CHERUB
Ezra 2:59. Neh 7:61

CHERUB
Gen 3:24. Ex 25:18-20, 22; 26:1, 31; 36:8, 35; 37:7-9. Num 7:89. I Sam 4:4. II Sam 6:2; 22:11. I Kgs 6:23-29, 32, 35; 7:29, 36; 8:6-7. II Kgs 19:15. I Chr 13:6; 28:18. II Chr 3:7, 10-14; 5:7-8. Ps 18:10; 80:1; 99:1. Is 37:16. Ezek 9:3; 10:1-9, 14-20; 11:22; 28:14, 16; 41:18, 20, 25. Heb 9:5

have two wings (Ex 25:20; I Kgs 6:24, 27) and one face (Ex 25:20). According to the chariot vision of Ezekiel, the expanse on which the throne reposes is supported by four composite creatures, each having four wings and four faces (Ezek 1:6). Two of their outstretched wings touch one another, and the other two cover their bodies (Ezek 1:23; cf the seraphim in Is 6:2). Their feet were like those of a calf and under their wings they had human hands (Ezek 1:7-8). These creatures whose faces included one of a man, a lion, an ox and an eagle (Ezek 1:10) were probably modeled after cherubim. And, in fact, Ezekiel actually substitutes the face of a cherub for that of an ox in a later chapter (Ezek 10:14).

In the Temple vision, however, the cherubim are pictured as having only two faces, a man's and a lion's (Ezek 41:18-19). The discrepancy between two and four faces in the earlier and later prophecies of Ezekiel has been explained either as a result of the adaptation of the cherub with two faces from the tabernacle and Temple design for his Temple vision or as being due to the two-dimensional portrayal of his chariot vision.

Eagle-faced cherub depicted on a bone incised handle from Hazor. 8th century B.C.

CHESALON (Josh 15:10) A city which fell to the lot of the tribe of Judah (Josh 15:1, 10). It was on the northwest of their territory, bordering on that of Dan. It is located on the site of present-day Kisla, west of Jerusalem.

View of the area in the vicinity of Chesalon, west of Jerusalem.

The village of Iksal identified with Chesulloth.

CHESED (Gen 22:22) The fourth of the children of Nahor (the brother of Abraham) by his wife Milcah (Gen 22:20); he is considered the forefather of the Chaldeans.

CHESIL (Josh 15:30) A city within the inheritance of the children of Judah. It was between Eltolad and Hormah (Josh 15:20, 30). Scholars believe it to have been situated in southern Judah. It may have been an alternate name for Bethul (Bethuel) (Josh 19:4; I Chr 4:30).

CHESTNUT See PLANTS

CHESULLOTH, CHISLOTH TABOR (Josh 19:12, 18) A town which fell to the lot of the tribe of Issachar (Josh 19:17) when Joshua divided the land among the Children of Israel (Josh 14:1). It is mentioned twice: the first time as Chisloth Tabor (Josh 19:12), the second time as Chesulloth (Josh 19:18). It was on the border separating the territory of Zebulun from that of Issachar. It is generally considered to be on the site of present-day Iksal, southwest of Tabor.

CHEZIB (Gen 38:5) The place where Shua, wife of Judah, bore her third son, Shelah; it is generally considered to be an alternate name for Achzib No.1.

CHIDON The place where Uzzah put his hand on the ark and was struck dead by the Lord (I Chr 13:9-10). It is referred to as "Chidon's threshing floor"; however the parallel story in II Samuel 6:6 calls it "Nachon's threshing floor".

CHILEAB The second son born to David in Hebron by his wife Abigail, the widow of Nabal the Carmelite (II Sam 3:3).

Some scholars believe Chileab to be an alternate name for Daniel, second son of Abigail according to I Chronicles 3:1, while others believe Chileab may have died in infancy.

CHILION Second son of Elimelech, an Ephrathite from Bethlehem, and of his wife Naomi (Ruth 1:2). Because "there was a famine in the land" (Ruth 1:1), he went, with his parents and brother, to Moab where he married a local woman, probably Orpah (Ruth 1:4); ten years later he died childless (Ruth 1:5).

CHILMAD A place mentioned by Ezekiel in his lamentation for Tyre (Ezek chap. 27) "the merchants of Sheba, Assyria and Chilmad were your merchants" (Ezek 27:23). Chilmad is believed to have been one of the main halts on the route of the caravans from the coastal cities of Phoenicia to the cities of Upper Tigris. Several locations have been suggested, most of them in northern Syria.

CHIMHAM

1. Son of Barzillai the Gileadite. When King David, in return for his many kindnesses, asked Barzillai to go with him to Jerusalem, the latter replied that, being 80 years old, he preferred to die in his own city, but suggested that the king take his son Chimham instead (II Sam 19:32-33, 37) and David agreed (II Sam 19:38). Later the king on his deathbed commended Chimham to his son Solomon (I Kgs 2:7).

2. A man upon whose land near Bethlehem Johanan the son of Kareah camped on his way to Egypt (Jer 41:17) when fleeing from the wrath of the Chaldeans after having "murdered Gedaliah the son of Ahikam whom the king of Babylon had made governor in the land" (Jer 41:18).

Some scholars have suggested that the two were identical.

CHINNERETH, CHINNEROTH

1. The name Chinnereth is to this day the Hebrew name of the Sea of Galilee. In the Scriptures the term "Sea of Chinnereth" is used twice when the border of the land of Canaan was delineated along its eastern shore (Num 34:11; Deut 3:17) (See GALILEE, SEA OF).

2. Fortified city within territory which fell to the tribe of Naphtali (Josh 19:32, 35) when Joshua divided the land of Canaan (Josh 14:1).

Gold disc, probably used as a pendant or belt-buckle, found in a tomb at Chinnereth. Early Bronze Age.

View from the Arbel mountains towards the plain south of Chinneroth.

Situated on the shore of the Sea of Galilee, it was mentioned among the cities conquered by Pharaoh Thutmosis III. When Jabin king of Hazor organized resistance to the approaching armies of Joshua, he sent messengers to the king "in the plain south of Chinneroth" (Josh 11:2); later Ben-Hadad king of Syria attacked "all Chinneroth" (I Kgs 15:20). It is located in Tell Oreimeh, 6 miles (10 km) north of Tiberias, recently a subject of extensive excavations where Bronze Age and Iron Age remains were uncovered.

CHIOS An island in the Aegean sea off the west coast of Asia Minor where Paul's ship anchored overnight on his journey from Troas to Miletus (Acts 20:15). Josephus (*Antiq.* XVI, 2, 2) relates that Herod the Great donated funds to rebuild the city's colonnades.

Part of the zodiac wheel depicted on the mosaic floor of the 6th-century synagogue at Bet Alfa in the Jezreel Valley with the sign of the Archer corresponding to the month of Chislev.

CHISLEV Hebrew month name derived from Old Babylonian *Kissilimu,* first occurring in Zechariah 7:1 where the phrase "which is Chislev" clarifies the older expression "of the ninth month" (i.e., November-December). In Nehemiah 1:1 "in the month of Chislev" has totally replaced the older designation. These late references support the rabbinic tradition that the Babylonian names of the months were introduced into the Jewish calendar by the returnees from Babylonia in the 6th century B.C. (See NISAN; TEBETH).

CHISLON The father of Elidad, from the tribe of Benjamin, who was appointed by the Lord to help Moses divide the land among the people of Israel (Num 34:21).

CHISLOTH TABOR See CHESULLOTH

CHIUN A deity mentioned by Amos among the gods that the dwellers of Samaria used to carry in sinful processions. It has been suggested that the name referred to the planet Saturn.

CHLOE ("green plant"). In his epistle to the Corinthians, Paul writes that he has been informed by members of "Chloe's household" that there were dissensions among the Christians in Corinth. Nothing further is known of her.

CHORASHAN See ASHAN

CHORAZIN A Jewish town in Upper Galilee, 3 miles (5 km) north of Capernaum, named with Bethsaida as one of the cities reproached by Jesus (Matt 11:20-24) and in Jewish literature in connection with the supply of grain to the Temple for ritual use.

(margin references)
CHIOS
Acts 20:15

CHISLEV
Neh 1:1.
Zech 7:1

CHISLON
Num 34:21

CHISLOTH TABOR
Josh 19:12

CHIUN
Amos 5:26

CHLOE
I Cor 1:11

CHORASHAN
I Sam 30:30

CHORAZIN
Matt 11:21.
Luke 10:13

Sculptured architraves from the synagogue at Chorazin.

Reconstructed synagogue at Chorazin. (Israel Dept. of Antiquities and Museums)

The synagogue of Chorazin was discovered as early as 1869 and was excavated in 1905-7, 1926 and in 1962-3. The synagogue, of the Galilean type, is situated in the center of the town, at its highest point, in the midst of some large buildings. The building, of local black basalt, is about 70 feet (21 m) by 50 feet (15 m) and its walls largely preserved. The three monumental entrances face south, towards Jerusalem. Among the finds in the synagogue was a basalt throne, decorated with a rosette on the back support. This is the "Throne of Moses", which was used during the reading of the Torah.

CHOZEBA (COZEBA) A village in Judah (I Chr 4:22) mentioned in the genealogy of Judah and generally considered to be an alternate form of Achzib.

CHOZEBA
I Chr 4:22

CHRIST See JESUS; MESSIAH

CHRONICLES, BOOKS OF The Books of Chronicles are the last two books of the Hagiographa in the printed Hebrew Bible. They were originally a single volume which, like the Books of Samuel and Kings, were divided into two scrolls in the Septuagint translation, where Chronicles appears among the historical books after the Book of Kings. This order is maintained in the Vulgate and in most modern translations.

The Books of Chronicles relate the history of Israel from the period of David to the decree of Cyrus. The first nine chapters serve as an introduction and largely contain genealogical tables of families and tribes; beginning with Adam, they show the origin of Israel and serve as the background to the Davidic monarchy. The main section of the introduction lists the tribes of Israel. The Chronicler focuses on the tribe of Judah, followed by Levi and Benjamin. The lists are taken from various sources, some of them known from other biblical books.

I Chronicles chapters 10-29 depict David's reign over all Israel, drawing mainly on the parallel chapters in the Book of Samuel. Some sections have been transferred almost verbatim, while others reveal large modifications, omissions and expansions. The account begins with the death of Saul at Mount Gilboa (I Chr chap. 10), followed in consequence by the anointing of David as king in Hebron (I Chr 10:13-11:3). Chronicles is interested in David only from that time on; all his previous deeds are almost entirely ignored. The book reveals a special concern for David's honor: his questionable family life is overlooked

Last page of the Second Book of the Chronicles. From the Keter Torah, *Palestine. 10th century. (Ben Zvi Institute, Jerusalem)*

and no reference is made to his faults and sins, the stress being placed instead on his positive sides and his extensive activities for the organization of the realm.

David's first acts were the capture of Jerusalem (I Chr 11:4-9) and the transfer of the ark from Kirjath Jearim. His intention to build a Temple for the ark having met with divine disapproval (the vision of the prophet Nathan, I Chr chap. 17), he concentrated his efforts upon the preparations for the building. Most of the information concerning these preparations has no parallel in the Book of Samuel (I Chr chaps. 22-29): David selected the site of the Temple (I Chr 21:18-22:1), prepared the plans, collected the necessary materials and assigned the craftsmen. He also organized the Temple personnel: the priests and the Levites, the musicians and the gatekeepers.

Solomon was thus left with nothing but execution of the predetermined plans, the project being depicted in six of the nine chapters devoted to him, which describe the Temple construction and furnishing, the installation of the ark and the dedication ceremony (II Chr 2:1-7:22). The history of Solomon's reign clearly derives from I Kings chapters 1-11. Nevertheless some changes are made: David's will is deleted as are the struggles attending Solomon's accession to the throne, the latter being depicted as effortless: "Solomon sat on the throne of the Lord as king instead of David his father, and prospered; and all of Israel obeyed him" (I Chr 29:23). No mention is made of Solomon's administrative activities such as the division of the country into districts and the list of his officers (I Kgs 4:1-19), this feature of the government being attributed to David. As in his treatment of David, the Chronicler glorified Solomon, emphasizing his wealth, and disregarding his later difficulties, his sins, his numerous foreign wives who led him astray, and his sacrifices at the high places (I Kgs 3:1-3; 11:1-13).

II Chronicles chapters 10-36 relate the history of the Kingdom of Judah from the division of the kingdom to the destruction of the land and the Temple. In contrast with the Book of Kings, Chronicles confines its narrative to the Kingdom of Judah, largely disregarding the affairs of the Northern Kingdom. The material is selected to create the impression that the Kingdom of Judah is the only legitimate legacy of David and Solomon, an attitude clearly expressed in the prophet Abijah's sermon on Mount Zemaraim (II Chr 13:4-12): The Lord gave eternal dominion over Israel to David and his sons. Yet Jeroboam the son of Nebat rose up and rebelled against Solomon. He and the "worthless rogues" (v. 7) who joined him thereby resisted the rule of the Lord as exercised through the sons of David.

The Lord's proper worship is carried on in Judah alone, while the priests of the North serve "things that are not gods" (v. 9). The division of the kingdom is a result of evil and disobedience (cf II Chr 10:19). Nevertheless the rebels are "the Children of Israel" (v. 12), and Abijah appeals to Jeroboam and all Israel to give up their revolt against the Lord. The Chronicler was of the opinion that the Northern monarchy, though conceived in sin and with no right to exist, was still an inseparable part of the people of Israel. The Book gives many details about Israel's history, some of them unknown from the Book of Kings, but they appear only in connection with the history of Judah: for example, the division of the kingdom (II Chr chap. 10), the war of Abijah and Jeroboam (II Chr 13:2-20), the war of Asa and Baasha (II Chr 16:1-6), Jehoshaphat's alliances with Ahab (II Chr chap. 18) and Ahaziah (II Chr 20:35-37), and Amaziah's war with Joash (II Chr chap. 25). The Chronicler gave special attention to four Judean kings: Asa, Jehoshaphat, Hezekiah and Josiah, all of whom carried out religious reforms. Asa removed the high places and the incense altars; he renewed the altar of the Lord and urged Judah to observe the Law (II Chr 14:2-4; 15:8-15). Jehoshaphat also removed the high places (II Chr 17:3-6), but the Chronicler's particular interest was in his judicial reform which had a strong religious emphasis (II Chr 19:4-11). Hezekiah purified and rededicated the Temple (II Chr chap. 29); during his reign all Israel completely destroyed the high places and altars (II Chr 31:1). Josiah cleansed Judah (II Chr 34:3-7, 29-33) and repaired the Temple (II Chr 34:8-13; compare also the repairs made by Joash, II Chr 24:4-14). The festival of Passover was celebrated during the time of Hezekiah (II Chr chap. 30) and Josiah (II Chr 35:1-19) with huge crowds of people, musicians and majestic splendor; the ceremonies took place at Jerusalem the cult center of the nation.

Nevertheless, the Chronicler made no attempt to idealize the kings of Judah, whose evaluation is based mainly on that of the Book of Kings. However, there are several changes, arising from the Chronicler's conception of God and history: God conducts his world according to the principle of justice and gives everyone his due. Any misfortune is conceived as punishment and every success as a reward. For example, the untimely end of Josiah, the good and pious king, is interpreted as punishment for his disobedience of the warning given by Necho on behalf of God (II Chr 35:20-24). On the other hand, Manasseh, who was an exceedingly wicked king, ruled over Judah 55 years, his unusual longevity being explained by his repentance (II Chr 33:12-13).

The Chronicler also had at his disposal information not found elsewhere concerning the activities of the kings. He offered details of the building projects of Rehoboam, Uzziah and Jotham, and of their military might (II Chr 11:5-12; 26:6-15; 27:3-5) and added new material concerning the wars and victories of Abijah, Asa and Jehoshaphat (II Chr 13:3-20; 14:7-14; chap. 20). Stressing that the house of God at Jerusalem was the only legitimate place of worship, the Chronicler described the ministry of the Temple in full detail. The chief cult officials were the priests, but the Levites are depicted with greater enthusiasm. At the Temple rededication ceremony under Hezekiah, the Levites received more attention than the priests, and were given special priestly prerogatives (II Chr chap. 29, see in particular v. 34). The Levites were the bearers of the ark, the gatekeepers and — above all — the singers.

They took a prominent part in the daily Temple service and in all the ceremonies and events connected with the Temple. In addition to those tasks they discharged other functions as teachers of the Law (II Chr 17:7-9), judges (II Chr 19:8-11) and prophets (II Chr 20:14ff). The prophets, too, play an important role in the Chronicler's account. The Davidic dynasty was founded by prophecy (I Chr 11:1-3) and destroyed by prophecy (II Chr 36:11-21). In between the history of the Judean kings was accompanied by a long succession of prophets exhorting and warning, calling for repentance and proffering encouragement. They generally appeared on critical occasions when divine help was desparately needed (II Chr chaps. 11-12; 15-16; 20; 28). The prophets were also historians: Chronicles refers to several written sources (now lost) bearing prophetic titles such as "the book of Nathan the prophet" (I Chr 29:29; II Chr 9:29) or "the annals of the prophet Iddo" (II Chr 13:22). Since the 19th century the general view has held Chronicles and Ezra-Nehemiah to have been one continuous composition written by a single author but this opinion is challenged by some scholars who claim that Chronicles and Ezra-Nehemiah represent two separate works written by different authors in different periods. The Book of Chronicles was composed during the Persian period, in about the 4th century B.C., after completion of the second division of the Hebrew Bible, the Prophets; consequently, it could neither be included along with the Books of Samuel and Kings nor replace them. Thus this somewhat parallel retelling of the history of Judah was placed in the third division, the Writings.

OUTLINE

I Chronicles
1:1-54	Genealogical lists
2:1-9:1	Lists of the Israelite tribes
9:2-44	Inhabitants of Jerusalem; Levitical functionaries; inhabitants of Gibeon
10:1-14	Death of Saul
11:1-29:30	The Story of David

II Chronicles
1:1-9:31	The story of Solomon
10:1-36:23	History of the kings of Judah to the Babylonian captivity

CHUB (CUB) A place, or a people, mentioned by Ezekiel together with "Ethiopia, Libya, Lydia, all the mingled people" (Ezek 30:5). The name occurs nowhere else and nothing is known about it. It has been suggested that it is a scribe's error. In some versions it is translated as "Libya".

CHUN (CUN) One of the cities of Hadadezer king of Zobah who was defeated by David (I Chr 18:3). From that city David took a large amount of brass or bronze (I Chr 18:8) later utilized by his son Solomon.

CHURCH The word used for church in the NT is *ekklesia* which means literally a calling out; then an assembly or meeting of an assembly; then a community, congregation or church, whether local or scattered over a wide area. The ancient Greeks had civic assemblies called *ekklesiai*. The OT root seems to be *kahal* or assembly of Israel as God's people, translated by the Septuagint as *ekklesia*. In the NT, church means the

CHUB
Ezek 30:5

CHUN
I Chr 18:8

gathering or community of the faithful, believers in Christ. It usually refers to the local congregation (e.g. Matt 18:17; I Cor 1:2) but also to the community of believers throughout the world (Matt 16:18; Eph 1:22).

The four gospels contain the word church only three times, all in Matthew. By contrast, it occurs frequently in the writings of Paul, especially in I Corinthians, Ephesians, in Acts of the Apostles, and in the first two chapters of Revelation. Paul was the great apostle of the Gentiles who founded and nourished churches throughout the Mediterranean basin. Acts tells the story of the early church, after Jesus' ascension. The Book of Revelation begins with letters to seven churches. But the rarity of the word in the gospels does pose the problem of whether Jesus founded a church. Much depends on what is meant by church; apart from Matthew 16:17-19, the gospels do not say, and that passage could be a post-Easter statement of the risen Christ. One tradition sets the birthday of the church at Pentecost (Acts chap. 2); alternatively, the church was said to have been born from the side of Christ, in the water (of baptism) and the blood (of the eucharist) that flowed from the open wound (John 19:34). Both of these traditions place the founding of the church after Jesus' public ministry.

It is clear from the gospels that Jesus gathered a circle of disciples around him (Matt 10:1-4; Mark 3:13-19; Luke 6:12-16). This gathering may have had something to do with the restoration of the twelve tribes of Israel as the full assembly of the people of God (Matt 19:28; Luke 22:29). In this sense, Jesus' public ministry may be said to have founded a community of believers which looked to the future restoration of all Israel (more than a local congregation) and the coming of the Kingdom of God. After Jesus' death and resurrection, this community developed into what the later NT calls the church.

Jesus' primary attention was devoted, not to the church as such, but rather to the imminent arrival of the Kingdom of God. On the basis of Matthew 13:41 some Christians have identified the Kingdom of God on earth with the church. Today this identification is commonly regarded as an incorrect interpretation of the main teaching of the Gospels. One text which is rather exceptional does make a connection between church and kingdom: Jesus tells Peter he will build his church on him, that it will endure despite opposition, and then he gives Peter the keys of the Kingdom of Heaven. Here is a link between church and Kingdom of Heaven (Matt 16:18-19). He goes on to add: "whatever you bind on earth will be bound (i.e., God shall bind) in heaven, and whatever you loose on earth will be loosed (i.e., God shall loose) in heaven." These strong words imply that the believer's relationship to the church on earth will in some way affect his relationship to the Kingdom of Heaven. In other words, the Kingdom of God and the church, while not identical, are related. The church is the community of those who hope and pray for the speedy coming of the Kingdom of God.

The Acts of the Apostles mentions a number of local churches but the special viewpoint of Luke in Acts comes out most clearly perhaps in 15:22 (cf v.4). "Then it pleased the apostles and the elders, with the whole church, to send chosen men of their own company to Antioch." This indicates a structured or ordered church. There is a twofold ministry or leadership structure made up of apostles and elders/presbyters/priests. (These elders reappear in Acts 20:17, and in 20:28 are said to be overseers or bishops.) But the whole church assembly participates in decision-making and the decision is missionary. The church has the power to commission men to preach the gospel, to carry on the work of the original apostles. Luke, in Acts chapter 15 and elsewhere, seems to have the idea of the apostles as a kind of governing college in Jerusalem. This picture of the church in Acts has brought up the matter of church ministry. The earliest list of ministries is perhaps to be found in I Corinthians 12:28. Here the top three ministries are apostles, prophets and teachers. (Another neglected list is in Matthew 23:34: "prophets, wise men and scribes", a purely OT list.) Paul's list is rapidly replaced by the Acts list, which is then supplemented in the pastoral epistles by a third ministry, the diaconate (I Tim 3:8, 12). The result is a threefold ministry of: bishop (as successor but not equal to the apostles); priest or elder; and deacon; which has remained classical and standard in the church ever since. But, as the complete list in I Corinthians 12:28 shows, this threefold pattern does not exhaust the range of ministries, nor does it spell out how they are to be worked out in practice.

Paul, the great founder of churches, makes further contributions to the NT understanding of church. He created a famous metaphor, the church as the body of Christ (Rom 12:5; I Cor 12:12-27; Eph 1:22-23; 2:16; 4:12; 5:23, 30; Col 1:18, 24, etc.). Extending the OT idea of the church as the people of God, this image fuses the scattered people into an organic unity in Christ, a single living organism. Paul thus had a very strong notion of Christian community. He believed that these communities of love would grow and attract new members, helping and strengthening one another. It is disputed how Paul acquired this image, whether from the moment of his conversion or from Roman stoicism; but it is a natural enough concept and certainly seems to be linked in his own mind with the birth of the church from Christ and the Holy Spirit in baptism (Rom 6:1-11; I Cor 12:12-13), and with the eucharistic body of Christ (I Cor 11:17-34). Consistent with this, Paul also deepened the understanding of Christian ministry as a share in the charisms or gifts of the Holy Spirit: he believed that every Christian was or could be endowed with such a charism. It is often thought that John chapter 15 with its image of Christ as the vine and his followers as the branches, is a way of expressing the same basic idea of organic unity as in the body language of Paul. Ephesians perhaps goes further than other epistles in suggesting a cosmic church which fills the universe as the body of the cosmic Christ (Eph 1:23).

Many characteristics of the church could be mentioned, but classically they are: unity (John 17:21; Eph 4:3-13); catholicity or universality (Matt 28:19-20); holiness (Eph 5:27) and apostolicity (Matt 10:40; Eph 2:20).

(bottom of page)
View of the Cilician Pass.

Cilicia

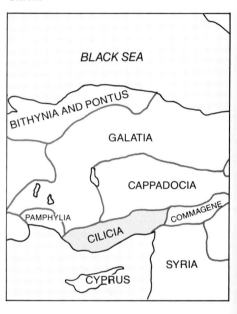

CHUZA
Luke 8:3

CHUZA A steward of King Herod whose wife Joanna was among the women "healed of evil spirits and infirmities" by Jesus and who "provided for him from their substance".

CILICIA
Acts 6:9; 15:23, 41; 21:39; 22:3; 23:34; 27:5. Gal 1:21

CILICIA District and Roman imperial province in the southeast corner of Asia Minor whose famous pass, the Cilician Gates, was traversed by the main route from Syria to western Asia Minor. Cilicia was made a province after Pompey's "pirate drive" in 67 B.C., and divided into two regions during NT times (Tracheia in the west and Pedias in the east); it was disbanded in the early 1st century A.D. Tracheia was a plateau in the Taurus range, valued only for its ship timber, and renowned from early times as the home of outlaws and pirates. In the 1st century A.D. it was divided between native rulers and the provinces of Galatia and Cappadocia. Pedias, a fertile plain producing flax, grapes, olives and wheat, lay between Mount Amanus in the south and Mount Taurus and the sea in the north. It was administered by Syria until A.D. 72, when the province was reunited by Vespasian.

This administration is accurately reflected in the NT, which combines

Coin of Datames, governor of Cilicia. 4th century B.C.

Cilicia with Syria (Acts 15:23, 41; Gal 1:21). Tarsus, the home of Paul (Acts 21:39; 22:3; 23:34), was the capital of Cilicia Pedias, which contained 15 other semi-autonomous cities. Jews from Cilicia disputed with Stephen in Jerusalem (Acts 6:9). See also KEVEH.

CINNAMON See SPICES AND PERFUMES

CIRCUMCISION The surgical removal of part or all of the foreskin which covers the glans of the penis. There is no agreement with respect to its exact purpose. Circumcision is known to have been a prevalent custom in antiquity when it was practiced by the Egyptians and many other peoples. Some peoples performed the rite shortly after the birth of the child, others at the attainment of puberty, still others shortly before marriage.

The Bible (Gen chap. 17) presents circumcision as having originated with Abraham, who, in fulfillment of God's command, circumcised himself at the age of 99 along with his son Ishmael and every male among his slaves. The divine behest makes the rite obligatory upon every male of the seed of Abraham and charges it with a highly religious significance, as a mark of everlasting covenant between God and Abraham's descendants throughout all generations (Gen 17:10-11). It further states that the operation should be performed at the age of eight days, and prescribes a penalty of excision from the community for those who fail to perform the rite (Gen 17:12-14; see also Lev 12:3). Abraham circumcised his son Isaac eight days after his birth and that became the Jewish custom (Gen 21:4).

Circumcision assumed a distinctive religious and national character among the Hebrews, as is clearly evidenced by Jacob's sons who insisted that the Hivites undergo circumcision as a necessary condition for intermarriage with them (Gen chap. 34). To give their sister Dinah to an uncircumcised man, they contended, would be a disgrace for them (Gen 34:13-17). Indeed the term "uncircumcised" is repeatedly used in the Bible as an opprobrious epithet, applied mainly to the Philistines (Judg 14:3; I Sam 14:6; 17:26; 31:4; Ezek 32:21). It is also applied figuratively to the unclean (Is 52:1), to the rebellious heart (Lev 26:41; Deut 10:16; Jer 4:4; 9:25), and to the obstinate ear (Jer 6:10).

The rite of circumcision may not have been strictly followed by the Israelites during their bondage in Egypt. Moses failed to circumcise his son, a fact which triggered God's wrath and almost brought about his death. His life was redeemed by his wife Zipporah, who performed the rite upon her son with a flint stone, and declared Moses " a husband of blood" (Ex 4:24-26). The practice was totally neglected during the period of the wilderness. Joshua renewed the rite *en masse*, following the crossing of the Jordan (Josh 5:2-7).

Circumcision later became firmly established among the Hebrews as an indispensable act of national consecration, invested with the profoundest religious significance. Chapter 15 of the pseudepigraphic Book of Jubilees states that the uncircumcised belong not to the "children of the covenant" but to the "children of destruction". When Antiochus Epiphanes, the Seleucid monarch, issued a prohibition against circumcision (I Macc 1:48), he was met with defiance by many Jewish mothers. Two of these mothers were publicly paraded about the city with their babies hanging on their breasts and then thrown down from the top of the city wall (II Macc 6:10).

John the Baptist and Jesus were circumcised on the eighth day after their birth (Luke 1:59; 2:21) and as shown by these NT passages, by that time sons were named at the circumcision ceremony. If the eighth day after birth fell on a Sabbath, circumcision was nevertheless performed on that day (John 7:21-24). The Christian apostles and elders in

Jerusalem disagreed over the question of whether or not Gentiles required circumcision in order to be saved (Acts 15:1-12).

Paul taught that circumcision was necessary for Jews (he himself was circumcised) but superfluous for Gentiles (Phil 3:3-5). He said "Was anyone called while circumcised? Let him not become uncircumcised. Anyone called while uncircumcised; let him not be circumcised" (I Cor 7:18).

Although circumcision is not required of Gentiles, the term was used symbolically by Paul, suggesting that their acceptance as members of the covenant with God through Jesus' life and death constitutes their circumcision (Col 2:11).

The eighth day after Christmas (January 1 in the western church) is celebrated by the church as the Feast of the Circumcision of Jesus.

CITRON WOOD See PLANTS

CITY OF DAVID See JERUSALEM

Jewish ritual circumcision implements. (Israel Museum)

CITY OF
DAVID
II Sam 5:7, 9;
6:10, 12, 16.
I Kgs 2:10;
3:1; 8:1; 9:24;
11:27, 43;
14:31; 15:8,
24; 22:50.
II Kgs 8:24;
9:28; 12:21;
14:20; 15:7,
38; 16:20.
I Chr 11:5, 7;
13:13; 15:1,
29. II Chr 5:2;
8:11; 9:31;
12:16; 14:1;
16:14; 21:1,
20; 24:16, 25;
27:9; 32:5, 30;
33:14. Neh
3:15; 12:37

CITY OF
REFUGE
Num 35:6, 11-15,
25-28, 32.
Josh 20:2, 4;
21:13, 21, 27,
32, 38. I Chr
6:57, 67

CITY OF REFUGE Six cities were assigned by Moses to serve as havens for accidental homicide (Num 35:13; Deut 19:9). These were populated towns in which the manslayer would be immune from pursuit by the blood avenger (Num 35:12). Moses himself established Bezer, Ramoth and Golan as refuge cities in Transjordan (Deut 4:43), and Joshua established Kedesh, Shechem and Hebron to the west of the Jordan (Josh 20:7-8). These six were all Levitical cities (Num 35:6); later, 42 additional Levitical cities functioned in much the same way (Josh chap. 21; I Chr 6:54-81), their purpose being to intercede between the manslayer and the avenger of blood, "that the manslayer may not die until he stands before the congregation in judgment" (Num 35:12). In this way the innocent blood of the accidental manslayer would not be shed in the avenger's passion to right a perceived wrong (Deut 19:10), and blood vengeance would be controlled.

Information as to the actual internal functioning of the cities of refuge is almost totally absent in the Bible. However, biblical accounts provided the basis for the following reconstruction by the rabbis of the Talmud: after the homicide the killer fled to the nearest city of refuge, where he presented himself to the elders at the city gate, to be assigned accommodation (Josh 20:4). He would later be taken under escort to court where his degree of guilt was determined. If found guilty of premeditated murder, he would be executed; if the manslaughter were unpremeditated, he would be sheltered at the city of refuge until the death of the then officiating high priest (Num 25:25, 28). He was not allowed to leave the precincts of the city under any circumstances. Once released from the refuge city, he was free to go anywhere. If the avenger then killed him, the avenger would be guilty of murder.

Talmudic literature also states that life in the refuge city was made as normal as possible for the killer (Deut 4:42; 19:5), who was allowed to earn his livelihood and even permitted to hold positions of honor. Certain trades were banned in cities of refuge for fear of stimulating commercial intercourse which could attract the avenger. There were differences in procedure between the initial six cities of refuge and the other Levitical cities. In the former, asylum was automatic while in the latter, it had to be requested. The original cities granted the fugitive housing as a right, whereas in the other cities he would have to pay rent. Despite all attempts to minimize the discomfort of living in these cities, the law requiring the manslayer to remain there stresses the underlying punitive nature of his confinement.

In the ancient world, (e.g. Phoenicia, Syria, Greece, Rome) certain shrines or sacred places were regarded as providing absolute security to fugitives. On arrival at a sacred place and claiming the protection of the

The cities of refuge.

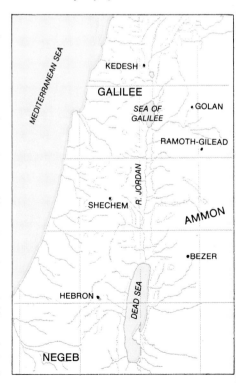

Seal impression from a wine-jar handle from Cnidus found at Tell Dor. Hellenistic period. (Tell Dor Excavations Project)

(top of page) Emperor Claudius.

god, both innocent and guilty were placed beyond the reach of revenge and justice. In Israel the altars likewise served as places of asylum (I Kgs 1:50-53; 2:28-34), but like the cities of refuge, for the innocent alone. The deliberate murderer was to be taken from his asylum at the altar to be executed (Ex 21:14). The altar offered temporary shelter for the accidental killer; from there he would be taken under escort to a city of refuge. Several instances of killers seeking refuge at the altar are recorded in the Bible (I Kgs 1:50; 2:28-30).

Many scholars date the actual establishment of these centers to the period of the United Monarchy under David and Solomon.

CLAUDA (CAUDA) A small island near Crete where the ship carrying Paul as a prisoner to Rome, sheltered during a tempest.

CLAUDIA One of the followers of Paul in Rome. She sent greetings to Timothy. It has been suggested that she was the mother of Linus, mentioned in the same text.

CLAUDIUS Roman emperor (ruled A.D. 41-54). He was poisoned by his wife and niece Agrippina, and succeeded by Nero. His reign was marked by a famine which had been predicted by Agabus, a prophet who came to Antioch from Jerusalem (Acts 11:28). Claudius issued a decree ordering all Jews to leave Rome (Acts 18:2).

CLAUDIUS LYSIAS See LYSIAS CLAUDIUS

CLEMENT ("mild"). A man of Philippi, one of the followers of Paul who preached the gospel with him.

CLEOPAS One of the two disciples who met Jesus on the road to Emmaus after the resurrection. Sometimes identified with Clopas.

CLOPAS The husband of Mary No.5 who stood by the cross with the mother of Jesus.

CNIDUS A city on a promontory on the southwestern coast of Asia Minor sighted by Paul on his voyage to Rome.

COBRA See ANIMALS

COCK See ANIMALS

COINS AND CURRENCY In prehistoric and early historical times the economy was based on barter — commodities were exchanged for other commodities. At a later stage certain goods, such as hides, cattle, and sheep or grain, served as fixed units of value and formed the basis of primitive commercial negotiations. As this method did not prove practicable in all cases, a better one had to be devised. In Palestine the Canaanites were using a much more progressive system before the arrival of the Hebrews; it was based on rare, and therefore costly, metals. In fact even at this stage there was a double system: in the villages the old method of bartering still prevailed, while in the ports and the larger cities metal was used as a token of exchange. When Abraham bought the cave of the field of Machpelah he weighed out 400 shekels of silver as payment to Ephron the Hittite (Gen 23:16). The money was weighed since this was still long before the minting of coins began.

Only once in the Bible are gold shekels referred to as a monetary unit (I Chr 21:25). Silver was used as a unit of value as may be inferred from the calculation of fines in shekels (Ex 21:32). Wherever a shekel is mentioned in the Bible a unit of weight is meant.

During the 6th and 5th centuries B.C. the dramatic change from barter money into coinage took place and Persian, Greek and Phoenician coins were put in circulation in the Holy Land.

In the 4th century B.C. the local Jewish authorities minted small silver coins bearing the legend *Yahud*, the name for the province of Judea in the Persian period. Minting of coins in Palestine did not become regular practice until the beginning of the Hellenistic period.

CLAUDA
Acts 27:16

CLAUDIA
II Tim 4:21

CLAUDIUS
Acts 11:28;
18:2

CLAUDIUS LYSIAS
Acts 23:26

CLEMENT
Phil 4:3

CLEOPAS
Luke 24:18

CLOPAS
John 19:25

CNIDUS
Acts 27:7

Alexander the Great founded a mint at Acco that produced gold and silver coins. The Jewish autonomy in Jerusalem minted small silver coins in the city inscribed "Yehuda" under Ptolemy II.

Jewish minting returned with the Hasmonean Dynasty under Alexander Jannaeus (103-76 B.C.). All coins bore Hebrew, or Hebrew and Greek, inscriptions, with the king's name and title and that of the High Council of the Jews. Common symbols on these coins were anchors, stars, palm branches, cornucopiae, and pomegranate flowers. All Hasmonean coins were bronze with the temporary emission of lead coins under Alexander Jannaeus.

Part of an ancient mold for making flans of coins.

(right and left)
Two hoards of silver ingots discovered in a cooking-pot at En Gedi. Late 7th century B.C.

A "banker", depicted on a Roman relief. (Belgrade Museo Nazionale)

Roman coin stamped with images of the ancient mintmaster's tools.

The next series of coins was that of the Herodian Dynasty. Herod the Great (37-4 B.C.) minted coins bearing Greek legends and pagan and Jewish symbols. Herod's immediate heirs, who inherited parts of their father's territories, used the same range of symbols: palm branches, anchors, bunches of grapes, prows of galleys, and so on. Only Philip (4 B.C.-A.D. 34), who reigned in the northeastern part of the kingdom beyond the Jordan where most of the population was non-Jewish, minted coins with portraits of Roman emperors as well as his own. Herod Agrippa I (A.D. 37-44) minted coins in which his dependence on the Romans is expressed. For the purely Jewish parts of the kingdom his coins bore symbols that would not offend the Jews. He founded the mint at Caesarea, which was to last for about 200 years. When Judea

Coin struck in Tiberias in A.D. 41, with a portrait of Gaius Caligula on one side, and Germanicus in a quadriga on the other side, with the unusual inscription "A coin of King Agrippa".

was directly ruled by the Roman procurators, they also minted coins.

Minting by the procurators continued until the First Jewish Revolt (A.D. 66-70). At that time the Jewish authorities minted coins of large denominations in silver. The coins were shekels and half-shekels in silver, with smaller denominations in bronze. They bore legends in the ancient, already antiquated, Hebrew script ("Jerusalem the Holy", "Shekel of Israel", "The Freedom of Zion" or "For the Redemption of Zion"), with dates according to the era of the revolt and symbols such as chalices, vine leaves, amphorae, citrons, palm branches and palm trees. When the revolt had been crushed the emperors Vespasian, Titus and Domitian minted coins to commemorate their victory over the Jews.

COL-HOZEH Father of Shallun, leader of the district of Beth Haccerem who repaired the Fountain Gate at the time of Nehemiah (Neh 3:15) and head of a family of the tribe of Judah who dwelled in Jerusalem (Neh 11:4-5).

COL-HOZEH
Neh 3:15; 11:5

It has been suggested that these were two different persons.

COLOSSE (COLOSSAE) A city of Phrygia c. 10 miles (16 km) east of the modern town of Denzili in Turkey. Situated on the banks of the river in the unusually fertile but earthquake-prone Lycus valley, it has never been excavated. In the 1st century A.D. its former glory had begun to wane under competition from the growing political power of Laodicea and the rising religious popularity of Hierapolis, the two other cities in the valley. It had degenerated to the status of a minor town on the trade-route from Ephesus to the interior of Asia Minor. Its chief source of prosperity was the production of dyed woollen goods.

COLOSSE
Col 1:2

The majority of the population was Phrygian, but the Epistle to the Colossians supposes the presence of a Jewish colony. In 62 B.C. there were at least 11,000 adult male Jews in the district of which Laodicea

Cliff-formation at Hierapolis, a few miles from ancient Colosse, formed by lime flowing from the hot springs for which the place was famous.

was the capital. These were the descendants of the 2,000 families transported from Babylon by Antiochus III in about 213 B.C.

Colossae was not evangelized by Paul himself, but by Epaphras, who had probably been converted by Paul during his long ministry in Ephesus (Acts chap. 19). Due to the uncertainty of the manuscript tradition of Colossians 1:7, it is not clear whether Epaphras was Paul's delegate in this mission or whether he was acting independently; in the light of Colossians 1:2 the latter would appear to be the more probable.

The city was destroyed by an earthquake in the reign of Nero (44-69) and never recovered.

COLOSSIANS, EPISTLE TO THE Epistle sent by Paul to Colossae.

Its authenticity has been disputed. Reputable scholars have denied that it was written by Paul on the grounds of theological content, language and style, which is cumbersome and verbose. Many new terms are used (e.g. "fullness"), several noted Pauline themes are missing (e.g. righteousness, justification, law), and Pauline concepts are presented in a different way (e.g. the Body of Christ). All these difficulties, however, can be accounted for if the purpose of the letter is kept in mind. It is essentially a polemic treatise designed to counter the influence of false teachers. It could be expected, then, (a) that Paul's thought should have evolved under the pressures of new difficulties, (b) that he should emphasize only what was relevant to his purpose, and (c) that he should to some extent adopt the terminology of his adversaries. The objections to Pauline authorship, therefore, are not decisive, and many scholars accept the traditional adscription to the Apostle of the Gentiles.

At the time of writing Paul was a prisoner (4:3, 10), which limits the place of composition to Ephesus (I Cor 15:32) in the winter of A.D. 53-54, to Caesarea (Acts 24:27-25:4) in the years 56-58, or to Rome (Acts 28:30) during the following two years. Rome is the most probable, because it best accounts for the development in Paul's thought.

The false teaching that Paul combats in this letter was certainly Jewish in origin because it concerned the calendar, dietary regulations, and possibly circumcision. In addition it assigned a salvific role to angels. This latter feature points to a rather esoteric version of Judaism, and the development of the concepts of mystery, revelation, knowledge and perfection, particularly when taken in association with the ritual and ascetic practices. It has been suggested that it referred to the type of Judaism practised by the Essenes, or perhaps to a form of gnosticism.

The kernel of the Epistle is the baptismal hymn which Paul expands in 1:15-20. Traditional Pauline themes (e.g. Christ as the image of God, the community as the Body of Christ) are here set in a new context. All things have been created in and for Christ in whom the Fullness dwells; he is the Head of the Body; the reconciliation effected by Christ has a cosmic dimension. Paul also articulates in a new way his central idea of the communal aspect of salvation.

OUTLINE

1:1:1-14	Opening greeting and thanksgiving
1:15-23	Christ as redeemer
1:24-2:5	Paul's mission to the Gentiles
2:6-23	Doctrinal matters
3:1-17	Significance of baptism
3:18-4:1	Practical advice, especially in family context
4:2-6	General instructions
4:7-18	Reference to emissaries; salutations

CONANIAH
II Chr 35:9

CONIAH
Jer 22:24, 28; 37:1

COLT See ANIMALS

CONANIAH See CONONIAH No.2

CONIAH A name used by the prophet Jeremiah for Jehoiachin son of Jehoiakim king of Judah. See JEHOIACHIN.

CONONIAH, CONANIAH

1. A Levite appointed by King Hezekiah over the collectors of tithes and offerings (II Chr 31:12) and directed the overseers together with his brother Shimei (II Chr 31:13).

2. A leader who gave offerings to the Levites for Passover at the time of Josiah king of Judah.

CORBAN The Hebrew word for sacrifice, which is mentioned untranslated in the Gospel of Mark (7:11). Mark 7:3-13 depicts a disagreement between Jesus and the Pharisees over the relations between God's commandment, which is the law, and the tradition of the elders, which is its authoritative oral interpretation; Mark's account represents the Pharisees neglecting the former in favor of the latter.

Jewish tradition forbids the dedication to God of money needed for supporting one's parents, but according to this passage some Pharisees were in the habit of circumventing the ban by making a vow (Corban seems to be part of the formula used in giving gifts to the Temple). Jesus opposed this ruse because it contradicted the commandment to honor one's father and mother (Mark 7:12-13).

CONONIAH, CONANIAH 1
II Chr 31:12-13

CONONIAH, CONANIAH 2
II Chr 35:9

CORBAN
Mark 7:11

Fragment of a stone jar found at the southwest corner of the Temple area in Jerusalem, bearing a drawing of two doves and the inscription "Corban"; 1st century B.C.

A coin of Corinth depicting Pegasus and Athena; c. 325 B.C.

CORIANDER See PLANTS

CORINTH The magnificent site on the Isthmus joining the Peloponnese to Greece and commanding two seas, the Corinthian Gulf and the Saronic Gulf, was settled about the 10th century B.C. That city, whose energetic exploitation of its strategic commercial location won for itself the title "wealthy Corinth" (Homer, Pindar), was destroyed by the Romans in 146 B.C. The city that Paul knew was the Roman colony founded by Julius Caesar in 44 B.C. on the same site and officially named *Colonia Laus Julia Corinthiensis*.

The settlers sent by Julius Caesar were for the most part freed slaves, who had come originally from Greece, Syria, Egypt and Judea. By the end of the reign of Augustus its chief merchants were very rich men, who had already begun to endow the city with the magnificent monuments that have been brought to light by excavations.

The productive capacity of Corinth was of less importance than the employment generated by, and the taxes levied on, the trade across the Isthmus. A great proportion of the east-west trade of the Roman Empire used the ports of Lechaeum on the Corinthian Gulf and Cenchreae on the Saronic Gulf, because the sea-route around the southern tip of the Peleponnese was so dangerous as to be proverbial, "When you round Cape Malea forget your home!" From the 6th century B.C. there had been talk of a canal joining the two seas, but

CORINTH
Acts 18:1, 18; 19:1. I Cor 1:2. II Cor 1:1, 23; 6:11. II Titus 4:20

none of the plans came to anything. Larger vessels had to unload and send their cargo over to the other port, while smaller boats could be hauled across on a wheeled vehicle running on a grooved pavement. The atmosphere of Corinth was that of a frontier boom-town.

Indirect evidence indicates that Corinth was the capital of the senatorial province of Achaia, which was governed by a proconsul sent annually from Rome. Lucius Iunius Gallio, whom Paul met (Acts 18:12-16), was nominated for the year July 51-June 52, but probably served only the first four months of his term of office. The municipal government was a miniature of that of Republican Rome. Citizen voters elected four annual magistrates, who on retirement became members of the city council. The senior magistrates were the *Duoviri,* who were assisted by two *Aediles.* An inscription in a pavement east of the theatre reads "Erastus in return for his aedileship laid the pavement at his own expense." This man is identified with the Erastus, who was city treasurer at the time of Paul and a Christian (Rom 16:23).

The greatest honor that Corinth could bestow was the presidency of the Isthmian Games. Of the four great panhellenic festivals these ranked immediately after the Olympic Games, and were celebrated every two years in the spring at the sanctuary of Poseidon at Isthmia, several miles east of Corinth. Paul may have attended the games of A.D. 51; such contests certainly contributed to his theological imagery (I Cor 9:24-27). The tents needed for the thousands of participants and spectators, and the booths set up by the shopkeepers of Corinth, would have provided employment for Paul the tentmaker (Acts 18:3).

According to Philo there was a vital Jewish community in Corinth by the early 1st century A.D.. Their numbers were increased in A.D. 67 by the 6,000 prisoners-of-war sent by Vespasian from Judea to work on the abortive canal project of Nero. No material remains of this community have been found save an undated lintel with the inscription *[Syna]goge Hebr[aion]* "synagogue of the Hebrews". Other religious groupings are well represented. Temples dedicated to the cult of the emperor, to the various Greek deities, and to the Egyptian gods, highlight both the ethnic complexity and the religious diversity of the city that Paul was to make one of the most important centers of early Christianity.

Paul visited Corinth three times. On the founding visit (Acts 18:1-18) he stayed 18 months (spring 50-fall 51). His second visit was brief and unhappy, and must have taken place during the early summer of A.D.

Street leading from the center of Corinth to the port of Lechaum on the Corinthian Gulf.

(top left)
The temple of Apollo at Corinth.

(top right)
Decorated vase from Corinth with an inscription; early 6th century B.C.

54. Only with difficulty did he reestablish a relationship with the church, and there must have been much to do during the three months he spent in the city during the winter of A.D. 55-56 (II Cor 13:1-2). He wrote the Epistle to the Romans during this latter visit.

CORINTHIANS, EPISTLES TO THE There are two canonical letters, First and Second Corinthians. Paul in fact wrote at least five letters to Corinth. Their relative order is:

1. The Previous Letter (I Cor 5:9).
2. I Corinthians.
3. The Sorrowful Letter (II Cor 2:4).
4. II Corinthians 1-9.
5. II Corinthians 10-13.

The Previous Letter has not been preserved. It is known only through its mention in I Corinthians 5:9, which also indicates at least part of its content. It forbade believers to associate with immoral members of the Christian community. This letter may have been written in the summer of A.D. 53 in response to information about the Corinthian community brought to Paul in Ephesus by Apollos (I Cor 3:6; 16:12).

I Corinthians was written from Ephesus before Passover in A.D. 54. It is a complex reaction to two sets of data about the situation at Corinth. Chloe's employees (I Cor 1:11) went on business from Ephesus to Corinth, and there noticed things about the community which surprised them. Naturally, when they returned to Ephesus they spoke about them to Paul. There were divisions within the community (I Cor 1:12), which were exacerbated by the claim of some to possess wisdom. A believer was living in incest with his stepmother. Believers were suing one another in pagan courts, and some visited prostitutes. Much more disturbing were the goings-on at the liturgical assemblies. The way men and women dressed blurred the distinction between the sexes and raised suspicions of homosexuality. Among the participants at the love feasts some had overeaten whereas others were starving. There was also a group who denied the Resurrection.

These aspects of the life of their community apparently did not bother the Corinthians. Certainly, they were not among the problems about which they asked Paul's advice in the letter (I Cor 7:1) probably brought by Stephanas and others (I Cor 16:17). They raised questions about marriage and divorce, about the propriety of eating meat which had been offered to idols, about spiritual gifts, and about the collection for the poor of Jerusalem.

Such an array of problems, many of them extremely delicate issues, would have dismayed a lesser man, but Paul rose to the occasion magnificently. The Corinthians had made many mistakes, but they were the errors of enthusiasm. They were struggling to work out what it meant in practice to live as Christians, and they had no established tradition to guide them. Hence, although Paul at times cannot hide his shock and dismay, he never simply condemns them. He discusses all the issues thoroughly, using carefully calculated explosions of passion to ensure they pay attention to what he is saying. His guidance is clear and unambiguous, but he never imposes a solution. He simply expounds the authentic Christian perspective and trusts the Corinthians to draw the appropriate conclusions. From many points of view the letter is a masterful object lesson on the exercise of authority in a Christian community.

The Sorrowful Letter has also been lost, but it can be deduced that it was written from Ephesus in the late summer of A.D. 54 after Paul's second visit to Corinth (II Cor 13:2). On that occasion Paul was gravely insulted by a Christian who was not a member of the community and the Corinthians had not come to his defense. He left Corinth bitterly hurt, and did not return there as he had promised (II Cor 2:1) but continued to Ephesus via Macedonia (II Cor 1:16). In the letter he poured out his anguish and love. When he heard from Titus, who had brought the letter, that the Corinthians had repented, his relief knew no bounds, and prompted the writing of II Corinthians 1-9, which sealed the reconciliation between himself and the Corinthians.

While the unity of I Corinthians is usually acknowledged, the general opinion is that II Corinthians is made up of a compilation of a number of letters. Some scholars postulate as many as five letters: (1) 1:1-2:13 plus 7:5-16; (2) 2:14-7:4 minus 6:14-7:1; (3) 8:1-24; (4) 9:1-15; (5) 10:1-13:14. The arguments against the literary unity of II Corinthians chapters 1-9 are not convincing. The difficult transitions, which have been interpreted as "breaks" between different letters, can be explained once Paul's associative mode of thought is recognized and the nature of the opposition he had to face is accurately determined. Paul had to defend himself against attacks on his apostleship previously (I Cor chap. 9). That opposition continued but in II Corinthians chapters 1-9 a reconciliatory tone dominates. Clear hints show that Paul was fully aware of what was going on, but he is determined not to let it disturb his newly reestablished relationship with the Corinthians. The delicate firmness of his appeal for the poor of Jerusalem underlines how careful he is being (II Cor 8-9).

Remains of the agora at Corinth.

The tone changes radically in II Corinthians chapters 10-13, making it impossible that it should be the continuation of the same letter. Here we find a torrent of reproaches and stern warnings mixed with outbursts of sarcastic self-vindication. After having sent II Corinthians chapters 1-9 with Titus, Paul must have received information from Corinth that intruders preaching another brand of Christianity had won a favorable hearing there. Bitter anger at these "most eminent apostles" (II Cor 11:5) explains the vitriolic nature of his reaction. This letter was sent some months after II Corinthians chapters 1-9, probably in summer A.D. 55, from northern Greece (Rom 15:19).

Perhaps better than any of his letters the Corinthian correspondence reveals the subtle complexity of Paul's personality. It also graphically illustrates the problems that had to be faced as Christianity moved from Palestine into Europe.

OUTLINE

First Epistle

Second Epistle

The baptism of Cornelius depicted on a sarcophagus of the 14th century. (Musée Lapidaire Chrétien, Arles)

CORNELIUS A Roman centurion in the Italian cohort and a God-fearing man, stationed at Caesarea. In a vision he was told to send for Peter, who at the time was staying in Joppa (Jaffa) at the home of Simon the Tanner. About the same time, Peter himself also had a vision, cautioning him that it was not for him to call unclean what God counts clean, and thus preparing him for the visit of the "unclean" Gentile Cornelius. The latter was subsequently converted, thereby becoming the first Gentile to be accepted by the young Christian congregation.
CORNELIUS **Acts 10:1, 3, 7, 17, 21-22, 24-25, 30-31**

COS An island in the Aegean Sea to the west of Caria; Paul sailed past it on his way to Rhodes.
COS **Acts 21:1**

COSAM ("diviner"). Son of Elmodam and father of Addi in the genealogy of Jesus according to Luke.
COSAM **Luke 3:28**

COSMETICS See SPICES AND PERFUMES

COVENANT Many of Israel's religious ideas are expressed in the terminology of human society and politics. Thus God is thought of as "Father," or as a "King," who gives "laws." One of the most original, pervasive and fruitful of these metaphors from human society is the idea that between God and man there is a covenant, that is, an explicit sworn agreement defining the terms of their relation. Very prominent in the Hebrew Scriptures, "covenant" also gives its name to the two parts of the Christian Bible, the "Old Covenant," and the "New Covenant." Rediscovery of the ancient political world in which Israel lived has set in motion an active restudy of biblical covenant ideas which has clarified and vivified the faded religious metaphor. Three points now seem fundamental. (a) The Bible presents no single unified covenant idea, but rather two principal — and almost converse — conceptions. One, the covenant of obligation is binding only upon the human partner; the other, the covenant of grant binds God to carry out a solemn promise. (b) These ideas are related to different types of ancient political instruments: the first to the treaty between a great king and a subordinate king, and the second to the royal grant. (c) The conception of a religious covenant changed with the progressive modification of political forms.

At one pole is the covenant of obligation. On the basis of previous acts of salvation, and without undertaking any specific obligations himself, God binds the people to abide by certain stipulations. If obedient, they will experience rich blessings, but if they are unfaithful, they will bring on themselves calamitous curses. More than a mere idea, this covenant was at times a social and political reality of powerful unifying force, since it bound the individuals and tribes of Israel together in allegiance to a common God and observance of fundamental social obligations to one another, such as respect for property, life and justice.

The secular model for this conception of covenant has emerged from the study of ancient treaties, after recovery of political archives of the Hittites. The Hittite treaties, dating from a time shortly before the emergence of the nation of Israel (Late Bronze Age), represent only one branch of a treaty tradition shared in essentials by all areas of the ancient Near East. Evidence suggests that in many respects Hittite treaties were much like those that earliest Israel would have known.

The typical treaty has five main parts. First is a preamble giving the titles of the "Great King," who grants the treaty. Next is a historical prologue, where the Great King sets forth his past dealings with the vassal king, stressing the major power's favors towards the minor ruler and his royal house. Then comes a series of explicit stipulations, the actions to be performed or avoided by the vassal (though not applying to the Great King.). Fourth is a list of the pact's witnesses, the gods both of the Great King and of the vassal. Fifth is a list of blessings to come on the minor king if he obeys, and curses if he disobeys.

It has been shown that this format was the model for the Israelite covenant of obligation, that is, for the Sinai covenant (Ex chap. 20) or the early covenant described in Joshua chapter 24. God gives a covenant, based on his past acts of salvation ("I am the Lord your God, who brought you out of the land of Egypt"); God himself does not swear to any specific future undertaking, whereas the people of Israel are tied to specific obligations toward the deity and toward one another. The Ten Commandments, inscribed on the "tablets of the covenant," spell out what the obligations are; obedience to them offers great blessings but curses attend any transgression.

Along with such general analogies, scholars have detected similarities in detail between ancient treaties and biblical conceptions of a religious covenant. In Joshua chapter 24, the history of Israel before God is set as a prologue to the covenant, which is thereby vindicated as a grateful response to the divine king's past favors. Covenant blessings, and in even greater quantity, curses, abound in Leviticus chapter 26 and Deuteronomy chapter 28. Still other aspects of biblical thought, such as the "love" of God and the "knowledge" of God now appear to be derived ultimately from the political vocabulary having to do with loyalty to a treaty partner. The prophets of Israel, moreover, predict the doom of an unfaithful people in colorful terms which seem to be related to curses traditionally associated with treaties. If one is horrified by Jeremiah's words (Jer 19:9) "I will cause them to eat the flesh of their

Moses standing on top of the flaming Mount Sinai holding the tablets of the Law. To his left stands Joshua; the Israelites encircle the mountain. From the Sarajevo Haggadah, Spain; 14th century. (Sarajevo National Museum)

sons and the flesh of their daughters," one may at least reflect that he is echoing the terms of Assyrian treaties.

The covenant of grant is radically different, and follows a different ancient model. In the covenant with Noah, only God takes on an obligation: he will not again destroy the world by flood, and it is up to the deity to "remember" what he has promised. Similarly, God makes a covenant with the house of David. He will continue David's line forever; and not only is nothing demanded in return, but the divine favor will be maintained even if David's sons prove unfaithful (II Sam 7:1ff). The covenant with Abraham similarly involves a one-sided promise by God to grant his descendants the land of Canaan, circumcision being the "sign" of the covenant (see Gen chaps. 15 and 17). The "covenant between the parts" boldly depicts God, under the symbols of the smoking oven and the flaming torch, taking on a solemn sworn obligation by passing between the parts of severed victims, a dramatic transformation of the ritual performed by humans swearing to a covenant.

The function of this sort of covenant was to give stability and validity to important aspects of Israel's spiritual and social world: the natural order, the national home, and the divinely chosen royal dynasty. This type of covenant is based on the analogy with ancient royal grants of land and privileges.

Treaty forms and vocabulary changed over the centuries, and as the model changed, so did the religious vocabulary. Written not long before the end of Israel's first period of national independence, Deuteronomy echoes contemporary Assyrian treaties in structure, tone, and sometimes even words. "The skies above you shall be copper and the earth under you iron" is from Deuteronomy 28:23 — and echoes the vassal treaties of the Assyrian king Esarhaddon. Assuming that covenant ideas in Israel predate Deuteronomy, this illustrates how an ancient concept may be clothed in contemporary fashion. Even more radical adaptation is evident in St. Paul. Since the Greek word *diatheke,* used to translate the Hebrew *berith* ("covenant"), most commonly means "last will and testament," Paul plays on the meaning of the Greek legal term to prove that the covenant with Abraham is unchangeable, like a man's last will (Gal chap. 3).

In the NT, the OT concept is quoted and taken over. When Matthew at the end of the Sermon on the Mount quotes Jesus as speaking of two ways (Matt 7:13-14), and later in the same chapter of the two houses built on sand and rock (Matt 7:24-27), this is to be seen as an adoption and adaptation by Matthew of the Deuteronomic theology of covenant. Jesus, harking back to the blood of the covenant ceremony in Exodus chapter 24, speaks of the New Covenant in his blood at the Last Supper (Matt 26:28; Mark 14:23-25; Luke 22:20). The blood of Jesus is now the bond uniting the two parties to the covenant.

Even more than the early Christians, the Essenes, the people of the Dead Sea Scrolls, exploited the idea of a New Covenant fully, and with greater superficial fidelity to the ancient idea of a covenant of obligation. However a great shift in emphasis was involved therein, the Essenes thinking of themselves as initiating a covenant with God, not as accepting one from him; and the covenant blessings are to fall on those inside the sectarian group, with the curses reserved for those outside.

COW See ANIMALS

COZBI ("voluptuousness"). The daughter of Zur, the Midianite chief, who was slain by Phinehas, the grandson of Aaron, at Baal of Peor, when Zimri, son of Salu a Simeonite, was lying with her (Num 25:6-15).

CRANE See ANIMALS

COZBI
Num 25:15, 18

CREATION AND COSMOGONY There are four different accounts of creation in the OT: two in the Book of Genesis (chaps. 1-2); one in Proverbs (8:22-31), and remnants of a fourth in prophetic and psalmic literature.

The OT commences with a majestic prologue describing the creation of the universe by an exalted transcendent God. See also GENESIS, BOOK OF. According to this account, the world was created in six days by divine fiat which produced cosmic order out of primordial chaos. Unlike the prevalent assumption, this description does not infer creation out of nothing — an outlook absent from the OT and mentioned for the first time only in the apocryphal book of II Maccabees 7:28. The tale is rather one of harmonic orchestration, wherein the six days divide into a symmetrical pattern of three days each: the creation of light on the first day, sky on the second, dry land, seas and vegetation on the third is complemented by the creation of the luminaries on the fourth day, living creatures in both sea and sky on the fifth, and land animals and man on the sixth. After each completed

The Creation depicted on two pages in the Sarajevo Haggadah *(Sarajevo National Museum).*

(bottom left)
The creation of the world. From the Book of the Dead. Egypt, c. 1000 B.C. (Kunsthistorisches Museum, Vienna)

An omphalos, "navel" of the world; Delphi, Greece, 5th century B.C.

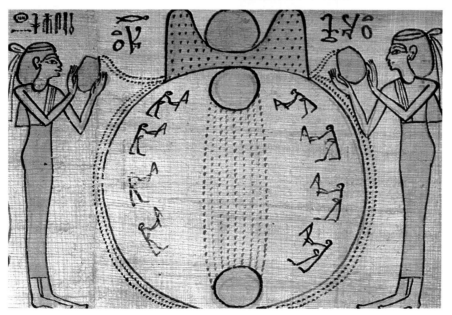

activity rings forth the refrain; "God saw that it was good." The culmination of creation is reached when the deity in a solemn declaration of purpose announces the creation of man: "Let us make man in our image, according to our likeness" (Gen 1:26). As God's representative on earth, man is then endowed with the unique blessing of sovereignty over all forms of life (Gen 1:28). After declaring that all this work was "very good", God thereupon ceases further creative activity on the seventh day, which he blesses and sanctifies (Gen 2:3).

The second creation account, Genesis 2:4-23, reflects an entirely different tradition and outlook, being more an anthropogeny than a cosmogony. In a highly anthropocentric version of the world, man was created first, formed from the dust of the earth and animated by divine breath. Woman was then formed from man's rib, and the two were placed in the Garden of Eden, where man's task was to till the garden.

These two traditional accounts of creation differ in many details: the names employed for deity, the generic name "God" (Gen chap. 1) versus his personal name Yahweh (Gen chap. 2); his transcendent (Gen chap. 1) versus immanent nature (Gen chap. 2); the sequence of creation, with man being created last (Gen chap. 1), or first (Gen chap. 2); the simultaneous creation of male and female in the divine image (Gen 1:27) versus woman's subsequent emergence from man's rib (Gen 2:21ff).

There are many points of contact between these two versions and earlier Mesopotamian tales of creation, in particular that of Enuma Elish. As in the first biblical account, existence of both water and wind is taken for granted; heaven and earth are created through separation of the waters by a firmament; the name for the watery abyss in Genesis is the cognate of the salty water goddess Tiamat; day and night precede the creation of the sun; the function of the luminaries is both to render light and regulate time, the creation of man is heralded by the deity stating his purpose to a divine council, and followed by divine repose. The order of events is identical in both: creation of the firmament, dry land, luminaries, man, divine repose. Even the concept of man's fashioning in the image of the deity has ancient Near Eastern prototypes, both in Mesopotamian and Egyptian literature.

The second story of creation also has one very distinct parallel in Mesopotamian stories; the shaping of man out of the dust of the earth. The fashioning of woman out of a rib may also reflect a Sumerian motif.

Egyptian analogues to these two accounts include the existence of primeval water and its subsequent division; the breathing of life into the nostrils of man; and the formation of man in the image of the deity.

Nevertheless, despite these blatant parallels, the biblical accounts reflect an entirely different world outlook in the vivid presentation of a preexistent god who is the single omnipotent creator. This monotheistic deity is not bound by, or subjugated to, any of the supra-divine realms of existence: nature, magic, destiny or time. He is completely free, and creation is the supreme act of his own absolute will. Man, in turn, is not an afterthought as in the Mesopotamian epic but rather the pinnacle of creation. The biblical accounts also differ from their earlier prototypes in that they have no political overtones, nor do they play any ritual role in the cult of Israel.

The third account of creation is reflected in Proverbs 8:22-31, where Wisdom relates that she is the oldest of all created things, and that she attended God during the various stages of creation. The fourth version contains allusions to a primordial struggle between a maritime monster and the supreme deity — a battle known from the earlier Mesopotamian and Ugaritic myths. This monster which represents the watery chaos, variously called Yam, Nahar, Leviathan, Rahab and Tannin, is either destroyed or placed under restraint by God whereupon creation can take place (Job 7:12; 26:10-13; 38:8-11; Ps 74:13-14; 89:10-11; 104:6-9; Prov 8:27-29; Is 27:1; 51:9-10; Jer 5:22; Hab 3:8).

It is of interest to note that four of the motifs in Genesis chapter 1: the existence of primordial material (Gen 1:2), God's working and resting, the council of God (Gen 1:26) and the creation of man in God's image (1:27), are contested and repudiated in the oracles of (Second) Isaiah (e.g. Is 40:14, 18, 25, 28; 45:7).

Early Christian writers affirm that time began when God created the world (Mark 13:19); the universe was fashioned by the word of God, so that the visible came forth from the invisible (Heb 11:3). Paul states in I Corinthians 11:9 "Nor was man created for the woman, but woman for the man." God is called simply "Creator" (Rom 1:25; I Pet 4:19) and the 24 elders laud God as worthy to receive "glory and honor and power, for you created all things; and by your will they exist" (Rev 4:11). The fact that God created something makes it good, to be enjoyed with thanksgiving (I Tim 4:1-5).

Consistent with an emerging Christology it began to be affirmed that Christ was active in creation, in the words of the writer to the Colossians "For by him all things were created that are in heaven and that are on the earth . . . all things were created through him and for him" (Col 1:16). Likewise the Epistle to the Hebrews affirms that it was through the Son that God created all orders of existence (Heb 1:2). Above all the early Christian community saw itself as Christ's own handiwork. For the writer to the Ephesians it is clear that they have nothing to boast of: "For we are his workmanship, created in Christ Jesus for good works, which God prepared beforehand" (Eph 2:10). There is relatively little interest in a doctrine of creation. In their doctrine of creation the NT writers followed the Jewish view on creation.

CRESCENS ("growing"). One of Paul's followers, who left him in order to work in Galatia.

CRETE, CRETANS The largest and southernmost of the Greek islands in the Mediterranean. According to Ezekiel (25:16) and Zephaniah (2:5), the Philistines would have originated in Crete (see CHERETHITES). Some scholars say the Cherethites of the Bible came from CAPHTOR. A Jewish community existed there in the time of Jesus (Acts 2:10). Paul was shipwrecked after sailing along the southern coast of Crete (Acts 27:7, 12). Paul quoted with approval a saying that Cretans were liars, evil beasts and lazy gluttons (Titus 1:12). Excavations have shed much light on the strong influence of Crete on the history and culture of the Mediterranean countries from the early 3rd millennium B.C. Numerous finds attest Crete's close cultural and commercial contacts with Asia Minor, Egypt, Phoenicia and Palestine.

CRESCENS
II Tim 4:10

CRETE,
CRETANS
Acts 2:11;
27:7, 12-13,
21. Titus 1:5,
12

(bottom left)
Crete (Caphtor)

(bottom right)
Remains of the Minoan palace at Knossos, Crete. 1750-1500 B.C.

Cretan pictographic inscription of the 3rd millennium B.C. (Cairo Museum)

CRICKET See ANIMALS

CRISPUS ("curled"). The head of the synagogue in Corinth; he was baptized by Paul along with Gaius.

CRISPUS
Acts 18:8.
I Cor 1:14

CROSS, CRUCIFIXION A form of punishment probably first used by the Persians, later adopted by the Greeks and Romans. Originally the "cross" was a simple stake on which was hung the corpse or head of the one just executed. This was intended as a public display for the purpose of humiliation (cf Deut 21:23; I Sam 31:9-10). In the Roman Empire crucifixion was not normally used for freemen or citizens, and it came to be known as the "slaves' punishment". The convicted man was usually tortured in some way, normally by flogging to the point of blood flow. This actually served to weaken the convict and hasten his death. The extent of the flogging could vary with the seriousness of the crime. He then carried a cross-beam to the place of execution where a vertical stake was already in place in the ground. The executioners laid him on the cross beam and tied or (less often) nailed him to it and then fastened it to the vertical stake — either on the top, forming a T or part way down, forming the more familiar cross. This must have been the shape of Jesus' cross, since the gospels indicate that an inscription was fastened above him on the cross (Matt 27:37; Luke 23:38). A small wooden block or peg was fastened half way up to support the body. Now unable to move, the victim was left to insects, weather and public abuse while the pain got increasingly worse. The noblewomen of Jerusalem, as a public service, used to provide a pain-relieving drug made of sour wine and myrrh. Death, nevertheless, was very painful and very slow, rarely taking less than 36 hours. Sometimes death was hastened by breaking the legs, for which reason crucifixion was also known to the Romans as "broken legs" (Cicero, *Philippicae* XIII 12 (27); cf John 19:31-33). Josephus, who calls it "the most wretched of deaths" (*War* VII 202ff) and records many crucifixions, also mentions that some victims were known to survive after some days on the cross (*Vita* 75).

The Monastery of the Cross in Jerusalem, built on the traditional site of the tree from which the Cross was made.

Altar in the Greek Orthodox Chapel in the Holy Sepulcher, Jerusalem, the traditional site of the Cross.

While Christian veneration of the actual cross of Jesus did not develop until about the 4th century, from the earliest times the cross became an important symbol in the Church. The NT writers, and Paul in particular, turn the despised symbol of an executed slave into a reason for pride and boasting (Gal 6:14). As the instrument by which God carried out his predetermined plan for sin's final atonement (Acts 2:23), the cross becomes the very symbol of redemption in all of its aspects (Col 2:13-14; I Pet 2:24) and the main focus of Paul's preaching (I Cor 1:17ff, 23; 2:2).

CUBIT See WEIGHTS AND MEASURES

CUCUMBER See PLANTS

CUSH

CUSH 1
Gen 2:13. Is 11:11; 45:14

1. A land which is mentioned by Isaiah (11:11; 45:14) among the countries of the world from which the exiles of Judah will be gathered. See ETHIOPIA.

(left)
A fettered Nubian and an Asiatic prisoner painted on the soles of two sandals. (Museo Egizio, Turin)

(right)
Terracotta head of a man from Nubia, (the biblical Cush) from the temple of Rameses III. 12th century B.C.

CUSH 2
Gen 10:6-8; I Chr 1:8-10

2. The first son of Ham, second son of Noah; he was the father of Nimrod the mighty hunter, and the ancestor of the Cushites.

The other sons of Cush were Seba, Havilah, Sabtah, Raamah and Sabtechah (Gen 10:6-8; some of these names are spelled slightly differently in I Chr 1:9).

CUSH 3
Ps 7:1

3. A Benjamite to whom David dedicated the seventh Psalm. Nothing is known about this Cush. It has been suggested that he was a foe David had defeated; that he was the Cushite who told David his son Absalom was dead (II Sam 18:21); that this was an alternate name for Kish, the father of Saul who became David's enemy.

CUSHAN
Hab 3:7

CUSHAN A term which occurs only once, in the Book of Habakkuk: "I saw the tents of Cushan in affliction, the curtains of the land of Midian trembled." It is thought to be an earlier name for Midian though it may have been the name of a wandering tribe living in the south of Israel and later integrated into Midian.

CUSHI An alternate name for CUSHITE.

1. Father of Shelemiah, grandfather of Nethaniah and great-grandfather of Jehudi (who was sent by the princes to Baruch with the scroll of the Lord) at the time of Jehoiakim king of Judah (Jer 36:4, 14).

2. Father of Zephaniah the prophet.

CUSHITE A man of Cush who was asked by Joab to bring the news of the death of Absalom to David his father. Some texts spell it Cushi (II Sam 18:21-23, 31-32).

CUTH, CUTHAH A Sumerian city dedicated to the god Nergal, lord of the underworld. When the Assyrian king Sargon conquered Samaria and deported the Children of Israel to Assyria, he brought in "men of Cuth" and settled them in the cities of Samaria in place of the Children of Israel (II Kgs 17:24, 30). The men of Cuth brought the cult of their god Nergal to their new country (II Kgs 17:30).

The site of Cuth has been identified as Tell Ibrahim, some 20 miles (32 km) northeast of Babylon.

CYPRESS See PLANTS

CYPRUS Island in the eastern Mediterranean. Some scholars maintain that it is to be identified with Elishah and Kittim mentioned in the OT. In the 3rd century B.C., the island came under Ptolemaic rule and its Jewish population grew rapidly, as reflected in the NT (Acts 4:36; 13:4-6; 15:39). Paul, Barnabas (who came from Cyprus) and John preached in various Cypriot synagogues, including the one in Salamis. The gospel had been brought to the island by Jewish Christians fleeing from Jerusalem after the stoning of Stephen (Acts 11:19ff). These attempts to spread Christianity were resisted by the Jews, one of whom, Bar-Jesus, described as a magician and false prophet, sought to prevent Paul and Barnabas from preaching to the island's governor. Barnabas twice revisited his native land and was finally martyred at Salamis and is thus considered by Christians as the apostle of the island.

CUSHI 1
Jer 36:14

CUSHI 2
Zeph 1:1

CUSHITE
II Sam 18:21-23, 31-32

CUTH, CUTHAH
II Kgs 17:24, 30

CYPRUS
Num 24:24. Is 23:1, 12. Jer 2:10. Ezek 27:6. Dan 11:30. Acts 4:36; 11:19-20; 13:4; 15:39; 21:3, 16; 27:4

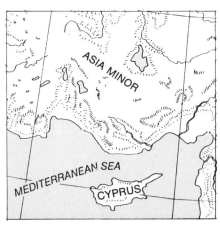

Cyprus.

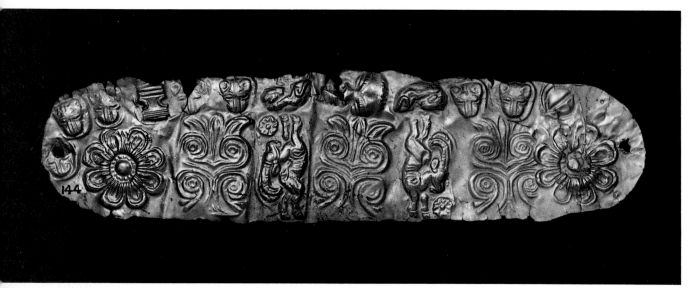

Gold diadem found in a tomb near Larnaka, Cyprus. 13th century B.C.

CYRENE Town in Libya, originally a Greek colony; in NT times, approximately 25 percent of its population were Jews. People of Cyrene were among those gathered in Jerusalem at the feast of Pentecost (Acts 2:10). Simon, who was pressed to carry Jesus' cross, originated from Cyrene (Matt 27:32; Mark 15:21; Luke 23:26). Lucius, one of the "prophets and teachers" in Antioch, was also from Cyrene (Acts 13:1). Cyrenian members of the Synagogue of the Freedmen in Jerusalem disputed with Stephen (Acts 6:9).

CYRENE
Matt 27:32. Acts 2:10; 11:20; 13:1

Aerial view of Cyrene.

CYRUS King of Persia, founder of the Achaemenian dynasty and the Persian empire; he reigned 559-529 B.C. Cyrus conspired against his grandfather, King Astyages of Media and seized Media in 550. He went on to conquer Lydia and his crowning success was the capture of Babylon in 539. His extended empire was the largest known until that time. He was finally killed in battle against one of the tribes in the north of his kingdom.

In the OT he is held up as a heroic figure, the messenger of God sent to redeem Israel. Second Isaiah (45:1ff) mentions him as God's "anointed" to save Israel, enabling the people to return to their land and rebuild the Temple. The prophet clearly foresees the defeat of Babylon at the hands of the Persian conqueror and thus regards Cyrus as the instrument of redemption. In Isaiah 44:28 Cyrus is praised as God's shepherd who will carry out the divine will and rebuild Jerusalem. In other parts of the book the prophet seems to refer to Cyrus, although he does not mention him specifically by name (Is 41:2, 25; 46:11).

It is usually thought that Cyrus' attitude to the Jews was part of his general policy towards all conquered peoples, and his respect for native religions and customs. This policy is reflected in his treatment of the Jews and in his edict to the Jews of Babylonia in 538 B.C., calling upon them to return to their ancestral land and to rebuild the Temple (Ezek 1:2-4; 6:3-5; II Chr 36:23). The first and last chapters of Daniel are dated to his reign (Dan 1:21; 10:1).

(bottom left)
The Cyrus Cylinder, 538 B.C., which tells how Cyrus captured Babylon and how he returned the former inhabitants to their cities.

The tomb of Cyrus II the Great.

D

DABBASHETH A hill town on the western boundary of the territory allocated to Zebulun. Its exact location is uncertain, but it has been identified as Tell esh-Shemman, opposite Jokneam, south of the Kishon River; or alternately, Dabsheh, a ruined site to the east of Acre.

DABERATH A city within the territory of Issachar, situated on the boundary between that tribe and Zebulun (Josh 19:12). It was assigned, with its suburbs, to the Gershonite Levites (Josh 21:28). It has been identified as the village of Daburiyeh, at the western base of Mount Tabor.

General view of the village of Daburiyeh on the slopes of Mount Tabor, identified with Daberath.

DAGON (Hebrew *dagan* — "grain"; popular etymology derives it from the Hebrew *dag* — "fish"). The chief deity of the Philistines worshiped in Samson's time at Gaza (Judg 16:21-23), and at Ashdod (I Sam 5:2-7); up to the Hasmonean period, when it was destroyed by Jonathan Maccabee in 147 B.C. (I Macc 10:83-85; 11:4) and at Beth Shan in the days of Saul and David (I Sam 31:10; I Chr 10:10). At a sacrificial festival in Gaza which the Philistines held for "Dagon their god" (Judg 16:23), Samson was brought forth and demonstrated his strength by pulling down the house upon himself and the Philistines gathered in it, proving the superiority of the Israelite God over Dagon. The same point is made in the narrative in I Samuel 5:1-7: where the image of Dagon in the temple at Ashdod is twice thrown down after the ark of the Lord has been brought into the temple and the head and hands of the divine image are broken off. Leaping over the threshold of Dagon's temple may have been a part of Philistine ritual (cf I Sam 5:4-5; Zeph 1:9). I Chronicles 10:10 tells how the Philistines hung up the head of Saul in the temple of Dagon after his death, and displayed his weapons at the sanctuary of Ashtaroth (I Sam 31:10, 12). Three place names, Beth

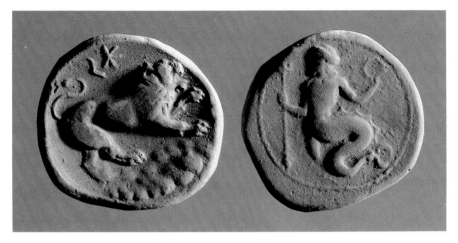

A coin of Askelon (?) with "Dagon" on one side and a lion on the other. 4th century B.C.

Dagon in Judah (Josh 15:41) (identified with modern Beit Dajan, southeast of Jaffa), Beth Dagon in Asher (Josh 19:27), and Beit Dajan east of Shechem, preserve the memory of the worship of Dagon. The god Dagon is well attested to in Akkadian sources and especially in the Mari texts. In the mythological texts from Ugarit (Ras Shamra), the name of the god "Dgn" appears as the father of Baal. The fact that the name is of Semitic origin indicates that Dagon was a god adopted by the Philistines from the neighboring Canaanites.

DALMANUTHA
Mark 8:10

DALMANUTHA A place north of Tiberias to which Jesus went by boat with his disciples after having fed the five thousand. It is otherwise unknown and the parallel passage in Matthew (15:39) reads Magadan. Many scholars feel it is identical with Magdala.

DALMATIA
II Tim 4:10

DALMATIA A region on the east coast of the Adriatic Sea. Dalmatia was part of the Roman province of Illyricum, which is mentioned by Paul as one of the areas where he preached the gospel (Rom 15:19). According to II Timothy 4:10 one of his collaborators, Titus, left Paul and departed for Dalmatia.

View of the coast of Dalmatia at Trogir on the Adriatic Sea.

DALPHON
Est 9:7

DALPHON One of Haman's ten sons. He was hanged by the order of Ahasuerus.

DAMARIS
Acts 17:34

DAMARIS An Athenian who believed in Jesus after hearing Paul's address to the Athenians at the Areopagus (Acts 17:22-34).

DAMASCUS.
DAMASCENES
Gen 14:15;
15:2. II Sam
8:5-6. I Kgs
11:24; 15:18;
19:15; 20:34.

DAMASCUS, DAMASCENES   Capital of Syria, in ancient times mentioned in Akkadian and Egyptian documents as an important caravan center at a fertile oasis in Southern Syria. The geographical position of Damascus, dominating the major trade routes, brought it economic prosperity in the biblical period (II Kgs 5:12; Ezek 27:18 mentions its trade in wine and wool). The patriarchal narratives

The street called Darb al-Mustaqim in Damascus today follows the same lines as the Straight Street mentioned in Acts 9:11.

(right) Remains of Roman columns in the Darb al-Mustaqim in Damascus.

Coin of Damascus portraying the city goddess on one side and the portrait of Antoninus Pius on the other. 2nd century A.D.

mention the city (Gen 14:15; 15:2). The desert oasis of Damascus became an important center for the Arameans at the end of the second millennium, and for some time was powerful enough to compete with Assyria. The city was captured and subjugated by David, during his campaigns against the Aramean confederation (II Sam 8:5-6; I Chr 18:5-6). It was conquered by Rezon, a former subject of the king of Zobah, who cast off Israelite sovereignty during Solomon's reign and made it the capital of the kingdom of Aram-Damascus (I Kgs 11:23 ff), which henceforth was often in conflict with Israel. It remained the capital until its destruction by the Assyrians in 732 B.C., reaching its height in the 9th century as an important political, economic and cultural center. Ben-Hadad I of Aram-Damascus broke his alliance with Baasha of Israel to make a league with Asa of Judah (I Kgs 15:18 ff). Damascus was forced to grant Israelite merchants special rights in the city, as indicated by King Ben-Hadad II's submission to Ahab of Israel (I Kgs 20:34). This same Ben-Hadad and his son Hadadezer fought against Ahab, who fell in battle at Ramoth Gilead in 853 B.C. (I Kgs chap. 22). Hazael killed Ben-Hadad III (II Kgs 8:7-15), who was succeeded by Ben-Hadad IV; the latter conquered almost all the northern kingdom of Israel, and his siege of Samaria was lifted only through the intervention of Elisha (II Kgs 6:24 ff). The Assyrian king Shalmaneser IV, weakened Damascus sufficiently to allow Jeroboam II, king of Israel, to impose his rule over it in 773 B.C. (II Kgs 14:28). During the Syro-Ephraimite War, Rezin of Damascus allied with Pekah of Israel against Ahaz of Judah, who in turn called upon Tiglath-Pileser III, king of Assyria, who captured Damascus (732 B.C.), carried the inhabitants captive to Kir and killed Rezin (II Kgs 16:5-9; Is 7:1-8; Amos 1:3-5) thereby reducing the city to the status of an Assyrian provincial center.

From the Assyrians, Damascus passed to the Chaldeans, from them to the Persians and then to the Macedonian Greeks. The city is mentioned several times in the Hasmonean era in connection with the conquests of Jonathan (II Macc 11:62). It was captured by the Roman general, Pompey, in 64 B.C. In NT times, a large and important Jewish community existed in Damascus, as did a Christian group. Saul (Paul) of Tarsus, while en route to persecute the Christians of the city, was smitten to the earth (Acts 9:2-3, 8-10; 22:6, 10-12; 26:12) and he escaped his Jewish enemies by being let down from the walls in a basket (Acts 9:24-25; 26:20; Gal 1:17). In Paul's day, the city was in the hands of Aretas, king of Arabia Petrea (II Cor 11:32). On the eve of the Roman war (A.D. 66) the Jews of Damascus were murdered by the Gentile inhabitants.

8:7, 9; 14:28; 16:9-12. I Chr 18:5-6. II Chr 16:2; 24:23; 28:5, 23. Song 7:4. Is 7:8; 8:4; 10:9; 17:1, 3. Jer 49:23-24, 27. Ezek 27:18; 47:16-18; 48:1. Amos 1:3, 5; 5:27. Zech 9:1. Acts 9:2-3, 8, 10, 19, 22, 27; 22:5-6, 10-11; 26:12, 20. II Cor 11:32. Gal 1:17

DAN, DANITES ("to judge", or "vindicate").

1. The fifth son of Jacob and the firstborn of Bilhah, Rachel's maid (Gen 30:1-6). In Jacob's blessing (Gen 49:16-18), which predicts the future destiny of his descendants, it is stated "Dan shall judge his people as one of the tribes of Israel... Dan shall be a serpent by the way, a viper by the path, that bites the horses' heels so that his rider shall fall backwards." In the Song of Deborah, the tribe is reprimanded for not participating in the war against the Canaanites, with the ironic question "...and why did Dan remain on ships?" (Judg 5:17).

According to Joshua 19:40-48 (cf Judg 1:34-35) the tribe was allotted the fertile area lying between Judah and the Mediterranean Sea, but the Danites' attempt to establish themselves in the coastal plain failed, as the place was occupied by Philistines and Amorites (Canaanites) who forced them up into the mountains. The Danites' failure to conquer their original inheritance made them move northward where, towards the end of the 12th century B.C. and the beginning of the 11th century B.C., they conquered Laish (alternately — Leshem) and renamed it Dan (Josh 19:47).

2. City (formerly called Laish) sacked and conquered by the Danites who settled there and renamed it (Josh 19:47; Judg 18:7, 27ff). From the time of the Judges, Dan was seen as the northernmost limit of the land of Israel, whose north-south span was described in the popular phrase "from Dan to Beersheba" (Judg 20:1, etc.). Jeroboam I built a temple and set up a golden calf to be worshiped in Dan and Bethel (I Kgs 12:29ff), evoking harsh criticism from the prophet Amos (8:14). The use of the name in Genesis 14:14 is anachronistic.

The territory of the Danites.

The high place at the Iron Age temple at Tell Dan.

Aerial view of Tell Dan.

Excavations on the mound, Tell Dan, 50 acres square (21 hectares) and 65 feet (20 m) in height, have shown that the town was established in the Early Bronze Age II. It was destroyed in a terrible conflagration in the 11th century B.C. but was soon rebuilt and a century later became the religious and administrative center of the region. Remains of the temple enclave set up by Jeroboam and enlarged by Ahab have been uncovered and the finds include a four-horned altar. The city was probably destroyed during the Babylonian conquest but was reoccupied at the end of the Persian period or the beginning of the Hellenistic era. The site continued to be occupied in the Roman and Byzantine periods.

Bilingual inscription (Greek and Aramaic) from Tell Dan mentioning the deity of Dan. Hellenistic period.

(bottom)
The story of Daniel and the lions depicted on the Armenian church at Aghtamar, Turkey. 11th century.

Daniel's tomb at Susa in Iran.

DANIEL ("God is my judge" or "God has judged").

1. David's second son by Abigail, he was born at Hebron (I Chr 3:1, called Chileab in II Sam 3:3).

2. A priest who signed the covenant in Nehemiah's time.

3. The exilic prophet, hero of the Book of Daniel, who was carried off with other captives by Nebuchadnezzar in the third or fourth year of Jehoiakim's reign (Dan 1:1; Jer 25:1), c. 605 B.C. The Daniel mentioned with Noah and Job in Ezekiel 14:14, 20 actually refers not to the prophet but to Danel, a king renowned in Ugaritic literature for judging the case of the widow and the cause of the fatherless. The same personality is alluded to in Ezekiel 28:3, where Tyre is mocked for considering herself "wiser than Daniel". This figure may very well have served as the prototype for the Book of Daniel.

DANIEL, BOOK OF In the Jewish canon, the Book of Daniel was not placed among the Prophets but instead was included in the Hagiographa. This was due to the book's final composition during the period of the Maccabean rebellion (around 168 B.C.), too late for it to be included in the Prophetic section which already had been closed and canonized.

The Book of Daniel divides into two clearly distinct parts:
(a) a collection of stories about Daniel and his friends (chaps. 1-6), written in Aramaic, except for chapter 1;
(b) a collection of apocalyptic visions predicting the course of world history (chaps. 7-12), written in Hebrew, except for chapter 7. It has been suggested that the entire book may originally have been composed in Aramaic, which had by the 3rd century B.C. become the language of the majority of Jews, with several chapters later being translated into Hebrew.

In the first section, chapter 1 depicts Daniel and his three friends, Hananiah, Mishael and Azariah — renamed respectively Belteshazzar, Shadrach, Meshach and Abed-Nego by Nebuchadnezzar's vizier — being trained for the king's service. Though living at the court, the young men nevertheless remained strictly observant of the dietary laws

DANIEL 1
I Chr 3:1

DANIEL 2
Ezra 8:2. Neh 10:6

DANIEL 3
Ezek 14:14, 20; 28:3. Dan 1:6-11, 17, 19, 21; 2:13-20, 24-27, 46-49; 4:8, 19; 5:12-13, 17, 29; 6:2-5, 10-11, 13-14, 16-17, 20-21, 23-24, 26-28; 7:1-2, 15, 28; 8:1, 15, 27; 9:2, 22; 10:1-2, 7, 11-12; 12:4-5, 9. Matt 24:15. Mark 13:14

in return for which God granted them such impressive knowledge and skill that they won the king's admiration.

Chapter 2 relates how Daniel interpreted Nebuchadnezzar's unpleasant apocalyptic dream which had left the Chaldean experts baffled. The colossal statue the king saw in his dream symbolized four

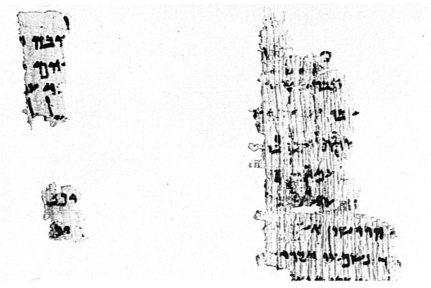

Fragments from the Book of Daniel found at Qumran (Shrine of the Book, Jerusalem)

successive pagan kingdoms — the Babylonian, Median, Persian and Greek. The stone uncut by human hand, which crushed the monstrous statue before itself becoming a mountain and filling the whole earth, represented the people of God. Upon hearing his dream explained, Nebuchadnezzar acknowledged the one true God and appointed Daniel and his companions to high ranking positions.

In spite of their promotion, the three pious friends refused to worship Nebuchadnezzar's golden idol, whereupon they were cast into the blazing furnace but emerged unharmed (chap. 3). The king again expressed his admiration for the God of the Jews and exalted the three Jewish officials.

Chapter 4 has Daniel interpreting Nebuchadnezzar's frightening dream in which a tree is hewn down and the king himself roams the field like a wild animal. Daniel explained these visions as foreshadowing Nebuchadnezzar's temporary insanity, a punishment for his overbearing arrogance; but as a reward for his repentance and conversion to the true God, the king's sanity and kingdom would be restored to him.

Chapter 5 describes Belshazzar's feast and Daniel's interpretation of the mysterious handwriting on the wall: "Mene" — the king's days were numbered; "Tekel" — the king had been weighed and found wanting; and "Parsin" — the kingdom had been divided up. That same night the king was slain and replaced by Darius the Mede. When Daniel ignored a royal prohibition on prayers addressed to anyone save the king for a period of one month, the plots of his jealous fellow ministers resulted in him being cast into a lions' den. But Daniel, who continued his thrice-daily prayers to God, remained untouched, whereupon his accusers were themselves thrown into the den and devoured instantaneously. Darius then decreed that Daniel's God must be revered throughout the kingdom.

The Book's second section consists of four apocalyptic visions: In chapter 7, Daniel sees four immense beasts emerging from the sea and seeks enlightenment from an angel who interprets his dream: the lion symbolizes the Babylonian kingdom; the bear, the Median; the leopard, the Persian; and the terrifying monster with the ten horns, the Hellenistic (Seleucid). Three of the horns are uprooted by an arrogant small horn, Antiochus IV Epiphanes, who oppressed the Jews for three and a half years. This beast is annihilated by God, and the fifth empire worldwide and everlasting will be that of the Jews. In this chapter God is anthropomorphically described as an old man with white hair, seated on a throne and called the "Ancient of Days".

Another of Daniel's symbolic visions is again explained by an angel (chap. 8): the two-horned ram represents the kingdoms of the Medes and Persians; the he-goat which breaks the rams' horns and totally subdues it is the Greek kingdom. The he-goat's big horn which eventually breaks off to be replaced by four conspicuous horns, represents respectively the kingdom of Alexander the Great and the four later kingdoms of Cassander (Macedonia), Lysimachus (Thrace), Ptolemy I (Egypt) and Seleucus I (Syria). The small horn which grows out of these four to blaspheme God and defile the pious sanctuary is Antiochus IV.

Chapter 9: After praying and fasting in an attempt to comprehend Jeremiah's prediction about the 70 years of Jerusalem's devastation (Jer 25:11-12; 29:10), Daniel learns from the angel Gabriel (chap. 9) that the 70 years are in reality 70 weeks of the years (490 years) at whose termination justice will be done and the Temple reconsecrated. Then will follow the roughly half week of years during which Antiochus IV abolishes sacrifices and defiles the Temple.

The last and longest apocalypse (chaps. 10-12) dated in the third year of Cyrus describes the course of events from Cyrus the Great in 538 B.C. to the death of the wicked Antiochus IV in 164 B.C. The angel shows Daniel a panoramic vista of history: four Persian monarchs; Alexander the Great; the four kingdoms following the breakup of Alexander's empire; the battles, intrigues and alliances that took place among the Seleucids and Ptolemies; the rise of the infamous Antiochus IV who brutally victimized the Jews and desecrated their Temple; the final vindication of Israel; and a concluding word of comfort. The rest of the book is concerned with an attempt to calculate the date of the end of the world and the OT's first mention of the partial resurrection of the dead.

Since no anti-Epiphanian propaganda is discernible in chapters 1-6, they can be assumed to antedate Antiochus IV Epiphanes' reign, and may be dated around 304 B.C. However, chapters 7-12 in their entirety are a product of the reign of Antiochus IV, and may stem, not from a single hand, but rather from several different apocalyptists.

Certain sections of Daniel are carefully dated by regnal years, but these statements do not always correspond with the usual knowledge of the history of this period, i.e., after Cyrus the Persian empire was ruled, not by three kings (11:2) but by ten. There never was a Darius the Mede (5:31; 6:1; 9:1; 11:1), and Belshazzar (5:1-2; 7:1), was never king of Babylon. The siege of Jerusalem is definitely dated in 597 B.C. after Jehoiakim had reigned 11 years; but Daniel 1:1 places the siege in his third year. Despite numerous discrepancies and historical problems, the book's spiritual lessons are clearer, surveying a continuous succession of world empires whose sequence is predetermined by God. The Book of Daniel, completed at a time when the very existence of God's people was threatened (under Antiochus IV Epiphanes), endeavors to show that God rules and that his purposes will be vindicated. The author viewed past, present and future as parts of a predetermined plan; by setting himself back into the era of Daniel, he presented the whole panorama of history in its true perspective.

OUTLINE

DAN JAAN
II Sam 24:6

DAN JAAN A town covered by David's census (II Sam 24:6), lying on the road between Gilead and Sidon (cf I Kgs 15:20; II Chr 16:4). It may be identical with Dan, the traditional extreme north of the country (cf Judg 18:28-29).

DANNAH
Josh 15:49

DANNAH A village in the hill country of Judah, in the district of Debir, near Hebron. Possibly to be identified with modern Idnah.

DARA, DARDA
I Kgs 4:31.
I Chr 2:6

DARA, DARDA Son of Zerah, of the tribe of Judah; he was famous for his wisdom which is compared to Solomon's (I Kgs 4:31). He is listed among the "sons of Mahol" which according to some scholars was an ancient musicians' guild.

DARDA
I Kgs 4:31

DARDA See DARA

DARIUS
Ezra 4:5, 24;
5:5-7; 6:1, 12-15.
Neh 12:22. Dan
5:31; 6:1, 6, 9,
25, 28; 9:1;
11:1. Hag 1:1,
15; 2:10.
Zech 1:1, 7;
7:1

DARIUS The name of three Persian kings of the Achamenid dynasty and of a ruler of uncertain identification mentioned in the Book of Daniel.

Darius I the Great (Hystaspes) (522-486 B.C.) succeeded Cambyses II. His account of the struggle for the succession to the throne of Persia appears in the famous trilingual Behistun inscription, where he tells how he defeated the impostor Gaumata who had usurped the throne in Cambyses' absence. This inscription, and that on his tomb at Naqsh-i Rustam, as well as his decree to cease further obstruction and promote

(left)
Remains of Darius' palace at Persepolis.

Darius the Great on his throne shown on the treasury building in Persepolis.

Gold coin of Darius the Great.

the rebuilding of the Temple in Jerusalem (Ezra 6:12; Hag 1:1-2, 15) afford an insight into Darius' tolerant attitude in matters of religion. The prophet Haggai's oracles are dated to the middle of 520 B.C., before Darius had succeeded in putting down the rebellion that had erupted throughout his empire, and while the future of the Persian empire was still in doubt. Haggai regarded the upheaval as foreshadowing God's imminent intervention, and therefore urged the community to rebuild the Temple (Ezra 5:1ff; 6:14). However, by the end of 520 Darius had crushed his foes and extended his empire. Zechariah, although his prophecies fall mainly after Darius' victories, continued to encourage his people in their efforts (Zech chaps. 1-8; note date in 7:1).

Darius II (Nothus) (442-404 B.C.). The reference in Nehemiah 12:22 may be to Darius II.

Darius III (Codomanus) (336-330 B.C.), the last king of Persia (cf "the fourth king of Persia" in Dan 11:2). Following his disastrous defeat at the hands of Alexander the Great he was murdered by Bessus, satrap of Bactria, and the Persian empire came to an end.

Darius the Mede: son of Ahasuerus (Dan 9:1) who according to Daniel 5:30-31 succeeded Belshazzar and preceded Cyrus as king of Babylon (cf Dan 6:28). Many historical difficulties have arisen from these references, causing much confusion (See DANIEL, BOOK OF). One explanation is based on the Achemenian concept of three world monarchies: the Chaldeans founded the first empire, the Medes the second, and the Persians the last. The Jews regarded Darius, who conquered Babylon, as a Median, successor to the Chaldean, Belshazzar, and predecessor of Cyrus the Persian.

DARKON A descendant of Solomon's servants, who headed one of the families returning with Zerubbabel from Exile.

DATHAN A son of Eliab of the tribe of Reuben, who, together with Abiram, led a revolt against Moses, joining the rebellion of Korah during the sojourn in the desert (Num 16:1-35; 26:9-11). It has been suggested that two separate accounts of rebellion against Moses' leadership have been woven together in Numbers chapter 16. The rebels complained that Moses had brought the Israelites out of the fertile land of Egypt to die in the wilderness, and that he had usurped princely authority over the community. The event served as a warning to Israel and as an example of divine justice, since Dathan, Abiram and their families and property were swallowed up by the earth (Num 16:25-33). The rebellion may have been connected with the Reubenite tribe's loss of its earlier position of preeminence.

DAVID The youngest son of Jesse, the great-grandson of Boaz and Ruth; born in Bethlehem of the tribe of Judah. He was Israel's second and greatest king and his united kingdom achieved the status of an intermediate power between Mesopotamia and Anatolia in the north and Egypt in the south. David's early years were spent as a shepherd, but later he joined the entourage of Saul, Israel's first king. Each of the three different accounts of David's appearance emphasize one of the qualities later to characterize him: I Samuel 16:1-13 stresses the anointment of David as chosen by God; I Samuel 16:14-23 describes David as an extraordinary musician and poet; and chapter 17 presents him as the warrior hero in the story of the slaying of Goliath the Philistine. Although at first Saul favored David, he became increasingly jealous (I Sam 18:8). Furthermore, Saul encouraged his son Jonathan, who had become David's closest friend to slay this potential threat, but Jonathan intervened on David's behalf, convincing the king of David's loyalty (I Sam 19:1-6). But the continuous attempts made on his life by the mentally disturbed king eventually forced David to flee the monarch's wrath. During his period as a political fugitive from Saul, Jonathan remained David's faithful companion assisting him in every way (I Sam chaps. 18-20, 23). David improved his position with different social groups within Judah (I Sam 22:20-23; 23:1-5; 25:1-43) and even among the Philistines with whom he sought refuge (I Sam 21:10-15; 27:2-12).

With the defeat of the Israelites and the death of Saul and his sons at the hands of the Philistines, David was anointed king over Judah (II Sam 2:4) at Hebron. David subsequently defeated Ishbosheth, Saul's son who had been crowned king of northern Israel at Mahanaim by Abner, Saul's commander. Thereafter, the northern tribes of Israel accepted David's leadership and by the eighth year of his reign, David felt himself strong enough to unite all tribes under an independent kingdom. Jerusalem, hitherto a Jebusite enclave, between Judah and the northern kingdom of Saul, was captured by David and became the political, military and religious capital of the United Kingdom when David brought the ark into the city. David resumed hostilities against the Philistines and in two decisive battles, at Baal Perazim and Rephaim near Jerusalem, they were defeated and forced to withdraw to the coastal plain, thus ceasing to pose a serious threat to Israel (II Sam 8:1).

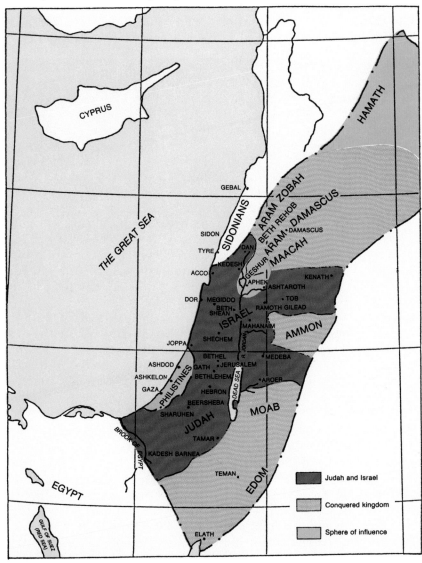

The kingdom of David.

However, Philistines were enrolled in his own personal guard, called the Cherethites and Pelethites, mercenary troops from independent Philistine cities, who joined David's ranks under the command of Benaiah son of Jehoiada.

David embarked on the creation of an empire, in five distinct phases: (a) Tribal kingdom: this period saw intense military activity combined with diplomatic marriages (II Sam 3:2-3; 10:7-19). (b) National kingdom: the alliance between David and the northern tribes of Israel. (c) Consolidated territorial state: having quelled the Philistines, David was free to attack the last strongholds and enclaves of the native Canaanites in the north: Megiddo, Beth Shean and Taanach. These were reduced, putting David in control of an integrated kingdom, comprising the territory of all the tribes. The Philistine monopoly of metal manufacture (I Sam 13:19-20) must also have fallen into Israelite hands at this stage. (d) Multinational state: having broken through the hostile western flank surrounding Israel, David then undertook a series of campaigns against the peoples around his borders: first the Moabites (II Sam 8:2) were defeated and subjugated, then Edom (II Sam 8:14), and finally the Ammonites (II Sam 12:30), from whom Ezion Geber was captured, giving the Israelites an outlet on the Red Sea. It was during the Ammonite war that David committed adultery with Bathsheba and sent her husband, Uriah the Hittite to his death. For this God rebuked David through Nathan the prophet who courageously confronted the king with his crime (II Sam 12:1-15) and imposed the penalty that the

Samuel anointing David, who stands with his hands folded. Wall painting from Dura-Europos synagogue on the Euphrates River. 3rd century.

sword should never depart from his house. Despite David's repentance (II Sam 12:13; Ps 51) the child of this adulterous union died. (e) Empire: the most remarkable territorial expansion was David's defeat of the Arameans and his annexation of Aram-Zobah and Damascus (II Sam 8:3-8), winning the vassal states of Aram-Zobah as well, so that the borders of his kingdom reached as far as the Euphrates River. Thus David forged a mighty empire (cf I Kgs 4:21; Ps 72:1, 8, 10-11).

In spite of David's overwhelming prestige, the old rivalries between the southern and northern parts of his kingdom continued. After nearly

8:1, 15-18, 20, 24-26, 66; 9:4-5, 24; 11:4, 6, 12-13, 15, 21, 24, 27, 32-34, 36, 38-39, 43; 12:16, 19-20, 26; 13:2; 14:8, 31; 15:3-5, 8, 11, 24; 22:50. II Kgs 8:19, 24; 9:28; 11:10; 12:21; 14:3, 20; 15:7, 38; 16:2, 20; 17:21; 18:3; 19:34; 20:5-6; 21:7; 22:2. I Chr 2:15; 3:1, 9; 4:31; 6:31; 7:2; 9:22; 10:14; 11:1, 3-7, 9, 11, 13, 15-18, 25; 12:1, 8, 16-19, 21-23, 31, 38-39; 13:1-2, 5-6, 8, 11-13; 14:1-3, 8, 10-12, 14, 16-17; 15:1-4, 11, 16, 25, 27, 29; 16:1-2, 7, 43; 17:1-2, 4, 7, 15-16, 18, 24; 18:1-11, 13-14, 17; 19:2-6, 8, 17-19; 20:1-3, 7-8; 21:1-2, 5, 8-11, 13, 16-19, 21-26, 28, 30; 22:1-5, 7, 17; 23:1, 5-6, 25, 27; 24:3, 31; 25:1; 26:26, 31-32; 27:18, 23-24, 31-32; 28:1-2, 11, 19-20; 29:1, 9-10, 20, 22-24, 26, 29. II Chr 1:1, 4, 8-9; 2:3, 7, 12, 14, 17; 3:1; 5:1-2; 6:4, 6-8, 10, 15-17, 42; 7:6, 10, 17-18; 8:11, 14; 9:31; 10:16, 19; 11:17-18; 12:16; 13:5-6, 8; 14:1; 16:14; 17:3; 21:1, 7, 12, 20; 23:3, 9, 18; 24:16, 25; 27:9; 28:1; 29:2, 25-27,

30; 30:26;
32:5, 30, 33;
33:7, 14; 34:2-3;
35:3-4, 15.
Ezra 3:10; 8:2,
20. Neh 3:15-16;
12:24, 36-37,
45-46. Ps
18:50; 72:20;
78:70; 89:3,
20, 35, 49;
122:5; 132:1,
10-11, 17;
144:10. Prov
1:1. Ecc 1:1.
Song 4:4. Is
7:2, 13; 9:7;
16:5; 22:9, 22;
29:1; 37:35;
38:5; 55:3. Jer
13:13; 17:25;
21:12; 22:2, 4,
30; 23:5;
29:16; 30:9;
33:15, 17, 21-22,
26; 36:30.
Ezek 34:23-24;
37:24-25. Hos
3:5. Amos 6:5;
9:11. Zech
12:7-8, 10, 12;
13:1. Matt
1:1, 6, 17, 20;
9:27; 12:3, 23;
15:22; 20:30-31;
21: 9, 15;
22:42-43, 45.
Mark 2:25;
10:47-48;
11:10; 12:35-37.
Luke 1:27, 32,
69; 2:4, 11;
3:31; 6:3;
18:38-39;
20:41-42, 44.
John 7:42.
Acts 1:16;
2:25, 29, 34;
4:25; 7:45;
13:22, 34, 36;
15:16. Rom
1:3; 4:6; 11:9.
II Tim 2:8.
Heb 4:7;
11:32. Rev 3:7;
5:5; 22:16

30 years of almost unchallenged supremacy over the Israelites, several major crises emerged over the questions of the succession (e.g. Absalom's revolt, II Sam chap. 15), and the actual unity of the kingdom (the rebellion of Sheba, II Sam chap. 20).

David undertook far-reaching reforms in national institutions and administration. He also began preparations for building a central sanctuary in Jerusalem, and chose the site of the future Temple. The worship of Israel's God became the official state religion, and the priesthood was organized under the chief priest who, along with other leading priests, became royal officials, members of David's court in Jerusalem (II Sam 8:17-18). David also laid the foundations for the division of the country into districts and for its administration through a sequence of officials, and also reorganized the army.

Biblical tradition relates that David initiated a cultural and literary revival which was continued by Solomon, and many Psalms are attributed to him, as well as the laments over Abner (II Sam 3:33-34), Saul and Jonathan (II Sam 1:17-27) and Absalom (II Sam 18:33).

As a result of his many conquests, the Israelites came into contact with the major powers and currents of civilization, particularly with the Phoenicians of Tyre and Sidon, who greatly influenced Israel's cultural development. David's personality, a fascinating mixture of historical fact and romantic legend, led Jewish national tradition to invest his name with a halo of mysticism and divine prestige, so that he became a powerful religious symbol and the focus of messianic dreams. These messianic traditions receive expression in the gospels in the person of Jesus descended from David (Matt 22:41-46; Mark 12:35-37; Luke 20:41-44; John 7:42), who is born in David's town of Bethlehem, and is frequently referred to as "son of David" or "seed of David".

DAY OF ATONEMENT Solemn festival observed on the tenth day of the month of Tishri. In biblical times, it was marked in the Temple by an elaborate ceremony. This consisted, firstly, of the sacrificial ritual in which the high priest uttered a confession of sins on behalf of all the people and entered the Holy of Holies (the only time during the year when this was permitted), sprinkled the blood of the sacrifice and offered incense. Secondly, two goats were taken, one was devoted to God, the other to AZAZEL. The sins of the community were figuratively transferred to the latter goat ("the scapegoat") which was sent out into the wilderness to die there.

The Day of Atonement was the annual day of purgation for the Temple and the people. This follows from the facts that its sacrifices consist solely of "sin" offerings (Ex 30:10; Num 29:11), and that the three sacrificial animals are offered on behalf of the priesthood (Lev 16:6, 11) and the people (Lev 16:5, 15). The biblical text expressly declares that the slain bull and goat purge the shrine of the (physical) pollution of the Israelites and their brazen sins (Lev 16:16; cf 16:19), and the scapegoat carries off their iniquities (Lev 16:22).

The purgation of the sanctuary rests on two complementary postulates: (a) The brazen defier of God's commandments is ineligible for sacrificial expiation (Num 15:30-31), but the Temple must be purged of his sins and impurities, and (b) since brazen sins possess the power not only to pollute the outer altar but to penetrate into the shrine, reaching even the holy ark, the entire Temple complex must be purged on the Day of Atonement.

The purgation-expulsion nexus essential to pagan magic survived in Israel's cult, but its meaning underwent a revolution. As scholars have noted, the purgation and Azazel rites on the Day of Atonement are distinct: the slain purgation offering purges the tabernacle, but the live

David playing the harp, portrayed in the Byzantine style, on a mosaic floor of a synagogue at Gaza. 5th-6th centuries. (Museum for Music and Ethnology, Haifa)

one carries off the people's sins. The reasons are clear: Israel, the holy people (Lev 11:44; 19:2; 20:26), needs the same purification as the holy place, so that "they shall not defile their camps in the midst of which I dwell" (Num 5:3). Moreover, the monotheistic dynamic is at work here: since the world of demons is nonexistent, the only source of rebellion against God is in the heart of man, and it is there that cathartic renewal must periodically take place.

Ordinarily, the hand-laying and confession must be performed by the offerer himself, but presumptuous, rebellious sin bars its perpetuators from the sanctuary, and they must be represented by the high priest. The latter's officiation, however, is not inherently efficacious. The people, though excluded from the rites, must submit to fasting and other acts of self-denial (Lev 16:29; 23:27-32; Num 29:7). Thus repentance purges man as the blood of the sacrifice does the sanctuary. This ethical achievement is unmatched in the ancient world. True, the Babylonian new year calls for a ritual of humiliation for the king, followed by his prayer of confession. But in contrast to Israel's high priest, whose confessional specifies where he and his people have failed, the Babylonian king appears arrogant and self-righteous.

Finally, atonement by sacrifice is efficacious only for sins against God. The Mishnah has captured the ethical import: "For the sins between man and God, the Day of Atonement effects atonement; but for the sins between man and his fellow, the Day of Atonement will effect atonement only if he has appeased his fellow" (M. Yoma 8:9). That this spiritual principle is not an innovation of the rabbis, but constitutes this legacy from biblical times, is shown by its explicit presence in the "guilt offering", where restitution to man must precede sacrificial expiation from God (Lev 6:1-7).

The Day of Atonement itself may not be as old as its ceremonial. For example, in distinction from all other festival prescriptions which give the date before the ritual (e.g. Lev chap. 23), here alone the date is not specified until the end (Lev 16:29). Evidence also points to the conclusion that originally this day was an emergency rite for purging the sanctuary (e.g. Lev 16:1-2). However, it seems likely that it was fixed as a regular purgation ritual for the Temple and nation on the tenth of Tishri — the seventh month — in pre-exilic times. Thus an ancient ritual for the purging of the sanctuary was reconstituted by Israel to include the purging of the nation's sins, which was then set as an annual observance.

DAY OF THE LORD A phrase recurring repeatedly in prophetic literature: in Amos, Isaiah, Joel, Obadiah, Zephaniah and Ezekiel. The phrases "on that day" and "the day of God's wrath", also frequent in the Prophets, are a reference to the Day of the Lord and serve as its synonym. All these terms designate the time in the future when God will manifest his universal rule and might by a series of destructive judgments on both the nations and Israel. The devastating destruction foreseen will be attended by frightening changes in the normal order of nature: a day of darkness (Amos 5:20); a day when the lights of the heavenly bodies will be dimmed (Joel 2:10; 3:15); "a day of trouble and distress, a day of devastation and desolation" (Zeph 1:15). Isaiah 13:6 warns: "...wail for the Day of the Lord is at hand". Joel (1:15) associates the term with the devastation brought on by a plague of locusts in his time, comparing the oncoming swarms of locusts to the armies of the Day of the Lord marching into battle (Joel 2:25).

The Day of the Lord will bring God's destruction of his enemies, the enemies of Israel (Is 13:6-11; Ezek 30:1 ff; Joel 3:1-8; Obad v. 15). The destruction of the wicked nations will also mark the passing of all idolatry (Is 2:18). This description of the Day of the Lord may have planted the notion in the popular mind that Israel will be totally exempt from the destruction the day will bring. But Amos, the first prophet to use this phrase, emphatically rejects such a view. "Woe to you who desire the Day of the Lord! For what good is the Day of the Lord to you? It will be darkness, and not light" (Amos 5:18). If the wicked nations will come to ruin, so will the wicked of Israel (Is 2:12; Zeph 1:7-16).

Ezekiel 34:12 regards the destruction of the Temple and the subsequent Exile as manifestations of the Day of the Lord. Similarly, the author of Lamentations bewails the destruction of the Temple and the misfortunes that accompanied it as manifestations of the day of God's "fierce anger" (Lam 1:12; 2:11). In the exilic period, the prophecies of destruction on the Day of the Lord were directed against specific hostile nations; against Babylonia (Is 13:6, 9, 13); against Edom (Is 34:8; 63:4); against Egypt (Jer 46:2-12). It is only among the exilic prophets, that the salvation aspect of the Day of the Lord was stressed. Thus, Isaiah (61:2-3) declares that the day of God's vengeance will witness God's consolation of the mourners of Zion. Likewise, Ezekiel 34:12 affirms that God will deliver Israel. The day will bring purification and salvation to those who fear God (Mal 3:2-3). But for the wicked, the day will be like a burning furnace that will consume them like straw. Before the coming of the "great and dreadful day", God will send the prophet Elijah who will reconcile fathers and sons (Mal 4:1-6).

In its apocalyptic vision of Armageddon, the final battle between the forces of good and evil that will engulf the present world and mark its end, Revelation 16:14 speaks of it as the "great day of God Almighty". For Luke, the day of the Lord is that on which Jesus will reappear on earth (Luke 17:24). Paul wrote that the Day of the Lord (the day of the reappearance of Jesus) will come like "a thief in the night" (I Thes 5:2). Elsewhere, (I Cor 1:8; 5:5; II Cor 1:14) he equated the OT Day of the Lord with "the day of our Lord Jesus Christ"; that is, the day of the Second Coming. II Peter 3:11-12 combines the rabbinic doctrine that man by his own good conduct hastens the Day of the Lord, with a Stoic-Platonic description of the final conflagration of the universe.

DEAD SEA The large lake in the lower part of the Jordan Valley lying between the hills of Moab to the east and the Judean Hills to the west. It is also referred to in the Bible as the "Sea" (Ezek 47:18) or the "Salt Sea" (Gen 14:3, etc.).

The Dead Sea is the earth's lowest point, lying about 1,200 feet (360m) below the level of the Mediterranean. At the north end its bed is about 2,400 feet (730m) below sea level. About 48 miles (77km) long, its maximum width is about 11 miles (18km). Most of the water reaches the lake from the Rivers Jordan, Arnon, Zered and Kidron and from

(bottom right)
View of the Dead Sea from En Gedi. (Nature Reserves Authority)

(bottom left)
Salt mounds on the surface of the Dead Sea.

The Dead Sea.

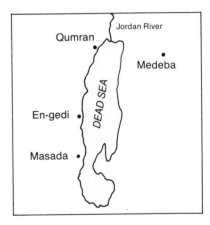

numerous other streams, which dry up in summer. In Herodian times a road to Moab passed through a part of the Dead Sea now under water. Of the natural resources of the Dead Sea only bitumen, used for embalming in Egypt, was exploited in ancient times. From the mountains on its southwestern shore salt was obtained. In Ezekiel's messianic vision (47:8-12) the lake was to be freshened by a river of water issuing from the Temple.

DEAD SEA SCROLLS The Dead Sea Scrolls are perhaps the greatest archeological discovery of the present century. The first seven scrolls were found by a Bedouin in a cave near the northwestern shore of the Dead Sea, in 1947. These are now kept in the Shrine of the Book in Jerusalem. Shortly after the first discovery several scholars, and larger numbers of Bedouins, began the hunt for more scrolls. Numerous additional ones were found in the vicinity of Khirbet Qumran, and some in four other caves to the north of that site.

The scrolls were mostly written on parchment; only a few were on papyrus. The writing was mostly in ink made of powdered charcoal, though a metallic ink was also used. One scroll was engraved on copper sheets. In the main the scrolls were written in the Hebrew square script. Paleographic analysis has divided this script into three chronological periods: pre-Hasmonean, Hasmonean and Herodian. Certain words, such as the names for God, were sometimes written in the ancient Hebrew script.

The importance of the discovery of these scrolls is that some of them are copies of certain books of the OT made between the 2nd century B.C. and the 2nd century A.D., and are thus earlier by about 1,000 years than any previously known copy of the OT. They are of great value in tracing the process of codification of the books of the OT. The scrolls fall into two main classes: manuscripts of the Bible and the APOCRYPHA; and the special writings of the Dead Sea sect.

Except for the Book of Esther, complete scrolls or fragments of all the books of the OT were found. The most complete texts were in cave 1, which yielded one complete scroll of Isaiah, another containing

(right)
General view of Qumran, where the Dead Sea Scrolls were found.

Clay jars in which the Qumran Scrolls were discovered. (Shrine of the Book, Jerusalem)

chapters 53-60 and fragments of others. One of the Isaiah scrolls differs from the current Hebrew text in the use of the full script (i.e. with all vowels, which were later partly replaced by dots below and above the letters) and also in certain grammatical forms. Other fragments of Isaiah are much closer to the present Masoretic (traditional) text. Cave 4 yielded numerous fragments of scrolls representing fourteen copies of Deuteronomy, twelve of Isaiah, ten of Psalms and eight of the twelve Minor Prophets. Of the Book of Exodus two copies, one of which is close to the Samaritan codex, were in the ancient Hebrew script, while six others were in the square Hebrew script, one being close to the text of the Septuagint. One copy of Numbers was written in red ink and is more detailed than the current text. Differences of this kind are found in other books from this and the other caves.

The Apocrypha includes fragments of the Hebrew or Aramaic texts of Jubilees, Enoch, Tobit, Testament of Levi, Testaments of the Twelve Patriarchs, the Wisdom of Ben-Sira, etc. It is not known whether these books were considered by the Dead Sea sect to be as sacred as the books of the Bible. What is certain is that, unlike the copies of the books of the Bible, they were not written by the sect's own scribes. The texts of the Apocrypha found in the Judean Desert caves settle once and for all some doubts concerning the original language of some of the books that were previously known only from late translations; they were found at Khirbet Qumran for the first time written in their original language. Still other books, such as the Genesis Apocryphon (written in Aramaic), were not known at all.

The writings of the Dead Sea Sect include many books peculiar to the Qumran community and other sects which dwelt in the Judean Desert. Some are Bible commentaries which include allusions to contemporary events and provide a glimpse into the history and beliefs of the sect. Most complete are the commentaries on the Book of Habakkuk. Other fragments concern the Psalms, Isaiah, Micah, Zephaniah and Nahum. One scroll book is a compilation of commentaries on verses from Genesis chapter 49, II Samuel chapter 7 and Psalms 2-3.

"Thanksgiving" Scroll. (Shrine of the Book, Jerusalem)

Other scrolls include the Scroll of Manuals, which contains the laws of the sect as well as a manual for the Last Days; the eschatological Scroll of the War of the Children of Light against the Children of Darkness; the Thanksgiving Scroll, a collection of hymns; the Damascus Document which contains religious rulings as well as historical material; the Copper Scroll with a list of hiding-places where the treasure had been concealed; and the Temple Scroll dealing with festivals, offerings and holy gifts, information on the Temple, Jerusalem and laws of uncleanness and purity.

In addition to the manuscripts found in the vicinity of Khirbet Qumran, documents of the Roman, Byzantine and Arab periods were discovered in the locality. The most important date from the time of the Bar-Kochba rebellion (A.D. 132-5) and the period immediately preceding it. They include fragments of biblical texts (Genesis, Exodus, Numbers, Deuteronomy, Isaiah, Amos, Obadiah, Jonah and Micah), which are very close to the Masoretic text now in use. This means that the editing of the books of the Bible must have been done by the generations following the destruction of the Second Temple.

DEATH Death is viewed as the natural, inevitable consequence of man having been created by God out of the dust of the earth: "...For dust you are, and to dust you shall return" (Gen 3:19; Job 10:9; cf Ecc 12:7). The possibility of living forever had been held out to Adam, but having disobeyed the divine command by eating the fruit of the tree of knowledge, immortality was forever barred to him (Gen 3:22-23).

The notion that at death the soul departs from the body is totally foreign to the Bible since body and soul are regarded as a single indivisible entity in both life and death. Hence, the Hebrew Bible refers to both the living (e.g. Gen 12:5) and the dead (e.g. Lev 21:1) as a *nephesh*. This is traditionally translated as "soul" but perhaps is better rendered "person". In death, man becomes a weak, vaporous substance and leads a shadowy existence in Sheol, the abode of the dead (Job 3:13-19).

The life span of human beings is limited to a maximum of 120 years (Gen 6:13). In Psalms (90:10), 70 years are said to be man's normal life span or, "by reason of strength...eighty years". "The death of the righteous" (Num 23:10) is described as a non-violent death at a good old age. Such death is part of the divine promise given to Abraham. "You shall go to your fathers in peace, you shall be buried at a good old age" (Gen 15:15; 25:8; cf 35:29; Job 42:17). This is evidence, moreover, that one has merited the fulfillment of the divine promise "I will fulfill the number of your days" (Ex 23:26). The Book of Job (5:26) describes such death as like "...a sheaf of grain [which] ripens in its season". Harvest is not the only biblical euphemism for death. More frequently it is spoken of as "going the way of all the earth" (Josh 23:14; I Kgs 2:2) or as "being gathered to his people" (Gen 25:8; 35:29; Judg 8:32). The inevitability of death is expressed by describing death as insatiable (Is 5:15; Hab 2:5). Death is not only insatiable, it is also "strong" (Song 8:6) and "bitter" (Ecc 7:26).

(right)
The dead confronted by gods and goddesses. Egyptian papyrus from Thebes. c. 1300 B.C.

The jackal-headed god of embalming, Anubis, preparing a deceased nobleman for burial. Fragment from the tomb of Sennutem. 12th century B.C. Thebes, Egypt.

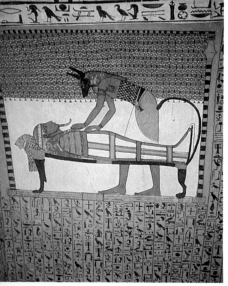

Biblical poetry includes distinct echoes of a mythological concept of death, particularly known from Ugaritic (early Canaanite) literature in which the god Mot is conceived as the King of Death (cf Is 25:8; Jer 9:20-22). His messengers who bring death to man are the demons occasionally mentioned in biblical poetry (Deut 32:24; Ps 91:6; cf Hos 13:14). In biblical prose narrative, however, the "destroying angel" is just a messenger subject to the will of God (Ex 12:23; II Sam 24:16; Job 33:22). It is God alone, who dispenses both life and death (Deut 32:39; I Sam 2:6; Ps 88:7). In one passage, (Is 25:8) God's eventual destruction of death itself is foreseen.

Death in the NT is regarded as a great evil and even as the last enemy (I Cor 15:26). Jesus grieves in agony at the prospect of his own death (Matt 26:38) and at the loss of his friend Lazarus (John 11:33, 35, 38). He uttered "vehement cries and tears" to God "to save him from death" (Heb 5:7). He even felt abandoned by God at the moment of his death (Mark 15:34 citing Ps 22:1). Paul regards death as punishment for Adam's sin (Rom 6:12).

On other other hand, Jesus and the early Christians shared the Pharisaic belief in the resurrection of the dead (Dan 12:2; Matt 22:23-28; Acts 23:6-9). Jesus raised the dead to life (Matt 9:18-26; Luke 7:11-17; John 11:38-44) and predicted his own resurrection (Mark 8:31; 9:31; 10:34). Paul regards Jesus' death as atoning for sin and his rising as mankind's justification (Rom 4:25). Paul's meditation on death and resurrection ends with a cry of victory over death (I Cor 15:54-57; cf Is 25:8; Hos 13:14). See also AFTERLIFE; BURIAL; MOURNING; RESURRECTION.

DEBIR

DEBIR 1
Josh 10:3

1. The king of Eglon, who, with a coalition of four other kings, attempted to halt Joshua's invasion.

DEBIR 2
Josh 10:38-39; 11:21; 12:13; 15:15, 49; 21:15. Judg 1:11. I Chr 6:58

2. Canaanite royal city located in the southern Judean hill country originally inhabited by the Anakim (Josh 11:21; 12:13) and also called Kirjath Sepher and Kirjath Sannah (Josh 15:15, 49). It was conquered by Othniel son of Kenaz, Caleb's nephew (Judg 1:11-13), though the author of the Book of Joshua attributes its capture to Joshua (10:38-39; 12:13). Debir is listed among the Levitical cities, which were administrative centers under the United Monarchy (Josh 21:15; I Chr 6:58). In the past it has been identified with Tell Beit Mirsim, but now with Khirbet Rabud, a large tell southwest of Hebron.

Khirbet Rabud in the Hebron region, identified with Debir.

DEBIR 3
Josh 15:7

3. A place on the northern boundary of Judah above the Valley of Achor between Jerusalem and Jericho. The modern name of Wadi al-Dabr most likely preserves the ancient name.

DEBIR 4
Josh 13:26

4. A place on the boundary of Gad in Gilead, believed to be the same as Lo Debar.

DEBORAH ("bee").

DEBORAH 1
Gen 35:8

1. The nurse of Rebekah, Isaac's wife. She is mentioned in a single verse only, where it is stated that she died and was buried in Bethel after Jacob's return to Canaan.

DEBORAH 2
Judg 4:4-5, 9-10, 14; 5:1, 7, 12, 15

2. A prophet, judge, military leader and poet in the period of the Judges (Judg chaps. 4-5); wife of Lapidoth (Judg 4:4). Her story commences at a time when the Israelites were under the yoke of King Jabin of Hazor (Judg 4:1-3). Deborah was a local judge within the Ephraim territory (4:4-5), her permanent seat being in an Ephraimite locality, between Ramah (Samuel's home town, I Sam 7:17) and Bethel. Like other judges including Samuel, her judicial duties included a military role in pursuance of which she summoned the warrior Barak and gave him a plan of action received through a divine oracle (Judg 4:6-7). Barak's response to her summons, together with his refusal to go to battle without her, reflect Deborah's prominence and popularity.

This explains her reply to his request, with the comment that the outcome of the battle would be decided by a woman (Judg 4:9). However, she accompanied Barak to his base in Kadesh. The army was recruited from the tribes of Naphtali and Zebulun, and the decisive battle took place by the Kishon River (Judg 4:11-16). Sisera, the commander of the opposing army, was slain by Jael, and this Israelite victory marked the beginning of the end for Canaanite hegemony in the center and north of the country (Judg 4:17-24).

Judges chapter 5 gives another account of the same events, with differences in several details. This chapter is a victory poem, usually considered one of the oldest in literature. Its composition is attributed to Deborah herself (Judg 5:1, 7, 12), although the editorial title cites Barak as co-author and singer. The following points in the poem stand in contrast to their parallels in the narrative account. In chapter 4 God conceives the plan of the battle, which is delivered to Barak by Deborah and henceforth carried out; in chapter 5 God himself fights for the Israelites from heaven (Judg 5:20). The poem claims that, in addition to the warriors from Zebulun and Naphtali, other tribes were also summoned and either came forth or refused to join (Judg 5:14-18). The poem makes no mention of Mount Tabor nor of Jabin: Sisera is presented as the Canaanite leader, with a court of his own. The outcome of the battle, however, is the same: the Canaanites are defeated, and Sisera is slain by Jael.

Deborah's poem alludes to her roles as judge and savior (Judg 5:6-7), although she does not actually refer to herself as "prophet". She calls herself "a mother in Israel" (Judg 5:7), which well defines her active role in the proceedings. It would seem that her significance as the initiator and mentor of the events is better accentuated by the poem than by the narrative.

DECALOGUE See TEN COMMANDMENTS

DECAPOLIS A league or group of ten Hellenistic cities with a Jewish minority, all (with the exception of Scythopolis) situated in Transjordan. The membership of the league was never constant. Pliny (*Nat. Hist.* v, 74) enumerates Damascus, Philadelphia (Rabbath-Ammon), Raphana, Scythopolis (Beth Shean), Gadara, Hippos (Susita), Dium, Pella (Pehel), Gerasa and Canatha (Kanath) but admits that other writers give a different list. Ptolemy (*Geography* v, 14, 18) lists different cities, omitting Raphana but adding Abila, Lysianae and Capitolias. Stephan of Byzantium (Gerasa) mentions 14 cities instead of the original ten.

DECAPOLIS
Matt 4:25.
Mark 5:20;
7:31

(bottom of page)
Colonnaded street at Gerasa (Jerash).

The ten cities of the Decapolis.

The earliest mentions of the Decapolis are in the NT (Matt 4:25; Mark 5:20). As most of the cities date their era from 64/62 B.C. it it evident that the foundation of the Decapolis was part of Pompey's settlement in the East, though the exact date is obscure.

DEDAN, DEDANITES An important Arabian people who established themselves in the region of Teima (their name is preserved in the nearby ruins of Daidan), in northwest Arabia, and are mentioned frequently in Assyrian and Chaldean sources. In the Bible they are descended from Raamah (also a place in southwest Arabia) son of Cush (Gen 10:7; I Chr 1:9), or alternately from Jokshan son of Abraham and Keturah (Gen 25:3; I Chr 1:32). The fact that Dedan and Sheba were regarded as brothers would indicate widespread trade throughout the Arabian peninsula. Isaiah alludes to their caravans (Is 21:13) and Ezekiel their commercial connection with Tyre (Ezek 27:3, 20). Reference to Dedan in oracles against Edom (Jer 49:7-8; Ezek 25:13), indicates that the Dedanites constituted the southern border of Edom, though there is no proof that Edom ever extended its territory so far south.

DEER See ANIMALS

DEHAVITES One of the groups in Samaria which tried to prevent the reconstruction of the Temple; they signed the protest letter dispatched to Artaxerxes (Ezra 4:9). Identified with the Persian tribe of Daoi, their original home was by the Caspian Sea. Some scholars say it is not a name but an Aramaic word meaning "namely, viz".

DELILAH A woman living near the Sorek River. Her name may derive from an Arabic root meaning "be amorous, coquettish, seductive". Delilah became Samson's mistress and, for a large sum of money delivered him into the hands of the Philistines with his Nazirite locks shorn and his supernatural power gone (Judg chap. 16).

DEMAS A fickle collaborator of Paul (Philem v. 24). Having shared the apostle's first imprisonment in Rome and after sending greetings to Philemon and his friends in Colossae through him (Col 4:14; Philem v. 24), Demas deserted Paul and went to Thessalonica "having loved this present world" (II Tim 4:10).

DEDAN,
DEDANITES
Gen 10:7;
25:3. I Chr
1:9, 32. Is
21:13. Jer
25:23; 49:8.
Ezek 25:13;
27:15; 27:20;
38:13

DEHAVITES
Ezra 4:9

DELILAH
Judg 16:4, 6,
10, 12-13, 18

DEMAS
Col 4:14.
II Tim 4:10.
Philem v. 24

Coin of Pella showing the portrait of Commodus on one side and the acropolis of the city on the other. 2nd century A.D.

*(top left)
A view of Roman remains at Pella in Transjordan.*

*(top right)
Roman columns at Hippos (Susita), on the east shore of the Sea of Galilee.*

DEMETRIUS

1. A silversmith of Ephesus, who manufactured silver shrines for the goddess Diana. When he discovered that Paul's preaching was harming his business, he incited a riot against the Christians.

2. A Christian, who received good testimonies from everyone.

DEMETRIUS 1
Acts 19:24, 38
DEMETRIUS 2
III John v. 12

DEMONS, DEMONOLOGY The ancient universal belief in demons is reflected in the Bible. In two passages (Deut 32:17; Ps 106:37) the Israelites are charged with having offered sacrifices to demons — a practice expressly condemned and forbidden. This proscribed worship is imputed to Canaanite influences. The demons are depicted as haunting ruined cities and deserts (cf Lev 16:10; Is 13:21).

Several demons are mentioned by name in the OT: *Seirim*, translated as "demons" or "wild goats", were probably hairy, goat-like demons (Deut 32:17; Ps 106:37; Is 13:21). *Keteb*, translated as "destruction" or "sudden death" (Deut 32:24; cf Is 28:2; Hos 13:14), has been identified as the bringer of a deadly plague. In the passage in Hosea, Keteb appears as a messenger of Sheol, the personified abode of the dead. *Reshef* was a god of plague in the ancient Near East. He has also been identified with the Akkadian deity Nergal who is compared to fire in Ugaritic literature. Translators have rendered Reshef both as "fever" and as "fiery lightning" or "sparks that fly upward" (Ps 78:48; Hab 3:5; Job 5:7). *Azazel* was a demon who lived in the wilderness, translated "scapegoat" in many versions (See AZAZEL) (Lev 16:8, 10, 26). *Lilith*, called "night creature" in Isaiah 34:14, was in ancient Mesopotamian and Jewish sources a female demon who tempts men sexually and strangles newborn babies. *Dever*, often translated "pestilence", joins Reshef in appearing before God as he is about to execute judgment on earth (Hab 3:5).

The OT antipathy to magic as practiced by the surrounding peoples meant that while demonology remained a folk-belief, it was excluded from the main line of religious thought.

An echo of the equation between demons and pagan deities found in the OT (Deut 32:17) is to be seen in the NT in such passages as Acts 17:18; I Corinthians 10:20 and Revelation 9:20. Demons are regarded in the NT as originators of evil, both physical and psychic. The mental disorders and physical ailments brought upon men by the entrance of demons (or "unclean spirits") into the human body include the loss of the power of speech (Matt 12:22), insanity (Luke 8:27-33), sickness (Matt 8:14-15), paralysis and lameness (Acts 8:7). The demons and "unclean spirits" are termed the ministers of Satan or Belial; the latter is occasionally called Beelzebub (Matt 10:25; 12:24, 27; Mark 3:22; Luke 11:15, 18-19). In these passages, the Pharisees charge Jesus with casting out demons by invoking the name of Satan or Beelzebub.

On a number of occasions, Jesus is reported to have expelled demons from people so afflicted and restored them to sanity or the normal use of their physical faculties (Matt 12:22; Mark 3:22; Luke 11:14). Jesus gives his twelve disciples the power over unclean spirits; that is, the power to cast them out (Matt 10:1: Acts 5:15).

DERBE A town in the Roman province of Galatia. When Paul and Barnabas visited this province they were not always made welcome, and they even had to flee from Iconium to Derbe and Lystra (Acts 14:1-6). According to the Acts (14:7) they preached the gospel at Derbe; there they also met Timothy, the son of a Jewish mother and a Greek father, whom Paul took along on his journeys (Acts 16:1).

DERBE
Acts 14:6, 20;
16:1; 20:4

DEUEL ("the Lord knows"). The father of Eliasaph No.1 leader or prince of the tribe of Gad (Num 1:14); the name is spelt Reuel in Numbers 2:14.

DEUEL
Num 1:14;
7:42, 47; 10:20

Bowl bearing a kabbalistic inscription, placed in the foundations of a building as protection against devils. 4th century A.D.

The Mount of Temptation (the mountain of Quarantal) overlooking Jericho where, according to tradition, Jesus was tempted by the devil (Matt 4:8-9).

DEUTERONOMY, BOOK OF The English name of the fifth book of the Pentateuch, Deuteronomy, is derived from the Greek translation of the Hebrew phrase, meaning "the second law" or "the repeated law" (Deut 17:18). Underlying this name is the supposition that Deuteronomy represents a recapitulation of the laws from Exodus through Numbers. It should be noted, however, that Deuteronomy repeatedly refers to itself as a unique law code (cf 1:5; 4:8; 17:19; 27:3, 8, 26; 29:20; 30:10; 31:26).

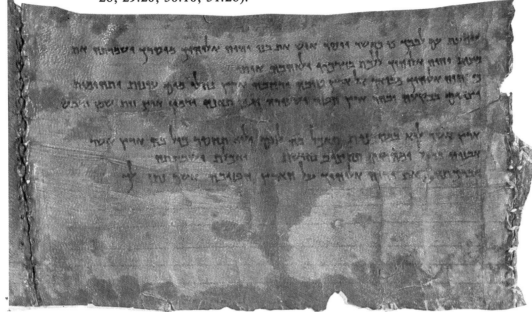

Fragment of the Book of Deuteronomy including the Ten Commandments; found at Qumran. (Shrine of the Book, Jerusalem)

A man touching a mezuzah *(scroll containing verses from Deuteronomy). Illuminated manuscript,* Rothschild Miscellany, *Italy c. 1470. (Israel Museum)*

In general terms, the book presents an organic structure. With a few scattered exceptions (e.g. 4:41-49; 27:1-26; 31:14-30), it is composed in the first person singular as a series of parting speeches delivered by Moses before his death. The book opens with two introductory discourses, the first of which emphasizes the lessons of Israel's history since leaving Sinai (1:6-3:29), and the second, God's uniqueness (4:1-40). Moses' third discourse, beginning with 5:1-11:32, starts with the acme of the law itself, namely the Decalogue, but instead of proceeding to the details of the law, Moses offers a multi-faceted exposition on the reasons for obeying the law. The third discourse continues with the body of the book, chapters 12-26, containing the Deuteronomic law code. This is followed by instructions regarding the manner and contents of the blessings and curses to be delivered at Shechem (on Mount Ebal and Mount Gerizim) in consequence of respective observance or neglect of the laws (chap. 27). Chapter 28 contains a longer catalogue of blessings and curses. The next three chapters of the book deal with Moses' official renewal of the covenant, his final exhortations, and his appointment of Joshua as successor (29:1-31:13). The book closes with a description of Moses' last day, on which he uttered a prophetic poem and blessings to the tribes of Israel before viewing the land of Israel from the heights of Mount Nebo.

On the surface, Deuteronomy presents itself as the last testimonies of Moses, who wished to impart the laws and exhortations which would be vital for the generation entering the promised land. The basic question, though, is: does Deuteronomy represent a complementary amplification of previous Pentateuchal law codes, or does it purport to be a completely new law code intended to supersede its forerunners? Either alternative presents an inherent difficulty, for if Moses was merely making some additions to the previous law codes, why had he not given all the laws at once at Sinai? Conversely, if the precepts of Deuteronomy were meant to revise or to update former laws, why would Moses have given those previous laws at all, if they were destined to be replaced forthwith?

Modern critical scholarship recognizes that Deuteronomy contains both additions to, and revisions of, earlier Pentateuchal laws, but it interprets this evidence as pointing to a legislator(s) later than Moses. In the critical view, the key to pinpointing the time frame of Deuteronomy lies in the repeated demand for centralization of cult, that is, the requirement that all sacrificial worship take place at the one central sanctuary (cf Deut 12:11, 13-14, 17-18; 15:20; 16:5-6). This concept was the hallmark of the reform of King Josiah of Judah in 622 B.C. (II Kgs chaps. 22-23), reportedly based on a recently discovered law book (II Kgs 22:8), which modern scholars have associated with Deuteronomy itself. At the same time, centralization of cult was unknown to earlier law codes (Ex 20:24) or to pre-7th century B.C. prophets (I Kgs 19:10); even the efforts of King Hezekiah to uproot the local "high places" in the late 8th century B.C. differed from the subsequent endeavors of Josiah, as he lacked possession of a law book (II Kgs 18:4). Significantly, the most crucial novelties in the Deuteronomic law revolve precisely around the issue of centralization. For example, Deuteronomy 12:14ff, assuming that only one town (implying Jerusalem) would have a sanctuary, sanctioned the non-sacrificial slaughter of meat for private consumption. This new law was a necessary relaxation of Leviticus 17:1-9, which required that people bring all animals intended for consumption to the sanctuary as formal sacrifices. In addition, Deuteronomy transformed the Passover celebration from a home observance to a national festival in the interests of centralization (Deut 16:1-8; cf Ex 12:21-27).

Assigning the focal point of the Deuteronomic legislation to the age of Josiah by no means implies that the entire book stems from the 7th century B.C. Many earlier elements are embodied in some of the laws, such as the provisions concerning the "holy war" (chap. 20). The two poems at the end of the book (chaps. 32-33) are generally viewed as deriving from an earlier time. Nevertheless, the 7th century B.C. still seems to be the most likely period for the compilation and editing of the book in its present form. Besides the internal biblical evidence surrounding the issue of centralization, there is also external testimony for the dating of the book. Comparative study has demonstrated the close affinities between Deuteronomy and Neo-Assyrian vassal treaties: examples include the shared contents and order of the curses found in Deuteronomy 28:23, 26-35, and the vassal treaties of Esarhaddon lines 528-531, 419-430. Likewise, some of Deuteronomy's key phrases such as "to love...with all your heart" (6:5; 11:13; 30:6), "to obey the voice of" (15:5; 28:1; 30:20), and "to fear" (4:10; 6:24; 10:12; 14:23; etc.), were especially prevalent in the 8th and 7th centuries B.C. as formulas of loyalty between vassal and suzerain. In short, Deuteronomy exhibits such close structural and linguistic resemblances to Neo-Assyrian vassal treaties, that it is hard to escape the conclusion that the book was purposely patterned after this model in order to state its theological message.

Deuteronomy is not merely a law code in the narrowest sense. Rather, the discourses attributed to Moses take on the character of a well-developed formula for national prosperity. God is Israel's sole sovereign. Thus, Israel's continued well-being in the promised land hinges on her unswerving fidelity to God's covenant. This cardinal statement is bolstered by some of the most unequivocal declarations of monotheism in the entire Bible (cf 4:28, 35, 39); by the ceaseless imploorations to love God, to fear him, and to walk in his ways (6:2, 5, 13, 24; 8:6; 10:12, 20; 11:1, 13, 22; 13:4-5; 19:9; 30:6, 16, 20); and by the repeated demands not to follow other gods (6:14-15; 7:4; 8:19-20; 11:16-17, 28; 13:2; 30:17-18). Indeed, it is the sin of idolatry, above all else, which carries the threat of national exile (4:25-26; 6:14-15; 8:19-20; 11:16-17; 29:23-28; 30:17-18). The writer took pains to stress that Israel's occupation of Canaan is not based on any natural right to this territory. Rather, the land is God's gift to Israel as her inheritance, much as he apportioned the surrounding lands to other nations (2:12, 21-22; 3:18; 8:10; 12:1). God chose this particularly good land for Israel (8:7-9) not because of her own righteousness, but because of the wickedness of its former inhabitants, and as a fulfillment of the promises made to Israel's forefathers, whom God loved (9:4-5; cf 7:7-8). At the same time, God can just as easily banish Israel from the land, if she proves to be undeserving (8:19-20). It is no accident that Deuteronomy was composed in the form and style of a vassal treaty, since the two-sided proposition entailing obedience and blessing or disobedience and curse stands at its very core. It is no less than a life and death choice (30:15-20).

Deuteronomy is set off from other biblical books by its expanded hortatory style. This style accounts for some of Deuteronomy's salient phraseology, such as serving God with all of one's "heart and soul" (4:29; 6:5; 10:12; 11:13; 13:4; 26:16), and "putting away evil" from the midst of Israelite society (13:5; 17:7, 12; 19:19; 21:21; 22:21-22, 24; 24:7). It also explains Deuteronomy's tendency to expound upon the moral significance of the law even within the law code itself (17:19-20; 19:8-9). This tendency, in turn, is part of a wider phenomenon found in the book, namely the mustering of logical arguments designed to persuade the people of the veracity of its message (4:35-40; 6:20-25). Besides the appeal to raw logic, however, Deuteronomy's arguments often take on a humanitarian note, such as the constant reminder that every Israelite was once in a lowly state of enslavement in Egypt (5:15; 15:15; 16:12; 24:18, 22).

On the basis of these unique features, as well as on factors discussed above, scholars have attempted to identify the circles from which Deuteronomy arose. According to some, the homiletical nature of the book and its peculiar covenantal structure demonstrate that the book stemmed from clerical circles, specifically Levites, who were responsible for preaching the law during presumed covenant renewal ceremonies. Subsequent research in the area of ancient Near Eastern treaties, however, has pointed to a political source, i.e., court scribes as those responsible for the promulgation of Deuteronomy. This also helps explain the book's many affinities with wisdom ideology (such as the appeal to logic noted above), a domain closely associated with the political aristocracy (cf Prov 25:1; 31:1).

The fact that Deuteronomy was not just a law book, but above all a religio-philosophical guideline, led to its profound influence on other biblical writers, in particular the historiographer(s) of Joshua, II Kings and the prophet Jeremiah. Deuteronomy provided these thinkers with a theological framework, through which it was possible to grasp the vicissitudes of Israel's experience during its settled days. In the Book of Kings, for example, the precept of centralization becomes a yardstick by which all the kings of Judah are measured (e.g. I Kgs 15:14; 22:43; II Kgs 12:3; 14:4; 15:4, 35). The concept of idolatry as the primary cause of national disaster finds expression throughout the Book of Judges (2:11ff; 6:7-10; 10:6ff; cf I Sam 12:9-10), and in a series of question and answer formulas in Kings and Jeremiah which are modeled after Deuteronomy 29:23-24 (I Kgs 9:8-9; Jer 5:19; 9:12-14; 16:10-11; 22:8-9). Finally, the conception of true prophecy as that which is communicated directly by God (Jer 1:7, 9; 14:14; 29:23), as well as that which is fulfilled in history (I Kgs 14:18; 16:7; 22:38; II Kgs 14:25; 17:23; 24:2), leans heavily on Deuteronomy 18:14-22 (especially vs. 18, 21-22).

OUTLINE

1:1-5	Introduction
1:6-3:29	Moses' first discourse: the lessons of Israel's history
4:1-40	Moses' second discourse: the uniqueness of God
4:41-49	Historical notices
5:1-11:32	Moses' third discourse: reasons for obeying the Law
12:1-26:19	The Deuteronomic law code
27:1-28:68	Blessing and curse
29:1-31:30	Concluding discourse; appointment of Joshua
32:1-52	The Song of Moses
33:1-29	The Blessing of Moses
34:1-12	The death of Moses

Diana-Artemis depicted on a coin of Gaza. 2nd century A.D.

DIANA The Roman name of Artemis, the goddess of hunt and vegetation. Her temple at Ephesus, one of the Seven Wonders of the World, housed her statue made of gold, silver and ebony, and believed to have come down from heaven (Acts 19:35). Diana was one of the deities most popular throughout the Hellenistic world. Thus, Paul's preaching against man-made gods (Acts 19:26), naturally considered highly blasphemous in this center of Diana worship, sparked off a riot whose immediate reason was, however, economic. The silversmiths, headed by Demetrius, feared for their main source of income, the manufacture of silver shrines and figurines of the goddess, should Paul succeed in converting the citizens of Ephesus to the new religion.

DIANA
Acts 19:24,
27-28, 34-35

DIBLAH (or Diblath). Place mentioned in Ezekiel 6:14 but otherwise unknown. As the Septuagint reads Diblah for Riblah in Jeremiah 52:10, it is thought that the references are a misreading for the important town of Riblah in Syria (See RIBLAH).

DIBLAH
Ezek 6:14

DIBLAIM ("lump of figs, raisin cakes"). The father of Gomer, the prostitute wife of the prophet Hosea.

DIBLAIM
Hos 1:3

DIBON, DIBON GAD A city in the high plain of Moab, about 10 miles (16 km) east of the Dead Sea, north of the Arnon River, retaining its ancient name in the modern Dhiban. It was wrested from Sihon king of the Amorites by the Israelites (Num 21:23-30; 32:3), rebuilt by the tribe of Gad (Num 32:34) and hence called Dibon Gad (Num 33:45-46; cf Joshua 13:17 where it is counted as belonging to the tribe of Reuben). Possibly Ehud freed it from subjugation by Eglon, king of Moab (Judg 3:12-30), and David conquered it (II Sam 8:2). It reverted to the Moabites when the Israelite kingdom was divided up. The Moabite Stone, discovered in 1868 at Dibon, and now in the Louvre, throws new

DIBON,
DIBON GAD
Num 21:30;
32:3, 34;
33:45-46. Josh
13:9, 17. Neh
11:25. Is 15:2.
Jer 48:18, 22

light on Moab-Israel relations during the reigns of Omri and Ahab kings of Israel, and Kemoshyt and Mesha kings of Moab, of which only partial information is given in II Kings 3:4-27. Archeological excavations carried out at Tell ed-Dhibon, the site of biblical Dibon, indicate that the city was not occupied during the Middle or Late Bronze Ages, but was settled and built up during the Iron Age.

Tell ed-Dhibon, the site of biblical Dibon

DIBRI
Lev 24:11

DIDYMUS
John 11:16;
20:24; 21:2

DIBRI ("loquacious"). A member of the tribe of Dan, whose grandfather was stoned to death in the wilderness for blaspheming the name of the Lord.

DIDYMUS ("twin"). Surname of the apostle Thomas.

DIETARY LAWS The Bible assumed man to have been a vegetarian originally (Gen 1:29-30), until the sons of Noah were permitted flesh (Gen 9:3). This concession was not granted without reservation: "But you shall not eat flesh with its life, that is, its blood" (Gen 9:4). Man's craving for meat is to be indulged, but he is to abstain from consuming the blood.

This blood prohibition, enjoined upon all men and not on the Israelites alone, is in stark contrast with the idolatrous practices of ancient Israel's environment, where blood was consumed as food. It may therefore be concluded that the blood prohibition was not a vestigial leftover of an ancient taboo; rather, it must have been the result of a rational, deliberate departure from prevalent practice. The reason for this departure becomes clear when it is recalled that the blood prohibition occurs within the same context in which the concession to eat meat is given for the first time (Gen 9:3ff). Man has no right to put an animal to death except by God's sanction. Hence he must eschew the blood, drain it, and return it, as it were, to the creator.

Certain animal foods are prohibited, in Leviticus chapter 11, the rationale being cited in verse 44: "sanctify yourselves, and you shall be holy; for I am holy". Relatively few individual Bible statutes are coupled with the demand for holiness, none of these feature the staccato emphasis and repetition characterizing the food prohibitions.

The Bible lays down various categories of forbidden food. In the story of Noah, the animals are already divided into "clean" and "unclean" categories (Gen 7:2) but it is only in the Mosaic Law that the criteria are defined: in Leviticus chapter 11 and Deuteronomy 14:3-21. "Among the beasts, whatever divides the hoof, having cloven hooves and chewing the cud — that may you eat" (Lev 11:3); a list of sanctioned quadrupeds is given in Deuteronomy 14:4-5. Fish have to have both fins and scales to qualify (Lev 11:9-12). For birds, no general rule is given, but a long list of forbidden fowl (many of which can no longer be certainly identified) is found in Leviticus 11:13-19. The implication is that those fowl not listed are permitted. With some exceptions in Leviticus 11:20-22, winged animals that creep on the ground are forbidden, as are all kinds of worms, snakes, snails, etc. (Lev 11:41).

Flesh may not be torn from a living animal (cf Gen 9:4); as a Noahide Law, this restriction applies to all mankind and not to the Israelites alone. The sinew of the hip is forbidden, this ban being ascribed to the story of Jacob wrestling with the angel (Gen 32:32). Part of the abdominal fat of the ox, sheep and goats is likewise forbidden (Lev 7:23). A kid may not be boiled in its mother's milk (Ex 23:19; 34:26; Deut 14:21); this regulation has recently been identified as a ban on pagan customs, as findings at Ugarit have shown that it was the custom there to boil a kid in its mother's milk as a lucky charm.

Another category of forbidden food relates to the fruit of trees during the first four years after planting (Lev 19:23-24) and food grown as the result of sowing diverse seeds together (Deut 22:9).

In the NT period, the dietary laws were interpreted with great strictness by the Pharisees. Jesus, in protest, belittled the laws, stating "Not what goes into the mouth defiles a man; but what comes out of the mouth, this defiles a man" (Matt 15:11ff; cf Mark 7:5ff).

DIKLAH ("palm tree"). Son of Joktan the son of Eber (grandson of Shem) (Gen 10:22-27). He lived "from Mesha as you go toward Sephar, the mountain of the east" (Gen 10:30) probably somewhere in the Arabian peninsula where palm trees abound.

DIKLAH
Gen 10:27. I Chr 1:21

DILEAN A Judean city in the coastal plain. Its precise location is unknown but it is thought to be in the Lachish area.

DILEAN
Josh 15:38

DIMNAH A Levitical city belonging to the tribe of Zebulun, identified with Rimmon No.4.

DIMNAH
Josh 21:35

DIMON A place mentioned in Isaiah's prophecy concerning Moab: "the waters of Dimon will be full of blood". It may be identical with Dibon. A suggested location is at Khirbet Dimnah 2½ miles (4 km) northwest of Rabbah.

DIMON
Is 15:9

DIMONAH A city in the southern part of Palestine, in the first district of Judah (Josh 15:22). It is tentatively located in the vicinity of a water source named Herabert Umm Dumneh, 5 miles (8 km) southeast of Aroer (identified with Arara). Others identify it with Dibon in Judah, mentioned in Nehemiah 11:25.

DIMONAH
Josh 15:22

DINAH The youngest child of Leah and Jacob (Gen 30:21); she was raped by Shechem the son of Hamor the Hittite, prince of the country (Gen 34:2). The young man wanted to marry her (Gen 34:8) and was ready to undergo circumcision to do so (Gen 34:15, 19) but later the sons of Jacob killed him and every other male from the city (Gen 34:25-26) to avenge the affront suffered by their sister, and they took her away from Shechem's home (Gen 34:26).

DINAH
Gen 30:21;
34:1, 3, 5, 13,
25-26; 46:15

DINAITES One of the tribes or groups brought by the Assyrians to Samaria to replace the Children of Israel sent into captivity. The Dinaites were among those who signed the letter to King Artaxerxes to protest the return of the Jews to Jerusalem and the rebuilding of the walls of the city. It has been suggested that the name is derived from the Hebrew *din* ("judgment").

DINAITES
Ezra 4:9

DINHABAH The city of Bela son of Beor, the first-known Edomite king. Its location is uncertain; Jerome identified it with Khirbet ed-Denn, a town in Moab, south of the Arnon River.

DIONYSUS See AREOPAGITE

DIOTREPHES A Christian mentioned in John's third epistle which complains about Diotrephes' domineering behavior.

DIPHATH See RIPHATH

DISCIPLES, DISCIPLESHIP Discipleship is the term used in the gospels to designate the condition of being followers of Jesus. The usage probably originated from contemporary Jewish school life (the *talmid* or "disciple of the wise"), perhaps through the circle of John the Baptist who had disciples (Matt 11:2); but Judaism in turn could have been influenced by Hellenistic gymnasium practice. The OT did not yet know this terminology (but see Is 50:4). Etymologically, disciple means learner and has an intellectual or academic connotation, correlative to the designation of Jesus as teacher. It is an important term because the whole life-style of the follower of Jesus is included in it. It is a gospel word which declined in importance in the rest of the NT when it was gradually replaced by other terms such as believer or Christian. One of the most difficult problems in understanding gospel use of the term is whether it refers exclusively to a closed group like the twelve apostles or is extended to all who hear Jesus sympathetically, for example, the crowds. Both usages seem to be present but it is difficult to be sure in each case which sense is meant.

Jesus taught his followers to make the pursuit of the Kingdom of God their highest priority (Matt 6:33). Discipleship is a lifestyle which first seeks the kingdom and its justice, follows Jesus wherever he goes and is willing to renounce all other interests to the extent that they become obstacles to these goals (see Rev 14:4; Matt 8:19-20; Mark 8:34-38; Luke 14:26; cf Matt 10:37; Luke 18:29; cf Matt 19:29; Mark 10:29-30). As this series of texts shows, at least some of Jesus' followers were urged to abandon parents, wife, children and property, and prepare themselves for martyrdom. Jesus' demands on his disciples were extremely radical, at times even harsh, as when he told someone who wanted to follow him to "let the dead bury their own dead" (Matt 8:21-22; Luke 9:59-60). This radical discipline was probably necessary to overcome the exaggerated family loyalty common in the Levant, and to insure the freedom for a life of itinerant preaching. It is also an application of the command to love God with one's whole heart, soul and might (Deut 6:5), interpreted in such a way that heart means all one's affective faculties, soul means life (to the point of martyrdom), and might means material possessions. Thus discipleship is a radical form of love.

In presenting the total picture of the disciple, each of the evangelists puts the accent on different aspects: Mark highlights life in the shadow of the cross (Mark 8:34) as well as the disciples' lack of understanding. Matthew stresses just the opposite; the good disciple is one who understands the teaching of Jesus (Matt 13:51-52). Matthew is the only evangelist to mention the church, and the disciples whom he usually identifies with the Twelve, have a role in it (Matt 18:1, 17-18). As church leaders, the disciples share in the authority of Jesus, even to the point of forgiving sins (Matt 9:8). Disciples obey the commandments of the earthly Jesus (Matt 28:16-20). They do not set themselves up as teachers independent of Christ (Matt 23:8-10). Luke distinguishes between the Twelve and the rest of the disciples (Luke 6:13; 10:1), some of whom are called elders in Acts 14:23. He lays great stress on the voluntary poverty and love of the poor which should characterize the disciples (Luke 12:13-21; 16:19-31; 19:1-10), yet he admits that the radical demands of the first period can no longer be applied without modification (Luke 22:35-38). For John discipleship is identical with being a Christian, through believing (John 2:11), abiding in the word (John 8:31), living in a community of mutual love, service and humility (John chaps. 13 and 15). It is sometimes said that there are no ranks among the disciples in John, but in fact many individual disciples are singled out, for example, Andrew, Simon Peter, Philip, Nathanael (John chap. 1); Mary, Martha and Lazarus (John chap. 11); Thomas (John chap. 20), and again, Simon Peter (John chap. 21). The Beloved Disciple is also an important and unique feature of the fourth gospel. The term disciple is mentioned in John 12:16, though this is often obscured in translation. John represents a spiritualizing of the concept of disciple, leaving out some of the harsh specific demands listed in the other gospels. Paul does not use discipleship terminology. He tends to replace it with more Hellenistic terms like imitation or mimesis of Christ. (I Cor 4:16; 11:1; Eph 5:1; Phil 3:17; I Thes 1:6; 2:14; II Thes 3:7, 9; Heb 6:12; 13:7).

DISHAN See DISHON No.1

DISHON

1. Some confusion exists with the names Dishon and Dishan which possibly represent two separate individuals, but are probably identical. The name designates a Hurrian (Horite) tribe whose eponym is the fifth (Gen 36:21) — or alternately the seventh (I Chr 1:38) — son of Seir, a native Horite clan chief in Edom (Gen 36:26, 30; I Chr 1:41).

2. The son of Anah, a Horite clan chief, or a grandson of Seir.

DISPERSION (DIASPORA). The term "Dispersion" is a translation of the Greek word "Diaspora," referring to the scattering and resettlement of Jews outside of the land of Israel. The earliest references to the idea of a dispersion are found in Leviticus 26:33; Deuteronomy 4:27; 28:64-68; Psalms 44:11; 106:27; Jeremiah 9:16; 13:24; and Ezekiel 12:13-16. Israel's unfaithfulness and disobedience to God's covenant were punishable by ruin and exile.

The history of the Diaspora can be dated from the Assyrian Exile (722 B.C.) when the ten tribes, deported to Assyria from the Northern Kingdom of Israel, were eventually assimilated; or from the Babylonian Exile (586 B.C.) when a large part of the population of Judah was sent to Babylonia where many remained even after being permitted to return by Cyrus the Great (539 B.C.). At the same time, a Jewish community began to develop in Egypt (Jer 44:1). The Diaspora grew extensively during the Second Temple era and by NT times extended from Cyrene to Rome (cf Acts 2:9-11). The travels of St. Paul and his visits to Jewish communities in various countries provide graphic evidence of the extent of the Diaspora in his time.

DIVORCE The law of writing and delivery of a writ of divorce by the husband is combined with the injunction forbidding the husband to remarry his divorced wife if, in the interim, she had married another man, been divorced by the latter, or been widowed (Deut 24:1-4). The grounds for divorce are given in the vague phrase "because he has found some uncleanness (others translate "unseemly" or "obnoxious") in her" (Deut 24:1). A distinct allusion to the law enjoining a man from remarrying his divorced wife once she has been remarried is to be found in Jeremiah 3:1. Isaiah (50:1) refers to a written bill of divorce when he declares: "Where is the certificate of your mother's divorce, whom I have put away?"

A legal formula of divorce appears in Hosea 2:2. "For she is not my wife nor am I her husband". The first half of this formula is known from ancient Babylonian documents, and the latter half is cited in the Talmud. The same legal terminology appears in an Aramaic writ of

DISHAN
Gen 36:21, 28, 30. I Chr 1:38, 42

DISHON 1
Gen 36:21, 26, 30. I Chr 1:38, 41

DISHON 2
Gen 36:25. I Chr 1:41

divorce dating from the middle of the 5th century B.C. The Code of Hammurabi provides for divorce by both the husband and the wife. The Bible, however, is silent on the right of the wife to divorce her husband. This silence can well be construed to mean that no such writ existed in biblical times.

Pentateuchal legislation provides for two instances in which a man cannot divorce his wife: if he has falsely charged her with not being a virgin at the time of marriage (Deut 22:19), and if the woman was raped (Deut 22:28-29). In both instances, it is declared "he cannot divorce her, all his days."

Malachi (2:14-16) denounces divorce on the moral ground that it is an act of betrayal. "Because the Lord has been witness between you and the wife of your youth...let none deal treacherously with the wife of his youth. For the Lord God of Israel says that he hates divorce." The Hebrew verb translated here as "divorce" is the same one as used to describe the act of divorce both in the Pentateuch (Deut 22:19, 29; 24:3) and by Jeremiah (3:1). An actual instance of divorce on a large scale is prescribed by Ezra where the women involved were non-Jewish (chaps. 9-10).

The Pharisees put the following question to Jesus. "Is it lawful for a man to divorce his wife for just any reason?" Jesus replied that the Creator said, "For this reason a man shall leave his father and mother and be joined to his wife and the two of them shall become one flesh...Therefore, what God has joined together, let not man separate." Whereupon, the Pharisees asked: "Then why did Moses command to give a certificate of divorce and to put her away?" Jesus' reply was: "Moses, because of the hardness of your hearts, permitted you to divorce your wives...I say to you whoever divorces his wife, except for sexual immorality, and marries another commits adultery" (Matt 19:3-9; cf the parallel passage in Mark 10:2-9). Similarly, to marry a divorced woman is an act of adultery (Matt 5:32). A woman who divorces her husband and marries another is an adulteress (Mark 10:11-12).

This view of Jesus on divorce accords with that of the rabbinical school of Shammai (Mishna Gittin 9:10) who interpret the phrase "because he found some uncleanness in her" (Deut 24:1) in a literal sense, as referring to adultery.

Bill of divorce. Aramaic papyrus of the 1st century found in one of the caves of the Judean Hills according to which a certain Joseph son of Joseph grants Miriam daughter of Jonathan, dwelling at Masada, this bill of divorce and deed of release. (Shrine of the Book, Israel Museum)

DIZAHAB
Deut 1:1

DIZAHAB A locality east of the Arabah cited in connection with the farewell addresses of Moses (Deut 1:1) Its location is uncertain, though several proposals have been made: Edh-Dheibeh east of Heshbon, or Rujm Umm edh-Dhahab near el-'Al. Dizahab may be identical with Mezahab, a district in Edom (Gen 36:39; cf Num 21:14).

Rujm Umm ed-Dhahab identified with Dizahab.

DODAI, DODO ("beloved").

1. A man of the tribe of Issachar, grandfather of Tola.

2. An Ahohite, and the father of Eleazar, one of David's three mighty warriors (II Sam 23:9). He was appointed by David as military commander for the second month (I Chr 27:4).

3. A man of Bethlehem whose son Elhanan was one of David's thirty "mighty men".

DODANIM A people descended from Javan. It has been suggested that the name should be emended to Rodanim, meaning "Rhodians", and referring to the people of Rhodes and of the neighboring Aegean islands; this is probable as Javan denotes the Greeks.

DODAVAH The father of the prophet Eliezer of Mareshah, who prophesied the destruction of Jehoshaphat's ships.

DOE See ANIMALS

DOEG The Edomite servant of Saul who informed the king of the priest Ahimelech's assistance to David at Nob (I Sam 21:1-9; 22:9-10). Saul's command to slay Ahimelech and his house was also carried out by Doeg because Saul's soldiers refused to kill the priests (I Sam 22:17-19).

DOG See ANIMALS

DONKEY See ANIMALS

DOPHKAH A station of the Israelites on the route to Sinai between the Red Sea and Rephidim. It has not been identified.

DOR (DORA) A coastal town, 8 miles (13 km) north of Caesarea; one of the important Canaanite city-states in the league of Jabin, king of Hazor (Josh 11:2). According to Egyptian documents it fell into the hands of the Zakkala, one of the Sea Peoples (Philistines) early in the 12th century B.C. It was among the cities of Manasseh in the territory of

DODAI, DODO 1
Judg 10:1

DODAI, DODO 2
II Sam 23:9. I Chr 11:12; 27:4

DODAI, DODO 3
II Sam 23:24. I Chr 11:26

DODANIM
Gen 10:4

DODAVAH
II Chr 20:37

DOEG
I Sam 21:7; 22:9, 18, 22. Ps 52:1

DOPHKAH
Num 33:12-13

DOR
Josh 11:2; 12:23; 17:11. Judg 1:27. I Kgs 4:11. I Chr 7:29

(right)
Aerial view of excavations at Dor showing levels from the 11th century B.C. to the Roman period. (Tell Dor Excavations Project)

(bottom)
Grotesque lamp depicting a satyr, found at Dor. Roman period.

Satyr-head ornamentation on Hellenistic pottery braziers from Tell Dor.

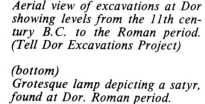

Asher, but according to Judges (1:27) it was not conquered by them. Solomon appointed the son of Abinadab as overseer of the region of Dor, which was the fourth district of his kingdom (I Kgs 4:11). Under the name of *Duru* it belonged to the Assyrian province of the same name.

In the Persian period, when the cities on the coast were granted autonomy, Dor became a Sidonian colony. In the early Hellenistic period it was a Ptolemaic royal fortress. Alexander Jannaeus acquired the city by negotiation. Under the Romans, the city was freed and it retained its freedom during the reign of Herod and his successors.

The excavations at Dor, which is identified with Tell el Burj near Tantura, have shown that it was founded by the Canaanites in the 20th century B.C. It was an important harbor, which, as indicated by the finds, had close connections with Cyprus and the Aegean countries. The most important remains, however, belong to the Hellenistic-Roman period. In the city itself temples to Zeus and Astarte were discovered, as well as a theater. According to Josephus a synagogue existed there before the destruction of the Second Temple. The Byzantine period is represented by a church.

DORCAS Also called Tabitha. A member of the Christian community, she lived in Joppa, where she was known for her acts of charity. When she died the disciples summoned Peter from nearby Lydda. He prayed, and revived her: "Tabitha, arise" (Acts 9:40).

DOTHAN A city on the boundary between the tribes of Manasseh and Issachar, at the southern extremity of the Jezreel Valley. Joseph was

DORCAS
Acts 9:36, 39

DOTHAN
Gen 37:17. II
Kgs 6:13

The Valley of Dothan.

(left) Tell Dothan.

sold here by his brothers to the Ishmaelites-Midianites whose caravan was on its way from Gilead in Transjordan to Egypt (Gen 37:17-28). The prophet Elisha dwelt in the walled city when it was besieged by the Arameans, in their attempt to capture the prophet (II Kgs 6:13ff). The apocryphal Book of Judith mentions it among the cities in the Jezreel Valley near Holofernes' camp (Judith 4:6; 7:3). It is identified with Tell Dothan, 3 miles (5 km) south of Jenin (En Gannim) and 13 miles (21 km) northwest of Shechem, at the head of the Valley of Dothan. Archeological excavations (1953-1960) uncovered rich remains from the Bronze and Iron ages including administrative buildings, private homes, walls and tombs.

DOVE See ANIMALS

DREAM A medium by which messages were believed to be communicated from the realm of the gods to humans. According to Numbers 12:6 the Israelite deity normally conveyed prophetic oracles through visions and dreams (cf I Sam 28:6 and Job 33:15-16). Only rare individuals were believed to have spoken directly with God as Moses is here characterized. It follows that most divine communication was enigmatic, requiring interpreters. In the ancient Near East specialists attended to the interpretation of dreams, thus creating dream books in Mesopotamia and Egypt. In Israel, too, gifted interpreters of dreams were known (Joseph, Daniel), but God is identified as the ultimate source of their knowledge.

The human desire to assure constant contact with the world of the supernatural gave rise to the practice of incubation, by which kings, priests, or commoners slept at a sacred place hoping to receive a favorable dream. The practice is known to have occurred in Babylonia and Ugarit, as well as in Israel (Solomon at Gibeon, I Kgs 3:4-15; II Chr 1:7-12; Jacob at Bethel, Gen 28:11-18, although here it seems unintentional; the boy Samuel, I Sam 3:1-15).

Two kinds of dreams can be distinguished: those which require no interpretation from a second person and those whose meaning is hidden from the dreamer. Solomon's dream at Gibeon is immediately transparent, although expressed in the language known from Egyptian royal novellae (e.g. "I am a little child; I do not know how to go out or come in" and, "give to your servant an understanding heart"). God promises the young king his heart's desire, and Solomon wisely responds in a manner that earns for himself wisdom, wealth and renown. Similarly, Jacob understood the implications of angels ascending and descending a ladder between heaven and earth (cf Gen 28:12). Similarly, in the NT, Pilate's wife grasped the import of her dream about Jesus (Matt 27:19). On the other hand, Jacob's dream about his goats (Gen 31:10-13) and Abimelech's dream about Sarah (Gen 20:3-7) are explained by an angel or God, although their meaning is obvious (cf Laban's dream, Gen 31:24).

Other dreams need interpretation: the barley cake that tumbled into the camp of Midian with devastating effects (Judg 7:13-15); dreams by the pharaoh's butler and baker (Gen 40:5-19), the pharaoh (Gen 41:1-36), and Nebuchadnezzar (Dan 2:1-45; 4:1-27). In several instances the person who had the dream was himself a specialist in interpreting such communications from the other world (Joseph's dreams about sheaves of grain and heavenly bodies, Gen 37:5-11); Daniel's dream about various animals, which represented different empires, and the Ancient of Days (Dan 7:1-28).

The widely acknowledged channel of divine communication with humans lent itself to abuse. The prophet Jeremiah denounces opposing prophets who claimed to have dreamed the divine will (Jer 23:16ff; 27:9). He associates these dreamers with diviners, soothsayers and sorcerers (cf Zech 10:2). It is no wonder that the author of Deuteronomy 13:1-5 prescribes the death penalty for those dreamers who lead Israel astray, given that book's stringent attitude toward a pure cult. Other thinkers emphasized the insubstantiality of dreams (Job 20:8; Ps 73:20; 90:5; 126:1; Ecc 5:7). Isaiah's use of this idea is especially poignant: the hungry person who dreams about eating awakes with hunger unabated, and the thirsty person who dreams of drinking awakes with unquenched thirst (Is 29:8). In some circles, however, hope was kept alive that some day God would restore the ancient mode of communicating with humans. Hence Joel envisions a day when God will pour out the Spirit on all flesh, enabling old men to dream dreams and young men to see visions (Joel 2:28-29). In this spirit Ananias responded to the summons to anoint a blind Saul (Acts 9:10-18) and the author of Revelation couched an apocalyptic message in visionary language. The story of Pentecost in the early church, which implies a reversal of the experience associated with the tower of Babel (Gen 11:1-9), assumes that the day which Joel anticipated has finally arrived (Acts 2:17-21).

Job's negative references to nightmares as divine punishment took root in Ecclesiasticus and Wisdom of Solomon, where they function to reinforce arguments about God's justice. Ecclesiasticus' claim that wicked persons suffer from excessive nightmares (Ecc 40:1-11) accords with a growing tendency to stress psychological anxiety during the 2nd century B.C. This trend culminates in the powerful description of anxiety that seized the Egyptians when God afflicted them but shielded the ancestors of Israel from harm (Wisd of Sol chaps. 17-18).

DRESS AND CLOTHING As no clothing has survived from the pre-biblical and OT periods we must turn to the neighboring countries, in which statues, reliefs and wall paintings have been preserved, to obtain an idea of how the ancient Israelite may have covered his body. An

Egyptian wall painting of the 12th Dynasty shows merchants coming from the east. They are wearing some kind of long tunic, covering the whole body from neck to ankles, while others wear something resembling a kilt that reaches from the hips to the thighs. These garments appear to have been made of plain white linen, but others were of multicolored wool, arranged in stripes. The longer garment is probably the kind worn by Joseph (Gen 37:3).

Canaanite men (above) and women (below) in a wall painting in an Egyptian tomb. 14th century B.C.

(top left)
Fragment of cloth of the 1st century found in the Judean Desert.

(bottom left)
Sandal from the 1st century found in the fortress of Masada, the last stronghold of resistance to the Romans after the fall of Jerusalem and the destruction of the Temple.

The Bible offers little information about clothing in the early Israelite period. Achan took "a beautiful Babylonian garment" (Josh 7:21); the Gibeonites wore old garments (Josh 9:13); Deborah speaks of a plunder of "garments embroidered and dyed" (Judg 5:30); in the story of Samson's marriage and his riddle, 30 "changes of clothing" are mentioned (Judg 14:12). There is a little more information about clothing in the period of the Israelite kingdom. The poor had one garment only (Ex 22:26; Deut 24:13). The richer people had more and better garments (Is 3:22; cf Luke 15:22). From the Hebrew text we may conclude that the clothing of that time consisted of some kind of undergarment covering the lower part of the body, with a garment of

Roman lady seated in a wicker chair having her hair combed by two other women; one of them holds up a mirror. Stone relief of the 1st century B.C. (Rheinisches Landsmuseum, Trier)

"many colors" worn on top (II Sam 13:18-19; cf John 21:7) to cover the entire body and part of the arms (cf Matt 10:10; Mark 6:9). In addition to these, women wore hoods, veils and other items of clothing which cannot be identified (cf Is 3:18-23). In the NT figurative use is made of the veil (Matt 27:51; II Cor 3:13ff; Heb 10:20).

There is much more evidence about the clothing of the Roman period. These garments do not differ basically from those worn along the whole Mediterranean coast at that time but the observance of the Mosaic Law, which forbade the mixing of wool and linen in the same garment, can be noted. The basic garment, according to these finds, was a tunic made of two identical lengths of woollen material joined at the top, with a slit so that it could be passed over the head. The tunic was decorated with two vertical stripes. The tunics were red, yellow or black, with contrasting stripes in this color range, or multicolored. The other garment found was a mantle (*tallit* in Hebrew, *pallium* in Latin and *himation* in Greek). This was also made of wool, consisted of one piece of cloth and was worn over a tunic. The mantles were yellow or brown and decorated with gammas or checkerboard patterns. Some of them had weavers' marks woven into them. There were also woollen kerchiefs decorated with fringes and made in a large range of colors.

Many leather sandals were also found in the Judean Desert Caves. These consisted of several pieces of leather stitched together. Strips of leather were attached at the heel and toe to ensure a firm grip on the foot and tied by straps (Is 5:27; Mark 1:7; Luke 3:16).

DROMEDARY See ANIMALS

DRUSILLA Youngest daughter of Herod Agrippa I and third wife of the Roman governor Felix.

DRUSILLA
Acts 24:24

DUMAH

1. An Arabian tribe descended from a son of Ishmael, apparently identical with the Adummatu / Adummu mentioned in Assyrian and Babylonian sources on the confines of the Syrian and Arabian deserts, in the region of the oasis Dumat al-Jandal (modern al-Jauf).

DUMAH 1
**Gen 25:14.
I Chr 1:30**

2. A village in the southern hill country of Judah whose ancient name is preserved in the modern el-Domeh southwest of Hebron.

DUMAH 2
Josh 15:52

3. A name occurring in "The burden against Dumah"(Is 21:11). Since the following passages refer to Seir, it may be a symbolic designation of Edom, whose coming destruction is foreshadowed.

DURA A valley in the land of Babylon where Nebuchadnezzar set up his golden image to be worshiped (Dan 3:1). Since the Akkadian *duru* means wall or walled place, it was a common place name in ancient Mesopotamia and therefore its identification is uncertain.

DYES AND DYEING Most of the earliest dyes were natural products, mainly obtained from colored earth or from certain plants and animals. Linen and wool were dyed in quite early times.

The curtains of the tabernacle were dyed blue, among other colors. Blue, or rather purple, was extracted from a secretion of the murex shellfish. To obtain the pigment the shellfish were crushed, cooked in salt and left in the sun for some time, so that the secretion would turn purple. This dye was used for coloring precious cloths (Est 8:15), as well as for the fringes of garments (Num 15:38). Purple, which is the color of the cloth cover of the altar (Num 4:13), is often mentioned together with blue (Ex 25:4). This pigment was made from the same shellfish but with the addition of another substance. Purple is also the most frequently mentioned color of cloth in the NT (Mark 15:17; Luke 16:19; John 19:2; Acts 16:14). Scarlet (Ex 25:4) was extracted from the eggs of certain lice (*Cocus vermilio* or *Cocus ilicis L.*). The eggs were collected with the female lice, dried and pounded into a red powder, which was then ready for use. Scarlet is mentioned together with precious cloths of other colors (Ex 28:5; Num 4:8).

Vermilion was used for staining wood (Jer 22:14; Ezek 23:14). This was probably made from red and yellow ochre, the natural iron oxide found in Palestine and used as early as the Chalcolithic period. From the Roman period onwards red oxide of lead was used in addition to the ochres to produce the red color.

In the realm of cosmetics, kohl was used for painting the eyelids (cf Ezek 23:40). This was basic carbonate of copper; in the Roman period galena, a sulphide of lead with the addition of other metallic substances, was also used.

Red and yellow pigments were extracted from the safflower (*Carthanus tinctorius L.v. inermis*) and in the Roman period a yellow dye was also made from the flowers of the crocus (*Crocus L.*). Blue was produced from isatis leaves (*Isatis tinctoria L.*), or in the Roman period indigo (*Indigofera tinctoria L.*) was used. Black was obtained either by painting red on blue or with the use of powdered charcoal. A green pigment was produced from powdered malachite, a hydrous carbonate of copper, which was also used in cosmetics. The same substance was used to produce a blue dye. White was made from ordinary chalk, carbonate of calcium, or gypsum, a sulphate of calcium.

Shellfish from which was extracted a fluid used in making dye.

E

EAGLE See ANIMALS

EAST GATE Apparently one of the gates of the Temple compound; it was guarded by Shemaiah the son of Shechaniah (Neh 3:29).

EBAL (MOUNT) A mountain rising 2,900 feet (882 m) above sea level, north of Shechem and opposite Mount Gerizim. Joshua built an altar of unhewn stones on its summit, as he had been commanded by Moses (Josh 8:30-32). The tribes of Israel then assembled on the slopes of Mount Ebal and Mount Gerizim, half on each, to hear the curses and blessings connected with the observance of the Law — the curses were read on Mount Ebal (Deut 11:29; 27:11-13; Josh 8:33-34). In ancient times there was some confusion about the location of both hills. In Deuteronomy (11:30) they are placed at Gilgal, "beside the terebinth trees of Moreh". Eusebius (*Onom.* 65, 9ff) disagrees with the Samaritans, who claimed that they were situated near Neapolis, ancient Shechem. On the Medaba map they are marked near Neapolis and later chroniclers accept this as correct.

EAST GATE
I Chr 26:14.
II Chr 31:14.
Neh 3:29

EBAL (MOUNT)
Gen 36:23.
Deut 11:29;
27:4, 13. Josh
8:30, 33. I Chr
1:22, 40

View of Mount Ebal in the foreground and Mount Gerizim in the background.

Punic votive inscription from Carthage including the name Ebed-Melech ("servant of the Lord/the King").

EBED ("slave", "servant").

1. Father of Gaal of Shechem who rebelled against Abimelech.

2. Son of Jonathan, from the family of Adin, among the exiles who came back from Babylon with Ezra.

EBED-MELECH ("servant of the Lord" or, "of the King"). An Ethiopian, one of the eunuchs who served in the court of King Zedekiah of Judah (Jer 38:7). He rescued the prophet Jeremiah who had been thrown in a dungeon (Jer 38:12-13); as his reward, Jeremiah promised him that he would escape the destruction of Jerusalem (Jer 39:16-18).

EBENEZER ("stone of help"). When Israel "went out to battle against the Philistines" in the time of Samuel, they encamped beside Ebenezer (I Sam 4:1). They were defeated (I Sam 4:2) and sent for the ark in Shiloh to save themselves (I Sam 4:4). The ark was taken into the camp and when the Philistines attacked, it fell into their hands (I Sam 4:11): "Then the Philistines took the ark of God and brought it from Ebenezer to Ashdod" (I Sam 5:1). Also the site where the men of Israel led by Samuel defeated the Philistines (I Sam 7:9-11). Samuel set up a victory stone "and called its name Ebenezer, saying, 'Thus far the Lord has helped us'" (I Sam 7:12). The stone was between Mizpah and Shen. The site has been recently located at a place called Izbet Zarta in the vicinity of Aphek.

EBED 1
Judg 9:26, 28,
30-31, 35

EBED 2
Ezra 8:6

EBED-MELECH
Jer 38:7-8, 10-
12; 39:16

EBENEZER
I Sam 4:1;
5:2; 7:12

Aerial view of Izbet Zarta identified with Ebenezer.

EBER ("Hebrew"). An alternate spelling of Heber.

1. Shem, firstborn son of Noah, is called "the father of all the children of Eber", or of the Hebrews.

2. Eber, great-grandson of Shem, father of Peleg and Joktan (Gen 10:24-25) in the genealogy of Noah. He was 34 when Peleg was born (Gen 11:16) and lived for 430 years afterwards (Gen 11:17).

3. Firstborn son of Elpaal of Benjamin.

4. A son of Shashak of the tribe of Benjamin.

5. A priest, head of a family of Amok at the time of Joiakim son of Jeshua.

EBEZ See ABEZ

EBIASAPH Alternate form of ABIASAPH

EBRON A place in the territory allotted to the tribe of Asher. It is generally identified with Abdon No.1.

ECCLESIASTES, BOOK OF Comprising 12 chapters it was traditionally attributed to King Solomon, although the language indicates a later date as it is much closer to Mishnaic than to classical Hebrew. If one ignores the superscription (1:1) and the two epilogues that have been added to the book (12:1-10, 11-14), perhaps for the purpose of making the radical views less objectionable by submitting them to traditional piety, Ecclesiastes opens with a thematic refrain (1:2) plus a poem (1:3-11) and closes with the same, in inverse order (refrain, 12:8; poem, 12:1-7). The initial poem characterizes the monotonous cycles of nature, while the concluding one describes the cycle of human life, that is, from youth through old age to death. Between the two remarkable poetic achievements the author offers a justification for the negative assessments of life's meaning encapsulated in the refrain, "Vanity of vanities, says the Preacher, all is vanity." This unusual conclusion arises from an examination of life as it unfolds under the sun. The author observes that death nullifies all human accomplishments, and that this enemy comes indiscriminately on good people and bad. Briefly adopting the literary fiction of royal authorship (1:12-2:26), for which Egyptian parallels exist in the Instructions of Ptahhotep, Merikare and Amenemhet, the author claims to have tested life's supreme rewards (fame, fortune, work, pleasure) and to have found them wanting. Since one cannot secure a profit from human endeavor, given the unpredictability and inevitability of death, Ecclesiastes concludes that humans ought to enjoy life insofar as that is possible. Close parallels to this advice (9:7-9) occur in both the Babylonian Epic of Gilgamesh, where the innkeeper Siduri counsels

EBER 1
Gen 10:21.
Num 24:24

EBER 2
Gen 10:24-25;
11:14-17. I
Chr 1:18-19,
25. Luke 3:35

EBER 3
I Chr 8:12

EBER 4
I Chr 8:22

EBER 5
Neh 12:20

EBIASAPH
I Chr 6:23, 37;
9:19

EBRON
Josh 19:28

Page from the Book of Ecclesiastes, from the De Castro Bible, *Germany, 14th century. (Israel Museum)*

Gilgamesh to enjoy his wife and children, wear festive garments and anoint himself with the finest oils, as well as in the Egyptian Harper's songs. The literary form by which Ecclesiastes arrives at this advice is typical of the Wisdom Literature, specifically the use of collected sayings (aphorisms, "better" sayings, biographical narrative, anecdote, instruction, allegory and so forth) from the school tradition. The author of Ecclesiastes often refutes older sayings, thus giving the book the appearance of a dialogue. In a word, Ecclesiastes reflects contradictory understandings of events, and this feature of the book has led to theories of editorial glosses. Related texts come from Mesopotamia (The Dialogue between a Master and his Slave) and from Egypt (The Dispute of a Man with his Soul). The biblical author's rejection of divine justice goes beyond the position found in the Book of Job, for Ecclesiastes finds no resolution to the vexing problem. The radical teachings of Ecclesiastes place him on the outer edges of the canon. The author acknowledges that God is creator, but no evidence convinces the skeptic that the remote deity is also redeemer. The book thus marks a crisis within biblical wisdom. Earlier claims about wisdom's power to steer humans successfully through life's dangers are declared to be mistaken, for none can discover the secrets of the universe that would lead to safe passage. As for life after death, the author denies the possibility or registers profound doubt in the rhetorical question: who knows? For the moment, the celebrated life under the sun is carried on under the shadow of death, and existence therefore is the ultimate emptiness. The Hebrew name bestowed on the author, Koheleth, often wrongly translated "the Preacher", designates an office related to the assembling of people or proverbs. It has been suggested that the name Koheleth derives from the account in I Kings 8:1, 14 which reports that Solomon assembled the people and addressed them on the occasion of the dedication of the Temple. The book was actually written quite late, perhaps at the end of the 3rd century B.C. Some have even contended that the book was originally written in Aramaic and shortly thereafter translated into Hebrew. Fragments from Qumran date from the middle of the 2nd century, and distortions of the author's radical teachings seem to be attacked in the 2nd century Greek Wisdom of Solomon. Ecclesiastes belongs to the five festal scrolls and is read during the Feast of Booths (Tabernacles).

OUTLINE

1:1-3:15	Vanity of life, wisdom and earthly pleasures
3:16-21	Same fate overtakes man and beast
4:1-16	Vanity of toil
5:1-6:12	Vanity of wealth
7:1-29	Assorted wise sayings — but wisdom too must be moderated
8:1-9:16	Same fate overtakes the righteous and the wicked
9:17-10:20	Various maxims
11:1-8	Uncertainty of human work
11:9-12:8	Youth to be enjoyed; infirmities of age
12:9-14	Epilogue

ECCLESIASTICUS (or The Wisdom of Jesus the Son of Sirach). An apocryphal work, belonging to the Wisdom Literature, written by Jesus, the son of Sirach (Ben Sira) from Jerusalem (50:27). The book, composed in Hebrew, has been mainly preserved in Greek, Latin and Syriac translations. The discovery of ancient fragments of text in the Karaite Synagogue in Cairo and at Masada has permitted restoration of much of the Hebrew original. The work dates from the 2nd century B.C. Frequently quoted in the rabbinic literature of the first centuries A.D., Ecclesiasticus must have been an accepted "exterior book" in Judaism. It was included in the Septuagint from which it was incorporated in the Christian Bible.

Fragment of the Ben Sira Scroll found at Masada.

The book is divided into eight sections, each prefaced with a poem in praise of wisdom. The author, Jesus son of Sirach, was a highly regarded person (39:4), who traveled widely (34:11; 39:4) and studied Torah intensively (39:1-3). The central theme of the whole book is that "All wisdom comes from the Lord and is with him forever" (1:1). Wisdom cannot be obtained unless God grants it. The many facets of wisdom are praised as having been pre-existent (1:4; 24:8-9) and having dwelled on the whole earth wisdom is sent to settle in Israel (24:4-8).

Other subjects, directly linked with the theme of wisdom, are the fear of the Lord (1:11-2:18), Torah as the expression of God's wisdom for the people (24:23), liturgy (chap. 50), history of the Jewish people (17:11-14; chap. 24) and social behavior. Of the 51 chapters, the final seven are devoted to eulogies of great figures of the Bible. The author seeks to teach man the love of wisdom and, consequently, of a virtuous life based upon God's Torah.

EDEN ("pleasure/delight").

EDEN 1
II Chr 29:12

1. Eden son of Joah, a Levite of the Gershonite family (II Chr 29:12) who participated in the cleansing of the House of the Lord in the time of Hezekiah king of Judah (II Chr 29:15).

EDEN 2
II Chr 31:15

2. A Levite who assisted Kore the son of Imnah in the distribution of the offerings of the Lord at the time of Hezekiah (II Chr 31:5). Possibly identical with No.1.

EDEN, GARDEN OF
Gen 2:8-10, 15-16; 3:1-3, 8, 10, 23-24; 4:16; 13:10. Is 51:3. Ezek 28:13; 31:8-9; 36:35. Joel 2:3

EDEN, GARDEN OF The name Eden is derived either from the Hebrew root meaning "to be fruitful, plentiful" or from a Sumerian word meaning "steppe, flatland". The biblical "Garden of Eden" motif occurs in three basic contexts: the second creation story (Gen 2:8-9, 15-16; 3:1-10, 23-24); a related, more mythologically oriented version of that story, concerning primeval times, which tells of a guardian angel who is later struck down by God because of his sins and wrongdoing (Ezek 28:12-16); and in two main similes — the first in an oracle of

A lush garden, depicted on a wall painting from the tomb of Sennutem, 13th century B.C. A bountiful land watered by irrigation channels was the epitome of blissful afterlife for the ancient Egypt.

The Greek Orthodox Church in the Shepherds' Field, east of Bethlehem, built near the remains of a watchtower known as Eder Tower (Tower of the Flock), where according to tradition the shepherds received the first tidings of the Nativity.

consolation referring to the rebuilding and recultivating of the land that had previously been laid waste (Ezek 36:35), and the second, in an oracle of rebuke alluding to the fertile condition of the land before its destruction (Joel 2:3). Other related passages include the listing of the irrigation sources responsible for Eden's lush fertility (Gen 2:10-14) which provides an etiological origin for the Garden of Eden concept; a geographical note regarding the banishment of Cain to the land of Nod, east of Eden (Gen 4:16); and additional similes and extended comparisons (Gen 13:10; Is 51:3; Ezek 31:8-9, 16, 18). Not all of the above passages include the exact phrase "Garden of Eden". As indicated by the parallelism in Isaiah 51:3 and Ezekiel 28:13 (cf Ezek 31:91), the phrase "Garden of Eden" may be replaced by its synonyms "Garden of the Lord" (Gen 13:10; Is 51:3) and "Garden of God" (Ezek 28:13; 31:8-9). While the second biblical creation story contains many unique elements, and in its entirety has no complete ancient Near Eastern counterpart, the cosmological motif of a paradise-like garden with lush, well-irrigated vegetation somehow connected with creation, is present in ancient Near Eastern literature, especially in Sumerian mythology. Many scholars believe that in the light of geographical information provided in Genesis 2:10-14, Eden is to be located near the Persian Gulf, maybe Bahrein, which is also the assumed location of the mythical garden, Dilmun, in the Sumerian myth.

EDER

1. A Levite, second son of Mushi son of Merari, at the time of King David.

2. Son of Beriah from the tribe of Benjamin who dwelled in Aijalon, in the genealogy of King Saul.

3. A city "at the limits of the tribe of the children of Judah, towards the border of Edom in the South" generally considered here to be an alternate spelling for Arad.

EDER, TOWER OF After the death of Rachel, Jacob went on and "journeyed beyond the tower of Eder" (Gen 35:21). Jewish tradition placed this "tower" close to Bethlehem, on the site of present-day Khirbet-el-Bireh. However, early Christian tradition sought to link the

EDER 1
**I Chr 23:23;
24:30**

EDER 2
I Chr 8:15

EDER 3
Josh 15:21

EDER,
TOWER OF
Gen 35:21

birth of Jesus to the place and identified the "tower of the flock" (Hebrew *eder*) with the Shepherds' Field, east of Bethlehem. There is another mention of "the tower of the flock" in Micah 4:8.

EDOM, EDOMITES The name of a country and a people to the east of the Arabah, bordered by Ammon to the north, the Dead Sea and the Arabah to the west and the desert to the south and east. In the early 4th millennium B.C. the land was inhabited by semi-nomadic peoples who practiced primitive forms of agriculture. These early cultures came to an end in about 1900 B.C. In the Middle and Late Bronze Ages, when Palestine and northern Transjordan were densely populated, the south was almost uninhabited and none of its sites is mentioned in Egyptian documents. The country emerges from obscurity again in the 13th century B.C. when Edom is specifically mentioned in a list of Sethos I of about 1215 B.C. Together with Moab and the Negeb it is also mentioned in the records of a punitive campaign organized by Rameses III.

Of Semitic stock, the Edomites must have penetrated the area as early as the 14th century B.C. Archeological surveys have shown that the country flourished mainly from the 13th to the 8th century B.C., declined, and was finally destroyed in the 6th century B.C. Surveys have found remains of fortified towns and of numerous villages. Agriculture was highly developed and so was the local pottery. The list of tribute which Edom paid to Esarhaddon suggests that it was richer than other countries in the vicinity. In part at least, it apparently owed its wealth to the exploitation of copper. The country was clearly strongly fortified at an early stage, since the Israelites could not use the roads passing through Edom on their way to Canaan (Num 20:17-21).

The first Israelite king to conquer Edom was David, who stationed garrisons all over the country (II Sam 8:14; I Kgs 11:15-16). Edom revolted in the days of Joram and the Edomites put up a king of their own (II Kgs 8:20-22), who probably also conquered Ezion Geber. About 100 years later Amaziah took Sela in Edom and renamed it Joktheel (II Kgs 14:7). The reconquest of Edom was later completed by King Amaziah of Judah (II Kgs 14:22; II Chr 26:1-2). It was not until the days of Ahaz that the country finally regained its independence (II Kgs 16:6). In the 6th century B.C. Edom was conquered by the Babylonians, and in the centuries following its downfall new nomadic tribes penetrated the country, pressing the Edomites westward into Judah, where they settled south of Hebron. Among the newcomers were the Nabateans, who are not heard of before the late 4th century B.C. but

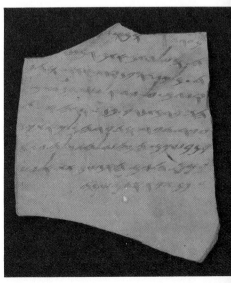

(left)
A view of Edom, the mountainous region east of the Dead Sea.

Ostracon from Arad, late 8th century B.C., in which the commander of Arad is warned against Edom. (Israel Dept. of Antiquities and Museums)

Coin of Adraa (Edrei) depicting a personification of the Jarmuk River. The Greek inscription reads: "Ieromykes, of the people of Adraa".

An Egyptian official and his wife. Wood carving 3rd millennium B.C. (Louvre, Paris)

who had established their kingdom in the former territory of Edom by the first half of the 2nd century B.C. Pushed back by the Nabateans, the Edomites occupied southern Judea, including the region of Hebron, which became known as Idumea. They were conquered by John Hyrcanus (135-105 B.C.) who forcibly converted them to Judaism; henceforth, they were part of the Jewish people. Herod was of Edomite origin.

EDREI

1. A city in the kingdom of Bashan, where Og king of Bashan was defeated by Moses (Num 21:33-35). Giants were reputed to have dwelled there (Josh 12:4). It was later allotted by Moses to the clan of Machir from the half-tribe of Manasseh (Josh 13:31) east of the Jordan River. It has been identified with Danah in the northern part of Jordan.

2. A city which fell to the lot of the tribe of Naphtali (Josh 19:32, 37) when Joshua divided the land of Canaan among the Children of Israel (Josh 14:1).

EGLAH ("heifer"). One of the wives of David and the mother of his sixth son, Ithream, born in Hebron.

EGLAIM A place or city in Moab mentioned by Isaiah in his proclamation against Moab (Is 15:8); it was probably on the southern border of the country. Several sites have been suggested but the location is unknown.

EGLON ("calf ?").

1. An Amorite city whose king allied himself to the kings of Jerusalem, Hebron, Lachish and Jarmuth to fight against Joshua. He was defeated and killed (Josh 10:5, 10, 16, 26). Later Joshua took the city and destroyed it (Josh 10:35). It was included in the domain of the tribe of Judah (Josh 15:39) when Joshua divided the land of Canaan among the Children of Israel (Josh 14:1).

Several sites have been suggested but no positive identification has been made.

2. King of Moab. In alliance with Ammon and Amalek, he defeated Israel (Judg 3:12-13), who remained under his yoke for 18 years (Judg 3:14) until Ehud the son of Gera killed him by trickery while bringing tribute (Judg 3:16-22). When he told the king that he had a message from God, Eglon, who was "a very fat man" rose from his chair as a mark of respect, and Ehud "took the dagger from his right thigh, and thrust it into his belly".

EGYPT, EGYPTIANS A land situated along the southeastern shore of the Mediterranean, bordered by the Red Sea on the east and Libya on the west. Its southern boundary altered in different periods. The territory falls naturally into two parts: Lower Egypt, which included the Nile Delta, and Upper Egypt, from Cairo southwards. In biblical times, as now, populated areas closely followed the Nile valley and its delta. Though its influence waxed and waned according to the rise and fall of successive empires and dynasties following the ongoing rivalry between Lower and Upper Egypt, it was throughout the biblical period, one of the great empires of the Middle East, whose only rival was in Mesopotamia (Sumeria, Assyria, Babylonia). Indeed the history of Palestine in biblical times must be seen against the background of that rivalry. On various occasions the Egyptians invaded and occupied Palestine. Many excavations attest their occupation.

Throughout the biblical period the relationship between Egypt and Israel remained unique. Egypt plays such a central part in biblical history that the name occurs more than 750 times in the Scriptures while "pharaoh" (the title of the Egyptian ruler) is mentioned over 200 times. However, only in a very few instances is the pharaoh mentioned by

EDREI 1
Num 21:33.
Deut 1:4; 3:1,
10. Josh 12:4;
13:12, 31

EDREI 2
Josh 19:37

EGLAH
II Sam 3:5. I
Chr 3:3

EGLAIM
Is 15:8

EGLON 1
Josh 10:3, 5,
23, 34, 36-37;
12:12; 15:39

EGLON 2
Judg 3:12, 14-
15, 17, 24

**EGYPT,
EGYPTIANS**
Gen 12:10-12,
14; 13:1, 10;
15:18; 16:1, 3;
21:9, 21;
25:12, 18;
26:2; 37:25,
28, 36; 39:1-2,
5; 40:1, 5;
41:8, 19, 29-
30, 33-34, 36,
41, 43-46, 48,
53-57; 42:1-3;
43:2, 15, 32;
45:2, 4, 8-9,
13, 18-20, 23,
25-26; 46:3-4,
6-8, 20, 26-27,
34; 47:6, 11,
13-15, 20-21,
26-30; 48:5;
50:3, 7, 11,

**14, 22, 26. Ex
1:1, 5, 8, 13,
15, 17-19;
2:11-12, 14,
19, 23; 3:7-12,
16-22; 4:18-21;
5:4, 12; 6:5-7,
11, 13, 26-29;
7:3-5, 11, 18-
19, 21-22, 24;
8:5-7, 16-17,
21, 24, 26;
9:4, 6, 9, 11,
18, 22-25;
10:2, 6-7, 12-
15, 19, 21-22;
11:1, 3-7, 9;
12:1, 12-13,
17, 23, 27, 29-
30, 33, 35-36,
39-42, 51;
13:3, 8-9, 14-
18; 14:4-5, 7-
13, 17-18, 20,
23-27, 30-31;
15:26; 16:1, 3,
6, 32; 17:3;
18:1, 8-10;
19:1, 4; 20:2;
22:21; 23:9,
15; 29:46;
32:1, 4, 7-8,
11-12, 23;
33:1; 34:18.
Lev 11:45;
18:3; 19:34,
36; 22:33, 43;
24:10; 25:38,
42, 55; 26:13,
45. Num 1:1;
3:13, 17; 9:1;
11:5, 18, 20;
13:22; 14:2-4,
13, 19, 22;
15:41; 20:5,
15-16; 21:5;
22:5, 11;
23:22; 24:8;
26:4, 59;
32:11; 33:1, 3-
4, 38; 34:5.
Deut 1:27, 30;
4:20, 34, 37,
45-46; 5:6, 15;
6:12, 21-22;
7:8, 15, 18;
8:14; 9:7, 12,
26, 10:19, 22;
11:3-4, 10;
13:5, 10;
15:15; 16:1, 3,
6, 12; 17:16;
20:1; 23:4;
24:9, 18, 22;
25:17; 26:5-6,
8; 28:27, 60,
68; 29:2, 16,
25; 34:11.**

name. There are more details and information on the life and customs of the Egyptians in the Scriptures than on any other external country or people and several Egyptian words and titles found their way into the Bible. For example Joseph is given the Egyptian name "Zaphnath-Paaneah", ("the god speaks and he [the one who bears the name] lives", Gen 41:45). Even the name of Moses is derived from the Egyptian verb "to be born".

The biblical image of Egypt is a contradictory one. On the one hand, it was the country where the Children of Israel were held in bondage and treated as slaves until divine intervention led to their miraculous escape through the Red Sea and eventually to the conquest of the land of Canaan. Because of this, its memory — as conserved for example in the Passover service — was execrated. On the other hand it was frequently a hospitable land, offering sanctuary and refuge in time of need. Very

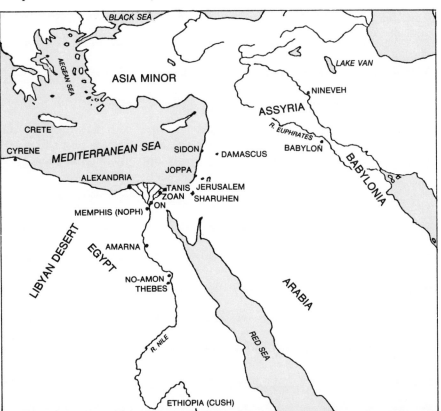

Egypt and the Middle East.

Aerial view of Abu Simbel, lower Egypt, where some of the most famous rock temples built by the pharaohs of Egypt (Rameses II in particular) have stood for over three thousand years.

often the Children of Israel turned to Egypt in periods of crisis or adversity, looking for a safe haven or, more simply, for food during a famine. "Now there was a famine in the land and Abraham went down to sojourn there, for the famine was severe in the land" (Gen 12:10). He was made welcome and when he went back to the land of Canaan he "was very rich in livestock, in silver and in gold" (Gen 13:2). Another famine drove Joseph's brothers to Egypt, following the advice of their father Jacob: "I have heard that there is grain in Egypt; go down to that place and buy for us there, that we may live and not die." (Gen 42:2). As the famine continued in the land of Canaan, Jacob and his whole family settled in Egypt under the protection of Joseph. Sold into slavery by his brothers, Joseph had been kindly received by Pharaoh and had risen to an exalted position. Pharaoh "set him over all the land of Egypt" (Gen 41:43) and gave him the daughter of a high priest for a wife. It was indeed the prosperity and expansion of the Children of Israel in Egypt after the death of Joseph (who, like his father, was embalmed after the custom of the Egyptians, Gen 50:2, 26) which led a new pharaoh, who had not known Joseph, to fear for his regime: "And he said to his people: 'Look, the people of the Children of Israel are more and mightier than we; come, let us deal wisely with them, lest they multiply, and it happen in the event of war, that they also join our enemies and fight against us'" (Ex 1:9-10).

The story of the ensuing plight of the Children of Israel in Egypt; the long years of bondage and suffering, the emergence of Moses as a leader, the ten plagues, the hurried meal of lamb and unleavened bread (Ex 12:3-20) which the Jews commemorate each year at Passover, the Exodus from Egypt by way of the Red Sea (Ex chap. 14), and the wandering in the Sinai desert where the Children of Israel received the Ten Commandments and the Mosaic law, were basic events in the crystallization of the Israelite people and the Jewish religion. "Thus says the Lord God of Israel: 'I brought up Israel out of Egypt, and delivered you from the hand of the Egyptians'" (I Sam 10:18); "I led you up from Egypt and brought you to the land of which I swore to your fathers" (Judg 2:1 etc.).

However, there was no lasting enmity between the Hebrews and the Egyptians following the Exodus. Indeed when Moses set up the statutes which were to rule the Children of Israel, the Egyptians were given a more favorable status than the other peoples: "You shall not abhor an Egyptian, because you were an alien in his land; the children of the third generation born to them may enter the congregation of the Lord" (Deut 23:7-8).

No reference is to be found in Egyptian sources to the sojourn of the Israelites in Egypt or to their exodus. It has been suggested that the period of the Hyksos, a group of Semitic peoples who overran Egypt after the destruction of the Middle Kingdom and who ruled c. 1720-1580 B.C., might provide the background for the story of Joseph, both because of the Semitic affinity and the appropriate chronology. The close involvement of Egypt at a slightly later period with the land of Canaan is clearly seen in the El Amarna Letters (1375-1300 B.C.). The pharaoh of the Exodus has been identified by many scholars with Rameses II (1198-1166 B.C.) of the 20th Dynasty.

The first mention of the people of Israel appears in Egyptian literature in the so-called "Israel Stele", when Pharaoh Merneptah (1224-1214) declares that "Israel is laid waste, he has no offspring".

After the establishment of the Monarchy, relations between Egypt and Israel fluctuated. For long periods they were friendly. King Solomon married a daughter of Pharaoh, who brought the town of

An Egyptian scribe. Detail of an Egyptian wall painting from a tomb at Beni Hassan, Egypt. 19th century B.C.

Josh 2:10; 5:4-6, 9; 9:9; 13:3; 15:4, 47; 24:4-7, 14, 17, 32. Judg 2:1, 12; 6:8-9, 13; 10:11; 11:13, 16; 19:30. I Sam 2:27; 4:8; 6:6; 8:8; 10:18; 12:6, 8; 15:2, 6-7; 27:8; 30:11, 13. II Sam 7:6, 23; 23:21. I Kgs 3:1; 4:21, 30; 6:1; 8:9, 16, 21, 51, 53, 65; 9:9, 16; 10:28-29; 11:17-18, 21, 40; 12:2, 28; 14:25. II Kgs 7:6, 17:4, 7, 36; 18:21, 24; 21:15; 23:29, 34; 24:7; 25:26. I Chr 2:34; 11:23; 13:5; 17:21. II Chr 1:16-17; 5:10; 6:5; 7:8, 22; 9:26, 28; 10:2; 12:2-3, 9; 20:10; 26:8; 35:20; 36:3-4. Ezra 9:1. Neh 9:9, 18. Ps 68:31; 78:12, 43, 51; 80:8; 81:5, 10; 105:23, 38; 106:7, 21; 114:1; 135:8-9; 136:10. Prov 7:16. Is 7:18; 10:24, 26; 11:11, 15-16; 19:1-4, 12-25; 20:3-5; 23:5; 27:12-13; 30:2-3, 7; 31:1, 3; 36:6, 9; 43:3; 45:14; 52:4. Jer 2:6, 18, 36; 7:22, 25; 9:26; 11:4, 7; 16:14; 23:7; 24:8; 25:19; 26:21-23; 31:32; 32:20-21; 34:13; 37:5, 7; 41:17; 42:14-19; 43:2, 7, 11-13; 44:1, 8, 12-15, 24, 26-28, 30;

Gezer as her dowry (I Kgs 9:16); but towards the end of his reign, his arch-rival Jeroboam found refuge in Egypt (I Kgs 11:40). After Jeroboam became king of Israel (I Kgs 12:20), the Egyptian ruler Sheshonk I (935-914 B.C.), the biblical Shishak, attacked Rehoboam's southern kingdom and destroyed numerous cities there (I Kgs 14:25; II Chr chap. 12).

After the fall of the Kingdom of Israel, Judah was increasingly drawn into the power struggle between Egypt and the Assyrian and Babylonian empires. Josiah was killed in 609 B.C. in a futile attempt to check the advance of Pharaoh Necho through his kingdom. His successor Jehoahaz was deported by the Egyptians who enthroned Jehoiakim in his place (II Kgs 23:34). King Hezekiah allied himself with Egypt against the Assyrian king Sennacherib despite the warning of the latter's general, "You are trusting in the staff of this broken reed, Egypt..." (Is 36:6). Zedekiah sided with Egypt in the rebellion against Nebuchadnezzar; but the Egyptian attempts failed and Judah was overrun by the Babylonian armies (II Kgs chap. 25). After the destruction of Jerusalem, some of the inhabitants who had not been sent into exile fled to Egypt, not heeding the warnings of Jeremiah: "For thus said the Lord of Hosts, the God of Israel: 'as my anger and my fury have been poured out on the inhabitants of Jerusalem, so will my fury be poured on you when you enter Egypt'" (Jer 42:18). However, Jeremiah too was forced to go to Egypt where he rebuked the Israelites for adopting the Egyptian worship of the "queen of the heaven" (Jer chap. 44). The Persians under Cambyses later conquered Egypt (525 B.C.) as they had the whole of the Middle East. The country became a vassal of the Persians, then of Alexander the Great, and then of the Greeks and of the Romans. The Jewish community, dating from the time of Jeremiah, prospered and grew rapidly until it numbered a million in the 1st century A.D. Here the Bible was first translated into Greek (the Septuagint, 3rd century B.C.).

In the NT, Egypt once more was a place of sanctuary. Joseph in Bethlehem was awakened by the Angel of the Lord who told him: "Arise, take the young child and his mother, flee to Egypt and stay there until I bring you word" (Matt 2:13). Thus the infant Jesus escaped from the Massacre of the Innocents (Matt 2:16).

EGYPT, BROOK OF The Brook of Egypt, which is identified with Wadi el-Arish, signifies the southwestern boundary of Canaan in many passages of the OT (Num 34:5; I Kgs 8:65; II Kgs 24:7; II Chr 7:8; Is 27:12; Ezek 47:19; 48:28). It usually appears along with the "entrance of Hamath" which includes the northern boundary of Canaan.

EGYPT, RIVER OF The River of Egypt (most likely the Nile or Wadi el-Arish) delineates the southern boundary in the divine promise of territory to the descendants of Abraham (Gen 15:18).

EHI Son of Benjamin in the list of the Children of Israel who went to Egypt with Jacob (Gen 46:8, 21). The name occurs only once and some scholars consider it to be a scribe's error.

EHUD

1. Son of Gera the Benjamite. Ehud, a left-handed man, was chosen by the Lord to deliver the Children of Israel from the yoke of King Eglon (Judg 3:15). Having made a special double-edged dagger (Judg 3:16), Ehud went to the king, bringing the usual tribute (Judg 3:17). He gained admittance to the king's private chamber by pretending to be the bearer of a secret message (Judg 3:19-20). When they were alone, he told the king the message was from God and as Eglon rose as a mark of respect Ehud thrust the dagger into his belly (Judg 3:20-21). Making his escape before the deed was discovered, Ehud blew the trumpet as a signal to the

The Rosetta Stone. An Egyptian stela of basalt inscribed in hieroglyphic, Demotic and Greek, which refers to Ptolemy V Epiphanes in his 9th year, 196 B.C. The stone was discovered in 1799 and played a vital role in deciphering the ancient Egyptian writing systems. (British Museum)

Assemblage of clay, iron and bronze utensils found in the building of the oil press at Ekron. End 7th century B.C.

Children of Israel and then led them to victory over Moab (Judg 3:26-29). He is mentioned between two minor judges, Othniel and Shamgar.

2. Third son of Bilhan, son of Jediael in the genealogy of Benjamin; it has been suggested that he was identical with Ehud No.1.

3. Father of Naaman, Ahijah and Gera in the genealogy of King Saul.

EKER The third son of Ram, firstborn of Jerameel, from the tribe of Judah.

EKRON, EKRONITES The northernmost of the five major Philistine cities (Josh 3:3) and one of the two situated inland. Originally a Canaanite town, it lay south of the Sorek River, on the western border of the coastal plain. Assigned to the tribe of Dan (Josh 19:43) it passed to Judah after Dan's migration (Josh 15:1, 45-46). The Bible preserves a tradition according to which the city was captured by Judah, together with other parts of Philistia (Judg 1:18), but that seems unlikely, especially at such an early stage in the settlement process. After the decisive battle between the Israelites and the Philistines at Aphek and Ebenezer, Ekron was one of the cities to which the recaptured ark was brought (I Sam 5:10). According to I Samuel 7:14, Samuel restored to Israel parts of Philistia, including Ekron, but this tradition, again, is doubtful, as Ekron still appears as a Philistine city at a later date (I Sam 17:52). It is possible, however, that the Israelites succeeded in conquering part of the expanded territory of Ekron. It is likewise probable that the passage describing David's capture of Philistia (II Sam 8:1) refers actually only to its northern part — that is, the land of Ekron.

During Ahaziah's reign, when the king was ill, he chose to address Baal-Zebub, the deity of Ekron (II Kgs 1:2-16). The city was denounced by several of the prophets (Jer 25:20; Amos 1:8; Zeph 2:4; Zech 9:5, 7).

EHUD 2
I Chr 7:10

EHUD 3
I Chr 8:6

EKER
I Chr 2:27

EKRON,
EKRONITES
Josh 13:3;
15:11, 45-46;
19:43. Judg
1:18. I Sam
5:10; 6:16-17;
7:14; 17:52.
II Kgs 1:2-3,
6, 16. Jer
25:20. Amos
1:8. Zeph 2:4.
Zech 9:5, 7

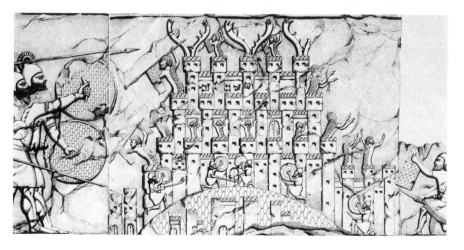

Airview of the excavations at Tell Miqne, the site identified with Ekron. (The W.F.Albright Inst. of Archaeological Research, Jerusalem)

Relief from the palace of Sargon II depicting the siege of Ekron.

Ekron was probably among the cities captured, together with Ashdod, by Sargon, king of Assyria. Later the city joined Ashkelon's rebellion against Assyria. In his famous punitive campaign, Sennacherib took Ekron and executed the rebels. It seems probable that Northern Philistia, including Ekron, was annexed by Judah during the reign of Josiah.

Ekron is identified with Tell Miqne (Khirbet el Muqanna) on the southern bank of Nahal Timnah $12\frac{1}{2}$ miles (20 km) east of Ashdod. Excavations have yielded remains from the Chalcolithic period to the 8th century B.C. A Canaanite city preceded the Philistine levels. The Philistine city was constructed in the 12th century B.C., at the time of the Philistines' penetration of the inner coastal plain and evidence indicates a long period of continuous occupation during the 12th-11th centuries. The last Iron Age level contained pottery of the late 7th century B.C., representing the city conquered by Nebuchadnezzar in 603 B.C.

Niche with horned altar from Ekron in the oil industrial complex. End 7th century B.C.

ELADAH (ELEADAH) *I Chr 7:20* — The son of Talath, son of Bered, son of Shuthelah, son of Ephraim in the genealogy of the family of Ephraim (I Chr 7:20). He was killed with other members of his family by the men of Gath "because they came down to take away their cattle" (I Chr 7:21) and "Ephraim their father mourned many days" (I Chr 7:22).

ELAH ("terebinth tree").

1. A chief of Esau in Edom (Gen 36:41, 43; I Chr 1:52). He is mentioned together with Pinon, which is a town and it has been suggested that Elah is also a town, perhaps Elath.

2. The father of Shimei, one of Solomon's governors assigned to the district of Benjamin.

3. A king of Israel, son of Baasha (I Kgs 16:6, 8, 13) who succeeded his father and reigned in Tirzah for two years (I Kgs 16:8). He was murdered by his servant Zimri while "he was in Tirzah drinking himself drunk" (I Kgs 16:9-10). King Elah reigned from 883 to 882 B.C.

4. Elah father of Hoshea, king of Israel (II Kgs 15:30).

5. The son of Caleb (I Chr 4:15) and the father of Kenaz in the genealogy of the family of Judah (I Chr 4:1).

6. Elah the son of Uzzi, one of the exiles who returned from Babylon and settled in Jerusalem in the time of Nehemiah.

ELAH, VALLEY OF *I Sam 17:2, 19; 21:9* — The place where Saul and the men of Israel encamped and "drew up in battle against the Philistines" (I Sam 17:2). There David met Goliath and killed him (I Sam 21:9). It is generally considered to be on the site of Wadi es-Samit, west of Bethlehem.

ELADAH
I Chr 7:20

ELAH 1
Gen 36:41. I
Chr 1:52

ELAH 2
I Kgs 4:18

ELAH 3
I Kgs 16:6, 8,
13-14

ELAH 4
II Kgs 15:30;
17:1; 18:1, 9

ELAH 5
I Chr 4:15

ELAH 6
I Chr 9:8

ELAH, VALLEY OF
I Sam 17:2,
19; 21:9

The Valley of Elah, looking east.

ELAM

1. Firstborn son of Shem (Gen 10:22; I Chr 1:17) and ancestor of the Elamites. See ELAM, ELAMITES.

2. Son of Shashak, a Benjamite, and an ancestor of King Saul.

3. A Korahite, son of Meshelemiah, a gatekeeper at the time of King David.

4. A town in Judah which was settled after the Restoration, known as "the other Elam" (Ezra 2:31; Neh 7:34) to distinguish it from the land of Elam. Not identified.

5. Member of the priestly choir at the dedication of the walls of Jerusalem in the time of Nehemiah (Neh 12:42).

6. Head of a family that returned from the Babylonian Exile with Zerubbabel (Ezra 2:7; Neh 7:12) and a signatory to Ezra's covenant (Neh 12:42).

ELAM, ELAMITES The biblical name of a hilly country, east of the River Tigris (Hiddekel) bordered by Assyria and Madai on the north, the Persian Gulf on the south and Persia on the east and southeast. Its capital was Susa (Shushan). Most of our knowledge of it derives from Sumerian, Babylonian and Assyrian sources. There was a constant state of war between Elam and the kingdoms of Lagash and Assyria. By the end of the 2nd millennium B.C. the Elamites had succeeded in deposing the Sumerian Dynasty of Ur. According to Genesis chapter 14, Chedorlaomer, king of Elam, ruled over all the countries which were formerly under the yoke of Babylon, and the countries on the Jordan were his tributaries. At the beginning of the 12th century B.C. the Elamites invaded Babylon, and the stone on which Hammurabi wrote his code of laws was captured by them and taken to Susa, where it was found in 1902. The rise of Assyria in the 8th-7th centuries B.C. led to clashes between the two kingdoms. Sargon II, Sennacherib and Ashurbanipal conducted continuous military campaigns against Elam.

ELAM 1
Gen 10:22.
I Chr 1:17

ELAM 2
I Chr 8:24

ELAM 3
I Chr 26:3

ELAM 4
Ezra 2:31.
Neh 7:34

ELAM 5
Neh 12:42

ELAM 6
Ezra 2:7; 8:7;
10:2, 26. Neh
7:12; 10:14

ELAM,
ELAMITES
Gen 14:1, 9.
Ezra 4:9. Is
11:11; 21:2;
22:6. Jer
25:25; 49:34-39.
Ezek 32:24.
Dan 8:2. Acts
2:9

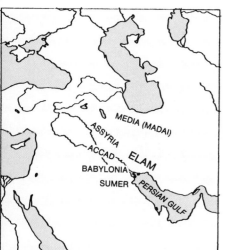

Elam.

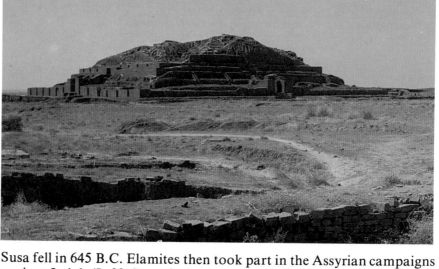

The great ziggurat of Choga-Zanbil in Khuzestan, built in the 13th century B.C. by the Elamite king Untash Gal.

Susa fell in 645 B.C. Elamites then took part in the Assyrian campaigns against Judah (Is 22:6), and after the fall of Nineveh Elam regained its freedom. Isaiah prophesied the unification of Elam and Media, which was to bring about the conquest of Babylon (Is 21:2, 9). The fall of Elam was foretold by Jeremiah (49:34-39) and by Ezekiel (32:24-25). During the period of the Persian empire Elam was one of the satrapies, with Susa as its capital. Elamites settled in Samaria impeded the Jews who returned from the Babylonian Exile (Ezra 4:8-9).

ELASAH ("made by God").

1. Elasah the son of Shaphan, one of the two messengers chosen by King Zedekiah of Judah to carry the letter of Jeremiah the prophet to Nebuchadnezzar, king of Babylon (Jer 29:1, 3).

2. Elasah son of Pashur (Ezra 10:22), one of the sons of the priest who had taken alien wives (Ezra 10:18) and had to repudiate them upon the command of Ezra (Ezra 10:19).

ELATH (ELOTH) A coastal town at the northern end of the northeastern arm of the Red Sea, mentioned frequently in conjunction with Ezion Geber; both were stations on the route of the Exodus (Deut 2:8). In the days of the United Monarchy Elath became an important harbor through which the trade with Arabia and Ophir flowed (I Kgs 9:26-28), but it may be inferred that in the days of Joram, son of

The Bay of Elath.

Jehoshaphat, it was taken by the Edomites (II Kgs 8:20-22). Amaziah, king of Judah, subdued Edom, and his son Azariah rebuilt Elath (II Kgs 14:22). In the days of Ahaz, Rezin, king of Aram, took it once more; according to the Bible it was never in Israelite hands again (II Kgs 16:6). Elath is identified with modern Akaba. See also EZION GEBER.

ELDAAH The fifth and last son of Midian, son of Abraham by Keturah (Gen 25:1-2, 4).

ELDAD One of the two elders (along with Medad) of the Israelites who started prophesying in the wilderness together with 70 elders because the spirit of the Lord rested upon them (Num 11:26-27). Joshua the son of Nun wanted Moses to silence them (Num 11:28) but Moses answered "Oh that all the Lord's people were prophets" (Num 11:29).

ELEAD A member of the family of Ephraim, perhaps his son (I Chr 7:21). He was killed with other members of the family by the men of Gath "because they came down to take away their cattle" (I Chr 7:21) and "Ephraim their father mourned many days" (I Chr 7:22).

ELEALEH A town on the east bank of the Jordan River, not far from Heshbon. It was part of the territory conquered from Sihon king of the Amorites which the children of Gad and Reuben wanted for their

View of the region of Elealeh on the east bank of the Jordan River.

livestock (Num 32:1-4). Moses gave it to them (Num 32:33) and the town of Elealeh was allotted to the children of Reuben who rebuilt it (Num 32:37). It fell later to Moab (Is 15:4) and Isaiah predicted its destruction together with that of the whole kingdom (Is 16:9).

ELEASAH ("made by God"; the Hebrew spelling of Eleasah is identical to that of Elasah).

1. The son of Helez and the father of Sismai, in the genealogy of the family of Jerahmeel, firstborn son of Hezron the grandson of Judah.

ELEASAH 1
I Chr 2:39-40

2. Son of Raphah (or Rephaiah) and father of Azel in the genealogy of King Saul.

ELEASAH 2
I Chr 8:37;
9:43

ELEAZAR ("God has helped").

1. The third son of Aaron, the high priest (Ex 6:23). After the death of his two older brothers (Lev 10:12) Eleazar was placed in a position of special importance and assumed a number of leadership responsibilities. He was titular head of the entire tribe of Levi (Num 3:32) and he performed some of the high priest's functions even during Aaron's lifetime (Num 19:4). On the death of his father, Eleazar succeeded him as high priest (Num 20:28; Deut 10:6). He assisted Moses in the census of the people (Num 26:1-3) and was responsible, together with Moses and Joshua, in planning and then executing the division of the land among the tribes of Israel (Num 34:17; Josh 14:1).

ELEAZAR 1
Ex 6:23, 25;
28:1. Lev 10:6,
12, 16. Num
3:2, 4, 32;
4:16; 16:37,
39; 19:3-4;
20:25-26, 28;
25:7, 11; 26:1,
3; 26:60, 63;
27:2, 19,
21-22; 31:6,
12-13, 21, 26,
29, 31, 41, 51,
54; 32:2, 28;
34:17. Deut
10:6. Josh
14:1; 17:4;
19:51; 21:1;
22:13, 31-32;
24:33. Judg
20:28. I Chr
6:3-4, 50;
9:20; 24:1-6.
Ezra 7:5

Eleazar was the father of Phinehas the priestly zealot (Num 25:10-13) and the ancestor of most of the priestly families including the family of Zadok (I Chr 24:3-18).

Coin from the time of Bar-Kochba, with the inscription "Eleazar the priest". A.D. 133.

2. Son of Abinadab. He guarded the ark of the Lord when it was brought to Kirjath Jearim.

ELEAZAR 2
I Sam 7:1

3. Son of Dodo (Dodai in I Chr 27:4). He was one of the "mighty men" who helped David in his battle against the Philistines.

ELEAZAR 3
II Sam 23:9.
I Chr 11:12

4. Son of Mahli, a Levite; he had three daughters who were married to their kinsmen.

ELEAZAR 4
I Chr
23:21-22;
24:28

5. A priest, son of Phinehas, who helped weigh the gold and silver in the Temple.

ELEAZAR 5
Ezra 8:33

6. Son of Parosh. He was one of those forced to repudiate their foreign wives at the decree of Ezra.

ELEAZAR 6
Ezra 10:25

7. A Levitical musician at the time of the dedication of the Temple walls.

ELEAZAR 7
Neh 12:42

8. Son of Eliud and father of Matthan; listed in the genealogy of Jesus.

ELEAZAR 8
Matt 1:15

ELEPH City of Benjamin (Josh 18:28). It may be part of the name Zelah which precedes it.

ELHANAN ("God was merciful").

1. Elhanan, son of Jair (I Chr 20:5) or Jaare-Oregim (II Sam 21:19) the Bethlehemite, who killed Goliath "whose spear was like a weaver's beam" (II Sam 21:19) or the brother of Goliath (I Chr 20:5). This heroic deed bears an intriguing resemblance to the tale of David and Goliath, and it has been suggested that these are two versions of the same event.

2. Elhanan the son of Dodo in Bethlehem, one of David's thirty "mighty men" (II Sam 23:24; I Chr 11:26). It has been suggested that he was identical with Elhanan No.1 since both were from Bethlehem and lived at the same time.

ELI ("[the Lord is] exalted"). High priest of the line of Ithamar and "judge" of Israel at Shiloh for 40 years. He was present at Hannah's vow (I Sam 1:9-18) and it was to him that her son Samuel was entrusted (I Sam 1:21ff).

Although apparently a pious man, Eli failed to curb the scandalous behavior of his sons, the priests Hophni and Phinehas (I Sam 2:12-17, 22). For this the future downfall of his progeny was predicted and a sign given that his sons would both die on the same day (I Sam 2:27-36). This prophecy was confirmed by a vision of Samuel (I Sam 3:11-14), and accepted by Eli as God's will. His sons were killed as they accompanied the ark of the covenant into battle against the Philistines. When Eli, then 98, heard that Shiloh and the ark had been captured and his sons killed, he fell backward from his seat, broke his neck, and died.

Eli's descendants continued in the office of high priest (I Sam 14:3) until the time of Solomon, when Abiathar, who had supported Adonijah's bid for the throne, was replaced by Zadok (I Kgs 2:22, 35). I Kings 2:27 identifies this as the fulfillment of the prophecy against the house of Eli.

ELIAB ("God will provide").

1. Eliab the son of Helon, a Zebulunite (Num 1:9) delegated by the Lord to assist Moses and Aaron in taking a census of the Children of Israel in the wilderness (Num 1:2, 4). Later appointed leader of the tribe of Zebulun (Num 2:7); on behalf of his tribe he presented an offering to the tabernacle set up by Moses (Num 7:24-29). He led the Zebulunites when the Children of Israel set forth in the wilderness (Num 10:12, 16).

2. Eliab the Reubenite, son of Pallu, father of Nemuel, Dathan and Abiram (Num 26:8-9) according to the second census of the Children of Israel taken by Moses and Eleazar (Num 26:1-2). His sons Dathan and Abiram rebelled against Moses and Aaron (Num 16:1, 12).

3. Firstborn son of Jesse (the grandson of Ruth and Boaz) and thus elder brother of David (I Chr 2:13). Eliab was the first to catch the eye of Samuel when the latter was sent by the Lord to Bethlehem to search for a king among the sons of Jesse (I Sam 16:1). Samuel found him tall and good looking, but the Lord told him he had refused Eliab (I Sam 16:7). Eliab was with King Saul when the Israelite army faced Goliath and the Philistines (I Sam 17:13). He became very angry with his younger brother David for abandoning his flock of sheep to come to the battle. Eliab's daughter, Abihail (II Chr 11:18), married Jerimoth son of David; their daughter Mahalath married King Rehoboam.

4. Son of Kohath (I Chr 6:27), and one of the ancestors of the prophet Samuel in the genealogy of the family of Levi (I Chr 6:1).

5. The third of the Gadites, "mighty men of valor", who joined David in Ziklag after a series of daring deeds (I Chr 12:9).

6. A Levite of the second rank at the time of David (I Chr 15:18); appointed to be a singer before the ark using a string instrument.

Bone Hebrew seal inscribed "[Belonging] to Eliakim [son of] Uzza]": 7th century B.C. (Israel Museum)

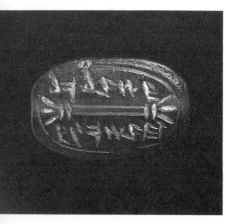
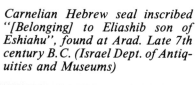

Carnelian Hebrew seal inscribed "[Belonging] to Eliashib son of Eshiahu", found at Arad. Late 7th century B.C. (Israel Dept. of Antiquities and Museums)

ELIADA ("the Lord knew"; the spelling of the name in Hebrew is identical to that of Eliadah below).

1. One of the sons born to David in Jerusalem.

2. A "mighty man of valor" from the tribe of Benjamin, and a captain in the army of Jehoshaphat king of Judah; he had "two hundred thousand men armed with bow and shield".

ELIADAH Father of Rezon, one of the enemies of Solomon and the founder of the reigning family of the Aramean kingdom of Damascus.

ELIAH An alternate form of Elijah used in Ezra 10:26.

ELIAHBA A Shaalbonite, one of David's thirty "mighty men".

ELIAKIM ("God raises up").

1. The son of Hilkiah, Eliakim was in charge of the household of King Hezekiah of Judah (II Kgs 18:18); his accession to that important office had been foretold by Isaiah (Is 22:20-21). He was involved in the bitter dispute with the emissary of the king of Assyria who mocked the Lord (II Kgs 18:37).

2. Eliakim second son of Josiah king of Judah (II Kgs 23:34); he was made a puppet king and renamed Jehoiakim by Pharaoh Necho after the latter had deposed his brother Jehoahaz (II Kgs 23:31-34; II Chr 36:4). (See also JEHOIAKIM).

3. One of the priests who participated in the dedication of the wall of Jerusalem by Nehemiah (Neh 12:27, 41).

4. Son of Abiud and grandson of Zerubbabel; father of Azor in the genealogy of Joseph the husband of Mary.

5. Father of Jonan and son of Melea in the corresponding genealogy given by Luke.

ELIAM

1. Father of Bathsheba, wife of Uriah the Hittite and later of David (II Sam 11:3). Though he is called Ammiel in I Chronicles 3:5 it is generally considered to be the same name, with the letters rearranged.

2. Son of Ahithophel the Gilonite, one of David's "mighty men". Some scholars believe Nos. 1 and 2 to be identical.

ELIASAPH ("whom God has added").

1. Eliasaph the son of Deuel (Num 1:14) or Reuel (Num 2:14), a man of Gad appointed by the Lord to help Moses and Aaron take a census of the Children of Israel in the wilderness (Num 1:2, 14). Later appointed leader of the tribe of the children of Gad (Num 2:14); on their behalf he presented an offering to the tabernacle set up by Moses (Num 7:1) on the sixth day (Num 7:42-47) and he led them when the Children of Israel set out from the wilderness of Sinai (Num 10:12, 20).

2. Eliasaph son of Lael, leader of the Gershonites in the family of Levi according to the census taken by Moses in the wilderness of Sinai (Num 3:14-15).

ELIASHIB ("God gives back").

1. The second of Elioenai's seven sons, and a descendant of Zerubbabel (I Chr 3:24) in the genealogy of the family of David (I Chr 3:1).

2. A priest, descendant of Aaron, and head of the 11th division of priests at the time of King David.

3. A high priest in the time of Nehemiah, he helped rebuild the Sheep Gate and consecrate it (Neh 3:1); probably identical with No.4.

4. A priest who allied himself with Tobiah against Nehemiah (Neh 13:4, 7) probably identical with No.3. He was the son of Joiakim (Ezra 10:6; Neh 12:10) and the father of Joiada (Neh 13:28) and Johanan (Neh 12:23).

5. A singer, one of the men who had taken an alien wife at the time of Ezra and had to repudiate her (Ezra 10:18, 24).

ELIADA 1
I Chr 3:8. II Sam 5:16

ELIADA 2
II Chr 17:17

ELIADAH
I Kgs 11:23

ELIAH
Ezra 10:26

ELIAHBA
II Sam 23:32.
I Chr 11:33

ELIAKIM 1
II Kgs 18:18, 26, 37; 19:2.
Is 22:20; 36:3, 11, 22; 37:2

ELIAKIM 2
II Kgs 23:34.
II Chr 36:4

ELIAKIM 3
Neh 12:41

ELIAKIM 4
Matt 1:13

ELIAKIM 5
Luke 3:30

ELIAM 1
II Sam 11:3

ELIAM 2
II Sam 23:34

ELIASAPH 1
Num 1:14;
2:14; 7:42, 47;
10:20

ELIASAPH 2
Num 3:24

ELIASHIB 1
I Chr 3:24

ELIASHIB 2
I Chr 24:12

ELIASHIB 3
Neh 3:1-2, 20-21

ELIASHIB 4
Ezra 10:6.
Neh 12:10, 22-23; 13:4, 7, 28

ELIASHIB 5
Ezra 10:24

6. The son of Zattu, one of those who had taken an alien wife at the time of Ezra and had to repudiate her (Ezra 10:18, 27).

7. The son of Bani, another of the men who had taken an alien wife at the time of Ezra and had to repudiate her (Ezra 10:18, 36).

ELIATHAH ("thou art my God"). Head of the 20th division set by David over the service of the Temple (I Chr 25:27) he was the son of Heman (I Chr 25:4) from the tribe of Levi.

It has been suggested that this is not a name, but a prayer, according to the translation from the Hebrew.

ELIDAD Elidad son of Chislon (Num 34:21) a man of Benjamin appointed by the Lord to help Moses divide up the land of Canaan (Num 34:16-18).

ELIEL ("the Lord is my God").

1. Head of a family of Manasseh dwelling on the east bank of the Jordan River (I Chr 5:23); "a mighty man of valor" (I Chr 5:24). However, having proved unfaithful to the God of his fathers (I Chr 5:25) he was punished by being taken into captivity by the king of Assyria, Tiglath-Pileser (I Chr 5:26).

2. Son of Toah and father of Jeroham, one of the Levites, sons of the Kohathites, appointed by David over the service of song in the Temple (I Chr 6:31, 33-34).

3. One of the sons of Shimei in the genealogy of King Saul.

4. One of the sons of Shashak in the genealogy of King Saul.

5. A Mahavite, one of the thirty "mighty men" of David.

6. Another of the thirty "mighty men" of David.

7. The seventh man of Gad to join David in Ziklag, a "mighty man of valor" (I Chr 12:8, 11).

8. A Levite, the chief of the sons of Hebron (I Chr 15:9) who was summoned by David to help carry the ark.

9. A Levite, one of the overseers in the Temple at the time of King Hezekiah of Judah.

ELIENAI ("my eyes are turned towards the Lord"). One of the heads of the tribe of Benjamin who settled in Jerusalem with their family, in the genealogy of King Saul.

ELIEZER ("God is my help").

1. Eliezer of Damascus, Abraham's servant and, up to the birth of Isaac, his prospective heir.

2. The second son of Moses by his wife Zipporah (Ex 18:4) the daughter of Jethro. Father of Rehabiah (I Chr 23:17).

3. Son of Becher of the tribe of Benjamin.

4. A priest who blew the trumpet before the ark at the time of King David.

5. The son of Zichri; leader of the Reubenites at the time of David.

6. The son of Dodavah of Mareshah, he prophesied against Jehoshaphat king of Judah because he had allied himself with Ahaziah king of Israel.

7. One of the leaders sent by Ezra to Iddo in Casiphia to bring back Levites for the House of the Lord (Ezra 8:15-17).

8. A priest of the family of Jeshua son of Jozadak who had taken an alien wife and had repudiated her upon the command of Ezra.

9. A Levite who had taken an alien wife and had to repudiate her.

10. A son of Harim who had taken an alien wife and had to repudiate her at the command of Ezra.

11. Father of Jose and son of Jorim in the genealogy of Joseph according to Luke.

ELIHOENAI ("my eyes are turned towards the Lord").

1. Son of Zerahiah, from Pahath-Moab, one of the heads of families

who came back from Babylon with Ezra; he brought with him "two hundred males".

2. An alternate spelling for Eljehoenai in some versions.

ELIHOREPH The son of Shisha who, together with his brother Ahijah, was appointed official scribe by King Solomon.

ELIHU ("God is the one").

1. Grandfather of Elkanah the father of Samuel (I Sam 1:1); also called Eliel (I Chr 6:34) and Eliab (I Chr 6:27).

2. One of the men of Manasseh who defected and joined David in Ziklag.

3. One of the sons of Shemaiah the Korahite (I Chr 26:7) a gatekeeper at the time of David.

4. One of the brothers of David (I Chr 27:18) but is probably meant here for Eliab No.3.

5. The son of Barachel the Buzite, of the family of Ram, who in chapters 32 and 33 of the Book of Job attempted to convince Job of the justice of God's ways.

ELIJAH ("Yah is my God"). A Tishbite, from the region of Gilead; the foremost prophet in Israel during the reigns of Ahab, Ahaziah and Jehoram. The Bible depicts him as a lonely figure with no settled home, roaming the countryside, appearing and vanishing unexpectedly (I Kgs 18:12). All his life Elijah was active in the defense of his God. His teachings brought him into constant conflict with the kings of Israel, and on at least one occasion, he had to flee for his life. In his campaign against the cult of Baal, he clashed frequently with Ahab's Phoenician wife Jezebel, who had introduced the pagan cult in Israel. Following his victory over the 850 prophets of Baal and Asherah on Mount Carmel (I Kgs chap. 18), Elijah fled from Jezebel's anger to the south of Judah, eventually reaching Horeb, the mount of God, where God revealed himself to him (I Kgs chap. 19). The story follows the lines of the revelation to Moses at Mount Sinai, with Elijah representing an ancient Mosaic tradition still surviving in Israel. While on the mountain, Elijah was commanded to anoint Hazael as king of Aram, and Jehu as king of Israel, and appoint Elisha as his own successor. Elijah carried out only the last of these tasks, while it fell to his disciple Elisha, to anoint the two kings. It may have been the pro-Phoenician tendencies of Ahab which caused the prophet to direct his endeavors against the dynasty of Omri, but what probably exceeded all else in moving Elijah to lay his curse on the whole house of Ahab was the episode of Naboth's vineyard (I Kgs chap. 21; II Kgs 9:25-26). The king was shown up for his flagrant injustice and cruelty, while Elijah emerged as the champion of tradition in the social and economic life of Israel.

The stories about Elijah are full of wonders and miraculous acts (I Kgs 17:1-6, 8-24); when his own life came to an end he was gathered up to heaven in a whirlwind (II Kgs 2:11). Specific magic powers were ascribed to Elijah's mantle (II Kgs 2:8-14) similar to those of Moses' rod. His powerful personality, which made an unforgettable impact on his own and later generations, and his demise, no ordinary mortal death but an ascent to heaven in a fiery chariot, combined to accord Elijah a special role in Jewish traditions about the End of Days (Mal 4:5-6). In the Dead Sea Scrolls he appears as one of the forerunners of the messiah. Elijah remains one of the most intriguing of the prophets of Israel, thus meriting the role in Jewish tradition as the herald of the messiah who would miraculously settle all controversies and make for more peace in the world.

In the NT many identified John the Baptist with Elijah the forerunner of the messiah (Luke 1:17; John 1:21). Some thought Jesus to be Elijah

ELIHOREPH
I Kgs 4:3

ELIHU 1
I Sam 1:1

ELIHU 2
I Chr 12:20

ELIHU 3
I Chr 26:7

ELIHU 4
I Chr 27:18

ELIHU 5
Job 32:2, 4-6; 34:1; 35:1; 36:1

ELIJAH
I Kgs 17:1, 13, 15-16, 18, 22-24; 18:1-2, 7-8, 11, 14-17, 21-22, 25, 27, 30-31, 36, 40-42, 46; 19:1-2, 9, 13, 19-21; 21:17, 20, 28. II Kgs 1:3-4, 8, 10, 12-13, 15, 17; 2:1-2, 4, 6, 8-9, 11, 13-15; 3:11; 9:36; 10:10, 17. I Chr 8:27. II Chr 21:12. Ezra 10:21. Mal 4:5. Matt 11:14; 16:14; 17:3-4, 10-12; 27:47, 49. Mark 6:15; 8:28; 9:4-5, 11-13; 15:35-36. Luke 1:17; 4:25-26; 9:8, 19, 30, 33, 54. John 1:21, 25. Rom 11:2. James 5:17

The hill of Sartaba, overlooking the Jordan Valley where it is said that Elijah ascended to heaven in a fiery chariot.

The Cave of Elijah on Mount Carmel, thought to be one of the places where the prophet took refuge from persecution by Ahab and Jezebel.

(Matt 16:14; Mark 6:15; 8:28; Luke 9:8, 19) but Jesus rejected this, attributing the role to John the Baptist (Matt 11:14; 17:11ff; Mark 9:12ff). Elijah, with Moses, flanked Jesus at the Transfiguration (Matt 17:3; Mark 9:4; Luke 9:30).

ELIKA Elika the Harodite, one of the thirty "mighty men" of David.
ELIKA
II Sam 23:25

ELIM The second halt of the Children of Israel on their way to the promised land. They found there "twelve wells of water and seventy palm trees" (Ex 15:27). From Elim they went on to the Red Sea (Num 33:10).
ELIM
Ex 15:27; 16:1. Num 33:9-10

ELIMELECH ("God is my king"). A man of Bethlehem in Judah who went to sojourn in Moab (Ruth 1:1) with his wife Naomi (1:2) and his two sons, Mahlon and Chilion (Ruth 1:2). The sons married two Moabite women, Orpah and Ruth. Elimelech died in Moab (Ruth 1:3) along with his two sons (Ruth 1:5). His widow Naomi returned to Bethlehem with her daughter-in-law, Ruth (Ruth 1:19).
ELIMELECH
Ruth 1:2-3; 2:1, 3; 4:3, 9

ELIOENAI ("my eyes are turned towards the Lord").
ELIOENAI 1
I Chr 3:23-24

1. A descendant of Zerubbabel, son of Neariah (I Chr 3:23) father of Hodaviah, Eliashib No.1, Pelaiah, Akkub, Johanan, Delaiah and Anani in the genealogy of the family of David.

ELIOENAI 2
I Chr 4:36

2. One of the leaders of the tribe of Simeon.

ELIOENAI 3
I Chr 7:8

3. A son of Becher in the genealogy of Benjamin.

4. An alternate spelling for Eljehoenai in some versions.

5. A son of Pashhur; a Levite who had taken an alien wife and had to repudiate her upon the decree of Ezra.

6. A son of Zattu who had taken an alien wife and had to repudiate her upon the decree of Ezra.

7. A priest who participated in the thanksgiving prayers at the dedication of the wall of Jerusalem by Nehemiah.

ELIPHAL One of the thirty "mighty men" of David; he was the son of Ur (I Chr 11:35). May be an alternate form of Eliphelet (II Sam 23:34).

ELIPHAZ

1. The eldest son of Esau by his wife Adah, daughter of Elon the Hittite (Gen 36:2-4). He was the father of Teman, Omar, Zepho (or Zephi), Gatam and Kenaz (Gen 36:11) and his concubine Timna bore him Amalek (Gen 36:12). He and his brothers were leaders of Edom (Gen 36:15-16).

2. Eliphaz the Temanite, the oldest of the three friends of Job (Job 2:11), who accused Job of multiple wrongs (Job chaps. 4-5, 15, 22). In the end he was rebuked by the Lord for his arguments (Job 42:7) and had to offer a burnt offering to appease the Lord (Job 42:7-9).

ELIPHELEH (ELIPHELEHU) A Levite of the second rank who was appointed among the singers in front of the ark (I Chr 15:16, 18). He "directed with harp on the Sheminith" (I Chr 15:21) at the time of King David.

ELIPHELET (the Hebrew spelling is the same as that of Eliphal).

1. Eliphelet the son of Ahasbai, the son of the Maacathite, one of the thirty "mighty men" of David.

2. One of the sons born to David in Jerusalem; he is mentioned twice in the same list, possibly by error.

3. Third son of Eshek the brother of Azel in the genealogy of Saul.

4. One of the sons of Adonikam and the head of a family of exiles who returned from Babylon with Ezra (Ezra 8:1, 13).

5. A Levite; one of the sons of the priest Hashum who had taken pagan wives and had to repudiate them upon the decree of Ezra.

ELISHA ("God is salvation"). Prophet from Abel Meholah in Gilead. He lived in the Northern Kingdom of Israel during the reigns of Jehoram, Jehu, Jehoahaz and Jehoash, and prophesied in the context of the wars between Aram and Israel. Initially Elisha was Elijah's disciple and attendant, then while on the Mount of Horeb (I Kgs 19:16) Elijah obeyed a divine command by laying his mantle upon Elisha (I Kgs 19:19; II Kgs 2:11, 15). With the ascent of Elijah (II Kgs chap. 2), Elisha took Elijah's mantle and thus commenced his own prophetic career, related in a collection of narratives, which though unconnected are all linked to the events of the time (II Kgs 3:11-8:15). The sons of the prophets, a group of zealous upholders of the purity of religion who opposed irreligious government policies, deferred to Elisha for decision in all matters (II Kgs 6:1-3). Elisha employed the techniques of early prophecy (II Kgs 3:15). Among the many miracles attributed to him were the multiplication of the oil (II Kgs 4:1-7), the restoration to life of the son of the Shunammite woman (II Kgs 4:8-37) and the cure from leprosy of Naaman, general of the ruler of Damascus (II Kgs 5:1-19). For the latter's cure Elisha refused payment: when his servant Gehazi, subsequently accepted a gift from Naaman, the prophet cursed him (II Kgs 5:20-27).

In times of war it was customary among the sons of the prophets to forget their differences with the king and follow the armies into the field proffering encouragement (I Kgs 20:13ff, 35-43). In this manner, Elisha accompanied the joint forces of King Jehoram of Israel and King

Elisha's Spring near Jericho which the prophet "healed" by casting salt in it (II Kgs 2:19-22)

Jehoshaphat of Judah, in their attempt to subjugate the rebellious Moab, and transmit the word of God. Elisha's rejection of Jehoram reflected religious objections to the house of Ahab, in view of Ahab's contempt for ancestral religion and customs. It was on Elisha's instructions that Jehu was anointed king over Israel (II Kgs 9:1-13). According to II Kings 8:7-15 Elisha also anointed Hazael king of Aram, though the historical truth of this story is doubted by some scholars. In spite of the inevitable legendary character of some of the stories, Elisha emerges as a man of courage and passionate convictions devoted to the preservation of the Israelite faith and its deliverance from all foreign pressures.

ELISHAH

1. The firstborn son of Javan (great grandson of Noah), in the line of Japheth.

2. A place from which "blue and purple" dye came, probably Cyprus.

ELISHAMA ("the Lord heard").

1. The son of Ammihud, from the family of Ephraim, who was delegated by the Lord to help Moses take a census of the Children of Israel (Num 1:2, 10); later was appointed leader of the tribe of Ephraim (Num 2:18) on whose behalf he presented the offering to the tabernacle set up by Moses, on the seventh day (Num 7:1, 48-53). He led the tribe of Ephraim when the Children of Israel set out from the wilderness of Sinai (Num 10:22).

He was the father of Nun and grandfather of Joshua (I Chr 7:27).

2. One of the sons born to David in Jerusalem.

3. Father of Nethaniah and grandfather of Ishmael, a member of the royal family who killed Gedaliah the governor of Judah.

4. Son of Jekamiah and grandson of Shallum, last descendant of Sheshan by the Egyptian husband of his daughter in the genealogy of Jerahmeel.

5. An alternate spelling for Elishua.

6. A priest; Jehoshaphat king of Judah sent him to teach in the cities of Judah (II Chr 17:7-9).

7. The royal scribe at the time of Jehoiakim king of Judah; in his chambers was stored the scroll of Jeremiah the prophet, later destroyed by the king (Jer 36:12, 20-21).

ELISHAPHAT ("the Lord has judged"). The son of Zichri. Elishaphat, a captain, helped Jehoiada instal Joash on the throne of Judah after he overthrew Athaliah.

ELISHEBA Wife of Aaron and mother of his sons Nadab, Abihu, Eleazar and Ithamar. She was the daughter of Amminadab and the sister of Nahshon.

ELISHUA ("the Lord is salvation"). One of the sons born to King David in Jerusalem (I Chr 14:5; II Sam 5:15); in I Chronicles 3:6, spelt Elishama.

ELIUD ("God of Judah"). Son of Achim and father of Eleazar in the genealogy of Jesus according to Matthew.

ELIZABETH ("my God has sworn"). The wife of Zacharias the priest, and mother of John the Baptist (Luke 1:5 ff). She is described as a descendant of Aaron, and bore the name of Aaron's wife (Elisheba in Hebrew) (Ex 6:23). Elizabeth conceived after an angelic apparition to Zacharias, although she had been barren and was advanced in years. During her pregnancy she was visited by her cousin Mary of Nazareth (Luke 1:39-40). Tradition places this meeting, and the home of Elizabeth, at the village of Ein Karem, just west of Jerusalem.

ELIZAPHAN ("God has hidden / protected").

1. The son of Uzziel, Elizaphan was the head of the Kohathites

Black limestone Hebrew seal inscribed "[Belonging] to Hoshaiah [son of] Elishama". Late 7th-6th centuries B.C. (Israel Museum)

The Church of the Visitation in Ein Karem, built on the spot where, according to tradition, Mary visited her cousin Elizabeth during her pregnancy — hence the name of the church. The well, below, is said to have been used by Elizabeth.

(descendants of the second son of Levi) who camped south of the tabernacle in the wilderness of Sinai (Num 3:30). In the Book of Exodus his name appears as Elzaphan (Ex 6:22). Together with his brother Mishael he took away the bodies of Nadab and Abihu after they had been smitten by the fire of the Lord in the camp (Lev 10:4).

I Chr 15:8.
II Chr 29:13

2. Elizaphan the son of Parnach, a leader from the tribe of Zebulun, one of the men delegated by the Lord, with Joshua and Eleazar, to help Moses divide up the land of Canaan (Num 34:16-17, 25).

ELIZAPHAN 2
Num 34:25

ELIZUR ("my God is a rock"). A man of the tribe of Reuben, son of Shedeur appointed by the Lord to help Moses take a census of the Children of Israel in the wilderness of Sinai (Num 1:1-2, 5). He was later appointed leader of the tribe of Reuben (Num 2:10) on whose behalf he presented the offering to the tabernacle set up by Moses, on the fourth day (7:30-35). He led the Reubenites when the Children of Israel set out from the wilderness on their way to the promised land (Num 10:18).

ELIZUR
Num 1:5; 2:10;
7:30, 35; 10:18

ELJEHOENAI ("my eyes are turned towards the Lord"). The seventh son of Meshelemiah son of Kore, a gatekeeper in the time of David (I Chr 26:1-3). Sometimes spelled Elihoenai.

ELJEHOENAI
I Chr 26:3

ELKANAH ("God has created").

1. The second son of Korah (Ex 6:24; I Chr 6:23). There is confusion about Korah's children, as three different lists are given in the same chapter (I Chr 6:23, 25, 27, 36).

ELKANAH 1
Ex 6:24. I Chr
6:23, 25-27

2. Father of Samuel the prophet. He was the husband of both Peninnah and Hannah. Whereas the former bore him children, the latter was childless for a long period of time. Hannah made a vow to the Lord, and finally bore her husband a child, Samuel.

ELKANAH 2
I Sam 1:1, 4,
8, 19, 21, 23;
2:11, 20

3. The son of Joel, a Kohathite, who, together with his sons, ministered "with music before the dwelling place of the tabernacle of meeting until Solomon had built the house of the Lord in Jerusalem".

ELKANAH 3
I Chr 6:34-36

4. Father of Asa and grandfather of Berechiah "who lived in the villages of the Nethophatites", a Levite.

ELKANAH 4
I Chr 9:16

5. Doorkeeper to the ark at the time of David.

ELKANAH 5
I Chr 15:23

6. A Korahite, one of David's thirty "mighty men". He was among the Benjamites who joined David in Ziklag and could use both the right and left hand to hurl stones and shoot arrows.

ELKANAH 6
I Chr 12:6

7. A high official, during the reign of King Ahaz of Judah, who was killed by Zichri when Pekah son of Remaliah rebelled against the king.

ELKANAH 7
II Chr 28:7

ELKOSHITE A man from Elkosh; the home of the prophet Nahum. It is generally supposed to have been in Judah.

ELKOSHITE
Nah 1:1

ELLASAR The kingdom of Arioch who allied himself with Chedorlaomer king of Elam (Gen 14:1) and was defeated together with him.

ELLASAR
Gen 14:1, 9

ELMODAM Son of Er and father of Cosam in the genealogy of Jesus according to Luke.

ELMODAM
Luke 3:28

ELNAAM ("God is pleasantness"). Father of Jeribai and Joshaviah, of David's thirty "mighty men". According to the Septuagint, he too was one of the "mighty men".

ELNAAM
I Chr 11:46

ELNATHAN ("God has given").

1. A man of Jerusalem, father of Nehushta who was the wife of Jehoiakim king of Judah and the mother of Eliakim (Jehoiakim); may have been identical with No.2.

ELNATHAN 1
II Kgs 24:8

2. The son of Achbor. He was among the men sent by King Jehoiakim to Egypt to bring back the prophet Urijah to be executed (Jer 26:22); he was a prince (Jer 36:12) and was among those who implored the king not to burn the scroll of Jeremiah (Jer 36:25). Perhaps identical with No.1.

ELNATHAN 2
Jer 26:22;
36:12, 25

3. Three men of this name are among those sent by Ezra to Iddo in

ELNATHAN 3
Ezra 8:16

Red limestone Aramaic seal inscribed "[Belonging] to Elnathan". 8th-7th centuries B.C. (Israel Museum)

Casiphia "to bring us servants for the house of our God", that is Levites; two are called leaders and the third, "a man of understanding".

ELON

1. The second son of Zebulun and head of the family of the Elonites according to the second census of the Children of Israel taken by Moses and Eleazar (Num 26:2, 26).

2. A Hittite, father-in-law of Esau; his daughter is called Basemath in Genesis 26:34 and Adah in Genesis 36:2.

3. Elon the Zebulunite, a judge in Israel; he succeeded Ibzan, was judge for ten years, and at his death "was buried at Aijalon, in the country of Zebulun" (Judg 12:10-12).

4. A city which fell to the lot of the tribe of Dan (Josh 19:40, 43) when Joshua divided the land among the Children of Israel (Josh 14:1). It was near Timnah (Josh 19:43) but its present location is unknown.

ELON BETH HANAN A city in the second administrative district of Solomon probably in the territory of Dan. Its present location is unknown, though it may have been an alternate name for Elon No.4.

ELONITE The family of Elon No.1, second son of Zebulun, according to the second census of the Children of Israel taken by Moses and Eleazar.

ELPAAL ("God of action"). The second son of Shaharaim by his wife Hushim (I Chr 8:11); in the genealogy of Benjamin.

ELPALET, ELPELET One of the sons born to David in Jerusalem; alternate names for Eliphelet.

ELPARAN The farthest point to be reached by the invasion of Chedorlaomer, beyond the mountains of Seir; it was in the wilderness (Gen 14:6). There is no other mention of the place in the Scriptures; it has been suggested that this is an alternate name for Elath.

ELTEKEH A place which fell to the lot of the tribe of Dan (Josh 19:40, 44) when the land of Canaan was divided by Joshua among the Children of Israel (Josh 14:1); it was later handed over to the Levites (Josh 21:3, 23). Some of the battles between Sennacherib and the Egyptians were fought there and the Assyrian king destroyed the town in 701 B.C. Its present location is unknown beyong the fact that it was on the coastal plain, between Timnah and Gibbethon.

ELTEKON A city which fell to the lot of the tribe of Judah (Josh 15:20, 59) when the land of Canaan was divided by Joshua among the Children of Israel (Josh 14:1). Its location is unknown beyond the fact that it was in the vicinity of Halhul in the mountains of Judah.

ELTOLAD A city which fell to the lot of the tribe of Judah (Josh 15:20, 30) when Joshua divided the land of Canaan among the Children of Israel (Josh 14:1). It was later included in the territory of Simeon (Josh 19:1, 4). Probably one of the ruined cities south of Beersheba, in the Negeb.

ELUL The sixth month of the year; it is mentioned once in the Bible, as the month in which Nehemiah completed the building of the wall of Jerusalem.

ELUZAI ("the Lord is my strength"). A man of Benjamin who came to David in Ziklag (I Chr 12:1, 5). He was a mighty warrior equally proficient in using right and left hand "in hurling stones and shooting arrows" (I Chr 12:2). The name may be an alternate form of Eliezer or Eleazar.

ELYMAS See BAR-JESUS

ELZABAD ("God has given").

1. The ninth of the 11 men of Gad who joined David in Ziklag and "whose faces were like the faces of lions, and were as swift as gazelles on the mountains" (I Chr 12:8, 12).

2. The fourth son of Shemaiah (I Chr 26:7) from the family of Obed-Edom (I Chr 26:8), a Levite and gatekeeper at the time of David.

ELZAPHAN An alternate spelling for Elizaphan in Exodus 6:22 and Leviticus 10:4.

EMEK KEZIZ A Benjamite city, possibly located in the Jordan Valley near Jericho.

EMIM Ancient inhabitants of the land of Moab, regarded as giants (Deut 2:10-11). They were attacked by King Chedorlaomer and his allies in Shaveh Kiriathaim in the time of Abraham (Gen 14:5).

EMMANUEL See IMMANUEL

EMMAUS A town in Judea, on the border of Judah in the Persian period, when it was also known as Hamthan, a name which means "hot springs"; this is a reference to the springs near the city which are mentioned in the Jewish sources. Judas Maccabee won a great victory over the Seleucid army of Gorgias and Nicanor near here in 166 B.C. After the middle of the 1st century B.C. it became the capital of a district. In A.D. 68, following the destruction of Jerusalem, Vespasian settled soldiers of the Legio V. Macedonica there. In A.D. 221 Elagabalus conferred the status of a *polis* on Emmaus, renaming it Nicopolis, "the City of Victory".

Remains outside the house identified as the house of Cleopas at Emmaus.

After the Crucifixion two of the disciples, who were on their way from Jerusalem, met the risen Christ there without recognizing him (Luke 24:13ff). This episode is one of the most important in the gospels in explaining the transformation which the disciples of the earthly Jesus underwent after his resurrection. From being mere eyewitnesses they became heralds of the risen Christ whom they recognized in the breaking of the bread (Luke 24:35) and in the study of the Scriptures (Luke 24:32, 45). This combination became the basis for the principal form of worship of the new faith.

Excavations on the site have unearthed remains of the Hellenistic, Roman, Byzantine and later periods. To the Byzantine period belong ruins of a basilical mono-apsidal church built on the foundations of a more ancient house, identified as the house of Cleopas. On the ruins of

ELZABAD 2
I Chr 26:7

ELZAPHAN
Ex 6:22. Lev 10:4

EMEK KEZIZ
Josh 18:21

EMIM
Gen 14:5. Deut 2:10-11

EMMAUS
Luke 24:13

this church a Crusader church was built that is still standing. Emmaus is identified with Imwas, about 18 miles (29 km) northwest of Jerusalem.

ENAM A village in the territory allotted to the tribe of Judah.

ENAN Father of Ahira, a man of Naphtali and leader of his tribe in the time of Moses.

EN DOR, ENDOR A city in lower Galilee, south of Nazareth, identified with present-day Indur, 4 miles (6 km) south of Mount Tabor.

It was within the domain of the half-tribe of Manasseh (Josh 17:11) when Joshua divided the land of Canaan among the Children of Israel (Josh 14:1). The Canaanites who dwelled in the city were not driven out but were made to work for the conquerors (Josh 17:12-13). Endor was the home of the witch consulted by King Saul (I Sam 28:7-25) before the battle of Gilboa. According to Psalm 83, Endor was the place where Jabin and Sisera perished (Ps 83:9-10).

View of Endor with Mount Tabor in the background.

EN EGLAIM A place on the Dead Sea mentioned in the vision of Ezekiel (Ezek 47:10), where fishermen will spread their nets, "their fish will be of the same kind as the fish of the Great Sea, exceedingly many" (Ezek 47:10). Though several locations have been suggested (e.g. Ain Hogla, Ain Feshka) it is now considered that En Eglaim was on the southeastern shore of the Dead Sea.

The southeastern shore of the Dead Sea where En Eglaim is said to have been located.

EN GANNIM

1. A city in the lowlands of the territory which fell to the lot of Judah (Josh 15:34); its present location is not known but it should be near Beth Shemesh.

2. A city in the territory of Issachar, assigned as a Levitical city (Josh 21:29). It is referred to as Anem in I Chronicles 6:73.

EN GEDI (ENGEDDI) An oasis on the western shores of the Dead Sea, named after the copious spring which waters it and mentioned together with the "city of salt" as part of the territory of Judah (Josh 15:62). On his flight from Saul David dwelt in the strongholds of En Gedi (I Sam 23:29; 24:1). The battle between Jehoshaphat, king of Judah, and the Ammonites and Moabites began at Hazezon Tamar "which is En Gedi" (II Chr 20:1 ff). In antiquity En Gedi was already known for its aromatic plants mentioned in the Song of Solomon (1:14). The site became still more renowned in the period of the Second Temple. Josephus relates that the finest palm trees and the opobalsamum (balsam) grew there (*Antiq.* IX, 7). At that time it was the capital of a district (*War* III, 55). It was raided by the Sicarii after they conquered Masada in A.D. 68 (*War* IV, 402). Pliny (*Nat. Hist.* v. 73), who wrote somewhat later, says: "Lying below the Essenes was formerly the town of Engedi, second only to Jerusalem in fertility of its groves of palm trees, and now like Jerusalem a heap of ashes".

EN GEDI
**Josh 15:62.
I Sam 23:29;
24:1. II Chr
20:2. Song
1:14. Ezek
47:10**

(right)
Nature reserve park at En Gedi.
(Nature Reserves Authority)

Waterfall at En Gedi known as the Fountain of the Kids or David's Fountain.

Excavations in the 1960-70's uncovered various layers of settlement going back to the time of Josiah, king of Judah. This settlement was destroyed c. 582 B.C. Later layers were from the Persian period, destroyed c. 40 B.C.; and from the 1st century A.D. when it consisted of a fortress, devastated by the Romans in A.D. 68. A synagogue from a later Jewish settlement has also been uncovered.

(bottom right)
Mosaic at the synagogue at En Gedi.

The so-called Window at En Gedi.

EN HADDAH A city which fell to the lot of the tribe of Issachar (Josh 19:17, 21) when Joshua divided the land of Canaan among the Children of Israel (Josh 14:1). It was in the northeastern part of their territory.

EN HAKKORE The spring which appeared when Samson, thirsty after a fight with the Philistines, asked the Lord for water.

EN HAZOR A fortified city which fell to the lot of the tribe of Naphtali (Josh 19:32, 35, 37) when Joshua divided the land of Canaan among the Children of Israel (Josh 14:1).

It should be in Upper Galilee but its location is not known.

EN MISHPAT An alternate name for KADESH.

ENOCH

1. The eldest son of Cain, and father of Irad; the world's first city was named after him (Gen 4:17).

2. Son of Jared and father of Methuselah. He lived 365 years (some have suggested that he was a solar hero). The cryptic statement which relates to Enoch as a man who "walked with God and he was not, for God took him" (Gen 5:24) gave rise to various mystical and esoteric interpretations, suggesting a miraculous translation of Enoch alive from earth to heaven, where he enjoyed an intimate fellowship with God, as did Elijah later on. In Ecclesiasticus 44:16 he is described as a "sign of knowledge to all generations", implying that he was the source of esoteric knowledge. The idea that Enoch was transported alive to heaven is prevalent in later Judaism and Christianity (see Heb 11:5).

View of En Haddah, east of Mount Tabor.

ENOCH, BOOKS OF Several ancient Jewish writings are attributed to Enoch No.2. Chief among these are the two pseudepigraphic works: the Ethiopic Enoch (I Enoch) and the Slavonic Enoch (II Enoch). The Ethiopic Enoch is a composite work constituting a compilation of disparate fragments and representing cycles of traditions of diverse origin and date. The book was originally written in Hebrew or in Aramaic and was later translated into Greek. Both the original text and the Greek translation were lost. Fortunately, the entire work has been preserved in an Ethiopic translation, which is regarded as canonical by the Ethiopic church. In its present form it contains 108 chapters and is divided into five sections.

Fragment of the Book of Enoch I, found at Qumran. (Shrine of the Book, Jerusalem)

The Slavonic Enoch has been preserved only in the Slavonic version of a lost Greek original. The book exists in two recensions. Generally speaking, both works have an apocalyptic thrust dealing with such characteristically eschatological aspects as heavenly visions, cosmology, angelology, judgment, the messiah, resurrection and bizarre symbolism. During his journey through heaven and earth Enoch is initiated into the secrets of the universe, and the course of the divinely predestined human events is disclosed to him.

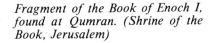

The Book of Enoch is the largest book of the Pseudepigrapha and the most significant of all the apocalyptic works. Not only does it provide important material for the study of the mystical and religio-historical atmosphere prevailing among the Jews of the Maccabean era, but it is also a richly stored repository of eschatological and folkloristic knowledge. The book played a highly significant role in the development of Christian gnosticism and of certain aspects of Jewish eschatology.

ENOS, ENOSH Son of Seth and grandson of Adam (Gen 5:3, 6); when he was 90 years "he begot Cainan" (Gen 5:9) and lived on for another 815 years, and begot sons and daughters (Gen 5:10). During his time, it is recorded that the worship of Yahweh began (Gen 4:26).

EN RIMMON A place where some of the exiles returning from Babylon settled in the time of Nehemiah (Neh 11:14). Most scholars believe this to be an alternate name for two neighboring cities, Ain and Rimmon, north of Hebron.

EN ROGEL A spring in Jerusalem on the border of the territories of Judah and Benjamin (Josh 15:7; 18:16).

Jonathan and Ahimaaz hid there, waiting for news, during the rebellion of Absalom against David his father (II Sam 17:17). Later Adonijah, younger brother of Absalom, sacrificed "by the stone of Zoheleth, which is by En Rogel" during his unsuccessful bid for the throne (I Kgs 1:9).

En Rogel has been identified with the "Well of Job", Bir Ayyub, at the junction of the Kidron Valley and the Hinnom Valley. It is conjectured that the place was a spring until partially blocked by an earthquake which turned it into a well.

EN ROGEL
Josh 15:7; 18:16. II Sam 17:17. I Kgs 1:9

En Rogel, a spring, southeast of Jerusalem at the confluence of the Hinnom and Kidron Valleys.

En Shemesh, east of the Mount of Olives.

EN SHEMESH A spring on the border of the territories of Judah and Benjamin between Gilgal and En Rogel (Josh 15:7; 18:17) usually identified with Ain el Houd, near Lazaryeh, east of the Mount of Olives.

EN SHEMESH
Josh 15:7; 18:17

EN TAPPUAH A city on the border of the territories of Manasseh and Ephraim (Josh 17:7), an alternate name for Tappuah.

EN TAPPUAH
Josh 17:7

EPAENETUS ("laudable"). In his epistle to the Romans Paul sends greetings to "my beloved Epaenetus, who is the first fruits of Achaia to Christ". Nothing further is known about the man.

EPAENETUS
Rom 16:5

EPAPHRAS ("charming"). A man of Colossae, "faithful minister of Christ" (Col 1:7), who was imprisoned in Rome with Paul.

EPAPHRAS
Col 1:7; 4:12. Philem 23

EPAPHRODITUS ("charming"). A Christian from Philippi in Macedonia, called by Paul "my brother, fellow worker and fellow soldier, but your messenger and the one who ministered to my need" (Phil 2:25). When Epaphroditus was seriously ill his friends were extremely worried, and on his recovery Paul sent him back from Rome to Philippi.

EPAPHRODITUS
Phil 2:25; 4:18

EPHAH

1. The firstborn son of Midian, fourth son of Abraham by Keturah.

2. A concubine of Caleb, son of Hezron, who bore him Haran, Moza and Gazez.

3. The fifth son of Jahdai in the genealogy of Caleb.

4. A place noted for its young camels.

EPHAH 1
Gen 25:4. I Chr 1:33

EPHAH 2
I Chr 2:46

EPHAH 3
I Chr 2:47

EPHAH 4
Is 60:6

EPHAI A Netophathite whose sons were among the survivors in Jerusalem after Nebuchadnezzar had broken down the walls and destroyed the city (Jer 39:1, 8); they joined Gedaliah at Mizpah (Jer 40:8).

EPHAI
Jer 40:8

EPHER

EPHER 1
Gen 25:4. I
Chr 1:33

EPHER 2
I Chr 4:17

EPHER 3
I Chr 5:24

EPHES DAMMIM
I Sam 17:1

1. Second son of Midian, fourth son of Abraham by his wife Keturah.
2. Third son of Ezrah in the genealogy of Judah.
3. Head of a family of the half-tribe of Manasseh east of the Jordan.

EPHES DAMMIM Site of the Philistine camp before the fight between David and Goliath; it was in the territory of Judah "between Sochoh and Azekah". Its present location is unknown.

EPHESIANS, EPISTLE TO THE The tenth book of the NT.

A letter attributed to the apostle Paul but differing from his other letters in its complete lack of personal references and of controversy. The letter reads in part like a long prayer of thanksgiving to God and for

The Arcadian Way at Ephesus.

this reason is much appreciated for its inspiration and its devotional value. Although the historical background of the letter remains partially unclear, some consensus seems to be emerging in contemporary scholarship. In the earliest and best manuscripts, the introductory verse 1:1 does not contain the words "in Ephesus". This means the letter is without a specific address, a fact supported by the general nature of its contents. The language is in many ways very close to Paul's and yet the use of many terms, as well as the style, differs from his. This has led many scholars to deny that it was written by Paul himself, but rather by a disciple of his who wished to summarize Paul's basic ideas for a new generation. The author did this by removing the

Remains of the temple of Artemis at Ephesus.

polemical references in the original Pauline letters, and by generalizing and universalizing their main contents around a new theme: the unity of the Church (as the body of Christ) in Christ. The letter develops this theme by stressing the role of the Spirit and of mutual love among Christians, particularly the love that should exist between husband and wife. If the letter is indeed the work of a disciple of Paul, then it is valuable in its information concerning the development in the Pauline churches in the period A.D. 80-100, after the death of the apostle but before the Pastoral Epistles, when the old controversy which had bedeviled Paul's ministry — that between Gentile and Jewish Christian missionary policies — had quieted, and when the church had become an object of reflection in its own right. The letter has an evenly balanced structure. The doctrinal part is contained in the first three chapters, and the moral part in the last three chapters.

OUTLINE

1:1-14	Doxology attaching cosmic significance to Christ
1:15-2:22	Reflections on the Christian mystery which is God's plan of salvation, specifically that Jews and Gentiles, formerly divided, are now united peacefully in Christ
3:1-13	Reflections on the mystery of the Church
3:14-21	Prayer for the Christian community
4:1-6	Appeal for unity in body of Christ
4:7-16	Invitation to grow in the diverse graces of Christ to full maturity
4:17-5:20	Appeal to leave pagan ways
5:21-6:9	Appeal for good order in the household including reflection on the theology of Christian marriage (5:22-33)
6:10-17	Description of the divine armor of the Christian
6:18-24	Conclusion

EPHESUS Capital of 16 Roman provinces of Asia and one of the largest (and wealthiest) cities in the eastern Mediterranean area. Located some 3 miles (5 km) from the Mediterranean on the left bank of the River Cayster in western Asia Minor, Ephesus was a link between East and West, and a junction of overland and sea routes (Acts 18:19-24; 19:1, 26; 20:16-17; I Tim 1:3; II Tim 1:18; 4:12). Under Roman rule, which started around 133 B.C., Ephesus became a melting-pot of peoples, one of the cosmopolitan centers of the Roman Empire and a meeting-place of religions.

From the time of Croesus of Lydia (in the 6th century B.C.) the city's religious life was controlled by the fertility goddess, identified by the Greeks with their goddess Artemis and by the Romans with Diana, who was worshiped in a temple where prostitution was legally permitted. This temple was one of the wonders of the ancient world (Acts 19:35). According to Acts 19:13-19 there were also many exorcists and quacks, who "took it upon themselves to call the name of the Lord Jesus over those who had evil spirits, saying, 'We adjure you by the Jesus whom Paul preaches'". Inscriptions discovered on excavated walls have

EPHESUS
Acts 18:19, 21, 24; 19:1, 17, 26, 35; 20:16-17. I Cor 15:32; 16:8. Eph 1:1. I Tim 1:3; II Tim 1:18; 4:12. Rev 1:11; 2:1

A general view of Ephesus.

shown a strong belief in superstition. Paul alludes to this in his Epistle to the Ephesians (4:18; 5:3-12) which does not in fact seem to have been written to the Ephesians (the most important NT codices do not mention the words "in Ephesus" (Eph 1:1)).

On the mountain of Pion stood the massive theater, seating 24,000, venue of the protest meeting organized by the silversmith Demetrius whose business was affected when Paul's preachings caused a sharp drop in his sales of Artemis-statues (Acts 19:24-29). The Ephesians were so impressed by the speech of Demetrius that they took Paul's companions, Gaius and Aristarchus, and tried to capture Paul too but some of the officials of Asia, who were his friends, begged him not to venture into the theater (19:31). These chiefs of Asia, sympathetic towards Paul, were Roman officials charged with promoting worship of the emperor and organizing public festivals.

In the cosmopolitan atmosphere of this city, its inhabitants were open to Paul's preaching. They went to hear him at the synagogue (Acts 19:8), at the school of Tyrannus (Acts 19:9), in private houses and in the market-places. Paul knew that Ephesus was an important center of idolatry: "You see and hear that not only at Ephesus, but almost throughout all Asia, this Paul has persuaded and turned away many people, saying that gods which are made with hands are not gods" (Acts 19:26). Paul lived in Ephesus for two years (c. 56-58) and there wrote the first Epistle to the Corinthians and probably other epistles also.

Priscilla and Aquila worked in the community of Ephesus (Acts 18:18) as did Apollos (Acts 18:24), Erastus (Acts 19:22) and John the Apostle. A comparatively positive description of Ephesus is given in Revelation 2:1-7. Ephesus became a noted center of Christianity and at the Council of Ephesus in 431, Pelagianism and Nestorius were condemned.

A coin of Ephesus depicting a bee, a deer and a palm tree. c. 325 B.C.

EPHLAL
I Chr 2:37

EPHLAL A man of Judah, son of Zabad and father of Obed in the genealogy of the family of Jerahmeel.

EPHOD
Num 34:23

EPHOD A man of Manasseh who was appointed by the Lord to help Joshua and Eleazar divide the land (Num 34:17, 23).

EPHOD
Ex 25:7; 28:4, 6, 8, 12, 15, 25-28, 31; 29:5; 35:9, 27; 39:2, 5, 7-8, 18-22. Lev 8:7. Judg 8:27; 17:5; 18:14, 17-18, 20. I Sam 2:18, 28;

EPHOD ("garment"). One of the eight garments worn by the high priest. It was loose-fitting, and worn over the blue tunic (Ex 28:31), being secured by two shoulder straps and a belt around the middle. The shoulder straps bore two precious onyx stones with the names of the 12 sons of Jacob, six on each stone (Ex 28:5-14). The front of the ephod carried the breastplate with the Urim and Thummim which the high priest used as mantic symbols for purposes of divination (Ex 28:30). Occasionally the term ephod comprised the garment together with the breastplate and the Urim and Thummim. Some scholars believe that consultation through the Urim and Thummim was discontinued as

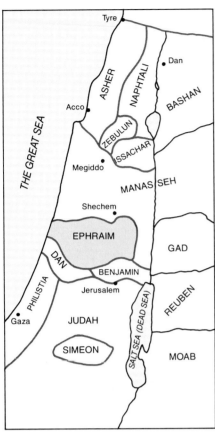

The territory of the tribe of Ephraim.

early as the First Temple period but the high priest continued to wear the ephod throughout the annals of both Temple periods.

The ephod was made of blue, purple and scarlet fine linen, distinguished only by strands of gold thread from the tabernacle curtains and veil of the ark (Ex 39:2-3). It thus helped to symbolize the close relationship of the high priest to the tabernacle and the Holy of Holies.

It is reported that Samuel wore a linen ephod (I Sam 2:18) as did David when the ark was brought to Jerusalem (II Sam 6:14).

EPHPHATA A word used by Jesus when healing the deaf mute. It means "be opened" in Aramaic.

EPHRAIM

1. The younger son of Joseph and of Asenath, daughter of the high priest of On (Gen 41:50-52); the ancestor of the tribe of Ephraim. The Hebrew name derives from a root meaning "fruitful", and according to Genesis 41:52 Joseph so named his younger son "because God has caused me to be fruitful in the land of my affliction." Before his death, Jacob adopted his grandchildren Ephraim and his older brother Manasseh to be equal with his own sons (Gen 48:5). He gave precedence to the younger Ephraim even though he linked Ephraim and Manasseh together as paradigms for future generations. In the chronicles of the tribes, Ephraim takes precedence over Manasseh in all matters such as the order of marching in the wilderness (Num 2:18-20), the consecration gifts for the tabernacle (Num 7:48, 54), and the order of the allocation of territory (Josh 16:5).

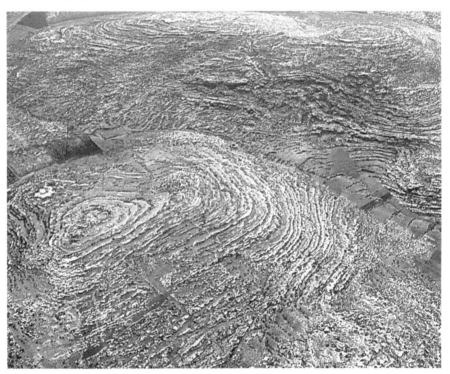

An aerial view of Samaria in the territory of Ephraim.

In the records of the divided kingdom, the name Ephraim often denoted the Northern Kingdom and its territory (Is 7:17; 11:13; Jer 7:15; 31:9; Ezek 37:16; Hos 4:17; 5:3). The tribe was allocated its land in the central hill country of Palestine, including some parts of the fertile valley (Josh 16:1-8). The Ephraimites were located south of the other Joseph tribe of Manasseh (Josh 17:10), and since the land of Ephraim was part of the wider unit, it is difficult to determine the precise borders of Ephraim's territory.

Living in central Palestine, it would seem that Ephraim was relatively free from clashes with Canaanites who consistently gave trouble to the other Israelite tribes. This freedom from foreign conflict led the tribe to develop without serious interference from the outside. As a result the Ephraimites became somewhat aggressive and proud. They encroached on the territory of their northern neighbor Manasseh (Josh 17:8-9), and also southward into the lands of the tribes of Benjamin and Dan.

Their touchy tribal pride is illustrated in their argument with Gideon (Judg 8:1-3) and in their conflict with Jephthah (Judg 12:1-6). The curious difficulty of the Ephraimites in pronouncing the word "Shibboleth" would indicate that they retained a strong local dialect (Judg 12:5-6).

Some scholars attribute the boastful pride and arrogance of the Ephraimite tribe to various other factors. Joshua, the leader of Israel at the time of the settlement, was of the tribe. The prime central position of Ephraimite territory, which included the religious shrine of Shiloh, gave the tribe a certain feeling of superiority and even the claim to leadership. To have been passed over by Gideon and Jephthah in the wars against the Midianites and the Ammonites (Judg 8:1; 12:1) must therefore have been a very painful slight to their tribal honor.

Ultimately, this tribal pride contributed to the division of the United Kingdom after the death of Solomon. The leader of the revolt and the first king of the breakaway Northern Kingdom was Jeroboam son of Nebat of the tribe of Ephraim (I Kgs 11:26).

2. A town near Bethel (II Sam 13:23).

3. A forest on the east side of the Jordan River, where King David's rebellious son, Absalom was killed by Joab (II Sam 18:6-17). Once possessed by the tribe of Ephraim, this area of land was claimed by the Gileadites, who defeated the Ephraimites in battle (Judg 12:1-7).

4. One of the gates of Jerusalem. When Jehoash, king of Israel, captured Amaziah, king of Judah, he destroyed the city walls from the Gate of Ephraim to the Corner Gate (II Kgs 14:13; II Chr 25:23).

EPHRAIMITES See EPHRAIM No.1

EPHRAIN A city of Israel taken by Abijah from Jeroboam.

EPHRATH The place near which Rachel gave birth to Benjamin, and where she died (Gen 35:16) and was buried "on the way to Ephrath (that is, Bethlehem)" (Gen 35:19; 48:7). Here too Caleb buried his wife Azubah (I Chr 2:19). Ephrath and Bethlehem may originally have been two separate places; later Ephrath was absorbed by Bethlehem.

Ephrath "on the way to Bethlehem".

EPHRATHAH

1. The place of origin of Elimelech and Naomi (Ruth 4:11). A place by this name is also mentioned in Psalm 132:6 and, again, together with Bethlehem in Micah 5:2. It is probably identical with Ephrath.

2. Second wife of Caleb.

EPHRATHITE An inhabitant of Ephrath or Ephrathah.

EPHRON

1. Ephron the son of Zohar, a Hittite living in Hebron (Gen 23:7-8, 10) who owned the cave of Machpelah and the surrounding land (Gen 23:9). When Abraham sought to bury his wife, Sarah (Gen 23:8), he offered to buy the site from Ephron. The Hittite was ready to let him use it without payment (Gen 23:15) but Abraham insisted on buying it to ensure possession of a burial place for himself and his family (Gen 23:16-20).

2. Mount Ephron, on the border of the territory of Judah, between Nephtoah and Kirjath Jearim. There is no other mention of this mountain.

Mount Kastel, identified with Mount Ephron.

EPICUREANS, EPICUREANISM Greek school of philosophy founded by Epicurus (342-270 B.C.). He taught freedom from fear and from desire through knowledge as the natural and pleasurable life. Rhetorical literature falsely accused Epicurus of materialistic hedonism. As the Epicureans did not believe in a world to come nor in the resurrection of the dead, they ridiculed Paul: "Then certain philosophers of the Epicureans and the Stoics encountered him. And some said, What does this babbler want to say? Others said, he seems to be a proclaimer of foreign gods: because he preached to them Jesus and the resurrection" (Acts 17:18). They took him to the Areopagus for a debate, and their challenge led to one of his most famous speeches (Acts 17:22-31).

ER ("watchful").

1. Firstborn son of Judah by his Canaanite wife Shua (Gen 38:3) and husband of Tamar (Gen 38:6). For his wickedness he died childless.

2. Son of Shelah and father of Lecah in the genealogy of Judah.

3. Son of Jose and father of Elmodam in the genealogy of Jesus.

ERAN Founder of a family of the clan of the sons of Shuthelah, from the tribe of Ephraim.

ERANITES A family of the clan of Shuthelah founded by Eran, a man of Ephraim.

ERASTUS ("beloved").

1. A companion of Paul sent by the apostle to Macedonia.

2. The treasurer of the city of Rome. May be identical with No.1. Alternatively II Timothy 4:20 may apply to No.2.

EPHRATHAH 1
Ruth 4:11. Ps 132:6. Mic 5:2

EPHRATHAH 2
I Chr 2:50; 4:4

EPHRATHITE
I Sam 17:12. Ruth 1:2

EPHRON 1
Gen 23:8, 10, 13-14, 16-17; 25:9; 49:29-30; 50:13

EPHRON 2
Josh 15:9

EPICUREANS
Acts 17:18

ER 1
Gen 38:3, 6-7; 46:12. Num 26:19. I Chr 2:3

ER 2
I Chr 4:21

ER 3
Luke 3:28

ERAN
Num 26:36

ERANITES
Num 26:36

ERASTUS 1
Acts 19:22. II Tim 4:20

ERASTUS 2
Rom 16:23

327

ESCHATOLOGY

ERECH A city in the land of Shinar, mentioned in the Table of Nations as one of the cities of Nimrod (Gen 10:10). In the Babylonian sources it is known by the name of Uruk. The city was in existence as early as the 4th millennium B.C. To the earlier levels of occupation belong a ziggurat, temples and a city wall which was strengthened with hundreds of towers. The city endured for thousands of years until its decay in the Hellenistic period.

ERI ("watchful"). The fifth son of Gad, founder of a family of the clan of Gad.

ERITES Belonging to the family founded by Eri the son of Gad.

ESARHADDON ("[the god] Asshur has given a brother"). King of Assyria and Babylonia, son of Sennacherib, ruled c. 680-669 B.C. According to the Bible he ascended the throne after his brothers Adrammelech and Sharezer had murdered Sennacherib their father (II Kgs 19:37; Is 37:38). Esarhaddon pursued his father's policy of mass deportation and resettlement of populations within his empire (Ezra 4:2). According to one of his stelae, King Manasseh of Judah was his vassal and paid him tribute. Esarhaddon's empire extended into Egypt, whose armies he defeated in 671 B.C. It was on his way to Egypt to quell an uprising that the Assyrian ruler met his death.

ESAU Firstborn son of Isaac and Rebekah, and ancestor of the Edomites (Gen chap. 36). Popular etymologies (see Gen 25:25, 30) relate the name Esau to *se'ar* (hairy) "he was like a hairy garment all over; so they called his name Esau" (cf Seir, another name for the land of Edom) and to *admoni* (ruddy) and *adom* (red) "the first came forth red" (cf Edom).

Before Esau's birth, it was prophesied that Rebekah's elder son would serve the younger (Gen 25:23). In addition, Esau was born with his twin brother holding his heel, which was interpreted as a sign that Jacob would supplant him. This he did on two occasions: Jacob sold a bowl of lentils to Esau in exchange for the latter's birthright (Gen 25:29-34); and later, with Rebekah's help, he tricked Isaac into giving him the blessing intended for Esau, the firstborn son. Instead of receiving a blessing, Esau's fate was to dwell in the wilderness, live by the sword, and for a time serve his brother Jacob. Some have suggested that this destiny was realized when the Edomites "became David's servants" (II Sam 8:14) in the 10th century, but rebelled successfully against Judean rule (II Kgs 8:20) in the 9th.

In contrast to Jacob the shepherd, Esau was a "skilful hunter, a man of the field" (Gen 25:27), whose venison his father Isaac loved to eat. Esau vowed to kill Jacob (Gen 27:41ff), but when the two met some 20 years later, Esau, at the head of a 400-man army, forgave his brother.

At the age of 40 Esau married two Hittite women Judith and Basemath (Gen 26:34; but according to Gen 36:2, Adah and Aholibamah). This displeased his parents (Gen 26:35), whereupon Esau also married an Ishmaelite, Mahalath (Gen 28:9; possibly an alternative name for Basemath), a granddaughter of Abraham (28:6-9).

The destruction of "Esau" (the land of Edom) is foretold in Jeremiah 49:7ff; cf Obadiah and Malachi 1:2ff.

The NT Letter to the Hebrews (12:16) points to Esau as an example of an immoral and irreligious man. Paul (Rom 9:10-13) cites the rejection of Esau, before either twin was born or had done good or evil, as an example of God's election.

ESCHATOLOGY A word referring to the doctrine of the "last things", based on the Greek *eschaton* (last thing). In some texts its meaning is restricted to the historical arena (horizontal eschatology) while in other texts its use ranges wider still to embrace a concept of eternal salvation

The Lion Hunt Stele, found at the site of biblical Erech.

Stele showing Esarhaddon holding by a leash the king of Egypt and Ethiopia and a bearded captive.

(vertical eschatology). Moreover, the eschatological age is pictured as both present and future, for its essential idea was that of divine coming. Even the individual's participation in the eschaton is understood differently, especially where apocalyptic thinking introduces the idea of a resurrection to renewed life on earth (Is 26:19; Dan 12:2) or for eternity (I Cor chap. 15).

Eschatological hope arose from a fundamental conviction about the nature of the deity. God intended good for the covenant people and could be trusted to fulfill every promise (cf Ps 73). As the list of promises grew, so did the consciousness of disparity between promise and fulfillment. Therefore a residue of hope formed a vision for the future, usually understood as the immediate future. Glorious moments in past history became paradigms for anticipated victory in the future (e.g. the Exodus from Egypt and the day of Midian: Is 9:4, referring to Judg chaps. 7-8). Thus belief in a day of the Lord arose, as did the conviction that God would raise up a deliverer (messiah) who would play a prominent role in inaugurating a kingdom of peace. To be sure, Israel's prophets sometimes questioned such hopes, announcing instead that the day of the Lord would be darkness rather than light (Amos 5:18-20) and calling for military action in place of peace (Joel 3:10). The underlying assumption was that the enemies of God must be destroyed before the deity could take up residence among humankind.

A classical eschatological text occurs both in Isaiah and in Micah (Is 2:2-4; Mic 4:1-4), where a vision of universal peace emerges. In the latter days the mountain of God will be established as a center for pilgrimage by nations from afar, and the heavenly judge will bring peace ("They shall beat their swords into plowshares, and their spears into pruning hooks", Is 2:4). The messiah comes to the forefront in several eschatological passages, especially in Isaiah. This wondrous child-prince will remove the yoke of bondage and remove every reminder of war (Is 9:1-7). According to Isaiah 11:1-9, the Spirit of the Lord will rest on the "stump" from Jesse, who will judge wisely and inaugurate an era of tranquillity when the original paradise will be restored. The notion of a surviving REMNANT occurs with considerable frequency in the Bible.

These fundamental hopes were altered over the years. A forerunner of the messiah was expected (Mal 3:1), and certain human actions were believed to have actualized the eschaton. For example, the construction of the Temple in the days of Haggai and Zechariah led to the crowning of Zerubbabel as messianic ruler (Zech 4:6). Ezekiel believed that the spirit would revive a dead nation, and he envisioned a life-giving stream flowing from the restored Temple in Jerusalem. Jeremiah also thought the Lord would renew the human heart, replacing a heart of stone, and instituting a new covenant (Jer 31:31-34). Daniel, the Son of man, would descend from the clouds and exercise dominion over the earth. That sovereignty was bestowed on him by the Ancient of Days (Dan 7:9-14), an expression for deity.

By the 1st century A.D. various groups believed they were living in the last days. The Essene community at Qumran and the early Christians expected the end of history at any moment. The former group compiled a text that provided a guide for the final conflict ("Wars of the Sons of Light against the Sons of Darkness"), while the Christians did their best to reconcile the fact that the expected return of Jesus did not in fact take place. Paul and various other believers expected Jesus to return during their lifetime. A confession (or prayer) was even preserved in Aramaic ("Come, Lord Jesus" / *Maranatha,* Rev 22:20), and a special ethic characterized Christians during the supposed interim between the resurrection of Jesus and his return for the faithful.

Opinions differed on whether Christians received eternal life at the moment of death or at a later time when the universal judgment would occur.

Ancient Israelite concepts of the eschaton were largely communal. Individuals participated in the blessings of life because of their solidarity with the group. A few exceptions arose in late apocalyptic, which imagined a resurrection. Christians placed the emphasis on individual salvation, but acknowledged that the good life had communal implications which commended voluntary poverty. Jesus was thought to have believed that the Kingdom of God had already dawned, although he also expected further manifestation of heavenly authority.

The initial act of deliverance from Egypt supplied the basic vocabulary for an anticipated deliverance from captivity to a human power or to sin's effect. Occasionally, a foreign ruler is pictured as assisting in this drama of salvation (for example, the Persian ruler, Cyrus). Within certain circles a vision of universal participation in Zion's benefits offers a partial corrective to the prevailing nationalism within the descriptions of the last things. Other thinkers stressed a terrible day of wrath and a cosmic confrontation (Ezek chaps. 38-39; Zeph chap. 1). Whereas some individuals tried to calculate the date of the end (Dan 12:5-13), Jesus warned his followers that God alone knew that day and hour.

ESDRAELON See JEZREEL

ESDRAS, I (=3 Esdras in Vulgate). A Jewish work dating from the Hellenistic period, preserved in the Apocrypha. It certainly dates from before A.D. 50 since it was used by Josephus as the basis for his account of the Return to Zion from Babylonia (*Antiq.* 11:1-158). The work is a compilation from biblical passages (II Chr chaps. 35-36; the Book of Ezra and Neh 7:72-8:13) translated into Greek with some additional material that does not appear in the Scriptures, the most significant of which is the story of non-Jewish origin, concerning Zerubbabel. The Persian King Darius I gave a banquet at which three of his bodyguards engaged in a contest to name the strongest thing imaginable. The winner was Zerubbabel who answered that "women are the strongest, but truth is victorious over all" (I Esd 3:8-12). As the winner, Zerubbabel made the request that the Jews be permitted to rebuild Jerusalem and restore the Temple vessels (4:43-46) and this was granted by Darius (4:47-58). The Jewish author of I Esdras (Ezra) probably revised a Gentile story using it to depict one of the most crucial moments in Jewish history — the Return to Zion from the Babylonian Exile.

The work describes the final years of the First Temple, from the Passover celebration of King Josiah to the destruction of the Temple (1:1-55). Chapter 2 relates the edict of Cyrus and the first return of Jews to Jerusalem, their work on the new Temple and the problems encountered (2:1-25). Then comes the legend of Zerubbabel, followed by the preparations for the return of the Babylonian exiles, their arrival in Jerusalem and the reconstruction of the Temple (3:1-7:15). The last chapters center around Ezra's activities and his reading of the Law in Jerusalem (8:1-9:55).

I Esdras probably served didactic purposes: a Greek-reading public was taught the theological lesson of Ezra-Nehemiah that truth is all-powerful and that God watches over those who serve him.

ESDRAS, II (also known as the Apocalypse of Ezra, IV Ezra or IV Esdras). A Jewish work ascribed to Ezra (in Greek, Esdras), and preserved in different ancient versions (including Latin, Syriac, Ethiopian, Armenian, Arabic and Coptic). The work was included in the Vulgate — the Bible of the Latin Church — and in the Protestant Apocrypha, but it is not found in the Septuagint; the Greek version, with the exception of a few passages, was lost.

Originally written in Aramaic or Hebrew, the work was composed in Palestine at the end of the 1st century A.D. The dating is based upon the identification of the three heads of the eagle in chapters 11-12 with the Flavian emperors. The work comprises seven visions around the central theme of the destruction of the Temple and Jerusalem, and the consequent theological problems. Seeking consolation for the Jewish people, the author's first three visions posed questions concerning the justice of God's management of the world (3:28) and God's purpose in, and responsibility for, the creation of sinful humanity (8:14). These questions receive an answer in three symbolic visions (4th-6th visions), mainly expressing eschatological expectations including a rebuilt Jerusalem (the vision of the mourning woman, 9:38-10:59), the last fourth of the wicked empire, symbolized by the eagle (chap. 11), or the Davidic messiah (chap. 13). In the final vision (chap. 14) Ezra receives the Torah, the 24 books of the Bible and the 70 books with secret knowledge.

Scholars are divided as to whether or not the work is a unity. Largely following traditional rabbinic thinking, it does not betray sectarian ideas.

ESEK The name given to a well dug by Isaac's herdsmen in Gerar.
`ESEK Gen 26:20`

ESH-BAAL The fourth son of King Saul (I Chr 8:33); an alternate name for Ishbosheth.
`ESH-BAAL I Chr 8:33; 9:39`

ESHBAN The second son of Dishon and a Horite chief in the land of Edom (Gen 36:26).
`ESHBAN Gen 36:26. I Chr 1:41`

ESHCOL ("cluster of grapes").

1. The brother of Aner and Mamre the Amorite, and one of the allies of Abraham (Gen 14:13) who helped him defeat King Chedorlaomer.
`ESHCOL 1 Gen 14:13, 24`

2. A brook and its valley near Hebron; there the spies sent by Moses "cut down a branch with one cluster of grapes" hence the valley was called Eshcol (Num 13:23-24).
`ESHCOL 2 Num 13:23-24; 32:9. Deut 1:24`

ESHEAN A city which fell to the lot of the tribe of Judah (Josh 15:20, 52) when Joshua divided the land of Canaan among the Children of Israel (Josh 14:1). It was in the district of Hebron. Its present location is uncertain.
`ESHEAN Josh 15:52`

ESHEK Brother of Azel and father of Ulam, Jeush and Eliphelet No.3 in the genealogy of King Saul.
`ESHEK I Chr 8:39`

ESHTAOL A city which fell to the lot of the tribe of Judah (Josh 15:33) when the land of Canaan was divided by Joshua among the Children of Israel (Josh 14:1), but was later given to Dan (Josh 19:41). It was halfway between Zorah and Eshtaol that the spirit of the Lord began to stir Samson (Judg 13:25) and here the mighty hero was buried (Judg 16:31). It is generally considered to be on the site of present-day Eshua, near Hartuv.
`ESHTAOL Josh 15:33; 19:41. Judg 13:25; 16:31; 18:2, 8, 11`

ESHTAOLITE (ESHTAULITE) A family or clan originating from Kirjath Jearim.
`ESHTAOLITE I Chr 2:53`

ESHTEMOA

1. The son of Ishbah the son of Mered and Pharaoh's daughter Bithiah in the genealogy of Judah.
`ESHTEMOA 1 I Chr 4:17`

2. Eshtemoa the Maachathite, the son of Hodiah by his wife the sister of Naham, in the genealogy of Judah.
`ESHTEMOA 2 I Chr 4:19`

3. A city in the domain of the tribe of Judah which was later given to the family of Aaron the priest (Josh 21:14) and made into a city of refuge (I Chr 6:57). Its inhabitants helped David in his fight against Saul and he rewarded them by sending bounty "from the spoils of the
`ESHTEMOA 3 Josh 21:14. I Sam 30:28. I Chr 6:57`

View of the region of Eshtaol and Zorah, northeast of Beth Shemesh.

enemies of the Lord" (I Sam 30:26, 28). It has been identified with present-day Sammua, 9 miles (14 km) south of Hebron, where important remains have been found, including those of a synagogue dating back to the Roman period.

ESHTEMOH An alternate form for Eshtemoa.

ESHTEMOH
Josh 15:50

ESHTON Son of Mehir, father of Beth-Rapha, Paseah and Tehinnah in the genealogy of Judah.

ESHTON
I Chr 4:11-12

ESLI Son of Naggai and father of Nahum in the genealogy of Jesus according to Luke.

ESLI
Luke 3:25

ESSENES A Jewish sect. Its origin is uncertain but it is first attested in the 2nd century B.C. and it remained active to the end of the 1st century A.D. According to Philo of Alexandria, the Essenes numbered some 4,000 and lived in the towns and villages of Judea; they owned no property and were engaged in agriculture. They lived together in organized communities, their homes being open to men of similar views. Their treasury, expenses, clothing and meals were all communal. A detailed description of the Essenes is provided by Josephus (*War* II, 119ff). According to him the priests had a special place in their prayers and in the blessings offered at their meals. There were both celibate and married men among them. One of their largest settlements was near the Dead Sea, but they lived elsewhere as well. In Jerusalem, for example, there was an "Essene" Gate.

Hoard of silver scrap, dross and jewelry, found at Eshtemoa. Israelite period.

(top left)
Portico of the synagogue at Eshtemoa.

(top right)
A menorah (seven-branched candelabrum), depicted on the mosaic floor at the synagogue of Eshtemoa.

General view of Qumran near the Dead Sea where the Essene community lived.

Josephus placed them on an equal footing with the Pharisees and Sadducees. Although "pacifists", they were swept along by the wave of national enthusiasm and fought in the anti-Roman revolt of A.D. 66.

The Essenes were strict in their observance of the Torah. They emphasized ritual punctiliousness, especially in observance of the Sabbath and the Levitical laws of holiness. They met at dawn for traditional prayers, worked through the greater part of the morning, then gathered together, clothed themselves in white linen garments, and bathed in cold water (Josephus, *Wars* II, 129). They ate their midday meal together and after working until evening, again dined together, in total silence.

Part of the "Order of the Community" (Book of Serakim, or Regulations) found in one of the Qumran caves.

They studied the Bible and explained it in their own way. After the discovery of the Dead Sea Scrolls, most scholars concluded that the documents emanated from an Essene community, identified with those who lived in Qumran on the shores of the Dead Sea. One problem in making a definite determination is that it is not known how the Essenes called themselves (the word "Essenes", of uncertain meaning, was applied to them by others). It is clear that the Essenes separated themselves from normative Judaism of their day, including the services in the Jerusalem Temple. This separation had partly to do with their rules of purity and perhaps also because of differences in their calendar. New members of the community were recruited by admitting candidates after a probationary period. It could take years before one was accepted as a full member of the sect.

There is no direct reference to the Essenes in the NT but only indirect hints, such as Luke 16:8; where Jesus refers to the Essenes as "the sons of light", a title which the Dead Sea Sect used for themselves, opposed to "the sons of darkness", which were the wicked people outside the Essene world. The belief in a dualistic predestination was very much stressed among the Essenes. It seems probable that John the Baptist was influenced by the sect of Essenes. Some scholars believe that the early Church incorporated Essene elements into its structure; after the destruction of the Temple in A.D. 70, nothing more is heard of the Essenes.

ESTHER Heroine of the biblical book which bears her name; daughter of Abihail of the tribe of Benjamin, cousin and adopted daughter of Mordecai. On the orders of the Persian king Ahasuerus, Esther replaced Vashti as queen. Together with Mordecai, she was subsequently

ESTHER
Est 2:7-8,
10-11, 15-18,
20, 22; 4:4-5,
8-10, 12-13,

15, 17; 5:1-7, 12; 6:14; 7:1-3, 5-8; 8:1-4, 7; 9:12-13, 25, 29, 31-32

instrumental in saving the Jews of Susa and the rest of the Persian empire from a royally decreed pogrom instigated by the vizir Haman, whose downfall she engineered (See ESTHER, BOOK OF).

Esther's Hebrew name was *Hadassah* ("myrtle tree"). Her foreign name seems to reflect the Mesopotamian goddess Ishtar (as Mordecai reflects the name of the Babylonian god Marduk). Another interpretation derives the name Esther from a Persian cognate meaning "star".

ESTHER, BOOK OF The Book of Esther is one of the "Five Scrolls" in the Hagiographa section of the OT and is read in the synagogue on the festival of Purim. It contains a narrative of events reported to have occurred during the reign of the Persian king Ahasuerus (Xerxes I, 486-465 B.C.).

The story runs as follows: King Ahasuerus, enraged by the refusal of his queen Vashti to appear before his court at the end of a six-month feast, follows the advice of his counselors by deposing the queen and launching a search throughout the 127 provinces of his empire for a replacement. In the fortress-city of Shushan (Susa) lives a beautiful Jewish girl, Esther, ward of her cousin Mordecai. Esther is brought to the court, and chosen to be queen. At Mordecai's behest, she conceals her Jewish birth. Mordecai later overhears and reports a plot to assassinate the king, but is not rewarded for saving the king's life.

The king appoints one Haman as chief minister. Mordecai alone refuses to do obeisance to Haman. Haman, discovering that his foe is a Jew, resolves to exterminate all Jews, and secures the king's permission to perpetrate a general massacre at the year's end on the 14th of Adar. The decree is published and disseminated throughout the empire. At the behest of his wife and companions, Haman builds a gallows upon which to hang Mordecai.

Tomb revered as that of Esther and Mordecai at Susa in Iran.

Illuminated Scroll of Esther, 18th century.

Urged on by Mordecai, Esther acts to foil the plot. At a banquet to which she invites the king and Haman, she dramatically reveals that she is Jewish, that the Jews are destined to be massacred, and that the villain is none other than Haman. Haman's last-minute appeal to the queen's mercies is misinterpreted by the king as an attempt at seduction, and the king orders Haman hanged on the very gallows built for Mordecai.

After Esther and Mordecai are awarded Haman's estate, Esther reminds the king that the decree of extermination is still in effect. Ahasuerus informs her that a royal edict cannot be revoked, and instead issues a counter-edict, permitting the Jews to arm and defend themselves on the fateful day. When the day arrives, the Jews are so successful in killing their would-be destroyers that they observe a feast day on the morrow. Within the precincts of Shushan, they are granted an extra day to continue the killing, postponing the feast until the next day. In commemoration of these events, Esther and Mordecai institute the annual festival of Purim and Mordecai is named chief minister.

Ahasuerus and Esther, enthroned, receive a report of the numbers slain in Shushan. Wall painting from the synagogue of Dura-Europos. 3rd century A.D.

The theme of the story is stated in 9:1: "On the day that the enemies of the Jews had hoped to overpower them, the opposite occurred, in that the Jews themselves overpowered those who hated them." The narrative is pervaded with such reversals of the expected: Haman plots a massacre of the Jews; instead they stage a counter-attack. Haman is compelled to honor Mordecai with the pomp and circumstance he had planned for himself, and later is hanged on the very gallows upon which he had plotted to hang Mordecai — following which Mordecai assumes Haman's former position of honor in the court. A date intended to mark a national calamity for the Jews is transformed into a yearly feast of merrymaking.

The events narrated are not corroborated by any outside source. In fact, historical knowledge occasionally conflicts with the book's account: Xerxes I had no queen by the name Esther; indeed, he was prohibited by law from marrying any but the daughters of certain noble families. Mordecai is described as having been exiled from Judah with King Jehoiachin (597 B.C.), which would make him at least 114 years old in the third year of Ahasuerus' rule (483 B.C.). Further, such occurrences as a half-year feast, an empire-wide beauty contest, and the slaying of 75,000 Persians in one day, seem exaggerated. The occasional correspondence with Persian and Babylonian mythology, the general folkloristic nature of the narrative, and the use of traditional wisdom themes (cf Ps 7:16-17; 37:12-13; Prov 26:27; Eccl 10:8) have led to the suggestion that a kernel of historical fact was subjected to substantial literary embellishment in order to communicate a religious teaching.

Familiar religious concepts such as revelation, prophecy, law, recompense and covenant are not alluded to in the book; God himself is never mentioned. The central theological point is placed in the mouth of

Mordecai who affirms God's providence, and his omnipotent direction of all earthly events (Est 4:13-14). In retrospect it is apparent that what seemed to be a chain of happy coincidence is evidence of God's guiding hand shaping history to protect and deliver his people.

In the larger canonical context, the story of Esther serves as an episode in the continuing drama of God's unending war with Amalek. This war was declared "from generation to generation" after Amalek's sneak attack on Israel at the time of the Exodus (Ex 17:8-16). Later, Saul was ordered to attack and utterly destroy the Amalekites and their King Agag (I Sam chap. 15). By denoting Haman as an "Agagite" (Est 3:1, etc.) and associating Mordecai with the family of Kish, Saul's father (2:5), the author of Esther seems to be identifying the current foe with Israel's arch-enemy and reaffirming the command to avenge his crime.

The events related in the Book of Esther are depicted as giving rise to the Jewish feast of Purim. The name Purim seems at first to have been taken from an inconsequential detail — the lots (Babylonian *pūru* "fate, lot") cast by Haman to fix the date for the slaughter (3:7; 9:24, 26). However, in light of the central message of the book — God's control of human fate as opposed to the arbitrary fall of lots — the name of the festival is not at all insignificant. The narrator has also taken care to use the tale to account for the strange custom of celebrating Purim on separate, consecutive days in the provinces and in Shushan.

Initially, at least, Esther was not accepted unanimously into the biblical canon. Ben Sira and Josephus probably did not consider it canonical. Esther alone is unrepresented among the Qumran scrolls. The reason for the controversy surrounding Esther may be surmised from Talmudic statements to the effect that the story of a Jewish counter-pogrom aroused the anger of the Gentiles. Some sages also objected to the institution of a festival not proclaimed by Moses. The absence of explicit mention of God may also help to account for the ambivalent stance of tradition regarding the book.

Similarly, Esther's status in the Church has not been unanimously upheld. The Eastern Church lagged far behind the Church of Rome in recognizing the book as canonical. Only by viewing Queen Esther as a prefiguration of the Church, or of the Virgin, was early Christian tradition able to accept the book. As late as the age of the Reformation, Luther stated his own wish that the Book of Esther "did not exist at all".

OUTLINE

1:1-22	Ahasuerus' feast. Vashti is dethroned
2:1-23	Esther is chosen for queen
3:1-4:17	Haman becomes vizier and decrees the killing of all Jews in the Empire
5:1-7:10	Esther's banquets for the king and Haman. She reveals Haman's plot. Haman and his sons are hanged
8:1-10:3	The Jews kill their would-be destroyers the festival of Purim is instituted. Mordecai appointed vizier in Haman's place

ESTHER, BOOK OF (ADDITIONS TO THE) Six passages in the Greek translation of the Book of Esther that are not found in the Hebrew version. Jerome's Latin translations removed these additions, appending them together at the end of the canonical book. According to one of the additions, the Greek translation was made by "Lysimachus the son of Ptolemy, one of the residents of Jerusalem" (11:1), which indicates that the translation dates to c. 1st century B.C.

One of the purposes of these apocryphal additions could have been the introduction of certain religious elements absent in the Hebrew text, such as the name of God and some prayers. Some additions contradict the Hebrew text. For example, according to the Hebrew, Mordecai discovered the plot against King Ahasuerus in the seventh year of his reign (Est 2:16, 21), whereas an addition suggests that this occurred in the second year (11:2).

The first addition is Mordecai's dream foreshadowing the victory of the Jews (Est Add. 10:4-13; 11:2-12:6) and the discovery by Mordecai of the conspiracy of two eunuchs against the king, for which he is rewarded by appointment to serve in court. The second addition (13:1-7) gives the text of Artaxerxes' edict to destroy the Jews. The prayers of Mordecai and Esther form the third addition (13:8-14:19). In the next addition Esther risks her life by appealing to the king (15:1-16). The fifth addition contains the king's edict revoking his earlier decree (16:1-20). The last addition gives the interpretation of Mordecai's dream and the conclusion that God remembered his people and that his loving kindness should always be remembered (16:21-24).

ETAM

1. Etam, brother of Jezreel, Ishma and Idbash; his sister was Hazelelponi in the genealogy of Judah.

ETAM 1
I Chr 4:3

2. A city originally within the territory of Judah (Josh 19:1) later transferred to Simeon; home of the sons of Shimei (I Chr 4:32) the grandson of Simeon. In the cleft of a nearby rock Samson rested for a while after the fight with the Philistines in which he avenged the death of his wife (Judg 15:8). Its exact location is unknown.

ETAM 2
Judg 15:8, 11.
I Chr 4:32

3. A city between Bethlehem and Tekoa in Judah which was fortified by King Rehoboam after the rebellion of Israel (II Chr 11:5-6). Probably present-day Ain Etan, near Arta, 2 miles (3 km) southwest of Bethlehem.

ETAM 3
II Chr 11:6

ETHAM The place on the edge of the wilderness where the Children of Israel camped after having left Succoth (Ex 13:20). From there they "turned back to Pi Hahiroth" (Num 33:7) and then spent three days in the "wilderness of Etham" before stopping at Marah (Num 33:8). This wilderness was part of the wilderness of Shur. The present location of Etham is not known; among the possibilities suggested, the Egyptian fortress of Silou, on the edge of the Sinai desert, in the vicinity of present-day El Kantara on the Suez Canal.

ETHAM
Ex 13:20.
Num 33:6-8

ETHAN ("the strong one").

1. Ethan the Ezrahite, whose wisdom was surpassed only by that of Solomon (I Kgs 4:31). According to the superscription, he was the author of Psalm 89. He is listed together with Zimri, Heman, Calcol and Dara as a son of Zerah (the son of Judah by his daughter-in-law Tamar, the widow of Er; I Chr 2:6). He is the father of Azariah (I Chr 2:8).

ETHAN 1
I Kgs 4:31. I
Chr 2:6, 8. Ps
89

2. Father of a Levite who was among the men appointed by David over the service of song in the House of the Lord (I Chr 6:31, 42); he had accompanied the ark to Jerusalem.

ETHAN 2
I Chr 6:42;
15:19

3. Son of Kishi and member of the Merari clan; he was among the men appointed by David over the service of song in the House of the Lord (I Chr 6:31, 44). He had been among those who accompanied the the ark to Jerusalem.

ETHAN 3
I Chr 6:44;
15:17

ETHANIM The seventh month of the calendar and the occasion of a great feast. The name was later changed to Tishri.

ETHANIM
I Kgs 8:2

Ain Etan southwest of Bethlehem.

337

ETHIOPIA

ETHBAAL
I Kgs 16:31

ETHER
Josh 15:42;
19:7

ETHIOPIA,
ETHIOPIANS
Num 12:1.
II Kgs 19:9.
II Chr 12:3;
14:9, 12-13;
16:8; 21:16.
Est 1:1; 8:9.
Job 28:19. Ps
68:31; 87:4. Is
18:1; 20:3-5;
37:9; 43:3. Jer
13:23; 38:7,
10, 12; 39:16;
46:9. Ezek
29:10; 30:4-5,
9; 38:5. Dan
11:43. Amos
9:7. Nah 3:9.
Zeph 2:12;
3:10. Acts 8:27

ETHBAAL King of the Sidonians and father of Jezebel, the wife of Ahab king of Israel, during the first half of the 9th century B.C.

ETHER A city which fell to the lot of the tribe of Judah (Josh 15:20, 42) when the land of Canaan was divided by Joshua among the Children of Israel (Josh 14:1); however it is also mentioned as being in the domain of Simeon (Josh 19:7). It has been suggested that these are two different cities but many scholars disagree. It was in the eastern lowlands of Judah but its present location is unknown.

ETHIOPIA, ETHIOPIANS The name of the country and the people by which the English OT sometimes translates Cush. The name Aethiopia was employed in the Septuagint. In the NT the Ethiopian queen Candace is mentioned (Acts 8:27), apparently meaning "dark-faced". According to the OT, Ethiopia borders upon Egypt to the south (Ezek 29:10), and they are frequently mentioned together (Ps 68:31; Is 11:11). An Ethiopian is a dark-skinned man, living in a distant country (Jer 13:23).

Egypt shared a border with Ethiopia from the times of the Old Kingdom. With the decline of Egyptian power in the period of the 20th Dynasty, Ethiopia became semi-dependent, and from the middle of the 9th century B.C. it gained full independence. In the last two decades of the 8th century B.C. the Ethiopians conquered Thebes and a decade later they ruled Egypt as pharaohs of the 25th Dynasty. Tirhakah, the last Ethiopian pharaoh, is mentioned in the Bible (II Kgs 19:9). To Isaiah (20:3-5; 43:3) and Ezekiel (30:9), Egypt and Ethiopia are identical. After the Assyrian conquest c. 660 B.C. Ethiopian rule declined, and towards the end of the 6th century B.C. Egypt itself was conquered by the Persians.

Taxpayers from Cush (Ethiopia) depicted on an Egyptian wall painting from Thebes. c. 1200 B.C. (British Museum)

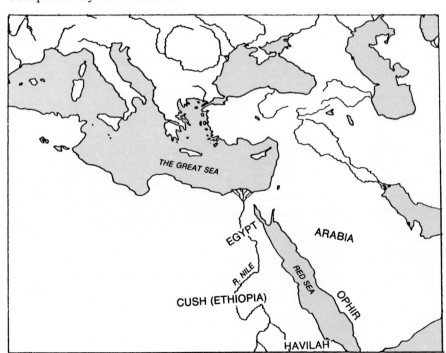

Ethiopia.

Ethiopian mercenaries served in the Egyptian army. In the El Amarna Letters they are mentioned by the name of Kashi, and some of them were among the soldiers who garrisoned Jerusalem. Ethiopians were in the army of Shishak who campaigned against Rehoboam (II Chr 12:3), and alongside soldiers from Libya, they served in the Egyptian army in the 6th century B.C. (Jer 46:9; Ezek 30:5). Ethiopians were also in the service of the kings of Judah (II Sam 18:21; Jer 38:7).

ETH KAZIN A place or city on the border of the territory of Zebulun. Nothing is known about it or its name.

ETH KAZIN
Josh 19:13

ETHNAN ("gift price"). Third son of Ashur by his wife Helah in the genealogy of Judah.

ETHNAN
I Chr 4:7

ETHNI The son of Zerah and the father of Malchijah, Ethni was a descendant of Gershon the firstborn son of Levi, and one of the musicians in the house of the Lord in the time of King David.

ETHNI
I Chr 6:41

EUBULUS ("well-advised", "prudent"). A Christian of Rome who sent greetings to Timothy.

EUBULUS
II Tim 4:21

EUNICE ("victorious"). A Jewish Christian, the mother of Timothy (Acts 16:1; II Tim 1:5). She was praised for her genuine faith, in Paul's second letter to her son.

EUNICE
II Tim 1:5

EUODIA A Christian woman of Philippi. The ill-will between her and Syntyche was so much a cause of scandal that Paul singled these two out for a reprimand in his epistle to the community.

EUODIA
Phil 4:2

EUPHRATES One of the largest rivers of western Asia, about 1,700 miles (2,700 km) long. In the Bible it is referred to by several names, among them the "great river" or just "the river".

EUPHRATES
Gen 2:14;
15:18. Deut
1:7; 11:24.
Josh 1:4.
II Sam 8:3.
II Kgs 23:29;
24:7. I Chr
5:9; 18:3.
II Chr 35:20.
Jer 13:4-7;
46:2, 6, 10;
51:63. Rev
9:14; 16:12

The Euphrates is formed by the confluence of two rivers, the Murad-su, which comes down from Armenia, and the Karasu, flowing from the Anti-Taurus. At first the river runs through a deep narrow gorge, but as they descend towards Babylon, the Euphrates and the Tigris (Hiddekel) form the broad plain of Mesopotamia. The rivers join at the head of the Persian Gulf to form the Shat al-Arab, though this union is quite recent. The Euphrates has a very strong current and for this reason was navigable only in its lower reaches. Along it flourished some of the important cities of Mesopotamia, the greatest of which was Babylon. Another, Carchemish, was an important road junction and a river-crossing for the caravans coming from the Far East. Some of the great battles of history took place on the Euphrates, notably the battle between Nebuchadnezzar II and Pharaoh Necho II of Egypt, in 605 B.C. (Jer 46:2).

Two views of the Euphrates River.

In the Bible the Euphrates is named among the four rivers which flowed from the Garden of Eden (Gen 2:14), and it formed the northeastern limit of the promised land (Gen 15:18). Throughout all periods it was the boundary between east and west, between the spheres of influence of Assyria and Egypt, and each of the great empires attempted the conquest of the borderland of Syria and Palestine. This is also true of the Persian period (Ezra 4:10, etc.). In the Hellenistic and Roman periods the Euphrates served as the boundary between the kingdoms of Armenia and Cappadocia, Sophene and Commagene. In the early Roman period it separated Rome from Parthia.

EUTYCHUS ("fortunate"). A young man of Troas who dozed off during a long talk by Paul, and fell from a third-floor window. Paul broke off his discourse briefly to revive him (Acts 20:9-12).

EVE The first woman, wife of Adam, mother of Cain, Abel and Seth. The Bible gives a popular etymology for her name, deriving it from the Hebrew for "life" or "living" because she was "the mother of all living" (Gen 3:20). Others have explained the origin of the name as related to an Aramaic and Arabic word for "serpent" which would be a sly echo of the narrative. Eve was created in the Garden of Eden from the rib of the first man, Adam, who interpreted this as her being "bone of my bones and flesh of my flesh"; the Bible adds that because of this origin, a man leaves his parents and is "joined to his wife and they shall become one flesh" (Gen 2:23-24).

Eve was persuaded by the serpent to eat of the fruit of the forbidden tree and took the initiative in leading Adam astray (Gen chap. 3) for which she was punished with the pains of childbirth and subjugation to her husband (Gen 3:16), contrary to the original intention of sexual equality. After the expulsion from Eden, Eve is mentioned only in connection with the birth of her children. She is not referred to again in the OT. In the NT she is mentioned twice: in I Timothy 2:11-15 as an example of woman's vulnerability, requiring her submissiveness; and in II Corinthians 11:3, where Paul cites her as an example of one easily led astray. See also FALL.

EVI ("love"). One of the five kings of the Midianites killed by the Children of Israel led by Phinehas the son of Eleazar (Num 31:8). He was allied to Sihon the king of the Amorites (Josh 13:21).

EVIL-MERODACH King of Babylon; in the first year of his reign he released Jehoiachin former king of Judah from prison in the 37th year of his exile granting him an ample food portion (II Kgs 25:27). He succeeded his father Nebuchadnezzar to the throne in 562 B.C. but less than two years later fell victim to a conspiracy led by his brother-in-law Neriglassar, who then ascended the throne.

EXODUS, BOOK OF The second book of the Pentateuch, so-called after Israel's Exodus from Egypt. It describes the deliverance of the Israelites from slavery, their flight to the desert, the conclusion of their covenant with God at Mount Sinai and the construction of the tabernacle.

The book opens with a description of Israel's enslavement after Joseph's death (the link with the preceding Book of Genesis); the gradual deterioration of their lot, culminating in Pharaoh's order to throw all newborn boys into the Nile, and the birth of the liberator Moses, who was placed in the Nile by his mother, but saved and brought up by Pharaoh's daughter (2:10).

The story of Adam and Eve shown in relief on the exterior wall of the Armenian church at Aghtamar, Turkey. 11th century.

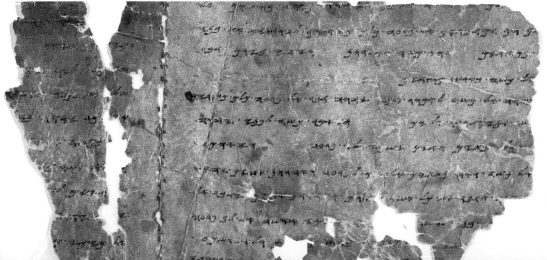

Fragment of Exodus 6:25-7:17 found at Qumran. (Shrine of the Book, Jerusalem)

After Moses' flight to the desert the Lord revealed himself to Moses and instructed him to present himself before Pharaoh to convey the divine command that the people of Israel be set free (3:1-4:17). Moses returned to Egypt, where, joined by his brother Aaron, he informed the Israelites of the divine purpose (4:18-31). Moses and Aaron then presented themselves before Pharaoh and communicated the divine command to let the Israelites go. Pharaoh, however, would not relent and even increased the workload of the Israelites, who blamed Moses and Aaron (chap. 5). In contrast with these expressions of disbelief, the narrative proclaims the greatness of the divine purpose: the Lord informed Moses that he would harden Pharaoh's heart so that only terrible afflictions would convince him of God's power and majesty (6:1-7:7).

This revelation opened the pericope of the Plagues (See PLAGUES) (7:8-12:30). At first Moses and Aaron demonstrated God's power by casting the rod which turned into a snake; but because the Egyptian magicians were able to perform the same miracle, Pharaoh did not yield, even after Aaron's rod had swallowed all their staffs (7:8-13). Nor was he convinced by the first three plagues (blood, frogs and lice, 7:14-8:19). However, the fourth plague (swarms of flies), made Pharaoh show a readiness for concessions. But after Moses' prayer put an end to

Page from the Book of Exodus, from the De Castro Bible, *Germany, 14th century. (Israel Museum)*

this plague, Pharaoh reneged on his promise (8:20-32). Two further plagues (pestilence and boils) likewise produced no change in his attitude. Only the seventh plague made him repent; but when the affliction was lifted, he again changed heart (9:13-35). Afflicted by locusts and by darkness, Pharaoh once again showed readiness to make concessions; but he was only ready to permit Israel to leave for a short period of time and without their women, children and cattle (10:1-29). Pharaoh's resistance was only broken by the last plague, whose circumstances are described in detail — the death of the firstborn son in every Egyptian family (11:1-12:33). The Israelites were ordered to mark their houses with a special apotropaic token (the blood of a slaughtered lamb) in order that the Lord would pass over and spare them (12:13). Thus the narrative indicates the origin of the "Passover" sacrifice on the 14th of the first month (12:1-14, 21-28, 43, 50), interweaving the account of the Exodus with prescriptions for its commemoration in the celebration of Passover when unleavened bread is eaten to commemorate the fact that the fleeing Israelites did not have sufficient time to let their dough rise (12:15-20, 34, 39; 23:15; 34:18).

The literary units dedicated to the flight from Egypt (12:37-42; 13:17-15:21) emphasize divine protection and guidance, the Israelites being led on their way by the Lord who took the form of a pillar of cloud by day and a pillar of fire by night (14:19-20; cf Num 10:33-36), and effected the miraculous rescue at the Red Sea (14:1-15:21). Informed of the Israelites' flight, Pharaoh pursued them with his chariots (14:1-9). Stricken with terror by the sudden appearance of the Egyptians, the people complained to Moses (14:10-14), but were immediately protected by the deity whose cloud and angel separated them from Pharaoh's army. When Moses stretched out his staff, a strong east wind dried up the sea, thus allowing the Israelites to pass through safely. As the Egyptians resumed their pursuit, Moses again stretched out his staff; the water rushed back and the Egyptians were drowned (14:15-30). By this dramatic event the power of the Lord was demonstrated to Israelites and Egyptians alike (14:31). It greatly strengthened the trust of the people in God and Moses' authority (14:11-12; 15:21). The miraculous delivery was celebrated by Moses and the Children of Israel in a hymn (15:1-21) regarded by most scholars as one of the most ancient OT poems.

After this deliverance, Moses led the people on their desert trek whose numerous difficulties evoked loud complaints (bitter water, 15:23-24; hunger 16:2-3; lack of water 17:1-3). In each instance, the Israelites were saved by divine providence: in answer to Moses' prayers, the well of water was made sweet (15:24-26); the Lord provided manna (16:4-36); and Moses brought forth water from the rock (17:4-7). An Amalekite attack was thwarted while Moses held the divine staff on high (17:8-16).

After three months of wandering, the Israelites reached Mount Sinai (19:1; cf 3:12; 5:1). Here the Lord declared that if Israel kept his covenant, they would be a holy nation (19:2-6). This call was motivated by reference to their liberation from Egyptian slavery and the divine providence which protected them in their journey through the desert ("How I bore you on eagles' wings"; 19:4). Moses conveyed the divine proposals to the elders of Israel who accepted them. Thereupon he was ordered to present the people before God (19:7-15). After three days the Lord revealed his glory. As the people stood at the foot of the Mount, he descended upon it in fire (19:17-25), and proclaimed the Ten Commandments (20:1-17). The people, terrified by the overwhelming power of the theophany, begged Moses to serve once again as their intermediary and to learn God's instructions on their behalf (20:18-21). God then communicated his law to Moses (20:22-23:33). This earliest collection of biblical law (the "Book of the Covenant") opens and closes with ordinances concerning the worship of God and its purity (20:22-26; 23:32-33). Many laws concern issues of everyday life; form and content are reminiscent of ancient Near Eastern law (21:1-22:15). The main theme of the Book of Exodus, i.e., the liberation from slavery, is reflected in the beginning of this corpus which opens with the regulations concerning the freeing of the Hebrew slave (21:2). Other prescriptions concern justice in the practice of law (23:1-3, 6-8), in society (22:20-26; 23:4-5, 9) and the regulations concerning the worship of God (22:17-19, 27-30; 23:10-19). This phase closes with Moses' proclamation of the law to the entire corporate body of Israelites, their acceptance and the covenant ceremonies at the foot of the Mount (24:3-8) and on the mountain before God (24:9-11; cf chaps. 1-2).

Afterwards Moses was again summoned to ascend the mountain to receive the tablets with the commandments: on this occasion he remained there 40 days and nights (24:12-18; 31:18). His long absence caused the people great anxiety and they begged Aaron to make them a surrogate god to guide them on their wilderness trek, whereupon Aaron made the Golden Calf and ordered festivities to be held (32:1-6). Moses, warned by the Lord, descended from the mountain and broke the tablets as a sign of the annulment of the covenant (32:7-19). After destroying the idol and severely punishing the sinners (32:20-30), he intervened and prayed for the people (32:11-14, 31-33:23). He erected a Tent of Meeting outside the camp for communication with God (33:7-11).

Afterwards Moses ascended the mountain once again (34:1-4), and the Lord proclaimed his divine attributes. Moses responded by a plea for atonement (34:5-9), whereupon the Lord reaffirmed his covenant with Israel (34:10-27).

The covenant idea gave expression to the permanency of the bond between God and Israel. Its permanent expression was the sanctuary which Moses was instructed to build, so that the Lord "may dwell among" Israel (25:8). This sanctuary was to be movable and would include objects necessary for the worship of God (25:10-27:19).

Moses was also shown how to prepare the priestly robes and how to consecrate the priests, Aaron and his sons, for their task (28:1-29:46; cf Lev chaps. 8-10).

After completion of the work and the erection of the tabernacle (40:1-33), the tent was covered by the divine cloud and the glory of the Lord filled the tabernacle (40:34-38).

The Book of Exodus is a crucial source for the origins of the Jewish people and contains the basic themes of Judaism: the birth of the nation, the revelation of the divine Torah at Sinai, the covenant between God and the Israelites — with the divine promise and the peoples' commitment — and the foundation of central institutes including the priesthood, the sanctuary and the forms of worship. For the literary structure and sources, see PENTATEUCH.

OUTLINE

1:1-22	The enslavement and persecution of the Israelites in Egypt
2:1-25	Advent of Moses; his flight to Midian
3:1-4:31	Moses' call
5:1-6:30	Moses and Aaron's first call to Pharaoh
7:1-11:10	The Plagues
12:1-13:16	The slaying of the firstborn and the first Passover
13:17-15:21	The crossing of the Red Sea
15:22-17:16	Problems between the Red Sea and Mount Sinai
18:1-27	Jethro's visit
19:1-20:21	The revelation on Sinai; the Ten Commandments
20:22-23:23	Miscellaneous ordinances
24:1-18	The covenant ceremony
25:1-31:18	Ordinances concerning the tabernacle
32:1-34:35	The golden calf
35:1-40:38	Construction of the tabernacle

EXODUS (ROUTE) After having lived for four generations under the Egyptian yoke, the Children of Israel set out on their long trek to the land of Canaan. The Exodus commenced at Rameses (Ex 12:37; Num 33:5), one of the two cities which the Israelites had been forced to build (Ex 1:11). From Rameses they went to their first station at Succoth (Ex 12:37; Num 33:5), proceeding next to Etham, at the edge of the wilderness (Ex 13:20). They were then instructed to turn back and to encamp before Pi Hahiroth, between Migdol and the sea, over against Baal Zephon, so that Pharaoh might be afflicted with the great calamity which God had in store for him (Ex 14:1-4). The sea near which they were instructed to camp is the Red Sea (in Hebrew *yam-suph*), or "the sea of reeds" (Ex 14:22). Consequently the course the Israelites followed ran from west to east, without reaching a sea: they had to move either northward or southward from the edge of the wilderness, to come to a sea situated in the vicinity of the three above-mentioned places. The sea was crossed miraculously (Ex 14:21-30) and from there they went on to the wilderness of Shur, where they failed to find water (Ex 15:22). Next came a three day march in the wilderness identified in Numbers 33:8 as the wilderness of Etham, which they had traversed previously: this indicates that their route had been circular. Their next stop was at Marah, but the water there was bitter (Ex 15:23).

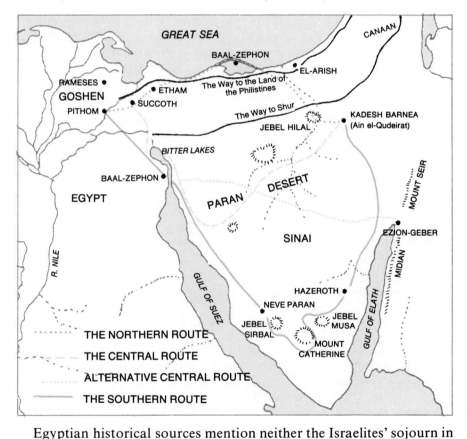

Possible routes of the Exodus.

Egyptian historical sources mention neither the Israelites' sojourn in Egypt nor their departure, but some Egyptian documents contain details which may help in elucidating the background of the Exodus. In the Anastasi I papyrus (late 13th century B.C.), a scribe officiating in an Egyptian fortress reported permission being granted to Edomite nomads to cross the border into Egypt with their herds. Concluded without requesting explicit authorization from Pharaoh, this seems to have been normal procedure. The construction of Pithom and Rameses, which is a historical fact, was accomplished under Pharaoh Rameses II, who built the new capital of Pi-Rameses (i.e. House of Rameses). According to Egyptian sources, this place was at the head of two roads. The first one, was the main route to Palestine running northeast to Qantara, from there to ancient Sile, and along the coast to Gaza. The second route to Palestine ran from the Qantir district (where Rameses is located) to the southeast, across semi-desert terrain, lying between the main Palestine road on the north and Wadi Tumilat on the south. This would have brought the Israelites to the region of Tell Maskhute; identified with Succoth, it lies near modern Ismailia, on the west bank of Lake Timsah. As the Israelites were prevented from using the Via Maris, the coastal highway, this was their only way to the wilderness of Sinai (cf Ex 13:18).

Numbers 33:3-15 gives the fullest list of stations on the route of the Exodus. In fact there is no general consensus on this point, and even the location of the "Red Sea" is far from agreed. An early Christian tradition of the 4th century A.D. locates the sea crossing at a site north of the Gulf of Suez, from which a road is mentioned as running southeast to Jebel Musa and Mount Catherine. This may find support in the preference of the wilderness road to the main highway as mentioned above, and would indicate that the Israelites wandered along the western coast of Sinai. It would also coincide with the 11 day trek "from Horeb by the way of Mount Seir unto Kadesh Barnea" (Deut 1:2), which is the actual length of the march from Jebel Musa in southern Sinai to Ain el-Qudeirat with which Kadesh Barnea is identified.

Against this view numerous objections have been raised. The southern part of the Sinai peninsula is stony and barren, and could have offered little food for such great multitudes of people. On the other hand, arable land may be found in the north only. During their wandering in the desert the Israelites ate manna (Ex 16:35), a substance which must have formed on trees. But trees are very rare in the southern part of Sinai, and much more frequent in the north; the other food, quails, which the Israelites ate before their arrival at and on their departure from Horeb (Ex 16:13; Num 11:31-32) is likewise found along the coast in the north, and not in the south. These considerations led to the proposition to identify Mount Sinai with Jebel Hilal south of el-Arish and east of Kadesh Barnea. To these materialistic objections, scholars have added further arguments based on literary grounds. However, none of these is well-founded. The fact remains that the name Paran, so closely connected with the Exodus (Num 13:3, 26; Deut 33:2), by which the whole wilderness of Sinai was named, is still preserved in one of the major wadis in the southern part of the peninsula, where it was crossed by an important west-east road, and where pre-Christian and Christian traditions venerated sacred mountains.

No less disputed than the route of the Exodus is its date. Scholars in the 19th century suggested that Thutmosis III was the Pharaoh of the oppression, and that the Exodus took place in the reign of Amenhotep II (c. 1440 B.C.). More scholars, however, prefer a later date, placing the Exodus in the period of the 19th Dynasty, which would make Rameses II the pharaoh of the oppression, and Merneptah the pharaoh of the Exodus. The conquest of Canaan would thus have begun at about 1200 B.C.

EZBAI Father of Naarai, one of David's thirty "mighty men".

EZBAI
I Chr 11:37

EZBON ("finger").

1. The fourth son of Gad (Gen 46:16) and one of the Children of Israel who settled in Egypt.

EZBON 1
Gen 46:16

2. The firstborn son of Bela, firstborn son of Benjamin, in the genealogy of the family of Benjamin.

EZBON 2
I Chr 7:7

EZEKIEL ("may God strengthen"). The third of the so-called major prophets, the other two being Isaiah and Jeremiah. From the scarce and scattered references to his life, usually embedded in his prophecies, we learn that he was the son of Buzi, probably from the priestly family of Zadok. In 597 B.C. he was carried to Babylon by Nebuchadnezzar along with King Jehoiachin and the Judean aristocracy. He settled in or near Tel Abib, a Jewish colony by the Chebar Canal, where he beheld the throne-chariot of God and was consecrated as a prophet. Ezekiel's prophetic activity began in the fifth year of Jehoiachin's exile (597 B.C.) and extended through 22 years (the latest date indicated in his book is 571 B.C.). See EZEKIEL, BOOK OF.

EZEKIEL, BOOK OF The book, which is presented in the first person, consists of 48 chapters; notwithstanding the occasional interweaving of heterogenous prophetic utterances, it may be thematically divided into the following sections: (a) Chapters 1-24: Denunciations addressed against Judah and Jerusalem. Ezekiel portrays a very gloomy picture of the entire history of Israel, as that of continuous sinfulness and rebellion against God. Consequently, his message is essentially one of utter and inevitable doom. The dramatic representations and bizarre symbolic acts which often accompany his utterances give color and forcefulness to his message. Notable among the acts representing the impending

Fragments from the Book of Eze-kiel found at Qumran (Shrine of the Book, Jerusalem)

doom are the eating of a scroll in which "lamentations and mourning and woe" are inscribed (chaps. 2:9-3:3); the drawing of the city of Jerusalem on a clay tablet and raising a siege against it as a symbol of its fate (4:1-8); baking barley loaves over human excrement, representing the unclean food which the Israelites will eat in exile (4:12-13); shaving his head and beard with a sharp razor, and burning one third of the hair in the fire, striking another third with the sword and strewing the last in the wind. Even the death of the prophet's wife and his dramatic abstention from mourning serve as a powerful symbol of doom (24:15-23). The prophet also employs parables, one of which depicts Israel as a nymphomaniacal and depraved adultress (chaps. 16 and 23). It is hardly surprising that Ezekiel's denunciation and his dramatic representations, though attracting a wide audience, were looked upon as a sort of entertainment (33:31-32). (b) Chapters 25-32: Oracles of doom against foreign nations: Ammon, Moab, Edom, Philistia, Sidon, Tyre and Egypt — all severely denounced for their attitude toward Judah, particularly after the destruction of Jerusalem in 586 B.C. Most of the oracles are, however, directed against Tyre and Egypt. The acts of chastisement against the foreign nations are intended to achieve a grand divine purpose: the sanctification of God's name and the magnification of his glory. Indeed each of the oracles against the nations includes variations on the well-known Ezekielian recognition formula: "That they may know that I am the Lord God". (c) Chapters 33-48: Oracles of consolation and restoration. These chapters include the celebrated vision relating to the revival of the dry bones, symbolizing the Israelites in exile (chap. 37) and the Gog and Magog Oracles (chaps. 38-39). The last nine chapters of the Book (40-48) provide visions of the new Jerusalem and a sketch of the constitution of the new Israel, centered around the newly restored sanctuary, to which the glory of God returns. It should be noted that this last section employs a new literary genre, already introduced in previous contexts (3:14; 8:3): the transportation vision, in which Ezekiel feels lifted to Jerusalem by the spirit of God and guided by an angelic being. This literary category becomes more prominent in post-exilic writings (cf Zechariah and Daniel) and particularly in the apocalyptic literature.

Wall painting at the synagogue of Dura-Europos portraying Ezekiel's vision of the dry bones. 3rd century.

Ezekiel is noted for the introduction of unusual themes, some being unique to him, others the products of elaboration and forceful articulation of scattered biblical notions. Among these are:

(a) The restoration of Israel, an overriding theme in biblical prophecy, is presented as a coercive act on the part of God; it will be forced upon the people of Israel, along with God's kingship, not for their own sake but for the sake of God himself. Israel's suffering and wretchedness, explains Ezekiel, not being commensurate with its attributes as "the people of the Lord," are understood by the nations as a sign of God's impotence and consequently greatly discredit God's reputation, causing his name to be profaned. Israel's redemption, a demonstration of God's supreme power, will, therefore, serve a grand divine purpose: the vindication of God's power and sanctification of his name (chap. 36).

(b) A total rejection of corporate responsibility and a strong emphasis on the individual's responsibility for his own deeds. There will be no vertical or horizontal bequeathal of sins or merits, declares Ezekiel: a son shall not suffer for the iniquity of his father, nor shall the father suffer for the iniquity of his son (18:20). Each will be judged according to his own ways. Ezekiel goes on to say that a person will not be judged by his past actions but by his new state of attitude toward God: a wicked person who casts off his past transgressions and carefully observes God's laws shall be forgiven. None of the sins he committed shall be held against him. Thus Ezekiel enunciated a powerful message of a highly rewarding repentance.

(c) The Gog Prophecy (chaps. 38-39), although spun with threads of motifs already familiar from other biblical contexts, is nevertheless one of the most enigmatic prophecies in the Bible. The prophet envisions a gigantic invasion of Gog and his hordes, who will advance against the restored people of Israel like a sudden storm, like a cloud to cover the earth (38:9), lured by wanton lust for spoil and stimulated by the prospect of easy victory against a people securely living in their habitation. The annihilation of the invaders on the mountains of Israel serves to reassert God's superiority. This resumption of hostilities, as well as the necessity of vindicating God's name after the restoration of Israel is, however, alien to the whole picture of the restoration as depicted in the Hebrew Scriptures, which envision the redemption of Israel as inaugurating a new age of perpetual peace, never to be disturbed again by hostile activities. It is also in disharmony with Ezekiel's own concept of the process of Israel's redemption (see e.g. Ezek 34:25-28). Moreover, the content, mood and outlook of the prophecy seems to be quite different from the rest of the Book of Ezekiel, which is usually anchored in a historical and realistic background. Even the visions of the restoration, despite their imaginative elements, are marked with clarity and precision, featuring such particulars as precise measurements and detailed cultic rules. In contrast, the Gog Prophecy embodies the totally unrealistic and imaginative. The elements of exaggeration and fantasy are so dominant that all logic and discipline of consistent thought are markedly absent. The prophecy does not supply any clue as to a time setting that can correspond to the historical events known to us, nor with any data that may correspond to any known historical context. The figure of Gog himself, the chief protagonist of this prophecy, has always been one of the enigmas of biblical prophecy. All the details of the prophecy indicate that Gog is to be perceived, not as a historical figure, but as a personification of the Foe of the North, embodying both cosmic destructiveness and demonic powers opposed to God, and historical enemies of Israel who appear in Israelite history in various guises. The prophecy, replete with obscurities and symbolic language, exhibits an esoteric character. It falls within the literary domains of the apocalyptic; there are suggestions that it is a product of post-exilic times and thus a late interpolation in the Book of Ezekiel.

The legal, ritual and theological teachings contained in the Book of Ezekiel conflict in a number of points with those of the Torah. For example, Ezekiel's statement that only priests who are descendants of Zadok may minister before God, and his relegation of all other priests to serve as Temple servants (44:10-15), is clearly in sharp contrast with the Deuteronomic and priestly codes, which place all the descendants of Aaron on an equal footing. The rabbis were troubled by the many divergences exhibited to the book and only admitted it to the Canon after long discussions.

Scholars over the past century have disputed the unity and authorship of the book with views ranging from a strictly traditional approach, affirming its unity, to a highly critical view questioning its unity, authorship and date. Recent studies tend to a basically conservative approach, adhering to the book's own assertions concerning the time and place of the prophet's proclamations while maintaining that portions of the text have been disfigured by corruptions and are therefore badly confused.

NT traces of the teachings of Ezekiel can be discerned most strikingly in the Book of Revelation (compare Rev 21:16 with Ezek 48:16, 30 and Rev 22:1 with Ezek 47:1), although there are no direct quotations.

OUTLINE

1:1-3:21	Ezekiel's call
3:22-24:27	Prophecies directed against Judah and Jerusalem prior to the destruction of Jerusalem
25:1-32:32	Oracles of doom against seven foreign nations
33:1-39:29	Prophecies of Israel's restoration
40:1-43:12	Vision of the future Temple
43:13-46:24	The restored cult
47:1-23	The river of holiness
48:1-35	The holy land

EZEL A stone at which Jonathan arranged to meet David.

EZEM ("fortress"). An alternate spelling for Azem, a village or place in the territory of Simeon (Josh 19:3; I Chr 4:29) also mentioned among the cities of Judah (Josh 15:29). Not identified but should be located in the southern part of the country near Beersheba.

EZER Name of several biblical characters; the Hebrew spelling of their names is not identical.

1. Ezer son of Seir the Horite and a chief of Edom; father of Bilhan, Zaavan and Akan (Gen 36:21, 27, 30) or Jaakan (I Chr 1:42).

2. Ezer ("help") son of Hur (the firstborn son of Ephratah the father of Bethlehem) and father of Hushah in the genealogy of Judah.

3. A son of Ephraim killed by the men of Gath because he had stolen their cattle (I Chr 7:21); his father "mourned many days" (I Chr 7:22).

4. The first of the Gadites to join David in Ziklag (I Chr 12:9) "mighty men of valor trained for battle, who could handle shield and spear, whose faces were like the faces of lion and as swift as gazelles on the mountain" (I Chr 12:8).

5. Ezer son of Jeshua, leader of Mizpah, who repaired a section of the wall of Jerusalem at the time of Nehemiah.

6. A priest who sang at the dedication of the wall of Jerusalem.

EZION GEBER (EZION GABER) An Ezion Geber and an Elath of the time of the Exodus are mentioned in the Bible (Num 33:35; Deut 2:8), but no archeological traces of either site of that period have been discovered. Ezion Geber reemerges in history in the time of Solomon, and is to be identified with the small low mound of Tell el-Kheleifeh, which lies at about the center of the north shore of the Gulf of Elath. Its position corresponds in general terms to the description in I Kings (9:26), where it is said to lie "beside Elath, on the shore of the Red Sea, in the land of Edom". Ezion Geber could have existed on one of the hills overlooking the oasis and town of Akaba, or it could be buried under the modern city.

Ezion Geber was Israel's southern gateway to Arabia, Africa and India. It was the home port for Solomon's fleet of ships of Tarshish voyaging to Ophir and back (I Kgs 10:11, 22). Later on, Jehoshaphat's newly rebuilt fleet came to grief nearby, shattering his hopes of renewing the Red Sea maritime trade instituted by Solomon (I Kgs 22:48; II Chr 20:36-37). The fortunes of Ezion Geber/Elath rose or fell depending upon whether or not Israel and/or Judah controlled the Negeb and the

Jezirat Far'un also known as Pharaoh's Island in the Gulf of Elath. It has been identified by some with Ezion Geber.

EZEL
I Sam 20:19

EZEM
Josh 15:29;
19:3. I Chr
4:29

EZER 1
Gen 36:21, 27,
30. I Chr 1:38,
42

EZER 2
I Chr 4:4

EZER 3
I Chr 7:21

EZER 4
I Chr 12:9

EZER 5
Neh 3:19

EZER 6
Neh 12:42

EZION GEBER
Num 33:35-36.
Deut 2:8.
I Kgs 9:26;
22:48. II Chr
8:17; 20:36

Arabah and exploited the latter's mineral resources. Copper mining and smelting were carried out here in the Late Chalcolithic and Middle Bronze I periods, and much later in Nabatean times down to the Byzantine era.

The excavations of Tell el-Kheleifeh revealed five periods of occupation, extending from the 10th to the 5th-4th centuries B.C. This time-span covers the history of Ezion Geber and of the Elath that subsequently replaced it on the same site. Period I dates to the time of Solomon, in the 10th century B.C. Period II represents a reconstruction, perhaps by Jehoshaphat of Judah (c. 870-848 B.C.), with a massive double fortification wall, and an elaborate city gateway. This enlarged settlement may have been destroyed by the Edomites in the middle of the 9th century B.C., during their successful rebellion against Jehoram, son of Jehoshaphat. Period III may be attributed to Uzziah, who "built Elath and restored it to Judah" (II Kgs 14:22; II Chr 26:1-2), probably shortly after the first quarter of the 8th century B.C. Period IV belonged to the Edomites, who regained control of Elath from Uzziah's grandson, Ahaz (II Kgs 16:1, 6). With its various subperiods it lasted approximately from the end of the 8th century to the end of the 6th century B.C. Period V has few remains but Aramaic (5th-4th centuries B.C.) and late Phoenician ostraca and black, glazed Greek pottery were found. The site was abandoned after this.

EZNITE An epithet affixed to Adino, one of David's "mighty men".

EZRA ("[God] helps").

1. The leader of a group of Jews returning to Jerusalem from the Babylonian Exile in 458 B.C., during the reign of the Persian King Artaxerxes I, as told in the Book of Ezra (7:7-9). Although of high-priestly stock (Ezra 7:1-5), Ezra did not officiate in the cult, nor did he hold specific political office. His function was that of a "skilled scribe in the law of Moses", officially recognized by the Persian emperor (Ezra 7:6). When Ezra learned that the renewed Jewish community in Judah lacked spiritual direction, he received permission from the king to lead 1,754 exiles to Judah, to give a firm foundation to Mosaic law there. Intent on fortifying the returned exiles' awareness of their Jewish identity, Ezra convened the people for a public reading of the Law (Neh 8:1-12), and a celebration of the Tabernacles festival culminating in a solemn prayer. Subsequently, the leaders of the community approached Ezra on the matter of mixed marriages: by prayer and a public fast, Ezra eventually encouraged the dissolution of alliances contracted between Jewish men and alien wives (Ezra 10:18-44). Ezra's memoirs end early in 457 B.C. after about one year of active leadership. See EZRA AND NEHEMIAH, BOOKS OF.

Ezra the Scribe portrayed in the so-called Northumbrian Bible. c. A.D. 715

2. A priest who returned to Jerusalem with Zerubbabel from the Babylonian Exile (Neh 12:1, 13); he is also called Azariah in Nehemiah 10:2.

3. A priest during the time of Nehemiah (Neh 12:33).

EZRA AND NEHEMIAH, BOOKS OF The Books of Ezra and Nehemiah comprise the main source of information for the crucial period of the return from the Babylonian Exile. This was a formative time of transition between the biblical age of the First Temple (destroyed in 586 B.C.) and the emerging Jewish commonwealth of the Second Temple period. The picture which emerges from these books can be supplemented by information and impressions from the books of the post-exilic prophets, Haggai, Zechariah and Malachi. The men of that period highly esteemed the traditions of Israel's past, and endeavored to utilize them as the base for shaping the reborn Jewish society. The acts and decrees of Ezra and Nehemiah convey an ongoing reinterpretation of tradition, and its application to changing circumstances, inspired by a genuine creativity in the fields of literature, religious thought and cultic organization. Here also are the beginnings of the exegetical and hermeneutical techniques of the *midrash* later applied by the sages of the Second Temple period to the interpretation of biblical literature.

Although early traditions viewed Ezra-Nehemiah as one work, written for the most part, along with the Books of Chronicles, by Ezra the scribe (in the Vulgate, the Latin Translation, Ezra is I Esdras and Nehemiah is II Esdras), recent linguistic and stylistic studies show the three works to be separate compositions. Historically, Ezra-Nehemiah are a sequel to Chronicles, since they open at Cyrus' decree, with which Chronicles ends. However, in most manuscripts and printed editions, Ezra-Nehemiah directly precede Chronicles in the biblical canon. Chronicles was probably transferred from its original place to the end of the Hebrew Bible because it was regarded as a summary of the whole sacred story.

In their present arrangement, the Books of Ezra-Nehemiah span approximately a century, from the decree of Cyrus the Great, emperor of Persia, in 538 B.C. (sanctioning the return of the exiles and the eventual rebuilding of the Temple in Jerusalem) — to about 420 B.C., the beginning of the reign of Darius II.

A page of the Book of Ezra from the Codex Leningrad *of the early 11th century, the oldest complete manuscript of the Bible. (Jewish National and University Library, Hebrew University, Jerusalem)*

From the point of view of internal Jewish history, the books cover three main periods, which may be identified by the personalities who exerted influence and leadership over the Jewish people in those times: Sheshbazzar and Zerubbabel, with the prophets Haggai and Zechariah; Ezra the scribe, and Nehemiah, governor of the Persian province of Judah.

In the absence of clear chronology in Ezra chapters 2-4, the relationship between Sheshbazzar and Zerubbabel is problematic, the same information being reported of the two. Both men were of royal descent, and both were governors of Judah (Ezra 1:8; Hag 1:1, etc.). If Sheshbazzar is an alternate form of Shenazzar (1 Chr 3:18), then Sheshbazzar was Zerubbabel's uncle, and both were of the line of David. Zerubbabel, however, was especially invested with messianic (regal) glory, as leader of the major wave of returning exiles (Ezra 2:1-2), while Sheshbazzar received the restored Temple vessels from the Persian treasury on behalf of the Jewish community (Ezra 1:7-8).

The return may have occurred in two stages: the first led by Sheshbazzar in 538 B.C., and the larger one led by Zerubbabel a few years later. Both leaders are credited with laying the foundations for the new Temple (Ezra 3:8-10; 5:16), but the reference to Sheshbazzar is dubious here; it would seem that the project belonged wholly to Zerubbabel who, however, did not complete the Temple, for he is not mentioned in the account of the dedication (Ezra 6:14-18).

The relationship beween Ezra and Nehemiah has been the subject of much scholarly debate. The biblical sources (Ezra chap. 7; Neh chap. 2) indicate that Ezra came to Jerusalem "in the seventh year of Artaxerxes" (458 B.C.) and Nehemiah 13 years later (445 B.C.). Some scholars have tried to prove, from chronological inconsistencies, that Nehemiah must have come before Ezra. However, in the light of recent archeological evidence, including Aramaic seal-impressions from the Persian period, the traditional view seems most credible: Ezra preceded Nehemiah as a functionary of the Persian regime in Judah during the reign of Artaxerxes I (464-424 B.C.).

From a literary point of view, Ezra-Nehemiah are a compilation of diverse sources and documents, as can be clearly seen through the interweaving of Hebrew and Aramaic accounts in Ezra chapters 1-6. The books are composed of three main blocks of material: the Sheshbazzar-Zerubbabel section, the Ezra memoirs and the Nehemiah

A page of the Book of Nehemiah from the Codex Leningrad *of the early 11th century, the oldest complete manuscript of the Bible. (Jewish National and University Library, Hebrew University, Jerusalem)*

memoirs. All three blocks show a similarity in structure and in the literary types of which they are composed: (a) Documents: e.g. the Aramaic edict of Cyrus and its Hebrew variant (Ezra 6:3-5; 1:2-4). (b) Letters: correspondence between officials in Palestine and the Persian court (Ezra 4:8-22; 5:7-17; Neh 6:2-9). (c) Lists: these include inventories of the Temple vessels (Ezra 1:9-11; 8:26-27); rosters of returnees (Ezra 2:1-70; Neh 7:7-72); lists of repatriates who married alien wives (Ezra 10:18-44); rebuilt the walls of Jerusalem (Neh 3:1-32); resided in Jerusalem (Neh 11:3-24); resettled Judah and Benjamin (Neh 11:25-36); served as priests and Levites (Neh 12:1-26); and signed Nehemiah's covenant with all of its obligations (Neh 9:38-10:27; 10:28-39. (d) Prayers: of Ezra (9:6-15) and Nehemiah (1:5-11).

These and other sources were woven together through a multi-phase literary process. Although the editor of Ezra-Nehemiah did not inform his readers of the considerations which guided him in his work, a study of the text's style and structure reveals traces of the basic components of the books and of the process of compilation. Taken together with historical and archeological investigations, they serve as guidelines in an attempt to rearrange the constituent units, and achieve a clearer picture of the period: (1) The era of Sheshbazzar and Zerubbabel: (Ezra 1:1-4, 5-11; 2:1-67; 2:68-69, 70; 3:1-3, 4-6, 7, 8-9, 10-13; 4:1-3, 4-5, 6-12; 5:1-2; 5:3-6:13, 14-15, 16-18, 22). After the dedication of the Temple (515 B.C.) there is a narrative hiatus of some 70 years, a gap bridged somewhat by the transposition of Ezra 4:6-22 as suggested above. The history continues with Ezra's return in 458 B.C.; (2) Ezra's leadership: (Ezra 7:1-8:36; Neh 8:1-9:37; Ezra 9:1; Neh 13:1-3; Ezra 6:19-22; 9:2-10:44); (3) Nehemiah's term of office: (Neh 1:1-7:73; 9:38-10:39; 11:1-12:26, 27-43; 12:44-47; 13:4-29; 13:30-31).

OUTLINE

EZRA

1:11	The decree of Cyrus
2:1-70	List of those who returned under Zerubbabel
3:1-13	Renewal of sacrifice and foundation of Second Temple
4:1-24	Samaritan measures to disrupt the building and countermeasures
5:1-6:22	Completion of the wall
7:1-28	Ezra leaves for Jerusalem
8:1-14	List of exiles who returned with Ezra
8:15-36	Journey of Ezra and his company to Jerusalem
9:1-10:44	Problem of intermarriage

NEHEMIAH

1:1-2:10	Nehemiah receives permission to go to Jerusalem and build the walls
2:11-4:17	Rebuilding of the walls
5:1-19	Community problems
6:1-7:3	Completion of the wall
7:4-73	List of those who returned from the Exile
8:1-9:38	Ezra proclaims the Law
10:1-39	The covenant
11:1-12:26	Repopulation of Jerusalem
12:27-47	Dedication of the wall
13:1-31	Correction of abuses after Nehemiah's return from Babylon

EZRAH A descendant of Judah and father of Jether, Mered, Epher and Jalon. **I Chr 4:17**

EZRAHITE A descendant of Zerah. Ethan and Heman the wise belonged to this family. **I Kgs 4:31. Ps 88:1; 89:1**

EZRI Son of Chelub; he was appointed by David "over those who did the work of the field". **I Chr 27:26**

FAIR HAVENS A harbor through which Paul sailed together with other prisoners on their voyage to Rome. It is identified with a bay 4-5 miles (6.5-8 km) east of Cape Matala in southern Crete.

FALCON See ANIMALS

FALL The Fall refers to the sin of Adam and Eve who disobeyed the divine edict by eating of the tree of knowledge of good and evil, whereupon they were expelled from the Garden of Eden (Gen chaps. 2-3). The concept of the Fall was developed by post-biblical Christian theologians who held that this "original sin" involved mankind in an inherent sinfulness from which it can only be saved by a special act of divine grace. This doctrine is based on Pauline passages such as Romans 5:12; Ephesians 2:3. The concept of the Fall is attractive because it proposes a view of a perfect primeval time when life was not marred by imperfection or sickness. In this idyllic state, when mankind enjoyed unblemished relations with the deity, with other humans and with nature, there was no evil and God's intention for humans was perfectly met. However, the option of disobedience existed, and when the opportunity was grasped, the couple "fell": from grace, from the favor of God or from perfect communion with him. Where once the human couple felt at ease with each other, they now shied away from their creator and covered their nakedness. This myth captured the imagination principally by explaining the origin of evil, illness and toil.

The OT has no doctrine of the Fall and those writers who subsequently drew on OT texts to support their dramatic notions have for the most part misrepresented them. Certainly the reference to Lucifer in Isaiah 14:12 has nothing to do with the fall of an angel but rather is a clever satire mocking the pomp and glory of the king of Babylon who must now exchange his bed of ivory for one of worms. If an identical act could be attributed to either God (II Sam 24:1) or Satan (I Chr 21:1), and if Satan could appear along with the sons of God (Job chap. 1), this probably indicates that the biblical writers had not finally resolved the question of the origin of evil. One solution is provided by Zechariah chapter 3 where Satan is depicted as taking one attribute of God and pushing it beyond any proportion, and in essence this is evil: lack of balance. In any case, Hebrew writings, treating good and evil as ever present, give little attention to the question of the Fall.

The same is true in the writings of the early Christians. Paul makes use of the Adam myth in Romans chapter 5 and uses a word (*paraptoma*) which has been translated as "fall" (Rom 5:15). But in the writings of the early Christians the idea of a fall is never sustained through recourse to the Genesis story. The belief in human depravity is supported by continuing evidence, not by myths of the past. Classical theology based its view of the Fall and human depravity on Romans 5:12 but it was a mistranslation from Greek into the Latin: the verse should be translated "inasmuch as all men sinned". Any notion of total depravity finds no anchor in the biblical texts, either Jewish or Christian, for the classical texts of both religions affirm the release from bondage and do not revel in the Fall or any view of it which consigns humans to a situation of despair. Paul's interest is not in depicting human depravity but rather in demonstrating that it is within God's power to redeem that depravity — that in fact, the grace of God has been so much more abundantly demonstrated than the evil humans can devise.

FASTING In the Bible, almost any situation that aroused deep emotion could provide an occasion for fasting. These included grief in bereavement, distress in the face of impending danger and urgent supplication in distress for divine aid and compassion. The ritual of

The stone in a grotto in the monastery believed to be the spot where Jesus sat when he fasted.

(right)
The Monastery of Quarantal, on a steep mountainside in the Judean Desert, commemorates the forty days and nights that Jesus fasted in the desert.

mourning normally included fasting. The men of Jabesh Gilead fasted for seven days after burying the remains of Saul and his sons (I Sam 31:13); David fasted on hearing the news of the death of Saul and Jonathan (II Sam 1:12) and on receiving word that Abner had been slain (II Sam 3:35). A striking exception was the behavior of David who fasted and prayed when his son by Bathsheba was stricken by illness; yet, on learning that the child had died, he abandoned his fast. The astonishment of his servants at his behavior, so contrary to the accepted norm, elicited the response: "While the child was still alive, I fasted and wept; for I said, 'Who can tell whether the Lord will be gracious to me, that the child may live? But now he is dead; why should I fast?...I shall go to him, but he shall not return to me'". (II Sam 12:22-23).

Several examples are found of fasting on the eve of impending danger and threatening disaster. Saul fasted on the eve of a crucial battle with the Philistines (I Sam 28:20, 22); Ahab fasted on hearing Elijah pronounce a prophecy of doom upon him and his offspring (I Kgs 21:27). Jehoshaphat fasted when he learned that hostile nations were on the march to do battle against him and his people (II Chr 20:3-4). The classic example of a collective fast is that of the people of Nineveh (Jonah 3:4-5) in response to Jonah's forecast of divine destruction of their city. Here, as in similar instances, the fast was part of an expression of repentance that might hopefully avert the disaster.

Actual disaster, too, could serve as an occasion for fasting. Thus the Israelites fasted when defeated in battle by the Benjamites (Judg 20:26). A devastating plague of locusts moved the prophet Joel to proclaim a public fast (Joel 1:14). With the possible exception of the fast of the Day of Atonement (Lev 23:27, 29; Num 29:7), there were no stated public fast days in the period of the First Temple. Fasts were proclaimed by the prophet or king *ad hoc*.

However, fasting by individuals is frequently referred to in Psalms. These fasts were voluntarily observed in response to occasions of personal distress or danger (Ps 35:13; 69:10; 109:24). Voluntary fasts were observed by Daniel (Dan 9:3ff; 10:3), Ezra (Ezra 10:6) and Nehemiah (Neh 1:4).

The prophets' attitude towards fasting is highly informed by the demand for sincerity, true repentance, and a reversal towards ethical conduct, cf Joel's saying (2:12-13) "...turn to me with all your heart, with fasting and weeping; and rend your heart and not your garments." Isaiah declared that compassionate moral conduct is more acceptable to God than fasting attended by strife and contention (Is 58:4-7). Zechariah declared that neither fasting nor eating are for the sake of God, but the word of God is to be found in ethical conduct (7:5-10).

The situation in regard to public fasts underwent a radical change with the destruction of the Temple and the Babylonian Exile. No less than four fast days were instituted in commemoration of these events: the fast of the fourth month (the ninth day of Tammuz when the walls of Jerusalem were breached by the Babylonians); the fast of the fifth month (Ab, when the Temple was put to the torch and burned from the seventh to the tenth day of the month); the fast of the seventh month (Tishri, in memory of the assassination of Gedaliah, murdered on the New Year — see Jeremiah 41:1-2); and the fast of the tenth month (Tebeth, the ninth day when Jerusalem was put under siege by the Babylonians (Zech 8:19).

Since fasting was a prominent element in the piety of 1st century Judaism, it is natural that the practice is referred to fairly frequently in the NT, particularly among the disciples of John the Baptist (Mark 2:18). Jesus is reported to have "prayed and fasted" as a prelude to his healing activities. However, he declared that fasting must not be used to win the admiration of men. "...when you fast, anoint your head and wash your face, so that you do not appear to men to be fasting, but to your Father who is in the secret place" (Matt 6:17; cf Luke 18:12).

Like the prophets, Jesus emphasized contrition and repentance as the true essence of fasting. When asked why his disciples did not fast, Jesus replied: "Can the friends of the bridegroom fast while the bridegroom is with them? As long as they have the bridegroom with them, they cannot fast. But the days will come when the bridegroom will be taken away from them, and then they will fast in those days" (Mark 2:18-20). Jesus himself fasted at times of spiritual crisis. When he was led into the desert and tempted by Satan, "He fasted forty days and forty nights" (Matt 4:1-2; cf Mark 1:12-13). The Anatolic writings mention fasting on rare occasions: in conjunction with a prayer for divine help (Acts 13:2ff) and the appointment of Church Elders in Asia (Acts 14:23).

Two coins of the Roman procurator Antonius Felix. A.D. 54.

FAWN See ANIMALS

FEASTS AND FESTIVALS See DAY OF ATONEMENT; NEW YEAR; PASSOVER; PENTECOST; PILGRIM FESTIVALS; PURIM; TABERNACLES

FELIX Marcus Antonius Felix, freedman of the Emperor Claudius, was Roman procurator in Judea from A.D. 52- c. 60. His cruelty and harsh misgovernment contributed to the unrest of his Jewish subjects, and led to a state of permanent Jewish rebellion against Rome. As governor at the time of Paul's arrest (Acts 23:24), Felix granted him an interview, apparently out of curiosity (Acts 24:24). It is typical of Felix that all he saw in Paul was an opportunity to solicit a bribe (Acts 24:26).

FELIX
Acts 23:24, 26;
24:3, 22, 24-25,
27; 25:14

FESTUS Porcius Festus was appointed procurator of Judea c. A.D. 60 when his notorious predecessor Felix was recalled to Rome (Acts 24:27). Festus seems to have been a sincere man, who made genuine efforts to resolve the growing enmity between the Jews and the Roman occupation. In Paul's case, he made efforts to ensure a proper trial, and when Paul appealed to Caesar, Festus gave orders that he be escorted to Rome (Acts 25:12 ff).

FESTUS
Acts 24:27;
25:1, 4, 9, 12-
14, 22-24;
26:24-25, 32

FIG See PLANTS

FIRSTBORN The term "firstborn" of an animal always refers to that of the mother. For human beings the term can refer either to that of the mother or of the father, or even as a metaphor (e.g. Ex 4:22). The designation "the first issue of the womb", naturally refers exclusively to the firstborn of the mother. The firstborn of the mother occurs in three limited instances: (a) to stress the child's sanctity (Ex 34:19); (b) to emphasize that he is not his father's firstborn (I Chr 2:50); and (c) to underscore the mother's status at the time of his birth (Deut 25:6; Luke 2:7). In all other instances, the firstborn is of the father.

The genealogical lists point up the importance of the firstborn male. He is first in the list, even if the genealogical line is given for all the sons (I Chr 6:16-30). The family line is continued through the firstborn, even if other sons are named (I Chr 7:1-4); at times, the firstborn is the only one named (Gen 11:12-13). Daughters, even the firstborn, are listed at the end (I Sam 14:49).

The hegemony of the firstborn is reflected in the early narratives (Gen chap. 27; 37:22; cf 29:32). More important, it is concretized in his rights of inheritance. In Israel, the law of Deuteronomy 21:15-17 ordains that the firstborn should receive double the portion allotted to each of his brothers. Though a younger brother might gain the birthright he never acquired the title firstborn (cf I Chr 26:10). The reason for this may be that in Israel the firstborn held a sacred status. Thus the transfer of the birthright — even without the title — is generally recorded as taking place, not by the whim of the father or intrigue of the brothers, but solely by the intervention of God (e.g. Jacob, Gen 25:23; Solomon, I Kgs 2:15; David, I Chr 28:4).

The laws declaring the sanctity of the firstborn consist of a general statement (Ex 13:1-2, 12; 34:19; Num 18:15) and a threefold application: to pure animals, impure animals and human beings (Ex 13:13; 34:20; Num 18:15-18; cf Ex 22:29-30; Lev 27:26-27; Deut 15:19-23). In the case of the pure animal the law codes differ: in Exodus 13:12-13; 22:29-30; 34:19, the firstborn is transferred to the Lord, i.e., sanctified either as a burnt offering or as a well-being offering of the priest; according to Numbers 18:8, 17 it is the priest's well-being offering; whereas Deuteronomy 15:20 maintains it is the owner's (Deut 15:20). The law codes also differ in the case of the impure animal: Exodus requires that only the donkey be ransomed (Ex 13:13), while Numbers (18:15) extends the ransom requirement to all impure animals. (The regulation is absent from Deuteronomy.)

The Hebrew verbs used in the laws of the human firstborn clearly indicate that the firstborn male is the property of the deity. Thus the Bible may be preserving the memory of the firstborn bearing a sacred status, and his replacement by the Levites (Num 3:11-13, 40 ff; 8:14-18) may reflect the establishment of a professional priestly class.

In the NT the term firstborn is chiefly applied to Jesus, who is called the firstborn of Mary (Matt 1:25; Luke 2:7). When the term is applied to Jesus in broader senses, it implies a certain exalted status and divine sonship, as in Hebrews 1:6. It can also connote a priority over, and oneness with, man, in starting the new era of risen life (Col 1:18); "firstborn from the dead" (Rev 1:5); "the firstborn among many brethren" (Rom 8:29). It can also refer to Jesus' preexistence, as in Colossians 1:15 "firstborn over all creation". John uses instead the term "only begotten Son", (e.g., John 1:18; 3:16, 18).

FIRST FRUITS In the OT, the first issue of all life whether from the womb (See FIRSTBORN) or the soil, was considered intrinsically holy. It had to be transferred to the deity, the rightful owner, before human beings were permitted to use the crop. Moreover, its transfer to the deity was considered a prerequisite for the assurance of divine blessing on the remainder of the crop. Both factors, the intrinsic holiness of the first fruit and its pragmatic purpose, are exemplified by the law of the first edible yield of fruit trees: "but in the fourth year all its fruit shall be holy, a praise to the Lord. And in the fifth year you may eat its fruit, that it may yield to you its increase" (Lev 19:24-25). Similar is the law of the first fruits of the barley harvest: "You shall bring a sheaf of the first fruits of your harvest to the priest...to be accepted on your behalf' (Lev 23:10-11).

The gift of the first fruits is due not only from the first ripe crops of the soil but also from certain foods processed from these crops, i.e. grain, new wine, new (olive) oil, fruit syrup, leavened food and bread dough. Thus, "All the best of the oil, all the best of the new wine and of the grain, their first fruits which they offer to the Lord, I have given them to you. Whatever first-ripe fruit is in their land, which they bring to the Lord, shall be yours" (Num 18:12-13; cf Ezek 44:30); grain, wine and oil as well as fruit syrup, leaven and dough and wool (Num 15:20-21; Deut 18:4; II Chr 31:5). The most significant festival involving the first of a crop to ripen was that of the first-ripe wheat, which was made to coincide with the Pentecost or Feast of Weeks (Ex 23:16; 34:22; Lev 23:15, 21; Num 28:26; Deut 16:9-12). In a figurative sense Israel is called the first fruits of God (Jer 2:3). In the NT, Jesus — the first to rise to a new life — is the first fruits of the dead (I Cor 15:20). Even in this life, Christians possess the first fruits of the spirit. The first generations of the Church were the first fruits of God (James 1:18; Rev 14:4) while the first Christians to be converted are also referred to as first fruits (Rom 16:5; I Cor 16:15).

FISH
GATE
II Chr 33:14.
Neh 3:3;
12:39. Zeph
1:10

FISH GATE One of the gates of Jerusalem, built by King Manasseh of Judah (II Chr 33:14); it was repaired after the return from the Babylonian Exile by the sons of Hassenaah (Neh 3:3), and mentioned together with the Gate of Ephraim, the Old Gate and the Tower of Hananea (Hananeel, Neh 3:1) in conjunction with the thanksgiving ceremony marking the completion of the work (Neh 12:39). It is identified by some with the Gate of Ephraim in the northern wall of the city. The name apparently derives from the nearby fish market (Neh 13:16).

FLAX See PLANTS

FLEA See ANIMALS

FLOOD The biblical flood story (Gen 6:5-9:17) relates how, in the tenth generation from Adam, God found that mankind's evil had reached proportions beyond toleration. As a result, God resolved to wipe out the human race and begin again with the only virtuous person in that entire generation, Noah, and his family. God revealed his fateful plan to Noah alone, ordering him to build a huge ark for himself and his family to ride out the flood in safety, along with representatives of every species of animal, so that they, too, could be regenerated after the calamity (Gen 6:14-20). Noah obeyed all of God's orders punctiliously. The flood came and destroyed all earthly life save the small party in the ark. After seven and a half months the ark came to rest upon the mountains of the Ararat region, in Armenia (Gen 8:4). Noah opened his window and sent out birds to see whether the earth had dried. He made four probes, once with a raven and three times with a dove; on the final occasion the dove failed to return (Gen 8:7-12). A year after the onset of the flood, God commanded Noah to leave the ark. Noah built an altar and offered sacrifices to God in gratitude for his deliverance (Gen 8:15-20). Upon smelling the sacrifices, God swore never again to doom the world because of man; just as he had commanded humanity at the beginning so he now commanded Noah, "be fruitful and multiply", so that the world would be repopulated (Gen 9:1). The reason for God's forswearing the future destruction of humanity is because "the imagination of man's heart is evil from his youth," (Gen 8:32). Realizing that, given human nature, the same problem was likely to arise again, God decided that repeated floods would be futile, whereupon he adopted a new approach: he gave man laws, spelling out what is prohibited, and ordering man himself to punish violators. He now permitted man to eat meat (without the blood) and prohibited murder, ordering that "whoever sheds man's blood, by man his blood shall be shed." (Gen 9:1-6). He then placed a rainbow in the clouds as a token of his covenant never again to destroy the human race by flood (Gen 9:12-17).

Because of certain inconsistencies in the account of the flood (e.g., the number of animals Noah was to take, the chronology of the flood), critical scholars are of the opinion that the present biblical text amalgamates two originally separate narratives which shared the same outline but differed from each other in formulation and certain details.

The biblical account of the flood has much in common with one from Mesopotamia which is known in several versions. The oldest and fullest versions are a Sumerian one in which the survivor is called Ziusudra ("life of long days"), an Akkadian one in which he is called Atrahasis ("exceedingly wise"), and, borrowed from the latter, another Akkadian one in the *Gilgamesh Epic*, where the survivor of the flood is called Utnapishtim (probably meaning "he found life").

The Mesopotamian stories contain many similarities to the biblical account. The flood marks a turning point in primeval history. It is brought on by divine decision as a punishment for man's sins against the gods. One man, the favorite of a god, is singled out for salvation. To save his family and representatives of all living creatures, he is to build a vessel caulked inside and out with pitch. The flood results from a rainstorm. After the devastation of the flood, the vessel comes to rest on a mountain peak. Birds are dispatched to discover whether dry land has appeared. When the hero leaves the boat he offers a sacrifice. The gods express their sorrow over what has happened.

All these similarities leave little doubt that there is a very close relationship between the biblical and Mesopotamian accounts of the flood; extensive floods being common in the Tigris-Euphrates Valley, but not Palestine, and the Mesopotamian texts being centuries older than the biblical ones, there is no doubt that the Israelites were the borrowers, though it cannot be said whether they drew on the known Mesopotamian texts, other texts or oral tradition. (A fragment of the flood story found at Ugarit shows that the Mesopotamian story was known in the Syro-Palestinian region by about the 14th century B.C.). This indebtedness is not surprising since biblical tradition traces the early Hebrew back to Mesopotamia, where they undoubtedly learned many traditions about early human history. But the borrowing did not take the form of unreflecting imitation. Probably feeling that key parts of the Mesopotamian version were highly improbable, the Israelites revised the account in accordance with their own views of what is believable. Consequently, despite its similarities to the Mesopotamian myth, the biblical version radically transforms the raw materials in light of original Israelite religious values.

In the polytheistic Mesopotamian version, the flood is brought on when the gods' sleep is disturbed by mankind's bellowing and uproar, which reached intolerable levels after humanity had multiplied. The idea is that too many people produce too much noise. That is why the gods sent all the plagues: to reduce the human population to a size which would not produce such a racket. This explanation was unacceptable to the Bible, for two reasons. First, God was not opposed to increases in the human population; his first utterance to man was "Be fruitful and multiply" (Gen 1:28), a blessing repeated immediately after the flood (Gen 9:1, 7). Second, the Bible rejects the notion that God sleeps and can be awakened by noise: "he who keeps Israel shall neither slumber nor sleep" (Ps 121:4), and Elijah used this as an accusation against Baal in mocking those who believed in him (I Kgs 18:27). The

(left)
Part of a tablet on which the Epic of Gilgamesh, the Babylonian version of the Flood, is recorded. c. 2000-1800 B.C.

People drowning in the Flood. Detail of a Spanish illuminated manuscript of the 8th century. (Library of the Cathedral of Gerona, Spain)

historicity of the flood itself was not doubted, but the event had to be interpreted in a manner compatible with the Israelite view of the way God operates. And since that view held that God judges the human race for actions in the moral sphere, it followed that the human offense which led to the flood must have been a moral breach, not a noisy violation of mythic divine repose.

A second biblical innovation involves the question of who is to be punished. In the Mesopotamian version, although mankind offended the gods, it is clear that the chief god was not interested in whether any humans were virtuous. After the flood was over, he was scolded by a fellow god, who said "Punish the sinner for his sin" (i.e. and not the innocent). In contrast, the biblical version takes great pains to show that all those punished were really guilty, by stating explicitly that man's devisings were nothing but evil and that the earth was filled with injustice (Gen 6:5). Even the seemingly naive statement that " all flesh had corrupted their ways" (Gen 6:12) emphasizes that not even a dumb beast would suffer undeservingly; if the animals died in the flood, they, too, must have sinned.

A third innovation is the reason for the protection of the hero. The Mesopotamian versions seem to stress that Atrahasis was a pious king favored by his god. His moral qualities are not emphasized, nor is his piety explicitly given as the reason for his salvation. In contrast, the Bible stresses that Noah was saved because he was a man who walked

Few settlements of the Persian period have been excavated, so that detailed knowledge of its fortifications is limited. The best example is the Phoenician settlement at Tell Megadim (Cartha), where the city was laid out to a rectangular plan and surrounded by a wall, mostly of the casemate type.

During the Hellenistic-Roman periods a city was nearly always surrounded by a stone wall. Excavations of such walls have been undertaken at Samaria, Mareshah, Jerusalem and Gerasa. Fortresses have been unearthed at Beth Zur, Arad, Herodium, Nessana and other places.

At the beginning of the Hellenistic period in Samaria the Israelite wall was reused to surround the acropolis, but huge towers were added. In about the 2nd century B.C. a new wall was built. The entire Roman wall was traced, encircling an area of about 170 acres (71 hectares). The gateway was protected by two round towers standing on square bases. The Roman wall (apparently built by Herod with additions in the time of Septimus Severus) consisted of stones with heavy projecting bosses with comb-picked margins on all four edges, laid in courses of headers (at right angles to the wall) and stretchers (sideways to the wall). At Mareshah, the town wall had buttresses and four corner towers. There are two walls, the inner at the edge of the mound and the outer a few feet down. Some of the towers are built of thin brick-like blocks of soft limestone dressed with a broad chisel, often diagonally. On the northeastern and part of the northern side the stones are set in mud with wide joints, roughly flaked and with no distinct dressing. Between the inner and outer wall there was a revetment, in order to strengthen the inner wall, which was built on debris.

Lower part of one of the towers fortified by Herod the Great in the Citadel in Jerusalem.

FORTUNATUS ("fortunate"). A Christian of Corinth who was with Paul in Ephesus when the apostle wrote his first epistle to the Corinthians.

FOUNDATION GATE One of Jerusalem's gates, mentioned in conjunction with the execution of Athaliah (II Chr 23:1-15), and also named "the way of the horses' entrance to the king's house" (II Kgs 11:16). Possibly one of the gates connecting the king's palace with the Temple compound.

FOUNTAIN GATE One of the gates of Jerusalem repaired after the

FORTUNATUS
I Cor 16:17

FOUNDATION
GATE
II Chr 23:5

FOUNTAIN
GATE
Neh 2:14;
3:15; 12:37

48:27-28, 34.
Rev 7:5

One of David's famous thirty "mighty men" was Bani the Gadite (II Sam 23:36). Gadites aided David at Ziklag while he was in hiding from Saul. They were "men trained for battle" with "the faces of lions" and were "swift as gazelles" (I Chr 12:8).

The Arameans later overran the territory of Gad and subsequently the Assyrians took its inhabitants to Assyria as captives (II Kgs 15:29); the land was then occupied by the Ammonites. Gad's portion is foreseen in Ezekiel's prophecy of the division of the land (Ezek 48:27-28).

In the NT Gad appears along with other tribes in the list of the sealed (Rev 7:5).

GAD 2
I Sam 22:5.
II Sam 24:11,
13-14, 18-19.
I Chr 21:9, 11,
13, 18-19; 29:29.
II Chr 29:25

2. A seer. He advised David who was in flight from Saul, to return to Judah (I Sam 22:1-5) and later to build the altar on the threshing floor of Araunah (II Sam 24:18; I Chr 21:9ff). He is also accredited with helping to organize the Levitical musicians in the Temple (II Chr 29:25).

There was also a book (now lost), called the "Chronicles of Gad the seer" which was utilized by the author of Chronicles (I Chr 29:29).

GAD 3
Is 65:11

3. A foreign deity of good fortune worshiped by some Israelites in the period after the Exile (Is 65:11). In a bilingual Aramaic-Greek inscription from Palymra the deity is identified in Greek as "fortune".

GADARA A city south of the River Yarmuk, identified with the ruins of Umm Keis. In Hellenistic times it was one of the centers of Greek culture in Transjordan. When, under Ptolemaic rule, the Assyrian-Persian provinces were split up, Gadara became capital of the biblical district of Gilead, later called Galaaditis. After Antiochus III's victory over the Ptolemies at Paneas it passed to the Seleucids and received

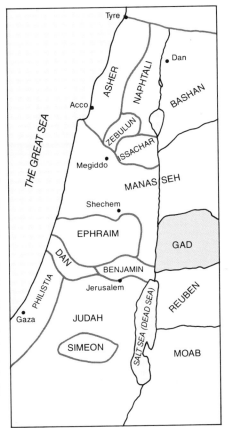

The territory of the tribe of Gad.

Roman columns at Gadara.

additional names, Antiochia and Seleucia. The Hasmonean Alexander Jannaeus conquered it in his first campaign. Under the Roman general, Pompey, it was rebuilt and made a member of the Decapolis. Gadara was one of several Greek cities granted to Herod by Augustus. At the time of the division of Herod's kingdom it was placed under the proconsul of Syria.

Gadara is mentioned in the gospels as the scene of the healing of men possessed with devils, though not all scholars agree on its location (See GERGESA) (Matt 8:28; AV: "Gergesenes"; Mark 5:1-2; Luke 8:26-7).

In the north the territory of Gadara extended across the River Yarmuk to include the famous hot springs of Hammath-Gader and in the west as far as the River Jordan, and possibly to the Sea of Galilee (Matt 8:28).

GADARENES
Mark 5:1.
Luke 8:26, 37

GADARENES See GADARA

GADDI The son of Susi, a man of Manasseh from the tribe of Joseph, one of the men sent by Moses from the wilderness of Paran to spy out the land of Canaan (Num 13:1, 11, 17).

Note: the Hebrew spelling is identical to that of Gadi.

GADDIEL ("my happiness is in the Lord"). Gaddiel the son of Sodi, from the tribe of Zebulun (Num 13:10) was among the men sent by Moses from the wilderness of Paran to spy out the land of Canaan (Num 13:2-3).

GADI The father of Menahem king of Israel.

The Hebrew spelling is identical to that of Gaddi.

GADITES See GAD No.1

GAHAM The second of the four children of Nahor, the brother of Abraham, by his concubine Reumah.

GAHAR A family of Nethinim (Temple servants) listed among those who returned from the Exile in Babylon with Zerubbabel and settled in Jerusalem.

GAIUS

1. A Macedonian traveling-companion of Paul, who was seized by the mob in Ephesus (Acts 19:29); perhaps identical with Gaius who was Paul's host at Corinth (Rom 16:23), and was baptized by him (I Cor 1:14). Another Gaius, from Derbe, accompanied Paul to Macedonia — he too has been identified by some scholars with the Macedonian traveling-companion.

2. The addressee of the Third Epistle of John.

GALAL

1. Descendant of Asaph. He was a Levite living in Jerusalem after the return from the Babylonian Exile.

2. Son of Jeduthun and father of Shemaiah (Shammua in Nehemiah 11:17); he lived in Jerusalem at the time of Nehemiah.

GALATIA, GALATIANS A region of Asia Minor which included the cities of Antioch, Iconium and Lystra. The name derives from the Gauls who conquered the area in the 3rd century B.C. The Galatians became a client state of the Roman Empire in 64 B.C. The Romans established the province of Galatia in 24 B.C.; this was considerably more extensive than the previous kingdom of Galatia. Paul's Epistle to the Galatians was written to the communities in the province. The apostle Peter also addressed an epistle to the "pilgrims of the Dispersion in Pontus, Galatia" etc. (I Pet 1:1). From the Epistle to the Galatians it appears that the communities addressed consisted mainly of Gentile Christians (Gal 4:8; 5:2). Paul visited Galatia on his first (Act 13:50-14:28), second (Acts 16:6) and third (Acts 18:23) missionary journeys. The churches of Galatia contributed to the upkeep of the Jerusalem community (Gal 1:2).

GALATIANS, EPISTLE TO THE The ninth book of the NT. While there is general agreement that Paul is the author of the Epistle to the Galatians, considerable debate has revolved around its date and recipients. The region of Galatia in Asia Minor covered a wide area, and scholars have been divided over whether it was the northern or southern part of the province that Paul traversed on his mission to found churches. Until the work of Ramsay in the latter part of the 19th century, the northern Galatia view held sway, but in more recent times it has largely been replaced by the southern view. This debate also has bearing on the dating of the letter. Since Paul definitely did not travel north on his first missionary journey, the letter must have been written after the second journey (i.e., c. A.D. 53) and more likely after the third (c. 56). While either of these dates would account for the similarities between the epistle and Paul's letter to the church at Rome, they leave

GADDI
Num 13:11

GADDIEL
Num 13:10

GADI
II Kgs 15:14, 17

GADITES
Deut 3:12, 16; 4:43; 29:8. Josh 1:12; 12:6; 13:8; 22:1. II Sam 23:36. I Chr 5:16, 18, 26; 12:8, 37; 26:32

GAHAM
Gen 22:24

GAHAR
Ezra 2:47. Neh 7:49

GAIUS 1
Acts 19:29; 20:4. Rom 16:23. I Cor 1:14

GAIUS 2
III John 1

GALAL 1
I Chr 9:15

GALAL 2
I Chr 9:16. Neh 11:17

GALATIA, GALATIANS
Acts 16:6; 18:23. I Cor 16:1. Gal 1:2; 3:1. II Tim 4:10. I Pet 1:1

Galatia.

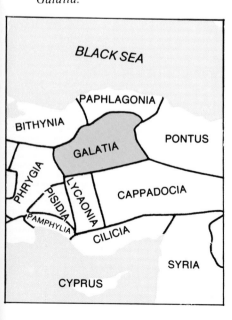

Aramaic text of Paul's Epistle to the Galatians from a 7th century manuscript now at St.Mark's monastery in Jerusalem.

one great difficulty. At the Jerusalem Council in the year 49 (Acts chap. 15) the main point at issue was whether or not non-Jewish believers were obliged to keep commandments of the Mosaic covenant. It is precisely this question which lies at the heart of the Epistle to the Galatians and yet Paul makes no reference to the Council's decisions (which concurred with his own view). This omission argues for a date of composition before the Council i.e. in 48 or 49, and would make this the earliest of Paul's extant letters having been written soon after his return to Antioch from his first missionary journey. Here he met Judaizing teachers from Jerusalem (Acts 15:1; Gal 2:12); finding they had been preaching in the very churches he had just founded, exhorting their Gentile members to keep the Law, he reacted with an immediate letter followed by the trip to Jerusalem (Acts chap. 15). This dating also gives an early date of c. 33 for Paul's conversion (based on the statements in Galatians 1:18 and 2:1). One fact regarding the addressees of the letter is quite clear: they were Gentiles, not Jews.

More than most of Paul's letters, the Epistle to the Galatians is a monograph. It was written to address a specific problem: whether or not Christians from among the Gentiles were to keep the commandments of the Mosaic law. Central to the discussion is the issue of circumcision. Briefly stated, the unspoken question which Paul sets out to answer is this: In order to be made righteous, was a Gentile believer in Jesus required to convert to Judaism and keep the commands of the Law of Moses? Paul's reply, an unequivocal "No", is summed up in 2:21, "if righteousness (i.e. salvation) comes through the Law then Christ died in vain." Paul's approach to the problem is systematic. First he reminds his readers of certain biographical details about himself as a means of establishing his authority to answer the question. This is done evidently to counter claims of authority by those preaching circumcision (which symbolizes entrance into the covenant of the Law with its concomitant requirements). This assertion of his authority takes almost one third of the letter and includes a section where Paul even stood up to Peter (Cephas) in Antioch. Paul is dependent for his revelation on none but Jesus himself (1:11ff). However, he has coordinated the gospel he preaches with other leaders (2:2-10).

Next Paul proceeds to establish that righteousness comes, not through the actions done in accordance with the Law, but rather through faith. For proof of this he speaks at length of the case of Abraham, who was declared righteous for his faith long before the Law was given (Gen 15:6). It is faith which was God's first approved way, and the Law was only given as a kind of child-conductor to lead those participating in its covenant to Abraham's promised seed, the messiah. In the end it is faith again, faith in the messiah, which is God's requirement for righteousness. Paul draws on several symbols to illustrate the precedence and superiority of faith in Jesus over the covenant of the Law: Abraham's two sons, one born of the slave girl, the other of the free woman; the two wives themselves; and two mountains, Sinai where the Law was given and (implicitly) Zion representing the heavenly Jerusalem (cf Heb 12:18-24). These multiple comparisons naturally lead to a discussion of the flesh and the spirit, and this provides the last major theme of the letter.

The epistle shows signs of having been written in what might be called a somewhat cooled passion. It lacks Paul's customary giving of thanks to the addressees as well as any personal greetings. Missing too for the most part are any practical counsels, so usual in most of his letters.

OUTLINE

1:1-5	Introduction
1:6-9	Another gospel?
1:10-2:10	Autobiographical information; Paul's
5:1-26	Flesh and spirit
2:11-21	Paul opposes Peter at Antioch
3:1-18	Abraham justified by faith, not by the Law
4:1-8	Sons or slaves?
4:9-20	Paul's appeal to them
4:21-31	Two covenants, two women, two mountains, two Jerusalems
5:1-26	Flesh and Spirit
6:1-18	Practical exhortation and closing

GALBANUM See SPICES AND PERFUMES

GALEED ("heap of testimony"). A name given by Jacob to a heap of stones gathered by him and Laban as testimony to their peace treaty and a boundary division between their countries. See JEGAR-SAHADUTHA.

GALEED
Gen 31:47-48

GALILEE The northern part of Palestine, also called Galilee of the nations after the Assyrian conquest (Is 9:1), possibly because of the many nations which dwelt in that part of the country before the Israelite conquest. Galilee is bordered by the Jezreel Valley on the south, the Sea of Galilee on the east, Lebanon on the north and the Plain of Acre on the west. It is the highest and coolest region in the country, well watered by the winter rains and with numerous and abundant springs. A deep valley divides the area into two, Upper Galilee rising to a height of more than 3,000 feet (915 m) above sea level.

The main road connecting the Mediterranean coast with the lands to the east of the Jordan ran through this declivity. Broad valleys, especially in Lower Galilee, provide very fertile soil for agriculture, which was the basis of the rich economy of this region.

GALILEE
Josh 20:7;
21:32. I Kgs
9:11. II Kgs
15:29. I Chr
6:76. Is 9:1.
Matt 2:22;
3:13; 4:12, 15,
23, 25; 17:22;
19:1; 21:11;
26:32, 69;
27:55; 28:7,
10, 16. Mark
1:9, 14, 28,
39; 3:7; 6:21;

When the Israelites conquered the territory, Galilee was densely settled with Canaanite city-states, and for a long time the tribes of Asher, Naphtali, Zebulun and Issachar dwelt among them. Kedesh, "in Galilee in the mountains of Naphtali", was one of the cities of refuge (Josh 20:7; 21:32). In the time of Solomon the area comprised four of the administrative divisions of his kingdom (I Kgs 4:12, 15-16). The land of Cabul in Asher (Josh 19:27) was ceded by Solomon to Hiram, king of Tyre, as part payment for his help in building the Temple (I Kgs 9:11-12).

In 732 Tiglath-Pileser III conquered the important cities of Galilee: Ijon, Abel-Beth-Maachah, Janoah, Kedesh and Hazor. The region then became an Assyrian satrapy, known in Assyrian documents as the satrapy of Megiddo, the seat of its governor. In the Persian period Galilee was outside the Jewish autonomous state. It seems that at that time Galilee and Samaria were a single district; at any event this was the case in the Seleucid period, when the district, called an eparchy, included also Judea. Under the Ptolemies Galilee formed a separate hyparchy. In this period the region was inhabited by many Greeks and Phoenicians, but there were also some Jewish settlements. In 104-103

Landscape in Galilee.

B.C. Galilee was conquered by Aristobulus and added to the Hasmonean kingdom, and when Palestine was conquered by Pompey in 64 B.C. it remained in Jewish territory. Later it formed part of Herod's kingdom. The capital of the district was Sepphoris, the other important towns being Magdala and Gush-Halav. After Herod's death Galilee became part of the territory of Herod Antipas, who founded the city of Tiberias, the new capital of Galilee. After his deposition in A.D. 39 Galilee was given to Agrippa I and after his death it formed part of the kingdom of Agrippa II.

Galilee was the scene of the early ministry of Jesus. He lived in Nazareth of Galilee (Matt 21:11; Mark 1:9) and performed his first miracle at Cana (John 2:1-11; 4:46).

For the earlier gospels of Mark and Matthew, Galilee, geographically a green and pleasant land, has a certain connotation of the happy days at the beginning of Jesus' public ministry, when the crowds heard him gladly (Mark 12:37), in contrast with stony Judea where he was put to death. It was there, Jesus told them at the Last Supper that, after he had been raised, he would go before them to meet them (Mark 14:28). The young man in the empty tomb told the women to inform the disciples that Jesus had preceded them in Galilee where they would see him as he had promised (Mark 16:7). Thus Galilee became a kind of promised land.

During the war against the Romans Galilee was fortified by Josephus, and the first battles against the Romans took place there. After the quelling of the revolt it formed part of the Roman province of Judea. Some of the larger cities, such as Tiberias and Sepphoris, were made autonomous and their territories enlarged. The area flourished after the period of the Second Jewish Revolt (A.D. 132-135). It was densely populated, with numerous towns and villages, some of which were the seats of the Jewish priestly orders.

The great prosperity of the region is evident from the numerous ruins of synagogues dating from the 2nd, 3rd and 4th centuries A.D., while the beautiful mosaic pavements of the churches attest its prosperity in the Byzantine period.

GALILEE, SEA OF A freshwater lake in the north of Palestine. It is 13 miles (21km) long and about 8½ miles (14km) across at its widest point, with a maximum depth of 150 feet (46m). Lying 640 feet (195m) below sea level, it is surrounded by mountains 1,200-1,500 feet (365-460m) high, rising close to the shore except for short stretches on the south,

GALILEE,
SEA OF
**Matt 4:18;
15:29. Mark
1:16; 7:31.
John 6:1**

The ancient synagogue of Bar Am in Upper Galilee.

(right)
The Sea of Galilee.

southwest and northwest. The lake is fed from the north by the River Jordan and by numerous lesser streams, as well as by underwater springs, some of them hot, to which medicinal properties have been attributed. Emerging from the southern end of the lake, the Jordan carries the outflow to the Dead Sea.

The great abundance of water and fish, its fertile soil and hot climate turned this region into a real paradise, which attracted settlers as early as prehistoric times. Some of the most important cities in Palestine flourished along its shores, such as Beth Yerah in the Canaanite period and Tiberias in the Roman period. Israelite towns on its shores included Rakkath, Chinnereth and Hammath (Josh 19:35). The western and southern shores were occupied by the tribe of Naphtali (Josh 19:35; Deut 33:23), while the territory of Gad extended from the southeastern shore (Deut 3:17; Josh 12:3; 13:27).

The area was very prosperous in the Hellenistic, Roman and Byzantine periods. Early on, under the Ptolemies, the fort of Philoteria was built on the site of ancient Beth Yerah and served as the capital of a district, developing into a large Jewish city in the Roman period. The shores of the Sea of Galilee were the scene of the early ministry of Jesus. From Nazareth he went to preach in the synagogues, some of them in cities close to the sea, such as Capernaum and Chorazin. It was from these shores that he called the fishermen, Simon and Andrew, and James and John "to become fishers of men" (Matt 4:18-21), and at the water's edge that he fed the multitude with two loaves and five fishes (Matt 14:19-20). Tradition places the site of this miracle at Heptapegon, where the early Church of the Loaves and Fishes was built. Both Jewish and Christian communities flourished along the shores of the lake during the whole of the Roman and Byzantine periods. Excavations made on many sites round the lake, such as Beth Yerah, Tiberias, Hammath, Heptapegon and Capernaum, have revealed much evidence of the splendor and prosperity of the region in all periods.

GALL See PLANTS

GALLIM The birthplace of Palti, son of Laish, the second husband of Michal, Saul's daughter (I Sam 25:44); conquered by Sennacherib on his way to Jerusalem (Is 10:30). Not identified.

GALLIO Proconsul of the province of Achaia (capital: Corinth), probably in A.D. 52-53. He was a brother of the Roman philosopher Seneca, and like him, was sentenced to death by Nero. He is mentioned in an inscription, found in Delphi, which is part of a letter by the Emperor Claudius. Paul was accused by the local Jews and brought before his court, but he dismissed the case as an unimportant dispute between Jews.

GAMALIEL

1. Son of Pedahzur, and a leader of the tribe of Manasseh.

2. Also known as Gamaliel I or the Elder, an outstanding Pharisee scholar and teacher (Paul was one of his pupils, Acts 22:3), known for his tolerance and wisdom. He introduced several reforms designed to adapt Jewish law to the economic and political conditions of the time. His tolerance is in evidence in the story in Acts 5:33-40, where he tried to prevent the persecution of the early Christians and warned the Sanhedrin that these people would not be overthrown if their belief came from God, although adding that "if this plan or this work is of men, it will come to nothing" (Acts 5:38). The later and entirely unsupported Christian legend that Gamaliel was a secret Christian probably has its origin in this story.

GAMMAD The Hebrew *gammadim* is a word of uncertain meaning mentioned in Ezekiel's lamentation over Tyre. Most scholars take it as meaning "men of Gammad" which they identify with Kumidi, a town mentioned in the El Amarna Letters and located on the Phoenician coast. Others have read it as the "Zemarites" (Gen 10:18) or as a noun meaning "watchmen" or "dwarfs".

Entrance to the tomb of Rabbi Gamaliel at Beth Shearim.

GAMUL ("who benefited from the Lord"). A descendant of Aaron, head of the 22nd division of Levites serving the House of the Lord at the time of King David (I Chr 24:6, 17, 19).

GAREB

1. Gareb the Ithrite, one of David's thirty "mighty men".

2. A hill, a turning point in the walls of Jerusalem to the west which, according to Jeremiah the prophet, shall be rebuilt. Its exact location is not clear.

GARLIC See PLANTS

GARMITE An epithet affixed to the name of Keilah, son of Hodiah.

GATAM The fourth of the five sons of Eliphaz No.1, son of Esau by his wife Adah (Gen 36:10-11). He was a chief in Edom (Gen 36:16).

(top left)
Model of gate at Megiddo of the time of Ahab.
(top right)
Remains of Solomonic period gate at Megiddo.
(bottom left)
A gate of the Iron Age at Tell Dan.
(bottom right)
The East Gate at Shechem (Tell Balata). 17th century B.C.

GATES In Israelite cities, as in their Canaanite counterparts, the gate, beyond its defensive function (see FORTIFICATIONS), also served as an important center of public life. The gates were suspended on posts, and closed by bars and locks (Judg 16:3; Neh 3:14) and were roofed over (II Sam 18:24). In front of the gate there was an open place (II Chr 32:6; Neh 8:1, 3, 16), lined with benches where the elders sat, and economic and judicial activities took place. Great crowds gathered in the field in front of the gate, the usual site of the threshing ground (cf I Kgs 22:10). The inner gate was dominated by two towers (II Chr 26:9), containing chambers (II Sam 18:33). Above the roof of the gate watchmen were posted to oversee the road (II Sam 18:25-27); in case of emergency, they would sound trumpets (Ezek 33:2-3). Within the gate, on both sides of the passage, were chambers where the guards could rest; these also served as storage spaces (Ezek 40:7; cf I Kgs 14:28). The gates were often richly embellished. The gates of Solomon's Temple in Jerusalem were decorated with "cherubim, palm trees and open flowers on them and overlaid them with gold applied evenly on the carved work" (I Kgs 6:35; cf Ezek 41:25).

In the Canaanite cities, the gate was the seat of the elders, and every important issue was negotiated there: it was at the city gate that Abraham bargained with Ephron the Hittite over the cave of Machpelah (Gen 23:10, 18). A man who had killed unintentionally and consequently requested admission to a city of refuge was first interrogated by its elders at the gate (Josh 20:4). The gate remained an important center of urban activity up to the end of the Israelite kingdom, but its judicial functions were transmitted to a special building, or a room in the governor's palace, or in a temple (Deut 17:8-12; I Kgs 7:7). Public punishment was administered at the gate to certain transgressors, such as persons who served other gods (Deut 17:5); a rebellious son (Deut 21:19-21); or a man who lay with a betrothed girl (Deut 22:23-24).

GATH The name means "winepress" but may designate a fortified agricultural complex. As a toponym, a second element (usually an ethnic designation) was normally appended to specify the particular Gath in question; thus in the Bible, Gath of the Philistines, Gath Hepher, Gath Rimmon, Moresheth Gath or Gittaim. When these identifying terms are omitted it is sometimes difficult — even from the context — to decide which Gath is meant.

1. GATH OF THE PHILISTINES has generally been recognized as the Gath *par excellence.* Its earliest appearance may be in the EL AMARNA LETTERS, written to the Egyptian pharaohs Amenhotep III and Amenhotep IV (Akhnaton) in the first half of the 14th century B.C.

Gath, along with Gaza and Ashdod, was remembered as a stronghold of the Anakim ("giants"), while Goliath the Gittite (I Sam 17:4, 23) was one of at least four warriors renowned in Israelite tradition who were counted among the Rephaim (II Sam 21:18-22; I Chr 20:4-8). With the arrival of the Philistines the pentapolis came into being, consisting of the Philistine city-states Gath, Gaza, Ashdod, Ashkelon and Ekron (Josh 13:3; I Sam 6:17), each ruled by a "lord" *(seren).* Elsewhere, however, Achish is called "king" of Gath (I Sam 21:10; 27:2), while the other lords are ranked as "princes" or "ministers" (I Sam 29:3-4). Moreover, Gath was called a "royal city" by David (I Sam 27:5). Gath was considered in early Israelite tradition (together with the rest of Philistia) as part of "the land that yet remains" (Josh 13:1-6; Judg 3:1-3), i.e. a region beyond Israelite settlement. In the battle of Eben-Ezer (c. 1050 B.C.) the ark of the covenant fell into Philistine hands (I Sam chap. 4). When it passed from Ashdod to Gath there was a plague (I Sam 5:8-9), whereupon the ark passed to Ekron.

David sought refuge with Achish in Gath twice, at first unsuccessfully (I Sam 21:10-15, and the superscription to Ps 34 and 56). Later, David returned to Achish and was well received (I Sam chap. 27). He was made a mercenary chieftain, given the border fortress city of Ziklag and charged with protecting Achish's southeastern flank facing the Judean and related clans in the Negeb. David deceived Achish by reporting that he had been raiding Judean-occupied territory (I Sam 27:10), when in reality he had been defending the Israelites by attacking their enemies and patrolling their frontier.

The mound of Tell es-Safi, identified with Gath of the Philistines.

When David firmly secured himself as king he began a series of wars with the Philistines in general, and the Gittites in particular (II Sam 21:18-22; I Chr 20:4-8). According to I Chronicles 18:1, David took Gath and its satellite cities from the Philistines. But a parallel passage (II Sam 8:1) substitutes "Metheg Ammah" for Gath. Since Achish still ruled Gath early in Solomon's reign (I Kgs 2:39-41) it seems unlikely that David occupied the city. (That Gath could be Gittaim; cf below). David had a mercenary force from Gath headed by Ittai the Gittite (II Sam 18:19).

Rehoboam's list of fortresses (II Chr 11:5-12) includes Gath among the 15 cities situated at strategic points in Judah. It is likely, however, that the reference is to Moresheth Gath (probably located at Tell Judeidah (Tell Goded), an important Israelite fortress).

In c. 815 B.C., Hazael, king of Aram Damascus, conducted a campaign, and conquered Gath (II Kgs 12:17), but opinions differ whether this was Gath of the Philistines or Gittaim.

In the mid-8th century B.C., Uzziah, king of Judah, set out on a sweeping campaign against Philistia, and conquered Gath (II Chr 26:6). The contemporary prophet Amos refers to Gath as an example of a mighty stronghold that had succumbed to siege (Amos 6:2). Later references to the Philistine cities ignore Gath (Jer 25:20; Zeph 2:4; Zech 9:5-7).

The location of Philistine Gath is uncertain — practically no biblical references to Gath provide any precise topographical information. It is identified by some with Tell es-Safi (Tell Zafit) which stands about 4 miles (6.4 km) west of the Judean Plain and guards the mouth of Wadi 'Ajjur, a continuation of the Valley of Elah (Wadi es-Sant), which leads into the Judean Hills. The mound is the most prominent site within the whole northeastern Philistine plain.

2. GATH (GITTAIM) (Gath with dual suffix). A city in the northern Shephelah commanding the strategic crossroads northwest of Gezer. In the time of Saul, the non-Israelite inhabitants of Beeroth — a city reckoned in Benjamin — fled to Gittaim, situated on the southwest fringes of Israelite territory, and apparently populated by non-Israelites (II Sam 4:2-3). Gittaim is mentioned among the cities of Benjamin during the return of the exiles from Babylonia (Neh 11:33). **GATH 2 / II Sam 4:3 / Neh 11:33**

There appear to be instances in the Bible where Gath implies Gittaim; scholars are divided, however, over which cases. One tradition — reflecting the migration of Ephraim from the hill country to the northern Shephelah and the Valley of Aijalon — seems to apply to Gath (Gittaim) and concerns the Ephraimites killed by the men of Gath who were born in the land, because the former were cattle rustling (I Chr 7:20-21). Afterwards, the wife of Ephraim bore Beriah, who appears together with Shema as clan heads in Benjamite Aijalon, who drove out the inhabitants of Gath (Gittaim) (I Chr 8:13).

According to Roman-Byzantine sources, Gittaim was situated between Antipatris (biblical Aphek — Tell Ras el-'Ain) and Jabneh, near present-day Ramleh. It has been located at Ras Abu-Humeid, a low tell of over 25 acres (10 ha).

GATH HEPHER A town in the territory of Zebulun; the birthplace of Jonah the prophet (II Kgs 14:25). **GATH HEPHER / Josh 19:13. / II Kgs 14:25**

GATH RIMMON

1. One of four Levitical cities in the tribal allotment of Dan (Josh 21:24; I Chr 6:54). The clan of Kehath was settled in Gath Rimmon among a local population that was probably mostly non-Israelite, and charged with administering what became royal lands after their conquest, including collecting taxes (cf I Chr 26:30-32). In the list of **GATH RIMMON / Josh 19:45; / 21:24-25. / I Chr 6:69**

Danite cities (Josh 19:41-46) Gath Rimmon is listed after Jehud and Bene Berak and before the Jarkon River (Mejarkon).

Tell Jerishe (Tell Gerisa), named after a former nearby Arab village, and popularly known as "Napoleon's Hill", has been identified as Gath Rimmon. It lies near Tel Aviv close to the southern bank of the Jarkon River.

"Napoleon's Hill", identified with Gath Rimmon.

2. A Levitical city of the Kehath clan, situated in the territory of Menasseh, near Taanach (Josh 21:25). The Septuagint version of this verse, however, lists Ibleam in place of Gath Rimmon and it is widely believed that there was a copying error in the Hebrew text. If not, this Gath Rimmon may possibly be identified with present-day Rumaneh, near Taanach.

GAZA, GAZITES A city on the coast of Palestine on the route to Egypt, the last halt before entering the desert. A caravan point of strategic importance from the earliest times, it was constantly involved in the wars between Egypt and Palestine, Syria and the Mesopotamian powers, and appears frequently in Egyptian and Assyrian records.

The Roman city extended to the seashore, but modern Gaza is about 3 miles (5 km) from the coast. It seems certain that the medieval and modern city stand on the site of the ancient one. For about 350 years

General view of Gaza.

A coin of Gaza. 4th century B.C.

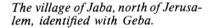

The village of Jaba, north of Jerusalem, identified with Geba.

the city was under Egyptian rule. It is mentioned as a Canaanite city in the early Table of Nations (Gen 10:19). From the 12th century B.C. it became one of the five Philistine coastal cities (I Sam 6:17) and appears in the story of Samson (Judg chap. 16). Dagon was worshiped there (Judg 16:21-30). It was Israelite from the time of David but became Assyrian under Tiglath-Pileser III and Sargon II (around 730 B.C.). In the 7th century it again came under Egyptian control, but in the Persian period (6th-4th centuries B.C.) it enjoyed a certain independence and was a flourishing city.

Alexander the Great conquered Gaza in 332 B.C. after a siege of five months. Belonging at first to the Ptolemaic kingdom, it passed after 200 B.C. to the Seleucids. In the 1st century B.C. and the first half of the 1st century A.D., it was the Mediterranean port of the Nabateans, whose caravans arrived there from Petra or from Elath on the Red Sea. In 96 B.C. the Hasmonean Alexander Jannaeus attacked the city. The inhabitants hoped for help from the Nabatean king, Aretas II, but when this did not come the city surrendered after a siege of a year. Jannaeus slaughtered the population and destroyed the city. Under Pompey it was refounded and rebuilt by Gabinius. In the NT Gaza is mentioned as being on the caravan route to Egypt (Acts 8:26). Granted to Herod by Augustus it formed a separate unit within his kingdom, and Cosgabar, the governor of Idumea was in charge of its affairs. On the division of Herod's kingdom it was placed under the proconsul of Syria. In the Roman period it was a prosperous city and received grants and attention from several emperors, especially Hadrian.

GAZELLE See ANIMALS

GAZEZ ("the shearer", or "shearing of sheep"). The name Gazez occurs twice in the same verse, first as the third son of Caleb by his concubine Ephah, and then as the son of the firstborn of Caleb by Ephah (I Chr 2:46). Some scholars believe the repetition is due to a scribe's error, but others maintain that the recurrence of the same name in a family is very common in the Scriptures.

GAZEZ
I Chr 2:46

GAZITES See GAZA

GAZZAM A family of Nethinim (Temple servants) who returned from the Exile in Babylon with Zerubbabel and settled in Jerusalem.

GAZITES
Josh 13:3.
Judg 16:2

GEBA A town in the territory of the tribe of Benjamin (I Chr 8:6; Josh 18:24 where it is called Gaba), identified with the modern village of Jaba, 5½ miles (9 km) north of Jerusalem. Geba was allotted to the descendants of Aaron, the high priest (Josh 21:17; I Chr 6:60). It served as the base for the Israelite forces of Saul and Jonathan during the battle with the Philistines at Michmash (I Sam 13:16; 14:5).

GAZZAM
Ezra 2:48.
Neh 7:51

Geba is next mentioned as a night-station on the route of the Assyrian army to Jerusalem (Is 10:29), while in the description of Josiah's religious reforms, it marks the place of the northernmost *bamah* (high place) defiled by that king (II Kgs 23:8). It has, however, been suggested that the town here named, as well as that mentioned in Zechariah 14:10, is a more northerly Geba which marked the northern border of Judah in late First Temple times.

GEBA
Josh 21:17.
Judg 20:33. I
Sam 13:3;
14:5. II Sam
5:25. I Kgs
15:22. II Kgs
23:8. I Chr
6:60; 8:6. II
Chr 16:6. Ezra
2:26. Neh
7:30; 11:31;
12:29. Is
10:29. Zech
14:10

Following the Babylonian Exile, the inhabitants of Geba were among the first to return to their town (Ezra 2:26; Neh 7:30), and they are later numbered among the inhabitants of Benjamin by Nehemiah.

There appears to be some confusion between Geba and Gibeah, both of which are in the territory of Benjamin, and it has been suggested that some of the biblical references to Geba in fact refer to Gibeah, commonly identified with Tell el-Ful (Judg 20:33; I Sam 13:3; II Sam 5:25; I Kgs 15:22; II Chr 16:6). On the other hand, it has been argued that the two names refer to one and the same site.

GEBAL, GEBALITES (commonly known as Byblos). Situated north of Beirut, Lebanon, Gebal was the most important port on the Phoenician coast in the 3rd and 2nd millennia B.C. By the time of the Israelite settlement in Canaan and the establishment of the kingdom, its importance had declined, and it receives only passing mention in the Bible, which records that Gebalites participated in Solomon's work force (I Kgs 5:18) and that they were considered experts in the caulking of ships (Ezek 27:9). Gebal was never conquered by the Israelites (Josh 13:5), and it is mentioned by the psalmist (Ps 83:7) among those seeking to destroy Israel.

For centuries, Gebal was the main port for trade between Egypt and the Levant. Its exports included various kinds of wood, including the famed cedar of Lebanon, which were vital for Egyptian architects, shipbuilders and craftsmen, and resins of great ritual importance, used in the process of mummification. In return, Gebal received a wealth of Egyptian luxury items, and gifts to its rulers and temples.

Frequent mention of Gebal in Egyptian texts, and the incorporation of Baalat Gebal — Gebal's patron goddess — into the Egyptian pantheon as the Asian Hathor testify to the close relations between Egypt and Gebal. In latter years, the declining position of Egypt in Asia was well documented in the EL AMARNA LETTERS from Gebal (14th century), and in the Tale of Wen-Amun (11th century).

Over 50 years of excavations at Gebal have revealed virtually continuous settlement at the site from the Neolithic to the Crusader period. The outstanding finds include massive fortifications of the 3rd millennium B.C., a series of temples to the local deities with rich foundation deposits, and inscriptions in syllabic and alphabetic scripts, the most notable being that of King Ahiram (cf Hiram), of the 11th century B.C.

A coin of Gebal-Byblos, depicting a winged Kronos with a Phoenician inscription "Gebal the holy". 82 B.C.

GEBER ("man").

1. Father of the governor of the sixth administrative district of Solomon. He was in charge of the towns of Jair in Gilead and the region of Argob in Bashan.

2. The son of Uri, Geber was governor of the 12th administrative district of Solomon, "in the country of Sihon king of the Amorites and Og king of Bashan".

GEBIM A place mentioned only in Isaiah's description of the route taken by the Assyrian army on its march to Jerusalem. According to some scholars it was a Benjamite city.

GECKO See ANIMALS

GEDALIAH ("God is mighty").

1. A Levite, son of Jeduthun. He appears in a list of singers from the time of David.

2. Son of Amariah, grandfather of the prophet Zephaniah.

3. Son of Pashur. A minister in Judah in the time of King Zedekiah.

Agate Hebrew seal inscribed "[Belonging] to Gedalyahu son of Samach". Late 8th-7th centuries B.C. (Israel Museum)

He was among those in favor of continuing the rebellion against Babylon and advised King Zedekiah to sentence the prophet Jeremiah to death for his oracles advocating surrender to Babylon.

4. Son of Ahikam (Jer 40:6). A member of a family of ministers and high functionaries in the Kingdom of Judah. After the fall of Jerusalem to the Babylonians and the destruction of the First Temple (586 B.C.) Gedaliah was appointed as the governor of Judah, with a small force of Babylonian soldiers seconded to him (II Kgs 25:23). Gedaliah chose the city of Mizpah as his residence and issued a general amnesty to the remnants of the army of Judah and its commanders. He was subsequently murdered by Ishmach, son of Nethaniah, who was aided by Baalis, king of the Ammonites (II Kgs 25:25). This assassination spelled the end of self-government in Judah for a long period. In commemoration of this event a fast day was instituted in the Jewish calendar, falling the day after the *Rosh Hashanah* (New Year) festival.

GEDALIAH 4
II Kgs 25:22-25. Jer 39:14; 40:5-9, 11-16; 41:1-4, 6, 9-10, 16, 18; 43:6

5. One of the priests who divorced his alien wife at the decree of Ezra.

GEDALIAH 5
Ezra 10:18

GEDER A place in Canaan; the king of Geder is mentioned among the 21 Canaanite kings vanquished by Joshua, listed after the king of Debir, and before the kings of Hormah and Arad (Josh 12:13-14). The site of the city is unknown. It could have been located either in the vicinity of Gezer, which would place it on the western slopes of the Judean Hills, or further south, in the region between the southern Judean Hills, and the northern Negeb.

GEDER
Josh 12:13

GEDERAH ("fence", "hedge").

1. A city or place which fell to the lot of the tribe of Judah when the land of Canaan was divided among the tribes. It was in the northern plain of Judah but its exact location is unknown. May be the same as Gederoth.

GEDERAH 1
Josh 15:36

2. Gederah is mentioned again in the genealogy of the family of Judah (I Chr 4:23) but most scholars believe the word should be read as the name of a person and not of a place.

GEDERAH 2
I Chr 4:23

GEDERATHITE A man of Gederah No.1; the home of Jozabad, one of David's "mighty men".

GEDERATHITE
I Chr 12:4

GEDERITE A man of Geder, or perhaps Gederah; the home of Baal-Hanan, a state official at the time of King David.

GEDERITE
I Chr 27:28

GEDEROTH A city in the Judean western hill country (Shephelah) (Josh 15:41). Gederoth was one of the cities seized from Judah by the Philistines in the time of King Ahaz.

GEDEROTH
Josh 15:41. II Chr 28:18

GEDEROTHAIM This city appears in a list of towns in the tribe of Judah. It follows the town of Gederah, leading to suggestions that the name may be a dittography. However, if such a city did exist, it should be placed in the vicinity of Gederah.

GEDEROTHAIM
Josh 15:36

GEDOR

GEDOR 1
Josh 15:58

1. A city in the mountainous region of Judah located about 7 miles (12 km) north of Hebron.

GEDOR 2
I Chr 4:4

2. Son of Penuel of the family of Judah.

3. Son of Jered, likewise descended from Judah.

GEDOR 3
I Chr 4:18

4. A valley rich in pasture lying in the territory of Simeon.

5. Son of Jeiel, member of the tribe of Benjamin; he lived in Gibeon.

GEDOR 4
I Chr 4:39

6. A city in Judah, possibly located at Khirbet el-Gudeira, about 10 miles (16 km) northwest of Jerusalem. Joelah and Zebadiah, who joined the fugitive David's army, were sons of Jeroham of Gedor.

GEDOR 5
I Chr 8:31; 9:37

GE-HARASHIM ("the valley of craftsmen").

1. A valley occupied by a Kenazite clan of craftsmen, whose father (or founder) was Joab, of the tribe of Judah (I Chr 4:14).

GEDOR 6
I Chr 12:7

The place may be located in the northern part of Wadi el-Arabah which was rich in copper and iron mines during ancient times.

GE-HARASHIM 1
I Chr 4:14

GE-HARASHIM 2
Neh 11:35

2. A place near Ono and Lod resettled by the Benjamites, at the time of Nehemiah (Neh 11:35); probably identified with Sarafand el-Kharab in the Plain of Sharon.

GEHAZI
II Kgs 4:12, 14, 25, 27, 29, 31, 36; 5:20-21, 25; 8:4-5

GEHAZI The servant of the prophet Elisha. He is mentioned in only three episodes. In the story about the Shunammite woman, it was Gehazi who suggested to the prophet, that the birth of a son would be a reward for her hospitality (II Kgs 4:12-14). Later he ran before Elisha to put the prophet's staff on the face of her dead child (II Kgs 4:25-31). Gehazi is mentioned again in the story of Naaman, where Elisha cursed him with leprosy for taking the gifts which the prophet had rejected (II Kgs 5:20-27). Later Gehazi told Jehoram, king of Israel, of all the great deeds his master had accomplished (II Kgs 8:4-5).

GEHENNA According to the NT and rabbinic literature, a place where the dead are to be judged; the abode of the wicked.

The name (given as hell in the KJV) is derived from the Valley of the Sons of Hinnom, southwest of Jerusalem. In biblical times this was the site of a cult where children were burned as offerings to the god Moloch (II Kgs 23:10). The prophet Jeremiah, condemning these idolatrous practices, predicted that the valley would be known as the "Valley of Slaughter" (Jer 7:31; 19:5-6).

The Valley of Hinnom, southwest of Jerusalem.

In the NT Gehenna (hell in the KJV) is seen as a place of unquenchable fire (Matt 5:22; Mark 9:43-47). God has the authority to cast wicked men into this hell (Matt 10:28; Luke 12:5) in whose fire he can destroy the soul and the body. Jesus taught that it is better to forfeit vital limbs or organs than to lose the whole body by being flung into hell (Matt 5:29; Mark 9:43). According to Mark, Gehenna is a place where the devouring worm never dies and the fire is not quenched (Mark 9:47). Only the wicked will be thrown into the blazing furnace, the place of wailing and gnashing of teeth (Matt 13:50). Although it is full of fire, there is no light in Gehenna, but only darkness (Matt 8:12).

See ABADDON, HADES, SHEOL.

GELILOTH
Josh 18:17

GELILOTH See GILGAL No.4

GEMALLI
Num 13:12

GEMALLI A man of Dan, father of Ammiel (Num 13:12) who was among the men chosen by Moses in the wilderness of Paran to spy out the land of Canaan (Num 13:2-3, 17).

GEMARIAH ("the Lord has accomplished").

GEMARIAH 1
Jer 29:3

1. The son of Hilkiah; Zedekiah king of Judah sent him to Nebuchadnezzar king of Babylon to carry a letter to the exiles.

2. The son of Shaphan the scribe (Jer 36:10). It was in his chamber — "in the upper court at the entry of the New Gate of the Lord's house" — that Baruch read from the scroll of Jeremiah (Jer 36:10). Later he vainly implored the king not to burn the scroll (Jer 36:25). He was the father of Michaiah (Jer 36:11).

GEMARIAH 2
Jer 36:10-12, 25

GENESIS, BOOK OF The first of the five books of the Pentateuch; it derives it name from the Septuagint reference to the opening theme of the entire book. Its 50 chapters cover the period from the creation of the world until the death of Joseph.

The book itself does not ascribe its composition to anyone, but its divinely-inspired Mosaic authorship, accepted by Jews, was taken over by Christianity. However, anachronisms within the text, duplications of stories (sometimes with marked differences) and differing names for God, have led modern critical scholars to deduce that the book is a composite work based on three main sources or traditions. One source, called P, contains material of priestly origin. The two others, designated J and E (J, representing material from Judah, employs the tetragrammaton Jehovah (Jahweh); E, stemming from Ephraim, northern Israel, employs the Hebrew generic term for God, Elohim), are of non-priestly origin. These various documents (oral and written) contain differences of language, style and religious standpoint which can be traced elsewhere in the Pentateuch (See PENTATEUCH). Some think that each source represented a different stream or school of thought in Israel, and there is still wide debate over their time of composition.

Fragments from the Book of Genesis found at Qumran. (Shrine of the Book, Jerusalem)

The book is divided into three sections: the first concerns the history of the universe and God's relation to it, as well as primordial human history (chaps. 1-11); the second, the history of the patriarchs (chaps. 12-36); and the third, the Joseph saga (chaps. 37-50).

The first section, chapters 1-11, opens with chapters 1-2:3, (ascribed to P) recording the creation of the world. The process is described as spanning seven days with the creation of light on the first day (1:3-5), the sky on the second (1:6-8), the sea, land and vegetation on the third (1:9-13), the heavenly bodies on the fourth (1:14-19), fish and birds on the fifth (1:20-23), land animals and man on the sixth (1:24-31), and on the seventh day when all was complete, God rested from all his work, blessed the day and sanctified it (2:1-3).

The beginnings of the human race are described in the story of the Garden of Eden (2:4-3:24), (assigned to J — E), along with another account of the creation of man and woman and a description of their surroundings. Man's freedom was put to the test (3:1-8), and after both man and woman had sinned by eating the forbidden fruit of the tree of knowledge, they were cursed (3:9-12), and expelled from the Garden (3:22-24). Chapters 4 and 5 concern the children of Adam and Eve including the murder of Abel by Cain (4:1-16).

The great flood is the subject of chapters 6:9-9:29 (See FLOOD).

Chapter 10 traces the nations of the earth to the three sons of Noah. The principal races and peoples known to the Israelites are arranged as if they were different branches of this one family. Chapter 11:1-9 describes the building of a tower in Babylon for which God punished men with the division of the hitherto universal language into various languages (See BABEL).

The first part of the second section, chapters 12-36, deals with the life of the patriarch Abraham (then called Abram) (12:1-15:18), beginning with his call by God to migrate from Mesopotamia to Canaan (12:1-9). As a result of a famine he was forced to move to Egypt where his wife Sarah (then called Sarai) was taken by the pharaoh, who released her only after being stricken by a mysterious plague. After this incident Abraham returned to Canaan (12:10-20). His nephew Lot, who migrated with him, left his company and settled in Sodom following a dispute over grazing lands (chap. 13).

Chapter 14 describes the war of the kings during which Lot was captured. Abraham organized a rescue party and succeeded in freeing his nephew. Chapter 15 vividly describes the pact between God and Abraham, in which, among other matters, the latter was promised an heir. The following chapter describes the circumstances of the birth of Ishmael by Abraham's concubine, Hagar. Abraham entered into a second covenant with God, which he symbolized by circumcising himself, his son Ishmael, his servants and slaves, as well as undertaking circumcision for his descendants. At this point God changed his name to Abraham and that of his wife to Sarah.

Chapters 18 and 19 concern the destruction of the cities of Sodom and Gomorrah. This story begins with the visit of three angels to Abraham (18:1-16) and their confirmation of God's promise of a child for Sarah. Abraham, informed of the impending destruction, interceded for Sodom asking that the city be saved on the merit of the righteous (18:17-33). The angels then proceeded to Sodom where they met Lot; warning him of the imminent calamity, they persuaded him to escape with his family. Only his wife and daughters fled with him, but his wife turned into a pillar of salt when she looked back at the city (19:26).

When Sarah gave birth to Isaac, difficulties arose between Sarah and Hagar, ending in the dismissal of Hagar and Ishmael from Abraham's household (21:1-21).

Chapter 22 describes how God put Abraham's fidelity to the test by ordering him to offer up his son Isaac as a sacrifice. Abraham responded to the request which, however, was withdrawn at the last moment, a ram being sacrificed instead.

Chapter 23 concerns the death and burial of Sarah. Abraham purchased from Ephron the Hittite the cave of Machpelah to serve as her burial site. Subsequently Abraham's servant was sent to find a wife for his master's son, Isaac; divine guidance led him to Rebekah (chap. 24). Abraham died at the age of 175 and was buried alongside his wife Sarah (25:8-10).

The section concerning the third of the patriarchs begins with the

GENNESARET
Matt 14:34
Mark 6:53
Luke 5:1

GENUBATH
I Kgs 11:2

GERA 1
Gen 46:21

GERA 2
I Chr 8:3,

GERA 3
I Chr 8:7

GERA 4
II Sam 16
19:16, 18.
Kgs 2:8

GERA 5
Judg 3:15

GERAR The most important city district in the western Negeb lying in the valley of Gerar, near the southern border of Canaan.

The patriarchs found pasture for their flocks in the land of Gerar whose king, Abimelech desired Sarah, but sent her away after discovering her relationship to Abraham; he granted Abraham permission to dwell in his country (Gen chap. 20). A similar incident is described when Isaac sought refuge at Gerar during the drought. After clashes with the local herdsmen over water sources, Isaac concluded a covenant with Gerar's king, likewise named Abimelech (Gen 26:28). The term "Philistine" used in this context is anachronistic.

It is probable that the Septuagint reading "Gerar" for Mount Gedor (I Chr 4:39) is correct. The passage describes the expansion of the tribe of Simeon into the rich pastures of the land of Gerar. The only other mention of Gerar in the OT is in II Chronicles 14:13-14. Zerah the Ethiopian, defeated near Mareshah, is pursued by Asa as far as Gerar.

Gerar is identified with Tell Abu Haseireh (Tell Haror) c. 12 miles (20 km) west of Beersheba. Excavations have uncovered remains from the Chalcolithic period, Bronze and Iron Ages and the Persian period.

GERGESA A place on the eastern shore of the Sea of Galilee, between Susita and Bethsaida, "the country of the Gergesenes", where according to some readings of Matthew Jesus cast out devils (Matt 8:28 ff), (See GADARA). Gergesa was known by the name of Kursi in Jewish sources. Origen and Eusebius (*Onom.* 73:14) mention a village by the name of Gergesai near the Lake of Tiberias, in which the swine drowned. A large monastery and church have been excavated at Kursi which make it probable that in Byzantine times this was regarded as the scene of the incident.

GERGESENES See GERGESA

GERIZIM Mount Gerizim, about 2,900 feet (880 m) high, towers over the valley of Shechem, which lies between it and Mount Ebal to the north. It was at this place that the Israelites were commanded to assemble in order to hear the blessing pronounced on Gerizim, and the curse on Ebal (Deut 11:29; 27:12; Josh 8:33); from Gerizim Jotham offered his parable to the elders of Shechem in the town below (Judg 9:7).

GERAR
Gen 10:19;
20:1-2; 26:1,
6, 17, 20,
26. II Chr
14:13-14

GERGESENES
Matt 8:28

GERIZIM
Deut 11:29;
27:12. Josh
8:33. Judg 9:7

Remains of a 6th-century church at Kursi (Gergesa).

View of the summit of Mount Gerizim where remains of a Byzantine church can be seen.

In later times, Gerizim became the Samaritan religious center, and the biblical traditions of the altar built by Joshua on Ebal were transferred there.

A Samaritan temple, probably built to rival the Second Temple in Jerusalem, existed there during the Persian and Hellenistic periods, and was destroyed by John Hyrcanus in 129 B.C. (recent excavations on Gerizim have uncovered a monumental structure of the Hellenistic period which could be this temple). The existence of this religious center is reflected in the story of the visit by Jesus to Samaria (John chap. 4), on his way to Galilee; here he is told by the Samaritan woman that her fathers "worshiped on this mountain" that is, Mount Gerizim (John 4:20).

Mount Gerizim depicted on a coin of Neapolis (Shechem). 3rd century A.D.

GERSHOM, GERSHON (The names interchange but are apparently identical).

1. Firstborn son of Levi and the father of a family of Levites, the Gershonites, who carried the external appurtenances of the tabernacle (Num 3:25-26; 4:24-26).

2. Eldest son of Moses and Zipporah, born in Midian. He was the forbear of Jonathan who was the father of a family of priests at the altar in the city of Dan. His name should be read Gershom son of Moses instead of Manasseh.

3. A descendant of Phinehas; he was among those who returned with Ezra from Babylonian Exile.

GERSHONITES The clans and family houses descended from Gershon, the eldest son of Levi, by his sons Libni (Laadan, I Chr 23:7; 26:21) and Shimei (Ex 6:17; Num 3:18; I Chr 6:17, 20). Of the three Levite families, the Kohathites, Merarites and Gershonites, the latter are generally listed first, thus indicating their predominant status (Gen 46:11; Ex 6:16-17; Num 3:17; 26:57; I Chr 6:1, 16; 23:6). Thus they appear first in the census notation (Num 26:57) and in the list of functionaries in the Temple (I Chr 23:7-11ff). However, in a few passages the order is changed and the Kohathites lead the list (e.g. Num chap. 4; I Chr 15:4-7).

In the tent of meeting in the wilderness, the Gershonites were in charge of the external properties of the tabernacle: the tent, the covering, the screen for the door and the hanging of the court (Num 3:25-26; 4:24-26). In the census taken by Moses in the desert, they numbered 7,500 males from one month old and upward (Num 3:21-22). In Canaan they received 13 cities inclusive of their pasture lands from the tribes of Issachar, Asher, Naphtali and the half-tribe of Manasseh (Josh 21:27-32).

The Gershonites are mentioned for the last time in the list of those who cleansed the Temple in the days of King Hezekiah (II Chr 29:12). They do not appear in the list of Levites who functioned in the days of Josiah (II Chr 34:12).

GESHAM See GESHAN

GESHAN Third son of Jahdai in the genealogy of Caleb. The name is sometimes spelt Gesham.

GESHEM ("the Arab"). Among the opponents of Nehemiah, in collusion with Sanballat the Horonite and Tobiah the Ammonite (Neh 2:19). Together they opposed the rebuilding of the walls of Jerusalem and planned several ways of harming Nehemiah, who, however, evaded their traps (Neh 6:1-2).

GESHUR, GESHURITES

1. A region near Bashan (Deut 3:14) not conquered by Joshua (Josh 13:13). When the Kingdom of Judah was established a small Aramean state was founded at Geshur. David married the daughter of Talmai,

king of Geshur (II Sam 3:3) and Absalom found refuge there after killing Amnon (II Sam 13:37-38). The Geshurite kingdom had ceased to exist by the 9th century B.C. Its territory is identified with the area which extends along the eastern shore of the Sea of Galilee and the northern bank of the River Yarmuk.

2. Inhabitants of a land in the territory of the Philistines (Josh 13:2). Their land was raided by David while he was a fugitive from King Saul (I Sam 27:8).

GETHER Third son of Aram, the fifth son of Shem (Gen 10:23) or the eighth son of Shem (I Chr 1:17). Nothing is known about him.

GETHSEMANE A garden on the Mount of Olives, (John 18:1). Jesus went there from the place of the Last Supper (Matt 26:30, 36; Mark 14:26-32). The name derives from the Hebrew *gath shemanim* ("oil presses"). Tradition places the garden to the east of the Temple Mount, on the slope above the Kidron Valley.

13:37-38;
14:23, 32;
15:8. I Chr
2:23; 3:2

GESHUR,
GESHURITES 2
Josh 13:2.
I Sam 27:8

GETHER
Gen 10:23. I
Chr 1:17

GETHSEMANE
Matt 26:36.
Mark 14:32

Gethsemane on the Mount of Olives.

GEUEL Son of Machi, from the tribe of Gad (Num 13:15); he was among the men chosen by Moses in the wilderness of Paran (Num 13:3) to spy out the land of Canaan (Num 13:2).

GEZER One of the most important cities in the coastal plain, situated at a junction on the roads from Egypt to Syria, and from the sea coast to the mountains. Under the name of Gazri, it is mentioned in the El Amarna Letters, and in Pharaoh Merneptah's list of conquests in Canaan on the eve of the Exodus.

King Horam of Gezer came to the help of Lachish when Joshua made war against that city (Josh 10:33), and is later mentioned among the 31 kings of Canaan subdued by Joshua (Josh 12:12). Despite this, Gezer still remained a Canaanite city within the territory of Ephraim, though it was required to pay tribute (Josh 16:10; Judg 1:29). David smote the Philistines "as far as Gezer" (II Sam 5:25; I Chr 14:16). In Solomon's time, "the pharaoh king of Egypt had gone up, and taken Gezer, and burnt it with fire, and slain the Canaanites that dwelt in the city, and given it for a present unto his daughter, Solomon's wife" (I Kgs 9:16); Solomon built one of his royal cities at Gezer (I Kgs 9:15, 17). The city declined in the later days of the Kingdom of Judah, apparently after its destruction by Pharaoh Shishak. The conquest of Gezer is subsequently described in the reliefs of Tiglath-Pileser III. It was repopulated by

GEUEL
Num 13:15

GEZER
Josh 10:33;
12:12; 16:3,
10; 21:21.
Judg 1:29.
II Sam 5:25.
I Kgs 9:15-17.
I Chr 6:67;
7:28; 14:16;
20:4

Assyrians and settlers belonging to other nations, as well as remnants of Israelite farmers. Under Persian rule and at the beginning of the Hellenistic period Gezer recovered, becoming an important border town between the satrapies of Ashdod and Judah (I Macc 14:34). In 142 B.C. it was conquered by Simon Maccabee, who fortified the city and built his home there (I Macc 13:43-48). In the Roman period it declined and was abandoned.

Gezer was first excavated at the beginning of the century, with important epigraphic finds, such as the "Gezer Potsherd" written in Proto-Sinaitic script (early 2nd millennium B.C.), cuneiform tablets from the El Amarna period and the Neo-Assyrian period (7th century B.C.) and the Hebrew Gezer Calendar from the late 10th century B.C. Six border stones inscribed with the name "Gezer" in Hebrew and Greek, belonging to the Hellenistic period were also uncovered. More recent excavations have investigated the city's fortifications of the

Middle Bronze Age IIc (c. 1600 B.C.), Late Bronze Age I, Solomon's casemate walls and gate, and the Maccabean fortifications. The "Gezer High-Place", uncovered at the beginning of the century, was excavated again. It consists of ten enormous stone stelae, some more than 9 feet (3 m) high, set in a north-south line on an open square; it is now dated to c. 1600 B.C.

Gold Astarte found at Gezer. 14th century B.C.

(left)
Standing stones on a Bronze Age "high place" at Gezer. They are part of a row of ten monoliths probably used for cultic purposes.

Gibbethon, west of Gezer.

GIBBAR
Ezra 2:20

GIBBAR ("hero"?). The people of Gibbar, 95 in number, are listed among the captives who returned from Babylon with Zerubbabel. The parallel text in Nehemiah reads the "people of Gibeon" (Neh 7:25). Scholars disagree as to which form is correct, and whether this is the name of a family or place.

GIBBETHON
Josh 19:44;
21:23. I Kgs
15:27; 16:15,
17

GIBBETHON A west central city that lay on the border between Israel and Philistia. It was annexed to Israel at the expense of Philistine territory in the 10th century B.C. It appears in the list of the cities allotted to the tribe of Dan (Josh 19:44) and was one of the four Levitical cities in Dan (Josh 21:23). The clan of Kehath was settled in Gibbethon among the mainly non-Israelite population, and administered what became royal lands after their conquest as well as collected taxes (cf I Chr 26:30-32). After the destruction of the United Monarchy, Jeroboam expelled the Levites, who returned to Judah (II Chr 11:13-14). After the partition, Gibbethon is twice mentioned in the

Book of Kings as a Philistine city that was besieged by the Israelites, first by Nadab son of Jeroboam, king of Israel (I Kgs 15:27). At the end of the reign of Elah son of Baasha, news of Zimri's revolt reached the Israelite forces encamped against Gibbethon, who then raised their commander, Omri, as king (I Kgs 16:15-28). In 712 B.C. it was conquered by Sargon, king of Assyria.

Gibbethon has been identified with Tell Melat, a $2\frac{1}{2}$ acre (1 ha) mound, located 3 miles (5 km) west of Gezer.

GIBEA ("hill"). A city or place founded by Sheva, the son of Caleb by his concubine Maachah. May be the same as Gibeah.

GIBEAH ("hill" or "height").

1. A city of the Benjamites which lay on both sides of the main highway along the watershed that linked the land of Judah and Jerusalem to the hills of Ephraim (Judg 19:11-13). The Book of Judges ends with the story of a fraternal war between Benjamin and the other Israelite tribes following the rape of the concubine of a Levite at the hands of the people of Gibeah, or "Gibeah which belongs to Benjamin", during which Gibeah was destroyed. While the story reflects the general situation in the period of the Judges (cf Judg 21:25) the historical circumstances of the war remain obscure.

Saul came from Gibeah and I Samuel 10:26 states that Saul went home to Gibeah immediately after he was proclaimed king. Messengers were sent from Jabesh Gilead to Gibeah of Saul (I Sam 11:4).

During the Philistine hegemony a Philistine garrison was stationed at Geba (I Sam 13:3), also known as Gibeath-Elohim ("the hill of God") (I Sam 10:5). It was assaulted by Jonathan, son of Saul, during the early part of his father's reign, and served to signal the Israelite revolt against the Philistines in the central hill country. Geba-Gibeath-Elohim is variously identified with Gibeah and Gibeon. After his military victory over the Philistines, Saul made Gibeah his capital and its name became Gibeah-Saul (I Sam 15:34).

Ithai, the son of Ribai, from Gibeah of the Benjamites was one of David's warriors (II Sam 23:29; I Chr 11:31), and according to I Chronicles 12:3, Ahiezer and Joash, the sons of Shemaah of Gibeah were among those of Saul's kinsmen who joined David in Ziklag. Micaiah, the daughter of Uriel, who was the mother of Abijah, king of Judah, was from Gibeah (II Chr 13:2). Isaiah envisioned Gibeah-Saul

GIBEA
I Chr 2:49

GIBEAH
Josh 15:57.
Judg 19:12-16;
20:4-5, 9-10,
13-15, 19-21,
25, 29-31, 34,
36-37, 43.
I Sam 10:26;
11:4; 13:2, 15-
16; 14:2, 5,
16; 15:34;
22:6; 23:19;
26:1. II Sam
21:6; 23:29.
I Chr 11:31. II
Chr 13:2. Is
10:29. Hos
5:8; 9:9; 10:9

Gibeah identified with Tell el-Ful, north of Jerusalem.

standing in the path of the Assyrian army's advance from the north on Jerusalem during Sennacherib's campaign in 701 B.C. (Is 10:29).

Little is known about Gibeah from later periods. According to Jerome, Gibeah was "a town destroyed to the ground".

There is virtual agreement that Gibeah of Saul (or Gibeah-Saul) is to be located at Tell el-Ful, 3 miles (5 km) north of Jerusalem. Archeological excavations have revealed a series of superimposed fortresses, beginning in the 11th century B.C. In all, five major periods of occupation were discovered.

2. A city in the hill country of Judah (Josh 15:57; cf I Chr 2:49), whose suggested location has been proposed as el-Jeba, $7\frac{1}{2}$ miles (12 km) southwest of Bethlehem; however, it should probably be sought in the Judean Hills south of Beth Zur and Hebron.

GIBEATH See GIBEAH No.2

GIBEATHITE Appellation of Shemaah who came from Gibeah No.1.

GIBEON, GIBEONITES One of the most ancient Canaanite cities. In the Bible it is referred to as one of the four Hivite cities (Josh 9:17), a great city, one of the royal cities, "greater than Ai, and all its men were mighty" (Josh 10:2). Although the Gibeonites were condemned by Joshua to perpetual bondage (Josh chap. 9), he nevertheless made an

The hill of el-Jib, the site of Gibeon, north of Jerusalem.

alliance with the city (Josh 9:17-18). The king of Jerusalem and his allies were vanquished by Joshua at Gibeon (Josh chap. 10) and it was on that occasion that Joshua made the sun stand still (Josh 10:12-13). "They drove back the army of the Philistines from Gibeon as far as Gezer" (I Chr 14:16). The men of Joab and of Abner fought each other near the pool of Gibeon, at a place called Helkath Hazzurim "the Field of Sharp Swords" from then on (II Sam 2:12-17). There was a great high place at Gibeon where Solomon offered a sacrifice and prayed for wisdom (I Kgs 3:4 ff; II Chr 1:3 ff). Johanan, son of Kareah, fought Ishmael, son of Nethaniah, "by the great pool that is in Gibeon" (Jer 41:11-12). After the return from Babylon the Gibeonites took part in rebuilding the walls of Jerusalem (Neh 3:7).

Gibeon is identified with el-Jib, about 8 miles (13 km) northwest of Jerusalem, on the way to Beth Horon, which was excavated in 1957-62. Except for some traces of settlement in the Late Bronze Age all the remains on the site are from the Iron Age and later periods. The main discoveries were the fortifications, a large pool, two water tunnels, wine cellars, some houses and a large amount of epigraphic material which confirms the identification of the site.

GIBEATH
Josh 18:28

GIBEATHITE
I Chr 12:3

GIBEON,
GIBEONITES
Josh 9:3, 17; 10:1-2, 4-6, 10, 12, 41; 11:19; 18:25; 21:17. II Sam 2:12-13, 16, 24; 3:30; 20:8; 21:1-4, 9. I Kgs 3:4-5; 9:2. I Chr 8:29; 9:35; 12:4; 14:16; 16:39; 21:29. II Chr 1:3, 13. Neh 3:7; 7:25. Is 28:21. Jer 28:1; 41:12, 16

The Pool of Gibeon.

The rock-cut pool is 37 feet (11 m) in diameter and 82 feet (25 m) deep. A spiral stairway of 79 steps, also cut into the rock, leads down to the bottom. The excavators believe that the pool was used either for storing rain-water or to provide better access to the water-table. It may possibly be identified with the one referred to in II Samuel (2:12-17) and Jeremiah (41:12). The two water tunnels lie at a short distance from the pool. At the spot where the large spring of Gibeon gushed out from the mountain a small reservoir in the form of a cave had been excavated below the surface level of the flowing water. From this reservoir a tunnel was excavated to the source of the spring itself, which is 180 feet (55 m) inside the mountain. Thus a good supply of water was ensured in times of war, while water could be drawn from the spring in times of peace. In order to ensure safe access to the spring in emergencies, a second tunnel was excavated from within the city wall. The excavators date this water-supply system to the 10th century B.C. The spring is still used today.

The finding of numerous jar handles stamped with the seal of Gibeon led to the discovery of wine cellars, consisting of a number of simple winepresses, each with a treading floor on the rock and a basin to collect the juice. The wine was made in 11 wine cellars. The capacity of some of the wine cellars was up to 5,000 wine jars and their total storage capacity was about 25,000 gallons (approx. 94,500 liters).

GIDDALTI A Levite; one of the sons of Heman (I Chr 25:4); the word is probably a verb which is part of a hymn and not a proper name. Having drawn the 22nd lot (I Chr 25:29) he headed the 22nd group of 12 musicians who served in the House of the Lord in the time of King David.

GIDDALTI
I Chr 25:4, 29

GIDDEL The name of two families of exiles:

1. A family of Nethinim (Temple servants) who returned from the Exile in Babylon together with Zerubbabel and settled in Jerusalem (Ezra 2:43, 47).

GIDDEL 1
Ezra 2:47.
Neh 7:49

2. A family of "the sons of Solomon's servants" (Ezra 2:55-56) who returned from the Exile in Babylon with Zerubbabel and settled in Jerusalem.

GIDDEL 2
Ezra 2:56.
Neh 7:58

GIDEON ("he who casts down"). The son of Joash the Abiezrite from Ophrah (Judg 6:11); Israel's fourth major judge in the period between the death of Joshua and the institution of the monarchy. Fulfilling no judiciary role, the judges were individuals imbued with the spirit of God who headed military campaigns to free Israel from periodic foreign oppression.

GIDEON
Judg 6:11, 13,
19, 22, 24, 27,
29, 34, 36, 39;
7:1-2, 4-5, 7,
13-15, 18-20,
24-25; 8:4, 7,
11, 13, 21-24,
27-28, 30, 32-
33, 35. Heb
11:32

Gideon had several wives, and it is related that he had 70 sons, one of them, Abimelech, by a concubine in Shechem (Judg 8:30-31). He was also known as Jerubbaal, "let Baal contend" (Judg 6:32; I Sam 2:11), a name he acquired after overturning an altar to Baal which had been built by the Israelites (Judg 6:24-32). For this idolatrous behavior, it was held, God had set the Midianites against Israel (Judg 6:11).

Gideon was called to be a judge by an angel and later by a miracle involving wet and dry fleece (Judg 6:11-24, 36-40). His task was to deliver Israel from the Midianites, the Amalekites and the children of the East (Judg 6:3). With an army of 300 men, selected out of 22,000 by means of several selective tests, Gideon defeated the Midianites in a night attack (Judg 7:3-25). The Midianite princes Oreb and Zeeb were captured and beheaded (Judg 7:25), and Gideon also pursued the kings Zebah and Zalmunna until he captured and killed them (Judg 8:5-21).

After the pursuit Gideon returned to Succoth where he took the elders of the city and tortured them with the thorns of the wilderness because the men of Succoth and Penuel, out of fear of Zebah and Zalmunna, had refused to provide Gideon's men with bread (Judg 8:5-

8, 16). Gideon beat down the tower of Penuel and slew the men of the city (Judg 8:17). His victory over the Midianites was remembered for many generations as the "Day of Midian" (Is 9:4).

The men of Israel requested Gideon to be their ruler, but he refused saying that only God is the ruler of Israel (Judg 8:22). Instead he returned to his home and lived to an old age. He was buried in Ophrah in the sepulcher of Joash his father (Judg 8:29-32).

GIDEONI The father of Abidan who was the head of a clan of the tribe of Benjamin and led the tribe in the wilderness.

GIDOM The place where 2,000 of the best warriors of Benjamin were killed in the course of the punitive war waged by all the tribes of Israel against Benjamin following the crime in Gibeah. The exact location of the place is unknown though it was close to the rock of Rimmon.

GIFT In the Hebrew Bible, the idea of gift is mostly expressed by the verb *ntn* (which appears more than 2,000 times). The giver is first of all God: man, or the people of God, is the principal receiver. This conviction appears in the various theophoric names, like Nathan, Natanael, Natanayah(u), Jonatan, Elnatan ("God, or Yhwh, gives"). God's gifts are realized in creation and in history. The Creator gives to men breath (Is 42:5); the days of life (Ps 39:5; Ecc 5:12); food (Gen 1:29; 9:3; Ps 136:25); and happiness in this life (Job 1:21; Ecc 5:18). But the gift of God is still more manifest in history. To the seed of Abraham, God gives the land of Canaan (Gen 12:7), and he confirms his promise by an oath (Gen 15:18). Deuteronomy repeats as a refrain that this land is given (Deut 4:40; 5:31; 6:23; 7:13; 8:10; 11:17; 12:1; etc), without any merit of the people (Deut 9:6). God also gives the Law to his people (Ex 24:12; 31:18; 34:32; Deut 5:22; Neh 9:13). When the people become unfaithful, God gives them up to their enemies (Neh 9:27, 30), but, in his mercy, he announces his gift of the interiorized law (Jer 31:33); a new life (Ezek 37:6); a new heart (Ezek 36:26); and his own spirit in them (Ezek 36:27; 37:14). To certain members of the people, God concedes special gifts: wisdom to Solomon (I Kgs 3:12); his judgment to the king (Ps 72:1); and the book of prophecies to Ezekiel (Ezek 3:3).

A man has some things to give to God in exchange: the firstborn of his sons will be consecrated to God, and the firstborn of his flock will be given in sacrifice (Ex 22:28-29). Nobody will appear before the Lord empty-handed (Ex 23:15); however, the verb 'give' is rarely used of a man's gift to God (Ps 51:18; Lev 22:22).

Between themselves, members of the people ought not to give a bribe (Ex 23:8; Is 5:23), but honest gifts confirm the mutual covenant (Gen 32:13-14; II Sam 17:27-29). They must give generously to the poor (Deut 15:7-11; Prov 3:27-28).

In the NT the concept of gift is mostly expressed by the Greek verb *didomi* (which appears 400 times). Again the gift of God is emphasized: "every perfect gift is from above" (James 1:17). Jesus urges man to acknowledge the gift of God (John 4:10). In love, God gives his only son (John 3:16), to whom he gives all things (John 3:35). To him he gives the disciples (John chap. 17). On his side, Jesus gives himself; his life (Matt 20:28; John 15:13), and his flesh for the world's life (John 6:51). He gives his new commandment of love (John 13:34). After his departure, his Father gives the Spirit to the disciples (John 14:16-17). In the community, "the manifestation of the Spirit is given to each" for the common good (I Cor 12:7; Eph 4:7). On his side, the disciple is invited to give to him who begs (Matt 5:42), and to give without pay (Matt 10:8). To the rich, searching for perfection, Jesus proposes that he give all his wealth to the poor and follow him (Matt 19:21). "It is more blessed to give than to receive" (Acts 20:35).

The Spring of Gihon.

GIHON

1. One of the four rivers flowing from the Garden of Eden, "which encompasses the whole land of Ethiopia" (Gen 2:13). It is most probably a legendary river, although some suggest that it should be identified with the Nile.

2. A spring in the valley of Kidron, the most important source of water for Jerusalem in ancient times, today called ed-Darag. It was the site of Solomon's coronation (I Kgs 1:33). As early as the pre-Israelite period an attempt was made to connect the spring by a tunnel with the city, but this was not completed. Later it is related that "Hezekiah also stopped the upper watercourse of Gihon, and brought it straight down to the west side of the city of David" (II Chr 32:30). This ensured a supply of water to the city during the Assyrian siege and at the same time prevented the use of the spring by the enemy (II Chr 32:3-4). The tunnel ascribed to Hezekiah can still be seen today; it is about 1,600 feet (490m) long and terminates at the Pool of Siloam. The making of the tunnel is commemorated by the famous Siloam inscription. See SILOAM.

GIHON 1
Gen 2:13

GIHON 2
I Kgs 1:33, 38, 45. II Chr 32:30; 33:14

The Kidron Valley, and the Spring of Gihon below the houses at right center.

GILALAI A Levite, a musician who was in the thanksgiving choirs (Neh 12:31, 35-36) at the time of the dedication of the wall of Jerusalem by Nehemiah.

GILALAI
Neh 12:36

GILBOA A ridge of mountains southeast of the Jezreel Valley, rising some 1,500 feet (400m) above sea level. Saul fought his last battle with the Philistines here and the Israelites were defeated (I Sam 28:4 ff; 31:1-6; II Sam 1:6-10). On hearing of this disaster David cursed the mountains of Gilboa (II Sam 1:21).

GILBOA
I Sam 28:4; 31:1, 8. II Sam 1:6, 21; 21:12. I Chr 10:1, 8

GILEAD

1. The central part of the territory east of the Jordan, which consisted of three regions: the plain, Gilead and Bashan (Deut 3:10). Gilead extends from the Sea of Galilee in the north to the Dead Sea in the south. The name probably derives from Galeed "heap of testimony" (Gen 31:47). After the Israelite conquest it was divided between the tribes of Reuben and Gad and half of the tribe of Manasseh (Deut 3:12-13). The name Gilead is sometimes applied to certain portions of this region (cf Deut 3:15-16; I Kgs 4:19), which was rich in pasture and was therefore a place for cattle-raising (Num 32:1, etc.). It was also famous for its balm (Jer 8:22).

GILEAD 1
Gen 31:21, 23, 25; 37:25. Num 26:29; 32:1, 26, 29, 39-40. Deut 2:36; 3:10, 12-13, 15-16; 4:43; 34:1. Josh 12:2, 5; 13:11, 25, 31; 17:1, 5-6; 20:8;

Archeological surveys have shown that the area was settled as early as the 24th-23rd centuries B.C. After a long period of abandonment it was resettled in the 13th century B.C. at the time when the kingdoms of Edom and Moab were founded in its southern part. Most of Gilead, however, was occupied by the kings of the Amorites and later conquered by the Israelite tribes (Num 32:1ff, etc). Jephtath the Gileadite fought Ammon in Gilead (Judg chap. 11). Later Saul defeated the Ammonites who attempted to take Jabesh Gilead (I Sam chap. 11). After the division of the kingdom Gilead was in Israel, but its northern part was soon conquered by the Arameans and another part was taken by the Ammonites (Amos 1:13). In 814 B.C. Hazael captured the whole of Gilead (II Kgs 10:32-3), but when Damascus was assailed by the Assyrians it returned to Israel (II Kgs 13:25). In 732 B.C. the country was conquered by Tiglath-Pileser III and many of its inhabitants were deported to Assyria (II Kgs 15:29). The southern part of Gilead was then in the hands of the Ammonites (Josh 13:24-25; Jer 49:1), while in the northern part an Assyrian satrapy by the name of Galaza was formed.

The Gilboa Range overlooking the Valley of Jezreel.

After the return from the Babylonian Exile Gilead was outside Jewish territory.

During the early Hellenistic period it was a separate district under the name of Galaaditis. Later in the same period, under the Seleucids, Jews settled in a few towns in the district. Some of these were conquered a little later by Judas Maccabee (I Macc 5:17-45). In two campaigns early in his reign Alexander Jannaeus conquered the whole of Gilead. When the country was conquered by the Roman general Pompey (in 63 B.C.) the whole region was divided into fairly small units and distributed among the larger cities some of which were members of the Decapolis. During the reign of Herod and his successors Galaaditis remained outside their kingdoms. After A.D. 106 it was part of the Provincia Arabia.

2. Son of Machir, grandson of Manasseh; he gave his name to the territory of Gilead.

3. Father of Jephthah.

4. A Gadite, son of Michael and father of Jaroah. The family lived in Gilead No.1.

GILEADITES See GILEAD No.1

GILGAL

1. A site west of the Jordan, the last station on the route of the Exodus, where Joshua set up 12 stones to commemorate the crossing of the river (Josh 4:19-20). Here, in the plain of Jericho, the Children of Israel were circumcised (Josh 5:3-9), the name Gilgal denoting that there the Lord "rolled away" (*galloti*) "the reproach of Egypt from you" (ibid). After the conquest of Canaan, Gilgal remained a holy place where Samuel judged Israel (I Sam 7:16) and Saul was crowned king (I Sam 10:8; 11:14ff). After the division of the kingdom, it was a sanctuary of the Northern Kingdom, to the outrage of Hosea (4:15) and Amos (4:4; 5:5). In Second Temple times, it was called Beth Gilgal and populated by Levites descended from Temple singers (Neh 12:29). The site has been tentatively identified in the region of Jericho.

2. Another Gilgal, near Shechem, is mentioned in Deuteronomy 11:30. Its location is uncertain.

3. Gilgal mentioned in the story of Elisha (II Kgs 2:1-2; 4:38-44) has been located by some scholars at Jaljuliya, north of Ramallah. Others identify it with Gilgal No.1.

4-5. Gilgal, referred to as lying on the borders of Judah in Joshua 15:7 has not been identified; nor has another town of that name whose king was defeated by Joshua (Josh 12:23). Both offer textual problems: the former is called Geliloth in Joshua 18:17 and the latter is translated as "Galilee" in the Septuagint.

GILOH A city in the Judean hill country, birthplace of Ahithophel the Gilonite, advisor to David (II Sam 15:12), and his son, Eliam, one of David's warriors (II Sam 23:34). Giloh's identification is problematical, but it seems to have been either north or south of Hebron.

GILONITE Appellation applied to inhabitant of Giloh. Such were Ahithophel, the counselor of David (II Sam 15:12) and his son Eliam, one of David's "mighty men" (II Sam 23:34).

GIMZO One of the towns conquered by the Philistines in the days of Ahaz (II Chr 28:18). Known also in the Roman period, it is identified with Jimzu, southeast of Lydda.

GINATH Father of Tibni, pretender to the throne of Israel in opposition to Omri.

GINNETHOI, GINNETHON One of the priests who, with his family (Neh 12:16), returned from the Exile in Babylon with Zerubbabel (Neh 12:4). Probably the same man was among those who sealed the covenant at the time of Nehemiah (Neh 10:6).

GIRGASHITE One of the peoples or nations who lived in Canaan prior to the Israelite conquest, alongside the Hittites, the Ammonites, the Perizites and the Jebusites. According to most scholars, the Girgashites were introduced into the area by their Hittite allies, during their campaign against the Egyptians under Rameses II. Some of the Girgashites settled there after the war.

GIRZITES Inhabitants of a land near Egypt which was raided by David during his stay with the Philistines.

GISHPA One of the two leaders of the Nethinim (Temple servants) who dwelt on Ophel at the time of Nehemiah.

GITTAIM See GATH No.2

GITTITES Inhabitants of part of the Philistine territory still unconquered by Joshua, but promised by God to the tribe of Manasseh. In the OT, three people, Obed-Edom, Ittai and Goliath, are referred to as Gittites, a term for the inhabitants of the Philistine city of GATH.

GIZONITE An epithet affixed to the name of Hashem, whose sons were among David's thirty "mighty men"; it may indicate a village or town from which the individual came.

Remains of an Israelite period fortress excavated at Giloh.

(above)
The region of Jericho where Gilgal is said to have been.

GILGAL 1
Josh 4:19-20; 5:9-10; 9:6; 10:6-7, 9, 15, 43; 14:6. Judg 2:1; 3:19. I Sam 7:16; 10:8; 11:14-15; 13:4, 7-8, 12, 15; 15:12, 21, 33. II Sam 19:15, 40. Neh 12:29. Hos 4:15; 9:15; 12:11. Amos 4:4; 5:5. Mic 6:5

GILGAL 2
Deut 11:30

GILGAL 3
II Kgs 2:1; 4:38

GILGAL 4-5
Josh 12:23; 15:7

GILOH
Josh 15:51. II Sam 15:12

GILONITE
II Sam 15:12; 23:34

GIMZO
II Chr 28:18

GINATH
I Kgs 16:21-22

GINNETHOI, GINNETHON
Neh 10:6; 12:4, 16

GIRGASHITE
Gen 10:16; 15:21. Deut 7:1. Josh 3:10; 24:11. I Chr 1:14. Neh 9:8

GIRZITES
I Sam 27:8

GISHPA
Neh 11:21

GITTAIM
II Sam 4:3. Neh 11:33

GITTITES
Josh 13:3. II Sam 6:10-11; 15:18-19, 22; 18:2; 21:19. I Chr 13:13; 20:5

GIZONITE
I Chr 11:34

Glass Phoenician amphora and necklace of "eye beads."

GLASS The first examples of man-made glass date to the last quarter of the 3rd millennium B.C. when glass beads were first made in Mesopotamia and Egypt. A formative era in the history of glass-making is marked by the appearance of the first glass vessels in the middle of the 2nd millennium B.C. again in Mesopotamia and Egypt. The heyday of Egypt's glass industry came in the El Amarna period (first half of the 14th century B.C.).

Glass vessels were rare in Palestine and Syria in the Late Bronze Age, and only princes and the very rich could afford them. Some vessels were dedicated to temples and shrines (e.g., at Lachish and Beth Shean); others were found in tombs (e.g., at Beth Shemesh, Megiddo). All these vessels seem to have been imported from Egypt.

The process of casting glass in molds was also invented in the mid-2nd millennium B.C. A homogenous group of blue glass pendants in the shape of a nude female (possibly a fertility goddess) is represented in such widely separated sites as Nuzi (northern Mesopotamia), Alalakh (Plain of Antioch), Beth Shean, Megiddo and Lachish. They originated either in northern Mesopotamia or in Syria. There is no evidence that glass vessels were made in Palestine in the Late Bronze Age.

A decline set in with the end of the New Kingdom in Egypt and the end of the Middle Assyrian period (end of the 2nd millennium B.C.). For the subsequent period there is no positive evidence and it is only in the late 8th and 7th centuries B.C. that glass vessels are found again. The sole remarkable finds of this period from Palestine are glass inlay pieces found with the famous ivories in the palaces of the kings of Israel at Samaria. The role of the Phoenicians in producing or trading in glass in this and subsequent periods is a matter of controversy because of the lack of adequate data. The sole OT mention of glass is in Job 28:17.

Small amphoriscs, aryballoi, alabastra and juglets were produced on a large scale from the 6th to the 4th centuries B.C. The center for this production seems to have been on the island of Rhodes. Vessels of this type, common all over the Mediterranean area, have been found in Palestine. Alexandria was apparently the leading center of glass-making in the Hellenistic period but very few of its luxury products have been found in Palestine. In the NT, glass is mentioned only in the Book of Revelation (4:6; 15:2; 21:18, 21).

GNAT See ANIMALS

GOAT See ANIMALS

GOATH A place named by Jeremiah in his prophecy of the rebuilding of Jerusalem.

GOATH
Jer 31:39

GOB ("well"?). The site of a battle between David and the Philistines; it is not identified.

GOB
II Sam 21:18-19

GOD The creator of the universe and redeemer of its creatures. Rarely does the Bible reflect on the divine being as such, although discussions of God's essential nature do occur: e.g., Abraham's probing into the appropriateness of wholesale destruction of the cities of Sodom and Gomorrah (Gen 18:16-33); the prologue to the Book of Job (Job chaps. 1-2); the interchange beween Jonah and God over the justice of sparing a wicked, though repentant, city (Jonah 4:2-11); the divine proclamation to Moses of the 13 attributes of the deity (Ex 34:6-7). The common theme of these reflections on God's nature is the problem of the theodicy. Given the fundamental goodness of God, how can life's anomalies be explained? The Bible is full of attempts to find an adequate solution to this vexing issue.

Perhaps nothing speaks so eloquently about the personal bond between the biblical God and human beings as these passages which wrestle with divine justice (cf Jer 12:1; Hab 1:1-3). The complaints of injustice assume a loving deity, and the protests concerning God's absence presuppose the deity's desire to dwell among humans. That is why moments of apparent injustice are acknowledged to be temporary and educative. Even when the prevalence of evil seems to compromise God's wisdom, goodness, or power, the Israelite and the Christian find comfort in a hopeful certainty that is grounded in the nature of God.

Above all else, God wishes to be known. That is, the deity takes the initiative and unveils the mystery of holiness. Otherwise, nothing could be known about God, for the human intellect cannot penetrate the veil. A few texts do intimate that a tiny aperture exists through which the naked eye can catch fleeting glimpses of truth (e.g., Rom 1:18-25), but such general revelation is declared to be inadequate for salvation. Some texts go further in denying the appropriateness of penetrating the darkness which shields the deity (Deut 29:29; cf Ecc 7:24; 8:17, where it is said that the intellect cannot even understand God's activity on earth).

Special revelation is therefore necessary for genuine knowledge of God, but the deity's voluntary self-limitation does not compromise transcendence. Nothing in all of creation accurately portrays the divine likeness — hence the prohibition of images — and sin results in human blindness *vis à vis* God. Only the pure in heart can hope to see the Father (Matt 5:8), who mercifully protects the viewer from harm (Ex 33:22). Although Christians spoke of incarnation, they were careful to preserve the otherness of God even at the expense of a subordinate view of Jesus.

The knowledge which God reveals is personal; it creates a relationship of trust. The Bible uses the word "know" in an intimate sense; it can even have the connotation of election (Amos 3:2). To know God is to act faithfully within an intimacy often symbolized by marital or familiar imagery. The prophet Hosea described the bond between Israel and God in terms of a husband-and-wife relationship. Divine pathos is nowhere depicted so poignantly as in Hosea's attempt to express the effect of infidelity on the deity's benevolence (Hos 11:8-9). Jesus took over this language of intimacy to indicate his special relationship with the Father, whom Jesus addressed with the child's expression of absolute trust: *Abba*. Only once in the NT is the abstract word for deity used, and it occurs in a philosophical context (Acts 17:29) where the purpose is to locate a point of contact between the biblical God and pagan understandings of deity.

How did the hidden one communicate the basis for personal relationship? The chief medium of revelation was the spoken word, which often accompanied theophanies but also came to chosen individuals apart from spectacular manifestations such as earthquake, wind and fire (compare the theophanies to Moses and Elijah at Sinai with prophetic oracles). In ancient Israel the Lord's presence was associated with specific objects (the ark and the tent of meeting, which represented presence and distance respectively), persons (the angel as messenger) and qualities (the face of God, the glory and the name, the latter of which is characteristic of Deuteronomy). Occasionally, divine attributes were almost personified (for instance, word and spirit). In the case of wisdom, personification is actually achieved (Prov chap. 8; Eccl chap. 24; Wisd of Sol chap. 7). The NT understands Jesus as the self-revelation of God; in some circles this revelation is described as an emptying, by which it is meant that God freely became incarnate (cf the Gospel of John in particular, but also Pauline intepretations of the Christ event).

The God of Israel was both holy and compassionate; hiddenness and presence characterized the deity. The qualities of justice and mercy generate considerable tension within the Bible. Whenever one aspect seems to be threatened, the other comes to the forefront for a time. To some extent the historical situation dictates the emphasis: in periods of prosperity and neglect of common decency prophets like Amos and Isaiah emphasized the judgment of God, while periods of defeat at the hands of enemies evoked prophetic comfort (Second Isaiah; cf the changes in Ezekiel's message after Jerusalem's fall). The NT also recognizes both divine attributes, wrath and love. As a matter of fact, the frequent claim that the God of the OT is wrathful and that of the NT is loving completely distorts the truth. The loving-kindness of God pervades the Hebrew Bible, and wrath is fully at home in the NT (besides the frequent threats of hell, the awful portents in Revelation show just how pervasive was the theme of punishment for sinners).

A remarkable feature of biblical revelation is its exclusivity. Although ancient Israel acknowledged the existence of deities other than Yahweh, they were subordinated to the level of ministering angels. In time the claims that the biblical God was unique (cf Second Isaiah's formula for divine incomparability, Is 45:21ff) resulted in a denial that any other deity existed. That conviction, taken for granted in NT times, became the occasion for martyrdom at the hands of Romans. During the early days of the Maccabean revolt, many Jews likewise gave their lives because of a refusal to acknowledge the claims of Seleucid deities. Those peoples accustomed to allegiance to numerous gods found it difficult to appreciate what they interpreted as obstinacy and irreverence on the part of Jews and Christians.

The unique God was thought to have chosen a specific people through whom the divine purpose for humanity would become known. It follows that an incipient eschatology lies at the heart of all knowledge of God. The aim of revelation was to establish community, and no effort on the part of sinful creatures could ultimately prevent God's attainment of the desired goal. The sovereign of the universe controls historical events, using foreign nations as instruments of punishment for faithlessness of Israel's part. Eventually, God will inaugurate an era of peace on earth. This vision continues into the NT, which speaks of God's kingdom as present reality and future hope. The goal is not mystical absorption into the deity, but a dwelling with God in circumstances where perfect obedience is possible. It is noteworthy that Israelites and Christians described themselves as children, thereby recognizing a relationship of absolute dependence on the Father.

NAMES OF GOD: Although God was believed to have been unique, many names were used to designate this reality. The exclusive name for God, known as the tetragrammaton, was Yahweh. Within the Bible various theories exist about its precise origin (during the days of Enosh [Gen 4:26] or later still in Moses' day [Ex 3:6; 6:2-3]). Moreover, the explanation of this name may conceal something at the same time it divulges truth, so that it is capable of more than one meaning (e.g., "I am", "I cause to be", "I shall be present", Ex 3:14). It is also possible that a shorter form of the name was original (*Yah* or *Yahu*) and that it arose as an exclamation: "Oh that one!" This would identify the deity as the self-revealing Lord who appears in theophany. Second Isaiah seems to echo such usage in the expression: "I am he" (Is 41:4).

Numerous other names for God occur in the Bible, many of which call attention to an attribute; this is especially true of combinations with *El*: Shaddai (strength, Gen 17:1), *elyon* (majesty, Gen 14:17-21), *olam* (eternity, Gen 21:33), *ro'i* (protective watchfulness, Gen 16:14; 22:14), *elohe yisrael* (patronage, Gen 33:20); others point to a relationship: Rock (Deut 32:18; Ps 18:31), Father (Is 63:16; Jer 31:9), Shield (Ps 3:3; 84:11), Redeemer (Ps 19:14; Is 63:16), Fear (Gen 31:42, 53), King (Ps 47:7, cf Judg 8:23), Judge (Is 33:22) and Shepherd (Gen 49:24; Is 40:11). The numerous epithets and metaphors indicate how the biblical faith drew from personal and national experience in order to describe Yahweh.

In addition to the above names, God was described by certain expressions such as, "The Living God" (I Sam 17:26; II Kgs 19:4), "The First and the Last" (especially Is 41:4; 44:6), "The Alpha and Omega" (Rev 1:8), "The Ancient of Days" (Dan 7:9, 13, 22) and "Rider of Clouds" (Deut 33:26; Is 19:1). Some of these descriptive titles were shared with other peoples of the ancient world (e.g. "Rider of Clouds" in Ugaritic literature). A distinct characteristic of the biblical religion, as reflected in the numerous titles of God, was its revelatory capacity of the "God of Israel".

IMAGE OF GOD: Genesis 1:26-27; 5:1-3; 9:6 affirm that God created man in his own image and likeness. This is clearly a positive statement about man, but the texts do not specifically define what constitutes the image of God in man, and numerous opinions about the exact meaning of this expression have been suggested.

Some, based on the usual meaning of the Hebrew word *tzelem* "image", conclude that the image refers to a physical similarity between man and God; others, noting that God is a spiritual being, reject the physical interpretation and identify the image with immaterial aspects or functions of man such as reason, will, moral perception, the capacity for relationship, self-determination, immortality or dominion over creation.

The use of "image" in this positive affirmation about man is surprising. Israel's religion prohibited images and both the Torah and the Prophets strongly denounced their use. There seems to be nothing in the biblical understanding of images that would give substance to this statement about man, and some content for understanding the term may have to come from the concept of images that existed outside Israel. Both in Egypt and Mesopotamia the king was sometimes referred to as the image of God. It is very possible that Israel's use of this term stemmed from familiarity with ancient Near-Eastern imagery applied to kings; however, the Bible emphasized that all men, not merely royalty, were created in God's image.

While there is disagreement over what in man constitutes the image of God, there is general agreement as to the significance of this description of man. A number of indicators make it clear that the creation of man is the climax and crown of God's creative activity. Man alone is said to be "in the image of God"; the image of God sets man apart from everything else that God created, giving him a preeminent position and, no doubt, establishing both his right and ability to exercise dominion over creation (Gen 1:28). In Genesis 9:6 the image of God in man clearly gives man a dignity and worth not possessed by the animals; man may kill animals for food but the life of another human being is not to be taken because "in the image of God he (God) made man."

Genesis 5:1-3 and 9:6 indicate that the image of God in man was not lost because of the Fall. Genesis 5:1-3 affirms that both male and female are in the image of God. By recording that Adam fathered a son in his likeness and image, the passage suggests that succeeding generations inherited the image of God.

The term is also found in the NT where several passages employ it after the manner of the OT (I Cor 11:7; James 3:9). It is applied to Jesus in II Corinthians 4:4; Colossians 1:15, and the context makes it clear that the term refers to the mode of Jesus' revelation to man of the attributes and character of God. A similar idea is expressed in Hebrews 1:3 where Jesus is said to reflect the glory of God and to bear the very stamp of his nature. Believers are said to "be conformed to" the image of Christ in several passages (Rom 8:29; Eph 4:24 and Col 3:10). This last use of the term in the NT implies that the image of God in man, while not lost as the result of the Fall, was damaged.

GOG

GOG 1
Ezek 38:2-3, 14, 16, 18, 21; 39:1, 11. Rev 20:8

1. Political and military leader of the nations Meshech and Tubal in the land of Magog (Ezek 38:2). After the nation of Israel will have been restored from its Exile, Gog will come to the land of Israel from the northernmost part of the world with a huge army (Ezek 38:15). The defeat of Gog and his cohorts and the survival of Israel as an independent nation will have the following consequences: (a) All people will recognize that Israel's previous military and political setbacks resulted not from the Lord's inability to defend Israel but from the Lord's having found it necessary to punish Israel for his transgressions (Ezek 39:23); (b) Israel will recognize the sovereignty of the Lord and will obey him forever; (c) The Lord will no longer hide his face from Israel when the latter is in difficulty. Ezekiel's choice of the name Gog may have been inspired by the exploits of the 7th century B.C. Gyges, king of Lydia, who appears in the annals of Assurbanipal of Assyria as Gugu. In the NT (Rev 20:7-9) both Gog and Magog are leaders of the armies mustered by Satan against God's people.

GOG 2
I Chr 5:4

2. The son of a certain Joel and the founder of one of the subdivisions of the tribe of Reuben.

GOLAN
Deut 4:43. Josh 20:8; 21:27. I Chr 6:71

GOLAN A city of refuge in the territory of Manasseh in Northern Transjordan (Deut 4:43), later allotted to the Levites (Josh 21:27). The town, as yet unidentified, has given its name to the region between the

Formation of hexagonal basalt pillars surrounding a small pool through which a stream flows down from the Golan Heights to the Sea of Galilee.

(right)
General view of the Golan region.

Jordan and Yarmuk Rivers to the west and southeast, and Mount Hermon to the north (later called Gaulanitis). The small kingdoms of Geshur and Maachah occupied this region in the 2nd and early 1st millennia B.C.

Surveys and excavations over recent years have revealed prehistoric sites, a unique Chalcolithic village culture, and nomadic and semi-nomadic sites of the Early Bronze periods. More permanent settlements appear to have been established in the Middle Bronze period, and some of them evidently continued to exist in the Late Bronze Age. A marked increase of sites in the Iron Age indicates the growing importance of the area as reflected in the Bible.

The later history of the Golan in Hellenistic, Roman and Byzantine times as attested in historical sources, and archeological investigations have revealed a dense settlement which lasted into medieval times, including important Jewish and Christian sites.

GOLDEN CALF Israelite object of worship. The golden calf was actually the representation of a young bull made of wood and overlaid with a plaiting of gold (see Ps 106:19-20). It appears in two separate periods, the first when Moses was receiving the Ten Commandments on Mount Sinai and the second during the reign of King Jeroboam I of Israel. In the former narrative, the golden calf was made by Aaron in response to the request of the Israelites for a god to lead them as they awaited the delayed return of Moses from the top of Mount Sinai (Ex 32:1-4). This calf was made of golden ornaments collected from the people, melted and molded and then worshiped amidst dancing, feasting and playing. When Moses returned after 40 days, he broke the tablets, destroyed the calf and forced the people to drink its remains mixed with water. The Levites then slew 3,000 of the worshipers and the Lord sent a plague upon the people for their sin.

The second case of calf building was during the reign of King Jeroboam (I Kgs 12:27) when two calves were erected in the northern temples of Bethel and Dan. Jeroboam's intention was to prevent the people from worshiping in the Temple of Jerusalem.

Not only are the general features of the two stories similar, but the explanatory formula in Exodus 32:4, — "This is your god, O Israel, that brought you out of the land of Egypt" — is virtually identical to that used in I Kings 12:28. This has given rise to the question of the chronological relationship between the two accounts with some

GOLDEN CALF
Ex 32:4, 8,
19-20, 24-25.
Deut 9:16, 21.
I Kgs 12:28,
32. II Kgs
10:29; 17:16.
II Chr 11:15;
13:8. Neh.
9:18. Ps
106:19. Hos
8:5-6; 10:5;
13:2. Acts 7:41

Bronze calf of the Canaanite period.

scholars holding the I Kings incident to be dependent on the Exodus story and others holding the view that the Exodus story presupposes that in I Kings. In any event, Jeroboam's initiative could not have succeeded without some ancient tradition as precedent. In this context, it should be noted that bulls occupied a prominent place in the cultic practices of various regions of Egypt. The bull also appears in the art and religious texts of the ancient Near East. The Syrian storm-god, Hadad-Rimmon, is frequently represented as standing on a bull.

In the case of the Exodus story, Aaron probably intended the calf to represent the vacant throne of God and not the deity himself, similar to the function of the cherubim in the tabernacle. However, the calf was popularly hailed as the representation of God who had brought the people out of Egypt. It is plausible that Jeroboam's calves were similarly designed as functional correspondences to the cherubim of Solomon's Temple. However, whereas the cherubim were kept in the Holy of Holies, inaccessible to the public, Jeroboam's calves were placed in the public courts of the Temple, where the people could see and kiss them (Hos 13:2).

GOLGOTHA
Matt 27:33.
Mark 15:22.
John 19:17

GOLGOTHA The site of the Crucifixion (Matt 27:33; Mark 15:22; John 19:17). The name derives from the Aramaic *golgolta*, meaning "skull" or "place of a skull". Early Christian tradition places the site west of the city of Jerusalem. From the Latin translation of Luke 23:33, it also became known as Calvary. In the 2nd century A.D., when Aelia Capitolina (Jerusalem) was built, a temple of Aphrodite was set up on the site by the Romans. After the Council of Nicea (A.D. 325) the Emperor Constantine felt it his duty "to make the most blessed spot, the place of the Resurrection, visible to all and given over to veneration". In A.D. 330 the remains of the temple of Aphrodite were torn down, the

The Garden Tomb lies beneath a rise outside the walls of Jerusalem and is said to resemble a human skull — Golgotha in Aramaic. It is believed by many Protestants to be the site of Calvary.

*(right)
The altar in the Greek Orthodox Chapel of Golgotha in the Church of the Holy Sepulcher traditionally marks the place where the cross stood.*

Mycenean warrior carrying a shield and a spear, and wearing a horned helmet and leather body armor, as in the biblical description of Goliath. From the "Warrior's Vase". 16th century B.C.

area cleansed and the great Church of the Holy Sepulcher built. It included the last stations on the Way of the Cross, Golgotha and the Holy Sepulcher.

The present church, built by the Crusaders, includes extensive remains of Constantine's structure.

GOLIATH A giant from Gath; the Philistine champion whom David killed with a sling-shot at Ephes-Dammim (I Sam chap.17) after he had struck terror in the hearts of Saul's soldiers for 40 days. David dedicated Goliath's huge armor to the Lord (I Sam 21:9). The priest Ahimelech later restored Goliath's sword to David when he was fleeing from Saul (I Sam 22:10). According to II Samuel 21:19, however, it was a Bethlehemite named Elhanan who slew Goliath. A parallel verse, I Chronicles 20:5, harmonizes the two versions by crediting Elhanan with a victory over Goliath's brother Lahmi.

GOMER

1. The first of the seven sons of Japheth son of Noah and the father of Ashkenaz, Riphath and Togarmah (Gen 10:2-3; I Chr 1:5-6). This branch of the Japhethites appears among the allies of Gog of the land of Magog in Ezekiel 38:6. This Gomer probably represents the Anatolian ethnic group known in Assyrian sources as Gimirraya and in Greek and Latin sources as Cimmerians.

2. Daughter of Diblaim, a "wife of whoredom", whom God commands the prophet Hosea to marry in order that the sorry state of the prophet's domestic life might symbolize the sad state of the covenant between God and Israel, which had been profaned by Israel's flirtations with Baal, the Phoenician god of rain. She bore the prophet three children — Jezreel, Lo-ruhammah and Lo-ammi — each of whose symbolic names is connected with the Lord's temporary rejection of Israel. Since the children bear symbolic names, scholars have suggested that the name Gomer might also be symbolic.

GOMORRAH One of the five Canaanite cities (Gen 10:19) in the Jordan Valley (Gen 13:10). Their location is very much disputed. See also SODOM.

GOPHER See PLANTS

GOREN ATAD A place close to the River Jordan; the name means "the threshing floor of Atad". Here Jacob's funeral cortege stopped for seven days of mourning while en route from Egypt to the Cave of Machpelah. When the Canaanites saw the mourning they called its name "Abel Mizraim" (Gen 50:7-13), which means literally "Mourning of Egypt". Opinions are divided as to its location.

GOLIATH
I Sam 17:4, 23; 21:9; 22:10. II Sam 21:19. I Chr 20:5

GOMER 1
Gen 10:2-3. I Chr 1:5-6. Ezek 38:6

GOMER 2
Hos 1:3

GOMORRAH
Gen 10:19; 13:10; 14:2, 8, 10-11; 18:20; 19:24, 28. Deut 29:23; 32:32. Is 1:9-10; 13:19. Jer 23:14; 49:18; 50:40. Amos 4:11. Zeph 2:9. Matt 10:15. Mark 6:11. Rom 9:29. II Pet 2:6. Jude v. 7

GOREN ATAD
Gen 50:10-11

GOSHEN

1. The name of a place and a region in Judah (Josh 11:16) in the southern part of the hill country (Josh 15:51). Not identified.

2. A region in Egypt, rich in pasture, where the Children of Israel settled (Gen 46:34), "the best of the land" (Gen 47:6, 11). The Septuagint identifies Goshen with Pithom, which is identified today with Tell er-Ratabeh in Wadi Thumeilat. The Bible also refers to the land of Goshen as the "land of Rameses" (Gen 47:11), which was the later name for Zoan (Tanis), to the north. Egyptian sources also mention the granting of grazing rights in the region of Pithom.

GOSPEL The verb "to announce the good news" (*euangelizesthai* in Greek) occurs 54 times in the whole NT, of which 25 times it is in the Lucan writings and 21 times in the Pauline letters (including the letter to the Ephesians). The noun derived from this verb, gospel (*euangelion*), occurs 76 times altogether, of which 56 times are in the writings of Paul (including Ephesians and Colossians).

Typical landscape in Goshen, Egypt.

The concept sums up the essence of early Christian preaching in one apt word. The background of the word's content lies especially in what scholars call "Second Isaiah" (see Is 52:7 in the Septuagint translation) and in a specific messianic expectation of early Judaism. In the new age to come the people of God will be comforted by good tidings: justice will be brought to all nations and peace will be published by the servant of God. The phrase "good news" developed its theological richness in contrast to the term's half-religious, half-political use in the Hellenistic-Roman world with its widespread cult of the emperor. The central concept of gospel refers to the onset of the messianic age. According to the unanimous testimony of the NT it concisely describes the new reality of life which Jesus, the messiah, represents, evokes and guarantees. The term reflects humanity's longing for ultimate deliverance from a world of constraints and power-connections. Accordingly it is a message which expresses the divine victory over the constricting evil forces of the old creation having "passed away" (II Cor 5:17), which the believer can now experience as freedom and deliverance.

In early Christian tradition, the term in all probability goes back to Jesus himself. His message of the impending Kingdom of God, connected with his activity and joined to his mission, presupposes a certainty that the promises are now being fulfilled (Matt 5:2-11). The thought patterns of "Second Isaiah" were of enormous importance for Jesus. In this sense, the earliest witnesses have aptly summarized the essence of his character and mission. The apostolic presentation of Jesus' life is based both exclusively and completely on the fundamental idea of "good news" having taken unique shape in the word and mission of Jesus. From the beginning he is attested and proclaimed as God's messenger of joy (Luke 4:16ff) who, by word and deed, breaks through the forces of the old creation. The difference from the Baptist's preaching of judgement is as fundamental as the difference between the old and new eras. The witness of the Saying-Source is in this sense unambiguous (see Matt 11:1-5; Luke 7:18-23). The pre-Pauline (Jewish-Christian) tradition builds on this basic insight. It explains the event of cross and resurrection on the level of a historical revolution of salvation. Very early explicit material gives a glimpse of the heart of the tradition, which may stem from the earliest baptismal instruction (see I Thes 1:5; I Cor 15:3ff; Rom 1:3ff; 3:25ff).

Paul in his turn thought through the concept of gospel in a comprehensive fashion. He underlines the inner connection of word and spirit, of matter and content, in order finally to define the gospel as "the power of God to salvation for everyone who believes" (Rom 1:16).

Earlier convictions, arising against the background of a thorough questioning of the OT (Rom 10:1-21), are then brought to a wider synthesis. The new insight expresses itself in an abundance of compact definitions. Paul speaks of the "gospel of Christ" (Rom 15:19; I Cor 9:12, 18), of "Christ's gospel" (II Cor 2:12), and of the "gospel of his Son" (Rom 1:9), to designate especially the unique basis of the new message. But he also frequently employs other descriptions which try to express the essential content of the witness, for example, "the word of the truth" (Col 1:5), "gospel of the glory" (II Cor 4:4), "gospel of your salvation" (Eph 1:13), "gospel for the uncircumcised" (Gal 2:7) and so on. Sometimes the apostle speaks quite pointedly of "my" gospel, which means the message must be distinguished from false demands. Again and again, at the risk of his life, he stood up for its original and pure form (Rom 2:16; 16:25; also II Tim 2:8; cf Gal 1:6 and 2:11). Under the strong impact of his unique character, Paul's disciples regarded him as the gospel messenger *par excellence*. He was considered the "good teacher" and venerated as the outstanding model of faithful service to the point of sacrificing his own life (II Tim 2:8-10).

The missionary stamp on the concept is most clearly seen in Mark's gospel. The term "gospel" denotes the message to be proclaimed by Christ's disciples in this world (Mark 1:1, 14; 8:35; 10:29 and 14:9). According to the last discourse (Mark 13:10) Jesus wants the gospel "that must first be preached to all nations". The view that proclaiming the gospel and following the cross essentially belong together (Mark 8:34) is reminiscent of Paul.

In Matthew's presentation, the preaching of the gospel is even more closely bound up with Jesus' message of the Kingdom of Heaven (Matt 4:23; 9:35). The "gospel of the kingdom will be preached in all the world, as a witness to all the nations; and then the end will come" (Matt 24:14). The historical place of the gospel of salvation is established for the catechetical and homiletic work of the Matthean community.

In Luke the content of the gospel is massively fused with the person of Jesus (Luke 4:16ff; Acts 10:36). The content of the gospel is the redeemer himself. In the third gospel it is as though the missionary is preaching and the theology of the Gentile Christian community is speaking.

John stressed the idea of the revelation of the word shining in the darkness (John 1:1-5). There is no explicit use of the term gospel in his writings but the idea of the divine function of the testimony of the Son nevertheless predominates. Apocalyptic thoughts form the basis for I Peter 4:17 and Revelation 14:6. The latter text appeals to the universal (endtime) character of the message of Christ. The gospel is represented in an idealizing way as an "eternal" message, administered by an angel and hence a heavenly word for "all nations and languages".

The secondary annex to Mark (16:9-20) also shows the same typical tendency (v. 15) of underlining the gospel's cosmic importance: "Go into all the world and preach the gospel to every creature".

The concept of the gospel originally denoted its character as living word and announcement. Only in the post-apostolic period did the word gospel come to mean the literary extract of the early Christian oral tradition about Jesus, i.e. a book. Mark 1:1 still refers to the older meaning in the form of a prophetic promise (Is 40:3). Later on in the 2nd century A.D. Justin Martyr (around 160) uses the term technically in respect to the "memoirs of the apostles". Even in these decades the oldest Gentile Christian communities began to reserve the term for the four familiar (canonical) gospels, whose origins and mutual interdependence give an insight into the recognized necessity of preserving the earliest narratives of apostolic testimony during the transitional stage of the post-apostolic period. Scholars generally agree that the order of their composition runs as follows: Mark (shortly before A.D. 70), Matthew (between 70 and 80), Luke (between 80 and 90), John (around A.D. 100). Some Jewish-Christian gospels were rejected because of their controversial contents; their few surviving fragments give a rough idea of their partially gnostic-heretical nature. Irenaeus of Lyon (around A.D. 180) represents a certain conclusion to the history of the early Christian canon. The fourfold number of the gospels, including the relatively late Gospel of John, is provided with a definitive salvation-historical support. The subsequently popularized symbols of the four evangelists (Mark, a lion; Matthew, an angel or a man; Luke, an ox; John, an eagle) are derived from the vision of the four creatures in Ezekiel 1:13ff. Even with this background the theological explanation could insist upon the divine origin of the new message rejecting speculative heretical ideas. See also NEW TESTAMENT.

GOURD See PLANTS

GOZAN An Aramean city-state in northwestern Mesopotamia, on the southern bank of the River Khabur. Assyrian documents of the early 9th century B.C. state that it was subject to Assyria. In 732 B.C. Tiglath-Pileser III deported the Reubenites, Gadites and half the tribe of Manasseh to Halah, Habor, Hara and to the River Gozan (I Chr 5:26). The same fate was also suffered by the inhabitants of Samaria after its conquest in 721 B.C. (II Kgs 17:6). Isaiah knew of the fate that befell Gozan at the hands of the Assyrians (Is 37:11-12).

Gozan is identified with Tell Halaf, where the remains of the Aramean city built in the 10th century B.C. occupied an area of about 150 acres (61 ha), its temples, a palace and other buildings provided very

GOZAN
**II Kgs 17:6;
18:11; 19:12.
I Chr 5:26. Is
37:12**

Relief from Gozan showing a slinger. 10th-9th centuries B.C. (British Museum)

rich finds uncovered in excavations. On the ruins of this city another was built to which the Israelites were deported by the Assyrians. Documents found in the later city that refer to this period contain Hebrew names, probably of the deportees.

GRAPE, GRAPEVINE See PLANTS

GRASSHOPPER See ANIMALS

GREAT SEA See SEA

GREECE, GREEKS, GRECIANS In the biblical Table of Nations, Javan is Japheth's fourth son (Gen 10:2, 4). Javan is the Hebrew name for Greece, derived from Iaonie, the land of the Greeks. Ezekiel's prophecy concerning Tyre, dating from 594 B.C., mentions Javan/Greece among the nations trading with Tyre (Ezek 27:13, 19). Joel's prophecy accusing Tyre, Sidon and the Philistines of selling captives from Judah into slavery to the Greeks (Joel 3:6) probably belongs to the time of Ezekiel's prophecy. Isaiah's prediction that Greece would be among the lands from which the exiles would return (Is 66:19) is of uncertain date but must precede the Hellenistic period. The term of Greek rule over Palestine is apparently reflected in Zechariah's prophecy "and raised up your sons, O Zion against your sons, O Greece" (Zech 9:13) which is attributed to the years before the Hasmonean uprising. Daniel's prophecy on the first prince of Greece refers to the time of that uprising (Dan 10:20).

The Greek era in Palestine began in 333 B.C. when Alexander the Great defeated Darius III of Persia, opening up the way for the conquest of Syria and Egypt. After his death, his kingdom was divided among his generals and Palestine was controlled either by the Egyptian-based Ptolemids or the Syria-based Seleucids. Greek culture (Hellenism) now became predominant throughout the entire region and the Jewish struggle was largely directed against those of its features incompatible with Judaism. The climax came with the decrees of Antiochus IV (175-162 B.C.) against the observances of Judaism and his desecration of the Temple in Jerusalem. The Hasmonean rising, led

GREAT SEA
Num 34:6-7.
Josh 1:4; 9:1;
15:12, 47;
23:4. Ezek
47:10, 15, 19-
20; 48:28. Dan
7:2

GREECE, GREEKS,
GRECIANS
Dan 8:21;
10:20; 11:2.
Joel 3:6. Zech
9:13. Mark
7:26. Luke
23:38. John
7:35; 12:20;
19:20. Acts
14:1; 16:1, 3;
17:4, 12; 18:4,
17; 19:10, 17;
20:2, 21;
21:28, 37.
Rom 1:14, 16;
2:9-10; 3:9;
10:12. I Cor
1:22-24; 10:32;
12:13. Gal 2:3;
3:28. Col 3:11.
Rev 9:11

(bottom of page)
Alexander the Great fighting the Persians depicted on a mosaic from Pompeii.

Greece

View of the temple of Apollo at Delphi with Mount Parnassus in the background.

by Judah the Maccabee, led to the reconquest of Jerusalem and the expulsion of the Syrian forces but Hellenistic influences were still to be found not only among the Gentile population but also among certain Jewish elements. In the NT, the term "Greeks" occurs most frequently in relation to the journeys of Paul: in each city he spoke to the Jews and the Greeks (meaning the non-Jewish population). To Paul, the characteristic of the Greeks was their pursuit of wisdom (I Cor 1:18-2:16). In the course of time, Paul came to the conclusion that there was no distinction between Jew and Greek when it came to salvation through belief in Christ (Rom 10:12).

The NT was written in Greek, although parts were based on Aramaic originals which have not been preserved. Greek was the language of the Christian Church until the mid-2nd century.

GUDGODAH One of the halts of the Children of Israel on their way to the promised land; it lay between Moserah (where Aaron died and was buried) and Jotbathah, "a land of rivers of water" (Deut 10:7). An alternate form, Har Hagidgad (the mountain of Gidgad), is used in Numbers (Num 33:32-33). Its location is unknown.

GUNI

1. The second son of Naphtali (Gen 46:24) son of Jacob by Rachel's maid Bilhah, and ancestor of the Gunites (Gen 30:7-8; Num 26:48).

2. Father of Abdiel and grandfather of Ahi in the genealogy of Gad.

GUNITES A family of Naphtali descended from Guni No.1.

GUR King Ahaziah of Judah, fleeing the men of Jehu, was shot by an arrow "at the ascent to Gur". The precise location is unknown but it must have been in the vicinity of Megiddo.

GUR BAAL A place in southern Judah where "Arabians" dwelled; they were defeated by King Uzziah. It is not identified.

GUDGODAH
Deut 10:7

GUNI 1
Gen 46:24.
Num 26:48. I
Chr 7:13

GUNI 2
I Chr 5:15

GUNITES
Num 26:48

GUR
II Kgs 9:27

GUR BAAL
II Chr 26:7

HAAHASHTARI Fourth son of Naarah, the second wife of Ashhur in the genealogy of the family of Judah. In some versions the name appears as Ahashtari.

HABAIAH ("the Lord has hidden / protected"). A family of priests who returned from Exile with Zerubbabel but who "could not identify their father's house or their genealogy" (Ezra 2:59) and were therefore "excluded from the priesthood as defiled" (Ezra 2:62) until their fate was decided (Ezra 2:63).

HABAKKUK Prophet of Judah whose date is uncertain but may have lived in the time of Kings Josiah and Jehoiakim. Nothing is known of him. The name may be derived from the Akkadian word for a type of a plant. See HABAKKUK, BOOK OF.

HABAKKUK, BOOK OF Eighth among the Minor Prophets in the OT canon, the book is set about the time of the Chaldean ascent to the status of a world power in 612 B.C. when Nabopolassar, founder of the neo-Babylonian (=Chaldean) empire, conquered Nineveh, the Assyrian capital. Comprising three chapters (totaling 56 verses), it is traditionally divided on the basis of its contents, into two sections: the narrative (chaps. 1 and 2) and the psalm (chap. 3). The narrative consists of a series of five prophetic utterances, the psalm contains the recollection of God's deeds and a prayer.

HAAHASHTARI
I Chr 4:6

HABAIAH
Ezra 2:61.
Neh 7:63

HABAKKUK
Hab 1:1; 3:1

Fragment of the commentary of the Book of Habakkuk, one of the Dead Sea manuscripts found at Qumran.

In the first oracle (1:1-4) Habakkuk complains to God for allowing the unchecked violence and injustice that fills the land. "How long, O Lord" (1:2) is a cry for help. There is an ambiguity in this section leading scholars to differ as to whether the prophet is describing the domestic situation in Judah, or the Chaldeans, who are known to have acted with total disregard for the rights of other nations in their attempt to conquer the then-known inhabited world.

In the second oracle (1:5-11), the prophet declares that the Chaldeans are the instrument of God, being wielded in response to the domestic problems referred to in the first oracle. The instrument, however, is unable to turn injustice into justice and the prophet's original question remains. The Chaldeans function, consequently, both as the answer to the prophet's complaint against his own people and as the cause for his complaint in and of itself.

In the third oracle (1:12-17), the prophet turns to protest. How can God allow the wicked to devour the righteous? Even if the Chaldeans are to be viewed as the chastisement of Judah, how can God endure to watch them swallowing an evidently more righteous people (1:13).

The fourth utterance (2:1-5), answers the question posed above both in its local and universal formulation. The truth is stated in two parts: one whose deeds are unjust will fail; and "the righteous (person or nation) shall live by his faith" (v. 4).

The first biblical reference to "the end" in its apocalyptic sense occurs here (2:3); its only other appearance in the OT is in the Book of Daniel (8:19; 11:13, 27, 35; 12:4-13).

The fifth oracle (2:6-17) takes the form of five parables, each beginning with the words, "woe unto him". Some of these parables are found differently phrased in other books of the Bible, e.g. Isaiah chapters 14, 51 and Jeremiah 22:13. This attests their popularity among the people of Judah. While the meaning of the individual parable was of necessity veiled, every Judean would know what was intended, thus finding an expression for his own pent-up indignation against the Chaldeans.

The first woe (2:6-9) describes Nebuchadnezzar's desire for tribute from the conquered nations in terms of a merciless creditor. The second (2:9-11) depicts Chaldean pillage and plunder as being directed towards the construction of an empire strong enough to be unchallengeable. The third woe (2:12-14) continues the theme of the previous parable, adding the aspect of the Chaldeans' cruelty in their use of captives. The fourth parable (2:15-18) teaches that the evil perpetrated by the Chaldeans will eventually redound upon themselves, while the fifth (2:19-20) contrasts the brilliantly ornamented, but lifeless idols with the glory of God.

Chapter three is divided into four sections; the first and fourth sections (3:1-2, 16-19) are a prayer and the second and third (3:3-7, 8-15) recall God's deeds. The prayer refers to God's deeds at the time of the Exodus from Egypt (3:3-4) while his destructive power is described in mythological terms (3:5-7), with God battling the power of chaos (3:8-11). Judah's enemy, the Chaldeans, are now the object of God's destructive forces (3:12-15), and this knowledge overwhelms the prophet (3:16). The conclusion is one of triumph and trust in God (3:17-19).

The link between the book's final chapters and the earlier two poses a difficult problem. One of the Dead Sea Scrolls contains a commentary on Habakkuk (which identifies the Chaldeans with the Macedonians). This does not include chapter 3, which, being unconnected with the other two, is seen by scholars as not part of the original work, but as having been taken from some psalms collection. Others, however, consider the entire book to be a single, continuous literary work, with the third chapter a response to the question posed in the first.

OUTLINE

1:1-4	Complaint against violence and oppression
1:5-11	Chaldeans as instruments of God
1:12-17	The prophet protests concerning the oppressor
2:1-5	The righteous shall live by faith and the wicked shall perish
2:6-20	Five woes against oppressors
3:1-19	God will come to save his people

HABAZZINIAH ("the Lord has enriched me"). Father of Jeremiah and grandfather of Jaaziniah, from the house of the Rechabites (Jer 35:3) in the days of Jehoiakim the son of Josiah king of Judah (Jer 35:1).

HABOR The name of a river, where the ten tribes were settled after their deportation (II Kgs 17:6; 18:11, etc.). Identified with the River Khabur, which rises in the Kharga Dag mountains and flows between the Euphrates and the Tigris through a fertile plain about 200 miles (320 km) long before uniting with the Euphrates. Some of the important cities of Mesopotamia, such as Gozan, flourished along its banks. In the 16th-14th centuries B.C. the Horite kingdom of Mitani held sway along the river, and in the 10th century B.C. the Arameans invaded the area and built riverside towns. In the 8th century B.C. it became an Assyrian satrapy, but the constant uprisings and subsequent deportations of the Aramean population led to the decline of this region, leaving space for the Israelites who were brought there from Samaria.

HACHALIAH, HACALIAH Father of Nehemiah; sometimes spelled Hacaliah.

HACHILAH A hill to the south of Jeshimon, not far from Jerusalem. It was on this hill that David hid while King Saul "sought him every day" (I Sam 23:14, 19). Its location is unknown.

HACHMONI ("the wise one"?). Father of Jehiel, an official at the court of King David who "was with the king's sons".

HACHMONITE The family of Jashobeam, chief of the captains of David.

Note: the Hebrew spelling is identical to that of Hachmoni.

HADAD, HADAR

1. The eighth of the kings of Edom (Gen 36:39), who preceded the establishment of the monarchy in Israel (Gen 36:31). His capital was Pau, and he married Mehetabel. The name is given as Hadar in some manuscripts but in others, both Jewish and Samaritan, he is called Hadad, the name given in I Chronicles 1:50.

2. Another king of Edom.

3. The eighth son of Ishmael, who is called Hadad in I Chronicles and Hadar in standard editions of the Hebrew Bible at Genesis 25:15. The form Hadad is found in the Samaritan recension and in many manuscripts of the Jewish version also at Genesis 25:15.

4. A member of the royal house of Edom. He fled to Egypt when David captured Edom, subsequently returning to lead a revolt against Solomon.

HADADEZER ("Hadad is help"). Son of Rehob and king of Zobah (II Sam 8:3), defeated several times by David, although hostilities had already begun in the reign of Saul. He was a shrewd and powerful ruler, who put Assyria's temporary weakness (under Ashurrabi II — 1012-972 B.C.) to his full advantage by seizing former Assyrian territory in the Upper Euphrates region. According to one biblical account, Joab, David's army commander defeated a coalition of Aramean rulers, including Hadadezer, who had come to the aid of the besieged Ammonites at Rabbah (II Sam 10:6-1; 11:1). On another occasion, the Arameans were forced to make peace with David after their defeat at Helam (II Sam 10:15-18). The account in II Samuel 8:3-8 which tells of yet another defeat inflicted on Hadadezer "as he went to recover his territory at the River Euphrates" may be a different version of the same campaign, although some scholars maintain that each account describes a separate battle.

HADAD RIMMON A place in the valley of Megiddo mentioned in the Book of Zechariah as the site of a public mourning.

HADAR See HADAD

HADASHAH ("the new one"?). A city or place which fell to the lot of the tribe of Judah when the land of Canaan was divided among the tribes (Josh 15:37). It was in the central plain of Judah but the exact location is not known.

HADASSAH ("myrtle"). Queen Esther's original name.

HADATTAH A city or place which fell to the lot of the tribe of Judah when the land of Canaan was divided among the tribes (Josh 15:25). It was in southern Judah. Many scholars believe the word should be read together with the preceding one "Hazor Hadattah" i.e., "the new court".

HADES According to Greek mythology, the god ruling the underworld, which he received when the world was divided between him and his brothers Zeus and Poseidon. Hades also came to denote the underworld itself. Hades in the NT corresponds to the word Sheol in the OT, representing the final abode of the dead. In several passages Hades appears as a frightening place, located in the depths (Matt 11:23; Luke

Coin depicting the rape of Persephone by Hades, god of the underworld, on a coin of Acco-Ptolemais. 3rd century B.C.

The "Harrowing of Hell" depicted in an Armenian illuminated manuscript dated 1265. (Hromkla Library of St Thoros, Jerusalem)

10:15), locked by gates (Matt 16:18), the keys of which will be possessed by the coming redeemer: "I have the keys of Death and Hades" (Rev 1:18). The dead abide in Hades until the end of days, when each one shall face judgment.

See ABADDON; GEHENNA; SHEOL.

HADID A town in the Plain, close to Lod and Ono, where the people who returned from the Babylonian Exile settled (Ezra 2:33; Neh 7:37). In the Hellenistic and Roman periods it was a fortress that had been built by Simon Maccabee (I Macc 12:38). Identified with el-Haditheh, east of Lydda.

HADLAI ("heavyset", "fat"). Father of Amasa, one of the leaders of the tribe of Ephraim at the time of Pekah son of Remaliah.

HADORAM ("great is the god Ram").

1. The fifth son of Joktan son of Eber (the grandson of Shem) in the genealogy of the family of Noah.

2. The son of Tou king of Hamath (I Chr 18:9-10). His father sent him

to King David with many presents in gold, silver and bronze (I Chr 18:10) because David had defeated their common enemy Hadadezer (I Chr 18:10).

3. An official of King Rehoboam of Israel who was in charge of the corvée labor. When the king sent him to the Israelites, they stoned him to death. Identical with Adoram (I Kgs 12:18) and Adoniram (I Kgs 4:6). HADORAM.3
II Chr 10:18

HADRACH The name of a town and country in Aram mentioned only once in the Bible (Zech 9:1). It is heard of for the first time in the inscription of Zachar, king of Hamath (c. 800 B.C.), and then reappears in the Assyrian documents of the 8th century B.C., which mention a satrapy called Hatarikka. In 738 B.C. it was conquered by Tiglath-Pileser III. The prophecy of Zechariah seems to refer to the great revolt against Assyria which took place in 720 B.C., in which Hadrach joined with Israel, Hamath and the Phoenician and Philistine cities. Its exact location is not known. HADRACH
Zech 9:1

HAGAB ("grasshopper"). A family of Nethinim (Temple servants) who returned from the Exile in Babylon with Zerubbabel and settled in Jerusalem. HAGAB
Ezra 2:46

HAGABA ("grasshopper"). A family of Nethinim (Temple servants) who returned from the Exile in Babylon with Zerubbabel and settled in Jerusalem; may be identical with Hagabah. HAGABA
Neh 7:48

HAGABAH ("grasshopper"). A family of Nethinim (Temple servants) who returned from Babylon with Zerubbabel and settled in Jerusalem. HAGABAH
Ezra 2:45

HAGAR Sarah's Egyptian slave-girl. As Sarah was childless she gave Abraham Hagar, who bore his first son Ishmael (Gen 16:1-4). HAGAR
**Gen 16:1, 3-4,
8, 15-16; 21:9,
14, 17; 25:12.
Gal 4:24-25**

Hagar's story is actually the story of Ishmael's birth, his mother's conflict with her mistress about the son's inheritance, and the exclusion of both mother and son from the paternal household and the divine promise of land and national uniqueness given to it. According to some scholars it is transmitted in two slightly different versions in Genesis chapters 16 and 21. In the NT, Paul refers to the Hagar story symbolically (Gal 4:21-31) to argue the freedom of Christians from the obligations of the law.

HAGARITES, HAGERITES, HAGRITES A tribe or clan of pastoral nomads (I Chr 5:10) and tent dwellers who raised camels, sheep and donkeys (I Chr 5:21). They inhabited the region east of Gilead (I Chr 5:10) and were listed among the enemies of Israel, together with the Moabites, Edomites and Ishmaelites (Ps 83:6). During the reign of Saul, the Hagrites were defeated by the tribe of Reuben and their territory was appropriated (I Chr 5:10). It is also related that the Reubenites, the Gadites and half-tribe of Manasseh fought against the Hagrites and the Ishmaelite tribe of Jetur, Naphish and Nodab and inhabited their territories until the Exile (I Chr 5:19-22). These narratives may refer to the same historical event and preserve two separate traditions. HAGARITES,
HAGERITES,
HAGRITES
**I Chr 5:10, 19-
20; 27:31. Ps
83:6**

Jaziz the Hagerite is listed as one of David's stewards, in charge of the flocks (I Chr 27:31).

HAGGAI Hebrew personal name derived from the Hebrew word *hag* meaning "festival". The name is borne only by the 6th century B.C. prophet mentioned in the Book of Haggai and in the Book of Ezra. Most likely the prophet was given the name Haggai because he was born on a festival (cf Hodesh). HAGGAI
**Ezra 5:1; 6:14.
Hag 1:1, 3,
12-13; 2:1, 10,
13-14, 20**

HAGGAI, BOOK OF The tenth book of the twelve Minor Prophets. It is built upon four prophetic revelations experienced by Haggai during the second regnal year of Darius I of Persia i.e., 520 B.C. These revelations are dated as follows: (a) the first day of the sixth month (later Elul, i.e., August-September; Hag 1:1); (b) the twenty-first day of the seventh month (later Tishri, i.e., September-October; Hag 2:1); (c) the twenty-fourth day of the ninth month (later Chislev; Hag 2:10); and (d) later that same day (Hag 2:20). Unlike the Books of Jeremiah and Ezekiel, in which the prophets often speak about themselves in the first person, this book invariably refers to Haggai in the third person (Hag 1:1, 12-13; 2:1, 10, 13, 20).

According to the author of the Book of Ezra, the Second Temple, whose foundations had been laid in 537 B.C. (Ezra 3:8-13), was still uncompleted as late as 520 B.C. because the returned exiles were intimidated by "the people of the land" (Ezra 4:4-5). Apparently unaware of this explanation, Haggai attributes the delay in rebuilding the Temple to the returned exiles' sheer neglect of their responsibility to the Lord, and preoccupation with their own material advancement. When asked why they had not rebuilt the Temple, they said that they were awaiting the divinely appointed time. This argument provoked the Lord's anger (Hag 1:1-4); the people's neglect was punished by a drought, which led to the near economic collapse of Judah (1:5-11). The Lord's rebuke through the agency of Haggai brought about the desired result when, three weeks after its delivery, on the twenty-first day of the

Fragments from the Book of Haggai found at Qumran. (Shrine of the Book, Jerusalem)

sixth month, the people and their leaders took up in earnest the task of rebuilding the Temple (1:12-15). In Haggai's second prophecy the Lord consoles the people of Judah over the fact that the Temple now being built is much less impressive than Solomon's Temple (2:1-9). The Lord promises that he himself will in due time make the new Temple more glorious than the first. In his third prophecy (2:10-19) Haggai returns to a central theme of classical prophecy — the primacy of morality. Lest the people think that the building of the Temple then in progress is the be-all and end-all of Israelite religion, Haggai reminds the people that the Temple cannot confer holiness on a people whose deeds are impure. On the contrary, just as sacrificial meat and bread and wine and oil do not transmit holiness but are susceptible to defilement, so is the Temple incapable of sanctifying the impure deeds of Israel and is itself susceptible to defilement by those deeds. The prophecy concludes with a promise of prosperity. Haggai's final prophecy (2:21-23) asserts that the Persian empire is about to be toppled by civil war and that Zerubbabel, the grandson of King Jehoiachin of Judah, who has been serving as Persian governor of Judah, is about to become the Lord's regent on earth. This short, unfulfilled prophecy may have been inspired, in part, by the series of revolts, which shook the Persian empire between the death of Cambyses (529-522 B.C.) and Darius' restoration of order, and in part by the curse of Jehoiachin in Jeremiah 22:24, 27. Haggai 2:21-23, like Isaiah chapter 11, and their prophetic passages, anticipates the arrival of a divinely appointed Davidic regent of the world.

OUTLINE

1:1-8	Exhortation to rebuild the Temple
2:1-9	Encouragement to the builders
2:10-19	Promise of prosperity to accompany work of restoration
2:20-23	Messianic promise to Zerubbabel

HAGGI The second son of Gad (Gen 46:16), seventh son of Jacob by Leah's maid Zilpah (Gen 30:9-11). He was the founder of the Haggite family (Num 26:15). The name is derived from the Hebrew *hag*, "festival", and may indicate that the bearer was born on such a day.

HAGGIAH ("born on a festive day"?). A Levite, son of Shimea and father of Asaiah in the family of Merari, third son of Levi.

HAGGITES A family founded by Haggi, the second son of Gad.

HAGGITH ("born on a festive day"?). One of the wives of King David and mother of his fourth son, Adonijah, born in Hebron (II Sam 3:4).

HAGIOGRAPHA ("holy writings"). A term designating the third and final division of the Hebrew Scriptures, the "Writings". The Hebrew Bible, whose order differs from the sequence of most English Bibles (which instead follow the Greek) includes in this section: Psalms, Proverbs, Job, Song of Songs, Ruth, Lamentations, Ecclesiastes, Esther, Daniel, Ezra-Nehemiah and I-II Chronicles.

The Hagiographa was the last part of the OT to be canonized, the status of some books still being debated in the late 1st century A.D. The NT does not refer to the Hagiographa as a group, although the normal designation of the OT scriptures as "the Law and the Prophets" appears once as "the Law of Moses and the Prophets, and the Psalms" (Luke 24:44).

HAGRI The father of Mibhar, one of David's thirty "mighty men".

HAGRITES See HAGARITES

HAHIROTH See PI HAHIROTH

HAKKATAN ("the small one"). A man of the family of Azgad, father of Johanan (Ezra 8:12), one of the men who returned from the Exile of Babylon with Ezra (Ezra 8:1).

HAKKOZ ("the thorn"). A Levite, head of the seventh division of priests serving the House of the Lord in the time of King David. An alternative name for Accoz, Koz.

HAKUPHA Head of a family of Nethinim (Temple servants) who returned with Zerubbabel from the Exile in Babylon (Ezra 2:1-2) and settled in Jerusalem (Neh 7:53).

HALAH A place to which Tiglath-Pileser III deported the people of northern Transjordan (I Chr 5:26). The inhabitants of Samaria were also exiled there by the king of Assyria (II Kgs 17:6; 18:11). Halah is identified with Khalakhkha in Assyria, north of Nineveh.

HAGGI
Gen 46:16.
Num 26:15

HAGGIAH
I Chr 6:30

HAGGITES
Num 26:15

HAGGITH
II Sam 3:4. I
Kgs 1:5, 11;
2:13. I Chr 3:2

HAGRI
I Chr 11:38

HAGRITES
I Chr 5:10,
19-20

HAHIROTH
Num 33:8

HAKKATAN
Ezra 8:12

HAKKOZ
I Chr 24:10

HAKUPHA
Ezra 2:51.
Neh 7:53

HALAH
II Kgs 17:6;
18:11. I Chr
5:26

HALAK (MOUNT) A mountain marking the southern limit of Joshua's conquest. Commonly identified with Jebel Halak, in the central Negeb.

HALHUL A town in the territory of Judah, in the mountains of Judah. In the Second Temple period it was part of Idumea. It is identified with the modern village of Halhul, about 4 miles (6 km) north of Hebron. The Moslems venerate the tomb of the prophet Jonah shown there,

General view of Halhul.

whereas a Jewish tradition of the Middle Ages pointed out the tomb of the seer Gad at Halhul.

HALI A town in the territory of Asher, mentioned together with Helkath, Beten and Achshaph (Josh 19:25). Most of the identifications which have been suggested are outside the territory of Asher, and lack archeological confirmation.

HALLELUJAH, ALLELUIA A cultic expression meaning "Praise Yah, i.e. "Praise the Lord". It was probably used as a shout or prayer at a point of great joy or rejoicing. The phrase appears in 16 psalms beginning with 104:35 where it closes the hymn (also Ps 105; 106; 113; 115-17; 135; 146-150); while it serves as an introduction to Psalms 106; 111-13; 135; 146-150. Psalms 146-150 are known as the "Hallelujah Psalms". The Greek and Latin versions do not translate the expression but simply transliterate it as a single word, "hallelouia" from which it passed into European languages. It also appears in the Book of Revelation in chapter 19.

HALLOHESH ("the whisperer"). Father of Shallum (leader of half the district of Jerusalem) who helped repair the wall of Jerusalem at the time of Nehemiah (Neh 3:12) and one of the men who sealed the covenant made by Nehemiah (Neh 10:24).

HAM

1. The second son of Noah, who with his wife joined his father and two other married brothers in the ark. Noah, Genesis 9:20-27, tells how Ham saw his father intoxicated and naked, and informed his brothers of what he had seen. As a result, Canaan (Ham's son) came under a curse which condemned him to be the slave of his brothers, foreshadowing the later subjugation of the Canaanites.

Ham was the father of Mizraim, Put and Canaan (Gen 10:6). The identification of Canaan as Ham's son is often explained as an attempt to harmonize divergent traditions of the names of Noah's sons, or as a recollection of Egyptian control over the land of Canaan.

In poetry "Ham" is sometimes used as a synonym for Egypt (Ps 78:51, etc.).

2. A city of the Zuzzim east of the Jordan River, which was attacked by Chedorlaomer, king of Elam, in the time of Abraham.

HAMAN The son of Hammedatha the Agagite (Est 3:1, 10; 8:3, 5; 9:24); the chief minister at the court of Ahasuerus, king of Persia and Media.

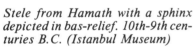

Haman leading Mordecai in triumph through the streets of Shushan. Scene from the Book of Esther from a wall painting at the synagogue of Dura-Europos. 3rd century.

The king acquiesced to his plan to destroy the Jews throughout the kingdom (Est 3:5-7). Haman's hatred for Mordecai and the Jews is explained by Mordecai's refusal to bow down before him. The plot was foiled by Esther and Mordecai, and Haman was hanged on the gallows he had prepared for the latter (Est 7:5-10). Haman's ten sons were also executed (Est 9:7-10). For Jews, Haman became the archetypal antisemite.

9:10, 12-14, 24-25

HAMATH, HAMATHITES One of the major cities on the Orontes, in northern Syria, the capital of a district and an Aramean-Hittite kingdom under the name of Hamath the Great (Amos 6:2, etc.). It was conquered by David (II Sam 8:9) and Solomon built a store city there (II Chr 8:4). According to the Assyrian sources Hamath was one of the countries of the "land of the Hittites" that joined forces with the neighboring states to oppose Assyria in 853 B.C. and succeeded in halting Shalmaneser III near Karkar. At the beginning of the 8th century B.C. it formed part of a larger country, that was a vassal of Assyria. After rebelling again it was conquered in about 740 B.C. by Tiglath-Pileser III, then finally destroyed by Sargon in 720 B.C. The people of Hamath were deported to Israel (II Kgs 17:24), and those of Samaria were taken to Hamath (Is 11:11-12). Known today as Hama.

The phrase "entrance to Hamath" actually refers to a town, modern Lebweh, within the jurisdiction of Hamath. It designated the northern boundary of Canaan (Num 34:8; Ezek 47:15) and was usually paired with the southwestern boundary, the Brook of Egypt.

HAMATH, HAMATHITES
Gen 10:18. Num 13:21; 34:8. Josh 13:5. Judg 3:3. II Sam 8:9. I Kgs 8:65. II Kgs 14:25, 28; 17:24, 30; 18:34; 19:13; 23:33; 25:21. I Chr 1:16; 13:5; 18:3, 9. II Chr 7:8; 8:4. Is 10:9; 11:11; 36:19; 37:13. Jer 39:5; 49:23; 52:9, 27. Ezek 47:16-17, 20; 48:1. Amos 6:2, 14. Zech 9:2

HAMATH ZOBAH An alternate name for ZOBAH, a city conquered by King Solomon.

HAMATH ZOBAH
II Chr 8:3

HAMITES See HAM No.1

HAMITES
I Chr 4:40

HAMMATH

1. Father or founder of the Rechab family or the home of the Kenites of the family of Rechab.

HAMMATH 1
I Chr 2:55

2. A fortified town which fell to the lot of Naphtali when the land of Canaan was divided among the tribes. Probably the same as Hammoth Dor, a city of the Levites (Josh 21:32). In Roman and Byzantine times it appears in Jewish sources as Hamtha ("hot baths"), or Ammatous in the Greek form. It was renowned for its hot springs, to which medicinal

HAMMATH 2
Josh 19:35

Stele from Hamath with a sphinx depicted in bas-relief. 10th-9th centuries B.C. (Istanbul Museum)

properties were ascribed. Identified with Hamman Tabariyeh, south of Tiberias.

HAMMEDATHA Hammedatha the Agagite was the father of Haman, archenemy of the Jews at the court of King Ahasuerus.

HAMMOLEKETH ("the queen"). Sister of Gilead and daughter of Machir the son of Manasseh (I Chr 7:17-18). She bore three sons: Ishdod, Abiezer and Mahlah (I Chr 7:18).

HAMMON

1. A town on the western border of the territory of Asher, south of Tyre (Josh 19:28). It has been suggested that the ancient name of the site is preserved in the name of Wadi Hamul, between Ran en-Naqura and Ras el-Abyad.

2. A Levite town in the territory of Naphtali, awarded to the family of Gershon (I Chr 6:76). It is apparently identical with Hammoth Dor (Josh 21:32), or Hammath (Josh 19:35). Unidentified.

HAMMOTH DOR See HAMMATH No.2

HAMONAH ("multitude"). The symbolic name of a city in the Valley of Hamon Gog, in whose vicinity Ezekiel prophesied that the armies of Gog and his allies would be defeated in their struggle with Israel (Ezek 39:16).

HAMON GOG, VALLEY OF Ezekiel 39:11 reads "And it shall come to pass in that day, that I will give Gog a burial place there in Israel, the valley of those who pass by east of the sea ... there shall bury Gog and all his multitude. Therefore they will call it the Valley of Hamon Gog." The name is probably symbolic.

HAMOR ("donkey"). Hamor the Hivite was the ruler of Shechem when Jacob arrived there from Padan Aram. Hamor's son, Shechem, falling in love with Jacob's daughter Dinah, raped her. Later father and son were killed, together with all the men of Shechem, by Dinah's brothers Simeon and Levi. Jacob built an altar on land purchased from Hamor's sons (Gen 33:19-20); and the bones of Joseph were buried there (Josh 24:32; cf Gen 48:21; Acts 7:16).

HAMRAN First son of Dishon, the son of Anah, in the genealogy of the family of Seir.

An alternate spelling for Amran and Hemdan.

HAMUEL ("the Lord protected"). Son of Mishma and father of Zecchur in the genealogy of the family of Simeon.

HAMUL (perhaps a shorter form of Hamuel). Second son of Perez, the fourth son of Judah (Gen 46:12) and the founder of the Hamulite family (Num 26:21).

HAMULITES A family descended from Hamul the second son of Perez according to the second census of Israel.

HAMUTAL Daughter of Jeremiah of Libneh, she was the wife of Josiah king of Judah (II Kgs 23:30-31) and the mother of Jehoahaz who succeeded his father as king, and of Mattaniah who reigned later under the name of Zedekiah (II Kgs 24:18).

HANAMEEL The son of Shallum, uncle of Jeremiah (Jer 32:7). Visiting the prophet in prison while Jerusalem was under the siege of the Babylonians, Hanameel offered to sell him his field in Anathoth so that it would remain in the family (Jer 32:7-8). Jeremiah bought the field for 17 shekels of silver (Jer 32:9).

HANAN (a shorter form of Elhanan).

1. One of the sons of Shashak (I Chr 8:23) son of Beriah (I Chr 8:14, 16) in the genealogy of King Saul.

2. The sixth and youngest son of Azel son of Eleasah No.2 in the genealogy of King Saul.

3. Hanan the son of Maachah, one of David's "mighty men".

HAMMEDATHA Est 3:1, 10; 8:5; 9:10, 24

HAMMOLEKETH I Chr 7:18

HAMMON 1 Josh 19:28

HAMMON 2 I Chr 6:76

HAMMOTH DOR Josh 21:32

HAMONAH Ezek 39:16

HAMON GOG Ezek 39:11, 15

HAMOR Gen 33:19; 34:2, 4, 6, 8, 13, 18, 20, 24, 26. Josh 24:32. Judg 9:28. Acts 7:16

HAMRAN I Chr 1:41

HAMUEL I Chr 4:26

HAMUL Gen 46:12. Num 26:21. I Chr 2:5

HAMULITES Num 26:21

HAMUTAL II Kgs 23:31; 24:18. Jer 52:1

HANAMEEL Jer 32:7-9, 12

HANAN 1 I Chr 8:23

HANAN 2 I Chr 8:38; 9:44

HANAN 3 I Chr 11:43

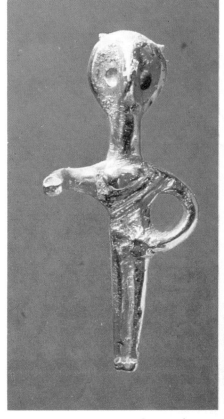

Gold-plated bronze Canaanite figurine from Hamath. 14th-13th centuries B.C. (Israel Dept. of Antiquities and Museums)

Carnelian Phoenician seal inscribed "[Belonging] to Hanan". In the center is a figure with hands raised in prayer. 8th-7th centuries B.C. (Israel Dept. of Antiquities and Museums)

4. The head of a family of Nethinim (Temple servants) who returned from Exile with Zerubbabel (Ezra 2:46) and settled in Jerusalem (Neh 7:49).

5. A Levite, one of the men who "helped the people understand the Law" (Neh 8:7) and was among those who sealed the covenant of Nehemiah (Neh 10:10).

6. Another man who sealed the covenant of Nehemiah.

7. A third man of that name to seal the covenant of Nehemiah.

8. Son of Zaccur and grandson of Mattaniah who was appointed assistant to the treasurers of the Temple.

9. Hanan the son of Igdaliah; the chamber of his sons adjoined the chamber of the princes in the house of the Rechabites.

HANANEAL, HANANEEL The name of a tower in Jerusalem at the time of Nehemiah, probably at the northwest corner of the Temple Mount. Its origin is unclear.

HANANI (a shorter form of Hananiah).

1. One of the sons of Heman the king's seer, head of the 18th group of singers in the House of the Lord at the time of King David.

2. The father of Jehu the prophet (II Chr 19:2) at the time of Baasha king of Israel and Jehoshaphat king of Judah.

3. A seer who went to Asa king of Judah and reproved him for his alliance with the king of Syria, telling him he should put his trust in the Lord alone (II Chr 16:7). This angered the king who imprisoned him. It has been suggested that this Hanani was identical with No.2.

4. A son of Immer, a priest, who had taken an alien wife and had to repudiate her following the decree of Ezra.

5. A brother or kinsman of Nehemiah who came from Judah to visit the prophet in his exile in Shushan to tell him of the great distress of the Jews in Judah and in Jerusalem (Neh 1:2). Later Nehemiah put him in charge of reconstructed Jerusalem (Neh 7:2).

6. A musician who led one of the two choirs in the thanksgiving ceremonies marking the completion and dedication of the wall rebuilt by Nehemiah (Neh 12:27, 36).

HANANIAH ("the Lord has been gracious").

1. A commander in the army of King Uzziah of Judah.

2. Son of Azur; a prophet who, in a controversy with Jeremiah, wrongly predicted the downfall of Babylon within two years.

3. Father of one of Jehoiakim's officials during the time of Jeremiah.

4. Grandfather of the sentry who arrested Jeremiah on the charge of deserting to the Babylonians.

5. Son of Zerubbabel.

6. A Benjamite descended from Shashak.

7. Son of Heman and one of David's chief musicians.

8. Son of Bebai; an Israelite who repudiated his alien wife at the command of Ezra.

9. Member of the perfumers' guild who assisted in rebuilding Jerusalem's wall.

10. Son of Shelemiah who helped rebuild the walls of Jerusalem.

11. Commander of Jerusalem's citadel under Nehemiah.

12. A leader of the people under Nehemiah; he was among those who signed the pledge of reform.

13. Head of a priestly family in the days of the high priest Joiakim.

14. A priest and trumpeter in the time of Nehemiah.

15. The Hebrew name of Daniel's companion Shadrach.

HANES An Egyptian city mentioned by Isaiah; its ruins are to be found on the east bank of the Nile River, some 15 miles (24 km) northeast of present-day Beni Suef.

HANAN 4
**Ezra 2:46.
Neh 7:49**

HANAN 5
**Neh 8:7;
10:10**

HANAN 6
Neh 10:22

HANAN 7
Neh 10:26

HANAN 8
Neh 13:13

HANAN 9
Jer 35:4

HANANEAL
HANANEEL
**Neh 3:1;
12:39. Jer
31:38. Zech
14:10**

HANANI 1
I Chr 25:4, 25

HANANI 2
**I Kgs 16:1, 7.
II Chr 19:2;
20:34**

HANANI 3
II Chr 16:7

HANANI 4
Ezra 10:20

HANANI 5
Neh 1:2; 7:2

HANANI 6
Neh 12:36

HANANIAH 1
II Chr 26:11

HANANIAH 2
**Jer 28:1, 5,
10-13, 15 17**

HANANIAH 3
Jer 36:12

HANANIAH 4
Jer 37:13

HANANIAH 5
I Chr 3:19, 21

HANANIAH 6
I Chr 8:24

HANANIAH 7
I Chr 25:4, 23

HANANIAH 8
Ezra 10:28

HANANIAH 9
Neh 3:8

HANANIAH 10
Neh 3:30

HANANIAH 11
Neh 7:2

HANIEL ("the Lord is grace"). Second son of Ulla in the genealogy of the family of Asher (I Chr 7:39); a great leader and a "mighty man of valor" (I Chr 7:40).

Note: the Hebrew spelling is identical to that of Hanniel.

HANNAH ("grace"). Wife of Elkanah, who preferred her to his other wife, Peninnah. The fertile Peninnah made life a misery for Hannah who was barren. Hannah directed strenuous effort towards the seemingly impossible goal of becoming a mother. She went to the Shiloh temple and vowed that if God granted her a son, she would dedicate him to God as a Nazirite (I Sam 1:11). The priest Eli observed her prayer and assured her that it would be answered (I Sam 1:12-17). Samuel was duly born, and when three years old he was brought to the sanctuary and placed under the care of Eli (I Sam 1:21-28). Eventually, he grew up to be a priest, judge and leader. Hannah's supreme sacrifice of separation from her long-awaited child was amply rewarded: her son became a great man and God granted her additional children, both male and female (I Sam 2:21).

I Samuel 2:1-10 is a thanksgiving hymn attributed to Hannah who supposedly composed and recited it after placing her son at the Shiloh sanctuary. The attribution may refer to the verse which states that God can make a barren mother give birth to many children (I Sam 2:5).

HANNATHON A town in Galilee, in the domain of the tribe of Zebulun. Hannathon is also mentioned in the El Amarna Letters of the 14th century B.C., and in the list of towns conquered by Tiglath-Pileser in 732 B.C. The tell of Hannathon, identified in the Bet Netofa Valley, has yielded sherds dating from the Bronze Age through medieval times.

HANNIEL ("the Lord is grace"). The son of Ephod, Hanniel, a man of Manasseh, was one of the ten leaders chosen by the Lord to help Joshua and Eleazar divide the land of Canaan among the Children of Israel (Num 34:16-17, 23).

Note: the Hebrew spelling is identical to that of Haniel.

HANOCH, HANOCHITES

1. Third son of Midian (a son of Abraham by his concubine Keturah).

2. Firstborn son of Reuben (the firstborn of Jacob) and founder of the Hanochite family.

HANUN

1. The son of Nahash king of Ammon, Hanun ascended to the Ammonite throne upon his father's death (II Sam 10:1). King David sent him a message of condolence but Hanun insulted and mocked the messengers (II Sam 10:3-4). David then made war against him; his captain Joab captured the king's capital, Rabbah (I Chr 20:1), and brought Hanun's crown to David. King David then appointed Hanun's brother Shobi to rule in his stead in Rabbah (II Sam 17:27).

2. Sixth son of Zalaph, he was among those who repaired the wall at the time of Nehemiah and is probably identical with the other Hanun mentioned earlier (Neh 3:13) as having repaired the Valley Gate.

HAPHRAIM A town in the territory of Issachar (Josh 19:19), mentioned after Jezreel, Chesulloth and Shunem, and before Shion and Anaharath. The order of the towns listed in the description of the territory of Issachar is not entirely clear. The identification of Haphraim would appear to depend on the identification of its neighbors in the list, but even this is not certain. It is difficult to decide whether it belongs to the group including Shion and Anaharath, which lie outside the Jezreel Valley, or to the group of Chesulloth and Shunem, situated within it. The phrase "and their territory went to Jezreel" (Josh 19:18) may also denote towns at the southern border of the territory of Issachar, bordering on the Valley of Jezreel. Several identifications have

Detail of a stele from Haran showing Nabonidus, the last Babylonian king, worshiping the moon god, Sin. 6th century B.C. (Urfa Museum, Turkey)

been suggested. One is at et-Taiyiba, 9½ miles (15 km) northwest of Beth Shean, a site also identified as Ophrah (Judg 6:11): the names of Haphraim and Ophrah are sometimes interchanged.

HAPPIZZEZ A priest, descendant of Aaron, who headed the 18th group of priests doing duty in the House of the Lord at the time of King David. The name is sometimes spelt Aphses. **HAPPIZZEZ I Chr 24:15**

HARA According to I Chronicles 5:26, Tiglath-Pileser king of Assyria deported the tribes of Reuben, Gad and half of the tribe of Manasseh to Halach, Habor and Hara, and to the River Gozan. In II Kings 17:6 "the cities of the Medes" replaces Hara. In the Septuagint in II Kings 17:6 "the mountains of the Medes" appears instead of Hara. The text in I Chronicles 5:26 thus seems to be corrupt. In any case, no place by the name of Hara is known. **HARA I Chr 5:26**

HARADAH A halt on the journey of the Children of Israel to the promised land, between Mount Shepher and Makheloth. Its location is unknown. **HARADAH Num 33:24-5**

HARAN

1. A city in the upper reaches of the Balih Valley, a commercial and cultural center from the 2nd millennium onwards. It lies on an ancient caravan route from Mesopotamia to Cappodocia, Syria, Palestine and Egypt. Terah, the father of Abraham, settled there with his family (Gen 11:31), and it was an important center in the early history of the Hebrew nation. Abraham sent to Haran to find a wife for his son Isaac (Gen 24:4) and Jacob went there after escaping from Esau (Gen 28:10). **HARAN 1 Gen 11:31-32; 12:4-5; 27:43; 28:10; 29:4. II Kgs 19:12. Is 37:12. Ezek 27:23. Acts 7:2, 4**

Haran is mentioned in the Mari archives as a religious center for the West Semitic tribes, who worshiped at the temple of the moon god, Sin.

From the 15th to the 13th centuries B.C. Haran was part of the Horite kingdom of Mitanni; with the collapse of the kingdom it was conquered by Assyria (c. 1270 B.C.) It was subsequently held temporarily by the Arameans and then recaptured by the Assyrians. When Nineveh was captured by the Medes (Madai) and the Chaldeans (612 B.C.), Haran became the capital of the kingdom of Madai for a brief period. At about this time it is mentioned by Ezekiel as one of the cities trading with Tyre (Ezek 27:23).

Haran is identified with Sultan Tepe. Excavations made in the vicinity of the town have uncovered an important library of the later Babylonian period.

2. Son of Terah and brother of Abraham and Nahor. He was the father of Lot, Milcah and Iscah. Haran died in Ur "his native land", while his father was still alive. **HARAN 2 Gen 11:26-29, 31**

3. Son of Caleb and his concubine Ephah; and father of Gazez. **HARAN 3 I Chr 2:46**

4. A Levite, son of Shimei and head of his father's house. **HARAN 4 I Chr 23:9**

HARARITE A tribe, possibly from the hill country of Judah. Three sons of the Hararites were numbered among David's "mighty men": Shammah son of Agee (II Sam 23:11), Jonathan son of Shammah (II Sam 23:32-33; son of Shageh in I Chr 11:34), and Ahiam son of Sharar (II Sam 23:33, son of Sacar in I Chr 11:35). **HARARITE II Sam 23:11, 33. I Chr 11:34-35**

HARBONA, HARBONAH One of the seven eunuchs who served as chamberlains at the court of King Ahasuerus (Est 1:10). When the king decided to put Haman to death, Harbona drew his attention to the gallows Haman had prepared for Mordecai, and there Haman was hanged. **HARBONA, HARBONAH Est 1:10; 7:9**

HARE See ANIMALS

HAREPH A son of Hur, firstborn of Ephrathah (I Chr 2:50-51) in the genealogy of the family of Caleb. The founder of Beth Gader (I Chr 2:51). **HAREPH I Chr 2:51**

HARHAIAH Father of Uzziel, a goldsmith, who participated in **HARHAIAH Neh 3:8**

repairing the walls of Jerusalem at the time of Nehemiah.

HARHAS Father of Tikuah and grandfather of Shallum, whose wife was Huldah the prophetess.

HARHUR Head of a family of Nethinim (Temple servants) who returned with Zerubbabel from the Exile in Babylon.

HARIM ("consecrated to the Lord").

1. A descendant of Aaron, a priest, head of the third division of Levites who officiated in the House of the Lord at the time of King David.

2. The head of a family who returned from the Exile in Babylon with Zerubbabel (Ezra 2:32) and settled in Jerusalem (Neh 7:35). This family, or another of the same name, is mentioned again in the same chapters (Ezra 2:39; Neh 7:42); and Harim appears twice in the list of those who sealed the covenant at the time of Nehemiah (Neh 10:5, 27).

3. No less than ten sons of Harim are listed among those who had taken pagan wives and had to repudiate them upon the decree of Ezra (Ezra 10:18-19, 21, 31).

4. Father of Malchijah; he was among those who repaired a section of the wall of Jerusalem.

5. A Levite who returned from the Exile in Babylon with Zerubbabel.

HARIPH The head of a family who returned in the first return from the captivity in Babylon (Neh 7:24); a member of that family was among those who sealed the covenant of Nehemiah (Neh 10:19).

HARMON A word which occurs only once and whose meaning is unknown.

HARNEPHER The second son of Zophah in the genealogy of the family of Asher.

HAROD The site of a well or spring at the foot of Mount Gilboa, where Gideon and his men camped before the battle against the Midianites.

The Spring of Harod at the foot of Mount Gilboa.

HARODITE An epithet affixed to the name of two of David's "mighty men": Shammah and Elika. Most scholars believe that there is no connection with Harod and that the two men came from the territory of Judah.

HAROEH ("the seer"). The son of Shobal, the founder of Kirjath Jearim, in the genealogy of the family of Caleb.

Coin of Kir Harosheth - Harosheth Hagoyim, showing an altar and a priest. 3rd century A.D.

HARORITE See HARODITE

HAROSHETH HAGOYIM The location of Sisera's home (Judg 4:2), the place where the army of Jabin, king of Hazor, assembled under Sisera's command before the battle with Barak and Deborah (Judg 4:13), and to which it subsequently fled in defeat (Judg 4:16). It has been suggested that, rather than a specific site, the name Harosheth Hagoiim (the Woodland of the Nations) represents the wooded hill country of Galilee.

HARSHA A family of Nethinim (Temple servants) who returned from the Exile in Babylon with Zerubbabel (Ezra 2:52) and settled in Jerusalem (Neh 7:54).

HARUM Father of Aharhel in the genealogy of the family of Judah.

HARUMAPH ("man with a mutilated or truncated nose"?). Father of Jedaiah, one of the men who helped to repair the walls of Jerusalem at the time of Nehemiah.

HARUPHITE An epithet affixed to the name of Shephatiah, one of the men of Benjamin who defected from the armies of Saul and joined David in Ziklag (I Chr 12:1, 5); they were equally adept in using right and left hands to hurl stones and shoot arrows (I Chr 12:2).

HARUZ The father of Meshullemeth, wife of Manasseh king of Judah and mother of his son Amon who reigned after him (II Kgs 21:18-19).

HASADIAH The fourth son of Zerubbabel, grandson of Jeconiah in the genealogy of David.

HASHABIAH Name of several biblical characters, most of them Levites.

1. A Levite from the line of Merari (third son of Levi), father of Malluch and son of Amaziah; he is one of the ancestors of Ethan No.3, the singer (I Chr 6:44-45).

2. Another Levite from the line of Merari, father of Azrikam and grandfather of Hashub No.4.

3. Another Levite, son of Jeduthun (perhaps an alternate name for Ethan No.3); together with his brothers and his father he "prophesied with a harp to give thanks and to praise the Lord" (I Chr 25:3). The 12th turn of duty in the House of the Lord in the time of King David was allotted to the Hashabiah family (I Chr 25:19).

4. A man of Hebron; King David put him in charge of the administration of the west side of the Jordan.

5. Son of Kermuel, appointed by David to lead the tribe of Levi.

6. A leader of the Levites at the time of Josiah king of Judah.

7. A Levite from the line of Merari who was living at Casiphia in the time of the Babylonian Exile; he was among the men who joined Ezra the prophet "by the river that flows to Ahava" (Ezra 8:15, 17-19) and was later among the 12 men put in charge of the treasures of the Temple (Ezra 8:24).

8. A Levite, leader of half the district of Keilah. He was among the men who repaired the wall at the time of Nehemiah; perhaps identical with No.7.

9. A Levite who was among the leaders who sealed the covenant at the time of Nehemiah; perhaps identical with Nos. 7 and 8.

10. Father of Bani No.5 and grandfather of Uzzi (overseer of the Levites in Jerusalem at the time of Nehemiah).

11. A priest, head of the Hilkiah family at the time of the high priest Joiakim (Neh 11:12, 21).

12. One of the leaders of the Levites.

HASHABNAH A Levite, one of the leaders of the people; he was among those who placed their seal on the covenant at the time of Ezra and Nehemiah.

HARORITE
I Chr 11:27

HAROSHETH
HAGOYIM
Judg 4:2, 13, 16

HARSHA
Ezra 2:52.
Neh 7:54

HARUM
I Chr 4:8

HARUMAPH
Neh 3:10

HARUPHITE
I Chr 12:5

HARUZ
II Kgs 21:19

HASADIAH
I Chr 3:20

HASHABIAH 1
I Chr 6:45

HASHABIAH 2
I Chr 9:14.
Neh 11:15

HASHABIAH 3
I Chr 25:3, 19

HASHABIAH 4
I Chr 26:30

HASHABIAH 5
I Chr 27:17

HASHABIAH 6
II Chr 35:9

HASHABIAH 7
Ezra 8:19, 24

HASHABIAH 8
Neh 3:17

HASHABIAH 9
Neh 10:11

HASHABIAH 10
Neh 11:22

HASHABIAH 11
Neh 12:21

HASHABIAH 12
Neh 12:24

HASHABNAH
Neh 10:25

HASHABNIAH

1. Father of Hattush No.3 (one of the men who repaired the walls of Jerusalem at the time of Nehemiah).

2. A Levite who participated in the great fast (Neh 9:1) held before the sealing of the covenant (Neh 9:38); he was one of the eight men who said the prayer to the Lord (Neh 9:5).

HASHBADANA One of the men who stood by Ezra when he read the Law to the people who had returned from the Exile of Babylon.

HASHEM The sons of "Hashem the Gizonite" are listed among David's thirty "mighty men".

HASHMONAH A halt in the journey of the Children of Israel to the promised land, between Mithkah and Moseroth; generally believed to have been in the wilderness of Paran south of present-day Elath.

HASHUB, HASSHUB

1. A son of Pahath-Moab who repaired a section of the wall of Jerusalem at the time of Nehemiah. He also took part in the repairs of the Tower of the Ovens.

2. Another of the men who repaired the walls; he worked on a section which was opposite his house.

3. One of the leaders of the people who sealed the covenant at the time of Nehemiah.

4. A Levite, son of Azrikam and father of Shemaiah, one of the men of the Merari clan who settled in Jerusalem after their return from the Exile in Babylon.

HASHUBAH ("important" or a shorter form of Hashabiah). One of the sons of Zerubbabel, grandson of Jeconiah in the genealogy of the family of Jeconiah.

HASHUM ("broad nose"?). Head of a family of exiles who returned from the Exile in Babylon with Zerubbabel (Ezra 2:1-2, 19) and numbered 223 persons according to Ezra (Ezra 2:19) and 328 according to Nehemiah (Neh 7:22). Hashum was among the leaders who sealed the covenant (Ezra 10:33; Neh 10:18); and he stood by Ezra when the Law was read to the congregation (Neh 8:4).

HASRAH An alternate spelling for Harhas (II Kgs 22:14). Father of Tokhath (II Chr 34:22) or Tikvah (II Kgs 22:14) and grandfather of Shallum, the husband of Huldah the prophetess (II Chr 34:22).

HASSENAAH (sometimes rendered as Senaah). The sons of Hassenaah are listed among the men who repaired the walls of Jerusalem at the time of Nehemiah; they were in charge of the section of the Fish Gate and "they laid its beams and hung its doors with its bolts and its bars".

HASSENUAH

1. A man of Benjamin, father of Hodaviah, grandfather of Meshullam the father of Sallu who settled in Jerusalem after the return of the exiles from Babylon.

2. Father of Judah who was an official in Jerusalem at the time of Nehemiah. Given as Senuah in Nehemiah 11:9.

HASSHUB An alternate spelling for Hashub.

HASUPHA Head of a family of Nethinim (Temple servants) (Ezra 2:43) who returned from the Exile in Babylon with Zerubbabel (Ezra 2:1-2).

HATHACH (HATACH) One of the eunuchs who were chamberlains at the court of King Ahasuerus; appointed to take care of Esther the queen (Est 4:5). He acted as a go-between for Esther and Mordecai; through him the queen learned of Haman's plot to destroy the Jews and plunder their property.

HATHATH Firstborn son of Othniel the firstborn son of Kenaz in the genealogy of the family of Judah.

HATIPHA ("snatched, captive"). Head of a family of Nethinim

(Temple servants) who returned from the Exile in Babylon with Zerubbabel (Ezra 2:1-2, 54).

HATITA ("small, insignificant"). Head of a family of gatekeepers who returned from the Exile in Babylon with Zerubbabel (Ezra 2:1-2, 42).

HATITA
Ezra 2:42.
Neh 7:45

HATTIL Head of a family of "the sons of Solomon's servants" (Ezra 2:55, 57), who returned from the Exile in Babylon with Zerubbabel (Ezra 2:1-2).

HATTIL
Ezra 2:57.
Neh 7:59

HATTUSH

1. Firstborn son of Shemaiah son of Shechaniah (I Chr 3:22) in the genealogy of the family of Jeconiah; perhaps related to No.2.

HATTUSH 1
I Chr 3:22

2. Son of a certain David, Hattush was head of one of the families who returned from the Exile in Babylon with Ezra (Ezra 8:1-2) maybe related to No.1.

HATTUSH 2
Ezra 8:2

3. Son of Hashabniah No.1; he was among those who repaired the wall of Jerusalem in the time of Nehemiah.

HATTUSH 3
Neh 3:10

4. One of the leaders of the people who sealed the covenant at the time of Nehemiah.

HATTUSH 4
Neh 10:4

5. A Levite who returned from the Exile in Babylon with Zerubbabel.

HATTUSH 5
Neh 12:2

HAURAN A region in the northeastern part of Transjordan, on the border of the country described by Ezekiel (47:15-18). Conquered by Shalmaneser III in 841 B.C. and later turned by Tiglath-Pileser III into an Assyrian satrapy under the name of Hauranu, the region became important in the Hellenistic and Roman periods. Early in the Hellenistic

HAURAN
Ezek 47:16, 18

Landscape in Hauran.

period the large Persian satrapy of Karnaim was divided into smaller districts, one of which was known in Greek, as Auranitis. By the end of the 2nd century B.C. this region formed part of the Iturean kingdom. Augustus gave Hauran to Herod the Great. In this period many Nabatean colonies were established there. Hauran remained under Jewish domination in the time of Herod's successors, until the death of Agrippa II when, together with the rest of the north of the country, it was annexed to the Provincia Syria. The region today comprises Jebel ed-Druz and the fertile plain of Nuqra.

HAVILAH

1. Second of the five sons of Cush, the son of Ham, the second son of Noah (Gen 10:7; I Chr 1:9). The association of this Havilah with Cush, which often designates Ethiopia, conforms with the identification of the place name Havilah (see No.3) with a district in Ethiopia.

HAVILAH 1
Gen 10:7.
I Chr 1:9

2. The 12th of the 13 sons of Joktan, a descendant of Shem son of Noah (Gen 10:29; 1 Chr 1:23). The association of this Havilah with

HAVILAH 2
Gen 10:29.
I Chr 1:23

Hazarmaveth (Gen 10:26), Uzal (Gen 10:27) and Sheba (Gen 10:28) suggests a location in southern Arabia.

3. According to the Garden of Eden narrative, a country completely surrounded by the Pishon River (Gen 2:11), which is noted for its gold, bdellium and onyx (Gen 2:12). Opinions vary as to its exact location. Some identify it with a district in Ethiopia which is called Aualis in Greek and Latin sources.

4. In Genesis 25:18, "Havilah", near Shur which is close to Egypt, is the western boundary of the encampments of the Ishmaelites. It was in this location that Saul defeated the Amalekites (I Sam 15:7). Presumably this Havilah was in the southern part of Palestine.

HAVOTH JAIR A group of small towns in the pastureland in the hilly part of Transjordan, along the bank of the River Yarmuk. The region was seized by Jair, son of Manasseh, from the Amorites (Deut 3:14) or in Bashan (Josh 13:30). In the time of Solomon, Argob in Bashan was a district under the command of the son of Geber (I Kgs 4:13). The region lies south of the Yarmuk, southeast of the Sea of Galilee.

HAWK See ANIMALS

HAZAEL ("God sees"). King of Aram-Damascus (842-798 B.C.), a contemporary of Jehu and Joram, kings of Israel, and Athaliah, Jehoahaz and Joash of Judah. He assassinated Ben-Hadad I (see BEN-HADAD and HADADEZER) and usurped the throne after Elisha had informed him that he was to be anointed king of Damascus (II Kgs 8:13-15). Upon assumption of the throne, he attacked Israel at Ramoth Gilead, as Elisha had predicted, and seriously injured Joram of Israel (II Kgs 8:28-29). An aggressive king, and mighty warrior, he succeeded in conquering all the Israelite lands east of the Jordan (II Kgs 10:32-33; Amos 1:3), and after Jehu's death he invaded Israel, reaching the borders of Judah (II Kgs 12:17-18). He only stopped his advance on Jerusalem when King Joash sent him an enormous bribe obtained by stripping his palace and Temple (II Kgs 12:17-18; II Chr 24:23-24). Israel and Judah suffered at his hands, and Adad-Nirari III, king of Assyria, was acclaimed a deliverer when he resumed his expeditions against Aram (II Kgs 13:5). He was succeeded by his son Ben-Hadad II (II Kgs 13:24).

HAZAIAH ("the Lord has seen"). A man of Judah from the Shiloni family (Neh 11:4-5). He was son of Adaiah and father of Col-Hozeh (Neh 11:5) and was among those who settled in Jerusalem when the exiles returned from Babylon (Neh 11:5).

HAZAR ADDAR An alternate name for Hezron.

HAZAR ENAN A city or place on the northeastern border of the land of Canaan. It has been suggested that it is an alternate name for Hazar Hatticon. However nothing is known about its actual location.

HAZAR GADDAH A city allotted to Judah when the land of Canaan was divided among the tribes (Josh 14:1; 15:1, 27). It was "towards the border of Edom in the South" (Josh 15:21). Its location is not known.

HAZAR HATTICON ("middle court" or "region"?). A place on the border of Hauran marking the northern limit of the land of Israel. Perhaps an alternate form of Hazar Enan or Henon.

HAZARMAVETH ("the court of the Lord of Death"). Third son of Joktan, the great-grandson of Shem; father or founder of the tribe of the same name in the southern Arabian peninsula (Hadramaut).

HAZAR SHUAL A city variously attributed to Judah (Josh 15:28) and to Simeon (Josh 19:3. I Chr 4:28). Some of the returning exiles settled there at the time of Nehemiah (Neh 11:27). Although nothing is known about its exact location, it must have been in the vicinity of Beersheba since all four texts mention them together.

HAVILAH 3
Gen 2:11

HAVILAH 4
Gen 25:18.
I Sam 15:7

HAVOTH JAIR
Num 32:41.
Deut 3:14.
Judg 10:4

HAZAEL
I Kgs 19:15,
17. II Kgs 8:8-
9, 12-13, 15,
28-29; 9:14-15;
10:32; 12:17-
18; 13:3, 22,
24-25. II Chr
22:5-6. Amos
1:4

HAZAIAH
Neh 11:5

HAZAR ADDAR
Num 34:4

HAZAR ENAN
Num 34:9-10.
Ezek 47:17;
48:1

HAZAR GADDAH
Josh 15:27

HAZAR HATTICON
Ezek 47:16

HAZARMAVETH
Gen 10:26.
I Chr 1:20

HAZAR SHUAL
Josh 15:28;
19:3. I Chr
4:28. Neh
11:27

Hazael, king of Aram-Damascus. Ivory carving from Arslan Tash, Syria.

HAZAR SUSAH, HAZAR SUSIM A city allotted to Simeon (Josh 19:5) when the land of Canaan was divided among the tribes (Josh 14:1). Its location is unknown.

HAZAZON TAMAR, HAZEZON TAMAR A town of the Amorites, south of the Dead Sea, taken by Chedorlaomer and his allies (Gen 14:7). According to II Chronicles (20:2) it is identified with En Gedi. If it is the same as Tamar, as some experts think, then it should be identified with Ain Husb, in the Arabah.

HAZELPONI Alternate spellings: Hazelelponi, Hazzeleponi. Sister of Jezreel, Ishma and Idbash in the genealogy of the family of Judah.

HAZEROTH One of the desert stations on the route of the Exodus (Num 11:35, etc.), where Miriam and Aaron spoke to Moses about the Ethiopian woman whom he had married (Num 12:1). Identified with Ain Hadra by those who believe that the Israelites took a southerly route on their way from Egypt.

HAZIEL ("vision of God"). The second son of Shimei, a Levite from the family of Gershon (the firstborn son of Levi; I Chr 23:6-7, 9). He headed one of the divisions of the priests in the House of the Lord at the time of King David.

HAZO (a shorter form of Hazon, "vision"). The fifth son of Nahor the brother of Abraham (Gen 22:22) by his wife Milcah, Lot's sister (Gen 11:26, 29).

HAZOR

1. One of the most important cities in the Holy Land. The ruler of Hazor is mentioned in the Egyptian Execration Texts of the 19th century B.C. During the period of the Egyptian Middle Kingdom the city was a renowned political and commercial center remaining important in the era of the New Kingdom. Hazor's status is well defined in the Bible: Jabin, its king, headed a coalition of all the kings of the north formed to fight Joshua (Josh 11:1-5), but "Joshua turned back at that time and took Hazor, and struck its king with the sword; for Hazor was formerly the head of all those kingdoms. And they struck all the people who were in it with the edge of the sword, utterly destroying them. There was none left breathing. Then he burned Hazor with fire" (Josh 11:10-11). After the conquest Hazor was allotted to Naphtali (Josh 19:36); it was one of the royal cities in Solomon's kingdom (I Kgs 9:15). Hazor was apparently one of the cities conquered by Ben-Hadad of Damascus (I Kgs 15:20; II Chr 16:4). The city was rebuilt by Omri

HAZAR SUSAH, HAZAR SUSIM
Josh 19:5.
I Chr 4:31

HAZAZON TAMAR, HAZEZON TAMAR
Gen 14:7.
II Chr 20:2

HAZELPONI
I Chr 4:3

HAZEROTH
Num 11:35;
12:16; 33:17-18.
Deut 1:1

HAZIEL
I Chr 23:9

HAZO
Gen 22:22

HAZOR 1
Josh 11:1, 10-11,
13; 12:19;
19:36. Judg
4:2, 17. I Sam
12:9. I Kgs
9:15. II Kgs
15:29

(right)
Excavations at Tell Hazor.

Clay mask from Tell Hazor.

Stone pillars from a storehouse at Hazor. 8th century B.C.

and destroyed in the course of the campaign of Tiglath-Pileser III in 732 B.C. (II Kgs 15:29), it was still in ruins when Jonathan the Hasmonean camped in the Valley of Hazor on his way to the north (I Macc 11:67).

The city of Hazor has been identified at the huge mound of Tell Hazor 9 miles (14 km) north of the Sea of Galilee. The ancient site comprises an elevated mound extending over an area of 30 acres (12.5 ha), and a lower city 175 acres (73 ha) large, 3,000 feet (910 m) long and 2,100 feet (640 m) wide. The earliest settlement at the Lower City is from the mid-18th century B.C. This large area was encompassed by an earthen rampart, by which it was fortified. In order to study this enormous area, the site was excavated in nine different sections. In some of these, sacred compounds were uncovered including a temple built in the 17th-16th centuries B.C. In the 15th century B.C. the floor of the temple was raised; the courtyard at its front was surrounded by a wall and adjoined by another paved court containing a high place, in whose vicinity cult objects and bones from animal sacrifices have been found. Among the cultic objects there was a clay liver, used in divination. In the 14th century B.C. the plan of the temple was entirely changed. It had consisted of a porch with two pillars, a hall and a Holy of Holies. The interior of the porch and the Holy of Holies was lined with smooth basalt orthostats, one in the form of a lion. This temple was continuously used until the 13th century B.C. when the city was destroyed by Joshua. In other sections houses were discovered with infant burials in clay jars placed under the floors.

In order to study the history of settlement on the higher mound a deep section was made. A settlement was built on bedrock in the Early

Aerial view of the entrance to the water supply system at Hazor.

Two vases with Mycenean style decorations found at a Late Canaanite period temple at Hazor.

Bronze Age II-III (29th-24th century B.C.) and henceforth, the site was continuously occupied until the Hellenistic period (2nd century B.C.) for about 2,000 years.

Solomon fortified the city with a casemate wall comprising a most imposing gate, of the same type he built at Megiddo and Gezer. During the period of the Israelite house of Omri the casemate wall was replaced by a solid wall. The Israelite citadel was destroyed by Tiglath-Pileser III. The Assyrians, and the Persians and the Hellenistic rulers after them, built their own fortresses on the site.

The Israelite city of Hazor was served by a magnificent water supply system. The spring, on which the city depended, was situated at the lower slope of the mound, outside the city's fortifications. In order to reach it safely in times of emergency, a large shaft (40 x 55 feet (12 x 17m) at its upper end) was excavated near the wall. From the bottom of the shaft a tunnel (15 x 15 feet) (5 x 5m) led down to the spring a distance of more than 90 feet (c. 30 m). At the end of the tunnel a small pool was made for the collection of water. This system is dated to the 10th century B.C.

2. A city of Judah in the Negeb. It may be identified with el-Jabariyeh, about 9 miles (19.5 km) southeast of el-Auja.

3. Same as HEZRON

4. A Benjamite city outside Jerusalem, resettled after the Exile. The name is preserved in nearby Khirbet Hazzur.

5. A place in the Arabian desert. Jeremiah 49:28-33 prophesies its conquest by Nebuchadnezzar.

HEAVEN See AFTERLIFE

HEBER

1. One of the sons of Beriah, of the children of Asher (Num 26:45). From the genealogical list of the children of Heber (I Chr 7:32-39) it appears that this clan was the best known family of the tribe of Asher. Its importance is accentuated by the mention of Heber among the 70 descendants of Jacob who went to Egypt (Gen 46:17).

2. Heber the Kenite, one of the sons of Hobab, Moses' father-in-law. Heber "had separated himself from the Kenites, and pitched his tent near the terebinth tree at Zaanaim" (Judg 4:11); he was the husband of Jael, who killed Sisera, the captain of Jabin's army (Judg 4:17; 5:24).

3. Heber the father of Sochoh. His genealogy is not clear.

4. A member of the tribe of Gad who dwelt in the Bashan.

5. One of the sons of Elpaal, of the tribe of Benjamin.

HEBERITES See HEBER No.1

HEBREWS The term Hebrew (Hebrews) in the Bible is connected with several events prior to the time of David. These are (a) Joseph and his brothers in Egypt (Gen 39:14, 17; 40:15; 41:12; 43:32); (b) the bondage in Egypt (Ex 1:15-16, 19; 2:6-7, 11, 13; Lord God of the Hebrews: Ex 3:18; 5:3; 7:16; 9:1, 13; 10:3; Hebrew slave: Ex 21:2; Deut 15:12; Jer 34:9, 14); (c) the Israelites' wars against the Philistines (I Sam 4:6, 9; 13:3, 7, 19; 14:11, 21; 29:3). An early isolated case of the use of this term is "Abram the Hebrew" (Gen 14:13).

The name Hebrew distinguishes members of the Israelite people from other nations: "because the Egyptians could not eat food with the Hebrews" (Gen 43:32); "be strong...you Philistines, that you do not become servants of the Hebrews" (I Sam 4:9); Jonah answers the question "and of what people are you?" with "I am a Hebrew" (Jonah 1:8-9).

Although the name "Children of Israel" is usually used in the story of the bondage in Egypt (Ex 1:9), the term Hebrews nevertheless occurs occasionally. The Lord God of Israel is also called God of the Hebrews

HAZOR 2
Josh 15:23

HAZOR 3
Josh 15:25

HAZOR 4
Neh 11:33

HAZOR 5
Jer 49:28, 30, 33

HEBER 1
Gen 46:17. Num 26:45. I Chr 7:31-32

HEBER 2
Judg 4:11, 17; 5:24

HEBER 3
I Chr 4:18

HEBER 4
I Chr 5:13

HEBER 5
I Chr 8:17

HEBERITES
Num 26:45

HEBREWS
Gen 14:13; 39:14, 17; 40:15; 41:12; 43:32. Ex 1:15-16, 19; 2:6-7, 11, 13; 3:18; 5:3; 7:16; 9:1, 13; 10:3; 21:2. Deut 15:12. I Sam 4:6, 9; 13:3, 7, 19; 14:11, 21; 29:3. Jer 34:9, 14. Jonah 1:9. Acts 6:1. II Cor 11:22. Phil 3:5

(Ex 5:1, 3); there are Hebrew midwives and Hebrew women (Ex 1:1, 15-16). The persistent use of the term may reflect the close link between the traditions concerning the Israelite Exodus and those of the Hebrew patriarchs, the fathers of the nation. The Bible identifies the Hebrews with Israel and there is hardly any doubt that in the period of the kingdom, if not earlier, the name "Hebrew" designated affiliation with the Israelite people. On the other hand, some scholars, acting on the belief that this designation is broader than that of Israel, have sought, without firm basis, a distinction between the biblical use of the two terms.

It has been suggested to connect the term Hebrew with the Habiru, or Apiru, mentioned in Assyrian and Babylonian cuneiform tablets. These were a nomadic people who roamed the countries of the Fertile Crescent in the 2nd millennium B.C., having been forced to leave their country of origin, and seek sustenance elsewhere. Those who support this hypothesis cite the Septuagint in Genesis 14:13 where Hebrews is translated as *perates* derived from the Greek word "to move from place to place", which would befit a nomadic group. The main difficulty in identifying the Hebrews with Habiru-Apiru lies in the fact that the latter were considered an inferior class of people, comprising various ethnic elements. Moreover, there is no evidence that they amalgamated into a single tribal or racial entity. Attempts have been made to bridge these difficulties by assuming that "Hebrew" too was at first a designation for a certain class of people, and the designation "Hebrew slave" is a man who belongs to this inferior class. Another possible explanation of the name "Hebrews" is based on the Greek translation *perates*, originating in the word *peran*, i.e. "the other side" (of the river) (cf Hebrew *eber*), a designation common in the Persian period for the countries on the other (western) side of the Euphrates.

Whatever the case, the verses in the Bible in which the name Hebrew or Hebrews is found, clearly relate to the areas through which the ancestors of the Children of Israel roamed.

HEBREWS, EPISTLE TO THE The 19th book of the NT. Since the latter part of the 2nd century A.D., this book has been attributed to the apostle Paul. However, unlike all of Paul's acknowledged letters, Hebrews makes no mention of its author's name in the text, nor is any author given in the title appended to the letter in the earliest manuscripts. Numerous other factors, such as style, vocabulary, subject matter and level of Greek, cast much doubt on the viability of holding Paul to be its author. At the same time a not inconsiderable school tenaciously maintains the Pauline authorship. Even some of those who deny that Paul was the author have attributed Hebrews to someone close to him, thus weakening some of the arguments of the pro-Paul school. Among those suggestions have been Barnabas, Luke, Silvanus, Priscilla, Apollos (see Acts 18:24-28) and Clement of Rome.

From the greeting in 13:24 it seems clear that the Epistle was written in Italy, and tradition has usually connected it specifically with Rome. The date is not so easily determined. The earliest quotations from Hebrews are probably to be found in the letter of Clement of Rome to the Corinthians, written in about A.D. 95; accordingly Hebrews must have been composed earlier than that, but how much earlier is a matter of some debate. Given its central argument that the priesthood and sacrifice of Jesus have replaced those of the Levitical priests, it is of interest that Hebrews contains no hint of the destruction of the Temple in Jerusalem. This would point to a date earlier than A.D. 70. However, those who would date it later point out that Hebrews in fact makes no reference whatsoever to the Temple cult. The focus is entirely on the tabernacle in the wilderness, as if the Temple had never existed. Nonetheless, had the author known of the destruction of the Temple and the cessation of the Levitical sacrifices, it is hard to imagine that he would not have found some way of referring to it in support of his argument. If the Timothy of 13:23 is Paul's companion in Acts, then a very late date is precluded. The recipients of the letter seem to be second-generation Christians who have already seen some of their leaders die and have experienced some hard times (2:3; 10:32ff; 13:7). It has been suggested that the repeated references in chapters 2 and 3 to Israel's 40 years in the wilderness are a veiled hint at the length of time which had elapsed since the redemption brought by Jesus. This would place the composition of the book in the later 60's.

Stylistically Hebrews is one of the best-organized and -written of the NT books; indeed its Greek is commonly acknowledged to be the best in the NT. OT quotations, of which there are many, are almost always from the Septuagint. Properly speaking the writing is not strictly a letter; although it contains many personal references to the readers (e.g. 5:11-12; 6:9; 10:32ff; 13:3, 7, 18-24), it lacks other characteristics of a letter, such as the name of the writer or an introductory greeting. All of these factors are better incorporated if we see Hebrews as a kind of exhortatory sermon, and this is indeed precisely what the author calls it at 13:22. While it was written to a specific audience, the writer seems to have had an eye on a wider potential readership.

No other NT book outside of the gospels has a greater focus on Jesus. From start to finish he is presented as the center of God's purposes, the goal of God's dealings with Israel and with all men. The first words set a very high Christology: Jesus is the "brightness of his glory, and the express image of his person". It is through him that all things were made, by him that all things are maintained, to him that all things will ultimately devolve. Here are words in line with the strongest in the NT, such as John's prologue or Paul's Epistle to the Colossian church.

OUTLINE

1:1-3	Christ, greater than the prophets
1:4-14	Christ, greater than the angels
2:1-4	Exhortation
2:5-16	Christ, greater than Satan
2:17-3:6	Christ, greater than Moses
3:7-4:13	Exhortation
4:14-5:10	The high priesthood of Jesus
5:11-6:20	Exhortation, on falling away
7:1-28	The superiority of Jesus' priesthood over
10:32-11:40	God's heroes of faith
8:1-6	Jesus' superior ministry
8:7-10:18	The superior covenant brought with Jesus' priesthood
10:19-31	Exhortation to perseverance
10:32-11:40	God's heros of faith
12:1-17	God's discipline and its results
12:18-24	Sinai and Zion contrasted
12:25-29	Exhortation
13:1-25	Practical advice and closing words

The primary focus on Christ, however, is in his role as high priest. Introduced near the end of the second chapter (2:17), the priesthood of Jesus forms the hub from which all central arguments radiate. The writer strives to demonstrate that unlike the priesthood of the descendants of Aaron, that of Jesus is new and yet ancient, and superior in all aspects. With a new priesthood came a new covenant with a new sacrifice. Unlike the sacrifices under the former covenant, which were offered repeatedly, Jesus' sacrifice was offered only once to be forever valid. And while he is the officiating priest, he himself is also the sacrificial victim.

Spaced through Hebrews are a series of warnings or exhortations directed at his audience. These should be seen not as detours but rather as an integral part of the author's plan and purpose in writing.

HEBRON
Gen 13:18;
23:2, 19;
35:27; 37:14.
Ex 6:18. Num
3:19; 13:22.
Josh 10:3, 5,
23, 36, 39;
11:21; 12:10;
14:13-15;
15:13, 54;
20:7; 21:11,
13. Judg 1:10,
20; 16:3.
I Sam 30:31.
II Sam 2:1, 3,
11, 32; 3:2, 5,
19-20, 22, 27,
32; 4:1, 8, 12;
5:1, 3, 5, 13;
15:7, 9-10.
I Kgs 2:11.
I Chr 3:1, 4;
6:55, 57;
11:1, 3; 12:23,
38; 29:27. II
Chr 11:10

HEBRON One of the most ancient cities of Judah, on the way from Jerusalem to Beersheba where roads leading east and west converge; a city of the Levites, and a city of refuge (Josh 21:13). Also named Kirjath Arba (Gen 23:2, etc.), possibly after Arba, who was a great man among the Anakim (Josh 14:15, cf also 15:13-14). Another explanation of this name is that the town had four suburbs (*arba* meaning four in Hebrew), one of which could have been Mamre (Gen 35:27).

According to Numbers (13:22) Hebron was built seven years before Zoan in Egypt. Zoan was founded in about 1720 B.C., so Hebron would have been settled at the beginning of the 18th century B.C. It was owned by the sons of Heth (Gen 23:1-7). Abraham was "a foreigner and a sojourner." among them (Gen 23:4); he built an altar here (Gen 13:18) and saw the Lord (Gen 18:1). From Ephron, the son of Zohar, Abraham bought the Cave of Machpelah which was on Ephron's land (Gen 23:9-17). Joshua defeated Hoham, king of Hebron, at Gibeon (Josh 10:1 ff), and later the city was allotted to Caleb, who had conquered it (Josh 15:13; Judg 1:20). Because of its connection with the Hebrew patriarchs Hebron has had an important place in national tradition since its conquest by Joshua. After Saul's death David and his two wives dwelt here (II Sam 2:1-3); it was here that David was anointed king over the house of Judah (II Sam 2:4). David made a covenant with the people and reigned at Hebron for seven years and six months (II Sam 5:5; I Chr 3:4). It was fortified by Rehoboam (II Chr 11:10).

After the return from Babylonian Exile, Hebron was resettled (Neh 11:25). In this period the southern region of Judah was settled by Edomites and was known as Idumea, a district extending from the southern hills of Judah to Beersheba. During the first years of the

Excavated walls at Tell Rumeideh, the site of biblical Hebron.

Partial view of Hebron with the Cave of Machpelah in the center.

Hasmonean revolt Hebron was conquered (I Macc 5:65) and became part of Judea. Hebron is not mentioned in the NT.

The identification of Hebron with modern el-Khalil is accepted by all experts. The ancient site is located in Tell el Rumeidah on top of one of the hills of the modern town. Recent excavations there uncovered strata dating to the Canaanite and Israelite periods. The beautiful wall which surrounds the traditional site of the Cave of Machpelah belongs to the time of Herod.

HEBRON, HEBRONITES A family or clan descended from Hebron the son of Kohath.

HEGAI A eunuch at the court of King Ahasuerus. He was "custodian of the women" (Est 2:8) and gave Esther advice and "beauty preparations" (Est 2:9) to help her please the king.

HELAH ("necklace"). One of the two wives of Asshur, a man of Judah and ancestor of Tekoa (I Chr 4:5); she bore him three sons: Zereth, Zohar and Ethnan (I Chr 4:7).

HELAM A place on the east bank of the Jordan River, where David defeated the army of King Hadadezer.

HELBAH A Canaanite city in the territory allotted to the tribe of Asher; its population was allowed to stay on. May be identical with Ahlab, mentioned in the same text.

HELBON A city or place north of Damascus, famous for its wine, mentioned by Ezekiel in his lamentation for Tyre. It was on the site of present-day Helbun.

HELDAI

1. Head of the 12th division of David's troops, captain of the entire army in the 12th month of the year (I Chr 27:1, 15); he was from Netophah, a town in Judah, and belonged to the family of Othniel (I Chr 27:15).

He is probably identical with Heled, one of David's thirty "mighty men" (I Chr 11:30) spelled Heleb in II Samuel 23:29.

2. One of those who returned from the Exile in Babylon and settled in Jerusalem at the time of the prophet Zechariah and brought gold and silver for the crown of the high priest Joshua.

HELEB, HELED The son of Baanah No.2, a Netophathite, that is a man of Netophah, a town in Judah, is listed among David's thirty "mighty men". Many scholars believe that this is an alternate name for Heldai No.1.

HELEK ("portion", "lot"). Son of Gilead (the son of Machrir, son of Manasseh, the firstborn of Joseph), he was the founder of the Helekite family (Num 26:30).

HELEKITES A family founded by Helek the son of Gilead, the great-great-grandson of Joseph.

HELEM

1. Brother of Shemer and son of Heber (the grandson of Asher) in the genealogy of the family of Asher.

2. An alternate spelling for Heldai No.2.

HELEPH A city on the border of the territory allotted to the tribe of Naphtali. Its location is unknown.

HELEZ ("he has rescued").

1. One of David's thirty "mighty men". In II Samuel he is called "Helez the Paltite" (i.e. from Bet Pelet); while in I Chronicles 11:27 he is referred to as "the Paltite". He was in charge of the seventh division of the troops of King David (I Chr 27:10) and commanded the entire army during the seventh month of each year.

2. Son of Azariah and father of Eleasah No.1 in the genealogy of the family of Jerahmeel.

HEBRON,
HEBRONITES
**Num 3:27;
26:58. I Chr
6:2, 18; 15:9;
23:12, 19;
24:23; 26:23,
30-31**

HEGAI
Est 2:3, 8, 15

HELAH
I Chr 4:5, 7

HELAM
II Sam 10:16-17

HELBAH
Judg 1:31

HELBON
Ezek 27:18

HELDAI 1
I Chr 27:15

HELDAI 2
Zech 6:10

HELEB, HELED
**II Sam 23:29.
I Chr 11:30**

HELEK
**Num 26:30.
Josh 17:2**

HELEKITES
Num 26:30

HELEM 1
I Chr 7:35

HELEM 2
Zech 6:14

HELEPH
Josh 19:33-34

HELEZ 1
**II Sam 23:26.
I Chr 11:27;
27:10**

HELEZ 2
I Chr 2:39

HELI ("summit"). Son of Matthat and father of Joseph No. 6 in the genealogy of Jesus according to Luke.

HELKAI (shorter form of Hilkiah). A priest, head of the Meraioth family (Neh 12:15) during the time of the high priest Joakim.

HELKATH A city which fell to the lot of the tribe of Asher and was later allotted to the Levites.

HELKATH HAZZURIM ("the field of sharp swords"). A place by the pool of Gibeon where 12 men of Benjamin, led by Abner the son of Ner, fought an equal number of David's servants, led by Joab the son of Zeruiah; hence its name (II Sam 2:12-16).

HELL See ABADDON, AFTERLIFE, GEHENNA, HADES, SHEOL

HELLENISTS A group of people mentioned in Acts (6:1; 9:29; 11:20). Scholars are uncertain as to the precise significance of the term. Some suggest that it was a group distinguished from other Jews only by its use of Greek. Others suggest that the difference was more profound and that the Hellenists were deeply influenced by all aspects of Hellenistic culture.

HELON A man of Zebulun, father of Eliab No.1 (who was chosen to lead his tribe by the Lord).

HEMAM, HOMAM The second son of Lotan, firstborn son of Seir the Horite (Gen 36:20, 22); the name is also spelled Homam (I Chr 1:39).

HEMAN ("faithful"). Two biblical characters who may be related.

1. Heman, "son of Mahol", who was greatly reputed for his wisdom; only Solomon was wiser (I Kgs 4:31). Another text lists him as a son of Zerah (I Chr 2:6), second son of Judah by Tamar (I Chr 2:4). Psalm 88 is ascribed to him.

2. A Levite from the line of Kohath; son of Joel and grandson of Samuel. Heman was a singer in the House of the Lord at the time of David (I Chr 6:33; 15:17, 19), and was also called a "seer". He gave thanks to the Lord and played "trumpets, cymbals and the musical instruments of God" (I Chr 16:41-42). He had 14 sons and three daughters (I Chr 25:5). His descendants Jehiel and Shimei helped cleanse the House of the Lord at the time of Hezekiah, king of Judah (II Chr 29:14); others took part in the Passover celebration at the time of Josiah, king of Judah (II Chr 35:15).

HEMDAN Firstborn son of Dishon the Horite chief who dwelled in the land of Seir (Gen 36:26, 30). The name is spelled Hamran in the parallel text (I Chr 1:41).

HEMLOCK See PLANTS

HEN Son of Zephaniah mentioned by Zechariah among those who were to retain the crown of Joshua the high priest. In Zechariah 6:10 the name is Josiah.

HENA A town mentioned as having been conquered by Assyria when King Sennacherib attempted to persuade King Hezekiah not to resist him.

HENADAD ("favored by Hadad"?). Head of a family of Levites who was listed among those who "oversee those working on the House of God" at the time of Zerubbabel (Ezra 3:9). His son Bavai was leader of the half district of Keilah and helped repair the wall (Neh 3:18); another of his sons, Binnui No. 1, repaired another section of the wall (Neh 3:24) and was among the leaders who sealed the covenant (Neh 10:9).

HENNA See SPICES AND PERFUMES

HEPHER

1. Son of Gilead (firstborn son of Machir, the grandson of Joseph) and founder of the Hepherite family (Num 26:28-32). He was the father of Zelophehad (Num 26:33) who had no sons but five daughters.

2. Second son of Naarah, one of the two wives of Ashur.

Marble sculpture of the Greek god Hermes found at Tell Dor. Hellenistic period. (Tell Dor Excavations Project)

3. Hepher the Mecherathite, one of David's thirty "mighty men".

4. A Canaanite town west of the Jordan River not far from Tappuah; its king was defeated by Joshua (Josh 12:17). The town was included within the borders of the tribe of Manasseh and was later part of the third administrative district of King Solomon (I Kgs 4:10). Today located in Tell Hepher in the Sharon Plain.

HEPHERITES A family founded by Hepher the son of Gilead.

HEPHZIBAH

1. Wife of King Hezekiah of Judah and mother of King Manasseh.

2. A symbolic name, used by Isaiah the prophet along with Beulah, to describe the salvation of Zion.

HERES See KIR HARASETH

HERESH A Levite, one of the men who returned from the Exile in Babylon and settled in Jerusalem.

HERETH A forest to which David escaped from Saul (I Sam 22:5). No plausible identification has been suggested.

HERMAS A Christian of Rome to whom Paul sent greetings. His name is probably derived from the name of the god Hermes.

HERMES

1. A Christian of Rome to whom Paul sent greetings.

2. A Greek god, the messenger of the gods, the equivalent of Mercury in the Latin pantheon. When Paul and Barnabas visited Lystra, Paul was taken for Hermes because he was the spokesman of the two.

HERMOGENES A Christian from Asia who deserted Paul.

HERMON (MOUNT) A mountain range on the northern border of Palestine, marking the limit of the conquests of Moses and Joshua on the east of the Jordan, and of the Israelite expansion (Deut 3:8; 4:48; Josh 11:17, etc. Judg 3:3). The Hermon rises above the valley of Lebanon (Josh 11:17) and above the land of Mizpeh (Josh 11:3-8). The Amorites called it Shenir, while to the Sidonians it was known as Sirion (Deut 3:9), the name by which it is mentioned in the Execration Texts and in the documents of Ugarit.

The name Hermon referred only to the southern part of the Anti-Lebanon. The highest peak rises to about 8,500 feet (2,800 m) above sea level. The mountain range is about 18 miles (29 km) long and is separated from the northern Anti-Lebanon by the deep gorge of the River Barada. It is known in Arabic as Jebel esh-Sheik or Jebel et-Talg ("mountain of snow") because it is snow-covered for most of the year.

Like most of the higher mountains in Palestine Mount Hermon was the seat of the local Baal, Baal Hermon (Judg 3:3; I Chr 5:23).

HEPHER 3
I Chr 11:36

HEPHER 4
Josh 12:17.
I Kgs 4:10

HEPHERITES
Num 26:32

HEPHZIBAH 1
II Kgs 21:1

HEPHZIBAH 2
Is 62:4

HERES
Judg 1:35;
8:13. Is 16:11;
48:31, 36.

HERESH
I Chr 9:15

HERETH
I Sam 22:5

HERMAS
Rom 16:14

HERMES 1
Rom 16:14

HERMES 2
Acts 14:12

HERMOGENES
II Tim 1:15

HERMON (MOUNT)
Deut 3:8-9;
4:48. Josh
11:3, 17; 12:1,
5; 13:5, 11.
I Chr 5:23. Ps
42:6; 89:12;
133:3. Song
4:8

Snow-capped Mount Hermon.

HEROD
(THE GREAT)
Matt 2:1, 3, 7,
12-13, 15-16,
19, 22. Luke
1:5

HEROD (THE GREAT) Son of the Idumean Antipater; he was procurator of Judea under Julius Caesar and king under Augustus. He reigned as king of the Jews for 33 years from 37-4 B.C. The major historical source is the account provided by Josephus (*Antiq.*, XV, XVI, XVII) which depends largely on the record kept by Herod's court historian, Nicholas of Damascus.

Though in theory an independent monarch, Herod understood that the exercise of his power was dependent upon knowing his place in relation to Rome. This relationship had to be maintained at all costs and the fact that he remained in power so long, is a testimony to his cunning and political genius.

Two major sources of resentment against Herod were evident throughout his reign. In the first place, though Jewish by religion he was only half Jewish by virtue of his Edomite ancestry; in addition, he was a friend of Rome, a fact which did not endear him to his subjects. The second source of hostility emanated from the manner whereby he had secured his claim to the Judean throne, which had required the overthrow and execution of a Hasmonean king. Although Herod had contracted an alliance with the Hasmonean family through his marriage to Mariamne, this did not heal the deep sense of grievance. Indeed, the obsessive hatred for him borne by Alexandra, mother of Mariamne, eventually brought sorrow and disaster to her children.

With Octavian's victory over Antony and Cleopatra at the Battle of

(left)
Aerial view of Herodion, the palace-fortress built by Herod the Great.

(bottom right)
Central tower at Herodion viewed from inside the fortress.

Head found in Egypt and thought to represent Herod the Great.

Coin of Herod the Great.

Portrait of Agrippa I on one side of a coin struck at Caesarea; on the other side is a depiction of the Tyche of Caesarea. A.D. 43.

Actium (31 B.C.), Herod adjusted with consummate skill to this new Roman ruler. Even though he had secured Octavian's goodwill, Herod's perception of intrigue and betrayal surrounding him wrought havoc in the lives of those who came under suspicion. Such suspicion led to the murder of the elderly Hyrcanus, the last of the Hasmoneans; to the execution of Mariamne in 29 B.C.; and in the following year to the death of Alexandra who was probably plotting his downfall. Distrust and jealousy pervaded the whole family. Antipater, Herod's son by his first wife Doris, was determined to turn his father against Alexander and Aristobulus, his two sons by Mariamne. They were eventually put on trial and executed for treason. Antipater, however, did not live to succeed his father, being put to death by Herod a few days before the latter's death in 4 B.C.

In the NT (Matt chap. 2) Herod is commemorated for his barbaric role in the "slaughter of the innocents" adding further to this gruesome picture of "Herod the Great", though the episode is not mentioned by any other source.

Herod's outrages are undeniable. There is, however, another side to his reign. He made what is universally acclaimed as a truly outstanding contribution to the architecture of his day. His building enterprises can be mainly dated to the period 25-13 B.C. At Samaria and Caesarea he founded whole cities and rebuilt many others; temples and amphitheaters were constructed both within and beyond his kingdom; he erected fortress strongholds, often named after members of his family, such as Cypros, Herodium and Antipatris, while refortifying and embellishing others such as Masada. His most magnificent achievement, however, was the reconstruction of the Temple in Jerusalem commenced in 19 B.C. and eventually completed only seven years before its destruction in the year A.D. 70.

HEROD AGRIPPA I Grandson of Herod the Great and son of Aristobulos and Bernice. He was four years old when his father was executed by Herod in 7 B.C. After having spent some time in prison under Tiberius, his fortunes changed when Caligula became emperor. In A.D. 37 Caligula granted him the territories which had been under the tetrarchs Philip and Lysanius, and he was given the title of king. His close friendship with Caligula kept him secure and in due course his kingdom expanded when Herod Antipas was sent into exile in A.D. 39. An important part of his policy was to nurture good relations with his Jewish subjects, who are said to have considered him more as a Hasmonean king than as a descendant of the Edomites. This policy may also have been responsible for his suppression of the early Jerusalem church as recorded in Acts 12:1 ff (where he is called Herod). Herod Agrippa died suddenly in A.D. 44, the event being recorded by Josephus (*Antiq.* xix. 343 ff) and in Acts 12:21-23.

HEROD AGRIPPA II Great-grandson of Herod the Great and son of Herod Agrippa I; only 17 when his father died in A.D. 44, he was considered too young to succeed, whereupon Judea reverted to rule by procurators. In 50, however, the emperor Claudius gave Herod Agrippa the kingdom of Chalcis and in 53, he exchanged this for the territories of Abilene, Galilee, Iturea and Trachonitis over which his father had been made king by Caligula. Later this kingdom was extended to include the cities of Tiberias, Tarichea and Bethsaida Julias. The younger Agrippa is considered a weaker character than his father. However, in the events leading up to the outbreak of the Jewish revolt which was to lead to the capture of Jerusalem by Titus, he did attempt to divert the contending parties from the catastrophic consequences of all-out war. The NT narrative records Paul's famous speech before King Agrippa in Acts

HEROD
AGRIPPA I
Acts 12:1, 6, 11, 19-21

HEROD
AGRIPPA II
Acts 25:13, 22-24, 26; 26:1-2, 7, 19, 27-28, 32

chapter 25. After the Roman War (66-70), Agrippa ruled his territories until about the end of the century.

HEROD ANTIPAS Son of Herod the Great by Malthace, a Samaritan. As "Herod the tetrarch" (Matt 14:1) he ruled over Galilee and Perea for over 40 years (4 B.C.-A.D. 39). The NT and Josephus' *Antiquities* xviii constitute the main historical sources for Herod Antipas, who is commonly remembered for his role in the execution of John the Baptist (Matt 14:1-12). He inherited his father's political cunning, which may have been why Jesus referred to him as "that fox" (Luke 13:32). Like his father, Herod Antipas had a great love for magnificent architecture and was responsible for the building of Tiberias in A.D. 22. He also took after Herod the Great in his pragmatic approach to Judaism: neither father nor son allowed their heads to be copied as images on coins, and Antipas was part of the delegation which protested to Pilate about the placing of the votive shields.

Herod Antipas married a daughter of the Nabatean king Aretas IV. When he divorced her in order to marry Herodias (the daughter of his late half-brother Aristobulos who was earlier married to another half-brother Herod Philip) he incurred the wrath of Aretas and the condemnation of John the Baptist (Matt 14:4; Mark 6:18; Luke 3:19). When Antipas was defeated by Aretas (A.D. 36), Josephus reports that many of his subjects perceived this as divine punishment for his behavior towards John the Baptist.

It was to Herod Antipas that Jesus was sent after his arrest by Pilate; as a Galilean, he fell under Herod's jurisdiction. When Jesus refused to answer his questions, Herod mocked him and returned him to Pilate (Luke 23:7-12).

After Caligula became emperor in 37, Herod Antipas was accused by his rival Herod Agrippa I, of plotting subversion against Rome and in 39 was banished to Lyons in Gaul. Herodias voluntarily accompanied him.

HEROD ARCHELAUS Ruler of Judea; the son of Herod the Great and his wife Malthace. After the death of Herod in 4 B.C., his kingdom was divided among his three sons: Herod Antipas, Archelaus and Philip. Archelaus was never given the title of king, but only that of ethnarch. His tyrannical rule, and his oppression of the Jews and Samaritans, induced his brothers and his subjects to complain to Rome. He was banished to Gaul (A.D. 6) where he died in A.D. 18.

Archelaus became ruler while Joseph, Mary and the infant Jesus were in Egypt. Upon their return, Joseph settled his family in Galilee, rather than live under Archelaus' rule in Judea.

HERODIANS A group of people mentioned in the NT; scholars are divided on the question of their identification. The Gospels of Matthew and Mark describe them, together with the Pharisees, as challenging Jesus on several topics, e.g., concerning the payment of tribute to Caesar (Matt 22:16; Mark 12:13). It has been suggested that the Herodians were loyal to the foreign rulers of Idumean origin, beginning with Herod the Great who reigned in Judah 37-4 B.C. Another hypothesis about the Herodians is that they were a group who reinforced the foreign, Greek element in the country. The Herodians are also sometimes identified as belonging to the Boethusians, a Jewish religious political party which was considered a branch of the Sadducees and was loyal to Herod the Great.

HERODIAS (a feminine form of Herod). The daughter of Aristobulus and granddaughter of Herod the Great and Mariamne. Herodias inherited the ruthlessness of her grandfather and the royal blood of her grandmother's Hasmonean forbears. She was first married to Herod

A coin of Herod Antipas struck at Tiberias with the name of Herod the Tetrarch and a palm-branch. A.D. 28

A coin of Herod Archelaus, depicting a galley on one side and a cornucopia on the other, struck in Jerusalem. 4 B.C.

Philip (not the tetrarch mentioned in Luke 3:1, but another relation of the Herodian family), and they had one daughter, Salome. Later (about A.D. 28), she met and married Herod Antipas, tetrarch of Galilee, Philip's half-brother and her own uncle. This was a scandalous union (cf Lev 18:16; 20:21), and was the occasion of John the Baptist's public denouncement of Herod and Herodias (Mark 6:18), which made her seek his death. Through the famous ruse of Salome's dance, Herod was eventually compelled to order John's execution (Matt 14:3ff; Mark 6:17ff).

Sometime after A.D. 37, when Emperor Caligula exiled Herod Antipas to Gaul, Herodias accompanied him (an uncharacteristic gesture of loyalty) into historical oblivion.

HERODION A Christian of Rome to whom Paul sent greeting.

HEROD PHILIP See PHILIP No.2

HERON See ANIMALS

HESHBON The capital of Sihon, king of the Amorites, formerly in the land of Moab (Num 21:26). Heshbon was among the cities of Sihon, for which the Reubenites and the Gadites asked Moses (Num 32:3). It was given to Reuben (Num 32:37). One of the cities of the Levites in the

A coin of Esbus (Heshbon), depicting the city goddess in a temple, on one side and the bust of Elagabal on the other. 3rd century A.D.

(right)
View of Hesban, identified with the site of Heshbon, a short distance from Medeba in Transjordan.

HERODION
Rom 16:11

HEROD PHILIP
Mark 6:17.
Luke 3:1

HESHBON
Num 21:25-28, 30, 34; 32:3, 37. Deut 1:4; 2:24, 26, 30; 3:2, 6; 4:46; 29:7. Josh 9:10; 12:2, 5; 13:10, 17, 21, 26-27; 21:39. Judg 11:19, 26. I Chr 6:81. Neh 9:22. Song 7:4. Is 15:4; 16:8-9. Jer 48:2, 34, 45; 49:3

territory of Gad (Josh 21:39), it was presumably taken by Mesha, king of Moab. Isaiah (15:4; 16:8-9) and Jeremiah (48:2, 34, 45, etc.) prophesied its destruction. Some time after the beginning of the Hasmonean revolt, in 129 B.C., the town was conquered by Simon Maccabee. It was part of the Hasmonean kingdom in the time of Alexander Jannaeus, but was returned to the Nabateans by Hyrcanus II. It was conquered again by Herod the Great, who founded a military colony there which he named Esbous. Identified with Hesban, 8 miles (13 km) north of Medaba. Excavations on this site revealed strata from the Iron Age to the Muslim periods.

HESHMON Settlement in the Negeb (Josh 15:27). By its listing, it should lie in the region of Beersheba, but its location is unknown. The name is omitted in the Septuagint.

HETH The son of Canaan and ancestor of the Hittite people (Gen 10:15; I Chr 1:13). In Genesis chapter 23 and 25:10, the Hittites are referred to as "the sons of Heth". Jacob married a "daughter of Heth" thus displeasing his mother Rebekah (Gen 27:46). See HITTITES.

HETHLON The northern border of the land of Canaan is described as "on the north: from the Great Sea, by the road to Hethlon, as one goes to Zedad" (Ezek 47:15) while the territory of Dan is given as "From the northern border along the road to Hethlon, at the entrance of Hamath" (Ezek 48:1). In the parallel description of the northern border (Num 34:7) Mount Hor replaces Hethlon. The "road to Hethlon" is apparently the road leading up from the Mediterranean coast to Mount

HESHMON
Josh 15:27

HETH
Gen 10:15; 23:3, 5, 7, 10, 16, 18, 20; 25:10; 27:46; 49:32. I Chr 1:13

HETHLON
Ezek 47:15; 48:1

Lebanon, which formed the natural border between the Egyptian territory of Canaan and the Hittite empire. Thus, Hethlon could be identified with Khaithala, situated northeast of Tripolis, 10 miles (16 km) north of the sea coast, between Nahr el-Kabir and Nahr Aqqar.

HEZEKIAH ("Yah is my strength").

1. Son of Ahaz, the weak and wicked king of Judah, and Abi (II Kgs 18:1-2; II Chr 29:1). He ruled 727-698 B.C. Hezekiah ascended the throne at a crucial time in Judah's history: Assyria had recently conquered Aram (in 732 B.C.) and the early period of his reign saw Assyria's conquest of Israel (722/1 B.C.). Judah itself had to pay a heavy annual tribute to Assyria which severely weakened the kingdom whilst its borders were under continual threat from both the Edomites and the Philistines. This situation led Hezekiah to realize that without political and religious reform, Judah's fate would be that of the surrounding nations. With the encouragement of the prophet Isaiah, he undertook a religious reform which included the elimination of idolatrous elements from Israelite worship, the cleansing and sanctifying of the Temple and the restoration of the Temple cult including the celebration of the Passover holiday (II Kgs 18:3-4; II Chr

Clay Hebrew seal impression inscribed "[Belonging] to Yeho-zarah son of Hilk [ia] hu servant of Hezekiahu". 8th-7th centuries B.C. (Israel Museum)

The Siloam inscription. It describes how King Hezekiah's tunnel was dug by two teams of miners starting at opposite ends, working toward each other and meeting in the middle.

chaps. 29-30). This national religious awakening throughout Judah was also expressed in literary activity (e.g. Prov 25:1). Hezekiah strengthened Judah politically and expanded the borders of the kingdom to include Philistia (I Chr 4:34-43). In 701 B.C. he rebelled against Sennacherib, king of Assyria, in his attempt to achieve absolute political independence (I Kgs 18:7). Among the preparations for the siege of Jerusalem, he built a tunnel to bring the waters of the Gihon spring within the walls of the city, and the Siloam inscription bears witness to this extraordinary engineering feat (II Kgs 20:20; II Chr 32:30; Is 22:9-11). Jerusalem was spared when a plague wiped out the Assyrian camp, which forced Sennacherib to return to his country (II Kgs 19:35; II Chr 32:21; Is 37:36), although not before Sennacherib had exacted a heavy tribute from Hezekiah who, in order to obtain the exhorbitant sum, stripped the doors and pillars of the Temple (II Kgs 18:13-16). The Assyrian inscription left by Sennacherib speaks of his capturing 46 cities and refers to Hezekiah as a "bird locked up in a cage," a vivid description of the siege of Jerusalem. While the biblical account does not present a clear order of events, it seems that the tribute was collected as a result of the siege. However, some scholars adopt the hypothesis of two campaigns carried out by Sennacherib against Hezekiah, the first in 701 B.C. and the second some time later, with the accounts being telescoped into one. In foreign affairs, Hezekiah was particularly adept in diplomatic relations, allying himself with Egypt (II Kgs 18:21; Is 36:6), Merodach-Baladan, king of Babylon (II Kgs

On the left, the tomb of the Bene Hezir in the Kidron Valley. Second Temple period.

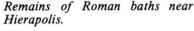

Remains of Roman baths near Hierapolis.

20:12-15; Is 39:1-4); Luli, king of Sidon and Sidka, king of Ashkelon (the latter known from Assyrian inscriptions). After Hezekiah's death, his son Manasseh ascended the throne (II Kgs 20:21; II Chr 32:33).

2. One of the sons of Neariah, a descendant of King David.

3. Name of several members of a family who returned with Nehemiah from the Babylonian Exile. A Hezekiah is included among those who sealed the covenant.

4. An ancestor of the prophet Zephaniah.

HEZION Father of Tabrimmon and grandfather of Ben-Hadad I who was king of Syria in the time of Baasha king of Israel and Asa king of Judah.

HEZIR

1. A descendant of Aaron; he was head of the 17th division of priests who served in the House of the Lord in the time of King David (I Chr 24:1, 3, 15).

2. One of the leaders of the people who sealed the covenant in the time of Nehemiah.

HEZRAI Hezrai the Carmelite, one of David's thirty "mighty men" (II Sam 23:35). He came from Carmel, a small city in Judah. The parallel text in the Chronicles lists him as Hezro (I Chr 11:37).

HEZRO An alternate name for Hezrai.

HEZRON A city located between Kadesh Barnea and Adar (Josh 15:3); also called Hazar Addar in Numbers 34:4. Its location helped to mark the southern border of Judah and Israel during the time of the Judges.

HEZRON, HEZRONITES

1. Son of Reuben and an eponym of the tribe of Reuben.

2. Son of Perez, grandson of Judah, and an eponym of the tribe of Judah.

HIDDAI Hiddai from the brooks of Gaash (II Sam 23:30), one of David's thirty "mighty men". In the parallel text of Chronicles, he is called Hurai (I Chr 11:32).

HIDDEKEL Hebrew name for the Tigris, one of the two large rivers of Mesopotamia which, according to Genesis (2:14), flowed from the Garden of Eden. It is formed by the confluence of two rivers that draw their waters from the mountains of Armenia. On its way southwards from Lake Van it receives some large tributaries, the most important of which are the Greater and Lesser Zab and the Diyala. In early times the courses of the Tigris and the Euphrates were separate — their confluence before they flow into the Persian Gulf is quite recent. The Tigris has a greater volume of water than the Euphrates and flows faster, so that no upstream navigation was possible. The prosperous cities of Nineveh, Calah and Ashur flourished along its shores.

HIEL A man of Bethel who rebuilt Jericho during the reign of Ahab king of Israel. His firstborn son, Abiram, and his youngest, Segub, died while the foundations and the gates were being set up (I Kgs 16:34). This was seen as the fulfillment of the curse of Joshua: "Cursed be the man...who...builds up this city Jericho; he shall lay its foundation with his firstborn, and with his youngest he shall set up the gates" (Josh 6:26).

HIERAPOLIS ("sacred city"). An important city in the southwest of Asia Minor, near Colossae and Laodicea; it is mentioned by Paul in his Epistle to the Colossians as the home of a Christian community. It was noted for its hot springs and its ancient baths have been uncovered in excavations, as have a number of early Christian churches.

HIGH PLACES A cultic installation, situated on a high elevation, such as a mountain top, a raised platform or the like (Deut 12:2; I Kgs 14:23; Jer 3:6).

HEZEKIAH 2
I Chr 3:23

HEZEKIAH 3
Ezra 2:16.
Neh 7:21;
10:17

HEZEKIAH 4
Zeph 1:1

HEZION
I Kgs 15:18

HEZIR 1
I Chr 24:15

HEZIR 2
Neh 10:20

HEZRAI
II Sam 23:35

HEZRO
I Chr 11:37

HEZRON
Josh 15:3, 25

HEZRON,
HEZRONITES 1
Gen 46:9. Ex 6:14. Num 26:6. I Chr 5:3

HEZRON,
HEZRONITES 2
Gen 46:12.
Num 26:21.
Ruth 4:18-19.
I Chr 2:5, 9, 18, 21, 24-25;
4:1. Matt 1:3.
Luke 3:33

HIDDAI
II Sam 23:30

HIDDEKEL
Gen 2:14

HIEL
I Kgs 16:34

HIERAPOLIS
Col 4:13

High places comprised both open-air and covered sanctuaries of various kinds (I Kgs 12:31; 13:32; II Kgs 17:32; 23:9). They contained altars for sacrifices, incense, stone pillars, *asherot* or cult poles and water. The high places were large and complex installations as evidenced from the ceremonial activities conducted at them (I Sam 9:13-14, 19, 25; 10:5, 10, 13, etc.). There is even mention of a dining chamber in the high places (I Sam 9:19-22). The pre-Israelite high place in the temple precincts at Megiddo, is a well preserved example. It is a large circular platform of stones, with stairs leading to it, with the altar most probably standing on top of the high place. Sacrifices, even at the covered sanctuaries, probably took place at some open-air section of the installation.

At the high places sacrifices and incense were offered. Worshipers ate, wept and prayed at the high places (I Sam 9:13; Is 15:2; 16:12). The shrines were frequented by priests, some of whom resided there (II Kgs

Canaanite high place at Gezer.

(left)
Canaanite high place at Tell Megiddo.

23:5), as did prophets (I Sam 10:5-13). There were also places suitable for private devotions, as well as centers for official ceremonies and feasts as evidenced in I and II Kings.

High places were an essential part of Canaanite worship from as early as the second half of the 3rd millennium. They later became Israelite sanctuaries, situated on high hills and frequently located outside the cities.

The legitimacy of these Israelite high places in monotheism is problematic. There were frequent moves to rid the country of the high places although in certain cases their legitimacy is not questioned. One example of this is Solomon's legitimate offering at the "great high place" at Gibeon (I Kgs 3:4), even though the ark had already been brought to Jerusalem. It is assumed by some scholars that the high places used only for Israelite worship came into disrepute about the time of the Assyrian conquest of the Northern Kingdom in the last quarter of the 8th century B.C. Josiah's reform (622 B.C.) is generally considered the serious turning point in this regard. Josiah dismissed priests who had officiated at the high places, and destroyed such shrines in Jerusalem and its environs, as well as in other cities in Judah. The important high place at Bethel, which had undoubtably kept many from worshiping in Jerusalem, was also destroyed (II Kgs chaps. 22-23).

The illegitimacy of the high places is affirmed in various places in the OT. They were the object of the Lord's wrath (Lev 26:30), and the Israelites were instructed to destroy them on entering Canaan (Num 33:52; Deut 33:29). They were partially removed by Kings Asa, Hezekiah and Josiah (II Chr 14:3; II Kgs 18:4; 23:8). No less than six kings were admonished for not having removed the high places during their reigns: Asa (I Kgs 15:14), Jehoshaphat (I Kgs 22:43), Jehoash (II Kgs 12:3), Amaziah (II Kgs 14:4), Azariah (II Kgs 15:4) and Jotham (II Kgs 15:35). In defiance of the prohibition, numerous high places were built by Solomon (I Kgs 11:7), Rehoboam (I Kgs 14:23) and many of the kings of Northern Israel. Manasseh is cited as having restored the high places (II Kgs 21:3).

The origins of the high places are a matter for speculation. One suggestion is that they were originally erected as funeral installations which later took on other cultic functions.

HIGH PRIEST See PRIESTS

HILEN, HOLON A priestly town in the territory of Judah (Josh 21:15, Holon; I Chr 6:58, Hilen). In Joshua 15:51 Holon is mentioned together with Goshen and Giloh among the towns of the sixth district of Judah, north of the district of Hebron. It is identified with Khirbet Alin northwest of Beit Jala, which apparently preserved the ancient form of the names Hilen and Giloh.

HILKIAH ("my portion is Yah").

1. A Merarite Levite, the son of Amzi.

2. A gatekeeper serving under David and a descendant of Merari.

3. Father of Eliakim, a court officer of King Hezekiah.

4. A high priest during the reign of King Josiah who discovered the Book of the Law while the Temple was being renovated.

5. A supporter of Ezra's reforms who stood next to Ezra at the time of the public reading of the Book.

6. Head of a family of priests that returned with Zerubbabel from the Babylonian Exile.

7. Father of Jeremiah the prophet.

8. Father of Gemariah, a messenger sent by King Zedekiah to the Babylonian king Nebuchadnezzar.

HILLEL ("he has praised"). Hillel the Pirathonite (from Pirathon in the land of Ephraim) was the father of Abdon who was judge in Israel after Elon the Zebulunite.

HINNOM, VALLEY OF A valley on the border betweeen the territories of Benjamin and Judah (Josh 15:8; 18:6), it lies to the south and

The Valley of Hinnom, a continuation of the Kidron Valley in Jerusalem.

southwest of Jerusalem and is a continuation of the Kidron Valley. Also known as Ge-Hinnom, the valley later became synonymous with hell (See GEHENNA). It served as Jerusalem's main cemetery in biblical times, as is confirmed by recent archeological research.

HILEN, HOLON
Josh 15:51; 21:15. I Chr 6:58

HILKIAH 1
I Chr 6:45

HILKIAH 2
I Chr 26:11

HILKIAH 3
II Kgs 18:18, 26, 37. Is 22:20; 36:3, 22

HILKIAH 4
II Kgs 22:4, 8, 10, 12, 14; 23:4, 24. I Chr 6:13; 9:11. II Chr 34:9, 14-15, 18, 20, 22; 35:8. Ezra 7:1. Neh 11:11

HILKIAH 5
Neh 8:4

HILKIAH 6
Neh 12:7, 21

HILKIAH 7
Jer 1:1

HILKIAH 8
Jer 29:3

HILLEL
Judg 12:13, 15

HINNOM, VALLEY OF
Josh 15:8; 18:16. II Kgs 23:10. II Chr 28:3; 33:6. Neh 11:30. Jer 7:31-32; 19:2, 6; 32:35

HIRAH A man of Adullam ("a town in Judah") who was a friend of Judah; at his house Judah met the Canaanite Shua whom he married (Gen 38:1-2).

HIRAM

1. King of Tyre (961-936 B.C.), the first of three kings of Tyre, who bore the name Hiram. He established diplomatic and commercial relations with King David and King Solomon. He sent cedar wood and craftsmen to build a palace for King David soon after the latter conquered Jerusalem from the Jebusites (I Chr 14:1). According to I Kings chapter 5, it was again Hiram who took the initiative in renewing diplomatic and trade relations with Israel upon Solomon's accession to the throne; but II Chronicles 2:3 reports that it was Solomon who first approached Hiram. In return for cedar and cypress wood Solomon agreed to give Hiram an annual payment of 20,000 *kor* (100,000 bushels) of wheat and 20,000 *baths* (110,000 gallons) of pressed oil (I Kgs 5:11; cf II Chr 2:10). When Solomon's building ventures had emptied Israel's treasury, Hiram lent him 120 talents (c. 5 tons) of gold (I Kgs 9:10-14), receiving as collateral 20 cities in Galilee. The report in II Chronicles 8:2 concerning the cities, which Hiram gave to Solomon, has been interpreted to mean that the 20 towns were returned to Israel's sovereignty when Solomon managed to repay the loan from his share of the income produced by the fleet of merchant ships he chartered jointly with Hiram (I Kgs 10:22; II Chr 9:21), where the name is given as Huram.

2. Son of a Tyrian coppersmith and an Israelite widow of the tribe of Naphtali, both unnamed; he was brought from Tyre by King Solomon to make all the burnished bronze artifacts for the Temple (I Kgs 7:1-47 and II Chr 2:13; 4:11-16 where he is called Huram). In addition to fashioning the right and left columns at the portico of the great hall, he gave them their respective names: Jachin and Boaz (I Kgs 7:21).

HITTITES Ancient people named as offspring of Heth, Canaan's second son (Gen 10:15; I Chr 1:13; cf Gen 23:3). They are listed among the peoples who dwelt in Canaan before its conquest by the Israelites (Gen 15:20; 26:34; Ex 3:8; Deut 7:1; Josh 3:10; 9:1; Judg 3:5; I Kgs 9:20; II Chr 8:7; Ezra 9:1; Neh 9:8). Ephron the Hittite sold Abraham the field and cave in which he buried Sarah (Gen chap. 23). Esau married Judith and Basemath, both Hittite women (Gen 26:34), but Rebekah objected to Jacob's attempt to marry a Hittite (Gen 27:46). The Hittites lived in the mountains (Num 13:29; Josh 11:3) and joined King Jabin of Hazor in his battle with Joshua (Josh 11:1-12). God ordered their destruction together with the other Canaanite peoples (Deut 20:17). After the conquest of Canaan the Israelites dwelt among the local peoples including the Hittites, taking their daughters for wives (Judg 3:5-6). Relations between Israelites and Hittites must have been close. When David was still in the wilderness Ahimelech the Hittite was one of his men (I Sam 26:6) and after he became king, Uriah the Hittite, husband of Bathsheba, was one of his thirty warriors (II Sam 11:3ff). King Solomon's numerous alien loves included Hittite women (I Kgs 11:1) and the Bible mentions Hittite kings as his contemporaries (I Kgs 10:29; II Chr 1:17). When the king of Israel waged war against the Syrians, Hittites were his allies (II Kgs 7:6). Scholars are of the opinion that the name Hittites was applied to all the peoples of Syria during the epoch of the kings of Israel.

As far back as the 19th century, documents were discovered in Boghazkoy in Asia Minor, written in a new and hitherto unknown hieroglyphic script; they were identified as Hittite, pertaining to a nation whose name also figures in Egyptian and Assyrian sources. The

The sarcophagus of Ahiram found in the tomb at Byblos. The carved sarcophagus bears on its lid a Phoenician funerary inscription of the Sidonian king.

(top)
The so-called tomb of Ahiram (Hiram) at Byblos.

Two Hittite dignitaries drinking, depicted on a stone bas-relief from Boghazkoy. 14th century B.C.

earliest documents, known as the Cappadocian tablets, comprise legal and commercial letters, written by Assyrian merchants who established commercial colonies in Asia Minor in about the 19th century B.C. Later Hittite literature attributes the foundation of their kingdom to Mursilis I. Labarnas, his heir, conquered Babylon (16th century B.C.). Shuppululiumas the Great, who reigned in 1380-1350 B.C., founded the Hittite empire. He established Hittite rule over Asia Minor and waged war against northern Syrian city-states. He subdued the kingdom of Mitani and made his sons kings at Carchemish and Aleppo. Hittite power posed a serious threat to Egypt, and under Rameses II the Hittites signed "a treaty of eternal friendship" with Egypt, the pact being engraved on the walls of Egyptian palaces and written on tablets found at Boghazkoy. Later the country was invaded by a wave of "Sea Peoples" and the Hittite cities were razed. The subsequent Late Hittite period was one of decline, with the formation of new kingdoms in Asia Minor, such as the Phrygian kingdom.

The Hittite kingdom was a divine establishment, the king and queen ministering side by side at religious ceremonies.

The Hittite pantheon consisted of numerous gods and goddesses, headed by the god of thunder and the sun goddess; their children and grandchildren were gods of storm. In addition, there were gods of mountains, rivers, springs, heaven and earth, clouds and winds. The gods were the masters and men their slaves. Initially, the gods were

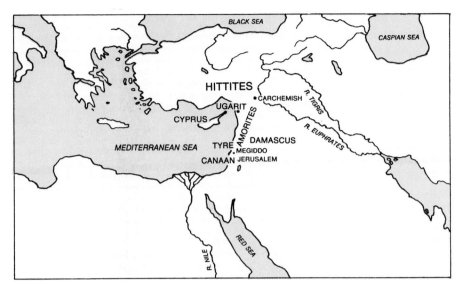

The Hittite empire.

View of the ruins of the great Hittite temple at Hattushash, (present-day Boghaskoy, Turkey), the ancient capital of the Hittite empire. 13th century B.C.

represented by simple stones. The god of storm subsequently assumed the form of a bull and later still, was given a human likeness. Other gods were symbolized by lions, stags and horses. Hittite ritual included solemn feasts and the sacrifice of animals. Divination was common and well organized, with questions submitted to an oracle whose answers were recorded on tablets.

The Hittite legal code consisted of two sections, each containing 100 laws. There were laws relating to assault and violence, slavery, marriage, theft, adultery, etc. Capital punishment was confined to special offenses, such as sorcery and defiance of the king.

Hittite farmers produced wheat, barley, grapes and other fruits. Their domestic animals included horses, cattle, sheep and goats, swine, dogs, fowl and honey bees. Manufacture of pottery by means of a potter's wheel began about 2000 B.C. The Hittite pottery is mostly monochrome, highly burnished with beautiful shapes featuring elaborate spouts and handles.

Hittite literature included myths and epics, Sumerian-Akkadian-Hittite dictionaries; prescriptions for divination by the hour of birth and by examination of the liver, kidney, facial features and the constellations of the stars. From Mesopotamian literature, they translated lists of temples, incantations, medical texts, hymns to various gods, prayers, renderings of the Gilgamesh Epic and a fable about the great kings of the Akkadian dynasty.

Numerous gigantic works of art, some sculptured in rock have been discovered. Dating to the Hittite empire and later periods, they are mostly reliefs depicting gods, kings and lions, the majority engraved on the orthostats which lined the walls of temples, palaces and tombs. Hittite architecture inclined to simplicity, houses being built of mud bricks set in wooden frames. Minor arts are represented by a large number of cylinder seals, decorated with animals, humans, gods, as well as ring seals made of silver. With the fall of the Hittite kingdom in 700 B.C. all traces of Hittite art vanish.

HIVITE(S) One of the subdivisions of the Canaanites, i.e., one of the peoples resident in the land of Canaan at the time of the conquest by Joshua (Gen 10:17; I Chr 1:15). This people is mentioned in the Bible among inhabitants of the land of Israel prior to the Israelite conquest, but otherwise does not appear in any of the ancient Near Eastern records. The Hivites are specifically associated with the towns of Shechem (Gen 34:2), Gibeon, Chephirah, Beeroth and Kirjath Jearim (Josh 9:17) in the land of Israel, and with Mount Lebanon (Judg 3:3) and the region called Mizpah at the foot of Mount Hermon (Josh 11:3). Scholars have sought to identify the biblical Hivites with (a) the Greek Achaeans known from Homer; (b) the Hurrians — one of the most important peoples in the ancient Near East — who are otherwise unmentioned in the Hebrew Bible; or (c) settlers, who went to Shechem and the other six locations mentioned above from Cilicia, a region in Asia Minor, which is called Kue in the Bible (I Kgs 10:28) and *huwi* in cuneiform sources.

HIVITE(S)
Gen 10:17; 34:2; 36:2. Ex 3:8, 17; 13:5; 23:23, 28; 33:2; 34:11. Deut 7:1; 20:17. Josh 3:10; 9:1, 7; 11:3, 19; 12:8; 24:11. Judg 3:3, 5. II Sam 24:7. I Kgs 9:20. I Chr 1:15. II Chr 8:7

HIZKI ("my strength"). One of the sons of Elpaal in the genealogy of King Saul; he dwelled in Jerusalem at the time of Nehemiah.

HIZKI
I Chr 8:17

HOBAB Son of Reuel the Midianite. According to one tradition Hobab was the father-in-law of Moses (Num 10:29); according to others, Jethro (Ex 3:1; 18:1) and Reuel (Ex 2:18) are each named as his father-in-law. He was the father of Heber the Kenite (Judg 4:11). Moses asked Hobab to guide the Children of Israel through the wilderness (Num 10:29-31).

HOBAB
Num 10:29. Judg 4:11

HOBAH Name of place north of Damascus to which Abraham pursued the captors of his nephew Lot (Gen 14:15).

HOBAH
Gen 14:15

HOD ("majesty"). One of the sons of Zophah in the genealogy of the family of Asher.

HOD
I Chr 7:37

HODAVIAH ("give thanks to the Lord"). Sometimes spelled Hodaiah.

1. Head of a family of the half-tribe of Manasseh dwelling on the east bank of the Jordan River, between the land of Bashan and Mount Hermon (I Chr 5:23-24). A "mighty man of valor" but unfaithful to God, he was carried into captivity by Tiglath-Pileser, king of Assyria (I Chr 5:26).

HODAVIAH 1
I Chr 5:24

2. Father of Meshullam and son of Hassenuah, from the tribe of Benjamin (I Chr 9:7); his grandchildren were among the settlers in Jerusalem after the return from the Babylonian Exile.

HODAVIAH 2
I Chr 9:7

3. A Levite whose family, 74 persons in all, returned with Zerubbabel from the Exile in Babylon and settled in Jerusalem (Ezra 2:1, 40); he is called Hodevah in the parallel verse in Nehemiah (Neh 7:43).

HODAVIAH 3
Ezra 2:40

4. Firstborn son of Elioenai No.1 and a descendant of Zerubbabel (I Chr 3:19, 24) in the genealogy of the family of Jeconiah.

HODAVIAH 4
I Chr 3:24

HODESH The wife of Shaharaim the Benjamite (I Chr 8:9). Her name, which means "day of the New Moon", probably indicates her birth on that day.

HODESH
I Chr 8:9

HODEVAH An alternate name for Hodaviah used in Nehemiah 7:43.

HODEVAH
Neh 7:43

HODIAH ("the splendor of the Lord"). A man of Judah, married to the sister of Naham, and grandfather of Keilah the Garmite and Eshtemoa the Maachathite in the genealogy of the family of Judah.

HODIAH
I Chr 4:19

HODIJAH ("the splendor of Yah"). An alternate spelling for Hodiah (the Hebrew spelling of the two names is identical).

1. One of the leaders who helped the people understand when Ezra read the Law (Neh 8:7); he was among those who led the prayers on the day of the great fast (Neh 9:5).

2. Two Levites of that name are listed among the leaders who put their seal to the covenant at the time of Ezra (Neh 10:10, 13); one of them is probably identical with No.1.

3. One of the "leaders of the people" who put their seal to the covenant at the time of Ezra.

HOGLAH ("partridge"). Third daughter of Zelophehad the son of Hepher, who had no sons (Num 26:33). Like her sisters she married a son of a brother of her father (Num 36:11) so as to keep her inheritance in her father's tribe (Num 36:11).

HOHAM King of Hebron at the time of Adoni-Zedek; he joined the coalition of the five Amorite kings which was defeated by Joshua at Gibeon.

HOLINESS The Hebrew root for holiness is *k.d.sh.*, which means "distinguished, set apart"; it is the unique stamp of the divine.

In primitive Semitic religions the holy was intrinsic to objects, sites, rites and persons. Seldom was the quality of holiness attributed to a deity. In contradistinction, the holiness concept is extrinsic in biblical tradition, with God the prime and ultimate source of holiness. There is mention of holy garments (Ex 28:2, 4; 29:21; 31:10), holy offerings (Ex 28:36; Lev 19:8), even holy food (Lev 22:14). All of these, as well as other rites and sites, derive their holiness from their relationship to God.

Not only does holiness inhere in God, but it constitutes his very essence. This extends still further to God's acts in history, the election of Israel and human conduct and experience. Certain times are even deemed to be holy both by virtue of being decreed so by God, and by Israel's consecration of them as holy in response (Ex 20:8; Lev 23:2). The nation of Israel is sanctified and commanded to be holy because it has entered into a covenantal relationship with the holy God (Ex 19:6; Lev 11:44; 19:2; 20:7; Deut 7:6; 26:19).

A number of elements in the concept of holiness are common to ancient Near Eastern religions and to the Bible. In both traditions, the holy exists in various degrees: there are objects, places and experiences, that have a greater or lesser degree of holiness. The holy in both traditions has a contagious, communicable character; a biblical example being the altar that sanctifies those that touch it (Ex 29:37; 30:29; Lev 6:18, 27). In both traditions there is mortal danger in an unauthorized approach to the holy. To gaze on the divine manifestations, or even only sacred vessels when they are not in use, may cause death (Ex 33:20; Num 4:20; Judg 13:22; cf I Kgs 19:13).

The Bible's understanding of holiness frequently involves the employment of fear-associated terms. The site of an encounter with the divine is described as "awesome" (Gen 28:17). This motif persists throughout the OT. God is holy, great and awesome (Ps 89:7; 99:3; 111:9), and holy in his terrible works (Ex 15:11; II Sam 7:23; Ps 66:3, 5; 145:6; Is 64:3). This attitude to the holiness of God is described in the verse "Who is able to stand before this holy Lord, God?" (I Sam 6:20). This fear is also occasioned by God's unrelenting demand for exclusive virtue (Josh 24:19).

It is often erroneously claimed that the association of God's holiness with his moral perfection is the contribution of the prophets. However, the earlier priestly writings already point to this association as evidenced in the holiness code (Lev chaps. 17-26). The liturgy reflected in the Psalms stresses that only "he who has clean hands and a pure heart" can stand on God's holy mountain (Ps 24:3-4). Amos associates oppression of the poor and sexual decadence with desecration of God's holy name (Amos 2:7). On the other hand it would be equally incorrect to equate perfection or righteousness with holiness. There is much that is considered holy, but has no moral content, such as the ark.

Early Christian definitions of holiness are clearly based on Jewish notions which preceded them. At the same time there is probably no area in which Jesus clashed so openly with his contemporaries as in his view of holiness. On most major points he was a faithful practicing Jew but he differed with his coreligionists in his view of the Temple as a place of prayer for all (Mark 11:17), and in allowing his disciples to eat unclean food without washing of hands (Matt 15:1-20; Mark 7:1-8). His life pointed to a concept of holiness unlike that practiced by either his pagan or his Jewish compatriots.

Jesus declared: "There is nothing that enters a man from outside which can defile him; but the things which come out of him, those are the things that defile a man" (Mark 7:15). While Mark applies this to foods, the reference can evidently be wider. What defiles is listed: evil thoughts, acts of fornication, of theft, murder, adultery, ruthless greed, and malice, fraud, indecency, envy, slander, arrogance and folly (Mark 7:21-23).

Jesus' contemporaries called him the "holy one of God" (Mark 1:24; Luke 4:34; cf John 6:69), and the Christians were most often referred to as "saints" or "holy ones." The term was derived from Hebrew words whose primary meaning is a person set apart for special devotion to God.

Essential to an understanding of holiness or sainthood is the fact that the term "saint" appears only once (Phil 4:21) in the singular form. To be a Christian involved belonging to a body of people. The only text in which Paul applies the verb "sanctify" to the action of one person upon another is in the context of marriage (I Cor 7:14) where it refers to what happens to children in a marriage where even one partner is Christian, or to an unbelieving spouse when married to a believer: in both cases, that person is drawn closer to the orbit of God's holiness and presence. It is the will of God that we should be holy and that means integrity of action towards one's own body, towards one's spouse and towards one's business partner (I Thes 4:3-8).

Furthermore the Epistle to the Hebrews warns that without holiness no one will see God (12:14) and that we are dealing with ultimate issues. The urgency of living a holy life, or being holy as God himself is holy (Heb 12:10, 14) is heightened under the lordship of Christ. Jesus tried to extend the Torah's demands and intensify their significance for his contemporaries. Paul simplified the Law for his Gentile converts, limiting it to its ethical precepts (Rom 13:8-10; cf Acts 15:20, 29). Both Christians and Jews were united in their commitment to the quest for holiness. They parted ways in their understanding of the relation of Torah to holiness, and in their interpretation of the command: "Be holy, for I am holy." (Lev 11:44; I Pet 1:15-16).

HOLON

1. A town in the plain country of Moab (Jer 48:21), mentioned together with the towns of Jahazah, Mephaath, Dibon and other places in Moab. It has been tentatively identified with Aliyan, 7 miles (11 km) northeast of Dibon. It is located at the eastern border of Moab, and seems to have been a border fortress.

2. See HILEN.

HOLY OF HOLIES See TEMPLE

HOLON 1
Jer 48:21

HOLON 2
Josh 15:51;
21:15

HOLY SPIRIT The Spirit of God, that manifestation of the one God working in creation and especially in human beings. The Holy Spirit is referred to in the OT about 80 times and about 240 times in the NT. It is the Spirit of God moving over the surface of the water (Gen 1:2) who is active in the creation (cf Ps 104:30). The Spirit is frequently described in the OT as "came upon" or "clothing" or simply "resting upon" men. Whenever this happens the person so affected is then enabled to perform some designated task for God. Thus Bezalel is able to fashion the tabernacle and its utensils (Ex 35:30ff), Gideon summons the Israelites to battle (Judg 6:34ff), Samson kills a lion and his Philistine enemies (Judg 14:6; 15:14ff), and King Saul prophesies (I Sam 10:10ff). The Holy Spirit is the source of the strength of mighty men (Judg 14:6, 19; 15:14; I Sam 11:6), the inspiration of rulers (I Sam 16:13; Is 11:2) and prophets (Mic 3:8; cf Num 11:25-26; I Sam 10:6, 10), often producing unexpected results (I Kgs 18:12; II Kgs 2:16; Ezek 8:3; 11:24), and the gift of intellectual and artistic endowments (Dan 5:14). In eschatological prophecies the Holy Spirit is associated with divine judgment (Is 4:4), the ideal ruler (Is 11:2), the renewal of the covenant with Israel (Is 32:15; Ezek I1:19; 36:26; Joel 2:28) and future repentance (Zech 12:10ff).

The NT writers quite noticeably expand the role of the Holy Spirit, who is mentioned by all but James and three of the shortest of the epistles. As in the OT, the NT also identifies the Holy Spirit as God himself, once again in a manifestation active in the affairs of men. It is the Holy Spirit who effects the conception of Jesus in Mary (Matt 1:18, 20; Luke 1:35); who descends upon Jesus at his baptism; and who then leads him to his wilderness testing (Matt 3:16; 14:1). By the power of the Holy Spirit Jesus works miracles (Matt 12:28; Acts 10:38) and teaches his disciples (Acts 1:2). John records Jesus' promise to his disciples that the Holy Spirit would be sent to them to remind them of Jesus' words and to enable them to bear witness of him (Acts 14:16ff; 15:28; 16:6ff). This came to pass immediately after the resurrection (John 20:22) and then in a fuller way 47 days later on the Day of Pentecost (Acts 1:8; 2:1-4). This latter event has often been considered the birth of the Church. The Acts of the Apostles (q.v.) place a special emphasis on the activity of the Holy Spirit and for this reason have sometimes popularly been known as "the Acts of the Holy Spirit". Another appellative for the Holy Spirit in the NT is "the Spirit of Jesus" or "the Spirit of Christ" (Acts 16:7; Rom 8:9; Phil 1:19; I Pet 1:11-12). The NT teaches that the Holy Spirit is active in the believer in Jesus; to give him new birth (Titus 3:5; cf John 3:5-8); to endow him with spiritual gifts for the good of the entire body of believers (I Chr 12:4-11); and to produce in him those traits of character which will make him like Jesus (Gal 5:22-25). For these purposes, the Spirit of God is said to "dwell in" every person who believes in Jesus (Rom 8:9-11).

HOMAM
I Chr 1:39

HOMAM Second son of Lotan, firstborn son of Seir the Horite (I Chr 1:39) the name is sometimes spelled Hemam (Gen 36:22).

HOOPOE See ANIMALS

HOPHNI
I Sam 1:3;
2:34; 4:4, 11,
17

HOPHNI A priest at Shiloh, son of the high priest Eli in the time of Samuel. Hophni and his brother Phinehas flagrantly abused their priestly positions by taking portions of meat from an animal before the sacrifice was dedicated to God and by having intercourse with women who served at the sanctuary (I Sam 2:12-17, 22). Their sins brought a curse on the house of Eli whose rebuke they ignored, and a prophecy that they would both die on the same day (I Sam 2:34). They were slain by the Philistines while escorting the ark of the covenant in a battle at Aphek (I Sam 4:11).

HOPHRA ("the heart of the god Ra endures"). King of Egypt of the 26th Dynasty (588-568 B.C.); an ally of Zedekiah, king of Judah during the Judean revolt against the Babylonians (Jer 37:5). After Jerusalem was captured by Nebuchadnezzar and the Babylonian-appointed governor Gedaliah, assassinated, the remaining Jews, including the prophet Jeremiah, fled to Egypt (Jer 43:5-7). There Jeremiah foresaw Hophra's death at the hand of his enemies (Jer 44:30). He was killed by one of his relatives who assumed the throne.

HOPHRA
Jer 44:30

HOR (MOUNT)

1. The name of a hill on the border between Canaan and Edom. One of the stations on the route of the Exodus, where the Israelites camped near a source of water. From here they tried to penetrate the land of Canaan but were forced to retreat to the desert. Aaron died here (Num 20:22-29). Tentatively located to the northeast of Kadesh Barnea.

HOR
(MOUNT) 1
Num 20:22-23,
25, 27; 21:4;
33:37-39, 41.
Deut 32:50

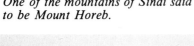
Jebel Harun in Edom, traditionally believed to be Mount Hor.

One of the mountains of Sinai said to be Mount Horeb.

2. A place on the northern border of the land of Canaan (Num 34:7). Not identified.

HOR
(MOUNT) 2
Num 34:7-8

HORAM King of Gezer; he went to the rescue of the town of Lachish attacked by Joshua, but was defeated.

HORAM
Josh 10:33

HOREB Another name for Mount Sinai, the mountain of God, encountered by Moses while tending Jethro's flock (Ex 3:1). Along the Exodus route, Moses smote the rock of Horeb which gave forth water to quench the thirst of the Children of Israel (Ex 17:6). It took 11 days to journey from Horeb via Mount Seir to Kadesh Barnea (Deut 1:2). Horeb is identical with Mount Sinai (Deut 1:6; 4:10, 15), and there God made a covenant with his people (Deut 5:2; 29:1). At Horeb, Moses placed the two tablets in the ark of the covenant (I Kgs 8:9; II Chr 5:10). For identification see EXODUS ROUTE.

HOREB
Ex 3:1; 17:6;
33:6. Deut 1:2,
6, 19; 4:10,
15; 5:2; 9:8;
18:16; 29:1.
I Kgs 8:9;
19:8. II Chr
5:10. Ps
106:19. Mal
4:4

HOREM A fortified town in the territory of Naphtali. Its precise location is unknown.

HOREM
Josh 19:38

HOR HAGIDGAD One of the stations on the route of the Exodus in the desert (Num 33:32-33), also named Gudgodah (Deut 10:7), from which the Children of Israel came to Jotbathah, a land of rivers of water. Various identifications have been proposed but without any basis.

HOR
HAGIDGAD
Num 33:32-33

HORI

1. Firstborn son of Lotan, a descendant of Esau.

HORI 1
Gen 36:22.
I Chr 1:39

2. A Simeonite; father of Shaphat, one of the spies sent by Moses to Canaan.

HORI 2
Num 13:5

HORITES The Horites probably originated in the hills of Zagrus and

HORITES
Gen 14:6;

36:21, 29-30.
Deut 2:12, 22

Armenia. They are first heard of in a document from the time of Sargon of Akkad (24th century B.C.), when they already had a kingdom beyond the Tigris (Hiddekel). From this kingdom they began their slow but steady penetration along the valleys of the Mesopotamian rivers southward. Early in the 19th century B.C. they had already occupied the land north of Ashur (Mesopotamia). A study of names shows how deeply the Horites penetrated into upper Mesopotamia. This movement of Horites, who were of non-Semitic stock, coincided with the appearance of the West Semites, the two elements subsequently constituting the bulk of the population in Syria and Palestine. By the 15th century B.C. the Horites formed the majority of the population in northern Syria. Towards the 14th-13th centuries B.C. they were an important element in the ruling classes of southern Syria and Palestine.

The exact date of the arrival of the Horites in Palestine and Egypt is still in dispute. It is thought by some experts to have coincided with the conquest of Egypt by the Hyksos in the 18th century B.C, but others date it a century later. Both in Egypt and in Palestine, the Horites and the Hyksos made up the ruling nobility, the *maryannu,* who introduced the horse and chariot into warfare. Together with other elements, such as the nomadic Habiru, they formed the population which the Israelites, and Sea Peoples (Philistines) had to face when they arrived in the land of Canaan in the 13th century B.C.

The Horites are not mentioned frequently in the Bible. Those living in Mount Seir (Edom) were defeated by Chedorlaomer (Gen 14:5-6), but they remained in the region (Gen 36:20) until they were destroyed by the descendants of Esau (Deut 2:12, 22). Scholars believe that the Jebusites and the Hivites, as well as some other ancient peoples mentioned in the Bible, were of Horite descent.

HORMAH
Num 14:45;
21:3. Deut
1:44. Josh
12:14; 15:30;
19:4. Judg
1:17. I Sam
30:30. I Chr
4:30

HORMAH A town in the northeastern Negeb, close to Arad. It was in the south of the land of Canaan and is connected with the first attempt to penetrate Canaan (Num 14:45; Deut 1:44). At that time it was a Canaanite city-state held by the king of Hormah. It was conquered and

Tell Malkhata in the eastern valley of Beersheba, one of the places believed to be at the site of Hormah.

destroyed by Judah and Simeon (Judg 1:17) and appears in the list of 31 kings vanquished by Joshua (Josh 12:14). It was later included in the territory of Judah (Josh 15:30) and given to Simeon (Josh 19:4). Hormah was one of the cities to which David sent presents after his victory over the Amalekites (I Sam 30:30). It does not apear in later biblical sources. Identified with Tell el-Meshash, about 8 miles (13 km) southeast of Beersheba.

HORNET See ANIMALS

HORONAIM A city in Moab, mentioned in the lamentation on Moab (Is 15:5; Jer 48:3, 34). It was at the foot of a descent (Jer 48:5). From its mention together with Zoar and the waters of Nimrim, it may be assumed that it is located in southern Moab. It has been identified with el-Iraq, 6 miles (10 km) south of Kir Moab (el-Kerak), where there are numerous caves.

HORONAIM
Is 15:5. Jer
43:3, 5, 34

HORONITE An epithet for Nehemiah's archenemy Sanballat, and native of Beth Horon.

HORONITE
Neh 2:10, 19;
13:28

HORSE See ANIMALS

HORSE GATE A gate in the eastern wall of Jerusalem, opposite the Kidron Valley, by which Athaliah came to the king's house (II Kgs 11:16). It faced the palace (Jer 31:40), and was restored by Nehemiah (Neh 3:28).

HORSE GATE
II Chr 23:15.
Neh 3:28. Jer
31:40

HOSAH

1. A man of Merari who was a gatekeeper at the ark in the time of King David and later in charge of the West Gate when the ark was brought to Jerusalem. He had 13 children.

HOSAH 1
I Chr 16:38;
26:10-11, 16

2. A town on the border of the territory which fell to the lot of the tribe of Asher when Joshua divided the land of Canaan among the Children of Israel. It is generally assumed to be in the vicinity of Tyre.

HOSAH 2
Josh 19:29

HOSANNA The Greek form of the Hebrew phrase *hoshana*, "hosanna" was the term used by the people to acclaim Jesus on his entry into Jerusalem on Palm Sunday. In Psalm 118:25, it is translated "save now" and, as in the gospels, is followed by the phrase "Blessed is he who comes in the name of the Lord." Psalm 118 was used liturgically at the Feast of Tabernacles, and verse 25 was the cue for the waving of the palm branches. In the NT and later rabbinic Judaism, the phrase no longer denoted a prayer for safety and success but rather a proclamation of religious enthusiasm coupled with the waving of palm branches. By the end of the 1st century A.D. the term had become merely an utterance of praise and exaltation in the Christian liturgy.

HOSANNA
Matt 21:9, 15.
Mark 11:9-10.
John 12:13

HOSEA (HOSHEA) ("may the Lord save"). (The Hebrew Bible mentions five different persons named Hoshea. The KJV and subsequent English versions call the prophet, Hosea, and the others Hoshea.)

HOSEA
Hos 1:1-2

Hosea the prophet was the son of Beeri (Hos 1:1). The information that Hosea experienced his revelation during the reigns of Uzziah (769-733 B.C.), Jotham, Ahaz, Hezekiah (727-698 B.C.), kings of Judah (Hos 1:1) appears to contradict the continuation of the verse which states that Hosea experienced prophetic revelation during the reign of Jeroboam II son of Joash (784-748 B.C.). The two statements have been explained as a conflation of the dates given to Isaiah in Isaiah 1:1 and to Amos in Amos 1:1. According to Hosea 1:2, the prophet's inaugural vision commanded him to marry a harlot and thereby symbolize Israel's disloyalty to the Lord. Hosea thereupon married Gomer, who bore him three children, given the symbolic names Jezreel, Lo-Ruhamah and Lo-Ammi (Hos 1:3-9). In a later vision, Hosea was commanded to befriend a woman who, while befriended by a companion (i.e., the prophet), consorts with others, just as the Lord befriended the Israelites, "who look to other gods" (Hos 3:1). Hosea then contracted with an unnamed woman that she should "not play the harlot" nor "have a man" for a long time (Hos 3:2). This arrangement is said to symbolize a period during which Israel would be without a king or any cultic installations (Hos 3:4). Thereafter Israel will repent and be duly rewarded (Hos 3:5). No further biographical information about Hosea is contained in the Bible.

HOSEA, BOOK OF The first and longest (14 chapters) book of the Minor Prophets. Notwithstanding the attribution in Hosea 1:1 of the entire book to the latter half of the 8th century B.C., the most likely setting of Hosea chapters 1-3 is the period beginning with King Ahab when the worship of Baal was officially sanctioned by the Israelite monarchy (I Kgs 16:30-33) and the prophets of the Lord were persecuted (I Kgs 18:4). According to II Kings 10:28 the worship of Baal was eradicated from Israel sometime during the reign of Jehu. The reference to the punishment on the house of Jehu for the bloodshed of Jezreel in Hosea 1:4 suggests that the *terminus ad quem* for Hosea

Fragment of a commentary of the Book of Hosea, found at Qumran. (Shrine of the Book, Jerusalem)

chapters 1-3 precedes Jehu's eradication of the worship of Baal, and the canonization of the view that Jehu's destruction of the survivors of the house of Ahab in Jezreel (II Kgs 10:11) was so pleasing to the Lord that four generations of his descendants were allowed to rule Israel (II Kgs 10:30).

The first three chapters of Hosea compare Israel's flirtation with Baal, the Phoenician god of rain, to an adulterous wife's flirtation with her paramours. In a prophecy of rebuke (Hos 2:4-13), these transgressions are to be punished by the cessation of the land's fertility and the abolition of all joyous festivals; this is linked with a prophecy of consolation (2:1-3, 14-23) promising Israel numerous progeny (1:10), the reunification of Judah and Israel (1:11), peace and security (Hos 2:20) and fertility of the land (2:22-23). These prophecies allude to ideas and images contained in the biographical accounts of Hosea chapters 1 and 3, which are discussed in the entry Hosea. Hosea 1-3 makes an important contribution to biblical thought by the comparison of God's relationship with Israel to a marriage, and the comparison of Israel's flirtation with other gods to the behavior of an adulterous wife. These ideas were taken over and elaborated upon by Jeremiah, Ezekiel and (Second) Isaiah.

Hosea chapters 4-14, in which the prophet is never named, contain oracles addressed to the Northern Kingdom, which is called both Israel and Ephraim, during the reign of King Menahem (746-737 B.C.). Like Isaiah (see Is 31:1; 39:5-7), the prophet believes that Israel's alliances with foreign powers — specifically Assyria or Egypt — constitute disloyalty to the Lord (Hos 5:13; 7:11; 12:1; 14:4). Like Jeremiah whom he influenced (see Jer 9:2), he condemns Israel for not "knowing the

Lord", and he equates "knowing the Lord" with observance of the ethical prohibitions found in the Ten Commandments (Hos 4:1-2, 6; 5:4; 6:3, 6). Similar to Amos (see Amos 2:7), Jeremiah (Jer 5:8), and Ezekiel (Ezek 18:11; 22:11; 33:26), he castigates Israel for sexual license (Hos 4:2, 10-15; 5:3; 6:10; 7:14; 9:1). Highlighting the supremacy of morality, he declares that immoral acts are not mitigated by the culprits' performance of religious rituals; on the contrary, their immorality makes such religiosity an abomination; see also Amos 2:8; Isaiah 1:10-17. Unlike the first three chapters, the latter portion of the book no longer uses harlotry as a metaphor for idolatry, referring to the worship of Baal only as a sin of the past (9:10; 13:1). With the author of I Kings 12:28, the prophet shares the view that the calves, which Jeroboam I erected at Bethel and Dan to serve, like the cherubim in Solomon's Temple, as symbolic thrones of the Lord, are an abomination tantamount to idolatry (8:4-6; 13:2). Hence he calls Bethel, denoting "House of God", Beth Aven, which means "House of Delusion" (4:15; 5:8; 10:5). He also condemns the cult of the angel of Bethel (12:4-6; cf Gen 31:11-13; 48:16), contending that it is foolish for the descendants of Jacob to rely for help on the very angel whom Jacob, a mere mortal, had overpowered (Gen 32:24-32). He is the first prophet to assert that the worship of the Lord at a multiplicity of altars is an abomination (Hos 4:13; 8:11). Later, under the influence of the scroll of the Torah found in the Temple at Jerusalem in the time of Josiah (see II Kgs chaps. 22-23), this idea became a fundamental teaching of Jeremiah, Ezekiel and the editor of the Book of Kings.

(bottom)
Opal Hebrew seal inscribed "[Belonging] to Hoshayahu son of Shelemyahu". Late 8th-7th centuries B.C. (Israel Museum)

Limestone Hebrew seal inscribed "[Belonging] to Hoshayahu [son of] Ahimelech". 7th-6th centuries B.C. (Israel Museum)

OUTLINE

1:1:9	Hosea's marriage to an unfaithful wife
1:10-11	The restoration of Israel
2:1-23	God the spouse of Israel
3:1-5	Hosea's marriage
4:1-5:7	Rebukes against corrupt priests, superstitious people and idolatry
5:8-6:6	Rebuke of Israel and Judah
6:7-9:10	Rebuke of Israel for various sins including idolatry, civil strife and lack of trust in God
9:11-10:15	Oracles based on historical sins of Israel
11:1-12	God's love for Israel
12:1-14:9	Divine judgment and call for repentance

HOSHAIAH ("the Lord has saved").

1. A leader of Judah who led one of the two thanksgiving choirs at the dedication of the wall of Jerusalem rebuilt by Nehemiah.

2. Father of Jezaniah (Jer 42:1) or Azariah (Jer 43:2) who was a high official, perhaps a minister, in the period which immediately followed the destruction of Jerusalem.

HOSHAMA One of the seven sons of King Jeconiah.

HOSHEA

1. Son of Elah, last king of Israel, 733-724 B.C., he ascended the throne after assassinating Pekah son of Remaliah (II Kgs 15:30). Because of the exile of most of the Kingdom of Israel and its division into

Assyrian provinces, Hoshea's kingdom was confined to the hill country of Ephraim. In the Assyrian king Tiglath-Pileser III's annals Hoshea is mentioned as his vassal whom he placed upon the throne. During the reign of the former's son, Shalmaneser V, Hoshea rebelled against Assyria and was supported by Egypt (II Kgs 17:3-4). As a result the Assyrian king took him prisoner, Samaria was besieged, the Kingdom of Israel was eventually overthrown and most of its inhabitants deported to Assyria. His fate is not recorded.

HOSHEA 2
Num 13:8, 16

2. The original name, changed by Moses, of Joshua son of Nun.

HOSHEA 3
I Chr 27:20

3. Son of Azaziah. An officer of David in charge of the Ephraimites.

HOSHEA 4
Neh 10:23

4. One of the leaders of the people who sealed the covenant in Nehemiah's time.

5. See HOSEA

HOSTS, LORD OF HOSTS A divine title of might and power most commonly found in military or apocalyptic contexts. It occurs some 300 times in the OT, especially in Isaiah, Jeremiah, Zechariah and Malachi, and twice in the NT. As a name for God, it has three nuances in the OT: most commonly, as Lord of the angelic hosts who wage war in the heavenly realms (Jer 5:14; Amos 3:13ff); as the Lord of the armies or hosts of Israel (I Sam 17:45); and in cultic settings without any military connotation (I Sam 1:3), where it is associated with the sanctuary at Shiloh (I Sam 1:3, 11; 4:4). In the Greek translation of the Bible, the term is either transliterated as "Sabaoth" or translated as "almighty". In its two NT occurrences (Rom 9:29; James 5:4), Sabaoth, while used as a title of God, may perhaps retain a nuance of God as Lord of the angelic realms as well as champion of the oppressed. (See also GOD, [NAMES OF]).

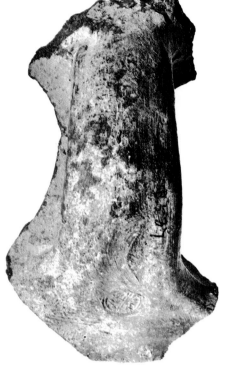

Hebrew Seal impression on a pottery jar-handle, inscribed "Hoshea Safan". 7th-6th centuries B.C.

HOTHAM ("seal").

HOTHAM 1
I Chr 7:32

1. Third son of Heber, son of Beriah and grandson of Asher (I Chr 7:32). His name is Helem in I Chronicles 7:35.

HOTHAM 2
I Chr 11:44

2. Hotham the Aroerite (from the town of Aroer) father of Shama and Jeiel, two of David's "mighty men".

HOTHIR
I Chr 25:4, 28

HOTHIR ("the Lord gave in plenty"?). One of the sons of Heman No.2; he was head of the 21st division of musicians in the House of the Lord at the time of King David.

HOUSE OF THE FOREST OF LEBANON
I Kgs 7:2; 10:7, 21. II Chr 9:16, 20. Is 22:8

HOUSE OF THE FOREST OF LEBANON A dwelling which King Solomon built for his own use (I Kgs 7:1-12). It was in the form of a large hall of wooden supports, hence its name. It was 100 by 50 cubits, and 30 cubits high. The cedar pillars, totalling 45, were arranged in four rows and supported cedar beams. The hall was illuminated by three rows of windows. Scholars have suggested that the house of the forest of Lebanon was Solomon's armory (cf I Kgs 10:17, 21; II Chr 9:16, 20; Is 22:8); others that it was the royal guardhouse and served as an entry for ceremonial processions. Whatever the case, the unusually lengthy description given of the structure reflects its importance, and its innovative design.

HOZAI
II Chr 33:19

HOZAI The writer of a history of Manasseh king of Judah (II Chr 33:19). Some scholars interpret Hozai as a common name (Hebrew, "seers").

HUKKOK
Josh 19:34

HUKKOK A city on the southern border of the territory allotted to Naphtali (Josh 19:34) when the land of Canaan was divided among the tribes (Josh 14:1). It was toward the territory of Zebulun. Its location is unknown.

HUKOK
I Chr 6:75

HUKOK A city allotted to Asher when the land of Canaan was divided among the tribes; it was later assigned to the Gershonite Levites (I Chr 6:71, 75). It has been suggested that this is an alternate name for Helkath but most scholars now reject that theory.

The triple Huldah Gates in the southern wall of the Temple Mount, Jerusalem. Traditionally they are said to have led to the academy of Huldah the prophetess in Jerusalem.

HUL Second son of Aram the son of Shem (Gen 10:23) or seventh son of Shem (I Chr 1:17).

HULDAH ("weasel"). Prophetess, wife of Shallum, the "keeper of the wardrobe," who lived in Jerusalem. In the course of the repairs to the Temple undertaken in the 18th year of King Josiah of Judah (622 B.C.), the high priest Hilkiah discovered a scroll of the Torah. Its contents suggested that for longer than anyone remembered affairs of state and the Temple had not been conducted "according to the book". The king urged Hilkiah and his officials "to inquire of the Lord" (II Kgs 22:13; II Chr 34:21), which means "consult a prophet" (see I Sam 9:9). They promptly went to consult Huldah who quoted the Lord as decreeing disaster for Jerusalem and its inhabitants as punishment for their idolatry.

However, since Josiah's immediate response to the reading of the Law was to rend his clothing, and weep, the disaster would be delayed until after the king had died (II Kgs 22:15-20; II Chr 34:23-28). Huldah's prophecy induced Josiah to undertake the reform described in II Kings 23:1-25 (cf II Chr 34:29-33).

HUMTAH A town in the region of Hebron, in the territory of Judah (Josh 15:54). Its location is unknown.

HUNTING AND FISHING Hunting was not practiced to a great extent but it is mentioned in the Bible: Nimrod was famed as a hunter (Gen 10:9); and so was Esau (Gen 27:5). The Jewish dietary laws restricted the kinds of animal that could be eaten as well as the manner in which they might be slaughtered. These limitations may have had an effect on hunting. Some scholars believe that if it was practiced at all it was purely for reasons of self protection or to prevent damage to fields and other property by wild animals. The trapper's methods are portrayed in Job (18:8-10). The implication is that the trap was some kind of a net; a bigger and stronger one would be used for catching larger game and one of finer mesh for birds (cf also Ecc 9:12; Ezek 12:13; 17:20; Amos 3:5). Larger animals could also be caught by the very ancient method of digging a hole in the ground and concealing it with branches (Jer 48:44).

HUL
Gen 10:23.
I Chr 1:17

HULDAH
II Kgs 22:14.
II Chr 34:22

HUMTAH
Josh 15:54

Gold bowl from Ugarit depicting a hunt in chariots. 14th century B.C.

Netting wild geese. Wall painting in the tomb of Nakht, scribe and priest of Thutmosis IV. 15th century B.C.

A hunted animal could be eaten only if it was ritually clean and if the blood had been properly drained from it (Lev 17:13). Hunting an animal with a bow and arrow, or with a spear, as in numerous Assyrian and Egyptian reliefs and wall paintings, was very rare in Palestine (cf I Sam 17:34-36). On the other hand, Solomon's daily diet included much ritually clean game, which must have been hunted by such methods (I Kgs 4:23). In the neighboring countries hunting was an accepted sport and some of the Assyrian monarchs kept large game reserves. It

Lion hunt on a mosaic floor at Beth Shean.

Hunting scene from a mosaic floor at Kissufim, northern Negeb.

continued to be a very common sport in the Persian, Hellenistic and Roman periods, when it was also used to obtain combat animals, mainly war elephants. In the Roman period hunting also supplied the circuses with wild animals for the popular contests with men.

There is not much evidence of fishing in the Bible and it was less common than in Egypt (Num 11:5; Is 19:8). The conquest of the coast of Palestine by the Hasmoneans encouraged the Jews to fish. The NT (Matt 4:18-22, etc.) provides evidence of fishing in the Sea of Galilee in the Roman period. There was no way of keeping fish fresh for more than a very short time, so it had to be salted and dried if it was to be preserved. One of the major salting centers on the Sea of Galilee was at Taricheae (Magdala), a Greek name which means "fish salting". The earlier, Aramaic name of the same place was Migdal Nunayah — "Tower of the Fishermen". Some of the kitchen refuse of ancient towns in the Negeb contains considerable quantities of fishbones from fish that must have been brought from the Red Sea. This may be taken as evidence that fish was also salted there.

Assyrian relief showing a man fishing. (British Museum)

Fishermen in Palestine, as elsewhere, used either a hook and a line or nets (Is 19:8); fishing from boats with dragnets was also known (Ezek 26:5; Hab 1:15; Luke 5:4). Clay or stone weights were used to make the net sink. Quantities of these were found at Roman Caesarea and on other sites along the coast.

HUPHAM Son of Benjamin and founder of the Huphamite family (Num 26:39) sometimes called Huppim (Gen 46:11).

HUPHAMITES A family founded by Hupham the son of Benjamin.

HUPPAH ("canopy"). Head of the 13th division of priests serving in the House of the Lord at the time of King David (I Chr 24:13, 19).

HUPPIM

1. A son of Benjamin; in Numbers 26:39 he is called Hupham.

2. A son of Ir, grandson of Benjamin; his sister Maachah married Machir son of Manasseh.

HUR

1. A Judahite ancestor of Bezalel, son of Caleb and Ephrath; possibly identical with Ashhur of I Chronicles 2:24; 4:5.

HUPHAM
Num 26:39

HUPHAMITES
Num 26:39

HUPPAH
I Chr 24:13

HUPPIM 1
Gen 46:21

HUPPIM 2
I Chr 7:12, 15

HUR 1
Ex 31:2;

2. One of the five Midianite rulers killed by the Israelites, in the war ordered by Moses.

3. An assistant of Moses, who, together with Aaron, presided over the Israelites in Moses' absence (Ex 24:14). During the battle against the Amalekites, Hur and Aaron supported Moses' upraised arms (Ex 17:10, 12).

4. Father or ancestor of the administrator in charge of the Mount Ephraim district during Solomon's reign: the name is given as Ben-Hur.

5. Father of Rephaiah, who governed half of Jerusalem and helped construct its city wall.

HURAI Hurai from the "brooks of Gaash" (I Chr 11:32) one of David's thirty "mighty men". In the parallel text of Samuel he is called "Hiddai from the brooks of Gaash" (II Sam 23:30).

HURAM

1. Son of Bela, a Benjamite.

2. See HIRAM No.1

3. See HIRAM No.2

HURI Son of Jaroah and father of Abihai from the family of Gad.

HUSHAH A place founded by Ezer son of Hur. It may be an eponym for a clan or a father's house that settled there (I Chr 4:4).

Sibbecai the Hushathite, one of David's "mighty men", came from Hushah. It is possibly to be identified with Husan, southwest of Bethlehem (II Sam 21:18; I Chr 11:29; 20:4; 27:11).

HUSHAI

1. A member of the family of the Archites. During the reign of David he served as the "king's companion" and took part in the administrative organization of the kingdom (I Chr 27:33). At the time of Absalom's rebellion, Hushai remained loyal to David and was anxious to join him when he fled Jerusalem (II Sam 15:32ff), but, at David's request, he remained in the city, to keep him informed and frustrate the plans of Absalom's adviser, Ahithophel. Hushai therefore joined Absalom as a royal counselor. Absalom mocked him, saying, "Is this your loyalty to your friend?" (II Sam 16:17). Nevertheless Hushai managed to gain Absalom's confidence (II Sam 16:17-20) and when Ahithophel proposed a plan for attacking David, Hushai counseled that the attack be delayed, thus affording David time to escape (II Sam 17:1-16, 22).

2. The father of Baanah, who was one of the regional governors of King Solomon (I Kgs 4:16). Probably identical with No.1.

HUSHAM Husham "of the land of the Temanites" was the third king of Edom.

HUSHATITE Appellation of Mebunnai, a native of the village of Hushah, and one of David's thirty "mighty men" (II Sam 23:27).

HUSHIM

1. The son of Dan (he is called Shuham in Num 26:42).

2. Son of Aher in the genealogy of the family of Benjamin.

3. Second wife of Shaharaim of Benjamin, who later repudiated her after she bore him Abitub and Elpaal.

HUZ Firstborn son of Nahor the brother of Abraham by his wife Milcah (Gen 22:20-21); an alternate form of Uz.

HYACINTH See PLANTS

HYENA See ANIMALS

HYMENAEUS ("pertaining to Hymen", the god of marriages). A Christian who had lost the faith and been excommunicated (I Tim 1:20). He is probably the same man who taught that the resurrection had already occurred (II Tim 2:17).

HYRAX See ANIMALS

HYSSOP See PLANTS

I

Entrance to the Iron Age water system at Ibleam. (Israel Dept. of Antiquities and Museums)

IBHAR ("the Lord chooses"). One of the sons born to David in Jerusalem.

IBHAR
II Sam 5:15.
I Chr 3:6; 14:5

IBLEAM A city located on the road leading from the ascent of the Jezreel Valley to the Samarian hills and Shechem.

IBLEAM
Josh 17:11.
Judg 1:27. II
Kgs 9:27

Although located in the tribal district of Issachar, Ibleam was reckoned among those cities of Issachar and Asher allotted to Manasseh, and were in fact Manassite enclaves (Josh 17:11). However, in the 12th century B.C., as in the case of other cities, the Canaanites could not be driven out of Ibleam (Josh 17:12-13; Judg 1:27-28). After their conquest by David they were put under tribute, and the extensive areas became royal property. It is probable that Ibleam was a Levitical city; identical with Bileam (I Chr 6:70, where the Septuagint transcription reads "Ibleam"). In Joshua 21:25 the Septuagint lists Ibleam as one of the cities allotted to the Levites, but the Hebrew text reads in its place Gath Rimmon.

During the revolt of Jehu (II Kgs 9:14ff), which brought down the Omride dynasty, Ahaziah, king of Judah, was mortally wounded by Jehu's forces at the ascent of Gur, near Ibleam, while fleeing from Jezreel. It is also possible that Zechariah, son of Jeroboam II, king of Israel, was assassinated by Shallum in Ibleam (II Kgs 15:10, on the basis of a Septuagint manuscript). A later, abbreviated form of the city's name is retained in the Book of Judith (4:4; 7:3).

Today, Wadi Bel'ameh, which descends from Jenin to the Jezreel Valley, preserves the ancient name Ibleam. Adjacent to it is Khirbet Bel'ame, ancient Ibleam, situated at the edge of a spur, isolated on three sides and encompassing 22½ acres (9 ha).

An archeological survey of the site has yielded pottery from the Canaanite period onward.

IBNEIAH ("Yah will build"). A man of Benjamin, son of Jeroham, who resided in Jerusalem after the return of the exiles from Babylon.

IBNEIAH
I Chr 9:8

IBNIJAH ("Yah will build?"). A man of Benjamin, one of the ancestors of Meshullam No.6 who settled in Jerusalem after the return of the exiles from Babylon.

IBNIJAH
I Chr 9:8

IBRI ("Hebrew"). A Merarite Levite son of Jaaziah, at the time of David.

IBRI
I Chr 24:27

IBSAM See JIBSAM

IBZAN ("swift"). One of the so-called minor judges; a man of Bethlehem who judged Israel for seven years; he had 30 sons and 30 daughters. He was buried in his city.

IBZAN
Judg 12:8, 10

ICHABOD ("lack of glory, [or pride]"). Grandson of Eli and son of Phinehas; both men died when the ark of God was captured by the Philistines. Phinehas' wife was so distraught at the news that she died in childbirth, but not before giving her son his name. He was the brother of Ahitub.

ICHABOD
I Sam 4:21;
14:3

ICONIUM A city in the Roman province of Galatia (in modern Turkey). In the days of Paul it was a flourishing center, located along the trade route between Syria and Ephesus.

ICONIUM
Acts 13:51;
14:1, 19, 21;
16:2. II Tim
3:11

On their first missionary journey, Paul and Barnabas, having been expelled from Antioch (Acts 13:50-51), went to Iconium where they spoke in the synagogue. As elsewhere, the apostles' mission in Iconium was only partly successful: numerous Jews and Greeks accepted their teaching but others sought to stone them and the apostles had to flee to Lystra and Derbe (Acts 14:5-6). Hostile elements from Iconium and Antioch followed the apostles to Lystra and again stoned Paul "and dragged him out of the city", supposing he was dead (Acts 14:19). Nevertheless Paul returned to Iconium "strengthening the souls of the disciples, exhorting them to continue in the faith" (Acts 14:22).

The "brethren who were at Lystra and Iconium" spoke favorably of Timothy, which weighed well with Paul (Acts 16:2). As Paul relates in the Second Epistle to Timothy, his visit to Galatia was difficult as it was filled with persecutions and afflictions at Antioch, Iconium and Lystra (II Tim 3:11).

IDALAH A town allotted to Zebulun when the land of Canaan was divided among the tribes (Josh 14:1; 19:15). It has not been identified.

IDBASH A man of Judah, brother of Hazelelponi; the son of Etam.

IDDO

1. The father of Ahinadab who supplied food to King Solomon's household.

2. A Levite, descendant of Gershon.

3. The son of a certain Zechariah; he was a leader of the half-tribe of Manasseh in Gilead during the time of King David.

4. A seer who lived during the reigns of Solomon, Rehoboam and Abijah. His deeds were recorded "in the book of Shemaiah the prophet, and of Iddo the seer" (II Chr 12:14-15).

5. The grandfather of the prophet Zechariah (Zech 1:1, 7). In Ezra 5:1 and 6:14, he is given as the father of Zechariah.

6. The head of a family of priests who returned from the Babylonian captivity.

7. The leading figure at Casiphia, to whom Ezra dispatched a delegation with the request to send Levites for the Temple, no Levites having returned up to that time from Babylonian captivity.

IDUMEA The region of south Judea, which in the Persian period was settled by Edomites. It included the southern hills of Judah, its southern border being north of Beersheba. In the early Hellenistic period Marissa (Mareshah) became its capital. During the reign of the Seleucids Idumea was enlarged to include the district of Ashdod (Josephus, *Antiq.* XII, 308). After the death of Antiochus VII (129 B.C.) John Hyrcanus subdued the Idumeans and converted them to Judaism by force. During the reign of Alexander, Jannaeus Antipas, grandfather of Herod, was appointed ruler over this district. After Herod's death the district was in the territory of Archelaus, Herod's eldest son, and from A.D. 41 it formed part of the kingdom of Agrippa I.

IGAL ("may [the Lord] redeem").

1. A man of Issachar, son of Joseph; one of the 12 men sent by Moses from the wilderness of Paran to spy out the land of Canaan.

2. The son of Nathan of Zobah; he was one of David's "mighty men".

3. The second son of Shemaiah No.2 in the genealogy of the family of Jeconiah.

IGDALIAH A Judean prophet, and father of Hanan; his grandsons had their chambers in the Temple at the time of Jehoiakim king of Judah.

IJE ABARIM One of the stations on the Exodus route. After the detour around Edom, the Children of Israel camped at Oboth, and halted at Ije Abarim from where they went to the valley of Zared (Num 21:11-12). More specifically in Numbers 33:44-45: "And they departed from Oboth, and camped at Ije Abarim, in the border of Moab. And they departed from Ijim, and camped at Dibon Gad". This description indicates a location on the southern border of Moab. Various identifications have been proposed.

Ije Abarim and Ijim (Num 33:44-45) are apparently two different localities, the second being a station at which the Children of Israel camped before crossing the River Arnon. Ijim in Hebrew apparently denotes a heap of stones marking a river crossing, and the addition of Abarim was to distinguish between the southern and the northern crossings.

Marginal references (left column):

IDALAH
Josh 19:15

IDBASH
I Chr 4:3

IDDO 1
I Kgs 4:14

IDDO 2
I Chr 6:21

IDDO 3
I Chr 27:21

IDDO 4
II Chr 9:29;
12:15; 13:22

IDDO 5
Ezra 5:1; 6:14.
Zech 1:1, 7

IDDO 6
Neh 12:4, 16

IDDO 7
Ezra 8:17

IDUMEA
Mark 3:8

IGAL 1
Num 13:7

IGAL 2
II Sam 23:36

IGAL 3
I Chr 3:22

IGDALIAH
Jer 35:4

IJE ABARIM
Num 21:11;
33:44

Rock-crystal Hebrew seal inscribed "[Belonging] to Joezer Igdaliahu". 7th century B.C. (Israel Museum)

One of the waterfalls along the course of the Ijon River, south of the site of the ancient town of the same name.

IJIM (IIM) A place in the Negeb, at the southern border of the territory of Judah (Josh 15:29). Its identification is uncertain.

IJON A town in the north of the Kingdom of Israel, in the territory of Naphtali, conquered by Ben-Hadad in the time of Baasha, king of Israel (I Kgs 15:20). During the reign of Pekah, king of Israel, it was conquered again by Tiglath-Pileser III and its inhabitants were deported to Assyria (II Kgs 15:29).

Identified with Tell Dibbin in the valley of Merg Ayun, which has preserved the ancient name.

IKKESH A Tekoite, father of Ira, one of David's thirty "mighty men", and the head officer of David's militia for the sixth month of each year (I Chr 27:9).

ILAI An Ahohite, one of David's thirty "mighty men". In the parallel list (II Sam 23:28) he is called Zalmon.

ILLYRICUM An extensive district to the east of the Adriatic Sea. Paul "fully preached the gospel" of Christ there (Rom 15:19).

IMLA, IMLAH (probably "he will be full", or "prosperous"). The father of the prophet Micaiah at the time of Ahab, king of Israel.

IMMANUEL ("God is with us"). A symbolic name given by the prophet Isaiah (Is 7:14; 8:8), to a child to be born of a young woman (the Hebrew noun *almah* refers only to a chronological description, i.e., a young woman, and does not of itself denote a virgin).

In 734 B.C., Rezin king of Aram and Pekah king of Israel, proposed to form a coalition with Judah against Tiglath-Pileser III, king of Assyria. When Ahaz king of Judah refused to join them, they threatened to dethrone him and replace him by a certain son of Tabeel; in pursuit of this threat, they actually laid siege to Jerusalem (Is 7:1-6). In this dire situation Ahaz wanted to appeal for help to Tiglath-Pileser. Isaiah, by God's command, met Ahaz and encouraged him not to fear his enemies' assault (Is 7:4), the prophet also gave him a sign: a young woman would conceive and bear a son to be named Immanuel; in a very short time, before the child could distinguish between good and evil, God would save Judah (Is 7:14-17).

In addition to this promise of salvation, Isaiah's prophecy also warned Ahaz of the Assyrian danger. Ahaz, however, did appeal for help to Assyria (II Kgs 16:7-10). Tiglath-Pileser readily consented, and proceeded to Damascus, exiling its people and killing Rezin; but Judah, in turn, became a vassal of Assyria.

In the NT (Matt 1:22-23), Isaiah's prophecy was interpreted as predicting the virgin birth of Jesus, and of his role as "God with us" (Matt 18:20; 28:20). "Almah" is given as virgin in the Jewish Greek translation of Isaiah and this is quoted by Matthew.

IMMER

1. The father of Zadok, who made repairs in the Temple after its reconstruction by Nehemiah.

2. The father of Pashhur the priest.

3. Father of Meshillemith, who was among those exiled to Babylonia.

4. A priest listed as a contemporary of David.

5. The ancestor of exiles who returned with Zerubbabel from the Babylonian captivity to Jerusalem and Judah.

6. The father of Hanani and Zebadiah, who had taken foreign wives, although being the sons of a priest. They were forced by Ezra to repudiate their wives.

7. A place in Babylonia; the Jewish exiles who returned from there were unable to authenticate their genealogy.

IMNA Son of Helem and descendant of Asher.

IJIM
Num 33:45.
Josh 15:29

IJON
I Kgs 15:20.
II Kgs 15:29.
II Chr 16:4

IKKESH
II Sam 23:26.
I Chr 11:28;
27:9

ILAI
I Chr 11:29

ILLYRICUM
Rom 15:19

IMLA, IMLAH
I Kgs 22:8-9.
II Chr 18:7-8

IMMANUEL
Is 7:14; 8:8.
Matt 1:23

IMMER 1
Neh 3:29

IMMER 2
Jer 20:1

IMMER 3
I Chr 9:12.
Neh 11:13

IMMER 4
I Chr 24:14

IMMER 5
Ezra 2:37
Neh 7:40

IMMER 6
Ezra 10:20

IMMER 7
Ezra 2:59.
Neh 7:61

IMNAH

1. See JIMNA

2. A Levite, father of Kore, who was a gatekeeper of the Temple in the time of Hezekiah king of Judah.

IMRAH A son of Zophah, a descendant of the tribe of Asher.

IMRI (contraction of Amariah: "the Lord has said", or, "Lord has promised").

1. Ancestor of Uthai, who returned to Jerusalem from Exile in Babylon. He is possibly to be identified with Amariah (Neh 11:4).

2. The father of Zaccur, who was among those who helped to repair the walls of Jerusalem during the time of Nehemiah.

INCENSE The Hebrew for "incense" derives from a verb meaning "to cause to smoke", and is used to denote the smoke from a sacrifice burnt on the altar (I Sam 2:15-16; Ps 66:15). Primarily, though not exclusively, incense was employed in conjunction with the sacrificial cult.

There were two types of incense; one consisted entirely of frankincense (Lev 2:1, 15) and was used in conjunction with certain meal-offerings. The incense of frankincense together with a handful of fine flour mixed with oil was offered on the outer altar of the sanctuary. Frankincense was also an ingredient of the offering of the showbread (Lev 24:7).

The other incense was compounded of equal measures of various aromatic spices: stacte, onycha, galbanum and frankincense (Ex 30:34-35). This was brought twice daily, once in the morning and once towards evening to a special altar within the Holy of Holies which was designated the "altar of incense" — a gold-overlaid table with horns, measuring one cubit by one cubit by two cubits (Ex 30:1-8). This offering also constituted part of the high priest's ritual prescribed for the Day of Atonement when he entered the Holy of Holies (Lev 16:12-13). The incense was either burned on the altar or was brought in a special fire pan and sprinkled on live coals (Lev 16:12).

Only the priests were permitted to offer incense (Num 17:5). The special efficacy of the incense offering as well as the ban on its being brought by an unauthorized person are reflected in two episodes. Numbers 17:11-15 relates how, at Moses' command, Aaron used incense to stay a plague caused by divine wrath that had broken out among the rebels. The other (Lev 10:1-3) tells how Nadab and Abihu, the two sons of Aaron, were consumed by fire when they brought an incense offering of "strange fire". Moreover, King Uzziah (II Chr 26:16, 19), who in his arrogance presumed to bring an incense offering in the Temple, was punished with leprosy. According to Jeremiah 41:5, even after the destruction of the Temple, men came from Samaria bearing a meal-offering and incense. Twelve incense vessels, each weighing ten shekels of gold are mentioned in Numbers 7:84-86; I Kings 7:50; II Chronicles 4:22; 24:14. They were taken by the Babylonians as plunder when they destroyed the Temple in 586 B.C. (II Kgs 25:14; Jer 34:25; 52:18-19). Jeremiah especially mentions the offering of incense in worship (Jer 1:16; 11:13; 19:13 and elsewhere).

Although incense was primarily used in conjunction with the sacrificial cult, its use for secular purposes is also attested. This may be inferred from the prohibition (Ex 30:37) on copying for personal use the compound of incense offered in the sanctuary. It can also be seen in the description of the lover "coming up out of the wilderness like columns of smoke, perfumed with myrrh and frankincense" (Song 3:6). Guests were honored by the burning of incense (Ezek 6:13; 23:41; Dan 2:46).

The costliness of frankincense in NT times is shown by its being coupled with the gold brought as gifts by the Magi to the infant Jesus

Clay incense burners from Tell Safit and Tell Amal. 10th century B.C.

(top of page)
Incense burner decorated with snakes, from Beth Shean. Late Canaanite period.

Incense shovels found in caves of the Judean Desert. 1st century A.D. (Israel Museum)

(Matt 2:11). It was while offering incense at the altar that the priest Zechariah, father of John the Baptist, was vouchsafed a vision (Luke 1:5-22, where he is called Zacharias). Revelations 5:8; 8:34 describes a vision of an angel with a golden censer offering incense at the heavenly altar.

INDIA A country in Asia, mentioned in the Book of Esther as the limit of Ahasuerus' kingdom to the east. The country referred to in the OT is not the Hindustan peninsula but the territories surrounding the Indus.

INDIA
Est 1:1; 8:9

INSCRIPTIONS Since the second half of the 19th century numerous inscriptions have been found in the Middle East whose contents are of great importance in the study of the Bible and its period. The inscriptions are sometimes more important than the classical historical accounts in our possession, since later editors very often changed the original texts to suit their views.

Present knowledge of the history of the New Kingdom of Egypt derives mainly from archeological finds. In the Bronze Age period the Egyptians conducted numerous campaigns in order to tighten their hold over the Canaanite city-states. Thutmosis III mentions in his list no less than 119 cities conquered by him in Palestine and Syria, thus providing an indication as to which were the important cities in the 15th century B.C.

Many details relating to the political situation in Canaan in the period preceding the Israelite conquest may be ascertained from the letters discovered in the archives of Pharaohs Amenophis III and Amenophis IV (Akhenaten), found at El Amarna.

From the stele of Pharaoh Merneptah (c. 1220 B.C.) we learn of the arrival of the Israelites as a unified tribal group. Among other things this stele records: "Plundered is Canaan with every evil; carried off is Ashkelon; seized upon is Gezer; Yenoam is made as that which does not exist; Israel is laid waste, his seed is not".

In comparison with the finds in Egypt and Mesopotamia those of Palestine are far less numerous, though they also contain material of great importance. The clay tablets found at Taanach and elsewhere, complete the knowledge gained from the El Amarna Letters, and from them it has been possible to glean certain facts concerning social patterns in Canaan during the 15th century B.C.

The ruler of the New Kingdom of Egypt also put up their stelae and statues in the conquered Canaanite cities. At Beth Shean two statues of Pharaoh Sethos I were unearthed in the course of the excavations. The conquest of Beth Shean and the neighboring cities is described on one of these.

(right)
Palimpsest from the 8th century B.C. found at Wadi Murabaat in the Judean Desert. (Israel Dept. of Antiquities and Museums)

Egyptian hieroglyphic inscription.

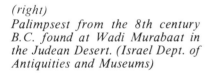

The Akkadian and Egyptian inscriptions of the Israelite period provide numerous details which supplement the information in the Bible. To this group belongs Pharaoh Sheshonk's (biblical Shishak's) list of cities found on the walls of the temple of Karnak, indicating that his campaign in Palestine took place in the fifth year of Rehoboam, king of Judah (I Kgs 14:25; II Chr 12:2).

One of the inscriptions of Shalmaneser III mentions Ahab as one of the chief participants in an anti-Assyrian league.

Jehu is also mentioned, 12 years later, as tributary to Shalmaneser III, king of Assyria. The Assyrian material also refers to the destruction of Samaria, and especially to Sennacherib's campaign against Judah. It recounts that Sennacherib surrounded Hezekiah like a "bird in a trap". Sennacherib established his headquarters at Lachish, as known both from the biblical account and from the Assyrian reliefs in Sennacherib's palace at Nineveh which depict the siege and conquest of Lachish.

A number of important Hebrew inscriptions of the time of the First Temple have been found. In the excavations at Gezer a seven-line inscription, was discovered. Known as the Gezer Calendar, it is considered to be the most ancient Hebrew inscription, dating from about 950-900 B.C., i.e., the days of Solomon. Eight agricultural seasons are listed on this calendar.

The Second Book of Kings (chap. 3) records the revolt of Mesha king of Moab against Israel's suzerainty from the Israelite perspective. The Moabite story has been preserved on the Mesha stele, discovered in 1868 and now in the Louvre, Paris. It was written in the Moabite dialect, which is close to biblical Hebrew but differs in some details from the language of the Hebrew inscriptons. (See MESHA).

Another famous inscription was found in the tunnel of the pool at Siloam dating from the time of Hezekiah, recording the completion by the workers of the digging of the tunnel (See SILOAM). In the village of Siloam itself three inscriptions were discovered, engraved on facades of tombs of the time of the First Temple. Paleographic research has shown that they too should be attributed to the time of Hezekiah.

The humid climate in most parts of Palestine caused the decay of organic writing materials such as parchment or papyrus, and mostly only inscriptions written on stone or pottery sherds have survived. Nevertheless, a papyrus was found recently at Wadi Murabaat, close to the Dead Sea which dates back to the 7th century B.C. As papyrus was a fairly expensive material it was frequently used twice. Such a double inscription is known as a palimpsest. The papyrus found at Wadi Murabaat is of this kind.

(left)
Sherd inscribed by an unskilled hand. First Temple period.

Samaritan inscription, c. 4th century A.D. (Israel Dept. of Antiquities and Museums)

A find of direct biblical interest was of 20 inscribed sherds discovered at Lachish ("the Lachish Letters"). Most of them are letters written to Yaush, the commander of the soldiers who were stationed at Lachish. One of the subjects with which these letters deal is the activities of an unnamed prophet who undermines the morale of the warriors. It is possible that the event alluded to was that in which King Jehoiakim and the prophet Urijah from Kirjath Jearim were involved (Jer chap. 26). Others throw light on the period described in Jeremiah 34:7.

The documents so far described are among the most important Hebrew inscriptions of their period, though some shorter ones, no less instructive, have also been found. Sometimes they were written on complete vessels, not just sherds, in which case they were inscribed before the jar was fired. The inscriptions consist mainly of names signifying ownership or responsibility for the capacity of the vessel.

About 800 impressions of royal seals were found bearing the inscription *lamelek*, the name of one of three cities: Hebron, Sochoh (Socoh) or Ziph, and the disputed name *Mmst*, which some interpret as "of the government". (See SEALS).

All these inscriptions were written in the Hebrew script, which developed from the proto-Canaanite. The proto-Canaanite script was an alphabetic script with about 30 acrophonic pictographic letters, such as a bull's head *(aleph)* or a house *(beth)*. These symbols developed between about 1500B.C. and the 11th century B.C. into linear letters, and finally into the classical Phoenician script. The Israelites accepted this script in the 12th or 11th century B.C., by which time the alphabet did not contain more than 22 letters. By the 9th century B.C. the Phoenician and Hebrew scripts had developed independently. The Arameans adopted the Phoenician script in the 11th or 10th century B.C. and used it for some 200 years before they began to develop their own independent script in the 8th century B.C. This process was very rapid, the reason being that the Assyrians chose Aramaic as the official language, since it was easier to read and write than the Assyrian cuneiform. It thus served as the means of communication between the Assyrian provinces and later became the language of international diplomacy.

The international status of the Aramaic script continued in the neo-Babylonian and Persian periods, but the conquest of Alexander the Great resulted in the Aramaic language being replaced by Greek, which was used in Palestine and Egypt for official documents. Nevertheless, Aramaic was so deeply rooted in Palestine and the neighboring countries that it continued to be used by Jews, Nabateans and Palmyrenes (Tadmor), and in large parts of Syria. Most of the epigraphic finds from the time of the Second Temple are written in Aramaic script and in the Jewish script developed from it. The most important collection of Aramaic documents from the Persian period is that of the Jewish military colony at Yeb (Elephantine). Similar legal documents were found at Wadi Daliyeh, east of Samaria; they belonged to the Samaritan governor's family, who had fled from the Macedonian conqueror but were intercepted and died in a cave at Wadi Daliyeh. The earliest document of this group is of 375 B.C. and the latest of 335 B.C.

The most important of the inscriptions of the time of the Second Temple are the DEAD SEA SCROLLS. Apart from these the most important Hebrew and Aramaic epigraphic material consists of epitaphs. One of these, found on Jason's tomb in Jerusalem, belongs to the end of the Hasmonean period, but all the rest are of the time of the Herodian Dynasty. The epitaphs were written either on the facades of the rock-cut tombs or on the blocking-stones of the *loculi*. To this class belongs the

Aramaic inscription which announces: "Here were brought [to burial] the bones of Uzziah, king of Judah. Not to be opened." This inscription testifies that in the time of Herod, or somewhat later, the bones of Uzziah, who died of leprosy (II Chr 26:23), were removed to a new burial place.

Most of the epitaphs, however, were found on ossuaries. There are many Greek inscriptions in this class, but others were written in the Jewish script, either in Hebrew or in Aramaic. These ossuaries have been found in Jerusalem and on other sites in Judea. Some names occur on them that are known from other sources, for example the name, in Greek, of Nicanor "who made the doors". This, without doubt, was the burial place of Nicanor, the man who made the gates of the Temple. This ossuary was found on Mount Scopus near Jerusalem.

An inscription mentioning Pontius Pilate was found at Caesarea Maritima. The donor's inscription for a synagogue in Jerusalem was found in 1913. The donor was a man named Theodotus and the inscription is interesting because it lists the functions of a synagogue as a place of worship, as a house of study and reading of the Scriptures, and as an inn for travelers, probably referring to pilgrims who flocked to Jerusalem for the three great pilgrim feasts. See also MARI; NUZI; UGARIT.

IPHDEIAH ("may the Lord ransom"). A Benjamite, the seventh son of Shashak, a head of a Benjamite family who dwelt in Jerusalem.

IPHTAH See JIPHTAH

IR ("young ass"). Father of Shuppim and Huppim in the genealogy of the family of Benjamin.

IRA ("young ass"). The name of three contemporaries of King David.

1. Ira the Jairite, a chief minister under King David.

2. Ira the son of Ikkesh the Tekoite, one of David's thirty "mighty men", later captain of the sixth division of the king's army.

3. Ira the Ithrite, another of David's thirty "mighty men".

IRAD Son of Enoch the son of Cain, and father of Mehujael; one of the ancestors of mankind.

IRAM A chief of an Edomite clan.

IRI A Benjamite, one of the sons of Bela.

IRIJAH The son of Shelemiah. An officer at the gate of Benjamin in Jerusalem who arrested Jeremiah, accusing him of seeking to desert to the Chaldeans.

IR NAHASH (IRNAHASH) A city or place mentioned only once in the Scriptures; it was founded by Tehinnah the son of Eshton. Though some scholars translate its name as "city of the serpent", the majority take it to mean "the copper city", or a place where there were copper mines. However its exact location is in dispute.

IRON One of the fortified cities of Naphtali (Josh 19:38). The name is preserved in the village of Yarun in Upper Galilee, today inside Lebanon. It is situated on a hill 2,400 feet (700 m) above sea level, 3 miles (5 km) south of Bint Jebeil.

IRPEEL A city allotted to Benjamin when the land of Canaan was divided among the tribes (Josh 14:1; 18:27). Its location is unknown.

IR SHEMESH A city of the territory of Dan lying in the Sorek Valley (Josh 19:41). Identical with BETH SHEMESH No.1.

IRU Son of Caleb, in the genealogy of Judah.

ISAAC The second patriarch of Israel, son of Abraham and Sarah and father of Jacob and Esau.

In the chronicles of Abraham, Isaac figures as the young child of his aging father, whereas in the Jacob stories he himself is the elderly father; in neither is he presented as a major personality in his own right.

Isaac was born to Abraham and Sarah in their old age, following a

IPHDEIAH
I Chr 8:25

IR
I Chr 7:12

IRA 1
II Sam 20:26

IRA 2
II Sam 23:26.
I Chr 11:28;
27:9

IRA 3
II Sam 23:38.
I Chr 11:40

IRAD
Gen 4:18

IRAM
Gen 36:43. I
Chr 1:54

IRI
I Chr 7:7

IRIJAH
Jer 37:13-14

IR NAHASH
I Chr 4:12

IRON
Josh 19:38

IRPEEL
Josh 18:27

IR SHEMESH
Josh 19:41

IRU
I Chr 4:15

ISAAC
Gen 17:19, 21;
21:3-5, 8, 10,
12; 22:2-3,
6-7, 9; 24:4, 14,

special divine promise (Gen 17:17-19; 18:10-14; 21:1-3). His name (Hebrew *Yitzhak*, from the root meaning "to laugh") is explained as a reference to the miraculous circumstances of his birth: Abraham and Sarah being of advanced age, their incredulity at the divine promise made them laugh (Gen 17:17; 18:12); similarly, anyone hearing of the belated birth would laugh at Sarah (Gen 21:6). After Isaac was weaned, his half-brother Ishmael found himself banished, as Isaac alone was designated as Abraham's heir (Gen 21:10-12), although after Abraham's death, the two half-brothers cooperated in his burial (Gen 25:9-10). Isaac's destiny was confirmed when Abraham proved willing to comply with the divine command to sacrifice his son on Mount Moriah. Isaac accompanied his father, carrying the wood for the sacrifice. When he asked Abraham about the offering, his father answered that God would provide the sacrificial lamb (Gen 22:6-8). As Abraham was about to slaughter his son, an angel from heaven stopped him and Abraham offered a ram as a substitute.

After the death of Sarah, Abraham sent a slave to his family in Mesopotamia to procure a wife for Isaac (Gen 24:1-10). The latter was 40 years old at the time of his marriage to Rebekah, who was childless initially, but after Isaac's prayers, bore twins, Esau and Jacob (Gen 25:21-26).

During a famine, Isaac went to dwell in the Philistine town of Gerar (Gen 26:1-7), where, like his father Abraham in similar circumstances, he feared that the local men would kill him to seize his wife. He therefore passed her off as his sister (Gen 26:6; cf 12:12-13; 20:2, 11-12). Unlike Sarah, however, Rebekah was not taken away from her husband but the king, Abimelech, rebuked Isaac for what might have happened and immediately warned his men not to touch her (Gen 26:8-11).

In Gerar Isaac's success as a farmer brought him such wealth that the local people sent him away out of envy (Gen 26:12-16). He became involved with the Philistines again in a conflict concerning his father's wells, which he had restored and the new wells which he had dug (Gen 26:17-22). Later he returned to the region of Beersheba, where again like Abraham, he concluded a covenant with the king of Gerar (Gen 26:26-31; cf 21:22-32).

In his old age Isaac grew blind (Gen 27:1). With the imminence of his death he wanted to give his blessing to his favorite elder son, Esau, the hunter who always brought him venison (Gen 27:1-2; cf 25:28). He sent Esau to catch some game over which to give him his final blessing (Gen

62-64, 66-67; 25:5-6, 9, 11, 19-21, 26, 28; 26:1, 6, 8-9, 12, 16-20, 25, 27, 31-32, 35; 27:1, 5, 20-22, 26, 30, 32-33, 37, 39, 46; 28:1, 5-6, 8, 13; 31:18, 42, 53; 32:9; 35:12, 27-29; 46:1; 48:15-16; 49:31; 50:24. Ex 2:24; 3:6, 15-16; 4:5; 6:3, 8; 32:13; 33:1. Lev 26:42. Num 32:11. Deut 1:8; 6:10; 9:5, 27; 29:13; 30:20; 34:4. Josh 24:3-4. I Kgs 18:36. II Kgs 13:23. I Chr 1:28, 34; 16:16; 29:18. II Chr 30:6. Ps 105:9. Jer 33:26. Amos 7:9, 16. Matt 1:2; 8:11; 22:32. Mark 12:26. Luke 3:34; 13:28; 20:37. Acts 3:13; 7:8, 32. Rom 9:7, 10. Gal 4:28. Heb 11:9, 17-18, 20. James 2:21

The "foundation stone" in the Dome of the Rock on Mount Moriah, Jerusalem; traditionally the place where Abraham was ordered to sacrifice his son Isaac.

The sacrifice of Isaac depicted on the mosaic pavement of the synagogue of Beth Alpha in the Jezreel Valley. Early 6th century.

27:3-4). Rebekah, however, preferred Jacob, a quiet home-loving man (Gen 25:27-28). Hoping to make Jacob the heir, she persuaded him to bring his father two kids which she would prepare, so that he, and not his brother, would obtain the blessing (Gen 27:5-13). Even though Isaac was suspicious, the ruse was not discovered because Rebekah covered Jacob's hands and the hairless part of his neck with goatskin to make him resemble his hirsute brother when touched by Isaac (Gen 27:14:29). Thus Jacob obtained the blessing originally meant for Esau, and when the latter returned from the field, he received a lesser blessing (Gen 27:30-40).

Rebekah, fearing that Esau would kill Jacob in revenge for this strategem, persuaded her younger son to leave for Mesopotamia to marry a woman from their family, while Esau married Hittite women, much to the displeasure of his parents (Gen 26:34-35; 27:41-46). Thus Isaac blessed Jacob again and sent him off to the house of Laban and Bethuel (Gen 28:1-4).

Isaac died at the age of 180 and was buried by his two sons (Gen 35:28-29).

In the Book of Amos (Gen 7:9, 16) the name of Isaac is applied to Israel in a pejorative sense. Paul uses Isaac as a type for the Gentile Church for what he calls "children of the promise" (Rom 9:6-13; Gal 4:28-31).

ISAIAH ("Yah is salvation"). One of the major prophets of the Hebrew Bible. Modern scholars maintain, however, that the Book of Isaiah was written by more than one prophet and that only Isaiah chapters 1-39 are the work of Isaiah the son of Amoz from Jerusalem. Isaiah prophesied in the late 8th century B.C. in Judah, during the reign of four kings of Judah; Uzziah, Jotham, Ahaz and Hezekiah, at a time when the Southern Kingdom came under great external pressure from the alliance of Syria and Ephraim (735 B.C.) and from the expansion of Assyria (701 B.C.).

Isaiah was the son of Amoz (Is 1:1) and had a wife who was a prophetess (Is 8:3). Two sons of Isaiah are mentioned and both, through their names, play a symbolic role in Isaiah's prophecies (cf Hos 1:4-9). The first son was Shear-Jashub (Is 7:3), which means "a remnant shall return." The name was given to convey hope to King Ahaz that Judah would survive the attack of Syria and Ephraim. The second name, Maher-Shalal-Hash-Baz (Is 8:1-4) means "the spoil speeds, the prey hastens" and probably refers to the coming destruction of Syria and Ephraim by the Assyrians.

ISAIAH
II Kgs 19:2, 5-6, 20; 20:1, 4, 7-9, 11, 14, 16, 19. II Chr 26:22; 32:20, 32. Is 1:1; 2:1; 7:3; 13:1; 20:2-3; 37:2, 5-6, 21; 38:1, 4, 21; 39:3, 5, 8. Matt 3:3; 4:14; 8:17; 12:17; 13:14; 15:7. Mark 7:6. Luke 3:4; 4:17. John 1:23; 12:38-39, 41. Acts 8:28, 30; 28:25. Rom 9:27, 29; 10:16, 20; 15:12

Green malachite Hebrew seal inscribed "[Belonging] to Yeshayahu (Isaiah) Amaryahu". (Israel Dept. of Antiquities and Museums)

There is only limited information about the background of Isaiah. According to Isaiah 6:1, he began prophesying in the year that King Uzziah died (733 B.C.). Isaiah chapter 6 goes on to recount a typical call narrative: the encounter with God (Is 6:1-2) when the prophet realized God's magnificence and his own inadequacy (Is 6:3-5); the cleansing or acceptance of the prophet by God (Is 6:6-7); the sense of compulsion on the part of the prophet (Is 6:8); and the divine commission of the prophet (Is 6:9). Based on this call narrative, especially on the description of the inner sanctuary of the Temple (Is 6:1-2), it has been suggested that Isaiah may have been a priest (since only priests would have access to the Holy of Holies); this contention is supported by the fact that Isaiah showed an intimate awareness of Temple functions (Is 1:10-17), and enjoyed easy access to religious and civil authorities (Is 8:2; 7:3-6; 37:1-2).

Following his call, Isaiah prophesied during the reign of Jotham (742-735 B.C.), only briefly during the time of Ahaz (733-727 B.C.; cf Is 8:16-18), and returned to full prophetic activity in the reign of Hezekiah (727-698 B.C.). However, there is no evidence of any activity on his part after Sennacherib's attack upon Jerusalem in 701 B.C. Isaiah is one of the few prophets about whom it is said that he had disciples (Is 8:16; see also Jer 35:4).

According to later Jewish tradition, Isaiah was killed by King Manasseh (698-642 B.C.). This tradition appears in the Pseudepigraphical work of the "Martyrdom of Isaiah" (5:11), and is perhaps based on II Kings 21:16 and alluded to in Hebrews 11:37.

ISAIAH, BOOK OF The Book of Isaiah is generally regarded as two works combined under one name. First Isaiah (or Isaiah I), chapters 1-39, written in the late 8th century B.C. focuses primarily on prophecies of woe to Judah. Second Isaiah (or Deutero Isaiah), composed of Isaiah chapters 40-66, dates from the early post-exilic period, and, in contrast to Isaiah chapters 1-39, presents prophecies of weal and consolation. Two scrolls of Isaiah have been discovered at Qumran. One is virtually complete (IQISa) but differs from the more fragmentary second scroll (IQISb). However, it is this second scroll which more nearly matches the Masoretic (i.e. traditional) Hebrew text for whose continuity the scrolls provide excellent evidence, also demonstrating that while the Qumran community may have considered the Book of Isaiah as accepted scripture, they had not canonized a particular text.

The author of Isaiah chapters 1-39 is identified as Isaiah, the son of Amoz (1:1; 2:1; 13:1). Isaiah had a wife (8:3), children (7:3; 8:3) and disciples (8:16). Beyond this, little is known about the man (See ISAIAH).

The historical period of Isaiah's prophecy spans three significant events. The earliest (735 B.C.) is the Syro-Ephraimite war (7:1-8:15) when Aram (Syria) and Ephraim (Israel) tried to coerce Judah into joining their campaign against Assyria. Isaiah used this occasion to prophesy against relying on foreign alliances instead of depending upon God (chap. 7). When Aram and Ephraim failed to gain Judah's help both kingdoms fell to Assyria, Aram in 734 B.C. and Israel in 722. Isaiah used these events as an object lesson when he tried to convince Judah to change its sinful ways lest it suffer a similar fate (9:8-10:4). Assyria continued its territorial expansion and in 701 B.C. Jerusalem was besieged and nearly captured. Isaiah again warned against seeking assistance from Egypt rather than trusting in God (30:1-17), and claimed that Jerusalem was saved only after King Hezekiah repented and turned to reliance upon the God of Israel (chaps. 36-39).

The book's complex composition contains at least six different

Part of a page from the Dead Sea Scroll of the Book of Isaiah, found at Qumran. 1st century B.C. (Shrine of the Book, Jerusalem)

literary units (chap. 1; chaps. 2-12; chaps. 13-23; chaps. 24-27; chaps. 28-35; chaps. 36-39), ranging from oracles against foreign nations (chaps. 13-23), to historical narratives (chaps. 36-39), to "woe" oracles (chaps. 28-35), to prophecies about Judah (chaps. 2-12). In addition, there are three different types of material: oracles from the prophet (1:2-31); autobiographical accounts (chap. 6); and stories about the prophet (chap. 7). All of this suggests a long process by which the Book of Isaiah attained its current form.

Like many other prophets, Isaiah condemned the ethical practices of the people (1:4; 10:1-4), calling upon them to repent and mend their ways (1:18-20). He used the elaborate allegory of the vineyard to elucidate this point (5:1-7). However, his pleas seeming to fall on deaf ears (5:8-23), Isaiah began to talk about a coming "Day of the Lord" (2:6-22) — not in any definitive eschatological sense, but in the firm belief that sinfulness would not go unpunished (3:1-17).

Isaiah 10:5-14 depicts God using Assyria as his "rod of anger" to chastise Israel and Judah. Subsequently, God turned against the king of Assyria for the latter's pretentious assumption that his conquests demonstrated his own power and not that of God (10:12-13).

In spite of his pessimism, Isaiah saw hope in two directions. One was the remnant (4:3; 10:20-23), the faithful who would survive the punishment and form the basis for a new beginning. The other hope was in a new king. Having lived through the sinful reign of Ahaz, Isaiah looked forward to a new anointed one ("messiah") of the Lord. This is the background for the messianic oracles in Isaiah chapters 7, 9, 11, primarily concerned with the coming of Hezekiah as a new king for Judah. Christian interpretation of these passages as anticipating Jesus, has resulted in a misunderstanding of the Hebrew text of Isaiah 7:14 which mentions a "young woman", and not a "virgin"; the child whose birth is foreseen is probably awaited by the wife of the king.

The middle portion of Isaiah chapters 1-39 is composed of oracles against the nations (chaps. 13-23) and the Isaiah Apocalypse (chaps. 24-27). The first section anticipates the turning of God's hand against the enemies of Judah. The Isaiah Apocalypse, which pertains to the eschatological end of time, is viewed by many scholars as a later addition.

Isaiah chapters 28-35 is a series of oracles concerning Judah and Ephraim. The oracles about Ephraim grow out of anger toward Ephraim for turning against Judah, and, more importantly, against

God. The oracles regarding Judah feature a strong streak of Zion theology (29:1-8; 31:4-9): since God resides in Jerusalem, the city is inviolable, for he will defend it from all attackers.

Isaiah chapters 36-39 relates the attack of the Assyrian king Sennacherib upon Jerusalem; the account of Hezekiah's repentance (37:1-4) leading to the city's miraculous salvation (37:36-38), strongly reinforces the Zion theology of the previous section. However, the parallel account in II Kings 18:13-20:19, contains a slight but significant variation: II Kings 18:14-16 records the payment of a tribute by Hezekiah to Sennacherib in order to save Jerusalem. This account is also found, in strikingly similar language, in the annals of Sennacherib, casting doubt upon the accuracy of Isaiah's version. However, no matter what actually happened, the saving of the city was interpreted by Isaiah as an example of God's action in the world.

The author of chapters 40-66 is unknown, but is clearly not identical with the writer of the first 39 chapters. Historical background, prophecies and theological perspective all point to a different author.

The historical background of Isaiah chapters 40-55 is reflected in references to the victorious Babylonians (Chaldeans) who did not rise to power until 605 B.C., and to their demise which took place in 538 (cf Is 43:14; chaps. 46-47; esp. 47:1-3); the Israelites have been conquered, their Temple is in ruins but will be rebuilt (44:24-28) and they are to return from captivity in Babylon (48:20). All of this points to events which occurred after the fall of Jerusalem in 586 B.C. There are two references to Cyrus, king of Persia (44:28; 45:1) who defeated the Babylonians in 539 and allowed the Israelites to return to their homeland and rebuild their Temple. This indicates that the author's historical frame of reference was the early post-exilic period.

Unlike Isaiah chapters 1-39, the whole tenor of Isaiah chapters 40-55 stresses hope, consolation and reconciliation. The difficulties are past and it is time for a new beginning (40:1-2). The harsh invective of First Isaiah is absent. There is even the moving reassurance that despite the people's suffering, God cannot and will not forget them (49:14-18).

The theological perspective seeks to reinforce this sense of reconciliation and solace, and assert important claims about God. On the one hand, there are passages which emphasize God as the omnipotent creator. Having just experienced the traumatic events of the Exile, the people need to be reassured by the knowledge that their sufferings — punishment for former sins — were brought about by God (40:2). Similarly, the elaborate "creation hymns" assert God's power over the created order (40:12-31; 42:5-9), including control of political events not only in Judah but throughout the world. It is God who sent Cyrus (41:2-4), calls Cyrus his shepherd (a common title for a king) whom God used for his purpose (44:28), and his messiah (anointed) whom God led against the nations (45:1).

These reassurances are reinforced by an important understanding of the universalism of God. No longer can the Lord be perceived as an exclusively Israelite God who coexists with gods of other peoples. The God of Israel is now hailed as the only God (44:6; 45:5, 18; 46:9-11). This claim includes challenges to the viability of other gods (41:21-24) and satirical passages about the futility of idolatry (44:9-20).

Comprehension of Isaiah chapters 40-55 depends on deciphering the role and identity of the "Servant". There are four "Servant Songs" in Second Isaiah (42:1-4; 49:1-6; 50:4-11; 52:13-53:13), and many other references to a Servant (e.g. 41:8; 43:10; 44:1; 45:4; 48:20): Whether the Servant Songs are integral to Isaiah chapters 40-55 is still a point of major disagreement. It is the identity of the Servant which is the larger and more highly debated issue. One position is that the Servant somehow represents a group, and Israel is the main candidate. Passages such as 44:21 and 49:3 clearly support this perspective, but on the other hand, how can Israel be its own servant or teacher (50:4-11)? Such difficulties have led to modification of this collective interpretation; the Servant is an ideal Israel or a select, faithful portion of Israel, or the group is represented by an individual (as a corporate personality).

Others, citing such passages as 50:4-11; 52:13-53:13, argue that the Servant is an individual, whether historical or ideal. Among the historical figures proposed have been Moses, Hezekiah, Isaiah and the author of Second Isaiah, himself. If it is an ideal individual, the foremost candidate is the king. Having lost their sovereign with the fall of Jerusalem, the people look forward to a new king who, like all former kings, will be God's anointed, his messiah (this is the basis for "messianic expectation"). The main difficulties with this understanding of the king as the Servant are dealt with by accepting the idea of corporate personality, where the king becomes the personification of the nation. The problem of identification, however, still remains. The NT writers took the Songs out of their original context and re-interpreted them as referring to Jesus. The remaining chapters, 56-66, are usually dated slightly later than Isaiah chapters 40-55, relying on references to the rebuilding of the Temple (56:5, 7; 60:7, 10). There is no clear reference to an author, but ties to Isaiah chapters 40-55 warrant the attribution to the semi-anonymous prophet.

The oracles express a consistent concern for the anticipated future intervention of God. Its glory and magnificence are detailed, and its delay is considered a disturbing reality, for which chapter 59 blames the sins of the people. Reference to corruption among the people (56:9-57:13) indicates the source of the problem; the legalism of Isaiah 56:1-8 proffers guidelines to correct their sinfulness. An eloquent plea for deliverance (63:7-64:12) anticipates the glorious intervention of God, which will come to Zion and the faithful people (chaps. 60-61). This glorious future will include all nations together at last; Jew and Gentile will both worship and serve God (56:3-8; 66:18-23).

OUTLINE

1:1-6:13	Denunciation of sins of Israel
7:1-11:16	Encouragement to look to God as savior from Assyrian armies
12:1-6	Hymn of thanksgiving
13:1-23:18	Prophecies against Babylon, Philistia, Moab, Syria, Egypt, Arabia and Tyre
24:1-27:13	Universal prophecies
28:1-35:10	Prophecies of consolation and rebuke
36:1-39:8	Historical section on Sennacherib's siege of Jerusalem
40:1-41:29	Prophecies of comfort and salvation
42:1-44:28	The Servant of the Lord passages
45:1-48:22	God's power demonstrated through Cyrus and fall of Babylon
49:1-55:13	Hymns of Jerusalem and Zion
56:1-59:21	The cultic concerns of the restored community
60:1-22	Glory of the new Jerusalem
61:1-62:12	Consolation of Zion
63:1-64:12	God's vengeance and hymn of lamentation
65:1-66:24	God destroys idol-worshipers but saves the faithful

ISCAH A daughter of Haran, sister of Milcah the wife of Nahor.

ISCARIOT See JUDAS

ISHBAH A descendant of Caleb, father (or founder) of Eshtemoa. The text is not clear; he may have been the son of Mered by his wife Bithiah the daughter of Pharaoh.

ISHBAK The fifth son of Abraham and Keturah.

ISHBI-BENOB A Philistine giant who attacked David and was slain by Abishai son of Zeruiah. It was then decided that David would no longer risk his life by going out to battle (II Sam 21:16-17).

ISHBOSHETH ("man of shame"). A son of Saul. His original name is commonly thought to be Esh-Baal ("man of Baal" — I Chr 8:33; 9:39). But since Baal, "master", later became identified with the name of the chief Canaanite deity, the word became offensive and was changed to Bosheth ("shame"). After his father's death, Ishbosheth was proclaimed king of Israel at Mahanaim by Abner the chief commander. As David grew stronger Ishbosheth lost all his supporters and was subsequently assassinated by two of his officers.

ISHHOD A man from the tribe of Manasseh, son of Hammoleketh.

ISHI ("God has saved").

1. A Jerahmeelite, the son of Appaim.

2. A man of Judah, whose family is unknown.

3. A Simeonite, whose sons went with 500 men to Mount Seir and smote the Amalekites.

4. A chief of the half-tribe of Manasseh in Transjordan.

ISHIAH A man of Issachar, grandson or great-grandson of Tola.

ISHIJAH (ISSHIJAH) One of the sons of Harim who, having taken alien wives, had to repudiate them following the decree of Ezra.

ISHMA ("[God] may hear"). A descendant of Judah, perhaps one of the sons of Hur.

ISHMAEL

1. See ISHMAEL, ISHMAELITES.

2. One of six sons of Azel of the tribe of Benjamin.

3. Father of Zebadiah, and the "ruler of the house of Judah" during the time of King Jehoshaphat.

4. Son of Jehohanan, a "captain of hundreds" who made a covenant with the priest Jehoiada to assist Joash to attain the throne.

5. Son of Nethaniah; a member "of the royal family," he was one of the ten men who killed Gedaliah, his fellow Jews and the Chaldean soldiers at Mizpah (II Kgs 25:25). He later also killed 70 of the 80 men who had come from Shechem, Shiloh and Samaria with offerings and incense for the Temple. The other ten were saved by offering him the treasures they had brought with them (Jer 41:4-8). Ishmael then took the rest of the citizens of Mizpeh as captives. They, in turn, were rescued by Johanan "the captain of the forces". Ishmael escaped to the Ammonites with eight of his men (Jer 41:10-15).

6. Son of Pashhur; he was amongst those who repudiated their foreign wives at the decree of Ezra.

ISHMAEL, ISHMAELITES ("may God hear"). Ishmael, the son of Abraham and his Egyptian handmaid, was born when his father was 86 years old. He was blessed by God: "I...will make him fruitful, and will multiply him exceedingly; he shall beget twelve princes, and I will make him a great nation" (Gen 17:20). Genesis 25:13-15 gives the names of the sons of Ishmael: "the firstborn of Ishmael, Nabajoth; then Kedar, Abdeel, Mibsam, Mishma, Dumah, Massa, Hadar, Tema, Jetur, Naphish and Kademah". The biblical story in which Hagar was driven away at Sarah's request, explains the meaning of the name Ishmael ("because the Lord has heard [your affliction]" Gen 16:11), while the

ISCAH
Gen 11:29

ISCARIOT
Matt 10:4; 26:14. Mark 3:19; 14:10. Luke 6:16; 22:3. John 6:71; 12:4; 13:2, 26; 14:22

ISHBAH
I Chr 4:17

ISHBAK
Gen 25:2. I Chr 1:32

ISHBI-BENOB
II Sam 21:16

ISHBOSHETH
II Sam 2:8, 10, 12, 15; 3:7-8, 14-15; 4:5, 8, 12

ISHHOD
I Chr 7:18

ISHI 1
I Chr 2:31

ISHI 2
I Chr 4:20

ISHI 3
I Chr 4:42

ISHI 4
I Chr 5:24

ISHIAH
I Chr 7:3

ISHIJAH
Ezra 10:31

ISHMA
I Chr 4:3

ISHMAEL 2
I Chr 8:38; 9:44

ISHMAEL 3
II Chr 19:11

ISHMAEL 4
II Chr 23:1

ISHMAEL 5
II Kgs 25:23, 25. Jer 40:8, 14-16; 41:1-3, 6-16, 18

ISHMAEL 6
Ezra 10:22

ISHMAEL, ISHMAELITES
Gen 16:11, 15-16; 17:18, 20, 23, 25-26; 25:9, 12-13, 16-17; 28:9; 36:3; 37:25,

expulsion to the desert explains the nomadic way of life to which the Ishmaelites were destined. On the one hand, there were to be hardships: "He shall be a wild man; his hand shall be against every man, and every man's hand against him" (Gen 16:12); but there would also be advantages: "I will multiply your descendants exceedingly, so that they shall not be counted for multitude" (Gen 16:10). Ishmael, who was circumcised at the age of 13 (Gen 17:25), became an archer and lived in the wilderness of Paran. He married an Egyptian woman (Gen 21:20-21) and joined Isaac in burying Abraham their father (Gen 25:9). He was 137 years at the time of his death (Gen 25:17).

The Ishmaelites, who trace their descent from Ishmael, are mentioned as spice traders, who travel on their camels from Gilead to Egypt (Gen 37:25, 28; 39:1). The Midianites, the Amalekites and all the children of the east smitten by Gideon are identified as Ishmaelites (Judg 8:24). Obil the Ishmaelite was appointed in charge of David's camels (I Chr 27:30). One of David's friends was Jether the Ishmaelite, the husband of Abigail, David's sister (I Chr 2:17). The Ishmaelites are also associated with Edom, Moab, the Hagrites and Amalek (Ps 83:6-7). It is therefore obvious that they belonged to the desert tribes who harassed the Israelites in the times of the Judges, but they are not mentioned later than the time of David.

Some of the Arab tribes who are listed in the Bible (Gen 25:12-16) are known also from Assyrian sources of the 9th-5th centuries B.C. Thus Nebajoth and Kedar, the two elder sons of Ishmael, are mentioned in the annals of Esarhaddon and Ashurbanipal as fighting against the Assyrian kings. These two tribes are frequently mentioned at the end of the First Temple period and in the time of the return from the Babylonian captivity (Is 42:11; 60:7; Jer 49:28; Ezek 27:21). The third son, Adbeel, is mentioned in the Assyrian sources of the times of Tiglath-Pileser together with Massa and Tema, the latter is also the name of a famous oasis and caravan center in northeastern Arabia. Similarly, Dumah is apparently identical with Adumatu, an oasis and fortress in the Syrian desert, conquered by Sennacherib. Mibsam and Mishma are unknown from other sources, but they appear among the families of Simeon who settled at the southern part of the tribe's territory and were probably close to the desert tribes. On the other hand Jetur and Naphish, the youngest sons together with Kademah, are mentioned in I Chronicles 5:19 with the Hagrites, with whom the border tribes of Israel were at war. Assyrian sources connect some of the Ishmaelite tribes mentioned in the Bible with the Arabians.

ISHMAIAH ("the Lord hears").

1. A Gibeonite. One of the Benjamite warriors who joined David at Ziklag. He was one of the leaders of David's thirty "mighty men".

2. Son of Obadiah, the chief of the tribe of Zebulun during David's reign.

ISHMERAI ("may [God] preserve"). A Benjamite, the son of Elpaal.

ISHPAN A Benjamite, the son of Shashak.

ISH-TOB ("man of Tob"). Name of an Aramean city and its environs north of Gilead. It is mentioned in connection with Jephthah who fled to Tob, when he was driven away by his half brothers (Judg 11:3-5). Later, the country, (with other Aramean countries) took part in the war against David (II Sam 10:6, 8) to which Tob sent 12,000 warriors.

ISHUAH, ISHVAH The second son of Asher.

ISHVI, JESUI A son of Asher.

ISMACHIAH ("the Lord may sustain"). One of the Temple officers at the time of Hezekiah king of Judah.

ISPAH A Benjamite, son of Beriah.

Mosaic inscribed "Peace to Israel" uncovered at Jericho. 5th-6th centuries A.D. (Israel Dept. of Antiquities and Museums)

ISRAEL The term is applied in the Bible as:

(a) an alternate name for the biblical patriarch Jacob, given to him after his struggle with the angel where the name is explained as meaning "for you have struggled with God" (Gen 32:28).

(b) the collective name for the twelve tribes who traced their ancestry back to Jacob (Gen 32:32; 49:16, 28; Ex 1:9). It designated the Jewish people until the division of the kingdom under Rehoboam.

(c) the Northern Kingdom which rebelled against Solomon's son Rehoboam and chose Jeroboam I as king, to be distinguished from the Southern Kingdom (of Judah), which remained loyal to the house of David (II Kgs chap. 12).

ISRAEL, KINGDOM OF The northerly of the two kingdoms into which Solomon's United Monarchy divided under his son and successor, Rehoboam (I Kgs 11:43). In the south Rehoboam's accession was taken as a matter of course, so firmly rooted was the dynastic principle in David's own domain. But this was not the case in the north. In accordance with the pattern of monarchy established by David, the king had to be recognized separately by both Judah and Israel, and therefore Rehoboam went to Shechem, the center of the disaffected tribes, in order to parley with them. The heavy economic burden placed upon the northern tribes by Solomon (I Kgs 9:15-19; 11:26-27) led the assembly of Israel to demand of the new king a reduction of taxes as a condition for their acceptance of his rule. Unable to find a suitable way of complying with these demands without risking his prestige, or causing adminstrative dislocations and loss of control, Rehoboam rejected the request (I Kgs 12:1-14). The king's defiant reply led to open revolt. The elders of Israel crowned Jeroboam son of Nebat, a member of the traditionally anti-Davidic Ephraim tribe, who had returned from exile in Egypt (I Kgs 2:20). Severing their ties with Jerusalem, the people of Israel renewed the slogan that had characterized the revolt of Sheba son of Bichri: "What portion have we in David? We have no inheritance in the son of Jesse" (I Kgs 12:16). Thus the north seceded and established the Kingdom of Israel, in contradistinction to the Kingdom of Judah in the south. The Southern Kingdom consisted of the territories of the tribes of Judah, Simeon and Benjamin whereas the Northern Kingdom included all the territories of the remaining tribes, and of the subjugated nations of Moab and Ammon. Unlike Judah, which maintained the continuity of the Davidic dynasty, the monarchy

ISRAEL
See end of book

in Israel was dependent upon the continued support of the ten tribes which had brought about its establishment. Intertribal rivalries naturally led to instability, as opposed to the dynastic continuity of the Southern Kingdom.

The Kingdom of Judah and the house of David continued to regard the seceders as rebels, and their action as illegal and sinful, a view also held by the biblical historiographer. Fierce military clashes resulted, and the fratricidal war lasted throughout Rehoboam's reign. Jeroboam was determined to detach Israel from Judah, both politically and religiously. Fearing that if the people sacrificed in Jerusalem, there would be a resurgence of loyalty to Rehoboam (I Kgs 12:27), Jeroboam insisted on a ritual totally different from that practiced in Jerusalem. In order to discourage pilgrimage to the Jerusalem Temple, Jeroboam changed the festival calendar (I Kgs 12:33; cf II Chr chap. 30). He appointed priests not of the traditional priestly tribe of Levi, who had been part of the administration of the United Kingdom, and were thus suspected of loyalty to the house of David. In so doing, he brought about the collapse of the administrative system in Israel, resulting in a severely disorganized and weakened kingdom. Jeroboam selected Shechem as his capital, and established Penuel in Transjordan and Tirzah as supplementary capitals or royal retreats (I Kgs 12:25; 14:17), perhaps in order to form a satisfactory balance between stable monarchy and tribal traditions. He revived the ancient cultic centers at the borders of his kingdom, Bethel and Dan, in an attempt to lead the people back to the idea of religious decentralization. However, the very prophetic circles which had supported Jeroboam were alienated from him when he placed two golden calves in the royal shrines. Ahijah the Shilonite, who had symbolically prophesied Jeroboam's rise to power (I Kgs 11:29-39), now predicted the imminent fall of his dynasty.

Five years after the division, Pharaoh Shishak of Egypt invaded Judah (I Kgs 14:25-26), but according to a record of the campaign on the wall of the temple of Amon at Karnak, Shishak also destroyed the largest Israelite cities and devastated the most fertile areas of the Northern Kingdom. War between the two hostile sister kingdoms continued during the short reign of Rehoboam's son Abijah (II Chr 13:13-19), and the Philistines threatened Israel. The wars and fortifications strained Israel's resources to the limit and Jeroboam was compelled to increase taxes, thus undermining the verv reason for Israel's secession from the United Monarchy.

The cities conquered by Shishak (Sheshonk I) in Judah and Israel listed on a stone relief at Karnak, Egypt. 10th century B.C.

Jeroboam's dynasty came to an end when his son Nadab was assassinated by Baasha, son of Ahijah of the tribe of Issachar, who founded a dynasty of his own (I Kgs 15:25-34) thus ending the hegemony of the tribe of Ephraim over the Northern Kingdom. The new king sought to win over the Aramean king Ben-Hadad I, but he was outbid by King Asa of Judah, with the consequence that several districts in the extreme north had to be ceded to the king of Damascus (I Kgs 15:9-22). The new dynasty in Israel was as short-lived as that which it had destroyed.

With Baasha's death, civil war broke out in Israel and a few ministers struggled to obtain the throne. Baasha's son, Elah, was assassinated in a plot instigated by Zimri, one of his captains, who then mounted the throne. Another officer, Omri, won the support of the army for himself, and marched against Zimri who, unable to hold out, set fire to the palace and perished in the flames (I Kgs 16:15-20). However, the nation remained divided, part of it supporting Tibni son of Ginath, and only after several years of conflict did Omri succeed in consolidating his position (I Kgs 16:22).

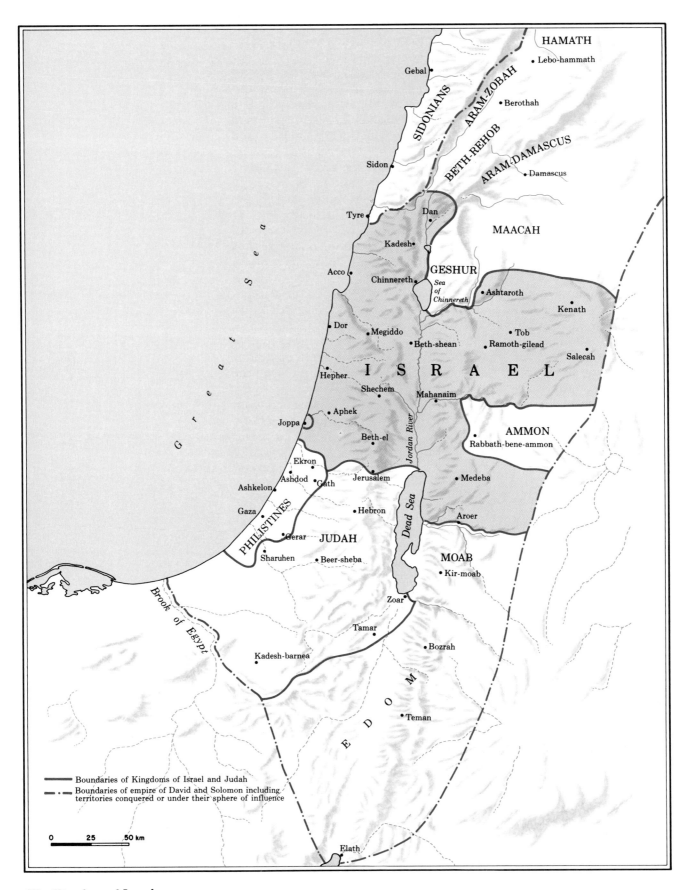

The Kingdom of Israel.

The accession of Omri to the throne was the initial step in consolidating the Northern Kingdom and raising it to the rank of a power in the ancient Near East. Omri was an able and energetic ruler. He founded a new capital in Samaria (I Kgs 16:24), and established a dynasty that prospered for over 40 years. So outstanding were his, and his son Ahab's achievements, that even after the fall of the Omride dynasty, Assyrian inscriptions referred to the Kingdom of Israel as the house of Omri. The Israelite king resolutely met the difficulties bequeathed by the former dynasties. He managed to end Philistine molestation, and to reduce Moab once again to a state of vassalage, exacting an enormous annual tribute from its king. However, Omri was apparently subject to heavy Aramean pressure, forcing him to grant special economic privileges to the Arameans in Samaria and possibly to recognize the sovereignty of Ben-Hadad (I Kgs 20:34). Eventually, Omri succeeded in establishing an independent foreign policy, concluding a peace treaty with Judah thus bringing the strife between their two kingdoms to an end. He foresaw the need of an alliance with the Phoenicians, sealing it by the marriage of Ahab, the heir apparent, to Jezebel, the Sidonian king's daughter (I Kgs 16:31). The Israel-Phoenician alliance gave Phoenicia a tremendous economic, cultural, social and spiritual influence over Israel.

When Omri's son Ahab ascended the throne, the Kingdom of Israel had been consolidated both politically and economically. Ahab was concerned with the Aramean peril, and his reign was marked by numerous clashes with the northern power. Ahab had the political wisdom to hold fast to the policies inaugurated by his father; he beautified his capital with extravagant buildings and palaces (I Kgs 22:39); while, to please his Tyrian wife and her compatriots, he built a temple to the chief deity of Tyre, Baal-Melkart. The continuing process of social and religious integration with Phoenicia brought upon Ahab the wrath of the prophet Elijah, as well as that of the populace who bitterly resented the penetration of foreign cults, and regarded idolatry as the cause of all evil.

Elijah, realizing that the future of Israel's religion was in jeopardy, summoned a contest between the prophets of Baal and the prophets of the Lord, resulting in the slaying of the former (I Kgs 18:15-45). Exasperated by the slaughter of her prophets, Jezebel ordered Elijah's death, but he escaped to the wilderness. The fate of the house of Ahab was irrevocably sealed after the incident of Naboth's vineyard, which represented gross social injustice (I Kgs chap. 21). Due to this, Ahab is given a negative appraisal in biblical historiography, though his positive aspects as an able ruler who strengthened the solidarity between Judah and Israel are recognized. His military power is attested in the inscription of Shalmaneser III, king of Assyria, pertaining to the battle of Karkar (853 B.C.) where Ahab occupied a place of honor among the kings of Syria who allied themselves against the Assyrians. Israel's armored strength which supplied 2,000 war-chariots and 10,000 infantry, was the greatest among the allies. Ahab fell in the battle of Ramoth Gilead against his former allies, the Arameans (I Kgs 22:37). His reign had been a period in which Israel assumed a considerable position in the international affairs of the region.

Ahaziah, Ahab's son and successor, died after a reign of two years (I Kgs 22:51). He was succeeded by his brother Jehoram who invited Jehoshaphat, king of Judah, to join him in an ill-fated campaign, intended to reestablish Jehoram's authority over Moab, which had thrown off the Israelite yoke on the death of Ahab (II Kgs 3:4-27). Driven to desperation, Mesha king of Moab, offered his eldest son as a sacrifice to his national god Chemosh on the wall of the besieged city, at which point the allied kings raised the siege and returned home. Thus Israel lost control of Moab and later Ammon. A further defeat was suffered by Jehoram, now allied with Jehoshaphat's successor, Ahaziah, in their attempt to recapture Ramoth Gilead from Aram, which was hard pressed by Assyria (II Kgs 8:28).

These defeats, resulting in the loss of international prestige as well as the economic regression caused by the collapse of Israelite rule in Transjordan and the loss of principal trade routes, strengthened the opposition of the military leaders against Jehoram. This opposition was encouraged by the prophets, led by Elisha (II Kgs 9:1-10), who resented the house of Ahab because of its Phoenician idol worship, and was supported by the people who had suffered economic hardship. The time was ripe for rebellion, and when it came it was led by Jehu, an army officer who instigated the revolt by calling for reprisals against the house of Omri. With great cruelty he killed the royal family, its courtiers and every follower of the Baal cult (II Kgs 10:8-28). In so doing, he destroyed the economic and political base of his kingdom. Now vulnerable to the pressures of Hazael, the new and powerful king of Aram-Damascus, Jehu had no choice but to submit to Shalmaneser III, in order to save Israel. The Black Obelisk of the Assyrian monarch describes the payment of tribute from five different regions, and Jehu is portrayed as humbly prostrating himself before Shalmaneser, accompanied by Israelites bearing rich tribute.

When Assyrian pressure relaxed, Hazael king of Aram-Damascus renewed his aggressive policy, launching a harsh and cruel invasion of Israel. The distressing conditions furnished an opportunity for the smaller neighboring nations — Ammonites, Moabites, Edomites, Philistines and Tyrians to make predatory incursions. The misery reached its climax during the reign of Jehu's son, Jehoahaz when the Kingdom of Israel virtually lost its independence (II Kgs 13:7). Hazael's successor, Ben-Hadad III, besieged Samaria and brought the beleaguered population to the verge of famine. Some relief from the Arameans was provided by Adad-Nirari III, king of Assyria, who invaded Aram and besieged Damascus (802 B.C.) and was designated a "deliverer" in the biblical sources (II Kgs 13:5).

Jehoash, son of Jehoahaz, utilized the decline of Aram to recapture territories taken from Israel during the reigns of his predecessors (II Kgs 13:25). Aram's decline following her war with Assyria allowed the two sister kingdoms to fill the ensuing political vacuum. Thus the period of Jeroboam son of Jehoash was one of renewed prosperity for Israel (the Book of Amos reflects this period). II Kings 14:23-29 indicates that Jeroboam II extended the boundaries of Israel to include Aram-Damascus, Transjordan and even the kingdom of Hamath, as in the days of David. It seems that Jeroboam, working in harmony with Uzziah, king of Judah, who had reconquered Elath, now regained control of the trade routes to the Red Sea and Arabian ports, and in order to consolidate his rule to the east of the Jordan, distributed large pieces of land among his officers and followers. These individuals developed into wealthy owners of estates and played an influential role in the final days of the kingdom in the frequent changes which followed Jeroboam's death.

The dynasty of Jehu came to an end when Zechariah son of Jeroboam II was assassinated by Shallum. The conspirator held power for only a month, until he was deposed by Menahem (II Kgs 15:10-17). The civil war was precipitated by the contest of two rival parties, the one favoring Egypt, the other — Assyria.

Under Menahem the pro-Assyrian party won the ascendancy, the advances of the powerful Assyrian monarch Tiglath-Pileser III leaving no other choice. The biblical account of Menahem as having been forced to pay a heavy tax to Pul (i.e., Tiglath-Pileser III, II Kgs 15:19) is attested by the reference to "Menahem of Samaria" in an Assyrian inscription as one of those who paid tribute to the Assyrian monarch. It is possible that these taxes were collected in the form of agricultural products, as ostraca found in Samaria would tend to suggest.

However, the tribute paid by Menahem to preserve the entity of his declining kingdom was of no avail. His son Pekahiah lost control of affairs and fell in a conspiracy led by Pekah son of Remaliah (735-733 B.C.), one of his own officers (II Kgs 15:25). The anti-Assyrian party was now in control. Supported by the big landowners in Gilead, Pekah formed an alliance with Rezin of Aram, as well as with Tyre, Sidon and several Philistine towns, against the Assyrian threat. When Judah refused to participate, war was declared and the allied armies of Israel and Damascus marched into Judah. On the advice of the prophet Isaiah (II Kgs 16:7), Ahaz, king of Judah, appealed to the Assyrian king, who reacted by besieging Damascus and turning it into an Assyrian province. Israel was stripped of Gilead and Galilee and the population was deported to Assyria. This marked the beginning of the Assyrian captivity. Samaria was still left intact, because the opposition removed Pekah and placed his assassin, Hoshea, upon the throne (II Kgs 17:1).

With the death of Tiglath-Pileser III, revolt broke out throughout Syria and Israel, resulting in Shalmaneser V's punitive military campaign, in which he besieged Samaria for three years. The capital fell in 722 B.C., its inhabitants were exiled, and Samaria was turned into an Assyrian province by the next Assyrian king, Sargon II (II Kgs 17:6; cf 18:9-11). The last remnant of Israel was organized as the province of Samaria, and in place of the citizens of Ephraim and western Manasseh who were deported *en masse* to Upper Mesopotamia and other places throughout the Assyrian empire, Sargon colonized the land with foreigners from Babylonia, Hamath and elsewhere (II Kgs 17:24). This new influx mingled with the surviving Israelite population, and their descendants were known as Samaritans. Thus Israel's political life had ended, after an existence of just over 200 years.

See also JUDAH, KINGDOM OF.

The horrors of war depicted on an Assyrian relief from the giant bronze doors of the palace of Shalmaneser III. 9th century B.C. (British Museum)

KINGDOM OF ISRAEL — KINGS	
B.C.	
928-907	Jeroboam I
907-906	Nadab
906-883	Baasha
883-882	Elah
882	Zimri
882-871	Omri
871-852	Ahab
852-851	Ahaziah
851-842	Jehoram
842-814	Jehu
814-800	Jehoahaz
800-784	Jehoash
784-748	Jeroboam II
748-747	Zechariah
748-747	Shallum
747-737	Menahem
737-735	Pekahiah
735-733	Pekah
733-724	Hoshea

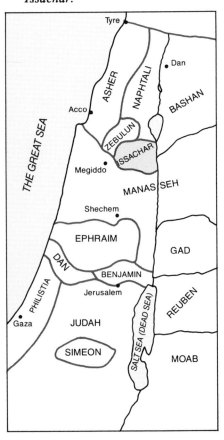

The territory of the tribe of Issachar.

ISRAELITES (CHILDREN OF ISRAEL) In the Pentateuch, the term is used to designate the members of the twelve tribes who traced their ancestry back to Jacob, (= Israel) i.e., the Children of Israel (Gen 32:32; 34:7; 49:16, 28). During the United Monarchy the term is used loosely to mean all their descendants in Israel (I Kgs 8:1; 9:7; II Chr 18:14 etc), whereas after the division of the kingdom, it specifically denotes residents of the Northern Kingdom of Israel, as opposed to the Judeans, residents of the Southern Kingdom of Judah (I Kgs 12:16; 14:7 etc). After the destruction of the Northern Kingdom in 722 B.C. and the exile of the majority of its inhabitants by the Assyrians, the term came to refer to those who remained in the Southern Kingdom.

ISSACHAR ("man of wages", or: "there is a reward" [for all my troubles]).

1. Ninth son of Jacob and fifth of Leah; the eponymous ancestor of one of the twelve tribes. Issachar is always mentioned together with Zebulun (Ex 1:3; I Chr 2:1); their territories adjoined, and they are mentioned together in the Blessings of Jacob (Gen 49:13-14) and Moses (Deut 33:18-19).

According to Joshua 19:17-23, Issachar's tribal territory lay between Mount Gilboa and the hills of Lower Galilee, at the eastern end of the Valley of Jezreel (Mount Tabor was included in this territory). Sixteen cities and their associated villages were assigned to the tribe.

Issachar is mentioned favorably in the Song of Deborah as one of the tribes taking part in the victorious campaign against the Canaanites which was conducted within its domain — Mount Tabor and the River Kishon. This victory broke the Canaanite domination of the area and Issachar gained an important position among the tribes. The tribe of Issachar produced one of the minor Judges, Tola son of Puah (Judg 10:1). According to one tradition, during the time of David the tribe gained a reputation for its wise men (I Chr 12:32).

In Solomon's arrangement of administrative districts, Issachar's territory formed an independent province (I Kgs 4:17).

ISRAELITES
Ex 9:7. Lev 23:42; 24:10-11. Num 25:14. Josh 8:24; 13:13. Judg 20:21. I Sam 2:14; 13:20; 14:21; 25:1; 29:1. II Sam 17:25. I Chr 9:2. Neh 9:2; 11:3. John 1:47. Rom 9:4; 11:1. II Cor 11:22

ISSACHAR 1
Gen 30:18; 35:23; 46:13; 49:14. Ex 1:3. Num 1:8, 28-29; 2:5; 7:18; 10:15; 13:7; 26:23, 25; 34:26. Deut 27:12; 33:18. Josh 17:10-11; 19:17, 23; 21:6, 28. Judg 5:15; 10:1. I Kgs 4:17; 15:27. I Chr 2:1; 6:62, 72; 7:1, 5; 12:32, 40; 27:18. II Chr 30:18. Ezek 48:25-26, 33. Rev 7:7

Baasha, king of Israel, also came from Issachar (I Kgs 15:27), and Jezreel, an Israelite royal residence, was situated in its territory (I Kgs 18:45).

The tribe is mentioned once more, when it went to Jerusalem to take part in the Passover feast, at the time of Hezekiah (II Chr 30:18).

ISSACHAR 2
I Chr 26:5

2. The seventh son of Obed-Edom; a Levite gatekeeper of the Temple during the time of David.

ISSHIAH (maybe "there is God").

1. Alternate form of Ishiah in some Bible versions.

2. Alternate form of Jisshiah.

ISSHIAH 3
I Chr 24:25

3. A Levite, the second son of Uzziel son of Kohath.

ISSHIAH 4
I Chr 24:21

4. A Levite, chief of the family of Rehabiah, and a descendant of Eliezer son of Moses (I Chr 23:17). In I Chronicles 26:25, Jeshaiah is the son of Rehabiah; this may be identical with Isshiah.

5. Alternate form of Ishijah.

ISUI
Gen 46:17

ISUI One of the sons of Asher; perhaps an alternate form of the name Ishvi.

ITALY.
ITALIANS
Acts 10:1;
18:2; 27:1, 6.
Heb 13:24

ITALY, ITALIANS A country in the Central Mediterranean, mentioned only four times in the NT, while the adjective Italian is mentioned once (Rome and Roman are used more often). The first mention of the country, in Acts 18:2, alludes to a Jew called Aquila who had been forced to leave Italy in A.D. 49 when the emperor Claudius decreed the expulsion of the Jews from Rome. Acts 27:1, 6 describes the beginning of Paul's final sea voyage to Italy which would take him to Rome for trial, since he was a Roman citizen. Hebrews 13:24 contains a mysterious reference to the brethren from Italy, perhaps the community from which the letter or exhortation arose. Acts 10:1 refers to the Italian Regiment, a military unit stationed in Caesarea Maritima but consisting of volunteers from Rome itself.

Italy.

ITHAI
I Chr 11:31

ITHAI (meaning unknown; perhaps "[God] is with me"). Son of Ribai of Gibeah, one of David's thirty "mighty men".

In the parallel list in II Samuel 23:29, he is called Ittai (See ITTAI No.2).

ITHAMAR
Ex 6:23; 28:1;
38:21. Lev
10:6, 12, 16.
Num 3:2, 4;
4:28, 33; 7:8;
26:60. I Chr
6:3; 24:1-6.
Ezra 8:2

ITHAMAR The fourth son of Aaron, ordained to the priesthood along with his brothers: Nadab, Abihu and Eleazar (Ex 28:1). After the death of Nadab and Abihu, he served as priest under Aaron and beside his brother Eleazar (Num 3:4; I Chr 24:2), who became high priest after Aaron's death (Num 20:28). Ithamar was supervisor over the work of the Gershonites and Merarites (Num 4:28, 33) in the tabernacle (see also: Ex 38:21).

The house of Eli was descended from Ithamar (I Sam 14:3; 22:9; I Chr 24:3). According to I Chronicles 24:1-6, David appointed to the regular priestly service eight families of the descendants of Ithamar, as compared to 16 families of Eleazar's offspring. A family of priests, descendants of Ithamar, returned with Ezra from Babylonian Exile (Ezra 8:2).

ITHIEL

ITHIEL 1
Neh 11:7

1. A Benjamite, ancestor of Sallu, who resided in Jerusalem after the Exile.·

ITHIEL 2
Prov 30:1

2. According to some interpreters, the proper name of a person whom Agur addressed.

ITHMAH
I Chr 11:46

ITHMAH A Moabite, one of David's thirty "mighty men".

ITHNAN
Josh 15:23

ITHNAN A city allotted to Judah when the land of Canaan was divided among the tribes (Josh 15:23). It was situated "towards the border of Edom in the South". It has been suggested that Ithnan may have been named after Ethnan, a man of Judah, son of Asshur by his first wife Helah.

ITHRA See JETHER No.2

Waterfalls at Banias (Panias) in Iturea, south of Mount Hermon.

ITHRAN, JITHRAN
1. One of the sons of Dishon of the family of Seir, and ancestor of a Horite family.

2. An Asherite, son of Zophah. In I Chronicles 7:38, he is called Jether.

ITHREAM The sixth son of David, born in Hebron from his wife Eglah.

ITHRITES One of the families of Kirjath Jearim; its members included two of David's "mighty men", Ira and Gareb.

ITTAI (meaning unknown; perhaps "[God] is with me").

1. A Philistine soldier from Gath, who with 600 men remained loyal to David, even during the rebellion of Absalom, when the king fled from Jerusalem. Ittai commanded a third part of David's forces in the battle against Absalom (II Sam 18:2, 5).

2. A Benjamite, son of Ribai of Gibeah, one of David's thirty "mighty men". In I Chronicles 11:31, he is called Ithai.

ITUREA A region south of Mount Hermon; in NT times it was part of the area ruled by the tetrarch Philip, son of Herod.

IVAH (IVVAH) A town which had been conquered by Assyria. Its fate was recalled during the siege of Jerusalem by the envoys of King Sennacherib who were trying to talk the city into surrendering.

Ivory stag drinking, from Samaria. 8th century B.C. (Israel Museum)

IVORY There is evidence in the Bible to suggest that the Phoenicians produced ivory. In a joint enterprise with Hiram king of Tyre, Solomon brought ivory from Tarshish (I Kgs 10:22; II Chr 9:21) and used it for his throne (I Kgs 10:18; II Chr 9:17). Ahab, king of Israel, an ally of Sidon, built the ivory house at Samaria (I Kgs 22:39). Houses of ivory (i.e., inlaid with ivory plaques) and beds of ivory are mentioned by Amos (3:15; 6:4). Single ivory carvings of the period have been found in Palestine and assemblages of Phoenician ivory carvings have been uncovered in Samaria, Hazor, Dor, Lachish and Ashdod. Ivories of the same style have also been found in Cyprus, Phoenicia, Syria and in the Assyrian palaces at Nineveh where they were brought as war spoil. These fine objects testify to the wealth of the ancient Israelite kings.

IZEHAR See IZHAR

IZHAR ("[may the deity] shine"). A Levite, son of Kohath and father of Korah.

IZHARITES A Kohathite family descended from Izhar.

IZRAHIAH, JEZRAHIAH ("may the Lord [God] shine").

1. An Issacharite, son of Uzzi, father of five chief men. The clan of his descendants mustered 36,000 soldiers (I Chr 7:4).

2. A leader of Temple singers at the time of Nehemiah.

IZRAHITE (probably: "may God shine"). Shamhuth the Izrahite was the officer charged with providing victuals for the king and his household during the fifth month.

JAAKAN The son of Ezer (I Chr 1:42) and an ancestor of Seir the Horite. Bene Jaakan are mentioned in Numbers 33:31-32; and Beeroth Bene Jaakan in Deuteronomy 10:6. Jaakan is probably to be identified with Akan in Genesis 36:27.

JAAKOBAH One of the officials of the tribe of Simeon.

JAALA ("ibex"). An eponym of a family of Solomon's servants, who returned from the Exile with Zerubbabel (Ezra 2:56).

JAALAM Son of Esau by his wife Aholibamah (Gen 35:5, 14; I Chr 1:35), and a chief of one of the Edomite clans (Gen 36:18).

JAANAI ("may [God] answer"). A Gadite who dwelt in Bashan.

JAARE-OREGIM Father of Elhanan of Bethlehem who slew the brother of Goliath the Gittite. The staff of his spear is described as resembling a "weaver's beam" (II Sam 21:19). The parallel passage in I Chronicles 20:5, relates that Elhanan the son of Jair slew Lahmi the brother of Goliath. According to some scholars, the Hebrew word *oregim* ("weavers"), however, is probably a dittography from the end of the verse (II Sam 21:19); and Jaare is identical with Jair of I Chronicles 20:5. The version in Chronicles would have been changed in order to adjust to the tradition that David slew Goliath (I Sam 17:40-51).

JAARESHIAH The son of Jeroham from the tribe of Benjamin.

JAASAI (JAASU) One of the sons of Bani, who, having married an alien wife, was forced by Ezra to repudiate her.

JAASIEL ("God will do").
1. A Benjamite, son of Abner, the leader of the tribe during the time of David.
2. A Mezoabite. One of David's thirty "mighty men".

JAAZANIAH ("God will hear").
1. Son of Jeremiah (not the prophet); the leader of the house of the Rechabites at the time of the prophet Jeremiah.
2. Son of the Maacathite (II Kgs 25:23); one of the officers who joined Gedaliah at Mizpah after the exile of Judah, mentioned as Jezaniah in Jeremiah 40:8.
3. The son of Shaphan, whom the prophet Ezekiel saw in his vision, among the 70 idolatrous elders of Israel.
4. Son of Azzur, one of the 25 officials of Israel whom Ezekiel saw in his vision.

The name Jaazaniah appears on Hebrew seals, seal-impressions and ostraca (Lachish, Arad) from the 8th to the 7th century B.C.

JAAZIAH A Levite, one of the sons of Merari (I Chr 24:26-27).

JAAZIEL A Levite appointed as musician when David brought the ark of God from the house of Obed-Edom to Jerusalem.

JABAL One of the sons of Lamech and his wife Adah. The forbear of all nomads and shepherds.

JABBOK A river east of the Jordan, the northern border of the kingdom of King Sihon of the Amorites (Num 21:23-24; Josh 12:2). After the Israelite conquest it was in the territory of the tribe of Gad. The river rises near Rabbath Ammon, flows in a wide curve to the northeast and then turns west, entering the Jordan near Adam; it drops from 2,700 feet (820 m) above sea level to 1,000 feet (306 m) below sea level in its course from the mountains to the Jordan Valley. Close to the Jordan it flows through the broad fertile plain of Succoth. One important route that followed the course of this valley was taken by Jacob on his way from Mesopotamia to Canaan (Gen 32:22-23).

JABESH ("dry"). The father of Shallum king of Israel (II Kgs 15:10, 13-14). Some scholars suggest that the term "son of Jabesh" means "a man of the town Jabesh" (Jabesh Gilead). In that case it would be a geographical, not a personal name.

J

(bottom of page)
The Jabbok River in Transjordan.

Onyx seal with the figure of a fighting cock, found at Mizpah, inscribed "[Belonging] to Jaazaniah servant of the king". (Israel Dept. of Antiquities and Museums)

Tell el-Maqlub, the site of Jabesh Gilead.

Ostracon found near Jabneh in a fortress of the First Temple period. This is a letter addressed by a reaper to the governor complaining that an officer has unjustly confiscated his garment. Late 7th century B.C.

JABESH GILEAD A town east of the Jordan in Gilead. Because the Jabeshites refused to participate in the war of the Israelites against the Gibeonites all the inhabitants of Jabesh Gilead were slain, except for 400 maidens who were given as wives to the Benjamites (Judg 21:6-14). In the days of Saul Jabesh Gilead was inhabited by Israelites and when it was attacked by the Ammonites Saul came to their aid (I Sam 11:1-13). When Saul was killed and his body exposed on the wall of Beth Shean, men of Jabesh Gilead took it down and buried it under a tree in their town (I Sam 31:11-13). Identified with Tell el-Maqlub, in the northeast of Gilead.

JABEZ

1. A city in Judah, the home of several families of scribes: the Tirathites, the Shimeathites and the Suchathites. It was probably in the vicinity of Bethlehem but its precise location is not known.

2. A man whose name occurs suddenly in the genealogy of the family of Judah, displaying no visible connection with the names preceding or following it. No satisfactory answer has been found to its occurence though some scholars tend to link Jabez the man with Jabez the city.

JABIN

1. King of Hazor, head of a coalition of Canaanite kings which fought against Joshua (Josh 11:1). The Canaanite kings gathered at the Waters of Merom in Upper Galilee and were defeated by Joshua (Josh 11:7-9), who burned Hazor and slew Jabin (Josh 11:10-11).

2. A Canaanite king who reigned in Hazor (Judg 4:2) and oppressed the tribes of Israel in that area for 20 years (Judg 4:3). A coalition of the northern tribes under the command of Deborah and Barak defeated his forces at the River Kishon. Jabin's commander-in-chief Sisera, was subsequently killed by Jael the wife of Heber the Kenite (Judg 4:21). The victory is recorded in detail in the Song of Deborah (Judg chap. 5), and briefly in Psalms 83:9.

JABNEEL

1. A city by the Mediterranean coast on the northwestern border of the territory allotted to the tribe of Judah. Generally identified with Yebna, 10 miles (16km) north of present-day Ashdod. Probably an alternate name for Jabneh.

JABESH GILEAD
Judg 21:8-10, 12, 14. I Sam 11:1, 3, 5, 9; 31:11-13. II Sam 2:4-5; 21:12. I Chr 10:11

JABEZ 1
I Chr 2:55

JABEZ 2
I Chr 4:9-10

JABIN 1
Josh 11:1

JABIN 2
Judg 4:2-3, 7, 17, 23-24. Ps 83:9

JABNEEL 1
Josh 15:11

Jabneh, north of Ashdod.

2. A city somewhere to the southwest of the Sea of Galilee on the southern border of the territory allotted to the tribe of Naphtali. Its location is disputed.

JABNEH A city conquered by King Uzziah of Judah (II Chr 26:6) in his war against the Philistines. Generally considered to be an alternate name for Jabneel No.1.

JABNEEL 2
Josh 19:33

JABNEH
II Chr 26:6

JACHAN An ancestor of one of the families of the tribe of Gad.

JACHIN, JACHINITES

1. Son of Simeon (Gen 46:10; Ex 6:15), ancestor of the family of the Jachinites (Num 26:12). In the parallel list (I Chr 4:24) he is replaced by Jarib.

2. Head of a priestly course at the time of David.

3. One of the priests who dwelt in Jerusalem at the time of Nehemiah.

JACHIN AND BOAZ Two bronze pillars which stood at the entrance vestibule of Solomon's Temple (I Kgs 7:21; II Chr 3:17). Their description is obscured by rare technical terms and discrepancies concerning their measurements and construction (I Kgs 7:15-22, 40-46; II Chr 3:15-17; cf II Kgs 25:17; Jer 52:21).

Archeological evidence of "free standing" pillars existing at the entrance of many ancient temples supports the idea that Solomon's pillars too were free standing and thus had no structural significance for the Temple. Their actual function, however, is still unclear. The names Jachin, "he will establish" and Boaz, "in strength", may refer to God or may be derived from inscriptions or biblical verses inscribed on the pillars.

JACKAL See ANIMALS

JACKDAW See ANIMALS

JACOB (later also called Israel), the third patriarch of Israel, son of Isaac and Rebekah, and twin brother of Esau (Gen 25:23-26).

From the outset there was a strong rivalry between the twins. Esau, born first, was entitled to the birthright as the eldest son; Jacob emerged clutching Esau's heel and folk-etymology explained his name Jacob (Hebrew *Yaakov*) from the Hebrew for "heel" (*akev*) (Gen 25:25-26). According to an oracle given to Rebekah before she gave birth, the younger son Jacob (Israel), was to hold sway over his older brother Esau (Edom) (Gen 25:22-23). The rivalry between Esau and Jacob has sociological dimensions: Esau represents the hunter and Jacob the husbandman who tends his flocks and tills the fields. It also has a national connotation: Esau, called "Edom" because this name is popularly explained as a form of the Hebrew word for "red" (*adom*, Gen 25:30), is inferior to his younger brother, as a sign of Israel's superiority and lordship over Edom.

Rebekah favored the homeloving Jacob, whereas Isaac preferred Esau the hunter who brought him game to eat (Gen 25:27-28). One day, when Esau returned home hungry from the hunt, he was persuaded by Jacob to sell his birthright for a pottage of lentils (Gen 25:29-34). Later, Jacob deceived his father into giving him the blessing of the firstborn, while Esau had to content himself with the second-best blessing (Gen chap. 27). Cheated by his brother, Esau vowed to kill Jacob (Gen 27:41), whereupon Rebekah intervened to protect her favorite, sending Jacob to her brother Laban in the Mesopotamian city of Padan Aram. At the outset of his journey, near Bethel, Jacob had a theophanous dream in which he saw a ladder reaching up to heaven. The Lord stood beside him and promised to grant him and his posterity possession of the country, as well as divine protection. Jacob consecrated the stone upon which he had laid his head, and thus founded the sanctuary of Bethel (Gen chap. 28).

Jacob was cordially received by Laban who offered him remuneration in return for work with his herd (Gen 29:10-15). Jacob wanted to marry Laban's younger daughter Rachel and agreed to work for seven years in order to earn her as his wife (Gen 29:16-20). After the seven years passed, Laban deceived Jacob by giving his eldest daughter Leah in marriage. In answer to Jacob's complaint, Laban explained

The twin pillars Jachin and Boaz embroidered on a velvet curtain for the ark housing the Scrolls of the Law in a synagogue. Germany, 1716. (Hechal Shlomo Synagogue Museum, Jerusalem)

Two scenes from the medieval Spanish illuminated manuscript, The Sarajevo Haggadah: one showing Isaac blessing Jacob; the other, illustrating Jacob's dream. c. 1400. (National Museum, Sarajevo)

that it was not the custom to marry the younger daughter before the elder one. Thus the themes of primogeniture (Leah, Esau) and preference of the youngest (Rachel, Jacob) reappear. This time it was Jacob who was tricked, and he had to consent to work another stint of seven years in order to obtain Rachel (Gen 29:21-29).

Rachel remained barren, whereas Leah bore Jacob four sons: Reuben, Simeon, Levi and Judah (Gen 29:30-35). Rachel's barrenness heightened tensions, and in accordance with a custom known from NUZI, she decided to let her maid, Bilhah, bear Jacob's children for her; Bilhah bore Dan and Naphtali (Gen 30:1-8). Leah likewise gave Jacob her maid, Zilpah, who bore him Gad and Asher (Gen 30:9-12). Afterwards Leah gave birth to two more sons, Issachar and Zebulun, and Jacob's only daughter Dinah (Gen 30:14-21). Only then did Rachel conceive, bearing Joseph (Gen 30:22-24). At this juncture Jacob decided to return home to Canaan. Laban was not agreeable to losing his daughters and the considerable flocks that Jacob had amassed but eventually they concluded a covenant (Gen 31:43-55).

Jacob now wanted to make up with his brother Esau. He sent messengers ahead, but was answered that Esau was coming to meet him, with 400 armed men (Gen 32:1-23). That night, after all his camp had crossed the Jabbok River, Jacob was attacked in his sleep by an angel of God who struggled with him until the break of dawn. At last the angel blessed him and gave him a new name: Israel, interpreted as "You have struggled with God" (Gen 32:24-29; cf 35:10).

The confrontation with Esau was less fearsome than anticipated. Jacob honored his brother like a king, and Esau, mollified by Jacob's gifts and by his skilful diplomatic maneuvering, left him in peace to proceed to the region of Shechem (Gen 33:1-20).

The later Jacob stories deal with his relations with his children: the incident of Dinah who was raped by Shechem, prince and eponym of the town by that name, and the revenge exacted by her brothers (Gen chap. 34); the birth of his last son, Benjamin, and Rachel's death in childbirth (Gen 35:16-22); and the story of Joseph, which culminated in Jacob and all his sons moving to Egypt (Gen 46:6; 47:1), where Jacob died at the age of 147 (Gen 47:28). Before his death he blessed Joseph's sons Ephraim and Manasseh (Gen 48:9-22) and pronounced a blessing on his own sons, anticipating the role played by the various tribes (Gen chap. 49). In accordance with his wishes, his body was taken back to Canaan to be buried in the Cave of Machpelah (Gen 49:29; 50:13).

In biblical literature the name Jacob occurs many times as an epithet for Israel (e.g. Num 23:7, 10; 24:5; Deut 33:4, 28), and the God of Israel is called the "king of Jacob" (Is 41:21). Hosea 12:4-13 contains many allusions to Jacob's relations with Esau as well as to his struggle with the angel (v. 4).

In the NT Jacob as the name for Israel, appears frequently: Israel is called "the house of Jacob" (Luke 1:33), and the Temple "the dwelling for the God of Jacob" (Acts 7:46). He is also mentioned frequently with Abraham and Isaac, the other patriarchs of the Jewish people (Deut 1:8; 9:27; II Kgs 13:23, etc).

JACOB'S WELL See SHECHEM

JADA ("God has known"). Son of Onam (I Chr 2:28), one of the Jerahmeelite family.

JADDAI (JADDU) One of the sons of Nebo, who, having married an alien woman, later repudiated her, at the decree of Ezra.

JADDUA ("he is known" [to God]).

1. One of the heads of the people, who sealed the covenant at the time of Nehemiah.

9:5, 27; 29:13; 30:20; 32:9; 33:4, 10, 28; 34:4. Josh 24:4, 32. I Sam 12:8. II Sam 23:1. I Kgs 18:31. II Kgs 13:23; 17:34. I Chr 16:13, 17. Ps 14:7; 20:1; 22:23; 24:6; 44:4; 46:7, 11; 47:4; 53:6; 59:13; 75:9; 76:6; 77:15; 78:5, 21, 71; 79:7; 81:1, 4, 8; 85:1; 87:2; 94:7; 99:4; 105:6, 10, 23; 114:1, 7; 132:2, 5; 135:4; 146:5; 147:19. Is 2:3, 5-6; 8:17; 9:8; 10:20-21; 14:1; 17:4; 27:6, 9; 29:22-23; 40:27; 41:8, 14, 21, 24; 43:1, 22, 28; 44:1-2, 5, 21, 23; 45:4, 19; 46:3; 48:1, 12, 20; 49:5-6, 26; 58:1, 14; 59:20; 60:16; 65:9. Jer 2:4; 5:20; 10:16, 25; 30:7, 10, 18; 31:7, 11; 33:26; 46:27-28; 51:19. Lam 1:17; 2:2-3. Ezek 20:5; 28:25; 37:25; 39:25. Hos 10:11; 12:2, 12. Amos 3:13; 6:8; 7:2, 5; 8:7; 9:8. Obad vs. 10, 17-18. Mic 1:5; 2:7, 12; 3:1, 8-9; 4:2; 5:7-8; 7:20. Nah 2:2. Mal 1:2; 2:12; 3:6. Matt 1:2, 15-16; 8:11; 22:32. Mark 12:26. Luke 1:33; 3:34; 13:28; 20:37. John 4:5-6, 12. Acts 3:13; 7:8, 12, 14-15, 32,

2. A high priest. The son of Jonathan, and a descendant of Eliashib (Neh 12:10-11, 22), he was the last high priest mentioned in the Bible. According to Josephus, Jaddua was high priest at the time of Alexander the Great.

JADON The Meronothite. One of the workers who repaired the walls of Jerusalem, at the time of Nehemiah.

JAEL ("mountain goat"). The wife of Heber the Kenite, she killed Sisera, the general of Jabin king of Hazor (Judg 4:17-22). After the defeat of the Canaanite forces by the coalition of the northern tribes under the command of Deborah and Barak, Sisera fled, taking refuge in Jael's tent. With a feeling of security inspired by her hospitality, he fell asleep. Jael then took a hammer and drove a tent peg through his temple (Judg 4:21). Thus, as already indicated in the prophecy of Deborah (Judg 4:9), Israel was saved by a woman. The victory entirely smashed the power of Jabin king of Hazor (Judg 4:23-24).

JAGUR A town on the southern border of the territory of Judah: "And the cities at the limits of the tribe of the children of Judah, toward the border of Edom in the South, were Kabzeel, Eder, Jagur" (Josh 15:21). The following verse mentions Kinah, Dimonah and Adadah. Some of the names in this list may have been rendered in a garbled form; thus Eder, mentioned before Jagur, is apparently a corruption of Arad, just as Adadah is a corruption of Ararah (the Hebew letters *resh* and *dalet* are easily interchanged). Jagur should therefore be sought in the region of the biblical town of Arad. Several identifications have been suggested; one of these locates Jagur at Khirbet Daragat, some 3½ miles (6 km) northwest of Arad, where there is a high mound, extending over an area of 5 acres (2 ha).

JAHALELEEL A descendant of Judah, mentioned in the list of the sons of Caleb.

JAHATH

1. The son of Reaiah, a descendant of Judah.
2. A Levite, a descendant of Gershon.
3. A Levite of the Izharite family, at the time of David.
4. A Levite, descendant of Merari, at the time of Josiah king of Judah.

JAHAZ, JAHAZA A town in Moab where the Israelites defeated Sihon, king of the Amorites (Num 21:23), in the territory of Reuben (Josh 13:18); a city of Levites (Josh 21:36). During the time of the Israelite kingdom it was in the hands of Moab (Is 15:4), as is confirmed by the Mesha Stele. Tentatively identified with Khirbet el-Medeiniyeh southeast of Medeba.

JAHAZIAH ("God will see"). The son of Tikvah, one of the four men who opposed Ezra's decree to repudiate their foreign wives.

JAHAZIEL ("God [El] will see").

1. A Benjamite, one of the warriors who joined David at Ziklag.
2. One of the priests charged with playing the trumpets before the ark of God in Jerusalem at the time of David.
3. A Levite, the third son of Hebron. Appointed by David to serve in the Temple.
4. A Levite, descendant of the family of Asaph, who prophesied to Jehoshaphat concerning the salvation of Judah from the threat of the Transjordanian people.
5. Father of Shechaniah, forebear of a family who returned from Exile.

JAHDAI ("God will guide"). A Judahite, mentioned in the list of the sons of Caleb.

JAHDIEL ("God will rejoice" [with the child]). One of the chiefs of the

Pottery decanter from the Hebron district, inscribed "[Belonging] to Jahaziahu, wine of Khl" (place-name). 8th-7th centuries B.C. (Collection R. Hecht, Haifa. Israel Museum)

half-tribe of Manasseh in Transjordan, who was exiled by Tiglath-Pileser III king of Assyria.

JAHDO A man of the tribe of Gad, the ancestor of Abihai.

JAHLEEL, JAHLEELITES The third son of Zebulun, the ancestor of the Jahleelite family.

JAHMAI Son of Tola and a descendant of Issachar.

JAHZAH Alternate form of JAHAZ.

JAHZEEL, JAHZEELITES Son of Naphtali and the ancestor of the Jahzeelite family.

JAHZERAH A priest from the family of Immer (I Chr 9:12), ancestor of Maasai and the priest Amashai (or Ahzai, Neh 11:13), who dwelt in Jerusalem at the time of Nehemiah.

JAHZIEL Another form of Jahzeel.

JAIR, JAIRITE ("may [God] enlight").

1. An eponym of a large family of Manasseh, who during the conquest of Transjordan, occupied several villages in the Bashan and Gilead and called them: "Havoth Jair".

2. A Gileadite, who judged Israel for 22 years. He had 30 sons and 30 cities in the Gilead, bearing the name "Havoth Jair" (Judg 10:4). See above, No.1.

3. A Benjamite, ancestor of Mordecai.

4. The father of Elhanan, one of David's heroes, who killed Lahmi the brother of Goliath. In II Samuel 21:19, his name is given as Jaare-Oregim, which might be a scribal error. Here the name Jair is written differently in Hebrew, meaning: "may [God] awaken".

5. Ira the Jairite, chief minister under David.

JAIRUS A "ruler" or president of the synagogue in Capernaum, whose daughter Jesus raised from the dead (Mark 5:21-43; Luke 8:40-56). In Matthew 9:18-26, Jairus is called simply "ruler".

JAKEH The father of Agur, whose words of wisdom are found in Proverbs No.30.

JAKIM ("may [God] establish").

1. A Benjamite.

2. Ancestor of the 12th course of priests, appointed by David.

JALON A Judahite, descendant of Caleb.

JAMBRES See JANNES AND JAMBRES

JAMES

1. Apostle, son of Zebedee, and the older brother of John (the two are always mentioned together). Like his father and brother, he was a fisherman (Matt 4:21; Mark 1:19; Luke 5:9-10). James was among the first apostles to be called by Jesus (Matt 4:22; Mark 1:20; Luke 5:10-11). He gave John and James the surname of Boanerges, i.e. sons of thunder (Mark 3:17). James and John asked Jesus to give them places of honor at his right and left hand and were willing to do anything for this privilege (Matt 20:20-24; Mark 10:35-41).

Together with Peter and John, James was a close confidant of Jesus, being present at many important events, including the resurrection of the daughter of Jairus (Mark 5:37; Luke 8:51), the transfiguration (Matt 17:1; Mark 9:2; Luke 9:28) and the agony in Gethsemane (Matt 26:37; Mark 14:33).

In the early period of the first Christian community James was killed "with the sword" by King Herod Agrippa (Acts 12:1-2).

2. Son of Alphaeus, he was also one of the twelve apostles (Matt 10:3; Mark 3:18; Luke 6:15; Acts 1:13). His mother's name was Mary (Matt 27:56; Mark 16:1; Luke 24:10). He is also called "the less" (Mark 15:40). Matthew (Levi) and Joses were probably his brothers (Mark 2:14; 15:40).

JAMES 2
Matt 10:3;
27:56. Mark
3:18; 15:40;
16:1. Luke
6:15; 24:10.
Acts 1:13

JAMES 3
Matt 13:55.
Mark 6:3. Acts
12:17; 15:13;
21:18. I Cor
15:7. Gal 1:19;
2:9, 12. James
1:1. Jude v. 1

After the ascension of Jesus, James was among those, who went from the Mount of Olives to Jerusalem into an upper room where they prayed and waited (Acts 1:13).

3. "The brother of the Lord" and first bishop of the church of Jerusalem. Paul explicitly identifies James as Jesus' brother (Gal 1:19) as do the gospel writers (Mark 6:3). This may mean that he was the son of Joseph and Mary, although such a possibility was rejected by St. Jerome and other Church Fathers from the 4th century onward in favor of the doctrine of the perpetual virginity of Mary. Various alternate suggestions have been made as to James' parentage. These include the possibility that he was the son of Joseph by a previous marriage or that he had other parents altogether and that "brother" is to be taken as meaning "cousin". James is portrayed as wavering in his belief in Jesus at some point before the latter's death (John 7:5), but he seems to have had a change of heart regarding his "brother", for he merited a special post-resurrection appearance (I Cor 15:7) such as was evidently reserved only for those who believed in Jesus; also described in the non-canonical but early "Gospel according to the Hebrews".

Perhaps because of this post-resurrection encounter and/or his kinship to Jesus, James soon became one of the recognized leaders in the church. This is evident from Peter's reference to him in Acts 12:17 (which is dated before A.D. 44) and from Paul's visit to him (Gal 1:19), which may have been even earlier. By the time the Jerusalem Council was convened in A.D. 49 (Acts chap. 15) James was clearly a leading figure in the church, not even deferring to Peter. His final appearance in the NT history is in Acts 21:18ff, on Paul's last visit to Jerusalem in about A.D. 57. Here he is clearly identified with the party of Jewish Christians who were zealous for the Law (cf Gal 2:9), and it is in this role that he achieves prominence in later apocryphal NT writings, especially the pseudo-Clementine "Recognitions". The Church Fathers of the 2nd and 3rd centuries speak of his exceptionally pious life, which earned him the appellation "James the Just". James is one of the few NT figures to be mentioned by a contemporary non-Christian writer. Josephus (*Antiq.* xx, 200) describes the occasion of his death in 62 at the hands of the high priest Anan ben Anan. Somewhat later Christian literature also tells the same story, albeit embellished, in one of the earliest Christian martyrologies. It is customary to identify James with the author of the canonical NT epistle by the same name.

4. James, the father of Judas.

JAMES 4
Luke 6:16.
Acts 1:13

JAMES, EPISTLE OF The twentieth book of the NT. The author identifies himself simply as "James, a servant of God and of the Lord Jesus Christ" (James 1:1). Of the several NT characters by that name (James), the most logical candidate for author of the epistle is James "the Lord's brother" (Gal 1:19), the leader of the church in Jerusalem (Acts 15:13; 21:18; see above JAMES No. 3). This is supported by comparing the letter's character and emphasis with the not-inconsiderable information available about this leader of early Jewish Christianity. As a well-known figure in the church, he needed no further introduction. James was martyred in Jerusalem in 62, so the letter must have been written before that date. From consideration of content (e.g. the position taken on faith and works, (James 2:14-26), and the primitive church organization referred to (3:1; 5:14)), many scholars have tended to assign an earlier date to the epistle, perhaps between 40 and 50, which would make it the earliest of the NT writings. The authorship of James and certain geographical hints (e.g., 5:7 "the early and latter rain", and cf 1:1) make it likely that it was composed in Palestine, probably in Jerusalem.

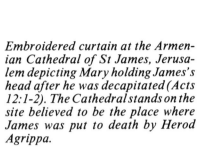

Embroidered curtain at the Armenian Cathedral of St James, Jerusalem depicting Mary holding James's head after he was decapitated (Acts 12:1-2). The Cathedral stands on the site believed to be the place where James was put to death by Herod Agrippa.

The Epistle of James was not included in lists of canonical Christian scriptures until the 3rd century, and Eusebius in the 4th indicated that some remained doubtful about it. However, by the middle of the 4th century it was universally recognized. Because of a misreading of James' position on the doctrine of justification by faith, Luther belittled the importance of the letter.

Some scholars have suggested that the composition, originally Jewish, was later adapted by a Christian writer with several cosmetic changes. While it is true that the author makes only two references to the "Lord Jesus Christ" (1:1; 2:1) and never refers to such central Christian doctrines as the incarnation, death, resurrection or atonement of Jesus, a less superficial reading of the epistle reveals numerous Christian (or Jewish Christian) elements. Among these are references to "elders of the church" (5:14), the rebirth of the believer (1:18) and a hint of Jesus' resurrection and ascension in calling him "the Lord of glory" (2:1). More weighty than any of these, however, is the fact that the letter so often quotes or echoes words of Jesus from the Sermon on the Mount and elsewhere in the gospels. Indeed, the short Epistle of James has been shown to preserve more words of Jesus than all the rest of the NT letters combined. Its eschatology also suggests that it was written by a Christian (5:7-9).

The letter is addressed to "the twelve tribes which are scattered abroad" (1:1), a clear reference to the Jewishness of the intended readers. While the phrase has been interpreted as referring to both Jewish and Gentile Christians, who are depicted as "spiritual Israel", this seems highly out of character in such a practical, non-spiritualizing letter. That the recipients were Jews is further supported by James's known position as the first leader of Jewish Christianity. The respect which he enjoyed generally in Jerusalem (Josephus, *Antiq.* xx, 200ff) leaves open the possibility that he at least had non-Christian Jews in mind while composing the letter.

As noted, this letter is extremely practical in its focus and deals with none of the central Christian doctrines. Instead the author treats such subjects as perseverance under testing, obedience to God's word, the evils of the uncontrolled tongue, the sin of partiality, the need for patience and humility. For James religion is nothing if not accompanied by practical action. This is "pure and undefiled religion...to visit orphans and widows" (1:27); "If a brother or sister is naked and destitute of daily food, and one of you says to them: 'Depart in peace, be warmed and filled', but you do not give them the things which are needed for the body, what does it profit?" (2:15-16).

This emphasis has given James the reputation as the epistle of works, and many have tried to see a reflection here of conflict between James and Paul, especially in the latter's letters to the Galatians and the Romans. The "conflict" is, however, more apparent than real. Verse for verse, James speaks of faith no less than any other NT letter, while the Epistle to Titus has more frequent references to works than does James. When Paul says (Rom 3:28; Gal 2:16) that no man is justified by works, and James seems to say exactly the opposite (James 2:21-24), the possibility must be weighed that the two are using the idea of justification differently. Paul is talking about an initial achievement of atoned perfection, the "righteousness" of Christ (I Cor 1:30; II Cor 5:21) whereas James, in a more Jewish way, is speaking of that growth of personal holiness which must accompany a life motivated by true faith.

OUTLINE

1:1	Salutation
1:2-16	The testing of faith
1:17-25	Be doers of the word
1:26-27	True religion
2:1-9	The sin of partiality
2:10-13	Obligation to keep all the law
2:14-26	Faith and works
3:1-12	The tongue
3:13-18	Wisdom from above and from below
4:1-5	The source of quarrels and strife
4:6-17	Humility and the sin of boasting
5:1-6	Judgment of the rich
5:7-11	Patient endurance
5:12	Do not swear
5:13-18	The effectiveness of prayer
5:19-20	Turning the sinner from his error

Janohah, south of Shechem.

JAMIN,
JAMINITES 1
**Gen 46:10. Ex
6:15. Num
26:12. I Chr
4:24**

JAMIN,
JAMINITES 2
I Chr 2:27

JAMIN,
JAMINITES 3
Neh 8:7

JAMLECH
I Chr 4:34

JANNA
Luke 3:24

JANNES
AND JAMBRES
II Tim 3:8

JANOAH
II Kgs 15:29

JANOHAH
Josh 16:6-7

JANUM
Josh 15:53

JAPHETH
**Gen 5:32;
6:10; 7:13;
9:18, 23, 27;
10:1-2, 21.
I Chr 1:4-5**

JAMIN, JAMINITES
1. The son of Simeon and the ancestor of the Jaminite family.
2. A Jarahmeelite, of the sons of Ram.
3. A Levite who expounded the law read by Ezra.

JAMLECH ("may [God] appoint as king"). One of the chiefs of the Simeonites.

JANNA A forbear of Joseph, in the genealogy of Jesus in Luke.

JANNES AND JAMBRES According to a Jewish tradition, these were the Egyptian magicians who strove with Moses (Ex 7:11 ff). Their names appear in II Timothy 3:8, as prototypes of those who "resist the truth". Ancient sources (including Origen) suggest that there existed an apocryphal Book of Jannes and Jambres, now lost.

JANOAH An Israelite city in northern Galilee, between Abel Beth Maachah and Kedesh (II Kgs 15:29). It was depopulated by Tiglath-Pileser III, king of Assyria, in 732 B.C. There is no certain identification.

JANOHAH A city on the eastern border of Ephraim (Josh 16:6-7); it is identified with Khirbet Yanun 7 miles (12 km) southeast of Shechem.

JANUM An Israelite city in the district of Hebron (Josh 15:53). It is not identified.

JAPHETH The third son of Noah (Gen 5:32; 6:10; 7:13; 9:18, 23, 27;

I Chr 1:4) who with his wife, two other brothers and their wives, joined Noah in the ark before the onset of the Flood. After the deluge, Japheth and his brother Shem covered the nakedness of their father when he lay drunk in his tent (Gen 9:23); for this virtuous act they were blessed. Japheth's blessing was that God would enlarge his territory and "he will dwell in the tents of Shem" (Gen 9:27). Some commentators interpret the word "he" as referring to God (who would dwell in the tents of Shem) and not to Japheth. The descendants of Japheth are recorded in Genesis 10:2-5; I Chronicles 1:5-7; most of them are identified as nations dwelling in northwestern regions such as Anatolia and the Aegean.

JAPHIA

1. King of Lachish; one of the five Amorite kings fighting under the leadership of Adoni-Zedek king of Jerusalem who were defeated by Joshua at the battle of Gibeon (Josh 10:3, 5, 10).

JAPHIA 1
Josh 10:3

2. One of the sons born to David in Jerusalem.

JAPHIA 2
II Sam 5:15.
I Chr 3:7; 14:6

3. A city 2 miles (3 km) southwest of Nazareth. It fell to the lot of Zebulun when the land of Canaan was divided among the tribes (Josh 14:1; 19:12).

JAPHIA 3
Josh 19:12

JAPHLET Firstborn son of Heber (grandson of Asher) and father of Pasach, Bimhal and Ashvath in the genealogy of the family of Asher.

JAPHLET
I Chr 7:32-33

JAPHLETITES A family or clan, related to Japhlet, whose territory marked the boundary of the inheritance of the children of Joseph.

JAPHLETITES
Josh 16:3

JARAH ("honeycomb"). Son of Ahaz and father of Alemeth, Azmaveth and Zimri (I Chr 9:42) in the genealogy of King Saul. In an earlier chapter he is called Jehoaddah (I Chr 8:36).

JARAH
I Chr 9:42

JAREB Title of Assyrian king meaning: "the great king". It has been misunderstood as the name of the king of Assyria, who received tribute from Israel.

JAREB
Hos 5:13; 10:6

JARED Father of Enoch, one of the early ancestors of mankind, in the genealogy of Seth.

JARED
Gen 5:15-16,
18-20. I Chr
1:2. Luke 3:37

JARHA An Egyptian servant of Sheshan the Jerahmeelite, who married the latter's daughter (I Chr 2:34-35). Thirteen generations descended from him are listed (I Chr 2:36-41).

JARHA
I Chr 2:34-35

JARIB ("God will contend").

1. A son of Simeon (I Chr 4:24). The name is missing in the list of Simeon's descendants (Gen 46:10; Ex 6:15; Num 26:12-13).

JARIB 1
I Chr 4:24

2. One of the chiefs sent by Ezra to Iddo at Casiphia (in Babylon), to bring Levites for the Temple service, before the return from Exile.

JARIB 2
Ezra 8:16

3. One of the priests who took an alien wife, and was forced by Ezra to repudiate her.

JARIB 3
Ezra 10:18

JARMUTH

1. A town in the Coastal Plain (Josh 15:35) which was a Canaanite city-state. Its king, Piram, took part in the war of the kings of the Amorites against Gibeon and was killed in battle (Josh 10:3-5). The town was rebuilt after the return from the Babylonian Exile (Neh 11:29) and was still inhabited in the Roman period. It is identified with Khirbet Yermuk, northeast of Beth Shemesh.

JARMUTH 1
Josh 10:3, 5,
23; 12:11;
15:35. Neh
11:29

Khirbet Yarmuk identified with the site of Jarmuth in the Coastal Plain.

JARMUTH 2
Josh 21:29

2. A town of Levites in the territory of Issachar (Josh 21:29), also called Remeth (Josh 19:21). Tentatively identified with Kaukab el-Hawa, where the large Crusader castle, Belvoir, is situated. If this identification is correct it might also be the site of Agrippina, where beacons were lit in the time of the Second Temple to announce the new moon.

Remains of the Crusader castle of Belvoir, at the site identified with Jarmuth, north of Beth Shean.

JAROAH
I Chr 5:14

JAROAH One of the ancestors of the tribe of Gad; he was son of Gilead and father of Huri in the genealogy of the family of Gad.

JASHEN
II Sam 23:32

JASHEN Apparently the father of some of David's heroes (II Sam 23:32); but the text is obscure. I Chronicles 11:34 says they were "sons of Hashem the Gizonite". Many scholars assume that the words "sons of" in both places are a dittography of the name Shaalbonite (in the same verse). In that case Jashen/Hashem is the proper name of the hero.

JASHER, BOOK OF ("the book of the upright/just"). A lost book of poetry, excerpts of which are preserved in Joshua's command to the sun and the moon not to set (Josh 10:12-13) and in David's lament over the death of Saul and Jonathan (II Sam 1:17-27). A third reference may be found in the Septuagint, (Greek) version, of Solomon's prayer at the dedication of the Temple, where the reader is directed to the "Book of Jashar".

JASHOBEAM

JASHOBEAM 1
I Chr 11:11;
27:2

1. Son of a Hachmonite, chief of David's leading trio of "mighty men" (I Chr 11:11). He killed no less than 300 men in one day. He is generally identified with the Jashobeam son of Zabdiel who was in charge of the 24,000 men of David's army who served for the first month of the year (I Chr 27:2).

JASHOBEAM 2
I Chr 12:6

2. One of the men of Benjamin who defected from the armies of Saul to join David at Ziklag. A mighty man, he could use both his right and left arm to hurl stones and shoot arrows.

JASHUB, JASHUBITES ("[God] will return").

JASHUB,
JASHUBITES 1
Num 26:24.
I Chr 7:1

1. The third son of Issachar, ancestor of the Jashubite family. In Genesis 46:13, his name is Job but this may be a scribe's error.

JASHUB,
JASHUBITES 2
Ezra 10:29

2. One of the sons of Bani, who married an alien wife and was forced by Ezra to repudiate her.

JASHUBI-LEHEM
I Chr 4:22

JASHUBI-LEHEM Name of a Judahite man or of a group of people. The text is obscure. Some scholars read: "and they returned to Lehem" (Beth-Lehem); others see in the words a shortened form of: "and Jesse of Beth-Lehem".

JASON
Acts 17:5-7, 9.
Rom 16:21

JASON (a popular Greek name, which was adopted by Hellenized Jews instead of Joshua or Jesus). A man living in Thessalonica, who received Paul in his house which was as a consequence attacked by a multitude

(Acts 17:6-7). Jason and his companions were brought before the authorities and charged with preaching another king — Jesus, in contradiction of Caesar's decrees (Acts 17:7). Jason was freed after giving a security (Acts 17:9). In the Epistle to the Romans, Paul mentions Jason as sending greetings from Corinth to the Roman community (Rom 16:21).

JATHNIEL The fourth son of Meshelemiah the Korhite, appointed by David as a gatekeeper in the Temple.

JATTIR A town of Levites in the south of the territory of Judah (Josh 15:48; 21:14). It was the birthplace of two of David's "mighty men," Ira and Gareb (II Sam 23:38), and David sent presents there after his victory over the Amalekites (I Sam 30:27). In the late Roman period it

Jattir, southwest of Hebron

Head of "The Charioteer of Pozylazes", from the temple of Apollo at Delphi, Greece. (Delphi Museum)

was a large Christian village identified with Khirbet Attir, about 14 miles (22.5km) northeast of Beersheba.

JAVAN Fourth son of Japheth in the Table of Nations (Gen 10:2, 4; I Chr 1:5). Javan (which is the same word as Iaonie, the land of the Greeks) is the Hebrew for Greece. See GREECE, GREEKS.

JAZER (JAAZER) An Amorite town east of the River Jordan, conquered by the Israelites (Num 21:32). The Gadites settled there, raised cattle (Num 32:1) and built a city (Num 32:35), which was one of the cities of refuge (I Chr 6:81). It was in the kingdom of David (II Sam 24:5). Isaiah (16:8-9) and Jeremiah (48:32) mention it as a Moabite town. At the time of the Second Temple it was Ammonite, but was later conquered by the Hasmoneans (I Macc 5:8). Tentatively identified with Khirbet es-Sar, about 8 miles (13 km) west of Amman.

JAZIZ The Hagerite. A royal steward appointed over the flocks during David's reign.

JEARIM, MOUNT The northern border of the territory of Judah ran from Baalah, another name for Kirjath Jearim, extending westward unto Mount Seir, "and passed along to the side of Mount Jearim, on the north (which is Chesalon), went down to Beth Shemesh" (Josh 15:9-10). See CHESALON for identification.

JEATHERAI A Levite, the son of Zerah and descendant of Gershom (I Chr 6:21). The name may be a corrupt form of Ethni.

JEBERECHIAH ("Yah will bless"). Father of Zechariah, who witnessed Isaiah's prophecy concerning the destruction of Damascus and Samaria (Is 8:2).

JEBUS, JEBUSITES One of the peoples that inhabited Jerusalem in ancient times. According to Genesis 10:16 the Jebusites were part of Canaan. They dwelt in Jerusalem and named their city Jebus (Judg

JATHNIEL
I Chr 26:2

JATTIR
Josh 15:48; 21:14. I Sam 30:27. I Chr 6:57

JAVAN
Gen 10:2, 4. I Chr 1:5, 7. Is 66:19. Ezek 27:13, 19

JAZER
Num 21:32; 32:1, 3, 35. Josh 13:25; 21:39. II Sam 24:5. I Chr 6:81; 26:31. Is 16:8-9. Jer 48:32

JAZIZ
I Chr 27:31

JEARIM, MOUNT
Josh 15:10

JEATHERAI
I Chr 6:21

JEBERECHIAH
Is 8:2

JEBUS, JEBUSITES
Gen 10:16; 15:21. Ex 3:8, 17; 13:5; 23:33; 33:2; 34:11. Num 13:29. Deut 7:1; 20:17. Josh 3:10; 9:1; 11:3; 12:8; 15:8, 63; 18:16, 28; 24:11. Judg 1:21; 3:5; 19:10-11. II Sam 5:6, 8; 24:16, 18. I Kgs 9:20. I Chr 1:14; 11:4-6; 21:15, 18, 28. II Chr 3:1; 8:7. Ezra

19:10-11). During the conquest of Canaan Joshua was unable to take the city and the surrounding land (Josh 15:8; 18:16). In the time of the Judges it was considered to be a "city of foreigners" (Judg 19:12), and it remained Jebusite in the time of Saul. David conquered the city and built an altar to the Lord on the threshing floor of Araunah the Jebusite (II Sam 24:16 ff).

JECAMIAH, JEKAMIAH ("Yah will fulfill" [his word]).
1. A Jerahmeelite, son of Shallum.
2. The son of King Jehoiachin of Judah.

JECHOLIAH (JECOLIAH) ("Yah is able"). The wife of King Amaziah of Judah and mother of his heir Uzziah (II Chr 26:3), also given as Azariah (II Kgs 15:1).

JECONIAH Another name for King Jehoiachin of Judah.

JEDAIAH ("Yah knows/has favored").
1. Descendant of the tribe of Simeon.
2. One who took part in the repairing of the wall of Jerusalem under Nehemiah.
3. Name of a priestly clan during the time of David. Jeshua, the high priest in Zerubbabel's time, was from this house.
4. One of the priests living in Jerusalem after the return from the Babylonian Exile.
5. A priest who returned from the Babylonian Exile.
6. Another priest who returned from Babylon.
7. One of the three representatives who brought gifts from Babylon for the community of Jerusalem.

JEDIAEL ([The man is] "known to God").
1. The third son of Benjamin.
2. A Levite, the second son of Meshelemiah, a gatekeeper at the time of David.
3. One of the chiefs of Manasseh who joined David at Ziklag.
4. The son of Shimri; one of David's heroes.

JEDIDAH ("God's friend" or "friendly", "beloved"). Mother of Josiah, king of Judah (II Kgs 22:1).

JEDIDIAH Personal name, meaning "the Lord's beloved", which was given to Solomon by the prophet Nathan.

JEDUTHUN Singer who sang liturgical music along with Asaph and Heman before the ark in Jerusalem in the days of David (I Chr 16:41). His name appears in the superscription to Psalm 39 verse 1. He is called a seer (II Chr 35:15). His sons were "keepers of the gate" (I Chr 16:42). Jeduthun and his six sons were assigned the role of "prophesy with harps, stringed instruments and cymbals" (I Chr 25:1, 3, 6). They and the other musical guilds mentioned in I Chronicles chapter 25 performed music at the dedication of Solomon's Temple. According to II Chronicles 5:12 it is asserted that they were Levites.

A descendant of Jeduthun named Abda or Obadiah was among the first to return to Judah from Babylonia after the promulgation of the Edict of Cyrus (I Chr 9:16; Neh 11:17).

Jeduthun also seems to be the name of a musical instrument, for the name appears in the formula "for the leader of the music upon a Jeduthun" (Ps 62:1; 77:1). Since in all other cases in the Bible Jeduthun is a musician, it has been suggested that these references (and possibly 39:1) denote a type of harp, flute or drum originated by Jeduthun.

JEEZER, JEEZERITES A son of Gilead who founded the family of the Jeezerites; an alternate form of Abiezer.

JEGAR SAHADUTHA ("heap of testimony"). The Aramaic name given by Laban to the heap of stones, erected by him and Jacob in witness of their peace treaty (Gen 31:47).

Limestone Hebrew seal inscribed "[Belonging] to Yekamyahu" (Jecamiah). 8th century B.C. (Rockefeller Museum)

JEHALELEL

502

JEHALELEL ("may Yah shine"). A Levite descendant of Merari (II Chr 29:12).

JEHDEIAH ("may Yah be glad").

1. A Levite, head of the Shubael clan at the time of David.

2. A Meronothite; one of the officers who were in charge of David's donkeys.

JEHEZEKEL ("may God strengthen"). Head of the 20th division of priests serving in the House of the Lord at the time of King David.

JEHIAH ("may Yah live"). A Levite, appointed gatekeeper to the ark of God, when it was brought by David to Jerusalem (I Chr 15:24).

JEHIEL, JEHIELI ("may God live").

1. A Levite, one of the musicians at the time of David.

2. A Levite, descendant of Gershom; chief of the house of Laadan (I Chr 23:8), and the ancestor of the Jehieli family (I Chr 26:21-22); in charge of the treasury during the time of King David (I Chr 29:8).

3. The son of Hachmoni; probably a tutor of David's sons.

4. The son of Jehoshaphat king of Judah.

5. A Levite, son of Heman, who purified the Temple during Hezekiah's reform (II Chr 29:14), and remained in service as an overseer (II Chr 31:13).

6. A priest (third in rank), at the Temple at the time of King Josiah.

7. Father of Obadiah, ancestor of the Joabite family, who returned from the Babylonian Exile.

8. Father of Shecaniah, who obeyed Ezra's order to repudiate his alien wife.

9. A priest of the Harim family who married an alien wife and was forced to repudiate her.

JEHIZKIAH ("God will show his strength"). The son of Shallum, one of the chiefs of Ephraim; he sided with the prophet Oded in demanding the return to Judah of the captives taken by Pekah of Israel. The name Jehizkio was found on coins in the Judah district (4th century B.C.).

JEHOADDAH A Benjamite, son of Ahaz, a descendant of King Saul, mentioned as Jarah in I Chronicles 9:42.

JEHOADDAN The wife of Joash and mother of Amaziah king of Judah.

JEHOAHAZ ("God has held firmly").

1. The youngest son of Jehoram (II Chr 21:17) and king of Judah (843-842 B.C.). Identical with Ahaziah (II Kgs 8:25-26, 29; 9:27; II Chr 22:1-2, 7-9).

2. The son of Jehu and king of Israel (814-798 B.C.), who reigned in Samaria (II Kgs 13:1). During his reign Aramean troops under the command of Hazael and his son Ben-Hadad, invaded Israel (II Kgs 13:3). The Israelite army was totally destroyed and the king pleaded for God's help (II Kgs 13:4). God sent a "deliverer" (II Kgs 13:5), most likely Adad-Nirari III king of Assyria, who renewed his campaigns in Syria, forcing Ben-Hadad to pay him tribute. Israel was saved but came under the yoke of the Assyrians.

JEHALELEL II Chr 29:12

JEHDEIAH 1 I Chr 24:20

JEHDEIAH 2 I Chr 27:30

JEHEZEKEL I Chr 24:16

JEHIAH I Chr 15:24

JEHIEL, JEHIELI 1 I Chr 15:18, 20; 16:5

JEHIEL, JEHIELI 2 I Chr 27:32; 29:8

JEHIEL, JEHIELI 3 I Chr 23:8; 26:21-22

JEHIEL, JEHIELI 4 II Chr 21:2

JEHIEL, JEHIELI 5 II Chr 29:14; 31:13

JEHIEL, JEHIELI 6 II Chr 35:8

JEHIEL, JEHIELI 7 Ezra 8:9

JEHIEL, JEHIELI 8 Ezra 10:2, 26

JEHIEL, JEHIELI 9 Ezra 10:21

JEHIZKIAH II Chr 28:12

JEHOADDAH I Chr 8:36

JEHOADDAN II Kgs 14:2, II Chr 25:1

JEHOAHAZ 1 II Chr 21:17

JEHOAHAZ 2 II Kgs 10:35; 13:1, 4, 7-10, 22, 25; 14:1, 8, 17. II Chr 25:17, 23, 25

Jasper seal inscribed "[Belonging] to Jehoahaz son of the king". Late 7th century B.C. (Israel Museum)

3. Fourth son and successor of Josiah, king of Judah (609-608 B.C.). His mother's name was Hamutal. He was made king by "the people of the land" (II Kgs 23:30; II Chr 36:1) at the age of 23 after Josiah's death at Megiddo. After reigning for three months he was removed by Pharaoh Necho king of Egypt, and brought to Riblah on the Orontes. He was made prisoner and then sent to Egypt where he died (II Kgs 23:33-34; II Chr 36:2-4). His exile to Egypt prompted the dirge of Jeremiah who summoned the people to lament for the king who would never return to Judah. In I Chronicles 3:15 and Jeremiah 22:11, he is called Shallum which is assumed to be his proper name whereas Jehoahaz was his throne name. The name Jehoahaz appears on a Hebrew seal from the 7th-6th centuries B.C.

JEHOASH, JOASH ("God has bestowed/donated").

1. The son of Shelah, descendant of Judah.

2. The father of Gideon, descendant of the Abiezrite family of the tribe of Manasseh, who dwelt at Ophrah (Judg 6:11). Joash had his own Asherah and an altar to Baal (Judg 6:25). When Gideon later destroyed these shrines (Judg 6:27), Joash protected his son from the anger of the people of the town (Judg 6:28-32).

3. A Benjamite, descendant of the Becher family.

4. The son of Shemaah of Gibeah. One of the Benjamite heroes who joined David at Ziklag.

5. One of the officials appointed by David to oversee the stores of oil.

6. The son of Ahab king of Israel, who imprisoned the prophet Micaiah in response to the latter's prophecy of doom before Ahab's campaign against Ramoth Gilead (I Kgs 22:14-27; II Chr 18:13-26).

7. The son of Ahaziah, and king of Judah (836-798 B.C.). He was concealed at the Temple for six years by his aunt, Jehosheba, the wife of Jehoiada the high priest, who protected him while Athaliah, the queen-mother, killed all the other members of the royal family and usurped the throne (II Kgs 11:1-3; II Chr 22:10-12).

When Joash was aged seven, Jehoiada rebelled against Athaliah and proclaimed Joash as the rightful ruler (II Kgs 11:4-20; II Chr 23:1-15). Joash reigned for 40 years (II Kgs 12:1; II Chr 24:1). Under the influence of Jehoiada he repaired the Temple and destroyed the cult of Baal (II Kgs 12:7-16; II Chr 24:6-14). After the death of Jehoiada, a dispute broke out between the king and the priesthood; pagan worship was renewed (II Chr 24:17-18), and Jehoiada's son Zechariah who resisted the cult of Baal, was killed on the king's orders (II Chr 24:20-22). During his reign, Judah suffered from Aramean invasions led by Hazael; Gath was captured and the Aramean army turned towards Jerusalem. In order to fend off an attack, Joash bribed Hazael with the Temple's treasure (II Kgs 12:17-18).

Joash was assassinated by two of his own servants (II Kgs 12:20-21; II Chr 24:25-26) and was buried in the City of David.

8. The son of Jehoahaz and king of Israel (800-784 B.C.). During his reign Israel came under pressure from three different nations: (a) the Assyrians, who received tribute from Israel, as confirmed also by extrabiblical sources, especially the stele of the Assyrian king Adad-Nirari III from Rimah, where the Israelite king is mentioned as "Iu'usu the Samaritan"; (b) the Arameans (II Kgs 13:3-4) who had already taken Israelite territories during the reign of his father Jehoahaz; (c) the Moabites who engaged in annual forays against Israel (II Kgs 13:20). Spurred on by the prophet Elisha (II Kgs 13:14-19) who, in a series of symbolic acts, forecast a threefold victory over Aram, Jehoash regained his lost territories from Aram after the latter had been weakened by the Assyrian invasion (II Kgs 13:25).

A coin of John Hyrcanus II the high priest (63-40 B.C.), with the name Jehohanan on one side and a double cornucopia on the other.

Towards the end of his reign Jehoash defeated Amaziah king of Judah who challenged him to war. He reached Jerusalem, broke down part of the city wall, and took the treasuries of the Temple and the royal house, together with hostages, back to Samaria (II Kgs 14:8-14; II Chr 25:17-24).

Joash was buried in Samaria (II Kgs 14:16), leaving a greatly strengthened kingdom to his son Jeroboam II.

JEHOHANAN ("God has been gracious").

1. A Levite, sixth son of Meshelemiah, a gatekeeper appointed by King David.

2. A captain, one of the warriors of Jehoshaphat, king of Judah.

3. Father of Ishmael, one of the captains who gathered the Levites from all their cities into Jerusalem by command of the high priest Jehoiada during the revolt against Athaliah.

4. The son of Eliashib to whose chamber Ezra retired in order to fast.

5. One of the Israelites who returned from Exile and was forced to repudiate his alien wife.

6. The son of Tobiah the Ammonite. His wife, a Jewess, was among those who helped repair the wall of Jerusalem during the time of Nehemiah.

7. A descendant of Amariah. One of the priests at the time of the high priest Joiakim.

8. A priest at the time of Nehemiah, who was present at the dedication of the wall of Jerusalem.

JEHOIACHIN ("God will establish"). Son of Jehoiakim and Nehushta, king of Judah (597 B.C.). He was also called Jeconiah (I Chr 3:16; Jer 24:1; 27:20; 28:4; 29:2) and Coniah (Jer 22:24, 28; 37:1). He became king at the age of 18 when Judah rebelled against Babylonia. Along with his mother, his wife, his officials and others, he was exiled by Nebuchadnezzar king of Babylon to Babylonia. Nebuchadnezzar appointed Jehoiachin's uncle Zedekiah, to be king in his place and exacted heavy tribute from the land. The historical events of Jehoiachin's short reign (three months, or three months and ten days), are described in II Kings 24:8-15; II Chronicles 36:9-20 and also in Babylonian inscriptions. After his captivity, a belief arose among the people that he would soon return and resume his kingship (Jer 28:3-4) and even the Jews in Babylonia reckoned their calendar by the years of his exile (Ezek 1:2; 8:1). On the other hand, Jeremiah, opposing another prophet Hananiah who declared that Jehoiachin would return within two years (Jer 28:3-4, 11), predicted the end of his reign and dynasty (Jer 22:24-30). While in exile throughout the reign of Nebuchadnezzar, Jehoiachin remained in prison. After the death of the Babylonian king, he was brought to the royal palace by the new king Evil-Merodach (II Kgs 25:27-30; Jer 52:31-34). Babylonian tablets record that Jehoiachin and his five sons were treated throughout as royal hostages receiving daily rations from the king at whose table he dined. Three stamps on jar handles, found in Judah with the inscription "to Eliakim servant of Yaukin", probably indicate that his property was preserved even when he was in exile.

JEHOIADA ("God has known").

1. A warrior from Kabzeel (I Chr 11:22) or a chief priest (I Chr 27:5), father of Benaiah one of David's heroes and chief officers (II Sam 8:18; 20:23; I Kgs 4:4).

2. A leader of the Aaronites who led his men to join David at Hebron and assist him in gaining the kingdom of Saul.

3. Son of Benaiah (presumably, grandson of No.1 above), one of David's counselors, replacing Ahithophel.

JEHOHANAN 1
I Chr 26:3

JEHOHANAN 2
II Chr 17:15

JEHOHANAN 3
II Chr 23:1

JEHOHANAN 4
Ezra 10:6

JEHOHANAN 5
Ezra 10:28

JEHOHANAN 6
Neh 6:18

JEHOHANAN 7
Neh 12:13

JEHOHANAN 8
Neh 12:42

JEHOIACHIN
II Kgs 24:6, 8, 12, 15, 17; 25:27, 29.
II Chr 36:8-9.
Jer 52:31, 33.
Ezek 1:2

JEHOIADA 1
II Sam 8:18; 20:23; 23:20, 22. I Kgs 1:8, 26, 32, 36, 38, 44; 2:25, 29, 34-35, 46; 4:4. I Chr 11:22, 24; 18:17; 27:5

JEHOIADA 2
I Chr 12:27

JEHOIADA 3
I Chr 27:34

4. The high priest in Jerusalem at the time of Ahaziah king of Judah and the brother-in-law of the king (II Chr 22:11). After the death of Ahaziah, the king's mother Athaliah, killed all the royal offspring and reigned herself. The infant Joash, the only survivor, was hidden by Jehoiada and his wife in the Temple for six years (II Kgs 11:3; II Chr 22:12). In the seventh year Jehoiada rebelled against Athaliah and restored Joash to the throne as the rightful king (II Kgs 11:4-21; II Chr chap. 23). During Joash's minority, Jehoiada ruled the country, destroying the Baal cult and reorganizing the Levites. Later, when Joash himself ruled, Jehoiada inspired him to repair the Temple (II Kgs 12:7-14; II Chr 24:6-14). Jehoiada died at the age of 130 (I Chr 24:15-16) and was buried in the City of David in the royal tomb.

5. A priest in Jerusalem at the time of the prophet Jeremiah.

6. The son of Paseah; he returned from the Exile with Nehemiah and was among those who repaired the old gate of Jerusalem (Neh 3:6). In Nehemiah 13:28 he is called Joiada.

JEHOIAKIM ("God will arise"). Son of Josiah and Zebidah, and king of Judah (608-598 B.C.). At the age of 25 he was made king by Pharaoh Necho in place of his brother Jehoahaz, who was deposed and exiled to Egypt. Necho changed his name from Eliakim to Jehoiakim (II Kgs 23:34; II Chr 36:4) and exacted heavy tribute from Judah (II Kgs 23:33; II Chr 36:3), which Jehoiakim collected by the imposition of crushing land taxes (II Kgs 23:35).

Jehoiakim is described as an evil and oppressive king (II Kgs 24:3; II Chr 36:5; Jer 22:18-23). In the fourth year of his reign (605 B.C.), Nebuchadnezzar king of Babylonia met Necho in battle at Carchemish. The Egyptian pharaoh was defeated and Babylonia took control of his countries including Judah (Jer 25:1; 46:2). At first Jehoiakim accepted the suzerainty of the new ruler but three years later, he rebelled (II Kgs 24:1).

Nebuchadnezzar sent Moabite, Syrian, Ammonite and Chaldean troops to invade Judah. Jerusalem was later captured (II Kgs 24:2) and a large number of the people along with part of the Temple treasure, were sent to Babylonia (II Chr 36:7). Many of these events are now attested by the extra-biblical source of the Babylonian Chronicle.

According to II Kings 24:6, Jehoiakim died peacefully. However, in Josephus' account (*Antiq.* x, 97) his body was thrown out over the gates of Jerusalem, as prophesied by Jeremiah (Jer 22:18-19; 36:30). It is recorded in Chronicles that Jehoiakim was sent to Babylon in fetters but no mention is made of his subsequent death (II Chr 36:6).

JEHOIARIB ("may the Lord contend"). Identical with Joiarib in Nehemiah 12:6, 19.

An eponym of a priestly family descended from Aaron, at the time of King David (I Chr 24:7). One member of the family returned from Exile and dwelt in Jerusalem at the time of Nehemiah (I Chr 9:10).

JEHONADAB, JONADAB ("God has donated").

1. The son of Shimeah, King David's brother, and a friend of Amnon (II Sam 13:3). He advised Amnon on how to seduce his half-sister Tamar (II Sam 13:5). Later on when Amnon was assassinated by Absalom, Jehonadab informed David that only Amnon (and not all of David's sons) was slain.

2. The son of Rechab, probably a Kenite (I Chr 2:55). He forbade his sons to dwell in houses, to cultivate the earth, to possess vineyards or drink wine (Jer 35:6-10). He assisted Jehu in his rebellion against the house of Ahab and in the destruction of the Baal cult in Israel (II Kgs 10:15-28).

The name appears on a Hebrew seal from the 6th century B.C.

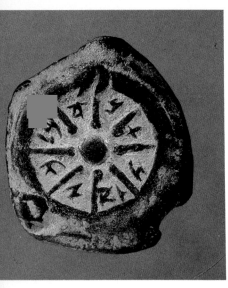

The name Jehonathan on a coin of Alexander Jannaeus (103-76 B.C.).

JEHONATHAN ("God has given").

1. The son of Uzziah; he was appointed by David to supervise the king's storehouses in the fields, cities, villages and castles.

2. A Levite, sent by King Jehoshaphat, with other Levites, to teach the Law in the cities of Judah.

3. A priest, head of the Shemaiah family (Neh 12:18), in the days of the high priest Joiakim (Neh 12:12).

4. Uncle of David; he was a scribe and counselor at King David's court.

JEHORAM, JORAM ("Yah is high").

1. A Levite descended from Moses who lived at the time of King David.

2. A prince of Hamath, son of King Toi, who was sent by his father with gifts to congratulate King David on his victory over Hadadezer king of Zobah (II Sam 8:9-11). In the parallel passage (I Chr 18:9-11), his name is given as Hadoram.

3. A priest who was sent by King Jehoshaphat to teach the Law in the cities of Judah.

4. The son of Ahab and Jezebel and the last king of the Omride dynasty (852-841 B.C.). He succeeded his brother Ahaziah (II Kgs 1:17), and reigned for 12 years (851-842 B.C.) according to II Kings 3:1; but extra-biblical sources (Assyrian inscription of Shalmaneser III) suggest that his reign may have been shorter.

Although he restricted the worship of Baal (II Kgs 3:2), he remained under the influence of the Tyrian cult introduced by his mother Queen Jezebel.

At the beginning of his reign, he faced a Moabite rebellion against Israel (II Kgs 3:4-27). Extra-biblical evidence of this revolt is documented in the Moabite Stone (Mesha Stele). With the help of King Jehoshaphat of Judah and of the ruler of Edom, Jehoram won a partial victory over the Moabites and destroyed a large part of their cities (II Kgs 3:24-25).

The long conflict between Israel and Aram continued during his reign as shown by the Elisha stories, although Jehoram is not mentioned by name, merely as "the king of Israel" (II Kgs 5:1-8; 6:9-7:20; 8:3-6). In one of his battles against Hazael king of Aram, at Ramoth Gilead, Jehoram was wounded and went to Jezreel to recover (II Kgs 8:28-29). While there he was killed by Jehu in a revolt against the Omride dynasty (II Kgs 9:15-26).

5. Son of Jehoshaphat and king of Judah (851-843 B.C.); he ascended the throne at the age of 32 and reigned for 8 years (II Kgs 8:17; II Chr 21:5). He married Athaliah the daughter of Ahab of Israel, and renewed pagan worship in Judah (II Kgs 8:18; II Chr 21:6). According to II Chronicles 21:4, he killed all his brothers, possibly in order to prevent a revolt against his foreign policy. During his reign, Edom and Libnah succeeded in their rebellion against Judah (II Kgs 8:22; II Chr 21:8-10), whereupon Jehoram lost control of the main routes from Arabia and the desert copper mines. Towards the end of his reign, Judah was invaded by the Philistines and Arabs who captured his wives, sons, except for his youngest, and all his property (II Chr 21:16-17).

Judah and sister of Ahaziah. She saved the child Joash from the assassins 8:24). In Chronicles, however, it is stated, that he was not buried "in the tombs of the kings" (II Chr 21:20).

JEHOSHABEATH, JEHOSHEBA Daughter of King Jehoram of Judah and sister of Ahaziah. She saved the child Joash from the assassins sent by the queen mother Athaliah, and hid him in the Temple for six years after King Ahaziah was killed.

JEHOSHAPHAT ("Yah has judged").

1. The son of Ahilud, the recorder (or: secretary) in the administrations of David (II Sam 8:16; 20:24; I Chr 18:15) and Solomon (I Kgs 4:3).

2. The son of Paruah, appointed over Issachar (I Kgs 4:17). He was one of 12 such officers, each of whom provided victuals for King Solomon's household for one month in a year (I Kgs 4:7).

3. Son of Nimshi and the father of King Jehu of Israel.

4. Son of King Asa and Azubah; he became king of Judah (873-849 B.C.) at the age of 35, and reigned for 25 years (I Kgs 22:42; II Chr 20:31) including a few years as a co-regent with his father.

During his reign he eradicated the pagan cults and sent priests and Levites all over the country to teach the law of God (II Chr 17:7-9). He reorganized the administration and appointed judges in the cities of Judah, with an appeal court in Jerusalem (II Chr 19:4-11). He fortified cities in Judah and placed standing garrisons in Ephraim (II Chr 17:1-2), built fortresses and store cities (II Chr 17:12-13) and strengthened the military forces (II Chr 7:14-19).

He was the first king to conclude a treaty with the Northern Kingdom of Israel which involved betrothing his son Jehoram to Ahab's daughter Athaliah (I Kgs 22:44; II Chr 18:1). The alliance between the two kingdoms brought prosperity to Judah, and overawed the surrounding nations: the Philistines and Arabs brought him tribute (II Chr 17:10-11) and even Edom came under his yoke (I Kgs 22:47), thereby granting him control over the copper mines in the desert and over the main routes from Arabia. Together with Israel and probably Tyre he attempted to build a navy in Ezion Geber (I Kgs 22:48-49; II Chr 20:35-37).

Jehoshaphat died in Jerusalem and was buried in the City of David.

JEHOSHAPHAT, VALLEY OF The valley where the Last Judgment is to take place (Joel 3:2), also called "the valley of decision" (Joel 3:14). Early traditions identify it with the valley of Kidron. Another early tradition held that the name Jehoshaphat ("God has judged") is symbolic and does not refer to an actual place.

The Valley of Jehoshaphat, part of the Valley of Kidron in Jerusalem, between the Mount of Olives and Mount Moriah.

JEHOZABAD, JOZABAD ("Yah had given" [a child]).

1. Son of Shomer, one of the two servants who assassinated King Joash of Judah (II Kgs 12:21). In the parallel passage (II Chr 24:26), he is called the son of Shimrith, a Moabite woman, thus stressing that the assassins were foreigners.

2. A Gederathite, one of the Benjamite heroes who joined David at Ziklag (I Chr 12:4).

3. Two of David's heroes from the tribe of Manasseh, who joined him at Ziklag (I Chr 12:20).

4. The second son of Obed-Edom who was appointed by King David as a gatekeeper in the Temple (I Chr 26:4).

5. A warrior from the tribe of Benjamin; commander of part of the Benjamite troops in the army of King Jehoshaphat of Judah (II Chr 17:18).

6. A Levite overseer in the Temple at the time of King Hezekiah of Judah (II Chr 31:13).

7. One of the chiefs of the Levites, at the time of King Josiah of Judah (II Chr 35:9).

8. Son of Jeshua; one of the Levites who weighed the treasures brought by Ezra, from Babylon to Jerusalem (Ezra 8:33).

9. A priest, a descendant of Pashhur who married an alien wife and was forced to repudiate her.

10. A Levite who married a foreign wife and was forced to repudiate her. He may be identical with No.8 above.

11. One of the Levites who explained the Law read by Ezra.

12. One of the chiefs of the Levites who dwelt in Jerusalem at the time of Nehemiah; appointed over the external dealings of the house of God.

JEHOZADAK, JOZADAK ("Yah has been just"). The son of Seraiah; he was exiled to Babylon by Nebuchadnezzar (I Chr 6:14-15). He was the father of Joshua (or Jeshua), the first high priest in the Second Temple (Ezra 3:2; Neh 12:26; Hag 1:1, 12, 14; 2:2, 4; Zech 6:11). His name is missing from the list of those who returned with Zerubbabel (Ezra 2:2) and it is therefore assumed that he died in Babylonia.

JEHU (a shortened form of: "Yahweh is he" [the Lord]).

1. Son of Obed, a descendant of the Jerahmeelite family of the tribe of Judah.

2. The son of Josibiah, the head of a Simeonite family at the time of Hezekiah king of Judah.

3. The Anathothite, one of the Benjamite warriors who joined David at Ziklag.

4. The son of Hanani, a prophet during the reign of Baasha king of Israel and Jehoshaphat king of Judah (I Kgs 16:1, 7, 12; II Chr 19:2; 20:34). He prophesied the end of Baasha's dynasty (I Kgs 16:2-4) and criticized Jehoshaphat for taking part in Ahab's war against the Arameans (II Chr 19:2-3). It is assumed that Jehu fled from Israel to Judah at the time of Jezebel and there chronicled Jehoshaphat's reign (II Chr 20:34).

5. The son of Jehoshaphat and grandson of Nimshi (II Kgs 9:2, 14; in parallel passages: the son of Nimshi — I Kgs 19:16; II Kgs 9:20; II Chr 22:7). He became king of Israel (842-814 B.C.), founding a new dynasty.

Jehu was a commander in the Israelite army and took the throne by force. His rebellion was supported by religious elements: the prophet Elisha, who dispatched one of the sons of the prophets to anoint Jehu (II Kgs 9:1-13), and the Rechabites (II Kgs 10:15-16), who were opposed to the cult of the Tyrian Baal and Astarte; and by army commanders (II Kgs 9:13) critical of King Joram's military policy (II Kgs 9:13), and by others dissatisfied with the country's economic and social situation

Seal impression from Lachish inscribed "[Belonging] to Jehucal son of Yeho[hai]". Early 6th century B.C. (Israel Museum)

(left)
Jehu (or his ambassador) prostrate at the feet of Shalmaneser III. Detail from "The Black Obelisk", a limestone monument. 9th century B.C. (British Museum)

27, 30-31;
10:1, 5, 11,
13, 15, 18-21,
23-25, 28-31,
34-36; 12:1;
13:1; 14:8;
15:12. II Chr
22:7-9; 25:17.
Hos 1:4

(II Kgs 4:1-7, 38-43). As described in II Kings chapters 9-10, Jehu went to Jezreel where King Joram was recuperating after being wounded in the battle at Ramoth Gilead (II Kgs 8:28-29); he killed both Joram and King Ahaziah of Judah (II Kgs 9:21-27; cf II Chr 22:9) as well as Jezebel the queen mother (II Kgs 9:31-35). Jehu executed Ahab's entire family with the aid of the officials in Samaria (II Kgs 10:1-11) thereby fulfilling the prophecy of Elijah (I Kgs 21:17ff). On his way to Samaria Jehu killed 42 brethren of Ahaziah (II Kgs 10:13-14; cf II Chr 22:8); reaching the city, he completed the destruction of the house of Ahab (II Kgs 10:17) and exterminated the priests and worshipers of Baal (II Kgs 10:18-28).

The downfall of the Omride dynasty severed the ties between Israel, Judah and Tyre. Israel was left isolated in her conflict with the Arameans who under Hazael captured parts of Israelite territories in Transjordan (II Kgs 10:32-33). Jehu reigned for 28 years and was buried in Samaria (II Kgs 10:35-36).

Extra-biblical sources complete the picture of the events during Jehu's reign. Israel came under the yoke of Assyria, as recorded clearly in the Black Obelisk of Shalmaneser III king of Assyria, where "Yau, son of Omri" is listed among the rulers who paid tribute. It also depicts Jehu as actually presenting this tribute to the king.

JEHUBBAH
I Chr 7:34

JEHUBBAH Third son of Shemer in the genealogy of the family of Asher.

JEHUCAL,
JUCAL
Jer 37:3; 38:1

JEHUCAL, JUCAL ("God will show his ability"). The son of Shelemiah. He was sent by Zedekiah the king of Judah, to beg the prophet Jeremiah to pray for the people during the Chaldean siege of Jerusalem (Jer 37:3). Later on, he was among those who urged the king to kill Jeremiah (38:1-4).

The name Jehucal appears on seal-impressions from Tell es-Safi and Lachish (6th century B.C.) and on an ostracon from Arad (7th century B.C.).

JEHUD
Josh 19:45

JEHUD A town in the territory of Dan, in the vicinity of Bene Berak and Gath Rimmon, east of Joppa (Josh 19:45). In the Hellenistic period it was named Iudaia, and Judas Maccabee fought one of his great battles there (I Macc 4:15).

The town is identified with el-Yahudiyeh, about 10 miles (16 km) east of Jaffa.

JEHUDI
Jer 36:14, 21,
23

JEHUDI ("Jew", or abbreviated form of "Judahite"). The son of Nethaniah, an officer in the court of Jehoiakim king of Judah. The officials ordered him to bring Baruch, the scribe of the prophet

Jeremiah, before the court to read the scroll of the prophet (Jer 36:14). Later on, Jehudi himself read the scroll to the king, who cut it up and burned it (Jer 36:21-23).

JEHUDIJAH ("Jewish", or "Judahite"). Probably one of the wives of Jered (I Chr 4:18). The word is not a proper name but means "woman of Judah", one of Jered's wives.

JEIEL ("may God bring life"). The name of several biblical figures:

1. A Reubenite, one of the chiefs of the tribe.

2. A Benjamite, ancestor of Gibeon, after whom the city of Gibeon was called, and of King Saul's family.

3. A Reubenite from Transjordan, son of Hotham the Aroerite; one of David's heroes. His name is missing in the parallel list in II Samuel chapter 23.

4. A Levite, appointed by King David to be a porter of the ark and a musician at the sanctuary.

5. Another Levite; a gatekeeper at the time of King David. It is assumed that he is to be identified with Jaaziel (I Chr 15:18) and Aziel (I Chr 15:20). He may also be identical with No.4 above.

6. A Levite, descendant of Asaph; great-grandfather of Jahaziel, who prophesied at the time of Jehoshaphat king of Judah.

7. The scribe of Uzziah king of Judah, who was responsible for the roster of the warriors.

8. A Levite, one of the sons of Elizaphan, who purified the Temple in Hezekiah's reform.

9. One of the chiefs of the Levites at the time of Josiah king of Judah.

10. One of the sons of Adonikam, who returned from Exile with Ezra.

11. One of the sons of Nebo, who married a pagan wife and was forced to repudiate her.

JEKABZEEL See KABZEEL

JEKAMEAM ("God [nation] will arise"). The fourth son of Hebron; a Levite at the time of King David.

JEKAMIAH See JECAMIAH

JEKUTHIEL The son of Mered and father of Zanoah, a descendant of Judah.

JEMIMAH One of the daughters of Job born to him after he regained his fortunes.

JEMUEL The first son of Simeon and ancestor of a Simeonite family (Gen 46:10; Ex 6:15). In the parallel list of the genealogy of Simeon he is called Nemuel (Num 26:12; I Chr 4:24).

JEPHTHAH ("God will open"). A Gileadite warrior (Judg 11:1), one of the judges of Israel. Being the son of a harlot, he was driven from his father's home by his brothers, the sons of the legitimate wife. He fled to the land of Tob where he became the leader of an outlaw band (Judg 11:2-3), who probably (like David subsequently) protected Israelite villages from the ravages of nomadic tribes.

Later on the elders of Gilead appealed to Jephthah to lead the war

JEHUDIJAH
I Chr 4:18

JEIEL 1
I Chr 5:7

JEIEL 2
I Chr 9:35

JEIEL 3
I Chr 11:44

JEIEL 4
I Chr 15:21;
16:5

JEIEL 5
I Chr 15:18

JEIEL 6
II Chr 20:14

JEIEL 7
II Chr 26:11

JEIEL 8
II Chr 29:13

JEIEL 9
II Chr 35:9

JEIEL 10
Ezra 8:13

JEIEL 11
Ezra 10:43

JEKABZEEL
Neh 11:25

JEKAMEAM
I Chr 23:19;
24:23

JEKAMIAH
I Chr 2:41

JEKUTHIEL
I Chr 4:18

JEMIMAH
Job 42:14

JEMUEL
Gen 46:10. Ex
6:15

JEPHTHAH
Judg 11:1-3,
5-15, 28-30,
32, 34, 40;
12:1-2, 4, 7.
I Sam 12:11.
Heb 11:32

Ammonite warriors on horseback. 8th-7th centuries B.C. (Amman Archaeological Museum)

against the Ammonites, promising him, by oaths before God in Mizpah, that he would remain the leader of the Gileadites after the battle (Judg 11:4-11).

At first Jephthah tried to solve the dispute with the Ammonites through diplomatic means, by sending messengers to the king of Ammon (Judg 11:12-27). This approach having failed, he went out to battle and decisively defeated the Ammonites (Judg 11:32-33), putting an end to their incursions up until the time of Saul.

The narrative of Jephthah's campaign is connected with his vow to offer up a sacrifice of whatever first came out of his house to meet him, if he should return from the war victorious (Judg 11:30-31). Tragically, it was his only daughter who came to greet him on his return, and in order to fulfill his vow, he had to sacrifice her (Judg 11:34-40).

The victory over the Ammonites led to a conflict with the Ephraimites who (according to Judg 12:1-3) were angry at not having been included in the war. In the ensuing fighting, they were defeated and massacred at the passages of Jordan (Judg 12:4-6). It has been suggested that this inter-tribal conflict may have been occasioned by the Ephraimites' desire (against the wish of the Gileadites) to gain control over Israelite Transjordan.

According to Judges 12:7, Jephthah judged "all Israel" for six years, but it is more likely to assume that he was only a local judge in the Gilead area.

JEPHUNNEH

1. A Judahite, the father of Caleb who was sent by Moses to search the land of Canaan (Num 13:6; Deut 1:36; Josh 14:6; I Chr 4:15). He is identified as a Kenizzite in Numbers 32:12.

2. An Asherite, son of Jether.

JERAH ("moon"). Fourth son of Joktan the son of Eber in the genealogy of the family of Adam; it is generally considered that the name denotes a place in the southern part of the Arabian Peninsula.

JERAHMEEL ("may God have compassion").

1. Firstborn son of Hezron of the tribe of Judah; he was the brother of Caleb and father of five sons.

2. Son of Kish; he is listed in the division of the Levites at the end of David's reign.

3. An officer under King Jehoiakim who, together with Seraiah and Shelemiah, was ordered to seize Baruch and Jeremiah.

JERAHMEELITES A people in southern Judah whose cities were attacked by David during his sojourn with the Philistines, when he was a fugitive from Saul. He later sent some of the spoils from these conquests to the elders of Judah.

JERED A man of Judah, "father of Gedor" or founder of that city.

JEREMAI One of the sons of Hashun who, having taken a pagan wife, had to repudiate her upon the decree of Ezra.

JEREMIAH

1. One of the three major prophets. He lived in Jerusalem and his long career coincided with the rise of Babylon to supremacy in the ancient Near East. Jeremiah's call occurred in 626 B.C., the year Nabopolassar captured Babylon. Four years later Judah's king, Josiah, launched a comprehensive reform based on legislation in Deuteronomy. In 612 Nineveh fell to Nabopolassar, and seven years later the rump state of Assyria was defeated at Carchemish by his son, Nebuchadnezzar. This king suppressed a revolt in Judah in 597, taking many Judeans who belonged to the upper social strata into Exile. Some ten years later Nebuchadnezzar crushed Judah, destroying its major cities, including Lachish and Jerusalem. This time the rebel king,

JEPHUNNEH 1
Num 13:6;
14:6, 30, 38;
26:65; 32:12;
34:19. Deut
1:36. Josh
14:6, 13-14;
15:13; 21:12. I
Chr 4:15; 6:56

JEPHUNNEH 2
I Chr 7:38

JERAH
Gen 10:26.
I Chr 1:20

JERAHMEEL 1
I Chr 2:9,
25-27, 33, 42

JERAHMEEL 2
I Chr 24:29

JERAHMEEL 3
Jer 36:26

JERAHMEELITES
I Sam 27:10;
30:29

JERED
I Chr 4:18

JEREMAI
Ezra 10:33

JEREMIAH 1
II Chr 35:25;
36:12, 21-22.
Ezra 1:1.
Jer 1:1, 11;
7:1; 11:1; 14:1;
18:1, 18;
19:14; 20:1-3;
21:1, 3; 24:3;

The village of Anata today, north of Jerusalem, near the ancient site of Anathoth, the birthplace of Jeremiah.

Zedekiah, was blinded and almost the entire population of Judah was taken captive. Jeremiah remained in Mizpah, where Gedaliah served as governor, but the murder of this ruler in 582 set events in motion that resulted in Jeremiah's being taken against his will to Egypt. There he ended his life; when last heard from he was still denouncing syncretistic worship and the people were resisting his words.

Born in Anathoth, a small village about 5 miles (8 km) northeast of Jerusalem, Jeremiah seems to have become a prophet at an early age. Associated with his call were two visions: a boiling cauldron and an almond rod. The first signified destruction from the North, and the second warned that the Lord was watching over Judah so as to destroy the nation. Jeremiah's virtual silence about Josiah's reform has prompted several interpreters to suggest that his call actually came as late as 609, the year of Josiah's premature death at the hands of Pharaoh Necho. It is noteworthy that not Jeremiah but a prophetess, Huldah, was consulted about the authenticity of the newly discovered Book of the Law (II Kgs 22:3-14). Perhaps Jeremiah's political views can best be summed up in the words: submit to Babylon and make the most of captivity. For this message he endured considerable persecution: he was thrown into prison, then into a cistern, and was finally held under house arrest. Another prophet, Hananiah, even opposed him, breaking a yoke that Jeremiah wore to symbolize captivity; moreover, the priest Pashhur beat him and put him in stocks. The same hostility greeted Jeremiah's radical religious views. After a sermon in which he denounced the Temple in Jerusalem and predicted its destruction like the earlier one at Shiloh, Jeremiah came very close to losing his life. Fortunately for him, an official named Ahikam lent his support, and a precedent for Jeremiah's views was remembered in the words of the prophet, Micah. Judah's kings seem to have tolerated the words of Jeremiah, although Jehoiakim destroyed the scroll that he dictated to his scribe, Baruch, and earnestly sought to kill the author of such denunciations. In return, Jeremiah predicted that the king would have the burial of an ass. One other king, Zedekiah, seems to have been unable to decide whether to heed Jeremiah's advice or not. At least he permitted an Ethiopian eunuch, Ebed-Melech, to rescue the prophet from almost certain death in a damp cistern. Another term that he used frequently was *sheker* (deception). In his view there was not a single righteous person in the land, and even the religious leaders were guilty of falsehood. This was especially true of the prophets, whom Jeremiah accused of immorality and deception. He tried to devise criteria by which the people could distinguish between a true prophet and a bogus

25:1-2, 13; 26:7-9, 12, 20, 24; 27:1; 28:5-6, 11-12, 15; 29:1, 27, 29-30; 30:1; 32:1-2, 6, 26; 33:1, 19, 23; 34:1, 6, 8, 12; 35:1, 12, 18; 36:1, 4, 5, 8, 10, 19, 26-27, 32; 37:2-4, 6, 12-18, 21; 38:1, 6-7, 9-17, 19-20, 24, 27-28; 39:11, 14-15; 40:1-2, 5-6; 42:2, 4-5, 7; 43:1-2, 6, 8; 44:1, 15, 20, 24; 45:1; 46:1, 13; 47:1; 49:34; 50:1; 51:59-61, 64; 52:1. Dan 9:2. Matt 2:17; 16:14; 27:9

Carnelian Hebrew seal inscribed "Yirmeyahu" (Jeremiah). 8th century B.C. (T. Kollek Collection, Israel Museum)

one, but that effort was not very successful. To strengthen the impact of his words, Jeremiah often acted them out (See JEREMIAH, BOOK OF). Jeremiah's message from the very beginning was unpromising: a foe from the North was poised to strike. By his own testimony he delivered that sort of word for more than two decades before putting it into writing.

Jeremiah's sense of values has commended itself to people of all ages: do not glory in wisdom, power or wealth, but glory in the fact that you know the Lord who practices justice (Jer 9:23-24).

2. A man of Libnah, father-in-law of King Josiah.

3. A mighty warrior, head of a family of Manasseh, east of the Jordan.

4. A Benjamite bowman who served under David.

5. Two Gadite warriors who enlisted with David.

6. A prince in the time of Nehemiah.

7. A priest who returned with Zerubbabel from the Babylonian Exile.

8. A Rechabite, father of Jaazaniah, who lived at the time of Jeremiah the prophet.

JEREMIAH, BOOK OF A prophetic collection of 52 chapters attributed to Jeremiah, whose activity covered over four decades during momentous events in the ancient Near East (c. 626-580 B.C.). Four distinct kinds of material make up the contents of the book: (a) poetic oracles of judgment in the first person, mostly in chapters 1-25; (b) sermons in prose, also in the first person (e.g., 1:4-10; chaps. 7; 11; 18; 21; 25; 32; 34); (c) biographical narratives in the third person (19:1-20:6; chaps. 26-29; 37-44); and (d) poetic oracles against foreign nations (chaps. 45-51). Much of this material displays similarities in style and language with literature from the Deuteronomic school, giving rise to various theories: Jeremiah used a style in vogue during the 6th century; Baruch, the prophet's faithful scribe, wrote some of the book in the style of the learned; later editors inserted their own materials into the authentic oracles from Jeremiah.

JEREMIAH 2
II Kgs 23:31;
24:18

JEREMIAH 3
I Chr 5:24

JEREMIAH 4
I Chr 12:4

JEREMIAH 5
I Chr 12:10,
13

JEREMIAH 6
Neh 10:2;
12:34

JEREMIAH 7
Neh 12:1, 12

JEREMIAH 8
Jer 35:3

Fragments from the Book of Jeremiah found at Qumran. (Shrine of the Book, Jerusalem)

The nature of the literature seems best explained in terms of a living tradition. The basic core of Jeremiah's prophecy was adapted over the years in a way that addressed new circumstances within the exilic community in Babylon. The prophetic utterances were originally oral, and that situation lasted for over two decades. The actual decision to write down his oracles came about because Jeremiah had incurred royal anger. As a result of King Jehoiakim's hostility toward him, the prophet did the only thing left to him. He dictated his oracles of judgment from the last twenty years to Baruch, who wrote them on a scroll and proceeded to read it before some chief officials and subsequently before the king. Jehoiakim showed his contempt for Jeremiah by cutting up the scroll and burning it. Thereupon, Jeremiah dictated the oracles once more, adding further words of similar content (see chap. 36). Scholars have tried, with little success, to discover the contents of the original scroll.

Two blocks of material within the present book have generated considerable discussion: the so-called confessions (11:18-12:6; 15:10-21; 17:14-18; 18:18-23; 20:7-18) and the Book of Consolation (chaps. 30-31). The former comprise five poignant laments that have frequently been mined for personal information about Jeremiah. For instance, they refer to attempts on his life by members of his own larger family at Anathoth, and they complain that God took advantage of his weakness and innocence (the actual term refers to rape). The little Book of Consolation, expressed in language akin to Deuteronomy, includes a promise that God will institute a new covenant, replacing the heart of stone with one of flesh. Another major literary complex within the book is the prose narrative about Jeremiah's suffering, which may have come from the hand of Baruch. Here is the beginning of a significant body of literature focusing on the trials and tribulations of holy persons, for which scholars have adopted the term martyrology. In this instance, however, Jeremiah escaped death at the hands of his enemies, but his suffering was nonetheless real and prolonged.

The major themes of the book are not easily perceived. One message stands out as singularly important: the nation Judah has rejected the fountain of living waters, hewing for themselves leaking cisterns, and the deity is determined to punish the sinners by sending Babylon against them. Unimpressed by the pro-Egyptian and nationalistic sentiments of his compatriots, Jeremiah urged capitulation to avoid a devastating siege. A central concept in the book is the word *shub*, "return". The future and hope for Judah lay in the exiles, who were called good figs, provided they repented and went in search of the Lord. But the possibility of turning arose from the fact that divine judgment had already fallen. Hence an equally important theme was the idea of impending doom, the "boiling pot" (1:13) or "disaster from the north" (4:6). Perhaps the supreme poetic achievement of the book, rivaled only by the lyrical laments, is the picture of the earth's return to chaos (4:23-26). Judging from the scope of material devoted to the subject of false prophecy, it is reasonable to conclude that this topic also loomed large in the eyes of those persons who compiled the book. It appears that conflicting opinions about what God was doing at the time separated Jeremiah from many of his fellow prophets. The struggle to legitimate a given message generated considerable heat on both sides, prompting Jeremiah to search for reliable criteria for distinguishing true prophets from false ones.

The prophetic word was deeply rooted in daily life. Even the proverbs of Judah left an impression on Jeremiah: "The fathers have eaten sour grapes, and the children's teeth are set on edge" (31:29), "The harvest is past, the summer is ended, and we are not saved" (8:20), and "I have neither lent for interest, nor have men lent to me for interest. Every one of them curses me" (15:10). It is little surprise that a prophet who appreciated the power of speech to this extent would resort to symbolic actions as well. The book therefore has several extensive accounts of prophecy being dramatized in the presence of onlookers: the burial of a linen waistcloth and its retrieval; refusal to marry; breaking a potter's vessel; purchasing a field during a siege of the city; offering wine to Rechabites who were opposed to the fruit of the vine.

OUTLINE

Chaps. 1-25	Words of Jeremiah written by himself or dictated to Baruch
1:1-19	Introduction
2:1-6:30	Reaction to current events, mostly in the reign of Josiah
7:1-20:18	Reaction to current events, mostly from the reign of Jehoiakim
21:1-25:38	Shorter prophecies, against the kings of Judah and false prophets
26:1-29:32	Biography of Jeremiah
30:1-31:40	Consolation for the Exile
32:1-44:30	Biography of Jeremiah, continued
45:1-5	Oracle promising deliverance to Baruch
46:1-51:64	Oracle against foreign nations
52:1-34	Appendix on the fall of Jerusalem

JEREMOTH, JERIMOTH
1. Fourth son of Bela, firstborn son of Benjamin.
2. Sixth son of Becher, second son of Benjamin.
3. Third of the many sons of Beriah in the genealogy of King Saul.
4. One of the men of Benjamin who defected from the armies of Saul and joined David at Ziklag. He could use both his right and left hand to hurl stones and shoot arrows.
5. A Levite, third son of Mushi, second son of Merari.
6. A Levite, the fifth of the 14 sons of Heman who played music in the House of the Lord at the time of King David; he was in charge of the 15th division of musicians.
7. Son of Ariel; leader of the tribe of Naphtali in King David's time.
8. A son of David, husband of Abihail; their daughter Mahalath married King Rehoboam of Judah.
9. A Levite who helped supervise the treasure of the Temple during King Hezekiah's reign.
10. A son of Elam who, having taken a pagan wife, had to repudiate her upon the decree of Ezra.
11. A son of Zattu who, having taken a pagan wife, had to repudiate her upon the decree of Ezra.
12. See RUMOTH No.1.

JERIAH, JERIJAH The firstborn son of Hebron the third son of Kohath; he headed the Hebronite family at the time of King David.
JERIBAI One of the two sons of Elnaam who were among David's "mighty men".

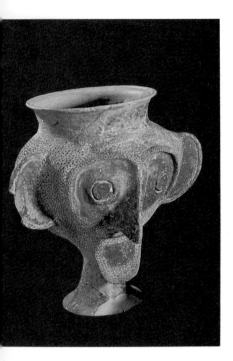

Clay anthropomorphic jar from Jericho. Middle Bronze Age.

(top right)
Excavations showing fortifications at ancient Jericho.

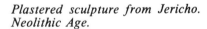

Plastered sculpture from Jericho. Neolithic Age.

JERICHO A city in the territory of Benjamin, near the Jordan, opposite the plains of Moab (Num 22:1); it gave its name to the valley of Jericho (Deut 34:3), and to the plains of Jericho (Josh 4:13); it was also known as the city of palm trees (Deut 34:3; Judg 3:13; II Chr 28:15). The hot climate, the plentiful water and the excellent arable soil attracted settlers as far back as the dawn of history; but despite its prominence at various periods, it is never mentioned in extra-biblical historical sources.

Jericho is situated near the Jordan River crossings on the way to Jerusalem and hence its strategic importance. For the Children of Israel Jericho was a key point in the penetration and conquest of Canaan, and for this reason the capture of the city is described in the Bible in greater detail than any other conquest. While still at Shittim, Joshua sent two spies to reconnoiter the land, with specific reference to Jericho (Josh 2:1). The city apparently had a single gate and was surrounded by a strong wall, with houses built into the wall, having windows looking out of the town (Josh 2:5, 15). After the spies completed their mission with the help of Rahab the harlot "About forty thousand prepared for war crossed over before the Lord for battle, to the plains of Jericho" (Josh 4:13). But "Jericho was securely shut up" (Josh 6:1) and could not be taken by assault. The Children of Israel compassed the city once a day for six days. On the seventh day they compassed it seven times: finally the priests blew their horns and the people were ordered to shout, whereupon the walls fell down and the city was stormed and set on fire (Josh 6:15, 20, 24), with only Rahab being saved (Josh 6:25). Joshua proclaimed "Cursed be the man before the Lord who rises up and builds this city Jericho; he shall lay its foundation with his firstborn and with his youngest son he shall set up its gates" (Josh 6:26).

At a later date King Eglon of Moab, in alliance with the Ammonites and Amalekites, conquered the city of palm trees, apparently wresting it from the hands of the Israelites who had a small settlement there (Judg 3:13). It was inhabited again in the time of David (II Sam 10:5). In the days of Ahab "Hiel of Bethel built Jericho. He laid its foundation with Abiram his firstborn, and with his youngest son Segub he set up its gates, according to the word of the Lord, which he had spoken through

JERICHO
**Num 22:1;
26:3, 63;
31:12; 33:48,
50; 34:15;
35:1; 36:13.
Deut 32:49;
34:1, 3. Josh
2:1-3; 3:16;
4:13, 19; 5:10,
13; 6:1-2,
25-26; 7:2;
8:2; 9:3; 10:1,
28, 30; 12:9;
13:32; 16:1, 7;
18:12, 21;
20:8; 24:11.
II Sam 10:5.
I Kgs 16:34.
II Kgs 2:4-5,
15, 18; 25:5.
I Chr 6:78;
19:5. II Chr
28:15. Ezra
2:34. Neh 3:2;
7:36. Jer 39:5;
52:8. Matt
20:29. Mark
10:46. Luke
10:30; 18:35;
19:1. Heb
11:30**

Joshua the son of Nun" (I Kgs 16:34). Nevertheless, by his act, the curse was apparently lifted, and the sons of the prophets were subsequently to be found there (II Kgs 2:5). Elijah sojourned at Jericho before his ascent to heaven (II Kgs 2:4). Elisha cured the malignant waters of Jericho (II Kgs 2:18-22). On the return from the Babylonian Exile, 345 men from Jericho went back to their city (Neh 7:36) and some of them participated in the building of the walls of Jerusalem (Neh 3:2).

Ancient Jericho has long been identified with Tell es-Sultan, near the copious spring of Ain es-Sultan, a mile (1.6 km) northwest of modern Jericho. The ancient mound extends over an area of 8 1/2 acres (3.5 ha). It is more than 4 miles (6.5 km) to the west of the Jordan and lies some 750 feet (c. 320m) below sea level.

The first excavations at Jericho were conducted over a hundred years ago, and these were followed by numerous teams of archeologists who aspired to find the fallen walls of Jericho, and to find a natural explanation for the biblical narrative. Another problem which intrigued the researchers was the date of the city's conquest by the Children of Israel. None of these aims has been satisfactorily achieved. However, excavations of early Jericho revolutionized knowledge of the development of civilization in the ancient Near East. Jericho is without doubt the earliest known city in the world.

Aerial view of Herod's palace south of present-day Jericho. (Courtesy Ehud Netzer)

In the Early Bronze Age, Jericho was a turbulent city, affected by frequent wars and earthquakes. Its walls were destroyed, repaired or rebuilt no less than 17 times in the course of the 3rd millennium B.C.

In the Middle Bronze Age I (2100-1900 B.C.) there was a period of decline apparently caused by the invasion of nomadic Semitic tribes who wrought devastation.

Jericho underwent drastic change in the Later Middle Bronze Age. The town was now surrounded by a massive glacis, a huge earth embankment, covered by plaster, over which mud brick walls were built. The destruction of this city is dated to the mid-16th century B.C. when the Egyptians reconquered the country from the Hyksos.

Nothing remains of the Late Bronze Age city which preceded the conquest by Joshua. There is no consensus among scholars as to the date of that conquest, although the dates suggested range between 1400 and 1250 B.C.

Stoa at Herod's palace, Jericho.

The finds pertaining to Iron Age Jericho (1200-330 B.C.) are not rich, but generally confirm the evidence of the Bible. It is doubtful if a settlement existed during the time of the Judges and at the beginning of the period of the Israelite kingdom. The city grew considerably in the 9th-7th centuries B.C.

By the end of the Israelite period (7th-6th centuries B.C.) the town expanded. Jericho suffered the fate of the other Judean towns when it was destroyed by the Babylonians in 587 B.C. In the period of the return from Babylonian captivity only a small portion of the northern and western parts of the mound was settled. Ancient Jericho was abandoned in the Hellenistic period, and the Hasmoneans and Herod built palaces at a new site to the south of the old town.

JERIEL Third son of Tola, firstborn son of Issachar.

JERIOTH ("tents"). Second wife of Caleb son of Hezron.

JEROBOAM ("may the people grow numerous").

1. Jeroboam I, son of Nebat from Zeredah in Ephraim (I Kgs 11:26); the first king of the Northern Kingdom of Israel (928-907 B.C.). Under Solomon he had been in charge of the corvée of the tribes of Ephraim and Manasseh but later rebelled against the king (I Kgs 11:26-28). The prophet, Ahijah the Shilonite, through the symbolic act of tearing his robe into 12 pieces and giving ten of them to Jeroboam, foretold that

Jasper Hebrew seal found at Megiddo showing a lion and inscribed "[Belonging] to Shema servant of Yeroboam" (Jeroboam). 8th century B.C. (Rockefeller Museum, Jerusalem)

The name Jeroboam appears on a coin struck in Samaria in the 4th century B.C.

Jeroboam would rule over ten of the twelve tribes of Israel after Solomon's death. When Solomon attempted to kill Jeroboam, the latter fled to Egypt and was protected by King Shishak until Solomon died (I Kgs 11:29-49). Upon his return after Solomon's death and the accession of Rehoboam, Jeroboam was appointed king by the leaders of the people at Shechem after Rehoboam had refused to ease the load on the people (I Kgs 12:20). Thus northern Israel became politically independent from the house of David and continual warfare persisted between the two kingdoms throughout his reign (I Kgs 14:30; II Chr 13:3-19). Among his varied activities Jeroboam fortified Shechem as his first capital, then Penuel in Transjordan (I Kgs 12:25), and finally made Tirzah his capital as alluded to by I Kings 14:17. He placed golden calves in Bethel and Dan, turning these places into holy shrines in competition with Jerusalem. According to I Kings 14:1-18, when his son Abijah fell sick, his mother went in disguise to the prophet Ahijah who predicted the boy's death and the eventual doom of Jeroboam's house. The kingdom was ravaged in the fifth year of Jeroboam's reign, by Shishak the king of Egypt (I Kgs 14:25-28; II Chr 12:2-12); and the inscription on the walls of the temple of Karnak in Egypt tells of this campaign. As Jeroboam's kingdom was weakened, Abijah, king of Judah, succeeded in conquering territories in southern Ephraim (II Chr 13:3-19).

13:1, 4, 33-34; 14:1-2, 4-7, 10-11, 13-14, 16-17, 19-20, 30; 15:1, 6-7, 9, 25, 29-30, 34; 16:2-3, 7, 19, 26, 31; 21:22; 22:52. II Kgs 3:3; 9:9; 10:29, 31; 13:2, 6, 11; 14:24; 15:9, 18, 24, 28; 17:21-22; 23:15. II Chr 9:29; 10:2-3, 12, 15; 11:4, 14; 12:15; 13:1-4, 6, 8, 13, 15, 19-20

2. Jeroboam II (reigned 789-748 B.C.). Son of Joash, king of Israel, the most important ruler of the Jehu dynasty. He continued his father's policy in campaigning against Aram-Damascus, and managed to reconquer Damascus and Hamath from them as a result of the weakening of the Aramean kingdom caused by the campaigns of Adad-Nirari III and Shalmaneser IV, kings of Assyria (II Kgs 14:23-28). These wars brought Israel into a new era — that of being a first-class political power in southern and central Syria. Peaceful relations existed during his reign between Israel and Judah, and the two kingdoms carried out a combined census in Transjordan (I Chr 5:17). The renewed prosperity led to the creation of a wealthy class of landowners, against whom the prophet Amos protested.

JEROBOAM 2 II Kgs 13:13; 14:16, 23, 27-29; 15:1, 8. I Chr 5:17. Hos 1:1. Amos 1:1; 7:9-11

JEROHAM ("may the Lord be compassionate").

1. A man of Ephraim, father of Elkanah and son of Elihu (I Sam 1:1; given as Eliel in I Chr 6:34); he was the father of Elkanah and grandfather of the prophet Samuel.

JEROHAM 1 I Sam 1:1. I Chr 6:27, 34

2. Father of Jaareshiah, Elijah and Zichri. Mentioned in the genealogy of King Saul, they were among those who dwelled in Jerusalem after the return from the Exile.

3. Father of Ibneiah who dwelled in Jerusalem after the return of the exiles; perhaps identical with No.2.

4. A priest dwelling in Jerusalem after the return from the Exile in Babylon; son of Pashur and father of Adaiah.

5. A man of Gedor, father of Joelah and Zebadiah, two men of Benjamin who defected from the army of Saul and joined David at Ziklag.

6. Father of Azarel, who led the tribe of Dan at the time of King David.

7. Father of Azariah, one of the captains of Jehoiada in the revolt against Queen Athaliah.

JERUBBAAL The name given to Gideon after he had destroyed his father's altar of Baal.

JERUBBESHETH Form of Jerubbaal (i.e. Gideon). The second element "Besheth" — "shame" was substituted for "Baal", interpreted as the name of the Canaanite deity.

JERUEL A wilderness; the scene of the defeat of the enemies of Judah — Ammonites, Moabites and Meunites — by the armies of King Jehoshaphat. It probably lay in the vicinity of Tekoa.

JERUSALEM Ancient capital of the Kingdom of Israel; located in the midst of the Judean hill range, bordering on the Judean desert. Geographically it consists of two ridges surrounded by the Kidron and Hinnom valleys; a valley in the center (the Tyropoeon or Valley of Cheesemakers) existed in biblical times but was subsequently filled in. It is some 2,600 feet (790m) above sea level and situated strategically at the crossroads leading from north to south and east to west.

The earliest mention of the city of Jerusalem is found in the Egyptian Execration (curse) Texts from the 19th century B.C. The name itself is apparently of western Semitic (Canaanite) origin, composed of two elements, *yeru*, from a root meaning "to establish, raise up", and *shalem*, the name of a Canaanite god. The El Amarna Letters, an archive of the correspondence of Canaanite kings with their Egyptian masters (14th century B.C.), contain six letters of the ruler of Jerusalem. Little is known of Jerusalem's pre-conquest history.

Jerusalem is first mentioned in the Bible (as Shalem) in Genesis 14:18 in the story of Melchizedek and Abraham. This story shows that Jerusalem was a royal city and cultic site for the worship of "the Most High God" in the patriarchal period.

The Book of Joshua mentions Adoni-Zedek, king of Jerusalem, as the head of a coalition of Amorite kings in the south of Canaan who fought against four Hivite cities and was later defeated by Joshua at Gibeon. No mention is made, however, of Jerusalem's capture. After recording Joshua's death, the Book of Judges contains an account of the Judahites' capture of Jerusalem (Judg 1:8), but most scholars cast doubt on the historical reliability of this source (or assume that the capture was only temporary) and date Jerusalem's conquest to the days of David. During the period of the settlement, Jerusalem was a city of the Jebusites (called Jebus, Judg 19:10-11; I Chr 11:4-5), an ethnic group which may have been related to the Hittites (cf Ezek 16:3), whose land lay on the border between the territories of Benjamin and Judah.

The accounts of David's conquest of Jerusalem are somewhat obscure (II Sam 5:6-9; I Chr 11:4-7). II Samuel 5:6-9 tells of the stationing of blind and lame people on the city walls in an apparent effort to ward off David's attack. The city's considerable defenses may

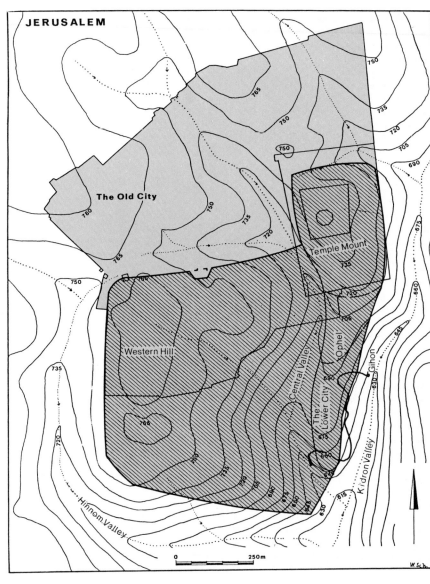

JERUSALEM

The Old City

Temple Mount

Western Hill

Central Valley

The Lower City

Ophel

Gihon

Kidron Valley

Hinnom Valley

0   250m

(right)
Jerusalem in the 8th-6th
centuries B.C.

General view of the City of David,
with the excavations on the left, the
El Aqsa mosque on the right and the
city walls in the background.

2, 4-6, 9, 13, 20, 23-24, 27, 30-31, 33, 36; 24:4, 8, 10, 14-15, 18, 20; 25:1, 8-10. I Chr 3:4-5; 6:10, 15, 32; 8:28, 32; 9:3, 34, 38; 11:4; 14:3-4; 15:3; 18:7; 19:15; 20:1, 3; 21:4, 15:16; 23:25; 26:29; 28:1; 29:27. II Chr 1:4, 13-15; 2:7, 16; 3:1; 5:2; 6:6; 8:6; 9:1, 25, 27, 30; 10:18; 11:1, 5, 14, 16; 12:2, 4-5, 7, 9, 13; 13:2; 14:15; 15:10; 17:13; 19:1, 4, 8; 20:5, 15, 17-18, 20, 27-28, 31; 21:5, 11, 13, 20; 22:1-2; 23:2; 24:1, 6, 9, 18, 23; 25:1, 23, 27; 26:3, 9, 15; 27:1, 8; 28:1, 10, 24, 27; 29:1, 8; 30:1-3, 5, 11, 13-14, 21, 26; 31:4; 32:2, 9-10, 12, 18-19, 22-23, 25-26, 33; 33:1, 4, 7, 9, 13, 15, 21; 34:1, 3, 5, 7, 9, 22, 29-30, 32; 35:1, 18, 24; 36:1-5, 9-11, 14, 19, 23. Ezra 1:2-5, 7, 11; 2:1, 68; 3:1, 8; 4:6, 8, 12, 20, 23-24; 5:1-2, 14-17; 6:3, 5, 9, 12, 18; 7:7-9, 13-17, 19, 27; 8:29-32; 9:9; 10:7, 9. Neh 1:2-3; 2:11-13, 17, 20; 3:8-9, 12; 4:7-8, 22; 6:7; 7:2-3, 6; 8:15; 11:1-4, 6, 22, 27-29, 43; 13:6-7, 15-16, 19-20. Est 2:6. Ps 51:18;

have been thwarted by the attackers having gained access through a tunnel, possibly that leading to the Gihon spring outside the city. I Chronicles 11:4-7, on the other hand, makes no mention of this stratagem and portrays the conquest rather idealistically as an act of military prowess.

The conquest of Jerusalem by David, who made it the capital of Israel, was an important step in consolidating his kingdom. The choice of a "neutral" site that is, one not belonging to a tribe, aided its acceptance as the royal capital and religious center for the entire kingdom, and demonstrates David's political foresight. Once the capital was established it became the civil and administrative hub of the kingdom. After building for himself a cedar palace, David aspired to build a temple for the God of Israel (II Sam chap. 7); but this was in fact carried out by his son Solomon (I Kgs chap. 6). Solomon's building activities made Jerusalem an international capital and the sanctified city and center for the worship of Israel's God.

Solomon's glory, however, was shortlived. The rapid internationalization of the kingdom brought with it the influx of foreign influences, reflected in the Bible in the shrines to the foreign gods Solomon built for his many wives. Solomon's extensive building projects made relations with the northern tribes tense and led them to complain of the heavy burden placed upon them (I Kgs 12:4ff). Thus the Bible provides both religious and political motivation for the division of the kingdom which occurred after Solomon's death. With the division, and up to the days of King Jehoshaphat, Jerusalem declined in importance. It was saved from Pharaoh Shishak's siege only by the payment of a heavy tribute from the treasuries of the Temple, which contained all the wealth accumulated by David and Solomon (I Kgs 14:25-26). A similar "bribe" had to be paid to Ben-Hadad, king of Syria, in order to encourage him to break his treaty with King Baasha of Israel who was threatening Jerusalem during the internecine conflict between the two divided kingdoms (I Kgs 15:16ff). The Bible mentions that King Asa tried to uproot the idolatrous worship that had taken hold in Jerusalem (I Kgs 15:12-13).

During King Jehoshaphat's reign, however, Jerusalem apparently returned somewhat to its former standing, according to the account in the Book of Chronicles (II Chr 17:7ff), and relations with the Northern Kingdom of Israel improved (II Kgs 8:18). But again, with improved relations with foreign countries — this time Tyre — idolatrous worship gained renewed ground in the holy city under the influence of Jezebel the Phoenician wife of King Ahab and their daughter, Athaliah, wife of King Jehoram of Judah (II Kgs 8:18, 27).

With King Joash's accession to the throne came a period of reform, with the help of the high priest Jehoaida, and the Temple was purified of the idols (II Kgs chaps. 11-12). But internal power struggles weakened the kingdom, and soon Jerusalem was again under siege from an invading army — this time that of Hazael, king of Aram (II Kgs 12:17-18). Joash was eventually assassinated by his servants, an indication of the condition of the court and the kingdom (II Kgs 12:20-21).

Fluctuations in Jerusalem's status continued until the days of King Hezekiah, who instituted extensive reforms and purges of foreign worship (II Kgs 18:1-6; II Chr chaps. 29-31). But again, in line with the pattern already established in the historiographical accounts of the Books of Kings, a foreign invader appeared on the scene — the powerful Assyrian army under Sennacherib, who in 701 B.C. laid siege to Jerusalem (II Kgs 18:13ff). Once again the Book of Kings presents the impending national disaster as punishment for the behavior of the king

(bottom of page)
Pottery heads from the City of David excavations: the three on the left are of the Iron Age II; the one on the right is of the Byzantine period.

Pottery vessels found in the "Bullae house", at the City of David. 586 B.C.

(II Kgs 20:12-18; Is 39:1ff). Sennacherib boasts of his siege of Jerusalem in one of his royal inscriptions that he held Hezekiah "like a bird in a cage". According to the biblical account, only divine intervention prevented the destruction of Jerusalem at this time. Hezekiah was forced to submit and became an Assyrian vassal, after paying a heavy tribute (II Kgs 18:14-16). This indication of divine protection of the city eventually brought about a belief among the people that the Holy City, with its Temple, was inviolable — a notion vehemently upbraided by the prophet Jeremiah who reminded them that their well-being depended only on their righteous and moral conduct (Jer chap. 7).

Under King Josiah, independence was regained and the infamous high places, which competed with Jerusalem and the Jerusalemite priesthood in the worship of the Lord, were finally destroyed. The Assyrian empire was inherited by the Babylonians, while within Judah, factions took sides either with Egypt or with Babylonia, playing one power against the other. King Jehoiakim succeeded in temporarily breaking loose from the yoke of Babylonia, only to be subdued again by its king, Nebuchadnezzar (II Kgs 24:1-2). Zedekiah, the last of the Davidic kings, also attempted to cast off Babylonian vassalage. His lack

Bullae from the end of the Judean kingdom, found in the destruction level at the City of David.

of success brought about the final destruction of Jerusalem in 586 B.C. after an extended final siege (II Kgs 25:1-21). The Babylonians razed the city and its Temple to the ground. After the destruction of the Temple and the looting of its treasures by Nebuchadnezzar, the history of Jerusalem entered a dark period.

No clear accounts of Jerusalem's history after the destruction have remained. Jeremiah tells of people with shaved beards and torn clothes who came from Shechem, Shiloh and Samaria to the ruined Temple with offerings to the Lord (Jer 41:5). The most poignant expression of the anguish over Jerusalem's fate is perhaps Psalm 137:5 "If I forget you O Jerusalem...". The day of the destruction, the ninth day of the month of Ab, became a day of fasting and mourning (Zech 7:3-7). Despite the destruction of the Temple and razing of the city, Jerusalem retained its standing as the holy city and the focus of hopes that the Temple would be rebuilt, as prophesied by the prophets Jeremiah and Ezekiel. On the other hand, Ezekiel castigated those who survived the catastrophe and remained in Jerusalem, thinking themselves to have been saved because of their righteousness (Ezek 11:1-13).

23:4; 24:2; 26:2; 33:21; 36:38. Dan 1:1; 5:2-3; 6:10; 9:2, 7, 12, 16, 25. Joel 2:32; 3:1, 6, 16-17, 20. Amos 1:2; 2:5. Obad vs. 11, 20. Mic 1:1, 5, 9, 12; 3:10, 12; 4:2, 8. Zeph 1:4, 12; 3:14, 16. Zech 1:12, 14, 16-17, 19; 2:2, 4, 12; 3:2; 7:7; 8:3-4, 8, 15, 22; 9:9-10; 12:2-3, 5-11; 13:1; 14:2, 4, 8, 10-12, 14, 16-17, 21. Mal 2:11; 3:4. Matt 2:1, 3; 3:5; 4:25; 5:35; 15:1; 16:21; 20:17-18; 21:1, 10; 23:37. Mark 1:5; 3:8, 22; 7:1; 10:32-33; 11:1, 11, 15, 27, 41. Luke 2:22, 25, 38, 41-43, 45, 4:9; 5:17; 6:17; 9:31, 51, 53; 10:30; 13:4, 22, 33-34; 17:11; 18:31; 19:11, 28; 21:20, 24; 23:7, 28; 24:13, 18, 33, 47, 49, 52. John 1:19; 2:13, 23; 4:20-21, 45; 5:1-2; 7:25; 10:22; 11:18, 55; 12:12. Acts 1:4, 8, 12, 19; 2:5, 14; 4:6, 16; 5:16, 28; 6:7; 8:1, 14, 25-27; 9:2, 13, 21, 26, 28; 10:39; 11:2, 22, 27; 12:25; 13:13, 27, 31; 15:2, 4; 16:4; 18:21; 19:21; 20:16, 22; 21: 4, 11-13, 15, 17, 31; 22:5, 17-18; 23:11; 24:11; 25:1, 3,

(top left and center)
Silver plaque, 7th century B.C., bearing a fragment of the Priestly Benediction (Numbers 6:24-26). It was found rolled up as a cylinder scroll in one of the burial caves in the Hinnom Valley.

(top right)
Pottery assemblage from the Hinnom Valley burial caves. 7th-6th centuries B.C.

(left)
Burial cave complex with burial niches of the First Temple period, in the grounds of the Monastery of St Etienne in Jerusalem.

(left)
Stone headrest for the deceased on a burial bench in the St Etienne tomb complex.

Two of the elaborate burial chambers at St Etienne, arranged one behind the other. Note the upper cornices and the benches with the headrests.

The Babylonian empire was conquered, in turn, by the Persians, who thus inherited the rule over Palestine as well. Persian policy differed greatly from the Babylonian and Assyrian policy of deportation and brute subjection, and actually encouraged the exiled Israelites to return to their homeland and rebuild the Temple. Cyrus' famous decree (538 B.C.), giving freedom to return to Israel and rebuild the Temple, is recounted in the first chapter of the Book of Ezra. At the head of the first returnees was Sheshbazzar, the prince of Judah, who drove a spike into the city's ruins as sign of the rebuilding work to come, reconsecrated the altar and laid the foundations of the Temple. A generation later, in the days of Darius I the number of returnees had significantly increased; motivation to rebuild the Temple was reawakened at the encouragement of the prophets Haggai and Zechariah. Leading the people were the Davidic descendant Zerubbabel and the high priest Jeshua. The opposition of various parties overcome, the rebuilding of the Temple was finally completed in 515/6 B.C., though it was of modest proportions. With the completion of the Temple Jerusalem gradually regained its status as the political and religious center of Israel, though with the eventual collapse of the Davidic lineage, the priestly classes became the effectual leaders of the people and Jerusalem became essentially a city of priests and Temple servants.

Conflicts arose with the Samaritans, who were not allowed to participate in the rebuilding of the Temple (Ezra 4:3), being considered an impure blend of races as a result of assimilation and mixed marriage with the populations relocated in Samaria by the Assyrians and Babylonians.

The real solidification of the spiritual and national life of the returned exiles in Jerusalem and Judah took place with the arrival of the priest and scribe Ezra, who was commissioned by the Persian king Xerxes to establish the laws of the Torah in Judah. Efforts were directed toward rebuilding the walls of Jerusalem, which was opposed by the Samaritans, who did their best to frustrate the refortification of the city (Ezra 4:7ff), and even informed the Persian authorities of the Judahites' intentions insinuating that the latter were preparing to rebel against Persian rule. This ploy succeeded in stopping the work for a time (Ezra 4:23), but when Nehemiah, one of Xerxes' Jewish ministers, heard about it, he asked the king for permission to return to Jerusalem, the city of his forefathers' graves, and rebuild it (Neh 2:5). The king granted his request and even appointed him governor with wide-ranging authority. Again, this did not go unopposed — the previous tactics were employed both from within and from without (Neh 6:6-14), but Nehemiah's strong personality and official position gave him the necessary advantage to overcome the difficulties. The builders of the wall had one hand on the bricks and the other on the spear (Neh 4:16-17). Finally, after 52 days' labor, the work was completed (Neh 6:15) and a great celebration was held (Neh 12:27ff). Nehemiah then set out to rebuild the city itself and repopulate it, casting lots and bringing one out of every ten from the cities of Judah to settle in Jerusalem (Neh 1:1-2). Jerusalem again became the religious and administrative capital of Judah and even prospered economically.

The last information the OT provides of the history of Jerusalem is the list of high priests who served in the time of Nehemiah (Neh 12:22-26), which indicates that the status of the high priest remained strong. Beyond this very little is known until the conquest of Palestine by Alexander the Great, when Jerusalem came within the Hellenistic orbit. An attempt was made by the Syrian rulers to establish a parallel Hellenized city on its western ridge. When Antiochus IV Ephiphanes

7, 9, 15, 20, 24; 26:4, 10, 20; 28:17. Rom 15:19, 25-26, 31. I Cor 16:3. Gal 1:17-18; 2:1; 4:25-26. Heb 12:22. Rev 3:12; 21:2, 10.

The excavations near the western side of the Temple showing "Robinson's Arch" and some of the Herodian remains.

attempted to impose Hellenism by force and desecrate the Temple, the revolt led by Judas Maccabee began. After two years of struggle, Judas finally succeeded in conquering Jerusalem and restored the Temple service (164 B.C.).

Steps once leading to the Gate of Huldah from the City of David.

In the Hasmonean period, Jerusalem again became the capital of the whole land of Israel and this lasted until 63 B.C. when the Roman general, Pompey, profiting from the fraternal warfare between the Hasmoneans was able to occupy Jerusalem. From 37 B.C. it was ruled by Herod as a Roman vassal, and he was responsible for grandiose building projects, especially the reconstruction and expansion of the Temple into a magnificent edifice. The seat of Roman government was in Caesarea but Jerusalem remained the national, economic and spiritual center of the Jews, home of the king and the Sanhedrin. After Herod's death and the deposition of his son and successor, Archelaus in A.D. 6, the country was ruled by Roman procurators. During the rule of one of these, Pontius Pilate, Jesus was crucified in Jerusalem. After his death, the city became holy not only to Jews but also to Christians.

Jerusalem is mentioned 144 times in the NT. The priest Zacharias was visited in the Temple in Jerusalem by an angel, who announced the birth of Jesus' forerunner John the Baptist (Luke 1:5-25). The wise men, having seen the star in the east, came to Jerusalem, the religious center, to seek the newborn "King of the Jews" (Matt 2:1-12). When the days for post-natal purification were completed, the infant Jesus was

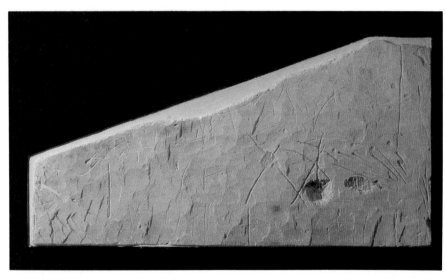

Graffito on the wall of a tomb chamber of the early 6th century B.C. This is the only known inscription from the First Temple period mentioning Jerusalem by name.

brought to Jerusalem to be presented to the Lord, as prescribed in the Mosaic law, since he was the firstborn male of his mother. Jesus' childhood and early manhood was spent, however, in Galilee.

When he was twelve years old, his parents who "went to Jerusalem every year at the feast of Passover" took him along. On the return journey they found he was missing and returned to Jerusalem where he was in the Temple listening to and questioning the Sages (Luke 2:41ff).

On his last journey to Jerusalem, around the time of Passover, Jesus, viewing the city from the Mount of Olives, expressed his feelings crying out "O Jerusalem, Jerusalem" (Matt 23:37-39; Luke 13:34-35) and later weeping over it, while prophesying its destruction (Luke 19:41-44; cf Is 29:3; Jer 6:6; Ezek 4:2), but not before making a triumphant entry into the city where he was proclaimed by his disciples (Luke 19:38). Jesus then proceeded to the Temple where, seeing the commerce in doves and the money-changers, he overturned their tables and cast them out. Afterwards, he continued teaching in the Temple, arousing the ire of the Pharisees and other religious parties. Jesus' final meal with his disciples was the Passover feast, which took place in an upper room in a private house in Jerusalem (Matt 26:18; Mark 14:13-15; Luke 22:10-12).

After the dramatic meal, Jesus together with his disciples went to the

Mount of Olives to pray (Luke 22:39ff). Here he was arrested and was brought the following day before the Jewish religious high court, the Sanhedrin, which had its seat in Jerusalem, and accused of blasphemy (Luke 22:66ff). He was subsequently taken before the Roman governor, Pilate, and the Jewish ruler, Herod Antipas, in Jerusalem.

Jesus was crucified, according to the law, outside the city gates (John 19:20). After his death on the cross, he was buried, presumably nearby, in the tomb of Joseph of Arimathea (Luke 23:50-53).

After the resurrection, Jesus is reported to have appeared repeatedly over a 40-day period to the apostles at Jerusalem (Luke 24:33-49; John 20:19-29; Acts 1:1-4), charging them to remain there until the day of Pentecost, when they were to be baptized in the Holy Spirit. Acts 1:12 tells of Jesus' ascension into the heavens as taking place on the Mount of Olives.

Virtually every site and event related to Jesus in Jerusalem came to be commemorated in some kind of shrine. Much controversy, however, surrounds these identifications, which have become fixed mostly by tradition. After Constantine the Great adopted Christianity, his mother Helena went to Palestine in 326 and her visit became associated with Constantine's building of the first great Christian churches, the Church of the Holy Sepulcher, the Church of the Nativity in nearby Bethlehem, and the Church of the Ascension on the Mount of Olives. From this time dates the beginning of organized Christian pilgrimage to Jerusalem.

The church came into being on the day of Pentecost in Jerusalem (Acts 4:23-31), and the first martyrdom took place outside the city gates (Acts 7:58). It is said that the early church met in private houses, breaking bread daily, as well as meeting in the Temple (Acts 2:42-47). Persecution, however, did not cease, and is illustrated in Stephen's martyrdom (Acts chap. 7). Acts 8:1 relates that in the wake of Stephen's stoning there was a great persecution against the church in Jerusalem, and its members were scattered.

The church in Jerusalem was for a time the center of the early church's activity, although apparently its authority did not override the autonomy of churches in other localities, nor did the apostles centered in Jerusalem exercise absolute authority, as witnessed in the case of Paul. Though there was a conference in Jerusalem (Acts 15:2ff), it took place there not because Jerusalem was the head church, but because it was the source of the problem (the demand for new members to be circumcised).

The destruction of Jerusalem in the NT comes to symbolize the end of the old order and the beginning of the church ages, though for the Jews, once again the symbol of their national and religious autonomy was destroyed by a foreign invader — this time Rome, in A.D. 70.

The Book of Revelation presents a picture of the "New Jerusalem" in which God will dwell with his people for eternity. Paul presents the "Jerusalem above, (which) is free", in contrast to the bondage of the Jerusalem below, as "the mother of us all", in an allegorical exposition of the story of Hagar and Sarah (Gal 4:21-31). The author of the Epistle to the Hebrews refers to the church as "the city of the living God, the heavenly Jerusalem" (Heb 12:22). These passages reveal a more spiritual and idealistic view of Jerusalem, which inspired thoughts of utopian perfection and messianic redemption.

Since the middle of the 19th century, numerous archeologists have excavated in and around Jerusalem. The one area where excavations have not been conducted is the Temple Mount, now a Moslem holy site where digging is forbidden.

The original site of Jerusalem was the City of David, southeast of the present Old City. This was a 15-acre (6 ha) area settled first by the Canaanites and then by David. Under Solomon, the Temple Mount was added, extending the area of the city to 37 acres (15 ha). Jerusalem was the royal center and structures have been discovered indicating the existence of monumental buildings. The Israelite acropolis was apparently built over its Canaanite predecessor.

Rich finds have been made from the later Israelite period (8th to 6th centuries B.C.) when the city with the addition of the western hill attained its greatest extent (137 acres, 55.5 ha). A section of the city wall has been uncovered from this time, 380 feet (120m) long and 15 feet (4.5m) wide. The plan for the reconstruction of the city evidently originated in the days of Hezekiah when the Siloam tunnel (see SHILOAH) was constructed to safeguard the water supply, which had always been problematic as the city was dependent on sources outside its walls. Evidence of the destruction of the city by Nebuchadnezzar shows total devastation.

A pillar commemorating the Tenth Roman Legion in the Old City of Jerusalem.

(right)
The so-called burnt house recently excavated in the Old City of Jerusalem; Second Temple period.

Recent excavations have thrown much light on the city in Second Temple times. In the Persian and Hellenistic periods the city was confined to the Temple Mount and the area of the City of David. Archeological finds of coins stamped with the name "Judah" apparently reveal that the province of Judah and Jerusalem maintained a status of autonomy within the Persian empire, with the right to mint its own coins. Under the Hasmoneans, the western hill was again incorporated. In the last century before its destruction, the city limits were expanded northward. Jerusalem was defended by three walls and protected on the south and west by steep valleys. The earliest foundations of the wall date back to the time of Hezekiah and it was reconstructed along the same course in the Hasmonean period. It contained 60 towers, one of which forms the base of the present Tower of David. Sections of this first wall have been uncovered. The second wall was built in the 1st century B.C. and enclosed a wider area than its predecessor. Under Herod, the Temple was doubled in size. The Western (or Wailing) Wall was part of its external enclosure. New

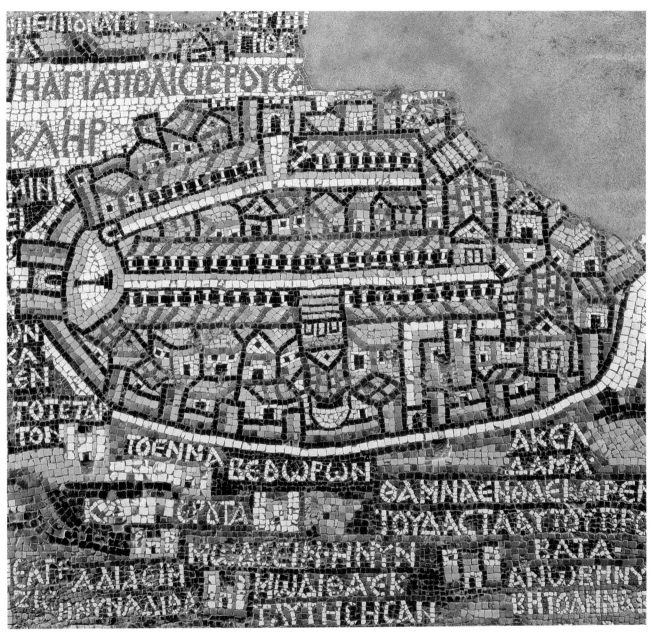

Jerusalem as it appears on the Medeba Map, discovered during excavations of the 6th-century St George's church at Medeba.

excavations have uncovered much of the rest of this western wall (which was 1,600 feet [490m] long), the southern wall — with the steps leading up to the Temple entrance — and the streets and building that adjoined them. The exact location of the Temple on the Temple Mount remains a subject of controversy.

Following the northern expansion in the 1st century, a third wall was built to enclose the northern side of the city. It has been explored for over half a mile (c. 1km) (only its foundations are preserved). The rebuilding of the Jewish Quarter after 1967 enabled extensive excavations in that area and many finds were made including the remains of houses destroyed by the Romans in A.D. 70. By that time the necropolis of Jerusalem surrounded the city on all sides, especially to the east (below the city and up the slopes of the Mount of Olives) and the north. About 700 tombs have been surveyed including those of the family of Herod. All these finds have thrown much light on the appearance of Jerusalem during the historic millennium from its capture by David until its destruction at the hands of the Romans.

Airview from the north of the Temple Mount with the Dome of the Rock in the center.

Airview of excavations along the southern side of the Temple area, looking west.

JERUSHA, JERUSHAH ("inheritance"). Daughter of Zadok, wife of Uzziah king of Judah and the mother of his son Jotham who succeeded him (II Kgs 15:32-33).

JERUSHA, JERUSHAH
II Kgs 15:33.
II Chr 27:1

JESHAIAH ("Yah has saved").

(Note: Hebrew spelling identical to that of Isaiah).

JESHAIAH 1
I Chr 25:3, 15

1. Third son of Jeduthun and head of the eighth division of musicians in the House of the Lord at the time of King David.

JESHAIAH 2
I Chr 26:25

2. Grandson of Eliezer the son of Moses; one of the Levites in charge of the Temple treasury.

JESHAIAH 3
I Chr 3:21

3. Second son of Hananiah, a descendant of Zerubbabel.

JESHAIAH 4
Ezra 8:7

4. Son of Athaliah and head of the family of the sons of Elam who returned from the Exile in Babylon with Ezra.

JESHAIAH 5
Ezra 8:19

5. A Merarite Levite, one of the men brought back from Casiphia to Ezra to serve in the Temple.

JESHAIAH 6
Neh 11:7

6. A man of Benjamin, ancestor of Sallu No.1 who settled in Jerusalem after the return of the exiles from Babylon.

JESHANAH
II Chr 13:19

JESHANAH One of the towns taken from King Jeroboam I of Israel, by King Abijah of Judah. It was in the mountains of Ephraim, by the northern border of Mount Beth El.

JESHARELAH
I Chr 25:14

JESHARELAH An alternate name for Asharelah; a musician who headed the seventh division of singers in the House of the Lord at the time of King David.

JESHEBEAB
I Chr 24:13

JESHEBEAB A Levite; he led the 14th division of priests in the House of the Lord at the time of King David.

JESHER
I Chr 2:18

JESHER ("[the Lord is] just"). Elder son of Caleb, the son of Hezron, by his wife Azubah.

JESHIMON
I Sam 23:19,
24; 26:1, 3

JESHIMON ("a waste" or "a desert"). A plain north of the wilderness of Maon and opposite the land of Hachilah where David hid from Saul. It is possibly located a few miles south of Hebron.

JESHISHAI
I Chr 5:14

JESHISHAI A man of Gad, father of Jahdo and son of Michael.

JESHOHAIAH
I Chr 4:36

JESHOHAIAH Head of a family of the tribe of Simeon.

JESHUA

JESHUA 1
I Chr 24:11.
Ezra 2:2, 36.
Neh 7:39

1. An Aaronite priest. The ninth of the 24 lots fell to him (I Chr 24:1, 11). He may be identical with the Jeshua listed as returning with Zerubbabel from the Babylonian captivity in Ezra 2:2, 36.

JESHUA 2
II Chr 31:15

2. A Levite who assisted King Hezekiah in distributing the offerings and tithes brought to the Temple.

JESHUA 3
Ezra 2:6. Neh
7:11

3. A branch of the Pahath-Moab family, some of whom returned with Zerubbabel from Babylonian captivity.

JESHUA 4
Ezra 2:40;
8:33. Neh
3:19; 7:43;
10:9; 12:8, 24

4. Members of a Levitical family or clan who returned from the Babylonian Exile. One member of this family, Ezer, worked on the construction of Nehemiah's wall and another was among those who signed the covenant of Ezra.

JESHUA 5
Ezra 3:2, 8;
4:3; 5:2; 10:18.
Neh 12:1, 7,
10, 26

5. Son of Jozadak (alternately Jehozadak) and high priest in Jerusalem, after the Babylonian Exile. Jeshua was the grandson of Seraiah who was the last high priest of the First Temple (I Chr 6:14-15). In Haggai and Zechariah his name is written "Joshua" (Hag 1:1, 12, 14; 2:2, 4; Zech 3:1, 3, 6, 8-9; 6:11).

Jeshua, head of the priestly family of Jedaiah (Ezra 2:36; Neh 7:39), helped organize the first group of exiles that returned to Jerusalem (Ezra 2:2; Neh 7:7).

The names of Jeshua and Zerubbabel are regularly mentioned together as the respective religious and civil leaders of the returning exiles (Ezra 3:2; Neh 2:1; Hag 1:1). They directed the rebuilding of the Temple and reestablished the sacrifices and the cult (Ezra 3:2-9; 5:2). When confronted by the Samaritans' request to join the rebuilding project, they declined the offer (Ezra 4:3).

Hebrew inscription on a sarcophagus of the 1st century A.D. It reads "Yeshua" (Jeshua). (Private Collection)

In the Book of Zechariah, Jeshua is a central figure in several of the visions of chapters 1-6. In chapter 3:1-10, he appears clothed in "filthy garments" and is called "a brand plucked from fire" (Zech 3:2). His old garments are exchanged for clean ones and he is installed into the service of God's house despite Satan's accusations. This vision depicts the purification and vindication of the new priestly line. The "brand plucked from fire" represents the survival of the priesthood in the wake of the destruction of the Temple and captivity.

In Zechariah 4:3, two olive trees appear which are identified as the "two anointed ones, who stand beside the Lord of the whole earth" (Zech 4:14). This is probably also a reference to Jeshua and Zerubbabel.

Finally, in Zechariah 6:9-14 Jeshua's name appears in a position that identifies him as "the Branch" — a term that bears messianic significance (Is 4:2; 11:1; Jer 23:5; 33:15). The passage refers to the ruling office that descends from the line of David, a position which Zerubbabel apparently occupied at the time of the book's writing. Later, this function was given to the high priest. Jeshua's name may have been substituted here in order to make this reference fit the later development. Some of his family are listed among those who took foreign wives during the time of Ezra (Ezra 10:18).

6. A Levite chief who helped oversee the building of the Temple after the return from the Babylonian Exile.

7. One of the Levites who helped explain the Law to the people at the time of Ezra and directed the public worship.

8. A town in southern Judah. It was occupied by some of the exiles returning from captivity (Neh 11:26).

It is identified with present-day Tell es-Sa'wi about 12 miles (20 km) northeast of Beersheba.

JESHURUN An appellation for the people of Israel which occurs only in poetic texts (Deut 32:15; 33:5, 26; Is 44:2). Many scholars derive the name from the Hebrew root meaning "upright".

JESIMIEL A man of Simeon, one of the leaders of the tribe.

JESSE A Bethlehemite from the tribe of Judah, son of Obed and grandson of Boaz and Ruth the Moabite; father of David. The phrase

JESHUA 6
Ezra 3:9

JESHUA 7
Neh 8:7; 9:4-5

JESHUA 8
Neh 11:26

JESHURUN
Deut 32:15; 33:5, 26. Is 44:2

JESIMIEL
I Chr 4:36

JESSE
Ruth 4:17, 22. I Sam 16:1, 3,

"son of Jesse" was apparently used by David's enemies to allude to his humble origins (I Sam 20:27, 30-31, etc.), but the term became a venerable one, so much so that it was predicted that the messiah would come from the "root of Jesse" (Is 11:10; cf 11:1; Rom 15:12). Jesse had eight sons (I Sam 16:10-11; 17:12). Seven are named in I Chronicles 2:13-15; and the eighth, Elihu, in I Chronicles 27:18.

Two sisters of David, Abigail and Zeruiah, are named in I Chronicles 2:16. Perhaps they were only step-daughters of Jesse, since Abigail is referred to as the "daughter of Nahash" (II Sam 17:25). It is twice mentioned that Jesse received a petition from King Saul to send David to the court (I Sam 16:14-23); and once he sent David to the battlefield to bring food supplies to his three eldest sons. This preceded David's famous duel with Goliath (I Sam 17:12ff). The circumstances of Jesse's death are unknown. I Samuel 22:3-4 says that when David's future was as yet unsure he placed his parents under the protection of the king of Moab. They are not mentioned again although verse 4 implies their return to Judah.

Jesse is named in the genealogies of Jesus (Matt 1:5-6; Luke 3:32) while Paul sees Jesus as fulfilling Isaiah's prophecy concerning the "root of Jesse" (Rom 15:12).

JESSHIAH The second son of Uzziel, a Levite.

JESUI, JESUITES (ISHVI, ISHVITES)

(Note: Hebrew spelling identical to that of Jishui).

A son of Asher, founder of the Jesuites family.

JESUS OF NAZARETH The central figure of, and the reason for, the NT and the Christian church.

While the gospels provide the great bulk of known information on the life of Jesus, some further knowledge has been preserved in the rest of the NT writings as well as in certain limited extra-biblical sources. The latter include non-canonical Christian writings, Jewish literature, and at least acknowledgement of Jesus' existence by some pagan historians. However, most of what appears in post-NT literature is either legendary fantasy or simply derivative from the gospel accounts.

Although probably composed prior to the appearance of any of the canonical gospels, Paul's epistles convey a modicum of information about Jesus: that he was descended from David (Rom 1:3), lived in the first half of the 1st century A.D., stood before the Roman governor Pontius Pilate (I Tim 6:13), died by crucifixion and rose from the dead. Paul never mentions Jesus' ministries of teaching, healing the sick or casting out of demons, and only rarely does he preserve a saying of Jesus.

Without the records of the four evangelists, biographical knowledge of Jesus of Nazareth would be sparse indeed. As it is, much remains untold. The Gospels of Matthew and Luke (the only two to give information on his life prior to baptism) relate that Jesus was a Jew, born in Bethlehem in the territory of the tribe of Judah, shortly before the death of Herod the Great (in 4 B.C.). His mother was Mary, at the time of the birth still a virgin and betrothed to Joseph (Matt 1:18), a carpenter of Judean descent living in Nazareth in Galilee. The exigencies of a census brought the family to Bethlehem where they found lodging only in a manger and there Jesus was born. His birth was accompanied by various signs and portents. The family with the young baby had to flee to Egypt because of Herod's "massacre of the innocents" (an incident unknown from any other source) and from there they returned to Nazareth, where Jesus grew up. Nothing is known of his childhood except for an incident at the age of 12 when he accompanied his parents to Jerusalem for the Passover feast (Luke 2:41

This 6th-century representation of Jesus is the oldest known hand-painted icon in the world. It is believed to have been inspired by the Holy Shroud of Edessa. (Santa Caterina Monastery Library, Sinai)

In the Grotto of the Nativity in Bethlehem this star marks the spot where Jesus was born. An inscription above reads: Hic de Virginie Maria Jesus Christus Natus Est — *"Here Jesus Christ was born to the Virgin Mary". Seventeen lamps above the star burn day and night.*

ff). The silence covering his early years continues until he is about 30 years old when he made his first public appearance in the Galilee region. Apart from the above-mentioned episodes, the entire story related in the gospels covers the events of the next two-three years. After his baptism by John the Baptist, a distant relative, and following a 40-day withdrawal to an unspecified "wilderness" for a period of spiritual testing, he began his ministry. Traveling to different parts of Galilee, he preached repentance and gathered a following of disciples, mostly lower-class Galileans. He evoked great popular enthusiasm from a populace eager for words of hope and prone to messianic expectations in view of their depressed circumstances under Roman rule.

Jesus' ministry was characterized by moral teaching largely in line with that of the Hillel school of Pharisaic Judaism. From a phrase used by Daniel and the rabbis, he took the name for his movement, the "Kingdom of God" or "of Heaven". He gave fresh meaning to this name as being any place or situation where God is actively reigning, and demonstrated this by healing numerous people of sickness and possession by devils. Among the miracles reported by the gospel writers are the multiplication of food to feed large numbers of people, walking on water, calming a storm with a word and raising the dead. Events such as these naturally gained him a reputation and a wide following.

The grotto below the Church of the Annunciation in Nazareth which, according to tradition, is the site where Mary, Joseph and Jesus lived. One of the columns shown here is called the "column of Gabriel", the other the "column of Mary". They mark the traditional spot where the Angel and Mary stood when the Annunciation of Jesus' birth took place.

After at least two years of this ministry, Jesus, accompanied by the more faithful of his followers, went to Jerusalem, predicting that he would die there. When he entered the city in the spring of A.D. 29 or 30, he was greeted by an enthusiastic crowd who had heard of his exploits, most recent of which was the raising of one, Lazarus, from the dead. However, he immediately encountered opposition from certain religious figures, foremost among them the leaders of the sect of the Sadducees, who denied the doctrine of resurrection and who felt threatened by the popular support for their revolutionary preacher and would-be reformer. These contracted with one of Jesus' disciples, Judas Iscariot, who offered to deliver Jesus into their hands. Fearing the reaction of the common people, who admired Jesus, the Sadducean leaders stipulated that the betrayal be accomplished discreetly. Judas chose the ideal time and place, outside the city, in the darkness of the night before Passover, when the masses were sure to be at home making preparations for the feast (or actually eating the Passover, depending on

the chronology adopted). Judas was accompanied by a "multitude" made up of elements from the Temple hierarchy and an indeterminate number of Roman soldiers. Taken first to the residence of the high priest for questioning, Jesus was finally condemned to death by the Roman procurator, Pontius Pilate. After being mocked and whipped and otherwise ill-treated by the soldiers, he was taken outside of the town and crucified. The common people, who awoke to this spectacle, were predictably dismayed (Luke 23:27ff, 48). After six hours on the cross at the "place of the skull" (Golgotha), Jesus died at about 3 p.m. on the 14th (or 15th) day of Nisan. He was buried by some of his followers in a nearby rock tomb. When some of his disciples visited the tomb on the following Sunday morning, they found it empty. They had already been told that Jesus was alive but refused to believe it (Luke 24:11; cf Mark 16:11-14). That same night they themselves saw Jesus, and spoke and ate with him. This was followed by a number of appearances of the risen Jesus to his disciples. On one occasion he was seen by more than 500 persons (I Cor 15:6). The final appearance came about on the Mount of Olives. Jesus gave last instructions to the apostles and then "was taken up... and a cloud received him out of their sight" (Acts 1:9).

Jesus' view of himself has been the subject of much controversy, primarily because, superficially at least, his own pronouncements seem less categorical than those made about him by Paul and others. It is a fact, for instance, that Jesus is never found uttering the bold claim "I am the messiah"; he does indeed answer in the affirmative when so asked (Matt 16:16ff; Mark 14:61ff; John 4:25ff; and cf Mark 9:39-41), but there are few instances even of this. The obvious conclusion is that Jesus refrained from making the claim because he did not think he was the messiah. An alternative — though less obvious — explanation is that his understanding of the messianic role was at such variance with the popular conception of the time that to use the title messiah would

The Holy Land in time of Jesus. The area outlined in green was governed by Herod Philip; the area outlined in red was ruled by Herod Antipas; the area outlined in gray was under the direct control of Roman governors.

The Church of the Primacy on the shore of the Sea of Galilee, which marks the site where it is believed that Jesus, risen from the dead, appeared to his disciples (John 21:1-25).

(right)
The Pool of Siloam in Jerusalem where Jesus restored his sight to a blind man (John 9:6-11).

The Chapel of the Angel in the Church of the Holy Sepulcher, Jerusalem. The tomb where Jesus was laid is reached through the very low door at the center.

actually have misled his listeners. They were expecting a political-military savior (See MESSIAH), but on those occasions when they tried to make Jesus king he fled from them (John 6:15; cf John 18:36ff and Acts 1:6ff).

Jesus' view of himself and his role is to be deduced from less direct statements. When he calls God "my Father" instead of "our Father", as was the custom of the time, he was echoing prophecies such as II Samuel 7:14, Psalms 2:7, and especially Psalms 89:26ff. His Nazareth synagogue reading of Isaiah chapter 61, followed by the declaration "Today this Scripture is fulfilled in your hearing" (Luke 4:17-21), was a messianic claim. When he forgave sins (e.g. Mark 2:5-10), probably using an OT word reserved only for God's forgiveness, his audience understood that he was saying things not permitted to the ordinary man. Similarly, his self-designation by Daniel's highly supernatural title "Son of man" (Dan 7:13-14) must have aroused disturbing associations in his hearers.

In the NT, Jesus is depicted as the Son of God, existing before creation and in fact active in the work of creation. He is Israel's promised messiah ("Christ", i.e., the anointed), God become man, a perfect man without sin, in order to be himself the redemptive sacrifice for sin. The NT writers see Jesus as clear fulfillment of OT prophecies and types, and references to these OT passages are legion in the NT. After the gospels, the NT writers place very little emphasis on the teachings of Jesus, and even such a central idea as the Kingdom of Heaven is referred to infrequently. As has been pointed out, the writers provide few of the normal biographical details, contrary to what might be expected with regard to one who so changed their lives. Instead the focus is on who Jesus was, and the redemption which God achieved through his demise. The death of Jesus is an act of atonement which has reversed the catastrophe of Eden; sin and death have been defeated, Satan has been subjected, and the way has been opened to restore man to a pre-sin pristine relationship with his Creator. This has all been accomplished by God's "Grace" and is applicable to all who will accept it by faith in the resurrected Jesus. The NT also sees Jesus in a strong eschatological light, looking forward to his return for judgment of sinners and the final salvation of all those who have followed him. In the meantime, the NT recognizes his active presence by the Holy Spirit, who represents him in the life of his believers.

JETHER (A shorter form of Jethro).

1. The firstborn son of Gideon. When instructed by his father to kill the Midianite kings, Zebah and Zalmunnah, who had murdered their kin, he could not bring himself to do it "because he was still a youth".

2. An Ishmaelite, husband of Abigail the sister of David, and father of Amasa who commanded the army of Judah at the time of King David. In II Samuel 17:25, he is called Ithre.

3. Great-grandson of Jerahmeel. He died without children.

4. Son of Ezrah in the genealogy of the family of Judah.

5. Son of Zophah and father of Jephunneh, Pispah and Arah in the genealogy of the family of Asher.

JETHETH A chief of Esau, prince in Edom (Gen 36:40, 43).

JETHLAH (ITHLAH) A city in the territory allotted to Dan when the land of Canaan was divided among the tribes (Josh 19:42).

JETHRO Priest of Midian and father-in-law of Moses. When Moses escaped from Egypt and stopped in Midian, he defended the priest's seven daughters from the shepherds who drove them away from the well. Their father invited Moses to live with them and gave him his daughter, Zipporah, in marriage (Ex 2:15-22). The name of the priest of Midian, according to Exodus 2:15-22, is Reuel. In Exodus 3:1, the father-in-law of Moses is called Jethro, "the priest of Midian". The names Reuel and Jethro probably represent two different traditions, referring to the same character. Another possible name for him is Hobab: Numbers 10:29 has Moses attempting to persuade "Hobab son of Reuel the Midianite, Moses' father-in-law" to join the Israelites on their way to the promised land.

The description of Jethro's encounter with Moses, during which the former blessed the Lord who "is greater than all gods" and offered sacrifices in the presence of Aaron and the elders of Israel (Ex 18:10-12), as well as Jethro's advice to Moses to appoint God-fearing men as officers, (Ex 18:18ff), have led scholars to suggest that Jethro was a polytheistic priest whose creed allowed him to worship several deities, including the God of Israel.

JETUR One of the 12 sons of Ishmael, the son of Abraham by Hagar the Egyptian (Gen 25:12, 15). He gave his name to a tribe on the east bank of the Jordan which later suffered defeat in its war against the tribes of Reuben, Gad and the half-tribe of Manasseh.

JEUEL ("may God bring life"). A Judahite, descendant of Zerah who dwelt in Jerusalem at the time of Nehemiah. His name is missing in the parallel list in Nehemiah 11:24.

JEUSH ("may [the Lord] help").

1. Firstborn son of Aholibamah, the second wife of Esau (Gen 36:2, 5); he was a chief in Edom (Gen 36:18).

2. Firstborn son of Bilhan, the grandson of Benjamin.

3. A Benjamite, son of Eshek, descendant of King Saul.

4. A Gershonite Levite in the time of King David.

5. Firstborn son of Rehoboam, king of Judah, by his wife Mahalath, daughter of King David and Abigail.

JEUZ Fifth son of Sharaim by his wife Hodesh in the genealogy of King Saul.

JEW, JEWS, JEWISH An ethnic designation variously applied in both OT and NT. Jacob's wife Leah named her fourth son Judah, saying "Now I will praise (or thank) the Lord" (Gen 29:35). The family or tribe descended from Judah was called by the same name, as was the geographic territory which they occupied after the conquest of the land by Joshua. As the split between north and south gradually began to develop, the entire southern area of Judah and Benjamin came to be

Interior of a Druze shrine in Galilee, assumed to be the burial place of Jethro. The leading prophet of the Druze sect, Nebi Shue'eib, is traditionally identified with Jethro.

known as Judah (cf II Sam 5:5; I Kgs 12:21ff). Later on the inhabitants of the region are called *Yehudim* (men of Judah, Judahites, Judeans, Jews; see II Kgs 16:6; 25:25). Among the earliest uses of the name are those which appear in the narrative sections towards the end of Jeremiah (Jer 34:9; 40:11-15; 44:1). A pattern can be discerned in the remaining OT uses (all in Ezra, Nehemiah and Esther plus twice in Daniel chapter 3 and once in Zechariah chapter 8) whereby the name "Jew" is used either by non-Jews, or Jews residing outside the land of Israel (Est 9:15-19; Dan 3:8; Zech 8:23). Jews inside the land used the name "Israel" (as does Ezra from the moment he arrives in the land. Cf Mark 15:26, where the Romans designate Jesus "King of the Jews", and Mark 15:32, where he is mocked by chief priests and scribes as "King of Israel").

By NT times the name had come into common use, and hence it appears far more often in the NT than in the OT. Especially to be noted are the uses of the word in the Gospel of John. Compared to a total of the 16 times the word *Ioudaios* appears in the Synoptic Gospels, John has it 71 times. Sometimes he intends it to describe Judeans as compared to Galileans (John 7:1; 11:7ff, 54; 18:36). At other places it is a substitute for Pharisees (John 1:19, 24; 8:13, 22; 9:13, 18. Here it is to be noted that at the time when John wrote — after the disaster of A.D. 70 — Judaism had effectively become exclusively Pharisaic Judaism). When foreigners are involved (John 4:22), the usage reflects the pattern of Ezra. Most frequently John uses the title "the Jews" to designate people in positions of authority (John 18:14 with 11:47-50; 19:6-7; and especially chaps. 7 and 8). In one passage (Rom 2:28-29) Paul speaks of "Jew" as something other than just an ethnic title. There he seems to play with the root meaning of the word, saying that the true Jew is one who is circumcised in heart and not just in flesh. Another non-standard usage is found in Revelation 2:9 and 3:9, which speaks of those "who say they are Jews, and are not, but lie".

JEZANIAH ("God hears"). An alternative form of Jaaziniah.

1. Son of a Maachathite; he was one of the captains who joined Gedaliah at Mizpah after the fall of Jerusalem.

2. Son of Hoshaiah; one of the captains who brought a petition to Jeremiah (Jer 42:1). May have been identical with No.1.

JEZEBEL Daughter of Ethbaal, king of Sidon and the Phoenicians; the wife of King Ahab of Israel and mother of his two sons, Ahaziah and Jehoram, who reigned after him. Jezebel's name contains the Canaanite element ZBL, which means "prince, master" and is often used as an attribute of the gods, especially Baal. The first element might have been tendentiously distorted by Hebrew tradition.

Ahab's marriage with Jezebel was very advantageous to him, politically as well as economically. It also paved the way for a growing Tyrian cultural-religious influence in his realm. Jezebel is depicted as patroness of the Phoenician Baal and Asherah cults, their priests and prophets, and an adversary of God's cult and prophets (I Kgs 16:31; 18:4; II Kgs 9:7, 22). Her influence was great: the Elijah and Elisha narratives blame her, more than Ahab, for the persecution of God's true prophets and the formal institution of Canaanite religious practices in Israel.

Jezebel's royal origin and education, together with her patronage of the Baal cult, must have been the base for her enormous political power during the reigns of her husband and her sons. She acted as reigning queen, although the Bible is careful not to refer to her by that title. She was the one who conceived and carried out the killing of Naboth, so that Ahab could have the latter's land (I Kgs chap. 21). Her planning of the

Opal Phoenician seal incised with several symbols and inscribed "izbl", the Phoenician form of the name Jezebel. 9th-8th centuries B.C.

38:19; 40:11-12, 15; 41:3; 44:1; 52:28, 30. Dan 3:8, 12. Zech 8:23. Matt 2:2; 27:11, 29, 37; 28:15. Mark 7:3; 15:2, 9, 12, 18, 26. Luke 7:3; 23:3, 37-38, 51. John 1:19; 2:6, 13, 18, 20; 3:1, 25; 4:9, 20, 22; 5:1, 10, 15-16, 18; 6:4, 41, 52; 7:1-2, 11, 13, 15, 35; 8:22, 31, 48, 52, 57; 9:18, 22; 10:19, 24, 31, 33; 11:8, 19, 31, 33, 36, 45, 54-55; 12:9, 11; 13:33; 18:12, 14, 20, 31, 33, 35-36, 38-39; 19:3, 7, 12, 14, 19-21, 31, 38, 40, 42; 20:19. Acts 2:5, 10; 9:22-23; 10:22, 28, 39; 11:19; 12:3, 11; 13:5-6, 42-43, 45, 50; 14:1-2, 4-5, 19; 16:1, 3, 20; 17:1, 5, 10, 13, 17; 18:2, 4-5, 12, 14, 19, 24, 28; 19:10, 13-14, 17, 33-34; 20:3, 19, 21; 21:11, 20-21, 27, 39; 22:3, 12, 30; 23:12, 20, 27, 30; 24:5, 9, 18, 24, 27; 25:2, 7-10, 15, 24; 26:2-4, 7, 17, 21, 23; 28:17, 19, 29. Rom 1:16; 2:9-10, 17, 28-29; 3:1, 9, 29; 9:24; 10:12. I Cor 1:22-24; 9:20; 10:32; 12:13. II Cor 11:24. Gal 2:13-15; 3:28. Col 3:11. I Thes 2:14.

affair shows legal knowledge, manipulative skill and determination.

Jezebel's political power did not come to an end with her husband's death. She carried the Hebrew title *Gevira* — "lady" (II Kgs 10:13). Her daughter, Athaliah, who became queen of Judah, was also regarded as having continued her mother's influence (II Kgs 8:18), and Jezebel probably acted as regent when her second reigning son Jehoram was killed by the rebel Jehu (II Kgs 9:14-28). Jehu himself was powerless to uproot the Baal cult from Samaria (II Kgs 10:18-28) until after he had killed Jezebel and safely buried her remains. Even in her death she remained the ruthless but royal woman. She "put paint on her eyes and adorned her head", defying Jehu with a powerful insult (II Kgs 9:30-37). Jezebel is depicted by biblical authors as ruthless, morally corrupt and sinful. Later tradition made her name a byword for a wicked woman. Elijah told Ahab that her influence was the chief reason for the fall of the dynasty of Omri (I Kgs 21:17 ff; II Kgs 9:36-37).

In Revelation 2:20, her name is used symbolically for a false prophetess who bewitches Christians into idolatrous practices.

JEZER, JEZERITES ("the Lord has created"). Third son of Naphtali (Gen 46:24) and founder of the family of the Jezerites (Num 26:49).

JEZIAH A man of Israel; one of the sons of Parosh who, having taken a pagan wife, had to repudiate her upon the decree of Ezra.

JEZIEL Son of Azmaveth. Along with his brother Pelet, he was among the men of Benjamin who deserted Saul's army and joined David at Ziklag; they were equally adept in using their right and left hands to hurl stones and to shoot arrows (I Chr 12:1-3).

JEZRAHIAH A leader of Temple singers at the time of Nehemiah. Identical with IZRAHIAH No.2.

JEZREEL

1. A town in the east of the hills of Judah (Josh 15:56), the birthplace of Ahinoam, one of David's wives (I Sam 25:43). Not identified.

2. A town on the border of the territory of Issachar, at the foot of Mount Gilboa (Josh 19:18, etc.). It was in the fifth district of the kingdom of Solomon (I Kgs 4:12) and an important city in the kingdom of Ahab (I Kgs 18:45), who had a palace there (I Kgs 21:1). It was the site of Naboth's vineyard (I Kgs 21:1ff). The descendants of the house of Ahab were slain at Jezreel (II Kgs 10:7, 11). It was finally destroyed by the Assyrians. In the Roman period there was a large village called Ezdraela. Identified with Zeriin, west of Beth Shean.

3. The Plain of Jezreel, which took its name from Jezreel No.2, extends across the breadth of the country, between Mount Carmel, Mount Gilboa and the hills of Lower Galilee. The River Kishon flows through its whole length to the Mediterranean. From early times the

(bottom of page)
The Plain of Jezreel.

View of Zeriin identified with Jezreel.

valley, known later as the Plain of Esdraelon or the Great Valley, was of the utmost importance to communications between the coast and the countries to the north and east. The fortified towns of Megiddo, Taanach, Ibleam and Beth Shean were built in order to guard the mountain passes leading into and from the plain. Some of the great battles in biblical history took place there, including the battle between Deborah and Jabin, king of Hazor (Judg chaps. 4-5); between Saul and the Philistines (I Sam 29:1; 31:1ff); and between Josiah and Pharaoh Necho (II Kgs 23:29-30). In the Hellenistic period the Ptolemies had large estates on the fertile plain, and from that time on it was mostly in the personal domain of the rulers. The Plain of Jezreel was conquered by the Maccabees and later formed part of Herod's kingdom.

4. The name of the eldest child of the prophet Hosea, by his wife Gomer. Hosea was instructed by God to give this name to his son in anticipation of the punishment to be inflicted upon the house of Jehu for the blood spilled at Jezreel when Jehu took power (cf II Kgs 9:17-26; 10:1-11).

5. A Judahite, son of Etam.

JEZREELITE Appellation of Naboth. He may have been an inhabitant of either Jezreel No.1 or No.2.

JEZREELITESS See JEZREEL No.1

JIBSAM An alternate form of Ibsam; the fifth son of Tola the firstborn son of Issachar and a "mighty man of valor".

JIDLAPH Seventh of the sons of Nahor, the brother of Abraham, by his wife Milcah (Gen 22:20, 22).

JIMNA, JIMNAH, JIMNITES Firstborn son of Asher (Gen 46:17) and founder of the family of the Jimnites (Num 26:44). In I Chronicles 7:30, his name is given as Imnah.

JIPHTAH A city of Judah in the Shephelah area. May be identified with Tarqumiya about 6 miles (10 km) northwest of Hebron.

JIPHTAH EL A valley which marked the boundary of the territory allotted to Zebulun with that of Asher. Location uncertain.

JISHUI Second son of Saul, called Abinadab in I Chronicles, 8:33; 9:39.

JISSHIAH A Korahite, a "mighty man" who joined David at Ziklag.

JITHRA See JETHER No.2

JITHRAN See ITHRAN No.2

JIZLIAH (IZLIAH, JEZLIAH) Son of Elpaal of the tribe of Benjamin. His name is given as Izliah or Jezliah in some versions of the Bible.

JIZRI The second son of Jeduthun (I Chr 25:3 where the name is spelt Zeri), he headed the fourth division of musicians in the Temple at the time of King David (I Chr 25:11).

JOAB

1. Commander-in-chief of David's army; he played an important role in the establishment, unification and consolidation of David's kingdom. Joab was the eldest son of David's sister, Zeruiah and brother of Abishai and Asahel (I Chr 2:16). Joab first appears in the civil war between the followers of David and those of Saul's son Ishbaal (Ishbosheth), who succeeded his father to the throne. In a battle at the Pool of Gibeon, David's adherents, led by Joab, defeated Ishbaal's men headed by Abner, son of Ner. The dead included Joab's young brother Asahel, killed by Abner (II Sam 2:12-23).

Joab helped to capture the well-fortified city of Jebus (Jerusalem) (II Sam 5:6ff; 8:16; 20:23; I Chr 11:4ff; 18:15). His military acumen gained him the position of commander-in-chief of David's army (I Chr 11:6), and he proved himself a shrewd tactician and resourceful general. He helped David crush the Philistines and subdue several of the neighboring nations, including the Arameans, Moabites and Edomites (II Sam 5:17-25; 8:1; 10:6-19; I Kgs 11:23-24; I Chr 14:10-16; 18:1-8).

Joab's loyalty to David was exemplary, at times verging on self-effacement. When, after fierce battles with the Ammonites and their allies, he was about to capture Rabbah, he asked David to come and lead the siege so as to receive credit for the conquest (II Sam 12:27-28). It was at this siege that Joab executed David's orders by stationing Bathsheba's husband Uriah in the forefront of the fierce battle and then pulling back, allowing Uriah to be killed (II Sam 11:14-17). Later, knowing of David's longing for his banished son Absalom, Joab concocted a scheme which brought about a reconciliation between the father and his son.

On the other hand, Joab was relentless and unscrupulous towards his enemies and rivals. He slew Abner perhaps out of rivalry or to avenge his brother. When Absalom revolted against his father, Joab killed him in stark violation of David's command to spare his life (II Sam 18:14). Jealous of his position, Joab later treacherously slew Amasa, who had been appointed by David to head the campaign against the Benjamite Sheba the son of Bichri; Joab proceeded to crush the revolt himself (II Sam chap. 20). He also conducted the census of the people ordered by David which took more than nine months (II Sam 24:1-9; I Chr 27:24).

In the dispute between Adonijah and Solomon over the succession to David's throne, Joab, unaware that David preferred Solomon, sided with Adonijah. When Solomon was established on the throne, he ordered the death of Joab; this was in accordance with David's command that Joab, who had shed innocent blood, must not be allowed to go down to the grave in peaceful old age (I Kgs 2:5-6). Joab met his death at the sanctuary, where he had sought refuge by seizing the altar's horns.

2. Son of Seraiah, from the tribe of Judah, and father of the Ge-Harashim.

3. The name of a Judean family which returned to Judah from the Babylonian Exile during the times of Zerubbabel (Ezra 2:6; Neh 7:11) and Ezra, when the head of the family was Obadiah the son of Jehiel.

JOAH ("Yah is brother").

1. A son of Obed-Edom who served as a Levitical gatekeeper at David's time.

2. Son of Zimmah. Descendant of the Levitical family of Gershon who served at the time of King Hezekiah's reform.

3. Son of Asaph. A court official who was part of the deputation sent by Hezekiah to the Assyrians.

4. One of the treasurers responsible for the repair work in the Temple under Josiah.

JOAHAZ Alternate form of Jehoahaz, "Yah has grasped". A recorder in the time of King Josiah, and father of Joah.

JOANNA The wife of Chuza, Herod Antipas' steward; one of the women healed of evil spirits and infirmities by Jesus. She was among 14 women who went on the first day of the week to the sepulcher of Jesus to anoint the body and found the stone rolled away. Two angels in shining garments told them that Jesus was risen, and the women informed the disciples.

JOANNAS (JOANNAN) Ancestor of Joseph, according to the Gospel of Luke (3:27). He was the grandson of Zerubbabel.

JOASH See JEHOASH

JOB A pious figure from early folklore who lost his vast possessions and family but continued to praise his God. According to Ezekiel 14:14, 20, Job belonged to the same type of hero as Noah and Daniel, who are mentioned alongside him as ancient great worthies. Noah is, of course, the survivor of the flood, but the Hebrew spelling of Daniel's name points to Dan'el, a pious king known from Ugaritic literature rather than to the later biblical interpreter of dreams and survivor in a lion's den. Apart from these two references in Ezekiel, there is only one other explicit mention of Job outside the book by that name. The NT Epistle of James holds up the steadfastness of Job as an example to all people, one that was met with divine compassion (James 5:11). Outside the Bible there is one notable work, The Testament of Job, which greatly amplifies the biblical record. Most of this material resembles the extensive pious legends about Job within Jewish and Arabic literature, for his misfortune evoked much reflection. Since it is stated that Job was from the land of Uz which is located in the territory of Edom, he may have been an Edomite. His name, attested to elsewhere in the ancient Near East, is derived from a verb that designates enmity or hostility. It probably suggests one whose enemy is God, or who was in enmity with God, a natural assumption about a person who suffered the way Job did. One may speak of two distinct portrayals of Job's character. The prose prologue and epilogue narrative depicts him as a patient hero who did not sin by word or deed, though he had sufficient cause to do so. The poetic sections, however, view matters differently, for here Job is a rebel who shakes a fist in God's face, denounces divine justice and complains bitterly, until the Lord finally appears in a storm-wind and brings him to his knees. According to the Bible, Job was married with a family of seven sons and three daughters. Though these children died when a storm destroyed the house they were in, they were later replaced by an equal number (by twice as many according to the Greek text of Job). In the Bible Job's wife is rebuked for foolish talk, but later legend gives her a name and has her sell her hair to buy bread for her husband. The Testament of Job salvages her reputation completely.

JOB, BOOK OF A poetic dialogue (3:1-42:6), that is enclosed within a prose framework (chaps. 1-2; 42:7-17), both of which probe the mystery of disinterested righteousness and explore the question of correct responses to suffering. The story contains both a prologue and an epilogue. The former consists of five scenes which alternate between earth and heaven, whereas the epilogue takes place on earth, the action however, being shaped by a heavenly being.

The opening scene introduces the hero, a man from the land of Uz, perhaps Edom. This man receives highest marks for moral integrity and religious devotion (1:1-5). Job's virtue naturally brings benefits, namely great wealth and a large family. Scene two tells about a convention in heaven that soon will shatter Job's bliss (1:6-12). The divine agent who was assigned the task of testing the sincerity of human spirituality, and who is identified here as the "adversary" (satan) registers skepticism about all religious acts, prompting the Lord to put forth Job's name as a test case. The third scene describes Job's rapid loss of possessions and children, which called forth in him an unforgettable expression of faith: "Naked I came from my mother's womb, and naked shall I return there; the Lord gave, and the Lord has taken away; blessed be the name of the Lord" (1:13-21). This scene opens with a reference to the children eating and drinking, thereby giving the illusion that all is well. The calamities that befall Job's possessions are orchestrated by the satan, although the agents of destruction alternate from human enemies to nature's fury: Sabeans destroy oxen and asses; fire from heaven consumes sheep; Chaldeans slay camels; a great wind fells the house in which Job's children are banqueting. Two refrains drone away amid the reports of atrocities: "I alone have escaped to tell you", and "while he was still

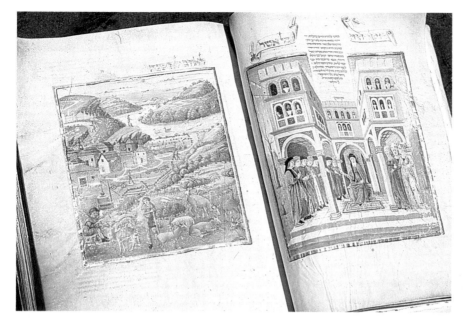

Two pages from an illuminated manuscript depicting Job's second family and his property. From the Rothschild Miscellany, Ferrara (?), c. 1470. (Israel Museum)

speaking, another also came and said". A narrator's observation that Job has escaped sin signals the conclusion of the first test (1:22). The fourth scene largely repeats the information in scene two, but once again the satan manages to persuade the Lord to deliver Job into alien hands (2:1-6). The adversary's earlier argument that loss of possessions would elicit a curse from Job now goes deeper: "Skin for skin! Yes, all that a man has he will give for his life". The last scene in the prologue describes a diseased Job, who spurns his wife's advice to curse God and die, and who remains faithful to the end (2:7-10). Once again the story teller intrudes to announce that Job's lips have not offended. The epilogue ties together all loose ends: Job intercedes for his three friends, whose visit is reported at the end of the prologue, whereupon the Lord restores Job to his former glory, doubling his wealth but letting him settle for seven sons and three beautiful daughters.

The poetic dialogue functions on two levels. First, there is a dispute between Job, on the one hand, and on the other, his three friends, Eliphaz the Temanite, Bildad the Shuhite and Zophar the Naamathite (chaps. 3-27). Then God, the silent partner in the earlier dispute, enters the debate and evokes repentant words (38:1-40:5). Once again God speaks from the stormwind, and once more Job submits (40:6-42:6). During this dispute the three friends remain silent. Between these two disputes a monologue occurs (chaps. 32-37) in which a young interlocutor, Elihu, attempts to silence Job and his friends. Elihu's speech comes when one expects the deity to appear, inasmuch as Job has just taken his life in his hands and pronounced an oath of innocence (chap. 31). This negative confession contains remarkable ethical consciousness going beyond the outward manifestation to the inner thought. Preceding this oath of innocence is a hymn about the inaccessability of wisdom (chap. 28) and a description of Job's way of life before his misfortune struck (chap. 29) and after it fell (chap. 30).

The initial debate takes place in three cycles, set into motion by Job's opening curse on the day of his birth (chap. 3). Job's speeches occur in chapters 3, 6, 9, 12, 16, 19, 21, 23, 26, 27:1-10. His friends are allocated considerably less space as individuals. Eliphaz speaks in 4-5, 15 and 22, Bildad in 8, 18 and 25, Zophar in 11, 20 and 27:11-23 (the last speech is wrongly attributed to Job).

The unity of the book has been questioned, and many scholars view chapters 28 and 32-37 as secondary, the former because the poem about a hidden wisdom seems to offer a premature answer to the problem of the book, and the latter because Elihu is otherwise unmentioned in the prologue and epilogue sections. In addition, differences in style and content between these chapters and the rest of the book are frequently noted. Some inconsistencies also occur in the prose story, as well as between it and the poetry. Many critics therefore think the poet used an old folktale about an innocent paragon of virtue who lost everything but retained his piety, the story being adapted by the poet to set the stage for a reexamination of the possibility of virtue without rewards.

The problem of the book is just this: does disinterested righteousness exist on earth? A secondary issue that receives extensive discussion concerns the proper response to innocent suffering. The various answers to these two problems are examined in great depth. The prose tale affirms disinterested virtue while undercutting it by restoring Job's earlier fortune. At the same time it describes a deity who acts with no regard for ethical standards that humans take for granted. The poetry has Job attack God in no uncertain terms; here the patient Job has become completely impatient as he charges the deity with cruelty beyond measure. The friends defend God, but in doing so they distance the deity from humans, who amount to nothing. God's speeches from the whirlwind fail to address the issue at a single point, for power rather than justice is the theme. Even Job is caught in a trap. He must accept the thesis of divine justice in order to protest against it. All the time he destroys the foundation on which he stands, for if the principle of reward and punishment is an illusion, then Job has no grounds for complaint. Perhaps that is what he finally realizes; he therefore repents before divine freedom. What, then, is the answer to the primary problem of disinterested righteousness? The poet contends that if it does not exist, neither can piety; for sooner or later all believers encounter unexplainable mystery that cannot fit into any rational system. The paradox of Job's experience was that he fled from divine fury at the same time that he searched for the hidden God. While in Job's case repentance brought divine solicitude, the poet does not encourage believers to expect the same, for claims about God's compassion are no less presumptuous than assertions about divine justice.

When was the Book of Job written? The theology that characterizes the Book of Deuteronomy and Israel's historical record seems to have created the situation against which the poet protests. The optimism associated with King Josiah's reform in 622 B.C., which had as its motto that God rewards virtue and punishes vice, was dealt a severe blow by Josiah's death at the hands of Pharaoh Necho (609 B.C.) and by the subsequent fall of Jerusalem. The 6th century is therefore the earliest possible date of the book, though its final composition may very well have been later. A later date is also reinforced by the developing concept of satan, which is in its early stages here compared to the allusions in Zechariah 3:1-2 and I Chronicles 21:1 and by the book's late Hebrew which has many affinities with the Aramaic language. It should be noted that some of the issues dealt with in the Book of Job have parallels in earlier Mesopotamian literature. Besides an ancient Sumerian poem entitled "A Man and His God", there are two other texts written in Babylonian: "I Will Praise the Lord of Wisdom", and an acrostic poem, "The Babylonian Theodicy". The Sumerian poem admitted that humans are born sinful and hence cannot accuse the gods of injustice. The second text describes the suffering of an innocent person in language somewhat similar to the Book of Job, likewise beginning the debate with a mythological introduction and resolving the problem by divine manifestation. Before doing so, however, the poem recognizes that humans cannot know what pleases the gods. In this text the cult plays a significant role. Finally, the "Babylonian Theodicy" takes refuge in mystery, although acknowledging minor iniquities.

OUTLINE

1:1-5	The prosperity of Job
1:6-12	Satan's challenge
1:13-2:13	The trials of Job; the arrival of the friends
3:1-26	Job's lament
4:1-14:22	First cycle of dialogue between the three friends and Job
15:1-21:34	Second cycle
22:1-27:23	Third cycle
28:1-28	In praise of wisdom
29:1-31:40	Job's final speech
32:1-37:24	The speeches of Elihu
38:1-42:6	Speeches of God and the submissions of Job
42:7-16	Job's prosperity is restored

JOBAB

1. Son of Joktan, a descendant of Shem (Gen 10:29; I Chr 1:23); the name may be connected with the Arabian town Juhaibab, mentioned in Sabean inscriptions.

2. The second king of Edom, who came from the city of Bozrah.

3. King of Madon in northern Palestine; he was defeated by Joshua (Josh 11:2; 12:19).

4. Son of Shaharaim, a descendant of the tribe of Benjamin.

5. Son of Elpaal, a descendant of the tribe of Benjamin.

JOCHEBED ("Yah is glory"). The daughter of Levi, wife and aunt of Amram and mother of Aaron, Moses and Miriam (Ex 6:20; Num 26:59). In Exodus 2:1, she is called simply "daughter of Levi".

JOED ("the Lord is my witness"). A man of Benjamin, son of Pedaiah father of Meshullam and grandfather of Sallum; he resided in Jerusalem during the time of Nehemiah.

JOEL ("Yah is God").

1. The firstborn son of the prophet Samuel. Joel and his brother Abijah (See ABIJAH No.1) were judges in Beersheba (I Sam 8:2). I Samuel 8:45 suggests that they would have succeeded Samuel as leader of the Israelites, had they not taken bribes to pervert justice. Joel was the father of Heman the musician (See HEMAN No.2) (I Chr 6:28; 15:17).

2. Ancestor of the prophet Samuel. He was the son of Azariah, the son of Zephaniah, a descendant of Korah.

3. Son of Jehiel and brother of Zetam (I Chr 26:22); he headed the Gershomite division of the Levites in the time of King David (I Chr 15:7). He was among the 130 to whom King David assigned the task of bringing the ark to Jerusalem (I Chr 15:11-15; cf II Sam chap. 6). Joel and Zetam were in charge of the Temple treasury (I Chr 26:22).

4. Son of Azariah the Kohathite; one of the chief Levites involved in

King Hezekiah's purification and reconsecration of the Temple.

5. Subdivision of the tribe of Reuben.

6. Prince of a subdivision of the tribe of Simeon.

7. First of the seven subdivisions of the tribe of Gad.

8. Chief of one of the principal divisions of the tribe of Issachar.

9. Son of Pedaiah; chief of the western half of the tribe of Manasseh in the time of King David.

10. Brother of Nathan; and of King David's thirty "mighty men" (II Sam 23:36; I Chr 11:38). In II Samuel 23:36 he is called Igal the son of Nathan.

11. One of the Israelites forced to repudiate his foreign wife by the decree of Ezra.

12. A son of Zichri. The reference Nehemiah 11:9 is ambiguous and has been given various interpretations: (a) the head of the group of Benjamites who acceded to Nehemiah's request for volunteers to settle in Jerusalem; (b) the mayor of Jerusalem; (c) the chief of police of Jerusalem; or (d) the chief officer of the non-priestly and non-Levitical population of Jerusalem.

13. The only biographical information known concerning the prophetic author of the Book of Joel (q.v.) is his name, and that of his father, Pethuel.

JOEL, BOOK OF The second of the twelve books of the Minor Prophets. Chapters 1-2 depict a plague of locusts and a promise of deliverance. Four responses to the calamity are recorded. In 1:2-3 the people are exhorted to take note of the disaster, which has overtaken them. In 1:8-18 the prophet calls upon the priests and the people to appeal to the Lord for help by means of mourning, fasting and prayer. Verses 19-20 contain the prophet's own prayer of supplication over the calamity. Another prayer, which the prophet composed for recitation by the priests, is found in 2:17. Chapters 2:28-3:21 is an apocalyptic poem. The Lord promises the repentant — both Jew and Gentile — deliverance from disaster, warns of punishment against the nations who had wronged the Jews (chap. 3) — specifically Tyre, Sidon, the Philistines, Egypt and Edom. In 3:14 "the Day of the Lord," when the Lord shall summon the heathen nations to the "valley of decision", denotes the impending punishment of the enemies of the Jews, in contrast to the parallel term which is denounced as a misconception (Amos 5:18-20). However, elsewhere in the Book of Joel "the Day of the Lord" refers to a disaster either present (Joel 1:15) or impending (2:1-2, 11, 31), which is to overtake those Jews who remain unrepentant. The book concludes by portraying a golden age when Jerusalem will be protected from all future attacks and the land blessed with great fertility, culminating in the promise that "Judah shall abide forever, and Jerusalem from generation to generation" (3:17-21).

Support for a late date for the composition of the Book of Joel has been sought in the reference to Greeks in 3:6. However, this reference actually argues against a Hellenistic date, for the Greeks are portrayed here, not as a political power in Palestine, but as a distant people to whom the Philistines and Phoenicians sold Jews as slaves. The references to past invasions of Jerusalem (3:7), to the functioning of the Jerusalem Temple in the prophet's own time (Joel 1:13; 2:17), and to the existence of Sidon, Tyre and the Philistines as independent nations (3:4), all support a date of composition subsequent to the rebuilding of the Temple (515 B.C.) and prior to the conquest of Sidon by the Persians (c. 348 B.C.). The portrayal of the Jerusalem Temple as the sole sanctuary, and the references to "elders" (1:2, 14; 2:16) and "priests" (1:9, 13; 2:17), combined with the absence of any mention of a king of

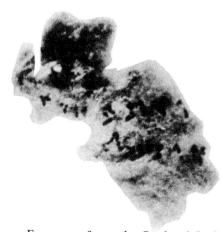

Fragment from the Book of Joel found at Qumran. (Shrine of the Book, Jerusalem)

JOEL 5
I Chr 5:4, 8

JOEL 6
I Chr 4:35

JOEL 7
I Chr 5:12

JOEL 8
I Chr 7:3

JOEL 9
I Chr 27:20

JOEL 10
I Chr 11:38

JOEL 11
Ezra 10:43

JOEL 12
Neh 11:9

JOEL 13
Joel 1:1. Acts 2:16

Judah, support the dating of the book's composition in the Persian era. Influenced by Amos, Isaiah, Zephaniah, Ezekiel and Obadiah, the author of the Book of Joel may, in turn, have influenced Zechariah in chapters 8-14 (See ZECHARIAH, BOOK OF). Joel's declaration that in the future all people will be prophets (2:28-29) provides the apostle Peter with an interpretation of the speaking in tongues on Pentecost (Acts 2:14-21).

OUTLINE

1:2:17	The plague of the locusts, description, lamentations, calls to repentance
2:18-27	Oracle of deliverance
2:28-3:15	The Day of the Lord, portents, judgment of the nations
3:16-21	Deliverance of Israel

JOELAH
I Chr 12:7

JOELAH A man of Benjamin; one of the sons of Jeroham of Gedor who joined David in Ziklag; he was equally adept in using his right and left hands to hurl stones and shoot arrows.

JOEZER
I Chr 12:6

JOEZER ("Yah is help"). One of the men of Benjamin who defected from the army of Saul to join David at Ziklag.

JOGBEHAH
Num 32:35.
Judg 8:11

JOGBEHAH A fortified city in the territory of Gad (Num 32:35), where Gideon defeated the armies of Zebah and Zalmunna (Judg 8:10-11). From the order of listing of the cities of Gad in Joshua 32:35, Jogbehah seems to have been the northernmost town in the Transjordanian plateau, but in Judges it is referred to as the easternmost city. For this reason scholars are inclined to seek it on the northeastern border of the territory of Gad. It is thus identified with the group of mounds named Jubeihat, some 7 miles (11 km) northwest of Amman. The Arabic name of the site, which recalls the ancient form, and the topographical surroundings, make this identification plausible.

JOGLI
Num 34:22

JOGLI A man of Dan, father of Bukki, who was appointed by the Lord to help Moses divide the land of Canaan among the tribes.

JOHA 1
I Chr 8:16

JOHA

1. One of the sons of Beriah in the genealogy of King Saul.

JOHA 2
I Chr 11:45

2. A Tizite, son of Shimri; along with his brother Jediael, he was among David's thirty "mighty men".

JOHANAN 1
I Chr 12:4

JOHANAN ("Yah has been gracious").

1. One of the Benjamites who joined David at Ziklag.

JOHANAN 2
I Chr 12:12

2. A Gadite military chief who joined David at Ziklag (I Chr 12:12, 14).

JOHANAN 3
I Chr 6:9-10

3. A priest, the son of Azariah, son of Ahimaaz, and father of Azariah the priest who served in the Temple at the time of Solomon (I Chr 6:9-10).

JOHANAN 4
II Chr 28:12

4. An Ephraimite; his son Azariah was among the Ephraimite leaders who tried to convince the Israelites to release the 200,000 women and children of Judah whom they had captured (II Chr 28:8, 12-13).

JOHANAN 5
I Chr 3:15

5. The firstborn of King Josiah.

JOHANAN 6
II Kgs 25:23.
Jer 40:8, 13,
15-16; 41:11,
13-16; 42:1, 8;
43:2, 4-5

6. The son of Kareah and brother of Jonathan. He was among those encouraged by Gedaliah, governor of Judah, to settle in the land of Judah and to serve the king of Babylon (II Kgs 25:23-24; Jer 40:8-9) during the time of Jeremiah the prophet. Johanan warned Gedaliah of a

plot against him by King Baalis of the Ammonites, but Gedaliah rejected the warning and was subsequently murdered by Ishmael son of Nethaniah, who was asking for Baalis (Jer 40:13-41:3). When Johanan heard of the murder, he and all the captains of the armed bands attacked Ishmael, who managed to escape (Jer 41:11-15). Johanan was among the remnant of Judah who asked Jeremiah to pray for them and to advise them whether or not to stay in Judah. The prophet advised them to stay, promising them on God's behalf that they would prosper, but they preferred to leave for Egypt (Jer 42:1-43:7).

7. One of the seven sons of Elioenai, descended from Solomon.

8. Son of Hakkatan of the family of Azgad. He returned from the Babylonian Exile with Ezra.

9. A high priest and head of a priestly family; the grandson of Eliashib the high priest (Neh 12:22). In Ezra 10:6 and Nehemiah 12:23, he is listed as a son of Eliashib. In the genealogical list of the high priests in Nehemiah 12:9-11, he is called Jonathan but this is probably a scribal error for Johanan.

Johanan the high priest is mentioned in the Elephantine Papyri of the 17th year of Darius II (423-404 B.C.).

JOHANAN 7
I Chr 3:24

JOHANAN 8
Ezra 8:12

JOHANAN 9
Neh 12:22-23

JOHN THE APOSTLE One of the twelve apostles, traditionally the author of five of the books of the NT. A member of a Galilean fishing family, John first appears with his brother James and their father Zebedee mending the nets (Matt 4:21). The two brothers may have been rather young and energetic at the time, as is perhaps indicated by the epithet "Boanerges" ("Sons of Thunder", Mark 3:17). Jesus called them from their father and the nets, and they soon appeared, together with Peter (and sometimes his brother Andrew), as a kind of inner circle around Jesus. As a member of this group John was with Jesus at some of the most dramatic moments of Jesus' career (See Matt 17:1; Mark 5:37; 13:3; 14:33). If it is accepted that John was the author of the fourth gospel, and that he was "the disciple whom Jesus loved", a view widely doubted by scholars today (See JOHN, GOSPEL OF), he enjoyed a special relationship with his master. For it was the "beloved disciple" who leaned back on Jesus' breast at the Last Supper (John 13:23), who was "known to the high priest" and therefore followed Jesus right into the high priest's courtyard (John 18:15ff), who was entrusted by Jesus with the care of his mother Mary (John 19:26ff), and who outran Peter to the empty tomb (John 20:2-4). After the resurrection, John appears as one of the leading figures of the early church (Acts 3:1ff; 4:13, 19; 8:14; Gal 2:9). According to a tradition passed on by one of his disciples, Papias, John later went to Ephesus, was exiled under the Emperor Domitian to the island of Patmos, and there wrote the Revelation (Rev 1:9). Under Nerva he returned to Ephesus and there composed the Gospel and the Epistles. Other traditions find him engaged in disputes with some of the church's earliest heretics. John reportedly died at a very old age shortly after the turn of the century.

JOHN THE BAPTIST The forerunner of Christ. His conception and birth (parallel to those of Jesus) are depicted in detail in Luke 1:5-80, in a story redolent of the OT with barrenness, prayer, promise and fulfillment. Like Samuel and Samson, John the Baptist was to be a Nazirite (Num 6:1-4), abstaining from wine or strong drink but "filled with the Holy Spirit" (Eph 5:18). The OT allusions underline John the Baptist's role as ushering in the NT economy and his birth to the elderly Zechariah and his barren wife Elizabeth (a parallel to Abraham and Sarah) served to indicate the divine origin of his conception. His relation to Jesus is emphasized even before they were born: when Elizabeth heard Mary's greeting, her baby leaped in her womb (Luke

John the Baptist dressed in goat skin, with a lamb in a medallion. From a carved ivory plaque of the 16th century. (Museo dell'Arcivescovado, Ravenna)

1:41). Even John's name (meaning "God shows grace") was given to him by the angel Gabriel.

Although he was the son of a priest, entitled to wear the ephod and to partake of the priestly portions, John the Baptist grew up in the wilderness (Luke 1:80), wearing a garment of coarse camel's hair with a leather girdle, and eating locusts and wild honey (Matt 3:4). This was also in fulfillment of Isaiah 40:3 — a voice crying in the wilderness. The portrayal is intended to signify that John's message was something absolutely new, foretold by the prophet, and far removed from previous culture and religion.

John's preaching too was in the wilderness (Matt 3:1), far from the Temple precinct or the holy city of Jerusalem with its religious and cultured people. His message was "repent, for the kingdom of heaven is at hand" (Matt 3:2).

John baptized his followers to signify the drowning of their old life and their emergence from the water into a new life. Significantly, John is mentioned particularly as baptizing in the Jordan River, through which the twelve tribes of Israel passed into the promised land. John, like Jesus later, immediately ran into conflict with the Pharisees and Sadducees for whom he had sharp words (Matt 3:7-12). The Gospel of John relates that they asked him who he was; when John answered that he was neither the Christ nor the prophet Elijah, they queried his baptizing activities. John replied that he was baptizing in water only ("unto repentance", Matt 3:11), but that he was to be followed by one who would baptize with the Holy Spirit and fire (that is, eternal punishment, cf Matt 3:11-12; John 1:19-28). When John saw Jesus, he proclaimed him "the Lamb of God who takes away the sin of the world" and testified that he saw the Spirit descending as a dove out of heaven and abiding in him (at Jesus' baptism) going so far as to declare that "this is the Son of God" (John 1:29-34).

Jesus himself appraised his forerunner in Matthew 11:7-15: John was much more than a prophet, surpassing his predecessors in greatness, and comparable to Elijah. Nevertheless, John's generation did not accept him, alleging instead that he was demon-possessed (Matt 11:17-18), as was later said of Jesus himself. John was beheaded c. A.D. 29 by the tetrarch Herod Antipas who imprisoned him in revenge for John's condemnation of his incestuous marriage to his brother's wife Herodias (Luke 3:19-20). Herodias' daughter, danced for Herod, who rewarded her by offering her whatever she wished. On the advice of her mother, she requested the head of John the Baptist on a platter. Herod, who enjoyed listening to John (Mark 6:20) was grieved at being required to execute him; but having given his oath before witnesses, he commanded that it be done (Matt 14:1-13; Mark 6:14-29). Luke 9:7-9 relates that

Machaerus, east of the Dead Sea, where Herod the Great built a fortress and palace. According to Josephus, Herod Antipas imprisoned and beheaded John the Baptist at Machaerus.

The tomb at the traditional burial site of John the Baptist at Samaria.

when Herod later heard that Jesus was being identified with the resurrected John, he became curious about the subject of the rumor.

Recent scholarship has found parallels between the teachings of John and those of the Dead Sea Sect, leading to suggestions that he may have belonged to the sect for a time before breaking away.

JOHN, GOSPEL OF The fourth of the NT gospels. Composed in a comparatively loose narrative fashion, it is a work which is intended to relate the signs that communicate knowledge of Jesus as the Christ. "And truly Jesus did many other signs in the presence of his disciples, which are not written in this book; but these are written that you may believe that Jesus is the Christ, the Son of God, and that believing you may have life in his name." (20:30-31).

John differs strikingly from the other three canonical gospels, even from Mark, with which it has some affinities. The great majority of biblical critics agree that it was in circulation by the end of the 1st century A.D. and that it is a composite work. Analyses of its composition vary. It is firmly established in the scholarly consensus that chapter 21 is a kind of appendix, though it is conceivable that the author intended to bring together the tradition of the risen Lord's appearances in Jerusalem (chap. 20) and in Galilee (chap. 21). Chapter 21 seems also to be designed to present the "beloved disciple" as the author (21:20-24), whereas there is no such indication earlier. It is also widely accepted that the tale of the woman taken in adultery (8:1-11) does not belong to the text as originally circulated because it is not found in most of the ancient manuscripts. Apart from these two passages, exegetical conclusions diverge widely, some interpreters seeing earlier sources and others seeing evidence of different schools of thought in the Johanine tradition.

Although John 21:24, taken with 21:20, identifies the "beloved disciple" as the author, this identification does not give any factual information about the latter. The beloved disciple, also mentioned in 13:23; 19:26; and 20:2, is not named. There is no evidence that it is the apostle John, son of Zebedee. Moreover, if chapter 21 is an appendix to the Gospel, one must ask whether the description of the beloved disciple as witness and writer refers to chapter 21 only or to the entire work. And even if the entire work is meant, that ascription may be at variance with the previous 20 chapters. In fact, it is possible that the beloved disciple is an allegorical figure, representing perhaps the church of the future.

The Gospel of John has little in common with the Synoptic Gospels (Matthew, Mark, Luke) with respect to theological outlook, sources, and style. John was written toward the end of the 1st century A.D. when the conflict of the church with its Jewish matrix had intensified in some areas. The Jews are viewed in John as enemies of mythical proportions (e.g. 8:44; 16:2), whereas the conflict in the synoptics has to do primarily with rivalry among claimants to authority in the same tradition. The author of the fourth gospel knew some of the sources used by the synoptic evangelists, and was evidently familiar with the Gospel of Mark. There are ten to 15 passages, depending on how one counts, in which John parallels Mark. But in spite of certain parallels and similarities, John has only about ten percent of its material in common with the first three gospels.

The Gospel of John is based around the central paradox, the paradox of the incarnation: the divine word, the divine light and truth, has completely entered into human existence. Jesus as the Christ is simultaneously a human being and the "only begotten" of God the Father. Time and eternity are here united, creator and creature are here joined. If one asks how this could be, the answer of the fourth gospel is, in effect, that the transcendence or sacred otherness of God includes the divine nearness in Christ and in creation as a whole. The essential reality of everything is the logos or divine word (1:1-19). Plato, for example, could bring together the unchangeable being of the Good and the realm of perishing, only through the myth of the Demiurge, who is a divine artisan that shapes resistant matter into forms according to patterns of the Good. John's witness is that "the Word became flesh and dwelt among us" (1:14), the very Word that says, "Before Abraham was, I am" (8:58). One cannot adequately speak of this incarnation of God in human being apart from symbols. It is truly known, according to the fourth gospel, only through the kind of participation in the divine reality that Jesus claims for himself and requests for his followers (see 17:20-21). The author, recognizing that one cannot approach the meaning of the God-Man directly, engages in an approach of indirection which expresses itself in an ironic style, the use of multiple metaphors and an emphasis on signs. The primary departure from this approach of indirection resides in Jesus' recurring self-affirmation, "I am", especially where it is not qualified in any way (see 8:58, cited above; also 6:20; 13:19; 18:5).

The fourth gospel views Jesus as the human form of the divine son, the incarnation of the Word. He is the heavenly stranger. The world did not know him, his own did not receive him. With this theological perspective John bears certain affinities with the gnostic writings found at Nag Hammadi, especially the Gospel of Truth. The implication of John is that Pilate's question to Jesus, "Where are you from?", can be answered only by believers, those who have true knowledge. It is therefore the height of irony when certain people in Jerusalem say, "Yet we know where this man comes from; and when the Christ appears, no one knows where he is from" (7:27). They think they know "where" he comes from, but they do not. He is "from above" (3:31; 8:23).

The one from above, who is before all things, has no predecessor. John the Baptist is not the Elijah prophesied by Malachi, as in the Synoptic Gospels, nor does he baptize Jesus as in Matthew and Mark (1:19-34). Jesus Christ is not from this world, but he comes into the world teaching and working signs. These signs, like the wonders and miracles of the first three gospels, involve the transformation of the ordinary course of things, such as changing water into wine (2:1-11) or healing a dying boy (4:46-54). But the word for sign, semeion, carries a special connotation, one particularly characteristic of John's gospel. It conveys the implication of communication. Something is made known which leads to belief. On the other hand, those who are prepared for a higher spiritual level will not need signs (6:1-59; 20:24-29).

John's view is that God is present in the historical reality of Jesus, but he has no interest in either the historical Jesus or the course of history as such. Jesus is completely severed from his Jewish background, and the Hebrew Bible, though important for John, is not understood as the

The Gospel of John from the Codex Sinaiticus. 4th-century manuscript found at Mount Sinai.

account of a history of salvation leading up to the Christ. John is the one NT source that could be seen as "anti-Semitic", although this judgment should be partially mitigated by knowledge of the struggle beginning to develop in the late 1st century A.D. between the synagogue and the young church.

History is really collapsed into the present for John, the present of salvation. The Savior is depicted as the stranger whose advent is a crisis for the world, a moment of turning and decision which leads to judgment or salvation. "And this is the condemnation (*krisis*), that the light has come into the world, and men loved darkness rather than light..." (3:19). John's representation of the Christ thus functions to invoke and support the believers' sense of strangeness in the world. The Christian has no roots or home except in God and in the One whom he has sent. The Hebrew Scriptures are understood not as a Jewish book but as a universalistic witness to the eternal divine word. To those who would believe, the purpose of the Gospel of John is to show the means whereby they may make their way to their true home (see 14:1-7). Indeed, through accepting the Stranger Son they are already "there".

OUTLINE

1:1-18	Prologue: The preexistent and incarnate Word
1:19-51	Revelation and ministry of Jesus to the world
2:1-4:54	Beginnings of the manifestation and ministry of Jesus
5:1-12:50	Ministry of Jesus
13:1-17:26	Christ's revelation of himself to his disciples
18:1-20:31	The Passion and Resurrection
21:1-25	Appearances after Resurrection

JOHN, THE FIRST EPISTLE OF The 23rd book of the NT. No name is given in the text of the letter, nor is there any personal information which might facilitate his identification. Early church tradition (Irenaeus, who, through Papias, represents a direct line to John) assigned it to the apostle John. This same tradition included the fourth gospel and the two shorter epistles which follow this one. On grounds of style, vocabulary, and what might be called literary personality, this letter would seem to have been written by the same person who composed the fourth gospel or by someone closely related to him (see JOHN, GOSPEL OF). If this man be identified with John the apostle, relevant biographical details would place the writing of the letter near the end of the 1st century A.D. in Ephesus. An earlier date is not, however, out of the question.

The occasion of writing was probably to combat an incipient split in the church being addressed — "They went out from us" (2:19). While the exact teaching of the heretical group is not stated, it is usually considered to have been some early form of Gnosticism. Adherents to this teaching claimed to have special revelatory knowledge, which was limited to a privileged few (cf 2:20, "But you have an anointing from the Holy One and you all know"). Gnostics rejected the material as evil, consequently denying that Jesus had actually "come in the flesh". The author addresses this idea directly, claiming that anyone who so denies the true humanity of Christ has the spirit of Antichrist (4:2-3; cf 2:22). One corollary to the esoteric approach to Christian belief was that the specially enlightened can attain a state of sinlessness. This problem is addressed at some length. We all sin, and we all need to confess so that we can receive God's forgiveness (1:7-10). Provision has been made for atonement for these sins by the death of Jesus (2:1-2). But the author goes on to emphasize that the true followers of Jesus should be gaining control over their penchant for sinning. That which is divine in them through their new birth cannot sin, and it is that side which should be dominant in their lives, not the things of the world and the devil (2:14-17; 3:3-10; 4:4ff).

The Epistle devotes much attention to love as the essence of God's new commandment (2:4-11; cf John 13:34; II John 5ff). He who truly loves God will necessarily love his brother, and in fact, if he does not love his brother, he has no right to say he loves God (4:7-21). This love, to be valid, must be practical and manifested in action (3:17ff).

OUTLINE

1:1-4	The writer's testimony and reason for writing
1:5-2:2	God, the forgiver of sins
2:3-6	Knowing God and keeping his commandments
2:7-11	The new commandment of love
2:12-14	Children, young men and fathers
2:15-17	Do not love the world
2:18-23	Warning against antichrist teachings
2:24-29	Abide in him as his word abides in you
3:1-10	Children of God
3:11-18	Practical love enjoined
3:19-24	Our confidence in God
4:1-6	Test the spirits
4:7-21	Love one another
5:1-5	Overcoming the world
5:6-13	The witness of God concerning Jesus
5:14:15	Asking according to God's will
5:16-17	Sin not unto death
5:18-21	Removed from the power of the evil one

JOHN, THE SECOND AND THIRD EPISTLES OF The 24th and 25th books of the NT. The author calls himself only "the elder". While difficulties attend any attempt to determine his identity more precisely, he is generally regarded as identical with the writer of the previous Epistle (q.v., also for date and provenance). None of the three individuals named in III John can be positively identified, therefore offering no assistance in assigning these letters.

These two short letters are unpretentious personal correspondences of a sort common in both the ancient world and the modern. They may be considered as a unit. In both of them the writer expresses his pleasure at good things he has heard about the recipients. In II John this is followed by a brief exhortation to "love one another", while in III John, Gaius "the beloved" is praised for his hospitality. Both letters then contain rather stern warnings against deceivers and troublemakers. One suggestion has been that both deal with the same problem situation, the first in general terms and the second (after the first had failed to achieve its purpose) with explicit naming of names. They close with a familiar explanation of the brevity of the letter and an expression of hope soon to visit the recipients.

OUTLINE
II John

vs. 1-3	Salutation
vs. 4-6	The old/new commandment of love
vs. 7-11	Warning against deceivers
vs. 12-13	Closing

III John

vs. 1-2	Salutation
vs. 3-8	Gaius' good reputation
vs. 9-12	Warning against evil men and praise of good men
vs. 13-14	Closing

JOIADA

1. Son of Eliashib No. 4 and father of Jonathan No. 9. He was a Levite at the time of Nehemiah.

2. See JEHOIADA No.6.

JOIAKIM A priest, son of Jeshua and father of Eliashib; he was among those who returned with Zerubbabel from the Babylonian Exile.

JOIARIB ("may the Lord fight on my side").

1. A "man of understanding" among those sent by Ezra to Iddo in Casiphia to bring back servants for the House of the Lord before the return from the Babylonian Exile.

2. Son of Zechariah and father of Adaiah, a man of Judah who dwelled in Jerusalem after the return of the exiles from Babylon.

3. A priest, father of Jedaiah who dwelled in Jerusalem after the return of the exiles from Babylon.

4. A Levite, among those who returned from Exile with Zerubbabel.

5. A Levite, father of Mattenai; he was among those who returned from the Exile in Babylon and settled in Jerusalem; perhaps the same as No.4.

JOKDEAM A city within the territory which fell to the lot of Judah when the land of Canaan was divided among the tribes (Josh 14:1; 15:56). Nothing is known about it and it has been suggested that it might be an alternate name for Jorkeam.

JOKIM (a shortened form of Jehoiakim, "may Yah establish"). A man of Judah from the family of Shelah.

JOKMEAM A city in Ephraim assigned to the Levites. May be identical with Kibzaim.

JOKNEAM Town situated some 9 miles (12 km) northwest of Megiddo, on the fringes of the western Jezreel Valley, commanding one of the most important junctions on the coastal road leading from Egypt and the land of Israel to Phoenicia. The traveler on this road would have diverged from the great highway to Damascus, which crossed the Carmel range via Wadi Ara and Megiddo, in order to take the northern passage via Wadi Milh and Jokneam and thus continue northwards to the coastal town of Tyre and beyond.

The earliest record of the site is in a topographical list from the time of

JOIADA 1
Neh 12:10, 11, 22

JOIADA 2
Neh 13:28

JOIAKIM
Neh 12:10, 12, 26

JOIARIB 1
Ezra 8:16

JOIARIB 2
Neh 11:5

JOIARIB 3
Neh 11:10

JOIARIB 4
Neh 12:6

JOIARIB 5
Neh 12:19

JOKDEAM
Josh 15:56

JOKIM
I Chr 4:22

JOKMEAM
I Chr 6:68

JOKNEAM
Josh 12:22; 19:11; 21:34. I Kgs 4:12

Aerial view of the excavations at Jokneam.

Thutmosis III (1482-1450 B.C.). It is also mentioned in the Book of Joshua as one of the Canaanite towns conquered by Joshua (Josh 12:22) and later apportioned to the Levites (Josh 21:34), being on the border of the inheritance of the tribe of Zebulun (Josh 19:11).

Archeological investigations of recent years have shown that the 10-acre site was almost continuously occupied from the Early Bronze Age (c. 3000 B.C.) until the Mameluke period (14th century A.D.). The most impressive finds to date are the massive fortifications and adjacent water system of the Israelite town, dating from the 10th to 8th centuries B.C., which crown the steep slopes of the mound. Other finds include domestic buildings of the Middle Bronze Age II through the Iron Age II, and remains of fortifications and a church of the Crusader period.

Jonah swallowed by the whale, shown on a bas-relief of the 9th century. (Archaeological Museum, Istanbul, Turkey)

JOKSHAN The second of the sons of Abraham by his wife Keturah (Gen 25:2); father of Sheba and Dedan (Gen 25:3).

JOKTAN The youngest son of Eber the grandson of Shem, and father of 13 sons or peoples.

JOKTHEEL

1. A village in Judah, mentioned between Mitzpah and Lachish (Josh 15:38). It has not been identified.

2. A stronghold in Edom whose name King Amaziah of Judah changed from "Sela" after his defeat of the Edomites (II Kgs 14:7). See SELA.

JONADAB See JEHONADAB

JONAH ("dove").

1. A prophet, son of Amittai from Gath Hepher in the territory of Zebulun. His prophecy of consolation promised the restoration to the Kingdom of Israel of territories that had been occupied by the Aramean kingdom of Damascus. According to II Kings 14:25, this prophecy was fulfilled during the reign of King Jeroboam II of Israel.

The historical Jonah is adopted as the main character in the Book of Jonah. (See JONAH, BOOK OF). Jonah in the latter role is referred to by Jesus in the expression "the sign of the prophet Jonah" (Matt 12:39). The three days Jonah spent in the belly of the great fish (Jonah 1:17) are depicted by Jesus as a prefiguration of his own three days' sojourn in Hades, between his death by crucifixion on Good Friday and his resurrection on Easter Sunday (Matt 12:39-41).

2. The father of the apostles Peter and Andrew. In some manuscripts he is also called John. Nothing is known about him.

JONAH, BOOK OF The fifth of the twelve books of the Minor Prophets, the Book of Jonah, unlike the other books in that collection, is not a collection of prophetic speeches but a short story. The author's hero is the prophet, Jonah, the son of Amittai. The plot of

Fragment from the Book of Jonah found at Qumran. (Shrine of the Book, Jerusalem)

the story may be summarized as follows: called by God to go east and summon the people of Nineveh to repentance, the prophet Jonah takes off in the opposite direction, booking passage at Joppa on the first ship bound westward to Tarshish. God, however, stirs up a great storm which threatens to capsize the boat. Unlike the sailors who pray to their various gods for deliverance, Jonah remains fast asleep. Only after lots are cast to determine who is the cause of the storm does Jonah confess that his desertion of his prophetic commission has caused God to send the violent storm. The sailors at first attempt to save his life, but finally decide to avoid shipwreck by throwing Jonah into the sea, whereupon the storm immediately subsides. The sailors, hitherto followers of a variety of gods, are so impressed that they acknowledge the Lord, and offer sacrifices to him (chap. 1).

The Lord now summons a large fish to swallow Jonah. After being in its belly for three days and three nights Jonah prays to the Lord (2:2-9) whereupon the fish spews him up onto dry land. When the Lord again commissions Jonah to call Nineveh to repentance (3:1-2), the prophet immediately proceeds to Nineveh to proclaim the city's destruction within 40 days (3:3-4). The people and king promptly respond with fasting, prayer, repentance and good deeds, hoping thereby to induce the Lord to relent (3:5-9).

Impressed by the Ninevites' response to Jonah's message, the Lord rescinds his decree. Jonah, however, is thoroughly chagrined (4:1) and now defends his flight to Tarshish before the Lord by arguing that he wanted Nineveh to receive its just deserts: knowing God's grace and compassion, he did not wish the Lord to change his mind (4:2). The remainder of the book (4:3-11) describes the Lord's attempt to convince Jonah that people and other living creatures are sufficiently dear to the Lord to justify divine clemency. When Jonah wants to die because of the Lord's decision God causes a large plant to spring up to protect him from the heat of the desert. The plant in turn is destroyed by a worm and Jonah again longs for death.

A major message of the Book of Jonah is that rigidity and the need for consistency are human attributes, whereas the ability to change course is a God-like virtue (see also Ex 32:14; Num 14:20; I Sam 15:11; etc.). In Jewish tradition the Book of Jonah is read in its entirety in the afternoon of the Day of Atonement. In that context the Book of Jonah is meant to remind the Jews of the efficacy of repentance, prayer and fasting — the three central activities of the Day of Atonement. The Book of Jonah illustrates the independent will of the Israelite prophet (cf Ex chaps. 3-4; Jer chap. 1; Ezek 4:14), and it shows that prophecies of doom are aimed at bringing about repentance.

Scholars have observed that certain linguistic features of the Book of Jonah point to the Second Temple period as the date of composition, the earliest possible date being the established date of the hero, Jonah — the 8th century B.C. (cf II Kgs 14:25). Jesus refers to Jonah's sojourn of three days and three nights in the "belly of the whale" as a prefiguration of the time between the crucifixion and the resurrection (Matt 12:39-41).

OUTLINE

1:1-3	Jonah flees from his mission and embarks for Tarshish
1:3-16	Jonah is blamed for the storm and thrown into the sea
1:17-2:10	He is swallowed by a fish, prays to the Lord from its belly and is vomited forth on dry land
3:1-4	Jonah goes to Nineveh, foretells its destruction
3:5-10	The people of Nineveh repent and the Lord relents
4:1-5	Jonah calls on the Lord to fulfill his original intention
4:6-11	The Lord explains to Jonah why he relented

JONAN Son of Eliakim and father of Joseph in the genealogy of Jesus.

JONATHAN ("Yah has given").

1. A Levite from the city of Bethlehem, employed as a personal priest in the home of Micah the Ephraimite (Judg 17:7-12) and later persuaded to accept the offer of a "Danite" priesthood (see Judg 18:27, 30).

2. The eldest son of Saul, the first king of Israel (I Sam 14:1). As a result of his military achievements in the war against the Ammonites (I Kgs chap. 11) he was given command of one-third of his father's army stationed at Gibeah during the campaign against the Philistines (I Sam 13:2, 16). In a bold, surprise attack on the large and powerful Philistine garrison, Jonathan spread panic throughout the enemy camp which allowed Saul and his forces to pursue the confused and disorganized foe down to Aijalon. The victory, however, was dampened by Saul's curse on any who should eat food during the pursuit. Unaware of this oath, Jonahan chanced upon wild honey and ate some, for which his father would have had him put to death, had not the Israelites, in recognition of his courage that had brought them the victory, interceded on his behalf (I Sam 14:38-45). Jonathan's wisdom is demonstrated by his statement that had his father allowed the troops to partake of the food spoils of the enemy, they would have had the energy to follow up their victory. After the slaying of Goliath, Jonathan came to admire David and made a brotherly covenant with him, despite Saul's forecast that David would eventually be king in their stead (I Sam 20:31). Jonathan's love for David was steadfast, and he intervened for his friend when

Saul's jealousy drove him to expel David from his court (I Sam 19:1-7), and more than once he risked his life for him. Saul, angered at what he understood as Jonathan's unfilial conduct, threw a javelin at him, as he had done several times at David. Fearing that his father's animosity towards David would lead to hostilities and thus jeopardize their friendship, Jonathan exacted an oath from David to the effect that the latter would spare Jonathan and his successors. At their last meeting, in the wilderness of Ziph, the two friends entered into a further covenant which stated that David would be king and Jonathan his first minister (I Sam 23:16-18). While remaining faithful to David, he also conformed as much as possible to his father's wishes, thus proving a noble example of filial piety. Jonathan was killed together with his father and two brothers, Abinadab and Malchishua, in the battle against the Philistines at Mount Gilboa (I Sam 31:2). Their corpses were despoiled and then hung by the Philistines on the wall of Beth Shan, from where they were rescued by the men of Jabesh Gilead. David bitterly mourned Saul and Jonathan (II Sam 1:17-27). In his dirge he lamented, "I am distressed for you, my brother Jonathan: you have been very pleasant to me. Your love to me was wonderful, surpassing the love of women." David honored their covenant and showed kindness to Jonathan's only son, Mephibosheth, sparing him the harsh fate that befell Saul's other sons (II Sam 9:1-13).

3. Son of Abiathar the priest.

4. A member of the tribe of Judah and father of Peleth and Zaza.

5. Son of Shimea, David's brother.

6. Son of Shammah (or Shageh) and one of the thirty "mighty men" of David.

7. Father of Ebed in the list of those returning with Ezra.

8. Son of Asahel who opposed Ezra's plan for marriage reforms.

9. A post-exilic high priest (Neh 12:11) whose name appears as "Johanan" in Nehemiah 12:23 and as Jehohanan in Ezra 10:6.

10. A priest who was the head of the priestly family of Malluchi.

11. A priest, son of Shemaiah and father of Zechariah.

12. A scribe whose house served as Jeremiah's prison.

13. Son of Kareah and brother of Johanan. See JOHANAN No.6.

JOPPA A port city (modern Jaffa) in the territory of Dan, on the coast of the Mediterranean (Josh 19:46), conquered by the Philistines and not included in Israelite territory. Solomon brought timber to Joppa from the Lebanon for building his Temple (II Chr 2:16) and cedar wood was also brought to the "sea at Joppa" after the return from Babylon (Ezra 3:7). The prophet Jonah sailed from Joppa to Tarshish (Jonah 1:3). In 701 B.C. Joppa was conquered by Sennacherib, king of Assyria, who took it from Sidka, king of Ashkelon. In the Persian period it was given to the Sidonians.

In the days of the Ptolemies Joppa was granted autonomy, with the right to mint coins. In 144 B.C. the city was conquered by Simon Maccabee, who drove out the alien inhabitants and settled his soldiers there so that he could use it as an opening to the sea (I Macc 10:76; 12:33-34; 13:11; 14:5). Jewish sovereignty over Joppa was disputed for some time but the Jews held it *de facto*. So important was the city for the economy of the Hasmonean kingdom that Alexander Jannaeus struck a large series of coins with marine symbols to commemorate its conquest. With the decline of the Hasmonean kingdom and the subsequent conquest of Palestine by Pompey in 64 B.C. Joppa was rebuilt and detached from Judea. This was a great blow to the Judean economy, but in 30 B.C. Augustus returned it to Herod. Herod conferred the rights of a *polis* on the city, and it became the capital of a small district.

Inscription on a Jewish tomb of the Byzantine period found at Jaffa (Joppa).

Excavations showing remains of the Hellenistic period at Jaffa.

*(left)
View of Jaffa from the sea.*

Joppa is mentioned several times in the NT. It was here that Tabitha, a disciple of Jesus and woman "full of good works and charitable deeds" died and was revived by Peter (Acts 9:36 ff) and also here that he saw his vision of the beasts (Acts 10:5 ff).

Excavations in the ancient mound of Jaffa have revealed remains of fortifications and habitations of all periods from the Bronze Age to Byzantine and Arab times. Of great interest are the remains of typical Hyksos fortification and a gate of the Egyptian town of the Late Bronze Age, on the jamb of which a hieroglyphic inscription was found.

JORAH Ancestor of a family which returned from the Babylonian Exile with Zerubbabel (Ezra 2:18).

JORAI Head of a Gadite family.

JORAM See JEHORAM

JORDAN The largest river in Palestine, flowing along the geological Syro-African rift. The river is formed by the confluence of three streams in the foothills of Mount Hermon, at a height of 250 feet (76m) above sea level. As it descends to the Huleh region it divides again into several streams. In the next 10 miles (16km) before it enters the Sea of Galilee it descends 850 feet (260m). Along this part of its course the banks are rocky and precipitous, leaving no margin at the water's edge. From the Sea of Galilee the river winds its way southwards on a meandering course 104 miles (170km) long, although the direct distance to the Dead Sea is only 65 miles (104km). On its passage southwards the Jordan receives numerous tributaries, mainly from Gilead, notably the Yarmuk and the Jabbok. The plain through which the river flows, referred to in the Bible simply as the Plain (Josh 12:1), or the Plain of Jordan (I Kgs 7:46), forms two shelves, one above the other. The southern part has different names: Plains of Moab (Num 22:1) and Plains of Jericho (Josh 4:13). The "cities of the plain" were located here (Gen 19:29).

The Jordan Valley is overgrown with thick vegetation and was rich in wild life, including boar; lions were also to be seen there in biblical times (Jer 49:19). The river was not important to the economy of the country, however; its steep banks prevented its waters being used for irrigation, while its winding course, obstructed by rocks in places, was not fit for navigation. It formed a geographical obstacle between the territories on either side of it, since there were few natural crossing places (there were no bridges in biblical times and swimming was kept only for emergencies). Although there were over 20 fords north of the Sea of Galilee, there were few in the middle reaches and only five closer to the Dead Sea. For this reason there were frequent struggles at these points. Thus the people of Jericho attempted to cut off the way of retreat near

Waterfall at Banias, one of the sources of the Jordan River.

Two views of the Jordan River.

the ford opposite Jericho (Josh 2:7); and after the defeat of Eglon, king of Moab, the Israelites took the fords of the Jordan towards Moab (Judg 3:28). This happened several times (Judg 7:24; 12:5-6). In the conquest of the land of Canaan the Israelites crossed the Jordan, an event considered no less miraculous than the crossing of the Red Sea (Josh chaps. 3-4). In some places in the Bible the Jordan was considered to be the eastern limit of Canaan (Num 13:29; 34:12). After the conquest the river completely separated the tribes on the east from those on the west (Judg 5:17).

The sanctity of the river goes back to early biblical times. Elijah miraculously divided its waters by smiting them with his mantle, and so did Elisha (II Kgs 2:8, 13-14). Naaman, the leprous captain of the host of Syria, dipped seven times in the river, "and his flesh came again like unto the flesh of a little child, and he was clean" (II Kgs 5:14). The holiness of the river was further accentuated when John the Baptist preached and baptized in its waters (Matt 3:5 ff; Mark 1:5 ff), and Jesus himself was baptized by John near Bethabarah (John 1:28-33).

JORIM Son of Matthat No.2 and father of Eliezer No. 11 in the genealogy of Jesus according to Luke.

JORKOAM A place or city founded by Raham the grandson of Hebron; perhaps the same as Jokdeam. Probably somewhere southeast of Hebron.

JOSE A man who appears in the genealogy of Jesus according to the Gospel of Luke (3:29). The name is a variation of Joses, Joshua or Jesus.

JOSEPH ("may [God] increase").

1. Son of Jacob and Rachel. As the firstborn son of his mother, the favorite wife of Jacob (Gen 30:22-24), Joseph received preferential treatment which angered his ten older brothers, their jealousy increasing further after Joseph confided to them his dreams forecasting his future ascendancy over his brothers and father (Gen 37:5-11).

When Joseph came to visit them in the fields near Dothan, the brothers decided to avenge themselves upon him (Gen 37:12-18). The proposal to kill him on the spot was rejected by the eldest, Reuben, who urged his brothers to cast Joseph into an empty well. Afterwards, in Reuben's absence, and at the suggestion of another brother, Judah, they sold him to a caravan of Ishmaelite traders who were on their way to Egypt (Gen 37:19-28). According to another tradition he was hauled

II Kgs 2:6-7, 13; 5:10, 14; 6:2, 4; 7:15; 10:33. I Chr 6:78; 12:15, 37; 19:17; 26:30. II Chr 4:17. Job 40:23. Ps 42:6; 114:3, 5. Is 9:1. Jer 12:5; 49:19; 50:44. Ezek 47:18. Zech 11:3. Matt 3:5-6, 13; 4:15, 25; 19:1. Mark 1:5, 9; 3:8; 10:1. Luke 3:3; 4:1. John 1:28, 3:26; 10:40

JORIM
Luke 3:29

JORKOAM
I Chr 2:44

JOSE
Luke 3:29

JOSEPH 1
Gen 30:24-25; 33:2, 7; 35:24; 37:2-3, 5, 13, 17, 23, 28-29, 31, 33; 39:1-2, 4-7, 10-11, 20-23; 40:3-4, 6, 8-9, 12, 16, 18, 22-23; 41:14-17, 25, 39, 41-42, 44-46, 49-51, 54-57; 42:3-4, 6-9, 14, 18, 23, 25, 36; 43:15-

19, 24-26, 30;
44:2, 4, 14-15;
45:1, 3-4, 9,
16-17, 21, 26-
28; 46:4, 19-
20, 27-31;
47:1, 5, 7, 11-
12, 14-17, 20,
23, 26, 29;
48:1-3, 8-13,
15, 17-18, 21;
49:22, 26;
50:1-2, 4 7-8,
14-17, 19, 22-
26. Ex 1:5-6,
8; 13:19. Num
1:10, 32;
13:11; 26:28,
37; 27:1;
32:33; 34:23;
36:1, 5, 12.
Deut 27:12;
33:13, 16.
Josh 14:4;
16:1, 4; 17:1-
2, 14, 16-17;
18:5, 11;
24:32. Judg
1:22-23, 35.
II Sam 19:20.
I Kgs 11:28.
I Chr 2:2; 5:1-
2; 7:29. Ps
77:15; 78:67;
80:1; 81:5;
105:17. Ezek
37:16, 19;
47:13; 48:32.
Amos 5:6, 15;
6:6. Obad v.
18. Zech 10:6.
John 4:5. Acts
7:9, 13-14, 18.
Heb 11:21-22.
Rev 7:8

out of the well by Midianites (Gen 37:28). On their return home, the brothers told their father that Joseph had been devoured by a wild animal; in support of their story, they displayed Joseph's coat which they had dipped in blood (Gen 37:29-36).

In Egypt Joseph was sold to Potiphar, the captain of Pharaoh's guard, who rewarded Joseph's success in all his tasks by appointing him overseer of his house. Joseph's charm induced Potiphar's wife to attempt to seduce him (Gen 39:1-6); but finding her advances rejected she in turn accused him of trying to rape her, an accusation for which his master put him in prison (Gen 39:7-20). There he was entrusted with the care of two of Pharaoh's imprisoned officers, his chief butler and his chief baker (Gen 39:21-40:4), whose dreams he interpreted.

The chief butler was subsequently reinstated. When Pharaoh had two disturbing dreams which seemed to defy interpretation, the butler told him about Joseph. Joseph was brought before Pharaoh, and interpreted his dreams as foretelling seven years of plenty to be followed by seven years of famine (Gen 41:8-32). Joseph also suggested how to put this foreknowledge to good use: during the seven bountiful years, a fifth of all agricultural produce was to be stored in Pharaoh's warehouses for distribution during the years of famine. Pharaoh charged Joseph, then age 30, with the task of implementing his own suggestions and gave him the rank and authority of a viceroy (Gen 41:33-44; cf 47:13-26). He also gave him an Egyptian name (Zaphnath-Paaneah) and a wife (Asenath), who bore him two sons, Manasseh and Ephraim (Gen 41:45, 50-53).

When the famine came, it also affected the land of Canaan, whereupon Jacob sent all his sons, except for Benjamin, to Egypt in order to buy corn (Gen 42:1-5). There they met Joseph who directed the distribution. He recognized them, but concealed his identity: accusing them of espionage, he put them in prison for three days. Afterwards he ordered them to bring their youngest brother, Benjamin (Joseph's full brother) to Egypt. Simeon was to remain in prison as a hostage (Gen 42:6-24). Despite his misgivings, Jacob had to approve of a second expedition and Judah took upon himself the responsibility for the safety of Benjamin (Gen 43:1-15).

On the brothers' return, Joseph still kept his identity hidden from them. When they left for home, all the money which they had brought with them was returned to their sacks, and Joseph's silver goblet was placed in Benjamin's luggage. Joseph then sent guards to bring them back, accusing them of stealing his favorite cup (Gen 44:1-15). After Judah in self-defense told the story of their family, recounting all the ills which had befallen Jacob (Gen 44:18-34), Joseph could no longer maintain the pretense. Weeping, he finally revealed his identity, explaining to them that his deportation to Egypt was actually an act of divine providence, whereby it befell to him to take care of his family. He ordered them to return home to fetch his father (Gen 45:1-24), and upon their return they were given land in Goshen (Gen 47:4, 11-12).

In accordance with Jacob's wishes, Joseph undertook the responsibility for his father's burial in Canaan (Gen 47:28-31; 49:29-33; 50:1-14). When Joseph himself died, at the age of 110, he made his family swear to restore his bones to Canaan (Gen 50:22-26).

The Joseph cycle forms the transition between the stories of the patriarchs and the Israelite enslavement in Egypt (Ex 1:6-8). At the time of the Exodus, Moses fulfilled Joseph's last wish by taking along his bones (Ex 13:19). Joseph was finally buried near Shechem in the field of Jacob (Josh 24:32).

In biblical literature the name "Joseph" (or "house of Joseph", "children of Joseph", etc.) denotes the tribes Manasseh and Ephraim

Entrance to the tomb of Joseph in Shechem.

Joseph forced into a pit by his brothers. On the right hand side of the illustration, Joseph's brothers bargain the sale of their brother. Page from a French 13th century psalter. (Bibliothèque Nationale, Paris)

(Josh 17:14-17; I Kgs 11:28; Ps 78:67); or the kingdom of the northern tribes (Amos 5:6; 6:6); or even Israel in general (Ps 80:1; 81:5).

The story of Joseph allows for interpretation on several levels. From the personal point of view, it is a story of the suffering and greatness of Joseph himself, the epitome of wisdom in government and in things divine (interpretation of dreams, Gen 40:8; 41:25, 28, 32) as well as of temperance (as e.g. Gen 39:8-12; 50:14-21). On the national plane, the Joseph narrative reflects the relations between the tribes; the powerful tribes of the house of Joseph (Ephraim and Manasseh) are exalted (cf Gen 48:19-20; 49:22-26) as is Benjamin; Judah is cautiously honored (Gen 37:26-27; 43:3-10; 44:18-34), whereas Reuben is shown to be well-intentioned but powerless (Gen 37:21-30; 42:22-37).

In the NT, Joseph was referred to by Stephen in his speech of defense before the Sanhedrin (Acts 7:9 ff); in the Epistle to the Hebrews he is mentioned among the heroes of faith (Heb 11:22).

2. Father of Igal, of the tribe of Issachar, one of the spies sent to scout the land of Canaan.

3. A Levite musician in the Temple and one of the sons of Asaph.

4. A son of Bani who repudiated his alien wife in accordance with Ezra's decree.

JOSEPH 2
Num 13:7

JOSEPH 3
I Chr 25:2, 9

JOSEPH 4
Ezra 10:42

5. A priest at the time of Joiakim, and head of the house of Shebaniah.

6. Son of Jacob (Matt 1:16), or of Heli (Luke 3:23). The gospels refer to Joseph as Jesus' father, through whom his family tree is traced back to David and Abraham (Matt chap. 1) or to Adam (Luke chap. 3). Joseph lived in Nazareth and worked there as a carpenter (Matt 13:55). Betrothed to Mary, he married her at the instigation of an angel, who informed him of her pregnancy by the Holy Spirit. At the time of the census during the rule of Quirinius, Joseph, being a descendant of David, was required to undergo registration in David's city, Bethlehem, and it was there that Jesus was born. With his wife Mary and the infant Jesus, Joseph subsequently fled to Egypt, fearing Herod's wrath; after the latter's death they returned to Nazareth. Joseph and his family went up to Jerusalem on two occasions, once to present Jesus in the Temple after Mary's "days of purification" were completed (Luke 2:22) and again, during Passover when Jesus was 12 years old. Joseph is not mentioned during the period of Jesus' public ministry and may have died previously.

7. Joseph of Arimathea. A rich man, a member of the Sanhedrin (Mark 15:43) and a follower of Jesus, to whom Pilate delivered the body of Jesus. Joseph owned the tomb in which Jesus was interred (Matt 27:57ff). According to Luke 23:50 Joseph was "a good and just man"; John adds (19:38) that he secretly feared the Jews.

8. The name of several otherwise unknown persons, mentioned in the genealogy of Jesus in Luke chapter 3.

9. One of the two disciples mentioned as successor of Judas Iscariot. He was also known as Barsabas, and bore the added name of Justus.

JOSES (Greek form of Joseph). Called Joseph in some manuscripts but Joses in others.

1. A brother of Jesus.

2. A brother of James the Less. His mother Mary stood by the cross of Jesus.

3. See BARNABAS.

JOSHAH Son of Amaziah and leader of one of the families of Simeon.

JOSHAPHAT ("Yah has judged").

1. Joshaphat the Mithnite, one of David's thirty "mighty men".

2. One of the priests who blew the trumpet before the ark in the time of King David.

JOSHAVIAH One of the two sons of Elneam who were among David's thirty "mighty men".

JOSHBEKASHAH One of the sons of Heman the singer; he was in charge of the 17th division of musicians in the House of the Lord at the time of King David. However, the word may not denote an individual but most probably is part of a liturgical prayer.

JOSHEB-BASSHEBETH See JASHOBEAM No.1

JOSHIBIAH ("may Yah cause to dwell"). The son of Seraiah of the tribe of Simeon (I Chr 4:35).

JOSHUA ("Yah is salvation").

1. The son of Nun of the tribe of Ephraim; Moses' successor as the leader of Israel. He was the head of the army during Moses' decisive battle against the Amalekites (Ex 17:8-16). Elsewhere Joshua is linked with Moses in various contexts (Ex 24:13; 32:17; 33:11), though always in a subordinate role. Of the 12 spies, only Joshua and Caleb gave an encouraging report of their mission, affirming the feasibility of conquering the land of Canaan (Num 13:6, 8; 14:6-8); the two men were rewarded with permission to enter the country (Num 14:30, 38; 26:65; 32:12) which even Moses could only view from afar.

One of the tombs inside the Church of the Holy Sepulcher in Jerusalem, traditionally said to be the tomb of Joseph of Arimathea.

The battle for Jericho, from the so-called Joshua Roll, showing seven priests blowing horns, while Joshua encourages the men entering the city. On the left are three priests bearing the ark of the covenant. 10th century. (Vatican Library, Rome)

Joshua led the Israelites in the conquest of Canaan but his contribution may have been more modest than the prevailing claims in the book that celebrates his accomplishments. Though almost all of the victories are ascribed to him, the conquest was a much more complicated process and many battles later accredited to him were in fact conducted by others. Joshua is said to have settled in the hill country of Ephraim; his village is called Timnath Serah (Josh 19:50; 24:30) and Timnath Heres (Judg 2:9). Two accounts of his death at the age of 110 have survived (Josh 24:29; Judg 2:8).

He is remembered for military exploits, but his liturgical leadership is also celebrated, especially the assembly at Shechem (Josh chap. 24) and the reading of the Law at Mount Ebal and Mount Gerizim. Joshua's original name, which was changed by Moses, was Hoshea (Num 3:8, 16).

Later literature identified Joshua as Moses' successor (Eccl 46:1) and a judge in Israel (I Macc 2:55). His power of intercession impressed one author (II Esdras 7:37), as did his role in transmitting the Torah (Pirke Avot 1:1). The unknown author of Hebrews reasons that the respite achieved for Israel by Joshua was only of limited duration, otherwise God would not have promised a rest at a later time (Heb 4:8). See JOSHUA, BOOK OF.

2. See JESHUA No.5

3. The owner of a field in Beth Shemesh (I Sam 6:14) through which the ark was brought from the Philistines.

4. A governor of Jerusalem in King Josiah's time.

JOSHUA, BOOK OF The story of Israel's conquest of Canaan and allocation of the land among the Israelite tribes. The book records the miraculous victory over Jericho and the defeat of Ai (chaps. 1-8). It reports that some Gibeonites carried out a successful ruse that tricked Joshua into a covenant relationship (chap. 9), although these people were relegated to a subservient role in society. The thread of the narrative weaves a fabric of victorious engagements on the battlefield, first against five Canaanite chieftains in the south (chap. 10) and subsequently in the north (chap. 11). A summary of Joshua's achievements brings to a close the account of holy wars against the native population (chap. 12). Having successfully seized the land, Joshua's next undertaking was to divide it among the tribes. Moreover, he is credited with having instituted six cities of refuge to which persons guilty of accidental killings could flee; he also designated 48 cities as the inheritance of the Levitical priests (chaps. 13-23). The book concludes with an account of a solemn ceremony of covenant renewal in which the people affirm exclusive allegiance to their victorious God (chap. 24).

The prevailing depiction of the conquest elevates Joshua by comparing him to Moses. Nevertheless, the real hero of the account of the conquest is Joshua's God, who demonstrates awesome power with

2:1, 23-24; 3:1, 5-7, 9-10; 4:1, 4-5, 8-10, 14-15, 17, 20; 5:2-4, 7, 9, 13-15; 6:2, 6, 8, 10, 12, 16, 22, 25-27; 7:2-3, 6-7, 10, 16, 19-20, 22-25; 8:1, 3, 9-10, 13, 15-16, 18, 21, 23, 26-30, 35; 9:2-3, 6, 8, 15, 22, 24, 27; 10:1, 4, 6-9, 12, 15, 17-18, 20-22, 24-29, 31, 33-34, 36, 38, 40-43; 11:6-7, 9-10, 12-13, 15-16, 18, 21, 23; 12:7; 13:1; 14:1, 6, 13; 15:13; 17:4, 14-15, 17; 18:3, 8-10; 19:49, 51; 20:1; 21:1; 22:6-7; 23:1-2; 24:1-2, 19, 21-22, 24-29, 31. Judg 1:1; 2:6-8, 21, 23. I Kgs 16:34. I Chr 7:27. Neh 8:17. Acts 7:45. Heb 4:8

JOSHUA 2
Hag 1:1, 12, 14; 2:2, 4. Zech 3:1, 3, 6, 8-9; 6:11

JOSHUA 3
I Sam 6:14, 18

JOSHUA 4
II Kgs 23:8

minimal assistance from Israelite soldiers. This feature of the book is no extraneous afterthought, but permeates the story from first to last. The deity is pictured as eager to eradicate the native population; the rationale for such hostility is the threat their religion presents to the Israelites. In the eyes of the author, this danger fully justified wholesale slaughter of Canaanites. For this reason, the cities are placed under the *herem*, the ban in holy war when everything and every person is utterly destroyed. Even Israelites who violate this ban for personal gain become subject to its grim sentence, as Achan and his family experience to his horror (7:1-26). The fall of Jericho is attributed to the deity alone, and this God is said to have actively entered into conflict at Gibeon, hurling hailstones upon the Canaanites and altering the course of the heavenly bodies for Israel's benefit ("Sun, stand still over Gibeon, and Moon in the valley of Aijalon" 10:12).

Some passages in the book indicate that the description of unified conquest is highly exaggerated (chaps. 14-19). Clearly, large native populations survived undefeated by the Israelite army. This view is also characteristic of Judges 1:1-2:5, which originally concluded the Book of Joshua. Instead of a sweeping military conquest, Israel's influx was probably a much more complicated process, consisting of local conquests of the individual tribes, along with gradual and peaceful infiltration into the unoccupied highlands and, later, into the more fertile sections of the country, also acquired by intermarriage and covenant relationships. Israel's failure to dislodge the Canaanites immediately is blamed on religious disobedience (Judg 1:28, 33, 35; 2:3). As these conflicting accounts show, the Book of Joshua lacks unity and contains contradictions and inconsistencies. There are the two reports of Joshua's dismissal of the people and of his death (chap. 24). Other indications of multiple composition are: Jerusalem was captured and was not (Josh chap. 10 as against 15:63); Israelites were faithful to the deity and were not (5:2-12· 8:30-35; 24:14 etc.); a memorial stone was set up on the Jordan River and within the land. Moreover, the stories about Jericho and Ai contain awkward inconsistencies, and the report about Rahab's family is loosely attached to the narrative. Even chronology presents some difficulty: if the crossing of the Jordan took place on the tenth day (3:11 ff; 4:19) and the Passover celebration on the 14th (5:10), how could mass circumcision have occurred between the two dates without rendering all males ritually impure?

An obvious explanation for these discrepancies must be sought in the literary origins of the book. Two theories have emerged in the forefront of discussion, one based on an assumption of sources and the other focusing on the history of tradition. The former is that the four sources or traditions underlying the Pentateuch continue into the Book of Joshua,

The traditional site of the tomb of Joshua, southwest of Shechem.

justifying the term Hexateuch. It is argued that without Joshua the Torah is truncated, for the fulfillment of God's promise of land occurs here. According to an alternative proposal the first four books of the Torah form a Tetrateuch, and Deuteronomy through Kings comprise a single work, called the Deuteronomistic history. It is the latter which portrayed the conquest in the grand sweeping manner that permeates the book.

OUTLINE

1:1-5:12	Crossing the Jordan; preparations for the conquest
5:13-8:35	Conquests in the south (Jericho, Ai)
9:1-10:27	Conquests in the center
10:28-43	Campaign in the south
11:1-12:24	Conquests in the north
13:1-19:51	Division of the land among the tribes
20:1-21:4	Cities of refuge and levitical cities
22:1-34	Departure of the tribes living in Transjordan
23:1-24:33	Joshua's last days, farewell address, death and burial

---

JOSIAH ("may Yah give"). Son of Amon, who was proclaimed king of Judah upon the assassination of his father. He came to the throne at the age of eight and reigned for 31 years (639-609 B.C.) (II Kgs 22:1; II Chr 34:1). His reign was the last surge of political independence and religious revival before the disintegration of the Kingdom of Judah, which ended with the destruction of Jerusalem in 586 B.C. The biblical accounts of the national and religious revival initiated by Josiah vary considerably. The Book of Chronicles records several stages: in the eighth year of his reign he rejected the gods of his Assyrian overlord and began to seek out the God of David (II Chr 34:3). In the 12th year Josiah began to purge Judah and Jerusalem, and continued in Manasseh, Ephraim and Naphtali (II Chr 34:3-7), thereby indicating that he expanded the borders of Judah to include almost all of the former territory of the Northern Kingdom of Israel. This was possible only after the Assyrian king, Ashurbanipal's death, c. 630 B.C., and the subsequent revolts in Assyria, which would explain both Assyria's weakened control over the former Northern Kingdom's territories, and the opportunity for Josiah to assert his independence and begin a reformation. In the 18th year of his reign he carried out far-reaching political and religious reforms following the discovery of the "Book of the Law" in the Temple (II Chr 34:8-33; 35:1-19). The Book of Kings, on the other hand, mentions only the reformation in the 18th year (II Kgs 22:3-20; 23:1-25) although it is stated that the kingdom extended beyond the borders of Judah (II Kgs 23:19). Archeological finds bear witness to the expansionist attempts of Josiah.

This great national-spiritual upsurge found expression in cultic reform including the purification of worship throughout Judah, and its centralization in Jerusalem. Although the details of the actual discovery of the "Book of Law" in the Temple are uncertain and pose many

JOSIAH
I Kgs 13:2.
II Kgs 21:24, 26; 22:1, 3; 23:16, 19, 23-24, 28-30, 34.
I Chr 3:14-15.
II Chr 33:25; 34:1, 33; 35:1, 7, 16, 18-20, 22-26; 36:1.
Jer 1:2-3; 3:6; 22:11, 18; 25:1, 3; 26:1; 27:1; 35:1; 36:1-2, 9, 37:1; 45:1; 46:2. Zeph 1:1. Zech 6:10. Matt 1:10-11

questions, many scholars adopt the position that this code now forms the kernel of the present Book of Deuteronomy (see DEUTERONOMY). According to the biblical account it was the reading of this book that caused Josiah to rend his clothes, since apparently the observance of the Law had been neglected in preceding decades. Huldah the prophetess warned the people of the impending judgment awaiting them because of this neglect. Thus Josiah, fearing divine punishment, was moved to sweeping religious reform, and because of this he ranks with Jehoshaphat and Hezekiah in the biblical account as an outstanding righteous ruler. However, his leadership was abruptly ended in 609 B.C. when he was mortally wounded in battle against Necho II pharaoh of Egypt at the Megiddo pass, while on his way to aid Assyria in her deteriorating struggle against the Babylonians (II Chr 35:20-25).

JOTBAH
II Kgs 21:19

JOTBAH A village in lower Galilee about 5¹/₂ miles (9 km) north of Sepphoris, also called Jodephat. The birthplace of Meshullemeth, daughter of Haruz, the mother of Amon, king of Judah (II Kgs 21:19). It is identified with Khirbet Jefat and archeological surveys made on the site show that it was inhabited as early as the Late Bronze Age. In the

Khirbet Jefat identified with Jotbah.

Mishnah it is listed among the walled cities dating back to the time of Joshua, son of Nun. Mentioned by Josephus as Jotapata, it was fortified by him when he prepared the defense of Galilee against the Romans (*War* III, 141-288). After a siege of 47 days Vespasian conquered the fortress in A.D. 67 (*War* III, 316-38).

JOTBATHAH
Num 33:33-34.
Deut 10:7

JOTBATHAH One of the stations of the Children of Israel on the route of the Exodus; it is mentioned between Moseroth, Bene Jaakan, Hor Hagidgad, Abronah and Ezion Geber (Num 33:33-35). Except for Ezion Geber, the location of which is definite, none of the other stations has been identified. In Deuteronomy 10:7 Jotbathah is "a land of rivers of water", which makes the identification still more difficult, because such rivers exist neither in Sinai nor the Negeb, where this place should be sought. Some identify Jotbathah with Sabhat (salt marshes) et-Taba site of the spring of Ain et-Taba, some 20 miles (32 km) north of Ezion Geber (Eilat); others suggest Ain Ghadian, a place rich in springs in the northern part of the same region, where recently a fortress of the 12th/11th century B.C. was found, giving further weight to the latter identification.

JOTHAM ("may Yah complete").

JOTHAM I
Judg 9:5, 7,
21, 57

1. The youngest of the 70 sons of Gideon (Jerubbaal). He was the only survivor of the massacre carried out by Abimelech and the men of Shechem (Judg 9:5).

After learning that Abimelech had been crowned at Shechem, Jotham ascended Mount Gerizim and addressed the people of the city. He berated them by recounting a fable about trees that sought to anoint a king over them: the olive, fig and vine all turned down kingship, but the worthless bramble accepted it (Judg 9:7-15). Jotham's interpretation of the fable spells out his anger at the people's treatment of Gideon; his attitude toward the institution of the monarchy echoes

Gideon's point of view (Judg 8:23). Jotham ended his words with a prophetic curse and fled for his life (Judg 9:21).

2. The son of King Uzziah (Azariah), of Judah, and of Jerusha the daughter of Zadok. He succeeded his father as king of Judah at the age of 25. According to II Kings 15:33 and II Chronicles chapter 27 he reigned for 16 years (758-743 B.C.). This span probably includes the eight years during which he functioned as regent because his father, smitten with leprosy, was unable to perform his royal duties. Jotham is mentioned as a contemporary of Jeroboam II (I Chr 5:17). He fought against the Ammonites, defeated them and forced them to pay a very heavy tribute (II Chr 27:5). He extended his father's building projects (II Chr 26:6) particularly in the hill-country of Judah (II Chr 27:4), constructed the upper gate of the House of the Lord (II Kgs 15:35) and built extensively on the wall at Ophel (II Chr 27:3). He also erected forts and towers on the wooded hills (II Chr 27:3-4).

3. The son of Jahdai, descendant of Jerahmeel of the tribe of Judah.

JOZABAD See JEHOZABAD

JOZACHAR Son of Shimeath and one of those who participated in the assassination of King Joash. He is called Zabad in II Chronicles 24:26.

JOZADAK See JEHOZADAK

JUBAL The son of Lamech and Adah and the brother of Jabal. He was the "father of all those who play the harp and flute" (Gen 4:20-21).

JUBILEE The jubilee year concluded a 50-year cycle and followed the seventh sabbatical year (See SABBATICAL YEAR). After 49 years, the land reverted to its original owner from whomever had been leasing it.

The word comes from the Hebrew *yobel*, probably meaning a ram's horn, the jubilee year being ushered in by the ram's horn sounded on the tenth day of the seventh month, the Day of Atonement (Lev 25:9).

Several characteristics distinguished the jubilee year:
(a) Being considered holy, it had the same agricultural restrictions as the sabbatical year when sowing, reaping or harvesting were forbidden (Lev 25:11-12). The land was to remain fallow, even though the previous year had been, by definition, a sabbatical year.
(b) It was a year of "release" when people returned to their homes and property reverted to its ancestral owner. In all land sales, the price took into consideration the time remaining until the eventual return of the land to its original owner (Lev 25:15-17).

A person who sold land could redeem it at any time; should he be unable to pay the redemption price, the land would nevertheless automatically revert to him at the jubilee. For other kinds of property,

JOTHAM 2
II Kgs 15:5, 7, 30, 32, 36, 38; 16:1. I Chr 3:12; 5:17. II Chr 26:21, 23; 27:1, 6-7, 9. Is 1:1; 7:1. Hos 1:1. Mic 1:1. Matt 1:9

JOTHAM 3
I Chr 2:47

JOZABAD
I Chr 12:4, 20. II Chr 31:13; 35:9. Ezra 8:33; 10:22-23. Neh 8:7; 11:16

JOZACHAR
II Kgs 12:21

JOZADAK
Ezra 3:2, 8; 5:2; 10:18. Neh 12:26

JUBAL
Gen 4:21

JUBILEE
Lev 25:9-13, 15, 28, 30-31, 33, 40, 50, 52, 54; 27:17-18, 21, 23-24. Num 36:4

Model of a granary with twelve silos from El Kab, Upper Egypt. 2600-2500 B.C. (Dagon Museum, Haifa)

the rules are as follows: (1) A house within a walled city could be redeemed for period of one year; if unredeemed, it did not revert to the original owner at jubilee, but remained in the permanent possession of the purchaser. (2) A house in an unwalled city was treated as a field. (3) Houses in Levitical cities had perpetual right of redemption (Lev 25:25-34).

(c) An Israelite selling himself into bondage due to poverty must be released in the jubilee year. The slave could redeem himself earlier, the redemption price taking into consideration the time span remaining until the jubilee year (Lev 25:39-55).

The books of the Prophets make no specific reference to observance or non-observance of the jubilee but there are two references to the year of release. Jeremiah tells of Zedekiah's proclamation of freedom for all slaves (but not in the context of the jubilee year, Jer 34:8-16), and Ezekiel's utopian vision which portrays restoration of property in the year of release (Ezek 46:17).

Many of the legal concepts of the jubilee year are familiar from ancient Near Eastern literature. The innovation of the Hebrew Bible was in assimilating these concepts into the relationship between God and the people of Israel. By virtue of the jubilee, God allows all people to begin their careers afresh with equality restored. One has no right to sell his ancestral land because "the land is mine" (Lev 25:20-23). One cannot enslave his fellow Israelite permanently, for the Children of Israel were brought out of the land of Egypt in order to be "my servants" (Lev 25:55).

JUCAL
Jer 38:1

JUCAL See JEHUCAL

JUDAH

JUDAH 1
See end of book

1. The fourth son of Jacob and Leah. The folk etymology of his name is derived from the verb "to praise" (Gen 29:35). He married the daughter of Shua (or possibly her name was Bath-Shua), a Canaanite, who bore him three sons (Gen 38:1-5). Judah's intimacy with his disguised daughter-in-law Tamar (Gen 38:12-18) resulted in the birth of Perez and Zerah, the main ancestors of the tribe of Judah. In the Joseph story, Judah plays an important role as the family spokesman (Gen 37:26; 43:3, 8; 44:14, 16, 18; 46:28). He is the eponym of the tribe of Judah.

The first judge of the period of the conquest and settlement was Othniel who belonged to the tribe of Judah (Judg 3:7-11), which was to be the main tribe in southern Canaan. It is seldom mentioned before the period of the monarchy. In the wilderness, it numbered 74,600 in the census described in Numbers 1:27 and 76,500 according to Numbers 26:22. During the process of settling the mountains, the Plain and the pasture lands of the wilderness of Judah, the Judahites came into contact with the Philistines, and it would seem that at first the Judahites had the upper hand in border skirmishes. However, the Philistines eventually succeeded in imposing their authority over the whole of the Shephelah (Judg 15:9-11). Their possibilities for westward expansion checked, the Judahites turned to the north, wresting extensive areas from the Jebusites, while finally penetrating into the area of the former Danite inheritance, which brought them into conflict with the Benjamites. This rivalry led to fratricidal war between Benjamin and its two neighbors, Ephraim to the north and Judah to the south. Judah participated actively in the struggle against the domination of the Philistines, who now ruled over almost the entire mountain area of western Israel (c. 1050 B.C.).

The territory of the tribe of Judah delineated in Joshua 15:1-12, included part of the Negeb region, the coastal plain, the Shephelah and

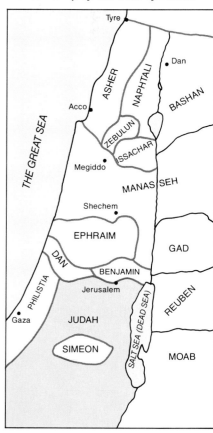

The territory of the tribe of Judah.

JUDAH 2
Luke 3:26

JUDAH 3
Luke 3:30

JUDAH 4
Ezra 3:9

JUDAH 5
Ezra 10:23

JUDAH 6
Neh 11:9

JUDAH 7
Neh 12:8

JUDAH 8
Neh 4:10, 16;
12:34

JUDAH 9
Neh 12:36

JUDAH, KINGDOM
OF
See end of
book

(bottom of page)
Seal impression on a jar handle, inscribed "to the king of Hebron". 8th-7th centuries B.C. (Israel Department of Antiquities and Museums)

Clay jar bearing the inscription "to the king of Hebron" on each of its handles. 8th-7th centuries B.C. (Israel Department of Antiquities and Museums)

the hill country of Judah, the wilderness of Judah, small areas of the Jordan plain (north of the Dead Sea) and the Arabah (south of the Dead Sea). The great importance of Judah stems in the first place from David. With the rule of David and Solomon, stemming from the tribe, Judah took a central role. After the split in the monarchy, Judah was predominant in the Southern Kingdom which was even known as the Kingdom of Judah. In the NT the tribe of Judah appears at the head of the list of the sealed.

2. Son of Joannas and father of a certain Joseph, in the genealogy of Jesus.

3. Son of a Joseph and father of a Simeon, in the genealogy of Jesus.

4. A Levite whose sons were overseers of the rebuilding of the Temple in the time of Ezra. Alternatively identified as Hodaviah (Ezra 2:40).

5. A Levite who repudiated his foreign wife at the decree of Ezra.

6. A son of Senuah from the tribe of Benjamin who dwelt in Jerusalem after the return from the Exile.

7. One of the Levites who returned from the Exile with Zerubbabel.

8. A leader of the tribe of Judah at the time of Nehemiah's dedication of the wall (Neh 12:34). Probably identical with the characters mentioned in Nehemiah 4:10, 16.

9. A priest and musician at the dedication of the wall.

JUDAH, KINGDOM OF The southerly of the two kingdoms into which Solomon's United Monarchy divided under his son and successor, Rehoboam. On his accession, Rehoboam did not enjoy his father's and grandfather's popularity with the people, and was faced with a growing wave of strong demands from the tribes to ease the economic burdens placed on them by Solomon (I Kgs 9:15-19; 11:26-27). In accordance with the pattern of the monarchy established by David, he had to be recognized separately by both Judah and Israel. After his coronation in Jerusalem, he traveled to Shechem. The assembly of Israel saw the time as favorable for putting pressure on the new king, and demanded a reduction of their territory's tax burden as a condition for their acceptance. The elder ministers advised the king to yield, but his younger counselors, who had been reared in the atmosphere of an absolute monarchy, advised him to reject. The king's defiant reply led to open revolt in the north. Adoram, the hated overseer of the corvée, who had been sent to quell what Rehoboam thought was a minor insurrection, was stoned to death, and the king himself barely escaped with his life (I Kgs 12:18). Jeroboam, who had been exiled under Solomon, returned and was proclaimed king in Shechem.

The Kingdom of Judah and the House of David did not accept the secession of the ten tribes, regarding the move as illegal. This viewpoint finds expression in biblical historiography: the author of the Book of Kings describes the history of the Kingdom of Israel in a negative light, whereas the Book of Chronicles almost completely ignores the existence of the Northern Kingdom.

Two generations of fierce military clashes between the two sister kingdoms followed the division of the United Monarchy. This fratricidal war severely weakened both kingdoms, and Judah lost control over Ammon, Moab and probably over Edom as well. The Davidic dynasty now ruled over a shrunken territory that consisted of the areas of the tribes of Judah, Simeon and Benjamin (which appears to have broken its connections with the northern tribes during the period of the United Monarchy.)

In addition to internal and external problems, Rehoboam had to face the aggressive Pharaoh Shishak (Sheshonk I) of the 22nd Dynasty of Egypt, who had been Solomon's enemy and had consistently supported

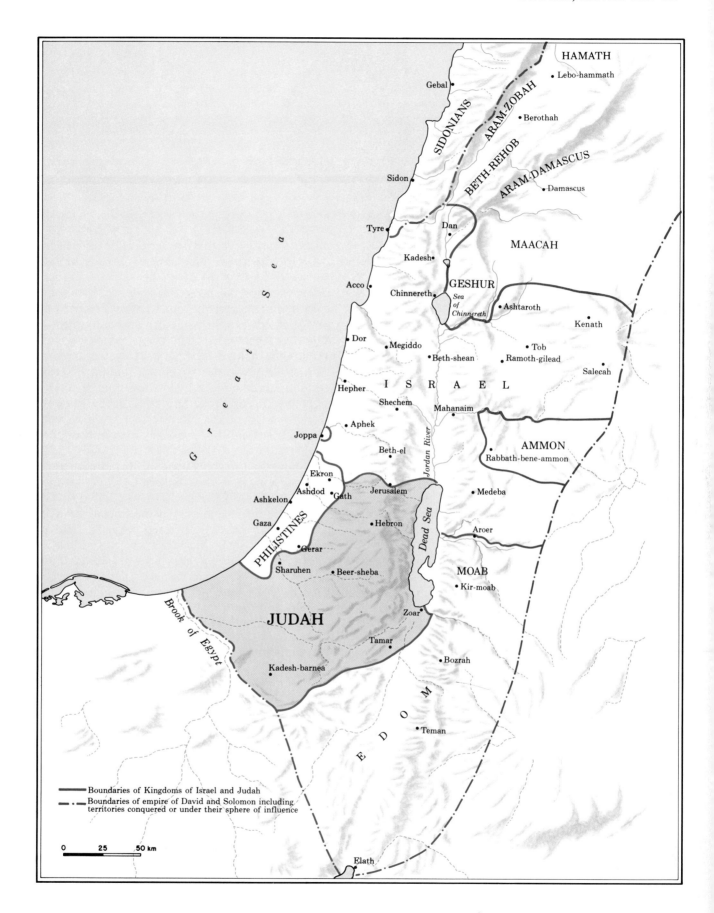

HAMATH

• Lebo-hammath

Gebal •

ARAM-ZOBAH

• Berothah

SIDONIANS

BETH-REHOB

ARAM-DAMASCUS

Sidon •

• Damascus

Tyre •

Dan •

Kadesh •

MAACAH

G r e a t   S e a

Acco •

GESHUR

Chinnereth •

*Sea
of
Chinnereth*

• Ashtaroth

Kenath

Dor •

• Megiddo

• Tob

Salecah

• Beth-shean

Ramoth-gilead

Hepher •

I S R A E L

Shechem •

Mahanaim •

• Aphek

Joppa •

Beth-el •

Jordan River

AMMON

Ekron •

Rabbath-bene-ammon •

Ashdod •

• Gath

Jerusalem •

Ashkelon •

• Medeba

Dead Sea

Gaza •

PHILISTINES

• Hebron

• Aroer

MOAB

• Gerar

JUDAH

• Kir-moab

Sharuhen •

• Beer-sheba

Zoar •

Brook of Egypt

Tamar •

• Bozrah

• Kadesh-barnea

E D O M

• Teman

——— Boundaries of Kingdoms of Israel and Judah
—·—·— Boundaries of empire of David and Solomon including
          territories conquered or under their sphere of influence

0   25   50 km

Elath •

The Kingdom of Judah

The name of the province "Jehud" on a coin struck in Jerusalem in the 4th century B.C.

all foes of the Davidic dynasty (I Kgs 11:14ff). After the division of the kingdom, Jeroboam called on Shishak, his former patron, to raid Judahite towns. According to I Kings 14:25-26 he invaded Judah, captured several fortified towns and besieged Jerusalem. Rehoboam was forced to pay a heavy tribute, surrendering to him Temple and palace treasures. A record of the campaign appearing on the southern wall of the Temple of Amon at Karnak lists 150 places which Shishak claims to have taken, but does not include Jerusalem. However, it seems that the largest Israelite cities were also destroyed and the most fertile areas of the Northern Kingdom damaged, so by encouraging Shishak's attack on Judah, Jeroboam apparently invited his own disaster as well.

After the withdrawal of the Egyptians, Rehoboam took care to prevent a further invasion by fortifying the exposed cities in the south (II Chr 11:5-12; cf 12:13).

War with Israel continued during the short reign of Rehoboam's son Abijah (called Abijam in Kings), who advanced his father's expansionist aims in the hill country of Ephraim (II Chr 13:13-19). The success of Abijah's large-scale offensive against Jeroboam was perhaps due to the good relations which his father fostered with the tribe of Benjamin, through his marriage with Maachah from Gibeah of Benjamin (II Chr 13:2). As a result, Judah's territory was extended not only over the territory of Benjamin but also over the southern part of Ephraim, with the conquest of the important towns of Bethel, Jeshanah and Ephraim. I Kings 15:19 may allude to a treaty that Abijah had concluded with Hadad son of Tabrimmon, king of Damascus, directed against Jeroboam. It was unfortunate that the successors of David and Solomon resorted to the short-sighted policy of inviting Aramean

Landscape in the Judean hills.

intervention in the affairs of the divided nation. It merely led to Aram-Damascus becoming the main beneficiary of the rivalry between the two sister kingdoms, which in the long run was to affect the Southern Kingdom disastrously.

Abijah reigned only three years and was succeeded by his son Asa. During the first 15 years of his reign, it would seem that Maachah, Asa's grandmother (according to II Chr 15:16, she was his mother), exerted considerable influence over affairs of state and forms of worship, and may even have acted as regent until Asa attained his majority. The first decade of Asa's reign was peaceful (II Chr 14:1) and was devoted to fortifying the country and training the army (II Chr 14:6-8). This proved worthwhile: when Zerah the Cushite later invaded the country, reaching Mareshah, Asa was successful in defending the south of Judah, and not only did he regain the territories Judah had lost in Rehoboam's time, he also expanded them (II Chr 14:9-14). Once all danger from the south had been removed, Asa turned his attention to internal reforms. Idolatrous practices had crept in during his grandmother's regency; Asa ordered the image she had set up in honor of Asherah destroyed, and removed her from her place of authority. With the help of the prophet Azariah he abolished all foreign religious rites and sanctuaries in Judah (I Kgs 15:12-13; II Chr 15:8). He was, however, powerless to put down the worship in the rural sanctuaries, for even in Judah religious decentralization was rampant and the high places' opposition to the Temple's claims to sole recognition continued to be tolerated.

While the process of internal religious reformation was taking place, Baasha king of Israel began a military campaign against Judah, in Asa's 36th year. He penetrated almost as far as Jerusalem, posing a serious threat of isolation to the capital of Judah. Asa was forced to turn to Ben-Hadad I, king of Damascus and succeeded in getting him to break off his treaty with Baasha, and in provoking the penetration of the Arameans into the northern parts of the Kingdom of Israel (I Kgs 15:16-22; II Chr 16:1-6). Baasha was compelled to withdraw from Judah in order to protect his own kingdom, and Asa fortified his northern boundary, thus abandoning whatever hopes there had been for the reunification of the two kingdoms. Asa, who had the support of popular and prophetic circles for his religious reforms, appears to have lost this support when he allied himself with the king of Aram-Damascus, and II Chronicles 16:7-10 implies that he oppressed his own people. Asa died after 41 years of rule (II Chr 16:12-13), and it is possible that during his last years, his son Jehoshaphat acted as regent.

Jehoshaphat, realizing the political and economic benefits which would accrue to Judah if it joined with the now-powerful Northern Kingdom, concluded a treaty with Ahab, the king of Israel (I Kgs 22:44; II Chr 18:1). As a result of this alliance, which was strengthened by the marriage of the crown prince, Jehoram, son of Jehoshaphat, to Athaliah, daughter of Ahab and Jezebel, Judah enjoyed a relatively long period of peace. Jehoshaphat exploited these conditions by resuming his ancestor's expeditions to Ophir. Judah's renewed control over Edom (I Kgs 22:47) made trade with Arabia and the Red Sea countries possible, bringing the country to new heights of prosperity. The copper mines in the Arabah were now worked. The fleet which was built, however, to increase Jehoshaphat's overseas trade, was wrecked before it set sail (I Kgs 22:48). After this setback, Jehoshaphat refused Ahaziah, king of Israel's offers to try again. Jehoshaphat devoted much attention to internal policy. He introduced a new juridical system (II Chr 17:7-9; 19:4-11), thus establishing firm foundations for the royal and administrative offices which had been undermined because of the

A stone with triangles carved in relief, found among the remains of the building. It was probably part of the palace decorations.

Remains of a royal building or palace of the Kingdom of Judah from Ramat Rachel near Jerusalem. 8th-6th centuries B.C.

frequent warfare between them since the division of the kingdoms. He also reorganized the regular army and the reserve forces and expanded the system of fortified cities and fortresses (II Chr 17:12-19). Jehoshaphat joined his forces with those of Ahab in the battle of Ramoth Gilead (I Kgs 22:4), perhaps because the king of Judah feared that an Aramean penetration into Transjordan would endanger his bases there and subsequently also the land routes to the south on which Judah's material prosperity depended. Thus, when Jehoram, Ahab's son, appealed to Jehoshaphat to come to his aid after Moab's revolt against Israel (II Kgs 1:1), the latter readily responded, himself leading the Judahite and Edomite troops (II Kgs 3:7-9). However, as a result of the ill-fated campaign, as well as the victory of Aram at Ramoth Gilead, Edom broke free of Judah, and Moabite, Ammonite and Edomite bands breached Jehoshaphat's borders and prepared to storm Jerusalem. Judah was saved, apparently due to dissension among the invaders (II Chr 20:23-24). Jehoshaphat died shortly after these events, and was succeeded by his son Jehoram.

Following Jehoshaphat's death, Athaliah, Jehoram's wife, became an influential figure in the royal court, advancing Phoenician culture and religious syncretism in Judah. The early part of Jehoram's reign was marked by internal upheavals, as attested by the murder of his brothers and several ministers by Jehoram himself (II Chr 21:4). Jehoram was unsuccessful in his attempt to regain Edom, so necessary for commerce with Arabia, and Judah also lost control of the Arabah and the northern Negeb (II Kgs 8:20-22). These losses brought about the collapse of the economic, administrative and military structure set up by Jehoshaphat, but the alliance between the Kingdoms of Judah and Israel remained intact. Jehoram combined his forces with those of Israel in a renewed treaty with the Syrian kings against Shalmaneser III. During the absence of Judah's army, the country was invaded by Philistines, Arabian tribes and Cushites, who were able to capture the king's family and treasures (II Chr 21:16-17). It was a much shrunken kingdom that Jehoram left to his only surviving son and successor Ahaziah, who reigned for just one year, influenced by his mother Athaliah.

Ahaziah changed none of his father's internal or foreign policies, even joining Jehoram son of Ahab in a war against Aram at Ramoth Gilead, where the Israelite king was wounded. During his visit to convalescing Jehoram at Jezreel, Ahaziah was killed in Jehu's revolt against the House of Omri (II Chr 22:6-9). Upon the news of her son's death, Athaliah seized power (Jehoram had killed all his brothers and their supporters in order to eliminate possible rivals). Her first act was to kill every member of the Davidic house who might oppose her rule. According to II Kings 11:1-3, only Joash escaped the massacre, and was hidden in the Temple for six years by Ahaziah's sister, Jehosheba, thus assuring the continuity of the Davidic dynasty. Because of Athaliah's unprecedented action and her tyrannous rule, she did not enjoy much popular support, and when the opportunity came, the people rose against her, led by Jehoiada, the chief priest. Athaliah was put to death and Joash son of Ahaziah was made king of Judah; the temple of Baal, with its altars and images, was demolished and Mattan, the chief priest of Baal, was slain (II Kgs 11:4-21; II Chr chap. 23).

Until Joash attained his majority, Jehoiada (who was married to Jehosheba) acted as regent, considerably strengthening the status of the priesthood. When Joash came of age, his coronation was accompanied by a covenant made between God and the king and the nation, and between the king and the people, the king assuming direct responsibility for the administration of the Temple which was restored to its former glory, repaired by funds raised from the people (II Kgs 12:10-11). In the 23rd year of Joash's reign, Judah was invaded by Hazael, king of Aram, and Joash was forced to pay a heavy tribute, which was taken from the Temple treasury (II Kgs 12:17-18; II Chr 24:23). This weakened Judah's political position and encouraged its neighbors to invade its borders. With the death of Jehoiada the priest, a struggle broke out between the priesthood and the secular administration over positions of power in the court. The conflict between the king and the priests assumed serious proportions, and when the king, who now supported the newly-risen secular power, ordered Zechariah, son of Jehoiada, put to death (II Chr 24:17-22) he himself was assassinated (II Chr 24:24-25).

The lack of stability continued during the reign of his son Amaziah. The new king allayed tensions by not avenging the descendants of his father's murderers (according to Mosaic Law), though he punished the murderers themselves (II Chr 25:1-4). Early in his reign, he defeated Edom in a military campaign at the Valley of Salt (II Kgs 14:7; II Chr 25:11-12), although it appears that he was unable to conquer the whole of that country. His victory over Edom led Amaziah to hope of renewing the union between Israel and Judah, but he miscalculated his own strength and that of Jehoash, king of Israel. In the 15th year of his reign, Amaziah was defeated by Jehoash, king of Israel, who entered Jerusalem, destroyed some of its fortifications, looted the Temple and

Typical agricultural terraces in Judah.

palace treasures, imposed economic sanctions and took hostages away with him (II Kgs 14:8-14; II Chr 25:17-24). As a result of this, Amaziah became a vassal of Israel, which the people of Judah could not tolerate; eventually they rebelled against his rule and assassinated him.

Nevertheless, the people of Judah remained loyal to the Davidic dynasty, and placed Uzziah (Azariah) son of Amaziah on the throne, while in Israel, Jehoash was followed by his son Jeroboam II. During the next half century these two kings, by reason of the favorable political situation, were able to restore the territories of Israel and Judah almost to their previous extent in the times of David and Solomon. In the absence of external disturbances Uzziah recovered the port of Elath from the Edomites (II Kgs 14:22: II Chr 26:2). He reorganized the army of Judah, supplied it with new weapons and fortified Jerusalem (II Chr 26:9ff). By the end of Uzziah's reign, Judah had expanded far beyond its former frontiers, penetrating deep into Philistia, which gave it control of the main trade route to Egypt. Uzziah also strengthened his sovereignty over Transjordan, the Negeb and Arabah by expanding agriculture and pasturing operations to meet the needs of the royal economy, as well as setting up a chain of fortifications for communications and defense. These measures were probably undertaken as part of the anti-Assyrian war preparations following Tiglath-Pileser III's invasion of Syria, thus explaining the mention of "Azriau from the land of Yaudi" (i.e., Azariah [Uzziah] from the land of Judah) in the Assyrian inscription as the leader of a group of allies who fought the armies of Assyria in northern Syria and were defeated in 738 B.C.

II Chronicles 26:16-21 would imply that Uzziah's cultic activities were rejected by the priesthood; at any rate, the Bible attributes his leprosy to his attempts to secure special privileges for himself in the Temple service. As a result of the king's infirmity his son Jotham acted as regent, taking part in the adminstration of the kingdom. When Uzziah died, he was not buried in the City of David, but "in the field of burial which belonged to the kings, for they said 'he is a leper'" (II Chr 26:23). The inscription on a stone bearing Uzziah's name, found on the slopes of the Mount of Olives, bears out the biblical tradition.

Jotham acted in accordance with the guidance and direction of his father. He succeeded in bringing Ammon under the rule of Judah (II Chr 27:5), and as a result of this victory was able to enlist the aid of the Israelite king Jeroboam II in a campaign into Transjordan. Jotham is also credited with the fortification of Jerusalem and cities of Judah and with the building of fortresses. He was succeeded by Ahaz. The allied kings of Israel and Aram, who had won over the Edomites by recovering for them the port of Elath (II Kgs 16:6), made ready to annex Judah and to place upon the throne an anti-Assyrian monarch. Encouraged by the prophet Isaiah (Is 7:1-9), Ahaz withstood the siege of Jerusalem; following Uzziah's policy, Ahaz sent tribute to the Assyrian emperor asking for aid (II Kgs 16:7-8). In 733-732 B.C. the Assyrians captured Damascus, and conquered portions of eastern Transjordan, Galilee and the Valley of Netophah, perhaps reaching as far as Ashkelon (II Kgs 15:29).

Ahaz had accomplished his immediate purpose, but at the price of complete submission to Assyria. Judah, like Israel, was now a vassal state. After a reign of six years, Ahaz died leaving a tiny kingdom, whose national religion was eclipsed, as a sequel to the king's pro-Assyrian policy so vigorously opposed by Isaiah. The prophet now put his faith in Ahaz's successor Hezekiah to redeem his people from foreign rule and restore the worship of the Lord (Is 9:1-7).

During the first part of Hezekiah's reign, Judah enjoyed a period of relative quiet, possibly because of its submission to Assyria. However, as soon as the Assyrian danger had passed, Hezekiah began to purify the cult from foreign and popular elements (II Chr 28:24; 29:3). He was disposed to break with Assyria at the earliest possible moment, and that opportunity came with the death of Sargon II in 795 B.C. Judah joined the anti-Assyrian rebellion led by Merodach-Baladan, the Chaldean (II Kgs 20:12; Is 39:1). The cities of the Sidonians, headed by Tyre, Ashkelon and Ekron in Philistia, rebelled first, supported by the Nubian kings of Egypt. Sennacherib, son of Sargon II, crushed the rebellion and in 701 B.C. turned against the rebellious kingdoms. To prepare Jerusalem for the siege, Hezekiah built the Siloam tunnel to carry the waters of the Gihon spring into the capital. He also fortified the walls of the capital (Is 22:10) and reorganized the army (II Chr 32:5-6). The Assyrian army entered Judah, captured its cities, distributing them among the Philistine kings, and exiled many of the people. Jerusalem was left to face the mighty conqueror single-handed. During the siege of Jerusalem, Hezekiah was "locked up like a bird in a cage" in the words of Sennacherib, who commemorated his victory in several inscriptions and reliefs. Hezekiah sent the Assyrian king a heavy tribute, but with the encouragement of the prophet Isaiah, refused to open the gates of the city to Sennacherib. The subsequent activities of the Assyrian monarch are not clear, and the various biblical accounts of the siege of Jerusalem (II Kgs 18:14-19:37; Is chaps. 36-37) and Sennacherib's inscription differ in many details. It appears that Sennacherib left Judah suddenly, thereby saving Jerusalem from ruin. Hezekiah remained on his throne as an Assyrian vassal. He left to his son Manasseh, a small kingdom totally dependent on the mercy of Assyria.

The subjugation to Assyria continued during Manasseh's long reign, and his was a period of reaction, both politically and religiously. The reforms of the previous reign were wiped out; the reformers paying for their obstinacy with their lives. Manasseh introduced a host of pagan cults into Jerusalem and Judah (II Kgs 21:1-9; II Chr 33:2-9), even making his own son pass through the fire in the Valley of Hinnom, as Ahaz had done. Assyrian documents mention him, together with other kings, as a faithful vassal of Assyria. Assyria's power and grandeur reached its peak under Esarhaddon and Ashurbanipal. Manasseh was reconciled to vassalage under Assyria; he paid his tribute regularly, and Judean contingents fought among the Assyrian expeditionary force in Egypt. The conquest of Egypt, under Psammetichus I, proved illusory, for while Ashurbanipal was busy in Elam, his own brother revolted in Babylon, straining all of his fighting resources. The Medes began threatening from the east, as did Gyges, king of Lydia, from the west. The Assyrian power rapidly began to decline, and perhaps the events related in II Chronicles 33:11, describing Manasseh's unsuccessful rebellion against Assyria, took place during this mutinous period. Evidently for political reasons the Assyrians returned him to the throne, after he had been taken captive in chains to Babylonia (II Chr 33:14-16).

Manasseh was succeeded by his son Amon who was assassinated, apparently because he continued his father's policy of submission to Assyria. The "people of the land" placed upon the throne Amon's son, Josiah, who was only eight years old (II Chr 33:25).

Events in world history during the reign of King Josiah were significant not only for Judah, but also for all the nations of the ancient Near East. Babylon began to rise as an independent power — the neo-Babylonian empire; the Medes and Scythians were making aggressive advances, in Egypt the strong 26th Dynasty emerged with its first vigorous kings Psammetichus I and Necho II. The Assyrian empire, which was already breaking up, was eventually to fall victim to these new powers. All the undertakings of King Josiah were connected with the pattern of world politics in his time, which offered him the possibility of new independent domestic and foreign policies. The voice of prophecy was once more heard in Judah: Nahum and Zephaniah foresaw the oncoming of Nineveh's downfall. Restored independence and the expansion of Judah's territory were accompanied by religious reforms which are described in the Bible in two separate accounts. In II Kings chapters 22-23 the reformation is described as a one-time act, the result of the finding of the Book of Law while the Temple was under repair. According to II Chronicles chapter 34, however, the reformation was the expression of a national renaissance and took place in several stages. It appears that Assyria's decline was the motivation behind the removal of foreign religious elements from Judah's worship. In his 18th year Josiah ordered the Temple restored (II Chr 34:8), in the process of which the Book of the Law (according to some scholars the Book of Deuteronomy) was found by the high priest, Hilkiah. As a result of the reproofs read in the book, Josiah assembled the people and established a covenant with the Lord (II Kgs 23:3; cf II Chr 34:29-32). Josiah raised Jerusalem to the rank of sole and exclusive center for all those faithful to the Lord (II Kgs 23:19). However, the developing political situation prevented Josiah from completing his reforms.

A typical view of the hilly Hebron region in Judah.

In 612 B.C. Nineveh fell before the combined attack of Babylonians, Medes and Scythians. Josiah was killed in 609 B.C. at Megiddo in an attempt to stop Pharaoh Necho II, who had just succeeded his father Psammetichus and was hastening to join forces with his former enemy, Assyria, in order to advance on the emerging neo-Babylonian empire. The death of Josiah put an effective end to the renewed prosperity of the Judean kingdom.

He was followed by his son Jehoahaz, who could be trusted to continue his father's anti-Egyptian policy. However, after a reign of three months, Necho deposed him and installed on the throne Jehoahaz' pro-Egyptian brother, Eliakim, changing his name to Jehoiakim (II Kgs 23:34). Jehoiakim's reign was a step backward from the religious aspect: the cult of the "queen of heaven" was openly pursued. However, shortly after the pharaoh's defeat and the Babylonians' rapid advance, Jehoiakim became a vassal of Babylon (II Kgs 24:1). The prophet Jeremiah foretold the Babylonian destruction of Judah and strongly recommended moderation in national policies. His advice was rejected and, fearing that his prophecies would dishearten the people, King Jehoiakim ordered the prophet's arrest, whereupon he went into hiding for a time. Jehoiakim mercilessly suppressed opposition, but the prevailing crisis led to the undermining of economic life and to serious tensions among the population (Jer 22:18ff).

When the king of Babylonia, Nebuchadnezzar, attacked Jerusalem, Egyptian aid never reached Judah (II Kgs 24:7). Jehoiakim died during the attack and his son Jehoiachin was exiled to Babylonia in 597 B.C. The fate of Jehoiachin in Babylon is recorded both in the Bible and in Babylonian inscriptions discovered in the palace of Nebuchadnezzar and according to the latter he was well treated in exile, even retaining his royal title.

In place of the exiled Jehoiachin, the king of Babylonia crowned Zedekiah, the son of Josiah and Jehoiachin's uncle. At first, he was loyal to Babylonia, but at a later period he summoned an anti-Babylonian conference, thus rebelling against the power which had enthroned him (Jer 27:3). In the ninth year of Zedekiah's reign, Nebuchadnezzar arrived in Judah to crush the rebellion. An Egyptian force was rushed to Judah at that time, providing some temporary relief from the siege of Jerusalem, but the Chaldeans defeated the Egyptian army and in 586 B.C., after Jerusalem had withstood one and a half

View of the village of Bet Sahur with Herodium on the horizon, on the border of the Judean Desert.

years of siege, the capital was conquered and destroyed, along with the Temple (II Kgs 25:1-10). Zedekiah and his entourage were captured and punished while trying to escape. Some of the population was led captive to Babylonia; others escaped, seeking refuge in neighboring countries. With the Judean fighting strength destroyed or in exile, Nebuchadnezzar appointed Gedaliah son of Ahikam to govern the remaining inhabitants of Judah. However, he was murdered by conspirators from among Judah's former officials and the assassins escaped. Those who were left behind feared the reprisals of Nebuchadnezzar, since the Babylonian garrison at Mizpah had been butchered (II Kgs 25:22-26). They fled to Egypt, much against the advice of Jeremiah, whom they dragged with them into involuntary exile. The territory of Judah became an administrative unit of Babylon. With the fall of Jerusalem and the total destruction of the palace and the Temple, the Davidic dynasty came to an end, and Judah was divested of its independence and sovereignty for generations to come.

A view of the Judean Desert, part of the Kingdom of Judah.

KINGDOM OF JUDAH — KINGS

B.C.	
928-911	Rehoboam
911-908	Abijah
908-867	Asa
867-846	Jehoshaphat
846-843	Jehoram
843-842	Ahaziah
842-836	Athaliah
836-798	Jehoash
798-769	Amaziah
769-733	Uzziah
758-743	Jotham (regent)
758-743	Ahaz (regent)
733-727	Ahaz
727-698	Hezekiah
698-642	Manasseh
641-640	Amon
639-609	Josiah
609	Jehoahaz
608-598	Jehoiakim
597	Jehoiachin
596-586	Zedekiah

JUDAS

1. Judas Iscariot ("man of Kerioth").

The son of Simon (John 6:71; 13:26) and one of the twelve disciples of Jesus (Matt 10:4; Mark 3:19). As the treasurer of the Twelve (John 12:4, 6; 13:29), he considered it a waste of money when Mary anointed Jesus' feet with precious oil; but, John said this was not out of solicitude for the poor, but because he was a thief (John 12:4ff).

After Jesus and his disciples went to Jerusalem, "Satan entered into" Judas (Luke 22:3) and he approached the priests, offering to deliver Jesus into their hands for thirty pieces of silver (Matt 26:14-15, cf Zech 11:12-13). At the Last Supper, Jesus foretold Judas' betrayal (Matt 26:25). Judas betrayed Jesus with a kiss in the Garden of Gethsemane (Matt 26:47ff; Mark 14:43ff; Luke 22:47-48). After Jesus' arrest, Judas was seized by remorse; he returned the money and hanged himself (Matt 27:3-5). With the money the priests bought a piece of land, which became known as "Field of Blood" (Aceldama). The story in Acts (1:16ff) tells that Judas bought the land himself, then fell down and burst his guts.

2. A brother of Jesus.

3. The son of James, one of the twelve apostles elected by Jesus from among his disciples (Luke 6:16). Some commentators identify him with the author of the Epistle of Jude, although the latter calls himself the brother of James.

4. The Galilean; leader of an ill-fated revolt against the Romans, "in the days of the census". The story of his revolt is told in detail by Josephus (*Antiq.* XVII, 271ff; *Wars* II, 56) and he was regarded as one of the founders of the extreme Jewish nationalist movement, the Sicarri. Judas is mentioned by Gamaliel in his warning to the Sanhedrin to leave the apostles alone, for if their belief is of human origin, like that of Judas, it will collapse without the Sanhedrin's interference, but if it is from God it cannot be overthrown (Acts 5:37).

5. Judas of Damascus. Paul, then still called Saul, stayed at Judas' house in the Straight Street, after his vision on the road from Jerusalem to Damascus.

6. See BARSABBAS No.2

JUDE See JUDAS No.3

JUDE, EPISTLE OF The 21st book of the NT. The author of this short letter is identified in the first verse as the "brother of James". This has led to varying interpretations. The fact that one of the twelve apostles is called "Judas of James" (Luke 6:16; Acts 1:13) has led to the author's identification with that apostle (See JUDAS). Another interpretation is that the James mentioned is the one named by Paul as "the Lord's brother" (Gal 1:19). This would make Jude himself a brother of Jesus, and indeed one of Jesus' "brothers" is so named (Mark 6:3. See JAMES). On this view, the writer of the Epistle has chosen the humbler title of "brother of James" while indicating his relationship to Jesus only as "bond-servant". The provenance of the Epistle, which cannot be determined from internal evidence, must depend on the identification of the author. The Epistle of Jude is classified among the "General Epistles" as it is addressed to no particular church.

The first clear reference to Jude is to be found in the later 2nd century. It is customary, however, to assign it a date in the second half of the 1st century. No mention is made of the destruction of the Temple in 70, a reference which would have been appropriate to the author's argument (especially at vs. 5-7). Another consideration in dating is its close similarity to II Peter, which probably made use of Jude. If Peter's authorship of II Peter be accepted (which many hesitate to do), then a date for Jude in

The Grotto of the Betrayal on the Mount of Olives which traditionally marks the spot where Judas Iscariot singled out Jesus by giving him a kiss.

the early sixties is necessary. While individuals like Tertullian and Clement of Alexandria recognized the canonicity of Jude, its general acceptance came relatively late. Jude was written to counteract certain heresies which were infiltrating the church. While these are not named, those who propounded them are attacked in the strongest language. They are linked with a rogues' gallery which includes the Egyptians, Sodom and Gomorrah, Cain, Balaam, Korah, fallen angels and the devil himself. The letter is characterized by frequent references to other scripture: sometimes to the OT as in the case of the above figures, at least twice to pseudepigraphical literature (I Enoch and the Assumption of Moses), and even to the teaching of the apostles (v. 17ff).

OUTLINE

vs. 1-3	Introduction
v. 4	Statement of the danger
vs. 5-16	Description of the dangerous men
vs. 17-23	Exhortation and practical advice
vs. 24-25	Doxology

JUDEA Name for the territory covered by the ancient Kingdom of Judah, an adjective meaning "the Jewish" (land). The name only came into use in Roman times. Around the beginning of the 1st century A.D., Judea and Samaria together formed a Roman province under a proconsul. This is the Judea referred to in Luke 5:17 and John 4:3. Later, from A.D. 44 onward, Galilee also belonged to the Roman province of Judea, so that the name then embraced all Jewish territory, that is, the whole of Palestine. This is the usage found in Paul's letters.

JUDGMENT, DAY OF See ESCHATOLOGY

JUDGES, BOOK OF The second book in the Prophets section of the OT. It is named for the charismatic leaders active between the death of Joshua and the institution of the monarchy. The judges' rule was temporary and none of them had the allegiance of all of the tribes. With the exception of Deborah (4:4-5), they were not judges in the legal sense of the word, but rather, inspired heroes who led single tribes or groups of tribes in military campaigns against various foreign enemies.

The contents of the book may be divided into three sections: (a) the completion of the conquest of Canaan (1:1-2:5); (b) the careers of the earlier and later judges (2:6-16:31); (c) the tribe of Dan's migration to the north and the war against the Benjamites (17:1-21:25).

Chapters 1:1-2:5 contain a brief summary of the conquest and final settlement of Canaan after the death of Joshua (1:1). The initial conquest of the land is attributed to a united Israel under the leadership of Joshua, with the mopping-up operations described here as the concern of individual tribes. The southern invasion was accomplished by the tribe of Judah, together with its clans Caleb and Othniel, the tribe of Simeon and friendly non-Israelites (1:1-21). The account of the settlement of the central and northern tribes deals with the conquest of Bethel (vs. 22-26), the Canaanite strongholds not yet conquered (vs. 27-33), and the struggles that took place on the southern border of the central territory (vs. 22-36).

Joshua chapters 1-11 and Judges chapter 1 are two different accounts

The so-called Judea capta coin showing a Roman soldier near a palm-tree (the palm was a common symbol of Judea). The soldier is guarding a woman sitting on a pile of weapons and weeping. The inscription reads Judaea capta *(Judea captured).*

of the Israelite conquest, according to many modern scholars. They generally favor the account in Judges which explains the conquest as a series of independent battles conducted by the separate tribes for their individual portions of land, in preference to Joshua with its unified conquest account which is considered to be a later ideological reconstruction of the events.

Chapters 2:6-3:6 function as an introduction to the central themes of the time of the judges. The Israelites lapsed into idolatry, were attracted to false gods and punished by God who subjected them to foreign oppressors. When they realized their misdeeds and repented, a judge was sent to rescue them. Some time after the death of the judges the people relapsed again and the cycle was repeated.

The first of the judges was Othniel (3:7-11). As a young man he participated in the general conquest and was credited with the capture of Debir (1:11-13). The next charismatic leader, Ehud (3:12-30), was a Benjamite hero who rescued his own and other tribes from the long oppression of Eglon the Moabite.

Chapter 4 depicts the victory of the judge Deborah and her commander, Barak, over the Canaanites, followed by Deborah's famous song of triumph (chap. 5). The fourth major judge, Gideon, rates the longest narrative devoted to any of the military leaders (chaps. 6-8), recounting his defeat of the Midianites. When, as a result of these exploits, Gideon was offered the kingship, he declined stating that it belonged to God (8:23).

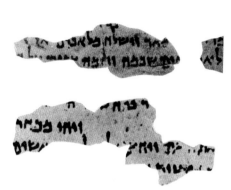

Fragments from the Book of Judges found at Qumran. (Shrine of the Book, Jerusalem)

The tragic account of the life of Abimelech (chap. 9), is supplementary to the Gideon narratives. A son of Gideon by a Shechemite concubine (8:31), Abimelech used Temple money to hire killers to murder his 70 half-brothers. The only surviving brother, Jotham, related a parable of the trees electing a worthless bramble bush to rule them, applying it to Abimelech. Jotham predicted that Abimelech's reign would be brief and that his Shechemite supporters would desert him. This prediction came true: Abimelech was mortally wounded by a millstone hurled by a woman. In order to avoid the humiliation of death at a woman's hands, he asked his armor-bearer to kill him. He ruled for only three years.

Two of the five minor judges, Tola and Jair (10:1-5) are mentioned as having judged Israel after Abimelech and before Jephthah. Their leadership spans a successful 45-year period.

The fifth major judge, Jephthah (10:17-12:7) made a name for himself as a warrior in the land of Tob, thereby attracting the notice of the elders of Gilead who sought to recruit his military skills against Ammon. Having earlier been expelled by these elders because of his illegitimacy, Jephthah only consented to undertake the military leadership on condition that he remained ruler in peacetime too. His terms accepted, Jephthah entered into a diplomatic correspondence with Ammon. When these overtures failed he prepared for war taking a solemn vow that, if victorious, he would make a burnt offering to God of whatever first came from his home to welcome him (11:31). On his return from a successful battle, the first to greet him was his virgin daughter and it was she whom he sacrificed. Her death became the subject of an annual commemoration by the women of Gilead.

The remaining three minor judges, Ibzan, Elon and Abdon (12:8-15), are portrayed in a manner recalling the accounts of the other two minor judges. Samson (chaps. 13-16) differed from the other judges in many respects. He did not go to war as a judge, nor did he lead an army; rather he relied upon his superhuman strength to wage war against the enemies of his people. Samson was a "war-Nazirite", whose uncut hair was believed to protect him. His weakness for Philistine women led to several clashes with the Philistines and ultimately to his death in the temple of Dagon (16:23-30).

Chapters 17-21, the book's concluding section, depict the migration of the tribe of Dan, and the bitter inter-tribal war against the Benjamites. There are no introductory statements to connect this portion with the rest of the book and the only expression linking the various sections is the recurring "In those days there was no king in Israel; everyone did what was right in his own eyes" (17:6; 18:1; 19:1; 21:25). Subjected to the pressures of the Philistines in the south, the Danites migrated northwards and settled there: on the way they stole sacred objects from the sanctuary of Micah for use in their own sanctuary at Laish (chaps. 17-18).

The war against the Benjamites commenced with an incident when the people of Gibeah assaulted a Levite wayfarer, surrounding his house and demanding that he submit to homosexual practices (19:22). When he sent out his concubine in his stead, she was abused to death (19:25). The man cut her body up into 12 pieces and sent one to each of the tribes, demanding revenge for the foul deed (19:25-29). In the subsequent inter-tribal war, Benjamin was decisively defeated. The Israelites took a vow not to marry Benjamites (21:1); but, fearing that one of the tribes would vanish, the people nevertheless continued to effect marriages with them, resorting to subterfuges to avoid breaking their vows.

The Book of Judges is of great historical value. It offers information on a period of Israelite history which would otherwise be practically unknown. It preserves fragments of literature of great antiquity, and offers insight into the social and political conditions that prevailed in the period between the conquest of Canaan and the foundation of the monarchy.

OUTLINE

1:1-2:5	Conquest and settlement of Canaan
2:6-3:6	Introduction to period of Judges
3:7-11	Othniel
3:12-30	Ehud
3:31	Shamgar
4:1-5:31	Deborah
6:1-8:35	Gideon
9:1-57	Abimelech
10:1-5	Tola and Jair
10:6-12:7	Jephthah
12:8-15	Ibzan, Elon and Abdon
13:1-16:31	Samson
17:1-18:31	Micah and the tribe of Dan
19:1-21:25	The war against the Benjamites

JUDITH A daughter of Beeri the Hittite; Esau married her when he was 40 years old, to the great distress of his parents Isaac and Rebekah.

JUDITH, BOOK OF Book of the Apocrypha; it dates from Persian times, but was probably rewritten in the Hasmonean period. It was

JUDITH
Gen 26:34

originally composed in Hebrew, but is extant only in four Greek versions. Judith is included in the Septuagint, the Bible canon of the Catholic and Greek churches, and in the Protestant Apocrypha. Although a prose work, it contains two poems of thanksgiving voiced by the heroine Judith.

The story depicts the crisis confronting Israel after Nebuchadnezzar overthrew Arphaxad, his enemy to the east (1:13). Nebuchadnezzar ordered his chief captain, Holofernes, to invade the west country, which had refused to join him in battle (2:6). The Israelites prepared for resistance, seeking divine help through fasting, prayer and mourning (chap. 4). But when the enemy appeared, they became greatly concerned

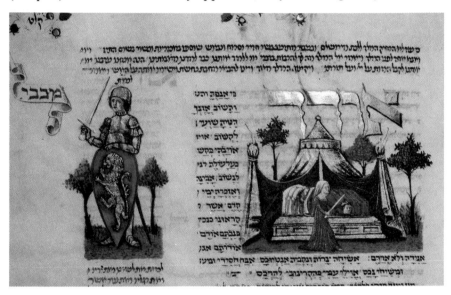

Judah Maccabee on the left, and Judith holding Holofernes' head, on the right, depicted in a Hebrew illuminated manuscript. Rothschild Miscellany, *Italy. c. 1470.* *(Israel Museum)*

(7:4), and in their panic cried to God (7:19). The turning point of the story is the appearance of Judith (chap. 8), a Jewish widow, described as wise, beautiful and of great faith. After praying to the Lord to prove that he, and not Nebuchadnezzar, is God (9:7-9), she laid her plan (10:1-5). By means of stealth, and helped by her beauty (chaps. 11-12), Judith seduced Holofernes. Plying him with liquor (12:16-13:2) she then beheaded the drunken general with his own sword (13:8-9). The book ends with Judith's song of thanksgiving which stresses the theme that, by the hand of a woman (16:6), God has won the battle (16:3) and that he is invincible (16:13).

The book is of interest because it mentions numerous Jewish religious customs practiced at the time of its composition. Judith herself is described as a devout woman in a state of mourning (8:4-6), who prayed regularly (9:1), abstained from Gentile food (10:5; 12:2), and washed herself every evening in running water (12:7-9). Other important aspects in the book are the conversion of Achior (14:10), who as an Ammonite, was barred by the Torah from adherence to the Israelite nation (Deut 23:3); wisdom, a frequent theme in apocryphal literature, in this case ascribed to Judith; and the fact that the author chose a woman as the hero.

The book dates from the Second Temple period. Some hold that it was written shortly after the return from the Babylonian Exile; others have placed it as late as the Hasmonean period.

JULIA
Rom 16:15

JULIUS
Acts 27:1, 3

JULIA A Christian woman of Rome who received a greeting from Paul.
JULIUS A Roman centurion who was responsible for the safe passage of Paul from Caesarea to Rome by ship. His name reflects an affiliation of loyalty to the Roman imperial family, the "gens Julia", of which

Caesar was a member. The noble manner of Julius is emphasized throughout the story of the stormy sea voyage (Acts chap. 27), and especially in his intervention to save Paul's life (Acts 27:42-43).

JUNIA A Jewish convert to Christianity, who was imprisoned together with Paul (Rom 16:7). Some versions read here "Julia", and other ancient commentators see Andronicus and Junia as man and wife. In view of the context, however, it is unlikely that Junia is a woman. JUNIA
Rom 16:7

JUNIPER See PLANTS

JUSHAB-HESED One of the descendants of Zerubbabel. JUSHAB-HESED
I Chr 3:20

JUSTIFICATION To be justified, means to be made righteous, and just actions towards other human beings must flow from those who have been made right. In the NT the verb "to justify" appears much more frequently than the nouns "justification" or "justice". It is most often used in Paul's letters to the Romans and Galatians. Fundamentally, the concern is with justice and being in a relationship with God. The just person is one who has been justified, is accepted by God, and lives in harmony with God's will.

For classical Judaism the ways and means by which one is justified are not simplified. Bildad the Shuhite cynically asks, "How then can man be justified before God?" (Job 25:4) to which Job replies that he will not give up his integrity (Job chap. 27), even in his darkest hours, but will build his case on the mystery and revelation of God and his own record (Job 26:14; 27:6). The Psalmist in a note of despair, hardly normative for Judaism, concludes: "in your sight no one living is justified" (Ps 143:2) and yet the whole Psalm is a cry to have an answer based on God's righteousness (Ps 143:1, 11) and is a clear affirmation "in you do I trust...for I lift up my soul to you" (Ps 143:8).

Early Christians accepted this, but, in the Pauline discussions in Romans and Galatians, there was a change of focus. Paul in these letters is engaged in a polemic with those who insist that male Gentile converts must be circumcised. Paul asserts that faith in the saving work of Christ on the cross and in the resurrection suffices to enter the covenant of salvation (Rom 4:24-5:1). Often Paul links this way of salvation with baptism (Rom 6:3-8; I Cor 6:11; Col 2:11-14). Paul uses other terms for salvation besides justification, e.g., redemption, reconciliation, adoptive sonship (see SALVATION).

Paul describes the person who has been "justified freely by his grace" (Rom 3:24) and who has accepted God's way of righting wrong, as one who also embodies in life the justice of God for God is "both just and the justifier of the one who has faith in Jesus" (Rom 3:26). The early Christians spoke of the harvest of justification or righteousness (Phil 1:11) and saw the relationship as that between seed and fruit; at times justice was the fruit and peace the seed and at times their relationship was reversed (James 3:18). In this manner they affirmed that justification which brings peace (Rom 5:1), and justice, are intimately related (Rom 14:17).

Present-day Yatta, south of Hebron, identified with the site of Juttah.

JUSTUS

1. Joseph Barsabbas Justus was one of two candidates for election to the rank of apostle. JUSTUS 1
Acts 1:23

2. Titius Justus (in most versions simply Justus), a proselyte of Corinth, to whose house Paul moved when his preaching was not accepted at the synagogue. JUSTUS 2
Acts 18:7

3. Jesus Justus, a Jewish Christian, whom Paul mentions as one of his fellow-workers. JUSTUS 3
Col 4:11

JUTTAH A city in the territory allotted to Judah when the land of Canaan was divided among the tribes; it was later given to the Levites of the sons of Aaron. Identified with present-day Yatta, south of Hebron. JUTTAH
Josh 15:55;
21:16

KABZEEL, JEKABZEEL A town in the Negeb of Judah, on the border of Edom (Josh 15:21), the birthplace of Benaiah, son of Jehoiada, one of David's "mighty men" (II Sam 23:20). Resettled after the return from Babylonian Exile, when it was named Jekabzeel (Neh 11:25). Tentatively identified with Khirbet Gharreh, 8 miles (13km) east of Beersheba, where an Israelite fortress was discovered.

KADESH See KADESH BARNEA

KADESH, KADESH BARNEA Place in the wilderness of Zin which was the principal station on the Israelites' 40-year journey to the promised land (Deut 1:46). It was from here that the 12 men were sent to spy out the land of Canaan" (Num 13:1-33; 32:8; Josh 14:7), here that the Israelites despaired and were condemned to remain in the desert until the generation of those who had been slaves in Egypt should perish (Num 14:21-23), and here that Moses brought upon himself the punishment of not being permitted to enter Canaan, after striking the rock to bring forth its waters (Num 20:12). And it was from Kadesh Barnea that the Israelites finally set out for Canaan (Num 12:22). After the conquest, Kadesh Barnea served as a marker of Judah's southern border (Num 34:4; Josh 15:3).

The identification of the site of Kadesh Barnea was long the subject of controversy. Following various unsatisfactory attempts, Woolley and Lawrence proposed the oasis of Ain el-Kudeirat as the most likely site for biblical Kadesh Barnea. This proposal, now widely accepted, was supported by the existence of the ruins of an ancient fortress, which lay both near the oasis and near the major highway from Egypt to Canaan — the Way of Shur.

Following small excavations in 1914 and in 1956, thorough excavations of the site were carried out between 1976 and 1982. In these excavations, remains of three superimposed fortresses of the Israelite period were uncovered. The earliest, of the 10th century B.C., was in the form of a connected circle of rooms around a courtyard with further structures nearby, and has been associated with the building activities of Solomon. After the destruction of this settlement, perhaps by Shishak, a new fortress was erected. This fortress, built perhaps during the reign of Hezekiah, shows superb planning and execution. It is rectangular, 65 feet by 195 feet (20 by 60 m), has six rectangular towers and is surrounded by a moat and glacis system on three sides, the fourth being protected by the wadi. Its interior is divided by alleyways into four parts, containing living quarters, administrative and perhaps religious areas, grain storage areas and a sophisticated water system. This fortress was destroyed around the end of the 8th century B.C., and several decades later a third fortress was constructed. The builders of

(left)
The oasis of Ain el-Kudeirat, identified as Kadesh Barnea in the Wilderness of Zin.

Clay figurine dated to the 8th-7th centuries B.C. from Kadesh Barnea.

Model of the Israelite fortress at Ain el Kudeirat (Kadesh Barnea) from the period of the Kingdom of Judah consisting of a casemate-wall fortified with towers. (Israel Dept. of Antiquities and Museums)

the third fortress followed the plan of the second one, building thin-walled casemates on top of the 4 m (13 ft) thick walls of the earlier fortress. This last fortress too was destroyed, probably by Nebuchadnezzar's army, at the beginning of the 6th century B.C.

The finds of Kadesh Barnea include much pottery and other everyday items, organic remains — including charred grain and apples — and inscribed sherds which show that the inhabitants of the fortress probably spoke Hebrew but used the Egyptian numerical system.

A problem left unsolved by the excavations is the lack of any remains in or near the fortress of the Late Bronze or Early Iron ages — the presumed period of the Israelites sojourn at Kadesh Barnea after the Exodus. This lack leaves a lingering doubt as to the identification of Ain el-Kudeirat with biblical Kadesh Barnea.

KADMIEL (the "ancient one God"). The head of a family of Levites, who returned with Zerubbabel from Babylon (Ezra 2:40; Neh 7:43; 12:8, 24). He appears among those who signed the covenant (Neh 10:9).

KADMONITES A nomadic people, associated with the Kenites and Kenizzites, whose land was promised by God to Abram and his offspring.

KAIN

1. A collective name for the Kenites. It appears in the oracle of Balaam (Num 24:21) and also in Judges 4:11.

2. A city of the district of Judah, inhabited by the Kenites. It is identified with modern Khirbet Yakin, southeast of Hebron.

KALLAI A priest, head of a family in the time of Joiakim.

KANAH

1. A ravine, mentioned as lying on the border of Ephraim and Manasseh (Josh 16:8; 17:9). Most scholars identify it with Wadi Qana, southwest of Shechem, one of the main brooks of the River Yarkon.

2. A city on the northern boundary of Asher (Josh 19:28), it is identified with the modern village of Qana, 6 miles (10 km) southeast of Tyre.

KAREAH ("bald"). The father of Johanan and Jonathan, captains of the army at the time of Jeremiah, who escaped deportation by Nebuchadnezzar. In II Kings 25:23 he is called Careah.

KARKAA A city or place near Azmon, on the southern boundary of the territory allotted to the tribe of Judah when the land of Canaan was

Wadi Qana southwest of Shechem, identified with Kanah.

KADMIEL
Ezra 2:40; 3:9. Neh 7:43; 9:4-5; 10:9; 12:8, 24

KADMONITES
Gen 15:19

KAIN 1
Num 24:22

KAIN 2
Josh 15:57

KALLAI
Neh 12:20

KANAH 1
Josh 16:8; 17:9

KANAH 2
Josh 19:28

KAREAH
Jer 40:8, 13, 15-16; 41:11, 13-14, 16; 42:1, 8; 43:2, 4-5

KARKAA
Josh 15:3

divided among the tribes (Josh 14:1; 15:3). The place is mentioned only once and its present location is unknown.

KARKOR A city on the eastern bank of the Jordan River; the site of Gideon's victory over Zebah and Zalmunna the kings of Midian (Judg 8:10-11). Its present location is unknown.

KARNAIM The capital of Bashan under Aramean and Assyrian rule, after the decline of neighboring Ashtaroth, whose name it annexed, being known as Ashtaroth Karnaim. In the Hellenistic period it was called Karnein (II Macc 12:21). Identified with Sheikh Saad, northeast of Ashtaroth, where an inscription bearing the name of Rameses II was found.

KARTAH A city in the territory of Zebulun which was later allotted to the Merarite Levites. Its present location is unknown.

KARTAN A city in the territory of Naphtali later allotted to the Gershonite Levites. Generally considered to be an alternate name for Kirjathaim.

KATTATH A city which fell to the lot of the tribe of Zebulun when the land of Canaan was divided among the tribes. Its present location is unknown.

KEDAR

1. The second son of Ishmael.

2. An Arabian tribe or league of nomadic tribes in the Syro-Arabian desert which engaged in breeding sheep, goats and camels (Is 60:7; Jer 49:29, 32; Ezek 27:21). Its members lived in tents (Ps 120:5; Song 1:5; Jer 49:29) or villages (Is 42:11).

The Bible contains very little information about the sons of Kedar, but ancient historical sources shed more light. Assyrian sources, mainly of the 8th century B.C. refer to certain kings of the Arabs as kings of Kedar.

The stele of Tiglath-Pileser III (737 B.C.) mentions Kedarites among the tribute-paying peoples. In 691-689 B.C. Sennacherib fought King Hazael of Kedar at Duma in Arabia. In 653 B.C. the Kedarites, under the leadership of Yutha son of Hazael launched marauding raids across the borders of Transjordan and Syria, but were beaten back by the

The king of Assyria fighting the Kedarites shown on a 7th-century relief.

Moabite and Assyrian garrisons stationed along the frontier from Lebanon to Edom. In 652-646 B.C., the Kedarites, together with the sons of Nebajoth (the firstborn son of Ishmael, Gen 25:13) and other nomadic tribes, exerted pressure on the western borders of the Assyrian empire. This forced the king of Assyria to conduct a campaign against an Arabian confederation in 645. The Arabian defeat by Nebuchadnezzar is reflected in Jeremiah 49:28ff.

With the disintegration of the Transjordanian kingdoms in the first half of the 6th century B.C., the Kedarites and other Arab tribes invaded the settled lands. In the 8th-5th centuries B.C., Kedarite territory extended over the whole of the Syrian desert and northern Sinai, from western Babylon to the confines of Egypt. The latest reference to the Kedarites is from the turn of the era, and Pliny (*Nat. Hist.* v 65) mentions the Kedarites together with the Nabateans as living in northern Arabia.

KEDEMAH ("toward the east"). One of the 12 sons of Ishmael and the name of an Arabian tribe.

KEDEMAH
Gen 25:15. I Chr 1:31

KEDEMOTH A place in the territory of Reuben (Josh 13:18), one of the cities given to the Levites of the family of Merari (Josh 21:37; I Chr 6:79). From the wilderness of Kedemoth, Moses sent messengers to Sihon king of Heshbon, seeking permission to pass through his land (Deut 2:26). The place is not identified, but it must be north of the River Arnon, at the extremity of the wilderness.

KEDEMOTH
Deut 2:26. Josh 13:18; 21:37. I Chr 6:79

KEDESH

1. A Canaanite city in Galilee, in the territory of Naphtali, whose ruler was one of the 31 monarchs vanquished by Joshua (Josh 12:22). To distinguish Kedesh from other cities with the same name it was also referred to as "Kedesh in Galilee, in the mountains of Naphtali" (Josh 20:7). The city was given to the Levites and was a place of refuge (Josh 21:32). It was conquered by Tiglath-Pileser III, king of Assyria (II Kgs 15:29) who deported its inhabitants. Kedesh is mentioned in the

KEDESH 1
Josh 12:22; 20:7; 21:32. II Kgs 15:29. I Chr 6:76

Ruins of a Roman temple at Kedesh in Galilee.

Hellenistic period and Josephus knew it by a different form of the name, as a village in the territory of Tyre (*Antiq.* II, 459, IV, 104-105). The area is identified with Tell Qades, 12 miles (19 km) north of Safed, where there are two ancient mounds, one of which was occupied from the 3rd millennium B.C. to the end of the Israelite period.

2. Kedesh-Naphtali, the seat of Abarak, son of Abinoam (Judg 4:6, 10). This Kedesh is identified with Khirbet Qedish near the Sea of Galilee.

KEDESH 2
Judg 4:6, 9-11

KEDESH 3
Josh 15:23; 19:37

3. A place in southeastern Judah, on the border of Edom (Josh 15:21, 23). Not identified.

4. A city in Issachar given to the sons of Gershon.

KEDESH 4
I Chr 6:72

KEHELATHAH A stopping place on the Israelites' route to the

KEHELATHAH
Num 33:22-23

promised land, between Rissah and Mount Shepher. Perhaps an alternate name for Makheloth.

KEILAH A fortified town in the Plain (Josh 15:44; I Sam 23:7). Mentioned in the El Amarna Letters, where it is related that the king of Keilah cooperated with the Habiru. David saved the city from the

Keilah, east of Beth Gubrin.

Philistines (I Sam 23:1-8) but was forced to abandon it (I Sam 23:12-13). In the time of Rehoboam it was conquered by Pharaoh Sheshonk, biblical Shishak. It was divided into two parts at the time of the return from Babylonia, each with its own ruler (Neh 3:17-18). It was a village in the Roman period and its Greek name was Kela. Identified with Khirbet Oila, east of Beth Gubrin near the Judean foothills.

KELAIAH One of the Levites who had married a foreign woman and was forced by Ezra to divorce her. His Aramaic name was Kelita. The name appears on a Hebrew seal from the 7th or 6th century B.C.

KELITA

1. The Aramaic name of Kelaiah mentioned above.

2. A Levite, one of the group who interpreted the Law read by Ezra (Neh 8:7), and who signed the covenant in the time of Nehemiah (Neh 10:11).

KEMUEL

1. The son of Nahor and father of Aram.

2. The son of Shiphtan, prince of the tribe of Ephraim (Num 34:24), who, with other princes, was appointed by Moses to divide the land of Canaan among the Children of Israel (Num 34:29).

3. A Levite, father of Hashabiah, contemporary of King David.

KENATH A city in Bashan, which was conquered by Nobah, who gave it his own name (Num 32:42). However, the city continued to preserve the name of Kenath and is so called in I Chronicles 2:23, where it is mentioned among the cities taken from the Israelites by Geshur and Aram.

The plural "Kenath and the villages" (Num 32:42; cf I Chr 2:23) indicates that it was an urban center in Bashan.

Most scholars identify it with Kanawat, 4 miles (7 km) northwest of es-Suweideh. (See also NOBAH).

KENAZ, KENEZZITES, KENIZZITE One of the non-Israelite peoples who inhabited southern Canaan during the period of the patriarchs (Gen 15:19). Their ancestor, Kenaz, appears as the son of Eliphaz, the eldest son of Esau (Gen 36:11; I Chr 1:36), and as one of the 12 rulers of Edom (Gen 36:15, 42; I Chr 1:53). An important Kenizzite family, the Caleb clan (Num 32:12), conquered Hebron (Josh 14:6, 12-14) and became part of Judah according to the commandment of God to Joshua (15:13). The Kenizzite origin of the Caleb clan is also emphasized in the information about Othniel son of Kenaz — the ancestor of the Kenizzites (I Chr 4:13). Othniel conquered Debir (Kirjath Sepher) and married Caleb's daughter (Josh 15:17; Judg 1:13). His brother Seraiah was the father of a clan of copper-and ironsmiths (I Chr 4:13-14).

KENITE(S) In some Semitic languages the name Kenite is the equivalent of "smith". This is the implication of "Tubal-Cain, an instructor of every craftsman in bronze and iron" (Gen 4:22). In II Samuel 21:16 the Hebrew *keino* stands for spear, or perhaps metal weapons in general. It seems that Tubal-Cain is to be identified with Tubal, a nation mentioned in the Bible (Ezek 27:13). It is also known from Assyrian documents, where it is said to produce metal objects and trade in copper in Asia Minor.

According to the Bible Moses' father-in-law was a Kenite (Judg 1:16). The Kenites were akin to the Midianites and wandered in Midian, Edom, Amalek, Sinai, the Negeb and northern Palestine. In Balaam's song there is a possible indication that the Kenites dwelt in the rock (Num 24:21) not far from Punon, one of the main sources of copper.

After the conquest of Canaan the Kenites, who were closely associated with the tribe of Judah, settled in the Negeb (Judg 1:16; AV: "south of Arad"), and part of that region was named after them (I Sam 27:10; Hebrew "Negeb of the Kenite"; AV: "south of the Kenites"). Saul warned them to separate themselves from the Amalekites before he attacked the latter (I Sam 15:6). Some Kenites settled in cities and received a gift of spoil from David after he came to Ziklag (I Sam 30:26-29). It thus seems that the Kenites, together with some other semi-nomadic tribes, dwelt in the south of the country and held some kind of monopoly of copper mining and the production of copper artifacts. A rare confirmation of their presence in that region is provided by a Hebrew ostracon discovered recently at Arad, in which a place by the name of Kinah is mentioned.

KEREN-HAPPUCH ("a ray of eye-paint" i.e. very beautiful eyes, or a cosmetic case in the shape of a horn). The youngest of the three fairest daughters of Job, born to him after his wealth was restored.

KERIOTH

1. A town in Judah (Josh 15:25). It is possible that Judas Iscariot, meaning "man of Cariot" (Matt 10:4, etc.), came from there. Tentatively identified with Khirbet el-Kariathein, north of Arad.

2. A town in Moab (Jer 48:24, 41), mentioned in the stele of Mesha, king of Moab, as a cult place of Chemosh and identified with el-Qureiyat, northwest of Dibon.

KEROS A family of the Nethinim — post-exilic Temple servants. The name is mentioned in the Arad Ostraca of the First Temple period.

KETURAH ("incense"). The second wife of Abraham. She bore him six sons: Zimran, Jokshan, Medan, Midian, Ishbak and Shuah (Gen 25:1-2; I Chr 1:32-33). In Genesis 25:6 and I Chronicles 1:32, she is called Abraham's concubine.

KEVEH (KUE) A region in southeastern Anatolia, named *Cilicia* by the Greeks. It is mentioned in the OT in connection with Solomon's trade in horses (I Kgs 10:28; II Chr 1:16). The country consists of a fertile coastal plain watered by two large rivers and a hill region, bordering on the Taurus Mountains to the west and northwest, on the Anti-Taurus to the northeast, and on the Amanus range to the east. The biblical kingdom of Keveh was founded in the 1st millennium B.C. Although no horses were bred at Keveh, the kingdom traded in animals from the north. Keveh is mentioned for the first time in 9th century B.C. Assyrian sources as part of a Neo-Hittite league, formed to defend the trade routes menaced by the Assyrians. Shalmaneser III conquered

KINGDOM OF GOD

593

cities in Keveh in 839 B.C. but only after his campaign in 833 B.C. was its principal city Tarsus, captured. After the fall of Assyria the Babylonians conducted a campaign against Keveh. The Persians conquered Hilaku, Cilicia's name in cuneiform documents. In 103 B.C. Cilicia was made a Roman province. Luke and Paul mentioned Cilicia together with Syria (Acts 15:23, 41; Gal 1:21); by that time the province had Jewish inhabitants (Acts 6:9) and Chrisitan communities (Acts 15:23).

KEZIAH ("cinnamon"). The second of the three daughters of Job, born to him after his wealth was restored.

KIBROTH HATTAAVAH ("graves of lust"). One of the stations of the Israelites in the wilderness between Sinai and Hazeroth (Num 11:34-35; 33:16-17; Deut 9:22). Numbers 11:34 gives an etiological explanation for the name, whereby all those who had tried to satisfy their craving for meat by eating too many of the quails provided by God, died there. The place has not been identified.

KIBZAIM A Levitical city in the territory of Ephraim (Josh 21:22). The parallel list, in I Chronicles 6:68, gives the name Jokmeam, which may however not be a corruption of Kibzaim, but the name of another Levitical city. Not identified.

KID See ANIMALS

KIDRON A valley running between the Temple Mount in Jerusalem and the Mount of Olives and extending through the Judean desert to the Dead Sea. On the western slope of the valley is the Spring of Gihon, the main permanent water source for Jerusalem. The eastern slope

Part of the Kidron Valley.

served as a necropolis in the times of the First and Second Temples. By the brook of Kidron, Asa, king of Judah, destroyed the idol made by Maachah (I Kgs 15:13) and Hilkiah the high priest burnt the vessels made for Baal (II Kgs 23:4). It was crossed by Jesus on his way to Gethsemane (John 18:1).

KINAH A city of Judah on the border of Edom (Josh 15:22), probably associated with the Kenites who dwelt in that area (Judg 1:16). Possibly to be identified with Khirbeth et-Taiyib, 3 miles (5 km) north of Arad.

KINGDOM OF GOD, OF THE HEAVENS The Kingdom of God is the central message of Jesus, from the beginning of his public ministry to

KEZIAH
Job 42:14

KIBROTH HATTAAVAH
Num 11:34-35; 33:16-17. Deut 9:22

KIBZAIM
Josh 21:22

KIDRON
II Sam 15:23. I Kgs 2:37; 15:13. II Kgs 23:4, 6, 12. II Chr 15:16; 29:16; 30:14. Jer 31:40. John 18:1

KINAH
Josh 15:22

the Last Supper. At the beginning he says: "Repent, for the Kingdom of Heaven is at hand" (Matt 4:17). At the end he says: "I will not drink of this fruit of the vine from now on until that day when I drink it new with you in my Father's kingdom" (Matt 26:29).

In many respects the expression "Kingdom of God" is original with Jesus. No other biblical teacher makes it the center of his message. It is true that the OT speaks of God as king, while the Book of Daniel speaks not only of God, as the Ancient of Days, giving the Kingdom to the Son of man (Dan 7:13-14) but also makes the Kingdom the theme of the entire work. This passage doubtless influenced Jesus; it further induced early Christians to think of Jesus as the Son of man sent from the Father to bring the Kingdom to his people.

Tracing the term through a single gospel — Mark — an idea can be obtained of the manner in which Jesus employed the concept. His first public preaching runs: "The time is fulfilled, and the Kingdom of God is at hand. Repent, and believe in the gospel" (Mark 1:14-15). The Kingdom is the content and purpose of the parables (Mark 4:11, 26, 30). It is the goal of death and the motive for ethical practice (Mark 9:1, 47). It must be approached as a child and is far from the rich (Mark 10:14-15, 23-25). One who knows that the great commandment is to love, is near to it (Mark 12:34). The eucharistic meal anticipates it and looks forward to it (Mark 14:25). The man who takes care of the body of Jesus is one who seeks the Kingdom (Mark 15:43). Thus the Kingdom of God is the ultimate horizon of the preaching of Jesus, the highest value, the goal of history and a symbol of eternity.

The meaning of the Kingdom of God in the preaching of Jesus may be listed under five characteristics. First, the Kingdom of God is a social reality, not individualistic. This is easy to see from the nature of the word "kingdom" itself, which suggests a territory and a people over which a king rules, a society ordered by a king; the Kingdom is something one enters (Matt 5:20; 7:21 etc.). Second, the Kingdom preached by Jesus is intended to be an earthly, political reality and not just heavenly. Thus he teaches the prayer: "Your Kingdom come, your will be done on earth as it is in heaven" (Matt 6:10). His will is a will for justice and peace: "Seek first the Kingdom of God and his righteousness" (Matt 6:33). Consider also the beatitudes of the poor in spirit, those who hunger for justice, the peace-makers and the persecuted (Matt 5:3, 6, 9-10). Third, the Kingdom of God is personalistic, not tyrannical or crushing of the individual person. It respects human dignity and the need for human rights and political freedom. "The Kingdom of God is within you" (Luke 17:21). Fourth, the Kingdom is universal, intended for all men and women, all peoples and nations: "Make disciples of all the nations" (Matt 28:19). All are invited to the feast (Matt 22:9). All stand under judgment (Matt 25:32). Fifth, the Kingdom of God is God's kingdom. In this sense it is connected with spiritual life and religious faith. It is a divine gift, i.e., it cannot be dissolved into pure human political arrangements. The best short definition of the Kingdom is by Saint Paul: "The Kingdom of God is...righteousness and peace and joy in the Holy Spirit" (Rom 14:17).

The Kingdom is Jesus' future hope for this world, as the resurrection was his hope for the next world, for heaven. That is why he prayed, "Your Kingdom come!"

KINGS, BOOKS OF The Books of Kings, which are the narrative continuation of the Books of Samuel, were originally a single work which was divided into two parts, known as I Kings and II Kings (in the Septuagint, where the Book of Samuel is called I and II Kings, the Book of Kings is III and IV Kings). They cover the end of the reign of King

Fragment from the Book of Kings found at Qumran. (Shrine of the Book, Jerusalem)

David, the accession to the throne of Solomon, and the split of the kingdom, and tell the parallel histories of the two kingdoms up to their fall.

I Kings chapters 1-11 cover the monarchy under David and Solomon. In David's old age, his son Adonijah attempted to usurp the throne on the grounds that he was the eldest living son (1:5-10). However, Nathan the prophet intervened and had Bathsheba, the mother of Solomon, make an appeal to the king on behalf of her son Solomon (1:11-21). David reassured Bathsheba and gave instructions to Zadok the priest and Nathan to anoint Solomon as the next king (1:28-37). When the news of the anointing reached Adonijah, his support melted away and he himself begged pardon from Solomon (1:38-53). After final deathbed instruction from David (2:1-12), Solomon began to systematically dispose of his enemies: Adonijah, Joab and Shimei each met their death (2:13-46).

The next task was the organization of the kingdom and the assignment of tasks and districts (4:2-19). Solomon's aim was to build and organize an empire extending beyond his own prosperous country (4:21-28). He planned the building of the Temple in Jerusalem, drawing on his friendship with King Hiram of Tyre to secure the required timber and artisans (5:1-12). For the first time, Israel experienced compulsory civilian service for the preparation of materials to be used in the building of the Temple (5:13-18). Chapter 6 describes the construction of the Temple; chapter 7 depicts the 13 year long construction of the royal palace, and details the Temple furnishings. The Temple was dedicated after the ark and holy vessels had been transported to Jerusalem (8:1-64).

The biblical account describes the visit of the Queen of Sheba (10:1-13) but, in contrast to the wealth, magnificence, exceptional wisdom, supreme power and influence exhibited by Solomon (10:14-29), chapter 11 describes his lapses and their consequences. These include polygamy with foreign women (11:1-3), who led him into apostasy (11:4-8). The end of this section presents the Ephraimite Jeroboam, detailing his early career, his abortive rebellion against Solomon, and his flight to Egypt (11:26-40); it also records the accession of Solomon's son Rehoboam to the throne on the death of his father (11:41-43).

I Kings chapter 12 - II Kings chapter 17 traces the annals of the two kingdoms; the split came when Jeroboam's demand for lightened taxation was rejected by Rehoboam (12:2-15), provoking a revolt which culminated in Jeroboam being made king over the northern tribes and consolidating his kingdom (12:16-20). He sponsored calf-worship in the north, appointed non-Levitical priests, and introduced a new Feast of Tabernacles (12:25-33).

When Jeroboam's son fell ill, his wife went to consult Ahijah the prophet, who predicted the child's death as well as the extinction of Jeroboam's house and kingdom, and the dispersal of Israel (14:1-16). Jeroboam died and was succeeded by his son Nadab (14:20).

In the meantime, Judah suffered invasion by Shishak king of Egypt (14:25-26). Rehoboam was succeeded by his son Abijam (Abijah) (14:29-31); Abijam, in turn, by his son Asa, who was pious and introduced religious reforms. Asa waged war against Baasha who was to be the next king of Israel (15:9-24). The entire house of Jeroboam was subsequently assassinated by Baasha (15:25-34).

Baasha was succeeded by his son, Elah (16:1-14). Elah was assassinated by the rebel Zimri who reigned for just one week (16:15-20) before being defeated in a civil war by Omri; the latter ruled for 12 years and founded the northern capital, Samaria (16:23-28). Omri was succeeded by Ahab, whose wickedness is described as unprecedented: he married Jezebel, the daughter of King Ethbaal of Sidon, and erected an altar to Baal in Samaria (16:29-33).

Chapters 17-18 are dominated by the appearance of Elijah, and various incidents concerning him culminating in his challenge to the prophets of Baal on Mount Carmel (18:1-40).

The evil of Ahab's reign is reflected in the episode of the vineyard of Naboth (21:1-29). The king, mortally wounded at the battle of Ramoth Gilead (825 B.C.), was succeeded by his son Ahaziah (22:29-40). The first Book of Kings ends with the reign of Jehoshaphat in Judah (22:41-50), and the beginning of the reign of Ahaziah of Israel (22:51-53).

II Kings opens with Ahaziah's attempt to capture Elijah and the miraculous fire from heaven which destroyed the king's troops. Chapter 2 describes Elijah's ascension to heaven in a whirlwind (2:7-11) and the beginning of the prophetic ministry of his successor Elisha. The king of Moab rebelled against Israel, but Elisha assured Jehoram, son of Ahab, of victory. Jehoram, with Jehoshaphat of Judah, defeated the Moabites and devastated their country (3:1-27).

Next come the miraculous deeds performed by Elisha; these include the widow's oil which unceasingly filled vessels (4:1-7), and a cure for the leprosy which afflicted Naaman, the commander of the Aramean army; Elisha floating on the Jordan, and his prediction of the death of Ben-Hadad, and the accession of Hazael to the Syrian throne (chaps. 5-8). The reigns of Jehoram of Judah and his son Ahaziah are then summarized (8:16-29).

Chapter 9 describes the revolt of Jehu, commander-in-chief of the army of Jehoram, his ascent to the throne of Israel, the murder of King Ahaziah of Judah, and the ignoble end of Jezebel (9:30-37). Jehu proceeded to wipe out the entire dynasty of Ahab (10:1-11) as well as eradicating the Baal worshipers of Israel (10:15-31).

After the death of Ahaziah, his mother Athaliah usurped the Judean throne (11:1-3), but seven years later, a plot of the priest Jehoiada (9:4-

16) led to her overthrow and replacement by her grandson Joash. Joash, while paying tribute to Hazael of Aram, led a pious life and regulated Temple income (chap. 12). He was assassinated in a palace revolt and replaced by Amaziah (12:19-21).

Chapter 13 recounts the reigns of Jehoahaz of Israel (13:1-9) and his son, Jehoash (13:10-13) as well as Elisha's last deed, his symbolic act of prophecy with arrows (13:14-19).

Amaziah of Judah executed his father's murderers and won a battle over the Edomites, but then challenged Joash of Israel with disastrous consequences (14:1-14).

Joash was succeeded by his son Jeroboam II (14:23-29), who was in turn succeeded by his son Zechariah. Chapter 15 describes the reigns of the last kings of Israel, Zechariah, Shallum, Menahem, Pekahiah and Pekah. The reign of Ahaz is recounted in chapter 16, including the Syro-Ephraimite war, his visit to Damascus and the building of a new altar in Jerusalem, followed by the final defeat and destruction of the Northern Kingdom and its last king Hoshea by the Assyrians (chap. 17), who banished the population (722 B.C.) replacing it with other exiled peoples.

II Kings chapters 18-25 record the annals of the Kingdom of Judah. Its king, Hezekiah played an important part in the destiny of the kingdom. He first instituted a cultic reform (18:1-8) and then appealed to Isaiah for support against the invading armies of the Assyrian king, Sennacherib; the prophet replied reassuringly (19:1-7). However, when Hezekiah received an embassy from the king of Babylon, Merodach-Baladan, Isaiah's resentment was aroused, and, speaking in the name of God, he predicted that Babylon would plunder and carry away all the wealth of the family of Hezekiah, and that his children would be their captives (20:12-19). The evil reigns of Manasseh (21:1-18) and his son Amon (21:19-26) were followed by the reign of Hezekiah's great-grandson, Josiah, who made arrangements for the repair of the Temple (22:3-7). It was during these repairs that the Book of the Law was discovered (22:8-13), whereupon Josiah undertook a major religious reform (23:4-14), which included the destruction of all idolatrous places, shrines and priests in Bethel and Samaria (23:15-20), the eradication from Judah of all superstitious practices (23:24) and centralization of all worship in Jerusalem. Josiah's premature death at the battle of Megiddo (23:26-30), was followed by the short reigns of Jehoahaz (23:31-34) and Jehoiakim (23:36-24:6).

The brief reign of the next king, Jehoiachin witnessed the capture and plunder of Jerusalem by Nebuchadnezzar, who led Jehoiachin into exile along with many other Judeans (24:8-16). Jehoiachin was succeeded by Zedekiah, whose revolt against **Nebuchadnezzar** resulted in the capture and destruction of Jerusalem (586 B.C.); the king was deposed, blinded and exiled (24:18-25:7); the Temple utensils were carried off, and prominent citizens and officers executed. Gedaliah was appointed governor, but he was assassinated by Ishmael (25:22-26). The book closes with Jehoiachin's transfer from prison in the 37th year of his exile; he was brought to the Babylonian palace where he lived with dignity at the table of the Babylonian king, Evil-Merodach.

Undoubtedly, the Book of Kings was taken from many distinct sources, three of which are mentioned by name: the Book of Acts of Solomon, the Book of the Chronicles of the Kings of Israel and the Book of the Chronicles of the Kings of Judah. The book's recurring theme is the centralization of worship as prescribed in Deuteronomy and enforced by Josiah. The Deuteronomic view, requiring the purity and centralization of religion, is reflected in the condemnation of these kings who introduce other forms of worship: they are blamed for the tragedies that befell the people.

OUTLINE

I Kings 1:1-11:43: The monarchy under David and Solomon
    1:1-2:46   Death of David and accession of
                  Solomon
    3:1-11:43   Reign of Solomon

I Kings 12:1-II Kings 17:41: The Two Kingdoms
    12:1-24   The Kingdom splits in two
    12:25-14:18 Reign of Jeroboam I of Israel
    14:19-16:16 Parallel history of Israel and Judah
    16:17-II Kings 10:31 House of Omri

II Kings 18:1-25:30: Judah alone
    18:1-20:21   Hezekiah
    21:1-26   Manasseh and Amon
    22:1-23:30   Josiah and his reforms
    23:31-25:30 The end of the Kingdom of Judah

KINGSHIP Government by a sole ruler, whether appointed or, more generally, hereditary, over a town (city-state, e.g., Tyre, Sidon or Ugarit), nation (e.g. Ammon, Edom) or empire ("King of Kings", e.g. Assyria, Babylonia, Persia). The king leads his people in war; he is responsible for upholding justice and maintaining the central administration and worship; international commerce also involved his participation. These functions require a central treasury, to be replenished by the taxes of the inhabitants and the tribute of subject nations. The institution of kingship, prevalent throughout the ancient Near East, was based on divine sanction.

In Israel, however, matters were arranged differently at the outset, when secular authority lay with the elders (the heads of the families), the people's leaders in war (Judg 11:5-11; I Sam 4:3) and representatives before God (Ex 19:7; 24:9-11).

Thus the very concept of royal authority is foreign to most of the laws and customs of the Pentateuch. Only Deuteronomy 17:14-15 considered the contingency of the Israelites electing to institute kingship. Characteristically, this possibility, while allowed for, is not obligatory nor considered meritorious. Moreover, the choice of a king, and his conduct, are subject to certain restrictions: he is not to be a foreigner; he is not to overindulge himself with gold and silver, costly horses or women (Deut 17:16-17); he is to have a copy of the Law of God, from which he shall read at all times (Deut 17:18-20).

Israel did not institute the monarchy lightly. Hereditary kingship was proposed to Gideon after his victory over the Midianites, but he refused, preferring God's rule (Judg 8:22-23). His son Abimelech became king of Shechem (Judg 9:1-21): his rule over "Israel" (Judg 9:22) was a passing episode at best.

Kingship was finally adopted in Israel at a time of crisis: the period of Philistine domination. The biblical narrative mentions two aspects of this crisis: the powerlessness of traditional structures *vis-à-vis* the Philistines (I Sam 9:16-17) and an erosion of Samuel's religious leadership because of the malpractices of his sons (I Sam 8:1-5). Even then, kingship was not accepted automatically: when the elders offered it to Samuel, he at first refused (I Sam 8:5-6). Although God commanded him to bow to the people's wishes he was instructed to warn them of the many prerogatives of the kings (familiar from other countries) and the dangers inherent in centralized power (I Sam 8:11-18). The elders, however, accepted these terms (I Sam 8:19-20), and Saul was publicly chosen as the first king (I Sam 10:17-25). But his act did not put an end to the opposition: some individuals, rejecting Saul's rule, refused to bring him tribute (I Sam 10:27). Thus the institution of the monarchy met with strong religious and social objections from the very outset.

On the other hand, kingship was also considered as God's grace. According to the story of Saul's anointment (I Sam 9:1-10:16), he was elected by God to save the people from Philistine oppression; indeed, his victory over the Philistines established Israel as an independent kingdom (I Sam 13:1-14:47). Saul is likewise celebrated as the savior of Jabesh Gilead, having defeated the Ammonites there (I Sam 11:1-12). Thus the king has a special position before the Lord: he is God's elect, as shown by the revelation to Samuel (I Sam 9:15-17) and by the oracle at the popular assembly (I Sam 10:20-24). He is even imbued with the "Spirit of God" (sometimes called "royal charisma" I Sam 10:6, 10; 11:6; cf 16:13). His position is symbolized by his anointment (a rite of purification and sanctification, I Sam 10:1) and the ceremonies at Mizpah and Gilgal (I Sam 10:17-25; 11:14-15).

This religious status, however, is not only a warrant for his legitimacy; it also carries an obligation. The king is responsible before God, as stressed in Samuel's farewell oration (I Sam chap. 12), where the prophet acknowledged the monarchy, but warned the king and people to observe God's commandments; should the king sin, retribution would be severe (I Sam 12:13-15). This principle is not unlike the rules laid down in Deuteronomy 17:14-20, but its formulation is more forceful. Thus the king is always considered as subject to the authority of God and his messengers, the prophets. Samuel was not only instrumental in enthroning Saul (I Sam 9:15-11:14), he also castigated him harshly (I Sam 13:13-14; 15:12-31), and even warned him that God was about to put an end to his kingdom (I Sam 13:14; 15:22-26, 28-29). David, in turn, was rebuked by Nathan and Gad (II Sam 12:1-14; 24:11-14). Ahijah the Shilonite prophesied the division of the kingdom and Jeroboam's future rule over the ten northern tribes (I Kgs 11:30-39). Elisha was involved in Jehu's insurrection (II Kgs 9:1-10). Thus the prophet was both an outspoken critic of the king and a "kingmaker".

At first, the king's authority over the people was relatively weak. Saul and David were elected by popular assent (I Sam 10:24; II Sam 5:1-3). From the outset Saul was patient with popular opposition (I Sam 10:27; 11:12-13; 14:45; cf 15:21). After his death the elders of Judah decided to part ways with his dynasty, whereupon they elected David (II Sam 2:4); David also made an agreement with the leaders of Israel (II Sam 5:3). It is quite possible that the "behavior of royalty", written down by Samuel when Saul was made king (I Sam 10:25), represents a similar agreement.

David and Solomon did much to consolidate their power, notwithstanding political upheavals (the rebellions of Absalom, Sheba and Jeroboam) and prophetic criticism (Nathan). In this they were greatly assisted by David's military successes and conquests. He created a standing professional army and a small empire; the latter in its turn contributed greatly to his royal treasury. He also strengthened the central administration, making Jerusalem his capital. The king owned royal domains (partly by conquest) out of which he granted prebends to his officials. The religious stature of his rule was considerably augmented when he transferred the ark of the Lord from Kirjath Jearim to Jerusalem (II Sam chap. 6; I Chr 15:5). The prophecy of Nathan further promised him the everlasting continuity of his dynasty ("the house of David", II Sam chap. 7). Solomon strengthened his position by building the Temple near his palace in Jerusalem (I Kgs chaps. 6-7). Popular opposition, however, did not weaken during Solomon's rule, most likely because of the heavy corvée service he exacted to further his building activities.

Jeroboam rebelled against Solomon, urged on by the prophet Ahijah (I Kgs 11:26-40). After Solomon's death his son Rehoboam was rejected by the ten northern tribes because of his refusal to lighten their burden (I Kgs 12:1-14). Only the tribe of Judah and part of Benjamin acknowledged Rehoboam as their new king (I Kgs 12:17-20). In religious terms, the division of the monarchy was attributed to Solomon's sins (his marriages to alien women, I Kgs 11:1-11). However, Rehoboam's continued rule in Jerusalem was seen as an expression of divine grace towards David (I Kgs 11:12-13, 32-36; 15:4-5).

In the north, dynasty followed dynasty, with military leaders and the citizen army taking an active hand in insurrection and kingmaking (I Kgs 15:17, 27; 16:9), as did the prophets (I Kgs 14:7-16; 16:1; II Kgs 9:1-10). Elijah, for example, severely castigated King Ahab and Jezebel for their murder of Naboth in order to procure his vineyard (I Kgs 21:1-19; II Kgs 9:25-26). The kings of both realms emulated David and Solomon in fostering religious worship. Jeroboam erected golden calves at the open-air sanctuaries of Dan and Bethel (I Kgs 12:26-31).

In Judah, by contrast, the house of David retained power, giving priority to the maintenance of the Jerusalem Temple. The Temple was restored by Jehoash and Josiah; Hezekiah and Josiah purged the cult of alien influences (II Kgs 18:3-4, 22; 22:8-13; 23:1-20). However, Judean kings were also castigated by the prophets for their shortcomings (Is 7:10-20; Jer 21:1-23:4).

Kingship, nevertheless remained an ideal. Many Psalms celebrate the anointed king as the God-given savior (Ps 2:2-11; 20:7-10; 21:1-8; 45:1-6; cf I Sam 2:10), upholder of justice (Ps 45:7-8; 72:1-4, 12-15), and conqueror of the nations (Ps 2:6-9; 72:8-11). It was the hope of the prophets that any future king would follow David, in faithful embodiment of these ideals (Is chap. 11; Jer 23:5-6; 33:14-22).

The NT does not stress the concept of Jesus as king. The title "King of the Jews" is ascribed to him already at birth (Matt 2:2) but Jesus is careful to avoid claims to an earthly kingship (Matt 4:8-10). In his discussion with Pilate on the nature of his kingship, Jesus accepts the title when challenged (Matt 27:11; Mark 15:2; Luke 23:3) but does not take the initiative in asserting the title. John 18:33-39 emphasizes that the kingdom is not of this world. However, the popular view took the title as a claim to this-worldly kingship (Matt 27:29, 37, 42 etc.). Jesus himself used the term, king, only for God (Matt 5:35; 18:23; 22:2). The kingship of Jesus mentioned in I Corinthians 15:24 is a reference to the end of days after all his enemies will have been subdued, while a similar eschatological concept is implied in Revelation (cf Rev 3:21; 14:14).

KIR

1. A Moabite city mentioned in Isaiah's prophecy against Moab (Is 15:1). May be identical with Kir Hareseth.

KIR 1
Is 15:1

2. Place in Mesopotamia from which the Arameans came to Syria (Amos 9:7). As Amos had prophesied (Amos 1:5), the Arameans returned to Kir as exiles after Tiglath-Pileser III invaded the Aramean capital Damascus "and took its people captive to Kir" (II Kgs 16:9).

KIR 2
II Kgs 16:9. Is 22:6. Amos 1:5; 9:7

KIR HARASETH, KIR HARESETH, KIR HERES The capital of Moab, a stronghold situated on top of a lofty mountain. Surrounded by a massive wall, it dominated the road from the Gulf of Elath to

View of el-Kerak identified with Kir Haraseth.

Damascus. Jehoram, king of Israel, and Jehoshaphat, king of Judah, attacked Kir Haraseth but could not take it (II Kgs 3:1, 25-26). The site is identified with el-Kerak.

KIRJATH See KIRJATH JEARIM

KIRJATHAIM (KIRIATHAIM)

1. A city on the Moabite plateau, conquered and rebuilt by the Reubenites (Num 32:37; Josh 13:19). It is mentioned as a Moabite city in the Mesha Stele (9th century B.C.), and also in Jeremiah's lamentation (Jer 48:1, 23) and Ezekiel's prophecy (Ezek 25:9) on Moab.

Some scholars identify it with Khirbeth el-Qureiya, 6 miles (10 km) west of Medeba.

2. A city of the Levites in the territory of Naphtali (I Chr 6:76). In the parallel passage (Josh 21:32), it is called Kartan.

Most scholars identify it with Khirbeth el-Qureiye, 7 miles (11 km) from Kedesh-Naphtali.

KIRJATH ARBA Original name of the city of Hebron, cf Joshua 14:15, "And the name of Hebron was formerly was Kirjath Arba for Arba was the greatest man among the Anakim". Elsewhere it is said of Kirjath Arba, "it is Hebron" (Gen 23:2; 35:27; Josh 15:54; 20:7). The city was conquered on behalf of the tribe of Judah by Caleb, who dispossessed Arba's three sons Sheshai, Ahiman and Talmai (Josh 15:13-14). It was designated as one of the six cities of refuge for the accidental manslayer (Josh 20:7; cf Num 35:9 ff; Deut 19:1-13) and as a Levitical city of the Kohathites (Josh 21:11; cf Num 35:1-8). The place name Kirjath Arba appears in narratives of the patriarchs (Gen 23:2; 35:27) and the conquest (Josh chaps. 14; 15; 20; 21; Judg chap. 1) and then disappears. It reappears in the list of districts settled by returnees from Babylonia in Nehemiah 11:25.

KIRJATH ARIM Alternative form of KIRJATH JEARIM.

KIRJATH BAAL See KIRJATH JEARIM

KIRJATH HUZOTH ("city of streets"). A city in Moab; the first place to which Balaam went with Balak in order to curse the Israelite tribes (Num 22:39). It is not identified.

KIRJATH JEARIM Town on the northern border of the territory of Judah. Its ancient names were Baale Judah (II Sam 6:2), Baalah (Josh 15:9) and Mount Baalah (Josh 15:11), attesting to the cult of Baal at this place. It was one of the cities of the Gibeonites (Josh 9:17) and later a town on the border of Judah (Josh 15:9-10, 60). It was the last place where the ark of the covenant rested before reaching Jerusalem (II Sam 6:2 etc.). The town was resettled after the return from the Babylonian Exile. According to Eusebius it is situated on the road between Jerusalem and Lod 9 miles (14.5 km) from Jerusalem, and the site is usually identified with the village of Abu Ghosh.

KIRJATH SANNAH See DEBIR No.2

KIRJATH SEPHER The ancient name of Debir (Josh 15:15; Judg 1:11).

KISH

1. A Benjamite of Gibeon, the son of Jeiel and brother of Ner. The latter was a forefather of Kish No.2 (I Chr 8:33; 9:39).

2. A Benjamite landowner and the father of King Saul. Kish is called the son of Abiel in I Samuel chapter 9, but according to I Chronicles chapters 8 and 9 his father was Ner, possibly referring to Kish's descent from the Ner mentioned above. Kish lived in Gibeah and was buried, together with Saul and Jonathan, in Zela.

3. A Benjamite, the father of Shimei, and an ancestor of Mordecai.

4. A Merarite Levite in David's day, the son of Mahli. His sons married the daughters of his brother, Eleazar.

5. The son of Abdi, a Merarite Levite who participated in Hezekiah's reform.

KISHI Identical with Kish No.5.

KISHION A city which fell to the lot of the tribe of Issachar (Josh 19:20) and was later allotted to the Gershonite Levites (Josh 21:28). It is identified with Tell Qasiun, south of Mount Tabor.

KISHON A river in the western part of the Jezreel Valley, which draws its water from the mountains of Gilboa and Nazareth. During the battle of Deborah and Barak, which took place in the winter, the river overflowed its shallow banks, bringing disaster to Sisera's chariots (Judg 4:7, 13; 5:21). It flows along the foot of Mount Carmel, where Elijah slew the prophets of Baal (I Kgs 18:40). The river mouth served as a harbor. Nearby is Tell Abu Hawan.

KITE See ANIMALS

KITHLISH A city which fell to the lot of the tribe of Judah when Canaan was divided among the tribes. Its present location is unknown.

KITRON A city which fell to the lot of the tribe of Zebulun when the land of Canaan was divided among the tribes. Its Canaanite inhabitants were allowed to stay. Its present location is unknown.

KITTIM As a proper name, Kittim appears as one of the sons of Javan (Gen 10:4; I Chr 1:7). The islands of the Kittim (Cyprus) are mentioned

Kirjath Jearim atop a hill northwest of Jerusalem.

53; 13:5-6.
II Chr 1:4.
Neh 7:29. Jer 26:20

KIRJATH SANNAH
Josh 15:49

KIRJATH SEPHER
Josh 15:15-16.
Judg 1:11-12

KISH 1
I Chr 8:30, 33;
9:36, 39

KISH 2
I Sam 9:1-3;
10:11, 21;
14:51. II Sam
21:14. I Chr
8:33; 9:39;
12:1; 26:28.
Acts 13:21

KISH 3
Est 2:5-6

KISH 4
I Chr 23:21-
22; 24:29

KISH 5
II Chr 29:12

KISHI
I Chr 6:44

KISHION
Josh 19:20;
21:28

KISHON
Judg 4:7, 13;
5:21. I Kgs
18:40. Ps 83:9

KITHLISH
Josh 15:40

KITRON
Judg 1:30

KITTIM
Gen 10:4.
I Chr 1:7

in Ezekiel 27:6 and the land of Kittim is mentioned in Isaiah 23:1. In Jeremiah 2:10 Kittim designates the West, as opposed to Kedar designating the East. Josephus (*Antiq.* 1, 6, 1) applies the name to Cyprus, modern scholars believing it to be preserved in the name of the city Kition (present-day Larnaka), presumably established at the beginning of the Phoenician expansion towards Cyprus in the 11th century B.C. Later, the term Kittim was expanded to embrace all the islands and seacoasts of the eastern Mediterranean.

The Kittim are mentioned in the Arad Ostraca from c. 600 B.C. probably as mercenaries. In the Book of Daniel the reference to Kittim is probably an allusion to Rome (Dan 11:30). (Kittim in Numbers 24:24 is translated in the Vulgate as "Italy", and in the Aramaic Targum of Onkelos as "Romans"). The name is also used in the Dead Sea Scrolls to refer to Rome.

KOA One of the people of Babylon, appearing together with Shoa.

KOHATH The second son of Levi; brother of Gershon and Merari (Gen 46:11; Ex 6:16; Num 3:17; I Chr 6:1, 16, 38; 23:6) and founder of the family of the KOHATHITES (Num 3:27). He was the father of Amram, Izhar, Hebron and Uzziel (Ex 6:18; Num 3:19; I Chr 6:2, 18; 23:12; 24:20-24), and the grandfather of Aaron, Moses and Miriam (Ex 6:18, 20; Num 26:58-59). He died at the age of 133 (Ex 6:18).

KOHATHITES Family of Levites; its members included Aaron, Moses and Miriam, making it the most important family descended from Levi. In the census taken by Moses in the wilderness, the Kohathites, comprising four major families, numbered 8,600 males from a month old and upward (Num 3:27-28). They also included 2,750 males in the 30 to 50 age-group eligible for service in the tent of meeting (Num 4:1-3, 34-37). In the desert, the Kohathites camped on the south side of the tabernacle (Num 3:29). They were in charge of the ark, the table, the lampstand, the altars, the vessels of sanctuary and the screen. They were very close to the sanctuary but God forbade them on pain of death to touch the holy objects which they were permitted to carry only after they had been covered by the sons of Aaron (Num 4:4-15, 17-20; 7:9).

The Kohathite descendants of Aaron received 13 cities by lot from the tribes of Judah, Simeon and Benjamin. The remaining Kohathites received ten cities from the tribe of Dan and half-tribe of Manasseh (Josh 21:4-5, 9, 26; I Chr 6:54-61, 66-70). David appointed 120 Kohathites under the leadership of Uriel to bring the ark up to Jerusalem and Heman represented them in the service (I Chr 6:33; 15:5). When the Moabites and Ammonites threatened to attack King Jehoshaphat of Judah, the Kohathites encouraged the army to give battle by voicing loud hymns of praise to the Lord (II Chr 20:14-19).

When Hezekiah instituted a cultic reform, he was assisted by two Kohathites, Mehath and Joel. Under Josiah, another two members of the family, Zechariah and Meshullam, supervised the Levites in repairing the Temple. After the Exile, the Kohathites were in charge of the preparation of the showbread every Sabbath (I Chr 9:32). The genealogical list of the descendants of Kohath in Exodus 6:20-24 differs from the list in I Chronicles 23:13:20.

KOLAIAH

1. An ancestor of Sallu of the Benjamites, who lived in Jerusalem in the time of Nehemiah.

2. The father of the false prophet Ahab.

KORAH

1. The youngest of the five sons of Esau (I Chr 1:35). He was the founder of an Edomite clan (Gen 36:18). His mother was Aholibamah and his two full brothers were Jeush and Jaalam (Gen 36:5, 14).

2. One of the seven Edomite clans, all of which were regarded as the lineal descendants of Esau's son Eliphaz and the latter's wife Adah (Gen 36:15-16).

KORAH 2
Gen 36:16

3. Leader of a rebellion against Moses. He was the son of Izhar, grandson of Levi, and a first cousin to Moses. Korah headed a group of 250 prominent men, who challenged the leadership of Moses and Aaron while the Israelites were in the desert (Num 16:1-2). The rebel faction is referred to as Korah and his company (Num 16:5, 32; 26:9; 27:3). Other leading conspirators were the Reubenites Dathan and Abiram, sons of Eliab, and On, son of Peleth (Num 16:1). Moses challenged Korah and his fellow rebels to a trial by ordeal. They all were to bring pans with incense and the Lord would choose who were to be his rightful leaders. A fire from the Lord then destroyed the conspirators, thus vindicating Moses and Aaron. When the earth opened to swallow the rebels (Num 16:31-35; 26:9-10), Korah's three sons — Assir, Elkanah and Abiasaph (Ex 6:24) — were spared, intimating that they may not have participated in the revolt. Later rabbinic tradition explained that this earned them their place of prominence in the Book of Psalms where the authorship of several psalms (Ps 42; 44; 45; 47; 48; 49; 84; 85; 87; 88) is attributed to "the sons of Korah", a guild of Temple singers. Some of these psalms refer to events falling centuries later than the Mosaic era, such as the Davidic dynasty (Ps 45) and the destruction of the Temple (Ps 84; 85; 87). The Korahites are also named alongside of the Kohathites as singers in II Chronicles 20:19. In Jude verse 11 Korah is named as the rebel par excellence.

KORAH 3
Ex 6:21, 24.
Num 16:1, 5-6,
8, 16, 19, 24,
27, 32, 40, 49;
26:9-11; 27:3.
I Chr 6:22, 37;
9:19; 26:19. Ps
42:1; 44:1;
45:1; 46:1;
47:1; 48:1;
49:1; 84:1;
85:1; 87:1;
88:1. Jude
v.11

4. One of the four sons of Hebron, according to the genealogy found in I Chronicles 2:43. His three brothers were Tappuah, Rekem and Shema.

KORAH 4
I Chr 2:43

KORAHITES, KORATHITES The relatives of Shallum, son of Kore, the son of Ebiasaph, son of Korah (See KORAH No.3); they were appointed by King David to guard the entrance to the tabernacle (I Chr 9:19; 26:1). According to I Chronicles 12:1-6, members of this family joined David at Ziklag while he was banished from Saul's presence. II Chronicles 20:19 relates that, during Jehoshaphat's battle with the Ammonites, the Korahites and the Kohathites "stood up to praise the Lord God of Israel with voices loud"; this led to Jehoshaphat's victory. The previously mentioned Shallum is called "the Korahite" in I Chronicles 9:13. In Exodus 6:24 Korahite refers to the three sons of Korah No.3 while in Numbers 26:58 and I Chronicles 26:19 it refers to their descendants collectively.

KORAHITES,
KORATHITES
Ex 6:24. Num
26:58. I Chr
9:19, 31; 12:6;
26:1; II Chr
20:19

KORE ("partridge").

1. A Levite, son of Imnah; he was in charge of the freewill offerings in the time of King Hezekiah.

KORE 1
II Chr 31:14

2. A Levite, the father of Shallum, who lived in Jerusalem during the restoration period.

KORE 2
I Chr 9:19;
26:1

The name Kore also appears in the Ohel Ostraca of the 7th century B.C.

KOZ ("thorn").

1. The father of Anub, listed in the genealogical list of Judah.

KOZ 1
I Chr 4:8

2. One of the priestly families who returned from Babylon with Zerubbabel; they were suspended from their priesthood duties on failing to find their genealogical documentation.

KOZ 2
Ezra 2:61.
Neh 3:4, 21;
7:63

KUE See KEVEH

KUSHAIAH A descendant of the Levitical family of Merari and father of Ethan, who was appointed as a singer in the Temple at the time of King David. It has been suggested that this may be an alternative form of the name Kishi.

KUSHAIAH
I Chr 15:17

LAADAH Son of Shelah the son of Judah; father of Mareshah.

LAADAN (LADAN)

1. The son of Tahan, a descendant of Ephraim.
2. The head of the Gershonites, a Levite clan.

LABAN ("white").

1. Son of Bethuel the Aramean (Gen 28:5) and, through his sister Rebekah (Gen 25:20; 27:43; 28:5), uncle of Jacob. Residing in Padan Aram (Gen 28:2) which is located in the province of Haran (Gen 27:43; 29:4) he is called Laban the Syrian (Gen 25:20; 31:24). He received Abraham's steward sent to arrange the marriage of Isaac to Rebekah (Gen 24:29ff). Years later, Jacob, fearing his brother Esau, fled to his uncle Laban (Gen 27:43 ff). He wed Laban's two daughters, Leah and Rachel, but had to serve Laban for 14 years in return. Laban's dealings with his son-in-law were deceitful but he was outwitted by Jacob, who left him to return to Israel with his wives and concubines and 11 sons (Gen 31:41). Laban pursued him and the two signed a covenant (Gen 31:44-45).

The documents uncovered in Nuzi provide striking parallels to these stories, including the nature of the teraphim (stolen by Rachel from Laban Gen 31:19, 31-35), the complaint of his daughters that he "consumed their money" (ibid v.15) and that whatever Jacob received from Laban belongs to the daughters and their sons and not to their brothers (v.16).

2. Place in the Sinai region. Its exact location is not known.

LACHISH An important ancient city in the foothills of the Hebron mountains, first mentioned in the El Amarna Letters of the 14th century B.C. and in a contemporary letter from Tell el-Hesi. Lachish played a prominent role at the time of the conquest of Canaan by the Israelites, when it joined four other cities in a coalition against Joshua. With the defeat of the coalition, Lachish was conquered (Josh 10:5, 26, 32-33), and its territory allotted to the tribe of Judah (Josh 15:39). After these events, nothing is heard of Lachish until its fortification by Rehoboam son of Solomon (II Chr 11:9). Amaziah king of Judea fled to Lachish from conspirators in Jerusalem, and was killed there (II Kgs 14:19; II Chr 25:27). When Sennacherib of Assyria conducted a campaign in Judea in the days of King Hezekiah in 701 B.C., the capture of Lachish was one of his chief victories. The siege of Lachish is documented in great detail in biblical sources (II Kgs chap. 18; Is chap.36; II Chr chap. 32), in Assyrian documents and in its outstanding representation in a series of reliefs which decorated Sennacherib's palace at Nineveh. Just over a century later, Nebuchadnezzar king of Babylon conducted a

(bottom left)
The site of Lachish today.
(bottom right)
Pottery bowl found at Lachish with a proto-Canaanite inscription. 13th century B.C. (Israel Dept. of Antiquities and Museums)

Gold sheet from Lachish showing Ashtoreth standing on a horse. 13th century B.C. (Dept. of Archaeology, Tel Aviv University)

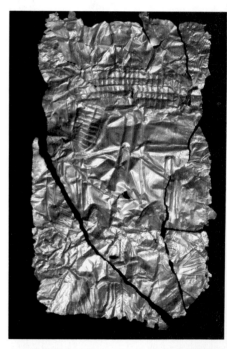

The siege of Lachish shown in a relief from Sennacherib's palace at Nineveh. (British Museum)

Proto-Canaanite inscription on the shoulder of an ewer dedicated to the shrine of Elat ("the Goddess") at Lachish by a certain Mattan. (Rockefeller Museum, Jerusalem)

campaign against Judah which extinguished the kingdom. Lachish and its neighbor Azekah were the last cities captured (Jer 34:7). Lachish was abandoned, but resettled after the return from Babylonia (Neh 11:30). After the Persian period, Lachish was abandoned forever.

The site of Lachish has been identified with Tell ed-Duweir, a prominent tell (mound) in the Shephelah. Excavations have revealed various layers of settlement. The mound was occupied from the Early Canaanite period. In the Middle Canaanite period a massive defensive earthwork was constructed around the mound and a large brick palace was built inside this fortified settlement. In the Late Canaanite period the previous fortifications went out of use. The outstanding structures of this time are two temples, one on the summit, the other in front of the earthwork fortifications.

The earliest Israelite occupation, in the days of King Rehoboam, was without a defensive wall; a square palace was built at its center. The following layer is a well-constructed Judean royal city, defended by massive fortifications. The palace was rebuilt, its size more than doubled, and supplemented by a large courtyard with two sets of storehouses on two of its sides. This city seems to have been destroyed by an earthquake, but was soon rebuilt. The city wall and its monumental gateway, with two gate houses enclosing a protected space, were in use, as was the palace now enlarged by an extension. This was the city of King Hezekiah, besieged and destroyed by Sennacherib. The immense conflagration that followed the capture of the city is evidenced in heavily burnt bricks and charred objects. Remnants of an Assyrian siege rampart, so clearly visible in the Lachish relief, were found at the southeastern corner of the mound. Other finds — numerous arrow heads, sling stones, scales or armor and even some crests of Assyrian helmets — testify to fierce fighting. Lachish was again rebuilt and fortified with a new wall and gate but the palace was not reconstructed. This city was destroyed by Nebuchadnezzar in 588/6 B.C. It was finally rebuilt in the Persian period, and may have been a provincial capital with a wall, a gate and a small palace.

Of the numerous objects found at Lachish, mention should be made of the exceptional number of inscriptions. The Lachish Ostraca — 21 inscribed pottery sherds found in a guardroom in the city gate — were

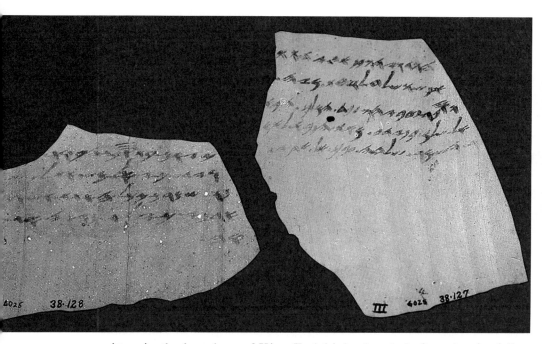

written in the last days of King Zedekiah, shortly before the city fell to the Babylonians. Most of the letters were addressed to "my lord Yaush", perhaps the military commander of Lachish, by a lower officer stationed somewhere in the vicinity.

LAEL ("belonging to God"). The father of Eliasaph, prince of the Gershonite clan of the Levites.

LAEL
Num 3:24

LAHAD The son of Jahath, one of the descendants of Judah who dwelt at Zorah.

LAHAD
I Chr 4:2

LAHMAS (LAHMAM) A village in the district of Lachish (Josh 15:40), usually identified with Khirbet el-Lahm, 2½ miles (4 km) south of Beit Jibrin.

LAHMAS
Josh 15:40

LAHMI Brother of Goliath; he was killed by Elhanan the son of Jair. He is mentioned as "the brother of Goliath" in II Samuel 21:19.

LAHMI
I Chr 20:5

LAISH ("lion").

1. Father of Palti(el) of Gallim to whom Saul gave his daughter Michal, the wife of David. She was later restored to David by Ishbosheth.

LAISH 1
I Sam 25:44.
II Sam 3:15

2. A Canaanite town conquered by the Danites, who changed its name to Dan (Judg chap. 18). The town, situated near the sources of the River Jordan, was apparently under Sidonian hegemony when it was

LAISH 2
Judg 18:7, 14, 27, 29

overrun by 600 members of the tribe of Dan, who were forced northwards by the expanding Philistines. See DAN No.2.

3. A Benjamite village, placed between Gallim and Anathoth in Isaiah 10:30. Its possible location is present-day el-Isawiyah, northeast of Jerusalem.

LAISH 3
Is 10:30

LAKKUM A town in the territory of Naphtali (Josh 19:33), identified by some with Khirbet el-Mansurah, west of the Jordan River.

LAKKUM
Josh 19:33

LAMB See ANIMALS

LAMB OF GOD Three strands go into this figure of speech: the lamb as apocalyptic lamb, as suffering servant and as paschal lamb. Of these, the last two predominate, in fact replacing the first which was probably the one held by John the Baptist.

The term "lamb of God" appears only twice in the NT, each time as a title John the Baptist bestows on Jesus. His role is here defined as "taking away the sins of the world" (John 1:29, 36). Comparisons are drawn between Jesus' bearing during his passion and the behavior of a lamb (Acts 8:32, quoting from Is 53:7; I Pet 1:19). As these usages indicate, the early Christians saw that Jesus' special relationship to God could be expressed in the terminology of self-sacrifice. They repeatedly affirmed that Jesus voluntarily gave up his life for his people. That point is lost in the image of the lamb, for no lamb consents to its death. While the term "lamb of God" does not appear in the Apocalypse, the image of the lamb "standing as slain" dominates that book in a very unusual fashion. For the lamb clearly holds the clue to history and until he emerges, John's only response to what he sees is tears (Rev 5:4).

The figure of the lamb is not unknown in Jewish apocalyptic writing (Testament of Joseph 19:8; Enoch 90:38). But whereas in other sources the lamb is transformed into a ram who exerts his authority and power over his enemies by fighting, the lamb in the Apocalypse of John is remarkable in never being portrayed as making war (in 17:14 he is attacked and in turn, in solidarity with his faithful followers, "overcomes"); he always conquers through the fact that he is worthy to take power and authority for "you were slain and have redeemed us to God by your blood out of every tribe and tongue and people and nation; and have made us kings and priests, to our God and we shall reign on the earth" (Rev 5:9-10). It is also important to note that the word used here for lamb is not (as above) *amnos*, but rather *arnion* — lamblet or lambkin. Yet the fury of the lamb (Rev 6:15-17) is described as the love of God rejected. The lamb is described as a lamp (Rev 21:23), a temple (Rev 21:22) and as getting prepared for a wedding (Rev 21:9).

LAMECH The son of Methushael (Gen 4:18-19; Methuselah in Luke 3:37) of the lineage of Cain, and seventh generation descended from Adam.

LAMECH
Gen 4:18-19,
23-26, 28, 30-
31. I Chr 1:3.
Luke 3:36

His wife Adah bore him Jabal, father of "those who dwell in tents and have livestock" (Gen 4:20) and Jubal, the father of "those who play the harp and flute" (Gen 4:21). By his other wife Zillah, he had Tubal-Cain, the forefather of all coppersmiths and blacksmiths, and a daughter Naamah (Gen 4:22). Lamech's song to his wives (Gen 4:23-24) is one of the most ancient pieces of Hebrew poetry. Its precise meaning and background, however, remain obscure.

According to another tradition, Lamech was also the son of Methuselah and seventh generation descended from Enosh. He lived for 777 years (Gen 5:31).

LAMENTATIONS, BOOK OF Book of the Bible consisting of five elegies corresponding to the five chapters of the book. The overall theological themes of these five poems are:

(a) The destruction of Jerusalem and its holy Temple (587/6 B.C.)

and the subsequent Exile are direct results of Judah's grievous sins against God and not an accident of history (e.g., Lam 1:5, 8, 17-18). Judah has sinned grievously even though the nature of the sin is not specifically indicated (e.g., Lam 1:8-9). Neither idolatry nor social injustice are referred to in this book. While the current generation is certainly not blameless (e.g., Lam 5:16), the sins of previous generations may be at least partially responsible for the destruction (e.g., Lam 5:7; cf Jer 31:29; Ezek 18:2).

(b) Prophets did not call Judah's faults to her attention (Lam 2:14), and, in general, misdeeds of prophets and priests contributed to the general sinful atmosphere (e.g., Lam 4:13; cf II Kgs 24:3-4).

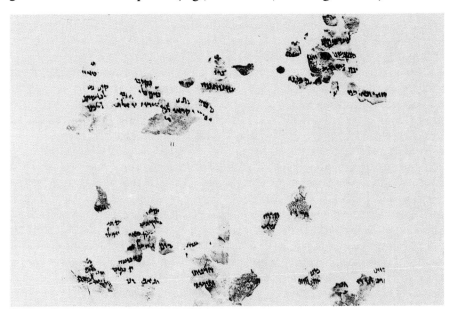

Fragments of the Book of Lamentations found at Qumran. (Shrine of the Book, Jerusalem)

(c) The people can only blame themselves for the destruction. The only road to redemption is through bettering themselves and genuine repentance (e.g., Lam 3:22-41; 5:21-22).

Though these five independent poems lament the destruction of Jerusalem and its Temple in general, chapter 3 deals mainly with the lamentations of an unfortunate individual who suffers illness, indignity and scorn at the hands of his fellow men, and chapter 5 is a liturgical confessional by the people confessing their sins, repenting and begging God for forgiveness. Thus chapters 3 and 5 may best be classified as individual and communal laments respectively, while chapters 1, 2 and 4 belong to the more specific genre of city laments, a genre which, in the Bible, is unique to this book. The inclusion of chapters 3 and 5 as part of Lamentations can be compared to the same phenomenon in several other biblical books e.g., I Samuel 2:1-10; II Samuel chapter 22; Jonah 2:3-10; Habakkuk chapter 3, where similar psalms relating to the book's general content are included. The poetic style of Lamentations resembles that of the rest of biblical poetry in that a majority of verses consists of a pair (or pairs) of parallel stichs. There are, however, two major distinguishing stylistic features in this book:

(a) A clear preference is discernible for the so-called "dirge" meter according to which the second stich in the Hebrew is made intentionally shorter than the first (e.g., Lam 3:58).

(b) Chapters 1, 2, 3 and 4 are alphabetic acrostics (1, 2 and 4 are single alphabetic acrostics consisting of 22 verses each corresponding to the 22 letters of the Hebrew alphabet, while chapter 3 is a triple alphabetic acrostic consisting of 66 verses), and chapter 5, though not being an acrostic, does consist of 22 verses, equaling the number of letters in the Hebrew alphabet. The traditional view which attributes Lamentations to Jeremiah is probably wrong concerning the authorship, but approximately right concerning the period of authorship, or at least the compilation of the book, i.e., the exilic period 587/6-538 B.C., when the horrors of the destruction and the upheaval caused by the Exile were still fresh in mind. Lamentations displays no knowledge of the ascent of Cyrus king of Persia, his conquest of Babylon (539 B.C.), or his subsequent edict allowing the Judeans to return to Israel and rebuild the Temple (538 B.C.), so that these later events serve as a convenient *terminus ad quem* for the dating of the book. The *terminus a quo* is, of course, the destruction itself in 587/6 B.C. The tradition that Jeremiah was the book's author, because of his major role as prophet of the destruction, already appears in the Greek Septuagint which prefixes the following words to its translation of 1:1 "And it came to pass after Israel had gone into captivity, and Jerusalem was laid waste, that Jeremiah sat weeping and composed this lament over Jerusalem and said...". Other ancient translations (e.g., the Aramaic Targum, the Latin Vulgate and the Syriac Peshitta) as well as the Babylonian Talmud (e.g., Bava Batra 15a) agree with this attribution. While there is no direct biblical evidence, reference is generally made to such verses as Jeremiah 8:21 and more specifically to II Chronicles 35:25 where it is stated that "Jeremiah also lamented for Josiah" (the Judean king who was killed in the Battle of Megiddo 609 B.C.). However, all this evidence is either late or circumstantial. Opposing it is the clear theological contradiction between the Books of Jeremiah and Lamentations: Jeremiah prophesied in advance that disaster would imminently strike Jerusalem as divine punishment for specific ethical shortcomings (Jer chap. 5; 9:1-10), while the Book of Lamentations, written after the destruction, still does not know the nature of Judah's sins.

As stated above, the genre of chapters 1, 2 and 4 is that of city laments, lamenting the fall of a city and the destruction of its Temple. Jeremiah 41:5; Zechariah 7:3-5; 8:19 etc. indicate that such mourning and fasting over the destruction of Jerusalem and the Temple had become regular especially during the month of Ab, from 587/6 B.C. Thus Lamentations could have been written in order to be read (or chanted) as part of the regular public mourning (which continues to this very day on the ninth day of Ab according to the Jewish calendar).

Oil lamp of the Hellenistic period. (Israel Museum)

OUTLINE

1:1-22	Desolation of Zion
2:1-22	God's wrath and Zion's ruin
3:1-66	Man's yoke of suffering
4:1-22	The agony of the holy city
5:1-22	O Lord, remember us and forgive

LAMPS The lamp, in the form of a small clay bowl in which oil was burned, was the most common form of domestic lighting from very early times. As olive oil was plentiful in Palestine, this was the fuel normally used in lamps (cf Ex 27:20; Lev 24:2); the wick was usually made of flax (Is 42:3). A much greater variety of oils was used for

Two lamps of the Roman period. (Israel Museum)

lighting in the Roman period. The shapes of lamps, and the materials from which they were made, are never specified in the Bible, but clay lamps are among the most common pottery vessels found in archeological remains, both in dwellings and in tombs.

The earliest identifiable lamps are those of the Early Bronze Age. These took the form of simple round bowls. In the Middle Bronze Age this was replaced by a simple bowl with a slightly inward-curving rim, pinched in one place only, and a rounded base.

Although the basic principle remained unaltered, there was much more variation in the Iron Age. The lamp of this period had a broad flat rim, a pronounced wick, spout and a flat base. Sometimes the lamp and the stand were two separate parts.

In the 5th century B.C., as closer contacts with the western world were established, Greek lamps began to appear. Greek potters had succeeded in producing a closed lamp, thus preventing the oil from spilling. The body of this type of lamp was round, the base concave, the rim slightly incurving, and the nozzle was a separate piece attached to the body. In the 5th and 4th centuries B.C. local imitations of this type were produced in the east; these were inferior in texture and glaze and were sometimes even unglazed.

Up to the late 4th century B.C. the clay lamp was invariably made on the potter's wheel. In the early Hellenistic period a basic change occurred with the introduction of the mold. This speeded up production and also provided a means of decorating the lamps. In the purely Jewish settlements the bowl lamp was still used, though its shape changed: the

Clay oil lamps from Dor. (Dor Excavations Project)

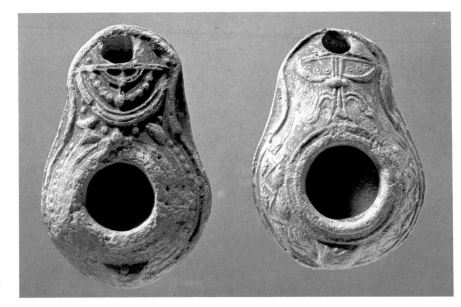

(right)
Two lamps from the Roman period.

Lamp of the Herodian period with ten wicks.

flat rim disappeared and the sides were completely pressed together to form a kind of cornucopia. At first molded lamps imitated those made on the wheel, the decoration consisting of simple geometric or vegetal designs; it was not until the Roman period that this great invention, which turned lamp production into an independent industry, was exploited to the full.

By the middle of the 1st century B.C. a new type of lamp had made its appearance in Palestine. It was not molded but made on the wheel. It is known as "Herodian", although it in fact made its appearance before Herod's accession and did not disappear until the 2nd century A.D. It was made of very finely powdered clay and had a clock-shaped body and a large filling-hole with a ridge around it. The nozzle was made separately and took the form of a splayed arch with a large wick-hole. Most of these lamps had no decoration. By the middle of the 1st century A.D. lamps with more decoration appeared, especially when they began to be molded again. This later type had a loop handle, and by the end of the 1st century was much more lavishly decorated.

In mixed or non-Jewish towns the Roman lamp, known as "Augustan", was common. This was round, had a very large disc with a small hole for filling and a triangular or bow-shaped nozzle. As they were made in a mold such lamps could be decorated in a wide variety of ways. The decoration ranged from simple rosettes to images of deities, scenes taken from everyday life, animals, birds, fairly coarse erotic scenes, political and religious propaganda and so on. Some lamps of this kind found on sites that were known to be Jewish had their decorative discs broken off, probably in accordance with the prohibition against graven images in the second commandment.

LAODICEA, LAODICEANS A city in southwestern Phrygia (western Asia Minor) near Colossae and Hierapolis (Col 2:1; 4:13) in the Roman province of Asia. It lay at the lower end of the Lycus River valley. The site is now abandoned; modern Denizli is situated near the springs. Laodicea lacked an adequate source of water, which was consequently piped from hot springs to the south via an aqueduct 6 miles (10 km) long, and apparently arrived at the city lukewarm. The city, of mixed population, quickly prospered through banking and trade, and was renowned as a medical center specializing in opthalmology and the production of glossy black wool garments. The Jewish community at Laodicea was established as the result of the settlement in Phrygia and

LAODICEA,
LAODICEANS
**Col 2:1; 4:13,
15-16. Rev
1:11; 3:14**

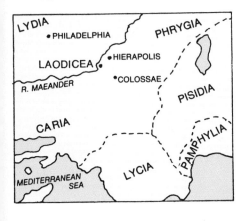

Laodicea.

Lydia of 2,000 Jewish families of soldiers by Antiochus III (*Antiq.* XII, 147 ff). The founder of the church at Laodicea is not known, though Epaphras has been suggested (Col 4:12-16). Laodicea is one of the seven churches addressed in Revelation chapters 1-3 where it was rebuked because, like its water, it was lukewarm. Laodicea was cautioned to recognize that, despite its financial prosperity, it was impoverished and in need of spiritual riches, and should buy gold, white garments and eye salve. Paul wrote a letter to the Laodiceans (Col 4:16), no longer extant. A 4th-5th century Latin forgery should not be confused with Paul's lost epistle.

LAPIDOTH
Judg 4:4

LAPIDOTH ("torch"). The husband of the prophetess Deborah.

LASEA
Acts 27:8

LASEA A city in Crete usually identified with ruins discovered in the 1850's, about 5 miles (8 km) east of Fair Havens. The vessel bearing Paul and other prisoners sailed near there on its way to Rome.

LASHA
Gen 10:19

LASHA A Canaanite border city (Gen 10:19), identified with Callirrhoe, a place on the eastern shore of the Dead Sea famous for its hot springs.

LASHARON
Josh 12:18

LASHARON A city or kingdom whose king was among those defeated by Joshua on the west bank of the Jordan River; perhaps the city of Sharon.

LAST SUPPER (LORD'S SUPPER) An expression for the last meal that Jesus ate with his disciples before being arrested. The term "Lord's Supper" appears only once in the Bible (I Cor 11:20). The dominant term for the meal which the early disciples practiced after Jesus' death was simply "the breaking of bread". This was at first a group experience without specific cultic or religious significance (Acts 2:42, 46) but then emerged as an event that took place on the Lord's Day (Acts 20:7). At the same time, the memory of the breaking of bread with Jesus became evidence of the risen Lord for it was through this that he became recognizable to the disciples (Luke 24:30, 35) and through eating with them, their doubts were removed (Luke 24:41-43; John 21:9-14; cf Mark 16:14).

Coin of Philippus Arabicus struck at Laodicea showing an eagle inside a domed shrine. A.D. 274.

(top of page)
Remains of a Roman aqueduct at Laodicea.

The word "communion" appears as a predicate, not a noun, (I Cor 10:16) and from all indications the Lord's Supper as practiced in Corinth was a real meal. The word "thanksgiving" or *eucharistia* was not used of the meal before Ignatius (c. 115). It is not known when the separation between the real meal and a memorial meal took place or when the various parts of the supper were isolated. Some have placed it

The Last Supper, shown on one of the carved plaques that were above the portals of the Holy Sepulcher. Jesus sits at a curved table flanked by his disciples. Judas Iscariot is in front of the table. The disciple whose head is held by Jesus is thought to be John.

The Coenaculum on Mount Zion, according to a tradition going back to the 5th century, this is the place where Jesus partook of the Passover feast with his disciples. The room is also associated with the events at Pentecost as related in the Acts of the Apostles (1:13).

as early as the year A.D. 100 or even earlier, between the writing of I Corinthians and Mark. The Eucharist soon developed in its own way, and the *agape* or love feast (see II Pet 2:13; Jude v. 12) continued to be practiced separately.

Primary sources provide different types of understanding for the meaning of the Lord's Supper. Paul (I Cor 11:23-34) shares with Mark 14:12-25 a division of the tradition into three parts: (a) the narrative: Jesus takes bread, gives thanks, breaks it, says an explanatory word about it, takes cup, gives thanks, provides an explanation; (b) formulas concerning bread and wine; (c) an eschatological saying (cf Mark 14:25; I Cor 11:26). There is no unanimity on the formulas concerning bread and wine in the texts and the words "Do this in remembrance of me" are found only in I Corinthians 11:24.

The Synoptic Gospels see the Last Supper as a Passover meal but not so John 18:28; 19:14. It is impossible to ascertain Jesus' intention for this meal, although an important element is his powerful assurance to the disciples of his presence for the days when he would no longer be with them.

The cup relates to the "new covenant" and represents therefore a tangible evidence of the new community Jesus established through his death. The admonition, moreover, to proclaim the Lord's death until he comes, provides the Lord's Supper with an eschatological dimension. The focus, however, is not merely on the future, for the prayer *Marantha* (I Cor 16:22) can mean either "our Lord is here now" or "may he come soon".

The abuse of the Lord's Supper caused Paul to focus on certain issues not present in the gospel narratives. To the latter it seems normal that all disciples, including those who would imminently deny Jesus or betray him, would be present. Paul, however, seeks to protect the Lord's Supper from abuse and urges that everyone partake of it in a worthy manner (I Cor 11:27) and not bring judgment upon themselves.

LAW The main source of law in the Bible is the Pentateuch, which, besides the Ten Commandments, contains more than 600 regulations said to have been dictated by God to Moses. They are interspersed among the historical narrative in three main collections: the Book of the

Covenant (Ex 20:22-23:33), the priestly rules (most of Lev, and Num 5:5-6:21; 15:1-30; 18:28-30; 35:9-34) and the Book of Deuteronomy (chaps. 12-26).

At first sight, these provisions present an impenetrable jumble of styles and subject matter, including regulations in the sacral or ritual sphere, or mere moral exhortations. This is because they combine material from different backgrounds, originally drafted for differing purposes, as revealed by comparison with the literature of ancient Israel's neighbors.

Thus direct commands, such as the Ten Commandments, were inspired by the model of international treaties, especially those between monarchs and their vassals. Breach of the Commandments therefore amounted to breach of the treaty between the people of Israel and God.

The sacral and ritual provisions derived from writings designed for the instruction of priests, as did medical regulations. Since illness could be a sign of divine punishment for an undetected crime, the cure lay in confession to the priest and expiatory sacrifice (e.g., Lev 5:11-16).

The rules settling everyday disputes and injuries were drawn from the "law-codes", a form popular in cuneiform literature, the most famous example being the Code of King Hammurabi of Babylon. These were not in fact legal codes in the modern sense, but scientific treatises on the law, consisting of a list of verdicts in prominent cases, elaborated by consideration of variations of the facts of the case, and all cast in what was considered the "scientific" style, the casuistic form of beginning "if a (man)..." (e.g., Ex 21:1-22:16).

The law in practice is illustrated by stories such as Abraham's purchase of the Cave of Machpelah (Gen chap.23), which reveals much about the law of property and contract, and by the prophetic works, in their use of metaphors drawn from legal institutions such as marriage to describe the relationship between God and his people (e.g., Ezek chap. 16).

Basic justice was administered by the local courts of elders, sitting at the city gate. Difficult cases came before the king (I Kgs 3:16-28). Moses is said to have set up a hierarchical system of courts in the desert (Ex 18:13-26) and King Jehoshaphat is credited with appointment of royal judges in the cities of Judah (II Chr 19:5).

The law of property centers on the ancestral estate. On the father's death, his sons divided the land into equal shares, the firstborn taking a double share. If one of the sons died childless before there had been a division, either because the father was still alive (Gen chap. 38) or because after the father's death the brothers had continued to hold the land in a kind of partnership ("brothers dwelling together"), the law of levirate applied: a surviving brother had to marry the deceased's widow and their offspring would take the place of the deceased, to preserve his share of the inheritance (Deut 25:5-10).

If a man died leaving daughters but no sons, the daughters were allowed to inherit the family land (Num 27:1-11; 36:1-12).

Various laws protected the family's ownership of their land. If poverty forced the owner to sell, he, or a rich relation, could redeem the land and thus bring it back into the family (Lev 25:25-27). If redemption was not possible, the land would automatically return to its owner at the Jubilee, which occurred every 50 years (Lev 25:28).

On the other hand, the person cultivating land bore social responsibilities. He had to set aside part of his crop for the poor (Lev 19:9-10; Deut 24:19-21) and, every seventh and fiftieth year, leave his land fallow (Ex 23:10-11; Lev 25:3-7), so that its produce could feed the poor.

The law made strenuous efforts to alleviate indebtedness. Interest was forbidden on loans to fellow Israelites (e.g., Ex 22:25). Although a creditor was entitled to distrain the debtor's goods or even his family (II Kgs 4:1), certain items, such as a millstone, could not be distrained at all (Deut 24:6); slaves, like land, could be redeemed (Lev 25:47-53) or gain automatic release after a number of years' service (Ex 21:1 and Deut 15:12, six years; Lev 25:54, in the Jubilee year). According to Deuteronomy 15:1-2, there was to be a general cancellation of debts every seventh year.

It has often been suggested that such laws were merely utopian. In fact, it was common practice for the kings of the ancient Near East to declare a cancellation of debts and the consequent release of slaves and property. This was regarded as one of the king's religious duties, although the timing was left to his discretion. The difference in the biblical law is its replacement of the king's role by an automatic cycle of seven or 50 years, which would render the measures less effective. King Zedekiah, at least, declared a slave-release (Jer 34:8-11).

Marriage was an alliance between families, in which the bride was the object of the transaction. The first step was an agreement between the groom (or his father) and the bride's father, who could demand a payment known as *mohar* for the hand of his daughter. Payment would normally be in money, but could, as in the case of Jacob, be in services. Once the *mohar* was paid the girl was betrothed, and although the marriage might still not take place, outsiders already regarded her as married (Deut 22:23-24). Divorce could be instigated by the husband alone. A special provision ruled that a wife, once divorced and remarried, could not return to her first husband if her second marriage ended (Deut 24:1-4).

Polygamy was permitted, but Leviticus 18:18 forbids marriage with two sisters. This had apparently not been the case in the time of the patriarchs, for Jacob married Laban's two daughters, Leah and Rachel. A man could also have concubines, and the patriarchal narratives record the custom of a wife giving her slave-girl to her husband, the offspring being adopted by the wife.

The famous dictum "an eye for an eye, a tooth for a tooth...", for all its apparent cruelty, must be seen in context. In the ancient Near East there were no police forces or prison sentences. The customary redress for crimes was revenge by the victim or his relatives on the perpetrator or even on his family. The latter could in turn buy off revenge by offering ransom-money. The criminal laws were therefore worded to regulate these practices, keeping revenge and ransom within reasonable limits. The cuneiform law-codes lay down either the maximum revenge to be inflicted or the maximum ransom to be demanded for each offense. In this respect, an "eye for an eye" restricts the right of revenge, since the alternative would be as in the boast of Lamech: "I have killed a man for wounding me, even a young man for hurting me" (Gen 4:23).

In biblical law, the relative of a murder victim (the "redeemer of blood") has the right to kill the murderer in revenge. Nonetheless, certain cities of refuge are appointed to which the latter can flee (Num 35:11-29; 4:41-43) and remain in asylum, if the killing had not been premeditated (Ex 21:13). Numbers 35:31-34 also forbids the redeemer of blood to take ransom-money, which was otherwise common practice.

If injury resulted in disfigurement, the talionic rule applied, (Lev 24:19-20), but non-permanent injury gave rise only to a claim in damages for medical expenses and recuperation (Ex 21:18-19). Abuse of a slave leading to disfigurement was grounds for his release (Ex 21:26-

27). Theft gave rise to a claim for multiple damages, the thief facing sale into slavery if unable to pay. A householder was entitled to kill a thief caught breaking in at night (Ex 22:2). One type of theft was more severely punished: the penalty for kidnaping was death.

Sexual offenses consisted of unnatural acts (homosexuality, bestiality, etc.), sexual relations within forbidden degrees (with relations of blood or by marriage) or with a woman married or betrothed to another. The penalty for the latter, whether by rape or seduction, was death — for the woman also, if she had consented (Deut 22:23-27). The rape or seduction of a single girl, on the other hand, carried only an obligation to marry her or pay compensation (Ex 22:16-17; Deut 22:28-29).

Treason was punishable by the death of the traitor and his family (I Kgs 21:13-15; II Kgs 9:26); the same punishment was applied to offenses which might be regarded as treason against God, such as apostasy (Deut 13:12-16).

Biblical law is characterized in general by several unique aspects: law has a divine authorship, and God is the ultimate source and sanction of law. Since law is a direct expression of the divine will, all crimes are also considered sins, with certain offenses ineligible for pardon by any human agency. In the biblical corpus, civil, moral and religious obligations are all interwoven. The law itself was given publicly to the corporate body of Israel, which shared equally in the responsibility for its observance. The will of the deity expressed in legal terms becomes the basis for the covenant relationship between God and Israel and determines the future of the nation.

In the NT, a distinction must be made between the attitude to the Law as expressed by Jesus and by Paul. The gospels depict Jesus as a practicing Jew who observed the Law — he attended synagogue on the Sabbath (Mark 1:21; 3:1), went to Jerusalem for the pilgrim festivals (Mark 11:1 ff; Luke 2:41 ff), wore the ritual fringes on his garments (Mark 6:56) and came "not to destroy but to fulfill" the Law (Matt 5:17). His critique is expressed, not in an antinomistic negation of the Law, but through a different interpretation (cf the healing of the woman on the Sabbath in Mark 3:1 ff). He opposes casuistry (Matt 23:14-33) and some rabbinic "oral" interpretation (e.g., Mark 7:5-13) but his criticism is made within the framework of the Law. The Law represents the will of God; it is not in itself sufficient to ensure salvation but reaches fulfillment only through the teaching of Jesus.

For Paul the Law is excellent and divine (cf Rom 3:2; 7:12, 14; Gal 2:21) but its impact on men is ambiguous as it reveals their sinfulness without providing delivery from it; the Law cannot therefore be seen as final. Its function is temporary and calls for another dispensation. This points towards the new era inaugurated by Christ (Gal 3:23ff; Col 2:17). Christians can attain justification (Gal 3:2) by faith, guided by love (Gal 5:14); Christ's death and resurrection mean that he has taken upon himself the curse invoked by the Law and therefore nobody is any longer bound by it (Gal 2:19; 3:13; Rom 7:4, 6). Both Gentiles and Jews were saved by the grace of Jesus (Acts 15:11). The purpose of the Law was not to save man but to lead him to Jesus the savior.

LAZARUS

LAZARUS 1
John 11:1-2, 5, 11, 14, 43; 12:1-2, 9-10, 17

1. Brother of Martha and Mary, of Bethany. He was raised from the dead by Jesus (John chap. 11). The priests, fearing the effect of his resurrection on the masses, plotted to kill him (John chap. 12). The modern Arabic name of the village of Bethany is Elazariya, a corruption of "Lazarus"

LAZARUS 2
Luke 16:20, 23-25

2. A poor man figuring in a parable of Jesus (Luke chap. 16).

Entrance to the shrine at the traditional site of Lazarus's tomb in Bethany.

LEAH ("cow"). Laban's elder daughter, who became Jacob's first wife and mother of six of his sons; the third matriarch of the Jewish people. Leah's history is given mainly in Genesis chapters 29-31. Jacob was in love with her younger sister Rachel and, to meet Laban's terms, invested seven years' labor as her brideprice. On the morning after the wedding he discovered that Leah had been substituted as bride. The deed being irreversible, Leah remained Jacob's wife while the latter devoted seven further years of work to obtain her younger sister. As if to compensate Leah for her husband's indifference, she, unlike the initially barren Rachel, was fertile, bearing Reuben, Simeon, Levi and Judah. When she stopped producing offspring, she gave Jacob her handmaid Zilpah; the latter bore two children (Gad and Asher), who were considered Leah's legal sons. Later still, Leah bore two more sons, Issachar and Zebulun, and a daughter, Dinah. Together with her sister, Leah stood by Jacob when he left Laban to return to Canaan and in his encounter with Esau (Gen chap. 31; 33:1-7). She is also mentioned in the genealogical list of Jacob's family (Gen 46:8-27), and in Jacob's last testament to his sons (Gen 49:31).

In biblical times the names of both Rachel and Leah were invoked to bless brides on their wedding day, as is attested by the blessing to Ruth when she married Boaz — "The Lord make the woman who is coming to your house like Rachel and Leah, the two who built the house of Israel". (Ruth 4:11).

Leah was buried in the family tomb of Machpelah in Hebron (Gen 49:30-31).

LEBANA, LEBANAH ("moon", "white"). Head of a family of Nethinim (Temple servants) that returned with Zerubbabel from the Babylonian Exile (Ezra 2:45; Neh 7:48).

LEBANON A range of mountains along the northern border of Palestine, 270 miles (430 km) long and 45 miles (72 km) wide, with peaks rising to a height of 10,000 feet (3,100 m). The tops of the mountains are covered with snow for most of the year (Jer 18:14) — hence its name, which in Hebrew means "white".

(right)
Bas-relief from Sargon's palace showing the transportation of timber from Lebanon by sea. 8th century B.C. (Musée du Louvre, Paris)

A cedar tree on the slopes of the Lebanon mountains.

Lebanon became famous for its cedars, cypresses and other splendid trees (Judg 9:15). In early historic times its timber was already being exported, especially to Egypt, which had no timber of its own for roofing and ship-building. The cedars of Lebanon were used in the building of the First Temple, for Solomon's palace and for the Second Temple in Jerusalem (I Kgs 5:6; 7:2, etc.). The Assyrian kings cut down trees in Lebanon for their buildings and palaces and used the tall cedars to make masts for their ships (Ezek 27:5). The area was also noted for its grapes and wine. At the end of the 1st century B.C. the Romans founded

LEAH
Gen 29:16-17, 23-25, 30-32; 30:9-14, 16-20; 31:4, 14, 33; 33:1-2, 7; 34:1; 35:23, 26; 46:15, 18; 49:31. Ruth 4:11

LEBANA, LEBANAH
Ezra 2:45. Neh 7:48

LEBANON
Deut 1:7; 3:25; 11:24. Josh 1:4; 9:1; 13:5-6. Judg 3:3; 9:15. I Kgs 4:33; 5:6, 9, 14; 7:2; 9:19; 10:17, 21. II Kgs 14:9; 19:23. II Chr 2:8, 16; 8:6; 9:16, 20; 25:18. Ezra 3:7. Ps 29:5-6; 72:16; 92:12; 104:16. Song 3:9; 4:8, 11, 15; 5:15; 7:4. Is 2:13; 10:34; 14:8; 29:17; 33:9; 35:2; 37:24; 40:16; 60:13. Jer 18:4; 22:6, 20, 23. Ezek 17:3; 27:5; 31:3, 15-16. Hos 14:5-7. Nah 1:4. Hab 2:17. Zech 10:10; 11:1

a colony of veteran soldiers at Berytus (Beirut) in order to seize Lebanon.

LEBANON (VALLEY OF) The valley between the mountains of Lebanon and the Anti-Lebanon, which extends from Laodicea to Chalcis, the northern limit of the conquests of Joshua (Josh 11:17). Known today as el-Buqeia, "the valley".

LEBBAEUS See THADDAEUS

LEB KAMAI A cryptogram for "Chaldeans" (Jer 51:1).

LEBONAH A city in the territory of Ephraim (Judg 21:19); identified with the village of el-Lubban, 2 miles (3 km) northwest of Shiloh.

The Plain of Lebonah between Shechem and Jerusalem.

LECAH Son of Er the grandson of Judah in the genealogy of the family of Judah. However it is generally considered that Lecah was the name of a city and Er was its father, i.e. its founder.

LEECH See ANIMALS

LEEK See PLANTS

LEHABIM An offspring of Mizraim.

LEHI ("jawbone"). A place in Judah near the border with the Philistines (Judg 15:9, 14). There Samson, having been betrayed by the people of Judah, armed himself with the jawbone of an ass and used it to kill thousands of Philistines; he then named the place Ramath Lehi(Judg 15:15-17).

According to most scholars, the place derived its name from something in its shape which resembled a jawbone; it was upon this resemblance that the popular story was based. The identification of Lehi with Khirbet es-Siyag, 4 miles (6 km) east of Timnah, has been accepted by most scholars.

LEMUEL King of Massa credited with the words of wisdom "which his mother taught him" (Prov 31:1-9). Some scholars have suggested, however, that "Lemuel" is not a proper name but a word of uncertain meaning, and that "Massa" should be translated not as a place name (Gen 25:14; I Chr 1:30 — referring to a North Arabian locality), but as a Hebrew word meaning "oracle".

LENTIL See PLANTS

LEOPARD See ANIMALS

LESHEM An alternate name of the town of Laish.

LETTER OF JEREMIAH See APOCRYPHA

LETUSHIM One of the three groups of tribes (along with Asshurim and Leummim), descended from the tribe of Dedan.

LEUMMIM A group of semi-nomads which, like the Asshurim and Letushim, were descended from the Dedanites.

LEVI (meaning uncertain; popular etymology in the Bible is "to be joined" [Gen 29:34; Num 18:2, 4]).

1. Third son of Jacob and Leah and eponymous ancestor of the tribe of Levi, the priestly Levites, and all subsequent priestly factions. In some lists Levi is one of the twelve tribes (Gen 29:31-30:24; Deut 27:12-13; I Chr 2:1-2); however, in other lists the tribe is replaced by Manasseh or Ephraim and not listed as one of the twelve (Num 1:5-15; 7:12-83; Josh 21:4-7).

In Genesis chapter 34 Levi, along with Simeon, killed Hamor and Shechem in retaliation for the rape of their sister Dinah.

The first descendants of Levi were Gershon (Gershom), Kohath and Merari (Gen 46:11; Num 3:17; I Chr 6:1), and all played a role in guarding and serving the tabernacle (Num 3:21-37). Moses is said to have been a descendant of Levi (Ex 2:1-2) as was Aaron, Moses' brother (Ex 4:14; I Chr 6:1-3) and Zadok (I Chr 6:1-8). Thus all three priestly groups, Levites, Aaronites and Zadokites, traced their ancestry to Levi. See LEVITES.

2. Levi, son of Alphaeus, was a tax collector and a follower of Jesus (Mark 2:14; Luke 5:27). In the synoptic parallel in Matthew (Matt 9:9), the tax collector is called Matthew not Levi. In addition, the writer of Matthew's gospel identified this Matthew as a tax collector and as one of the twelve disciples (Matt 10:3), unlike Mark (Mark 3:16-19) and Luke (Luke 6:13-16) where Levi never appears as one of the twelve, and the identification of him with Matthew is doubtful.

3. Levi, son of Melchi, an ancestor of Jesus in Luke's genealogy.

4. Levi, son of Simeon and father of Matthat, an ancestor of Jesus in Luke's genealogy.

LEVIATHAN A dragon-like creature mentioned in the Bible five times (Job 3:8; 41:1; Ps 74:13-14; 104:26; Is 27:1), always connected in one way or another to the demythologized battle between God and his rebellious helpers in primordial times. As part of the demythologization process, and with the aim of eradicating any possible hint that they might be independent deities fighting against God in order to achieve pantheon supremacy, as was the case in parallel ancient Near Eastern mythology, these rebellious creatures are specifically referred to as having been created by God himself (Gen 1:21). In Psalms 104:25-26, the psalmist speaks of God's creation of all creatures of the sea, "small and great" (v. 25), singling out the largest of them all, the sea-serpent "Leviathan, whom you (God) have made to play there" (v. 26). The term used in Genesis 1:21 (translated "serpent; sea creature"), occurs in parallelism or in association with the Leviathan of two of the above passages: Psalm 74:13-14 "You [God] divided the sea by your strength, you broke the heads of the sea-serpents in the waters; you broke the heads of Leviathan"; Isaiah 27:1 "In that day, the Lord with his severe sword, great and strong, will punish Leviathan the fleeing serpent, Leviathan that twisted serpent; and he will slay the reptile that is in the sea". Thus Leviathan, the many headed sea-serpent, represented the forces of evil in the First Temple period (cf also Is 51:9, from a later period). The origin of this symbol, however, goes back much earlier (2nd millennium B.C.) and is found in ancient Near Eastern mythology as the following Canaanite parallel from Ugaritic literature clearly demonstrates: "If

---

LESHEM
Josh 19:47

LETUSHIM
Gen 25:3

LEUMMIM
Gen 25:3

LEVI 1
Gen 29:34; 34:25, 30; 35:23; 46:11; 49:5. Ex 1:2; 2:1; 6:16, 19; 32:26, 28. Num 1:49; 3:6, 15, 17; 4:2; 16:1, 7-8, 10; 17:3, 8; 18:2, 21; 26:59. Deut 10:8-9; 18:1; 21:5; 27:12; 31:9; 33:8. Josh 13:14, 33; 21:10. I Kgs 12:31. I Chr 2:1; 6:1, 16, 38, 43, 47; 9:18; 12:26; 21:6; 23:6, 14, 24; 24:20. Ezra 8:15, 18. Neh 10:39; 12:23. Ps 135:20. Ezek 40:46; 48:31. Zech 12:13. Mal 2:4, 8; 3:3. Heb 7:5, 9. Rev 7:7

LEVI 2
Mark 2:14. Luke 5:27, 29

LEVI 3
Luke 3:24

LEVI 4
Luke 3:29

LEVIATHAN
Job 3:8; 41:1. Ps 74:14; 104:26. Is 27:1

thou smite Lotan ("Leviathan"), the Elusive Serpent, destroy the Twisting Serpent...of the seven heads". The remaining two biblical references to Leviathan are from the Book of Job, where scholarly attempts have been made to connect the two creatures, Leviathan (Job 41:1-34) and Behemoth (Job 40:15-24) with the crocodile and the hippopotamus respectively. The Book of Job, however, contains many references to the aforementioned demythologized battle (Job 3:8; 7:12; 9:13; 26:12-13), where not only Leviathan, but also such familiar figures as the Dragon Yam and the Elusive Serpent are all mentioned. Furthermore, Job 40:19 indicates that the Lord created Behemoth as the foremost of his creations in order to serve him as a sword bearer (Job 40:19); while Leviathan is described as a scaly monster of supernatural strength, breathing smoke from his nostrils and with flames blazing from his mouth (Job 41:11ff). Neither of these descriptions fit any natural creatures, but they are appropriate demythologized depictions of the dragon-like creatures who God created in primordial times to serve him, but who later rebelled and were destroyed by their creator. Another name for this mythological dragon is Rahab (Is 30:7; 51:9-10; Job 9:13; 26:12; Ps 89:10). In Psalms 87:4 and Isaiah 30:9, the name is used symbolically for Egypt.

LEVIRATE (from the Latin, *levir*, "husband's brother"). Marriage of the widow by the brother of the deceased husband.

Despite its wide variations in non-Israelite societies, it is generally agreed that the levirate has its *raison d'être* in the view that a wife is the exclusive property of the family by virtue of the dowry or the brideprice that was paid for her. Hence the family is entitled to inherit her along with the other possessions of her deceased husband. In order to retain the widow within the family's fold, she would usually be given to her brother-in-law, or to his next-of-kin, customs varying with different societies and circumstances.

To judge from the three extant biblical sources, the levirate in Israel gained its social sanction from the aim of raising up an offspring for the childless deceased as a means of carrying on his name (Deut 25:6). That this is the focal point of the institution is made clear from the command given by Judah to his son Onan, "Go in to your brother's wife and marry her, and raise up an heir to your brother." (Gen 38:8). Onan's resort to *coitus interruptus*, spilling his semen to the ground whenever he went in to his brother's wife, was prompted by his reluctance to raise up a seed which he "knew...would not be his" (Gen 38:9). The motive of the levirate, to beget an offspring for the childless deceased, is reiterated

Sandal from the 18th century used in the ceremony of halitzah *during which a widow pulls the sandal off the foot of her brother-in-law to release him from the levirate obligation. (Israel Museum)*

in Ruth, where Boaz views the marriage with Ruth as a pious act which will "raise up the name of the dead on his inheritance" (Ruth 4:5).

The extant sources pertaining to the levirate in ancient Israel (Gen chap. 38; Deut 25:5-10; Book of Ruth) do not reflect a uniform and well crystallized mode of operation. Rather, they are characterized by variations in details, and in some respects by vagueness and loose formulations. This is particularly true of the two narratives (Gen chap. 38 and the Book of Ruth) which provide a glimpse of the levirate in operation. Thus, for example, one may infer from the former that while the duty of the levirate rests mainly upon the brother of the deceased, it may also be performed by a next-of-kin (in this case, Judah, the father-in-law of Tamar). According to the Book of Ruth even a far-distant relative (Boaz) may assume the levirate obligation. This and several other differences make it abundantly clear that the levirate either existed in varied forms in ancient Israel or underwent various developments.

Both Genesis chapter 38 and Deuteronomy 25:5ff differ from Ruth in that they present the levirate as a sacred and mandatory obligation which should not and ought not be shirked or circumvented. Onan's attempt to evade his duty by resorting to *coitus interruptus* evoked the wrath of God, who brought death upon Onan (Gen 38:10). Deuteronomy, which formulates the levirate rites in legal terms, does not specify the death penalty for evasion of the duty. It does, however, view the refusal of a man to raise up seed for his deceased brother as a grave moral offense, for which the recalcitrant brother must endure an extremely humiliating public censure, known as the ceremony of *halitzah*, in which the widow pulls the sandal off his foot, spits in his face and declares, "So shall it be done to the man who will not build up his brother's house" (Deut 25:9). The recalcitrant brother is further stigmatized by the label "the house of him who had his sandal removed" (Deut 25:10), which would henceforth be attached to his family.

LEVITES A priestly group, whose origins are unclear but unambiguously reach back to the tribe of Levi. The Levites are priests of God yet there are conflicting accounts of their ordination and questions about their status before ordination. In the course of time their primarily priestly duties varied from preeminent priest to gatekeeper, musician and priest's assistant. This change reflects a continual struggle with other priestly groups intent both on supplanting the Levites and claiming descent from them. The tribe of Levi, and hence the Levites, having inherited no land, their fluctuating status called forth differing arrangements for their sustenance.

The Bible links the origin of the Levites with the tribe of Levi. In the wilderness this was the smallest tribe, numbering 22,000-23,000 males (Num 3:39; 26:62). They were a tribe like any other but, because of their special destiny, were not allotted any territory. Modern scholars have put forward different theories regarding their origin.

When the Song of Deborah (Judg chap. 5) lists the tribes that came together to fight the Canaanites, Levi is omitted as are Simeon and Judah. As the latter two were southern tribes, or at least claiming lands in the south, it has been suggested that Levi too may have been southern. Moses was a Levite (Ex 2:1-2) and his first encounter with God is placed in the land of Midian (Ex 3:1-6), a region south and east of Palestine. Some of the names of the Levites, such as Moses, Hophni and Merari are Egyptian in origin. Moreover, the name "Levi" appears in an Egyptian toponymic list of Rameses III (early 12th century B.C.) which locates the name in southwestern Arabia. Some scholars have therefore deduced that Levi, and hence the Levites, originated south and southeast of Palestine.

LEVITES
Ex 4:14; 6:25;
38:21. Lev
25:32-33. Num
1:47, 50-51,
53; 2:17, 33;
3:9, 12, 20,
32, 39, 41, 45-46,
49; 4:18, 46;
7:5-6; 8:6, 9-15,
18-22, 24, 26;
18:6, 23-24,
26, 30;
26:57-58;
31:30, 47;
35:2, 4, 6-8.
Deut 12:12,
18-19; 14:27,
29; 16:11, 14;
17:9, 18; 18:1,
6-7; 24:8;
26:11-13; 27:9,
14; 31:25.
Josh 3:3; 8:33;
14:3-4; 18:7;
21:1, 3-4, 8,
20, 27, 34,
40-41. Judg 17:7,
9-13; 18:3, 15;
19:1; 20:4.
I Sam 6:15.
II Sam 15:24.

Pentateuch-scroll "crown" of the 18th century from Germany, with hands raised in priestly blessing. (Israel Museum)

I Kgs 8:4. I Chr
6:19, 48, 64;
9:2, 14, 26,
31, 33-34;
13:2; 15:2, 4,
11-12, 14-17,
22, 26-27;
16:4; 23:2-3,
26-27; 24:6,
30-31; 26:17,
20; 27:17;
28:13, 21.
II Chr 5:4-5,
12; 7:6; 8:14-15;
11:13-14, 16;
13:9-10; 17:8;
19:8, 11;
20:14, 19;
23:2, 4, 6-8,
18; 24:5-6, 11;
29:4-5, 12, 16,
25-26, 30, 34;
30:15-17,
21-22, 25, 27;
31:2, 4, 9, 12,
14, 17, 19;
34:9, 12-13,
30; 35:3, 5,
8-11, 14-15, 18.
Ezra 1:5; 2:40,
70; 3:8-10, 12;
6:16, 18, 20;
7:7, 13, 24;
8:20, 29-30,
33; 9:1; 10:5,
15, 23. Neh
3:17; 7:1, 43,
73; 8:7, 9, 11,
13; 9:4-5, 38;
10:9, 28, 34,
37-38; 11:3,
15-16, 18, 20,
22, 36; 12:1,
8, 22, 24, 27,
30, 44, 47;

An understanding of the process by which the Levites became priests is complicated by the presence of divergent accounts and by the question of their status before ordination. In Exodus chapter 32 the sons of Levi sided with Moses against Aaron and the worshipers of the golden calf; having killed 3,000 of the apostates, the sons of Levi are said to have thereby ordained themselves into the service of God (Ex 32:28-29). A second account is given in Numbers; following a census in preparation for war (Num chaps. 1-2), the Levites replaced the firstborn as God's servants (Num 3:11-13). In Deuteronomy 10:7-9, after the death of Aaron, the tribe of Levi was set apart to carry the ark of the covenant and to minister to God. According to yet another tradition the Lord instructed Moses to bring Aaron and his sons — all descendants of Levi (cf Ex 4:14) to serve as his priests (Ex 28:1-4). Accordingly, a firm and consistent tradition depicts the Levites as set aside as God's chosen servants. As to what the Levites were before becoming priests of God, modern Bible scholars offer two answers. One is that they were originally a secular entity, like the other tribes; the other that they always occupied a priestly role. Passages such as Genesis chapter 34 and 49:5-7 which describe the military actions of the tribe without, however, according it any special status, taken together with the texts which describe its ordination to the priesthood, are the basis of the argument for a secular tribe subsequently turned priests. On the other hand, Levi's military activities provide insufficient ground on which to argue for a secular origin. In addition, prior priestly service is not precluded by the accounts of ordination which may merely reflect the point at which the Levites became priests of God.

The installation ceremony consisted of shaving the body, sacrifice, the laying on of hands and a solemn presentation to God (Num 8:5-15). According to Numbers 4:3 their period of service was from 30 to 50 years of age. The age of eligibility is lowered to 25 in Numbers 8:23-26 and to 20 in I Chronicles 23:24.

An analysis of the duties of the Levites shows both change and permanence. In early periods, as exemplified in Judges chapters 17-18 (especially 17:12) there was a distinct preference for a Levite as priest, and a Levite performed the priestly duties at Micah's sanctuary. Even Deuteronomy (cf 18:1-5; 33:8-11), makes no explicit differentiation between Levites and priests, as shown by the expression "the priests, the Levites" (Deut 17:9; 18:1; 24:8). The Levites were expected to perform the normal priestly functions: to teach the ordinances of God (Deut 33:10), to carry the ark of the covenant and to "stand before" God and "minister" to him (Deut 10:8). However, in the other traditions and in post-exilic material, Levites and priests are disparate groups (cf Num 18:25-32; I Chr 15:14; Ezra 6:16; 7:13) and subservient tasks are assigned to the Levites. Hence the Levites are to "minister" to Aaron, not God, and are to be a "gift" to Aaron (Num 18:1-6); their duties included the keeping of the gate (I Chr 9:18-19), playing music (I Chr 23:1-6; Ezra 3:10), counting and weighing the gold and silver of the treasury (Ezra 8:33-34), assisting Aaron (I Chr 23:26-32), caring for the courts and chambers of the sanctuary, cleansing the sacred vessels, preparing cereal offerings and singing praises (I Chr 3:28-32). They also had a teaching function as interpreters of the Law (Neh 8:7-9). The Levites' prime priestly tasks having been taken over by Aaron, they were now second-level functionaries. Numbering only several hundred, they were also numerically inferior to the priests whose ranks comprised several thousand (Ezra chap. 2; Neh chap. 7).

The Levites were not the only priestly family and their decline in status reflects a losing struggle with their rivals. In the monarchical period, the latter were primarily the Zadokite priests of Jerusalem, who possibly represented the Jebusite priestly community which officiated in the city prior to its conquest by David. The struggle for the succession to David, which pitted Adonijah against Solomon, also placed Abiathar and Zadok on opposing sides (I Kgs chaps. 1-2; cf II Sam 15:24). With Solomon's rise to power, it was Zadok who became chief priest while Abiathar was banished (I Kgs 2:26-27). Thus the Zadokites finally gained control, with the Levites turned out. This perspective on the conflict between Zadokites and Levites is further reflected in II Kings 23:8-9; centralization of worship in Jerusalem displaced the Levites who, as priests in the cities of Judah, forfeited their positions with the closing down of the local sanctuaries. This view is supported when Ezekiel makes a clear distinction between the Zadokites and the Levites, the latter having gone astray (Ezek 44:10-27). A similar struggle between Levite and Aaronites commenced when the Levites killed the followers of Aaron who built the golden calf (Ex chap. 32), and continued when Levites were explicitly denied appointment in the Northern Kingdom of Israel — Bethel was apparently a stronghold of the Aaronites, devotees of the golden calf (cf Ex 32:4-5 and I Kgs 12:28).

As a result of the Exile and the collapse of the pre-exilic religious perspective, the Aaronites were able to gain control of the priesthood making the Levites their servants. This division of roles is already evidenced in Leviticus chapter 8 where the Aaronites are priests and there is no reference to Levites at all; and in Numbers chapter 18 where the Levites are to serve Aaron and his sons. In spite of these struggles and the secondary status eventually accorded to the Levites, all priestly factions traced their ancestry to the tribe of Levi, legitimizing their claim to the priesthood by employing genealogies, such as the late composition in I Chronicles 6:1-30.

The changing status of the Levites, their ordination as priests, and their supposed dispersion, all created problems for their survival. In Joshua chapter 21 the Levites were awarded 48 "Levitical" cities (48 being 12 x 4, although not every tribe contributed 4 cities), which were dispersed throughout the land. There has been some speculation that the Levitical cities may have been garrison cities or at least religious outposts for the central government; but the inconsistent distribution pattern in the territories controlled by the monarchy makes this questionable. In these cities the Levites were given pasture land only,

13:5, 10, 13, 22, 29-30. Is 66:21. Jer 33:18, 21-22. Ezek 43:19; 44:10, 15; 45:5; 48:11-13, 22. Luke 10:32. John 1:19. Acts 4:36

being denied farm land. Deuteronomy 10:9 recognizes their landless status, making provision by categorizing them with the widow, the orphan and the resident alien (cf Judg 17:7, where the Levite is called a sojourner, i.e. resident alien) to be supported by society at large (Deut 14:28-29; 19:14; 26:12). In several instances, a portion of the tithe was given to the Levites for their sustenance. This could be an "informal" tithe such as described in Deuteronomy 18:3-4 or, the more "formal" regulations as explicitly laid out by the Book of Numbers. Since the Levites had no inheritance, they were to receive a tithe (Num 18:24) and, in turn, convey a tithe of the tithe to Aaron the priest (Num 18:25-28).

There are few references to Levites in the NT. One occurs in the famous story of the "Good Samaritan" (Luke 10:29-37) and another in the first chapter of John (1:19). Finally a Levite named Joses is reported to have sold his property and given the money to the apostles (Acts 4:36-37). Little is learned about the Levites from these passages. The only item of note is that the first two references clearly distinguish priests from Levites, a distinction which has its origin in the post-exilic writings of the Hebrew Bible.

LEVITICUS, BOOK OF Third book of the Pentateuch, called by the early rabbis "the Priests' Manual." The role of the priest is defined in pedagogic terms: to teach the distinctions "between the holy and unholy, and between unclean and clean" (10:10; cf Ezek 44:23). This is necessary to prevent Israel's moral sins and physical impurities from polluting the sanctuary and causing its eventual abandonment by God. The priests are therefore charged with a double task: to instruct Israel to purify themselves of their pollution, and to purge the sanctuary of its pollution. However, Leviticus is not just a collection of rituals; one may justifiably seek a moral basis behind every ritual act.

Chapters 1-7 depict the sacrificial system: chapters 1-5 list the sacrifices from the point of the donor: chapters 1-3, the spontaneously motivated sacrifices; chapters 4-5, the expiatory sacrifices. Chapters 6-7 regroup these sacrifices in order of their sanctity and frequency.

Part of the Book of Leviticus found at Qumran. (Shrine of the Book, Jerusalem)

Page from the Book of Leviticus, from the De Castro Bible, *Germany, 14th century. (Israel Museum)*

The sacrifices discussed in these chapters share the characteristic of responding to an unpredictable religious and emotional need; they are to be distinguished from the sacrifices connected with the public feasts and fasts as determined by the calendar (chaps. 9; 16; 23; cf Num chaps. 28-29).

The "burnt offering" must be chosen from male, unblemished and eligible species of the herd, flock and birds. Its function here is expiatory (Lev 1:4), but in the priestly texts, whenever it is offered by an individual, the motivation is joyful (cf 22:17ff; Num 15:1-11). In non-priestly texts, the burnt offering denotes a tribute brought by subjects to their overlords, whether human (Judg 13:15-18) or divine (I Sam 3:14). It could be either animal or vegetable (Gen 4:3; I Sam 2:13): in a priestly context, however, it is exclusively cereal, either choice flour or roasted grain (Lev 2:14-16). The restriction to cereal emphasizes that man's tribute to God should be from the fruit of his labors on the soil. The peace offering (chap. 3) is motivated solely by elation. Its rules are similar to those of the burnt offering. Being of lesser sanctity, its portions are assigned to the donor as well as to God. The choicest internal fats (suet) are turned to smoke. The purification offering removes the impurity inflicted upon the sanctuary by the inadvertent violation of prohibitive laws (chap. 4) or by the creation of severe physical impurity (chaps. 12-14, see below). The failure to cleanse minor impurity immediately upon its occurrence also requires the purification offering. The other exclusive expiatory sacrifice is the reparation offering prescribed for sacrilege against the property of God or man (5:14-6:7).

Chapters 8-10 depict the inaugural service at the sanctuary. The priests are inducted after the priestly vestments and the tabernacle are completed and consecrated (chap. 8). It is not Aaron, however, but Moses who dominates the scene. He is the one who conducts the inaugural service, consecrates the priests, and apportions all the tasks. Following the week of consecration, the priests commence their official duties. They offer up special sacrifices for the people "that the glory of the Lord may appear" (9:6; cf vs. 4, 23). Indeed, the whole purpose of the sacrificial system is revelation, the assurance that God is with his people. During the service the eldest sons of Aaron, Nadab and Abihu, are killed by a divine fire because they offered incense with "profane fire", most probably brought from elsewhere than the altar (cf 16:12; Num 16:46). The cereal and well-being offerings are eaten by the priests in accordance with Leviticus 6:16 and 7:28-34. But the procedure for the purification offering is switched from the individual (6:26) to the communal form (10:12); Aaron does not eat the sacrificial meat, but destroys it, because it has been doubly polluted by the sin and death of his sons (10:19).

Chapters 11-15 prescribe the laws of impurities, whose basic rationale is the binary opposition of life and death. Impurity is that which symbolizes death and hence must be avoided and eliminated.

Animal carcasses generate impurity (11:24-44) except for those declared fit for consumption (11:1-23). But the permitted species are so few that these laws clearly aim to limit Israel's access to animal flesh. This rationale is also implied by the explicit reason cited in the text: holiness (11:44-47; cf 20:22-26), a word which bears the dual connotation of "sanctification" (by emulating God's nature, 11:44) and "separation" (from the impurities of the pagans, 20:22-26). Holiness is the antonym of impurity; it represents the forces of life.

Blood and semen are forces of life. Thus their loss from the genital organs is declared an impurity. After the birth of a boy or girl, the parturient is impure for 40 or 80 days respectively, after which, sacrifices are offered (chap. 12). Natural discharges of men and women are purified by bathing (15:16-18, 19-24), but pathological discharges require sacrificial expiation (15:2-15, 25-30).

Chapter 16 gives the regulation for the Day of Atonement ritual.

Chapters 17-27 have been called the Holiness Source (designated as H) by scholars who suggest that it constitutes an independent code in which moral and ritual laws alternate, and whose motivation is holiness. Others, however, question this theory, pointing out that chapter 17, the alleged beginning of the code, is connected thematically and verbally with the preceding chapters while chapters 25-26, the alleged conclusion, form an independent scroll, to judge by their unique vocabulary (e.g. 25:18-19; 26:5), theme (25:8-13; 26:34-35, 43) and redaction (25:1; 26:46). Nonetheless, much of the language, ideas and premises in chapters 17-27 differ from the first part of Leviticus.

Chapter 17 states that whosoever kills a sacrificial animal outside the sanctuary is guilty of murder (17:3-4). Two ends are thus achieved: sacrifice to "demons" is abolished (vs. 5-9), and expiation for killing the animal is assured through the ritual by which its lifeblood is returned to its creator either upon the altar (vs. 10-12), or by being drained and covered by earth, in the case of game animals (vs. 13-14; cf Deut 12:16).

Chapters 18-20 are thematically united: chapter 20 prescribes the penalties for the illicit relations and homicidal cult practices of chapter 18 (cf 20:1-5) and for violating the ban on magic of 19:31 (cf 20:6). Moreover, the entire unit is framed by a single goal: dissociation from the Canaanites whose idolatry and criminal practices pollute the divinely chosen land (18:3, 24-30; 20:22-24).

The positive aspect of holiness — *imitatio dei*, the life of godliness — is spelled out in the ethical and ritual commands of chapter 19, reaching its climax in the commandment to love all persons (v. 18), including resident aliens (v. 34). Such love must be tangibly expressed in deeds: equality in civil justice (20:2-24:16, 22; cf Num 35:15), free loans (25:35-55; cf Deut 10:18) and free gleanings (19:9-10).

Defects which disqualify sacrifices also disqualify priests from officiating (chaps. 21-22). Chapter 23 contains a festival calendar; being addressed to the lay farmer rather than the priest, it omits the New Moon festival (when the Israelite has no special duties or prohibitions). Indeed, with the exception of verses 13 and 18-20, all requirements of the public cult are ignored, and only the offerings of the individual farmer are enumerated. Chapter 25 deals with the sabbatical and jubilee years.

A threat of total destruction and exile appears in chapter 26 as it does in three other books of the Bible: Deuteronomy, Jeremiah and Ezekiel (whose eschatology is largely based on this chapter). These also share with chapter 26 the pre-prophetic view that cultic sins alone determine the nation's collapse — idolatry (v. 1) and the neglect of the sabbatical system (vs. 2, 34-35) being specified here.

Chapter 27 discusses the commutation of gifts to the sanctuary. The organizing principle of this chapter is that gifts offerable on the altar may never be desanctified, but nonofferable gifts (with the exception of proscriptions) may be desanctified by their sale or redemption.

In comparison with the rest of the Pentateuch, Leviticus is relatively uncomplicated. Critical scholars attribute it to two priestly sources: an older source, P, which has been assimilated and redacted by a younger source, H. In the main, P is found in chapters 1-16 and H in chapters 17-26. However, traces are found of P within H (e.g. 17:3-4; 23:13, 18-20) and of H within P (e.g. 11:43-45; 16:29-34).

```
                        OUTLINE

    1:1-7:38      Laws governing sacrifice
    8:1-10:20     Installation of the priesthood
    11:1-15:33    Laws of ritual purity and impurity
    16:1-34       Day of Atonement
    17:1-16       Killing for food
    18:1-20:27    More laws of holiness
    21:1-22:33    Disqualification of priests and sacrifices
    23:1-44       A festival calendar
    24:1-23       Miscellaneous regulations
    25:1-55       Sabbatical and jubilee years
    26:1-46       A curse if the Law is disobeyed, a blessing
                  if kept
    27:1-34       Commutation of gifts to the sanctuary
```

LIBNAH

1. A Canaanite town in the Plain conquered by Joshua (Josh 10:29-30) and given to the priests; also a city of refuge (Josh 21:13). It resisted the onslaught of Sennacherib (II Kgs 19:8). Identified by some scholars with Tell es-Safi, but others suggest that it should be sought closer to Lachish c. 25 miles (40km) southwest of Jerusalem.

2. The tenth station from the Red Sea along the route of the Exodus (Num 33:20-21), possibly the same as Laban (Deut 1:1). It may be identified with Bir el-Beida, about 20 miles (32 km) south of Kadesh Barnea.

LIBNI ("of white [bright] skin"; or belonging to the place Libnah).

1. The eldest son of Gershon the son of Levi (Ex 6:17; Num 3:18, 21; I Chr 6:17, 20), and the head of the Libnites.

2. A Levite, the son of Mahli the son of Merari.

3. A family of Levite priests from the town of Libna.

LIBNITES See LIBNI No.3.

LIBYA, LIBYANS Called *Lubim* in the Hebrew Bible. A country and a people in the north of Africa, west of Egypt in what was later Cyrenaica. The Egyptians recruited mercenaries from among them (II Chr 12:3). Some scholars identify them with one of the Sea Peoples who attempted to invade Egypt in the 13th century B.C. According to this view, after their defeat by Rameses III they settled in the area to the west of Egypt, and the country was named after them. By the 10th century B.C. they had become strong enough to disrupt the rule of the 21st Dynasty and to put Pharaoh Sheshonk I (Shishak) the founder of the 22nd Dynasty, on the throne (see also CYRENE).

LICE See ANIMALS

LIFE The Bible's central concern and main issue is the paramount importance of life, and how to maintain and sanctify it.

The underlying concept for the biblical view of life is the creation of man in God's image (Gen 1:26). God breathed into the nostrils of the man the breath of life and man thereby became a living being (Gen 2:7). By this divine act man was set apart from all other creatures, to stand only a step lower than the angels (Ps 8:5). The divine likeness serves man, not to achieve immortality, but to attain sanctity; nevertheless, having been created in the divine image, one of man's prime tasks is the preservation of life. Since life is a divine gift, no one has the right to take either his own life or that of others (Ex 20:13; Deut 5:17).

LIBNAH 1
Josh 10:29, 31-32, 39; 12:15; 15:42; 21:13. II Kgs 8:22; 19:8; 23:31; 24:18. I Chr 6:57. II Chr 21:10. Is 37:8. Jer 52:1

LIBNAH 2
Num 33:20-21

LIBNI 1
Ex 6:17. Num 3:18, 21. I Chr 6:17, 20

LIBNI 2
I Chr 6:29

LIBNI 3
Num 26:58

LIBYA, LIBYANS
Jer 46:9. Ezek 27:10; 30:5; 38:5. Dan 11:43

Life in the biblical sense means to live according to God's way (*imitatio Dei*) which can be summarized in the command "You shall be holy: for I the Lord your God am holy" (Lev 19:2). In the Psalms and Proverbs, life is clearly connected with the observing of the commandments of God's laws: "keep my commands and live" (Prov 4:4; 7:2). To prolong one's life, it is required to fear the Lord (Prov 10:27). Prolongation of days is granted to all those who keep God's statutes and commandments (Deut 6:2). The Torah itself is seen as "a tree of life to those who take hold of her: and happy are all who retain her" (Prov 3:18).

Trust in God who sustains the world is likewise a basic theme in the NT: "Do not worry about your life, what you will eat or what you will drink; nor about your body, what you will put on. Is not life more than food and the body more than clothing?" (Matt 6:25; cf Luke 12:22-23). In the NT, as in contemporary rabbinic literature, life is seen in the double dimension: in this world and in the world to come (Matt 16:25; Mark 8:35; John 6:26-58; 8:12).

For the Gospel According to John, more abundant life for the believer is the whole goal of the coming of Jesus (John 10:10). It is the greatest existential theme of the entire gospel (John 20:31). Resurrection, eternal life and faith in Christ are closely related (John 11:25-26). According to Paul, Gentiles can fill their lives with the hope of salvation, which consists of being raised together with Christ (I Cor 15:23-28; I Thes 5:15-17, 23). While Christians await God's son (I Thes 1:10), they have the Holy Spirit manifest in spiritual gifts (Gal 5:22-26). Paul urges the Christians to remain pure and blameless until the Day of the Lord (I Cor 6:11). The messianic aspect of waiting actively by living according to God's will is common to both Jewish and Christian traditions.

LIKHI The third son of Shemida the son of Manasseh (I Chr 7:19). In the related lists of Numbers 26:30; Joshua 17:2, he is called Helek.

LILITH A female demon referred to as "the night creature", along with beasts of prey and spirits who will reside in the desolate places of Edom after its destruction (Is 34:14). The figure of Lilith can be traced back to Mesopotamian demonology (which also features a male counterpart, Lilu). Lilith was thought to prey upon women in childbirth and to strangle newborn babies, a role she retained in post-biblical literature, where she was also identified as the "first Eve" and seductress *par excellence*.

LILY See PLANTS

LIME See PLANTS

LINUS A follower of Paul who sent greetings to Timothy. Perhaps the son of Claudia who is mentioned in the same text; perhaps the Linus who, according to an ancient tradition, succeeded Peter as bishop of Rome.

LION See ANIMALS

LIZARD See ANIMALS

LO-AMMI ("not-my-people"). Symbolic name given by divine command to the third of the three children of the prophet Hosea and his wife Gomer. It refers to the Lord's temporary rejection of Israel because of Israel's flirtation with Baal, the Phoenician god of rain (Hos 1:9). In the prophecy of consolation in Hosea 1:10-11, 16-23 this symbolic name is applied collectively to the people of Israel.

LOCUST See ANIMALS

LOD See LYDDA

LO DEBAR A city in Gilead, probably near Mahanaim, where Jonathan's son, Mephibosheth, dwelt for a while, at the house of

LIKHI
I Chr 7:19

LINUS
II Tim 4:21

LO-AMMI
Hos 1:9; 2:23

LOD
I Chr 8:12.
Ezra 2:33.
Neh 7:37;
11:35

LO DEBAR
II Sam 9:4-5;
17:27. Amos
6:13

Machir son of Ammiel, (II Sam 9:4-5) who also befriended David on his flight from Absalom (II Sam 17:27). Lo Debar might be identical with Debir, mentioned in Joshua 13:26, as one of the cities in the territory of Gad.

Lo Debar is usually identified with Khirbet ed-Dabar at the south of Wadi el-Arab.

LOGOS ("word"). This Greek word has a long history, and conveys different meanings in Greek philosophy, in Jewish theology and in early Christianity.

In Greek philosophy, Logos means either the order of the universe, or the divine reason as the organizing force of the cosmos. In the Septuagint, the Greek translation of the Bible, Logos renders the Hebrew *davar*, the Word of God, whereas the 1st century Jewish philosopher Philo of Alexandria develops an entire theology of the Logos in his allegorical commentaries on scripture. In Christianity, finally, Logos becomes the name for the second person of the Trinity incarnated in Jesus of Nazareth.

In the 5th century B.C. the Greek philosopher Heraclitus of Ephesus, reacting against the materialism of the Ionian philosophers, introduced the Logos idea. The visible world is a symbolic system which conceals and reveals the reality. This reality is the divine soul of the world whose life is manifested in the endless cycle of the cosmos with its changes and renewals. There is one Logos in the world which can be seen as its imminent reason.

For the Stoics, the Logos is responsible for fashioning things. He is God himself as the organic principle of the cosmic process, which he directs to a rational and a moral end. Only man participates in it so fully that he may be regarded as an effluence of the deity. Since the one Logos is present in many human souls, men may have communion with each other through their participation in the same Logos.

In the OT the Word of God — *Davar* in Hebrew; *Logos* in Greek — is connected with creation, providence and revelation. It is the instrument that controls the cosmos (Ps 107:20; 147:18). God spoke and the world was created. His Spirit gives life to what the Logos creates. The Word of God also inspires prophecy and imparts the Law.

Philo of Alexandria blends Greek and Jewish ideas about the Logos and achieves a syncretism of divergent Greek conceptions. He believes in the Logos as revealed in the Bible, but he wishes to present the divine activity to the Hellenistic mind. The Logos he depicts is an intermediary between God and the world. Among the many titles he gives to the Logos, is the firstborn Son of God, the first of the angels, the image of God. Logos is sometimes called Wisdom. In other passages Wisdom is considered as the mother of Logos. In the mind of God Logos is going out of itself in creation. It represents the world before God as High Priest, Intercessor and Paraclete.

In the NT, the Gospel of John applies the title Logos to Jesus (cf John 1:1); but Paul also knows the whole doctrine of the Logos which he expresses in his letter to the Colossians.

The influence of Philo on the author of the fourth gospel, hitherto accepted by many scholars, has been questioned lately. If there are similarities between Philo and John, there are also many differences. Philo never thought of identifying the Logos with the messiah as John did. Moreover John clearly defines the relation of the Logos to God as the second person of the Trinity, distinct though eternally inseparable from the Father. In John's gospel the concept of Logos is more dynamic than in Philo. Christ as the Logos is the complete Revelation of God. Finally the main difference between Philo and John remains the idea of the incarnation of the Logos, in order that mankind might see his Glory.

LOIS
II Tim 1:5

LOIS The grandmother of Timothy, described in the NT as a woman of sincere faith (II Tim 1:5).

LORD See GOD

LORD'S PRAYER, THE The prayer "Our Father" taught by Jesus to the apostles. In the NT it is given in two slightly different forms: in Matthew 6:9-13, in the teaching of prayer in the Sermon on the Mount, and in Luke 11:2-4, where Jesus gives it to the disciples in answer to their request "Lord, teach us to pray." The form in Matthew is that universally used by Christians; that in Luke is shorter and is often thought to be the original form or closer to it. A concluding doxology was probably added in early times and taken over into some gospel manuscripts.

The Lord's Prayer is usually divided into the address and seven petitions, the first three asking for the glorification of God, the latter four being requests for the chief physical and spiritual needs of humanity. Since it was taught by Jesus himself, it has always been regarded by Christians as uniquely sacred.

Apart from the address "Father", which represents Jesus' characteristically intimate and trusting address to, and conception of God, the first part shows similarities with the Jewish Aramaic Kaddish prayer used in the synagogue liturgy. Its central petition is for the speedy coming of God's kingdom to earth, which means that his will (for peace and justice) be done. The second part, besides the basic petition for daily sustenance, centers on the prayer for forgiveness, another emphasis in Jesus' own ministry. Indeed, even though the prayer for the kingdom is in the Kaddish, it also is the main theme of the preaching of Jesus.

LO-RUHAMAH
Hos 1:6, 8;
2:23

LO-RUHAMAH ("not-accepted"). Symbolic name given by divine command to the second of the three children and the only daughter of the prophet Hosea and his wife Gomer. The name refers to God's temporary rejection of Israel because of Israel's flirtation with Baal, the Phoenician god of rain (Hos 1:8-9). In the prophecy of consolation in Hosea 2:23 the name Lo-Ruhamah is applied to Israel collectively. Similarly in Hosea 2:3, Hosea's daughter represents all the women of Israel.

LOT
Gen 11:27, 31;
12:4-5; 13:1,
5, 7-8, 10-12,
14; 14:12, 16;
19:1, 5-6, 9-
10, 12, 14-15,
18, 23, 29-30,
36. Deut 2:9,
19. Ps 83:8.
Luke 17:28-29,
32. II Pet 2:7

LOT The son of Haran and nephew of Abraham (Abram) (Gen 11:27). Terah took Abraham and Lot from Ur of the Chaldees to Haran, where they resided for a time (Gen 11:31). When Abraham was commanded by God to leave his country and to go to Canaan, Lot accompanied him (Gen 12:4-5), as he did again on the journey to and from Egypt in time of famine (Gen 12:10; 13:1).

The Lord's Prayer inscribed in over fifty languages at the Pater Noster Church in Jerusalem. The original edifice was built in the 4th century over the grotto, where according to tradition, Jesus traught his disciples the Lord's Prayer.

Landscape at the southern end of the Dead Sea on the way to Sodom. This cliff with the outline of a human figure is known as "Lot's Wife".

Abraham and Lot were so rich in cattle that "the land was not able to support them" (Gen 13:2-6), and after strife between their herdsmen, Abraham decided to separate, allowing Lot first choice of territory (Gen 13:8-9). Lot took the best part: the Jordan Valley as far as Sodom. The region, made fertile by its abundance of water (Gen 13:10) resembled "the garden of the Lord". Lot took up his abode in Sodom (Gen 14:12).

During the war between Chedorlaomer and the kings of Sodom and Gomorrah, the latter fled and Lot was taken captive, but Abraham liberated him (Gen 14:1-16). The Bible relates that Sodom was a depraved city. Two angels visited Lot, who received them in his home as his guests (Gen 19:1-3). When the men of Sodom demanded that the guests be handed over to them, Lot refused, preferring to surrender his daughters rather than offend against the rules of hospitality (Gen 19:4-10). The angels then took action, smiting their would-be assailants with blindness, and urging Lot to leave Sodom immediately, because God intended to devastate it (Gen 19:11-13). Lot was led out of the city together with his wife and two daughters; they were forbidden to look back as they escaped to the mountains (Gen 19:16-17). But during the ensuing destruction of Sodom and Gomorrah, Lot's wife did look back and was turned into a pillar of salt (Gen 19:24-26).

Lot and his daughters were the progenitors of the Moabites and the Ammonites (Gen 19:30-38). The Children of Israel were subsequently forbidden to conquer these people's lands, which had been promised to the descendants of Lot (Deut 2:9, 19).

The moral decay of Sodom and its final destruction by God was mentioned by Jesus when he taught about the unforeseen advent of the Kingdom.

The Second Epistle of Peter terms Lot a righteous man and describes him as vexing his righteous soul with the unlawful deeds of the men of Sodom (II Peter 2:6-8).

LOTAN The eldest son of Seir and chief of the Horites (Gen 36:20, 22, 29; I Chr 1:38-39).

LOTAN
Gen 36:20, 22, 29. I Chr 1:38-39

LOTUS See PLANTS

LOVE God's love for mankind is the fundamental tenet of the Hebrew faith (Deut 4:37; 7:8). The channel through which God expresses that love is, first and foremost, his people Israel. Prophets and historical writers agree in finding the basis of Israel's election and peoplehood in God's love for them (I Kgs 10:9; II Chr 2:11; 9:8; Is 43:4; 48:14; Jer 31:3; Hos 11:1; Mal 1:2). The human love of God and all acts of piety, devotion and service towards him, are subsumed under the command: "You shall love the Lord your God with all your heart" (Deut 6:5; cf Ex 20:6); this love is made possible by God himself (Deut 30:6). There is, in addition, love between humans although such love begins within the immediate family circle (Gen 24:67; 25:28; 29:20; Ruth 4:15), it branches out and includes the stranger in the midst and, even one's enemy (cf Ex 23:44ff; Deut 22:1-4; Prov 25:21). The tension between the love of God and the prophet's desire for vengeance against God's enemies, is clearly seen in the Book of Jonah and the book's inclusion in the canon affirms Judaism's transcendence over chauvinism and over any narrow notion of God's election.

An early and profound affirmation of God's love appears in the Book of Hosea. Using the model of a broken marriage (Hos chaps. 1-3), Hosea is the first to declare the relationship between God and Israel a special covenant love, dating back to the great formative event of Hebrew history, the Exodus, as interpreted by Moses.

Human love is strongly felt in the Song of Solomon where male and female lovers show little inhibition in expressing their delight in each other. It has been recognized as contributing significantly to a theology of love precisely because it lacks all prurient interest. Although throughout history there has been a tendency to resort to allegory to avoid the book's concrete literalness, the collection of love poetry in the Song of Solomon emphasizes the joy, innocence, mutuality and naturalness of the devotion of love. The light it throws on human love is in striking contrast to parallel Greek perceptions.

However mundane some aspects of human love may seem, it is related directly to God's love and the love shown towards God. Love for one's neighbor is part of loving God. Such love begins with the one near to us (the neighbor) but reaches out to those farther away and always includes the resident alien (Lev 19:34), the foreigner living within Israel's territory who, being denied civil rights, is particularly helpless and vulnerable to abuse (Deut 10:19).

The role of Israel was to serve as a light to the Gentiles so that the latter could experience not only the sovereignty of God but also his compassion and love.

Love is central in the message of the NT, although there is no foundation for the claim that its view of love is unique. While the verb "to love" appears in the gospels with some frequency, the noun does not, whereas in the epistles (with the exception of I John) the reverse is true. But it should not be concluded that love has become an abstract virtue, for its dynamic and active sense is always maintained.

Christian perceptions of love are grounded above all in the Jewish affirmation of God's election. All discussions of love begin with the premise that God first loved man and that act of free deliverance gave rise to the commandments: You must love the Lord your God with all your heart, mind and strength and your neighbor as yourself (Matt 22:37, 39; Mark 12:30-31; Luke 10:27). Jesus' fusion of these commandments was no innovation; his interpretation made him a participant in the debate already in progress among his Jewish fellow teachers. In the parable of the good Samaritan (Luke chap. 10) the element of surprise lies in the fact that an individual whose people were more renowned for molesting travelers rather than for assisting them, is portrayed as understanding the meaning of love for his neighbor. Though equally bound by the laws of purification, the Samaritan risked defilement in order to bring help to the wounded man.

Jesus taught that his disciples should love their enemies (Luke 6:27, 35). Here too he drew on his own Jewish heritage which, although it may not contain the explicit commandment, precisely prescribes what loving the enemy means: returning blessings for curses, praying for those who harm us, feeding the hungry enemy and quenching his thirst (Prov 25:21; Rom 12:20). The Jewish work The Testament of Joseph states: "If anyone seeks to do evil to you, do well unto him and pray for him, and you will be redeemed of the Lord from all evil".

Such behavior is grounded in the nature of God and is consistent with being his child (Matt 5:43-48). Some sources, both Christian and Jewish, promise that this course of action will lead to a dissolution of the enmity. Jesus offers no such easy assurance, while Paul holds out the hope that good is the only way to conquer evil (Rom 12:19-21).

A profound Christian view of love is to be found in I John. Not only is in the central theme (the word appears about 50 times in this short epistle) but the writer also affirms that it is mockery to speak of love for God unless love is expressed for one's brother (I John 4:20); the latter term is probably not restricted to "fellow Christian" even though that may be the primary reference point. Jesus' repeated urgings to relinquish family ties, stated in its most radical form in Luke 14:26: "If anyone comes to me and does not hate his father and mother, wife and children, brothers and sisters, yes and his own life also, he cannot be my disciple", are an invitation to place love for God first.

A high tribute to love is found in I Corinthians chapter 13 which has no reference to Jesus but faithfully describes the way he loved and lived. Perhaps some early Christian poet composed this tribute and Paul introduced it into his epistle in order to restore perspective to a church which had lost its sense of priorities. Affirming that all human accomplishments pale in the absence of love (I Cor 13:1-3), it depicts both the negative and the positive ways in which love is expressed and concludes with a tribute to its enduring quality (I Cor 13:8-13).

LUBIM See LIBYA, LIBYANS

LUCIFER ("bearer of light"). The planet Venus at dawn. In some Bible translations the name is used in Isaiah 14:12 "How you are fallen from heaven, O Lucifer, son of the morning!" originally meaning "the shining one" and referred to the king of Babylon. In the 3rd century A.D. the saying of Jesus: "I saw Satan fall like lightning from heaven" (Luke 10:18) was connected to Isaiah 14:12 and Lucifer was accepted as the name of Satan before his fall.

LUCIUS

1. A man from Cyrene, active as a teacher and prophet in the community of Antioch (Acts 13:1).

2. A man who sent greetings to the community in Rome, appending them to those of Paul who was writing from Corinth.

LUD Son of Shem (Gen 10:22; I Chr 1:17). Most scholars accept Josephus' identification of Lud (*Antiq.* I, 6, 4) with the Lydians, a non-Semitic nation settled on the west coast of Asia Minor, and known also from Assyrian documents of the 7th century B.C.

The list of nations in Isaiah 66:19, where Lud appears together with Tubal and Javan, supports this assumption. See LUDIM.

LUDIM Son of Mizraim, a descendant of Ham (Gen 10:13; I Chr 1:11). In Jeremiah 46:9 and Ezekiel 27:10; 30:5, Ludim is listed among African nations, leading to the suggestion that it is an unidentified African nation which some scholars emend to Lubim — Libyans. Most scholars identify the Ludim with Lud and the people as the Lydians.

LUHITH A city in Moab mentioned by Isaiah in his proclamation against Moab, and by Jeremiah in his judgment on Moab.

LUKE A doctor and traveling-companion of Paul, who is mentioned three times by name as "Luke, the beloved physician" (Col 4:14), and further in II Timothy 4:11 and Philemon v.24. The third gospel and the Acts of the Apostles, traditionally written by Luke, contain only indirect details of his life. Luke joined Paul on his second missionary journey in Troas. During Paul's third journey, Luke joined him in

LUBIM
II Chr 12:3; 16:8. Nah 3:9

LUCIFER
Is 14:12

LUCIUS 1
Acts 13:1

LUCIUS 2
Rom 16:21

LUD
Gen 10:22. I Chr 1:17. Is 66:19

LUDIM
Gen 10:13. I Chr 1:11

LUHITH
Is 15:5. Jer 48:5

LUKE
Col 4:14. II Tim 4:11. Philem v.24

Head of a Libyan depicted on a glazed tile from the temple of Rameses III. 12th century B.C. The Ludim are believed by some scholars to be the same people as the Libyans.

A view of Sedaya in Syria, Luke is held to have been a native of Syria.

Philippi (Acts 20:6) and went with him to Jerusalem (Acts 20:16). From the enumeration Paul gives of his fellow-workers in the Epistle to the Colossians, it appears that Luke was of heathen origin (Col 4:10-14). Because Luke the physician is generally identified with the writer of the third gospel, he is called "the evangelist". He had a good education, literary talents and skill in writing. He was well-traveled and versed in navigation (Acts chap. 27). Scholars assume that Luke wanted to mediate between the Jewish and the pagan world, and that he wrote for Greeks and Romans. Apart from their common concern about mission to the pagan world, Paul and Luke may have had a professional relationship, with Luke ministering to Paul's disease (cf II Cor 12:7; Gal 4:13-15).

LUKE, GOSPEL OF Luke is the third of the four gospels in the Christian canon. It was intended by its author as the first part of a two-volume work, the second book being the Acts of the Apostles which is an evident continuation of the Gospel of Luke, as attested by the writer's explicit statement (Acts 1:1), and by the literary style and theology.

Luke-Acts represents the earliest historiography written from a Christian point of view. It is also the first full-fledged theology of the imitation of Christ directed to the daily routine of ongoing historical existence. (Mark and Paul also teach the imitation of Christ, but for

Two pages from the Gospel of St. Luke from the Armenian Book of the Four Gospels of the 12th century. Hromkla Library, Jerusalem.

them historical existence is already all but brought to an end). In both these areas, historiography and the spirituality of the imitation of Christ, Luke-Acts had a great influence on subsequent Christian patterns of thought and conduct.

In the historical criticism that developed in the 19th century, Luke, like Matthew, was viewed as based on the Gospel of Mark and a circulating collection of Jesus' sayings. There were also oral and written materials unique to Luke, which he shaped to his own ends. After World War II prominence was achieved by a method of interpretation called "redaction criticism", which involves examination of the final "redaction" or editorial stage of the work, the one that we have, in order to determine the redactor's theological tendencies. Redaction critics also began to inquire into the audience, and the historical circumstances, for which the work was written. One conclusion commonly accepted about Luke-Acts was that the writer and his readers, living c. A.D. 75-90, were concerned about the delay of the parousia (the return of the Christ) as history continued its course and the church began to develop a sense of its tradition and definite structures of authority.

Luke bases his gospel upon his understanding of the church as a new historical order based on the earlier history of the Law and the prophets. The church is guided by the Spirit of God along a way, a path requiring prayer and patience. The pattern of conduct for the journey along this way is revealed in the teachings and deeds of Jesus. Jesus as the Christ is the perfect human, the divine man.

Luke traces the divine design as disclosed not only in the salvation history of the Jews, but revealed for all humankind. In the nativity story, peculiar in this form to Luke (compare Matt 2:1-12), the heavenly host exclaim to the shepherds, "Glory to God in the highest, and on earth peace, good will toward men!" (Luke 2:14). The genealogy in Luke, again quite different from Matthew's, is traced back through David and Abraham to "Adam, the son of God" (3:38). Luke clearly wants to present Jesus as a savior born for all humankind. This universalistic context thus lends a significance to Luke's description of Jesus' baptism where the heavenly voice, not mentioned in the other gospels, proclaims "You are my beloved Son" (3:22). In Luke's setting, this public announcement means that the God-given Son comes for all humankind and is sent to all men.

The continuity of Jesus and the church with the past of the Jews and the Gentiles is expressed in a definite history of salvation. Although the major focus is on continuity, there is a division into epochs viewed as distinct from one another. The first epoch is that of Israel, the Law and the prophets, which in effect is linked to creation and extends to John the Baptist. Not only does John's ministry predate that of Jesus, as it does in the other gospels; Luke even relates the story of his conception and birth, which precede the parallel account for Jesus (1:5-25, 57-66). However, John marks the end of an era, as Luke stresses in demarcating the period of John (Israel) from the ministry of Jesus. "The Law and the prophets were until John..." (16:16). Although the baptizing movement began with John, Luke has John in prison by the time Jesus is baptized (3:19-22; cf Matt 3:13; Mark 1:9). Thus the two are separated, even though they are also closely related.

Jesus comes as Lord and Christ in the second epoch of salvation history. He is the center of God's history. His teachings and deeds reveal no content essentially different from the Law or the prophets. Anyone will have eternal life who loves God wholeheartedly and his neighbor as himself (Luke 10:27). The good news is already given in principle through Moses and the prophets. "If they do not hear Moses and the prophets, neither will they be persuaded though one rise from the dead" (16:31). Jesus is not the messiah-teacher giving a new Torah as in Matthew, nor the secret Son of man whose death is a sacrifice as in Mark. He is rather the divine son in two basic respects: he discloses the pattern of faith and virtue required by God, and his ministry is directed to the Gentiles — in fact, to all "outsiders" — as well as to the Jews. To give but one indication of a Christ-pattern which the reader-hearer is to emulate: Jesus is portrayed as praying "without ceasing". There are seven references to Jesus praying in Luke (3:21; 5:16; 6:12; 9:18, 28-29; 11:1; 22:40-46). They cover the whole range of his ministry: baptism, retreat into the wilderness, choosing of the apostles, ministry in Gentile territory, transfiguration, teaching how to pray and passion. The first six instances occur only in Luke.

During the post-resurrection period, before the ascension into heaven, Jesus appears to the disciples and opens up the Scriptures to them (24:27, 32). Among the Synoptic Gospels, only Luke presents these resurrection appearances as occurring in Jerusalem and its environs. The way to and from Jerusalem is at the heart of his language of salvation and mission. The "way" is the chief metaphor of Luke-Acts (see Luke 9:57-62; 11:6; 24:32; Acts 9:2; 19:9, 23; 22:4; 24:14, 22). The way of the gospel is a journey from Galilee to Jerusalem and then out from Jerusalem. Having been instructed by the resurrected Lord, the apostles begin the work of witnessing to the gospel "in Jerusalem and in all Judea and Samaria and to the end of the earth" (Acts 1:8). Although Paul plays a prominent part in this mission to the Gentiles, it is striking that Luke does not call him "apostle". This probably does not imply Paul's lesser status in relation to the twelve, but reflects the clear distinction Luke makes between the second epoch, the time of Jesus, and the mission to the Gentiles that reaches out from Jerusalem and is therefore the third epoch of the salvation history. The writing of a history of the apostles through Paul's house arrest in Rome represents the strong sense that the church is becoming an institution in history. This sense of time, the image of a long way extending into the future, is the obverse side of another distinctive Lucan motif: the delay of the parousia. Mark expresses an air of urgency about the imminent transformation of all things with the advent of the Son of man. Matthew follows Mark in this, but somewhat attenuates the eschatological urgency with a gospel which is a foundation document of the church as an active messianic community in history. However, Luke-Acts foresees an indefinite delay in the end of all historical existence and the full consummation of God's rule. When Jesus begins his ministry in Galilee, he announces, not the imminent arrival of the Kingdom, but the divine Spirit present and working through his words and deeds (Luke 4:14; compare Mark 1:14-15). The seed sown in good soil does not produce an eschatological yield, but is a type of the one who bears fruit with patience (Luke 8:15; cf Matt 13:23; Mark 4:20). Jesus tells the parable of the pounds because some "thought that the Kingdom of God would appear immediately" (Luke 19:11; cf Matt 25:13-14). The eschaton (end) is delayed so that "the time of the Gentiles", i.e., the mission of the church to the Gentiles, might be fulfilled (Luke 21:24).

OUTLINE

1:1-4	Introduction
1:5-2:52	Infancy of Jesus
3:1-4:13	Preaching of John, baptism, temptation
4:14-9:50	Ministry of Galilee
9:51-13:21	Samaria, sayings, parables
13:22-21:38	Continuation of journey to Jerusalem, sayings, miracles, discourses
22:1-23:56	Passion
24:1-53	Resurrection

LUZ 1
Gen 28:19;
35:6; 48:3.
Josh 16:2;
18:13. Judg
1:23

LUZ

1. A Canaanite city which Jacob renamed Bethel, following his dream of the ladder and the setting up of the altar (Gen 28:19; 48:3).

In Joshua 16:2, Luz and Bethel are mentioned as two separate cities

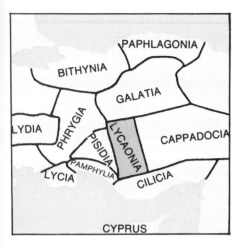

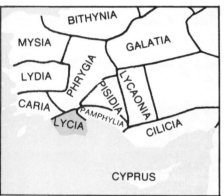

Lycaonia and Lycia in Asia Minor.

(top right)
Bethel identified with Luz.

Coin of Lod (Diospolis) depicting the head of Demeter on one side and Zeus-Heliopites on the other. A.D. 209.

situated in the territory of Joseph, but in all other instances Luz is identified with Bethel (Gen 35:6; Josh 18:13; Judg 1:23).

Scholars assume that Jacob applied the name Bethel exclusively to the place where he slept, and that the city only received the name after the conquest of Canaan. See BETHEL.

2. A city founded in the "land of the Hittites", by a citizen of Bethel or Luz, who was forced to leave the city after the Israelites had conquered it (Judg 1:24-26).

LUZ 2
Judg 1:26

The name "land of the Hittites", signifies here northern Syria and the place has been identified at Luweiz, 11 miles (18 km) southwest of Sidon, or with Khirbet Luweizie, west of Banias.

LYCAONIA, LYCAONIAN An ethnic district in southcentral Asia Minor traversed by the main east-west trade route from Asia Minor to Syria. It bordered the plains of Galatia and Cappadocia on the north and east and was bounded by hills on the west and south. Acquired by Rome in 190 B.C., it was divided among three Roman imperial provinces by Pompey in 64; the west went to Cilicia, the east to Cappadocia, and the north to Galatia. Eastern Lycaonia became independent of Cappadocia in 25 B.C. The mixed population included the native pagan Lycaonians, for whom the territory was named (Acts 14:11), and a sizeable Jewish population (cf Acts 16:1, Timothy and his family). The NT references deal with Lycaonia Galatica, that portion which lay within Galatia, whose major cities were Lystra and Derbe. Paul may have visited the region on three separate occasions (Acts chaps. 13-14, with Barnabas; 16:1-5, with Silas; and possibly 18:23).

LYCAONIA,
LYCAONIAN
Acts 14:6, 11

LYCIA A province in southwestern Asia Minor. Its main cities, Patara and Myra, were Mediterranean ports. Paul passed through Patara, where he embarked for Phoenicia (Acts 21:1-2). From Myra he later set sail to Italy (Acts 27:5-6).

LYCIA
Acts 27:5

LYDDA, LOD A town not mentioned in the Bible until the return from the Babylonian Exile (Ezra 2:33), though its inclusion in a list of the Egyptian pharaoh Thutmosis III testifies to its antiquity. It is situated between Jerusalem and Joppa, about 12 miles (19 km) from the latter. Its main importance lies in its role in Roman and Byzantine times. According to the NT the apostle Peter went to Lydda to visit believers who lived there (Acts 9:32). There he healed Aenas who had been paralyzed for eight years. In the time of Constantine, St. George, patron saint of England, was martyred at Lydda, and his shrine was venerated from the 4th century.

LYDDA, LOD
**I Chr 8:12.
Ezra 2:33.
Neh 7:37;
11:35. Acts
9:32, 35, 38**

LYDIA

1. A district in the center of the western coastal slope of Asia Minor,

LYDIA 1
**Ezek 27:10;
30:5.**

mentioned in both the OT and NT; it included the very fertile, cultivable Cayster and Hermus valleys and the Tmolos mountains (6,500 feet, 2,000 m). It bordered Mysia on the north, Phrygia on the east, and Caria on the south. Located on the main east-west trade route leading across Asia Minor to Syria, Lydia was a prosperous commercial center with gold, textile and carpet industries, woolmaking and dyeing, and perfume manufacture. Its principal cities included the capital Sardis, Thyatira, Philadelphia and Colophon. The coastal cities such as Ephesus and Smyrna were at times considered Lydian, at others, Greek. Lydia was independent and controlled all of Asia Minor until 546 B.C. when the Persian Cyrus defeated King Croesus and attached it to the Attalid kingdom of Pergamum. In 133 B.C. Lydia became part of the Roman senatorial province of Asia. Coinage was invented in Lydia in the 7th century B.C. The city's population was mixed. Antiochus III (223-187 B.C.) settled 2,000 Jewish familes from Babylonia and Lydia and Phrygia (Josephus, *Antiq.* XII, 147 ff). Friction arose between Lydia's Gentile and Jewish inhabitants over the dispatch of the half-shekel to the Temple of Jerusalem. The church grew rapidly in Lydia where three of the seven cities of the Book of Revelation (Thyatira, Sardis and Philadelphia) were located.

2. A woman, native of the city of Thyatira in Asia, who sold purple dye in Philippi and who had been converted to Judaism (Acts 16:14). When Paul arrived in Philippi she was overwhelmed by his preaching. She was baptized together with her household (Acts 16:15) and immediately invited Paul and Silas into her home. After their release from prison, they returned to her house.

LYDIA 2
Acts 16:14, 40

LYDIANS The inhabitants of the district of Lydia on the western coast of Asia Minor. The origin of the Lydian race is difficult to pinpoint. In Jeremiah 46:9 the Lydians are bow-carrying allies of Egypt. The Hebrew plural, *Ludim* occurs in Genesis 10:13 and I Chronicles 1:11 as descendants of Ham/Egypt. In this list, the "Ludim" are associated with Philistines and Caphtorim, who, like the Lydians, had their home in the northern Mediterranean.

LYDIANS
Jer 46:9

LYSANIAS The tetrarch of Abilene, the area north of Mount Hermon. He was a contemporary of Tiberius Caesar, Pontius Pilate and Herod, and officiated at the time that John the Baptist commenced his mission.

LYSANIAS
Luke 3:1

LYSIAS, CLAUDIUS A centurion in command of the Roman garrison in Jerusalem. After Paul's speech to the people, he was taken to Claudius, who had him brought into the castle (probably the Antonia Fortress) for examination under scourging (Acts 22:24).

Lysias himself was a Greek who had obtained Roman citizenship (Acts 22:28). When he discovered that Paul was also a Roman citizen, he prudently withdrew from the case, handing Paul over to the chief priests and the council (Acts 22:30) and later sending him to Felix the governor in Caesarea (Acts 23:17-33).

LYSIAS, CLAUDIUS
Acts 23:26; 24:7, 22

Lydia in Asia Minor.

(top of page)
Forecourt at the ancient synagogue of Sardis, the capital of Lydia.

Coin of Lydia, showing the foreparts of a lion and a bull facing each other. c.550 B.C.

LYSTRA A city in the Roman province of Galatia, in Asia Minor, where Paul and Barnabas preached and Paul healed a cripple. The citizens were so impressed that they said "The gods have come down to us in the likeness of men" and they called Barnabas Zeus and Paul Hermes (Acts 14:11-12). However, some Jews from Antioch and Iconium, feeling threatened by the message of Paul and Barnabas, stirred up the people in Lystra and "they stoned Paul and dragged him out of the city, supposing that he was dead" (Acts 14:19). Nevertheless Paul returned to Lystra (Acts 14:21; 16:1-2) where he met Timothy, the son of a Jewess and a Greek father, taking him on his journeys.

LYSTRA
Acts 14:6, 8, 21; 16:1-2.
II Tim 3:11

The site of Lystra has been located but no remains have been found of the ancient town.

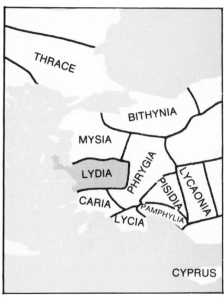

M

MAACAH Name of a place and several people.

1. Small Aramean kingdom in northern Transjordan (Josh 13:11) around the town of Abel Beth Maacah. Geshur and Maacah were situated between Gilead and Mount Hermon, bordering the kingdom of Og in Bashan (Josh 13:12). During the conquest of Canaan the Israelites did not expel them but dwelt among them (Josh 13:13). They fought against David in alliance with the Ammonites (II Sam 10:6-8; I Chr 19:6-7). After David conquered the Arameans and annexed Abel Beth Maacah, it became an Israelite city (II Sam 20:13-15).

2. Daughter of Talmai the king of Geshur; one of David's wives and mother of Absalom.

3. Wife of Jeiel the father of Gibeon.

4. See MAACHAH No.3

MAACATHITE(S), MAACHATHITE(S) Inhabitants of the kingdom of Maacah.

MAACHAH

1. The son of Nahor, Abraham's brother, born to him by his concubine Reumah (Gen 22:24). Eponym of the kingdom of Maachah (called MAACAH in II Sam 10:6, 8).

2. The father of Achish king of Gath (I Kgs 2:39); in I Samuel 27:2 he is called Maoch.

3. Granddaughter of Absalom and mother of Abijam the son of Rehoboam king of Judah (I Kgs 15:2; II Chr 11:20, 22). According to I Kings 15:10, 13, Maacah was the grandmother of King Asa son of Abijam but II Chronicles 15:16 states that she was Asa's mother.

4. The concubine of Caleb.

5. Wife of Machir (I Chr 7:16), also called his sister (v.15).

6. The father of Hanan, one of David's "mighty men" from east of the Jordan.

7. Father of Shephatiah, who was the chief officer of the Simeonites in the list of King David's officers.

MAADAI One of the sons of Bani, who married a foreign wife and was forced to repudiate her at the decree of Ezra.

MAADIAH A priest, who returned with Zerubbabel from Babylon.

MAAI One of the priest-musicians who took part in the dedication of the walls of Jerusalem in the time of Nehemiah.

MAARATH A town of Judah, in the hill district north of Hebron, mentioned together with Halhul, Beth Zur and Gedor (Josh 15:58-59). It has been tentatively identified with the modern village of Beit Imar, 3 miles (5 km) north of Halhul, and more than a mile (1.6 km) southwest of Jadur, a site where caves abound (*me'arah* means "cave" in Hebrew).

MAASAI A priest; son of Adiel, one of those who returned from the Babylonian Exile (I Chr 9:12). In the parallel verse in Nehemiah 11:13 the name appears as Amshasai son of Azriel.

MAASEIAH ("The works/creations of God").

1. A Levite musician among those who helped to bring the ark to Jerusalem, in the time of King David and played in the procession (v. 20).

2. The son of Adaiah. One of the military officers who assisted Jehoiada the priest in the rebellion against Queen Athaliah.

3. An officer, who helped assemble the military lists of the army of King Uzziah.

4. "The son of the king", first to be mentioned in a list of officials who were killed by Zichri, an Ephraimite hero, in the time of King Ahaz. He may have been the son of Ahaz.

5. The governor of Jerusalem in the time of Josiah; he was sent, along with other officials, to cleanse the Temple.

Hebrew limestone seal inscribed "[Belonging] to Maaseiah Ishmael". 7th century B.C. (Israel Museum)

MAACAH 1
II Sam 10:6, 8

MAACAH 2
**II Sam 3:3.
I Chr 3:2**

MAACAH 3
**I Chr 8:29;
9:35**

MAACAH 4
**II Chr 11:20-
22; 15:16**

MAACATHITE(S),
MAACHATHITE(S)
**Deut 3:14.
Josh 12:5;
13:11, 13.
II Sam 23:34.
II Kgs 25:23.
I Chr 4:19. Jer
40:8**

MAACHAH 1
**Gen 22:24.
I Chr 19:6-7**

MAACHAH 2
I Kgs 2:39

MAACHAH 3
**I Kgs 15:2, 10,
13**

MAACHAH 4
I Chr 2:48

MAACHAH 5
I Chr 7:15-16

MAACHAH 6
I Chr 11:43

MAACHAH 7
I Chr 27:16

MAADAI
Ezra 10:34

MAADIAH
Neh 12:5

MAAI
Neh 12:36

MAARATH
Josh 15:59

MAASAI
I Chr 9:12

MAASEIAH 1
I Chr 15:18, 20

MAASEIAH 2
II Chr 23:1

MAASEIAH 3
II Chr 26:11

MAASEIAH 4
II Chr 28:7

MAASEIAH 5
II Chr 34:8

6. The father of the false prophet Zedekiah.

7. A priest, son of Shallum. Keeper of the doors of the Temple, and father of Zephaniah, priest in the time of Jeremiah.

8-11. The name of four persons, sons of the families of Jeshua, Harim, Pashhur and Pahath-Moab, who married alien women in the time of Ezra and were forced to repudiate them.

12. The father of Azariah who took part in rebuilding the wall of Jerusalem in the time of Nehemiah.

13. One of the people who stood on the right side of Ezra when he read from the Book of the Law.

14. A Levite who helped the people understand the meaning of the Book of the Law, when Ezra read from it before the public.

15. One of the heads of the families who signed the covenant in the time of Nehemiah.

16. The son of Baruch, a Judahite, who settled in Jerusalem in the time of Nehemiah. In I Chronicles 9:5 his name is recorded as Asaiah.

17. Ancestor of Sallu the son of Meshullam, a Benjamite, who settled in Jerusalem in the time of Nehemiah.

18-19. Two of the priests who took part in the rebuilding of the wall of Jerusalem in the time of Nehemiah.

The name appears on several Hebrew seals and seal-impressions.

MAATH ("little"). Son of Mattathiah and father of Naggai in the genealogy of Jesus according to Luke.

MAAZ A Jerahmeelite, the son of Ram.

MAAZIAH ("God is my stronghold / shelter"). Eponym of a clan — the 24th division of the priests (I Chr 24:18). The name appears among the priests who signed the covenant in the time of Nehemiah (Neh 10:8).

I MACCABEES Book of the Apocrypha, extant in Greek but originally written in Hebrew, telling the story of the Hasmonean Revolt. Its Jewish author must have written this history during the reign of John Hyrcanus or shortly after his death (104 B.C.).

The book starts with a brief overview of the events preceding the Hasmonean Revolt: Alexander the Great's conquest, and the oppression of the Syrian ruler Antiochus Epiphanes who tried to stop Jewish religious life by persecuting those Jews who continued to observe their religious traditions, which included circumcision and the observance of the Sabbath and New Moon. Antiochus desecrated the Temple in Jerusalem and dedicated it to idolatry (1:1-64).

The main subject of I Maccabees, however, is the Jewish struggle for independence and the rebellion against idolatry. Mattathias, the head of the Hasmonean family, started the rebellion and the fortunes of his family are recorded until the time of his grandson John Hyrcanus (134-104 B.C.).

The book traces the history of a 40-year period (175-134) and is the main source of information about the Hasmoneans, a pious family (2:19-27), who fought to restore religious freedom and traditional

Hebrew seal impression inscribed "[Belonging] to Eliakim son of Maaseiah". 6th century B.C. (Israel Museum)

Hanukkah stone lamp from the Talmudic period (Israel Museum). According to tradition the Festival of Hanukkah was instituted by Judas Maccabee and his followers to commemorate the rededication of the altar in the Temple which had been defiled.

El Media identified with Modi'in, the birthplace of the Hasmoneans.

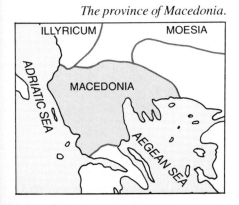

Traditional sites of the tombs of the Hasmoneans in the Modi'in region.

The province of Macedonia.

worship in Jerusalem. It tells the history of Judas, Jonathan and Simon, sons of Mattathias, all of whom fell in this struggle after a period of successful leadership. A central event is the rededication of the Temple in Jerusalem, under the leadership of Judas (4:36-58), who ordained that the anniversary of this occasion on the 25th of the month Kislev should be observed as a festival — the festival of Hanukkah (4:59).

II MACCABEES A book of the Apocrypha written in Greek probably in Alexandria during the 1st century B.C. It is a summary of a larger, lost five-volume work by the historian Jason of Cyrene, and tells the story of the Hasmonean revolt. It is more didactic in intent than the First Book of the Maccabees whose stress is historical. II Maccabees projects the concept of a God who cares for his people and punishes the wicked who do not keep the commandments. The enemies are not only Gentiles, like Antiochus IV and Nicanor, but also those Jews who became assimilated into the environment of Greek culture. Indeed a theme of the book is this inner Jewish struggle between the Hellenized priesthood and their sympathizers, and the people, who were tenacious in their beliefs preferring death to transgressing commandments.

The book starts with two letters addressed to the Jews in Alexandria with the request that the festival of Hanukkah be observed (1:1-9; 1:10-2:18). Its main content is summarized in the words: "Now as concerning Judas Maccabee, and his brothers, and the purification of the great Temple, and the dedication of the altar, and the wars against Antiochus Epiphanes and Eupator his son, and the manifest signs that came from heaven unto those that behaved themselves manfully to their honor for Judaism..." (2:19-21). The book expounds the causes of the religious persecution under Antiochus, which ended in martyrdom for many religious Jews. Chapter 7 relates the story of the mother with her seven sons, who were martyred for refusing to eat swine's flesh. The turning point is the appearance of Judas, assembling 6,000 men (8:1) and starting the revolt against the persecutors. Judas wins many battles and his activity culminates in the rededication and purification of the defiled Temple in Jerusalem (chap. 10). The final event is Judas' last victory over Nicanor, the Syrian general.

MACEDONIA, MACEDONIANS The northern part of modern Greece, stretching from the Adriatic to the Aegean Sea, centered on the plains of the gulf of Thessalonica and running up the great river valleys into the Balkan mountains. Though predominantly mountainous, the region has many fertile plains, and was a source of timber and precious metals.

The Macedonians were part of the Hellenic race. After the rise of Alexander in the late 4th century B.C., they dominated the eastern Mediterranean region until the rise of the Roman Empire. Macedonia became a Roman senatorial province in 146 B.C. Its most important cities lay on the Aegean coast and included Thessalonica (the seat of the proconsul from 44 B.C.), and Pella, as well as Berea, seat of the imperial cult and the place where the assembly of Greek states met. The region also boasted six Roman colonies, including Philippi. Jewish communities were found in Macedonia before the end of the 1st century A.D. (Philo, *Embassy to Gaius* 281).

In I Maccabees 1:1 Alexander the Great, a Macedonian, is identified as coming from the land of the Kittim (Cyprus) (cf Dan 11:30). The biblical place-name Javan is translated by the rabbis as "Macedonia".

Paul's first European ministry was conducted in Macedonia which he visited after seeing a vision of a Macedonian man imploring him to come there (Acts 16:6-10). Having founded strong churches at Philippi (where he was imprisoned for a time), Thessalonica and Berea, he

MACEDONIA, MACEDONIANS
Acts 16:9-10, 12; 18:5; 19:21-22, 29; 20:1, 3; 27:2. Rom 15:26. I Cor 16:5. II Cor 1:16; 2:13; 7:5; 8:1; 9:2, 4; 11:9. Phil 4:15. I Thes 1:7-8; 4:10. I Tim 1:3

moved on to Achaia, leaving Silas and Timothy responsible for the ministry in Berea (Acts 17:14; 18:5). Paul returned to Macedonia on his third missionary journey (Acts chaps. 19-20), receiving money from the church at Philippi on behalf of its Jerusalem counterpart (Rom 15:26). The churches of Macedonia were the only ones he permitted to contribute to his financial welfare (II Cor 8:1-4; Phil 4:15). Paul showed great affection for these churches (I Thes 4:10) which suffered persecution for the gospel's sake (II Thes 1:6-8).

MACHBANAI
One of the men of Gad, captains of the army and "mighty men of valor" who joined David at Ziklag.

MACHBENAH
Son of Sheva who was a son of Caleb by his concubine Maachah.

MACHI
Father of Geuel of the tribe of Gad, one of the 12 spies sent to the land of Canaan (Num 13:15). The name appears on a Hebrew seal impression from the 6th century B.C.

MACHIR, MACHIRITES

1. The only son of Manasseh and grandson of Joseph (Gen 50:23); father of the Machirites (Num 26:29); his wife's name was Maachah (I Chr 7:16). The Machirites conquered Gilead to the east of the Jordan and settled there prior to the conquest of Canaan (Num 32:39-40). In Joshua 17:1 Machir is mentioned as father of Gilead. Other references, however, name Machir among the tribes who settled to the west of the Jordan and who took part in the war against Sisera (Judg 5:14).

2. The son of Ammiel from Lo Debar in Gilead. He was probably related to King Saul's family, as Mephibosheth — the lame son of Jonathan — stayed in his house (II Sam 9:4-5). Machir is mentioned, together with Barzillai the Gileadite and Shobi the son of Nahash the Ammonite, as supplying David and his men with food and equipment when they fled from Absalom and found shelter in Mahanaim (II Sam 17:27).

MACHNADEBAI
One of the Israelites who married an alien woman and was forced to repudiate her at the command of Ezra.

MACHPELAH
The name of a field and a cave near Mamre (Gen 23:17), which is Hebron (Gen 23:19). It was bought by Abraham from Ephron the Hittite. Sarah (Gen 23:19), Abraham (Gen 25:9), Isaac, Rebekah and Leah (Gen 49:31) and Jacob (Gen 50:13) were buried here. An ancient tradition, which goes back to the time of the Second Temple, sites the Cave of the Machpelah, at a place in the Haram el-Khalil at Hebron, surrounded by a wall built in Herod's times. It is still venerated today by Jews, Christians and Moslems alike.

(left)
The edifice over the Cave of Machpelah at Hebron the "Haram al-Khalil" (The Shrine of the Beloved of God, i.e., Abraham).

Part of the Herodian wall over the Cave of Machpelah.

The Church of Mary Magdalene at Magdala.

Models of a cow's liver, made of clay, with inscribed omens; found at Hazor and dating to c. 1400 B.C. The liver of animals was used for divination and foretelling in ancient times, particularly by the Babylonians.

Nothing is known of the configuration of the burial cave, as entrance to it is forbidden. It has been suggested that it may originally have been a rock-cut shaft tomb, of the type common around 2000 B.C. Likewise, there is no knowledge of the mode of burial practiced by the patriarchs, except for the obvious fact that the cave was reused over several generations for successive burials. The massive Herodian walls that enclosed a large, rectangular open air temenos have remained intact. The open rectangle, however, was built up in later periods with a succession of churches and mosques, which produced the rather confusing structure now standing on the site. The cenotaphs and tombstones now standing in the mosque and pointed out as the burial sites of the patriarchs, are of the Mameluk period or later.

MADAI See MEDIA

MADMANNAH ("place of dung"). A place in the southern end of the territory of Judah (Josh 15:21, 31), founded by Shaaph the son of Jahdai (I Chr 2:47, 49).

MADMENAH A place, probably in Benjamin, mentioned in Isaiah 10:31 as lying on the route of the Assyrian army on its way to Jerusalem.

Most scholars believe that Madmenah may be Shu'fat, 1 mile (1.6km) north of Jerusalem; but that assumption has not yet been proven.

MADON A Canaanite town in Galilee. Its king, Jobab, was one of the allies of Jabin king of Hazor in his war against the Israelites.

MAGBISH Eponym of a family, whose 156 members returned from Babylon with Zerubbabel. In the parallel list in Nehemiah chapter 7 they are not mentioned.

MAGDALA Town on the western shore of the Sea of Galilee, about 3 miles (5 km) north of Tiberias, the birthplace of Mary Magdalene (Matt 27:56, 61). It is possible that it was visited by Jesus (Mark 8:10 "Dalmanutha"). In excavations remains of the Roman city, a small synagogue of the Galilean type and a monastic complex have been brought to light.

MAGDALENE See MARY

MAGDIEL One of the 12 chiefs of Edom.

MAGGOT See ANIMALS

MAGIC, DIVINATION AND WITCHCRAFT The Bible contains many references to witchcraft, but is strongly opposed to it. A person who practices this art is called a witch (Deut 18:10) or a magician (Ex 7:11, etc.). One of the terms by which the Egyptian magicians are referred to is *hartum* (Gen 41:24; Ex 8:7 "magicians"), the equivalent of the Egyptian *hrytp,* the name given to the most famous magicians. In Daniel (5:7) Chaldeans are mentioned together with astrologers and soothsayers, the reference being both to an ethnic group and to a class of magicians. Sorcery and witchcraft are also mentioned in the NT (Acts 8:9-11, etc.). The "wise men" (Matt 2:7), *magi* in the Greek, were an ethnic group (the term comes from Medes or Madai) and, like the Chaldeans, became synonymous with witchcraft.

The biblical view of witchcraft is quite clear: "There shall not be found among you anyone... who practices witchcraft, or a soothsayer, or one who interprets omens, or a sorcerer..." (Deut 18:10-21). All of these were considered to be sworn enemies of true religious belief, at the center of which stands a belief in one God and adherence to his ways. The true believer will accept whatever God has destined for him and will not make any attempt to change it. In complete opposition to this stands the belief that witchcraft may influence the supernatural. "You shall not permit a sorceress to live" (Ex 22:18). Saul had "put the mediums and spiritists out of the land" but in the end he had to resort to one himself (I Sam 28:3, 7-25).

MADAI
Gen 10:2.
I Chr 1:5

MADMANNAH
Josh 15:31.
I Chr 2:49

MADMENAH
Is 10:31

MADON
Josh 11:1;
12:19

MAGBISH
Ezra 2:30

MAGDALA
Matt 15:39

MAGDIEL
Gen 36:43.
I Chr 1:54

The attitude towards witchcraft expressed in the Bible had another purpose: to put a sharp distinction between Israel and the ways of the Canaanites, as encountered by the Israelites in the land of Canaan. In practice it seems that this purpose was not always achieved. Jezebel was known for her "witchcrafts" (II Kgs 9:22); Micah (5:12) mentions witchcraft and soothsayers; Manasseh, who "constructed altars for Baal", also "practiced soothsaying (and) used witchcraft." (II Kgs 21:3, 6); and the methods of a female sorcerer are described by Ezekiel (13:17-23). But these seem to be isolated instances, and when witchcraft is mentioned it is mostly when practiced by other nations, as with the prophecy of Isaiah (47:9-13) on Babylon. Still more typical is the prophecy of Ezekiel, who saw that "the king of Babylon stands at the parting of the road, at the fork of the two roads, to use divination: he shakes the arrows, he consults the images, he looks at the liver. In his right hand is the divination for Jerusalem..." (Ezek 21:21-22). This kind of military divination was much resorted to by the Romans at a later date. Simon Magus (i.e., Magician) and Bar-Jesus are mentioned as sorcerers in the NT (Acts 8:9-24; 13:6-12). In Ephesus, converts brought magical bodies to be burned (Acts 19:18ff) but Paul had to warn converts against magic (Gal 5:20).

MAGOG The second of the seven sons of Japheth (Gen 10:2; I Chr 1:5). Magog and the other Japhethites represent the peoples who lived to the north of the Fertile Crescent. In Ezekiel 38:2 "the land of Magog" refers to the place of origin of Gog, the leader of the nations Meshech and Tubal and the Lord says he will bring Gog from the north to attack Israel (Ezek 39:2). The choice of a political and military leader emanating from the far north to initiate the eschatological battle, which will culminate in many nations' knowing "that I am the Lord" (Ezek 38:23), reflects the folkloristic notion that agents of destruction emanate from the north (cf Jer 1:14; 4:6; 6:1; 13:20; 15:12; 46:20; 47:2; 50:3, 41; 51:48; Joel 2:20). When Gog's mission of destruction will have been accomplished, Magog too will be punished by fire "then they shall know that I am the Lord" (Ezek 39:6). In Revelation 20:9 Magog is not a nation or a country but a co-leader with Gog of the armies mustered by Satan against God's people.

MAGOR-MISSABIB ("terror on every side"). A symbolic name, given by Jeremiah to the priest Pashhur son of Immer, when the latter arrested him and put him in the stocks (Jer 20:3).

MAGPIASH One of those who signed the covenant of Ezra.

MAHALALEEL, MAHALALEL

1. The eldest son of Kenan, father of Jared, fifth generation to Adam.

2. A descendant of Perez the son of Judah, and an ancestor of Athaiah who settled in Jerusalem at the time of Nehemiah.

MAHALATH

1. The wife of Esau; she was a daughter of Ishmael, son of Abraham.

2. The wife of Rehoboam king of Judah and daughter of Jerimoth the son of David.

MAHALI, MAHLI

1. The eldest son of Merari the son of Levi. Eponym of a Levite family.

2. The son of Mushi and grandson of Merari.

MAHANAIM A city of Gilead, on the border between the territories of Gad and Manasseh (Josh 13:26, 30). This is the place where the angels of God met Jacob (Gen 32:1-2); one of the cities of the Levites (Josh 21:38). Abner, son of Ner, enthroned Ishbosheth, son of Saul, at Mahanaim (II Sam 2:8), and David fled there when Absalom revolted (II Sam 17:24). Solomon appointed Ahinadab, son of Iddo, over the district of which Mahanaim was the center (I Kgs 4:14). Identified with Tell edh-Dhahab el Gharbi, north of the Jabbok River.

MAHANEH DAN ("camp of Dan"). A place between Zorah and Eshtaol where the Spirit of the Lord began to move Samson (Judg 13:25). According to Judges 18:12, the Danites "went up and pitched in Kirjath Jearim, in Judah. Therefore they called that place Mahaneh Dan to this day. There it is, west of Kirjath Jearim". The geographical information is contradictory and there may have been two places by the same name. Unidentified.

MAHARAI A man of Netophah, and one of David's thirty "mighty men" (II Sam 23:28; I Chr 11:30). He is also listed as the head of the tenth division of David's army that served during the tenth month.

MAHATH

1. A Levite, son of Amasai, grandson of Elkanah and father of Elkanah.

2. Son of Amasai. One of the Levites who cleansed the Temple in the reforms of King Hezekiah.

3. A Levite, one of the officials responsible for the offerings that were brought to the Temple. Probably identical with No.2.

MAHAVITE Gentilic name imployed to describe Eliel, one of David's thirty "mighty men".

MAHAZIOTH A Levite, one of the sons of Heman, but the name may refer to a prayer rather than to a person.

MAHER-SHALAL-HASH-BAZ Symbolic name of the second son of the prophet Isaiah. It means "Pillage hastens, looting speeds", and refers to the imminent destruction of both Damascus and Samaria (Is 8:4). The prophet first wrote the words in the presence of two witnesses for all to see; and a year later, on the birth of his son, gave him the name.

MAHLAH

1. The eldest of the five daughters of Zelophehad who inherited the family territory after the death of their father.

2. Head of a clan of the tribe of Manasseh, brother of Abiezer and Ishhod.

MAHLITES Family of Levites, descended from Merari.

MAHLON One of the two sons born to Elimelech and Naomi in Bethlehem. As a result of a famine west of the Jordan the entire family went to live in Moab. After the death of Elimelech, Mahlon married the Moabite woman Ruth (Ruth 4:10) and his brother married another Moabite woman. Both Mahlon and Chilion died in Moab and when Naomi returned to her Bethlehem home, Mahlon's widow, Ruth, insisted on accompanying her.

MAHOL ("dance"). King Solomon is depicted as being wiser than any person; even wiser "than Ethan the Ezrahite and Heman, Calcol and Darda, the sons of Mahol," (I Kgs 4:31) and this contention is supported by pointing out that Solomon composed 3,000 proverbs and 1,005 songs. It appears, therefore, that the wisdom of the sons of Mahol consisted of their skills as song writers. Since the Hebrew word for "sons of" often means "members of a guild of" as in the expression "sons of the prophets" (II Kgs 6:1 etc.) and since the Hebrew noun *mahol* means "dance", it has been suggested that "the sons of Mahol" is a mistranslation which should read "members of the guild of dance musicians".

MAHSEIAH ("God is my shelter"). The grandfather of Baruch the scribe of Jeremiah (Jer 32:12), and of Seraiah who was an official of King Zedekiah (Jer 51:59).

MAKAZ The first town in the second district of Solomon's kingdom, ruled by the son of Dekar, the other towns being Shaalbim, Beth

MAHANEH
DAN
**Judg 13:25;
18:12**

MAHARAI
**II Sam 23:28.
I Chr 11:30;
27:13**

MAHATH 1
I Chr 6:35

MAHATH 2
II Chr 29:12

MAHATH 3
II Chr 31:13

MAHAVITE
I Chr 11:46

MAHAZIOTH
I Chr 25:4, 30

MAHER-SHALAL-
HASH-BAZ
Is 8:1, 3

MAHLAH 1
**Num 26:33;
27:1; 36:11.
Josh 17:3**

MAHLAH 2
I Chr 7:18

MAHLITES
**Num 3:33;
26:58**

MAHLON
**Ruth 1:2, 5;
4:9-10**

MAHOL
I Kgs 4:31

MAHSEIAH
**Jer 32:12;
51:59**

MAKAZ
I Kgs 4:9

Shemesh and Elon Beth Hanan (I Kgs 4:9). These towns were in the territory of Dan (Josh 19:41-42), and thus in the eastern part of the territory of that tribe. Makaz is identified with Khirbet Qazareh, 12½ miles (20 km) southwest of Beth Shemesh, or with Khirbet el-Mukheizin to the northwest.

MAKHELOTH One of the stations of the Children of Israel on the Exodus route (Num 33:25-26), perhaps identical with Kehelathah, mentioned in verse 22. The Hebrew name implies a place of assembly. The location is unknown, but it is identified by some with Quntilat Quraiya in the northeastern part of Sinai, some 31 miles (50 km) south of Kadesh Barnea.

MAKHELOTH
Num 33:25-26

MAKKEDAH A Canaanite city-state (Josh 15:41), conquered by Joshua (Josh 10:28). Close to it was the cave in which the corpses of five Canaanite kings were deposited (Josh 10:16-29). During the reign of Rehoboam it was conquered by Pharaoh Sheshonk I (Shishak). Identification not certain, but probably in the vicinity of Azekah and Beth Gubrin in the plain near the Judean foothills.

MAKKEDAH
Josh 10:10,
16-17, 21,
28-29; 12:16;
15:41

MAKTESH A residential district in Jerusalem, apparently lying to the west of the Temple Mount (Zeph 1:11), which was populated during the period of the Kingdom of Israel. It is possibly located on the lower ground, in the Tyropoeon Valley, between the eastern and western hills.

MAKTESH
Zeph 1:11

The Tyropoeon Valley in Jerusalem, identified as the site of the Maktesh.

MALACHI Possibly the personal name of the prophetic author of the last book of the Minor Prophets. It is also possible that the Hebrew *malachi,* which means "my messenger", refers to the prophet's divine mission (cf Mal 3:1) and that his given name is unknown. The Book of Malachi supplies no biographical details concerning the prophet. Hence the Talmudic rabbis, in accord with their tendency to identify less famous persons with their more familiar contemporaries, identified this last of the prophets with Ezra the scribe.

MALACHI
Mal 1:1

MALACHI, BOOK OF The Book of Malachi is the last book of the twelve Minor Prophets. Its contents indicate that it was written in the post-exilic period after the rebuilding of the Temple, but probably before the arrival of Ezra and Nehemiah. Especially worthy of note is this book's universalism: "For from the rising of the sun, even to its going down, my name shall be great among the Gentiles; in every place incense shall be offered to my name and a pure offering; for my name shall be great among the nations — says the Lord of hosts" (1:11).

The Book of Malachi consists of the following seven divisions: (a) 1:1-5 in which the Lord assures Israel of the permanency of his special relationship with the descendants of Jacob. (b) 1:6-2:9 in which Malachi denounces the priests for treating the Temple with contempt. 1:10 suggests that the Temple may as well be closed down if it is too burdensome for the priests and the people at large to present worthy offerings. (c) 2:10-16, in which God denounces both divorce and intermarriage with idolators. (d) 2:17-3:5, in which "the messenger of the covenant" of popular belief is transformed from Israel's guardian angel (cf Gen 48:16) to an agent of divine retribution for those who

Page from the Book of Malachi, from the Damascus Keter Torah, *Palestine, 10th century. (Jewish National and University Library)*

engage in sorcery, adultery, perjury and exploitation of the economically disadvantaged (for listing of these offenses cf Leviticus chapter 19). (e) 3:6-12, in which the Lord accuses the people of defrauding him of the tithe and the contribution prescribed in Numbers chapter 18, but promises that payment in full will be rewarded with a bountiful harvest. (f) 3:13-4:3 in which the Lord responds to the charge that the wicked and the arrogant tempt God and go free. The day is coming, it is stated, when the wicked will be destroyed and the obedient will prosper. (g) The book closes with an exhortation to be mindful of the Torah of Moses, for the prophet Elijah is about to herald "the Day of the Lord". A characteristic stylistic feature of the Book of Malachi is the disputation. While 3:5 reflects the influence of Leviticus chapter 19 and Malachi 3:8-10 refers to laws contained in Numbers chapter 18, the book's diction is most heavily influenced by Deuteronomy. Hence, for the prophetic author of this book, priests and Levites are synonymous (Mal 2:4-7), and the site of the granting of the Law is called Horeb (Mal 4:4; cf Deut 5:2) rather than Sinai (Ex chap. 19). Malachi is the first to suggest an eschatological role for Elijah (4:5). 4:4-6 has been interpreted not only as the end of this book but also as the culmination of the entire second major section of the Hebrew Bible, that of the Prophets.

```
                            OUTLINE
         1:1-5        Preamble
         1:6-2:9      Priests rebuked as responsible for spiritual
                      backsliding
         2:10-16      Denunciation of mixed marriages and of
                      divorces
         2:17-3:5     The approach of the Day of the Lord
         3:6-12       Denunciation of Jews for failing to pay
                      tithes to the Temple
         3:13-4:3     Condemnation of those who lack belief in
                      divine justice
         4:4-6        The coming of Elijah before the Day of the
                      Lord
```

MALCAM One of the heads of the clans of the tribe of Benjamin (I Chr 8:9). His mother's name was Hodesh.

MALCHIAH ("my king is God").

1. See MALCHIJAH No.3

2. Amongst those who put away their pagan wives during Ezra's reforms.

3. An official of King Zedekiah, whose title was "the son of the king"; he owned the cistern in which Jeremiah was imprisoned. The name appears on several Hebrew seals and seal-impressions from the end of the 8th to the 7th century B.C. and also on the Arad Ostraca.

MALCHIEL, MALCHIELITES ("my king is God"). The son of Beriah son of Asher and head of the Malchielite families.

MALCHIJAH ("God is king" or "God is my king").

1. A Levite, one of the ancestors of Asaph.

2. A priest or priestly family during the time of David.

3. Father of Pashhur. A priest that was one of King Zedekiah's officials. Also referred to as Malchiah in Jeremiah 38:1, and Melchiah in Jeremiah 21:1.

4. Member of the family of Parosh who had to repudiate their alien wives in the time of Ezra.

5. One of the sons of Harim who had to repudiate his alien wife in the time of Ezra (Ezra 10:31). He is also mentioned among those who took part in rebuilding the wall of Jerusalem (Neh 3:11).

6. The son of Rechab, governor of the district of Beth Haccerem, who took part in rebuilding the wall of Jerusalem in the time of Nehemiah.

7. A member of the goldsmiths' guild who took part in rebuilding the wall of Jerusalem in the time of Nehemiah.

8. One of the heads of the people who stood near Ezra while he read before the public from the Scroll of the Law.

9. Head of one of the priestly families who signed the covenant at the time of Ezra (Neh 10:3).

10. A priest who took part in the dedication of the wall of Jerusalem in the time of Nehemiah.

MALCHIRAM ("my king is exalted"). One of the sons of King Jeconiah.

MALCHISHUA ("my king is noble"). The youngest son of King Saul by his wife Ahinoam (I Sam 14:49; I Chr 8:33). He was killed by the Philistines together with his brothers and father on Mount Gilboa (I Chr 10:2).

MALCHUS The high priest's servant who accompanied Judas Iscariot and the mob to Gethsemane to arrest Jesus. The servant is given this proper name (which means "royal" in Hebrew) only in John 18:10. The story of the scuffle at the arrest is given in all four gospels (Matt 26:51; Mark 14:47; Luke 22:50-51; John 18:10). Each evangelist adds his own details. John adds the proper names Malchus and Simon Peter. In John it is Simon Peter who cuts off Malchus' right ear. In Luke the servant is healed. Later, when Jesus was brought to Caiaphas' house, one of Malchus' relatives recognized Peter, who denied for the second time being one of Jesus' disciples (John 18:26-27). It should be noted that the servant of the high priest was not an insignificant personage but the vice-president of the temple administration and, as such, suitable to be a representative of the high priest himself in the narrative.

MALCHUS
John 18:10

MALLOTHI One of the sons of Heman the singer; but the name may refer to the words of a prayer rather than to a person.

MALLOTHI
I Chr 25:4, 26

MALLOW See PLANTS

MALLUCH

1. A Levite of the Merarites, an ancestor of Ethan in Solomon's Temple.

MALLUCH 1
I Chr 6:44

2. One of the Meshullamites who married an alien woman in the time of Ezra and was forced to repudiate her.

MALLUCH 2
Ezra 10:29

3. One of the sons of Harim who married an alien woman in the time of Ezra and was forced to repudiate her.

MALLUCH 3
Ezra 10:32

4. Head of a priestly family who signed the covenant in the time of Ezra.

MALLUCH 4
Neh 10:4

5. One of the important families who signed the covenant in the time of Ezra.

MALLUCH 5
Neh 10:27

6. A priest who returned with Zerubbabel from the Exile.

MALLUCH 6
Neh 12:2

MALTA (MELITA) A small island in the center of the Mediterranean Sea, 60 miles (100 km) south of Sicily. In 218 B.C. the island passed from Carthaginian to Roman control, becoming part of the province of Sicily.

MALTA
Acts 28:1

Paul, accompanied by Luke on a journey from Crete to Rome, was shipwrecked on Malta for a period of three months (Acts 27:39-28:10). During this time he performed healings and was acclaimed by the people, whose hospitality he praised (Acts 28:2). He then continued to Rome (28:11-16). Luke refers to the inhabitants as "barbarous people" (AV: Acts 28:2) since they did not speak Greek (they probably spoke Punic). A local deity may have been *Dike* ("Justice" Acts 28:4). The site of Paul's shipwreck is traditionally held to be on the west side of St. Paul's Bay, 8 miles (13 km) northwest of modern Valetta and 4 miles (6 km) from the ancient capital of Vettia.

MAMRE Plain near Hebron, connected with the patriarchs. The Hebrew Bible uses the words *alonei mamreh*, which means "oaks of Mamreh", to refer to a grove of oaks named after Mamreh the Amorite, who dwelt near Hebron (Gen 14:13, 24). Abraham built an altar to the Lord there (Gen 13:18) and it was there that he learnt of the capture of his brother's son, Lot (Gen 14:13). The Lord appeared to Abraham there in a vision (Gen 15:1 ff) and it seems that the place where Abraham lived was soon sanctified. The Septuagint refers to "the oak of Mamreh", which would imply that one of the oaks was already being venerated as Abraham's altar. Isaac also lived there (Gen 35:27).

MAMRE
Gen 13:18;
14:13, 24;
18:1; 23:17,
19; 25:9;
35:27; 49:30;
50:13

An early tradition points to Ramat el-Khalil, 2 miles (3km) north of Hebron, as the site of Mamreh. Herod surrounded it with a beautifully built wall enclosing an area 150 feet (46m) by 200 feet (61m) in which the altar and the well of Abraham were shown. The site was destroyed during the war against the Romans (A.D. 66-70).

The miracle of Paul and the serpent at Malta shown on an 11th-century fresco at Canterbury Cathedral, England.

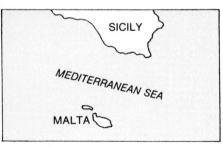

Malta.

Mamre with Herodian ruins.

MANAEN A leader of the church of Antioch; he had been a member of the court of Herod, the tetrarch (Acts 13:1). He prophesied or taught in the Antioch community.

MANAHATH

1. Second son of Shobal the second son of Seir the Horite; the ancestor of the family or clan of the Manahathites.

2. A place where people of Geb were exiled.

MANAHETHITES The name of two families or clans descended from Manahath No.1.

MANASSEH

1. The elder of Joseph's two sons by Asenath, daughter of Potiphera, the Egyptian priest of Heliopolis (the other son was Ephraim). According to I Chronicles 7:14 Manasseh had an Aramean concubine who bore Machir, the father of Gilead. The biblical account (Gen 41:51) derives the name Manasseh from the root meaning "to forget" and indicative of the joy that the newborn son brought to Joseph's life, causing him to forget the suffering he had endured. Joseph's two sons were awarded an exceptional status by their grandfather Jacob, who adopted them and accorded them equal footing with his own sons, thus making them progenitors of the two tribes named after them, Manasseh and Ephraim (Gen 48:5). Ignoring the prerogatives customarily accorded to firstborn, Jacob furthermore granted a preferential position to Ephraim, the younger son, declaring that he would surpass his brother in greatness (Gen 48:19). It is widely held, however, that this account has an etiological thrust designed to explain future historical realities.

Both tribes, Manasseh and Ephraim, hailed in the Blessing of Moses as the horns of the majestic wild ox which gores the nations (Deut 33:17), played a significant role in the history of Israel. In the account of the land of Canaan, there are numerous references to the significant contribution of Manasseh which along with the tribe of Reuben and Gad served as an armed vanguard. As a reward, Moses granted Manasseh permission to settle on the eastern side of the Jordan. It is further related that the tribe settled on both sides of the river, the eastern half north of Gad in the highlands east of Jordan, and the western half in the central highlands, north of Ephraim (Num chap. 32; Josh chaps. 13-14). A city of refuge was located in Golan, in the territory of the Manassites (Deut 4:43). Notable among the heroes listed as belonging to Manasseh are Gilead, Gideon and Jephthah, who subdued the offended men of Ephraim (Judg 12:1-4). Abimelech, who reigned over a

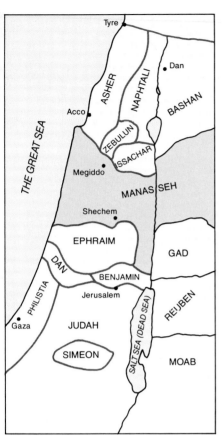

The territory of the tribe of Manasseh.

short-lived kingdom, was the son of Gideon. Manasseh was among the tribes deported by Assyria to Halah, Harbor, Hara and the River Gozan (I Chr 5:23-26), where they fell into oblivion.

2. Son of King Hezekiah of Judah. His mother was Hephzibah (II Kgs 21:1). Manasseh was 12 years old when he succeeded his father to the throne. His 55-year reign over Judah (c. 698-642 B.C.), the longest recorded in the chronicles of the Hebrew kings, is presented in both biblical accounts (II Kgs 21:1-18 and II Chr 33:1-10), as a period of precipitous religious and moral decline. In addition to abolishing the religious reforms effected by Hezekiah, Manasseh is said to have reintroduced alien cults, particularly the worship of Baal and astral deities. Furthermore, he is accused of having reestablished the rite of child sacrifice to Moloch in the Valley of Ben-Hinnom, where he immolated his own sons by fire; of having persecuted the prophets and their adherents; and of shedding innocent blood. Both accounts stress that Manasseh misled Judah into deeds of even greater evil than those of the Canaanites in pre-Israelite times.

The Book of Chronicles, however, adds a singular pericope, according to which Manasseh was captured by the Assyrians, and carried shackled in chains, to Babylon, where in his great distress he repented before the Lord, resulting in his restoration to his kingdom (II Chr 33:11-20). The historical validity of this episode is generally held to be precarious, being perhaps an attempt on the part of the Chronicler to justify the length of Manasseh's reign. It should be noted, however, that during Manasseh's time Judah was under Assyrian domination as a tribute-paying province headed by an essentially vassal monarch. This fact is well-attested in Assyrian inscriptions, one of which lists Manasseh along with 22 kings upon whom Esarhaddon imposed forced labor. He is also listed in one of Ashurbanipal's inscriptions pertaining to various armies which accompanied the Assyrian king on his campaign to Egypt. The political subordination of Judah might well account for the enormity of its relapse into idolatrous worship.

The Bible states that Manasseh's enormous sins prompted God's decision to wipe out Judah and Jerusalem (II Kgs 24:3).

3. The grandfather of Jonathan (Judg 18:30). In some Bible translations the name is given as Moses instead of Manasseh.

4. A descendant of Pahath-Moab, he was forced to repudiate his alien wife on the decree of Ezra.

5. A son of Hashum, he was forced to repudiate his alien wife on the decree of Ezra.

MANASSITES See MANASSEH No.1

MANDRAKE See PLANTS

MANNA The food eaten by the Children of Israel during their 40 years in the desert (Ex 16:14-31, etc.). It is described as "fine as frost on the ground...and the taste of it was like wafers made with honey (Ex 16:14, 31)...and its color like the color of bdellium [i.e. rock-crystal]...The people went about and gathered it, ground it on millstones or beat it in a mortar, cooked it in pans, and made cakes of it; and its taste was like the taste of pastry prepared with oil" (Num 11:7-8). Manna made its first appearance in the Wilderness of Sin when the Israelites protested to Moses and Aaron that they did not have sufficient food. God thereupon provided them with manna, commanding them to gather the required amount each day. On the sixth day they were to take a double portion as provision for the Sabbath. The daily supply of manna lasted until they arrived at the borders of Canaan (Ex 16:35), or, according to another tradition, when they entered the land of Canaan at Gilgal (Josh 5:12). To commemorate the manna, Moses commanded Aaron to put a

12:19-20, 31, 37; 26:32; 27:20-21. II Chr 15:9; 30:1, 10-11, 18; 31:1; 34:6, 9. Ps 60:7; 80:2; 108:8. Is 9:21. Ezek 48:4-5. Rev 7:6

MANASSEH 2
II Kgs 20:21; 21:1, 9, 11, 16-18, 20; 23:12, 26; 24:3. I Chr 3:13. II Chr 32:33; 33:1, 9-11, 13, 18, 20, 22-23. Jer 15:4. Matt 1:10

MANASSEH 3
Judg 18:30

MANASSEH 4
Ezra 10:30

MANASSEH 5
Ezra 10:33

MANASSITES
Deut 4:43. Judg 12:4

MANNA
Ex 16:31, 33, 35. Num 11:6-7, 9. Deut 8:3, 16. Josh 5:12. Neh 9:20. Ps 78:24. John 6:31, 49, 58. Heb 9:4. Rev 2:17

quantity (an *omer*) in a jar to be kept for all future generations (Ex 16:33).

Jesus referred to manna as the "bread of heaven", adding that he himself was the "living bread which came down from heaven". Anyone who partook of this bread would live forever (John 6:31-35; cf I Cor 10:3; Rev 2:17).

According to the most accepted interpretation, manna is the secretion of a scale-insect which feeds upon the sap of the tamarisk bush in the Sinai desert. The preservation of the name manna in Arabic may be taken as an indication of the accuracy of this identification. The honey-like excretion solidifies into dry and sticky drops. The secretion has a rough surface and is white at first, changing later to a yellowish-brown color. When kept for a long time it becomes sweet, like honey. The local Bedouins call it "manna of heaven" and cook it into a porridge which keeps for a long time. They gather it in the early morning, after the chill of the night, working in haste before it melts in the hot morning sun (cf Ex 16:21); it is then stored in tightly closed vessels to protect it from ants and prevent it from becoming infested with worms (cf Ex 16:20). In the rainy season a Bedouin can collect about 3 pounds (1.4 kg) in one morning.

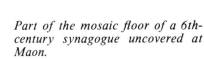

Tamarisk, believed by some scholars to be the source of manna, which is thought to be the sweet edible drops of fluid secreted by two kinds of insects living on the tree.

MANOAH ("peaceful, contented"). A man of the Danites, from Zorah, whose wife was barren until an angel of the Lord told her she would conceive a son (Judg 13:2-3). The child she bore was Samson (Judg 13:24). After his death Manoah was buried "between Zorah and Eshtaol" where his son was later brought to rest (Judg 16:31).

MANUHOTH, MANAHETHITES The name of a clan mentioned in the genealogy of the tribe of Judah. This family was related to the descendants of Shobai who dwelt in Kirjath Jearim (I Chr 2:52). Apparently half of the tribe dwelt in the territory of the clan of Salma, near Bethlehem (I Chr 2:54).

MAOCH See MAACHAH No.1

MAON, MAONITES

1. A town in the mountains of Judah (Josh 15:55) in the vicinity of the desert of Maon where David sought refuge from Saul (I Sam 23:24); it was also inhabited in the Roman period. Identified with Khirbet Main, southeast of Hebron.

MANOAH
Judg 13:2, 8-9, 11-13, 15-17, 19-22; 16:31

MANUHOTH, MANAHETHITES
I Chr 2:52, 54

MAOCH
I Sam 27:2

MAON, MAONITES 1
Josh 15:55.
Judg 10:12.
I Sam 23:24-25; 25:2

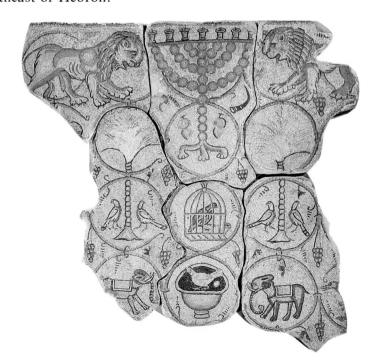

Part of the mosaic floor of a 6th-century synagogue uncovered at Maon.

2. A son of Shammai of the family of Caleb, and founder of the city of Beth Zur.

MARA ("bitter"). When Naomi returned with Ruth from Moab to Bethlehem, the whole city greeted her with the question, "Is this Naomi?" (Naomi means "pleasant"). Naomi replied, "Do not call me Naomi; call me Mara", i.e. "bitter", "for the Almighty has dealt very bitterly with me" (Ruth 1:20). Both of her sons, Mahlon and Chilion, died without progeny in Moab.

MARAH ("bitter"). One of the stations on the route of the Exodus, in the desert of Shur, where the Israelites found bitter water. Those who maintain that the Exodus took a southern course, generally identify Marah with the oasis of Ain Hauwarah, a pool of bitter water on the eastern shore of the Gulf of Suez. Those who believe that the Hebrews took a northern course look for it in the region to the east of the Sirbonian Lake (Sabhat Bardawil). Others still believe that it is identical with Kadesh Barnea.

MARALAH (MAREAL) A city which fell to the lot of the tribe of Zebulun; it was in the western part of the territory, near the boundary with Manasseh. Its location is unknown.

MARESHAH A town in the territory of Judah (Josh 15:44). Rehoboam converted Mareshah into a Judean stronghold, giving it a commander and storing food, oil and wine there (II Chr 11:8, 11). During the first half of the 9th century B.C. Zerah the Ethiopian attacked Judah, was defeated by Asa at Mareshah and was pursued as far as Gerar (II Chr 14:8-15). In the division of Judah into 12 districts (recorded in Josh chap. 15 but probably dating to the time of Jehoshaphat), Mareshah, together with Keilah, Achzib and nine other towns, formed one district.

The town was conquered by Sennacherib in 701 B.C. Although the biblical text describing his campaigns does not provide a detailed list of towns (II Kgs 18:13), Michah's lamentation over the destruction of the towns in the Plain refers to this campaign and does mention Mareshah (Mic 1:15). After 586 B.C. it fell to Idumea. From the Books of the Maccabees and from Josephus' account it is evident that Marissa was the largest and most important city of Idumea. A decline set in after its conquest by Hyrcanus in the last third of the 2nd century B.C. Although it was freed by Pompey in 63 B.C. and rebuilt by Gabinius in 57 B.C. it did not recover. During its conquest by the Parthians in 40 B.C. it was completely destroyed and was never afterwards resettled, its role being

MAON, MAONITES 2
I Chr 2:45

MARA
Ruth 1:20

MARAH
Ex 15:23.
Num 33:8-9

MARALAH
Josh 19:11

MARESHAH
Josh 15:44.
I Chr 2:42;
4:21. II Chr
11:8; 14:9-10;
20:37. Mic
1:15

Tell Sandahanna identified with ancient Mareshah.

taken over by nearby Beth Gubrin (Eleutheropolis). It is identified with Tell Sandahanna on the plain near the Judean foothills.

Excavations have revealed the Hellenistic city.

MARI One of the largest cities in Syria, on the right bank of the Euphrates, identified with Tell Hariri. Before the city had been identified, with the help of inscriptions found during the excavations, Mari was known from cuneiform texts found at Nippur and Kish, in southern Mesopotamia. It is also mentioned in the records of the campaigns of Sargon (middle of the 3rd millennium B.C.) and its capture is recorded in the letters of Hammurabi (c. 1792-1750 B.C.). This scanty evidence from external sources was much enriched by the large amount of information derived from documents found in the excavations.

The documents found in the archives of the palace of Zimrilim are of outstanding importance. They comprise some 25,000 cuneiform tablets inscribed with economic, legal and diplomatic texts. The diplomatic texts were letters sent to the Mari court by officials, neighboring kings, members of the royal family and ambassadors. These documents are dated to the first quarter of the 2nd millennium B.C. A number of the

The so-called Man of Mari, clothed in a fleece-like skirt.
Votive statue from the temple of Ishtar at Mari. Mid-3rd millennium B.C.

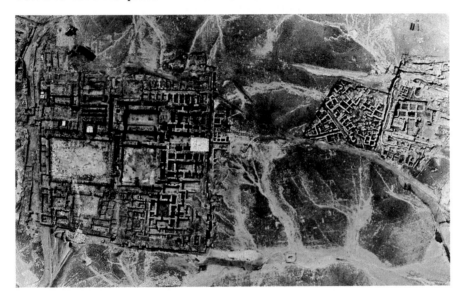

Aerial view of the excavations at Mari. (Musée du Louvre, Paris)

texts refer to the Habiru, and the tribe of the Benjamites also gets special mention. Both the Habiru and the Benjamites are linked by scholars with the early Hebrews. The economic documents relate mainly to foodstuffs supplied to the court or distributed by it, hundreds of them dealing with the daily menus of the king and his retinue. The legal texts deal mainly with sales and purchases, and loans of money and grain.

The Mari documents shed light not only on that flourishing kingdom, but also on the history of the ancient Near East and of the the early Hebrews.

Acts 12:12, 25; 15:37, 39. Col 4:10. II Titus 4:11. Philem v. 24. 1 Pet 5:13

MARK A Jew from Jerusalem, whose full name was John Mark (Acts 12:12). His mother was Mary, whose house served as a meeting place for the first Christians (Acts 12:12). Mark was a cousin of Barnabas (Col 4:10) whom he accompanied when Barnabas and Paul left Jerusalem after the persecution of Herod Agrippa (Acts 12:25; 13:1) and on their first missionary journey (Acts 13:5), but at a certain point he left them and went back to Jerusalem (Acts 13:13). Paul decided not to take him with them on the second journey although Barnabas disagreed: "And Barnabas was determined to take with them John, called Mark. But Paul insisted that they should not take with them the one who had departed from them in Pamphylia, and had not gone with them to the work" (Acts 15:37-38). Paul and Barnabas separated and Barnabas went with Mark to Cyprus (Acts 15:39). Years later Mark joined Paul again (Col 4:10), and it seems that Paul had forgiven him and he calls him a "fellow-laborer" (Philem v. 24). Mark probably assisted both Paul and Peter in Rome. A strong suggestion in this direction is contained in the Epistle of Peter "She (the church) who is in Babylon (Rome), elect together with you, greets you; and so does Mark my son" (I Pet 5:13). This passage shows the relationship between Peter and Mark, and that both had been working in Rome. It has therefore been suggested that the Gospel of Mark had its origin in Rome, written for the Roman Christians.

MARK, GOSPEL OF The second of the four gospels in the NT canon. Since it is placed second in the NT arrangement of writings, and contains fewer teachings of Jesus and less narrative cohesiveness than the gospels of Matthew and Luke, it was relatively neglected in the Christian tradition until the modern period. (John, the fourth gospel, is difficult to compare to the other three, which scholars call the "synoptics", because they are obviously related to one another in composition and can easily be compared).

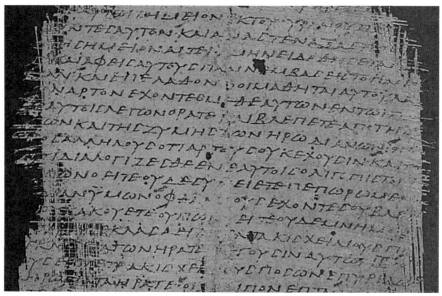

Entrance to St Mark's Church, built on the site believed to be that of Mark's house in Jerusalem.

(right)
Fragment of the Gospel of Mark (8:10-26) from a Greek papyrus of the 3rd century A.D. (Chester Beatty Library)

With the emergence of historical criticism in the 19th century, however, a documentary hypothesis postulated Mark to have been the first gospel written, subsequently being used, conjunctly with a collection of the sayings of Jesus, by Matthew and Luke. The importance of eschatology (message or doctrine of last things) in Mark was a key factor in the revised view of Jesus' message that came about in 20th century German scholarship.

But more recent interest, certainly in North America, has to do with Mark's literary and Christological peculiarities ("Christology" means doctrine concerning the Christ). The writer of Mark was a theologian who communicated his message of good news ("gospel") in story form. As a narrative theologian, Mark's style leaves much unspoken, and even the things that are expressed are often put in the form of allusion. In fact, it appears that the gospel writer deliberately created gaps in the narrative. Along with these gaps there are puzzling teachings of Jesus and a number of repeated episodes and motifs. It is coming to be recognized in current literary criticism of the Bible that Mark's way of shaping the narrative is bound up with the content of his theology, which is centered in God's presence in the suffering Son of man and the coming of the Son of man in the consummation of the Kingdom of God.

This style and theology cannot be adequately accounted for by the Christian tradition that John Mark (see Acts 12:12) was the interpreter of Peter's account of the sayings and deeds of the Lord. This tradition goes back to an exposition of Jesus' teachings written by Papias, bishop of Hierapolis, c. A.D. 140. The basic concern of the post-apostolic church was to link each of the gospels to one of the apostles. If Papias' account and certain other early traditions are accepted, then the Gospel of Mark was based on Peter's words and would have been written shortly after the latter's death during the Neronian persecution, c. A.D. 64-65. And in fact, modern criticism forms a consensus that Mark was written between A.D. 65 and 70. However, this gospel probably owes little to Peter's memories of Jesus. For one thing, Mark creates a very negative picture of the apostles, and of Peter above all. The total effect of Mark, if it is read carefully, is to undercut apostolic authority.

Indeed, one of the most troublesome features of Mark for those inclined to take it literally as "history" in the sense of modern factual historiography, is precisely the difficulty that the twelve disciples have in comprehending the mystery of the Kingdom of God (Mark 4:11-13). This mystery has its locus in the suffering of the Son of man. "Son of man" is a title of rather nebulous Jewish origins which occurs frequently in the gospels. Its usage was more or less dropped in the later tradition, probably because few people understood it. For Mark it was associated both with the imminent apocalypse (Mark chap. 13) and with the suffering of the Lord's chosen one. The suffering servant of the Lord (Is 52:13-53:12) is one of Mark's primary biblical paradigms. It is in the combination of the suffering and death of the messiah that the early believers departed from the mainstream Jewish tradition, and Mark makes a point of showing that the twelve have no comprehension of the Son of man's suffering (Mark 8:27-33; 9:9-13; 10:35-45). The "outsiders" are not supposed to understand the mystery of the Kingdom, but the disciples are (4:11). This mystery is concealed from the public until Jesus is brought before the high priest after his arrest (14:62), but the mystery revealed in the Son of man's suffering and death is stated "plainly" to the intimate followers (8:32). Still they do not comprehend.

This picture of the apostles is reinforced by the abrupt ending of the gospel. Three women go to the tomb where Jesus' body has been laid and there encounter a young man dressed in a white robe, who tells them, "Do not be alarmed. You seek Jesus of Nazareth, who was crucified. He is risen! He is not here. See the place where they laid him. But go and tell his disciples — and Peter — that he is going before you into Galilee; there you will see him, as he said to you." (16:6-7). But the women run away in fear — and there the gospel ends. Some interpreters hold it could not have terminated there; surely something has been lost which relates that the disciples were informed by the women and subsequently reunited with their risen Master. Their position is supported by some Greek manuscripts (especially *Codex Alexandrinus*) where there is a longer ending which, however, is absent from other important manuscripts, particularly *Codex Sinaiticus* and *Vaticanus*. Most modern critics conclude that the longer ending (16:9-20) is an attempt by some person(s) in the chain of tradition to give the narrative a satisfactory conclusion after the model of Matthew, Luke and John. In fact, however, the abrupt breaking off of the story at 16:8 is of a piece with the perspective and style of the rest of the gospel. Mark's style is characteristically enigmatic and abrupt, and he does not picture the apostles as the authentic link to Jesus and the meaning of his mission. That link is rather the written text of the Gospel of Mark. Mark's story implies that the gospel narrative itself is the best guide to the teachings of Jesus and his sacrificial death. This position, which includes a strong polemic against apostolic authority centered in Jerusalem, functions to counteract the influence of oral tradition and the many charismatic preachers that traveled about in the first century of Christianity.

It is certain that there was a vital oral tradition in early Christianity. This fact, taken with the peculiarities of Mark's style, has led most modern critics to the view that Mark is simply a collection of oral traditions strung together, with an occasional imposition of the editor's theological bias. However, in North America a very different approach became discernible in the 1960's and has blossomed since the 1970's. It may be characterized as "literary criticism" in a sense similar to the usage in literature faculties. From the standpoint of literary criticism, Mark is the work of one writer and is a deliberately plotted narrative. The author undoubtedly used many prior oral and written traditions, and the seams of these primitive stories and teachings show through. But in many instances what seem to be lacunae or inconsistencies really belong to the style of the writer.

The theology of the Gospel of Mark is informed by the overlapping motifs of (a) the coming Kingdom of God, which is associated with the advent of the Son of man and (b) the eternal Kingdom of God, which means that God is present in the present.

(a) Mark's language of rapid action and astonishment suggests the powerful and empowering presence of God in the person and work of Jesus. Jesus begins his ministry in Galilee by announcing, "The time is fulfilled and the Kingdom of God is at hand. Repent and believe in the gospel" (Mark 1:15). Perhaps the central signifier of the coming Kingdom in Mark is the final meal of Jesus with the twelve disciples (14:12-26). "Assuredly I say to you, I will no longer drink of the fruit of the vine until that day when I drink it new in the Kingdom of God" (14:25).

The blessing and breaking of the bread, which Jesus offers parabolically as his body (14:22), is prefigured in the two accounts of the feeding of the multitude (6:30-44 and 8:1-10). The great amount of bread and fish left over implies that the feeding will continue, the compassionate shepherd will not cease to guide and nourish his sheep. In these wilderness feeding episodes the use of the imperfect tense is striking in 6:41 and 8:6, which read literally: "and he was giving them [the broken loaves] to his disciples to set before the people". The use of the imperfect, surrounded otherwise by verbs expressing completed action in the past, indicates parabolically that this One keeps on giving to his people. The Kingdom of God comes as the divine power which gives and keeps on giving.

(b) If the Kingdom is future, it is also present. In Mark the presence of God presents itself above all in three sets of metaphors: (1) Sea and boat — Jesus teaches beside the Sea of Galilee (3:7; 4:1) and crosses the lake frequently with his disciples. These lake crossings "to the other side" (4:35 *passim*) both enframe the wilderness feedings (4:35-41; 8:10-21) and divide them (6:45-52). The lake crossings suggest, in a sort of metonymic function, the Presence that moves between life and death, that leads over deep waters into foreign territory (the other side of the lake was Gentile country). As Jesus crosses the deep and sometimes troubled waters to non-Jewish territory and returns then to Galilee, so also he endures suffering and death on the cross to rise and return to

Galilee. The boat in which he travels is the vessel of faith that transports the fellowship of the faithful. (2) The bread in the wilderness. The bread given by Jesus in the wilderness satisfies; it is a concrete expression of the divinely given life and redemption. Whoever belongs to the Son of man is a "companion" (according to its etymology, "sharer of bread"). (3) The body and blood. The ultimate parable of Presence is Jesus' act of associating the bread and cup with his body and blood, as enacted at the last meal. The broken bread is a reminder of the giving of bread in the wilderness, but also a token of the divine plenitude that is always "left over." The wine of the cup is a remembrance of the service of healing, exorcism and feeding, and above all, of the giving of divine life that many may be renewed in the "blood of the covenant". The fulfillment of this acted parable is narrated in the rest of chapter 14 and in chapter 15. With Jesus' death on the cross, the tearing of the Temple curtain, and the Roman centurion's outcry that "Truly this man was the Son of God" (15:37-39), the Presence moves out into the Gentile world. That is, the Gospel of Mark says in narrative fashion that the Presence, no longer confined to the inner sanctum of the Temple, now moves out into the world through the death of the suffering one "who serves many well" (Is 53:11, Greek translation).

OUTLINE

1:1-13	Beginning of the ministry of Jesus
1:14-7:23	Jesus' ministry in Eastern Galilee
7:24-9:50	His ministry in Northern Galilee
10:1-31	Journey to Perea
10:32-13:32	Journey to Jerusalem and the last days
14:1-15:47	The Passion
16:1-20	The Resurrection and Ascension

MAROTH
Mic 1:12

MAROTH A town on the western slopes of the Judean Hills, mentioned only once in the Bible, in Micah 1:12.

MARRIAGE The Bible regards marriage as the natural ideal and as a source of fulfillment and blessing. This concept is established at the outset in the first story of creation: "It is not good that the man should be alone; I will make him a helper comparable to him" (Gen 2:18) and "A man shall leave his father and mother, and be joined to his wife, and they shall become one flesh" (Gen 2:24).

Biblical references perceive a twofold purpose in marriage. The first is procreation — "Be fruitful and multiply" (Gen 1:28); when this is realized, it is a source of great blessing (Gen 9:1; 13:16; 22:17; Ps 127:3-5; 128) whereas childlessness is a tragedy and even a disgrace (Gen 16:4; 30:1-23).

In addition, marriage should be a source of satisfying companionship. "He who finds a wife finds a good thing" (Prov 18:22). The final chapter of Proverbs paints an idealized picture of the good wife and of her beneficial influence on her household. However, the Wisdom literature also contains a few uncomplimentary references to an unworthy wife (Prov 12:4; 14:1).

Wives assumed a position of significance; their views were respected and even accepted, for example, in the stories of Sarah and Rebekah (Gen 16:5-6; 21:12; 27:1ff). This is not to imply that there was equality between husband and wife, but to suggest that the wife's role could be quite central. However, the husband could revoke a vow that his wife had made to God (Num 30:10-14), and wives were occasionally classified along with chattel (Jer 6:12). In general they were subordinated to their husband who could determine their fate.

Polygamy was sanctioned in biblical times. Kings and the upper classes were permitted more than one wife (Gen 29:18, 25, 30; Deut 21:15; Judg 8:30; I Kgs 11:1-8; II Chr 11:21). The reasons for polygamy were love, desire for children, or political diplomacy. Yet there was an ideal of monogamy (Gen 2:24; Ps 128) as implied by many of the biblical laws (Ex 20:17; Lev 18:8, 16, 20; 21:13; Num 5:12; Deut 5:21; 22:22) and supported by the frequent description of God's relationship with his chosen people Israel through the metaphor of the husband-wife bond. Clearly such a literary device would have its point only within a monogamous framework.

There is reference to a covenant in marriage relations (Prov 2:17; Mal 2:14). Marriages were usually arranged by parents (Gen 21:21; 24:1-67; 28:2; 29:23, 28). In contracting a marriage, the bride's consent was also to be taken into consideration (Gen 24:5, 58). The husband paid the father of the bride for his daughter (Gen 31:15).

The first stage in marriage was betrothal, whereby both partners were mutually bound in a legal relationship which gave them married status, although the couple did not live together as husband and wife until the man took the woman to his home to consummate the marriage (Deut 20:7). But a betrothed woman was already under the ban of extra-marital relationships (Deut 22:23-26). At the wedding ceremony itself, the bride was veiled (Gen 24:65); she wore special wedding attire (Is 61:10); and the wedding feast lasted seven days (Judg 14:12).

Marriage was strictly within the clan or tribe (Gen 24:4; 28:2; 29:19). Basically, this exclusivity was important for religious reasons (Ex 34:16; Deut 7:3-5) although economic factors also demanded that women who inherited land should marry within their own tribe, to prevent tribal land passing to extra-tribal descendants (Num 36:1-13). However, marriages outside of the clan are also recorded (Gen 36:2; 41:45; Ex 2:21; Lev 24:10; Ruth 1:4). In the post-exilic period those who married alien women were forced to repudiate them (Ezra 10:1ff).

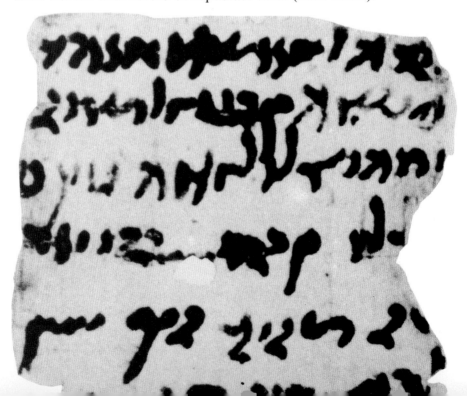

Marriage deed.

Biblical marriage law is conditioned by further regulations. Levirate marriage required a surviving brother to marry his deceased brother's childless widow (Deut 25:5ff). This seems to have been a very ancient and widespread practice (Gen 38:8; Ruth 3:12-13) serving to retain inherited property within the tribe, and perpetuate the name and line of the deceased. Should the surviving brother refuse to marry his widowed sister-in-law, she could obtain a "release" from him after which she was free to marry anyone else (Deut 25:7-10).

The Bible prohibits marriage with certain categories of individuals, such as blood relations, as well as the wives of blood relations, whether of the husband or wife (Lev 18:6-18; Deut 27:20-23). Biblical law also excludes certain other groups such as the sexually self-mutilated for idolatrous purposes, the issue of an act of incestuous union, and an Ammonite or a Moabite because of their historical cruelty to Israel (Deut 23:2-7).

The institution of marriage does not figure prominently in the NT writings. The fact that Jesus, John the Baptist and Paul were unmarried, constituted a deviation from normal Jewish practice. Certain sayings, notably Luke 14:26: "If anyone comes to me and does not hate his father and mother, wife and children, brothers and sisters, yes, and his own life, also he cannot be my disciple" place all institutions, including marriage, secondary to following Jesus or the Kingdom of God.

Jesus' views on marriage emerge from the decisions he was asked to render about divorce (Mark 10:2-9). He clearly affirmed that the marriage bond is rooted in the creative act of God himself; that the union is indissoluble; and that persons become an integral part of each other when they marry. His highest tribute to marriage is his use of it as a symbol to illustrate the nature of the Kingdom (Luke 5:34-35). The most positive contribution Jesus made to the institution of marriage derived from the place he allotted to women. By treating them fully as humans he gave an impetus to marriage unprecedented in history, for he revolutionized the institution of marriage by liberating one partner in it thus allowing the potential of such a union to be realized. Marriage was no longer seen as an institution for procreation but rather, as an aspect of the Kingdom and as a context in which people could serve the creator.

In Pauline congregations problems arose from implementing this radical view of a woman's role in marriage. There is moreover evidence that Paul had to practice accommodation to his society. Nevertheless, like Jesus, he used the wedding or marriage metaphor to illustrate the profoundest truths (Eph 5:25ff) and did not hesitate to prescribe the most detailed codes of conduct for married people including the frequency of intercourse (as often as either partner likes cf I Cor 7:2-5). While there are some indications that Paul saw marriage primarily as an anodyne for sexual drives (I Thes 4:1-6; cf I Cor 7:2), on the whole he perceived it as a partnership between two people committed to carrying out a higher will than their own. For this reason the household codes (Eph 5:22ff; Col 3:18ff) for which there was much precedent in his world, can be seen as fully integrated into his Christology for this is what it means to be "in Christ".

In the latter part of the NT, there is an apparently defensive attitude towards the institution of marriage (Heb 13:4), and even some hints favoring celibacy (Matt 19:12; Rev 14:4) but these views did not succeed. The overall position of the early church is that marriage and family are valid ways of serving the Lord and that whether one stays single or marries, both can be done fully in the Lord and each person must determine his or her calling. See also DIVORCE.

MARSENA One of the seven princes of the provinces of Persia and Media consulted by King Ahasuerus when Queen Vashti defied him.

MARTHA Sister of Mary No.3 and Lazarus. When Jesus visited them at their home in Bethany, it fell to Martha to serve him (John 12:2), while Mary sat at his feet. Martha asked him to tell her sister to help her to prepare the meal, but Jesus rebuked her for being "troubled about many things" while Mary had chosen "that good part" (Luke 10:38ff). Martha and her sister sent for Jesus when their brother Lazarus fell ill (John 11:3).

MARTHA
Luke 10:38,
40-41. John
11:1, 5, 19-21,
24, 30, 39;
12:2

MARY

1. Mother of Jesus. Mary was betrothed to Joseph (Matt 1:18; Luke 1:27; 2:5) when the angel Gabriel appeared to her and announced that she would bear a son, conceived by the Holy Spirit. Following the intervention of an angel of the Lord, Joseph nevertheless married her (Matt 1:20, 24). During her pregnancy she visited her cousin Elizabeth, the future mother of John the Baptist, who lived in a village in Judah, traditionally identified as Ein Kerem near Jerusalem. It was on this occasion that she praised the Lord in a hymn (Luke 1:39-56) which has become part of church liturgy as the *Magnificat.*

MARY 1
Matt 1:16, 18,
20; 2:11;
13:55. Mark
6:3. Luke
1:27, 30, 34,
38-39, 41, 46,
56; 2:5, 16,
19, 34. Acts
1:14

The chapel of Mary's Well below the Church of the Annunciation in Nazareth, said to be where Mary came to fetch water for her family.

After the birth of Jesus in Bethlehem (Luke 2:1-20), Joseph took his wife and child to Egypt to escape Herod's fury (Matt 2:14). After Herod's death, the family returned and settled in Nazareth in Galilee (Matt 2:22). According to Matthew (13:55) Mary had four other sons, as well as daughters (these are sometimes understood to be Jesus' cousins). She stood, together with two other Mary's (see Nos. 2 and 5 below) at the foot of the cross at the time of her son's crucifixion, and after his death she was taken into the home of "the disciple whom he loved" (John 19:25-27), usually assumed to be John. With her other sons and the disciples, Mary was among the people who gathered for prayer in Jerusalem after Jesus' ascension to heaven (Acts 1:14).

The apocryphal gospels (especially the Protevangelium of James) relate that Anna, "whose womb the Lord hath shut up", gave birth to Mary after Joachim her husband had fasted and prayed for 40 days and 40 nights in the wilderness. The veneration of Mary as the Virgin Mother of God was developed in these apocryphal writings as well as in the devotion of later Christians. See also VIRGIN BIRTH.

MARY 2
Matt 27:56,
61; 28:1. Mark
15:40, 47;
16:1, 9. Luke
8:2; 24:10.
John 19:25;
20:1, 11, 16,
18

2. A woman from Magdala (present-day Migdal) in Galilee, who, having been set free from evil spirits (Luke 8:2), became a faithful follower of Jesus. She was present at the crucifixion, "looking on from afar" (Matt 27:56; Mark 15:40; John 19:25) and was one of the women watching when Jesus was laid in his grave (Matt 27:61; Mark 15:47). On the third day she and others went to anoint Jesus' body (Mark 16:1), but found the grave empty. An angel told them that he had risen from the dead. According to John, Jesus himself appeared to her, but she did not recognize him until he called her by her name (John 20:14ff). The disciples at first did not believe her story (Luke 24:11).

3. Sister of Martha and Lazarus, who lived in Bethany, near Jerusalem (John 11:1). She was praised by Jesus for choosing "the best part" — sitting at his feet and listening to his words (Luke 10:42). When their brother Lazarus fell ill, Martha and Mary sent for Jesus (John 11:3). But Lazarus died before he came and Mary rebuked him: "If you had been here my brother would not have died" (John 11:32). After Lazarus was raised from the dead, Mary anointed Jesus' feet with myrrh and wiped them with her hair (John 12:1-8); however, the parallel story in Luke 7:37-38 seems to attribute the act to a different person.

4. Mother of John Mark. Peter came to her house after his miraculous escape from prison.

MARY 5
Matt 27:56,
61; 28:1. Mark
15:40, 47;
16:1. Luke
24:10. John
19:25

5. Mother of James and Joseph (Matt 27:56; Mark 15:40), called by Matthew "the other Mary" (Matt 27:61; 28:1). She had followed Jesus from Galilee, and watched from a distance, together with Mary, the mother of Jesus, and Mary of Magdala, when Jesus was crucified (Matt 27:55-56). She was also among the women who went to the grave to anoint his body (Mark 15:47; Luke 24:10). According to John (19:25) she was a sister of Mary, Jesus' mother, and the wife of Clopas.

6. A member of the Christian congregation in Rome "who labored much for us", to whom Paul sent his greetings.

MASH Son of Aram a grandson of Noah. In I Chronicles 1:17 he is called Meshech.

MASHAL Alternative spelling of MISHAL.

MASREKAH The city of Samlah, the fifth "of the kings that ruled in Edom before any king reigned over the Children of Israel". Its location is unknown.

MASSA Seventh of the 12 sons of Ishmael, the son of Abraham by Hagar the Egyptian.

MASSAH and
MERIBAH
Ex 17:7. Num
20:13, 24;
27:14. Deut
6:16; 9:22;
32:51; 33:8. Ps
81:7. Ezek
47:19; 48:28

MASSAH and MERIBAH Names of two places in Rephidim, so called because it was there that the Children of Israel tempted the Lord, saying "Is the Lord among us, or not?" (Ex 17:7). The cause of the quarrel (*massah* and *meribah* both mean quarrel in Hebrew) was the lack of water at Rephidim.

MATRED The mother of Mehetabel, the wife of King Hadar of Edom, in the genealogy of Edom.

MATRI A family or clan of the tribe of Benjamin. Saul the son of Kish, who was chosen by Samuel to be the first king of Israel, belonged to this family.

MATTAN ("gift of the Lord").

1. A priest of Baal in Jerusalem at the time of Athaliah; he was killed after her execution.

2. Father of Shephatiah, one of the leaders of Judah at the time of King Zedekiah.

MATTANAH One of the stations of the Children of Israel on the route of the Exodus (Num 21:18-19), to the east of the Jordan. Eusebius (*Onom.* 126:14) locates Mattanem on the bank of the Arnon, 12 miles (19 km) east of Medeba; it is consequently identified with Khirbet el-Medeyineh, southeast of Medeba, on the banks of Wadi eth-Thamad, a tributary of the Arnon, but this identification remains uncertain.

MATTANIAH ("gift of the Lord").

1. An uncle of King Jehoiachin of Judah, crowned in his stead by King Nebuchadnezzar of Babylon, who changed his name to Zedekiah. His mother was Hamutal, the daughter of Jeremiah of Libnah.

2. Name of some Levites, descendants of Asaph who returned from the Exile in Babylon and settled in Jerusalem; they participated in the thanksgiving choir.

3. One of the sons of Heman; he was in charge of the ninth division of musicians in the House of the Lord at the time of King David.

4. A Levite of the sons of Asaph, father of Jeiel and grandfather of Benaiah No.5. He helped cleanse the House of the Lord at the time of King Hezekiah of Judah.

5. A Levite also of the sons of Asaph who helped cleanse the House of the Lord at the time of Hezekiah, king of Judah.

6. A son of Elam who was among those who, having taken pagan wives, had to repudiate them according to the decree of Ezra.

7. Son of Zattu; he had to repudiate his pagan wife.

8. A son of Pahath-Moab who, having taken a pagan wife, had to repudiate her.

9. One of the sons of Bani who, having taken a pagan wife, had to repudiate her.

10. Father of Zaccur and grandfather of Hanan, he was one of the treasurers in the House of the Lord at the time of Nehemiah; perhaps identical with No.2.

11. A Levite gatekeeper in charge of guarding the storehouses of the gates in Jerusalem.

MATTATHAH ("gift of the Lord"). Grandson of David and father of Menan in the genealogy of Jesus according to Luke.

MATTATHIAH ("gift of Yah"). The name of two ancestors of Jesus in the genealogy of Luke.

MATTATTAH ("gift of [Yah]"). Son of Hashum, and one of the Israelites who divorced his foreign wife under Ezra's reform.

MATTENAI ("gift of the Lord").

1. A son of Hashum who, having taken a pagan wife, had to repudiate her according to the decree of Ezra.

2. One of the sons of Bani who, having taken pagan wives, had to repudiate them according to the decree of Ezra.

3. Head of the priestly family of Joiarib at the time of Joiakim the high priest.

MATTHAN ("present"). Son of Eleazar and father of Jacob who was the father of Joseph in the genealogy of Jesus according to Matthew.

MATTHAT ("gift of the Lord"). The name of two of the ancestors of Jesus in the genealogy according to Luke:

1. Son of Levi father of Heli and grandfather of Joseph.

2. Son of Levi and father of Jorim.

MATTHEW Apostle and evangelist. His name occurs in all four lists of the twelve apostles (Matt 10:3; Mark 3:18; Luke 6:15; Acts 1:13). In Matthew 10:3 he is described as a publican or tax-collector. The call of Matthew by Jesus is recorded in Matthew 9:9 (in the parallel passages in Mark 2:14 and Luke 5:27 the name of the person called is given as Levi).

According to the early Christian writer Papias, Matthew made a collection of Jesus' sayings in Hebrew. If, as is now often assumed, there is no basis for the traditional view that Matthew composed the first gospel (see following entry), then Papias' statement could be understood as crediting the apostle with collecting the sayings of Jesus

St Matthew portrayed as a scribe holding a parchment scroll in a Byzantine illuminated manuscript.

MATTANIAH 1
II Kgs 24:17

MATTANIAH 2
I Chr 9:15.
Neh 11:17, 22;
12:8, 35

MATTANIAH 3
I Chr 25:4, 16

MATTANIAH 4
II Chr 20:14

MATTANIAH 5
II Chr 29:13

MATTANIAH 6
Ezra 10:26

MATTANIAH 7
Ezra 10:27

MATTANIAH 8
Ezra 10:30

MATTANIAH 9
Ezra 10:37

MATTANIAH 10
Neh 13:13

MATTANIAH 11
Neh 12:25

MATTATHAH
Luke 3:31

MATTATHIAH
Luke 3:25-26

MATTATTAH
Ezra 10:33

MATTENAI 1
Ezra 10:33

MATTENAI 2
Ezra 10:37

MATTENAI 3
Neh 12:19

MATTHAN
Matt 1:15

MATTHAT 1
Luke 3:24

MATTHAT 2
Luke 3:29

MATTHEW
Matt 9:9;
10:3. Mark
3:18. Luke
6:15. Acts 1:13

in a hypothetical document partially preserved in Matthew and Luke and dubbed by scholars the "Sayings Source" or "Q". In that case the evangelist, i.e., the author of the final form of the first gospel in Greek, would be a different person from the apostle. This final evangelist may have penned his own portrait in Matthew 13:52.

According to Eusebius (*Church History* III 24) Matthew preached to the Hebrews. Other traditions about his later life conflict and are probably legendary. Thus his martyrdom has been located respectively in Ethiopia, in Persia and in Pontus. Salerno and other places have laid claim to his relics. In Christian symbolism Matthew has commonly been allotted the figure of a man (cf Rev 4:7) on the ground that he emphasizes the humanity of Christ.

MATTHEW, GOSPEL OF Heading the usual order of NT books, Matthew was also the gospel most influential in preaching and worship for most of Christian history. But many scholars today maintain that it was not the first gospel to be composed, nor was it written, in its final Greek form, by the apostle Matthew. The gospel as known is best understood as a work of mature synthesis, combining the oldest gospel, Mark, which it reproduces almost completely, with an early collection of sayings of Jesus ("Q") which it shares with the Gospel According to Luke. The final evangelist completed this combination with a special introduction and conclusion, as well as with supporting quotations from the OT and some explanatory matter. (Since Matthew derives from Mark on this hypothesis, it is unlikely that the gospel was written by an eyewitness who would find no need to copy from someone who was not. The apostle Matthew may, however, have been at the start of the gospel tradition if he gathered the sayings of Jesus together in a document which became "Q".)

The masterpieces of the gospel are its series of major discourses or speeches of Jesus (the Sermon on the Mount, chaps. 5-7, the mission

Jesus and his ancestry (Matt 1:1-17) as shown on the mosaic ceiling of the 14th-century Kariye Church in Istanbul, Turkey.

discourse in chap. 10, the parables of the kingdom in chap. 13, the discourse on Christian community living in chap. 18 and the final, endtime warnings in chaps. 23-25). These discourses, as well as other aspects of the gospel, show the hand of a master teacher. Little is known of this anonymous Christian scribe (see his autobiography in 13:52, rather than 9:9-13). Some have thought of him as a concerted rabbi and catechist. This may be presuming too much, but it can certainly be said that he had a good Jewish education, including both Bible and legal tradition, and that he was a lucid teacher with a concern for the church and its leaders.

His work has been described as a textbook for Christian leaders, but it is first of all a gospel, a presentation of the birth, ministry of teaching and healing, death and resurrection of Jesus Christ. Thus the gospel is a narrative enriched with instructional material for the contemporary church. It has also been suggested that it is the product of the first Christian school of higher biblical studies and that it was intended as a Christian response to the challenge represented by the codifying activities of the contemporary rabbis at Jamnia, but these are bolder theories.

The theological characteristics which distinguish Matthew's gospel are as follows. It is the gospel which has the strongest Jewish flavor. This works in two ways. Matthew employs Scripture texts to argue fine points of the law. But the gospel is also deeply involved in debate with contemporary Judaism and has harsh things to say about the Pharisees (cf chap. 23). It has been called the great gospel of the church. It is the only gospel to mention the word church (16:18; 18:17) and the promise to Peter (16:18-19) and, for the most part, it is concerned to put the disciples in a good light, to show them as usually understanding the Lord (13:51), and to transfer the authority of Jesus to them (9:8). One chapter is devoted to church order (18). It is an orderly gospel, didactic and catechetic for ready learning, and provides much of the teaching of Jesus, especially legal and ethical instruction. One of its major themes is justice (righteousness). It is interested in debating with the rabbis. Whereas Jesus had called God "Father" or "*Abba*", the gospel often writes "my (or: our) heavenly Father (or: who art in heaven)". It concentrates on Jesus as the son of David, Son of God, and Son of man, but neglects the Holy Spirit (in comparison with Luke or John), except indirectly through its interest in prophecy and fulfillment of prophecy and the rest of Scripture. In comparison with Mark and John it shows a special interest in angels.

It is not known when or where the gospel was first composed, nor for whom. If it was by an apostle it would most likely have been written shortly before A.D. 70, but its apparent awareness of the fall of Jerusalem which took place in that year (24:2, 28), and its dialogue with post-fall Judaism, now has it commonly dated between A.D. 75 and 85 or 90. Many places have been suggested as the site of its composition. Antioch (in modern Turkey) or somewhere else in Syria, preferably further south, as well as Tyre and Sidon in Lebanon, are often mentioned. Caesarea Maritima, the capital of Roman Palestine, should also be considered because of its closeness to the center of Pharisaic reform and because Jerome claims to have seen the Aramaic original of Matthew there. Other possibilities are Alexandria or Edessa. The audience of the gospel, the original community, must have been a mixed community, or a community in transition from being predominantly Jewish Christians to one which was not only Greek-speaking but accepted Gentile members and certainly was favorable to the Gentile mission (28:16-20).

Various outlines of the gospel are possible but this one shows the alternation of narrative (N) and sermon (S) in a series of concentric circles called ring composition.

OUTLINE

1:1-4:25	Genealogy, birth, beginning of the public ministry (N)
5:1-7:29	The Sermon on the Mount (S)
8:1-9:38	Ten miracles (N)
10:1-42	Missionary address to the apostles (S)
11:1-12:50	Rejection of Jesus by the Jews (N)
13:1-58	Seven parables of the Kingdom of God (S)
14:1-17:27	Christ acknowledged by the disciples (N)
18:1-35	Authority and forgiveness in the community (S)
19:1-22:46	Authority and invitation (N)
23:1-25:46	Woes against the Pharisees and eschatological discourse (S)
26:1-28:20	Passion, death, and resurrection; missionary command (N)

MATTHIAS
Acts 1:23, 26

MATTITHIAH 1
I Chr 9:31

MATTITHIAH 2
I Chr 15:18, 21; 16:5; 25:3, 21

MATTITHIAH 3
Ezra 10:43

MATTITHIAH 4
Neh 8:4

MEARAH
Josh 13:4

MEBUNNAI
II Sam 23:27

MECHERATHITE
I Chr 11:36

MECONAH
Neh 11:28

MEDAD
Num 11:26-27

MEDAN
Gen 25:2.
I Chr 1:32

MEDE
Dan 5:31; 11:1

MEDEBA
Num 21:30.
Josh 13:9, 16.
I Chr 19:7. Is 15:2

MATTHIAS ("gift of the Lord"). The disciple of Jesus chosen to fill the place of Judas among the twelve apostles after the betrayal. Nothing more is known of him.

MATTITHIAH ("gift of Yah").

1. Son of Shallum, a Levite, descendant of Korah (I Chr 9:31). Mattithiah was responsible for making the flat cakes of the meal-offering.

2. A Levite, son of Jeduthun, he became head of one of the groups of musicians in the sanctuary.

3. An Israelite among those who divorced their foreign wives under Ezra's reforms.

4. One of those who stood by Ezra at the public reading of the Law.

MEARAH A city or place belonging to the Sidonians and among the territories Joshua failed to conquer. Its location is unknown beyond the fact that it was in the vicinity of Sidon.

MEBUNNAI Mebunnai the Hushathite was one of David's thirty "mighty men". In I Chronicles 11:29; 27:11, the name appears as Sibbecai.

MECHERATHITE An epithet affixed to the name of Hepher, one of David's "mighty men". It should probably be Maacathite as in II Samuel 23:34.

MECONAH ("foundation"). One of the towns in southern Judah settled by the exiles who had returned from Babylon.

MEDAD ("beloved" [by God]). An Israelite who, together with Eldad, was among the 70 elders chosen to assist Moses in the desert. While all the others prophesied near the tabernacle, they prophesied in the camp (Num 11:26-27).

MEDAN Third son of Abraham by his wife Keturah.

MEDE See MEDIA

MEDEBA (MEDABA). A town in Moab siezed by the Israelites from Sihon the Amorite (Num 21:30); in the territory of Reuben (Josh 13:16).

A coin of Mattathias Antigonus, the high priest (40-37 B.C.), with a Hebrew inscription and a double cornucopia on one side and a Greek inscription around a wreath on the other.

Coin of Medeba depicting the chariot of the god Helios. A.D. 210.

(top right)
The Medeba Map showing part of Palestine, discovered in 1896 during excavations of the 6th-century St George's church at Medeba.

(top left)
Excavations at Medeba.

(left center)
View of the site of Medeba, south of Heshbon.

During the reign of David Joab fought the Ammonites and the Amorites there (I Chr 19:7 ff). Mesha, king of Moab, tells in his stele of Omri's conquest of Medeba and its subsequent release by Mesha. In the Hellenistic period it was in the hands of the Nabateans (I Macc 1:9, 31). Alexander Jannaeus seized the city from them, but it was returned to them by John Hyrcanus II. Nabatean inscriptions found at Medeba show that it was also in their hands in the Roman period. In 1896 a mosaic floor was discovered in a 6th-century church. This depicts a map of the biblical lands, accompanied by appropriate quotations from the Bible. It is known as the Medeba map and is an extremely useful source of information about the topography of the Holy Land.

MEDES See MEDIA

MEDIA, MEDES (MEDE) Madai, the Hebrew name for Media, is listed in the Table of Nations (Gen 10:2; I Chr 1:5) as the third son of Japheth, a people living east of Mesopotamia. Media and Medes are often mentioned together with Persia (Est 10:2; Dan 5:28; 8:20, etc.). The history of the Medes, a people apparently of Indo-Iranian origin, is reflected in Assyrian, Babylonian, Persian and Greek documents. In the 9th century B.C., Media was invaded by various Assyrian kings. At this time the Medes began to settle in towns administered by local rulers, without any central authority, which made it easy for the Assyrians to fight them but failing to subdue them, the Assyrians often resorted to large-scale deportations. The Median kingdom was founded by Diokes who united the seven Median tribes (best known of whom were the Magi, a tribe of priests) and ruled for 53 years (699-646 B.C.). The kingdom was consolidated under Phraortas (646-624) who headed a league that endangered the Assyrian hold over the Zagros mountains. Under his successor, Cyaxeres (625-585), a serious threat to the Median kingdom was posed by the Scythians; the latter were, however, eventually thrown back by the Medes in alliance with the Babylonians. As Babylonian power grew, the Medes too became a significant political and military factor. They were included in Jeremiah's enumeration of foreign peoples (Jer 25:25). The last king of the Medes was Astyages (585-550 B.C.); in 553 B.C., the kingdom was overthrown by Persia, its

MEDIA, MEDES
II Kgs 17:6;
18:11. Ezra
6:2. Est 1:3,
14, 18-19;
10:2. Is 13:17;
21:2. Jer
25:25; 51:11,
28. Dan 5:28,
31; 6:8, 12,
15; 8:20; 9:1;
11:1. Acts 2:9

former vassal, under Cyrus. The Bible depicts Media as the enemy of Babylon (Is 13:17-18; 21:1-10). The Book of Daniel considers Media and Persia as a single political unit, prophesying that this combined power will defeat Babylon (Dan 5:26-28).

MEDITTERANEAN See SEA

MEGIDDO One of the best known ancient cities in the Holy Land. Its renown largely stemmed from its exceptionally strategic location, at the Iron (Aruna) Brook's descent into the Jezreel Valley, where it dominated the international route between Egypt and Syria-Mesopotamia. Because of this position, many battles were fought in the immediate vicinity of Megiddo, until its very name — Armageddon — became synonymous with the site of the final battle to be fought at the end of the days between the forces of good and evil (Rev 16:12 ff). The city's repeated destruction and rebuilding has resulted in the accumulation of a high mound — Tell el-Mutesellim — the site of one of the largest and most famous archeological excavations ever undertaken in the country.

The first written mention of Megiddo is in connection with one of the best recorded military campaigns of ancient history. Thutmosis III (15th century B.C.) led an expedition against a coalition of Canaanite cities who rebelled against Egypt's rule. The battle, fought in the vicinity of Megiddo, was followed by a seven month's siege of the city itself. The Egyptian army was victorious in both stages and took large quantities of valuable booty. Thutmosis III then converted Megiddo into an important Egyptian stronghold, and the city retained its importance throughout the period of the Egyptian empire. It figures in the El Amarna Letters and in other texts of the period.

Megiddo was not initially taken over by the Israelites, remaining throughout the period of the Judges a foreign city in the territory of the tribe of Manasseh (Josh 17:11-13; Judg 1:27-28; I Chr 7:29). By the time of Solomon's rule, Megiddo had become an Israelite city and was fortified together with Hazor and Gezer. Shortly afterwards, in the fifth year of King Rehoboam (c. 925 B.C.), it was captured by Pharaoh

MEGIDDO
Josh 12:21;
17:11. Judg
1:27; 5:19.
I Kgs 4:12;
9:15. II Kgs
9:27; 23:29-30.
I Chr 7:29.
II Chr 35:22.
Zech 12:11

Aerial view of excavations at Tell Megiddo.

Remains of pillars from buildings at Megiddo thought to have been storehouses or barracks in Ahab's time.

(right)
Model of the city of Megiddo showing mainly Iron Age levels.

Shishak of Egypt. Centuries later it fell to Tiglath-Pileser III king of Assyria (733/32 B.C.), who made it the capital of the Assyrian province of Maggidu. After Josiah's battle against Pharaoh Necho in 609 B.C. at Megiddo (II Kgs 23:29; II Chr 35:22), the city is not mentioned again.

The mound of Megiddo was first excavated in 1903-1905 while more important excavations were carried out between 1925 and 1939. All in all, Tell Megiddo is built up of 24 layers of occupation numbered XX to I (some are subdivided into A and B). These layers cover a period of some 3,000 years, from about 3300 B.C. to about 350 B.C. The first six layers (XX to XV) cover the Early Canaanite period. The earliest settlement was humble with mud brick houses. Layer XIX already features a substantial settlement, with a building identified as a temple. This is the earliest of a long sequence of temples built on the same spot. The first known city wall was built in layer XVIII. It was an enormous stone wall, some 25 feet (8 m) wide and at least 13 feet (4 m) high. In the next layer a large building was erected adjoining the wall, and on the spot of the early temple a large circular altar of small rubble stones was constructed. This stone altar remained unchanged for a long time, and in the last phase of the Early Canaanite period three almost identical temples were built around it. One of these temples was also used in the next phase of occupation. The entire building was filled up with rubble, leaving only a square cella in the middle, used as a holy place.

Layers XIII to X represent the Middle Canaanite period (c. 2000-1550 B.C.). The earliest of these layers differs markedly from both the preceding and the succeeding layers. A new city wall was built, with a gate, or rather two narrow entrances set a right angles. The gate, being reached from the outside by a flight of steps, was no doubt designed for pedestrians. In layer XII the city took the basic shape it had for the next 650 years or so. Neighborhoods of private houses were identified in various parts of the city. In layer X a palace was built in the northern part of the city. It was rebuilt several times in the subsequent periods, first greatly enlarged, then reduced in size. Much of Megiddo's wealth, including hoards of gold and ivory objects, was discovered in the palaces. An imposing and well-built city gate on the northern side of the city, and the equally impressive fortified temple in the sacred area, may also have been first built in this phase.

The character of the city changed sharply in the 11th century B.C., after the last of the Late Canaanite period cities. The following phase was very poorly built, with the former sacred area no longer in use. This change is believed to indicate a new population. Matters improved later, with renewal of extensive building activity, perhaps by Megiddo's Philistine inhabitants, identified by their pottery vessels. Their city was destroyed by a great fire, attributed to King David.

In the Israelite period, the settlement was initially poor and unfortified, but in the time of King Solomon it became an administrative center with a city wall, a well-built gate with many interesting details and two palaces. This Solomonic city, being rather elusive, was only gradually understood by archeologists. The offset and inset wall, the stables, a city gate shorter than the Solomonic gate and a sophisticated supply system conveying water into the city from the spring at the foot of the mound, are all attributed to King Ahab. Ahab's city stood for about 150 years, until it fell to the Assyrians in 722/23 B.C.

Layer III is Assyrian Megiddo, built along new lines but reusing the old Israelite wall. This is the last phase of importance in the long history of Megiddo. Layers II and I were open, unfortified settlements, which survived into the Persian period.

MEHETABEEL ("God does good"). (Note: Hebrew spelling is identical to that of Mehetabel). Father of Delaiah and grandfather of Shemaiah who was a secret informer and a false prophet at the time of Nehemiah.

MEHETABEL ("God does good"). The wife of Hadar, king of Achbor and last king of Edom; she was the daughter of Matred and the granddaughter of Mezahab.

MEHIDA Head of a family of Nethinim (Temple servants) who returned with Zerubbabel from the Exile in Babylon.

MEHIR ("price, reward"). Son of Chelub and father of Eshton in the genealogy of the family of Judah.

MEHOLATHITE Appellation of Barzillai and his son Adriel.

MEHUJAEL Son of Irad the grandson of Cain and father of Methushael in the genealogy of the family of Cain.

MEHUMAN ("eunuch"). First of the seven eunuchs mentioned as chamberlains at the court of King Ahasuerus.

ME JARKON A river at the northern border of the territory of Dan (Josh 19:45-46). The River Jarkon is identified with Nahr el-Auja (it flows through present-day northern Tel Aviv). Next to the Jordan, the Jarkon is the most abundant river in western Palestine. Its sources are the copious springs of Rosh ha'Ayin and other springs to the north and south, as well as an intricate system of wadis draining the hill country on the east.

The Jarkon River.

The river follows a meandering course from east to west. Its fertile banks have supported intensive agriculture from early periods. During the time of Solomon and Zerubbabel, the river mouth appears to have served as a harbor for small craft with access from the towns along its banks by means of rafts. The River Jarkon bisects the coastal plain from the sea to the hill country, forming an important strategic obstacle.

MELATIAH ("the Lord saved"). A Gibeonite, one of the men who repaired the walls of Jerusalem at the time of Nehemiah.

MELCHI ("my king"). The name of two of the ancestors of Jesus in the genealogy according to Luke.

1. Son of Janna and father of Levi.
2. Son of Addi and father of Neri.

MELCHIAH See MALCHIJAH No.3

MELCHIZEDEK ("legitimate king"; later interpreted to mean "righteous king"). Gentile king of Salem called priest of the Most High, Creator of Heaven and Earth (Gen 14:18-20). Abraham used these epithets, which are applied in Ugaritic literature to El, the nominal head of the Canaanite pantheon, and applied them to the Lord (Gen 14:22).

After Abraham's victory over Chedorlaomer, Melchizedek greeted him with a gift of bread and wine (Gen 14:18). One of the two gave the other a tithe (Gen 14:20); most interpreters assume that Melchizedek, being a priest, was the recipient. In Psalms 110:4 the promise is made, "You are a priest forever according to the order of (or "because of the word of") Melchizedek." Most commentators take David as the addressee, and they see here an attempt to legitimize Jerusalem as the seat of God and king on the basis of Genesis 14:10-20. Salem is here identified with Jerusalem as in Psalms 76:2.

In the Dead Sea documents, Melchizedek is an angel who stands in judgment over the other angels and in time to come he will rescue the Children of Light from Belial. Scholars have suggested that this belief in Melchizedek as an angel inspired the author of the Epistle to the Hebrews to say of him: "He has no father, no mother, no lineage; his years have no beginning, his life no end. He is like the Son of God; remains a priest continually" (Heb 7:3). Taking Jesus as the addressee in Psalms 110:4, the Epistle to the Hebrews (5:1-8:2) sees Jesus as the successor of Melchizedek, whose priesthood is to replace the priesthood of the descendants of Aaron.

MELEA ("plenitude"). Son of Menan and father of Eliakim in the genealogy of Jesus according to Luke.

MELECH ("king"). Second son of Micah, the grandson of Jonathan, in the genealogy of King Saul.

MELICHU A family of priests who returned with Zerubbabel from the Babylonian Exile. Possibly identical with Malluch No.6.

MELITA See MALTA

MELON See PLANTS

MEMPHIS See NOPH

MEMUCAN One of the seven princes of Persia and Media who were among the closest confidants of King Ahasuerus; he was the one to advise the king to banish Queen Vashti.

MENAHEM ("comforter"). Son of Gadi, king of Israel. Menahem acceded to the throne after assassinating the usurper Shallum, who himself had slain Zechariah to become king only one month previously. It was perhaps in retribution for its support of Shallum that Menahem carried out the brutal subjugation of the city of Tiphsah (Tappuah, according to some Greek manuscripts) recorded in II Kings 15:16.

Before Menahem could secure his position on the throne, he was confronted by the seemingly unstoppable westward advance of Assyria.

MELATIAH
Neh 3:7

MELCHI 1
Luke 3:24

MELCHI 2
Luke 3:28

MELCHIAH
Jer 21:1

MELCHIZEDEK
Gen 14:18.
Ps 110:4.
Heb 5:6, 10;
6:20; 7:1, 10-
11, 15, 17, 21

MELEA
Luke 3:31

MELECH
I Chr 8:35;
9:41

MELICHU
Neh 12:14

MEMPHIS
Hos 9:6

MEMUCAN
Est 1:14, 16,
21

MENAHEM
II Kgs 15:14,
16-17, 19-23

Fragment of a pottery jar-handle bearing a Hebrew seal impression inscribed "[Belonging] to Menahem Yohanah" from Ramat Rahel. 7th century B.C. (Israel Dept. of Antiquities and Museums)

When Tiglath-Pileser III (Pul), the architect of the neo-Assyrian empire, reached Samaria, Menahem paid the huge tribute demanded, raising 1,000 talents of siver by a tax on wealthy Israelites. Assyrian inscriptions also record a tribute payment by "Menahem of Samaria" (*Me-ni-hi-im-me (al) Sa-me-ri-na-a-a*). The payment assured Menahem's retention of the throne, but consigned Israel to the status of a vassal state.

Menahem lived in Tirzah, perhaps as a military commander, before becoming king. Like the other northern kings, he is condemned in the Bible for perpetuating the illegitimate worship instituted by Jeroboam No.1.

Menahem ruled for ten years, beginning c. 747 B.C., although chronological problems regarding his reign remain unsolved. He died a natural death and was succeeded by his son Pekahiah.

MENAN (MENNA) Great-grandson of David and father of Melea in the genealogy of Jesus according to Luke.

MENE MENE TEKEL UPHARSIN This enigmatic expression appeared as an inscription written by a detached hand on the wall of the palace where Belshazzar, the Chaldean king, was giving a banquet (Dan 5:25). As he and his officers drank from the golden and silver vessels which Nebuchadnezzar had removed from the Temple in 586 B.C. and praised their gods of gold and silver, this writing suddenly appeared, defying the skills of the Chaldean astrologers, wise men or magicians to decipher it. Daniel was promptly summoned and immediately interpreted the inscription as follows (Dan 5:25-28):

Mene "God has numbered (the days of) your kingdom and brought it to an end;" *Tekel* "You have been weighed in the balance and found wanting;" *Peres* "Your kingdom has been divided and given to the Medes and the Persians."

Each word was explained by Daniel as related to a corresponding Aramaic verb. Together they indicated that God was about to put an end to the Chaldean dynasty, and indeed that very evening Belshazzar was assassinated (Dan 5:30). It has been shown that the words themselves originally referred to weights of monetary value. Thus *Mene* represents a *mina (60 shekels); Tekel* a *shekel* and *Peres* a half-*mina*. They, in turn, most probably indicate the rulers of the neo-Babylonian Chaldean dynasty; Nebuchadnezzar, Evil-Merodach, Nabonidus and Belshazzar.

Several suggestions have been offered to explain why the Chaldean wise men were unable to decipher the inscription: the inscription was written in Aramaic without word dividers; departing from the usual right to left direction, it was written in a different order, i.e. from left to right or in vertical columns; only the first initials were written down and not the complete words themselves.

MENI A deity of good luck, mentioned along with Gad in Isaiah 65:11.

MEONENIM The Hebrew Bible has Alon (i.e. terebinth, or oak) of Meonenim (Judg 9:37); and the KJV translation reads: "The Diviners' Terebinth Tree." The Hebrew text implies that this was a sacred tree, like the Oak of Mamre, and other sacred trees in the Holy Land.

MEONOTHAI ("the Lord is my refuge"). Second son of Othniel and father of Ophrah in the genealogy of the family of Judah.

MEPHAATH A town in Moab, in the territory of Reuben (Josh 13:18), awarded to Levites of the family of Merari (I Chr 6:63). Jeremiah (48:21) mentions it in his prophecy on Moab.

The site is apparently at Khirbet Jauwa 6 miles (10 km) south of Amman.

MEPHIBOSHETH (Probably an intentional modification of Merib-

Quartz Hebrew seal inscribed "[Belonging] to Menahem". Late 8th century B.C. (Israel Museum)

Baal (I Chr 8:34; 9:40) which substituted *bosheth* (shame) for the name of the pagan god Baal).

The name of two members of King Saul's family.

1. The son of Jonathan (II Sam 4:4; 21:7). In I Chronicles 8:34 and 9:40 he is called Merib-Baal which was probably his original name. He was crippled at the age of five when his nurse dropped him while fleeing from the palace on hearing of the deaths of King Saul and of the child's father (II Sam 4:4).

When David handed over the male members of Saul's family to the Gibeonites, he spared Mephibosheth because of his oath to Jonathan (II Sam 21:7).

Mephibosheth was in Transjordan at the house of Machir the son of Ammiel (II Sam 9:4) when he was invited by David to stay at his court and dine at his table. As a mark of indebtedness to Jonathan, David restored the property of the house of Saul to Mephibosheth, appointing Saul's steward Ziba to administer it (II Sam 9:7-11, 13).

During Absalom's rebellion, Mephibosheth remained in Jerusalem with Absalom, whereas Ziba assisted David in bringing him food and animals, and was consequently rewarded with part of Mephibosheth's property (II Sam 16:1-4). When David returned to Jerusalem, he discovered Mephibosheth in mourning clothes; although accepting his recantation, the king did not allow him to retain all his property, instead ordering it to be shared with Ziba (II Sam 19:24-30).

Mephibosheth had one son, Micha (II Sam 9:12) who founded a well-known family (I Chr 8:35; 9:41).

2. The son of Saul by his concubine Rizpah the daughter of Aiah. Along with his brother Armoni and the five sons of Saul's daughter Merab, Mephibosheth was handed over by King David to the Gibeonites (II Sam 21:8-9) in expiation of the massacres the latter had suffered at Saul's hands (cf Josh 9:15ff). The Gibeonites executed the prisoners, leaving the bodies unburied. Mephibosheth's mother stood guard over the corpses until they were interred by the order of David.

MERAB Saul's elder daughter (I Sam 14:49; 18:17). She was promised to David should he succeed in killing 100 Philistines, but although he fulfilled the condition, she was instead betrothed to Adriel the Meholathite (I Sam 18:17-19). The five sons she bore to Adriel (some Hebrew manuscripts present the five as sons of Michal) were among the seven offspring of Saul whom David handed over to the Gibeonites in expiation of Saul's sins against them (II Sam 21:8-9).

MERAIAH Head of the priestly family of Seraiah in the time of Joiakim the high priest.

MERAIOTH

1. Grandson of Uzzi and father of Amariah in the genealogy of the family of Levi.

2. Son of Ahitub and father of Zadok. One of his descendants, Azariah, was among the priests who settled in Jerusalem after the return of the Exile in Babylon.

3. A descendant of Eleazar and Aaron; one of the ancestors of Ezra.

4. Head of the priestly family of Helkai at the time of Joiakim the high priest.

MERARI, MERARITES The third son of Levi, younger brother of Gershon and Kohath (Gen 46:11; Ex 6:16; Num 3:17; I Chr 6:1, etc.), and head of a Levitical family — the Merarites (Num 26:57). During the Israelites' trek through the wilderness, the Merarites marched on the northern side of the tabernacle, being entrusted with carrying its less important components — frames, bars, pillars etc. — from station to station (Num 3:36-37; 4:29-33).

MEPHIBOSHETH 1
II Sam 4:4; 9:6, 10-13; 16:1, 4; 19:24-25, 30; 21:7

MEPHIBOSHETH 2
II Sam 21:8

MERAB
I Sam 14:49; 18:17, 19

MERAIAH
Neh 12:12

MERAIOTH 1
I Chr 6:6-7, 52

MERAIOTH 2
I Chr 9:11. Neh 11:11

MERAIOTH 3
Ezra 7:3

MERAIOTH 4
Neh 12:15

MERARI, MERARITES
Gen 46:11. Ex 6:16, 19. Num 3:17, 20, 33, 35-36; 4:29,

During Joshua's time, the Merarites were allotted 12 cities scattered throughout the territories of the tribes of Zebulun, Reuben and Gad (Josh 21:7; 34:40; I Chr 6:63, 77-81); these included one city of refuge (Josh 21:38). Two hundred and forty Merarites under Asaiah were among the Levites who brought the ark from Kirjath Jearim to Jerusalem during David's time (I Chr 15:6). Later, David appointed a Merarite — Ethan the son of Kushaiah — as a singer in the Temple.

Members of the family were among the Levites who took part in cleansing the Temple in the time of Hezekiah (II Chr 29:12); others helped repair it during the reign of Josiah (II Chr 34:12). During the return from Babylonian Exile, members of the family followed Ezra to Jerusalem (Ezra 8:18-19) where they ministered in the Temple.

MERATHAIM, LAND OF The land of Merathaim is mentioned in Jeremiah's prophecy on the destruction of Babylon. In Akkadian documents the Babylonian region of the Persian Gulf is called Marratum. But in the case of Jeremiah's prophecy the name Merathaim might have been a play on words: *meri* in Hebrew means rebellion, and the suffix may be understood as "double rebellion".

MERCY It is an attribute of God to show mercy both to the deserving as well as to the undeserving. While his wrath extends to the third and fourth generations of the sinful, his mercy extends to the thousandth generation of those who love him and keep his commandments (Ex 20:5-6). The attribute of mercy is proclaimed to Moses by God when he declares himself to be "merciful and gracious, long-suffering and abounding in goodness" (Ex 34:6).

Frequent appeals to God's mercy are expressed, especially on the part of penitent sinners (e.g., Ps 51:1, 3; 78:38; cf also Neh 1:5; 9:17; Ps 25:6; 103:8; 145:8-9; Is 63:9; Joel 2:17). The theme of God's mercy and compassion appears frequently in the Prophets (e.g., Jonah 4:2; Mic 7:18-19).

The quality of "long-suffering" attributed to God in some of the passages cited above is recommended to man (Prov 14:29; Ecc 7:8). However, God alone is called "gracious", a term connoting generosity of spirit and free giving (Gen 33:5, 11). Only God is called the Merciful One and bears the epithet "abundant in kindness" (Ex 34:6). The exact nuances of meaning between the latter term and its synonyms such as "mercy" and "pity" are difficult to establish. The nuances of meaning of the term "mercy" can only be approximated from the similes in which they occur. The invocation of familial relationships to express God's "kindness", "mercy" and "compassion" indicates that the mood in which they are cast is one of love.

The kindness of God, like that of man, is not mere feeling. It is manifested in deeds: by his repeated forgiveness, both to the individual and the community, by the restoration of Israel to its former relationship with God (Deut 13:17; II Sam 24:14; II Kgs 13:23), by his deliverance of Israel from its enemies (Neh 9:27-28), and by his future gathering of his exiled people and their restoration to their land (Deut 30:3; Is 14:1; 49:13; Jer 12:15; 33:26; Ezek 39:25). All these and their like are manifestations of God's mercy.

Two Greek words underlie the English word for mercy in the NT writings. The first, *eleeo*, means to receive something not earned and so the people who meet Jesus cry out for assistance from him (Matt 9:27; 15:22; 17:15; 20:30-31; Mark 10:47-48; Luke 16:24; 17:13; 18:38-39). The ultimate origin of mercy is God himself and he dispenses it solely through his sovereignty, "I will have mercy on whomever I will have mercy" (Rom 9:15). The phrase "obtain mercy" denotes that people have been redeemed by God (Rom 11:30-32) or saved (cf I Pet 2:19) and

Paul concludes his discussion of the salvation and special role of Israel with the words: "For God has committed them all to disobedience, that he might have mercy on all" (Rom 11:32). Paul in fact speaks of himself in his relationship to Christ as having received mercy (I Cor 7:25; II Cor 4:1; I Tim 1:13, 16). Since God has been merciful to the believers they in turn are urged to show "mercy with cheerfulness" (Rom 12:8) and the merciful are congratulated "for they shall obtain mercy" (Matt 5:7).

The second word, *oiktirmoi*, means tenderness and is used to describe God in James 5:11; the Lord is full of pity and compassion. The word comes from another realm, the cult. When the tax collector in the parable cries: "God, be merciful to me a sinner" (Luke 18:13) the word for mercy is related to expectation or propiation and may have been linked to the mercy-seat in the Temple. Fundamentally, Christians shared with Judaism the conviction that God's throne is a throne of grace where "we may obtain mercy and find grace to help in time of need" (Heb 4:16).

The name "Meremoth" inscribed in ink on an ostracon found at the temple at Arad. Late 8th century B.C. (Israel Dept. of Antiquities and Museums)

MERED Second son of Ezrah in the genealogy of the family of Judah, he married Bithia, the daughter of Pharaoh who bore him Miriam, Shabbai and Ishbah. | MERED
I Chr 4:17-18

MEREMOTH

1. Son of Uriah the priest; he weighed the silver and gold brought back from Babylon by Ezra for the House of the Lord. The family, initially unable to verify its priestly lineage, was subsequently acknowledged as legitimate and permitted to participate in the receipt of the Temple vessels and in the rebuilding of the wall of Jerusalem (Ezra 8:33; Neh 3:4, 21). | MEREMOTH 1
Ezra 8:33.
Neh 3:4, 21

2. One of the sons of Bani, who, having taken pagan wives, had to repudiate them according to the decree of Ezra. | MEREMOTH 2
Ezra 10:36

3. Family of priests at the time of the return from the Babylonian Exile. Its head returned with Zerubbabel and settled in Jerusalem; he was among the leaders who sealed the covenant. | MEREMOTH 3
Neh 10:5; 12:3

MERES One of the seven princes consulted by Ahauserus during his dispute with Vashti. | MERES
Est 1:14

MERIBAH See MASSAH AND MERIBAH | MERIBAH
Ex 17:7. Num 20:13, 24; 27:14. Deut 32:51; 33:8. Ps 81:7. Ezek 47:19; 48:28

MERIB-BAAL An alternate name for Mephibosheth the son of Saul. Several personal names originally compounded with "Baal", the Canaanite deity, were subsequently changed to "Bosheth", "shame". | MERIB-BAAL
I Chr 8:34; 9:40

MERODACH Hebraized form of the Akkadian "Marduk", the name of the patron god of the city of Babylon. The Akkadian name is contracted from Sumerian "Amarutuk," which means "calf of the sun-god Utu". Marduk's discomfiture is predicted in Jeremiah's prophecy concerning the fall of Babylon in Jeremiah 50:2. The divine name Merodach is found also as an element in the Babylonian royal names Merodach-Baladan and Evil-Merodach. | MERODACH
Jer 50:2

MERODACH-BALADAN (Hebraized form of the Akkadian *Marduk-apla-iddina,* which means "[the god] Marduk gave me a son"). | MERODACH-BALADAN
Is 39:1

A Chaldean chieftain from Bit-Yakin near the Persian Gulf, who, with the support of King Humbanigash of Elam, made himself king of Babylon in 721 B.C. He continued to rule Babylon until ousted from the throne by Sargon II of Assyria in 710. He returned to Bit-Yakin until 703 when he again made himself king of Babylon. On this occasion he attempted to organize an alliance of all anti-Assyrian forces. This effort provides the background for the dispatch by Merodach-Baladan of envoys to the court of King Hezekiah of Judah described in Isaiah 39:1 (cf II Chr 32:31). The parallel account in II Kings 20:12 calls the Babylonian ruler in question Berodach-Baladan. After ruling Babylon for nine months Merodach-Baladan was ousted by Sennacherib of

Assyria. He returned to his native Bit-Yakin, from where he was ousted by Sennacherib in 700 B.C. He fled to Nagitu where he remained until his death.

MEROM (THE WATERS OF MEROM, MERON) Place where all the kings of northern Canaan gathered under the leadership of Jabin, king of Hazor, and where they were vanquished by Joshua (Josh 11:5-7). It

MEROM
Josh 11:5, 7

was known as Meron in the period of the Second Temple but Josephus, who fortified it, refers to it as Meroth. It is still called Meron today, not far from Safed.

MERONOTHITE An appellation for Jehdeiah, the man in charge of the donkeys at the court of King David (I Chr 27:30) and for Jadon, who repaired the walls of Jerusalem in the time of Nehemiah. They were from the town of Meronoth, near Gibeah.

MERONOTHITE
I Chr 27:30.
Neh 3:7

MEROZ A town whose inhabitants refused to assist Deborah and Barak, son of Abinoam in the war against Sisera (Judg 5:23). Identified by some scholars with a place close to Kedesh (Naphtali), while others prefer the Arab village of Mazar on Mount Gilboa.

MEROZ
Judg 5:23

MESHA

1. A place which marks the boundary of the Joktanite territory.

MESHA 1
Gen 10:30

2. King of Moab, a contemporary of Kings Ahab and Jehoram of Israel and Jehoshaphat of Judah. According to II Kings 3:4, Moab was tributary to Israel, but during Israel's war against Aram, Mesha revolted against Jehoram. Aided by King Jehoshaphat of Judah and by Edom, Jehoram embarked on a punitive campaign (II Kgs 3:6), devastating Moab until, at the siege of Kir Hareseth, Mesha in despair offered his eldest son as a burnt offering upon the city wall, to his god Chemosh. The Israelites were so horrified that they lifted the siege and withdrew (II Kgs 3:25-27).

MESHA 2
II Kgs 3:4

A different account of relations between Israel and Moab and of Mesha's successful revolt is recorded on the "Mesha Stone" (also called the "Moabite Stone"), a large stele erected by Mesha in his capital at Dibon, and inscribed in a Moabite-Canaanite dialect similar to biblical Hebrew. The stele, discovered in 1868, sheds considerable light on Moab's history and religion. Dedicated to the Moabite national god Chemosh, it commemorates Mesha's revolt against Israel, apparently after the death of Ahab (II Kgs 1:1; 3:5), his recovery of independence

The site of Merom, in Galilee known today as Meron.

The Stele of Mesha or Moabite Stone, found at Dibon in Transjordan, commemorates Mesha's revolt against Israel and his rebuilding of several towns (Musée du Louvre, Paris)

Carnelian Moabite seal inscribed "[Belonging] to Mesha". 6th century B.C. (Israel Museum)

Moabite inscription found at Kir Moab mentioning Kmoshyt, king of Moab and son of Mesha. 9th century B.C. (Archaeological Museum, Amman)

for Moab, and his glorious and successful reign. The order of events mentioned in the stele conflicts with the biblical account: Mesha claims that he revolted 40 years after Omri began his oppression of Moab, in the middle of the reign of Omri's son, whereas II Kings 3:5 tells of Mesha's revolt against Israel after the death of Omri's son and successor Ahab. This contradiction may be reconciled if we take "son" to mean "grandson" (as in II Kgs 8:26). The horrifying account of the siege of Kir Hareseth (II Kgs chap. 3) is completely ignored in the stele, perhaps indicating that this took place after the stele was erected by Mesha. Several aspects of ancient western-Semitic religion are illuminated by the stele: Chemosh's anger against his people and the resultant punishment of Moab by Israelite domination under Omri parallel the biblical conception of divine punishment. Just as Israel's victories were attributed to divine intervention (Judg 11:24; II Kgs 3:18, etc.), so Moab saw hers as coming from Chemosh. The biblical custom of ban — devotion of spoils of war to God — was observed in Moab as in Israel. The biblical description of Mesha as a "sheepbreeder" (II Kgs 3:4) is borne out by Mesha's explicit claim in the stele that he placed "sheep-raisers" over the land. Although written in Moabite, the stele has been called the "earliest important Hebrew inscription," its import lying in its historical as well as paleographic significance.

3. The firstborn son of Caleb the grandson of Judah.

4. A son of Shaharaim, an ancestor of Saul.

MESHACH One of the young men of Judah taken along with Daniel, Shadrach and Abednego, to the court of Nebuchadnezzar. His original name was Mishael, but the chief of eunuchs at the court renamed him Meshach.

MESHECH

1. A people in Asia Minor. In the Table of Nations in Genesis chapter 10, Meshech is listed after Javan and Tubal as the sixth son of Japheth. It is generally identified with Mushki of Assyrian, and Moschoi of classical sources. The first known mention dates from 1116 B.C. in the first year of Tiglath-Pileser I, who vanquished the five kings of Mushki ruling in the southeastern part of Anatolia. They are mentioned again in Assyrian sources from the reign of Ashurnasirpal II (884-859 B.C.) as paying a tribute of copper vessels, cattle and wine. They do not appear in the Assyrian sources from the era of Assyrian decline, but are mentioned again in conjunction with clashes with Assyrians in the period of Shalmaneser V, reaching a climax in the reign of Sargon (722-705 B.C.). The Assyrian sources seem to identify Mita king of the Meshech with Midas of the Greek sources. This indicates that the peoples the Greeks called Phrygians are the Mushki of the Assyrians. The statement in Psalm 120:5 "Woe is me, that I sojourn in Meshech, that I dwell in the tents of Kedar" refers to Meshech as the border of the civilized world in the north, as Kedar was its southeastern extremity in the Babylonian and Persian periods, Meshech and Tubal denote the land of central Anatolia and its peoples (Ezek 32:26). Meshech, Tubal and Javan (i.e. Greece) traded in slaves and copper vessels (Ezek 39:1).

2. See MASH

MESHELEMIAH ("God will recompense"). A Levite, son of Kore and father of seven sons. He was head of a division of gatekeepers in charge of the East Gate at the time of King David. His firstborn son Zechariah was in charge of the North Gate.

In I Chronicles 26:14, he is called Shelemiah, a shortened form of the same name.

MESHEZABEEL ("God rescues").

1. Father of Berechiah and grandfather of Meshullam; he was among

MESHA 3
I Chr 2:42

MESHA 4
I Chr 8:9

MESHACH
Dan 1:7; 2:49;
3:12-14, 16,
19-20, 22-23,
26, 28-30

MESHECH 1
Gen 10:2.
I Chr 1:5, 17.
Ps 120:5. Ezek
27:13; 32:26;
38:2-3; 39:1

MESHELEMIAH
I Chr 9:21;
26:1-2, 9

MESHEZABEEL 1
Neh 3:4

the builders of the walls of Jerusalem at the time of Nehemiah.

2. One of the leaders who sealed the covenant of Nehemiah.

3. A man of Judah, father of Pethahiah, the king's deputy.

MESHILLEMITH Son of Immer and the ancestor of a priestly family who settled in Jerusalem after the return of the exiles from Babylon. In Nehemiah 11:13 he is called Meshillemoth.

MESHILLEMOTH ("the Lord gives peace").

1. An alternate spelling for Meshillemith.

2. Father of Berechiah, head of a family of Ephraim at the time of Pekah son of Remaliah.

MESHOBAB A Simeonite who with his clan helped settle an area called Gedor. The exact location is unclear (I Chr 4:34).

MESHULLAM ("[the Lord] grants peace"). The name of 21 biblical characters.

1. Father of Azaliah and grandfather of Shaphan the scribe of Josiah king of Judah.

2. Eldest son of Zerubbabel the grandson of Jeconiah.

3. Head of a family or clan of the tribe of Gad at the time of Jotham king of Judah and Jeroboam king of Israel.

4. One of the sons of Elpaal in the genealogy of King Saul of Benjamin.

5. A man of Benjamin, son of Hodaviah and grandson of Hassenuah; he was the father of Sallul No.1 who settled in Jerusalem at the time of Nehemiah.

6. A man of Benjamin, son of Shephatiah and grandson of Reuel, who settled in Jerusalem at the time of Nehemiah.

7. Father of Hilkiah and grandfather of Azariah, who was "officer over the House of God" at the time of Nehemiah.

8. Son of Meshillemith and father of Jahzerah the grandfather of Maasai who was head of a priestly family in Jerusalem at the time of Nehemiah.

9. A Levite of the sons of the Kohathites; he was among the men who supervised the repairs in the House of the Lord at the time of Josiah king of Judah.

10. One of the leaders sent by Ezra to Iddo at Casiphia to bring back priests and Levites for the House of God.

11. One of the men who supported Ezra's decision to order those who had taken pagan wives to repudiate them. Perhaps the same as No.10.

12. One of the sons of Bani who had taken pagan wives and had to repudiate them upon the decree of Ezra.

13. Son of Berechiah and grandson of Meshezabeel; he was among the men who helped repair the walls of Jerusalem at the time of Nehemiah. His daughter was married to Jehohanan the son of Tobiah.

14. A son of Besodeiah; he was among the men who repaired the walls of Jerusalem at the time of Nehemiah. He repaired the Old Gate.

15. One of the leaders of the people who stood to the left of Ezra when he read the Law to the people.

16. One of the leaders of the people who sealed the covenant at the time of Nehemiah; perhaps the same as No.15.

17. Another leader who sealed the covenant.

18. Head of the priestly family of Ezra at the time of Joiakim the high priest.

19. Head of the priestly family of Ginnethon at the time of Joiakim the high priest.

20. One of the gatekeepers of the House of the Lord at the time of Joiakim the high priest.

21. One of the leaders who participated in the thanksgiving choirs at

Fragment of a pottery jar-handle bearing a Hebrew seal impression inscribed "Meshullam Ahimelech", found at Lachish. Late 8th century B.C. (Rockefeller Museum, Jerusalem

The world at the time of Sargon (c.2300) depicted as a circle surrounded by water, with Babylon at its center, on a tablet from the 7th or 6th century B.C. (British Museum)

Mesopotamia.

the dedication of the wall repaired and rebuilt by Nehemiah.

MESHULLEMETH The daughter of Haruz of Jotbah, Meshullemeth was the wife of Manasseh king of Judah and the mother of his son Amon who reigned after him.

MESHULLEMETH
II Kgs 21:19

MESOPOTAMIA "The land between the rivers", the name first given by Polybius and Strabo exclusively to the lands lying between the Tigris and the Euphrates, is now applied to various regions. They are all bordered on the north by the mountains of Kurdistan, to the south by the marshes of the river delta, to the west by the Syrian steppes and deserts and to the east by the mountains of Iran. The northern and southern parts of Mesopotamia differ in many respects — geographically, culturally, and in other ways. But they can still be considered as two facets of the same historical entity that can properly be called Mesopotamia throughout its cultural development, which lasts from the beginning of the 3rd millennium B.C. down to the end of the Persian period.

MESOPOTAMIA
Gen 24:10.
Deut 23:4.
Judg 3:8, 10.
I Chr 19:6.
Acts 2:9; 7:2

The oldest known Mesopotamian civilization, at Jarmo in northern Iraq, belongs to the Neolithic period. In the south the earliest cultures have been unearthed at Tell el-Ubaid. The civilization of Tell-el-Ubaid

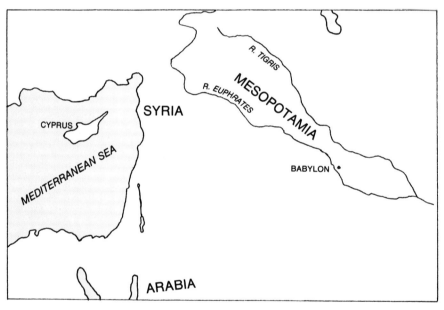

proper flourished in the 4th millennium B.C. From then until the emergence of the Assyrian kingdom the hegemony of Mesopotamia was established in the south. Tell el-Ubaid civilization was preceded by the Eridu civilization, the earliest known in southern Mesopotamia; it was succeeded by the Erech civilization, which was to establish the prototypes of the Mesopotamian culture: the appearance of writing, the cylinder seal and the building of ziggurats. This protohistoric era came to an end in about 3000 B.C. This period does, however, mark the beginning of a new era that has left behind written testimony — the Sumerian civilization. The early dynastic period of Sumerian civilization lasted about four centuries. The main sources for its history are a number of lists of kings, together with other documents that assist in identifying them, their dynasties and their deeds, although they provide a far from comprehensive picture of the period.

The advent of Sargon of Agade and the establishment of the Akkadian kingdom (2371-2230 B.C.) provided the first Semitic interlude in the history of Mesopotamia. Although it was brief and ended in catastrophe, it was considered by later generations to have been the most important because for the first time it gave shape to a great empire with a single central authority. Sargon led his campaigns upstream along the Euphrates and in all likelihood conquered northern Syria, before reaching the Mediterranean coast. Another important member of the Agade Dynasty was Naram Sin (2291-2255 B.C.), Sargon's grandson, who again ruled over vast territories. Although a number of kings are mentioned as his successors it seems that the decline of the Akkadian empire had begun in his own time with the invasions of barbaric tribes, who came from the Zagros Mountains in the east and ruled over almost the whole of Mesopotamia for about a century.

They were overcome by the king of Erech, Utu-Hegal (2120-2114 B.C.) whose successor, Ur-Nammu of Ur, founded the celebrated 3rd Dynasty of Ur, the place of origin of Abraham (Gen 11:31). This period, also known as the "Sumerian renaissance", is extremely well documented by finds from archeological excavations. The monarchs of this dynasty called themselves "Kings of Sumer and Accad", a title used from then onwards by all the great kings of Mesopotamia. The fall of the 3rd Dynasty of Ur was brought about by Semitic tribes who harried it from the west, as well as by invasions from the east and by a chain reaction of internal crises and revolts.

Upon the ruins of Ur sprang up a large number of independent city-states, ruled by kings from the west or from the east. The ruling class was either Amorite or Elamite. They adopted the civilization of the Sumerians, so a cultural continuity was maintained despite the political disintegration and the penetration of foreign elements and influences, mostly Semitic ones.

Our knowledge of this period is based mainly on the discovery of the archives of Mari, with thousands of clay tablets containing information about the events that preceded the capture of the town by Hammurabi (properly Hammurepi). Hammurabi overshadowed other rulers with great political shrewdness, founded the Babylonian kingdom that dominated southern and central Mesopotamia and also wielded some kind of influence over Assyria in the north.

Hammurabi's reign (1792-1749 B.C.) was an era of intense cultural activity and economic prosperity and survived in the memory of the following generations as the "golden age" of Babylon. His code of laws, although not the very earliest in Mesopotamia, is the most complete and perfect of them all and became the canon of law studied in the schools of Babylon. Hammurabi had no successor who was in any way comparable to him and his vast domain was eventually split into a northern and a southern kingdom. This dynasty did, however, contrive to remain on the throne of Babylon until the Hittites put an end to it in the year 1595 B.C.

(bottom left)
Babylonian seal impression.

The Laws of Hammurabi, king of Babylon, inscribed on a stele.

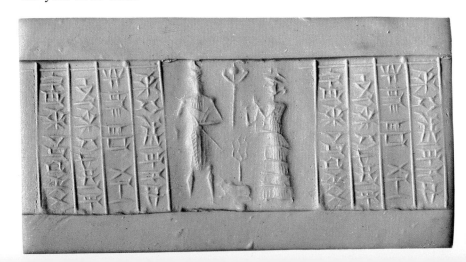

Clay prism bearing the names of the Sumerian kings, from Kish. 1800 B.C.

The invasions of the Hittites, and the Kassite conquest that followed, brought in their wake a dark age that is characterized by a complete absence of written documents concerning Babylon. These reappear in the 15th and 14th centuries B.C., heralding the Middle Babylonian and Middle Assyrian periods, which were to last until the end of the 2nd millennium B.C. During this time Assyria experienced a new ascendancy. Its rulers were considered to rank with the pharaohs of Egypt, the kings of the Hittites and the kings of Babylon under the Kassites. Babylon was in constant political decline throughout this period. Apart from a few revivals it continued to decline until the 8th century B.C.

Although politically inferior, Babylonian culture during this Middle Babylonian period exerted a great influence abroad, especially in Assyria, where its scholars were active at the courts. The Babylonian language was an international language and was used far beyond the borders of Mesopotamia.

At the end of the 2nd millennium B.C., Assyria itself suffered a period of decline and obscurity caused by Aramean invaders and the establishment of their kingdoms on its borders. It emerged from this eclipse only in the days of Ashurdan II (934-912 B.C.) and Adad-Nirari II (911-891 B.C.), the founders of the Assyrian empire. Ashurnasirpal II (883-859 B.C.) and his son Shalmaneser III (858-824 B.C.) were mighty conquerors who greatly extended the boundaries of their empire. It was during the reign of Shalmaneser III that the first encounter occurred between a king of Assyria and a king of Israel, at the battle of Karkar in northern Syria in the year 853 B.C. From that time onwards Assyria, and later Babylon, were to play a fateful role in the history of the kingdoms of Israel and Judah.

The Assyrian empire reached its peak during the Sargonid Dynasty founded by Sargon II (720-704 B.C.). This was the period of its greatest territorial expansion and its richest literary activity. It was now the most powerful empire the world had ever known. Yet its lines of communication were becoming much too long, while the conquered nations were awaiting any opportunity to shake off its yoke. Thus the Babylonians, the Medes and the Scythians united against Assyria in the summer of 612 B.C. and captured and destroyed Nineveh, the capital. The ultimate refuge of the Assyrians and of their last king, Ashurubalit II, was Haran. But that city too was captured in 610 B.C. and the remainder of the Assyrian army was finally destroyed at Carchemish on the Euphrates in 605 B.C.

The victor of Carchemish, Nebuchadnezzar, built the mighty neo-Babylonian empire, but after his death in 562 B.C. it quickly declined. Treachery and political and religious conflicts were the rule in Babylon. This was the situation when Cyrus, king of the Persians, entered world history. He had little difficulty in conquering Babylon in the year 539 B.C.: the city surrendered to him without a blow being struck. Although it was not destroyed, its capture marks the fall of Babylon and the decline of the Mesopotamian civilization. The city remained standing for some time but an entirely new era had already dawned, an era marking the end of a civilization that could boast of an uninterrupted tradition lasting over 2,000 years. See also ASSYRIA; BABYLONIA.

MESSIAH A Hebrew term which literally means "anointed". It denotes a person invested by God with special functions and powers. It was rendered in Greek as *christos*, from which the title "Christ" derives.

In the OT, the term could be applied to anyone set apart for a special function, such as the priest in Leviticus 4:3, 5, who is described as "the anointed priest." It was, however, used more particularly of the king,

MESSIAH
Dan 9:25-26.
John 1:41;
4:25

The twin portals of the Golden Gate, in Jerusalem, blocked for centuries. For the Jews, who call it the Gate of Mercy, it will be opened only when the messiah comes. To the Christians it symbolizes the entrance of Jesus into Jerusalem,

who was conceived of as being anointed by divine command (cf I Sam 10:1); and his person, as "the Lord's anointed," was held to be sacrosanct (I Sam 24:6). After the promise made to David through the prophet Nathan that the throne of his "seed" should be established "forever" (II Sam 7:12-13), the whole Davidic dynasty came to be regarded as specially chosen by God (II Sam 22:51; Ps 89:35ff). Nevertheless, the term could still be used for other people, such as the patriarchs (I Chr 16:22) or even the Persian king Cyrus (Is 45:1). Under the later monarchy, when the kingdom was threatened by Assyria and Babylon, the appearance of a future king of the house of David, whose rule would be glorious, wise and secure, was foretold by Isaiah and Jeremiah. After Jerusalem had fallen, the exiled Ezekiel had no doubt that the restored Israel in Palestine would be shepherded by "my servant David" (Ezek 34:23ff; 37:24ff). Immediately after the return from Exile it seemed possible that the kingship might be restored in the person of the Davidic prince Zerubbabel (cf Zech 6:12-13) in association with Joshua the high priest. This did not occur, however, and the high priests alone became the secular rulers until the time of the Maccabees, from whom (and not from the Davidic line) the Hasmoneans were descended. The Hasmoneans ruled Palestine from the middle of the 2nd century until the middle of the 1st century B.C., but the hope of a king who would be both "the Lord's anointed" and "the son of David" never died and is reflected, for example, in the pseudepigraphical Psalms of Solomon (17:23-38). In some of the Dead Sea Scrolls from Qumran, the Essene community seems to have expected two or three messianic figures: messiahs of David and Aaron (royal and priestly) and "a prophet like Moses" (cf Deut 18:15-19).

In the NT, the continued expectation of a deliverer who would be descended from the house of David and who would restore the Davidic independence, is seen in such passages as Matthew 2:4-6 and Acts 1:6.

According to the Synoptic Gospels, Jesus was expressly proclaimed as the Christ or messiah by the angels at his birth (Luke 2:11) and his fulfillment of this role is divinely attested before his birth (Luke 1:32-33) and, in different terms, at his baptism (Mark 1:11). In his public ministry his messiahship was acclaimed at first only by demoniacs (Luke 4:41), and suspected by John the Baptist (Matt 11:3). Jesus himself did not at this period openly acknowledge his messiahship. Peter's explicit confession of him as the Christ at Caesarea Philippi (Matt 16:16; Mark 8:29) seems to mark a turning-point; on this occasion Jesus did not disclaim the title and according to Matthew 16:17, he acknowledged it fully. He still, however, charged his disciples that they should not tell anyone that he was the Christ (Matt 16:20; Mark 8:30), perhaps because of the current political implications of the title and the need to prepare the disciples for its fulfillment through the passion and resurrection rather than the immediate establishment of a visible Kingdom of God. When at his trial Jesus was asked by the high priest the direct question, "Are you the Christ?" he replied in the affirmative (Mark 14:61ff). After his resurrection, he explicitly taught that he was identical with the messiah of the OT expectation (Luke 24:26ff). According to John's gospel Jesus acknowledged it at a comparatively early stage in his ministry (John 4:26).

METALS Asia Minor was rich in iron and had some copper. Copper was also mined in northern Syria, in a region known to the authors of the El Amarna Letters as the "Land of Copper". More important, however, were the copper mines of Cyprus, whence copper (late Latin: *cuprum*) took its name. Some iron and some copper were also found in Lebanon. In Palestine the important sources of copper were those of the southern Arabah, Sinai and Punon, east of the Arabah, which were exploited at different periods (the attribution of these mines to Solomon now seems very doubtful). Ezekiel knew that the metals used in Palestine were brought by Tyrian merchants from Tarshish (Ezek 27:12), and Solomon set up foundries in the Jordan Valley (I Kgs 7:46).

Knowledge of mining activities in the biblical period is limited. Surface veins of metal ore were exploited, and the possibility that tunnels were dug in order to reach richer deposits should not be excluded. Job 28:1-7 may have been alluding to such methods. Metals were probably brought to Palestine in bars, from which the finished products were produced locally. Crucibles for founding copper and iron have been discovered in several places in Palestine. Some of the installations used in metal-founding are mentioned in the Bible, examples being the iron furnace (Deut 4:20) and the furnace (Is 48:10). Precious metals were worked by beating, soldering, engraving and in the filigree technique. A vivid picture of the metalworker may be found in Isaiah (41:6-7).

GOLD This precious metal was mined in Egypt in early times. The Bible uses many different names for gold, some of which refer to its quality, such as "pure gold" (Ex 25:36, 38; I Kgs 6:20-21); "refined gold" (I Chr 28:18); and "hammered gold" (I Kgs 10:17). Gold is also associated with Ophir: "wedge of Ophir" (Is 13:12); "gold of Ophir" (I Chr 29:4) or, in Hebrew, just "Ophir" (Job 22:24). The Israelites most probably acquired the goldsmith's art while in Egypt. According to the Bible many of the vessels used in the tabernacle were made of gold.

There is no gold in Palestine, so it had to be brought from other countries including Tarshish, India or Arabia. The Phoenicians brought gold from Havilah (Gen 2:11), buying it from Arabian merchants (Ezek 27:22). Solomon sent a fleet to bring gold from Ophir. Gold coins were not minted before the Persian period; until then

Copper ingots from the Middle Bronze Age found at Tell Yeruham.

A goldsmith at his furnace. Detail of a wall painting from the tomb of Rekhmere. Thebes. c. 1470 B.C.

payments were made in metal (cf Josh 7:21). Gold was one of the gifts brought by the three wise men to the infant Jesus in Bethlehem (Matt 2:11).

SILVER A precious metal, known in very early times. In Palestine silver vessels have been found in archeological strata as early as the Middle and Late Bronze Ages. Silver was used for producing cups, bowls, plates and jewelry. The richest silver mines in the ancient world were in Spain. There were also silver mines in the mountains bordering the Red Sea and quantities of silver were found in Anatolia, which supplied the needs of Babylon.

This metal is rarely found in the pure state. The crude ore, which contains other elements, mainly lead, is refined by a process of smelting. At high temperatures the molten lead and other heavier substances sink, while the lighter silver floats (cf Jer 6:28-30; Ezek 22:17-22). Silver was highly esteemed because of its comparative rarity and because of its chemical and physical properties. Together with gold and copper it was used as payment, in barter (Gen 20:16, etc.) and for paying taxes (I Kgs 15:19). Images of gods were made of silver (Ex 20:23), as were jewelry and household utensils (Ex 3:22; 11:2, etc.). Together with gold, silver was much used in the tabernacle (Ex chap. 26) and in the Temple (II Chr chap. 2, etc.). Silver mines are mentioned in Job 28:1 and methods of refining it are often referred to (Prov 17:3; Zech 13:9). Solomon imported silver from Arabia (II Chr 9:14) and Tarshish (II Chr 9:21; Jer 10:9).

In the Hellenistic and Roman periods silver was freely used in everyday life and the art of the silversmith was soon highly developed (for the silversmiths of Ephesus, see Acts 19:24ff).

COPPER The metal referred to by this name in the Bible is bronze, which is an alloy of copper and tin. Copper in its pure form was rarely used. Bronze was the most useful and most important of metals from the beginning of the 3rd millennium B.C. down to the 13th century B.C. when iron began to supplant it. Weapons, agricultural implements, mining tools, household utensils and jewelry were all made of bronze. The Egyptians exploited the copper mines of Sinai, where smelting was also carried out. It was also mined in the Arabah (Punon) and, early in the Iron Age, at Timnah, northwest of the Gulf of Elath. The copper-bearing ore was ground in stone mortars and subsequently smelted in crucibles made of clay. Slag heaps abound in the southern part of Sinai and along the southern Arabah. According to I Kings 7:46 Solomon

Metal workers depicted on a wall painting from the tomb of Rekhmere, Thebes. c. 1470 B.C.

cast the copper vessels of the Temple between Succoth and Zaretan, but no traces of this have as yet been discovered there.

IRON Since iron is very hard to separate from its oxides, it was the last of the metals that the ancient world learned to produce, and was not used until about 2,000 years after bronze. The frequent allusions in the Bible to the use of iron in conjunction with copper are considered by many scholars to be anachronistic. The Egyptians knew the rare meteoritic iron as early as about 3000 B.C. and used it to produce weapons, but it was not until the 13th century B.C. that the secrets of separating iron from its oxides was discovered. The credit for this discovery goes to the Hittites, from whose territory it was brought by the merchants of Tyre to Syria and Palestine. The wanderings of the Sea Peoples (Philistines) brought more iron to the Near East. According to archeological data the metal was known in Palestine from about the time of their arrival in Canaan; iron weapons have been found in tombs of Philistine warriors, together with tools and jewelry made of the same metal. According to the Bible, its production was monopolized by the Philistines (I Sam 13:19-20). There was very little iron in Palestine, and its seems that the metal that was used was brought from abroad by Phoenician merchants. Iron ores are mentioned in the Sinai peninsula, but it is doubtful whether they were in fact exploited (cf Deut 4:20; I Kgs 8:51). Iron was also brought from Tarshish (Ezek 27:12), and a special kind came from Javan (Ezek 27:19). Bolts for gates (Is 45:2), nails (I Chr 22:3), agricultural implements (I Sam 13:20-1), weapons (Num 35:16), chains (Ps 105:18), chariots (Josh 17:16) and weights (I Sam 17:7) were all made of iron.

TIN In the Bible tin is mentioned in conjunction with copper (AV: "brass"), lead and iron (Num 31:22). According to Ezekiel (22:18-20) it was brought from Tarshish, together with silver, copper, iron and lead. In the Hellenistic and later periods it was obtained from Europe.

LEAD No lead is found in Palestine but there are comparatively rich deposits in Syria and Asia Minor. The Phoenicians brought it from Tarshish (Ezek 27:12). Although it is rarely found in the strata of the biblical periods its use was known (cf Ex 15:10; Amos 7:7). During the time of the Second Temple it was used for weights, slingstones, images of gods and as a binding material between stones used for building.

METHUSELAH The son of Enoch and grandfather of Noah in the genealogy of Seth (Gen 5:21-22, 25-27; I Chr 1:3). He lived 969 years, longer than any other biblical character.

METHUSHAEL ("man of God"). The son of Mehujael and father of Lamech in the genealogy of Cain.

MEUNIM, MEUNITES A people or a group of peoples, neighbors of Israel. Judges 10:12 names a number of peoples who were hostile to Israel: Sidonians, Amalekites and Maonites, and it is likely that the Maonites are the same as Meunim of I Chronicles 4:41 (translated in some versions as "dwellings"), mentioned as one of the nomadic peoples in the times of Uzziah and Hezekiah. The Meunim are difficult to

METHUSELAH
**Gen 5:21-22,
25-27. I Chr
1:3. Luke 3:37**

METHUSHAEL
Gen 4:18

MEUNIM,
MEUNITES
**I Chr 4:41.
II Chr 26:7.
Ezra 2:50.
Neh 7:52**

identify because they are not mentioned in any other biblical or extra-biblical source. None refers to Meunim among the other nomadic tribes in the periods of the conquest of Canaan, in the Judges, or even in the early days of the United Kingdom. The compilers of the Septuagint were aware of these difficulties and in Judges 10:12 translated Meunim as Midian.

II Chronicles 26:7 tells of the victory of Uzziah over the Philistines, Arabians and the Mehunims. The next verse relates that the Ammonites gave gifts to Uzziah, but the Septuagint reads Meunim and this would be logical. The same verse ends: "his fame spread as far as the entrance of Egypt". This may mean that the Meunim dwelt between Palestine and Egypt.

MEZAHAB ("golden waters" or "rain waters"). Mother of Matred and grandmother of Mehetabel. However, some scholars believe that Mezahab is the name of a man who was father of Matred.

MEZOBAITE An epithet affixed to the name of Jaasiel, one of David's thirty "mighty men".

MIBHAR The son of Hagri, he was one of David's "mighty men".

MIBSAM ("perfume").

1. Fourth son of Ishmael the son of Abraham.

2. Son of Shallum and father of Mishma in the genealogy of the family of Simeon.

MIBZAR One of the chiefs of Esau, princes of Edom.

MICAH ("who is like Yah?" implying "there is none like Yah").

1. An Ephraimite who used 200 pieces of his mother's silver to set up a private shrine complete with ephod and teraphim (Judg chaps. 17-18). Prominent features of this shrine were a sculptured image and a molten image. Micah, who was not a Levite, appointed one of his own sons as priest of the shrine. Micah's establishment of this shrine is presented by the author of Judges chapters 17-18 as proof that the period of the Judges was characterized by anarchy (Judg 17:6). A Levite from Bethlehem, named Jonathan son of Gershon, was later persuaded by Micah to assume the priesthood of the shrine. Members of the tribe of Dan subsequently stole the Ephraimite's cultic objects, and they persuaded the Levite to accompany them on their way to their new location on a the site of the former Canaanite city of Laish. At first Micah thought of defending himself but soon decided against risking his life in a vain attempt to recover his lost property. The Bible provides no further information concerning this Micah.

2. Great-grandson of Shemaiah son of Joel the Reubenite.

3. See MICHA, MICHAH No.1.

4. See MICHA, MICHAH No.2.

5. An official at the court of King Josiah. Having heard Shaphan read the Scroll of the Torah which had been found in the Temple, the king responded by rending his clothes and sending five people to consult a prophet concerning the fate that lay in store for the people of Judah for their generations-long failure to obey the laws contained in the scroll (II Chr 34:18-21). One of these was Abdon son of Micah. According to the parallel account in II Kings 22:11-13 the official in question was not Abdon son of Micah but Achbor son of Michaiah.

6. A prophet who is said to have received his revelations during the reigns of Jotham, Ahaz and Hezekiah, kings of Judah (Jer 26:18; Mic 1:1). In both these references Micah is referred to as having come from Moresheth, probably identical with the town near Gath called Moresheth-Gath, which is mentioned in the Bible only in Micah 1:14. Like his contemporary Amos, Micah was a native of the Kingdom of Judah who addressed his prophetic message to both Samaria (Mic 1:1;

5:7; chaps. 6-7; cf Amos 2:6ff) and Judah (Mic 1:1, 5, 8ff; chaps. 2-5; cf Amos 2:4-5; 6:1). Micah 7:14 intimates that the only Israelite territories then occupied by a foreign power (presumably the Arameans) were Bashan and Gilead, leading to suggestions that Micah's mission to Samaria belongs to the early years of King Jeroboam son of Joash king of Israel. Micah was the first prophet to foresee Jerusalem's destruction as a punishment for the city's sins against the Lord. A century later, during the early months of the reign of King Jehoiakim of Judah, it was recalled that Micah's prophecy "Zion shall be plowed as a field, Jerusalem shall become heaps of ruins, and the Temple Mount a shrine in the forest" (Mic 3:12), did not make King Hezekiah execute the prophet for blasphemy (Jer 26:17, 19). On the contrary, the king prayed to the Lord procuring a reprieve from the divine punishment. Micah's declaration that the Lord requires "only to do justice, to love mercy, and to walk humbly with your God" (Mic 6:8) became a favorite quotation. (See MICAH, BOOK OF).

MICAH, BOOK OF The sixth book of the twelve Minor Prophets. Ascribed to the Judean Micah the Moreshtite (see MICAH No.6) who prophesied concerning both Samaria and Jerusalem. The date and place of composition are given in the first verse which places the prophecy in the days of the kings of Judah, Jotham, Ahaz and Hezekiah (8th century B.C.).

The book contains three major divisions. Part I, corresponding to Micah 1:2-3:12, predicts the destruction of both Samaria and Jerusalem for their respective sins. The people of Samaria are accused of worshiping idols, which it is asserted, were bought with the income earned by prostitutes (1:7). Micah was the first prophet to predict the downfall of Jerusalem. According to him, the city was doomed because its beautification was financed by dishonest business practices, whereby numerous persons were impoverished (chaps. 2-3). He also attacked the prophets of his day whom he accused of accepting money for their oracles (3:5-12). Part II, corresponding to chapters 4-5, anticipates the destruction of the Judean state and promises its restoration more glorious than before. Micah 4:1-3 — the prophecy of an era of universal peace over which the Lord will preside from Jerusalem — appears to be take over almost verbatim from Isaiah 2:2-4. Contradicting Micah 4:1-2 which foresees all peoples acknowledging the Lord as their sovereign, 4:5 suggests a doctrine of religious tolerance, even extending to polytheists. Micah 5:1-5 announces that Israel shall be ruled by a descendant of David (cf Is chap. 11; Hos 3:5; Amos 9:11) and delivered by him from the Assyrians. Micah 5:9-15 declares that when the glory of Zion and Jacob is restored the Lord will force the Gentiles to abandon idolatry.

Fragment of the Book of Micah found at Qumran. (Shrine of the Book, Jerusalem)

In Part III, Micah chapters 6-7, dishonesty in the marketplace and corruption in government provide grounds for a prophetic rebuke of Samaria which is threatened with destruction (chap. 6). This part features the prophet's declaration (6:8) that the Lord requires of man only "to do justice, to love mercy and to walk humbly with your God".

Samaria's response to Micah's charges and threats consists of three parts: (a) an admission of guilt (7:1-6); (b) adversaries are forewarned that Samaria will rely on the Lord for forgiveness and deliverance (7:7-13); and (c) a prayer for forgiveness and deliverance (7:14-20). The final portion of the latter prayer (7:18-20) is the main text employed in the Jewish New Year rite of *Tashlikh* (meaning "you will cast out" Mic 7:19), which is performed near a body of water, with an appeal to God to hurl Israel's sins "into the depths of the sea" (7:19). In that context 7:18-20 is regarded as a paraphrase of the "thirteen attributes of God" contained in Exodus 34:6-7. Micah was so filled with the word of God that he dedicated his life to delivering his message, "but truly, I am full of power, by the Spirit of the Lord, and of justice and might, to declare to Jacob his transgression and to Israel his sin" (Mic 3:8).

OUTLINE

1:1-3:12	Threatening prophecies: sins of Israel and Judah; condemnation of rich oppressors, tyrannical rulers, false prophets
4:1-5:15	Promise of restoration of Zion, of the Temple, the ingathering of the Jewish exiles and the advent of the messiah
6:1-16	God's charges against Israel; the city threatened
7:1-20	The conquest of enemies and restoration of the exiles

MICAIAH
I Kgs 22:8-9, 13-15, 19, 24-26, 28. II Chr 18:7-8, 12-14, 18, 23-25, 27

MICAIAH Son of Imlah; a prophet during the reign of King Ahab. Before the battle of Ramoth Gilead (I Kgs chap. 22; II Chr chap. 18), Ahab, at the request of King Jehoshaphat of Judah, summoned 400 prophets to "inquire for the word of the Lord" (I Kgs 22:5). Their favorable reply did not satisfy Jehoshaphat who asked for further testimony and Micaiah, whom Ahab hated "because he does not prophecy good concerning me" (I Kgs 22:8), was brought before the court. His first prophecy was also favorable but Ahab disbelieved him and demanded the truth. Micaiah then told of Israel being "scattered on the mountains, as sheep that have no shepherd" (I Kgs 22:17; II Chr 18:16), and discredited the other prophets, in whose mouths "The Lord put a lying spirit" (I Kgs 22:23). In response, Zedekiah, one of the 400, struck Micaiah on the cheek after which he was imprisoned at the order of Ahab (I Kgs 22:24-28; II Chr 18:23-27).

MICHA, MICHAH 1
II Sam 9:12

MICHA, MICHAH ("who is like God").

The name of several biblical characters, spelled differently in different texts.

1. Son of Mephibosheth, grandson of Jonathan the son of Saul; he was the father of Pithon, Melech, Tarea and Ahaz. In I Chronicles 8:34; 9:40-41 he is given as Micah.

MICHA, MICHAH 2
I Chr 23:20; 24:24-25

2. Firstborn son of Uzziel, the youngest son of Kohath. He was head

of one of the divisions of Levites in the House of the Lord at the time of King David.

3. One of the leaders of the people who sealed the covenant at the time of Nehemiah.

4. A descendant of Asaph the singer and father of Mattaniah who was one of the first settlers in Jerusalem after the return from Babylon. In I Chronicles 9:15 he is given as Micah.

MICHAEL ("who is like God"?).

1. A man of the tribe of Asher; the father of Sethur, one of the 12 spies sent by Moses to explore the land of Canaan.

2. Ancestor of a clan of the Gadites.

3. The head of one of the chief families of the Gadites.

4. An ancestor of Asaph, a Levitical singer.

5. The son of Izrahiah of the tribe of Issachar.

6. The son of Beriah the Benjamite.

7. A man of Manasseh, one of the "captains of the thousands" who joined David at Ziklag.

8. Father of Omri; head of the tribe of Issachar at the time of David.

9. The sixth son of King Jehoshaphat of Judah (II Chr 21:2); he was slain by his brother Jehoram when the latter ascended the throne.

10. The father of Zebadiah head of the family of the sons of Sephatiah who returned to Jerusalem with Ezra.

11. An angel mentioned in the Book of Daniel; he is called "one of the chief princes" (Dan 10:13), or the "great prince" (Dan 12:1). Michael was the patron angel of Israel. According to the Book of Daniel, his tasks include the destruction of the sinners at the End of Days, he will also praise and glorify the righteous (Dan 12:1-3). There are references to Michael in the Apocrypha (as intercessor for the nations, and recording angel); the Dead Sea Scrolls (where he is mentioned as the first of the four angels and associated with Gabriel and Raphael); Talmudic and Midrashic literature; the NT (Jude v. 9; Rev 12:7) depicts his struggle with the Devil (Dragon) over Moses' body because of his responsibility for burying the dead; and later Christian writings.

MICHAH See MICHAH, MICHAH No.2.

MICHAIAH ("who is like God").

1. One of the leaders sent by Jehoshaphat king of Judah to teach in the cities of his kingdom

2. See MICAH No.5.

3. Son of Gemariah and grandson of Shaphan, he heard Baruch read the words of Jeremiah and repeated them to the princes of the court.

4. A priest in the time of Nehemiah. See MICHA, MICHAH No.4.

5. One of the priests who played the trumpet at the dedication of the wall of Jerusalem repaired by Nehemiah.

6. The mother of Abijah, king of Judah; the name is probably a corruption of Maacah.

MICHAL The younger daughter of King Saul (I Sam 14:49). Hearing that she loved David (I Sam 18:20-21) and hoping to rid himself of his young and popular rival, Saul offered him Michal for a wife, for the brideprice of 100 Philistine foreskins. David managed the feat, leaving Saul no choice but to fulfill his promise. When the king later sent men to murder David at home, Michal helped her husband escape thus saving his life (I Sam 19:11-18).

While David was a fugitive from Saul, Michal was betrothed to Palti son of Laish from Galim (I Sam 25:44). Later, when David was crowned in Hebron, his first condition for ending hostilities with Abner and the survivors of Saul's family was the restoration of his wife; this was duly done (II Sam 3:12-16).

When David brought the ark to Jerusalem and danced in front of it, Michal haughtily accused him of immodesty and even indecent exposure (II Sam 6:16-22).

Michal never had any children (II Sam 6:23) and a seemingly conflicting account that she bore five sons to Adriel of Meholah (II Sam 21:8), is probably erroneous; it was her elder sister Merab who was Adriel's wife (I Sam 18:19) and the mother of his children.

MICHMAS, MICHMASH A town in the territory of Benjamin, in the region of Bethel, north of Jerusalem, on the border of the desert. It was apparently founded during the conquest of Canaan by the Israelites. Saul assembled some of his men there (I Sam 13:2). It was also on the Assyrian army's route to Jerusalem (Is 10:28). It was resettled after the

View of the village of Mukhmas, the site of ancient Michmash.

return from Babylonia (Ezra 2:27). Jonathan the Hasmonean made the town his base after his victory over Bacchides (I Macc 9:73). It was a large village in the Roman period. Identified with Mukhmas, 4 miles (6.5 km) southeast of Bethel.

MICHMETHATH A place near Shechem on the border between Ephraim and Manasseh (Josh 16:6; 17:7). The site has been identified by some at Khirbet Makhneh el Foqa, about 2½ miles (4 km) south of Tell Balata. Others prefer the identification with Khirbet Ibn Nasir, 1½ miles (2.5 km) southeast of ancient Shechem. Michmethath is the name of a mountain or a valley in the region of Shechem.

MICHRI A man of Benjamin, father of Uzzi and grandfather of Elah No.6, head of one of the families of exiles who settled in Jerusalem at the time of Nehemiah.

MIDDIN A town in the wilderness of Judah, mentioned once in the Bible (Josh 15:61). It is listed among six other towns, the northernmost of which is Beth Arabah, and the southernmost En Gedi. In the Buqei'a valley in the Judean desert three ancient ruins have been discovered. One of these, Khirbet Abu Tabaq, has been identified with Middin. It is 3 miles (5 km) west of Qumran and about 9 miles (14 km) south of Jericho. At this place remains have been found of a fortified settlement which may perhaps be ascribed to Jehoshaphat (cf II Chr 17:12), or to Uzziah (cf II Chr 26:10).

MIDIAN

1. One of the sons of Abraham by Keturah; his father sent him to live in "the country of the east" (Gen 25:2-6).

2. A country in the northwestern part of the Arabian peninsula, along the Gulf of Elath bordered by Edom to the north and Arabian kingdoms to the south. At times the nomadic Midianites controlled parts of the Arabah, the Negeb and Sinai. It was in Sinai that Moses met

Drawing of a decoration on a Midiniate votive juglet from northwest Arabia. 12th century B.C.

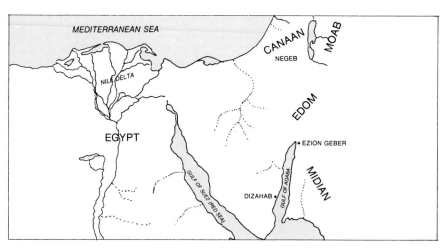

Midianite pottery vases from the 13th century temple at Timna. (Courtesy B. Rothenberg)

(top right)
The territory of the Midianites.

Section of an Egyptian fortress near Haruba in North Sinai. (Courtesy of Prof. E. D. Oren, North Sinai Expedition)

Jethro, the priest of Midian whose daughter, Zipporah, he married (Ex 2:15-3:1) and it was in Midian he experienced the vision of the burning bush (Ex 3:2). Like the Ishmaelites, the Midianites engaged in international trade (Gen 37:28). In the time of the Judges they marauded the settled areas (Judg 6:1-7), where they were soundly defeated by the Israelites under Gideon (Judg chaps. 6-8). Since they possessed camels (Judg 6:5), they could pursue their activities as warriors and traders and indeed they were the chief agents in the trade in gold and incense from Arabia (Is 60:6). In later periods the Midianites are still referred to as nomadic herdsmen (Judith 2:26). Midian is not mentioned in sources outside the Bible.

MIDIANITES See MIDIAN No.2

MIGDAL EL (MIGDAEL) ("tower or fortress of God"). A fortress town in the territory of Naphtali (Josh 19:38), close to Hazor, Kadesh and Iron, in Upper Galilee.

MIGDAL GAD A city which fell to the lot of the tribe of Judah when Joshua divided the land of Canaan among the tribes; it was in the Lachish district but its location is not known.

MIGDOL One of the halts on the route of the Exodus (Ex 14:2), before the crossing of the Red Sea. Identified with the Migdol fortress of

1:46. Ps 83:9. Is 9:4; 10:26; 60:6. Hab 3:7. Acts 7:29

MIDIANITES
Gen 37:28, 36. Num 10:29; 25:6, 14-15, 17; 31:2-3, 7. Judg 6:2-3, 6-7, 11, 13-14, 16, 33; 7:1-2, 7, 12, 23-25; 8:1

MIGDAL EL
Josh 19:38

MIGDAL GAD
Josh 15:37

MIGDOL
Ex 14:2. Num 33:7. Jer 44:1; 46:14. Ezek 29:10; 30:6

Excavations at the site of Migdol.

Sethos I and of Merneptah at Tell el-Heir, 13 miles (21km) northwest of Kantara. Recent excavations at the site of Tell el-Heir revealed an important Egyptian-Greek fortress dating to the 7th-6th century B.C.

MIGRON A town in the territory of Benjamin, where Saul and his men resided, while watching the Philistines' preparations for war (I Sam 14:2). In the description of the Assyrian army's march upon Jerusalem (Is 10:28), Migron is cited as a place where they made a stop.

MIJAMIN

1. Head of the sixth division of priests in the House of the Lord at the time of King David.

2. One of the leaders who sealed the covenant in the time of Nehemiah.

3. One of the priests and Levites who came back from the Exile in Babylon with Zerubbabel and settled in Jerusalem.

4. One of the sons of Parosh who had taken pagan wives and had to repudiate them at the decree of Ezra.

MIKLOTH

1. One of the sons of Jeiel, a man of Gibeon. He was the father of Shimeah (I Chr 8:32) or Shimeam (I Chr 9:38) who lived in Jerusalem. Mikloth was one of the great-grandparents of King Saul.

2. One of the captains of King David; he served in the second military division under the leadership of Dodai or Dodo the Ahohite.

MIKNEIAH A Levite who played the lyre at the time of King David.

MILALAI A Levite of the sons of Asaph the singer; he participated in one of the thanksgiving choirs at the dedication of the completed walls of Jerusalem at the time of Nehemiah.

MILCAH ("queen").

1. Daughter of Haran and sister of Iscah and Lot, she married Nahor the brother of Abraham (Gen 11:29). She bore him eight children: Huz, Buz, Kemuel, Chesed, Hazo, Pildash, Jidlaph and Bethuel (Gen 22:20-22). She was the grandmother of Rebekah (daughter of Bethuel).

2. Fourth daughter of Zelophehad the son of Hepher. Since Zelophehad had no sons, his daughters received his inheritance. Eventually they married sons of their father's brothers to keep the inheritance in the family.

MILCHAM See MILCOM

MILCOM Chief god of the Ammonites (I Kgs 11:5, 33; II Kgs 23:13). When King Solomon grew senile his Gentile wives influenced him to worship their gods, one of whom was Milcom (I Kgs 11:5). It was the

(left)
The Amman Citadel Inscription of the 8th century B.C. in which the name Milcom appears. (American Schools of Oriental Research)

Seal of "Mannu-ki- Inurta blessed by Milcom". 7th century B.C. (Israel Exploration Society)

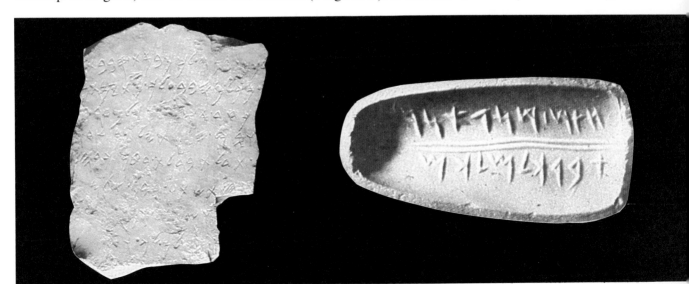

Judeans' cult of the gods of the neighboring peoples, including the Ammonite Milcom, that made the Lord strip Solomon's descendants of their sovereignty over the ten northern tribes of Israel (I Kgs 11:1-13).

Solomon surrounded Jerusalem with shrines dedicated to various deities including Milcom; these shrines remained in use until they were destroyed by King Josiah (II Kgs 23:13-14). Another reference to Milcom may be found in II Samuel 12:30 in the account of King David's conquest of Rabbah, the Ammonite capital: "Then he took the king's crown from his (the idol's) head..., and it was set on David's head." Here, however, the Masoretic text vocalized the Hebrew consonants *mlkm* as *malkam* "their king", which could refer instead to the mortal king of the Ammonites. Another reference to Milcom may be found in Zephaniah 1:5 where the Lord condemns those who swear both by the Lord and by "their king". Many scholars hold that the vocalization *malkam* "their king" ought to be corrected to Milcom. In this case Zephaniah 1:5, like the narrative concerning Elijah and the priests of Baal (I Kgs chap. 18), urges the people to choose between one of two deities; syncretism is unacceptable (cf Ex 20:3 ff). A final reference is found in the Septuagint translation of Jeremiah 49:1, 3. It is generally accepted that Milcom is a form of the common Semitic noun meaning "king" (Hebrew *melek*), and became an epithet of the head of the Ammonite pantheon. See also MOLECH.

MILETUS The southernmost of the 12 colonies forming the Ionian confederacy on the west coast of Asia Minor, Miletus flourished as a commercial center specializing in woolen goods and furniture. During

MILETUS
Acts 20:15, 17.
II Tim 4:20

Remains of the Roman theater at Miletus.

the 8th-6th centuries B.C. it established numerous colonies in the Black Sea region but was destroyed in 494 B.C. in the wake of the Ionian revolt against Persia and never regained its former glory as the harbor gradually silted up from deposits from the River Meander. During the Roman period the Jews of Miletus encountered opposition from the local inhabitants who objected to their observance of the Sabbath, religious rites and tithing (Josephus, *Antiq.*XIV, 244-6). An inscription in the ruins of the theater shows a place reserved for Jews and "god-fearing people". On Paul's final voyage to Jerusalem, he visited Miletus where he met with the Ephesian church leaders (Acts 20:15, 17).

MILLET See PLANTS

MILLO ("filling"). Millo is first mentioned in conjunction with David's building activities in Jerusalem (II Sam 5:9); the name apparently refers to the filling of the saddle uniting the southeastern hill of Jerusalem with Mount Zion. The king's house may have been built on this filling (II

MILLO
II Sam 5:9.
I Kgs 9:15, 24;
11:27. II Kgs
12:20. I Chr
11:8. II Chr
32:5

A view of the City of David and Temple Mount excavations. Below the corner of the wall to the left is the area which some believe may be the Millo. (City of David Excavations)

Sam 5:11). Solomon built the Millo using forced labor (I Kgs 9:15, 24). The Millo must have been one of the city's main fortifications; it was repaired by Hezekiah (II Chr 32:5). Joash was slain in the "house of the Millo" (II Kgs 12:20).

MINIAMIN One of the assistants of Kore the Levite who gathered the freewill offerings at the time of Hezekiah king of Judah.

MINJAMIN

1. Head of a priestly family in Jerusalem at the time of Joakim the high priest.

2. One of the priests who played the trumpet at the dedication of the wall of Jerusalem repaired by Nehemiah.

MINNI One of the three kingdoms defeated by Babylon which are mentioned by Jeremiah in his prophecy of the destruction of Babylon. Generally considered to be the land of the Manneans.

MINNITH A town in the land of Ammon, mentioned as the scene of one of the victories of Jephthah (Judg 11:32-3). Wheat was exported from here to Tyre (Ezek 27:17). Identified by some with Umm el-Khanafish, northeast of Heshbon.

MINOR PROPHETS The works of twelve prophets contained in the Prophets section of the OT. They are called "minor" in comparison with the much larger works of the three "major" prophets — Isaiah, Jeremiah and Ezekiel. The Minor Prophets are Hosea, Joel, Amos, Obadiah, Jonah, Micah, Nahum, Habakkuk, Zephaniah, Haggai, Zechariah and Malachi.

MINT See PLANTS

MIPHKAD GATE One of the gates of Jerusalem, mentioned in Nehemiah 3:31, as having been repaired by the merchants. It was apparently on the eastern side of the Temple compound.

MIRACLES Extraordinary events ascribed to divine or supernatural intervention in the ordinary course of events. In biblical times, man viewed both the world of nature and the human world as the area in which an omnipotent God frequently displayed his power and purpose by such acts so as to move men to marvel and to religious reverence. As the creator of both spheres God was not bound or limited by the fixed laws of nature.

The OT abounds with acts that, passing beyond the limits of the natural, bespeak God's power and control of events. Many ·of these miracles are meant to prove the divine character of the commission imposed by God on various special individuals. For example, the shepherd's staff Moses holds in his hand is converted into a snake and then converted back to a staff. On God's command, Moses thrusts his

The miracle of the healed paralytic carrying his bed on his back (Mark 12:10-12). From a wall painting at Dura-Europos.

hand into his bosom; upon withdrawing it, his hand has turned leprous. Again thrusting it back into his bosom, it resumes its ordinary appearance (Ex 4:2-8). The angel who appears to Gideon touches with his staff the meat and bread Gideon has placed on a rock and a flame consumes them (Judg 6:20-22). Gideon tests the veracity of God's promise to grant him victory over Midian and Amalek by placing a fleece of wool on the ground and asking that God perform a miracle with it (Judg 6:36-40).

The story of Korah and his followers being swallowed up by the earth is intended as proof that Moses has indeed been sent by God (Num 16:28-32). Similarly, the miraculous blossoming of Aaron's rod (Num 17:1-10) serves as evidence of Aaron's appointment by God as priest. The story of Elijah's contest with the prophets of Baal on Mount Carmel is similar in nature. The fire that descends from heaven and consumes Elijah's sacrifice is proof that the Lord, and not Baal, is the one and only God (I Kgs 18:20-39).

Miracles are also performed as evidence of the future fulfillment of a prophecy.

The divine promise that King Hezekiah will recover from his illness within three days is verified by the miracle of the shadow of the sun dial turning backwards ten degrees (II Kgs 20:8-11).

The ten plagues visited on the Egyptians (Ex 5:1-12:29) are described as wonders performed by God (Ex 3:20) to humble Pharaoh, for the Egyptian ruler had initially refused to recognize the God of Israel and do his bidding (Ex 5:2). The wonders serve as signs of God's power. The memory of them is repeatedly recalled in many passages throughout the Hebrew Bible, where they are called "signs" and "wonders" (Num 14:22; Deut 4:34; 29:3; Josh 24:17; Ps 78:43; Jer 32:21).

Beginning with the story of the parting of the Red Sea (Ex 14:26-29), the years of wandering in the wilderness are marked by a number of miracles the purpose of which is to teach the lesson of God's saving power. Among these, are the sweetening of the waters at Marah (Ex 15:22-25), the manna, the "bread from heaven" (Ex 16:4, 31), the quails (Ex 16:13; Num 11:31) and Moses' drawing water from a rock by striking it (Num 20:8).

The prophets Elijah and Elisha are related in terms of the miracles they performed or were performed by God through them. Elijah is fed by the ravens (I Kgs 17:3-7). He performs a miracle for the widow of Sidon by having her jars of flour and cruse of oil repeatedly refill themselves (I Kgs 17:8-16) and he restores her son to life when the latter is apparently dead (I Kgs 17:17-23). It is significant that in these three episodes, the prophet is but the instrument through which God performs his miracles. When Elijah calls down the fire from heaven that consumes the "captain of fifty" and his "fifty men" (II Kgs 1:10; cf 6:18), the miracle is ascribed to God, not the prophet. Like his master Elijah, Elisha is described as performing a series of miracles, some of them similar to those performed by Elijah (cf I Kgs 17:8-16 with II Kgs 4:1-7). Elisha too restores a child to life (II Kgs 4:8-37; cf I Kgs 17:17-23). He cures the Aramean captain Naaman of his leprosy by having him bathe seven times in the Jordan (II Kgs 5:1-14).

No miracles are reported as having been performed in the time of the literary prophets — a period of approximately three centuries. After this long lapse, however, we find two miracles being performed for Daniel. Daniel and his three companions are cast into a fiery furnace and emerge unscathed (Dan 3:24-25), and, Daniel is cast into a den of lions but remains unharmed (Dan 6:17, 23).

Miracles are an essential feature of the NT portrayal of Jesus.

Although earlier, more rationalistic scholarship had suggested that miracles were a later accretion on the gospel traditions about Jesus, today most scholars would concede that the miracles are integral to the gospel portrayal.

A wide variety of miraculous acts are ascribed to Jesus, more, in fact, than the number credited to any other figure in antiquity. Most of the miracles are "therapeutic": healings of various physical and psychological afflictions (e.g., leprosy, blindness, deafness, paralysis, epilepsy, etc.). The most radical form of the therapeutic miracle was the restoration of life to the dead (e.g., Luke 7:11-17). In the Synoptic Gospels, particularly in Mark, Jesus also performs exorcisms; powerful expulsions of evil spirits that hold human beings in bondage (e.g., Mark 5:1-20). The NT world often (but not always) attributed physical and

(left)
The miracle of the Multiplication of the loaves and the fishes commemorated in a mosaic uncovered at the church at Tabgha, on the shore of the Sea of Galilee.

One of the springs at Tabgha (Heptapegon, i.e. "Seven Springs") where tradition located the site of the miracle of the Multiplication of the loaves and fishes.

mental afflictions to the presence of demonic beings (see DEMONS), so that the line between healings and exorcisms is often very thin (as in the story of the cleansing of the leper in Mark 1:40-45). Another type of miracle has been labeled by some scholars as "nature" miracles. Examples would be the stilling of the storm (Mark 4:35-41), the walking on the water (Mark 6:45-52), the multiplication of the loaves (Mark 6:34-44), and the changing of water into wine (John 2:1-11). In these instances too, the intent of the miracle is ultimately therapeutic or salvific but the action of Jesus is focused on elements of nature: wind, sea, food, etc. Finally, there are a few miracle stories that are not immediately salvific in intent but seem more calculated to show the awesome power or authority of Jesus. This is the case with the story of the coin found in the mouth of a fish (Matt 17:24-27) or the cursing and withering of the fig tree (Mark 11:12-14, 20-21). Similar stories are told of the apostles in Acts (e.g., their miraculous escape from jail with the help of an angel, Acts 5:17-26). This type of story is exceptional in the NT and has a strong analogy with the type of wonders attributed to other figures of Greco-Roman antiquity.

The miracles of Jesus are given important theological meaning by the evangelists. In general the Synoptic Gospels view the healings and liberating nature of the miracle as part of Jesus' basic mission to inaugurate the rule of God. This is expressly stated in Matthew 12:28: "but if I cast out demons by the Spirit of God, surely the Kingdom of God has come upon you" (cf a similar saying in Luke 11:20). It is also evident in Mark: the first public activity of Jesus following his announcement of the Kingdom (Mark 1:14-15) is the expulsion of a demon in the synagogue of Capernaum (Mark 1:21-28). By freeing human beings from the threat of sickness, evil and death itself, Jesus reveals the nature of God's coming rule, the longed-for era of salvation when evil would be defeated and the fullness of life attained. Therefore the miracles disclose the ultimate meaning of Jesus' mission just as forcefully as his teaching. And, consequently, healing is considered an essential part of the disciples' mission, which is to take its inspiration and authority from that of Jesus (see Matt 10:7-8; Mark 3:13-15; 6:7).

The miracles also help define the scope of Jesus' redemptive mission. Because sickness could involve isolation and denial of access to social life and to the sacred, the healing activity of Jesus has an inclusive, boundary-breaking quality to it. God's redemption is extended to the ritually unclean (e.g., the leper), and to the foreigner (e.g., the daughter of the Syro-Phoenician woman in Mark 7:24-30). In this sense, the miracles serve as symbolic actions pointing to the universal horizon of the gospel.

Such acts also illustrate the God-given authority and power of Jesus. The acclamations that often follow a miracle of Jesus make this point: the crowds acclaim his unique authority (e.g., Mark 1:27), his identity as prophet (Luke 7:16), his divine power to forgive sins (Matt 9:8), etc. In other instances such as the stilling of the storm (Mark 4:35-41), Jesus' power is evocative of God's own power (e.g., authority over the chaos of the sea). Although the miracle stories are not exclusively apologetic in intent, it is clear that through these stories the gospels assert Jesus' identity as the messiah and the unique revealer of God.

In the Gospel of John miracles play a slightly different, if related, role. The fourth gospel refers to the miracles as "signs" (in the Synoptics they are usually termed "acts of power"). The miracles are transparently symbolic stories which demonstrate the unique identity of the Johannine Jesus. Thus the healing of the man born blind illustrates Jesus' identity as the "light of the world" (John 9:1-41); the raising of Lazarus gives force to Jesus' self-designation as the "resurrection and the life" (John 11:1-44). The miracles are "signs" in that they point to the profound identity of Jesus as the revealer of God.

For John and the Synoptics the miracles of Jesus are not recounted for their own sake but are meant to provoke a response of faith. Only if new insight is gained into the power of God revealed by Jesus' actions can the miracle be termed successful. Within the stories themselves the recipients of healing are usually called upon to express their faith in Jesus (e.g., Matt 10:27-31; Mark 10:46-52) and the same response is evidently expected of the reader or hearer of the narrative.

Miracles, therefore, play a major role in the NT. In Acts, Luke attributes miraculous powers to the great heroes of the early church. Paul himself acknowledges that he was gifted with extraordinary powers (e.g., II Cor 12:12) and gives miraculous healing a place among the gifts of the Spirit (I Cor 12:28) — aspects of Paul's ministry often overlooked.

MIRIAM

1. Prophetess (Ex 15:20); the sister of Moses and Aaron (Num 26:59; I Chr 6:3; Mic 6:4). She helped save the life of her infant brother Moses (Ex 2:4-8).

Tensions over issues of leadership and kinship pitted Miriam and Aaron against Moses (Num chap. 12). Moses' right to supreme leadership was contested by his brother and sister on two grounds: his marriage to a Cushite woman; and their contention that their own powers of prophecy, an indispensible ingredient of a leader's profile, were not inferior to his (Num 12:1-2). God quickly intervened,

MIRIAM 1
Ex 15:20-21.
Num 12:1, 4-5,
10, 15; 20:1;
26:59. Deut
24:9. I Chr
6:3. Mic 6:4

upholding Moses' supremacy as prophet and leader, and punishing Miriam by inflicting upon her a skin disease which rendered her ritually unclean. She was obliged to undergo a period of isolation outside the camp (cf Lev chaps. 13-14) until Moses' prayer removed the disease and Miriam was reinstated as a member of the community.

Another indication of her prominence is found in Exodus chapter 15: at the conclusion of the victory poem (Song of the Sea) celebrating the Israelites' salvation from their Egyptian pursuers by the Red Sea, Miriam led a female choir which repeated the beginning of the poem (Ex 15:20-21).

She died at Kadesh Barnea and was buried there, near the end of the Israelites' trek through the wilderness (Num 20:1).

MIRIAM 2
I Chr 4:17

2. A relative of Shammai and Ishbah.

MIRMAH
I Chr 8:10

MIRMAH Seventh and youngest son of Shaharaim by his wife Hodesh and head of a Benjamite family.

MISHAEL ("who belongs to the Lord").

MISHAEL 1
Dan 1:6-7, 11, 19; 2:17

1. One of Daniel's three companions, along with Shadrach and Abednego, taken to the court of Nebuchadnezzar and renamed Meshach.

MISHAEL 2
Ex 6:22. Lev 10:4

2. A Levite, firstborn son of Uzziel the grandson of Levi and brother of Elzaphan. The two brothers were ordered to remove the bodies of Nadab and Abihu, the sons of Aaron, who had been smitten by the Lord in the tabernacle of meeting on the journey of the Children of Israel toward the promised land.

MISHAEL 3
Neh 8:4

3. One of the leaders of the people who stood to the left of Ezra when he read the Law to the people.

MISHAL
Josh 19:26; 21:30

MISHAL A city of Levites on the border of the territory of Asher (Josh 19:26; 21:30). It appears as Msir in the Execration Texts and in the list of conquests of Thutmosis III. Identified either with Tell Kisan, Tell en-Nahl or Tell Abu Hawam, all in the Plain of Acco (Acre).

MISHAM
I Chr 8:12

MISHAM Second son of Elpaal the son of Shaharaim in the genealogy of King Saul. He participated in the building of Ono and Lod.

MISHMA 1
Gen 25:14. I Chr 1:30

MISHMA

1. One of the sons of Ishmael, the son of Abraham.

MISHMA 2
I Chr 4:25-26

2. Son of Mibsam and father of Hamuel in the genealogy of the family of Simeon.

MISHMANNAH
I Chr 12:10

MISHMANNAH Fourth of the Gadites who joined David in Ziklag; one of the "mighty men".

MISHRAITES
I Chr 2:53

MISHRAITES One of the families of Kirjath Jearim, forebears of the Zorathites and the Eshtaolites.

MISPAR, MISPERETH
Ezra 2:2. Neh 7:7

MISPAR, MISPERETH One of the exiles who came back from Babylon with Zerubbabel and settled in Jerusalem.

MISPERETH
Neh 7:7

MISPERETH See MISPAR

MISREPHOTH
Josh 11:8; 13:6

MISREPHOTH A place on the border of Sidon, which was not settled by the tribes of Israel at the time of Joshua (Josh 13:6). Part of the Canaanite army retreated there after they were defeated at the battle of the waters of Merom (Josh 11:8).

MITHKAH
Num 33:28-29

MITHKAH One of the halts of the Children of Israel on their way to the promised land, between Terah and Hashmonah. Its location is unknown.

MITHNITE
I Chr 11:43

MITHNITE An epithet affixed to the name of Joshaphat, one of David's "mighty men".

MITHREDATH 1
Ezra 1:8

MITHREDATH ("gift of Mithra").

1. Treasurer of Cyrus king of Persia; he gave back to Sheshbazzar, prince of Judah, the gold and precious articles taken by Nebuchadnezzar from the Temple of Jerusalem.

MITHREDATH 2
Ezra 4:7

2. A man of Samaria, a Persian official, who was among those who opposed the rebuilding of Jerusalem and signed the letter of protest to

King Artaxerxes which resulted in an order to stop the building work.

MITYLENE (MYTILENE). The capital of the island of Lesbos off the coast of Asia Minor, from which Paul crossed to Chios on his third missionary journey.

MITYLENE
Acts 20:14

MIZAR ("littleness"). Name of a mountain in the Hermon range or possibly just an adjective used to provide a contrast between Mount Hermon and a small mountain. It has not been identified.

MIZAR
Ps 42:6

MIZPAH (MIZPEH)

1. A town in Gilead, the home of Jephthah (Judg 11:34), and the place where the Israelites assembled to fight the Ammonites under his leadership (Judg 11:11). Mizpah's sanctity was of remote antiquity: Jacob and Laban set up a heap of stones (Galeed) as a witness at the site (Gen 31:48-49). Numerous identifications have been proposed.

MIZPAH,
(MIZPEH) 1
Gen 31:49.
Judg 10:17;
11:11, 34. Hos
5:1

2. A town in the northern part of the territory of Benjamin (Josh 18:26). It is mentioned in the account of the concubine at Gibeah (Judg chaps. 20-21). As the Israelites gathered at Mizpah before the battle against the Benjamites, it must have been a town of importance. Samuel made Mizpah a place of assembly (I Sam 7:5-12) and a center of his activities (I Sam 7:16-17). After the division of the kingdom Mizpah attained still greater importance as a border town between Judah and Israel. Following Abijah's conquests on Mount Ephraim and the fall of the house of Jeroboam, Baasha forced the border of Judah to the south of Ramah, fortifying Mizpah in order to secure his southern border. King Asa of Judah, taking advantage of the Aramean assault on Israel, prevented the fortification of Ramah, instead fortifying his own towns of Geba and Mizpah (I Kgs 15:17-22; II Chr 16:1-6). After the destruction of Jerusalem at the end of the First Temple period, Mizpah became the seat of Gedaliah son of Ahikam, whom the Babylonians appointed ruler over Judah (II Kgs 25:23; Jer chaps. 40-41). The town was resettled after the return from the Babylonian Exile (Neh 3:7). The two most likely identifications of Mizpah are en-Nebi Samwil, 5 miles (8 km) northwest of Jerusalem, and Tell en-Nasbeh 7½ miles (12 km) north of the city. Most scholars tend to accept the latter identification.

MIZPAH,
(MIZPEH) 2
Josh 18:26.
Judg 20:1, 3;
21:1, 5, 8.
I Sam 7:5-7,
11, 12, 16;
10:17. I Kgs
15:22. II Kgs
25:23, 25.
II Chr 16:6.
Neh 3:7, 15,
19. Jer 40:6,
8, 10, 12-13,
15; 41:1, 3, 6,
10, 14, 16

The site is on an elevated hill, 1,600 feet (500 m) above sea level. It has been excavated extensively and is one of the few places in Palestine where the whole of the Israelite city has been uncovered. Settlement on the site began in the Chalcolithic period and the Early Bronze Age (c. 3000 B.C.), but its main occupation was in the Iron Age. The earliest

Fortifications at Tell en-Nasbeh, the site of ancient Mizpah.

Israelite settlement is of the 11th-10th centuries B.C. but typically Philistine pottery points to a possibility that it was already occupied earlier. In the 9th century B.C. the frail wall was replaced by a formidable system of fortifications enclosing an area of some 8 acres (3.5 ha). Tombs of the Persian, Hellenistic, Roman and Byzantine periods were found in the vicinity of the mound.

3. A town in the plain of Judah, one of a group also including Lachish and Makkedah (Josh 15:37-41). It is generally identified with Tell es-Safi, 5 miles (8 km) northwest of Beth Gubrin (Eleutheropolis).

4. The land of Mizpah. A district under Mount Hermon, inhabited by Hivites (Josh 11:3), identical with Mizpah mentioned in verse 8.

5. Mizpah of Gilead where Jephthah passed on his way to fight the Ammonites (Judg 11:29). Although some scholars have identified it with Mizpah No.1, the Septuagint clearly indicates that the two were different. Its location is unknown.

6. Mizpah of Moab. A place where David fled from Saul, and sought refuge for his family with the king of Moab (I Sam 22:3). It has been identified with Rujum el-Meshrefesh, some 2½ miles (4 km) south of Medeba. Others, however, suggest that it should be sought further to the south, which would lead David away from the territories of Saul.

MIZRAIM In the Table of Nations in Genesis chapter 10, Mizraim, together with Cush, Put and Canaan, is listed among the sons of Ham (Gen 10:6). The sons of Mizraim are Ludim, Anamim, Lehabim, Naphtuhim, Pathrusim and Casluhim (Gen 10:13-14). Not all of these have been identified. Naphtuhim and Pathrusim are apparently peoples of Lower and Upper Egypt. Mizraim is identified with Lower Egypt.

MIZZAH Fourth son of Reuel, son of Esau by his wife Basemath; a chief of an Edomite clan.

MNASON A man of Cyprus, "an early disciple", at whose house Paul stayed on his last visit to Jerusalem.

MOAB, MOABITES The Bible ascribes the origin of this people to the incestuous union of Lot with his elder daughter who bore him a son, Moab (Gen 19:30-38). The Moabites' chief god was Chemosh and their land, whose early inhabitants were the Rephaim Zuzim and Emim (Gen 14:5), lies to the east of the Dead Sea between Edom and Ammon. Some scholars suggest that the earliest Moabites came from a group of nomadic tribes which lived in the Syrian-Arabian desert, and occupied the territory in the 14th century B.C. Moses died and was buried in Moab. There was constant enmity between Israel and Moab (Num

(bottom of page)
The mountains of Moab.

The first appearance of the name Moab inscribed in front of the temple of Luxor. 13th century B.C.

33. II Kgs 1:1;
3:4-5, 7, 10,
13, 18, 21-24,
26; 13:20,
23:13; 24:2.
I Chr 1:46;
4:22; 8:8,
11:22, 46;
18:2, 11.
II Chr 20:1,
10, 22-23.
Ezra 9:1. Neh
13:1, 23. Ps
60:8; 83:6;
108:9. Is
11:14; 15:1-2,
4-5, 8-9; 10:2,
4, 6-7, 11-14;
25:10. Jer
9:26; 25:21;
27:3; 40:11;
48:1-2, 4, 9,
11, 13, 15-16,
18, 20, 24-26,
28-29, 31, 33,
35-36, 38-47.
Ezek 25:8-9,
11. Dan 11:41.
Amos 2:1-2.
Mic 6:5. Zeph
2:8-9

Monument from Moab known as the Balu'ah Stele, with three figures in relief and an indecipherable inscription. 12th century B.C.

(top of page)
View of Moab in the region north of the Arnon River.

22:2ff; II Kgs 1:1; 3:4ff). The Reubenites and the Gadites conquered parts of the country of the Amorites that had formerly belonged to Moab (Num 21:25ff), and there was also a state of war between Israel and Moab in the time of the Judges (Judg 3:12). Saul fought Moab (I Sam 14:47) and David completed its conquest (II Sam 8:2), but there were friendly relations between the two kingdoms (I Sam 22:3ff; I Kgs 11:1, 7). According to tradition, David was descended from the Moabitess Ruth, a convert to the Israelite people and religion. After the division of the Kingdom of Israel, Moab regained its independence, only for Omri to then conquer the country, but it freed itself once more after Ahab's death (II Kgs 1:1; 3:4ff); this is confirmed by the stele of Mesha, king of Moab (see MESHA). Oracles against Moab were uttered by both Isaiah (Is chaps. 15-16) and Jeremiah (chap. 48), who also predicts its fall (Jer 9:25-26; 25:21). Sargon II speaks in his annals of the conquest of Moab and of the Moabite soldiers who afterwards helped the Assyrians in their wars against the Arabs. After Judah's defeat by Babylonia, Moab apparently joined in the plunder and seized some of its territory. Later it formed part of the Babylonian and Persian kingdoms. In about the 4th or 3rd century B.C. the Nabateans penetrated Moab after gaining control of Edom. After A.D. 106 Moab was part of the Provincia Arabia, whose cities, Rabbathmoba and Characmoba (Kir Moab), were administrative centers. The country flourished in the later Roman and Byzantine periods.

MOABITESS Appellation of Ruth.
MOABITE STONE See MESHA
MOADIAH Identical with Maadiah.
MOLADAH A town in the Negeb of Judah (Josh 15:26) and of Simeon. One of the places resettled after the return from Babylon Exile (Neh 11:2). Identification uncertain.
MOLE See ANIMALS
MOLECH, MOLOCH A god mentioned repeatedly in connection with idolatrous worship. The name is most likely a deliberate misvocalization of *melekh* ("king") (Is 30:33) using the vowels of *boshet* which means "shame". The name also appears as "Milcom" in I Kings 11:5, 33 and II Kings 23:13 and twice as "Moloch" in the Septuagint (II Kgs 23:10; Amos 5:26).

Child sacrifices are explicitly mentioned as characterizing the Molech cult. The Pentateuch and the Book of Kings use the phrase "Passing your son [or daughter] through fire to Molech" (Lev 18:21; Deut 18:10; II Kgs 16:3; 17:17; 21:6; 23:10). In the Prophets, stronger terms are employed such as "to slaughter" or "to burn" as well as "to cause to

MOABITESS
Ruth 1:22; 2:2,
21; 4:5, 10.
II Chr 24:26

MOADIAH
Neh 12:17

MOLADAH
Josh 15:26;
19:2. I Chr
4:28. Neh
11:26

MOLECH,
MOLOCH
Lev 18:21;
20:2-5. I Kgs
11:7. II Kgs
23:10. Jer
32:35. Acts
7:43

pass through fire" (Jer 7:31; 19:5; Ezek 16:21; 20:31; 23:37, 39). Some scholars interpret the "sacrificing and burning" of these children in a figurative sense, as understood by later traditions (Jubilees 30:7ff). The ritual would then be viewed as an initiation or consecration rite for dedicatory Temple service.

The cult of Molech was connected with the worship of the Ammonites (I Kgs 11:5, 7); but the Moabites worshiped a god named Chemosh who was closely associated with, or even easily substituted for, Molech (I Kgs 11:7, 33; Judg 11:24; cf also II Kgs 23:13). Molech and Chemosh may have been local variations of the same deity.

According to Jeremiah 32:35 the "high places of Baal" in the Valley of the Son of Hinnom was the location where sacrifices were made to Molech. This practice was firmly established during the reign of Manasseh and the location specifically referred to as "Topheth" (II Kgs 23:10; Jer 7:31; 19:6-7; cf also Is 30:33; Matt 5:22). During the reform of Josiah, this high place was defiled in order to prevent further sacrifices to Molech (II Kgs 23:10). Molech-worship had greatly penetrated Israelite culture. Solomon was influenced by his foreign wives to build altars for Chemosh and Molech (I Kgs 11:5); while Ahaz and Manasseh offered their children to Molech (II Kgs 16:3; 21:6). The prophets strongly condemned the people's continual participation in the cult, and the Mosaic laws made mention of it (cf also Acts 7:43).

MOLID Second son of Abishur by his wife Abihail in the genealogy of the family of Jerahmeel.

MONEY See COINS AND CURRENCY

MONKEY See ANIMALS

MOON In the minds and deeds of the peoples of biblical times, a prominent role was played by the moon. It was first and foremost, a luminary — "lesser light" than the sun, but nevertheless the ruler of the night (Gen 1:16), admired for its radiant whiteness (Song 6:10).

More important was the moon's function as timepiece. The moon, together with the other celestial bodies, was created "for signs and seasons and for days and years" (Gen 1:14). Its cycle was the basis for the Hebrew month, and, like their English equivalents, the Hebrew words for "moon" and "month" are related. The moon was the principal regulator of Israel's religious calendar. On each new moon special sacrifices were offered (Num 28:11-15), and trumpets were blown (Num 10:10). The full moon marked the beginning of Passover and the Feast of Tabernacles.

The reliability of the moon, "the faithful witness" (Ps 89:37) gave rise to its use as a symbol of permanence, as in Psalms 72:7, "peace until the moon is no more." Eschatological literature employs this symbol of constancy to emphasize the upheaval of the end times: the moon will not shine (Is 13:10); it will be turned to blood (Joel 2:31); one third of its light will be darkened (Rev 8:12). The moon also serves to show the wonder of the day of salvation: "the light of the moon will be as the light of the sun" (Is 30:26), and ultimately God himself will replace sun and moon as the everlasting light (Is 60:19-20; Rev 21:23).

In pagan religion moon worship was widespread. Abraham must have been acquainted with the cult of the Mesopotamian moon god Nanna (or Sin), which predominated in both Ur and Haran. At Ugarit, records testify to the worship of the moon god Yarah, and traces of this deity in Palestine remain in the names Beth Yerah and possibly Jericho. A stele from the end of the Canaanite period (13th century B.C.) found at Hazor depicts hands outstretched in supplication to the moon. Job asks rhetorically if he has ever blown a kiss in adoration of the sun or moon (Job 31:26-27). Influenced by Assyrian practices, Manasseh of

MOLID
I Chr 2:29

Canaanite stele found at Hazor showing two hands raised in prayer to the Moon crescent. 13th century B.C.

Judah built altars to the heavenly host in the Temple precincts (II Kgs 21:3-5); these were destroyed in Josiah's reform (II Kgs 23:12). Obeisance to the celestial bodies is mentioned among the sins which brought about the fall of Israel (II Kgs 17:16), and according to Deuteronomy 17:2-5 moon worship was punishable by death.

In popular belief the moon may have been thought capable of causing harm (Ps 121:6), but also of influencing fertility: moon-shaped pendants were worn by the women of Jerusalem (Is 3:18) and adorned the camels of the Midianites (Judg 8:21). In NT times the belief that the moon could cause insanity is reflected in the Greek term which corresponds to English "lunatic" or "moonstruck" (Matt 4:24; 17:15). See NEW MOON.

MORDECAI

1. One of those who returned from the Babylonian Exile with Zerubbabel.

2. A Benjamite, the son of Jair who lived in Susa (Est 2:5). He was the cousin and foster-father of Esther (Est 2:7, 15). He used to sit before the king's gate and there discovered a plot by two officials, Bigthan and Teresh, against the life of the Persian king Ahasuerus (Est 2:21-23). After the culprits were put to death by hanging, the event was written in the Book of the Chronicles of the Persian kings, and only later was Mordecai rewarded for this service (Est 6:10-11). Since he did not bow down and pay homage to Haman the Agagite, the king's vizir, he was

MORDECAI 1
Ezra 2:2. Neh 7:7

MORDECAI 2
Est 2:5, 7, 10-11, 15, 19-22; 3:2-6; 4:1, 4-7, 9-10, 12-13, 15, 17; 5:9, 13-14; 6:2-4, 10-13; 7:9-10; 8:1-2, 7, 9, 15; 9:3-4, 20, 23, 29-31; 10:2-3

Page from the Book of Esther, from the De Castro Bible, *Germany, 14th century. (Israel Museum)*

Interior of the tomb revered as that of Mordecai and Esther at Hamadan, Persia.

considered his personal enemy (Est 3:5). Highly insulted, Haman planned to kill Mordecai along with all the Jews in the Persian empire (Est 3:6). With the help of Esther Mordecai succeeded in thwarting the planned genocide, and Haman and his sons were executed (Est 7:10; 9:7-10, 12-14). The Jews, all over the empire were not only saved but were permitted by royal decree to take revenge on their enemies (Est 9:5, 15-16). To mark this event Mordecai sent letters to all the Jews to celebrate the 13th and 14th day of the month of Adar each year (the festival of Purim) (Est 9:20ff). Mordecai himself was promoted to the position of vizir at the court of King Ahasuerus (Est 8:2, 15; 9:4; 10:2-3), thereby replacing his enemy Haman.

There is a chronological problem concerning the age of Mordecai at the time of these events. According to Esther 2:6, he was exiled from

Jerusalem at the time of Jeconiah king of Judah (597 B.C.) which means that in the 12th year of King Ahasuerus (Xerxes I, 486/5-465 B.C.) he was more than 123 years old. Either the narrator did not concern himself with chronological details or the reference to the one who was exiled at the time of Jeconiah was not Mordecai but one of his ancestors.

MOREH

MOREH 1
Judg 7:1

1. The hill where the Midianites encamped for their attack on the Israelites, in the days of Gideon (Judg 7:1). Identified with Jebel ed-Dehi in the Jezreel Valley.

MOREH 2
**Gen 12:6.
Deut 11:30**

2. Abraham's first halt in the land of Canaan on his journey from Haran (Gen 12:4). Here he saw God and built an altar (Gen 12:7). This was also the place where Moses conveyed the divine blessing and curse on the eve of their entry into the promised land (Deut 11:26ff). The Hebrew Bible gives *alon*, which means "oak", and not "plain" as in the AV. It is thus possible that a sacred oak is meant.

MORESHETH,
MORESHETH-GATH
**Jer 26:18. Mic
1:1, 14**

MORESHETH, MORESHETH-GATH Town in the lowlands of Judah where the prophet Micah was born. Micah refers to it in connection with the destruction of towns in the region (Mic 1:14).

MORIAH
**Gen 22:2.
II Chr 3:1**

MORIAH The land that was designated to be the place of sacrifice of Isaac (Gen 22:2). It was also the site where God appeared to David and where the House of God was to be built by Solomon (II Chr 3:1). (See JERUSALEM.)

MOSERAH,
MOSEROTH
**Num 33:30-31.
Deut 10:6**

MOSERAH, MOSEROTH One of the stations of the Israelites in the desert (Num 33:30-31). According to Deuteronomy 10:6, Aaron died and was buried there, and his son Eleazar succeeded him in office. A second tradition states that Mount Hor was the place of Aaron's death and burial (Num 20:22-29; Deut 32:50).

MOSEROTH
Num 33:30-31

MOSEROTH See MOSERAH

MOSES
**Ex 2:10-11,
14-15, 17, 21;
3:1, 3-4, 6,
11, 13-15; 4:1,
3-4, 10, 14,
18-21, 25,
27-30; 5:1, 4,
20, 22; 6:1-2,
9-10, 12-13,
20, 26-30; 7:1,
6-8, 10, 14,
19-20; 8:1, 5,
8-9, 12-13, 16,
20, 25-26,
29-31; 9:1, 8,
10-13, 22-23,
27, 29, 33, 35;
10:1, 3, 8-9,
12-13, 16,
21-22, 24-25,
29; 11:1, 3-4,
9-10; 12:1, 21,
28, 31, 35, 43.
50; 13:1, 3,
19; 14:1, 11,
13, 15, 21,
26-27, 31;
15:1, 22, 24;
16:2, 4, 6, 8-9,
11, 15, 19-20,
22, 24-25, 28,
32-34; 17:2-6,**

MOSES The leader of the Israelites in the Exodus from Egypt and during their wanderings to the promised land.

Moses was the son of Amram and Jochebed from the tribe of Levi (Ex 2:1-2; 6:20) and the younger brother of Miriam and Aaron (Ex 7:7). At the time of his birth, the Israelites were experiencing severe oppression in Egypt. Pharaoh, having reduced the people to bondage (Ex 1:8-21), went one step further by giving instructions to cast all newborn males into the Nile (Ex 1:22). When Jochebed gave birth to a son, she tried to save him by placing him in the Nile reeds, in an ark, from which he was rescued by Pharaoh's daughter who named him Moses (Ex 2:5-10). The Hebrew form, *Mosheh,* is probably cognate to the Egyptian word for "to be born", although the name is popularly explained in Hebrew as "I drew him out of the water" (Ex 2:10).

Moses was forced to flee Egypt after killing an Egyptian overseer who had beaten a Hebrew slave. He escaped to the Sinai desert and was received by the Midianite priest Jethro after rescuing the latter's daughters from the hands of ruffians; he subsequently married one of them, Zipporah (Ex 2:11-22). The turning-point in Moses' life was the divine revelation of the bush which burned "but was not consumed" (Ex 3:1-6) from where God called him revealing his own personal name and affirming that he was identical with the Lord of the patriarchs, Abraham, Isaac and Jacob (Ex 3:6, 15). God ordered Moses to return to Egypt and lead his people out of bondage. When Moses shrank from this task, protesting his inadequacy and arguing that the Israelites would not believe him, God overcame his objections by giving him a number of signs in order to persuade the people of his divine mission. When Moses insisted that he lacked the eloquence to perform these duties, God designated his brother Aaron to accompany him as spokesman.

Moses taken from his floating ark. Fresco from the synagogue of Dura-Europos, on the Euphrates River, destroyed in the 3rd century A.D.

9-12, 14-15; 18:1-2, 5-8, 12-15, 17, 24-27; 19:3, 7-10, 14, 17, 19-21, 23, 25; 20:19-22; 24:1-4, 6, 8-9, 12-13, 15-16, 18; 25:1; 30:11, 17, 22, 34; 31:1, 12, 18; 32:1, 7, 9, 11, 15, 17, 19, 21, 23, 25-26, 28-31, 33; 33:1, 5, 7-9, 11-12, 17; 34:1, 4, 8, 27, 29-31, 33-35; 35:1, 4, 20, 29-30; 36:2-3, 5-6; 38:21-22; 39:1, 5, 7, 21, 26, 29, 31-33, 42-43; 40:1, 16, 18-19, 21, 23, 25, 27, 29, 31-33, 35. **Lev** 1:1; 4:1; 5:14; 6:1, 8, 19, 24; 7:22, 28, 35, 38; 8:1, 4-6, 9-10, 13, 15-17, 19-21, 23-24, 28-31, 36; 9:1, 5-7, 10, 21, 23; 10:3-7, 11-12, 16, 19-20; 11:1; 12:1; 13:1; 14:1, 33; 15:1; 16:1-2, 34; 17:1; 18:1; 19:1; 20:1; 21:1, 16, 24; 22:1, 17, 26; 23:1, 9, 23, 26, 33, 44; 24:1, 11, 13, 23; 25:1; 27:1, 34. **Num** 1:1, 17, 19, 44, 48, 54; 2:1, 33-34; 3:1, 5, 11, 14, 16, 38-40, 42, 44, 49, 51; 4:1, 17, 21, 34, 37, 41, 45-46, 49; 5:1, 4-5, 11; 6:1, 22; 7:1, 4, 6, 11, 89; 8:1, 3-5, 20, 22-23; 9:1, 4-6, 8-9, 23; 10:1, 13, 29, 31, 35; 11:2, 10-11,

Returning to Egypt, Moses easily convinced the Israelites of his mission. But his request to permit the Israelites to go into the desert and worship God met with a flat refusal from Pharaoh who responded by increasing their workload. Only after a series of divinely-ordained punishments did Pharaoh agree to set the Israelites free.

Moses, aged 80, then assumed a new role, leading the Children of Israel on their historic journey. As God's agent, Moses cared for the people's needs and defended them against their enemies. At the Red Sea, when the chariots of Pharaoh were about to overtake the fleeing Israelites, God instructed Moses to stretch his staff over the water, which parted, enabling the people to pass. When the Egyptians tried to followed them, Moses once again stretched out his staff, the waters returned and the Egyptians were drowned (Ex 14:1-31). This triumph further strengthened the people's belief in God and trust in Moses.

After three months' wandering the people arrived at the Mountain of God, Sinai (sometimes called Horeb). Moses ascended the mountain, where he was informed by God of a covenant to be concluded with Israel (Ex 19:3-6). Thus Moses became, as it were. the mediator in the negotiations between the deity and his people, serving simultaneously as a messenger of God and as Israel's advocate before God. He convened the people at the foot of Sinai, while the Lord descended on the mount in a terrifying theophany (Ex 19:9, 17-19; 20:18) to address the people with the Ten Commandments (Ex 20:1-14); the latter, overwhelmed by this revelation and unable to hear the divine voice directly, beseeched Moses to serve as intermediary and convey God's commands to them (Ex 20:18-21 a similar account is given in Deut 5:2-5). Moses now received the first collection of biblical Law, the so-called "Book of the Covenant" (Ex 20:20-23:33). The covenant ceremony concluded with the people's consent to the ordinances, and a sacrificial rite (Ex 24:3-8). According to another tradition the covenant was finalized at a joint repast held before the Lord by Moses, Aaron, Nadab, Abihu and 70 elders (Ex 24:1-2, 9-11). Moses again ascended the mount and received the Tablets of the Law (Ex 24:12-18), remaining there for 40 days and nights.

In the meantime the people, anxious over Moses' prolonged absence, implored Aaron to make a golden calf as a visible surrogate for worship. When Moses finally descended, he witnessed their reveling around the calf, and responded by smashing the tablets, which symbolized the breaking of the covenant (Ex 32:1-19). He then crushed the golden calf and made those responsible drink from its powdered dust (Ex 32:20-29). However, his special plea on behalf of the people succeeded in averting worse retribution (Ex 32:7-14, 30, also retold in Deut 9:8-21).

Moses was again summoned to appear before the Deity on the mount and received another set of tablets containing the Ten Commandments (Ex 34:1-28; also Deut 10:1-4).

He was also instructed to build a movable Temple, i.e. the tabernacle with all its appurtenances, where his brother Aaron and the latter's sons were consecrated to serve God (Ex 25:1-31:17).

After their prolonged stay at Sinai (nearly a year) the Israelites started their trek to the Holy Land. During this journey communication with God did not cease. Moses built a "Tent of Meeting" outside the camp (not to be confused with the tabernacle, in its center) where he consulted the Lord (Ex 33:7-11). When Moses complained of the people's grumbling, God ordered him to convene 70 wise men before the Tent of Meeting, where the Lord imbued them with Moses' spirit, thereby preparing them for leadership (Num 11:16-30). When Moses' authority was contested by Aaron and Miriam who considered themselves their brother's equals, God showed them that Moses was incomparable, for to him alone did God speak directly, rather than in visions or dreams. Miriam was punished with leprosy and Aaron had to humbly beg Moses to intercede for her (Num 12:1-15).

Moses faced occasional difficulties in his relations with the people, who became rebellious under the many perils and hardships they experienced. At the Red Sea they already began to complain against Moses' leadership out of fear of the approaching attack of Pharaoh's army (Ex 14:1-4). In the desert these difficulties were aggravated by lack of water and food (Ex 15:24; 16:3; 17:2-4) until Moses' prayer induced the Lord to provide them with manna for their daily food (Ex 16:11-36), and Moses was instructed to bring forth water from the rock (Ex 17:5-6). The people's worship of the golden calf marked a crisis point; only Moses' intercession prevented a major catastrophe (Ex 32:1-33:6). During the subsequent journey to the Holy Land these problems did not lessen. No longer content with manna, the Israelites desired meat (Num 11:4-9), whereupon God provided quails, but those who complained were smitten with a plague (Num 11:31-34). A grave challenge to Moses' authority arose with the mutiny of Korah the Levite and two members of the tribe of Reuben, Dathan and Abiram, who argued that the whole people was holy (Num 16:1-15). When summoned before Moses, Dathan and Abiram accused him of self-aggrandizement; they, as well as Korah, paid for their mutiny with their lives.

In some cases Moses succeeded in bringing relief from afflictions God imposed upon the Israelites. Through incense he and Aaron stopped the plague inflicted in retribution for the Israelites' complaints upon the death of Korah and his congregation (Num 6:46-50; 17:1-15). A plague of snakes, again caused by their discontent, was halted, when Moses, upon divine order, constructed a serpent of brass (Num 21:4-9). The magic staff he had been given at the burning bush, also provided a remedy for various difficulties; by striking the rock with it, he produced water (Ex 17:5-6); when holding it high, he ensured victory in the battle against the Amalekites (Ex 17:8-13). However, when instructed by God to produce water from the rock by addressing it, he preferred instead to strike it with his staff. For this act of disobedience he and Aaron were punished by being denied entry into the promised land (Num 20:7-12).

After witnessing the conquest of the eastern side of the Jordan, Moses

Moses holding a scroll. Fresco from the synagogue of Dura-Europos. 3rd century A.D.

was notified of his imminent death. Before parting from his people Moses conferred his authority upon Joshua (Deut 31:1-8). In his valedictory oration (Deut chaps. 29-31) he again set out the covenant obligations and bade his people to uphold their allegiance to God; the so-called Song of Moses (Deut 32:1-43) treats of the same theme.

Moses died at the age of 120, after being granted the privilege of seeing the land of Canaan from the mountain top of Pisgah (Deut 34:1-5). His death occurred in the Plains of Moab, but the place of burial is unknown (Deut 34:6), making it impossible for any cult to emerge about his grave site.

Later biblical tradition repeatedly mentions Moses as the author of the Book of the Law (Josh 8:31). He is named as the leader of the Exodus (I Sam 12:6, 8; Ps 77:20; Mic 6:4) and as intercessor (Jer 15:1; Ps 99:6); in addition, he is credited with the authorship of Psalm 90 (Ps 90:1).

The Bible gives little information on Moses' personal life. In Midian he was married to Zipporah, the daughter of Jethro the priest. Mention is also made of a Cushite (Ethiopian) woman (Num 12:1). His sons, Eliezer and Gershom, fade into insignificance. As to Moses' character, biblical tradition praises his humility and selflessness (Num 12:3). His killing of the Egyptian overseer (Ex 2:11-12) is often quoted as a sign of irascibility, borne out when he struck the rock instead of addressing it (Num 20:7-12). The biblical account, however, tends to disregard Moses' personality; and focuses upon his role. He occupies a unique position in the Bible for the multidimensional role which he filled. He was the great national leader who transformed a group of motley slaves into the nation of Israel. He was the prophet *par excellence* (Deut 34:10) to whom God spoke "face to face" (Ex 33:11). He was "servant of the Lord" (Num 12:7-8; Deut 34:5; Josh 1:1) who also interceded for his people. He was their great religious leader who mediated the covenant and both received and transmitted the laws of God to his people. In short, he became the founding father of the national-religious community of Israel, to whom many of the basic institutions may ultimately be traced. And above all, he turned the monotheistic faith of the patriarchs into the religion of a whole nation, thereby laying the foundation for three world religions, Judaism, Christianity and Islam.

In the NT, Moses is mentioned 80 times, usually as the lawgiver (e.g., Matt 19:7; Mark 10:3ff; John 7:22ff). However, while Moses brought the Law, Jesus brought grace and truth (John 1:17). Moses is seen as the prophet who points the way to Jesus (Luke 24:27, 44; John 5:45ff; Acts 3:22; 26:22). In the transfiguration, Moses representing the Law and Elijah representing prophecy stand with Jesus who is the fulfillment of both (Matt 17:1-8; Mark 9:2-8; Luke 9:28-36). On various occasions Moses' contribution is praised, but with stress on the superiority of Jesus (John 6:32; Heb 3:2ff etc.). At the same time, Jesus expresses his recognition of the laws of Moses which he has come, not to change, but to fulfill (Matt 5:17ff).

MOTH See ANIMALS

MOURNING On the death of an important personage (II Sam 3:31), when a calamity befell an individual (II Sam 12:15-16) or the whole congregation, or when bad tidings were received (Num 14:1-6), certain prescribed customs, common to the Israelites and to the other peoples of the ancient Near East, were observed. In addition to weeping and wailing, mourning involved rending one's clothes (Gen 37:29, etc.), walking barefoot and covering one's head (II Sam 15:30), girding one's loins with sackcloth (II Sam 3:31, etc.) and placing ashes on one's head (II Sam 13:19, etc.). The mourner would abstain from washing his feet,

Clay figurine of a mourner, found at Azor, near Jaffa.

14:6; 18:4, 6, 12; 21:8; 23:25. I Chr 6:3, 49; 15:15; 21:29; 22:13; 23:13-15; 26:24. II Chr 1:3; 5:10; 8:13; 23:18; 24:6, 9; 25:4; 30:16; 33:8; 34:14; 35:6, 12. Ezra 3:2; 6:18; 7:6. Neh 1:7-8; 8:1, 14; 9:14; 10:29; 13:1. Ps 77:20; 99:6; 103:7; 105:26; 106:16, 23, 32. Is 63:11-12. Jer 15:1. Dan 9:11, 13. Mic 6:4. Mal 4:4. Matt 8:4; 17:3-4; 19:7-8; 22:24; 23:2. Mark 1:44; 7:10; 9:4-5; 10:3-4; 12:19, 26. Luke 2:22; 5:14; 9:30, 33; 16:29, 31; 20:28, 37; 24:27, 44. John 1:17, 45; 3:14; 5:45-46; 6:32; 7:19, 22-23; 8:5; 9:28-29. Acts 3:22; 6:11, 14; 7:20, 22, 29, 31-32, 35, 37, 40, 44; 13:39; 15:1, 5, 21; 21:21; 26:22; 28:23. Rom 5:14; 9:15; 10:5, 19. I Cor 9:9; 10:2. II Cor 3:7, 13, 15. II Tim 3:8. Heb 3:2-3, 5, 16; 7:14; 8:5; 9:19; 10:28; 11:23-24; 12:21. Jude 9. Rev 15:3

trimming his beard, washing his clothes (II Sam 19:24) and from anointing himself with oil (II Sam 14:2). He might abstain altogether from meat and wine (Dan 10:3). Mourners would sit on the ground and tremble with grief (Ezek 26:16), shave their heads and cut their flesh (Jer 16:6). Some of these mourning signs, such as shaving the head, shaving a corner of the beard and cutting the flesh, all of which were very common among the heathen, were forbidden (Lev 21:5), but it seems that habit was stronger than the Law. Members of the family (Gen 23:2; 50:10; II Sam 11:26) and all others affected by mourning participated in the lamenting (I Sam 25:1; 28:3; II Sam 1:11-12; 2:31; I Kgs 13:29-30).

Mourning normally lasted for seven days (Gen 50:10), but on the death of an important personage it continued for 70 days, the first 40 being the period necessary for the completion of the process of embalming and the last 30 the actual mourning period (Gen 50:3). Aaron (Num 20:29) and Moses (Deut 34:8) were both mourned for 30 days. During the period of mourning people would come to eat with the mourners (II Sam 3:35). The funerary meal was observed by the Jews and other peoples in later times as well. To enhance the atmosphere of grief professional women mourners would be invited (Jer 9:17ff etc.). Egyptian wall paintings in which women are seen standing, weeping and tearing their hair indicate that this was also the practice among other nations in the ancient Near East.

According to Mark 16:1-2, the women mourning Jesus visited his tomb on the Sunday after his death to anoint the corpse with spices.

MOUSE See ANIMALS

MOZA

1. Second son of Caleb by his concubine Ephah.

2. Son of Zimri and father of Binea in the genealogy of King Saul.

MOZAH A town in the territory of Benjamin (Josh 18:26). Its name is mentioned on stamp jar-handles dating to the 6th century B.C.; known in the Roman period as Ammaous and later as Colonia, the name given to the town when Vespasian settled a colony of Roman veterans there. Identified with Mevasseret-Yerushalaim west of Jerusalem.

MULBERRY See PLANTS

MULE See ANIMALS

MUPPIM Eighth son of Benjamin; an alternate form of Shephupham.

MUSHI, MUSHITES The second son of Merari and ancestor of a major division of Levites (Ex 6:19; Num 3:20, 33; I Chr 6:19, 47; 23:21, 23; 24:26, 30). According to one of the earliest genealogy lists, the Mushites were settled around Hebron (Num 26:58).

MUSICAL INSTRUMENTS Since the dawn of civilization man has used musical instruments. Some have been found in excavations while others are known from Assyrian, Egyptian and other wall paintings and reliefs. Numerous musical instruments are mentioned in the Bible, which may indicate that music was important both in religion and in private life in biblical Palestine. Many of these instruments cannot be satisfactorily identified.

Alamoth (Ps 46:1). Identification unknown; probably an instrument that produced high soprano sounds.

Al Gittith (Ps 8:1; 81:1; 84:1). Identification not certain; perhaps the name of a group of instruments.

Halil ("flute", AV: "pipe"). A wind instrument made of cane, hollowed wood or bone. Its bright sounds were heard in holy day processions and at feasts (I Kgs 1:40; Is 5:12), but it could also produce a note of grief (Jer 48:36). It was used mainly by the common people and never in the Temple service. There were probably several kinds of flute in use during the biblical period.

Women mourning. Detail of a wall painting from a tomb. Egypt. 14th century B.C.

(bottom of page)
Coin of Bar Kochba depicting the kinor *of the Temple. A.D. 134*

Pottery jar-handle inscribed with the name of the region "Moza" and the name "Shual". The jar was probably intended for wine. 6th century B.C.

Blind harpist depicted from a wall painting in the tomb of Nakht, scribe and priest of Thutmosis IV. Thebes. 15th century B.C.

Hazozra ("trumpet"). An instrument made of metal. The trumpets mentioned in the Bible were of silver (Num 10:2), but most trumpets that have been found are made of brass and silver and are sometimes gold-plated. A continuous sound from two trumpets was the signal for the congregation to assemble at the tabernacle, while the sounding of only one marked the gathering of the princes and chiefs. There were other signals for gathering the congregation and for moving camp in battle. Trumpets were also used in the new moon festivities, on holy days and at the coronation of kings. The trumpet produced a sharp sound. It was made of a metal pipe with a mouthpiece narrower than the body.

Keren ("horn", AV: "cornet" Dan 3:5ff). A wind instrument made from the horn of an animal. Some scholars make no distinction between the *keren* and the *shofar*. Others believe the difference was that the *shofar* was made only from a ram's horn.

Kinnor ("harp"). A stringed instrument. According to the Bible, Jubal was the "father of all those who play the harp and flute" (Gen 4:21). The *kinnor* was much used in the biblical period, in the Temple service (I Chr 15:16; II Chr 5:12 etc.), at festivities and banquets (Is 5:12 etc.). Prophecies were made to the sound of its strings (I Chr 25:1) and it could raise one's spirits in moments of depression (I Sam 16:23). It was played alone, with string, wind or percussion instruments, or in an orchestra that contained them all. The number of its strings is unknown.

Kitaros ("harp"). A stringed instrument (Dan 3:5ff). The name derives from the Greek *kitharis* ("lyre").

Mahol Mentioned only in Psalms (150:4), among the many instruments that formed the orchestra of praise. See article MAHOL.

Menaaneim ("sistrums"). A percussion instrument played together with the timbrels (II Sam 6:5). It was probably made of metal plates that produced a sound when moved, as the Hebrew name implies. It has wrongly been identified with the cornet.

Meziltaim ("cymbals"). A percussion instrument made of copper. The Hebrew name implies a pair of instruments used together to produce a musical sound. They were sounded by the Levites, with other instruments, in the Temple service (I Chr 15:16, 28; Ezra 3:10 etc.). The cymbals may have been employed to mark the beginnings, endings and pauses in the chapters sung.

Minnim ("stringed instruments" Ps 150:4). Although it is certain that this was a musical instrument, its identification is not known.

Nebel ("lute", AV: "psaltery"). A stringed instrument, played solo (Ps 71:22), with the harp (Ps 150:3) or in a full orchestra (Is 5:12). It was in

(right)
Phoenician clay figure of a woman playing the cymbals. 7th century B.C. (Israel Museum)

(left)
Detail of a pottery incense stand showing a figure playing the double pipe. Ashdod. c. 1000 B.C. (Israel Museum)

use in the Temple and in secular life. The number of strings was not fixed but did not exceed ten. A psaltery of ten strings was called *nebel asor* (Ps 33:2) or simply *asor* (Ps 92:3), *asor* meaning ten. Some scholars, however, believe that the *nebel* was made of skin, like a bagpipe.

Neginoth ("stringed instruments"). A name that occurs in the opening lines of six of the Psalms (4, 6, 54, 55, 67, 76). Identification not known.

Psalterion ("psaltery"). Mentioned only once (Dan 3:5ff). The name derives from the Greek *psalter*. Its form is unknown.

Sabbah ("lyre" Dan 3:5). Not identified. Probably a seven-stringed instrument as the Aramaic name suggests. Some scholars, however, believe that its name derives from the Roman *sambucus*, a tree whose wood might have been used in its production. The identification with the sackbut or the trombone cannot be substantiated.

Shalishim ("musical instruments"). Some believe that it was a three-stringed instrument, or a triangular percussion instrument. Either theory can be supported by the Hebrew name (I Sam 18:6).

Sheminith (Ps 6:1). Thought by some scholars to be an eight-stringed instrument, as the Hebrew name may imply. Others suggest that it was an instrument pitched one octave higher than usual.

Shofar ("trumpet"). A wind instrument made of a ram's horn, used with stringed instruments (Ps 150:3), wind instruments (Ps 98:6) or both (I Chr 15:28). It was, and still is, much used in Jewish ritual.

Sumphonia. Word of Greek origin meaning "accompanying sound" (Dan 3:5ff). Some scholars believe that it was a bagpipe, while others think that it was not a specific instrument, but a whole orchestra. The identification with the dulcimer is very doubtful.

Tof ("timbrel/tambourine"). A percussion instrument with a membrane or timbrel, mentioned frequently in the Bible (Is 5:12; Ps 81:2, etc.). Timbrels varied in size and were played with the bare hand or sticks. Large ones were played by two people.

Ugab ("flute" Gen 4:21). The nature of this instrument is unknown. Some translators suggest it was a flute or a stringed instrument. The identification with the organ must be dismissed.

There is little evidence of musical life in Palestine in the later periods. In the Second Temple the rituals were accompanied by cymbals, harps, lyres and trumpets. An orchestra in the Temple consisted of six psalteries, an unlimited number of harps, one pair of cymbals and two trumpets.

There are few mentions of music in the NT (but cf Luke 7:32; 15:25; Matt 9:23). When Paul wrote to the Corinthians, he referred to their knowledge of music (I Chr 14:7ff). The author of Revelations speaks of harpists and singers (Rev 14:2-3) and also, foreseeing the end of Babylon (i.e., Rome), describes the end of music in its midst (Rev 18:22).

MUSTARD See PLANTS

MYRA
Acts 27:5
MYRA An ancient seaport on the River Andracus; lying in the province of Lycia on the southwest coast of Asia Minor, on a site now known as Dembre, it was a center of the grain trade. The name probably referred both to the harbor and the city proper situated on a hill about 3 miles (5 km) inland. As a prisoner bound for Rome, Paul sailed there from Caesarea by way of Sidon on an Adramyttian ship and reached Myra, where he was transferred to an Alexandrian ship.

MYRRH See SPICES AND PERFUMES

MYRTLE See PLANTS

MYSIA
Acts 16:7-8
MYSIA The northwest region of Asia Minor. Paul and his company passed through there on their way to Troas, being forbidden by the Holy Spirit to deviate northward to Bithynia, or southward to the interior.

Flute player in bronze from Byblos. 2nd millennium B.C. (Musée du Louvre, Paris)

(bottom of page) Mysia in Asia Minor.

Mosaic of the Byzantine period from Beth Shean showing a boy playing the flute.

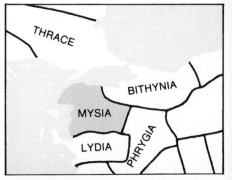

NAAM ("pleasant"). Third son of Caleb the son of Jephunneh in the genealogy of the family of Judah.

NAAMAH ("pleasant"). The name of two biblical women and of one place:

1. Daughter of Lamech by his second wife Zillah, and sister of Tubal-Cain.

2. An Ammonite princess, one of the wives of Solomon and the mother of his son Rehoboam who later became king.

3. A village which fell within the inheritance of the tribe of Judah when the land of Canaan was divided among the Children of Israel (Josh 15:41).

NAAMAN

1. A descendant of Benjamin and the founder of the Naamite family.

2. The commander of the army of the king of Aram, Naaman was a leper. When cured of his affliction by the prophet Elisha by bathing in the Jordan, he spontaneously offered up thanks and vows of loyalty to the God of Israel whom he swore to worship exclusively. When Jesus preached in the synagogue of Nazareth he cited this miracle as an example of God's care and concern for the non-Israelite.

NAAMATHITE An epithet affixed to the name of Zophar, one of the three friends of Job and taken to indicate that he was a native of Naameh, a place as yet unidentified.

NAAMITES See NAAMAN No. 1

NAARAH ("girl").

1. One of the two wives of Ashhur, a Judahite, father of Tekoa.

2. A city called Naarah on the eastern border of Ephraim, not far from Jericho, is mentioned in Joshua 16:7.

NAARAI The son of Ezbai, one of David's thirty "mighty men" (I Chr

Aqueduct and bridge in the region of Naarah near Jericho.

11:37). In the parallel list in II Samuel 23:35 he is called Paarai the Arbite.

NAARAN See NAARAH

NABAJOTH Alternative spelling of Nebajoth.

NABAL ("mean", "vile"). A wealthy Judahite from the family of Caleb (I Sam 25:3), he dwelt in Maon 8 miles (12km) south of Hebron, but his flocks pastured at Carmel (in the Judean desert; 25:2) and therefore he was also called Nabal the Carmelite (I Sam 30:5; II Sam 3:3).

As David's men roamed the wilderness of Judah, they used to protect Nabal's shepherds from robbers (I Sam 25:7). During the sheepshearing festival, David sent ten men to collect presents for his followers for their protective service (I Sam 25:8). When Nabal refused to pay and, in addition, insulted the messengers, David gathered 400 men to take revenge (I Sam 25:10-13). However, Abigail, Nabal's wife, brought food and wine thereby persuading him to abandon his plan (I Sam 25:18-35). Exerting her personal charm, she remarked: "Nabal ['fool'] is his name and folly is with him". When Nabal heard of his wife's deeds, he suffered a stroke and died ten days later (I Sam 25:37-38).

After Nabal's death, David married Abigail (I Sam 25:42; 27:3; 30:5; II Sam 2:2; 3:3).

NABATEANS A Semitic people who established their kingdom in the former territory of Edom and Moab. They reached Transjordan in the 3rd century B.C. and subsequently penetrated the Negeb. Excavations have shown the advanced level of Nabatean civilization: their capital city, Petra hewn out of rock in the desert, was a great trading center. Modern excavations have uncovered other Nabatean towns in the Negeb as well as revealing the Nabateans' ingenuity in desert agriculture.

In the reign of Herod (whose mother was of noble Nabatean descent)

Main street at Nabatean Petra.

(top, left to right)
Nabatean dam at Kurnub in the Negeb.
Remains of columns at Obodah, the main Nabatean city in the Negeb.
Nabatean remains at Petra, Transjordan.

(bottom, left to right)
Nabatean pottery from Mamshit, one of the Nabatean settlements in the Negeb.
General view of a line of royal tombs at Petra.

there was considerable tension between the Nabateans and the Jews, partly because the Romans granted Herod regions that had formerly belonged to the Nabateans.

In NT times, the Nabatean kingdom reached as far as Damascus. The Nabatean king Aretas IV is mentioned in II Corinthians 11:32: Paul only escaped from the governor of Damascus appointed by Aretas by being let down over the city wall in a basket. The Romans annexed the Nabatean kingdom in A.D. 106 but the Nabateans maintained their own culture until the area became Christian under Byzantine rule.

NABOTH Owner of a vineyard adjoining King Ahab's palace in Jezreel. When he refused to sell his inheritance to Ahab, probably out of a sense of responsibility to his family, Naboth was falsely accused of blasphemy and sedition and stoned to death. Ahab then confiscated the vineyard (cf I Sam 8:14). The murder was actually orchestrated by Jezebel (I Kgs. 21:7ff). Elijah forecast the bloody deaths of Ahab and Jezebel in retribution for the crime. In view of Ahab's repentance (I Kgs. 21:27ff), his punishment was transferred to his son Joram (II Kgs. 9:25-26) while Jezebel met the end prophesied by Elijah (II Kgs. 9:30-37).

NABOTH
I Kgs 21:1-4, 6-9, 12-16, 18-19. II Kgs 9:21, 25-26

NACHON (NACON) ("straight"). Owner of a threshing floor on the way between Baale Judah and Jerusalem. It was here that God killed Uzzah when he stretched out his hand to steady the ark of covenant while it was

NACHON
II Sam 6:6

being transferred by David to Jerusalem (II Sam 6:6). In I Chronicles 13:9, the name is given as Chidon.

NADAB

1. The second son of Aaron the high priest (Ex 6:23; Num 3:2; I Chr 6:3). Together with his brother Abihu, his father, Moses and 70 of the elders of Israel, he ascended Mount Sinai and beheld the Lord from afar (Ex 24:1). Later, he became a priest (Ex 28:1). He and his brother died before the Lord when they offered alien fire upon the altar. They were both childless (Num 3:4; I Chr 24:2).

2. The son of Jeroboam No.1, king of Israel, 907-906 B.C. Succeeding his father, he began to reign over Israel in the second year of Asa king of Judah. Although it is recorded that he reigned for two years, it must have been less as he was murdered by Baasha, the son of Ahijah, at Gibbethon, in the third year of Asa's reign (I Kgs 15:25-28). His death and the death of his family marked the end of the house of Jeroboam (I Kgs 15:29).

3. A descendant of Hezron; of the tribe of Judah. The son of Shammai and the father of Seled and Appaim (I Chr 2:28, 30).

4. A man of the tribe of Benjamin. The fifth son of Jeiel of Gibeon and his wife Maacah. The brother of Abdon, Zur, Kish, Baal, Gedor, Ahio, Zecher and Mikloth.

NAGGAI (NAGGE) ("illuminating"). Son of Maath and father of Esli in the genealogy of Jesus according to Luke.

NAHALAL, NAHALLAL, NAHALOL A city of Levites in the territory of Zebulun (Josh 19:15). Zebulun did not in fact conquer it and it remained Canaanite (Judg 1:30). It is identified today with the Arab village of Malul in the Jezreel Valley. Others identify it with Tell en-Nahl, in the southern part of the Plain of Acco.

NAHALIEL ("God's property", or: "God's river"). A place in Transjordan, one of the stations of the Israelite tribes before entering Canaan (Num 21:19).

Some scholars identify Nahaliel with Wadi el-Wala, the northern gorge of the River Arnon; others with one of the upper gorges of Wadi Zerqa Ma'in, which flows into the Dead Sea.

NAHAM ("[God will] comfort"). A Judahite, father of Keilah the Garmite.

NAHAMANI ("[God had] comforted me"). One of the people who returned with Zerubbabel from the Babylonian Exile (Neh 7:7).

NAHARAI (NAHARI) A Beerothite; one of David's thirty "mighty men". He was the armor bearer to Joab (II Sam 23:37; I Chr 11:39).

NAHASH ("serpent").

1. An Ammonite king in the time of Saul. Hoping to annex territories of Northern Gilead, he besieged the city of Jabesh Gilead (I Sam 11:1-2). Confident of victory he allowed the citizens to seek help, whereupon Saul gathered forces and defeated him (I Sam 11:3-11), thereby winning acceptance as king of Israel. It is assumed that as an enemy of Saul, Nahash sheltered David while the latter was in flight from the king (II Sam 10:2; I Chr 19:2).

Two sons of Nahash, Hanun and Shobi, are mentioned as rulers of the Ammonites during the reign of David (II Sam 10:1; 17:27; I Chr 19:1).

2. The father of Abigail, sister of Zeruiah (II Sam 17:25). However, in I Chronicles 2:16 Abigail and Zeruiah are listed among Jesse's children implying that Nahash may be the name of a woman (a second wife of Jesse), or may be a textual corruption.

NAHATH

1. An Edomite, clan chief, the first son of Reuel.

2. The grandson of Elkanah and one of the ancestors of Samuel in the genealogy of the family of Levi.

3. A Levite overseer in the Temple at the time of Hezekiah.

NAHBI Son of Vophsi, from the tribe of Naphtali; he was one of the 12 men sent by Moses from the wilderness of Paran to spy out the land of Canaan (Num 13:2-3, 14).

NAHOR

1. A city in Mesopotamia to which Abraham sent his servant to find a wife for his son Isaac. It occurs frequently in texts from Mesopotamia and is located in the upper Balih River.

2. The son of Serug, father of Terah and grandfather of Abraham, Nahor and Haran (Gen 11:22-26).

3. The son of Terah, brother of Abraham and Haran and the grandson of Nahor No.2. Nahor was married to Milcah, the daughter of his brother Haran (Gen 11:29). She bore him eight sons (Gen 22:20-22), while his concubine gave birth to another four (Gen 22:24).

In the time of the patriarchs a belief in the ancestral deities was still prevalent as is evident from the story of the covenant between Laban and Jacob: "The God of Abraham, the God of Nahor, and the God of their father judge between us" (Gen 31:53).

NAHSHON The son of Amminadab, a man of Judah, who was chosen by God to help Moses take the census of the Children of Israel (Num 1:2, 7). He was later appointed leader of his tribe and as such was the first to bring an offering to the tabernacle set up by Moses (Num 7:12). He led the army of Judah, which was at the head of the armies of Israel, out of the wilderness of Sinai (Num 10:14). Nahshon was the father of Salmon, the father of Boaz and thus an ancestor of David. He was the brother-in-law of Aaron who married his sister Elisheba (Ex 6:23). He is also listed as an ancestor of Jesus (Matt 1:4; Luke 3:32).

NAHUM ("comforted").

1. Judean prophet, author of the Book of Nahum.

2. An ancestor of Jesus.

NAHUM, BOOK OF Seventh of the books of the twelve Minor Prophets. The immediate background of this book is the fall of the Assyrian capital Nineveh to the allied armies of the Babylonians and the Medes in August 612 B.C. Scholars are divided as to whether the words contained in the Book of Nahum were first spoken before, during, or

NAHATH 2
I Chr 6:26

NAHATH 3
II Chr 31:13

NAHBI
Num 13:14

NAHOR 1
Gen 24:10

NAHOR 2
**Gen 11:22-25.
I Chr 1:26.
Luke 3:34**

NAHOR 3
**Gen 11:26-27,
29; 22:20, 23;
24:15, 24, 47;
29:5; 31:53.
Josh 24:2**

NAHSHON
**Ex 6:23. Num
1:7; 2:3; 7:12,
17; 10:14.
Ruth 4:20.
I Chr 2:10-11.
Matt 1:4.
Luke 3:32**

NAHUM 1
Nah 1:1

NAHUM 2
Luke 3:25

(bottom of page)
Fragment of a commentary on the Book of Nahum, from Qumran. (Shrine of the Book, Jerusalem)

Seal impression on a pottery jar-handle inscribed "[Belonging] to Nahum Abdi". 6th century B.C. (Rockefeller Museum, Jerusalem)

after that event. The designation of the book as "the burden of Nineveh" in 1:1 is a typical title of a prophetic pronouncement of doom concerning one of the nations of the world (cf Is 13:1; 15:1; 17:1; etc.). The content of the book may be subdivided as follows: (a) In 1:1-10 the prophet, speaking in his own name, says that God's justice is about to be made manifest in the world. In verse 11 an unnamed city, which must be Jerusalem, is told that he who conspired against the Lord, i.e., Assyria, is about to depart from her. (b) In 1:12-14 the prophet first quotes the Lord. Here he promises an unnamed city, which again must be Jerusalem, release from "his (i.e., Assyria's) yoke" (v. 13), and to another entity, which must be Assyria, he declares, "I will dig your grave for you are vile." (v. 14). (c) In 1:15-2:2 Judah is consoled that the enemy has been eliminated and that the honor of Israel is restored. (d) In 2:3-13 Nineveh is given a most vivid description as to how she is to be destroyed. (e) In 3:1-19 the prophet, speaking in the name of the Lord, tells Nineveh that her destruction is the just punishment of a nation that had engaged in brutality and intrigue. Like the tradition preserved in the works of the Greek historians Diodorus and Xenophon, Nahum (2:6, 8) suggests that a flood (of the Tigris) was a major factor in the fall of Nineveh. 1:2-10 contains (in the Hebrew) a partially preserved alphabetical acrostic. Other stylistic features of the

OUTLINE

1:1-10	God's vengeance and judgment
1:11-2:2	Threats against Assyria and promises to Judah
2:3-13	Attack on Nineveh
3:1-19	Sack of Nineveh

book include alliteration, metaphors (Nah 2:11-12; 3:13), and similes (Nah 3:12, 17-18). Nahum shares rare Hebrew expressions with Hosea and Joel, and is influenced by Isaiah (cf Is 9:2-4 with Nah 2:1; cf Is chap. 23 with Nah chap. 3).

NAIN A village in Galilee, southeast of Nazareth, called Naim in the

NAIN
Luke 7:11

later Jewish sources, where Jesus revived the widow's son (Luke 7:11-14). Eusebius (*Onom.* 140:3) names it Naeim, 12 miles (19 km) south of Mount Tabor near Endor. A place of some importance in the Byzantine period, when it was known as Kome Nais, the "village Nais", it is identified with Nein, about 6 miles (10 km) southeast of Nazareth. The ruins of the medieval church found there incorporate some remains of an earlier religious building, the exact nature of which has not been determined. Around the village there are rock-cut tombs of the time of the Second Temple.

NAIOTH A place, occupied by Samuel and a company of prophets to which Saul pursued David. The king sent messengers ahead and when they arrived at Naioth, they began to prophecy. A second group of messengers did likewise. When Saul approached, "the Spirit of God was

NAIOTH
I Sam
19:18-19,
22-23; 20:1

The village of Nein identified with Nain.

upon him, also, and he went on and prophesied until he came to Naioth in Ramah" (I Sam 19:23). Naioth is not identified.

NAOMI ("delight"). Wife of Elimelech and the mother of Mahlon and Chilion. To escape a famine they went from their native Bethlehem to Moab. After the death of Elimelech, the sons married the Moabite women Orpah and Ruth. When the two sons died, Naomi decided to return to Bethlehem. While Naomi was able to persuade Orpah to return to her Moabite family, Ruth insisted on accompanying Naomi to Bethlehem. There Naomi, due to the bitterness of her lot, insisted that she be called Marah, "bitter" (Ruth 1:1-20). Naomi later encouraged Ruth in the pursuit of her kinsman Boaz until he married her and redeemed the property of Elimelech (Ruth 4:9-10). When a son named Obed was born to Ruth and Boaz, "Naomi took the child and laid him on her bosom, and became a nurse to him...the neighbor women...(said) 'There is a son born to Naomi'". (Ruth 4:16-17). On the basis of both these sentences many scholars have concluded that Naomi adopted Obed. Others, however, understand Ruth 4:16 to mean only that Naomi hugged the baby and helped Ruth take care of him.

NAPHISH ("enormous", "numerous"). The 11th son of Ishmael (Gen 25:15; I Chr 1:31), and ancestor of a nomadic tribe. According to I Chronicles 5:19, the tribe wandered in Transjordan and was exterminated by the Israelite tribes of Transjordan, probably at the time of King Saul.

NAPHTALI The sixth son of Jacob, by Bilhah, Rachel's servant, and eponym of one of the twelve tribes. The child's name is derived from the folk etymology meaning "my struggle" and reflects Rachel's rivalry with Leah for bearing children to Jacob (Gen 30:1-8).

Naphtali was the second son that Bilhah bore to Jacob, the first being Dan (Gen 30:2-6). When the sons of Jacob are listed, Naphtali and Dan are usually grouped together with Gad and Asher, the sons of Leah's servant Zilpah (Gen 49:16-21; Ex 1:4; Deut 27:13; 33:20-25). The tribe of Naphtali's geographical relationship with the rest of the Rachel tribes who were in the south was very weak, being separated by the territories of Zebulun and Issachar. Some scholars think that Naphtali's wandering tendencies were being alluded to in the phrase of Jacob's blessing, "a deer, let loose" (Gen 49:21). Naphtali also appears in the list of Levitical cities (Josh 21:6; I Chr 6:62) and the cities of refuge (Josh 20:7).

The Naphtalites played an important part in the two conflicts led by Deborah and Gideon (Judg 4:6, 10; 5:18; 6:35; 7:23). Barak, the son of Abinoam, who commanded the armies under Deborah's direction, was from Naphtali (Judg 4:6). The song of Deborah praises Zebulun and Naphtali for their bravery in defeating Sisera and the Canaanites (Judg 5:18). When David became ruler over all of Israel after Saul's death, the tribe of Naphtali joined the new king at Hebron with a large army. They also brought food and provisions for the armies (I Chr 12:34, 39-40).

In the Blessing of Moses, Naphtali is mentioned as possessing "the west and the south" (Deut 33:23). This phrase describes the territory adjacent to the western shore of Galilee and extending northward (Josh 19:32-39). The western and southern borders were facing the lands of Asher and Zebulun. When Solomon divided the land into districts, he kept the area of Naphtali as one of the districts (I Kgs 4:15). Joshua 19:35 shows that there were many fortified cities in Naphtali.

Since Naphtali lay far in the north, and even though it had fortifications, it was easy prey for the invading Syrians during Baasha's reign (I Kgs 15:20). Later it was also conquered by Tiglath-Pileser, king of Assyria and many of its inhabitants were taken captive (II Kgs 15:29).

NAOMI
Ruth 1:2-3, 8, 11, 19-22; 2:1-2, 6, 20, 22; 3:1; 4:3, 5, 9, 14, 16-17

NAPHISH
Gen 25:15. I Chr 1:31; 5:19

NAPHTALI
Gen 30:8; 35:25; 46:24; 49:21. Ex 1:4. Num 1:15, 42-43; 2:29; 7:78; 10:27; 13:14; 26:48, 50; 34:28. Deut 27:13; 33:23; 34:2. Josh 19:32, 39; 20:7; 21:6, 32. Judg 1:33; 4:6, 10; 5:18; 6:35; 7:23. I Kgs 4:15; 7:14; 15:20. II Kgs 15:29. I Chr 2:2; 6:62, 76; 7:13; 12:34, 40; 27:19. II Chr 16:4; 34:6. Ps 68:27. Is 9:1. Ezek 48:3-4, 34. Matt 4:13, 15. Rev 7:6

The territory of the tribe of Naphtali.

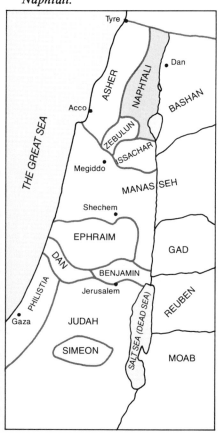

Isaiah alludes to the sufferings of Naphtali in his prophecies, and promises that they will once again see light and receive comfort (Is 9:1-7). An interpretation of this prophecy is later given in the NT, when Jesus initiates his ministry in the region of Galilee and calls his first disciples from its shores (Matt 4:13-22).

In the list of the sealed in Revelation (7:5-8), Naphtali appears in the fifth position.

Landscape in the region of the territory of Naphtali.

NAPHTUHIM In the ethnographic lists, Naphtuhim are mentioned among the sons of Mizraim (Gen 10:13; I Chr 1:11). The Naphtuhim are assumed to have been inhabitants of the Egyptian delta.

NARCISSUS A Roman whose household numbered several Christians; Paul sends them greetings in his Epistle to the Romans.

NATHAN ("God's gift").

1. Nathan the prophet: a contemporary of David and a prominent figure in three events which took place at David's court. In II Samuel 7:2 (I Chr 17:1), David complains to Nathan "I dwell in a house of cedars, but the ark of God dwells inside tent curtains!" Agreeing immediately with the king, Nathan provides the prophetic stamp of approval: "So do all that is in your heart, for the Lord is with you." (II Sam 7:3). In David's mind was the desire to build a Temple for God. However, the prophet misapprehended God's own view. That evening, in a prophetic vision he is instructed to notify David that he is not the person to build the Temple (I Chr 17:4ff). God would build a "house" for David (I Chr 17:12) — a reference to the dynastic monarchy but construction of the Temple would be left to David's son (I Chr 17:11-13). After David's scandalous adultery with Bathsheba, and his subsequent devious instigation of her husband Uriah's death in battle (II Sam chap. 11), Nathan, in his capacity as God's messenger, confronts David with his misdeeds (II Sam 12:1-15). Nathan's accusation is couched in the tale of a pauper whose only possession, a little ewe lamb, is stolen, slaughtered and served up for supper by a wealthy neighbor. David, exercising his royal judicial role, sentences the guilty man to death. When Nathan pronounces the words "You are the man!" (II Sam 12:7), David realizes that the "case" was a parable. Nathan goes on to inform David of the consequences of his sin: violent turmoil will pervade his household and his own wives will be publicly defiled by another man (II Sam 12:10-11). At David's remorse (see Ps 51:2ff), Nathan declares that God has commuted the sentence of death that David himself decreed, stating that the life of the son born to him by Bathsheba will be taken instead (II Sam 12:13ff).

Nathan's third and final appearance is not as divine messenger but as devoted and clever courtier (I Kgs 1:9ff). When David's son Adonijah proclaims himself successor to his aging father, Nathan allies himself with others to prevent Adonijah's ascension to the throne. Nathan persuades Bathsheba to approach the ailing king and "remind" him of his sworn oath to her that Solomon would reign upon his death. David is swayed to act accordingly and, in the presence of Nathan and Bathsheba, names Solomon his successor.

The Book of Chronicles makes reference to "the book of Nathan the prophet" (I Chr 29:29; II Chr 9:29). Along with David and Gad, Nathan also played a role in establishing the musical rite of the Temple (II Chr 29:25).

2. The third son of David born to him in Jerusalem (II Sam 5:14). According to I Chronicles 3:5, his mother was Bathshua. Since the same verse states that she was also Solomon's mother, she may be identified with Bathsheba. Thus Nathan is Solomon's brother. In one of his visions, the prophet Zechariah (Zech 12:12) mentions the descendants

of "the house of Nathan", apparently a reference to the same figure. The genealogy of Jesus in Luke is traced through this son of David (Luke 3:31).

3. Father of Igal, a native of Zobah: and one of David's thirty "mighty warriors" (II Sam 23:36); probably identical with Nathan the brother of Joel in the list of David's warriors in Chronicles (I Chr 11:38).

NATHAN 3
II Sam 23:36.
I Chr 11:38

4. The father of Azariah, an official in Solomon's administration, placed in charge of the prefects; and of Zabud, priest and companion of Solomon. (Perhaps identical with Nathan No.1).

NATHAN 4
I Kgs 4:5

5. Son of Attai, and father of Zabad mentioned among the descendants of Judah (I Chr 2:36).

NATHAN 5
I Chr 2:36

6-7. Either one or two contemporaries of Ezra. In Ezra 8:16 Nathan is mentioned among the members of a delegation dispatched by Ezra to Casiphia to petition a chief named Iddor for Temple attendants to be sent to join the returnees, as a way of making up for the lack of Levites. In Ezra 10:39, a Nathan is listed as one of the returnees who pledged to repudiate their alien wives.

NATHAN 6-7
Ezra 8:16;
10:39

NATHANAEL ("God has given"). A man of Cana mentioned in the Gospel of John. It is not clear whether or not he was a disciple of Jesus. In Galilee "Jesus saw Nathanael coming toward him and said of him, 'Behold an Israelite indeed, in whom is no guile'" (John 1:47). At first Nathanael did not believe in Jesus, doubting that anything good could come out of Nazareth; but after he met Jesus, Nathanael confessed that he was "the Son of God" and "the king of Israel" (John 1:48-49). Jesus assured him that he would see the heaven open, and angels ascending and descending upon the Son of man (John 1:51).

NATHANAEL
John 1:45-49;
21:2

Nathanael was among those to whom Jesus appeared at the Sea of Galilee after his resurrection (John 21:2).

Some scholars identify Nathanael with Bartholomew, supposing that the latter name was a patronymic and that Nathanael was his personal name.

NATHAN-MELECH ("the king has given"). A chamberlain at the time of King Josiah of Judah (II Kgs 23:11). His chamber in the suburbs housed the horses dedicated to the sun cult until the shrine's destruction by Josiah.

NATHAN-MELECH
II Kgs 23:11

NAZARENE A name or title frequently applied to Jesus of Nazareth, and, in one reference (Acts 24:5), to his followers (see next entry). While the English translations frequently render the name as "of Nazareth", it is far from certain that the title actually derives from that village. First of all, a person coming from Nazareth (*Natzrat* in Hebrew) would properly be called a Nazarethite (*Natzrati*), not Nazarene (*Notzri*) which is etymologically impossible. Secondly, it would have been uncommon to name a man's followers after his hometown.

NAZARENE
Matt 2:23.
Acts 24:5

Only Matthew 2:23 seems to derive Nazarene from Nazareth: "and dwelt in a city called Nazareth, that it might be fulfilled which was spoken by the prophets, 'He shall be called a Nazarene'". However, the prophecy quoted is not found in any extant book of the OT. Numerous attempts have been made to determine Matthew's source. The Septuagint at Judges 13:5 is reasonably close to Matthew's Greek, but this reference to Samson the Nazirite could be rejected on several grounds: it leaves no possible connection to Nazareth; Jesus was probably not a Nazirite (cf Luke 7:34); it is difficult to see how this reference could be construed as "that which was spoken through the prophets"; and it is not clear that Matthew saw Samson as a type of Jesus.

It is important to note that the first two chapters of Matthew use a similar phrase four times (Matt 1:22ff; 2:5ff; 2:15; 2:17ff). In each case he speaks of a singular prophet, in each case the verse cited can easily be found. However, in 2:23 he speaks of "prophets" in the plural, leaving open the possibility that he is thinking less of a single reference than of a common theme in the prophets. The most important prophetic theme for Matthew was the promised messiah under his various titles. This may provide the key to his enigmatic reference (cf Luke 24:27; Acts 3:24). Isaiah 11:1-10 is a passage frequently cited in Talmudic literature, invariably appearing in a messianic context. One name used by Isaiah there is "branch", in Hebrew *netzer*. The description of the promised messianic figure as a Branch (more usually the Hebrew *tzemaḥ*) is used by several prophets (Jer 23:5; Zech 3:8). Etymologically the title *notzri* (Nazarene) is easily derivable from Isaiah's *netzer*, and it has the advantage of being of the same Hebrew root as Nazareth. Thus the appellation Nazarene may be seen as a messianic title which also happens to be indirectly related to the name of the town from which Jesus came.

NAZARENES Acts 24:5

NAZARENES One of the earliest names given to the followers of Jesus. In Acts 24:5 the lawyer Tertullus calls Paul "a ringleader of the sect of the Nazarenes", and Paul subsequently (Acts 24:14) connects the epithet to the more common name, "The Way". At that point, the "sect" was in fact a sect of Judaism, in the same way that Essenes, Sicarii and Pharisees were sects of Judaism. In later centuries several Church Fathers refer to the Nazarene sect, but by that time it was considered a sect of the church, a sect of Jewish Christians. These post-NT Nazarenes left Jerusalem shortly before it was destroyed in A.D. 70 and fled to the Decapolis city of Pella. After the war some returned to Jerusalem while others moved further north, into Coele Syria. They are reported to have maintained a Christology compatible with that of the Nicene church (unlike their offshoot cousins, the Ebionites).

They continued to observe the commandments of the Mosaic covenant, however, for which they incurred the condemnation of the Church Fathers. Their continued existence as a distinct community can be traced clearly into the 3rd or perhaps the 4th century A.D.

NAZARETH Matt 2:23; 4:13; 21:11; 26:71. Mark 1:9, 24; 10:47; 14:67; 16:6. Luke 1:26; 2:4, 39, 51; 4:16, 34; 18:37; 24:19. John 1:45-46; 18:5, 7; 19:19. Acts 2:22; 3:6; 4:10; 6:14; 10:38; 22:8; 26:9

NAZARETH The small town in Galilee where Jesus spent his childhood and youth. It is not mentioned in the OT although excavations have shown settlement in the area from the Bronze Age, and tombs from the Iron Age down to the Hasmonean period. Joseph and Mary lived there

General view of Nazareth.

after their betrothal and the annunciation of Jesus' birth came to Mary in Nazareth (Luke 1:26).

Joseph may have moved his family there (Matt 2:23) because of the availability of carpentry work in the vicinity as Herod Antipas was building a Hellenistic city, Sepphoris, 7 miles (11 km) away. Although a small town, Nazareth lay on the Roman road to Jerusalem and thus had good communications with the larger world outside. Here Jesus grew up; from here he left for his baptism (Mark 1:9); he returned to Nazareth before going forth to preach (Matt 4:13). However, when attempting to preach his message in his home town, he was violently rejected and left Nazareth to make his center in Capernaum (Matt 13:54-58; Mark 6:1-6; Luke 4:16-30). There is no mention of his having returned to the town, but he remained associated with it (Matt 21:11) and was called "Nazarene", a title subsequently applied to his followers (Acts 24:5). In Jesus' time the town had a synagogue (Luke 4:16) and Jews were living there after the destruction of the Second Temple. Eusebius mentions a small village called Nazareth in the 4th century A.D. Its first church was built there in the time of Constantine.

The Mount of the Leap or Hill of Precipitation in Nazareth, traditionally identified as the place from which the angry people of the town wanted to throw Jesus (Luke 4:16-30).

NAZIRITE A man or woman who vows for a limited period of time to abstain from cutting his hair or imbibing beer, wine, beer vinegar, wine vinegar and all grape products, and to avoid defilement by a corpse (Num 6:3-7). The Israelite who made such a vow, and fulfilled it, thereby emulated the sanctity of the high priest while the latter was performing divine service (cf Lev 9:8-9; 21:1-6). If the Nazirite was inadvertently defiled by a corpse, he had first to undergo the week long purification ritual prescribed in Numbers 19:1-22 for such defilement. The purification was completed on the seventh day when the Nazirite shaved his hair (Num 6:9); the following day he presented a sin offering, a burnt offering and a guilt offering to expiate his violation of the vow. That same day he had to begin a new period of abstinence in fulfillment of the original vow; the days already observed did not count (Num 6:10-13). Upon completion of the full period of abstinence, the Nazirite presented an elaborate series of offerings, as described in Numbers 6:13-20.

Num 6:2, 13, 18-21. Judg 13:5, 7; 16:17. Lam 4:7. Amos 2:11-12

While Numbers chapter 6 conceives of the Nazirite as an adult who binds himself by a vow for a limited period, Judges chapter 13, and Samuel refer to a person who is dedicated from conception to death by divine decree. In Judges 13:3-7 (see also Judg 13:13-14) an angel commands the wife of Manoah to abstain from wine and beer and from eating anything unclean while she is pregnant with Samson. Moreover, the angel announces, no razor is ever to touch the child's head, "for the child shall be a Nazirite to God from the womb" (Judg 13:5; see also Judg 16:17). Hannah's vow concerning the still unconceived Samuel, "and no razor shall come upon his head" in I Samuel 1:11 suggests that Samuel too was a life-long Nazirite. This view is supported by the Septuagint translation and by the Hebrew version of the Book of Samuel found at Qumran. In both these versions Hannah prefaces the aforementioned promise with the words "and I shall present him to you as a Nazirite until his death all the days of his life". The Septuagint adds, "and he shall drink no wine or beer". Ben Sira 46:3 also calls Samuel "a Nazirite".

The prohibition against letting oneself be defiled by a corpse, which figures prominently in Numbers chapter 6, plays no part in the Samson narrative; hence rabbinic exegesis concludes that one who vows to be "a Nazirite like Samson" is exempt from the latter prohibition. Apart from Numbers chapter 6 and the Samson narrative, the OT mentions Nazirites only in Amos 2:11-12 where it is suggested that, just as declaring the word of the Lord is the characteristic of the prophet so abstaining from wine is the characteristic of the Nazirite. Amos reprimanded the Israelites equally for forcing the Nazirites to drink wine, and commanding the prophets not to prophesy. According to Acts 21:23-26 Paul was told that by accompanying four Nazirites as they went through the ritual purification and by underwriting the cost of their prescribed offerings, he could silence the rumors that he had been undermining the observance of the Law; and he complied with this suggestion.

NEAH Border town, part of the territory of Zebulun. Not identified.

NEAPOLIS The harbor of Philippi in Macedonia. Paul arrived there from Troas in Asia. From Neapolis he commenced his missionary journey in Greece.

The marshy coast near modern Kavalla in northern Greece, thought to be Neapolis.

NEARIAH ("servant of Yah").
1. The son of Shemaiah, a descendant of Zerubbabel.
2. The son of Ishi; one of the commanders of the tribe of Simeon. During the reign of King Hezekiah of Judah, he led 500 men to Mount Seir where he exterminated the remnants of the Amalekites and took it as his dwelling place (I Chr 4:42-43).

NEBAI One of those who signed the covenant of Ezra.

NEBAIOTH, NEBAJOTH An Arabian tribe which wandered along the fringes of the cultivated region. It claimed descent from the eldest son of Ishmael (Gen 25:13; 28:9; 36:3; Nabajoth in I Chr 1:29). In a list of nomadic tribes (Is 60:7), Nebaioth is mentioned together with Kedar, both sons of Ishmael, according to Genesis 25:13; I Chronicles 1:29. Nebaioth and Kedar are apparently identical with the Arabian tribes Nabaiti and Qidri mentioned in Assyrian documents from the time of Tiglath-Pileser III (8th century B.C.) and Ashurbanipal (7th century B.C.).

Some scholars assume the Nebaioth to be identical with the Nabateans; but as the latter are first mentioned in documents from the 1st century B.C., and the Hebrew spelling of the two names is different, the identification is highly improbable.

NEBALLAT One of the towns of the Benjamites, resettled at the time of the return from the Babylonian Exile (Neh 11:34). It is identified with Beit-Nebala 4 miles (6 km) northeast of Lod.

NEBAT An Ephraimite; father of King Jeroboam I of Israel.

One of the mountains of the Abarim range in Moab identified by some as Mount Nebo.

NEBO

1. The peak of the Abarim Mountains in Moab, where the Children of Israel camped (Num 33:47) and from which Moses beheld the land of Canaan before his death (Deut 32:49).

2. One of the nine cities in the regions of Jazer and Gilead, which Israel conquered from Sihon and Og and which were claimed by the Reubenites and Gadites (Num 32:3). Nebo is mentioned as one of 14 such cities and as one of the six cities rebuilt and inhabited by the Reubenites (Num 32:34-38). In Isaiah 15:2 and Jeremiah 48:1, 22, it appears as a Moabite city, having been conquered by Mesha king of Moab in the mid-9th century B.C. According to Ezra 10:43 "sons of Nebo" were among those who had married foreign wives.

3. Nebo is the Hebraized form of the Akkadian divine name *Nabu*. Some time after 1000 B.C. Nabu, the son of Marduk the patron god of Babylon, became the patron deity of Babylon's sister city, Borsippa. It is the close association of these two deities in the later Babylonian pantheon that accounts for their appearance together in Isaiah's oracle against Babylon: "Bel (i.e., an epithet of Marduk) bows down; Nebo stoops" (Is 46:1). The importance of Nebo in Babylonian religion during the neo-Babylonian period is also reflected in the many personal names which include the name of this deity, such as Nebopolassar, Nebuchadnezzar, Nebonidus, Nebushazban and Nebuzaradan.

NEBUCHADNEZZAR King of Babylon. The Hebrew name Nebuchadnezzar is an alternate form of the name Nebuchadrezzar appearing in Jeremiah and Ezekiel which is closer to the original Akkadian form of the name, *Nabû-kudurriusur,* meaning "Nabu, protect my boundary" (on the Babylonian god Nabu see NEBO). The biblical Nebuchadnezzar was the second ruler by that name in the history of Babylon; and is referred to in history books as Nebuchadrezzar II. The son of Nabopolassar (626-605 B.C.), the Chaldean ruler who liberated Babylonia from Assyria, Nebuchadnezzar ruled from 605 to 562 B.C. He expanded the neo-Babylonian empire so that it extended from the frontier of Egypt in the west to Elam in the east. He rebuilt temples throughout Babylonia, and enhanced the fortifications and public buildings of Babylon. As a consequence of Nebuchadnezzar's military campaigns in the west, beginning in 605 B.C. when he was still crown prince, King Jehoiakim of Judah paid tribute to Nebuchadnezzar and thereby acknowledged the Babylonian ruler as overlord (II Kgs 24:1). However, at the end of his reign in 598 B.C. Jehoiakim withheld tribute. Nebuchadnezzar

NEBO 1
Num 33:47.
Deut 32:49;
34:1

NEBO 2
Num 32:3, 38.
I Chr 5:8.
Ezra 2:29;
10:43. Neh
7:33. Is 15:2.
Jer 48:1, 22

NEBO 3
Is 46:1

NEBUCHADNEZZAR
II Kgs 24:1,
10-11; 25:1, 8,
22. I Chr 6:15.
II Chr 36:6-7,
10, 13. Ezra
1:7; 2:1; 5:12,
14; 6:5. Neh
7:6. Est 2:6.
Jer 21:2, 7;
22:25; 24:1;
25:1, 9; 27:6,
8, 20; 28:3,
11, 14; 29:1,
3, 21; 32:1,
28; 34:1;
35:11; 37:1;
39:1, 5, 11;
43:10; 44:30;
46:2, 13, 26;
49:28, 30;

marched against Judah and laid siege to Jerusalem. According to the Babylonian Chronicle, on the second day of Adar i.e., March 16, 597 B.C. Jerusalem fell to Nebuchadnezzar. Jehoiachin, who meanwhile had succeeded to the throne in Judah, was taken captive along with many of the most prominent citizens (II Kgs 24:14). Nebuchadnezzar installed Jehoiachin's uncle Zedekiah as king of Judah. When the latter rebelled against Babylon (Jer chap. 37), Nebuchadnezzar, who had been engaged in war against Elam, again marched against Judah. On the tenth day of the tenth month 588 B.C. he laid siege to Jerusalem. After holding out for more than a year and a half, the city fell on the seventh day of the fifth month 586 B.C. The Temple was destroyed, and most of Judah's polulation was exiled to Babylonia. Nebuchadnezzar made Judah a Babylonian province, over which he appointed as governor a Judean noble named Gedaliah son of Ahikam. Nebuchadnezzar is the king of Babylonia, at whose court Daniel served as interpreter of dreams (Dan chaps. 1-4). According to Daniel 5:2 Nebuchadnezzar was the father of Belshazzar.

NEBUSHASBAN (NEBUSHAZBAR) ([the God] "Nabu save me"). The chief eunuch of King Nebuchadnezzar of Babylon. He took part in the conquest of Jerusalem, and was among those who delivered the prophet Jeremiah from prison (Jer 39:13-14).

NEBUZARADAN (The name is the Hebraized form of the Akkadian personal name *Nabû-zēr-iddina,* which means "Nabu gave me offspring". On the god Nabu see NEBO No.1).

A high official at the court of Nebuchadnezzar, he was responsible for the destruction by fire of Jerusalem in 586 B.C., for the deportation of most of the population of Judah to Babylonia, and for the dispatch to Babylon of the Temple treasures (II Kgs 25:8-17). According to Jeremiah 52:30 Nebuzaradan deported another 750 Jews from Judah to Babylonia in 582 B.C. In the Hebrew Bible Nebuzaradan's title is *rav ha-tabbaḥim.* The Septuagint took this to mean "head of the cooks" and the Aramaic translation of the Bible "head executioner"; either rendering is plausible linguistically, but it is now known that the Hebrew is a translation of the Akkadian title "head of the cooks, director of food services".

NECHO Necho II (ruled 610/9-595 B.C.), king of Egypt in the 26th Dynasty, son of Psammetichus. In 609 B.C. he led his army to help the disintegrating Assyrian army in Haran (II Kgs 23:29). King Josiah tried to stop the Egyptians at Megiddo and was killed in the battle. Necho II continued northward to Haran; later, on his way back to Egypt, he stopped in Judah to depose Jehoahaz who had become king after Josiah's death. Necho replaced him with Eliakim, whose name was changed to Jehoiakim and who became a vassal ruler (II Kgs 23:33-34; II Chr 36:4). Necho II spent most of his reign fighting against the Babylonians. Battles took place in Haran, in the Euphrates area in Carchemish, in Hamath and in the south, close to the Egyptian borders. Necho II lost his domains in Syria, Israel and the coast to the Babylonians. However, he kept his throne in Egypt, as the Babylonians, under Nebuchadnezzar, never succeeded in crossing the Egyptian borders. The last battle between Necho and Nebuchadnezzar (Jer 46:2) took place in 601/600, after which the former concentrated mainly on internal affairs.

NEDABIAH ("Yah has donated"). One of the sons of King Jehoiachin of Judah (I Chr 3:18).

NEGEB A region extending southwards from the border of Judah. The name denotes "dryness" in Hebrew, but in the Bible it is sometimes used to refer to the south, and is often translated "South" where the Hebrew

Bible has "*negeb*" or "*negbah*". Geographically and from the point of view of climate the plain of Beersheba forms its northern border, but in the Bible the southern and southwestern foothills of Hebron were also included in it. It is bounded by the Arabah on the east and by the coastal plain and the wildernesses of Paran, Zin and Shur on the northwest and west. Most of the central and southern parts of the Negeb are mountainous. The central part is zig-zagged by deep wadis and craters, which form a serious obstacle to transport. For this reason no important international trade routes traversed the Negeb from north to south, and the two major international thoroughfares (the Via Maris and the King's Way) that skirted it were linked by a network of secondary roads. The more important of these were the biblical way of the mountains of the Amorites (Deut 1:7), which connected Kadesh Barnea with the southern Arabah, and "the way of Edom", which descended from Arad to the southern part of the mountains of Sodom (II Kgs 3:20). In the Hellenistic, Roman and Byzantine periods a road connected Petra, Oboda and Elusa with Gaza, while another ran from Aila (Elath) along the Arabah to Mampsis, Hebron and Jerusalem.

The Negeb was of little economic importance in biblical times. The northern plain and the banks of the wadis did, however, provide grazing for goats and sheep (I Sam 25:2 ff; I Chr 4:38-41; II Chr 26:10). Of greater economic importance was the establishment, in the period of the Israelite kingdom, of commercial relations with the South Arabian kingdoms, inaugurated by the visit of the Queen of Sheba, and the subsequent building of a merchant navy (I Kgs 9:26; 10:22 ff). This trade route was still used in the time of Jehoshaphat and Azariah (I Kgs 22:48-49; II Kgs 14:21-22).

There are copper mines in the southern part of the Negeb, in the vicinity of Timnah to the northwest of Elath; the initial working of these was formerly attributed to Solomon, but recent researches have shown that this dating is approximately two centuries too late. Abraham "dwelt between Kadesh and Shur and sojourned in Gerar" (Gen 12:9; 13:1; 20:1). Isaac also lived there (Gen 24:62; 26:20-21). In the 13th century B.C. the Negeb, together with Moab and Edom, was the

24:62. Num 13:17, 22, 29; 21:1; 33:40. Deut 1:7; 34:3. Josh 10:40; 11:16; 12:8; 15:19, 21. Judg 1:9, 15-16; 30:1. II Sam 34:7. II Chr 28:18. Ps 126:4. Is 30:6. Jer 13:19; 17:26; 32:44; 33:13. Ezek 20:46-47. Obad 1:19-20. Zech 7:7

The Wilderness of Zin, south of Kadesh Barnea in the Negeb.

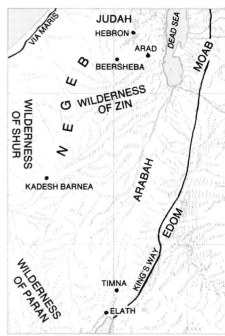

The Negeb.

(left)
The so-called Solomon's Pillars in the Negeb.

objective of several punitive campaigns by Rameses II. After the conquest of Canaan it was allotted to Simeon, although it was incorporated into the territory of Judah (Josh 19:1-9; I Chr 4:28-33). At the beginning of the period of the Judean kingdom the region came to be known as southern Judah (I Sam 27:10; II Sam 24:7).

In the first half of the 10th century the expansion towards the Gulf of Elath and the fortification of Ezion Geber took place (I Kgs 9:26). In the fifth year of the reign of Rehoboam (924 B.C.) Pharaoh Shishak led a campaign against Judah (I Kgs 14:25; II Chr 12:1-12) and the list of conquered sites found in the temple of Amun at Karnak includes the names of 85 places, all of which are believed to have been in the Negeb. During Jehoshaphat's reign the Negeb was again in Israelite hands (I Kgs 22:48-50; II Chr 20:35-37). To the northeast of Beersheba new fortresses and settlements were built in the 9th and 8th centuries B.C. and also in the time of Azariah, who conquered Edom and built Elath (II Kgs 14:22; II Chr 26:2). During the Assyrian campaigns against Judah the Judean kingdom lost the Negeb and Elath was conquered by the Edomites (II Kgs 16:6; in some versions "Syria").

There was no permanent settlement in the Negeb until late in the 4th and early 3rd centuries B.C. when it was occupied by the Nabateans. During the following centuries the Nabatean settlement expanded over larger areas in the Negeb. The Nabatean towns were abandoned before the middle of the 2nd century A.D., for reasons that are still obscure.

In the last quarter of the 1st century A.D. the Nabateans in the Negeb and the Hauran embarked on an agricultural enterprise, using their old knowledge of collecting rainwater into cisterns for irrigating terraced fields. It seems that they engaged in horse breeding and growing of barley first. Viticulture and the production of wine formed the last stage in the transition of the descendants of the Nabateans in the late Roman-Byzantine period to agriculture. It is possible that their renewed prosperity was in part due to renewed mining of turquoise and copper in southern Sinai.

NEHELAMITE
Jer 29:24, 31-32

NEHELAMITE The epithet of Shemaiah, a false prophet, one of the captives in Babylonia, who opposed Jeremiah's prophecies in letters he sent to Jerusalem (Jer 29:24, 31-32).

NEHEMIAH ("Yah has comforted").

1. Son of Hacaliah; cupbearer of the Persian king Artaxerxes I (464-424 B.C.); he played a decisive role in the rebuilding of Judah. In 444 B.C. the king appointed Nehemiah governor of Judah under the Persian empire and permitted him to go to Jerusalem in order to help his fellow Jews (Neh 1:1-2:8). Upon his arrival Nehemiah secretly inspected the city walls which were still in ruins (Neh 2:9-16). This became known to his two arch-enemies, Sanballat and Tobiah, who repeatedly acted to foil his plans for rebuilding the walls (Neh 2:17-20; 6:1-14); but despite their active opposition, Nehemiah succeeded in his building project, completing the work in 52 days (Neh chaps. 3-4; 6:15-19), and stationed guards at the city gates (Neh 7:1-3). In order to repopulate Jerusalem, the number of whose inhabitants had dwindled greatly, he ordered that one out of every ten Jews should take up residence in the capital. He also instituted a series of religious and social reforms including the commitment to avoid intermarriage, the cancellation of debts owed by the poor, the support of the Temple cult, and the payment of tithes drawn up and sealed in a covenant (Neh chap. 10) — and then returned to Persia.

In 432 B.C. Nehemiah revisited Jerusalem, drove Tobiah out of the Temple (Neh 13:4-9) and enforced several of the laws, such as the payment due to the Levites (Neh 13:10-14), the observance of the Sabbath (Neh 13:15-22) and the abolition of mixed marriages (Neh 13:23-27). He concluded his memoirs with a prayer to God to remember to his credit all of his efforts to strengthen divine law within Jerusalem (Neh 13:30-31). See EZRA AND NEHEMIAH, BOOKS OF.

2. One of the leaders of those who returned from the Babylonian Exile with Sheshbazzar (Ezra 2:2; Neh 7:7).

3. Son of Azbuk and "leader of half the district of Beth Zur"; he was among those who assisted Nehemiah in rebuilding the walls of Jerusalem (Neh 3:16).

NEHEMIAH, BOOK OF See EZRA AND NEHEMIAH, BOOKS OF

NEHUM One of those who returned from the Babylonian Exile with Zerubbabel (Neh 7:7). In the parallel list in Ezra 2:2, he is called Rehum.

NEHUSHTA ("serpent", or "bronze"). The daugher of Elnathan and wife of Jehoiakim, to whom she bore Jehoiachin, later king of Judah (II Kgs 24:8). She was exiled together with her son by Nebuchadnezzar king of Babylonia in 597 B.C. (II Kgs 24:12, 15; cf Jer 29:2).

NEHUSHTAN The name given by King Hezekiah of Judah, to a bronze serpent which according to II Kings 18:4, was the original one Moses made in the wilderness to heal all those who were bitten by snakes (Num 21:6-9). It was later placed in the Temple court where it was worshiped, probably as the embodiment of the snake-god.

Hezekiah, as part of his extensive religious reform, removed all the symbols of the Canaanite cult and smashed the serpent to pieces.

NEIEL The name of a border town in the territory of Asher, between Beth Emek and Cabul (Josh 19:27). Identified with Khirbet Ya'anin, about 2 miles (3 km) north of the Arab village of Cabul.

NEKODA

1. A family of Nethinim (Temple servants) who returned from the Babylonian Exile with Zerubbabel (Ezra 2:48; Neh 7:50).

2. A family which returned from the Babylonian Exile, but which could not prove its Israelite origin (Ezra 2:60; Neh 7:62).

NEMUEL, NEMUELITES

1. The son of Eliab, brother of Dathan and Abiram (Num 26:9) of the tribe of Reuben.

2. Son of Simeon and ancestor of the Nemuelite family (Num 26:12;

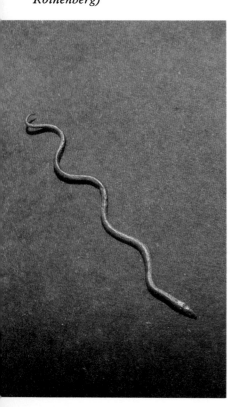

Votive copper serpent from the 13th century B.C. found at the Midianite temple at Timnah (Courtesy B. Rothenberg)

NEHEMIAH 1
Neh 1:1; 8:9; 10:1; 12:26, 47

NEHEMIAH 2
Ezra 2:2. Neh 7:7

NEHEMIAH 3
Neh 3:16

NEHUM
Neh 7:7

NEHUSHTA
II Kgs 24:8

NEHUSHTAN
II Kgs 18:4

NEIEL
Josh 19:27

NEKODA 1
Ezra 2:48. Neh 7:50

NEKODA 2
Ezra 2:60. Neh 7:62

NEMUEL, NEMUELITES 1
Num 26:9

NEMUEL, NEMUELITES 2
Num 26:12. I Chr 4:24

I Chr 4:24). In Genesis 46:10 and Exodus 6:15 he is called Jemuel.

NEPHEG

1. Son of Izhar, one of the tribe of Levi (Ex 6:21).

2. A son of King David, who was born in Jerusalem (II Sam 5:15; I Chr 3:7; 14:6).

NEPHISHESIM, NEPHUSIM A family of Nethinim (Temple servants) who returned from the Babylonian Exile with Zerubbabel (Ezra 2:50; Neh 7:52); they were probably descendants of Naphish, the son of Ishmael (Gen 25:15; I Chr 1:31).

NEPHTOAH Spring mentioned in the description of the border between the territories of Judah and Benjamin: "the fountain of the water of Nephtoah" (Josh 15:9), and "the spring of the waters of Nephtoah" (Josh 18:15). Joshua 18:16, reads "The border came down

The village of Lifta identified with the site of Nephtoah.

to the end of the mountain that lies before the Valley of the Son of Hinnom, which is in the Valley of the Rephaim on the north". This fits the identification of this spring with Ain Lifta, the large spring of the deserted village by the same name on the slopes of Wadi Beit Hanina, the upper stream of Sorek, the northern entrance to modern Jerusalem.

NER ("light"). A Benjamite, the son of Abiel (I Sam 14:51) and father of Abner commander of King Saul's army (I Sam 14:50; 26:5, etc.). Ner was related to the king, but it is not certain whether he was Saul's uncle (I Sam 14:51; I Chr 9:36) or his grandfather (I Chr 8:33; 9:39).

NEREUS (the name of a water-god). A Christian of Rome, greeted, together with his sister, by Paul.

NERGAL ("lord of the great city"). Mesopotamian deity (II Kgs 17:30), god of the underworld. His cult was brought to Israel by the people of Cuth who were deported and resettled by Tiglath-Pileser III in Samaria.

NERGAL-SHAREZER (NERGAL-SAREZER) ("Nergal protect the king!"). One of the officers serving under Nebuchadnezzar, king of Babylon. He participated in the conquest and destruction of Jerusalem (Jer 39:1-8) in the year 586 B.C. (Two people of the same name are mentioned in v. 3, but some scholars feel that the second reference is an error). Some identify him with King Neriglissar who reigned in Babylon from 559-556 B.C.

NERI The grandfather of Zerubbabel, an ancestor in the genealogy of Jesus.

NERIAH ("God is the light"). Son of Mahseiah and father of Baruch,

Agate Phoenician seal inscribed "[Belonging] to Neri". 8th century B.C. (Israel Museum)

Jeremiah's scribe (Jer 32:12, 16; 36:4, 8, 14, 32) and Seraiah, one of King Zedekiah's officials (Jer 51:59).

NETAIM A place in the plain of Judah where royal potters lived.

NETHANEAL ("God had given").

1. A priest, chief of the house of Jedaiah, at the time of the high priest Joiakim (Neh 12:21).

2. One of the priests and a musician, who was present at the dedication of the wall of Jerusalem, at the time of Nehemiah (Neh 12:36).

NETHANEEL ("God had given").

1. The son of Zuar, one of the chiefs of the tribe of Issachar, who gave offerings to the tabernacle (Num 1:8; 2:5; 7:18, 23; 10:15).

2. One of the priests appointed by King David to blow the trumpets before the ark of God (I Chr 15:24).

3. The father of Shemaiah, a Levite appointed by King David to make the roster of the priests (I Chr 24:6).

4. One of the officials of King Jehoshaphat of Judah, who was sent to teach the Law in the cities of Judah (II Chr 17:7).

5. One of the officials of King Josiah of Judah, who gave Passover offerings to the Levites (II Chr 35:9).

6. A priest, son of Pashhur who, having married an alien wife, repudiated her, at the time of Nehemiah (Ezra 10:22).

NETHANEL ("God had given").

1. One of King David's brothers, the fourth son of Jesse (I Chr 2:14).

2. The fifth son of Obed-Edom, appointed by King David as a gatekeeper in the Temple (I Chr 26:4).

NETHANIAH ("Yah has given").

1. Son of Elishama and father of Ishmael who assassinated Gedaliah at Mizpah (II Kgs 25:23, 25; Jer 40:8, 14-15; 41:2).

2. The son of Shelemiah and father of Jehudi, one of the officials of King Jehoiakim of Judah (Jer 36:14).

3. A Levite, descendant of Asaph, who was appointed over the fifth group of the Temple musicians (I Chr 25:2, 12).

4. One of the Levites sent by Jehoshaphat king of Judah, to teach the Law in the cities of Judah (II Chr 17:8).

The name Nethaniahu appears on Hebrew seals from the 7th century B.C.

NETHINIM A tribe, or a group of families, associated with the Israelites during the entire biblical period from the time of Joshua until Ezra. They were the lowest class of Temple servants.

Scholars hold different views about the origin and identity of the Nethinim. According to one view they were the descendants of the Gibeonites who tricked Joshua into making a treaty with them (Josh chap. 9). As a result, the Gibeonites were forced to become woodcutters and water carriers for the assembly of the people and for the altar (Josh 9:27). This view traces the name "Nethinim" to the Hebrew word "given" because the Nethinim were given over to the service of the priests and the Levites in the Temple. David is also said to have "appointed" the Nethinim to serve the Levites in their ministerial functions (Ezra 8:20). If this is the correct explanation, it would fit in with the practice widely followed in the ancient world whereby conquered peoples were subjected to some kind of forced labor in the sanctuaries of their conquerors.

The later biblical books suggest a change in the status of the Nethinim. The lists of those who returned from Exile to rebuild the Temple include the Nethinim, who were organized under family heads (Ezra 2:43ff; Neh 10:28; 11:21) among the priests, Levites, gatekeepers, singers and servants of the Temple (according to Nehemiah 3:26 many of them dwelt in the Ophel, in their own quarter by the Temple hall). On the basis of the above view, these Nethinim of the Second Temple were descendants of the earlier First Temple slaves. Support for this is found in the fact that the Nethinim listed bore foreign names (Ezra 2:43ff). Their changed status is evident in that they were recognized as part of the Temple congregation, and according to Ezra 7:24 even enjoyed the privilege of tax exemption, as did the priests and Levites. According to Nehemiah 10:28ff the Nethinim were loyal to the covenant of God's law and avoided mixed marriages.

A different view is held by other scholars who identify the Nethinim as a group of uncircumcised cult practitioners of the class referred to by Ezekiel when he strongly criticized Israel for entrusting them with the care of the Temple (Ezek 44:7ff): but his perception of the Nethinim is difficult to maintain in view of Ezra's apparently close association with them: an outspoken nationalist and religious dogmatist, he nevertheless recruited the Nethinim preparatory to his return to Jerusalem (Ezra 7:7; 8:20). All these sources make it clear that the Nethinim were accepted servants whose assistance in various duties connected with the Temple and its service was perfectly regular in the eyes of the religious leadership.

NETOPHAH, NETOPHATHITES A town in Judah close to Bethlehem, the birthplace of two of David's "mighty men" (II Sam 23:28-29), where families of Levites settled (I Chr 9:16). It was also inhabited at the time of the return from the Babylonian Exile (Ezra 2:22), when the "sons of the singers" (Neh 12:28) lived there, and in the Roman period.

NETTLE See PLANTS

NEW GATE Name of one of the gates of the Temple during Jeremiah's time. The people brought Jeremiah to this gate to accuse him before the magistrates (Jer 26:10). Its location is unknown.

NEW MOON A day of rejoicing and feasting (Hos 2:11), on which one refrained from work (Amos 8:5). It marked the beginning of the month with family meals (I Sam 20:5-6), visits to the prophet (II Kgs 4:23) and assemblies at the Temple (Is 1:13-15). On the New Moon special sacrifices were offered, their number being even greater than those for the Sabbath (Num 28:9-15).

According to Numbers 10:10 and Psalms 81:3, this holiday was proclaimed by the blowing of trumpets. In future days, both the New Moon and the Sabbath will be a time when all people will congregate to worship the one God (Is 66:23). Ezra read the Law to the people in Jerusalem at one of the New Moon holidays (Neh 8:2).

NEW TESTAMENT See CANON; OLD AND NEW TESTAMENT

NEW YEAR Festival celebrated on the first day of the seventh month of Tishri. The celebration of the New Year was an important religious occasion in the Middle East and it is surprising that it receives so little prominence as such in the Bible. The term "New Year" is mentioned only once in the Hebrew text of the OT in Ezekiel 40:1. Even there the exact day is problematical since the date in that verse is the tenth of the month. This has led some scholars to suggest that there was a span of ten days, from the first until the tenth of the seventh month, which constituted the period of the New Year.

The months of the year are in fact counted from the spring month (Ex 12:2). The references to the first day of the seventh month as a special festival day are found in Numbers 29:1 where it is described as a day "of blowing the trumpets". In Leviticus 23:24, it is a "memorial... a holy convocation". On this date a national assembly was convoked by Ezra to read the Law to the people who were so moved that they wept; whereupon Nehemiah said to them, "The day is holy to the Lord your God, do not mourn nor weep. For all the people wept, when they heard the words of the Law." Nehemiah went on to encourage them to observe the day with some joy and to distribute charity (Neh 8:1-10).

NEZIAH The head of a family of Nethinim (Temple servants) who returned with Zerubbabel from the Exile in Babylon.

NEZIB The name of a place in the plain of Judah, mentioned together with the towns of Libnah, Keilah, Achzib and Mareshah (Josh 15:42-44). It is identified with Khirbet Beit Nesib ash-Sharqiya.

NIBHAZ A deity worshiped by the Avites (II Kgs 17:31), who were exiled to Samaria by the Assyrians (722 B.C.).

NIBSHAN A town in the desert of Judah (Josh 15:62). Identified with Khirbet el Makari in the Buqeia Valley, near the Dead Sea.

NICANOR ("conqueror of man"). One of the men chosen, along with Stephen, to assist the apostles in Jerusalem.

NICODEMUS ("conqueror for the people"). One of the secret disciples of Jesus, probably a member of the Sanhedrin, who spoke on behalf of Jesus before the Council, and after the crucifixion helped to arrange Jesus' burial.

NICOLAITANS ("follower of Nicolas"?). Members of a heresy or sect in the very early church at Ephesus and Pergamum; the author of Revelation repudiates them, but nothing is known of their teachings.

NICOLAS ("conqueror for the people"). A Greek proselyte to Judaism from Antioch; one of the seven deacons chosen to assist the apostles in the Jerusalem church; apparently no connection with Nicolaitans.

NICOPOLIS A Roman city in Greece, where Paul spent a winter.

NIGER ("black"). The surname of Simeon, one of the "prophets and teachers" in the Christian community of Antioch. The Roman family name "Niger" is not necessarily an indication of African origin.

NILE (THE RIVER) The biggest river in Africa, about 3,800 miles (6,100km) long, which in its lower reaches flows through Egypt to a delta emptying into the Mediterranean. The economy of Egypt depends on the waters of the Nile. In the Bible the Nile is referred to simply as "the river" (Gen 41:1 etc.), a term sometimes used as a synonym for any

NEZIAH
Ezra 2:54.
Neh 7:56

NEZIB
Josh 15:43

NIBHAZ
II Kgs 17:31

NIBSHAN
Josh 15:62

NICANOR
Acts 6:5

NICODEMUS
John 3:1, 4, 9;
7:50; 19:39

NICOLAITANS
Rev 2:6, 15

NICOLAS
Acts 6:5

NICOPOLIS
Titus 3:12

NIGER
Acts 13:1

A coin of Nicopolis, depicting Nike. Struck in A.D. 219.

The Nile.

large river. It is also called Sihor (Jer 2:18). The seven cows came up "the river" in the dream of Pharaoh (Gen 41:2) and the infant Moses was found in the ark among the reeds along its bank (Ex 2:3). "The river" also symbolized the whole land of Egypt (Ezek chap. 29 etc.).

NIMRAH A Gadite city in the Jordan Valley (Num 32:3), also called

NIMRAH
Num 32:3

Beth Nimrah (Num 32:36; Josh 13:27). It may be identified with Tell Nimrim, 5 miles (8 km) east of the Jordan River.

JIMRIM, THE
VATERS OF
s 15:6. Jer
48:34
NIMRIM, THE WATERS OF A place in Moab, mentioned in Isaiah 15:6 and Jeremiah 48:34. Some scholars identify it with Wadi Nimrim, which flows into the Jordan 6 miles (10 km) north of the Dead Sea; others with Wadi en-Numeirah which flows into the Dead Sea, 6 miles (10 km) from its southern extremity.

NIMROD
Gen 10:8-9. I
Chr 1:10. Mic
5:6
NIMROD Son of Cush and grandson of Ham. In chapter 10 of Genesis it is related that he was the first mighty hero. His renown as a hunter made his name proverbial as "Nimrod, the mighty hunter before the Lord" (Gen 10:8-12; I Chr 1:10).

Nimrod is depicted as having established a great empire including Babylon, Erech, Accad and Calneh. He is also associated with Asshur and Nineveh; so Assyria itself was once being mentioned as the "land of Nimrod" (Mic 5:6).

Since his father's name (Cush) may refer to the nation of Kassites who once ruled Babylonia, many scholars have sought Nimrod's identification among Assyrian or Babylonian deities (e.g. Ninurta) or kings (e.g. Tukulti-Ninurta I of Assyria). However, there is no general consensus.

NIMSHI
I Kgs 19:16.
II Kgs 9:2, 14,
20. II Chr 22:7
NIMSHI The father of King Jehu of Israel (I Kgs 19:16; II Kgs 9:20; II Chr 22:7), or grandfather, according to II Kings 9:2, 14.

NINEVEH,
NINEVITES
Gen 10:11-12.
II Kgs 19:36.
Is 37:37.
Jonah 1:2; 3:2-
7; 4:11. Nah 1:1;
2:8; 3:7. Zeph
2:13. Matt
12:41. Luke
11:30, 32
NINEVEH, NINEVITES The last capital of the Assyrian empire, situated on the east bank of the Tigris (Hiddekel), opposite modern Mosul. The city was probably founded early in the 3rd millennium B.C. According to the Bible it was founded by Ashur (ancestor of the Assyrians) in the time of Nimrod (Gen 10:10-12). During the reign of Sargon II it became one of the capitals of the Assyrian kingdom, and it was the sole capital during the reign of Sennacherib (who was murdered there by his sons II Kgs 19:36-37; Is 37:37-38). Esarhaddon and Ashurbanipal adorned Nineveh with magnificent palaces. It is described in the Book of Jonah (Jonah 3:3) as "an exceedingly great city," with an enormous population and taking three days to traverse (Jonah 4:11). The Assyrian sources do not disclose how it was finally destroyed. Diodorus Siculus recounts that Arabaces the Scythian

A group of deportees — two men and a boy — carrying packs, and an Assyrian soldier urging them along. From a relief at Sennacherib's palace at Nineveh. (Musée du Louvre, Paris)

besieged the city for two years but could not take it. But in the third year the waters of the river rose and destroyed its fortifications; the king and his retinue committed suicide by throwing themselves into the flames and the city fell to the Scythians. According to a chronicle of the Babylonian king Nabopolassar the united forces of the Chaldeans (Ur) and the Medians (Madai) destroyed Nineveh in 612 B.C. Its destruction is mentioned by Zephaniah (2:13-15) and Nahum.

The remains of Nineveh are hidden in two mounds on either bank of the Hawsar River. One is Kouyunjik Tepe, where the palaces of Esarhaddon and Ashurbanipal were discovered, and the other, on the south bank is Nebi Younis (the prophet Jonah), where the palace of Sennacherib stood. These palaces were unusually large, built upon raised platforms about 75 feet (19m) high. At the gates of the palaces stood winged lions with human faces. On the walls were reliefs depicting the military campaigns of the kings of Assyria and their hunting expeditions, plus mythological and other scenes. Sennacherib's palace occupied the southeastern quarter of the city. It was here that the relief portraying the siege and conquest of Lachish was discovered. The city wall was more than 3 miles (5km) long and according to the king's description it had 15 gates. Sennacherib encircled the inner wall with an outer one which, in his words, "was like a mountain." The whole city was surrounded by gardens full of scented plants and irrigated by channels that drew water from the neighboring rivers. The great library of Ashurbanipal, containing 25,000 clay tablets dealing with historical, literary and religious matters, was found in Kouyunjik.

NISAN The first month of the year. The name, which is of Babylonian origin, is found in the Bible only in Nehemiah 2:1 and Esther 3:7. While the oldest Hebrew calendar referred to the first month of the year (March-April) as *Abib,* most biblical texts designate this month simply as "the first month" (e.g., Ex 12:2; 40:17; Lev 23:5; Num 9:1; 28:16; Ezek 29:17; etc). The Babylonian month names may have been introduced by the Jews returning from the Babylonian Exile.

NISAN
Neh 2:1. Est 3:7

NISROCH A deity worshiped by the Assyrians. Sennacherib, king of Assyria, was assassinated in Nisroch's temple at Nineveh (II Kgs 19:37; Is 37:38).

NISROCH
II Kgs 19:37. Is 37:38

NOADIAH ("the Lord has arranged an encounter"). Name of two persons — one of each sex — mentioned in the Bible during the first two centuries of the Second Temple period.

1. Noadiah son of Binnui. Upon the return to Jerusalem of the Temple vessels, which Nebuchadnezzar had carried away to Babylon and which Cyrus released in the care of Sheshbazzar, the priests Meremoth and Eleazar inventoried the vessels with the assistance of two Levites. One of these was Noadiah, the other, Jozabad.

NOADIAH 1
Ezra 8:33

2. The last clearly datable named prophetic personality in the Hebrew Bible. Noadiah was one of five prophetesses mentioned in the Hebrew Bible (the others being Miriam, Deborah, the wife of the prophet Isaiah [Is 8:3] and Huldah). "The prophetess Noadiah and the rest of the prophets" sought to intimidate Nehemiah when he was attempting to surround Jerusalem with a wall.

NOADIAH 2
Neh 6:14

NOAH

1. The hero of the Flood story. Two stories are related of Noah in the Book of Genesis — the man whose righteousness saved him from the destruction of his generation (Gen 5:28-9:19), and the drunken farmer (Gen 9:20-29).

Noah's birth is seen as an auspicious event. His father Lamech called him Noah, because "this one will comfort us concerning our work and the toil of our hands, because of the ground which the Lord has cursed",

NOAH 1
Gen 5:29-30, 32; 6:8-10, 13, 22; 7:1, 5-7, 9, 11, 13, 15, 23; 8:1, 6, 11, 13, 15, 18, 20; 9:1, 8, 17-20,

The month of Nisan represented by the sign of Aries (Taleh) in the wheel of the zodiac on the mosaic pavement of the synagogue at Bet Alpha.

(Gen 5:29, alluding to the curse of Gen 3:19). After the age of 500, Noah begot three sons, Shem, Ham and Japheth.

Because of its ubiquitous evil, the Lord decided to blot out the human race, with the exception of Noah — the one righteous and blameless person on the face of the earth: he and his family were to be spared. Noah was commanded to construct an ark, into which he would bring his family, as well as two or seven pairs of every species of animal and bird. Entering the ark in the 600th year of his life, Noah, his family and the animals, survived the 40-day deluge, while all other human and animal life on the face of the earth was destroyed.

The waters began to abate on the 150th day, allowing the ark to rest on the mountains of Ararat (in Armenia). After sending forth a raven and a dove which returned to the ark, Noah again released the dove which did not return, indicating that dry land had reappeared. After disembarking Noah offered a sacrifice to the Lord who blessed him with the same blessing given to Adam "Be fruitful and multiply, and fill the earth" — since mankind was being created anew. God now made a covenant — symbolized by the rainbow — that a universal flood would never recur. Noah and his sons were permitted to eat meat but forbidden to drink blood or commit murder (Gen 5:32-9:17).

Similar flood stories, both in Sumerian and in Akkadian, such as the Epic of Gilgamesh, were told in ancient Mesopotamia, but the Bible story contains major innovations. Noah was righteous while the rest of the world was corrupt and filled with injustice (Gen 6:5, 11-13). The Bible stresses that it was moral corruption that led to the destruction and only the moral individual was saved. No other ancient flood story has this moral emphasis.

The second Noah story is much more brief. Returning to dry land, Noah became a "tiller of the soil" and planted a vineyard, whose produce made him inebriated. Losing his senses, he "uncovered himself". His son Ham "saw his nakedness" and told his brothers, who immediately, walking backwards for modesty, covered up their father with a blanket. Upon recovering his sobriety, Noah cursed Ham's son Canaan and blessed Japheth and Shem (Gen 9:20-29). Noah died at age 950.

Noah was remembered as one of the three prototypes of righteousness along with Daniel (probably the Danel of Ugaritic renown) and Job (Ezek 14:14, 20). The only other reference to Noah in the Bible is Isaiah 54:9, where the Flood is recalled as the "waters of Noah".

Noah building the ark, shown on a carved ivory plaque of the 9th century (Cathedral of San Matteo, Salerno, Italy).

Noah's Ark on the mosaic floor of a Byzantine period church near Medeba.

In the NT, Noah was a symbol of the righteous man, who has faith in God and obeys him, especially in comparison with the surrounding world (Matt 24:37ff; Luke 17:26ff; Heb 11:7; II Pet 2:5). See FLOOD.

2. One of the five daughters of Zelophehad, who, in the absence of brothers, received their father's inheritance.

NO AMON The capital of Upper Egypt, and in certain periods also the capital of the whole country. No Amon meant "the city of the god Amun" and this is how most of the references to it in the Bible should be understood (cf Jer 46:25; Ezek 30:14; Nah 3:8). The identification of No Amon with Thebes, the center of the cult of the god Amun, is accepted by all. On the east bank the huge temple complexes of modern Karnak and Luxor were erected, while on the west bank lie the necropolis and the funerary temples. The greatest building activities date to the reigns of Hatshepsut, Thutmosis III and Amenophis III.

The large necropolis, or city of the dead, with its beautiful funerary monuments and temples extended along the west bank of the Nile. In a wadi nearby, known as the Valley of the Kings, the pharaohs were buried. One of the most famous tombs found here is that of Tutankhamun.

Of great importance are the reliefs found in the tombs and temples, which illustrate the daily life and historic events of their time. A relief in a temple at Karnak depicts Rameses II's conquest of Ashkelon. Another famous scene, found at Medinet Habu, portrays Rameses III's battle against the Sea Peoples (Philistines).

NOB A town in the territory of Benjamin which was the residence of Ahimelech and the priests, and apparently a sanctuary. David was given refuge here, and was given Goliath's sword which was kept there (I Sam chaps. 21-22). In retaliation Saul ordered the massacre of the priests of Nob. It was a place from which the Assyrians on their march from the north could view the city of Jerusalem for the first time (Is 10:32). After the return from the Babylonian Exile Nob was settled by Benjamites (Neh 11:32). Not identified.

NOBAH

1. A Manassite who conquered Kenath and its villages in Gilead, and named the city after himself (Num 32:42). According to I Chronicles 2:23, however, the city continued to preserve its original name, Kenath.

Scholars identify Kenath with Kanawat in the eastern part of Bashan and assume that Nobah is the name of the families who settled there.

2. A town located in Gilead, through which Gideon passed during his battle against the Midianites (Judg 8:11).

NOD ("wandering"). A land east of Eden where Cain dwelt after being banished by God (Gen 4:16). The name may be a pun: a place of "wandering" for the perpetual wanderer.

NODAB A nomadic tribe which, along with Jetur and Naphish, the sons of Ishmael, fought against the Israelites in Transjordan (I Chr 5:19).

NOGAH ("brightness"). Son of King David, born in Jerusalem.

NOHAH ("calmness", "tranquillity"). The fourth son of Benjamin.

NOPH (MEMPHIS) One of the most important cities of ancient Egypt, at the head of the Nile Delta. The name Memphis, which means "white wall" or "wall", is preserved in the name of the local citadel, Leukos Teichos as it was known to the Greeks. The city was built by Pharaoh Phiops I in the 24th century B.C. The pyramids of Gise, dating back to the 4th Dynasty, the most famous of which is that of Cheops, were found nearby as were other later monuments. During the New Kingdom Memphis was the second capital of Egypt and from the time of Thutmosis III onwards the pharaohs lived there. It became their

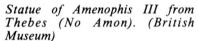

View of Thebes (No Amon).

Statue of Amenophis III from Thebes (No Amon). (British Museum)

NOAH 2
**Num 26:33;
27:1; 36:11.
Josh 17:3**

NO AMON
**Jer 46:25.
Ezek 30:14-16
Nah 3:8**

NOB
**I Sam 21:1;
22:9, 11, 19.
Neh 11:32. Is
10:32**

NOBAH 1
Num 32:42

NOBAH 2
Judg 8:11

NOD
Gen 4:16

NODAB
I Chr 5:19

NOGAH
I Chr 3:7; 14:6

NOHAH
I Chr 8:2

NOPH
**Is 19:13. Jer
2:16; 44:1;
46:14, 19.
Ezek 30:13, 16**

Alabaster sphinx at Memphis (Noph). It presumably represented Amenophis II and stood at the entrance to the temple of Ptah.

official residence at the end of the El Amarna period. In 730 B.C. the city was conquered by the Ethiopians, but was taken by Esarhaddon, king of Assyria in 671 B.C. and again by Ashurbanipal in 663 B.C. For the prophets it was a symbol of evil (Hos 9:6; Is 19:13; Jer 2:16) while its destruction is prophesied in Jeremiah 46:19 and Ezekiel 30:13, 16. During the wars of the Babylonians against Judah many Jews fled to Noph and Jeremiah directed prophecies against them (Jer 44:1ff).

NOPHAH
Num 21:30

NOPHAH A town in Moab, probably north of Dibon; it is mentioned in the poem about King Sihon of the Amorites (Num 21:30).

NUMBERS, BOOK OF The fourth book of the Pentateuch. The "numbering" of the tribes, to which its name refers, is by no means indicative of the contents of the book, since the counting only occupies chapters 1-4 and 26.

Though the book is a collection of many disparate elements, it can broadly be divided into three main sections:
(a) 1:1-10:10, the 19-day sojourn at Sinai; (b) 10:11-22:1, the trek from Sinai to the plains of Moab, which are reached in the 40th year of the Exodus (cf 10:11 with 33:38); (c) 22:2-36:13, in the plains of Moab, spanning less than five months.

The first four chapters of the book are concerned with the two types of service: the laity prepared for battle while the Levites were to carry the components of the portable sanctuary. The able-bodied males were numbered, and the tribes organized both for camping and for travel. The census achieved the same total as Exodus 38:26, namely 603,550 (Num 2:32).

Numbers 5:1-4 requires the removal from the camp of all those afflicted by bodily symptoms or discharges and verses 11-29 pertain to a cultic ordeal for determining whether a wife suspected of adultery is innocent or guilty.

This is followed by the institution of the Nazirite (6:1-21) which gives details of how an Israelite may undertake a limited period of strict observance. Chapter 7 describes in formulaic pattern the presents offered by the tribal leaders at the dedication of the tabernacle. Chapters 8-9 prescribe the consecration of the Levites, the installation

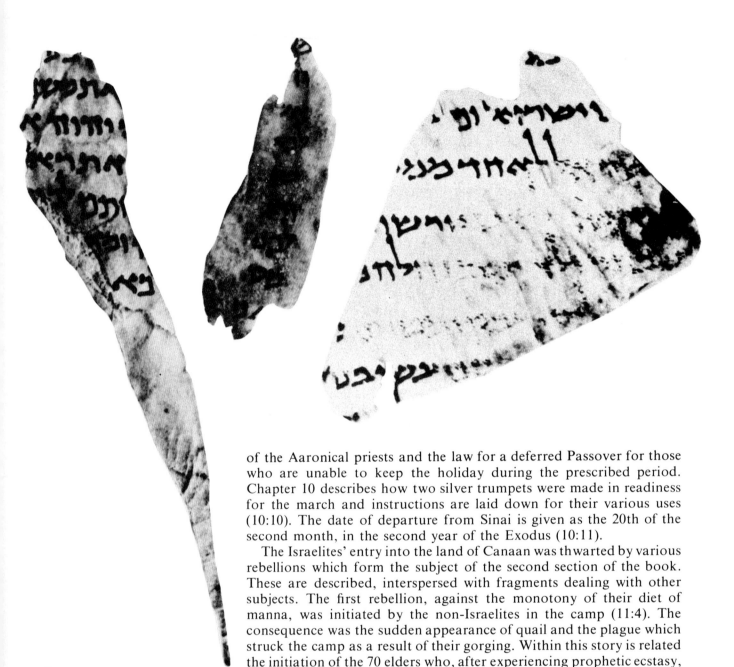

Fragments from the Book of Numbers found at Qumran. (Shrine of the Book, Jerusalem)

of the Aaronical priests and the law for a deferred Passover for those who are unable to keep the holiday during the prescribed period. Chapter 10 describes how two silver trumpets were made in readiness for the march and instructions are laid down for their various uses (10:10). The date of departure from Sinai is given as the 20th of the second month, in the second year of the Exodus (10:11).

The Israelites' entry into the land of Canaan was thwarted by various rebellions which form the subject of the second section of the book. These are described, interspersed with fragments dealing with other subjects. The first rebellion, against the monotony of their diet of manna, was initiated by the non-Israelites in the camp (11:4). The consequence was the sudden appearance of quail and the plague which struck the camp as a result of their gorging. Within this story is related the initiation of the 70 elders who, after experiencing prophetic ecstasy, began to function as leaders of the people.

The next instance of disobedience arose from the criticism leveled by Miriam and Aaron at Moses for having taken an "Ethiopian" (Cushite) wife (chap. 12). Miriam was punished by being smitten with leprosy. The most serious loss of faith arose in the episode of the twelve spies sent to reconnoiter Canaan (chaps. 13-14): their report made the Israelites reluctant to invade the land of Canaan from the south. This lack of faith resulted in that generation being decreed to die in the wilderness before the entrance to the promised land. The Korah rebellion, along with that of Dathan and Abiram, is the subject of chapters 16-17. This was actually an attack on the leadership of Moses and Aaron by a group of Reubenites and Levites, the latter complaining of their subordinate position to the Aaronic priests. Through divine intervention both parties were punished. The subsequent murmurings of the people against Moses and Aaron were punished by a plague halted only when Aaron carried a burning incense pan in front of the dying. This, together with the contest of the staves which ended with the budding of Aaron's rod, served to emphasize the authority of Aaron and the Levites to serve in the tabernacle.

The prescriptions of the red heifer to purify the ritually polluted (chap. 19) is followed by historical information including the death of Miriam and Aaron and an account of the end of the 40 years in the wilderness (chaps. 20-21).

Another rebellion is recorded (21:4-9); this one was punished by a plague of poisonous snakes, as an antidote to which Moses molded a copper snake and mounted it on a high pole.

The remainder of this section deals with the occupation of the land north of the Transjordanian states. It contains an account of two victories, one over the Amorite king Sihon and the other over Og, the king of Bashan.

Chapters 22-24 recount how the diviner Balaam was hired by Balak to curse the Israelites prior to battle. Though Balaam tried repeatedly to utter his curse, he only ended up each time blessing the Israelites and was finally dismissed by Balak. Subsequently, however, the Midianite women succeeded in enticing the Israelites into joining in their cultic worship. When a leader of the tribe of Simeon held public intercourse with a Midianite woman, he was killed by the zealous Phinehas, who thereby earned, for himself and his descendants the right of eternal priesthood (25:1-15).

Chapter 26 once again gives details of a census. The total, lower than in chapter 1, reflects the losses resulting from the various punishments which had meanwhile beset the Israelites.

The book continues with the episode of the daughters of Zelophehad and their claim to a share in the future allotment of the land. This case was exceptional because there were no males in the family; it was consequently decreed that the women could claim their land provided they did not upset tribal divisions by marrying out of their tribe (27:1-11). The chapter ends with the leadership passing from Moses to Joshua.

The narrative is again interrupted by prescriptions pertaining to festival sacrifices (chaps. 28-29) and the laws of vows made by women (chap. 30). It continues with the defeat of Midian (chap. 31) and the allocation of land in Amorite territory east of the Jordan to the tribes of Reuben and Gad and half of Manasseh.

A list of the stations on the wilderness trek is then recorded (chap. 33). This is followed by instructions on the conquest of the land and the names of those who will be in charge of its distribution by lot (chap. 34). Chapter 35 deals with the Levitical cities and the cities of refuge and the book concludes with prescriptions in the event of intermarriage between tribes (chap. 36).

The historical value of Numbers has long been questioned by some scholars who regard the meager elements as late and artificial. They suggest that the texts in 10:11-14:45 and 20:1-25:5 refer to two separate attempts to invade the land, undertaken by different groups of tribes at widely separate periods and that these two strands may well have been fused by a late tradition into a single and continuous movement of a nation, rather than of individual tribes.

The religious value of the book lies in its reinforcement of the conviction that God manifests himself in history, and that he demands obedience to his will. Moses emerges as a deeply compassionate leader who sympathized with others even when they sinned (12:13; 14:19). It also serves as a valuable text in the understanding of the historically-centered mentality of OT religion.

```
                              OUTLINE

          1:1-4:49       The census
          5:1-6:21       Miscellaneous laws (suspected wife,
                           Nazirite, etc.)
          7:1-89         Consecration of the altar
          8:1-26         Laws governing the Levites
          9:1-14         Passover laws
          9:15-23        The cloud over the tabernacle
          10:1-10        The silver trumpets
          10:11-11:35    Setting out for Canaan
          12:1-16        The rebellion of Miriam and Aaron
          13:1-14:45     The twelve spies visit Canaan
          15:1-41        Laws about offerings
          16:1-17:13     The rebellion of Korah, Dathan and
                           Abiram
          18:1-19:22     Priests and Levites
          20:1-21:22     Israel at Kadesh
          22:1-24:25     Story of Balaam
          25:1-18        Phinehas and his reward
          26:1-65        The second census
          27:1-11        Laws of inheritance for daughters
          27:12-23       Appointment of Joshua
          28:1-30:16     Festival sacrifices and vows
          31:1-54        The war against Midian
          32:1-42        Allotment of Transjordan
          33:1-35:34     Boundaries, cities of refuge etc.
          36:1-13        Laws for female heirs
```

NUN ("fish"). An Ephraimite; father of Joshua (Ex 33:11; Num 11:28; Deut 1:38; Josh 1:1 etc.).

NUTS See PLANTS

NUZI A city in northeast Iraq, approximately 5 miles (8 km) southwest of modern Kirkuk, near the foothills of southern Kurdistan. The Akkadian cuneiform texts discovered there in excavations from 1925-1931, contain much information on the native Hurrian population, especially in the realm of family law, and also have significance for the understanding of several of the social and legal customs reflected in the patriarchal narratives.

The situation described in Genesis 15:2-3, where the as yet childless Abraham proclaims his chief servant as his heir, follows the pattern of that society where an adopted son who provides both for the physical maintenance of his parents and for their proper burial, becomes the sole heir of the family estate. If, subsequent to the adoption, a natural son is born, the latter becomes principal heir and inherits a double share of the parental property (cf Gen 15:4).

The institution of concubinage (Gen 16:1ff; 30:3) was also an established legal custom at Nuzi, wherein a barren wife must provide her husband with a handmaid for the specific purpose of bearing children. Slave girls were also presented to new brides as was the case with Leah (Gen 29:24) and Rachel (29:29).

The transference or sale of the birthright (Gen 25:31-34) is also documented at Nuzi. In that society, as in the Bible, birthright was not so much a matter of chronological priority as of parental decree (cf Gen

NUN
Ex 33:11.
Num 11:28;
13:8, 16; 14:6,
30, 38; 26:65;
27:18; 32:12,
28; 34:17.
Deut 1:38;
31:23; 32:44;
34:9. Josh 1:1;
2:1, 23; 6:6;
14:1; 17:4;
19:49, 51;
21:1; 24:29.
Judg 2:8. I
Kgs 16:34. I
Chr 7:27. Neh
8:17

49:3-4 where Reuben is deprived of his birthright). This practice of parental favoritism was later prohibited by Israelite law (Deut 21:15-17). Deathbed declarations have legal validity both in Nuzi and in the Bible, and one such oral pronouncement begins with a formula similar to Genesis 27:2, "Behold now, I am old".

Rachel's appropriation of the teraphim — the household gods belonging to her father Laban — has been compared to these texts which indicate that the ancestral images were bequeathed to the principal heir as symbols of household unity. It is questionable, however, if their possession guaranteed a legal hereditary title to the parental estate.

Other analogues include the common phrase "to go to the gods" which, in both traditions, symbolizes a juridical ordeal pertaining to various stages of indebtedness and containing a specific injunction against the exactment of interest (cf Ex 21:6; 22:8; Lev 25:35-37), is echoed in Nuzi documents of loans without new interest charges. Another example from the familial sphere pertains to a disobedient and defiant son (Deut 21:18-21) who in both societies was summoned to judgment before the judges of his town.

NYMPHAS
Col 4:15
NYMPHAS A Christian at Colossae, to whom Luke and Demas sent greetings.

OAK See PLANTS

OATH In the biblical view, the spoken word is charged with intrinsic power to effect good or evil, blessing or curse. Hence, an oath carries with it an explicit or implicit curse, if the oath taken proves false or is violated. The words curse and oath are virtually synonymous and are used interchangeably (I Kgs 8:31).

The oath taken by the exiles concludes with the words: "Let my right hand forget her skill... Let my tongue cling to the roof of my mouth" (Ps 137:5-7). The phrase "God do so and more also," an introductory formula of an oath, is a distinct allusion to a self-imposed curse (I Sam 14:44; II Sam 3:9).

One may well conclude that every oath carried with it a curse either explicit or implied. The same may be said of the oath that ratified a covenant or treaty between two parties. Deuteronomy 29:14 speaks of "this covenant and this oath" as does Daniel 9:11. When Zedekiah violated his treaty with Nebuchadnezzar (Ezek 17:15), Ezekiel described the consequences in the following terms: "...can he break the covenant and still be delivered? As I live, says the Lord God, surely, in the place where the king dwells... whose oath he despised, and whose covenant he broke — with him in the midst of Babylon he shall die" (Ezek 17:15-16).

An oath could begin or end by invoking the name of God. A common introductory formula opens with the words: "By the life of Yahweh" (or, alternatively translated "As Yahweh lives" Judg 8:19; I Sam 14:39; 19:6; I Kgs 17:1). These phrases are elliptical and one must add "who will punish me if I swear falsely or fail to fulfill this oath". Somewhat less frequent was the locution "as you live, my Lord the king" (II Sam 11:11; 14:19). Occasionally, "as the Lord lives" and "as my Lord the king lives" were joined for emphasis as in II Samuel 15:21.

To swear in the name of a deity other than the God of Israel was tantamount to idolatry. Amos (8:14) denounced those who "swear by the sin of Samaria... And as the way of Beersheba lives". The Psalmist (Ps 16:4) proclaimed that he would not take the name of another god on his lips. This accords with the command (Deut 6:13-14) to swear in the name of God.

God himself is often described as taking an oath, e.g., Genesis 22:16; 26:3; Exodus 33:1; Numbers 14:23. All these refer to the divine oath that he will give the land to the descendants of Abraham. However, an oath by God may be elicited by a specific occasion or situation (I Sam 3:14; Jer 22:5). Psalm 89:4 refers to God's oath to David to establish his kingdom and his house forever.

An oath could be imposed upon an underling by someone in a superior position anxious to ensure that his charge be carried out. So Abraham adjured his servant, the elder of his house (Gen 24:2-4). Likewise, Jacob caused Joseph to swear that he would not bury him in Egypt but rather in the burying place of his fathers in the land of Canaan (Gen 47:29-31).

Mention is made of the gesture of raising a hand or hands heavenward while taking an oath: "Abraham said to the king of Sodom, I have lifted my hand to the Lord" (Gen 14:22). The phrase is the equivalent of taking an oath (Ezek 20:6; Dan 12:7).

Because pronouncing an oath is an act of holiness, its violation is a profanation of the name of God and subjects one to divine punishment. Both versions of the Ten Commandments proscribe swearing falsely (Ex 20:7; Deut 5:11). The commandment contains the additional phrase "for the Lord will not hold him guiltless who takes his name in vain". The injunction against a false oath is likewise found in Leviticus (19:12).

Even an oath violated through being unwittingly forgotten must be atoned for by means of a sin offering brought as a sacrifice (Lev 5:4-6). An oath must be kept even if it brings one harm (Ps 15:4).

Distinct from voluntary oaths are judicial oaths, mandatory in certain court procedures. When no decision can be reached by the judge, or if the accused cannot produce witnesses in his defense, recourse was found by subjecting the accused to an oath. Several such instances are grouped together in Exodus 22:6-11. Here the oath apparently terminated the case. Leviticus (6:2-5) prescribes the procedure to be followed in a civil case when a man admits to having sworn falsely. He must pay the value of the object claimed and add thereto a fifth of its value. Moreover, the offense having been committed not against his fellow man alone, but also against God, the offender's monetary restitution must be supplemented by a guilt offering (Lev 6:6-7).

The inviolability of an oath once uttered, even when elicited under false pretenses, is to be inferred from the account (Josh 9:2-19) of the covenant made by Joshua with the Gibeonites who claimed that they had come from a far-off country. When it was discovered that the Gibeonites lived nearby, the people protested and inclined to disregard the treaty. But Joshua and the princes reply: "... we have sworn to them by the Lord God of Israel, now therefore we may not touch them" (Josh 9:19).

Non-Israelites in the future will take an oath of allegiance to God to express their loyalty to him (Is 19:18; 45:23). Only Ecclesiastes contains a warning against taking an oath (Ecc 5:4-5), which is followed by Ecclesiasticus 23:9ff.

Jesus' condemnation of oaths (Matt 5:33-37) may be understood as referring to oaths in ordinary, everyday speech and not to judicial oaths. "...do not swear at all; neither by heaven... nor by the earth... nor by Jerusalem... nor shall you swear by your head." (The latter locution as an introductory formula for an oath is quite common in rabbinic sources). If, however, this condemnation is taken to include all oaths, then it differs substantially from that of rabbinic Judaism. While the latter condemned rash and needless oaths, it did not, on the whole, either condemn nor forbid all oaths. Jesus demanded of his followers (James 5:12) that "let your yes be yes, and your no no". A similar statement is also to be found in the Talmud. Finally, Jesus railed against the Pharisees to say "whoever swears by the Temple it is nothing; but whoever swears by the gold of the Temple, he is obliged to perform it" (Matt 23:16). Paul employed oaths to prove his truthfulness (Rom 1:9; II Cor 1:23; 11:31; Gal 1:20). See also vow.

OBADIAH ("servant of Yah").

1. Servant of King Ahab who protected the prophets of Israel from Queen Jezebel.

2. A descendant of David.

3. Son of Izrahiah and a chief of the tribe of Issachar.

4. Son of Azel, a Benjamite.

5. A Levite who returned with Zerubbabel (I Chr 9:16). He is called Abda in Nehemiah 11:17.

6. An officer in David's army from the tribe of Gad.

7. The father of Ishmaiah, a chief of Zebulun during the time of David.

8. An officer of King Jehoshaphat who was sent with priests and Levites to teach the people from the "Book of the Law of the Lord".

9. One of the Levites commissioned by Josiah to oversee the repairs to the Temple.

10. Son of Jehiel and head of a family clan that returned with Ezra from the Babylonian Exile.

OBADIAH 10
Ezra 8:9

11. One of the priests who sealed the covenant.

OBADIAH 11
Neh 10:5

12. A gatekeeper who guarded the storehouses during the time of the high priest Joiakim.

OBADIAH 12
Neh 12:25

13. The name of a prophet whose book of only one chapter which is a polemic against Edom, is the shortest in the OT. It is the fourth book of the Minor Prophets. Nothing is known of him. See OBADIAH, BOOK OF.

OBADIAH 13
Obad v.1

OBADIAH, BOOK OF The Book of Obadiah is the fourth of the twelve books of the Minor Prophets. It is the shortest book in the OT, consisting of only one chapter with 21 verses. It contains an anti-Edomite oracle (cf Gen 27:39-40; Ps 137:7; Is 34:5; Ezek 25:12-14; Mal 1:2-5), as well as a Day of the Lord prophecy (cf Is 2:12-22; Ezek chap. 7; Joel 1:15-2:11). When Jerusalem fell in 586 B.C., the Edomites not only exulted at the humiliation of the Judahites, but actively assisted their Babylonian foes by intercepting the fugitives, and occupying the Negeb (Ezek 25:12; 35:10; Lam 4:21). Toward the end of the 6th century B.C., Edom was invaded by the neighboring Arab tribes, who seem to have taken over the land in its entirety. Edom remained without a settled population throughout the Persian period.

Fragment from the Book of Obadiah found at Qumran. (Shrine of the Book, Jerusalem)

Against this background, the book opens with the brief superscription, "The vision of Obadiah," (v. 1) and an ecstatic cry. The prophet has heard a report from the Lord, and a messenger has been sent among the nations to call them to battle. From its lofty place in the "clefts of the rock", Edom is pulled down to earth, plundered and overcome (v. 3). On that day, Edom will be abandoned by her allies, and the Lord will destroy her wise men and her warriors. The reasons for this terrible fate are given in verses 11-14, and the meting out of justice in kind, is for what Edom has done to Judah. Verses 15ff describe the imminent Day of the Lord, when the tables shall be turned with the house of Jacob acquiring the possessions of Edom. Mount Zion will then rule Mount Esau (Edom), and the "Kingdom shall be the Lord's" (v. 21).

Scholarly views on the composition of the book are characterized by two principal approaches: one maintains the essential integrity of the book; the other regards it as comprising two separate works (vs. 1-10, 11-14, 15 (second half)) stemming from different periods, with an additional prophecy of the "Day of the Lord", 15 (first half) and 16-21. Some scholars assign Obadiah verses 1-10, and especially verses 1-7, to the reign of King Amaziah (c. 800 B.C.) since they contain no allusions to the events of 586 B.C. However, the call to the nations to rise in battle against Edom, the marauders in verse 5, and the alliance between Edom and Babylon in verse 7, are suggestive of the Arab incursions in the 6th century. The indication that the author of Jeremiah (Jer 49:7-22) knew only of Obadiah verses 1-11 suggests that this section was earlier than the rest of the book.

OUTLINE

vs. 1-16   The guilt of Edom and its punishment
vs. 17-21   The future restoration of Israel

OBAL One of the sons of Joktan, the great-grandson of Shem (Gen 10:28). In Chronicles the name is spelled Ebal (I Chr 1:22).

OBED ("slave, servant"?).

1. Firstborn son of Ruth and Boaz and the father of Jesse, who was the father of David.

2. Son of Ephlal and father of Jehu in the genealogy of the family of Jerahmeel.

3. One of David's "mighty men".

4. One of the sons of Shemaiah, firstborn of the house of Obed-Edom and a gatekeeper in the House of the Lord at the time of King David.

5. Father of Azariah, one of the captains who made a covenant with Jehoiada the priest at the time of Athaliah.

OBED-EDOM

1. The Gittite in whose house David placed the ark of the Lord following the death of Uzzah. After the ark remained in his house for three months, bringing blessing to him and to all his household, David decided to move it to Jerusalem (II Sam 6:10-12; I Chr 13:13-14; 15:25).

2. A gatekeeper; his sons and their sons and brothers numbered 62 able men (I Chr 26:4-8).

3. One of the gatekeepers and musicians appointed by David to serve before the ark (I Chr 15:16-24). According to I Chronicles 16:38, he was the son of Jeduthun the musician, but his name is absent from the genealogical list of Jeduthun.

4. A guardian of the Temple vessels. He was captured by King Joash of Israel in the war against King Amaziah of Judah.

OBIL ("camel driver"). An Ishmaelite in charge of the camels in the household of King David.

OBOTH One of the stations of the Children of Israel on the route of the Exodus (Num 33:43-44). Oboth, translated in the KJV as "new

Bone Hebrew seal inscribed "MY'MN son [of] Oded". 7th-6th centuries B.C. (Israel Museum)

wineskins" (Job 32:19), denotes water skins; in this case, it apparently refers to springs. The site has variously been identified at the springs of Ein el-Weiba, west of Punon, or, preferably, with Ain Husb northwest of that place.

OCRAN (OCHRAN) A man of Asher, the father of Pagiel who led his tribe (Num 2:27) in the wilderness of Sinai.

ODED

1. Father of Azariah, who was a prophet in Judah at the time of King Asa.

2. A "prophet of the Lord" in Samaria at the time of Kings Ahaz and Pekah; he persuaded the Israelites to repatriate Judean prisoners of war (II Chr 28:9-11).

OG Amorite king of Bashan in Transjordan, ruler of 60 towns; he engaged the Children of Israel in battle, after they had defeated King Sihon of Heshbon on their journey to Canaan. Og eventually saw his kingdom destroyed by Moses and the Children of Israel. The area of this kingdom which included the Hermon region to the north, and was bounded by the Jordan on the west, was repopulated by parts of the tribe of Manasseh (Num 21:33-35; Deut 3:1-13). Og is portrayed as a giant, one of the last of the awesome Rephaim; whose huge bedstead in Rabbath-Ammon was particularly impressive (Deut 3:11; Josh 12:4-6; 13:12). News of the defeat of their two powerful kings caused consternation among the Canaanites (Josh 2:10; 9:9-10), and encouraged the Israelites, who had hitherto gone in fear of the formidable Canaanite and Amorite monarchs (Ps 135:10-12).

OHAD The third son of Simeon; he was among those who accompanied Jacob on his journey to Egypt (Gen 46:5, 10).

OHEL ("tent"). One of the descendants of David listed in the genealogy of the family of Jeconiah.

OHOLAH A symbolic name used by Ezekiel to refer to Samaria, the older sister of Jerusalem, which he calls Oholibah (Ezek 23:4). The name can be translated "she who has her own tent". These two "sisters" are denounced by the prophet for their incessant political harlotry throughout history. As punishment they are to be delivered to their "lovers" for execution.

OHOLIBAH See OHOLAH

OIL The most common oil in biblical times was extracted from olives. Other oils were rare in Palestine. Together with grain and wine, oil symbolized divine bounty (Jer 31:12; Joel 2:19); should the nation be disobedient, these gifts were taken away (Deut 28:51; Joel 1:10; Hag 1:11). Oil was put to manifold uses: it served as a condiment (Judg 9:9; Hos 2:8); the taste of manna was compared to cakes baked in oil (Num 11:8); it was noted that oil made the face shine (Ps 104:15) and was a refreshing unguent, e.g. after a bath (Ruth 3:3; II Sam 12:20). Oil was given medicinal application in anointing wounds (Luke 10:34; cf Is 1:6). Olive oil was utilized for lighting lamps in the home (Matt 25:1-13)

OCRAN
Num 1:13; 2:27; 7:72, 77; 10:26

ODED 1
II Chr 15:1, 8

ODED 2
II Chr 28:9

OG
Num 21:33; 32:33. Deut 1:4; 3:1, 3-4, 10-11, 13; 4:47; 29:7; 31:4. Josh 2:10; 9:10; 12:4; 13:12, 30-31. I Kgs 4:19. Neh 9:22. Ps 135:11; 136:20

OHAD
Gen 46:10. Ex 6:15

OHEL
I Chr 3:20

OHOLAH
Ezek 23:4-5, 36, 44

OHOLIBAH
Ezek 23:4, 11, 22, 36, 44

(right)
Oil press from the 15th century.

(left)
Oil press from Gamla in the Golan.

Oil press from Tirat Jehuda.

(left)
Olive oil installation reconstructed by Erez Cohen.

and in the sanctuary (Ex 25:6). It served for ceremonial anointing of kings (I Sam 10:1; 16:1, 13), priests (Lev 8:30) or prophets (cf Is 61:1). Oil was an essential ingredient in various sacrifices, for example in the burnt offering and in cereal offerings (Lev 2:4). Olive oil was an important export (II Chr 2:10; Ezra 3:7).

OLD GATE

Neh 3:6; 12:39

OLD GATE One of Jerusalem's city gates; it was repaired by Jehoiada son of Paseah and Meshullam the son of Besodeiah (Neh 3:6). This gate was close to the goldsmiths' and perfumers' quarters (Neh 3:8). Some identify it with the corner gate mentioned in the defeat of Amaziah, king of Judah (II Kgs 14:13); they consequently locate it at the northwestern corner of the city. The gate apparently got its name by serving as the outlet to the road to the town of Jeshanah (Hebrew: "old") at the southern border of the district of Samaria (II Chr 13:19).

OLD AND NEW TESTAMENT As early as the 2nd century A.D. Christians divided the books of their Bible into two parts: Old and New Testaments. The word "testament" came from the fact that the Greek word for covenant (*diatheke*) in Latin versions had been translated *testamentum*. The new covenant referred to by Jeremiah 31:31 is an image employed to describe the time when God will inscribe his teaching upon the hearts of the Israelites. The same term was used by Jesus (Matt 26:28; Mark 14:24; Luke 22:20) and is firmly embedded in the early Christian tradition with respect to the Lord's Supper (I Cor 11:25). In other connections "new covenant" appears only once in Paul (II Cor 3:6) and most prominently in the Epistle to the Hebrews, the first early Christian text to speak of Jeremiah's new covenant as having "made the first obsolete" (Heb 8:13; cf 7:18).

A page from the Aleppo Codex, the oldest known complete manuscript of the Old Testament, dating from the 10th century.

Only Paul referred to the "Old Testament" as a written document (II Cor 3:14) and to the "oldness of the letter" in contrast to the new way of the Spirit (Rom 7:6).

See also CANON.

OLIVE See PLANTS

OLIVES (MOUNT OF), OLIVET A mountain to the east of Jerusalem (Zech 14:4), on the other side of the Kidron Valley, rising about 2,500 feet (800m) above sea level. It seems to have been sacred from early times (cf II Sam 15:30, 32; Ezek 11:23). Solomon built high places there for Ashtoreth, Chemosh and Milcom (II Kgs 23:13), but these and the images were broken by Josiah, king of Judah.

The Mount of Olives occupies a special place in early Christian tradition. According to Acts (1:9-12) it was "a Sabbath day's journey" (2,000 cubits) from Jerusalem, and it was also the place of the Ascension. On its slopes lay Bethpage, Bethany and Gethsemane. Jesus' Palm Sunday entry into Jerusalem began on the Mount of Olives (Matt 21:1ff; Mark 11:1ff; Luke 19:28ff). At the traditional site a Roman lady by the name of Pomenia built a church in about A.D. 387, but the present chapel dates from no earlier than the Crusader period. To the

OLIVES (MOUNT OF), OLIVET
II Sam 15:30.
Zech 14:4.
Matt 21:1;
24:3; 26:30.
Mark 11:1;
13:3; 14:26.
Luke 19:37;
22:39. John
8:1

One of the very ancient olive trees growing in the Garden of Gethsemane on the Mount of Olives.

(right)
The Mount of Olives as seen from the Garden of Gethsemane.

south of it the Emperor Constantine built the church of Eleona, on the site where Jesus traditionally foretold the destruction of Jerusalem (Matt 24:1-3; Mark 13:1-4). The church, of which little remains today, was destroyed by the Persians in A.D. 614 but was soon rebuilt. Further rebuilding took place in the middle of the 12th century. On the lower slope of the mountain, tombs of the time of the Second Temple and remains of additional churches were discovered.

OLIVET See OLIVES, MOUNT OF

OLYMPAS A Christian of Rome greeted by Paul.

OMAR Second son of Eliphaz, the firstborn son of Esau (Gen 36:4, 11) a prince of Edom (Gen 36:15).

OMEGA See ALPHA AND OMEGA

OMRI

1. King of the Northern Kingdom of Israel (882-871 B.C.) and a contemporary of Asa, king of Judah. The concise record accorded to his 12 year reign in I Kings 16:16-28 states that he had previously served as general of King Elah's army. With the assassination of Elah by another

OLIVET
Luke 19:29, 37;
21:37; 22:39.
John 8:1. Acts
1:12

OLYMPAS
Rom 16:15

OMAR
Gen 36:11, 15.
I Chr 1:36

OMEGA
Rev 1:8, 11;
21:6; 22:13

OMRI 1
I Kgs 16:16-
17, 21-23, 25,

27-30. II Kgs
9:26. II Chr
22:2. Mic 6:16

general, Zimri, and the latter's seizure of the throne in Tirzah, Omri was proclaimed king by the Israelite army while encamped against Gibbethon of the Philistines (I Kgs 16:15-17). Omri immediately set out for Tirzah and captured it. With the death of Zimri (who committed suicide by burning the royal palace over himself), Omri had to contend with yet another aspirant to the throne, Tibni the son of Ginath, who was supported by half of the people of Israel. The four-year civil war ended in Omri's victory and the death of Tibni (I Kgs 16:17-22).

The biblical account mentions one significant act of Omri: the transfer of his royal residence from Tirzah to a new capital, which he himself established on a hill named Samaria (I Kgs 16:24). The record concludes with a passing reference to other acts of Omri involving displays of might, without specifying the nature of these acts (I Kgs 16:26).

The Moabite Stone (the inscription of Mesha, king of Moab, now in the Louvre) affords some insight into Omri's military prowess; it shows that Omri subjugated the land of Moab and conquered the land of Medeba, north of Arnon. Furthermore, from the biblical account relating to King Ahab, Omri's son and successor, it can be inferred that Omri was hard pressed by the Assyrians who wrested from him a few cities and extraterritorial rights in Samaria (I Kgs 20:34). It is reasonable to assume that Ahab's marriage to Jezebel, daughter of King Ethbaal of Phoenicia (I Kgs 16:31), was initiated by Omri with the double aim of a politico-economic alliance between the two countries, and of countering the threat of growing Assyrian power. This, together with the royal marriage pact concluded between Ahab's daughter and Jehoram, king of Judah (II Kgs 8:18), must have enhanced the political, military and economic status of the Northern Kingdom.

Indeed the references in Assyrian records to the later kings of Israel (including Jehu, who annihilated the Omride dynasty) as the "house of Omri" and to the land of Israel as "the land of Omri", are indicative of his reputation and the strong impact which his reign had upon the region.

However, the marriage alliance with Phoenicia subjected the Kingdom of Israel to sweeping Phoenician cultural and religious influence, triggering a fierce and bloody opposition, later headed by Elijah and Elisha and evoking an extremely negative assessment of Omri on the part of the Deuteronomic historiographer.

OMRI 2
I Chr 7:8

2. A son of Becher from the tribe of Benjamin.

OMRI 3
I Chr 9:4

3. Son of Imri and father of Ammihud; a Judahite who dwelt in Jerusalem.

OMRI 4
I Chr 27:18

4. Son of Michael and head officer of the tribe of Issachar during the reign of King David.

ON

ON 1
Num 16:1

1. The son of Peleth, and a chief of the tribe of Reuben; he took part in the rebellion led by Korah against Moses (Num 16:1-2).

ON 2
Gen 41:45, 50;
46:20

2. The Hebrew name of the Egyptian city called Heliopolis by the Greeks, and mentioned as Aven elsewhere in the Bible (Ezek 30:17).

Asenath, the daughter of Poti-Pherah, priest of On, was given to Joseph as a wife (Gen 41:45).

See AVEN No.1.

ONAGER See ANIMALS

ONAM

ONAM 1
Gen 36:23.
I Chr 1:40

1. Fifth and last son of Shobal, second son of Seir the Horite; he was a chief of the Horites in the land of Edom (Gen 36:23).

ONAM 2
I Chr 2:26, 28

2. Son of Jerahmeel by his wife Atarah (I Chr 2:26); he was the father of Shammai and Jada (I Chr 2:28). Some believe he was related to No.1.

Slaves being freed; shown on a Roman relief of the 1st century A.D. (Musée Marienne, Bruxelles)

ONAN The second son of Judah by Shua the Canaanite. On the death of his elder brother Er, Onan was instructed to enter into a levirate marriage with the latter's widow, Tamar. To avoid raising a child for his brother, he practiced coitus interruptus, a sin for which the Lord killed him (Gen 38:4-10).

ONESIMUS A runaway slave converted by Paul in Rome. From Paul's letter to Onesimus' master Philemon in Asia Minor it appears that Onesimus had probably stolen something from his master before accepting the gospel from Paul (Philemon had accepted it some time before). Paul sent Onesimus back to his master with an accompanying letter, the canonical Epistle to Philemon. The name Onesimus, which means useful or profitable, gives Paul occasion for a play on words: "who once was unprofitable to you, but now is profitable to you and to me" (Philem v. 11). In the 2nd century Ignatius relates that Onesimus became bishop of Ephesus. Since the name was common, this must remain doubtful.

ONESIPHORUS A man of Ephesus who aided Paul.

ONION See PLANTS

ONO A town built by families of the tribe of Benjamin in the vicinity of Lod (I Chr 8:12). A site of that name is mentioned in the lists of Thutmosis III, but it is never again referred to in Egyptian or Assyrian sources, nor does it appear in the early books of the Bible. Ono was inhabited after the return from Babylonian Exile (Ezra 2:33; Neh 7:37) by the Benjamites (Neh 11:35). In the late Roman period it was the capital of a district. The site is identified with Kefr Ana, 6 miles (10 km) northeast of Lydda.

ONYCHA See PLANTS

OPHEL A name given to a certain part of a city, as in Jerusalem (II Chr 27:3; 33:14), or Samaria (II Kgs 5:24, given as "citadel" in the KJV). After the return from the Babylonian Exile the Nethinim (Temple servants) in Jerusalem dwelt in the Ophel (Neh 3:26). From Isaiah 32:14 (KJV "forts and towers") and Micah 4:8 (KJV "tower"), it can be deduced that this part of the city was strongly fortified. The word *ophel* in Semitic languages means "swell, rise" and hence the ophel was the elevated part of the town, containing the inner citadel, the acropolis, the seat of the king and the center of royal administration.

ONAN
Gen 38:4, 8-9; 46:12. Num 26:19. I Chr 2:3

ONESIMUS
Col 4:9. Philem v. 10

ONESIPHORUS
II Tim 1:16; 4:19

ONO
I Chr 8:12. Ezra 2:33. Neh 6:2; 7:37; 11:35

OPHEL
II Chr 27:3; 33:14. Neh 3:26-27; 11:21

The Ophel, north of the City of David in Jerusalem.

In Jerusalem the Ophel apparently included the City of David, the site of the former Jebusite castle of Zion (I Chr 11:5), located near the Water Gate, as well as the buildings which David and Solomon built higher up, towards the Temple Mount. The eastern slope, towards the

Kidron Valley, was fortified by a series of walls from as early as the Middle Bronze Age.

OPHIR

OPHIR 1
Gen 10:29.
I Chr 1:23

1. The son of Joktan and grandson of Shem. Ancestor of the people of Ophir. For the location of their territory see No.2 below.

Hebrew ostracon with an inscription referring to a consignment of gold from Ophir, found at Tell Qasile, on the north bank of the Yarkon River. 8th century B.C. (Israel Museum and Israel Dept. of Antiquities and Museums)

OPHIR 2
I Kgs 9:28;
10:11; 22:48.
I Chr 29:4.
II Chr 8:18;
9:10. Job
22:24; 28:16.
Ps 45:9. Is
13:12

2. In the Bible Ophir is referred to as a source of gold. Solomon brought 420 talents of gold from here (I Kgs 9:28), but Jehoshaphat failed to acquire any because his ships foundered in a storm at Ezion Geber (I Kgs 22:48). Ophir gold was considered to be of high quality (I Chr 29:4; Is 13:12). The location of Ophir is not known with certainty; many places are offered as possible candidates, including Arabia, East Africa and even far-away Sumatra. The coupling of Ophir with other identifiable places (Gen 10:29; I Chr 1:23) may perhaps point to southern Arabia.

OPHNI
Josh 18:24

OPHNI A town in the territory of Benjamin (Josh 18:24). In the time of the Second Temple its name was changed to Ophnah, or Beth Guphnin, which was the capital of a toparchy. After the destruction of the Temple the notables of Jerusalem were sent into exile there. A palace of the Roman period was discovered on the site. Identified with Jifneh, near Ramallah.

OPHRAH

OPHRAH 1
Josh 18:23.
I Sam 13:17

1. A town in the territory of Benjamin (Josh 18:23), prominent in the war between the Philistines and Israel (I Sam 13:17), known in the Roman period as Afairema, or Aifraim. It was in the center of the northern district of Judah from 145 B.C. until the conquest by Pompey. Identified with et-Taiyibeh, five miles (8 km) north of ancient Michmash.

OPHRAH 2
Judg 6:11, 24;
8:27, 32; 9:5

2. The town of Joash the Abiezrite where the angel of God appeared to Gideon, his son, and where he built an altar (Judg 6:11-12, 24) and was buried (Judg 8:32). Identified with several places in the Jezreel Valley; possibly Afuleh.

OPHRAH 3
I Chr 4:14

3. Son of Meonothai of the family of Judah.

OREB ("raven"). Name of a man and a place.

OREB 1
Judg 7:25; 8:3.
Ps 83:11

1. One of the two princes of the Midianites captured (along with Zeeb) by the men of Ephraim who executed them and brought their heads to Gideon. Their execution, along with the decisive defeat of the Midianites, became proverbial in Israel.

OREB 2
Judg 7:25. Is
10:26

2. The place where Oreb was killed was called the rock of Oreb. It was probably north of Jericho and west of the Jordan River.

OREN
I Chr 2:25

OREN ("fir tree"). A man of Judah, third son of Jerahmeel the son of Hezron.

Hoard of jewelry from the early Israelite period found at Beth Shemesh.

ORNAMENTS AND JEWELRY Ornaments and jewelry appear prominently in biblical stories, both in the literal and in the figurative sense. They were worn by men and women, warriors and princes; they were also part of the ceremonial dress of the high priest. The prophetic books of the OT as well as the NT use jewels and ornaments as symbols to convey their message.

Jewels were part of the daily life of the ancient Hebrews. They could be used as a betrothal present, as when the servant sent by Abraham to find a bride for his son, Isaac, gives Rebekah "A golden nose ring weighing half a shekel, and two bracelets for her wrists weighing ten shekels of gold" (Gen 24:22). When the parents of the girl agreed to the match "he brought out jewelry of silver, jewelry of gold... and gave them to Rebekah" (Gen 24:53). They were also used as a pledge: Tamar received from her father-in-law Judah a signet ring as a pledge (Gen 38:18). They were easily movable assets; before leaving Egypt the Children of Israel took the jewels of their Egyptian neighbors (Ex 3:22; 11:2; 12:35). In the desert, when the Children of Israel demanded — in the absence of Moses on Mount Sinai — that Aaron make them an image, he instructed them to "Break off the golden earrings which are in the ears of your wives, your sons and your daughters and bring them to me" (Ex 32:2) and with the gold that they brought he molded a calf (Ex 32:4).

There are some 25 different names referring to jewels in the Bible. They have not all been identified. Some occur only once and still puzzle scholars; others are translated as "ornaments" for want of a more precise word (II Sam 1:24; Jer 2:32). In a long tirade condemning the luxury of the women of Jerusalem, Isaiah lists their finery and many jewels (Is 3:18-22 in the NKJV translation which is not accepted by all scholars). A similar condemnation of costly jewels is to be found in the first epistle of Paul to Timothy (I Tim 2:9).

Among ornaments ordinarily worn by men were "ornaments of gold, armlets and bracelets and signet rings and earrings and necklaces" (Num 31:50). Isaiah writes approvingly of "a bride adorning herself with her jewels" while her bridegroom "decks himself with ornaments" (Is 61:10).

The exact difference between armlet and bracelet is not clear; the word bracelet sometimes means anklet. Scholars are also not sure of the exact difference between the various headdresses: headbands, crescents,

*(right)
Collection of Nabatean jewelry found in the cemetery of Mampsis in the Negeb. 1st to late 3rd century A.D.*

Necklace with crescent-shaped pendant from the 2nd century B.C. (British Museum)

Tutankhamon and his wife wearing broad heavy pectorals and bracelets of gold inlaid with stones. From the back panel of Tutankhamon's tomb which is made of sheet gold inlaid with silver-colored glass. 14th century B.C.

diadems, etc. mentioned in the Scriptures. It could be a single ribbon or veil embroidered with pearls or a gold ornament studded with precious stones.

Kings were fond of jewels and ornaments. They wore ornate crowns of gold set with precious stones (II Sam 12:30) and surrounded themselves with priceless objects (I Kgs 10:14-23). Solomon "made silver as common in Jerusalem as stones" (I Kgs 10:27).

One of the ornaments on the breastplate of judgment worn by the high priest on or over the ephod, is described in great detail (Ex 28:15-29). Both ephod and breastplate were made of rich material and lavishly covered with gold and precious stones.

Ezekiel compared Jerusalem to a beautiful woman "adorned with gold and silver" (Ezek 16:13) later stripped of her "beautiful jewelry" (Ezek 16:39) as a punishment because "you have taken your beautiful jewelry from my gold and my silver which I had given you, and made for yourself male images" (Ezek 16:17).

In the Book of Revelation Babylon is shown as "arrayed in purple and scarlet, and adorned with gold and precious stones and pearls"

(Rev 17:4). The city of New Jerusalem in the Book of Revelation is made of gold, pearls and precious stones (Rev 21:9-21).

The predilection shown by biblical figures for jewels and jewelry is backed by extensive archeological findings. The finds of the Late Bronze Age are especially rich, reflecting the prosperity of the area at the time. A rich collection of gold jewelry was found in Tell el Ajjul. Outstanding are a mother-goddess amulet with a female head, a pendant in the form of an eight-pointed star, crescent-shaped earrings with rich granular decoration, a gold pendant (used as an amulet) in the form of animals and faience beads depicting animals and flowers. Bracelets of gold and silver are numerous, as are pairs of simple earrings and finger-rings decorated with scarabs.In the Middle and Late Bronze Ages Egyptian influence is illustrated by numerous jewelry finds. From the Persian period onward the jewelry found belongs to types developed in such advanced cultures as those of Greece, Asia Minor, Phoenicia and Persia. Gold jewelry is common, much of it connected with religious belief and cult images.

ORNAN See ARAUNAH

ORNAN
I Chr 21:15, 18, 20-25, 28. II Chr 3:1

ORPAH A woman of Moab who married one of the two sons of Naomi and Elimelech (Ruth 1:2, 4). When Naomi returned to Bethlehem with Ruth after the death of her husband and of her sons, Orpah stayed in Moab (Ruth 1:14).

ORPAH
Ruth 1:4, 14

It has been suggested that the name should be translated "she who turned back".

OSNAPPER (OSNAPPAR, ASNAPPER) One of the kings of Assyria; he is mentioned only once in the Scriptures (Ezra 4:10) in connection with the letter sent to Artaxerxes by the foreign population settled in Judah, in protest against the rebuilding of Jerusalem and of the Temple. Many scholars believe the king referred to was Assurbanipal.

OSNAPPER
Ezra 4:10

OSPREY See ANIMALS

OSTRICH See ANIMALS

OTHNI (shorter form of Othniel). A Levite, firstborn son of Shemaiah, eldest son of Obed-Edom; he was a gatekeeper in the House of the Lord at the time of King David.

OTHNI
I Chr 26:7

OTHNIEL The son of Kenaz; the first of the judges who brought salvation to Israel. He defeated Cushan-Rishathaim, a king of Mesopotamia (Aram-Naharaim in Hebrew), who had enslaved Israel for eight years. After that, the land knew peace for 40 years (Judg 3:7-11). Achsah daughter of Caleb was awarded to him as a prize for his conquest of the city of Debir, formerly Kirjath Sepher (Josh 15:15-17; Judg 1:12-13). In Joshua 15:17 he is called "Othniel the son of Kenaz, the brother of Caleb" and in Judges 1:13, he is mentioned as "the son of Kenaz, Caleb's younger brother". It is not clear whether Caleb is the brother of Othniel or of Kenaz. It has therefore been suggested that Caleb and Othniel denote two clans of the tribe of Kenaz. Later they appeared in the genealogy of Judah.

OTHNIEL
Josh 15:17. Judg 1:13; 3:9, 11. I Chr 4:13; 27:15

Othniel's sons were Hathath and Meonothai (I Chr 4:13). His descendant Heldai the Netophathite was in charge of a division of 24,000 men in David's army (I Chr 27:15).

OWL See ANIMALS

OX, OXEN See ANIMALS

OZEM
1. The brother of David and sixth son of Jesse.

OZEM 1
I Chr 2:15

2. Fourth of the five sons of Jerahmeel, descendant of Judah.

OZEM 2
I Chr 2:25

OZNI, OZNITES Fourth son of Gad according to the census of the Children of Israel taken in the wilderness (Num 26:16); founder of the Oznite family.

OZNI, OZNITES
Num 26:16

ARAI
Sam 23:35

DAN,
DAN ARAM
en 25:20;
:2, 5-7;
:18; 33:18;
:9, 26;
:15; 48:7

DON
zra 2:44.
eh 7:47

GIEL
um 1:13;
27; 7:72, 77;
:26

HATH-MOAB
zra 2:6; 8:4;
:30. Neh
11; 7:11;
:14

I, PAU
en 36:39.
Chr 1:50

PAARAI Paarai the Arbite was one of David's thirty "mighty men". In I Chronicles 11:37 his name is Naarai.

PADAN, PADAN ARAM The land in which Nahor and his family lived (Gen 48:7, Padan; Gen 25:20; 28:2, etc. Padan Aram). The Akkadian word *padan* designates "field", and Padan is believed to symbolize Mesopotamia (Aram Naharaim of the Hebrew Bible).

PADON ("the Lord redeemed"). A family of Nethinim (Temple servants) who returned from Exile with Zerubbabel (Ezra 2:2, 44).

PAGIEL A man of Asher, the son of Ocran; he was appointed by the Lord to help Moses take the first census of Israel in the wilderness (Num 1:2, 13) and later became leader of his tribe (Num 2:27), on behalf of whom he presented an offering to the tabernacle set up by Moses (Num 7:72-77). Pagiel led the armies of the tribe of Asher when the Children of Israel set out on their journey from the wilderness of Sinai to the promised land (Num 10:26).

PAHATH-MOAB ("governor of Moab"). A family of Israelites who returned from the Babylonian Exile with Zerubbabel (Ezra 2:6; 8:4; Neh 7:11). Several members of the clan were listed among those who willingly divorced their wives at the decree of Ezra (Ezra 10:30). Hashub, who helped repair the city wall, was a member of this family (Neh 3:11).

PAI, PAU The residence of King Hadar of Edom (Gen 36:39; I Chr 1:50). In the Septuagint the name is rendered Fogor, which is identical with Peor (q.v.).

PALACES Apart from the "palace of Ai", which belongs to the Early Bronze Age, the first palaces unearthed are dated to the period of Hyksos domination. The general plan is like that of the usual oriental dwelling, with rooms arranged around a central court. The buildings had at least two stories, the lower one being used for domestic purposes and the accommodation of servants while the upper storey contained the living quarters proper. Excavators very often call a building a palace simply by reason of its size. But the quality of the architecture or a find of some importance — large numbers of scarabs, inscribed material, a

Herodian palace at Jericho.

Remains of the palace at Masada.

hoard of ivory plaques or of gold jewelry — would point to the fact that its inhabitants belonged to a privileged class.

The most famous palace ever constructed in Palestine was Solomon's royal palace in Jerusalem. Its several units are described in I Kings 7:1-12. This palace and the adjoining Temple were built under the influence of northern architecture. It was of a type that originated in Syria in the 2nd millennium B.C. The complex was entered through a portico with a single pillar, opening to an entrance hall, the "Hall of Pillars" (I Kgs 7:6) that led into the throne room or "Hall of Judgment" (I Kgs 7:7). Then came the living quarters, rooms surrounding "another court" (I Kgs 7:8). The "great court" (I Kgs 7:12) was apparently a huge court in front of the entrance. Built on similar lines, the palace of the Solomonic period at Megiddo has been identified as being of the same type. Another outstanding palace of the Iron Age was that of Omri and Ahab at Samaria, which followed the usual plan of rooms grouped around a central court. Its fame derives from the decoration of its furniture with ivory plaques in low or high relief or open-work; hence the reference to "the ivory house" in I Kings 22:39. A palace of the Late Iron Age, the first to be discovered in Judah, was found at Ramat Rachel and identified with the palace built by Jehoiakim (609-597 B.C.) and referred to by Jeremiah (22:13-14).

A palace of the Persian period, which was built late in the 5th century B.C., has been unearthed at Lachish. Of the outstanding palace of Roman Palestine, Herod's palace in Jerusalem, nothing remains, but its splendor can be imagined now that the two palaces at Masada have been excavated.

See BUILDING MATERIALS

PALAL The son of Uzai; he was among the men who repaired the walls of Jerusalem at the time of Nehemiah.

PALESTINE "Palaestina", the Greek word from which "Palestine" was derived, designated the southwest coast of Canaan as early as the time of Herodotus (5th century B.C.). The term is derived from "Philistina", which referred to the land of the Philistines. It was later used to designate the entire land of Israel under Hadrian's new title for the province, "Provincia Syria Palaestina", (2nd century A.D.) which replaced the former, "Provincia Judaea". The name was also used by other 1st century A.D. Greek writers such as Philo and Josephus. The usual name for the promised land in the Hebrew Bible is Canaan.

PALLU, PALLUITES Second son of Reuben, eldest son of Jacob and

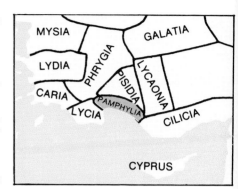

Pamphylia.

Leah (Ex 6:14); he founded the family of the Palluites (Num 26:5). He had one son, Eliab No.2.

PALM See PLANTS

PALTI ("God is my adviser").

1. Son of Raphu of Benjamin and one of the spies sent by Moses into Canaan.

2. Son of Laish, the Benjamite who was given David's first wife, Michal, after David fled from Saul's house (I Sam 25:44). She was later taken back from Palti. In II Samuel 3:15 he is called Paltiel.

PALTIEL

1. Son of Azzan of Issachar, he was appointed by Moses to help in the distribution of the land (Num 34:26).

2. See PALTI No.2

PALTITE Appellation of Helez, a native of Beth Pelet; one of David's "mighty men".

PAMPHYLIA A region on the south coast of Asia Minor with Perga as its capital; visited by Paul on his first missionary journey.

PAPHOS Port in the southwest corner of Cyprus, visited by Paul on his first journey.

PAPYRUS See PLANTS

PARABLES Parables are an important part of wisdom teaching having a decided didactic purpose. The English words stems directly from the Greek *parabole*. In the Aramaic that Jesus spoke, the common word was *matla*, a cognate of the Hebrew *mashal*. The latter word occurs in the Hebrew Bible with a broad range of specific connotations: it may express a proverb (cf I Sam 10:12; 24:13; Ezek 12:22-23; 16:44; 18:2-3), a popular derisive saying (Ezek 16:44), a taunt song (Num 21:27-30; Is 14:4; Mic 2:4), an oracular utterance (Num 24:3, 15, 20-21, 23) or an allegorical saying (Ezek 17:2-3; 24:3-4). The root idea is that of comparison: a likeness between two realities is indicated or implied. In other words, *mashal* is basically a kind of metaphor. The Jewish tradition of parable and proverb was characterized by dynamic juxtaposition of images, sharp and subtle wit, vital narrativity and keen insight into human affairs. The *mashal* as short tale and sometimes allegory, features in Jewish intertestamental literature and in rabbinical sources. The word was particularly associated with the sayings of the wise, as seen in the Hebrew title of the Book of Proverbs, "The Proverbs of Solomon". However, the Greeks showing greater analytical precision in vocabulary, their translation of the Hebrew Bible (the "Septuagint") renders *mashal* by other terms in addition to *parabole*.

An interest in parables has always been great in the Christian tradition owing to their important function in the Gospels of Matthew, Mark and Luke, where the parable is the characteristic teaching form of Jesus' ministry. The Gospels of Mark and Matthew relate that Jesus spoke entirely in parables to the crowds (Matt 13:34; Mark 4:33-34). The modern discovery of the Gospel of Thomas, one of the documents in Coptic preserved in the library of the Christians at Nag Hammadi in Egypt, has increased scholarly interest in the parables. Thomas is comprised of parables and sayings of Jesus placed within the barest narrative frame. Some of the material is quite similar to that found in the canonical gospels, and may even come from an older tradition, while some of the Thomas teachings have no parallel in the NT.

A coin of Paphos with a bull and an eagle. 5th century B.C.

The literary and religious role of parables in the gospels goes far toward accounting for their appeal. In fact, recent research raises the question of whether the parable was a form so closely associated with Jesus and had such an impact on early Christians that the narrative gospel as a literary form was partially shaped by characteristics of the parables ascribed to Jesus. Here we touch upon a more basic question: why were the parables of Jesus so striking and memorable in the first place?

On the one hand, Jesus clearly stands in this parable tradition. For example, parables like the hidden treasure (Matt 13:44) and the lost sheep (Luke 15:3-6; Matt 18:12-13) draw upon a repertory of parable elements in the tradition (cf Testament of Job chapter 18 and Testament of Solomon chapter 1).

On the other hand, the parables attributed to Jesus in the NT and Thomas typically develop a central metaphor to the point that it comes across either as paradoxical or as so exaggerated as to be ludicrous. This was not typical of the rabbis, who used parables as allegories to inculcate adherence to the Torah; and therefore excluded any sense of paradox or the absurd. But Jesus did otherwise, according to the portrayal of him in the NT gospels and Thomas. The literary phenomenon of paradox and exaggeration in the parables was the medium for announcing the Kingdom of God that comes without warning, overturning human establishments and shattering wordly security. The listener is invited to consider things from a radically different point of view, which is expressed both in the parables (short tales) and parabolic sayings. The Greek parabole covers both in the Synoptic Gospels. Since recent scholarly and lay interest has focused on the short tale form of parable, a few parables of this sort will be mentioned here. The parable of the Samaritan (Luke 10:30-35) begins in the world of the Jewish traveler who goes down to Jericho. The priest and the Levite are representatives of this established world, but they do not stop to help the victim after he is attacked and left half-dead by robbers. The robbers are a threat, as is always the case, to the established world. The Samaritan does not belong in this world, being despised by the Jews — a feeling the Samaritans reciprocated. But he acts as though it is his own world to travel in; he will even come back to reimburse for the care of the traveler-victim. The parable of the banquet (Luke 14:15-24; allegorized form in Matt 22:1-14) begins in the world of the rich man with his palatial home and (presumably) respectable neighbors. He is turned down by the first guests invited, so he sends his servant to fetch people from the streets, and those who have no means, cannot walk and cannot see are brought in. The parable of the sower (Matt 13:1-9; Mark 4:1-9; Luke 8:4-8) comes across as a typical situation: a farmer sows his seed and it grows successfully or not, depending on the kind of soil it lands in. But the yield is astonishing, especially as Mark presents it in the form of poetic ascending intensification: "But other seed fell on good ground and yielded a crop that sprang up, increased and produced: some thirtyfold some sixty and some a hundred" (Mark 4:8).

The parable is a form which invites one to spell out its meaning in a given context. The Synoptic Gospels do this in their own way, sometimes setting the parables within narrative frames that reflect the concerns of the early church as it sought to interpret the words of its Lord. The effect was sometimes to encase or rigidify a parable's meaning when other meanings are possible, and are really necessary in new situations. For instance, the narrative frame of the Samaritan parable in Luke turns it into an example story (Luke 10:25-28, 36-37; so the title "The Good Samaritan"), whereas the parable itself, verses 30-35, may be read as an invitation to see oneself as the traveler-victim who is graciously aided by someone he would have despised in ordinary circumstances. The parable thus suggests that the Kingdom of God is like life-saving aid received from a foreign, perhaps hated, agent.

PARADISE See EDEN, GARDEN OF

PARAH ("heifer"). A Benjamite village located between Jerusalem and Jericho (Josh 18:23). Jeremiah 13:4-7 may have been referring to this location as the place where he was commanded by God to symbolically bury his loincloth. The site is near the spring Ain Farah which supplied water to Jerusalem.

PARAN A desert in the Sinaı peninsula, south of Kadesh Barnea, lying between the land of Midian and Egypt (I Kgs 11:18). Ishmael lived here with his mother, Hagar the Egyptian (Gen 21:21). One of the stations of the Israelites on their way from Egypt to the promised land (Deut

Khirbet Abu Muserach, identified with Parah.

Landscape in the rocky region of Paran in the Sinai Peninsula.

33:2). Moses sent men from there to spy out the land (Num 13:3) and the Israelites remained there 40 days (Num 13:25-26). David found shelter in the wilderness of Paran after the death of Samuel (I Sam 25:1).

At an early date Christian tradition identified Paran with the great oasis of Feiran, in the southern rocky part of the Sinai peninsula, where Mount Sinai is shown at Jebel Musa. Early in the Byzantine period this region became a center of Christian monasticism, and it was there that the monastery of St. Catherine was built.

PARBAR A room or section of the courtyard on the west side of the Temple area. The word is of Persian origin.

PARMASHTA Seventh of the ten sons of Haman; along with his brothers he was killed by decree of King Ahasuerus (Est 9:1, 9).

PARMENAS One of the seven deacons appointed to assist the apostles ın the Jerusalem church.

PARNACH ("the bright one"). A man of Zebulun, father of Elizaphan who was appointed by the Lord to help Joshua divide the land of Canaan (Num 34:17, 25).

PAROSH

1. Name of a family or clan who returned with Zerubbabel from Exile in Babylon: they numbered 2,172 persons (Ezra 2:3). Seven members of the family are listed among those who, having taken pagan wives, had to repudiate them according to the decree of Ezra (Ezra 10:25). Another member was among those who repaired the wall of Jerusalem (Neh 3:25) while Parosh himself was one of the leaders who sealed the covenant (Neh 10:14).

2. Father of Zechariah mentioned among the heads of families who returned with Ezra from Exile (Ezra 8:3).

PARSHANDATHA Firstborn of the ten sons of Haman; along with his brothers he was killed by decree of King Ahasuerus (Est 9:1, 7).

PARTHIANS A people originating in nomadic tribes which in early antiquity invaded Asia Minor, and settled in the Seleucid province of Parthia in 248/7 B.C. In later periods the Parthians ruled from the Euphrates to the Indus, with Ecbatana as their capital. The declining power of the Seleucid kingdoms was the main cause for the rapid growth of the Parthian dominions. With the coronation of Mithridates I in 170 B.C. the borders of Parthia expanded in all directions, and the

Parthian coin of Mithridates IV. 2nd century A.D.

kingdom apparently traded directly with China. In the years 51/50 and 40 B.C. Parthians invaded Syria and Palestine, looting the whole country. After the formation of the Second Roman Triumvirate, Anthony, who was allotted the eastern provinces, defeated the Parthians, and the Romans succeeded in checking Parthian power by establishing a rival kingdom in Armenia.

PARTRIDGE See ANIMALS

PARUAH ("bloom"). Father of Jehoshaphat who was governor of the tenth administrative district of King Solomon.

PARVAIM Solomon adorned the Temple with "gold of Parvaim". In the Jerusalem Talmud, Parvaim is explained as referring to the quality of the gold, i.e., pure gold. However, later Jewish expounders of the Bible interpreted the term as denoting the place of origin of the gold. Some scholars have identified Parvaim with Sak el-Farwein in the western part of the Arabian peninsula, or with Farwa in Yemen, neither of which however is known to have had gold mines in antiquity.

PARZITES Descendants of Perez of the tribe of Judah.

PASACH Firstborn son of Japhlet the grandson of Asher in the genealogy of the family of Asher.

PASDAMMIM Identical with EPHES DAMMIM.

PASEAH

1. Second son of Eshton the grandson of Chelub in the genealogy of the family of Judah.

2. Head of a family of Nethinim (Temple servants) who returned with Zerubbabel from Exile in Babylon.

3. Father of Joiada who repaired the Old Gate in the walls of Jerusalem at the time of Nehemiah. May have belonged to the family of No.2.

PASHHUR, PASHUR

1. The son of Malchijah and father of Jeroham (I Chr 9:12). He was sent by King Zedekiah together with Zephaniah to seek an oracle from the prophet Jeremiah when the Babylonian king Nebuchadnezzar attacked Jerusalem (Jer 21:1-2). Jeremiah foretold that Jerusalem

Ostracon from the temple at Arad bearing the name Passhur. Late 8th century B.C. (Israel Museum and Israel Dept. of Antiquities and Museums)

would fall to the Babylonian king and that whoever remained in the city would die by the sword, famine and pestilence (Jer 38:2-3).

2. The ancestor of a priestly family which returned to Judah after the Babylonian Exile.

3. The son of Immer the priest. He was chief governor in the Jerusalem Temple (Jer 20:1). Upon hearing Jeremiah's prophecy, which foretold evil for Jerusalem, Pashhur "struck Jeremiah the prophet, and put him in the stocks". Jeremiah thereupon pronounced his judgment upon Passhur and the nation (Jer 20:2-6).

4. The father of Gedaliah; the latter was in the delegation sent to Jeremiah during the time of King Zedekiah.

5. One of the priests who sealed the covenant written in the time of Ezra.

PASHUR See PASSHUR

PASSOVER The first of the three major festivals in the Jewish liturgical calendars, celebrating the most significant event in Israel's history, the deliverance from Egypt. It begins on the 15th of the "first month", later named Nisan, and lasts for seven days, during which only unleavened bread may be eaten, in commemoration of an event linked with the Exodus. In their haste to leave Egypt, the Israelites took their dough before it was leavened, baking it into unleavened bread (Ex 12:34, 39). This bread, to which Deuteronomy 16:3 refers as "the bread of affliction," is known as *matzah*.

The Bible mentions the festival under two different designations: Passover and Feast of the Unleavened Bread. It has been suggested that originally, these two were distinct agricultural or pastoral feasts, perhaps harking back to pre-Israelite times. The Passover festival would then have resulted from a fusion of the components of these two semi-nomadic holidays, followed by the historicization of the integrated feast, associating it with the Exodus and its predominant

Illustration from the Darmastatd Haggadah, *showing a family celebrating the Passover. 15th century. (Darmstadt Landesbibliothek)*

idea of deliverance. While the origin of the Passover is far from being critically resolved, the biblical account (Ex chap. 12) associates the name with events relating to the tenth plague. When God passed through Egypt, smiting every firstborn in the land, he spared the firstborn of the Israelites, by "passing over" their houses whose door-posts and lintels he had ordered marked by the blood of the paschal lamb. Indeed the term for Passover is used both of the feast itself, and of the paschal lamb, offered as a sacrifice on the eve of the feast (Ex 12:21-48).

While the Israelites are enjoined to observe Passover at its prescribed time, a second Passover, also known as Minor Passover, was designated for the ritually disqualified (unclean) or those who had been absent on a journey, to be celebrated on the eve of the 14th of the "second month" (*Iyar*) in lieu of the first (Num 9:1-14). Thus, King Hezekiah, after cleansing the Temple, invited "all Israel and Judah" to come to Jerusalem to celebrate the Passover during the second month, "since they had not done it for a long time in the prescribed manner" (II Chr 30:5).

The laws of Passover are prescribed in the Pentateuch (Ex chap. 12; Lev chap. 23; Num chap. 9 and Deut chap. 16), but other biblical books provide numerous references to the actual mass celebration of the festival, which point to a repeated revival of the holiday. Thus the Passover was reinstated by Joshua at Gilgal (Josh 5:10-12), by Josiah (II Kgs 23:21-23), by Hezekiah (see above) and, after the return from captivity, by Ezra (Ezra 6:19). By the time of the Second Temple it was firmly established in Israel. Josephus and other sources give accounts of multitudes gathering in Jerusalem to celebrate the Passover and offer up the paschal sacrifice at the Temple. This feast was one of the three Pilgrimage festivals when all Israelite males are enjoined to appear before the Lord "in the place which he chooses" (Deut 16:16).

All four gospels state that towards the end of his life, Jesus wished to share a Passover meal with his disciples (Matt 26:2-19; Mark 14:1-16; Luke 22:1-15; John 11:55-12:2). The Synoptic Gospels identify the Last Supper with the Passover meal. At that meal Jesus gave instructions as to the nature of authority among his followers (Luke 22:24-28) and according to early Christian tradition, inaugurated the observance of a meal of thanksgiving (Eucharist) in which his disciples would remember his work and death until he came again.

Since the record is ambiguous some conclude that the disciples had a hurried meal with Jesus which anticipated the Passover. Clearly the Last Supper took place during the Passover season and ideas of the Passover must have filled the minds of both the disciples and Jesus himself. For the early Christians, the Last Supper became the new feast commemorating the deliverance effected by Christ.

The Passover for them was an important occasion by which to date events (Acts 12:3; 20:6) but its most important role was performed in the theological exposition of the death and resurrection of Christ in the Passover ritual perspective. In that sense Christ is called "our Passover" (I Cor 5:7; cf 15:20, 23: Christ the first fruits), and Paul used the diligent removal of all remnants of the leaven as a symbol of the new life and joy (I Cor 5:7-8).

PATARA A port in Lycia (Asia Minor) at which Paul called on his last journey to Jerusalem. Identified with present-day Gelemish.

PATHROS, PATHRUSIM A name for Upper Egypt which occurs chiefly in the prophets (e.g., Is 11:11), derived from the Egyptian *pa-ta-rsh* (land of the south). It is always mentioned together with Mizraim, which means Lower Egypt. In the Table of Nations in Genesis chapter 10, the Pathrusim are listed among the descendants of Mizraim and

Ezek 45:21.
Matt 26:2, 17-19. Mark 14:1, 12, 14, 16.
Luke 2:41; 22:1, 7-8, 11, 13, 15. John 2:13, 23; 6:4; 11:55; 12:1; 13:1; 18:28, 39; 19:14. Acts 12:4. I Cor 5:7. Heb 11:28

PATARA
Acts 21:1

PATHROS, PATHRUSIM
I Chr 1:12. Is 11:11. Jer 44:1, 15. Ezek 29:14; 30:14

PATMOS
Rev 1:9

mentioned among others together with Casluhim (from whom the Philistines descended), and Caphtorim (Gen 10:13-14; I Chr 1:12). The Pathrusim may have been people who dwelt in the region of Mount Cassius, east of Pelusium, i.e., in the northeastern Delta, between Egypt and the peninsula of Sinai.

PATMOS A Dodecanese island located 35 miles (56 km) southwest of Miletus. It is of irregular shape, 10 miles (16 km) long and 6 miles (10 km) wide at its widest point. The land itself is mountainous, dry and desolate, and consists of rocky volcanic outcroppings. Although its ancient history is unknown, during Roman times Patmos, along with other Aegean islands, served as a place of banishment. It is best known

as the place where John wrote the Book of Revelation after having been banished to the island from Ephesus by the emperor Domitian c. A.D. 95. The island's association with the Apocalypse of John lent Patmos a religious appeal during Roman and Byzantine times and a monastery was built there in A.D. 1088 near the cave where, according to tradition, he received the revelation.

A view of Patmos, a barren and rocky island in the Aegean Sea.

*(left)
St John's Grotto at Patmos where it is said that he had his vision.*

PATRIARCHS, THE The "patriarchs", Abraham, Isaac and Jacob, were the founding fathers of the Israelite nation. The term is sometimes used in a broader sense to include such figures as Enoch, Noah, Moses, David, etc. (Eccl chaps. 44-50; I Macc 2:51-60; Acts 2:29; Heb chap. 11). However, the patriarchal period usually denotes the time of the three patriarchs.

Study of that period has been aided by the discovery of thousands of tablets from Mari, Nuzi and Ugarit. Scholars are cautious, however, in drawing over-hasty parallels between these civilizations and the record of the patriarchs in Genesis.

Vital to the religion of the patriarchs was the covenant relationship and its two fundamental elements: the promise of the land and the assurance of innumerable descendants (Gen 12:7; 13:14-17; 15:4, 18; 22:16-18; 26:3; 50:24). The patriarchal religion was characterized by numerous titles for God, especially the distinct personal reference of the deity as "the God of my/your father...." (Gen 26:24; 31:42; 46:1, 3; 50:17; Ex 3:6), as well as the regular use of the Canaanite appellations, El ("God"), in such titles as *El Elyon* ("God Most High", Gen 14:18, 22), *El Shaddai* ("Almighty God", 17:1; 28:3; 43:14; 48:3; Ex 6:3) and *El Olam* ("Everlasting God", 21:33; cf 16:13; 31:13; 35:7). Emphasis on the appearance of the deity to individuals (Gen 12:1, 7; 28:12-13; cf 20:3; 41:25) and the identification of these theophanies with sacred trees (Gen

21:33; cf 12:6; 35:4; Deut 16:21), stone pillars (Gen 28:18, 22; 31:13; 35:14) and altars (Gen 12:7; 13:4; 22:9; 31:54; 33:20; 46:1) preserve the cultic norms of this early period and distinguish it from subsequent times.

PATROBAS One of the men greeted by Paul in his Epistle to the Romans.

PAU See PAI

PAUL (Saul of Tarsus). Apostle and founder of numerous churches; author of 13 books of the NT.

Paul was born in Tarsus of Cilicia in Asia Minor in the early 1st century A.D. His family, of the line of Benjamin (Rom 11:1; Phil 3:5), is reported in patristic literature to have stemmed from the area of Giscala (Gush Halav) in Upper Galilee. In circumstances which remain obscure, Paul's father had obtained Roman citizenship. Paul's education was mixed. He grew up in Jerusalem, where he studied Bible and Jewish tradition in the school of the elder Gamaliel (Acts 22:3), becoming a thoroughgoing and zealous Pharisee, like his father before him (Acts 23:6). However, Paul's writing indicates that he also received an education in Greek literature and culture. While his literary style is peculiarly his own, it is evident that Greek came naturally to him (cf Acts 21:37). This aspect of his education may belong to his Diaspora years before moving to Jerusalem. By profession he was a tentmaker (Acts 18:3).

Paul first appears in the NT as an active opponent of the nascent Christian movement, minding the cloaks of those who stoned Stephen (Acts 7:58; 22:20) and then himself zealously ferreting out other followers of Jesus, "breathing threats and murder" (Acts 8:3; 9:1). This phase as a persecutor of the church left a deep impression on Paul, and in his writings years later he frequently refers to it (I Cor 15:9; Gal 1:13; Phil 3:6; I Tim 1:13). While he himself does not say so it is not unlikely that — as in the case of Tertullian a century and a half later — his conversion was much influenced by the steadfastness of the testimony of the men and women he was persecuting. There is perhaps a hint of this in the description of his actual conversion just outside the walls of Damascus (Acts 9:1-8). The voice which he heard declared "It is I, Jesus, whom you are persecuting." This lays the foundation for one of Paul's central doctrines: the total identification of Christ and his church. This crisis experience left Paul temporarily blinded. For three days he fasted. Then he was healed, filled with the Holy Spirit, and baptized at the hands of one Ananias (Acts 9:17-19). The transformation was immediate and dramatic. The zealous personality did not change, but now the zeal to persecute the church was rechanneled into preaching the gospel.

Certain chronological difficulties attend any attempt to reconstruct the subsequent events of Paul's life. Such reconstruction must rest on an interweaving of events related in Acts chapters 9, 11 and 12 and Galatians I and II. It is possible that the conversion took place about the year 33 (See GALATIANS). Shortly afterwards Paul retired to the wilderness of Arabia and then returned to Damascus. In 36 he was forced to flee from Damascus (II Cor 11:32ff) going to Jerusalem where Barnabas introduced him to a church skeptical about rumors of his conversion (Acts 9:26ff; Gal 1:18). Again obliged to flee, Paul returned to his family in Tarsus. There follows a silent period of nine years until, in 45, Barnabas went to Tarsus to look for Paul and take him to Antioch (Acts 11:25ff). After a year of teaching together in Antioch, Barnabas and Paul were sent to Jerusalem with famine relief (Acts 11:27-30; 12:25; cf Gal 2:1ff). Returning soon afterward to Antioch, they were

Paul fleeing Damascus shown on an enamel plaque of the 11th century. (Victoria and Albert Museum, London)

commissioned by leaders of that church to preach the gospel (Acts 13:1 ff). This "First Missionary Journey" (Acts chaps. 13-14) took them to Cyprus and Lycaonia and lasted perhaps two years. During their time of rest back in Antioch, Paul and Barnabas became aware that certain men had been teaching that non-Jews (among whom the two apostles had enjoyed much success) must be circumcised before they could be considered part of the church (Acts 15:1ff; cf Gal 2:12ff). This led to a disagreement which brought about the convening of the "Jerusalem Council" in 48/49 to discuss the issue (Acts 15:4-29). Paul and Barnabas were prime witnesses on this occasion, and the council's decision — that observance of the commandments was not required of believers from among the Gentiles — was very much in their favor. Upon returning to Antioch, Paul and Barnabas had a sharp disagreement over a matter of traveling companions, so they parted ways. Paul now traveled with a larger group of men, including Silas, the young Timothy and the physician-historian Luke. He now embarked from Antioch on his "Second Missionary Journey" (Acts 15:40-18:22), which lasted perhaps five years; he visited churches earlier established and preached the gospel in Macedonia (including Philippi, Berea and Thessalonica) and Achaia (Athens and Corinth).

After another rest stop in Antioch (Acts 18:22ff), Paul set off in about 53 on the "Third Missionary Journey" (Acts 18:23-21:16), this one lasting almost four years and taking in much of Asia Minor with return visits to Macedonia and Achaia. It ended in 57 in Jerusalem, which witnessed the onset of the last phase of Paul's ministry as recorded in Acts. Opponents of Paul in Jerusalem stirred up a riot which resulted in his arrest by the Roman authorities (Acts 21:27-22:29). Various trials and hearings followed, and in the course of one of these, before the governor Festus, Paul exercised his right as a Roman citizen to appeal to the emperor (Acts 25:11). Thus, in 59/60 Paul was sent under guard

St Paul-Outside-the Walls, Rome, built on the site of the traditional tomb of the Apostle.

to Rome. After an eventful voyage ending in shipwreck on the island of Malta, Paul finally arrived in Rome where he was kept under light guard in his own quarters for two years (Acts 28:30ff).

Here the record of Acts ends. Further biographical data can only be surmised from Paul's own writings and small amounts of patristic tradition. One possible scenario of his last years would have him released after his hearing in Rome. This may have been followed by a trip to Spain (cf Rom 15:24, 28) and another journey including Crete (Titus 1:5), Asia Minor (II Tim 4:13) and Nicopolis (Titus 3:12). While any such reconstruction must entail considerable uncertainty, there is good patristic evidence for Paul's death by beheading in Rome under Nero in about 67.

Thirteen NT letters appear under Paul's signature. Some scholars question his authorship of various of these, most frequently the "Pastoral Epistles" of I and II Timothy and Titus. Other letters by Paul have been lost. These include one to the Laodiceans (Col 4:16) and perhaps one to the Corinthians (cf I Cor 5:9 and II Cor 7:8). There are those who would also attribute Hebrews to him. With the exception of Romans, all of Paul's letters were written to churches or individuals whom he knew personally. A precise dovetailing of his epistles into the Acts chronology is problematic, but several of them were clearly written during his imprisonment.

While most of Paul's epistles were penned to answer specific needs and questions, there are certain basic concepts and doctrines which characterize his writings generally. The same elements are evident in his recorded sermons in Acts. The focus of all of Paul's writing is Jesus, through whom God has effected redemption for all people regardless of ethnic or social background. Paul's interest in Jesus is selective, taking little notice of how he lived or what he taught, focusing instead on who he was and what his death and resurrection accomplished. For Paul, Jesus is God's son in a unique and absolute sense. By his death he made possible the reconciliation of sinful man with his holy Creator. In his death he took on all the sins of the world, in fact "became sin for us". Once this redemption was accomplished, God set his seal on it by raising Jesus from the dead. Paul's personal revelation of the risen Jesus permeates all of his thinking. The living, ascended Jesus sent the Holy Spirit as a guarantee of the sure fulfillment of all of God's promises to the

Paul's journey to Rome is shown in red.

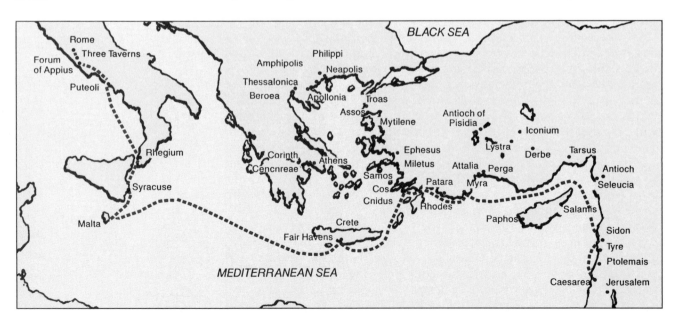

believer. Just as man fell from the image of God through sin, so Jesus took on humanity in order that men might be re-formed into the image of God's son. The collective company of all believers in Jesus is pictured by Paul as the body of Christ, or the bride, of whom Christ is the bridegroom; or the temple, of which Christ is the foundation stone. Whatever the type, Paul always sees close identification of Jesus and the Church, and a day will come when he will return to take that Church to himself. Though John is also very important, no other individual can be said to have contributed more to the formulation and expression of Christian doctrine than Paul. In the early centuries of church history (as also in later centuries), it was acceptance or rejection of Paul's gospel which often determined whether or not a new group would be considered truly Christian.

PAULUS See SERGIUS PAULUS

PAULUS
Acts 13:7

PEACE The word *shalom*, peace, occurs over 500 times in the OT, in both verb and noun form. Although much research has gone into the search for an understanding of its basic meaning, no unanimous conclusion has been reached. Clearly it is not merely the opposite of war (Ecc 3:8), and it is more comprehensive than "wholeness" (Hebrew *shalem*). It relates to the spheres of law, the cult and the social order, as well as to the military-political realms. Peace in the OT refers primarily to a state which allows the optimum conditions for life to unfold. When that happens, health and prosperity, freedom and security all exist together.

The Hebrews saw peace as part of the original plan of God. When peace was not manifest they called the existing condition chaos.

The Hebrews lived with this tension between peace and chaos, and although they affirmed that the Lord is peace (Judg 6:24) and recognized peace as a gift of God, they also saw human action and behavior, especially human unfaithfulness in carrying out covenant obligations, as the critical factor which determined whether there would be peace or war.

The Lord is depicted as battling against chaos and in so doing he gives strength and peace to his people (Ps 29:11). Jerusalem is a special object for prayer for peace (Ps 122:6-8; 147:14) and whoever draws near to God in the Temple will participate in this peace (Ps 125:5; 128:5-6; Num 6:24-27). Evidence of God's love and care is shown by the fact that he "has redeemed my soul in peace" (Ps 55:18). King Hezekiah praises God for having, through love, brought him back from "the pit of corruption" giving his spirit peace and taking away his bitterness and replacing it with prosperity (Is 38:16ff). Whoever stands on the side of peace will receive peace and life (Ps 34:13-15; 37:37 ff; Prov 12:20). Because evil-doers do not know the way of peace (Is 59:8) and even hate it (Ps 120:6), there is no peace for them (Is 48:22; 57:21). But whoever listens to the counsels of wisdom will receive a long life and peace in its fullness (Prov 3:2) for all the paths of wisdom lead to peace (Prov 3:17). It is the meek who will possess the land "and shall delight themselves in the abundance of peace" (Ps 37:11) and those who love the law will receive as their reward "peace" and no pitfalls will beset their paths (Ps 119:165).

In the realm of worship the idea of peace plays a special role in connection with blessing. The benediction of Numbers 6:24-26 ("the Lord lift up his countenance upon you and give you peace") and the prayers for the peace of Israel (Ps 125:5; 128:6) signify that peace is a gift and comes in the form of a blessing from God. The legal, wisdom and cultic dimensions unite in Leviticus 26:1-13 where in the holiness code the promise is made that if the covenant is kept "you shall eat your

Two warriors embracing as if to conclude a peace treaty, shown on a relief on a basalt ritual basin from a temple at Ebla of the Middle Bronze Age. (Aleppo Museum, Syria)

bread to the full and dwell in your land safely. I will give peace in the land, and you shall lie down and none will make you afraid" (Lev 26:5-6); nor will war ravage the land (Lev 26:6-7).

The peace greeting or blessing on meeting came from the view that as people meet they pray for peace for each other. From that it developed into a more or less standard greeting (e.g., I Sam 25:6; II Sam 18:28). One can also enquire about the peace or welfare of a person (Gen 37:14; 43:27; Ex 18:7), or a people (II Sam 11:7), of a city (Jer 15:5), of cattle (Gen 37:14) and even about the welfare of a war (II Sam 11:7).

One of the primary functions of the king is to establish peace in the political realm, even if such peace is attained by war. Solomon was legendary for his prosperity because "Now the Lord my God has given me rest on every side" (I Kgs 5:4). Psalm 2 makes it clear that the way in which the king will establish this peace is through the destruction of his enemies.

The prophets attribute absence of peace to decadent living. Only false prophets predict peace but their predictions are all lies (Jer 14:14; 23:11-15; 27:9-14, 16) for they are incapable of reading the times correctly and promise peace in return for a morsel of food (Mic 3:5).

For the exilic and post-exilic prophets, peace becomes an important designation of a future time when God will intervene and bring peace. The writer of Psalm 85 is convinced that God "will speak peace to his people and to his saints" (v.8) for "righteousness and peace have kissed each other" (v.10). The message of peace dominates in Deutero-Isaiah.The covenant of peace will not be removed (Is 54:10) and God's people will "go out in joy and be led out with peace" (Is 55:12), and "great shall be the peace of your children" (Is 54:13). Jeremiah also looks forward to the time after the exile, "For I know the thoughts that I think toward you,... thoughts of peace, and not of evil" (Jer 29:11). God will bring health to the city "and reveal to them the abundance of peace and truth" (Jer 33:6). When the Temple was restored Haggai declared "in this place I will give peace, says the Lord of Hosts" (Hag 2:9).

Increasingly, the idea of peace became a matter of eschatological hope. Isaiah looks forward to the time when "the spirit is poured upon us from on high... then justice will dwell in the wilderness,... the work of righteousness will be peace; and the effect of righteousness, quietness and confidence forever. My people will dwell in a peaceable habitation" (Is 32:15-18). Justice and peace are often seen as interchangeable. Ezekiel speaks of a covenant of peace (Ezek 34:25) which will be everlasting (Ezek 37:26).

While peace is mostly directed to the group or the community it is also directed to the individual: "Peace, peace to him who is far off, and to him who is near" (Is 57:19) but there is no peace for the wicked (Is 48:22; 57:21).

Peace for the OT writers was a personal as well as a corporate entity. It is seen as a social gift permeating community life and intimately attached to justice. Peace is always viewed as an ultimate goal of God's creation; he will bring it about in his own time and in his own way. God is to bear the major burden of dealing with the Israelites' enemies (Ex 14:14) and they can depend upon God to be their security and their peace (Deut 17:16; Ps 20:7-9; 44:7). The peace of which the OT speaks is a religious and a secular peace — but both have their source ultimately in God.

Fundamental to the understanding of peace in the NT is the use of the description of God as a "God of peace" which flourished in the NT community (Rom 15:33; 16:20; I Cor 14:33; II Cor 13:11; Phil 4:9;

I Thes 5:23). Closely related is the singular designation appearing in the earliest gospel tradition: "son of peace" (Luke 10:6). Here, this phrase is part of the commission of Jesus to his disciples and stands unique in the ancient world.

As the disciples go out as sheep among wolves, they are to proclaim peace by healing, exorcism, forgiving people, providing for their needs and by entering fully into the beatitude of being peacemakers (Matt 5:9). In doing so there is continuity between the life of the disciple and that of Jesus himself who made peace through the blood of his cross (Eph 2:15; Col 1:20). For this reason Jesus himself is described as "our peace" (Eph 2:14) and the peace of Christ is described as beyond human understanding (Phil 4:7). Although there are statements that Jesus came not to bring peace but a sword (Matt 10:34; Luke 12:51), the normative Christian affirmation is that with the coming of Jesus peace was announced to the world (Luke 2:14; 19:38), even though the offer of peace was not accepted (Luke 19:42) much to Jesus' sorrow. The characteristic greeting of Jesus to the sinner and the oppressed is: "Go in peace" (Mark 5:34; Luke 7:50; 8:48). Moreover, "Peace to you" is the phrase with which the risen Christ greets his disciples (John 20:19, 21, 26).

Linked with peace is grace, especially in the opening lines of Paul's letters, but also in the letters of Peter and in II John. Of major importance is the link between justice and peace, in which the early Christians follow the Hebrew prophets. Thus Paul defines the Kingdom of God as existing in justice, peace and joy in the Holy Spirit (Rom 14:17) and the writer of II Timothy 2:22 urges Timothy to pursue justice and peace. The profoundest relation between the two is seen by James when he writes: "Now the fruit of righeousness is sown in peace by those who make peace" (James 3:18).

The importance of peace is seen in the capsule summary of Acts 10:36: "The word which God sent... preaching peace through Jesus Christ". It is also apparent in the repeated admonitions of the followers of Jesus to "have peace with one another" beginning in the first group of disciples (Mark 9:50), extending to the early Christian communities (II Cor 13:11; I Thes 5:13) and the urge to pursue peace (II Tim 2:22; I Pet 3:11) within the community and with all people (Rom 12:18; Heb 12:14).

Peace is seen as a social reality by the NT writers. Only twice is reference made to having peace with God (Rom 5:1; II Pet 3:14). When the peace of Christ rules in the heart of the Christians (Col 3:15); there is more than absence of conflict. When that happens the true calling of the Christian has been attained: God has called them to the peace of Christ (I Cor 7:15; Col 3:16). This peace, since it has its origins in God himself, brings joy to the one who receives it (Rom 14:17; 15:13).

PEACOCK See ANIMALS

PEDAHEL ("God has redeemed"). A man of Naphtali, son of Ammihud, he was appointed to represent his tribe when Joshua divided the land of Canaan among the Children of Israel.

PEDAHZUR ("[the] rock has redeemed"). Father of Gamaliel who was leader of the tribe of Manasseh when the Children of Israel were in the wilderness.

PEDAIAH

1. Father of Zebida (wife of King Josiah and mother of his son King Jehoiakim).
2. Fourth son of Jeconiah and father of Zerubbabel and Shimei.
3. Father of Joel who was leader of the half-tribe of Manasseh at the time of King David.

Ammonite seal inscribed with the name of the owner "Peda'el". 7th century B.C. (Israel Museum)

4. A son of Parosh; he was among those who repaired the walls of Jerusalem at the time of Nehemiah.

5. One of the men who stood to the left of Ezra when he read the Law.

6. A man of Benjamin, son of Kolaiah and father of Joed; his grandson Sallu was among those who returned from Exile in Babylon and settled in Jerusalem (Neh 11:3, 7).

7. A Levite; he was among the four men appointed by Nehemiah as treasurers in the House of the Lord.

PEKAH ("[God] has opened [his eyes]"). King of Israel, 735-733 B.C. Son of Remaliah, one of the nobles of Gilead, he was a ruthless opportunist who took advantage of the upheavals so characteristic of the last decade of Samaria, to usurp the throne of Israel by slaying Pekahiah son of Menahem under whom he had served as an army commander (II Kgs 15:25). The cause of the conspiracy seems to have been dissatisfaction on the part of the Transjordanian Israelites with Assyrian domination of Israel. Thus when Pekah became king he entered into a treaty with King Rezin of Damascus, which was directed against Tiglath-Pileser III, king of Assyria (II Kgs 16:5-9). In an attempt

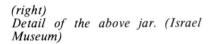
Pottery wine jar from Hazor inscribed "[Belonging] to Pekah Semadar". 8th century B.C.

(right)
Detail of the above jar. (Israel Museum)

to compel King Ahaz of Judah to join their coalition and abandon his pro-Assyrian policy, Pekah and Rezin stirred up rebellion in Edom and Philistia (II Kgs 16:6; II Chr 28:17-18) and advanced against Jerusalem. Ahaz in his plight turned to Tiglath-Pileser III, who in return for Judah's submission, invaded Damascus (734 B.C.) and besieged Israel, deporting many captives to Assyria. Pekah, who had brought disaster to the kingdom, was slain in a conspiracy by Hoshea son of Elah, who became king, and had his position confirmed by the Assyrian ruler. The biblical accounts in II Kings 15:29 ff; I Chronicles 5:26 are matched by a corresponding record in the annals of Tiglath-Pileser III.

PEKAHIAH ("the Lord opened [his eyes]"). Son of Menahem king of Israel, he became king at the death of his father in 737 B.C. He reigned for only two years, but "he did evil in the sight of the Lord" (II Kgs 15:24) and was assassinated in his own house in a plot led by Pekah son of Remaliah.

PEKOD A geographical name. In Jeremiah's prophecy on the destruction of Babylon it is mentioned along with Merathaim (Jer 50:21). Ezekiel refers to it — with Shoa, Koa, the Chaldeans and the Assyrians — among the lovers of Oholibah who are destined to punish her (Ezek 23:23). In Akkadian, Puqudu is the name of an Aramean tribe who dwelt in southern Babylon. The name of Pekod is found in Assyrian and Babylonian documents from the time of Tiglath-Pileser III onwards. Because they belong to the same geographic region, Pekod is mentioned by Ezekiel and Jeremiah along with the Chaldeans, the founders of the neo-Babylonian empire.

PELAIAH

1. Third son of Elioenai (No.1) in the genealogy of the family of Jeconiah.

2. A Levite; one of the men who helped the people understand when

Ezra read from the book of the Law; probably the same as No.3.

3. A Levite; one of the leaders who put his seal to the covenant in the time of Ezra, probably the same as No.2.

PELALIAH Son of Amzi, father of Jeroham and grandfather of Adaiah, a priest in the House of the Lord after the return from the Babylonian Exile.

PELATIAH ("Yah rescued").

1. Firstborn son of Hananiah and brother of Jeshaiah in the genealogy of the family of David.

2. A man of Simeon, a captain who led his men to victory over the Amalekites in the days of Hezekiah king of Judah.

3. A Levite; one of the leaders who sealed the covenant at the time of Nehemiah.

4. The son of Benaiah No.8; a prince of the people at the time of Ezekiel. He did not heed the prophet and died while Ezekiel was prophesying.

PELEG ("division"). Firstborn son of Eber the great-grandson of Shem, he lived 239 years and begot Reu and other sons and daughters.

PELET

1. Fourth son of Jahdai in the genealogy of the family of Caleb.

2. A man of Benjamin, one of the two sons of Azmaveth; he defected from the armies of Saul and joined David at Ziklag. Like his brethren he could use both right and left hands to hurl stones and shoot arrows.

PELETH

1. Father of On, one of the men who rebelled against Moses and Aaron in the wilderness.

2. Son of Jonathan, a Jerahmeelite.

PELETHITES See CHERETHITES

PELICAN See ANIMALS

PELONITE Appellation of Ahijah (I Chr 11:36), and Helez (I Chr 11:27; given as "Paltite" in II Sam 23:16); two of David's "mighty men".

PENIEL See PENUEL

PENINNAH One of the two wives of Elkanah (I Sam 1:2); the other was Hannah. Peninnah, the mother of an unspecified number of sons and daughters (I Sam 1:4), taunted Hannah concerning the latter's childlessness. However, Elkanah continued to prefer Hannah.

PENTATEUCH The first five books in the Bible (Genesis, Exodus, Leviticus, Numbers, Deuteronomy). The scope of these books extends from creation to the wanderings in the wilderness by the Children of Israel recently liberated from slavery under Moses' leadership. Interspersed within the story of liberation from Egypt and the journey to the promised land are several collections of laws which, it is stated, were revealed to Moses on Mount Sinai. The combination of redemptive story and divine stipulations for obedience became normative for post-biblical Judaism, so that the other two divisions of the Hebrew Bible, Prophecy and Writings, were subordinated to the Pentateuch (Torah).

Modern students of the Bible do not agree about the exact number of books that formed the original work. Some critics propose a four-fold unit (a Tetrateuch), joining Deuteronomy with the comprehensive historical work which follows (Joshua, Judges, Samuel, Kings). Other interpreters suggest that Joshua belongs to the first five books, comprising a Hexateuch. The primary reason for this claim is the otherwise incomplete character of the Pentateuch, inasmuch as the promise of land is not yet fulfilled.

The beginnings of biblical historical criticism focused on the

Pentateuch scroll case, decorated with silver-gilt designs on wood, from Baghdad, Iraq, 1852. The twin glass plates on the inside of the cupola are inscribed with biblical passages.

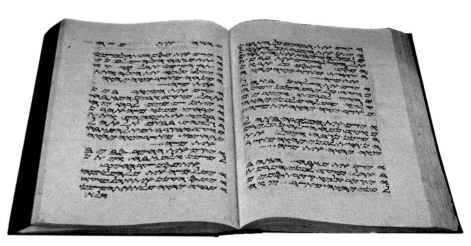

New Samaritan transcription of the Pentateuch.

Pentateuch. A medieval Jewish commentator, Abraham Ibn Ezra, recognized signs of inconsistency which could bring into question the belief of Mosaic authorship (e.g., the formula "until this day"; the admission that Canaanites had been dispossessed when the author wrote; anachronisms such as the late name for Kirjath Jearim; references to Moses' death). In the middle of the 18th century a French physician, Jean Astruc, wrote a treatise in which he argued that Moses used literary sources in compiling the Pentateuch. The use of different names for deity, *Yahweh* and *Elohim*, provided the decisive clue for this hypothesis.

There followed a century of source criticism during which a theory emerged that has served as an interpretative tool to the present day. This model goes by the name of the brilliant German scholar Julius Wellhausen who perfected and popularized it in the *Encyclopedia Britannica.*

In brief, it postulates the existence of four literary sources in the following sequence: JEDP. A relative chronology was achieved when D (Deuteronomy) was identified with the lost scroll that was said to have been discovered in Josiah's reign (7th century B.C.) and to have become the basis for this king's sweeping reform of the cult. The earliest source, J (the Yahwist) was thought to have come roughly from the time of David, while E (the Elohist) arose about a century later. These southern and northern sources respectively were joined together around 750 B.C. and to this larger work was added D somewhere around 550. Finally, P (the Priestly source) was integrated into the whole about 450. Various features of the Yahwistic and Priestly sources soon gave rise to theories about additional sub-units (a lay source and a legal source). It is still a matter of debate among source critics whether the growth of the Pentateuch is best described as the coming together of fragments or the supplementation of a basic literary source by several lesser ones. The fragmentary nature of E has prompted some critics to deny its existence, while others stress its influence on northern prophetic circles.

Another hypothesis about the origin of the Pentateuch has come from the school of form criticism. The emphasis here is on the liturgical setting of the material that eventually formed the Hexateuch. One significant hypothesis called attention to little credos in Deuteronomy 6:20-25; 26:5; Joshua 24:2-13, which are understood as the seeds from which the larger tree grew. In short, it is said that these liturgical confessions encapsulate the entire story of the Hexateuch, with a single exception, the Sinai legislation. The latter is therefore taken to be a later addition. The little credos were at home in the sanctuary at Gilgal, whence they came to assume representative capacity for all Israel. The essential point is that the Hexateuch arose within Israelite worship.

An alternative theory has emerged among tradition historians. In this view the Tetrateuch comprises units of oral tradition dealing with the exodus from Egypt, wanderings in the wilderness, primeval history, patriarchal narratives and the revelation at Sinai. A fundamental work combined the traditions of JE, to which a priestly emphasis was later added (P). Deuteronomy chapters 1-4 served as an introduction to another comprehensive work, which traced a history of failure from the time of Moses to the release and death of King Jehoiachin in 561. This Deuteronomistic history functioned as a theological explanation for the collapse of Samaria and Jerusalem. These cities fell because the people refused to heed prophetic warnings.

From this survey of competing hypotheses it can readily be seen that an adequate solution to the Pentateuch has not yet appeared. Conservatives have long rejected the documentary hypothesis in favor of Mosaic authorship. Several prominent Jewish interpreters have questioned the idea of sources, arguing instead for complementary story-telling akin to that which created rabbinic literature, or have insisted (e.g., Yehezkel Kaufman) that the Priestly source is much earlier than generally thought. It should be noted, however, that most interpreters distinguish between the age of the materials within a source and its actual composition (which is later).

Perhaps the concentration on sources should be replaced by emphasis on strata, thus avoiding the assumption of written documents. It is likely that the Hexateuch arose from many separate strata which were brought together in the interests of worship and celebration. The form critical acknowledgment that professional storytelling lies behind some narratives in Genesis commends itself, and the same can surely be said for portions of Exodus. Beyond that, one can certainly recognize motives behind many emphases, particularly those which seek to promote priestly interests. Then, of course, legal codifications will have arisen from precedent and in circles where absolute claims seemed to be more desirable than case law. In the end, however, the exact nature of the rise of the Pentateuch remains a mystery.

The heated debate over the origin of the Pentateuch has obscured its contents in certain scholarly circles to the extent that attention has been aimed at taking it apart verse by verse. The virtue of the form critical and tradition historical approaches is their attention to the larger narrative. One significant attempt to isolate the theme of the Hexateuch has emphasized promise and fulfillment. An arc of tension extends from the story about Abraham to the narrative about Joshua's conquest of the land and the settlement of Jacob's descendants in Canaan. Others have preferred to think in terms of themes, for it can rightly be said that many different themes combine to tell the sacred story.

Three significant blocks of tradition have received considerable attention of late, namely the primeval history, the patriarchal narratives and the Sinai legislation. The influence of Mesopotamian traditions of creation and flood has been examined in much detail, often with clarification of disputed points. Recent analysis of the patriarchal stories is of two kinds: one of which is primarily interested in historical accuracy, and another which attends primarily to theological issues, with insights derived from the history of religions. Important gains have come from comparative studies in law, which have led to distinctions between case laws and categorical laws. Although early claims that the latter were unique have not stood the test of time, the scope of these absolute expressions of the deity's will is impressive.

One trend in contemporary interpretation has yielded significant

Enamel plaque representing Pentecost at the Verdun Altar, 1180, and showing "divided tongues as of fire" upon each of the apostles (Acts 2:1-4). (Klosterneuburg Abbey)

analyses within the Pentateuch. That is the literary study of the Bible, an appreciation of its style and craft. Several discussions of stories in Genesis have enabled modern readers to appreciate the ancient text much better (e.g., the Joseph story; the episode of Judah and Tamar; the offering of Isaac; the story of creation and fall; the incident of the tower of Babel). In some cases these literary analyses have offered plausible explanations for elements that gave rise to a theory of multiple authorship.

PENTECOST ("fiftieth day"). The second of the three annual pilgrim festivals (along with Passover and Tabernacles) when every male was required to proceed on foot to the Temple in Jerusalem. It is also called the Feast of Weeks, because it was held after the counting of seven complete weeks after "the morrow of the Sabbath" when the barley sheaves were offered (Lev 23:15-20). The festival is then held on the 50th day, i.e. Pentecost. The Pharisees took the "morrow of the Sabbath" as the second day of Passover, while the Sadducees interpreted it as the first Sunday after the first day of Passover. The Pharisee interpretation was accepted as normative. The festival is also named the Feast of the Ingathering (Ex 23:16) and the Day of the First Fruits (Num 28:26).

All the pilgrim festivals possessed agricultural significance. Pentecost marked the end of the barley and the beginning of the wheat harvest, and two loaves, made of the finest wheat were "a wave offering before the Lord" in the Temple (Lev 23:17-20). The first fruits were also brought to the Temple on this occasion. Pilgrims used to assemble in large towns in each district, and would set out together in joyful procession to the Temple, where they were welcomed by the Levites. Historical connections were given to these festivals: Pentecost was associated with the revelation on Sinai, becoming known as "The Season of the Giving of our Torah" although the Bible gives the event no specific date; it was deduced by reckoning based on Exodus 19:1-2. The Book of Ruth, associated with the barley and wheat harvests, as well as with a proselyte who accepts the Torah, became part of the synagogue liturgy on this festival.

Christian tradition regarded Pentecost as of special significance in view of the events related in Acts chapter 2, which tells of the very beginning of the Church. On that day, the risen Lord sent the Spirit in accordance with the prophecy of Joel (Acts 2:16-21). The author of Acts (Luke) understands the experience of the Spirit in the context of the prophetic tradition: the Spirit realizes the new covenant promised by Ezekiel 36:26-27. Crowds who had come for the Pentecost feast were witnesses to the outpouring of the Holy Spirit on the apostles and some 120 disciples. Just as at Sinai, God addressed Moses from the midst of the fire, so now the Spirit of the Lord manifested itself with the symbol of tongues of fire. The disciples who experienced the Spirit speak in other tongues. In this way, Luke expresses the universality of the Christian message. He sees the truth of the Spirit forming the Church among all peoples through Peter's discourse which was understood by men of different nationalities.

PENUEL, PENIEL

1. A town to the east of the Jordan, near the ford of the Jabbok River (Gen 32:30-31; Judg 8:8-9, 17; I Kgs 12:25). Here Jacob wrestled at night with a man (an angel according to Hos 12:4), who finally blessed him and changed his name to Israel. Jacob named the place Peniel ("face of God") "for I have seen God face to face, and my life is preserved" (Gen 32:30); in the following verse the name is spelled Penuel.

Penuel is mentioned together with Succoth in the account of Gideon's

PENTECOST
Acts 2:1;
20:16. I Cor
16:8

PENUEL,
PENIEL 1
Gen 32:30-31.
Judg 8:8-9, 17.
I Kgs 12:25

pursuit of the Midianites (Judg 8:4-18). Because its people (like those of Succoth) refused to help Gideon, he destroyed the town's tower and killed all its inhabitants (Judg 8:17). Penuel regained importance when it was rebuilt by Jeroboam (I Kgs 12:25). The phrase "and he went out from there" is understood by some as indicating that he made Penuel his new capital city. Others suggest that Jeroboam fortified Penuel and made it an administrative and military center in Transjordan.

It has been tentatively identified with various places along the Jabbok River.

2. A Judahite; the father of Gedor.

3. Son of Shashak and ancestor of King Saul.

PEOR A high mountain in the land of Moab, the last of the three to which Balak directed Balaam so that he might curse Israel, and from which instead he proclaimed a blessing (Num 23:28). Eusebius identified this mountain between Livias (Bethsaida) and Heshbon. Peor is now variously identified with several mountains near Heshbon.

PERAZIM This location is called Baal Perazim in II Samuel 5:20 and I Chronicles 14:11, and Mount Perazim in Isaiah 28:21. David defeated the Philistines here after being anointed king of Israel; Isaiah refers to this victory in his prophecies. The area is identified with Sheikh Bedr, located northwest of Jerusalem.

PERESH A man of Manasseh, firstborn son of Machir by his wife Maachah.

PEREZ ("breach"). Son born from the union of Judah and his daughter-in-law Tamar. The twin brother of Zerah (Gen 38:29; I Chr 2:4); father of Hezron and Hamuel (Gen 46:12; Num 26:21; I Chr 2:5) and ancestor of the most important family of the tribe of Judah, the Perezites (Num 26:20).

The struggle for dominance within the tribe of Judah is probably reflected in the story of Perez' birth (Gen 38:27-30).

He is listed first in the genealogical list of the tribe of Judah, and his supremacy is linked to the tradition that he was an ancestor of David (Ruth 4:18-22; Matt 1:3; Luke 3:33). Four hundred and sixty-eight descendants of Perez are mentioned in the list of inhabitants to Jerusalem at the time of Nehemiah (Neh 11:6).

PEREZ UZZAH, (PEREZ UZZA) See UZZA, UZZAH No.3

PERGA A city located on the southern coast of Asia Minor in the province of Pamphylia. It was the province's principal native city, and its religious capital. Like Ephesus, its primary deity was an Artemis whose character was more Oriental than Greek and whose temple stood on a nearby hill. Paul passed through Perga twice on his first missionary journey, preaching only on his return (Acts 13:13-14; 14:25).

PERGAMOS A city in the district of Mysia in western Asia Minor located 15 miles (24 km) inland from the Aegean near the seaward end of the Caicus Valley. Pergamos was settled from early times and served as the capital of the Roman province of Asia from 133 B.C. to the 2nd century A.D. However, under the Romans, Pergamos retained only official and religious preeminence, as Ephesus became the commercial center. The city was renowned for its beautiful architecture and for its library, which rivaled that in Alexandria. The first temple of the imperial cult was built in Pergamos in 29 B.C. by Augustus' permission in honor of Rome and Augustus; later, imperial temples were erected to Trajan/Hadrian and to Caracalla. Pergamos also contained a complex of temples to Athena, Dionysus and Asclepius and a famous temple of Zeus.

Pergamos' church is the third of the seven mentioned in the Book of Revelation; the city is characterized as "where Satan's throne is" (Rev

(bottom of page)
The Red Church at Bergamo (Pergamos), Turkey.

View of Perga showing the site of the temple of Artemis and the modern town in the background.

2:13) — probably a reference to its role as the seat of imperial worship in the province. It was at Pergamos that Domitian put Christians to the test over the issue of participation in emperor worship — a major crisis for the church in Asia. Revelation mentions adherents of Balaam and Nicolaitans in Pergamos (Rev 2:14-15); this is evidently a reference to those within the church who maintained that, being powerless, they were entitled to attend pagan ceremonies to preserve their social position.

PERIDA, PERUDA Head of a family of the children of Solomon's servants who returned with Zerubbabel from Exile in Babylonia and settled in Jerusalem (Neh 7:57); the name is spelled Peruda in Ezra (Ezra 2:55).

PERIZZITES One of the peoples dwelling in the land between the river of Egypt and the Euphrates (Gen 15:20; Ex 3:8, etc.). They are mentioned as dwelling in the land of Canaan together with the Canaanites (Gen 13:7; 34:30; Judg 1:4-5), the Hivites and Jebusites (Josh 9:1; 12:8; Judg 3:5, etc.) and the giants (Josh 17:15). Remnants of the Perizzites are still mentioned among the people who did forced labor during Solomon's reign (I Kgs 9:20; II Chr 8:7). The Perizzites' origins are obscure, as is the location where they dwelt. They are mentioned in conjunction with the territories of the sons of Joseph (Josh 17:15; cf Gen 13:7; 34:30; Judg 1:4-5).

PERIZZITES
Gen 13:7;
15:20; 34:30.
Ex 3:8, 17;
23:23; 33:2;
34:11. Deut
7:1; 20:17.
Josh 3:10; 9:1;
11:3; 12:8;
17:15; 24:11.
Judg 1:4-5;
3:5. I Kgs
9:20. II Chr
8:7. Ezra 9:1.
Neh 9:8

PERSIA, PERSIANS Country in western Asia. In about the middle of the 2nd millennium B.C. the Indo-Iranian peoples migrated, apparently from Southern Russia, to Iran and India. By the 10th century B.C. numerous Iranian tribes had settled on the plateau, and in the 9th century B.C. they are mentioned in Assyrian documents. The Medes were among the first of these listed, followed by the Persian tribes although the date of the latter's arrival and the original place of their settlement, are not at all clear. It is not known what routes the Persian tribes followed, but they seem to have wandered in different parts of the plateau, and finally settled in the region of Pars in southwestern Iran before the 6th century B.C.

PERSIA,
PERSIANS
II Chr 36:20,
22-23. Ezra
1:1-2, 8; 3:7;
4:3, 5, 7, 9,
24; 5:6; 6:6,
14; 7:1; 9:9.
Neh 12:22. Est
1:3, 14, 18-19;

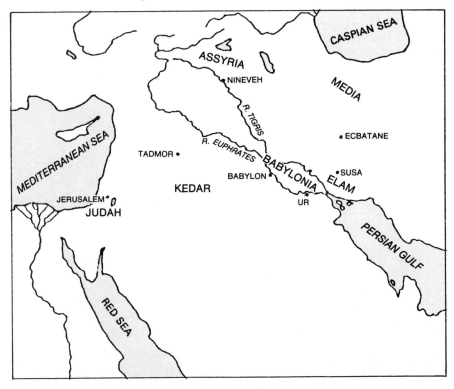

The Persian Empire.

):2. Ezek
7:10; 38:5.
an 5:28; 6:8,
2, 15, 28;
20; 10:1, 13,
); 11:2

The Achaemenid period in Persia began with the rise of Cyrus, who defeated King Astyages of Media and conquered his country (550/49 B.C.). In 547 Cyrus attacked the powerful kingdom of Lydia, conquering its capital Sardis.

After a long struggle, mighty Babylon's turn finally came in 539 in fulfillment of the biblical prophecies (Is 21:2, 9; 44:26; 45:7; Dan 5:28) and Persia became a universal empire, replacing the empires of Assyria and Babylon and also embracing Mesopotamia and Syria.

Cyrus' son and heir Cambyses ascended the throne in 525 B.C. His greatest achievement was the annexation of Egypt to the Persian empire. In his campaign Cambyses was helped by the Arabs of Sinai, who supplied the Persian army with water. Cambyses enthroned himself as a pharaoh, and as the legal heir of the Egyptian rulers.

He was succeeded by Darius I, who founded a new dynasty. Darius built the palaces at Susa, the ancient Elamite city, and his own capital at Persepolis; he also organized the administration of the huge empire, dividing it into satrapies and expanding it to the east. He even considered cutting a canal to connect the Mediterranean with the Red Sea. He set out to fight the Scythians in southern Russia, and on his way back conquered the Greek coastal cities of Asia Minor; however, the Persian expansion ended with the defeat at Marathon in 490 B.C.

With Darius' death in 486, his eldest son Xerxes ascended to the throne. In the second year of his reign Xerxes subdued the revolt in Egypt which had broken out under Darius. In 480 Xerxes defeated the Greeks at Thermopylae, but later the same year the Persian fleet was destroyed at Salamis. Shortly afterwards Xerxes was murdered, and Artaxerxes I (464-423 B.C.) became king. In the following years, Persia experienced uprisings in Egypt and in other satrapies. The last revival of the Achaemenid empire occurred under Artaxerxes III Ochus (359/8-338/7 B.C.) who subdued some of the rebellious satraps, conquered Phoenicia and renewed Persian rule over Lower Egypt. His murder was followed by the enthronement of the last Achaemenid king, Darius III (336/3-330 B.C.), who was defeated at Issus by Alexander the Great.

(bottom of page)
Remains of the palace of the Persian kings at Persepolis. 5th century B.C.

Ceramic aquamanille from Persia. c. 10th-8th centuries B:C. (Israel Museum)

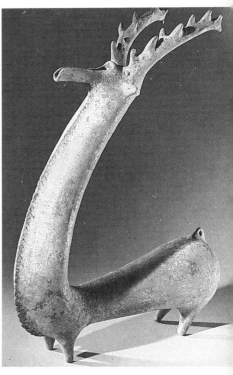

Gold drinking horn from Achmetha.

Persia was mentioned for the first time in the Bible by Ezekiel, who referred to Persian mercenaries in the Tyrian army (Ezek 27:10), as well as linking Persia with his prophecy on Gog king of Magog (Ezek 38:5). The OT's favorable view of Persia stemmed from the permission Cyrus granted to the deportees from Judah to return home and rebuild the Temple in Jerusalem (II Chr 36:23), a policy continued by his heirs (cf Ezra 9:9). Darius I ratified the permission to build the Temple, whose construction was completed in the 6th year of his reign. This positive attitude is also reflected in the Book of Esther which is set in Shushan, i.e., Susa.

PERSIS A Christian of Rome greeted by Paul.

PERUDA See PERIDA

PETER (SIMON) One of the original twelve apostles and their leader following Jesus' ascension. Originally from the village of Bethsaida on the northern shore of the Sea of Galilee (John 1:44). Peter was married (Mark 1:30; I Cor 9:5) and a fisherman by trade together with his brother Andrew (Mark 1:16). His home was in Capernaum (Mark 1:21, 29). When Jesus called him, he was given the added name Cepha (Aramaic: "stone", Greek: "Petros", hence Peter). With James and John and sometimes his brother Andrew, Peter was chosen by Jesus to be present on certain important moments of his ministry. As a member of this group he witnessed Jesus' transfiguration (Mark 9:2ff). He heard Jesus predict coming events (Mark 13:3ff), and was with Jesus in the Garden of Gethsemane (Mark 14:32ff). Peter first made a clear confession of faith in Jesus after observing the miracle at the Sea of Galilee (Luke 5:1-11); later it was he who answered Jesus' question "Who do you say that I am?" with the famous statement, "You are the Christ (messiah), the Son of the living God" (Matt 16:15-16).

One trait of Peter's character that stands out in the NT account is his impetuosity. Immediately after his confession of Jesus' messiahship and his receiving words of praise from his master, Peter rebuked Jesus for what seemed to him negative thinking, drawing Jesus' sharp reply, "Get behind me, Satan" (Matt 16:21-23). When he asked Jesus to allow him to walk on water he began to sink through fear. At the transfiguration, he was rebuked for suggesting they build booths for Moses and Elijah as well as for Jesus (Matt 17:1-5). Again, at the Last Supper, it was Peter who first refused to let Jesus wash his feet and then, hearing that having his feet washed will bring him closer to his Lord, requested that Jesus also wash his hands and head (John 13:6-9). On this same occasion Jesus predicted that all the disciples would fall away but again Peter was ready to argue with Jesus — he, Peter, would never fall away. Jesus then foretold Peter's very denial of the one he so loved. This threefold denial occurred only a few hours later in the courtyard of the high priest, and when Peter realized what he had done, Matthew records (Matt 26:75) that "he went out and wept bitterly". This, and the events of the next couple of days, affected Peter. He was perhaps no less impulsive at first (he stepped into the empty tomb while John hesitated outside), but the later picture is of a humbler man, willing to wait for God to use him. After Jesus' ascension, Peter was very clearly the leader. Jesus himself had foreseen this, as is perhaps indicated in the "Confession" scene in Matthew 16:13-20, and more definitely in Luke 22:31-32 (where the distinction between the singular and plural "you" is lost in modern English translations) and John 21:15-17. Peter was also granted the singular privilege of an individual post-resurrection appearance by Jesus (Luke 24:34; I Cor 15:5). The opening chapters of Acts leave no doubt about Peter's role as leader. He figures prominently in each of the first 12 chapters except for the two which tell of Stephen and his

PERSIS
Rom 16:12

PERUDA
Ezra 2:55

PETER (SIMON)
Matt 4:18;
8:14; 10:2;
14:28-29;
15:15; 16:16-18, 22-23;
17:1, 4, 24-26;
18:21;
19:27; 26:33,
35, 37, 40, 58,
69, 73, 75.
Mark 1:16,
29-30, 36;
3:16; 5:37;
8:29, 32-33;
9:2, 5; 10:28;
11:21; 13:3;
14:29, 33, 37,
54, 66-67, 70,
72; 16:7. Luke
4:38; 5:3-5, 8,
10; 6:14; 8:45,
51; 9:20, 28,
32-33; 12:41;
18:28; 22:8, 31,
34, 54-55, 58,
60-62; 24:12,
34. John 1:40-42, 44; 6:8,
68; 13:6, 8-9,
24, 36-37;
18:10-11, 15-18, 25-27;
20:2-4, 6;
21:2-3, 7, 11,
15-17, 20-21.
Acts 1:13, 15;
2:14, 37-38;
3:1, 3-4, 6, 11-12; 4:8, 13,
19; 5:3, 8-9,
15, 29; 8:14,
20; 9:32, 34,
38-40; 10:5, 9,
13-14, 17-19,
21, 23, 25-26,
32, 34, 44-46;
11:2, 4, 7, 13;
12:3, 5-7, 11,
13-14, 16, 18;
15:7, 14. Gal
1:18; 2:7-8,
11, 14. I Pet
1:1. II Pet 1:1

Model of St Peter's house. (Franciscan Museum, Jerusalem)

martyrdom (Acts chaps. 6-7). When the disciples addressed a crowd or the Sanhedrin, Peter was always the spokesman. He preached the first sermon to his fellow Jews (Acts 2:14-36) and then later to Gentiles (Acts 10:34-43). Under the power of the Holy Spirit, he healed the sick and raised the dead (Acts 3:1-8; 5:15; 9:32-41). In the first need for church discipline following the accusation made by Peter, the offenders dropped dead (Acts 5:1-10). He was later imprisoned by Herod Agrippa who was seeking to appease the Jews, and was released by an angel in about the year 44 (Acts 12:1-10).

While Peter's chief ministry was in the Holy Land, he made a trip to Antioch (Gal 2:1ff) and perhaps also to Corinth (I Cor 1:12). A reliable tradition relates that he later traveled to Rome and this indeed may be hinted at in I Peter 5:13 where Babylon refers to Rome. During the Neronic persecution in Rome in 64, Peter was martyred by crucifixion. He is said to have requested that he be crucified upside down so as not to die in the manner of his Lord.

The name of Peter appears as the author of two NT letters (q.v.). Papias, a disciple of the apostle John, wrote that Mark's gospel was based on Peter's own writings.

PETER, FIRST EPISTLE OF The 21st book of the NT.

Of the "Catholic Epistles", none is better or earlier attested than I Peter. It is quoted by several writers of the first decades of the 2nd century, and its authority was never called into question. But despite the fact that all extant manuscripts contain Peter's name in the first verse, there has been some doubt among scholars as to whether he actually wrote the letter. Two major objections have been raised. First, the Greek style of the letter seems to be far above what might be expected of an Aramaic-speaking Galilean fisherman. The facts that Greek was not uncommon in Galilee, and that Peter's brother had a Greek name, are not sufficient to explain the excellent command of the language so obviously possessed by the author of the epistle. One plausible and common explanation is that Silvanus (5:12) had a more direct input than that of mere carrier or scribe: it was not unknown in ancient times for a secretary to be given the task of stylizing letters dictated to him.

The second major objection to Peter as author stems from the letter's frequent references to persecution. Some have claimed that this must refer to official persecutions, which only occurred after Peter's death. However, the language of the letter, specifically 4:12ff, does not necessitate a formal policy of persecution "for the Name" (cf Acts 5:41). Indeed Peter's language can be explained on a background of pending trouble in Nero's time.

Reliable tradition has it that Peter died in Rome during the Neronic persecutions of the 60's. It is likely that he wrote this letter sometime between the death of James in 62 and the outbreak of troubles in the capital in 64. The only hint within the letter of its place of origin is in 5:13, where it is called "Babylon". This is clearly a symbolic reference to Rome (cf Rev 17:3-6). The addressees are churches in Northern Asia Minor, mostly in areas which had not been evangelized by Paul. While Peter describes them as "dispersed" (Greek: diasporas), his readers were Christians from among both Jews and Gentiles (cf 2:9-10).

I Peter contains numerous parallels to other NT texts, not least among them certain of Paul's writings. This is not surprising in view of Peter's relationship with Silvanus and Mark (5:12-13), both of whom worked closely with Paul. The letters to the Thessalonians, to which I Peter bears special affinities, were even co-authored by Silvanus. However, the epistle also includes a wealth of thought which develops along lines independent of other NT writers. Especially to be noted is

The Church of the Primacy (of St Peter) on the shore of the Sea of Galilee.

St Peter healing Tabitha shown on the capital of a column from the time of the Crusaders. Found at Nazareth.

Peter's emphasis on how present suffering is to be followed by future glory (1:7, 11; 4:13-17; 5:1, 10). Here are words of encouragement to fellow-believers facing hard times.

One suggestion which has gained a measure of acceptance is that I Peter 1:3-4:11 is a sermon intended to accompany a baptism, where an opening prayer and instruction (1:3-21) precede the rite, which is followed by further instruction and exhortation (1:22-4:11). This interesting and attractive theory, however, runs into several difficulties: (a) no satisfactory explanation is given for 4:12ff; (b) baptism is mentioned only once (3:21) and then only incidentally; and (c) I Peter is unquestionably a letter, and it is difficult to understand why such a sermon would be so incorporated into a letter.

OUTLINE

1:1-2	Salutation
1:3-12	The dynamics of salvation
1:13-17	Exhortation to holiness
1:18-21	Redemption through Jesus' blood
1:22-2:3	New birth through God's word
2:4-10	God's house of living stones
2:11-3:13	Submissiveness and good behavior exhorted
3:14-4:2	Partaking of Christ's sufferings
4:3-11	Christian conduct opposed to heathen conduct
4:12-19	Suffering for the sake of righteousness
5:1-4	Instructions to elders
5:5-7	Humble yourselves
5:8-11	Resist the devil
5:12-14	Closing greetings

The Tempietto in Rome, built in 1502 by Bramante, at the site where, according to tradition, Peter was crucified.

PETER, SECOND EPISTLE OF The 22nd book of the NT.

While no addressees are named in the letter, the author has written a previous letter to them (3:1) and seems to know them well (1:12ff). From the wording of the opening verse, they are sharers in the Christian faith, perhaps from Gentile background. The communication has been necessitated by the presence among them of certain false teachers who are characterized by immorality, insubordination, a denial of the authority of scripture, and, perhaps, unethical financial dealings. The core of the letter is a lengthy diatribe against men like these and includes several warnings to the readers to beware of them (chap. 2). The best guard against heresy is a healthy view of scripture and its authority (1:19-21; 3:14-16).

II Peter is cited by the Church Fathers less frequently than any other NT book; in fact, its first mention by name is by Origen in the 3rd century. It is, however, better attested than any non-canonical writing and was firmly fixed in the canon by the middle of the 4th century.

The opening words identify the writer as Simon Peter; if he was indeed the author, then the epistle was probably written shortly before his death in the mid-60's (cf 1:14). Many scholars, however, have objected to Petrine authorship for a variety of reasons. (a) The second chapter is generally judged to be dependent on the Epistle of Jude. It is clear at least that one used the other. If Jude used II Peter, then the date of the latter will be early. If, as is generally thought, II Peter derives from

Jude, then many see this as evidence that Peter could not have written it, since the greater would not have copied from the lesser. (b) In 3:15ff the writer seems to be acquainted with Paul's letters in some sort of collection, and to consider them authoritative. Since such a collection was probably not in circulation before about 90, the letter may have to be placed after that date. However, the writer may not be referring to a collection, and he may even have been familiar with letters of Paul which are no longer extant. As with the previous objection, the judgment on the position of respect afforded Paul's letters is a subjective one. (c) There are several apparent divergences, both in language usage and in doctrine, from I Peter. On the question of language, it is important to note the mention of Silvanus' involvement in the composition of I Peter (I Pet 5:12). If Peter used another amanuensis for the second epistle, this would account for both the differences, and the similarities in style between the two, especially if the two assistants were given considerable leeway in the actual wording. As to the variant doctrinal positions of the two letters, it must be remembered that the emphasis or reason for writing each is considerably different. It should be noted further that the two letters feature some common elements, both linguistically and doctrinally. (d) Finally, it is argued that the heresies combatted in the letter were in vogue in the 2nd century. While this is true, it cannot be ruled out that they may actually have had their roots much earlier. So, for example, the skeptics about the second coming of Christ (3:4) are akin to others familiar from letters universally accepted as early (cf I Cor 15:12; I Thes 4:13ff).

While the cumulative effect of these objections is impressive, none of them is definitive, and Peter's authorship must remain as one option.

If the letter is pseudonymous, i.e. written by a later Christian using Peter's name and authority, and dates from as late as A.D. 150, as is commonly thought today, it represents an interesting attempt to defend the old faith in the early return of Christ during a later generation when that hope had begun to wane. The doctrine then is traditional, but is expressed in language which is partly new and difficult, showing the influence of both non-canonical Jewish apocalyptic books (one is quoted in 2:10ff) and of Greek thought (the world is destroyed by fire in 3:7 and in Plato's "Gorgias"). The evaluation of Paul's writings in 3:15-16 shows some of the difficulties of early Christians in meeting the challenge of Gnosticism.

St Peter's Basilica on Vatican Hill, Rome, built on the site venerated since the year 160 as the burial place of the Apostle.

OUTLINE

1:1-2	Salutation
1:3-11	Growth in virtue by God's power
1:12-18	Peter's testimony
1:19-21	True prophecy
2:1-22	False prophets and teachers
3:1-13	The last days
3:14-18	Practical exhortation and closing

PETHAHIAH ("the Lord opens").

1. A Levite, head of the 19th division of priests serving in the House of the Lord in the time of King David

2. A Levite, among those who, having taken a pagan wife, had to repudiate her following the decree of Ezra

3. A Levite who was among those who led the people in the recitation of the blessing on the day of the great fast in the time of Nehemiah. May be identical with No.2.

4. A man of Judah, from the family of Zerah; son of Meshezabeel he was "the king's deputy in all matters concerning the people".

PETHOR Place to which Balak king of Moab sent messengers to Balaam son of Beor. It is described as "near the river in the land of the sons of his people" (Num 22:5). Deuteronomy 23:4 calls it "Pethor of Mesopotamia" (which is also the name rendered by the Septuagint). Pethor has been identified with Pittiru, a place mentioned in an inscription of the times of Shalmaneser III as situated on the right bank of the Euphrates, some 12 miles (19 km) south of Carchemish. The Hittites knew this place by the name of Pitru. They held the city until the 9th century B.C. when it was taken by Shalmaneser III.

PETHUEL Father of Joel the prophet.

PEULTHAI (PEULLETHAI) ("recompense of the Lord"). Eighth and last son of Obed-Edom, a Levite gatekeeper of the sanctuary.

PHANUEL The father of the elderly prophetess Anna.

PHARAOH An Egyptian word (literally "great house"), mentioned in Egyptian documents from as early as 2500 B.C. as one of the designations of the royal palace, and from 1500 B.C. as one of the Egyptian king's titles. In the Bible it appears 274 times as a descriptive name in various forms: "Pharaoh" (Gen 12:15, 17-18, 20; 37:36; 39:1;

Pharaoh on his chariot shown on a chest from Tutankhamon's tomb. 14th century B.C.

45:16; 50:7; Ex 5:2 etc.), "Pharaoh king of Egypt" (I Kgs 9:16; Ezek 32:2 etc.); "Pharaoh" plus "personal name" (for example: "Pharaoh Necho" — II Kings 23:33-34; "Pharaoh Hophra" — Jeremiah 44:30); and "Pharaoh" plus "personal name" plus the title "king of Egypt" (II Kgs 23:29; Jer 46:2).

There are still disagreements as to the historical identifications of the pharaohs who reigned at the time of Joseph, during the Egyptian bondage, and the Exodus from Egypt.

PHARISEES ("those who separated" [*perushim*] or "those who sanctify" [*perishut*]). Members of one of three major parties in Judaism from the last centuries B.C. until the destruction of the Second Temple in A.D. 70.

Christian tradition, beginning with the NT has generally perceived and presented the Pharisees as an antithesis to the life and teachings of Jesus. A closer examination, however, reveals that the NT picture of the

PETHAHIAH 1
I Chr 24:16
PETHAHIAH 2
Ezra 10:23
PETHAHIAH 3
Neh 9:5
PETHAHIAH 4
Neh 11:24
PETHOR
Num 22:5.
Deut 23:4
PETHUEL
Joel 1:1
PEULTHAI
I Chr 26:5
PHANUEL
Luke 2:36
PHARISEES
Matt 3:7;
5:20; 9:11, 14,
34; 12:2, 14,
24, 38; 15:1,
12; 16:1, 6,
11-12; 19:3;
21:45; 22:15,

Pharisees is much more complex than their one-sided presentation as "hypocrites". Indeed, Jesus was closer to this group than to any other, as indicated by his comments about them. On the one hand, in the Sermon on the Mount he said "For I say to you, that unless your righteousness exceeds the righteousness of the scribes and Pharisees, you will by no means enter the Kingdom of Heaven" (Matt 5:20), clearly affirming the view that the Pharisees are righteous people. On the other hand, certain discussions and disputes took the form of a confrontation between Jesus and some Pharisees, though more over matters of practice than of principle. Indeed it was the affinity between Jesus and the Pharisees which made such discussions possible. When Jesus tells the Pharisees "Woe to you Pharisees! For you love the best seats in the synagogues and greetings in the market places" (Luke 11:43), this must be read as criticism from within, and not as overall condemnation of the Pharisees as such.

The Pharisees are also described in the NT as people having the authority to expound the Torah. Jesus taught the people and his own disciples that "the scribes and the Pharisees sit in Moses' seat" (Matt 23:2), meaning that they interpreted the law in accordance with the Mosaic tradition. During the 1st century A.D. there were various schools within Judaism with different ways of interpreting the laws governing daily life. Because of this diversity many practical details remained fluid and open to discussion. Within this framework one should read the arguments in the gospels concerning the Sabbath. That one should refrain from work (Ex 20:10) was clear to all but what this meant in practice had yet to be decided and encoded in law. The Jewish literature of that time also contains such internal disputes, especially among the Pharisees who were the teachers. Thus, the Gospel of Luke describes the healing by Jesus on the Sabbath and in the house of a Pharisee, of a man suffering from dropsy. "And Jesus, answering, spoke to the lawyers and Pharisees, saying, 'Is it lawful to heal on the Sabbath?' But they kept silent. And he took him, and healed him, and let him go" (Luke 14:1-4). The reaction of the Pharisees is not so negative as is usually thought. Healing on the Sabbath was one of the matters still at issue among the rabbinical scholars. The Pharisees said nothing because there was still no clear verdict on this point. Instead of taking a negative attitude towards the Pharisees' discussions with Jesus, these exchanges should instead be seen as a useful source of information about the debates among Jewish teachers in this decisive century.

Jewish literature of the Second Temple period gives a broader and more realistic picture of the Pharisees. They emerge as successors to the group which tried from the time of Ezra onward, to make the Torah central to the life of the entire people, rather than confine it to the priests alone. The Pharisees stimulated prayer in the synagogues, alongside worship in the Temple. Communal life became more focal and the Pharisees tried to make the individual feel responsible for his own life and that of his community. The Pharisees generally adopted a lenient stand in matters of daily religious observance.

A comparison of the four gospels provides no clear picture as to the position of the Pharisees in the trial of Jesus. Throughout the trial, they are hardly mentioned, possibly indicating that just as the Jewish multitude sympathized with Jesus, so did most of the Pharisees. A positive attitude towards Jesus is displayed by the Pharisee Nicodemus (John 3:1; 19:39) and by Joseph of Arimathea (Matt 27:57; Mark 15:43; Luke 23:50-51), both of whom took an active part in Jesus' interment.

PHARPAR One of the two rivers of Damascus, mentioned by Naaman (II Kgs 5:12). Some identify it with Nahr el-Awaj, which takes its source

The Pharisee and the publican. From a Byzantine mosaic of the 6th century at San Apollinare in Classe, Ravenna, Italy.

from Mount Hermon, 8 miles (13 km) to the east of the city. Some suggest that it is Nahr Taura, the largest tributary of Nahr el-Barad; while others prefer the identification with Nahar Barbar, which flows to the south of Damascus, between the city and Nahr el-Awaj.

PHICOL General of the army of Abimelech, king of Gerar. According to both Genesis, chapter 21 and Genesis, chapter 26 Phicol accompanied Abimelech at the time of the exchange of oaths between Abimelech and the patriarch (Abraham in Gen chap. 21; Isaac in Gen chap. 26), which culminated in the naming of the city of Bcersheba.

PHILADELPHIA A city in the district of Lydia in the Roman province of Asia in western Asia Minor. It was situated near the upper end of a broad valley leading down through Sardis to the sea near Smyrna. Philadelphia handled the trade between the great central plateau of Asia Minor and Smyrna and specialized in textile and leather production. Philadelphia's church is one of the seven mentioned in the Book of Revelation, where it receives no reproach. The Philadelphia church, of whose foundation nothing is known, apparently encountered some opposition from the local synagogue (Rev 3:9). The modern city of Alasehir lies upon the ancient site.

PHILEMON See PHILEMON, EPISTLE TO

PHILEMON, EPISTLE TO Short letter from Paul to Philemon, a Christian from the area of Colossae or Laodicea, which now forms the 18th book of the NT. Paul met Philemon while preaching in the region and seems to have been the one to win him to faith in Jesus (cf v.19). Later, one of Philemon's slaves, Onesimus by name, ran away and evidently even took some of his master's property with him. By design or by accident, the runaway met Paul in Rome while the latter was imprisoned there. Perhaps he had met Paul in his master's home in Asia Minor and had for some reason searched Paul out. Whatever the case may be, Paul led him to faith in Jesus and convinced him to return to his master to face the consequences. But to ease the return, Paul wrote to Philemon to ask him to receive Onesimus back without retribution, "no longer as a slave but more than a slave, as a beloved brother". Absent here, as from all of Paul's letters, is any explicit attack on the institution of slavery. But implicitly Paul indicates that brotherly love must overcome and replace master-slave relations, that in the new brotherhood of the messiah "there is neither slave nor free (man)" (Gal 3:28; Col 3:11). The letter was probably sent by the hand of Onesimus himself, together with Tychicus, as an addition to the longer letter to the church at Colossae (cf Col 4:7-9). Subsequent church tradition has it that Philemon and his wife were martyred.

OUTLINE

vs. 1-7	Thanksgiving for Philemon's charitable deeds
vs. 8-11	Petition in behalf of Onesimus
vs. 12-25	Request to receive Onesimus not as a runaway slave but as a brother in Christ

PHILETUS ("beloved"). Cited by Paul as an example of men who were to be avoided because of their heretical views (Philetus maintained that resurrection had already taken place).

PHILIP ("horse lover").

1. One of the twelve apostles, he came from Bethsaida in Galilee. Jesus invited Philip personally to become his disciple: "Jesus wanted to go to Galilee, and he found Philip and said to him, 'Follow me'" (John 1:43). He became the sixth disciple of Jesus and introduced his friend Nathanael to Jesus (John 1:45-51). Philip was put to the test at the multiplication of the loaves and fishes: "Then Jesus lifted up his eyes, and seeing a great multitude coming toward him, he said to Philip, 'Where shall we buy bread, that these may eat?' But this he said to test him: for he himself knew what he would do" (John 6:5-6). A group of Greek Jews who were in Jerusalem for Passover and wanted to meet Jesus, turned to Philip to introduce them (John 12:20-22). According to the Gospel of John, Philip asked Jesus to show them the Father "Lord, show us the Father, and it is sufficient for us" (John 14:8-11). Together with others, Philip was present in an "upper room where they were staying: Peter, James, John and Andrew; Philip and Thomas...these all continued with one accord in prayer and supplication" (Acts 1:13-14) after the ascension of Jesus. Nothing is related of his subsequent life.

2. Philip the tetrarch 4 B.C.-A.D. 34; son of Herod the Great and Cleopatra of Jerusalem. Philip was educated in Rome, and after the death of his father he received the territory of Iturea and Trachonitis (Luke 3:1). He administered his territories effectively and peacefully. Philip founded the city of Caesarea Philippi near Paneas and the sources of the Jordan. He rebuilt the town of Bethsaida on the Sea of Galilee and called it Julias after Augustus' daughter Julia. Philip remained loyal to the Romans throughout his life. He was married to his niece Salome, granddaughter of Herod and Mariamne II, and died childless. After his death, his territory was incorporated into the province of Syria, but shortly afterwards, was given by Caligula to Agrippa.

3. Herod Philip. The first husband of Herodias and father of Salome.

4. Philip the evangelist. One of the seven appointed by the apostles, to take care of the growing Christian community and to look after their widows and needy (Acts 6:1-6). He was sent out, after being "ordained" through communal prayer and hands being laid on him, and he went down to the city of Samaria where he preached, and performed miracles (Acts 8:4-6). He converted Simon the magician "and when he was baptized he continued with Philip" (Acts 8:9-13). Philip received the message from an angel to go down to Gaza, where he met a man of Ethiopia, a eunuch of great authority under Queen Candace, and inspired the Ethiopian to be baptized (Acts 8:26-39). Later he lived in Caesarea, where he received Paul: "On the next day we who were Paul's companions departed and came to Caesarea, and entered the house of Philip the evangelist, who was one of the seven, and stayed with him" (Acts 21:8). According to Acts 21:9, Philip's four unmarried daughters "prophesied".

PHILIPPI, PHILIPPIANS A city in the northeastern Greek district of Thrace, on the east-west road between Neapolis (modern Kavalla) and Thessalonica. It was founded in 360 B.C. by colonists from Thasos, and named Krenides ("springs") after the abundant springs at the foot of the settlement. Four years later the city was annexed by King Philip II of Macedon, who changed its name to Philippi.

In 42 B.C. Philippi was the site of the decisive battle in which the forces of Octavian (later Augustus Caesar) and Mark Antony defeated the army of Brutus and Cassius. After the battle a colony for Roman veterans was established at Philippi. During the Roman period, Philippi was an important station on the Via Egnatia, the main east-west route through the empire to Rome.

Paralytic waiting to be healed; shown on a mosaic of the 14th century at the church of Kariye, Istanbul, Turkey.

Philippi was the first European city to hear the Christian gospel preached. This event occurred in the year A.D. 49, when Paul arrived in Philippi from Alexandria (Acts 16:12). Paul and his companions had sailed from Alexandria to Samothrace, where they spent one night. They then left for Neapolis, and walked directly from there to Philippi (Acts 16:11). Paul spent several days in Philippi where he founded the first church in the West (I Phil 4:15). While in Philippi, he and his companion Silas were imprisoned (Acts 16:23). Paul passed through Philippi once more, on his return to Palestine from Greece (Acts 20:6).

With the official establishment of Christianity, Philippi became a metropolitan seat with jurisdiction over five to seven dioceses. The remains of five churches of the Early Christian period attest the importance of the city at this time.

PHILIPPIANS, EPISTLE TO THE The 11th book of the NT.

Paul had founded the church in Philippi during his second missionary journey as described in Acts 16:9-40. In subsequent journeys he twice returned to the city to encourage the church (Acts 20:1-2, 6). He seems to have maintained some communication with his followers there, as is evidenced by the warm tone of the letter, which was probably carried by Epaphroditus (2:25-28). At the time of writing, Paul is also considering sending Timothy, and expresses the hope that he himself will be able to come to them (2:19-24).

Paul wrote from prison in an unstated location (1:7, 13ff, 16). The Book of Acts records three imprisonments of Paul: one in Philippi itself (Acts 16:23ff); one in Palestine, primarily in Caesarea (Acts 21:32-27:1); and finally in Rome (Acts 28:16, 30). There were, however, probably others (cf II Cor 6:5; 11:23). Earliest tradition assigned this letter to the Roman imprisonment, i.e. about the year 62. This is supported by Paul's mention of the praetorian guard and "Caesar's household" (1:13; 4:22) and by the absence of any mention of the possibility of appealing to Caesar, indicating that he is in fact awaiting Caesar's judgment. There have been those who posited Caesarea as the place of writing, but Paul's circumstances and state of mind in the letter do not fit well with what is known of his imprisonment there. In the 19th century it was proposed that this epistle may have been written from Ephesus. This view, still held by only a minority, has gained some respectable adherents. It would necessitate a dating of about 55-57 (Acts 19:10). There is no direct evidence of Paul having been imprisoned in Ephesus.

In the text Paul seems recently to have received a monetary gift from Philippi, and this letter includes words of thanks (4:10-19). He is also concerned that they be kept informed of his present circumstances (1:12ff) and perhaps of his still-tentative plans to visit them shortly (2:24) as well as of the coming of Timothy.

As is typical of most of Paul's letters, no systematic development of a theme is to be found here. However, several elements of the epistle stand out and deserve mention. Perhaps no other NT writing contains a clearer affirmation of the necessity of facing difficult circumstances with a joyful attitude. In this short letter, written from prison at a time when Paul even encountered opposition within the church (1:15-17), he employs various forms of the word "joy" no less than 16 times. In 2:18 he exhorts his addressees to rejoice; in 3:1 he repeats the exhortation and then defends the repetition; and in 4:4 he repeats it yet again. Here is the picture of a man matured by his experiences, a man at peace with himself and with God (1:12-19; 4:11-13), a man who has "learned in whatever state I am, to be content" and who can even hold himself up to his readers as an example to be emulated (4:8-9). Paul is also seen as totally dedicated to the task and vision to which God has called him (1:21-26; 3:7-14).

Perhaps no better statement exists in Paul's writings of his basic gospel of Christ than 2:5-11, the so-called "carmen Christi" or "song of Christ". Many scholars have felt that these verses preserve one of the oldest church hymns, perhaps not composed by Paul himself but certainly carrying his complete endorsement.

A Philistine depicted on an Egyptian glazed tile. The figure is wearing the typical Philistine head covering, but is dressed in the style customary in Syria and Palestine in that period. From the mortuary temple of Rameses III at Medinet Habu, Egypt. 12th century B.C.

OUTLINE

1:1-2	Salutation
1:3-11	Paul's thanks and prayer for them
1:12-26	Paul's circumstances
1:27-2:4	Exhortation to steadfastness and unity
2:5-11	The humbling and exaltation of Christ
2:12-18	Blameless conduct and joy enjoined
2:19-30	Timothy and Epaphroditus
3:1-14	Paul's testimony
3:15-4:1	Exhortation to follow Paul's example
4:2-3	Personal instructions
4:4-9	Joy, peace and right thinking
4:10-19	Contentment in all circumstances
4:20-23	Final greetings and benediction

PHILISTIA, PHILISTINES The Philistines were a tribe, one of the Sea Peoples, that appeared at the end of the Late Bronze Age in the southeastern sector of the Mediterranean. The Egyptian sources refer to them as mercenaries in the Egyptian army. "People of the Sea" are listed among those who collaborated with the Libyans in their revolt against Egypt during the reign of Merneptah. The Philistines are mentioned specifically in the time of Rameses III. They are vividly depicted in reliefs in the temple of Rameses III at Medinet Habu in Thebes. The Philistines are depicted as tall men, shaven and wearing feathered head-dresses secured by chinstraps. The captive Philistines wear a breastplate (or shirt), and in the naval battle they are shown wearing strap-shields. They have broad belts round their waists, and skirts.

In a later Egyptian source, that of Amen-em-Opet, of the late 12th or early 11th century B.C., three ethnic groups are mentioned among other nations — Sherden, Tjekers and Philistines — and also three towns — Ashkelon, Ashdod and Gaza — all of which were in Philistia.

The Egyptian sources give no clue as to the origin of the Philistines and the other Sea Peoples. On the other hand, Genesis 10:14 has: "Pathrusim, and Casluhim (from whom came the Philistines and Caphtorim)". This is usually understood to mean that the Philistines and the Cherethites were kindred people (Ezek 25:16; Zeph 2:5). Moreover, Jeremiah (47:4) and Amos (9:7) both state that the Philistines originated in Caphtor. It seems from the Bible that Caphtor and Cherethim were either identical or close to each other.

According to the Bible the Philistines were in the Negeb at the time of the patriarchs, and their king, Abimelech dwelt at Gerar (Gen 26:1). This tradition was set down in writing when the Philistines had already settled in Canaan, in the 12th or 11th century B.C. They are very

Philistine vase with geometrical designs and representations of birds.

prominent in the Bible in the period of the Judges, when there was an almost constant state of war between them and the expanding Israelites (Judg 3:31; 15:11, etc.). One of the main issues in dispute between the two peoples was the settlement of the Danites, whose territory bordered that of the Philistines. This serious clash terminated with the resettlement of the Danites in the north of the country (Judg chaps. 13-16). There was a strong and permanent encroachment of the Philistines onto the territory of Judah as well. Open hostilities began at Ebenezer (I Sam chap. 4) in the course of which the ark of God was captured by the enemy (I Sam chap. 5). Later, with the conquest of Beth Shean, the whole of the Via Maris was in the hands of the Philistines (I Sam chap.31). They established garrisons in Judah and Benjamin (I Sam 10:5; 13:3) and took steps to prevent the use of iron weapons (I Sam 13:19). In the latter part of the 11th century B.C. there was a change of fortune and the Philistines were defeated and driven out of Israelite territory (I Sam 13:4; 14:20 ff.) Another clash between the Philistines and the Israelites occurred in the Valley of Elah, where David slew Goliath (I Sam 17:49-50). This battle was decisive and the decline of the Philistines now began. David was later given shelter by Achish, king of Gath, who gave him the town of Ziklag (I Sam 27:6). Before the battle of Mount Gilboa Achish made David "one of my chief guardians" (I Sam 28:1-2) and in the battle Saul and his sons fell in one of the last clashes in the Jezreel Valley (I Sam 31:1-6). It was only after he became king of Israel that David finally defeated the Philistines (II Sam 8:1; I Chr 18:1), and even used them as mercenaries (II Sam 8:18). Uzziah, king of Judah, pushed the Israelite conquest further into Philistine territory, taking Gath, Jabneh (Jabneel) and Ashdod (II Chr 26:6-7). During the period of the Assyrian campaigns the Philistines were several times involved in alliances against the Assyrians and on the side of Egypt. Even up to the time of the return from the Babylonian Exile they retained some of their national characteristics, and spoke in the "speech of Ashdod" (Neh 13:24).

The five main Philistine cities are named in the Bible as Gaza, Ashkelon, Ashdod, Ekron and Gath, each being the capital of a lordship. Some smaller Philistine towns are also mentioned, such as Ziklag (I Sam 27:6), Timnath (Timnah) (Judg 14:1) and the fortified town of Jabneh (II Chr 26:6). It is also recorded that during their expansion further west and north the Philistines established garrisons at Geba (I Sam 13:3) and Beth Shean (I Sam 31:12). But archeological finds show that many other towns were also under Philistine influence or direct rule, for Philistine pottery has been found at places such as Megiddo, Joppa, Bethel and Beth Shemesh.

The Bible contains a great deal of information about the internal organization of the Philistines. At the head of each Philistine kingdom stood a lord (I Sam 5:11), or sometimes a king (I Sam 27:2), who was probably also the commander-in-chief of the army. At the head of these states was a military aristocracy which, since it was supported by an advanced military organization and superior arms, could impose its rule over a much larger local population. The army consisted of archers (I Sam 31:3), cavalrymen and charioteers (I Sam 13:5), and was divided into hundreds and thousands (I Sam 29:2). In battle the whole army would hold the front line and small units would be sent forward to attack. Another method, alien to the Hebrews was the use of a champion, such as Goliath (I Sam 17:4ff), who went into battle clad in a "bronze helmet" and a "coat of mail", with "bronze greaves on his legs and a bronze javelin between his shoulders, armed with an iron spearhead and preceded by a shield bearer".

21, 25, 27, 30; 19:5, 8; 21:9; 22:10; 23:1-5, 27-28; 24:1; 27:1, 7, 11; 28:1, 4-5, 15, 19; 29:1-4, 7, 9, 11; 30:16; 31:1-2, 7-9, 11. II Sam 1:20; 3:14, 18; 5:17-19, 22, 24-25; 8:1, 12; 19:9; 21:12, 15, 17-19; 23:9-14, 16. I Kgs 4:21; 15:27; 16:15. II Kgs 8:2-3; 18:8. I Chr 1:12; 10:1-2, 7-9, 11; 11:13-16, 18; 12:19; 14:8-10, 13, 15-16; 18:1, 11; 20:4-5. II Chr 9:26; 17:11; 21:16; 26:6-7; 28:18. Ps 60:8; 83:7; 87:4; 108:9. Is 2:6; 9:12; 11:14; 14:29, 31. Jer 25:20; 47:1, 4. Ezek 16:27, 57; 25:15-16. Joel 3:4. Amos 1:8; 6:2; 9:7. Obad v 19. Zeph 2:5. Zech 9:6

Lid of an anthropoid clay coffin, with the characteristic feathered headdress attributed to the Philistines. From Beth Shean. 12th century B.C.

(left)
Philistine captives shown on a wall relief from the temple of Rameses II at Medinet Habu, 12th century B.C.

The Philistines carried the images of their gods with them into battle (II Sam 5:21). The chief of these was Dagon (Judg 16:23), and there were temples to him at Gaza, Ashdod and Beth Shean. A statue of this god stood in the temple at Ashdod (I Sam 5:2-3), while at Ekron there was an oracle of Baal-Zebub, another Philistine god (II Kgs 1:3). The principal goddess was Ashtaroth, whose temple, the house of Ashtaroth, was at Beth Shean (I Sam 31:10).

Remains of the Philistine material culture have been found from the 12th and 11th centuries B.C. on many sites in the coastal plain south of the River Yarkon. These consist mainly of pottery, the most typical being bowls and jugs with a white wash and painted with a great variety of geometric patterns, birds and fishes. From the similarity of shape and decoration it is obvious that these had their origin in the sphere of the Mycenean culture, though local features and some Egyptian elements are also identifiable.

Peculiar to the Philistines was their disposal of the dead in anthropoid clay coffins. In their cemeteries at Beth Shean, Lachish and Tell el-Farah (south), as well as in some places in Egypt, clay coffins of this type were discovered with a cylindrical, elongated body and a cover made in the form of a human head framed by hands.

No written material of the Philistines has so far been found.

PHILOLOGUS
Rom 16:15

PHILOLOGUS A Christian of Rome to whom Paul sent greetings.

PHINEHAS

PHINEHAS 1
Ex 6:25. Num
25:7, 11; 31:6.
Josh 22:13,
30-32; 24:33.
Judg 20:28.
I Chr 6:4, 50;
9:20. Ezra 7:5;
8:2. Ps 106:30

1. The son of Eleazar, son of Aaron the high priest (Ex 6:3-4, 50; Ezra 7:1-5). When the Israelites, in Shittim, began to have intercourse with the daughters of Moab and to offer sacrifices to the Moabite god Baal of Peor, God inflicted a plague upon Israel. Phinehas, zealous for God, used his spear to kill Zimri son of Salu, who was sinning with a Midianite woman. This deed appeased God who stayed the plague (Num 25:1-15). In recognition of his zeal, God granted perpetual priesthood to Phinehas and his descendants (Num 25:10-13; Ps 106:30-31). Subsequently, when Moses sent 12,000 men to wage war against the Midianites, Phinehas was entrusted with the holy vessels and the trumpets of alarm (Num 31:6). Later, he led an Israelite delegation, consisting of ten tribal chiefs, sent to rebuke the two and a half tribes east of the Jordan for offending God by building their own altar (Josh 22:9-34). Phinehas served before the ark in Bethel when the Israelites came to inquire of the Lord whether to do battle against Benjamin (Judg 20:27-28). According to I Chronicles 9:20 Phinehas was superintendent of the gatekeepers.

Gershom of the family of Phinehas was among the heads of household who returned from the Exile with Ezra (Ezra 8:2).

2. Along with Hophni, one of the two sons of Eli who served as priests at Shiloh (I Sam 1:3). They were guilty of treating the Lord with contempt by tasting choice portions of meat before a sacrifice was offered to God. They were also in the habit of having sexual intercourse with the women who served in the sanctuary. For their gross misbehavior and their father's inability to check them, a man of God heralded the downfall of the house of Eli (I Sam 2:12-36). At the battle of Aphek they were killed and the ark of the covenant captured by the Philistines (I Sam 4:4-11).

PHINEHAS 2
I Sam 1:3;
2:34; 4:4, 11,
17, 19; 14:3

3. The father of Eleazar. The latter was an assistant to Meremoth, son of Uriah the priest who was in charge of the vessels and the silver and gold deposits in the Temple (Ezra 8:33).

PHINEHAS 3
Ezra 8:33

PHLEGON A Christian of Rome greeted by Paul.

PHLEGON
Rom 16:14

PHOEBE ("radiant, bright"). A deaconess from the church at Cenchrea who carried Paul's letter to the Romans from Corinth to Rome. She was a patron of Paul, among others, and he requested that the Roman church receive her and provide for her needs.

PHOEBE
Rom 16:1

PHOENICIA, PHOENICIANS The name given by the classical authors to the land extending along the coast of Lebanon and the northern part of Palestine, and to the peoples living there extending from Arvad on the north, to Acco on the south. The name Phoenicia was variously applied to different parts of that area, but at its peak it covered a region extending from Dora in the south as far as Ugarit in the north.

PHOENICIA
Acts 11:19;
15:3; 21:2

Phoenician coin minted at Tyre depicting on one side the Baal of Tyre riding a winged horse over the waves, with a dolphin in the sea below; and an owl on the other side.

*(right)
The coast at the Phoenician city of Dor.*

From early times maritime trade played a major part in its economy. Other relatively important elements were fishing and the extraction of purple dye from the murex, a shellfish that abounded on the coast. The earliest traces of human occupation on the Phoenician coast go back to the Paleolithic Age. In the Mesolithic period crops were cultivated and animals domesticated. During the Neolithic period man began to leave his caves and temporary dwellings and to build villages with houses made of mud. During the last quarter of the 5th millennium B.C. pottery made its first appearance at Ugarit and Byblos. The Chalcolithic culture, characterized by the use of copper weapons and painted pottery, was observed on both of these sites. By the time of the 3rd-6th Dynasties these trade relations with Egypt were well established and

Egyptian alabaster vases bearing the names of some Egyptian pharaohs were found at Byblos. These relations were, however, disturbed during the period of anarchy that prevailed in Egypt under the 8th-10th Dynasties, and Egypt's hold over Phoenicia was therefore interrupted.

The arrival of the Amorites brought destruction to Byblos and to other Phoenician centers in the south of the country. Ugarit, in the north, suffered destruction somewhat later at the hands of the Horites, who arrived from the northeast. During this period of unrest a new ethnic element, a people skilled in working bronze, arrived in Phoenicia from Anatolia, in the 21st century B.C. By the middle of the 20th century B.C. Phoenicia had again come under Egyptian control. The 19th and a great part of the 18th centuries B.C. was a period of great prosperity, but this was disrupted by the arrival of Hyksos, who ruled over Phoenicia from about 1730 to 1580 B.C.

Egyptian rule over Phoenicia was renewed with the rise of the 18th Dynasty. The influence of Egypt on Phoenicia was great in every field and even Phoenician art included many Egyptian elements. Egypt's ascendancy over Phoenicia was disrupted again with the arrival of the Sea Peoples (Philistines), who together with the Canaanites were to form the new Phoenician nation. Whereas in the period preceding the 12th century B.C. the inhabitants of the different city-states had been referred to by the names of their individual cities, from that time onwards they were known as Phoenicians. This period marks the beginning of the golden age of Phoenicia.

During the period between 1150 and 883 B.C. the Phoenician cities enjoyed independence. Tyre and Sidon and some other cities started up

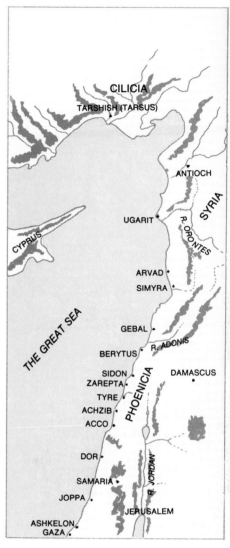

Phoenicia.

Phoenician red burnished pottery jugs and mask from Achzib.

their lively maritime trade and Phoenician colonies were founded along the Mediterranean coast, a process which culminated in the foundation of Carthage in about 814 B.C. At this period the Phoenician alphabetic script found its way to Greece. Trade expanded, and Hiram, king of Tyre, made a treaty with Solomon (I Kgs 5:12). Ties were still more closely knit when Ahab, king of Israel, married Jezebel, daughter of Ethbaal, king of Sidon (I Kgs 16:31).

During this period Assyria was gradually expanding towards the Mediterranean. Ashurnasirpal invaded Phoenicia in 883 B.C. and imposed a heavy tribute on Tyre, Sidon, Byblos and Arvad. During the remainder of the 8th and 7th centuries B.C. Phoenicia paid a heavy tribute to Assyria. Some Phoenician cities attempted from time to time to break the Assyrian yoke. One revolt instigated by a confederacy of Phoenician cities, under the leadership of Tyre, was severely crushed by Sennacherib. As a result Sidon was destroyed and its inhabitants were replaced by others who had been brought from far afield. Further revolts by the Phoenician cities were no more successful.

After the defeat of Assyria by the Babylonians and the Medes in 612 B.C. the Phoenician cities regained their independence, but after the defeat of Pharaoh Necho II, with whom the cities were allied in 605 B.C., Phoenicia was brought under direct Babylonian rule. Another revolt, in which Judah and Tyre took part, resulted in the destruction of Jerusalem and the capture of Tyre by Nebuchadnezzar. After the capture of Babylon by Cyrus in 539 B.C. Phoenicia became part of a Persian satrapy. At that time Sidon took the place of Tyre as its leading city. The large Phoenician navy took part in the wars of Darius and Xerxes against Greece.

Early in the 4th century B.C. Tyre, weary of the oppressive rule of the Persian satraps, joined the rebel Greek tyrant of Cyprus, while Tabnit, king of Sidon, rebelled later in the same century against the Persians. Artaxerxes III, king of Persia, besieged Sidon and set the city on fire. Many people, documents and works of art perished.

After the Battle of Issus in 333 B.C. the way was open for the conquest of Phoenicia by Alexander the Great. In 301 B.C., it was conquered by Ptolemy and annexed to Egypt. In 200 B.C. Antiochus III defeated Ptolemy V Epiphanes, and Phoenicia remained under Seleucid rule until the dissolution of their kingdom after the death of Antiochus IV Epiphanes.

By 112 B.C. all the Phoenician cities had regained their autonomy. In 64 B.C. Phoenicia was conquered by the Romans and turned by Pompey into a Roman province, although it retained full autonomy in internal affairs. Under Roman rule Phoenicia enjoyed no less prosperity than in former times. Glass-blowing was invented at Sidon, and brought additional wealth to the city. The arts and letters flourished both in Tyre and in Sidon. By the middle of the 1st century A.D. a Christian community was already in existence at Tyre.

PHOENIX A harbor on the island of Crete. The crew of the ship carrying Paul from Fair Havens, Cyprus, attempted, without success, to land at Phoenix in order to winter there (Acts 27:8-12). The harbor's precise location is uncertain, although Luke describes it as facing northwest and southwest (RSV, northeast and southeast). The western bay, though little used, is still known as Phinika. However, some scholars citing Strabo and Ptolemy, feel that ancient Phoenix lay on the east side of the island near modern Loutro, a harbor more suitable for large ships such as that which carried Paul.

PHOENIX
Acts 27:12

PHRYGIA A large district in central Asia Minor; a mountainous region, it lay in the western watershed of the great Anatolian plateau

PHRYGIA
Acts 2:10;
16:6; 18:23

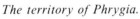
The territory of Phrygia.

THRACE

BITHYNIA

MYSIA

GALATIA

LYDIA

PHRYGIA

LYCAONIA

CARIA

PISIDIA

PAMPHYLIA

LYCIA

CYPRUS

and was best suited for grazing. From 116 B.C. most of the area was incorporated within the Roman imperial province of Asia; in 25 B.C. the eastern section, known as Phrygia Galatica, was included within the province of Galatia. Its major cities included Laodicea, Hierapolis and Colossae; the Phrygian cities of Pisidian Antioch and Iconium were located in Phrygia Galatica. The Phrygians were a European race who migrated from Thrace to Asia Minor c. 1200 B.C., displacing the Hittites wherever they settled. They are associated in Homer's *Iliad* with the Trojans to whom they were related.

Jews from Phrygia visited Jerusalem during the feast of Pentecost (Acts 2:1, 10) and Paul passed through Phrygia on all three of his missionary journeys (Acts chaps. 13-14; 16:6; 18:23). Having been forbidden by the Spirit to preach the gospel in the province of Asia (Acts 16:6-7), he did not personally found any churches in Phrygia, the churches in Colossae and Laodicea referred to in Colossians 2:1 must have had an origin independent of Paul's ministry. Epaphras and Archippus, members of the Ephesian church, are mentioned in Colossians chapter 4 and it has been suggested that these churches were founded as a result of zealous missionary activity by the church at Ephesus. John and Philip were also traditionally associated with these churches.

Phylactery found in one of the Qumram Caves in the Dead Sea region, dating from the 1st century A.D.

(top of page)
Façade of an unfinished monument in Midas City, which is, according to legend, the tomb of the mythological king Midas of Phrygia.

PHYGELLUS One of the Christians of Asia who turned away from Paul when the apostle was imprisoned in Rome.

PHYLACTERIES ("safeguard, amulet"). Called *tefillin* in Aramaic and Hebrew. Two black leather boxes, containing scriptural passages (Ex 13:1-16; Deut 6:4-9; 11:13-21), bound on the left arm and on the head by black leather straps, and worn for the morning services on all days of the year except Sabbaths and holidays by observant Jews. The scriptural basis for the custom is found in Exodus 13:9, 16; Deuteronomy 6:8; 11:18.

PI BESETH A city in the Delta of Egypt, mentioned in Ezekiel 30:17; its Egyptian name was *P(r)-bast(t)*, meaning "the city of the goddess Bast(t)" (*Boubastos* in Greek). Pi Beseth was in the 18th district of Lower Egypt, identified with Tell Basteh in the Delta, northeast of Zagazig.

Its history goes back to the Old Kingdom. The pharaohs of the 18th Dynasty built monuments in the city, which reached the peak of its importance when Shishak I, the founder of the 22nd Libyan Dynasty, made it his capital. Pi Beseth was also the capital of the 23rd Dynasty, and flourished greatly in the years 950-750 B.C. The city fell to ruin after being conquered by the Persians in 350 B.C.

As implied by its name, Pi Beseth was the center of the cult of the goddess Bastet, portrayed as a woman with a lioness' head.

PIGEON See ANIMALS

PI HAHIROTH One of the stations of the Children of Israel on the route of the Exodus, between Migdol and Baal Zephon (Ex 14:2, 9; Num 33:7-8). The numerous identifications suggested for this place are far from convincing. The main difficulty in identifying Pi Hahiroth lies in the fact that no Egyptian document mentions a place name resembling that given in the Bible.

PILATE See PONTIUS

PILDASH Sixth son of Abraham's brother Nahor, by his wife Milcah.

PILGRIM FESTIVALS Three festivals required a pilgrimage to the Temple in Jerusalem: the Feast of Passover, the Feast of Weeks (Pentecost), and the Feast of Tabernacles (Ex 23:14-17).

The obligation fell on all males, who were enjoined not to appear empty-handed but to bring, each according to his own means (Deut

A pilgrim's ship of the early 4th century A.D. painted on the wall of a chapel below the Holy Sepulcher with the Latin inscription Domine ivimus *(The Lord we went).*

16:16-17). The pilgrims brought a sacrifice as well as the second tithe of their produce which was to be eaten in Jerusalem.

In the period of the Judges, the pilgrimage was made to Shiloh (I Sam 1:3); following the building of the Temple, it centered on Jerusalem (I Kgs 8:65; II Chr 7:8-9). After the Babylonian Exile, the custom was reintroduced by Nehemiah on the occasion of the Feast of Tabernacles (Neh 8:13-18). Tabernacles was the most widely attended pilgrim festival because it fell at a season when the farmer was relieved of his work in the fields and freer to travel than on the other two occasions.

The NT records how Jesus journeyed to Jerusalem to observe pilgrim festivals in the Temple (John 2:23; 7:2-37); his last fateful pilgrimage to Jerusalem was to celebrate the Passover (Matt 26:17; Mark 14:12; Luke 22:8; John 13:1).

See PASSOVER; PENTECOST; TABERNACLES.

PILHA ("millstone"). One of those who sealed the covenant of Ezra at the time of Nehemiah.

PILHA
Neh 10:24

PILLAR OF CLOUD AND PILLAR OF FIRE The presence of God accompanying and protecting the Israelites throughout their 40-year desert wanderings, up until the time they entered the land of Canaan, was symbolized by a pillar of cloud during the day and a pillar of fire at night (Ex 13:21-22; 14:19, 24). On one occasion the pillar of cloud moved from before the camp to its rear to protect the Israelites from the attacking Egyptians (Ex 14:19-20). The pillar of cloud also descended upon the tent of meeting when Moses entered to converse with God (Ex 33:9-10; Num 11:25; 12:5). According to another tradition, the tabernacle was covered at all times by a cloud (and not a pillar) which took on a fiery appearance at night. It only lifted as a sign to Israel to break camp and continue on to their next station (Ex 40:34-38; Num 9:15-23; 10:11-12, 34; 14:14). A cloud also descended upon the Temple of Solomon symbolizing the presence of God (I Kgs 8:10-11). The origin of both the cloud and fire can be traced back to the revelation at Sinai when the appearance of God was accompanied by cloud, thunder and lightning, and fire (Ex 19:9). All these manifestations are also found in the descriptions of theophanies of gods in the literature of the ancient Near East.

PILTAI ("[God is] deliverance"). Son of Moadiah; one of the priests who returned from the Babylonian Exile with Zerubbabel.

PILTAI
Neh 12:17

PINE See PLANTS

PINON A chief of Esau, prince in Edom.

PINON
Gen 36:41. I Chr 1:52

PIRAM King of Jarmuth, and one of the five Amorite kings defeated by Joshua at Gibeon (Josh 10:3, 5, 9, 11).

PIRAM
Josh 10:3

PIRATHON, PIRATHONITE The birthplace and burial place of Judge Abdon, son of Hillel, in the land of Ephraim, in the mount of the Amalekites (Judg 12:14-15); the home town of Benaiah, one of David's "mighty men" (II Sam 23:30). Identified with the Arab village of Farata, southwest of Shechem.

PIRATHON, PIRATHONITE
Judg 12:13, 15. II Sam 23:30. I Chr 11:31; 27:14

PISGAH The highest part of the mountains of Abarim, close to the northeastern shore of the Dead Sea (Deut 3:27; 32:49; 34:1), with a view

PISGAH
Num 21:20; 23:14. Deut 3:17, 27; 4:49; 34:1. Josh 12:3; 13:20

The mountains of Abarim in Moab one of which is thought to be Pisgah.

over the wilderness (Num 21:20). On the field of Zophim, at the top of the Pisgah, Balak met Balaam (Num 23:14). From the peak of Pisgah, called Nebo, Moses saw a great part of the land of Canaan before his death (Deut 3:27; 34:1-4). Pisgah was the southern border of the land of Sihon, king of the Amorites (Josh 12:2-3). It is identified with Ras Siyagha, west of Mount Nebo.

PISHON The first of the four rivers of the Garden of Eden which "encompasses the whole land of Havilah, where there is gold" (Gen 2:11). Two of the four rivers, the Hiddekel (Tigris) and the Euphrates, have been identified, but the location of the other two is unknown. In the Table of Nations (Gen 10:7) Havilah is one of the sons of Cush, and for this reason the Gihon has been identified with the White Nile, and the Pishon with the Blue Nile. Others identified the Pishon with one of the other rivers of Mesopotamia. Still others have suggested identifying Havilah with India and the Pishon with either the Indus or the Ganges. As the same Table of Nations lists Havilah (Gen 10:29) among the sons of Jokthan, the Pishon was also sought in Southern Arabia. None of these identifications is well founded.

PISIDIA A district in the western Taurus Mountains of Asia Minor which bordered Pamphylia on the south, Lycaonia on the east and north, and Lycia and Caria or Phrygia on the west. This mountainous highland area, 120 miles (190 km) long by 50 miles (80 km) wide, was populated by outlaws and brigands who posed a constant threat to travelers and occupying armies from early times. The Persian and Hellenistic overlords of Pisidia were unable to subdue these mountain tribes. Antioch of Pisidia (See ANTIOCH No.1) (which lay in the district of Phrygia on the border of Pisidia and Phrygia) was founded by the Seleucid kings in order to stabilize the region. Augustus incorporated the area into the heavily occupied province of Galatia.

Paul, who passed through the dangerous area on his first missionary journey (Acts 13:14; 14:24), did not venture into the interior, only founding a church at the border city of Antioch. II Corinthians 11:26 which speaks of "perils of robbers...perils in the wilderness" may refer to this area. Christianity apparently made little impact in Pisidia in the 1st century.

PISPAH Second son of Jether, a man of Asher.

PISTACHIO See PLANTS

PITHOM A city in the land of Goshen in Egypt. The meaning of the name is "the house of the god Atum". Goshen was one of the treasure cities built for Pharaoh by the Children of Israel (Ex 1:11). It has been identified with Tell Mashute, at the western end of Wadi Thumeilat, where a temple of Atum was discovered. Although inscriptions of the times of the 1st and 6th Dynasties were found there, the city and its fortifications are not earlier than the days of Rameses II, when the Israelites built Pithom. Some of the structures found there were identified by the excavators as storehouses that might have been built by the Israelites. Some scholars suggest identifying Pithom with Tell er-Retabeh, 10 miles (16 km) west of Maskhute, where another temple of Atum was discovered.

PITHON Firstborn son of Micah, grandson of Jonathan, in the genealogy of King Saul of Benjamin.

PLAGUES, THE TEN Disasters inflicted by God on Pharaoh to persuade him to allow the Israelites to leave Egypt. The number of plagues in the account in Exodus is set at ten. 1. Blood (Ex 7:14-25): At the wave of Aaron's staff, the waters of the Nile and all the lesser bodies of water throughout Egypt are turned to blood. The Egyptians, in their thirst, dig around the Nile, searching for unbloodied water, and find

PISHON
Gen 2:11

PISIDIA
Acts 13:14;
14:24

PISPAH
I Chr 7:38

PITHOM
Ex 1:11

PITHON
I Chr 8:35;
9:41

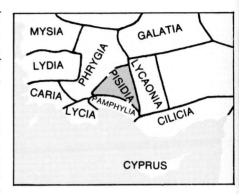

Pisidia in Asia Minor.

none. 2. Frogs (Ex 8:1-15): Aaron waves his staff and the Nile and its tributaries bring forth great swarms of frogs, so numerous that they "covered the land of Egypt", infesting the houses and persons of all the Egyptians. 3. Lice (Ex 8:16-19): Aaron strikes the ground with his staff, and the dust becomes lice, again infesting the entire land. 4. "Swarms" (Ex 8:20-32): The houses of Pharaoh and all of Egypt are infested with "swarms", generally taken to be a "mixture of wild beasts", alternatively — more likely, perhaps — swarms of flies. 5. Pestilence (Ex 9:1-7): God's hand afflicts all the Egyptian livestock with a deadly pestilence, decimating its numbers. 6. Boils (Ex 9:8-12): At God's command, Moses and Aaron throw handfuls of soot heavenward, which, when it settles, sets off a skin inflammation, infecting man and beast. 7. Hail (Ex 9:13-35): Moses calls down a hailstorm, accompanied by thunder and fire, which utterly destroys fields and crops, and kills all living things, man or beast, that fail to take cover. 8. Locusts (Ex 10:1-20): At a wave of Moses' staff, the east wind brings swarms of locusts, covering, indeed darkening, Egypt. What little vegetation was left untouched by the hail is consumed. 9. Darkness (Ex 10:21-29): Moses raises his hands, and a thick darkness descends, blackening Egypt for three days. 10. Death of the Firstborn (Ex chaps. 11-12), when all firstborn Egyptian males die.

The first nine plagues are grouped in threes: The first plague of each triad begins with God instructing Moses to warn Pharaoh at the Nile (Ex 7:15ff; 8:20ff; 9:13ff); the second begins with the command to confront Pharaoh in his palace (Ex 8:1ff; 9:1ff; 10:1ff); the final plague of each group is brought on unannounced. The tenth plague is climactic. A pattern of increasing severity can be detected in the plagues. The first several are distressing nuisances; the later plagues are fatal. The plagues are rooted in natural phenomena: the reddening of the Nile; the swarms of frogs and other creatures; hail — all are attested occurrences. The supernatural is to be seen in their dimensions (three days' darkness, swarms throughout Egypt; the death of all the livestock); their rapid succession; their arrival, and disappearance, at the prophet's command and their being confined to the Egyptians, never harming a single Israelite. The tenth plague alone is entirely outside the sphere of the natural, and can be understood only as the act of God himself, personally traversing the land of Egypt (Ex 11:4; 12:12). This plague finally brings Pharaoh to his knees.

On one level, the plagues are an attempt to inflict on Pharaoh enough suffering to coerce him into acceding to Moses' demand. Since that demand had been disguised as a request for a "three-days' journey" for the purpose of sacrificing to God (Ex 3:18; 5:1 etc.), it would appear that the plagues are also a last resort, inflicted only after Pharaoh has callously refused a reasonable request. Without Pharaoh's permission, the Israelites cannot leave Egypt; when he has had more than he can endure, he will finally yield.

The cause of Pharaoh's unrelenting obduracy, the narrative asserts, is God himself: "I will harden his heart", says God to Moses "so that he will not let the people go" (Ex 4:21). His purpose therein is in order that "I may multiply my signs and my wonders in the land of Egypt" (Ex 7:3; 11:9). God desires to exert and display his might and thus to proclaim his lordship. "The Egyptians shall know that I am the Lord, when I stretch forth my hand on Egypt" (Ex 7:5, etc.). Were not this the divine aim, Moses informs Pharaoh (Ex 9:16), God could have simply destroyed Pharaoh at any point and spared himself the trouble of further struggle.

God's action is thus first of all a response to Pharaoh's taunt "Who is the Lord, that I should obey His voice to let Israel go? I do not know the Lord, nor will I let Israel go." (Ex 5:2). Since Pharaoh's refusal stems from his failure to acknowledge the Lord, he must first be brought to know him; then he will let Israel go. But God's hardening of Pharaoh's heart, and the resultant barrage of signs and wonders, are equally a lesson for the Israelites: "and that you may tell in the hearing of your son and your son's son the mighty things I have done in Egypt, and my signs which I have done among them, that you may know that I am the Lord." (Ex 10:2). Bringing Pharaoh to recognize God is of temporary, functional importance; for the Israelites, on the other hand, the multiplicity and severity of the plagues are designed to provide an object lesson for all time.

This latter aim was achieved, as witnessed by the impression made by the plagues on biblical thought, and indicated by numerous other passages. Seldom is the Exodus mentioned without reference to God's strength of hand (Ex 13:3, 14, 16), great strength (Ex 32:11; Deut 9:29; see Num 14:13; Neh 1:10), strong hand and outstretched arm (frequently in Deut, Kgs and Jer), signs and wonders (Deut 4:34 etc.; Ps 135:9). Psalms 78:44-51 and 105:28-36 each contain lyric recollections of the plagues, the former as part of an exhortation not to forget God's favors, the latter as part of a hymn of praise recounting God's wondrous deeds. The psalms differ from each other, and from the prose account in Exodus, in their enumerations of the plagues, their number, their order and their effects, reflecting poetic license or variant traditions (or both), and bearing testimony to the richness of the tradition concerning God's archetypal manifestation of his strength.

PLAIN, THE (SHEPHELAH). The Plain, or lowland, *Shephelah* in Hebrew, is one of the geographical regions of Palestine frequently mentioned in the Bible (Deut 1:7; Josh 9:1; AV: "valleys"; 10:40; AV: "vale", etc.). It is an intermediate region between the higher mountains to the east and the coastal plain to the west. The Plain is a region of low hills 1,000-1,200 feet (305-365m) high. As a geographical term it is usually applied to the south of the country, adjoining the Judean Hills, bordering on the Sharon in the north and the Negeb in the south. A distinction is made in the Bible between this and the northern plain: "the mountain of Israel, and the valley of the same" (Josh 11:16). The conquest of the cities of the Plain is referred to in Joshua chapter 10. It was an area rich in olives and sycamores (I Kgs 10:27; I Chr 27:28). In the Hellenistic and Roman periods the name Sephela was applied to the region between Lod and Beth Gubrin (I Macc 12:38).

PLAIN
Deut 1:7. Josh 9:1; 10:40; 11:2, 16; 12:8; 15:33. Judg 1:9, 19. I Kgs 10:27. I Chr 27:28. II Chr 1:15; 9:27; 26:10; 28:18. Jer 17:26; 32:44; 33:13. Obad v. 19. Zech 7:7

The Plain in the region of Lod.

Acacia

Almonds in their shells

Aloes

PLANTS
**See end of
book**

PLANTS Given below in alphabetical order are the plants mentioned in the Bible. It is to be noted that translators differ as to the precise identification of some of them.

ACACIA Called *shittah* in Hebrew, the word given as acacia in the English Bible is identified with several species of this tree growing in Palestine. The most common species found today in the Sinai Peninsula is a thorny tree with yellow flowers. Its trunk is generally thin and this makes it difficult to identify it with the acacia of the Bible from which the wide boards of the tabernacle were made (Ex 26:16).

The acacia tree and its wood are mentioned almost exclusively in connection with the ark of the testimony, the altar and the tabernacle built by the Children of Israel (Ex 25:10, 13; 26:15; 36:20; 38:1, 6 etc.).

Several biblical place-names reflect the Hebrew name of the tree e.g., Abel Shittim, Beth Shittah and Beth Shittim, probably areas where the acacia was especially abundant. According to Isaiah 41:19 the acacia growing in the wilderness is part of God's promise to the Israelites.

ALMOND A tree common to the Near East, growing wild or cultivated in most Mediterranean countries. Its pink-white flowers, arranged in pairs, appear before the leaves, as early as January or the beginning of February. The almond fruit has an oblong shape, rounded at one end and pointed at the other, and has always been considered a delicacy. The kernel produces oil.

When Joseph's brothers returned to Egypt with Benjamin, their father Jacob included almonds among the gifts he sent with them (Gen 43:11). The cup of the branches of the gold lampstand of the tabernacle was designed like almond blossoms (Ex 25:33-34; 37:19-20). Aaron's rod was an almond-tree branch which miraculously blossomed overnight to yield ripe almonds (Num 17:23). In Ecclesiastes the white head of old men is compared to the blossoming almond tree (Ecc 12:5).

ALMUG A special kind of wood supplied to Solomon by Hiram of Tyre for the construction of the Temple. It was also used to make musical instruments (I Kgs 10:11-12). The almug wood imported from Ophir, has generally been thought to refer to sandalwood.

ALOES See SPICES AND PERFUMES

ANISE A plant of the parsley family which is cultivated for its seedlike fruits. Anise is mentioned in Matthew 23:23 as one of the plants for which the Pharisees were very punctilious in paying tithes while they failed, however, to observe moral values. Many scholars believe that anise here refers to dill.

APPLE The apple mentioned in the Bible has not been identified with certainty. The apple tree is described as a shady tree bearing fruit sweet to the taste; it is referred to poetically for its fragrance and beauty (Prov 25:11; Song 2:3, 5; 7:8; 8:5). In art and in later literature, the tree of knowledge in Genesis was interpreted as referring to the apple tree, but it is not identified as such in the Bible.

BALM See SPICES AND PERFUMES

BALSAM See SPICES AND PERFUMES

BARLEY An annual grain closely related to wheat and a most important source of food for man and beast. It was sown in outlying areas where wheat could not be cultivated. Barley is mentioned together with wheat and other field crops, among which it occupies a prominent place (Deut 8:8; Is 28:25; Ezek 4:9; Joel 1:11, etc.). Listed among the seven kinds of agricultural produce with which Israel was blessed (Deut 8:8), barley was one of the country's exports (II Chr 2:15); it also served as a cereal offering (Num 5:15; Ezek 45:13).

Barley ripens early (Ex 9:31) and its harvest begins in the month of Nisan (March-April), the *omer* ("sheaf") firstfruit offering being taken from the barley field on the day following the first Sabbath after Passover (Lev 23:9 ff). In Ruth 1:22 and II Samuel 21:9, the barley harvest serves as an agricultural time marker, as in the Gezer calendar.

Bread made from barley, poorer in quality and taste than wheat, was considered poor man's bread, and II Kings 7:1, 16, 18 puts its price at half that of wheat (cf Rev 6:6). Barley was used as fodder (I Kgs 4:28). Several of these OT characteristics of barley are recalled in John 6:1-14 where five barley loaves and two fish fed the 5,000.

BEANS A nutritious food grown in pods from a leguminous plant. Beans are mentioned twice in the Bible: along with other foods they were brought to David at Mahanaim during Absalom's revolt (II Sam 17:28), while in Ezekiel's portrayal of the siege of Jerusalem, beans are used as an ingredient for bread.

Dried broad beans

BITTER HERBS Bitter herbs were eaten along with the paschal lamb prior to the Exodus of the Israelites from Egypt (Ex 12:8; Num 9:11). In later rabbinic literature they were interpreted as a symbolic reminder of the bitter times that the Israelites had during their long period of bondage and slavery. The Hebrew noun most probably refers to a variety of different herbs.

BRIAR, BRIER, BRAMBLE Any of several wild prickly plants. A number of different Hebrew words are variously translated as briar, thorn and bramble since the plants they refer to have not been identified exactly. The briar symbolizes that which is worthless or evil (Mic 7:4), and is used figuratively of the enemies of Israel (Ezek 28:24) and the land (Is 5:6; 7:23-25; 55:13).

BROOM A shrub which grows in the desert. Elijah sheltered in its shade (I Kgs 19:4-5). The broom's roots and foliage were employed for fuel (Ps 120:4) and food (Job 30:4). Some translations render "juniper" rather than broom.

BULRUSH Common name for several kinds of tall grass growing by the water, used to translate two different Hebrew words and sometimes given as "reed". In at least one instance (the story of the infant Moses, Exodus 2:3), it has been suggested that it refers to the cyprus papyrus, the celebrated papyrus tree of Egypt, now almost extinct.

White broom

Cedar

CALAMUS See SPICES AND PERFUMES

CANE See SPICES AND PERFUMES

CAROB See PODS below

CASSIA See SPICES AND PERFUMES

CEDAR Tree of the pine family indigenous to Lebanon. The cedar tree is mentioned some 75 times in the OT. It was used in various religious ceremonies together with hyssop and scarlet (for the cleansing of lepers and their houses Lev 14:4, 6, 49, 51-52; and for the laws of purification Num 19:6). Cedar wood was imported to build Solomon's Temple (I Kgs 5:6; 6:9, 15-16, 18, 20, 36), being used in the supporting pillars and beams (I Kgs 7:2) and paneling (I Kgs 6:9, 15) and was "carved with ornamental buds and open flowers" (I Kgs 6:18). One of Solomon's buildings was called the House of the Forest of Lebanon because of its three rows of 15 cedar pillars (I Kgs 7:2-5).

Cedars were a symbol of strength and beauty and as such are used to demonstrate the power of the Lord: "The voice of the Lord breaks the cedars, yes the Lord splinters the cedars of Lebanon" (Ps 29:5; cf Is 2:13; Zech 11:1).

CHESTNUT A tree mentioned twice in the OT — first in the episode of Jacob and the spotted sheep (Gen 30:25-43) and then in Ezekiel, where the "chestnut trees" are compared to the greatness of Assyria (Ezek 31:3-8). Many scholars believe both references denote the plane tree, since chestnut trees are not indigenous to the area.

Cumin

Fig

Fig tree

CINNAMON See SPICES AND PERFUMES

CITRON WOOD One of the items mentioned in the prophecy of the fall of Babylon in Revelation 18:12; it was highly valued in biblical times for cabinet making.

CORIANDER A plant of the umbelliferous family, yielding small, globular seeds with an aromatic flavor. It is mentioned twice in the OT, in both cases to describe manna.

CUCUMBER This very common vegetable is mentioned twice in the Scriptures. While roaming the wilderness of Sinai, the Children of Israel recalled Egypt and the melons, leeks, onions, garlic and cucumbers they had eaten there (Num 11:5). In Isaiah's vision of a desolate Jerusalem he compares the city to a hut in a cucumber field (Is 1:8).

CUMIN, CUMMIN A caraway-like seed, commonly cultivated and used as spice and medicine. It is only mentioned once in the OT, when the prophet Isaiah, expounding on the teaching of the Lord, gives a detailed description of the planting and threshing of the cumin (Is 28:25, 27). In the NT, Matthew refers to it in his condemnation of the Pharisees "who pay tithe of mint and anise and cumin and have neglected the weightier matters of the law" (Matt 23:23).

CYPRESS Several different Hebrew words are rendered as cypress in the NKJV (RSV: "pine"); an evergreen coniferous tree with dark overlapping leaves. Hiram king of Tyre sent King Solomon cypress logs for the Temple (I Kgs 5:8, 10; 6:15, 34; II Chr 3:5). Isaiah prophesied that God would cut down the cedars of Lebanon in order to punish Sennacherib king of Assyria (II Kgs 19:23), and Babylon (Is 14:8). He reassured the Israelites of God's promise to protect the Children of Israel: the cypress tree will grow in the desert (Is 41:19) and "instead of the thorn shall come up the cypress tree" (Is 55:13; cf 60:13).

DILL See ANISE above

FIG A fruit-bearing tree indigenous to Palestine. It was the first tree referred to in the OT: "Then the eyes of both of them [Adam and Eve] were opened, and they knew that they were naked, and they sewed fig leaves together and made themselves coverings" (Gen 3:7). It is listed among the seven species with which the land of Canaan was blessed (Deut 8:8). Figs were used to make cakes (I Sam 25:18) and had curative properties: a poultice of figs was used to relieve King Hezekiah's sores (Is 38:21). It was also a symbol of peace and prosperity (I Kgs 4:25; II Kgs 18:31; Is 36:16; Joel 2:22; Mic 4:4; Hag 2:19; Zech 3:10), as well as fertility and as such was used by Jesus in one of his parables (Luke 13:6-9). It appears in Jotham's fable of the trees (Judg 9:7-15) in Jeremiah's parable about the exiles (Jer chap. 24) and in the story of Jesus cursing the fig tree (Matt 21:18-22; Mark 11:13-14, 20-24).

FLAX The oldest textile plant of the Near East, flax and its products were of great importance to the ancient world. The earliest biblical references are to the Egyptian crop that was destroyed by the plague of hail (Ex 9:31), and the drying stalks that provided a protective covering for the two spies on Rahab's Jericho rooftop (Josh 2:6). The combed fibers were used for lamp wicks (Is 42:3; 43:17), ropes (Ezek 40:3) and woven linen (Jer 13:1; Ezek 44:17-18; Prov 31:13). One of the qualities of the exemplary wife described in Proverbs 31:13 is that she looks for wool and flax and works with them with willing hands. Promiscuous Israel, in the image of a harlot, is said to have received her wool and her linen from her paramours; God will later take them away from her (Hos 2:5, 9).

The blue flowered plant, which grows to a height of 2 to 3 feet (c. 1m), is pulled from the ground when its seeds are ripe. The stalks are dried and its fibers combed while linseed oil is extracted from the shiny seeds.

FRANKINCENSE See INCENSE; SPICES AND PERFUMES
GALBANUM See SPICES AND PERFUMES
GALL A poisonous and bitter herb used to signify bitterness and misfortune (Ps 69:21; Jer 8:14); and often mentioned together with wormwood in this context (Lam 3:19; Amos 6:12). In the Song of Moses those who rebel against the word of God are condemned: "their grapes are grapes of gall".
GARLIC A bulbed vegetable. The pungent garlic was among the foods the Israelites craved for after the Exodus from Egypt (Num 11:5-6).
GOPHER WOOD Mentioned only once in the Bible as the material from which God instructed Noah to build the ark. A possible identification with the conifer or cypress has been suggested.
GRAPE, GRAPEVINE See VINE, VINEYARD
GOURDS In Hebrew, the distinction is made between the feminine plural (*pakka'ot*) and the masculine plural (*pakka'im*). The former is mentioned only once, in II Kings 4:39 as a wild, poisonous fruit that was added to a pot of stew during a time of famine. The stew was rendered edible by the prophet Elisha (II Kgs 4:38-41). It is believed that this strain of gourd might have been of the colocynth plant, a relative of the watermelon. The latter, translated as "ornamental buds", decorated the cedar paneling in Solomon's Temple (I Kgs 6:18). The plant, translated as "gourd" by the AV in Jonah 4:6ff, is in fact the castor.
HEMLOCK A poisonous plant. The name occurs only once in the Scriptures: "Thus judgment springs up like hemlock in the furrows of the field" (Hos 10:4). It may refer, however, to the wild poppy.
HENNA See SPICES AND PERFUMES
HYSSOP A small, strongly aromatic shrub which grows between cliffs and rocks; it has been identified with Majoraner Syriaca, a plant of the Labiatae family.

Hyssop is referred to in the Book of Exodus where, the Israelites, in order to distinguish themselves from the Egyptians, used the shrub to smear blood on their doorposts: when God plagued the Egyptians, the marked houses of the Israelites were left unharmed (Ex 12:22).

Other biblical references mention the hyssop together with the cedar. The Bible describes King Solomon, the wisest of all men as one who knew everything from "the cedar tree of Lebanon to the hyssop that springs out of the wall" (I Kgs 4:33). Both hyssop and cedar were used in preparing the ashes of the red heifer (Num 19:6) and in the sprinkling of water of purification (Num 19:18). Both were also employed in a house plagued by leprosy (Lev 14:49) and in the water of purification for the leper (Lev 14:4).

Psalms (51:7) contains another reference to the symbolic use of hyssop in a purification ceremony. According to Hebrews 9:19 hyssop was sprinkled over the people at the sealing of the covenant at Sinai. Hyssop with sour wine was sprinkled on Jesus while he was on the cross (John 19:29).
JUNIPER A low-growing tree found in the Sinai and the desert of Edom, called *aroer* in Hebrew. The Moabite city Aroer might have been named after this tree (cf Jer 48:6). The "shrub in the desert" mentioned in Jeremiah 17:6 is thought by some scholars to refer to the juniper.

It is to be noted that in the AV a different Hebrew word is translated as juniper, while the RSV gives "wild ass" for *aroer* in Jeremiah 48:6.
LEEK Vegetable of the onion family, which was craved for by the Israelites in the wilderness following the Exodus from Egypt.
LENTIL A legume, reddish-brown in color. Esau traded his birthright for a pot of lentil stew prepared by his twin brother, Jacob, and thus received his epithet *edom* ("red", Gen 25:29-34). Lentils were among the

Garlic

Hyssop (Marjoram)

Juniper

From left to right:
Almond tree
Almug/algum
Apple Blossom

From left to right:
Anise
Balm
Barley

From left to right:
Ripe barley
Broad bean blossom
Briar

From left to right:
Calamus
Citron
Cumin

From left to right:
Coriander
Flax
Garlic

From left to right:
Gourds
Hemlock (gall)
leeks

From left to right:
Lentils
Lily
Mallow

From left to right:
Mandrake
Common millet
Millet (sorghum)

From left to right:
Mint
Mulberry
Mustard

From left to right:
Myrrh
Nettle
Acorn

From left to right:
Oak tree
Olive tree
Onions

From left to right:
Palm dates
Pine tree
Pistachio

From left to right:
Pistachio nuts
Plane tree
Pods (Carob)

From left to right:
White poplar
Reeds
Rue

From left to right:
Saffron
Tamarisk
Thistles

From left to right:
Thorns
Weeds
Willow

Wild tulip (may refer to the lily)

Mandrake

Watermelon

food delivered to David at Mahanaim (II Sam 17:27-29), and Ezekiel made a bread of lentils and other grains when he simulated the siege of Jerusalem (Ezek 4:9).

LILY The word lily may refer to any one of several different flowers, among them, the narcissus, wild tulip, crocus and anemone. The capitals of the two pillars Jachin and Boaz, in Solomon's Temple were in the form of a lily (I Kgs 7:19, 22) as was the rim of the molten sea (I Kgs 7:26; II Chr 4:5). The "lily of the valleys" is referred to in Song of Solomon 2:1 (cf Song 6:11) and the lily is mentioned several other times in these love poems (Song 2:2, 16; 4:5; 5:13; 6:2-3; 7:2). In Hosea's image of the restoration of Israel, the nation will blossom as a lily (Hos 14:5).

The lily was a symbol of beauty, and, as such, was employed in the imagery of Jesus: "Consider the lilies of the field, how they grow: they neither toil nor spin; and yet I say to you that even Solomon in all his glory was not arrayed like one of these" (Matt 6:28-29; cf Luke 12:27).

LOTUS A thorny shrub or tree with small oval leaves, which is found in dry places. The word lotus occurs twice, but its identification is disputed and "lotus" may refer to the lily.

MALLOW This plant which has been identified as the shrubby orache, grows in the salt marshes of the Dead Sea and the Mediterranean. "Sons of vile men", who were "gaunt from want and famine" (Job 30:3-4, 8) ate from the mallow plant.

MANDRAKE A stemless perennial herb with a thick, branched taproot, blue or white winter flowers, and edible, plum-shaped orange-red springtime fruit. The fragrant plant (Song 7:13) has purgative, narcotic and emetic qualities, and was employed as an aphrodisiac and fertility aid from early times. This explains why the barren Rachel made an exchange with Leah for some mandrakes collected by Reuben (Gen 30:14-16).

MANNA See article MANNA

MELON A fruit mentioned only once in the OT. It was indigenous to Egypt: when the Children of Israel were suffering from hunger in the wilderness of Sinai they recalled the good foods, among them melons, which they had eaten in Egypt.

MILLET A grass seed cultivated for making a poor quality of bread. Ezekiel used millet seeds along with other grains to make a bread which symbolized the siege of Jerusalem (Ezek 4:9). Millet is also mentioned as an item of trade between Judah and Israel and Tyre in Ezekiel's lamentation for Tyre (Ezek 27:17).

MINT A sweet-smelling herb whose leaves and stems contain an aromatic oil employed for medicinal and food-seasoning purposes. The name occurs only twice in the NT in connection with the tithe on various plants (Matt 23:23; Luke 11:42).

MULBERRY Growing to a height of 20 feet (6m), the black mulberry tree, common in Israel, has a large crown, large lobed leaves, and produces a sweet, fleshy fruit. Jesus mentioned the mulberry tree in a parable on faith (Luke 17:6; sycamine in some editions).

The tree mentioned in II Samuel 5:23-24 and I Chronicles 14:14-15, is usually translated as mulberry, but the identification is still not exactly known.

MUSTARD In parables concerning the Kingdom of God and faith, Jesus drew upon the mustard plant, "which, when it is sown on the ground, is smaller than all the seeds on earth; but when it is sown, it grows up and becomes greater than all herbs, and shoots out large branches" (Mark 4:31-32). The black mustard is the most common of the several varieties found in the Near East; it grows rapidly, up to 15 feet (c. 5m) in height.

MYRRH See SPICES AND PERFUMES

MYRTLE An aromatic evergreen shrub. Myrtle branches were among the greenery covering the booths during the festival of Tabernacles (Neh 8:15), and its ceremonial use remains incorporated within the holiday as one of the "four species" (along with the willow branches, palm leaf and ethrog). In Isaiah's prophecy of future restoration "the myrtle and the oil tree" will flourish in the desert (Is 41:19) and "instead of the brier shall come up the myrtle tree" (Is 55:13). Zechariah, in one of his visions, sees "the angel of the Lord, who stood among the myrtle trees" (Zech 1:11). The original name of Queen Esther was Hadassah, which is the feminine form of the Hebrew word for myrtle (Est 2:7).

NETTLE Two different Hebrew words are used to refer to this wild plant, known for its covering of stinging hairs, which release a toxic liquid upon contact. One is thought to be wild mustard, while the other is accepted specifically as nettle. Both are used to describe scenes of neglect and poverty; the passages in Isaiah and Hosea highlight destruction as well.

Myrtle

NUT When Jacob's sons went down to Egypt a second time, Jacob told them to take a present of "some of the best fruits of the land" for the Egyptian governor who, unknown to them, was their brother Joseph (Gen 43:11). Included with the gift of balm, honey, spices and myrrh were pistachio nuts and almonds. The tree from which pistachio nuts grow is found in the rocky areas of Palestine and Syria. The "garden of nuts" mentioned in the Song of Solomon was probably a plantation of walnuts.

OAK A tree noted for its size and strength. The Amorite "was as strong as the oaks" (Amos 2:9). In Isaiah 6:13, the future remnant of Judah is compared to the stump of an oak tree. Idol worship was common in oak groves (Ezek 6:13), and Hosea charged the Children of Israel with burning incense under oak trees (Hos 4:13).

OLIVE An evergreen tree, which grows in all lands bordering the Mediterranean Sea. In Deuteronomy 8:8 the olive is listed as one of the seven plants characteristic of the promised land (cf Deut 6:11; 28:40). The olive tree is regarded in the Bible as a thing of beauty (Hos 14:6); hence Israel is personified as a leafy olive tree, beautiful with ripe fruit (Jer 11:16). The simile, "Your children like olive plants all around your table" (Ps 128:3), is based upon the observation that shoots springing from the roots of the olive tree protect the parent tree and, like children, survive the demise of the parent. In the Book of Job the death of the wicked is compared to the olive tree, which casts off "his blossom" in the spring (Job 15:33). The return of the dove to Noah's ark bearing in her mouth an olive branch (Gen 8:11) suggests the renewal of life after the deluge. This image then came to symbolize peace. According to Nehemiah 8:15 olive branches were among the species used in building the festival booths on the Feast of Tabernacles in the time of Ezra.

Olives

Walnuts in their shells

The most characteristic function of the olive in the biblical era was the extraction of oil from its ripe fruit. This oil was burnt for illumination (Ex 25:6; 27:20; Lev 24:2), and employed in cosmetics and anointing (Ex 30:25). It was an ingredient in food for human consumption and in certain obligatory (Ex 29:40; Num 28:5) and free-will offerings to the Lord (Lev 2:1-7). The finest grade of olive oil, called "pressed oil", was a major Israelite export from the reign of King Solomon (I Kgs 5:11; II Chr 2:14-15; Ezra 3:7; Hos 12:1).

Paul compares Gentile Christianity to a wild olive branch, which has been grafted on to a cultivated olive tree (i.e. Israel; Rom chap. 11).

ONION Member of the lily family and relative of the leek and the garlic, it was one of the foods craved by the Israelites in the wilderness.

Palm trees

Papyrus

Pomegranates

ONYCHA One of the ingredients in the incense used exclusively in the sanctuary; its origins remain unknown. Some think that onycha was derived from the closing valve flaps of certain mollusks. Others, questioning such unclean origins, hold that it was a vegetable product.

PALM The date palm is a tall, stately tree which grows in Palestine's coastal plain and the Jordan Valley. Its physical attributes, such as its upright stature and towering height, inspired the Psalmist to use it as a simile for the righteous man (Ps 92:12) and the lover in the Song of Solomon for his beloved (Song 7:7). Several women in the Bible are called Tamar, which is the Hebrew for the palm tree; the word also figures in place-names such as Baal Tamar (Judg 20:33), Hazezon Tamar (Gen 14:7) and Tadmor (I Kgs 9:18). Jericho is known as the city of palms (Deut 34:3). The palm branch is one of the four species with which the Israelites are commanded to celebrate the Feast of Tabernacles (Lev 23:40). According to rabbinic tradition, the honey with which the land of Israel was blessed (e.g. Deut 8:8) was date honey.

PAPYRUS A type of reed. Scholars think that the bulrushes mentioned in Exodus 2:3 refer to the papyrus. Papyrus was used in ancient Egypt in the construction of light boats or canoes because of the shortage of wood (Is 18:2). It was also a common writing material in Egypt from the 3rd millennium B.C. until well into the 1st millennium A.D. II John verse 12 refers to paper which was made from papyrus.

PINE A member of the conifer family of trees. The identification of conifers in the Bible, aside from the cedar of Lebanon, is a matter of dispute among botanists. It has been suggested that the pine trees mentioned in Isaiah might refer to fir, plane, or juniper trees.

PISTACHIO See NUT above

PODS Most probably the seed vessel of the carob tree. The word occurs only once, in the parable of the prodigal son.

POMEGRANATE Fruit with purple-red rind and pink juicy seeds which came to symbolize agricultural fertility. In Deuteronomy it is listed as one of the "seven species" of the land of Israel (Deut 8:8), and the Book of Numbers relates that the spies brought Moses some pomegranates as a specimen of the land's rich vegetation (Num 13:23). In contrast, the destruction of the land is reflected by the absence of the pomegranate (Hag 2:19; cf Joel 1:12). In addition to symbolizing the fertility of the land, it is a token of human fertility and love. In the Song of Solomon the pomegranate serves as an image of praise for both the beauty of the beloved (4:3, 13; 6:7) and the joy of spring (6:11; 7:12); it is also mentioned as the source of a delicious wine (Song 8:2).

So important and popular was the pomegranate that its shape inspired the embellishment of the robe of the high priest (Ex 28:33-34; 39:24-26). It also provided a model for decorating the capitals of the Temple pillars named Jachin and Boaz (I Kgs 7:18, 20; II Chr 3:16; 4:13).

POPLAR A white tree mentioned twice in the OT. Jacob spliced its branches along with the almond and plane trees in his scheme against Laban to increase his flocks (Gen 30:37). It is mentioned as growing with the oaks and terebinths in the hills (Hos 4:13).

RAISIN See VINE, VINEYARD below

REED The stalk of several types of tall aquatic grasses. Moses was placed in an ark "in the reeds by the river's bank" (Ex 2:3); and Job asks, "can the reeds flourish without water?" (Job 8:11). Psalm 68:30 makes an obscure reference to the "beasts of the reeds". The Assyrian king, Sennacherib, compares Egypt to a "broken reed" (II Kgs 18:21; Is 36:6), and the prophet Ahijah, in the time of Jeroboam I predicts that "the Lord will strike Israel, as a reed is shaken in water" (I Kgs 14:15).

The Lord's servant mentioned in Isaiah 42:3 and Matthew 12:20, will not break "a bruised reed". A reed is used as a measuring rod in Revelation (11:1; 21:15-16). The English word "canon" ultimately stems from the Hebrew word for reed, *kane*, which indicates the means by which something is measured.

Before Jesus' crucifixion, a reed was placed in his right hand (Matt 27:29), he was struck on the head with one (Mark 15:19) and a wine-soaked sponge on a reed was offered to him on the cross (Matt 27:48).

ROSE The flower (a member of the narcissus family) is mentioned twice in the OT: "I am the rose of Sharon" (Song 2:1), "And the desert shall rejoice and blossom as the rose" (Is 35:1). However, the identity of the flower is not clear in either text.

RUE A strong-smelling shrub with gray-green leaves and lemon-yellow clusters of flowers; used as a condiment and charm. It is mentioned in Jesus' criticism of the Pharisees: "For you tithe mint and rue and all manner of herbs, and pass by justice and the love of God" (Luke 11:42; cf Matt 23:23).

SAFFRON A plant and its product used in cooking and medicine. It is mentioned only once, in the Song of Solomon 4:14, where the beloved is described as a park containing fragrant flowers and spices.

STACTE One of the ingredients compounded to make incense for the tabernacle (Ex 31:34-36). Its source is uncertain but most scholars suggest the storax tree from whose bark a fragrant resin can be obtained. The tree, with its snow-drop white flowers, is found throughout Palestine.

SYCAMORE (SYCOMORE) A tree indigenous to Palestine where it grew along the coastal plain and in the Negeb. It was so common that King Solomon "made cedars as abundant as the sycamores which are in the lowland" (I Kgs 10:27). This tree belonged to the family of the fig tree and had nothing in common with the sycamore of North America. David appointed an overseer for these trees in the lowland (I Chr 27:28). Amos identifies himself as a "tender of sycamore fruit".

In the NT, the short-statured Zacchaeus climbs a sycamore tree in order to see Jesus (Luke 19:4).

TAMARISK A tree or shrub with scalelike leaves. Abraham planted a tamarisk in Beersheba (Gen 21:33). Saul sat under one in Gibeah (I Sam 22:6) and his bones were buried beneath a tamarisk in Jabesh-Gilead (I Sam 31:13).

TEREBINTH A large tree, common in Palestine, which grows to a height of 35 feet (10.5m). God appeared to Abraham after his circumcision "by the terebinth trees of Mamre" (Gen 18:1), and the angel of the Lord visited Gideon at the terebinth tree in Ophrah (Judg 6:11). Jacob hid his household idols under such a tree before returning to Bethel to live there; and his wife Rebekah's nurse, Deborah, was buried under a terebinth tree (Gen 35:4, 8). Terebinth trees also acted as boundary markers (Josh 19:33) and landmarks (I Sam 10:3). Abimelech was crowned beside one (Judg 9:6), and his attack on Shechem passed by the Diviner's terebinth tree (Judg 9:37). Absalom's revolt ended in his entanglement in one "and his head caught in the terebinth so he was left hanging between heaven and earth" (II Sam 18:9). Isaiah prophesied that Judah "shall be as a terebinth whose leaf fades" (Is 1:30) and that none but the "stump" shall remain (Is 6:13). Hosea charged the Children of Israel with burning incense under terebinths.

THISTLE, THORN Types of wild plant which have sharp projections on their stems, branches or leaves. Over 20 different Hebrew words are used to describe these plants, frequently mentioned together in the Bible.

Reeds

Sycamore

Terebinth

Thistles and thorns are figuratively employed to describe the results of sin (e.g. Gen 3:18; Hos 10:8). Elsewhere they denote worthlessness (II Sam 23:6; II Kgs 14:9); while in Matthew 7:16 they symbolize the evil of false prophets (cf Luke 6:44).

VINE, VINEYARD One of the most characteristic plants of Palestine. When Moses sent the spies into Canaan it "was the season of the first ripe grapes" (Num 13:20), and the spies returned with a cluster of grapes (Num 13:23). Nazirites were forbidden to drink "any grape juice" or eat "fresh grapes or raisins" (Num 6:3). Raisins or raisin cakes, made from dried grapes, could be kept for a long time and were therefore suitable food for journeys (II Sam 6:19) and military provisions (II Sam 16:1).

Bunch of grapes

The vine is employed in the OT to symbolize peace and security, "Judah and Israel dwelt safely, each man under his vine and fig tree" (I Kgs 4:25; cf Mic 4:4; Zech 3:10). Israel is compared to a vine which has taken "deep root" (Ps 80:8-9), but has "brought forth wild grapes" (Is 5:2). The inhabitants of Jerusalem will be devoured by fire like the "wood of the vine" (Ezek 15:2-8) because of their unfaithfulness.

In the NT, the most important symbolic use of the vine is Jesus' description of himself as "the true vine" (John 15:1). The connection between him and his followers is emphasized by his extension of this metaphor "I am the vine, you are the branches....without me you can do nothing" (John 15:5).

A detailed description of the planting of a vineyard is found in Isaiah 5:1-2. It was usually planted on a hill (Jer 31:5; Amos 9:13; Ps 80:10) and provided with a hedge for protection from boars (Ps 80:13), foxes (Song 2:15) and thieves (Jer 49:9). Each vineyard had a storehouse (Is 5:2). Vineyards could be rented out (Song 8:11; Matt 21:33-43) or cultivated by the owners or by hired laborers (Matt 20:1-16). In the Levitical laws dealing with the harvest, vineyards were not to be gleaned (Lev 19:10; cf Deut 24:21). A vineyard was the cause of a dispute between King Ahab and Naboth which ended in the latter's death (I Kgs 21:1ff).

Wheat

Willow tree

WHEAT One of the most important grains, along with barley; cultivated since prehistoric times. Wheat is listed among the seven blessings of the land of Canaan (Deut 8:8). There are many references in the Bible to the harvesting (I Sam 6:13; Ruth 2:23), threshing (Judg 6:11; I Chr 21:20), cleaning (II Sam 4:6) and winnowing (Matt 3:12) of wheat. Its harvest served as the beginning of the Feast of Weeks, one of the three annual pilgrim festivals (Ex 34:22; Num 28:26-31). Wheat served as an export item sent by Solomon to Hiram (I Kgs 5:10-11).

Is also appears in poetic images, for God's care for Israel (Ps 81:16; 147:14) and describes as well, one of the limbs of the beautiful body of a young girl (Song 7:2). In the NT it is employed both in allegory (Matt 3:12; Luke 3:17) and parable (Matt 13:25-30; Luke 16:7).

WILLOW Two different Hebrew words are rendered as willow, a tree found along water courses. The "willows of the brooks" (Lev 23:40; Job 40:22) are among the plants to be used for the Feast of Tabernacles. It was upon the willows "by the rivers of Babylon" that the exiles hung their harps and wept (Ps 137:1-2).

WORMWOOD A bitter plant indigenous to Palestine, yielding a juice with medicinal properties. It is mostly employed in metaphors: an "immoral woman" is "bitter as wormwood" (Prov 5:4). Jeremiah describes God's judgment as feeding the people wormwood and giving them water of gall to drink (Jer 9:15; 23:15). Amos condemns those who turn "justice to wormwood" (Amos 5:7; cf 6:12); and the prophet's anguish over the destruction of Jerusalem was like the bitterness of wormwood and gall (Lam 3:15, 19). In the Book of Revelation the blazing star which falls from heaven is called wormwood (Rev 8:10-11).

Pomegranate on a Jewish shekel, c. A.D. 68.

Arabia holding cinnamon sticks on a coin of the province. A.D. 106.

Cluster of grapes on a coin of Bar-Kochba. A.D. 134.

Palm tree on a coin of Bar-Kochba. A.D. 134.

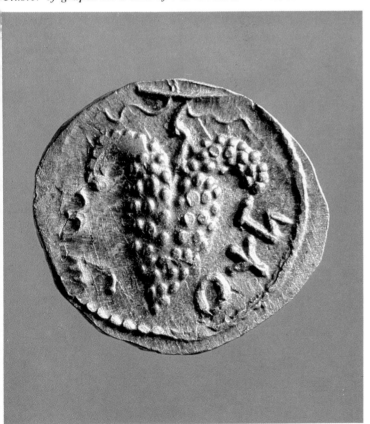

POCHERETH ("gazelle hunter"). Head of a family of Solomon's servants who returned from the Exile in Babylon with Zerubbabel.

PODS See PLANTS

POMEGRANATE See PLANTS

PONTIUS PILATE The fifth Roman procurator of Judea, appointed to that office by Tiberius in A.D. 26. His term lasted ten years.

Though under the general supervision of the legates of Syria, the procurators of Judea in fact operated with considerable independence, subject to intervention only in exceptional circumstances. Caesarea was their official place of residence with moves to Jerusalem during the main Jewish festivals when it was considered that maintenance of public order necessitated the procurator's presence in the city. Thus Pilate was in residence in Jerusalem during Passover when Jesus was arrested and put on trial and it was he who pronounced the sentence of death. All four gospels state that he did not think that Jesus was guilty and that he sought to free him.

POCHERETH
Ezra 2:57.
Neh 7:59

PONTIUS
PILATE
Matt 27:2, 13,
17, 22, 24, 58,
62, 65. Mark
15:1-2, 4-5, 9,
12, 14-15, 43-
44. Luke 3:1;
13:1; 23:1, 3-
4, 6, 11-13,
20, 24, 52.
John 18:29,
31, 33, 35, 37-
38; 19:1, 4-6,
8, 10, 12-13,
15, 19, 21-22,
31, 38. Acts
3:13; 4:27;
13:28. I Tim
6:13

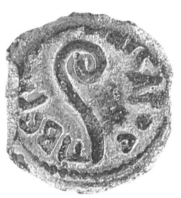

Bronze coin issued by Pontius Pilate with a litus (bent staff), the symbol of his office, and the name of Tiberius Caesar.

A stone found in the theater at Caesarea bearing a dedicatory inscription by Pontius Pilate procurator of Judea, in honor of the emperor Tiberius Caesar.

Of all the early procurators of Judea, Pilate is the one of whom most is known, not only through the NT account, but also because he is the only Roman governor discussed in any detail by the famous chroniclers of that period, Philo and Josephus. Philo describes him as "a man of inflexible disposition, harsh and obdurate" (*Legatio*, 38, 302). Pilate is further characterized as a person of cruel, selfish and malicious intent. Being the sole recorded character sketch from one of Pilate's contemporaries, this one is of particular interest.

Pilate's behavior towards the Jewish community exhibited a contempt which engendered protest, unrest and resentment. One of his first acts in office was to order the Jerusalem garrison to enter the city with their military standards bearing the emperor's image, which previous prefects had ordered removed to avoid offending the Jewish populace. This infringement of the second commandment evoked such determined protest that Pilate eventually had to back down and remove the images from Jerusalem (*Antiq.* XVIII, 3, 1, 55-9).

The force with which Pilate quelled riots often resulted in the loss of life, as, for example, when the people protested against the appropriation of sacred Temple treasures to defray the cost of building an aqueduct to Jerusalem (*Antiq.* XVIII, 3, 2, 60-62).

The NT mentions certain Galileans "whose blood Pilate mingled with their sacrifices" (Luke 13:1); some commentators interpret this as referring to pilgrims who had come to Jerusalem at a major festival to present their offerings at the Temple and lost their lives in the violent suppression of a riot. It was his brutal dispersion of a crowd of Samaritan pilgrims at Mount Gerizim which finally brought about Pilate's downfall (*Antiq.* XVIII 4, 1-2, 85-89). The Samaritan leaders protested to Vitellius, the legate in Syria, who ordered Pilate to return to Rome to answer for his conduct. Caligula banished Pilate to Vienne in Gaul, where he died in A.D. 41.

PONTUS The coastal strip of northern Asia Minor bordering the Black Sea and extending on the west from the Halys River in Bithynia to the highlands of Armenia in the east. This large mountainous area with fertile coastal plains had a mild climate and produced olives, grain and timber. Under Roman rule, the western part of Pontus was linked to Bithynia to form a Roman senatorial province, while the eastern part continued to be administered by Greek puppet kings.

Jews from Pontus, probably from the coastal Greek city-states, went to Jerusalem during the Feast of Pentecost (Acts 2:9). Aquila, companion, friend and co-worker of Paul, was a native of Pontus (Acts 18:2). The church there is addressed in I Peter 1:1 but its origin and growth are unknown.

POPLAR See PLANTS

PORATHA One of the ten sons of Haman; he was killed with his brothers at the order of King Ahasuerus (Est 9:2,8).

PORCIUS See FESTUS

PORCUPINE See ANIMALS

POTIPHAR ("he whom [the sun-god] Re has given") One of Pharaoh's officers (Gen chap. 39), whose title "head of the cooks" (various other translations are "captain of the guard" or "chief steward") is also applied to Nebuzaradan the Babylonian who held a military post (Jer 52:12). Potiphar appears to have been in charge of the royal prison. He bought Joseph as a slave from the Midianites (Gen 37:36) or from the Ishmaelites (Gen 39:1).

The account of the attempt by Potiphar's wife to seduce Joseph is similar in pattern to an Egyptian story, "The Tale of Two Brothers".

Potiphar's name is identical with that of Joseph's father-in law, Poti-Pherah priest of On (Gen 41:45).

POTI-PHERAH ("he whom Re has given"). The Egyptian name of Joseph's father-in-law. He was a priest of the Temple in On (Heliopolis, the center of the cult of the sun-god Re), and father of Asenath, whom Pharaoh gave to Joseph in marriage.

POTTERY The use of clay for manufacturing various kinds of vessels and other artifacts is one of the oldest crafts known to mankind. The raw material is abundantly found and pliable, the heat needed for firing is not so high as to require a complicated installation, the process of preparation is rather simple, and a considerable skill can be obtained after a short period of training. In addition, the softness of the material enables the creation of many shapes, and the chemical features of the clay make it possible to add to it painted decorations, seal impressions and various ornaments expressing religious ideas.

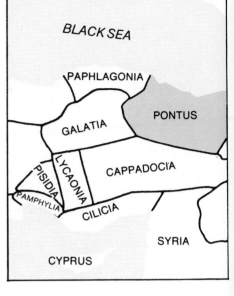

Pontus in Asia Minor.

Potter's wheel from Hazor. Canaanite period. (Israel Museum)

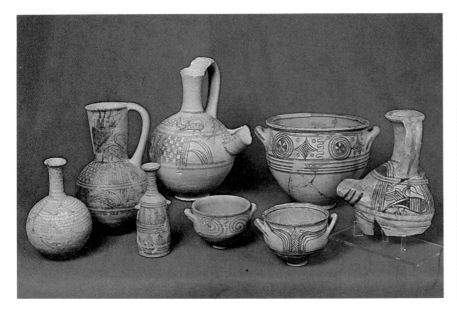

Pottery vessels were most common. Their main use was in dwellings, where they were utilized for cooking, baking and storing. However they were also utilized for public purposes. Storage jars were found in royal storehouses, where the supplies of the kingdom were kept. They were also used as containers for goods for international trade. Special types of vessels — ornamented stands, goblets, kernoi etc. — were made as cultic objects.

Pottery workshops were probably to be found in every region of ancient Israel. Different workshops created different shapes and had varying techniques. However, the art of pottery-making was rather similar throughout ancient Israel. Differences are noticeable mainly during the period of the divided monarchy. Constant connections with neighboring countries and with the coastal area led to individual influences on pottery making. The Phoenician style was introduced at the end of the 10th century B.C., the Syrian (Aramean) in the 9th and the Assyrian and Greek at the end of the 7th and the beginning of the 6th centuries B.C.

PRAETORIUM The term referred originally to the "tent of the commander, or *praetor*", and thus denoted military headquarters. By extension it came to refer to the officers and counselors who assembled in the praetor's tent, and, subsequently, the official residence of a provincial governor or procurator (John 18:28, 33). The praetorian were the special troops who acted as bodyguards for the emperor and

PRAETORIUM
Matt 27:27.
Mark 15:16.
John 18:28,
33; 19:9. Acts
23:35

Nabatean pottery. (Archaeological Museum, Amman)

(top left)
Collection of Philistine pottery. (Israel Museum)

(top right)
Model of a potter's workshop, Egypt 21st century B.C.

The Praetorium — Pilate's judgment hall — today in the grounds of the convent of Notre Dame de Sion in the Old City of Jerusalem.

other important military and civil leaders; in addition they would have custody of imperial prisoners in Rome.

In the NT the word refers to: (a) the judgment hall in Jerusalem where Pontius Pilate sentenced Jesus to death (Matt 27:27; Mark 15:16; John 18:28, 33; 19:9). The precise location of Pilate's Jerusalem headquarters, whether in the Antonia fortress or in Herod's palace, is undetermined; (b) the governor's residence in Caesarea where Paul was held in custody (Acts 23:35). Herod's palace at Caesarea served as the Roman praetor's headquarters; (c) the praetorium in Rome (Phil 1:13). Since the residence of the praetorian guard by the Porta Viminalis in Rome was not called the praetorium, the reference in Philippians 1:13 probably refers to the guard itself, rather than to their residence.

PRAYER Underlying the concept of prayer is the perception of God as a personal deity who hears and answers. Man created in the divine image (Gen 1:26-27) relates to his creator through this medium of prayer.

While the concept of prayer in the OT may be seen as largely uniform, differences manifest themselves in the various sources, schools and periods. In the Pentateuch, prayer is often depicted as a conversation

Bone sculpture representing a man in an attitude of prayer, from Beth Shean. 1600-1200 B.C. (Israel Museum, Jerusalem)

between God and man (Gen 3:8-19; 4:9-15; 15:1-16; 18:2-5; 20:3-7; 28:12-16; Ex 3:1-12). Man responds to these encounters by erecting a shrine (Gen 12:7), by obedience (Gen 12:1-4), by faith (Gen 15:1-16), or verbally with his questions or requests (Gen 15:2, 8; 18:23). Past acts of mercy are recalled as a basis for prayer (Gen 32:9-12; Ex 32:13).

The moral requirements of prayer were introduced by the 8th century B.C. prophets along with their clarification of the nature and demands of God. Prayer must consist of more than mere ritual and ceremony (Is 1:1-11; Hos 6:6; 8:11-13; 9:4; Amos 4:4-5, 5:21-25; Mic 6:6-8 etc.). Calamities were viewed as a call to return to God (Is 30:15; Hos 5:15-6:5; Amos 4:6-11), which is synonymous with moral living (Amos 5:14).

For the Deuteronomic school, prayer is strongly associated with recollection of the past deeds of God (e.g., Deut 9:25-29), and these memories are an inspiration to prayer (Deut 4:9, 32-39; I Kgs 8:23-27).

The covenantal theme is strong and prayer functions within this covenant (Deut 4:23). Noteworthy here is the life and personal prayers of Jeremiah. His prayers were not praise, confession or petition, but rather an intercourse with God best described as mediation and intercession.

In Second Temple times, individuals were prompted to mourn, fast and pray for days on end (Neh 1:4), and there are examples of spontaneous prayer at the confrontation with danger (Neh 2:4). The use of the "Amen" response first appears here (I Chr 16:36; Neh 5:13; Ps 41:13; 72:19; 89:52; 106:48) as does the practice of praying before reading the Law (Neh 8:6).

There are many different forms of prayer, petition, confession, thanksgiving, praise, recollection and intercession. In view of this wide variety, it is hardly surprising that numerous terms were employed. The most common word for prayer is *tephillah* (Is 1:15) based on the root which implies interposition and judgment, both of which are significant in the biblical conception of praying. Other verbs for praying mean literally "to cry or call out", "to seek" (the face of), "to request", "to inquire" (of an oracle), "to intercede", "to pour out (one's) heart".

Prayer reflects the varied range of man's concerns and moods. The nature of prayer seems to develop from a simple call in the name of the Lord (Gen 12:8; 21:33), to more complex and, later, more structured forms. The simple desire to know the future took the form of direct appeals to God for guidance (Gen 24:12-14), through the aid of a priest (I Sam 14:36-37) or a prophet (II Kgs 19:2). An outgrowth of this trend are the various prayers of guidance that are found in various parts of the OT (Num 6:24-26; I Kgs 3:6-9; Ps. 119:33).

Along a similar vein are the prayers intent on changing the future with God's help. The subject of the entreaty varies greatly. The concern could be for one's own personal satisfaction (Gen 28:20); for success on a mission (Gen 24:12-14); for the salvation of others (Gen 18:23-33); for forgiveness for the sins of the nation (Ex 32:31-32); for divine help in the hour of defeat (Josh 7:6-9); for deliverance from an enemy (II Kgs 19:15-19); for Israel's restoration (Dan 9:3-19); for the relief of the people's distress (Neh 1:4-11) or the intercessory appeal of the prophets on behalf of their people (Jer 14:1; 15:1; Amos 7:2). Interestingly enough there are times when intercession is forbidden (Jer 7:16; 11:14; 14:11).

Devout Jew wearing prayer-shawl and phylacteries, praying at the Western Wall in Jerusalem.

Prayer, unlike sacrifice, could be offered at any place (Gen 24:26; Dan 6:11; Jonah 2:2-10); yet sacred sites were favored. Thus the Temple at Jerusalem eventually became the major place of prayer (Is 56:7), and the focal point for those unable to be there (Dan 6:11). While communal prayer grew in importance, private prayer remained a feature of OT life.

Though no particular gestures or postures were necessary for praying, certain postures did develop which complemented the content of the prayer. These include standing (I Sam 1:26; I Kgs 8:22); kneeling (Dan 6:11; Ezra 9:5); prostration (Josh 7:6); head bowing (Gen 24:26; Neh 8:6); facing Jerusalem (Dan 6:11); stretching the hands out or up (I Kgs 8:22; Ps 28:2); placing the head between the knees (I Kgs 18:42); or simply sitting (II Sam 7:18). Prayers were often accompanied by fasting, mourning and weeping (Is 58:2-5; Joel 2:12) and later were offered thrice daily (Ps 55:17; Dan 6:11).

With the overall organization of OT religion, prayer was ordered in liturgies and, in many cases, given musical rendition (I Chr 16:5-36). This trend is exemplified by the Psalms, many of them including choral and instrumental directions.

Prayers were occasionally accompanied by some type of bargaining or promise for the fulfillment of the request. Hannah promised to dedicate Samuel to the service of the shrine (I Sam 1:9-28), and Jacob bargained with his faith (Gen 28:20-22).

It is an OT assumption that prayers are heard (Ps 77:1), but they could remain unanswered. Moses petitioned God to see Canaan, but was refused because of God's displeasure with the people for whom Moses was responsible (Deut 3:23-27). David failed in his prayer for the life of the child of his sin (II Sam 12:22). This underscoring of the non-magical nature of prayer sets OT worship off from pagan cults where the deity could be compelled to fulfill the worshiper's wishes (Is 29:12-14).

Within Greco-Roman society, prayer was primarily an object of ridicule, at least by the writers of the time, though the common people probably perceived it differently.

Both Judaism and Christianity agree in attributing a very high priority to prayer and it is in fact difficult to conceive of public worship without it. Jesus himself placed a high value on prayer. His disciples wanted him to teach them to pray even as John the Baptist had instructed his own followers (Luke 11:1).

Relatively little is known about the prayers of Jesus, for apart from the exclamatory prayers of the crucifixion, only two of his prayers are known (Matt 11:25ff, the exclamatory prayer; Mark 14:36ff, the prayer of Gethsemane). Three are added by the Gospel of John (11:41ff; 12:27ff; chap. 17, the so-called high priestly prayer).

Jesus prayed before sunrise (Mark 1:35) and he ascended a mountain to pray one evening (Mark 6:46); on at least one occasion he prolonged his evening prayer until dawn (Luke 6:12), presumably because of the gravity of his choice of the Twelve the next day. It can be assumed that Jesus followed the customs of his day in prayer. (Jewish prayers in the 1st century included the sunrise, afternoon and sunset prayers).

At the same time, Jesus also defied custom by not confining his prayers to stated times. Although Luke on numerous occasions adds a note on prayer to Mark's text (Luke 5:16; 6:12; 9:18; cf 3:21), his inducement to do so may well have come from reliable traditions about Jesus praying (cf Mark 14:32-42). Furthermore Jesus prayed in the vernacular Aramaic rather than Hebrew and taught his disciples to do likewise (Mark 14:36). Indeed it seems that he removed prayer from the sacred liturgical realm, into the realm of the mundane. Above all he warned that prayer was to be a private event and not performed in public to impress others (Matt 6:6). It is clear from Luke 11:1 that the disciples of Jesus requested a peculiar prayer style distinguished from the forms employed by John the Baptist, the Essenes or the Pharisees.

The church did indeed regard the Lord's Prayer as a substitute for the prayers they had practiced as Jews. The invocation of God as Father, while not new with Jesus, did have special prominence in his prayers. There was a new level of intimacy and the tone of prayer was dominated by thanksgiving.

The early church carried on the pattern of prayer established by Jesus. The Didache specifies the Lord's Prayer three times a day (8:3). But Paul went considerably further when he spoke of praying without ceasing, always, day and night, etc. It has been argued that to be "vigilant" in prayer (Col 4:2) and to pray "steadfastly" (Rom 12:12) means faithfully to observe the rite of prayer, as the Greek verb denotes in Acts 1:14; 2:42, 46; 6:4. But more likely the early church went beyond the bounds of stated times and seasons of prayer, perceiving the believer's relationship with the Holy Spirit, Jesus Christ and God the Father in an intimate light which made any time suitable for communion with God (cf Rom 8:15, 23).

To the first Christians, prayer implied petitioning, thanksgiving and praise. Intercession had an important role to play, requiring certain guidelines: the more specific a request, the greater the assurances that it would be met (John 16:23-24; I John 5:14-15). Prayers for the sick (James 5:13-18), for the erring (I John 5:16), and the return of the misguided, were recommended. All rulers were to be assured of the prayer of the early Christian community (I Tim 2:1-3) and enemies were to be included in believers' prayers and petitions (Luke 6:28-29). In this they followed Psalm 141:5 which also assumes that prayer has a particular power over enemies.

Prayer was a virtual dynamo which accounts, not only for the inner dynamic of the early church, but also sustained it in its purpose and guided its strategy. Repeatedly the early Christians concluded their admonitions with that which they felt to be the most important: prayer. The writer of the Epistle to the Ephesians concluded: "Take the helmets of salvation... praying always with prayer and supplication in the Spirit" (Eph 6:17-18). Such commitment to prayer is also wedded to joy (Phil 1:3-4, 9).

PRAYER OF AZARIAH AND THE SONG OF THE THREE YOUNG MEN An apocryphal addition to the ancient versions of the canonical text of the Book of Daniel. It was inserted into the Greek version of Daniel between 3:23 and 3:24, at the point where Shadrach, Meshach and Abed-Nego fall down bound in the midst of the burning furnace. The date of writing is the 2nd or 1st century B.C. It contains a penitential prayer of Abed-Nego (Azariah) and a song of praise of the Three Young Men.

The three youths in the furnace shown on a fresco of the 3rd century A.D. in the catacombs of St Priscilla, Rome.

A problem taken up by Jewish thinkers of the Greco-Roman period was the contradiction between Israel's covenant with God and its own existential misfortune. This idea is taken up in the prayer of Azariah (vs. 3-5), as it is in the Book of Baruch and the Psalms of Solomon. Although the prayer is uttered at a time when the speaker's life was in danger, it is not so much a plea for salvation from immediate threat as a confession of the nation's sins and a prayer for its deliverance.

The two poetic compositions were probably written originally in Hebrew. They transform the atmosphere of the story in the canonical Daniel into a dramatic, liturgical event. The early Church retained this liturgical element, and these additions were included in the collection of the "Odes", which was appended to the Book of Psalms in Greek manuscripts of the Bible written in the 5th century ff. They are still used in the liturgies of the Greek Orthodox Church, and the song of the Three Young Men is found in many Christian hymns.

PRAYER OF MANASSES Penitential prayer, included in the

Apocrypha and probably composed by a Jewish author. The date of writing is probably the 1st century B.C. and the original language was Hebrew, Aramaic or Greek. The prayer is attributed to the wicked King Manasseh, who according to II Chronicles 33:12-13, "humbled himself greatly before the God of his fathers, and prayed to him; and he received his entreaty, heard his supplication." This work gives the apocryphal words ascribed to Manasseh. The content is his repentance and his request for God's mercy.

The Prayer of Manasses is included in the Odes appended to the Book of Psalms in the Septuagint, and in the Protestant Apocrypha (although in the Geneva Bible of 1560, much used by Puritans, it was placed among the canonical works).

PRECIOUS STONES Man felt a great need to find an outlet for his aesthetic leanings at a very early stage in human culture. One of the ways of fulfilling this need was to acquire rare, gleaming stones. To some of these stones, of unusual shape or color, he would attribute magical or therapeutic qualities or the power of conferring fruitfulness. Much later these beliefs became deeply rooted among the Hebrews and other Semitic peoples, as well as among those of the neighboring countries. The Hebrews' love of precious stones is amply illustrated by many references in the Bible to the extraordinary properties of such stones, and by the large number of stones specifically named.

Very few of the precious stones referred to in the Bible are among the natural resources of Palestine, but in some cases their place of origin is mentioned. The main sources were the rich countries of Arabia, such as Havilah (Gen 2:11-12), where gold and *shoham* ("onyx") came from; Ophir (I Kgs 10:11; II Chr 9:10), whence, in addition to precious stones, came gold and precious timber; Sheba and Raamah ("gold and precious stones" Ezek 27:22); and topaz from Ethiopia (Job 28:19). The desire for precious stones was also common among the Canaanites, and many are mentioned in the El Amarna Letters. In excavated sites throughout the Middle East precious stones have been found, set into jewelry made of gold, silver and bronze, and into scarabs, weights and seals. The high priest's "breastplate of judgment" was set with 12 precious stones (Ex 28:17-20; 39:10-13), and most of these are enumerated by Ezekiel (28:13) as among the stones found in the Garden of Eden. A variety of precious stones are mentioned in the description of the wall of the New Jerusalem in the Book of Revelation (Rev 21:15-22).

The identification of the precious stones mentioned in the Bible with

Beads of different materials including precious and semi-precious stones, metal and glass; of different periods, but mostly from the 7th-6th centuries B.C. Found at Ketef Hinnom, Jerusalem.

those known today presents many difficulties. It is only now, with the development of chemistry, mineralogy and crystallography, that the classification of the various stones into groups and their attribution to distinct mineralogical families has become possible. In ancient times they were classified solely on the basis of external characteristics, especially color. Thus stones that are listed in the Bible as belonging to different groups sometimes form a single mineralogical family. The following list includes precious stones mentioned in the Bible with tentative identifications.

Ahlamah ("amethyst" Ex 28:19; 39:12). The identification of this stone is not certain. In the Septuagint it is rendered as "amethyst", one of the quartzes, which is purple or violet in color. Some scholars agree with this identification of the stone.

Bareket ("emerald" Ex 28:17). This stone has the same name in Akkadian. The Septuagint calls it *smaragdos*, and the identification with *smaragd*, emerald, is generally accepted. During the Hellenistic period this name was applied to a different stone, the "false emerald"or malachite, whose greenish shade is close to that of the true emerald. Real emeralds were extremely rare in the ancient world and could not be easily worked. Some scholars hold that *bareket* should be identified with jasper.

Dar The court of the garden of the Persian king was paved with *dar* ("alabaster, turquoise, white and black marble" Est 1:6). In Arabic *dar* means pearl, and some scholars believe that it should be identified with mother-of-pearl. Others believe that it was an orange-colored stone.

Ekdah ("crystal" Is 54:12). The Septuagint refers to this as *lithus crystallou*, which would be the equivalent of rock crystal. Some maintain that it should be identified with *carbunculus*, the garnet, a red stone.

Kadkod ("ruby"). Listed among the precious stones which the Aramean merchants brought to Tyre (Ezek 27:16). According to Isaiah (54:12) God will make the windows of the house of Jerusalem of *kadkod*. The Arabs give the name *karkund* to a red stone resembling the ruby, identified today with the pinel. Scholars are of the view that *kadkod* should be identified with hyacinth, the medieval name for a yellow stone with sorts of lilac and purple. It may possibly be one of the quartzes that the Greeks and Romans used for jewelry. Pliny says that it was blue and that it came from Gaul. Today, under the name of hyacinth, it is classified among the zircons, stones that range from a colorless quality to green, blue, red and golden yellow.

Leshem ("jacinth" Ex 28:19). The Septuagint has *ligurion*, a corruption of the *lyncurium* of the classical sources, which is a shining yellow color; probably the opal, which is multicolored or a glimmering orange. Some identify it with aventurine, a quartz containing very fine crystals of hematite, limonite or mica, which sparkle when the light catches them. Still others identify it with amber.

Nopheh ("turquoise" Ex 28:18; Ezek 28:13). The Septuagint has *anthrax*. Ancient Greek sources refer to it as a hard red stone, much used by jewelers. Pliny calls the same stone *carbunculus*. Some scholars identify it with turquoise; a sulfate of aluminum, the small percentage of copper it contains gives it a distinctive red color. It was very much used in jewelry.

Odem ("sardius" Ex 28:17; Ezek 28:13). Some identify it with the Akkadian *samtu*, a red stone, but it is more likely the carnelian. Others believe it was red jasper, an opaque stone found abundantly in Palestine and Egypt. The identification of the *odem* with the ruby cannot be sustained, because this was not known before the 3rd century A.D.

Pitdah ("topaz" Ex 28:17; Ezek 28:13). Most biblical commentators understand this to be a greenish stone. Pliny uses the name *topazion* for a stone known as chrysolithos or as olivine, but *pitdah* is now identified with plasma, a greenish semi-translucent stone, one of the chalcedonies. The *pitdah* of Ethiopia symbolizes the value of wisdom in Job 28:19.

Ramoth ("coral"Ezek 27:16; Job 28:18). The identification of this stone is not certain. Some suggest that it is not a stone at all, but a shell.

Sapir ("sapphire" Ex 28:18). In the OT this is referred to among the most precious stones (Job 28:16). Ezekiel sees the firmament as resembling the sapphire and his vision of the Garden of Eden includes the *sapir* (Ezek 28:13). It is also a symbol of beauty (Song 5:4). This is not to be mistaken for the sapphire of our day, which is the corundum, a stone that was not known in ancient times. Theophrastos, a Greek scholar, in his book on stones, refers to it as blue with gold-white specks, like lapis lazuli.

Shebo ("agate" Ex 28:19). The identification with agate is accepted by all scholars. It is believed that the agate of the OT was not the white stone, but a mixed black and white stone. White-grey agates were found in Egypt.

Shoham ("onyx" Ex 28:20; Ezek 28:13; Job 28:16). One of the stones brought from Havilah (Gen 2:11-12). It seems that onyx is the most appropriate identification. It comes from the East and has three colors arranged in three stripes: red, blue or brown and black or dark brown. To Job (28:16) it was a symbol of wealth.

Soheret ("black marble" Est 1:6). The identification is not known. Some scholars think that it was a black stone used for paving floors.

Tarshish ("beryl" Ex 28:20). Believed to have been identical with mother-of-pearl. To Ezekiel the wheels of his vision resemble *tarshish* (Ezek 28:13).

Yahalom ("diamond" Ex 28:18; Ezek 28:13). According to the Midrash this stone is white. Some identify it with anthrax or carbuncle, which is red, and others with onyx, which has different colors arranged in layers, or even with chalcedony, which was much used for beads and seals. However, its identification with the diamond should be rejected, as this stone was not known before the Middle Ages. Ezekiel (28:13) sees it as one of the precious stones in the Garden of Eden.

Yaspeh ("jasper" Ex 28:20; 39:13). A translucent green stone; but may refer to a present-day opaque red quartz. *Yaspeh* is mentioned in the El Amarna Letters as a royal stone.

Semi-precious stones of the Hellenistic period, from Tell Anafa. (Israel Museum, Jerusalem)

Another stone known in biblical times was the lapis lazuli. There were in fact two qualities of it in the ancient world: natural and artificial. The natural stone was found in Cyprus and Scythia. Chemically it is a silicate of aluminum and sodium, ultramarine blue in color. The artificial lapis lazuli was produced in Egypt and was an alkaline silicate in which the blue color came from copper carbonate. It was often set in rings and used for scarabs. Ground lapis lazuli was used as an ultramarine pigment.

In the NT, pearls (rendered as "rubies" in OT translations) are mentioned as items of women's jewelry (I Tim 2:9; Rev 17:4). The list of the 12 precious stones which adorn the foundations of the walls of the New Jerusalem (Rev 21:19-21) was influenced by the description of the high priest's breastplate (Ex 28:17-20; 39:10-13). The discrepancies between the two, however, show that the later list is not directly dependent on the first. The twelve gates of this city "were twelve pearls" (Rev 21:21). Some scholars have seen the use of twelve stones and gates as symbolizing the signs of the zodiac, the twelve tribes or the twelve apostles, but there is no general agreement on this.

PRIESTS The hereditary office of priesthood was filled by members and descendants of Aaron's family of the tribe of Levi; they alone were authorized to perform the sacred service in the tabernacle and Temple (Num 3:32; 25:11ff; 35:25, 38; Neh 12:10-12).

According to Exodus chapter 28, the priesthood was established in the wilderness soon after the revelation at Mount Sinai. The choice of the tribe of Levi to be God's servants in the tabernacle was, as recorded, a reward for their loyalty to Moses during the episode of the golden calf (Ex 32:26-29) (See LEVITES). The Temple priesthood survived effectively until the destruction of the Second Temple in A.D. 70.

However, there are various views of the origins of the priesthood which differ from the Exodus account. According to one view, the Deuteronomic Code entitles the entire tribe of Levi, and not just the Aaronites, to serve in the Temple (Deut 10:8-9 and possibly also 33:8-10). Other scholars suggest that while that right may have applied to the tribe in entirety, in practice, only the Aaronites who lived in Jerusalem exercised it. Furthermore, in the early stages of Israelite history any layman could and did offer sacrifices to God. The practice of the patriarchs (Gen 26:25; 31:54; 46:1) is repeated in one way or another after the Mosaic legislation.

Gideon (Judg 6:20-28) and Elijah (I Kgs 18:30-38) are clear examples of non-priestly personalities who offer up sacrifices. Some scholars view the institution of a cultic priesthood as a later development in the history of the monarchy. Against this view, more traditional scholars point to the difference between the altar and Temple, suggesting that while laymen did offer sacrifices on outside altars, the Temple cult was restricted to the priesthood. As a consequence of the religious reformation of King Josiah of Judah (622 B.C.), the outside altars were abolished and sacrifices confined to the Temple in Jerusalem.

According to the Pentateuch there were three levels of priesthood. The lowest grade consisted of the Levites in charge of the sanctuary's service. Above them were the regular priests and then came the high priest, sometimes called "the anointed priest" (Lev 4:3, 5, 16) because of the special ceremony of anointing reserved exclusively for him (Ex 29:7; Lev 8:12; 21:10). The installation ceremonies for both the regular priests and high priest lasted for one week (Ex 29:1-37; Lev 8:5-35).

All priests had to be free of any physical defects (Lev 21:17-24; 22:4). The priests wore special garments: tunic, breeches and turbans of white linen, along with a white linen girdle; the high priest was distinguished from the other priests by additional vestments (Ex 28:1-5, 40-43) including an ephod, a breastplate bearing the names of the twelve tribes of Israel, and a linen turban with a golden plate inscribed "Holiness to the Lord" (Ex 29:6; 39:30; Lev 8:9).

The daily service in the tabernacle and Temple, including the ritual aspects of the sacrifices could be performed by all priests. There were 24 priestly families who attended the Temple in a weekly rotation. Ordinary priests also carried out the duties connected with the Temple lamp, the showbread and the frankincense on the altar. However, the Day of Atonement service was performed exclusively by the high priest. He alone, wearing only linen garments, was permitted to enter beyond the veil into the Holy of Holies where he made atonement for the nation's iniquity and for himself (Lev chap. 16). The high priest also consulted the Urim and Thummim which he carried on his breastplate (Num 27:21); this mantic practice disappeared after the destruction of the First Temple. On the death of the high priest a manslaughterer's stay in a city of refuge was terminated (Num 35:25-28; Josh 20:6). Among other functions of the priesthood was the blessing of the people, part of the daily office in Temple times (Num 6:22-27). The priests were responsible for sounding the trumpets on festivals and other special occasions (Num 10:8). They carried the ark when it was moved to a new location (Deut 10:8; 31:9, 25). The priests also administered justice (Deut 17:8-9; 21:5; II Chr 19:8-11; Ezek 44:24). Further, disease being regarded as more than physical and pointing also to a condition of

"Breastplate" or shield, hanging from the staves of a scroll of the Law. It recalls the breastplate worn by the high priest. The one shown here is from Munich, 1816. (Israel Museum, Jerusalem)

spiritual impurity, it seemed natural for the priest to act as the diagnostician who helped to remove that impurity from the patient during his illness and after the symptoms had disappeared (Lev chaps. 13-15; Deut 24:8).

In addition to their other duties the priests also served as teachers to the people. Certainly, this task was not theirs exclusively, but they are described as teachers of the Law, which was a natural offshoot of their functions as priests of God (Deut 17:11; 33:10; Jer 18:18; Mal 2:6-7).

The priests owned no land. In compensation they were entitled to several perquisites. These included the breast and thigh parts of the peace offerings and a portion of the dough offering (Num 18:17-21). The priests also received the heave offering consisting of roughly two per cent of the layman's produce (Num 18:8ff); while the Bible mentions only wine, corn and oil, the commentators believed that these were merely symbolic, all farm produce being subject to the tax. A further priestly privilege was the right to all first fruits of the field and firstlings of those animals which were fit for sacrifice. The firstling of a non-sacrificial animal, like a human firstborn, was redeemed with a fixed sum of money paid to the priest (Num 18:15-16). The priest also received the showbread (Lev 24:5-9), almost all the cereal offerings (Lev 2:3, 10; 6:16; 10:12-13; Num 18:9) and sin offerings (Lev 5:13; 6:26; Num 18:9). A tenth of the people's tithes to the Levites was transmitted to the priests (Num 18:26-28).

During the period of the Second Temple, the high priest Joshua is mentioned side by side with Zerubbabel, the political leader, suggesting equal status (Hag 1:1, 12, 14; 2:2, 4). Together they began to rebuild the Temple (Hag chaps. 1-2; Ezra 3:1-2), and they shared the rule of the community as the "two anointed" (Zech 4:14; 6:9-15).

The priests were subject to rigorous laws of ritual purity; in the event of defilement they were barred from the Temple service until they had undergone a cleansing procedure. Contact with a corpse constituted a major source of defilement; a priest was not permitted to attend a burial except of that of a close relative such as wife, child, brother or sister or parent. The high priest was barred from all interments and forbidden to let his hair flow long or rend his clothing as a sign of mourning (Lev 21:1-5).

Another law restricted the priest's choice of a wife. A priest could not marry a divorcee or a proselyte. In addition, a high priest could not marry a widow (Lev 21:7). If he was found guilty of any sin, it was expiated by a specially regulated sin offering (Lev 4:3-12).

Israel, as the covenant people of God, is called a "kingdom of priests and a holy nation" (Ex 19:5-6). As such it must preserve a state of holiness (Lev 11:44ff; Num 15:40).

The NT also reflects the role of the priest as a recognized functionary of Judaism. In a parable related by Jesus, a priest is described as unwilling to assist the man who fell among thieves (Luke 10:31) perhaps because he feared defilement by a corpse. Throughout, the gospel narratives give the impression that it was the chief priests (Sadducees) who felt particularly threatened by Jesus' activities and consequently sought to take him into captivity.

The Book of Acts reports that in the time of Stephen, when the number of disciples was on the increase in Jerusalem, "a great many of the priests were obedient to the faith" (Acts 6:7).

Christianity abolished the priest's role as intermediary between God and man, a change facilitated by the destruction of the Temple in A.D. 70. The earliest Christians did not use the term "priest" to designate any special functionary because each Christian was considered a priest;

indeed the church itself was designated "a spiritual house, a holy priesthood, to offer up spiritual sacrifices acceptable to God" (I Pet 2:5; cf Ex 19:6) or a royal house, to serve as "the priests to his God" (Rev 1:6; 5:10; 20:6). Yet the priestly metaphor cannot be totally erased, as seen in Paul's reference to his ministry of grace to the Gentiles as "my priestly service is the preaching of the gospel of God, and it falls to me to offer the Gentiles to him as an acceptable sacrifice consecrated by the Holy Spirit" (RSV Rom 15:16). Earlier in the same epistle, he urged his readers to offer their very selves as a living sacrifice, dedicated and fit for his acceptance, the worship offered by mind and heart (Rom 12:1).

The Epistle to the Hebrews most fully spells out Jesus' own mission as that of the high priest who made, once-and-for-all atonement for his sins (2:17; 3:1; 5:10; 6:20). This epistle attempts to show that Jesus was the perfect priest who has rendered all others obsolete (7:12, 15-19). Jesus' priesthood had made all other mediators redundant (I Tim 2:5) and Christians' service for each other and for the world is a priestly ministry. Liturgical terms are used in Hebrews to instill awe in the assembly of the believers and to show that the numinous reality of God's living presence which the Temple symbolized and which the priest sought to make present had dawned in a totally comparable way with the coming of the "kingdom which cannot be shaken" (Heb 12:28). The response called for: "Let us have grace by which we may serve God acceptably, with reverence and godly fear; for our God is a consuming fire" (Heb 12:28-29). This endows the priestly metaphor with a power available to all.

Beyond the priest as temple officer, the NT knows of priests in another sense, as ruling elders in a church. Perhaps modeled on the governing board of a synagogue, Christian elders are mentioned in I Timothy 5:17, 19; Titus 1:5; James 5:14; I Peter 5:1, 5; II John verse 1; III John verse 1. In I Timothy priests as elders are mentioned along with bishops or overseers, and deacons or ministers as church officers. Eventually this three-fold pattern became standard in the church, and absorbed many other ministries mentioned in I Corinthians 12:28ff.

PRISCA See PRISCA

PRISCILLA The wife of Aquila, always mentioned in association with her husband (See AQUILA). The couple showed warm hospitality to individuals, and entertained congregational meetings of Christians in their home both in Rome and in Ephesus (Rom 16:3; I Cor 16:19). Priscilla is also referred to as Prisca (II Tim 4:19).

PRISON, COURT OF The open area used for detaining prisoners. Despite being confined there, Jeremiah was able to continue prophesying.

PRISONS Imprisonment as a punishment for criminal behavior is never referred to in the Pentateuch or in other ancient legal codes. Nevertheless, there are numerous terms in the Bible denoting places of imprisonment. The Hebrew Bible has no less than 11 such names (all rendered as "prison" in the AV), (I Kgs 22:27; II Kgs 25:27; Jer 52:31 etc.). Other terms used are "dungeon" (Gen 40:15; Jer 37:16) and "under guard" (Num 15:34). Not until the time of the return from the Babylonian Exile is imprisonment specifically mentioned as a punishment (Ezra 7:26). On the other hand it seems that detention before trial sometimes occurred (Num 15:32-35). Detention on political grounds is also frequently referred to, as for example in the cases of the prophet Micaiah (I Kgs 22:6-7); Hoshea, king of Israel (II Kgs 17:4); Jehoiachin, king of Judah (II Kgs 24:12); Jeremiah (Jer 37:15-21, etc.) and Zedekiah, who was detained until his death (Jer 52:11).

It seems that no special place was set aside for detention, the need being met as it arose. Thus Jeremiah was placed in prison in the house of Jonathan the scribe (Jer 37:15), transferred to the court of the prison (Jer 37:21) and later placed in the dungeon of Malchiah, in the court of the prison (Jer 38:6ff). Joseph was detained in a prison in the house of the captain of the guard (Gen 39:20-23; 40:3).

A prisoner would be bound in chains (Jer 40:1) of bronze (Judg 16:21) or of iron (Ps 105:18). Sometimes his feet would be placed in stocks (Job 13:27; Jer 20:2).

In the Roman period, as in biblical times, the law did not recognize imprisonment as a form of punishment. A man could be detained to await trial in order to make him available to the court, but once convicted he was expected to leave Rome and go into exile. It is only in the larger households that a prison for the detention of slaves has been found. The NT relates that John the Baptist (Matt 14:3), Peter (Acts 5:18), Paul and Silas (Acts 16:23) were put in the "common prison" or prison. According to Josephus (*Antiq.* XVIII, 119), John was imprisoned in Herod's palace at Machaerus. The prison referred to in Acts 5:18 was probably in the Temple, under the custody of the priests. Paul was imprisoned in the Antonia fortress in Jerusalem (Acts 23:10) and also in the palace of Herod at Caesarea (Acts 23:35). The NT also mentions prisoners having their feet put in stocks (Acts 16:24).

PROCHORUS One of the seven "men of good reputation" among the Hellenists chosen to help the apostles in Jerusalem in their lay work (Acts 6:1-6).

PROCHORUS
Acts 6:5

PROPHETS AND PROPHECY The institution of prophecy is founded on the basic premise that God makes his will known to chosen individuals in successive generations. A prophet is a charismatic individual endowed with the divine gift of both receiving and imparting the message of revelation. As the spokesman for the deity, he does not choose his profession but is chosen, often against his will, to convey the word of God to his people, regardless of whether or not they wish to hear it (Ezek 3:11). The prophet is consecrated to be set apart from his fellowmen and to bear the responsibility and burden of being chosen. An appointed messenger, he must translate his revelatory experience into the idiom of his people; for though the prophet is overwhelmed by the divine word, he does not lose his identity nor does he suffer from any effacement of personality. The prophetic experience is one of confrontation. The prophet is both a recipient and a participant. Armed solely with the divine word and as conveyor of the divine will, he becomes a radical iconoclast. He is concerned not with the being of God but with the designs of God. He has knowledge not about God but from God concerning his actions in history.

In the Jewish tradition, the second of the three sections into which the OT is divided, is called "The Prophets". It is subdivided into the "Former Prophets" — Joshua, Judges, Samuel, Kings and the "Latter Prophets" — Isaiah, Jeremiah, Ezekiel and the twelve Minor Prophets — Hosea, Joel, Amos, Obadiah, Jonah, Micah, Nahum, Habakkuk, Zephaniah, Haggai, Zechariah, Malachi. The two groups could also be characterized as preclassical popular prophets and classical literary prophets.

The former books consist primarily of biographical incidents in the lives of these well-known figures, while the latter contain primarily the oracles of the prophets themselves. It was formerly thought that the main differences between the two could be classified according to the following critera: unlike their preclassical forerunners, the classical prophets highlighted ethical monotheism and absolutely rejected all cult and ritual; they also substituted a universalist concept of the deity for the nationalist outlook of their predecessors; engaged in reproving the people and not in mantic behavior; appeared by themselves and not in groups or guilds; and delivered their oracles in clear control of their senses and not in an ecstatic state.

Today, however, it is commonly agreed that such a decisive distinction should not be made for there are many points of contact and continuation between popular and classical prophets. Both are called by the same technical term "prophet" and speak in the name of the God of Israel, who sends them to deliver his message to his people in order to preserve his covenant with Israel.

The preclassical prophets rebuke kings for primary infractions of the moral law: adultery and murder (Nathan — David in his conduct with Bathsheba and Uriah [II Sam 12:1 ff]; and Elijah — Ahab, in the story of Naboth's vineyard [I Kgs chap. 21]). The classical prophets, in turn, do not reject the cult as such any more than prayer or other forms of worship; however, cultic rites are merely means to an end and are thus secondary to, and dependent upon, the moral law which is an end unto itself. Exilic and post-exilic prophets view the cult very favorably. Nationalist and universalist outlooks are to be found in the writings of both sets of prophets; I Kings 20:28 and II Kings 5:15; 19:15 are examples of universalist themes in the preclassical prophets, while many nationalistic oracles are recorded in the classical prophets. The popular prophets were no mere predictors of the future, but also served as messengers and chastisers. Nor were they alone in their mantic utterances. The classical prophets likewise foretold the future: Isaiah for Hezekiah (Is 37:1 ff; 38:1ff) and Jeremiah for Zedekiah (Jer 32:4-5). Furthermore, even though Samuel, Elijah and Elisha were found in the company of bands of prophets (e.g., I Sam 19:18-24; II Kgs 2:3-15; 4:38-44; 9:1), when discharging their prophetic mission, they appear by themselves just as the classical prophets. The latter, too, had their followers (e.g., Jer 36:4). The phenomenon of ecstasy is not limited to the preclassical prophets (e.g., I Kgs 19:23-24). Both Hosea and, by direct implication, Jeremiah, are called "madman" (Hos 9:7; Jer 29:26), as was Elisha (II Kgs 9:11); and Ezekiel was subject to several ecstatic fits.

Both sets of prophets played an active role in society; they influenced the political destiny of Israel, performed symbolic acts, resorted to signs and wonders, had visions and suffered persecution for their dire predictions.

Nevertheless the classical prophets, who prophesied for over 300 years, from the middle of the 8th century B.C. to the middle of the 5th century, do represent a new phenomenon which cannot be entirely explained by their indebtedness to their predecessors and the traditions they shaped. The classical prophets were active during the period when three successive major empires dominated the world: Assyria (Isaiah, Hosea, Micah, Nahum, Zephaniah), Babylonia (Jeremiah, Ezekiel, Habakkuk), Persia (Second Isaiah, Haggai, Zechariah, Malachi). In a unique religious phenomenon, the later prophets interpreted these momentous political events in the light of their own religious outlook, whereby the Lord of Israel was director of this panoramic drama which focused almost entirely upon his main performer, Israel. The classical prophets provided an answer for both the "why" of punishment, destruction and exile, and the "how" of future restoration.

The prophets, dedicated and commissioned to their tasks, were often reluctant to accept their calling (Is 6:5; Jer 1:6; Jonah 1:1-3). Their burden was not easy to bear; their life was full of frustration and rejection and occasionally they were even subjected to persecution.

Jeremiah, in particular, also had to contend with false prophets (Jer chap. 23), who contradicted his very message (Jer chap. 28 — the confrontation with Hananiah son of Azzur). These false prophets lulled the people into false security (Jer 6:14; 8:11; 14:13; 23:17; 28:2 ff). Jeremiah charged that they had not been sent by God (Jer 14:14-15; 23:21, 32; 28:15; 29:9), were not admitted into the divine council and did not intercede with God on behalf of the people. The charges reflect the characteristics required of a true prophet: he who has truly stood in the Lord's council and heard his word acts, at times, as an intercessor on behalf of his people. This intercessory role which can be traced back to Abraham, Moses and Samuel, is clearly evident in the words of Amos and Ezekiel and dominates the life of Jeremiah. The prophets are known primarily as the spokesmen and messengers of God. Israel, chosen from among all the nations of the world, was thereby held responsible for all of its deeds and misdeeds (Amos 3:2).

From kings, priests, prophets, judges, women and wealthy landowners, down to the poorer classes, no one was impervious to prophetic chastisement. The prophets denounced corruption, dishonesty, harlotry, violence, cruelty, oppression, greed, debauchery, arrogance, apathy, lust for power and idolatry.

According to the prophets, the essence of God's demand is to be found, not in the cult, but rather in the moral and ethical spheres. Amos and many of the other prophets stressed the primacy of morality (Is 1:11-17; 66:1-4; Jer 6:20; 7:21-23; Hos 6:6; Amos 5:21-24; Mic 6:6-8). They did not abrogate the practice of sacrifice, but they adamantly opposed the absolutization of the cult. As a substitute for moral behavior, ritual was to be condemned; if performed by one whose character is blemished, any cultic practice was an abomination to the deity. These views understandably led to clashes with the priests of established religion (Jer 20:1-6; Amos 7:10ff).

The prophets depicted morality and rectitude as the decisive factors in shaping the destiny of the nation, whose very existence was dependent upon its ethical integrity. They warned the people to forsake their immoral behavior: repentance could offset the dire punishment, if it were effected wholeheartedly and in time. Correct actions and righteous behavior could tip the scales of justice and mercy (Jer 18:7-8; Joel 2:13; Amos 5:15; Jonah 1:6; 3:8-10; Zeph 2:3).

Some of the prophets expressed a novel idea: where man failed, God would initiate the process of return, to be finalized in a "new covenant". Man's heart of stone would be turned into a heart of flesh. God would implant his will directly into man's heart. Man's whole being would be filled with the "knowledge of God", rendering him incapable of rejecting or spurning the divine teachings. This new covenant engraved on the heart would be unbreakable and would presage final redemption (Is 11:9; 55:3; Jer 31:30-33; 32:38-41; Ezek 34:25-31; 36:26-38).

With the renewal of the covenant, the remnant of Israel which would have survived the Day of the Lord, would live in peace, untroubled by oppression, injustice or war (Is 2:1-4; 10:27; 11:1-9; 60:5-16; 61:4-9; Hos 2:21-23; Mic 4:3-4). All the nations of the world would finally reject their idolatry and worship the God of Israel alone (Is 19:18-25; Jer 12:16; Ezek 17:24; Mic 7:16-20; Hab 2:14; Zeph 2:11; Zech 14:16-21 etc.). Israel would become a light to the nations, bringing God's blessing and beneficence to the ends of the world (Is 45:22-24; 49:6).

Like John the Baptist (Matt 21:25-26), Jesus was considered to be a prophet (Matt 21:11, 46; Mark 6:15; 8:28; Luke 7:16; 24:19; John 4:19; 9:17), and he apparently accepted the title (Matt 13:57; Luke 13:33). The NT, however, never says that Jesus prophesied, though Mark chapter

13 can be understood as prophecies. The title was seen to be apposite only when used in an absolute sense, "the prophet" (John 6:14; 7:40), because this identified Jesus as the inaugurator of the end of days (cf Deut 18:15; Mal 3:1; 4:5-6).

The NT abounds in references to the OT prophecies, because Jesus and his church were seen as the fulfillment of the salvific plan of God of which the prophets spoke. The prophecies gave Christians categories with which to interpret their experience. They also encouraged hope because not all that had been predicted had yet come to pass.

The end of days (Eschaton) was to be characterized by an outpouring of the Spirit, one of whose manifestations would be an extension of the gift of prophecy (Joel 2:28-32; cf Num 11:29). This was seen to be verified at Pentecost (Acts 2:14-21), and the presence of the charismatic gift is well attested in the Pauline communities (I Cor chaps. 12-14; I Thes 5:20). The precise nature of the charisma cannot be defined. It appears to have been exercised in a liturgical context (I Cor 11:4-5; 14:26-33), and contributed to the edification, encouragement and consolation of the believers (I Cor 14:3-4). It also had a missionary dimension (I Cor 14:24-25). Inevitably, there was a tendency for those granted authority by possession of the gift of prophecy to retain power, and as time went on prophets emerged as a stable group within the church (Acts 13:1; Eph 4:11).

PROSELYTES The Jewish tradition, generally speaking, was favorable towards proselytes and it was seen as a holy duty to attract people to the Torah. Evidence points to widespread conversions to Judaism — in the Diaspora as well as in Israel — during the Second Temple period, especially its latter part. The existence of these proselytes is attested by Jewish and pagan literary sources and by tomb inscriptions in the land of Israel and elsewhere. Proselytes came from many backgrounds, ranging from slaves to royal personalities. The most famous converts were of the royal house of Adiabene in the Tigris region around the 1st century A.D.

Full conversion to Judaism required men to undergo circumcision and immersion, a court of three judges witnessing their undertaking to observe the commandments; women likewise underwent immersion and undertook to observe the commandments. As long as the Temple stood, conversion also entailed a pilgrimage to Jerusalem, since the

Notice in Greek and Hebrew forbidding non-Jews to enter the inner court of the Temple on pain of death. Herodian period.

proselyte had to bring a sacrifice. Some persons, while not converting, undertook to refrain from idolatry and to observe certain commandments; in Jewish and Gentile literature of the Second Temple period, they are called "God-fearers". When Paul traveled through Asia Minor and Greece, he preached and taught in synagogues, where Jews and God-fearers assembled. Jesus, referring to scholars and sages who undertook proselytizing missions, said "Woe to you, scribes and Pharisees, hypocrites! For you travel land and sea to win one proselyte; and when he is won, you make him twice as much a son of hell as yourselves" (Matt 23:15). This passage may well be hyperbolic; there were some Jewish missionaries, but most conversions took place because of the Gentile's own attraction to Judaism.

Some groups, influenced by the bitter experience of Jews with proselytes in times of war and persecution, discouraged proselytism. But this was always a minority view, while the mainstream of Judaism continued to maintain that the proselyte should be accepted "under the wings of the divine presence", conversion being equated with Israel's entry into the covenant. As long as the Temple stood, Jewish sages taught that "When a Gentile comes to you and wants to become a Jew, stretch out your hand, in order to bring him under the wings of the Divine Glory". Later, when Christianity attained predominance in the Roman Empire, proselytism was banned by the Christian emperors; Church canons likewise forbade proselytism and Christian rulers fiercely opposed any tendency to adopt Jewish religious customs. Nevertheless, there were always a number of proselytes who converted to Judaism.

PROVERBS, BOOK OF Book in Hagiographa consisting of nine collections, comprising 31 chapters of individual sayings and instructions from various historical periods. The individual collections consist of chapters 1-9; 10:1-22:16; 22:17-24:22; 24:23-34; 25-29; 30:1-14; 30:15-33; 31:1-9; 31:10-31). Two minor collections acknowledge their foreign origin (the sayings of Agur, 30:1-9; the teachings of King

Part of a page from the Book of Proverbs, from the 9th-century Aleppo Codex. (Courtesy of Prof. M. Goshen-Gottstein and the Hebrew University Bible Project, Jerusalem)

Lemuel's mother, 31:1-9), while yet another has recently been identified in 22:17-24:22 (eleven sayings from the Egyptian Instruction of Amenemopet, and perhaps also one aphorism from the Aramaic text, Ahikar). In addition, many individual sayings within chapters 1-9 betray Egyptian influence: the description of wisdom as an agent of creation (Prov chap. 8) and the notion of wisdom holding life in one hand, righteousness in the other, both of which depend on ideas associated with the goddess Ma'at; the concept of righteousness as the foundation of the royal throne; and the image of God weighing the heart in judgment. Close parallels in form and content to the entire Book of Proverbs are readily available in Babylonian proverb collections and their Sumerian predecessors, as well as in Egyptian Instruction literature and aphorisms.

The biblical claim that Solomon wrote most of the material in Proverbs rests on the account of his extraordinary wisdom, which is illustrated by three episodes: the dream at Gibeon (I Kgs 3:4-15); the king's resolution of a dispute between two harlots (I Kgs 3:16-28); and the visit by the Queen of Sheba (I Kgs 10:1-13). In addition, I Kings 4:29-34 reports that Solomon composed 3,000 proverbs and 1,005 songs. Actually, very few proverbs in the Bible treat the subjects mentioned here (trees, beasts, birds, reptiles and fish). Solomon may have sponsored learning in his court, whereupon his courtiers honored their king by attaching his name to their collected material, just as psalmists associated David's name with numerous psalms. Perhaps the mention of King Hezekiah's men as transcribers of chapters 25-29 is similar in function.

Though it is very difficult to date the different collections that comprise the Book of Proverbs, the book as a whole should be viewed as an anthology spanning several hundreds of years. There is, however, no reason to deny the antiquity of many of the individual proverbs which could well have originated during the Solomonic period.

Many literary forms occur throughout the Book of Proverbs, but the two major ones are those of instruction and saying (often called a "sentence"). The simple saying achieved considerable variety, for example numerical proverbs (30:15-16, 18-19), "better" sayings (15:16-17), allegory (5:15-19), anecdote (7:6-23) and alphabetic poem (31:10-31). Whereas individual sayings used parallelism, mostly antithetic or synonymous, one half verse either opposing or repeating in different words the idea in the other half verse, the instructions in chapters 1-9 comprise extended paragraphs devoted to a particular topic. Some favorite subjects are the contrasts between wise persons and fools; the importance of discipline, whether from parents or teachers or self-imposed; the value of eloquence; the dangers of drunkenness, laziness, and gossip; and the threat presented by the "foreign woman", sometimes personified as Madam Folly. The aim of instruction was to know the right word and act for the occasion, hence to master life. That goal could not be attained without controlling the passions, especially anger and lust.

Instructional texts such as these seem to have evolved within three distinct contexts, each in its own time. The family setting appears to lie behind most of the sayings in the book, and parents instructed their children in the inherited traditions that would secure their existence (cf 6:20-35). The royal court may also have served as a place for useful advice about how to cope with every eventuality, particularly alluring seductresses and angry rulers. Scribal schools offered a third context for instruction; it was probably here that a conscious effort to make these sayings even more religious took place.

(bottom of page)
A page from the Utrecht Psalter. *13th century.*

Fragment of the Book of Psalms (Psalm 82) dating from before A.D. 73, found at Masada. (Shrine of the Book, Jerusalem)

PSALMS, BOOK OF The initial book in the third division of the Hebrew Bible, Psalms represents the pulse of religious life in ancient Israel, primarily during the period of the monarchy, but also in exilic and post-exilic times. The voice of royalty and the cry of ordinary citizens come together in praise, thanksgiving, complaint and instruction. These psalms arose in daily experience; they therefore reflect life's ambiguities from first to last. Extremes of adoration and puzzlement, sighs and shouts, doubt and trust, find expression in them. So do opposing perspectives such as sentiments endorsing the Temple cult and others which consider it inappropriate (50). Sublime thoughts sometimes compete with altogether base desire for revenge on the children of one's enemies, and reflexions by fools amounting to practical atheism exist alongside traditional views about God.

The five collections (1-41, 42-72, 73-89, 90-106, 107-150) evolved over several centuries, each one eventually being supplied with a concluding doxology (41:13; 72:18-19; 89:52; 106:48, 150). The first two psalms function as a general introduction to the entire collection, and the final psalm serves as a conclusion. In time various superscriptions associate specific psalms with events in David's life (e.g. 3:34, 51); identify groups of psalms with a musical guild (Korah and sons, Ethan and Heman, 42-49, 84-85, 87-89), or an individual (Asaph, 50:73-83), Moses (90), Solomon (127); indicate the tune or supply musical comments.

Two additional superscriptions have occasioned considerable discussion. The first is *le-david*, which traditionally was thought to mean "belonging to David" in the sense of authorship. That older view seemed to be confirmed by the ancient traditions that David was a musician (Amos 6:5; II Sam 1:17-27; 3:33-34). The Qumran manuscripts indicate the vigor of this tradition, for David's psalms are numbered at 3,600 and his songs at 450. However, I Chronicles 15:16-24 implies that David's connection with psalms is that of royal patron. This suggests that *le-david* at times may mean "pertaining to David", hence written by various people for use in the royal cult, Davidic or post-Davidic.

The second superscription that has evoked much comment is "A Song of Ascents" (120-134). It has been thought that these psalms were sung while religious pilgrims made the journey from their villages to Jerusalem. It seems more likely that priests sang these 15 psalms as they made their way up the same number of steps within the Temple. Yet another superscription is *hallelujah*, introducing songs of praise (104-

106, 111-113, 117, 135, 146-150). Such clustering of kindred psalms even took place without any superscription (e.g. the enthronement psalms in 93-99).

A page from the Stuttgart Psalter. *9th century.*

The division into five books seems to derive from the fact that the Torah comprised five books. From Psalms 72:20 an older division may be postulated, for this verse observes that David's prayers have come to an end. In any case, some psalms certainly reflect a northern setting (cf 45, which, it has been suggested, may have been a wedding song for Ahab and Jezebel), where Canaanite influence was particularly weighty (cf 29:68). After the fall of Samaria in 722 B.C. these psalms must have made their way south to Judah. Curiously, one group of psalms (42-89) has replaced the name for God, *Yahweh*, in many verses with the more general name, *Elohim*. This fact can be seen clearly where duplicate psalms occur (14:53; 40:14-17, 70). Two psalms (19:1-6; 104) bear a close resemblance to Egyptian hymns; this is understandable in light of evidence that portions of an Egyptian instruction are incorporated within the Book of Proverbs (22:17-22:33 and *Amen-em-opet*). Many psalms from Israel's repertoire exist outside the Psalter (e.g. II Sam chap. 22=Ps 18; Gen chap. 49; Ex 15:1-18; Deut chaps. 32-33; Judg chap. 5; I Sam 2:1-10; Jonah 2:3-10; Hab chap. 3).

The precise dating of individual psalms is impossible. Only Psalm 137 yields specific clues that require a post-exilic date, for it looks back over the period of residence in Babylon. Many psalms can only be understood as having arisen during the monarchy, for they functioned in the royal cult. Occasions such as enthronement (24, 74, 93, 96-99), coronation (2:110), wedding (45) and consultation prior to battle (20) were sanctioned by appropriate psalms. Perhaps, too, the king spoke many of the laments on behalf of the people, especially during national catastrophes. One thing seems clear: comparison of biblical psalms with Maccabean psalms, the Qumran psalms scroll, and the Odes of Solomon justifies the tendency to date biblical psalms earlier than was the fashion a few decades ago. Most of them can be safely situated within the First Temple period.

Much discussion has arisen about the actual psalm types in the Bible. Four categories have commended themselves to critics: hymns, laments, songs of trust and didactic poems. The hymns usually celebrate the deity's role as creator and redeemer; they describe the saving deeds in Israel's behalf with lavish rhetoric. Laments, both individual and communal, complain about divine absence or wrath. The sufferer insists that personal distress is undeserved, and wonders whether the deity has forsaken one who is in need. The causes for anxiety are multiple: sickness, economic distress, physical abuse, warfare, drought, earthquake and the like. Structurally, laments consist of complaint and confession of confidence. What brings about the shift from complaint to trust? Two answers are often given to this question. The first takes its cue from Hannah's prayer, when the priest Eli offered a divine response (I Sam 1:17). Accordingly, it is claimed that a priest or prophet gave a response to the sufferer, and this assurance of divine deliverance gave birth to the expression of confidence. The second answer stresses the leap of faith in spite of all evidence to the contrary. That confidence was grounded in covenant faith.

The third literary type, song of trust, may not represent a distinct form, since it resembles the confession of confidence within the lament. Nevertheless, this component has become an entity in itself, ultimately contributing the title of the Qumran collection (Thanksgiving Psalms). Some of these biblical songs of trust have nourished the lives of countless Jews and Christians (e.g. 23). To be sure, echoes of life's dark side persist, but the dominant mood is positive. Sometimes this bright side is so overwhelming that it threatens to become the prevalent mood within laments (129).

The fourth type is didactic poem, whether learned psalmography (the retelling of Israel's history), reflexion on the Torah (1; 19:7-14; 119), examination of the problem of evil (37; 49; 73) or acrostics (9-10; 25; 34; 37; 111-112; 119; 145). The alphabetic psalms seem to represent the notion of completion, rather than functioning as magical incantations or as an aid to memory. The three psalms that deal with theodicy resemble the Book of Job, although Psalm 73 achieves a theological breakthrough by redefining the nature of the good (it is God's presence, not divine presents). The most striking feature of the Torah psalms is the positive attitude toward the Torah as an expression of divine love, an attitude that is diametrically opposed to that of the apostle Paul, from whom the law was a heavy burden that condemned humanity.

Not all of the psalms were restricted to royal ceremonies, although many of them functioned in that manner. Entrance liturgies, for example, arose for priestly (24) and private use (15). By far the majority of psalms served to articulate private sentiments (cf 121) ranging from the agony of despair to the ecstasy of triumph. During the days of Temple worship these personal expressions may have been largely submerged into official ceremony, but the songs outlasted the Temple and its cult. By that time their content had come to embody the very soul of the people toward God, and regular singing of hymns became common. The NT confirms this practice for Christians (Eph 5:19; Col 3:16) as rabbinic literature does for Jews.

OUTLINE

1-41	Book I	Psalms of David (except 1-2, which are introductory, 10, 33).
42-72	Book II	18 ascribed to David, 7 to the sons of Korah, 50 to Asaph, 72 to Solomon, and 4 are anonymous
73-89	Book III	73-83 attributed to Asaph, 84-85 and 87 to the sons of Korah, 86 to David, 88 to Heman the Ezrahite and 89 to Ethan the Ezrahite
90-106	Book IV	Which has one psalm attributed to Moses (90), two to David (101, 103) and the rest are anonymous
107-150	Book V	15 attributed to David and one to Solomon. Most of the others have no inscription. 120-134 are called "Songs of Ascent".

PSEUDEPIGRAPHA The Pseudepigrapha is a collection of ancient writings reflecting Jewish thought from c. 250 B.C. to A.D. 200. Many of these documents were eventually expanded or rewritten by Christians; a few seem to have been composed by Christians. The Pseudepigrapha are almost always influenced by the OT: many supply revelations reputed to have been received by prominent OT personalities, others are rewritten versions or expansions of biblical narratives; some are psalms modeled on the Davidic Psalter, and a few are compositions shaped by Jewish Wisdom literature. Although these writings were composed long after Abraham, Moses, David, Solomon, Jeremiah, Isaiah, Ezra and other famous men, they were often intentionally but incorrectly (pseudepigraphically) attributed to one of them.

The names of the Pseudepigrapha and their broadly conceived genres are as follows:

Apocalyptic Literature and Related Works

1 Enoch	Questions of Ezra
2 Enoch	Revelation of Ezra
3 Enoch	Apocalypse of Sedrach
Sibylline Oracles	2 Baruch
Treatise of Shem	3 Baruch
Apocryphon of Ezekiel	Apocalypse of Abraham
Apocalypse of Zephaniah	Apocalypse of Adam
The Fourth Book of Ezra	Apocalypse of Elijah
Greek Apocalypse of Ezra	Apocalypse of Daniel
Vision of Ezra	

Testaments (Often with Apocalyptic Sections)

Testaments of the Twelve Patriarchs	Testament of Moses
Testament of Job	Testament of Solomon
Testaments of the Three Patriarchs (Abraham, Isaac and Jacob)	Testament of Adam

Expansions of the OT and Legends

Letter of Aristeas	Ladder of Jacob
Jubilees	4 Baruch
Martyrdom and Ascension of Isaiah	James and Jambres
Joseph and Asenath	History of the Rechabites
Life of Adam and Eve	Eldad and Medad
Pseudo-Philo	History of Joseph
Lives of the Prophets	

Wisdom and Philosophical Literature

Ahikar	Pseudo-Phocylides
3 Maccabees	Syriac-Menander
4 Maccabees	

Prayers, Psalms and Odes

More Psalms of David	Prayer of Joseph
Prayer of Manasseh	Prayer of Jacob
Psalms of Solomon	Odes of Solomon
Hellenistic Synagogal Prayers	

Fragments of Judeo-Hellenistic Works

Philo the Epic Poet	Theodotus
Orphica	Ezekiel the Tragedian
Fragments of Pseudo-Greek Poets	Aristobulus
Demetrius.the Chronographer	Aristeas the Exegete
Eupolemus	Pseudo-Eupolemus
Cleodemus Malchus	Artapanus
Pseudo-Hecataeus	

PUAH ("girl, young woman").

1. One of the two Hebrew midwives who, along with Shiphrah defied Pharaoh's decree that all males born to the Hebrew women should be killed (Ex 1:15-22). Her name appears to be identical with that of the daughter of Danel in the Ugaritic myth of Danel.

2. Second son of Issachar (Num 26:23). Called Puvah in Genesis 46:13.

3. Son of Dodo and father of Tola the judge of Israel after Abimelech's downfall.

PUBLICAN, TAX COLLECTOR Minor officials appointed by the Roman governors to collect taxes from the populace. Denying the legitimacy of Roman rule, the Jewish population as a whole never submitted to the foreign yoke ("We are Abraham's descendants, and have never been in bondage to anyone", John 8:33) and there was consequent controversy over payment of the taxes demanded by the Romans. The Zealots considered it sinful to pay taxes to foreign rulers; others agreed in denouncing submission to the Romans but held payment of taxes to be legitimate because of *force majeure*. The Jews were also required to pay customs duties at the frontiers and ports, and there were even inland levies (on agricultural produce, for example, at the city gates of Jerusalem). These customs stations, where high duties were charged on imports such as perfumes or medicaments brought from Arabia, were manned by tax collectors; one such was Levi, also called Matthew, the son of Alfaeus (Matt 9:9; Mark 2:14). Seen as collaborators willing to help the Romans tighten their grip on the country, publicans were not popular among their fellow Jews, being equated with sinners or Gentiles (Matt 18:17; Mark 2:15). Jewish tradition even sanctioned a "false oath to publicans and robbers" (Mishnah Nedarim 3:4). For the people subjected to Roman taxes, publicans and robbers were synonymous.

According to the gospels, Jesus used to meet with publicans, as with other "sinners", not in condonation of their behavior but in constant hope for their repentance (Matt 9:13; Mark 2:17; Luke 5:32). He ate with the publican Matthew, who later became one of the twelve disciples (Matt 9:9-10; Mark 2:14-15; Luke 5:27-29). The NT also mentions Zaccaeus of Jericho who was the head of a group of publicans and renowned for his wealth: after meeting Jesus, he repented, giving half of his possessions to the poor and compensating fourfold those from whom he had taken by false accusation (Luke 19:1-10). Jesus stressed that he came to all, not the righteous alone but the sinners too; he warned the Jews that "tax collectors and harlots enter the Kingdom of God before you" (Matt 21:31).

PUBLIUS ("common"). A leading citizen of Malta who hosted Paul for

---

PUAH 1
Ex 1:15

PUAH 2
Num 26:23.
I Chr 7:1

PUAH 3
Judg 10:1

PUBLICAN,
TAX COLLECTOR
Matt 5:46-47;
9:10-11; 10:3;
11:19; 18:17;
21:31-32.
Mark 2:15-16.
Luke 3:12;
5:27, 29-30;
7:29, 34; 15:1;
18:10-11, 13;
19:2

PUBLIUS
Acts 28:7-8

three days during his ministry in Malta. His father fell sick and was healed by the apostle.

PUDENS ("ashamed"). A Roman Christian who sent greetings to Timothy.

PUL See TIGLATH-PILESER

PUNITES Descendants of Puah (written in Hebrew as Puvah) of the tribe of Issachar.

PUNON One of the stations on the route of the Exodus, between Zalmon and Oboth (Num 33:42-43). Identified with Feinan 30 miles (48km) south of the Dead Sea, it was known in the Roman period as Finon, or Fainon. The region is comparatively rich in water and arable soil, which contributed to its importance. The copper mines in the vicinity were worked in both early and later historical periods.

PUR See PURIM

PURAH A young servant of Gideon who went with him to spy upon the enemy camps of the Midianites and Amalekites.

PURIM A festival falling on Adar 14-15 celebrating the deliverance of the Jews from the genocidal decree of Haman. The Akkadian term *pur* meaning "lots", from which the name of the holiday is derived, appears eight times in the Bible, all in the Book of Esther, and is occasionally glossed by the Hebrew word which explains its meaning. Twice the term "pur" refers to the actual casting of lots before Haman in order to establish Adar as the month for exterminating the Jews (Est 3:7; 9:24); two other occurrences refer to the naming of the holiday as Purim (literally "lots" — plural form of *pur*) based on the aforementioned casting of lots (Est 9:26); the remaining four usages refer to the holiday Purim as an established Jewish festival (Est 9:28-29, 31-32). Purim and Hanukkah were the two main festivals to be added to the Jewish calendar after the return from the Babylonian Exile (after 538 B.C.). The foreign term employed to name the holiday and its nonreligious nature points to an ultimate non-Israelite source for the festival, whose origin is still unknown. The Book of Esther provides biblical authority for the Jewish practice of the Purim holiday, while the Talmudic tractate Megillah, delineates the rules and regulations for the synagogue reading of the Book of Esther on the eve and the morning of the holiday as well as for other aspects of the holiday's observance.

PURITY, IMPURITY The biblical concept of purity and impurity is to be sharply distinguished in one important respect from that prevalent in the paganism of antiquity. In the latter, the impure is conceived as hostile and dangerous to both man and the gods. In the Bible, on the other hand, there is no suggestion that the impure can inflict harm upon man, much less upon God. Nevertheless, impurity is regarded as incompatible with holiness. The person who has become defiled must be purified before entering the sphere of the holy even as the latter must periodically be cleansed of its impurities.

Certain creatures, objects and physical conditions are deemed impure and sources of defilement. The latter two categories become pure by means of a prescribed ritual of purification. Though the state of impurity is regarded as a kind of contagious infection, the ritual of purification is not a means of healing since it takes place only after the source and condition of impurity have disappeared.

Purity is an aspect of holiness just as impurity is an aspect of sin with which it is often equated. Since it is Israel's task and destiny to be a holy people (Ex 19:6; Lev 19:2; Num 15:40), it must rigorously exclude from its midst every form of impurity. Otherwise, God will turn away and doom Israel to exile and destruction (Lev 15:31; Ezek 39:24). Idolatrous cults and practices are deemed impure, and render Israel unclean (Ps

Ritual washing of the hands. Miniature from the Barcelona Haggadah. *Spain, 14th century. (British Museum)*

106:38; Is 30:22; Ezek 24:13; 36:25; 37:23). The presence of idolatry in foreign lands likewise makes them impure (Amos 7:17). Evil and idolatrous practices by Israel render its own land unclean (Ezek 36:17). The Temple in ruins and unrestored spreads impurity throughout Jerusalem (Hag 2:13-14).

Pagan worship defiles the Temple and the altar. So, Hezekiah, in his program of religious reform instructed the Levites and priests to purify the Temple of the idolatry introduced by Ahaz (II Chr 29:15-16). The sacrificial ritual of the Day of Atonement removed the pollution of the sanctuary caused by the sins and impurities of Israel during the past year (Lev 16:19,33).

An extension of the concept of ritual impurity is to be seen in the Prophets, Psalms and Wisdom Literature where the emphasis is placed on moral purity. In this literature, "cleanness of hand" means moral integrity (II Sam 22:21, 25). When Isaiah proclaimed (Is 1:16) "...wash yourselves, make yourselves clean", he equated uncleanness with evil and injustice. The Psalmist (18:20; 73:13) gave the same sense to the phrase "cleanness of hands". The latter is one of the moral prerequisites, in addition to a "pure heart", for him who would "ascend the mountain of the Lord and stand in his holy place" (Ps 24:3-4; 51:7ff).

A priest inspecting possible cases of leprosy for ritual impurity. Illustration from the title page of the Hebrew-Latin edition of the Mishnah, *published in Amsterdam, 1700-1704)*

Ritual impurity derives from certain physical states and objects, conceived as exuding impurity on contact. Among the former, is a person from whose body there is a discharge (probably, a gonorrheal flux). Such person defiles anyone with whom he or she comes in contact as well as any seat, bed or saddle (Lev 15:2-12). The same holds true for a menstruating woman (Lev 15:19). Sexual intercourse produces uncleanness in both the man and the woman (Lev 15:16-18). Another source is a persistent discharge of blood from a woman (Lev 15:25-30). Childbirth produces impurity for seven days following the birth of a male child and for 14 days if the child is female. In addition, for a further period of 33 days after the birth of a male and 66 days following the birth of a female, the woman is prohibited from touching holy things or entering the sanctuary (Lev 12:1-5). The most severe grade of impurity, that of a leper or of one who has had contact with a corpse, requires that the person so defiled be sent beyond the camp (Lev 13:46; 14:2-3; Num 5:2-4). If after an initial period of seclusion of seven days, the signs of leprosy have not spread, the person is secluded for an additional seven days and a final determination is made by the priest. If he is pronounced leprous, he is to dwell outside the camp. Analogous indications are given (Lev 13:47-58) by which the priest is to determine the cleanness or uncleanness of a wool or linen cloth or leather on the wall of a home in which a mold has appeared. Contact with the dead renders one unclean for a period of seven days (Num 19:11; Ezek 44:26). Uncovered vessels in a dwelling in which a corpse lay become unclean (Num 19:15). For each of the impurities mentioned above, a specific ritual of purification is prescribed; the more severe the impurity the more elaborate the ritual. Purification requires a waiting period of varying duration.

Purification requires the use of water (bathing), fire or the sprinkling of blood by the priest on the altar and on the cover of the ark (Lev 16:15). Again, the means used for purification depends on the severity of the impurity to be cleansed. Contact with someone or something with a primary degree of impurity, inflicts secondary impurity, for which bathing suffices, while a more severe form of impurity requires both bathing and washing one's clothes. A more elaborate ritual of purification is prescribed for the leper (Lev 14:2-20). The ritual for one who has been defiled by contact with a corpse is described in Numbers chapter 19. See RED HEIFER. Severe grades of impurity require the bringing of a sacrifice (Lev 12:6; 14:10). The purification of the leper requires the smearing of the blood of the sacrifice on the lobe of the ear, on the thumb of the right hand and on the right toe of the foot. Finally, the priest is to smear oil on these places on the body of the leper after having sprinkled some of the oil "seven times before the Lord" (Lev 14:14-18).

The concepts of ritual purity and impurity underwent a radical transformation in the NT parallel to those found in the Prophets and Wisdom Literature. The latter, however, did not repudiate the notion of ritual purity and impurity as did Jesus. "There is nothing that enters a man from outside which can defile him; but the things which come out of him, those are the things that defile a man" (Mark 7:15, 23). "From within, out of the heart of men, proceed evil thoughts, adulteries, fornications, murders,... all these evil things come from within and defile man" (Mark 7:21, 23; cf James 4:8). Paul (Rom 14:14-21) declared "that there is nothing unclean of itself". Yet, as a tactic, he advised to refrain from eating food (presumably impure) in the presence of a potential Jewish convert. It may offend and prove "a stumbling block" to his conversion to faith in Jesus.

Jesus cleansed lepers by a touch of his hand or by a mere word, then ordered the cleansed leper to "... go your way and show yourself to the priest, and offer the gift that Moses commanded, as a testimony to them" (Matt 8:2-4; Mark 1:40-45; Luke 5:12-15; 17:11-14). Jesus is described (John 15:3), as cleansing his disciples (of moral evil) by his word or by washing their feet (John 13:10). Paul wrote (Heb 10:22) "... our hearts sprinkled from an evil conscience and our bodies washed with pure water". These passages obviously reflect the bathing for the purpose of ritual purification found frequently in Hebrew Scripture. The notion that the blood of Jesus "cleanses us from all sin" is found in I John 1:7.

Remains of a temple of the 1st century B.C. in the ancient port of Pozzuoli, a few miles from Naples, and believed to be the town of Puteoli.

In one of his denunciations of the Pharisees, Jesus declared: "... first cleanse the inside of the cup and dish, that the outside of them may be clean also" (Matt 23:26; Luke 11:39). Yet, like the Pharisees, he implicitly acknowledged that the bones of the dead render one impure... "Pharisees... are like white-washed tombs which indeed appear beautiful outwardly but inside are full of dead men's bones and all uncleanness" (Matt 23:27).

In one significant respect, the NT departed from the OT concept of impurity when it attributed sickness, leprosy and insanity to "unclean spirits" that take possession of a man's body (Matt 10:8; 12:43; Mark 1:23-26; 3:11).

PUT

PUT 1
Gen 10:6.
I Chr 1:8

1. One of the sons of Ham (Gen 10:6; I Chr 1:8).

PUT 2
Nah 3:9

2. The name of a Libyan tribe, and later the name of the country to the west of Egypt. They are mentioned both as allies and foes of Egypt (Nah 3:9; cf Jer 46:9; Ezek 27:10; 30:5; 38:5).

PUTEOLI
Acts 28:13

PUTEOLI A harbor in the Bay of Naples on the west coast of Italy, modern Puzzuoli. Puteoli was Italy's most important port and trade center until the refurbishment of Ostia by Trajan.

It had a large Jewish population in ancient times. On Paul's way to Rome aboard an Alexandrian grain freighter he arrived in Puteoli where he found a Christian population already in existence. Part of the port's ancient pier is visible to this day.

PUTHITES
I Chr 2:53

PUTHITES A family of Judahites from Kirjath Jearim.

PUTIEL
Ex 6:25

PUTIEL Father-in-law of Eleazar, the son of Aaron; his daughter bore Eleazar a son, Phinehas.

PUVAH
Gen 46:13

PUVAH See PUAH No.2

QUAIL See ANIMALS

QUARTUS ("the fourth"). One of the early Christians in Rome.

QUEEN OF HEAVEN The designation of a specific form of idol worship denounced by the prophet Jeremiah, who castigated the people of Judah (especially the women) for burning incense and offering libations as part of cultic practice (Jer 7:18; 44:17-19, 25). The term "Queen of Heaven" is actually a Hebrew translation from the Akkadian where it appears as an epithet for Ishtar, the goddess of love and fertility. In an attempt to avoid the mention of this goddess in Jeremiah, the Masoretic Hebrew text altered the vocalization of the first word from "Queen of Heaven" to "Handiwork of Heaven".

QUEEN OF SHEBA See SHEBA

QUIRINIUS Governor of Syria, A.D. 6-11. His term of office included the census which brought Joseph and Mary to Bethlehem.

QUARTUS
Rom 16:23

QUEEN OF HEAVEN
**Jer 7:18;
44:17-19, 25**

QUEEN OF SHEBA
I Kgs 10:1, 4, 10, 13. II Chr 9:1, 3, 9, 12

QUIRINIUS
Luke 2:2

R

RAAMA, RAAMAH

1. A son of Cush in the genealogy of Ham (Gen 10:7; I Chr 1:9). His name is eponymous with the place.

2. An Arabian locality which traded with Tyre in spices, precious stones and gold (Ezek 27:22). It is linked by Ezekiel with "Sheba" (Sabeans) which occupied the southwest part of Arabia.

RAAMIAH One of the heads of families or clans who returned from the Exile in Babylon with Zerubbabel. Spelled Reelaiah in the Book of Ezra (Ezra 2:2).

RAAMSES, RAMESES The name of a town and a district in the eastern half of the Nile Delta, where Joseph settled his father and brothers (Gen 47:11); it was one of the treasure cities built by the Israelites for Pharaoh (Ex 1:11). In Egyptian it is known as "Per-Rameses" — "House of Rameses". It became the delta residence of the pharaohs from the reign of Rameses II. Some scholars identify Raamses with Tanis while others prefer an identification with Qantir, about 11 miles (18 km) to the south, where both Sethos I and Rameses II built palaces. The city of Raamses was much praised for its beauty and luxury.

RABBAH, RABBATH AMMON The capital of the Ammonites, on the border of the desert, near the sources of the River Jabbok; also called Rabbah (Josh 13:25) and surrounded by small villages, the "daughters of Rabbah" (Jer 49:3). It was an important junction for roads leading

(bottom of page)
Bronze bottle bearing the names of the last Ammonite kings. 8th-7th centuries B.C. (Archaeological Museum, Amman)

(left)
Excavations at Tell Rabbat Ammon.

A small Ammonite tower, part of the fortifications encircling the city of Rabbat Ammon.

from the Arabian peninsula in the south to Damascus in the north, and from the Syrian desert on the east to Palestine and the Mediterranean on the west. The city was built in two parts, the lower one containing the city's water supply (II Sam 12:27), and the upper being referred to as the "royal city" (II Sam 12:26). Joab conquered the lower city and waited for David to complete the conquest (II Sam 12:27-29). After the division of the United Monarchy, Rabbah became the capital of the independent kingdom of Ammon. At the beginning of the 6th century B.C. it was destroyed by "men of the east" who made it "a stable for camels" and "a resting place for flocks" (Ezek 25:4-5). This may refer to an Arabian tribe.

Ptolemy II Philadelphus (285-246 B.C.) rebuilt the city and renamed it Philadelphia. From 63 B.C., after the Roman conquest, it became part of the DECAPOLIS.

A coin of Philadelphia (Rabbat Ammon) depicting Demeter holding ears of corn. 2nd century.

(top right)
The Roman theater at Philadelphia.

(top left)
Excavations showing remains of Roman period temple at Philadelphia (Rabbat Ammon).

Extensive excavations have made finds from various periods. Near the top of the acropolis, tombs of the end of the Middle Bronze Age were discovered. At the site of Amman airport a temple was discovered; under its 6 feet (2 m) thick walls, built of unhewn stones, were found foundation offerings, including fowl and animals. There were also 40 gold objects deposited as offerings. The temple was built at the end of the 14th century B.C. and abandoned in the following century. In various parts of the city remains from the 9th century B.C. were found, including the only known Ammonite inscriptions. One inscription, engraved on a bronze bottle, mentioned Amminadab son of Hisael son of Amminadab, king of the Ammonites, dating to the 7th century B.C. Some short inscriptions were engraved on statues of gods or rulers. The city fortifications, including a wall and numerous towers, are also attributed to the Ammonite period.

Most of the remains are of the Roman period. Among the monuments are a nymphaeum, odeum and theater in the lower city, the propylaea and steps of the acropolis, and a temple of Zeus.

RABBITH A city allotted to Issachar when the land of Canaan was divided among the tribes; it was later assigned to the Levites. Some scholars believe it to be an alternate name for Daberath; however it is more generally considered to have been a different city, located somewhere in the vicinity of Gezer.

RABBITH
Josh 19:20

RABMAG The designation of an official at the court of the Babylonian king Nebuchadnezzar. The name may refer to a title or position.

RABMAG
Jer 39:3, 13

RABSARIS A high official or function at the Assyrian court and later in the kingdom of Babylon.

RABSARIS
II Kgs 18:17.
Jer 39:3, 13

RABSHAKEH An Akkadian loanword meaning "chief cupbearer", occurring in only one biblical context, the military campaign of Sennacherib, king of Assyria against Jerusalem in 701 B.C. (cf II Kgs 18:17ff; 19:4, 8; Is 36:2, 4, 11, 13, 22; 37:4, 8). Both II Kings chapter 18 and Isaiah chapter 36 indicate that Sennacherib sent him at the head of a high level Assyrian delegation, whose mission was to persuade King Hezekiah and all of Judah to surrender unconditionally to the Assyrian king. According to II Kings chapter 18, the Rabshakeh arrived in

RABSHAKEH
II Kgs 18:17,
19, 26-28, 37;
19:4, 8. Is
36:2, 4, 11-13,
22; 37:4, 8

Jerusalem accompanied by two other high ranking military commanders. According to Isaiah chapter 36, the Rabshakeh was the sole leader of the delegation (in both sources, only the Rabshakeh speaks). In a third source, II Chronicles chapter 32, the Assyrian officials are not referred to by title, but rather as Sennacherib's "servants" (vs. 9, 16), who were sent to speak in his name. It has been suggested that Rabshakeh's first speech (II Kgs 18:19-25, 27-35; Is 36:4-10, 12-20), contains neo-Assyrian elements which demonstrate its authenticity.

RACA A derogatory term; a form of the Aramaic word *reke* meaning "empty" or "worthless". Its use was condemned by Jesus.

RACHAL One of the cities of Judah. David sent some of the plunder taken from the Amalekites to its elders. Nothing further is known about it and it may have been an alternate name for Carmel (which is the form used in the Septuagint).

RACHEL ("ewe"). Laban's younger daughter and Jacob's second, but favored, wife.

Jacob first met Rachel by a well. Struck by her beauty, he fell in love with her, and pledged seven years of labor to her father as her brideprice. Having completed his term, Jacob was tricked into taking Rachel's elder sister Leah instead, but he then covenanted to work a further seven years to gain Rachel, and ultimately married her.

Rachel's tomb on the road between Jerusalem and Bethlehem.

*(left)
The tomb of Rachel (exterior). Photograph taken in 1908. (Collection Dr. N. Gidal, Jerusalem)*

However, Rachel remained barren while Leah was fertile (Gen chap. 29). After Rachel cried that she would die if she had no children, she was blessed with her first son, Joseph (Gen 30:22-24), and a second, Benjamin, at whose birth she died (Gen 35:16-18). Before she had children of her own, she had emulated Sarah and Leah, acquiring legal sons by giving Jacob her handmaid Bilhah, who bore for him two sons, Dan and Naphtali (Gen 30:3-8).

Although socially inferior as the younger sister and chronologically second to marry, and despite her persistent barrenness, Rachel always enjoyed her husband's love and preferential treatment. More often than not when she and Leah are mentioned together, her name comes first (e.g. Gen 31:4). Fearing hostility in his forthcoming encounter with Esau, Jacob ordered Rachel and her household to be stationed at the rear of the column to reduce the danger of harm to her (Gen 33:2). Rachel was the more spirited of the two sisters, as borne out by her successful removal of Laban's household gods (teraphim) prior to departure for Canaan, and her subsequent imprudent lie to her father about the affair (Gen 31:34ff). In the blessing for brides (Ruth 4:11) Rachel is named first although her sister's nominal domestic status and fertility ought to have gained her that position.

Rachel died on the way to Bethlehem and an ancient site became revered as her tomb. In biblical times she was already perceived as the tortured mother, whose untimely departure caused her to grieve continuously for her sons. As Jeremiah says: "Hark, lamentation is heard in Ramah, and bitter weeping. Rachel is weeping for her sons. She refuses to be comforted..." (Jer 31:15; cf Matt 2:16-18 in connection with the massacre of the infants by Herod). Rachel is regarded as the fourth matriarch of the Jewish people.

RADDAI Fifth of the seven sons of Jesse, and one of David's elder brothers.

RADDAI
I Chr 2:14

RAHAB

1. The prostitute who played a key role in the conquest of Jericho (Josh chaps. 2-6). Occupying a house upon the city wall (Josh 2:15), Rahab gave lodging to the two men sent into Jericho by Joshua on a reconnaissance expedition (Josh 2:1-12). When the king of Jericho learned about the two spies, he sent men to Rahab's house ordering her to hand them over (Josh 2:3). Rahab, however, hid them on her roof under stalks of flax, and told the king's servants that they had already left (Josh 2:4-6). Before letting the two men down through the window by means of a scarlet cord, Rahab asked them to remember her kindness by saving her family when they conquered the city (Josh 2:12-13) and the men swore to do so (Josh 2:14). When Joshua conquered Jericho and laid the town waste (Josh 6:24) Rahab's family was spared (Josh 6:22-25), and they dwelt in Israel from that time on (Josh 6:25).

RAHAB 1
Josh 2:1, 3; 6:17, 23, 25. Matt 1:5. Heb 11:31. James 2:25

Rahab is mentioned in the genealogy of Jesus as one of his ancestors (Matt 1:5), and is cited as a heroine of faith (Heb 11:31), and as one who was justified through righteous works (James 2:25).

2. A name of a mythological dragon, defeated by God in a primordial battle. See LEVIATHAN.

RAHAB 2
Ps 87:4; 89:10. Is 30:7; 51:9

RAHAM ("mercy", "love"). Son of Shema the son of Hebron, and father of Jorkoam.

RAHAM
I Chr 2:44

RAKEM One of the two sons of Sheresh, a man of Manasseh.

RAKEM
I Chr 7:16

RAKKATH A fortified town in the territory of Naphtali (Josh 19:35), situated between Hammath and the Sea of Galilee. It is identified with Tell Quneitra, $1\frac{1}{2}$ miles (2.5 km) northwest of Tiberias.

RAKKATH
Josh 19:35

RAKKON A river or brook on the northwestern border of the territory allotted to Dan (Josh 19:46) when the land of Canaan was divided among the tribes (Josh 14:1). Perhaps the Al Barideh brook, a tributary of the Eilon River.

RAKKON
Josh 19:46

RAM See ANIMALS

RAM ("tall").

1. A son of Hezron (grandson of Judah); father of Amminadab, the great-grandfather of Boaz and hence an ancestor of David.

RAM 1
Ruth 4:19. I Chr 2:9-10. Matt 1:3-4. Luke 3:33

2. The eldest son of Jerahmeel (firstborn son of Hezron) (I Chr 2:25) and the father of Maaz, Jamin and Eker.

RAM 2
I Chr 2:25, 27

3. Family of Elihu, son of Barachel the Buzite, who argued with Job in defense of God's justice.

RAM 3
Job 32:2

RAMAH (RAMA) ("height"). A geographical name given to several towns in ancient Israel.

1. One of the towns in the territory of Benjamin (Josh 18:25). Mentioned together with Gibeon and Beeroth, it is situated near Gebah, north of Gibeon, on the watershed (cf Judg 19:13; Is 10:29; Jer 40:1; Hos

RAMAH 1
Josh 18:25. Judg 4:5;

5:8; Ezra 2:26; Neh 7:30). The identification of this site with er-Ram $5\frac{1}{2}$ miles (9 km) north of Jerusalem, is accepted by most scholars and supported by archeological finds. This Ramah is apparently the town conquered and fortified by King Baasha of Israel "that he might not let none go out or come in to Asa king of Judah" (I Kgs 15:17), and the home of Samuel in the land of Zuph, also named Ramathaim Zophim (I Sam 1:1). It therefore seems that at the time of the narrative in Judges and the First Book of Samuel, Ramah was on the southern border of the territory of Ephraim, but it subsequently changed hands when the territory of Benjamin expanded. This then is also the Ramah mentioned in connection with Deborah (Judg 4:5).

Ramah stood on Sennacherib's line of advance from Samaria toward Jerusalem (Is 10:29); Jeremiah describes Ramah as the scene of Rachel's weeping for her children (Jer 31:15). With the return from the Babylonian captivity, some of the former residents went back to Ramah (Ezra 2:26; Neh 7:30).

2. Town on the border of the territory of Asher: "...as far as Sidon. And the border turned to Ramah, and to the fortified city of Tyre" (Josh 19:28-29). This Ramah should then be sought between Tyre and Sidon. The strong city of Tyre is apparently inland Tyre, known in Assyrian sources as Usu, which is identified with Tell er-Rasidiyeh; Ramah must have been located northwest of it, but the exact site is not known.

3. A town of Naphtali (Josh 19:36). The site has long been identified with a large village er-Rameh, 5 miles (8 km) west-southwest of Safed, on the slope of Jebel Khaidar, which is part of the high mountain range forming the natural border between Upper and Lower Galilee. This fits in well with the order of the towns of Naphtali between Upper and Lower Galilee. But no archeological remains earlier than the Hellenistic and Roman periods have been found within the bounds of er-Rameh. It thus seems that biblical Ramah is situated at Khirbet Zeitun er-Rameh, an ancient mound about $1\frac{1}{2}$ miles (2.5 km) southeast of er-Rameh.

4. A place listed among the villages of Benjamin (Neh 11:33) where it is mentioned between Hazor and Gittaim, and followed by Hadid, Zeboim and Neballat. This site was apparently located on the western slopes of the mountains, in the vicinity of Lod. This Ramah is apparently identical with Ramathaim, one of the districts whose annexation was confirmed by the Seleucids (I Macc 10:30, 38; 11:34), and with Arimathea, the home of Joseph, one of Jesus' disciples (Matt 27:57; John 19:38). Its identification with Rentis, 6 miles (10 km) northeast of Lod (Lydda), is plausible.

5. Ramah of the South (Negeb). One of the towns in the territory of Simeon (Josh 19:8). In I Samuel 30:26-27 Ramoth of the South is mentioned among the places to which David sent some of the spoils he had taken from "the enemies of the Lord" as a gift to the elders of the town. Ramath Negeb is mentioned in a Hebrew ostracon found at Arad and dating to the late period of the Kingdom of Judah. The site is identified either with Horvat Uzza, in the eastern part of the Negeb of Judah, or with Horvat Ira.

6. See RAMOTH GILEAD.

RAMATHAIM ZOPHIM An alternate name for Ramah, Samuel's place of birth and burial.

RAMATHITE A native or inhabitant of Ramah. The appellation is applied to Shimei, the supervisor of the vineyards of King David.

RAMATH LEHI See LEHI

RAMATH MIZPAH A city in Gilead allotted to Gad when the land of Canaan was divided among the tribes (Josh 13:26; 14:1). Its location is disputed.

Er-Ram, north of Jerusalem, the site of ancient Ramah.

RAMESES The name of several Egyptian kings. The Bible does not mention Rameses by name but the pharaoh referred to in Exodus is thought to be Rameses II or Rameses III.

Rameses II reigned for over 66 years (1290-1224 B.C.). Most of his reign is characterized by conflicts. His defeat by the Hittites in the famous battle at Kadesh affected the hegemony of these two empires over Canaan. Later, Rameses conducted several campaigns in Canaan and along the Phoenician coast in order to reestablish his sovereignty over these areas. He is also famous for his building activities in Egypt among which were the city of Raamses and the temples at Abu Simbel.

Statues of Rameses II in his temple at Abu Simbel.

Rameses III was closely involved with the Philistine presence in Canaan in the 12th century B.C. His naval and land battles against the invading Sea Peoples, including the Philistines are depicted in wall paintings and reliefs of the time. He ruled c. 1182-1151 B.C. during most of which period he kept parts of Canaan under Egyptian hegemony. Evidence of his activities are found in several Palestinian sites such as Beth Shan, Megiddo and Lachish.

RAMIAH ("Yah is exalted"). One of the sons of Parosh who, having taken a pagan wife, had to repudiate her following the decree of Ezra.

RAMOTH

1. One of the sons of Bani, he is given also as Jeremoth.

2. A city allotted to Issachar when the land was divided among the tribes (Josh 14:1). It was later assigned to the Gershonite Levites. Perhaps on the site of present-day Kochav Hayarden ("star of the Jordan") above the ruined Crusader castle of Belvoir.

3. See RAMAH No.5.

RAMOTH GILEAD An important city to the east of the Jordan. It was a city of refuge in the territory of Gad (Deut 4:43; Josh 20:8), assigned to the Levites of the family of Merari (Josh 21:38; I Chr 6:80). Under King Solomon's administration it was the seat of the son of Geber, the officer appointed over the sixth district, which apparently included the northeastern part of Gilead and Bashan (I Kgs 4:13). After Solomon's death and the conquest of portions of Golan, Bashan and Hauran by the Arameans, Ramoth Gilead was disputed by the Arameans and the Israelites, and the city changed masters from time to time (cf I Kgs 22:3-4). Ahab, king of Israel, seeking, in alliance with King Jehoshaphat of Judah, to capture the city, was mortally wounded there, and the armies of Judah and Israel had to disperse without achieving their aim (I Kgs chap. 22; II Chr chap. 18). Joram son of Ahab continued his father's war against Hazael king of Aram-Damascus over Ramoth Gilead (II Kgs 8:28), but he too was wounded in the war. It seems that Ramoth Gilead remained in the hands of the Arameans until the days of Jehoash son of Jehoahaz, who conquered the city from Ben-Hadad the son of Hazael (II Kgs 13:25). Jeroboam son of Jehoash established Israelite rule over the whole region (II Kgs 14:25-28). Ramoth Gilead was reconquered by the Arameans under Rezin, king of Damascus. In 733-732 B.C. Tiglath-Pileser III campaigned against Damascus and Samaria and conquered Ramoth Gilead (II Kgs 15:29; I Chr 5:6, 26). In his list of conquered cities he called it Galada.

Jewish sources locate Ramoth Gilead in the region of the Jabbok River and identify it with Gerasa. It should perhaps be sought in northern Gilead, and the most plausible identification is with Tell er-Rumeith, on the northeastern ridge of the Ajlun hills, dominating the Rabbath Ammon-Damascus highway, a site ideal for an Israelite stronghold against the Arameans. Excavations at Tell er-Rumeith revealed three strata from the Iron Age showing Israelite and Aramean occupation ending in 733 B.C. with the destructive campaign of Tiglath-Pileser III. Another strata showing remains of the Hellenistic, Roman, Byzantine and Arab periods have also been brought to light.

RAPHA (shorter form of Raphael, "the Lord heals"). The fifth son of Benjamin.

RAPHAH Son of Binea and father of Eleasah No.2; descendant of King Saul; the name is spelled Rephaiah in I Chronicles 9:43.

RAPHU (a shorter form of Raphael). A man of Benjamin, father of Palti who was sent by Moses to spy out the land of Canaan.

RAT See ANIMALS

RAVEN See ANIMALS

REAIAH

1. Firstborn son of Shobal the youngest son of Judah; father of Jahath in the genealogy of the family of Judah. He is called Haroeh in I Chronicles 2:52.

2. A man of Reuben, son of Micah, father of Baal; the leader of the Reubenites carried into captivity by Tiglath-Pileser.

3. Head of a family of Nethinim (Temple servants) who returned with Zerubbabel from the Exile in Babylon and settled in Jerusalem.

REBA One of the five kings of Midian killed by the armies of Israel led by Phinehas the son of Eleazar.

REBECCA See REBEKAH

REBEKAH (REBECCA) Bethuel's daughter and wife of the patriarch Isaac. Apart from a passing reference in a genealogical list of her family (Gen 22:23), Rebekah is first mentioned when Abraham's servant brought her to Canaan from Haran as the future bride of his master's son (Gen chap. 24). Though the match proved successful, Rebekah remained barren. However, following a prayer by Isaac, she conceived and gave birth to twin sons Jacob and Esau (Gen 25:21-23). Esau was

Isaac's favorite son, but Rebekah inclined towards Jacob, being particularly displeased by Esau's exogamic marriages (Gen 26:34-35). Rebekah helped Jacob in deceiving Isaac and eliciting the paternal blessing intended for Esau. This undoubtedly conformed to the divinely preordained plan as expressed in the birth oracle (Gen 25:23). The blessing being irrevocable, Esau, who had to be content with an inferior blessing, planned to kill his brother, but Rebekah resolved the sibling rivalry by sending Jacob to her family in Haran on the pretext of seeking a wife (Gen chap. 27).

In one episode, Rebekah was presented to a foreign king as Isaac's sister, for fear that the local inhabitants' lust for her would lead them to kill her husband (Gen 26:42ff). This story repeats a motif already related of Sarah and Abraham. Like Abraham, Sarah, and Isaac before her, (and Leah and Jacob subsequently) Rebekah was buried in the Cave of Machpelah in Hebron (Gen 49:31). She is regarded as the second matriarch of the Jewish people.

RECHAB, RECHABITES

1. Rechab ("rider"). A Benjamite, the son of Rimmon of Beeroth and a captain under Saul's son Ishbosheth during the latter's conflict with David. Rechab and his brother, Baaneh, killed Ishbosheth as he slept and presented his severed head to David. Instead of rewarding them, David had the pair executed and their mutilated bodies publicly displayed by the pool of Hebron.

2. Eponymous ancestor of the nomadic Rechabites and father or ancestor of J(eh)onadab. The Book of Jeremiah chapter 35 relates that the prophet summoned the Rechabites to the Temple and offered them wine. They refused, citing Jonadab's prohibition, more than two centuries earlier, upon drinking wine, planting or owning vineyards, or dwelling in houses. Jeremiah praised their loyalty and adherence to their forefather's command, held them up as examples to his disobedient fellow-Judeans, and predicted that the progeny of Jonadab would always survive to serve God.

Many scholars view the Rechabites' strictly nomadic lifestyle as a reflection of the age-old tension between herdsman and farmer, seen also in the conflict of Cain and Abel and in the contrast between the originally nomadic Israelites and their sedentary Canaanite adversaries.

The history of the Rechabites prior to Jonadab is not well known. They were apparently Kenites (I Chr 2:55), as was Moses' father-in-law, who also worshiped Yahwah. Jonadab, too, was a strict Yahwist who assisted in Jehu's purge of Baal-worshipers and descendants of Ahab (II Kgs 10:15-27). At some point, probably after the fall of Samaria, Jonadab's descendants moved south to Judah, and in the days of Jeremiah took refuge from Nebuchadnezzar's armies in Jerusalem.

Some Rechabites survived the Babylonian captivity. Malchijah son of Rechab repaired Jerusalem's Dung Gate in Nehemiah's time (Neh 3:14) and is called the leader of the district of Beth Haccerem. At some later point, three families of Rechabite scribes are mentioned as living in Jabez, in Judah (I Chr 2:55).

RECHAH A city or place in Judah; it was the home of Beth-Rapha, Paseah and Tehinnah.

REDEMPTION See SALVATION

RED HEIFER The law of the Red Heifer is detailed in Numbers 19:1-22. Although not strictly speaking a sacrifice, like any animal sacrifice it had to be free of any physical defect. Moreover, it could not previously have been used for any profane purpose. The animal was to be slaughtered beyond the limits of the camp and its blood sprinkled seven times by the priest. The entire carcass was then burned to ash. The

27:5-6, 11, 15, 42, 46; 28:5; 29:12; 35:8; 49:31

RECHAB, RECHABITES 1
II Sam 4:2, 5-6, 9

RECHAB, RECHABITES 2
II Kgs 10:15, 23. I Chr 2:55. Neh 3:14. Jer 35:2-3, 5-6, 8, 14, 16, 18-19

RECHAH
I Chr 4:12

RED HEIFER
Num 19:2, 5-6, 9-10, 17

priests who sprinkled the blood and burned the heifer, both became ritually impure and remained so until evening. A person who was ritually clean would then gather the ashes and put them in a "clean place" beyond the camp. The ash, mixed with spring water, was to be sprinkled by means of a bunch of hyssop on one who had been rendered impure by contact with a corpse. Exposed vessels in a dwelling in which there was a corpse likewise became impure and required the same ritual. A person who failed to undergo such purification and entered the sanctuary in a state of impurity, suffered excision from the congregation of Israel.

The "ashes of the heifer" which purified the flesh were compared in the NT to "the blood of Christ" which purified the "conscience from dead works" (Heb 9:13-14).

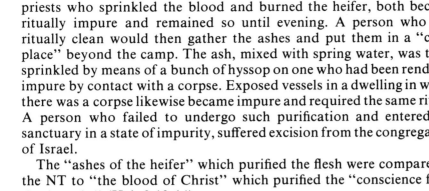

A view of the Red Sea.

RED SEA Long gulf between western Arabia and northeastern Africa. The Hebrew name for this sea is *Yam Suf*, meaning "sea of reeds". Its identification with the Red Sea is an ancient one, and most early translators and commentators of the Bible adopted it. Most biblical references to the Red Sea are directed to its northeastern branch, known as the Gulf of Elath or Aqaba, although reeds do not grow in these salty waters. The AV also translates *Yam Suf* as Red Sea (Num 14:25; 21:4; Deut 1:40, etc). The sea that the Israelites crossed on their way from Egypt to the land of Canaan is referred to as the Egyptian Sea (Is 11:15) or the Red Sea (Ex 13:18; 15:4, etc.), and its identification is very much disputed. Some scholars believe that the reference is to the northwestern branch of the Red Sea, known as the Gulf of Suez, but this would have involved a long and apparently unnecessary detour by the Israelites from the land of Goshen southwards, with the Egyptian chariots on their heels. Others suggest that it was one of the lakes that lay on the border of Egypt and Sinai, between Suez and the Mediterranean, where plenty of reeds still grow. Still others believe that it should be identified with Lake Sirbonis, which was once a continuation of the eastern arm of the Nile Delta.

Apart from the Exodus, the Sea is mentioned in connection with maritime enterprises such as those of Solomon (I Kgs 9:26) and subsequent kings. David secured access to the Sea which was lost with the division of the kingdom but regained by Jehoshaphat and Uzziah.

The Ptolemies were the first to establish forts and harbors along its western coast to serve as stations for the elephant hunters in East Africa. In the early Roman period it became a vital artery in the spice trade with southern Arabia and India.

REELAIAH An alternate name for Raamiah.

REFUSE GATE One of the gates of Jerusalem during the First Temple period; like the others it was badly damaged when the city was destroyed by Nebuchadnezzar. It was repaired at the time of Nehemiah (Neh 3:14). Some translations, including KJV, call it the "Dung Gate", which is also the name of a present-day gate in the walls of the Old City of Jerusalem. However, scholars do not believe the modern Dung Gate stands on the site of the biblical one. It has been suggested that the Refuse Gate is the same as the Potsherd Gate (KJV, East Gate) mentioned in Jeremiah 19:2 as being by the Valley of the Son of Hinnom, that is southwest of the City of David. The Refuse Gate was evidently the gate used to take garbage out of the city.

REGEM Firstborn son of Jahdai, a descendant of Caleb.

REGEM-MELECH One of the men sent by the people to the priests in the Temple at the time of Zechariah to ask for clarification about fasting rituals. However, the name may have been the title of one of the officials in the delegation.

RED SEA
Ex 10:19;
13:18; 15:4, 22;
23:21. Num
14:25; 21:4;
33:10-11. Deut
1:40; 2:1; 11:4.
Josh 2:10;
4:23; 24:6.
Judg 11:16. I
Kgs 9:26. Neh
9:9. Ps 106:7,
9, 22; 136:13,
15. Jer 49:21.
Acts 7:36. Heb
11:29

REELAIAH
Ezra 2:2

REFUSE GATE
Neh 2:13;
3:13-14; 12:31

REGEM
I Chr 2:47

REGEM-
MELECH
Zech 7:2

REHABIAH The only son of Eliezer the son of Moses, and the founder of a Levite family which officiated in the Temple in the time of King David.

REHOB

1. Place or geographic region marking the northern limit of the land of Canaan (Num 34:8; cf Num 13:21). It is mentioned in conjunction with the spies sent out by Moses (Num 13:21). The inhabitants of Rehob (II Sam 10:8) took part in the war of the Ammonites against David. It has been identified with Tell es-Sarm in the Jordan Valley.

REHABIAH
I Chr 23:17;
24:21; 26:25

REHOB 1
Num 13:21.
II Sam 10:8

The mound of Rehob in the Jordan Valley.

(right)
Inscription on the mosaic of the 7th-century synagogue at Rehob.

2. A town on the northern border of the territory of Asher (Josh 19:28) allotted to the Levites of the family of Gershom (I Chr 6:75). It was not conquered by the Israelites, and the Canaanites held it for a long time (Judg 1:31). Doubtfully identified with Tell el-Balat.

3. A town in the territory of Asher (Josh 19:30), identified with one of the numerous mounds in the Plain of Acco.

4. The father of Hadadezer king of Zobah.

5. One of the Levites who sealed the covenant at the time of Ezra.

REHOBOAM ("may the people be enlarged"). Son of Solomon and Naamah the Ammonitess, and first ruler of the Southern Kingdom of Judah. Rehoboam acceded to the throne at the age of 41, upon the death of Solomon. Shortly thereafter the northern tribes of Israel, prompted by Rehoboam's refusal to alleviate the burdens of taxation and forced labor which Solomon had laid upon them, seceded from the state, proclaiming Jeroboam as their king. Only the tribes of Judah and Benjamin remained under Rehoboam's rule. An initial plan to win back the northern tribes by force was abandoned in accord with a prophecy by Shemaiah (I Kgs 12:21-24). Nevertheless, there was continual warfare between the Northern and Southern Kingdoms during Rehoboam's lifetime (I Kgs 14:30).

Ecclesiasticus (47:23) blames the dissolution of the united kingdom of David and Solomon on the folly of Rehoboam, inasmuch as he preferred the counsel of his young friends to that of more seasoned advisors (II Kgs 12:8). Rehoboam's dispatch of his taskmaster Adoram to the north (where he was stoned to death, I Kgs 12:18) also suggests that Rehoboam did not inherit his father's wisdom. But Rehoboam's son explains more sympathetically that Rehoboam, being "young and

REHOB 2
Josh 19:28;
21:31. Judg
1:31. I Chr
6:75

REHOB 3
Josh 19:30

REHOB 4
II Sam 8:3, 12

REHOB 5
Neh 10:11

REHOBOAM
I Kgs 11:43;
12:1, 3, 6, 12,
17-18, 21, 23,
27; 14:21, 25,
27, 29-31;
15:6. I Chr
3:10. II Chr
9:31; 10:1, 3,
6, 12-13, 17-
18; 11:1, 3, 5,
17-18, 21-22;
12:1-2, 5, 10,
13, 15-16;
13:7. Matt 1:7

inexperienced", was unable to withstand the rebellion at the hands of Jeroboam and the scoundrels who collected around him (II Chr 13:6-7). In any case, it is evident that even before Rehoboam's accession to the throne, there was strong resentment in the north against the house of David. The fact that Rehoboam was required to go to the northern city of Shechem to be separately crowned by the northern tribes (I Kgs 12:1) shows that the latter were not well integrated into the kingdom.

Rehoboam's difficulties were not confined to the north. In his fifth year Pharaoh Shishak ravaged Judah, capturing many fortified cities

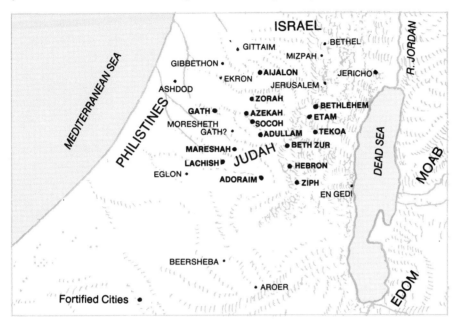

Map showing the cities fortified by Rehoboam.

and carrying off the treasures of the Temple and palace. Archeological excavations support the picture of a large-scale invasion at this time, as do the inscriptions of Shishak still visible at the temple of Amun in Karnak, Egypt. According to the inscriptions, the campaign was not directed exclusively against Judah, but included the conquest of cities in Israel, Philistia and Edom. A total of 150 captured cities are listed.

It was perhaps in the aftermath of this campaign that Rehoboam fortified the 15 strategically located cities named in II Chronicles 11:5-12. Rehoboam's activities may have produced the defenses uncovered at Azekah and Lachish. The distribution of the fortified cities — to the west, south and east, but not along the border with Israel — reflects a blend of concern over possible attack from Egypt with a concomitant refusal to accept the current northern frontier as a permanent border.

I Kings 14:22-28 implies that Shishak's invasion came as punishment for the sins of Judah; II Chronicles 12:1-2 explicitly states as much and includes Rehoboam among the wrongdoers. Nevertheless, Chronicles credits him with following God at the beginning of his rule. In particular, he gave refuge to the priests and Levites who left the Northern Kingdom during Jeroboam's reign (II Chr 11:13ff.).

Chronicles reports that Rehoboam (following the precedent set by his father) had 18 wives and 60 concubines, who together bore him 28 sons and 60 daughters. His rule lasted 17 years, from c. 928 B.C. He was buried in Jerusalem and succeeded by his son Abijam (or Abijah). Rehoboam is mentioned among the ancestors of Jesus (Matt 1:7).

REHOBOTH

1. Place in the Negeb where Isaac dug a well (Gen 26:22). Its identification is not known; Ruheiba in the central Negeb with which it

has been identified, has no remains earlier than the Roman period.

2. The capital city of King Saul of Edom; it is called "Rehoboth-by-the-river" probably to differentiate it from Rehoboth Ir. Nothing is known about it.

REHOBOTH IR One of the cities built in Assyria by Nimrod the mighty hunter. Nothing is known about it.

REHUM

1. Head of a family of exiles who returned with Zerubbabel from Babylon and settled in Jerusalem; the name is spelled Nehum in Nehemiah 7:7.

2. One of the officials of King Artaxerxes who signed a letter of protest along with Shimshai the scribe, against the rebuilding of Jerusalem after the return of the exiles; the letter caused the king to order all work to cease.

3. A Levi, son of Bani who repaired the walls of Jerusalem at the time of Nehemiah.

4. One of the leaders of the people who sealed the covenant at the time of Nehemiah.

5. One of the priests and Levites who returned with Zerubbabel from the Exile in Babylon and settled in Jerusalem, perhaps identical with No.3.

REI ("friend [of the Lord]"). One of David's "mighty men", he supported Solomon against Adonijah's unsuccessful bid for the throne.

REKEM

1. One of the five kings of Midian killed by the armies of Israel led by Phinehas the son of Eleazar.

2. Third son of Hebron and father of Shammai in the genealogy of the family of Caleb.

3. One of the cities which fell to the inheritance of the tribe of Benjamin; probably somewhere north of present-day Jerusalem.

REMALIAH The father of Pekah, king of Israel.

REMETH A town on the border of the territory allotted to Issachar. It may be identical with Ramoth and Jarmuth No.2.

REMNANT OF ISRAEL The doctrine that there will always remain a faithful few dedicated to God and to his teaching. The prophets preached warning messages of national disaster and destruction to be brought on by the sins of the people. On the other hand, they frequently offered words of comfort and encouragement, promising that the exiles would be returned, the land rebuilt and the people of Israel reestablished in its land in a state of security and peace.

The contradiction between these two messages was resolved by the prophetic concept of the remnant of Israel. Whatever the sorry state of mass disloyalty and the resultant national destruction, this small group of the faithful will continue to exist, to provide the seed of subsequent growth and national revival. Consequently the people of Israel will never be totally destroyed, since the loyal remnant will survive to rebuild.

This doctrine of the remnant of Israel is to be found in most of the prophets (cf Jer 23:3; Joel 3:2; Amos 9:9ff; Obad v.17; Mic 2:12). But the concept was particularly advanced by Isaiah who even called one of his sons Shear Yashub "a remnant shall return" (7:3) as a visible token of his conviction that this hope would be realized (8:18).

The community which constituted Israel after the Exile regarded itself as such a surviving remnant (Ezra 9:8, 14-15; Neh 1:2-3; Hag 1:12-14; 2:2; Zech 8:6, 11-12). The promise of a remnant is also applied twice to foreign nations in the order of Zechariah (9:7; 14:16).

The biblical doctrine can be connected with the teaching of God's

REHOBOTH 2
Gen 36:37.
I Chr 1:48

REHOBOTH IR
Gen 10:11

REHUM 1
Ezra 2:2

REHUM 2
Ezra 4:8-9, 17
23

REHUM 3
Neh 3:17

REHUM 4
Neh 10:25

REHUM 5
Neh 12:3

REI
I Kgs 1:8

REKEM 1
Num 31:8.
Josh 13:21

REKEM 2
I Chr 2:43-44

REKEM 3
Josh 18:27

REMALIAH
II Kgs 15:25,
27, 30, 32, 37;
16:1, 5. II Chr
28:6. Is 7:1,
4-5, 9; 8:6

REMETH
Josh 19:21

covenant relationship with Israel; even when the latter's sins bring dire punishment, God will ultimately remember his covenant with them and return those who survive (Lev 26:44-45). Paul quoted Isaiah's reading on the remnant and applied it to the Church (Rom 9:27).

REMPHAN
Acts 7:43

REMPHAN A false god referred to by Stephen (Acts 7:43) when he quoted Amos 5:26. His quotation comes from the Greek translation, the Septuagint, as the name does not appear in the original Hebrew; the latter mentions *kiyyun* (Chiun), an Assyrian star god associated with the planet Saturn. Some scholars have suggested that Repa, the Egyptian god of the planet Saturn, has replaced *kiyyun* in this passage. However, others feel that the Septuagint version is simply a corrupt reading of *kiyyun*.

REPENTANCE According to the OT, man's involvement, both in conscience and deed, is a *sine qua non* for securing divine forgiveness. It is not enough to hope and pray for pardon; man must humble himself, acknowledge his wrong and resolve to depart from sin (e.g., David, II Sam 12:13ff; Ahab, I Kgs 21:27-29). The Psalms provide ample evidence that penitence and confession must be integral components of all prayers for forgiveness (Ps 32:5; 38:18; 41:4; Lam 3:40-42). The many synonyms for contrition testify to its primacy in the human effort to restore the desired relationship with God; e.g., seek the Lord (II Sam 12:16; 21:1); search for him (Amos 5:4); humble oneself before him (Lev 26:41); and direct the heart to him (I Sam 7:3). The rituals of penitence, such as weeping, fasting, rending clothes and donning sackcloth and ashes, were unqualifiedly condemned by the prophets if the heart was not involved (Is 1:10ff; 29:13; Hos 7:14; Joel 2:12-13).

At the same time, inner contrition must be followed by outward acts, remorse must be translated into deeds. Two substages are involved in this process: first, the negative one of ceasing to do evil (Is 33:15; Ps 15), and then the positive, active step of doing good (Is 1:17; Jer 26:13; Amos 5:14-15). Again, the language used to describe man's active role in the process testifies to its centrality; e.g., incline the heart to the Lord (Josh 24:23); make oneself a new heart (Ezek 18:31); circumcise the heart (Jer 4:4); wash the heart (Jer 4:14) and break one's fallow ground (Hos 10:12). However, all these expressions are subsumed and encapsulated by one verb which dominates the penitential literature of the Bible, "turn, return" (Hebrew *shuv*). This root combines in itself both requisites of repentance: to turn from evil and to turn to good. The motion of turning implies that sin is not an eradicable stain but a straying from the right path, and that by the effort of turning, a power God has given all men, the sinner can redirect his destiny.

That the term for repentance is not a prophetic innovation but goes back to Israel's ancient traditions, is clear from the fact that Amos, the first writing prophet, used it without bothering to explain it (Amos 4:6-11). Moreover, the concept of repentance was also assumed in the early narratives about Pharaoh (Ex 7:3-4; 10:1; 11:10) and the sons of Eli (I Sam 2:25); these accounts say that God deliberately blocked their repentance. The motif of repentance occurs in the tales of the early heroes: David (II Sam 12:13-14; 24:10-14), Ahab (I Kgs 21:27-29) and Josiah (II Kgs 22:18-20).

It must be noted that the repentance of these early narratives is not the same as that taught by the prophets. First, repentance in the narratives is ineffectual. At best it mitigated retribution (e.g., David) or postponed it (Ahab, Josiah). On occasion it was of no avail (e.g., to Moses himself; Deut 3:23-26). Repentance can only terminate the punishment but cannot prevent its onset (Lev 26:40-42; Deut 4:29-31; 30:1-10). The limited scope of repentance in these texts can best be appraised by contrasting it with the success of the people of Nineveh in averting their doom (Jonah 3:1-10).

Secondly, wherever repentance occurs in the early narratives, it is a human virtue. God does not call upon man to repent or upon his prophet to rouse him to repentance. Moses interceded for Israel so that God would annul his evil decrees (e.g., Ex 32:11-13, 31-34; 34:9; Num 12:11-13; 14:13-19; Deut 9:16-29), but not once was he expected to bring his people to repentance so that they might merit divine forgiveness. Other intercessors are also recorded in the early narratives, e.g., Abraham (Gen 18:23-33), Samuel (I Sam 7:5-9; 12:19-25), Elijah (I Kgs 17:17-23), Elisha (II Kgs 4:33; 6:15-20) and Job (Job 42:7-9). These righteous leaders, just like Moses, appealed to God to ask for pardon but not to man to urge repentance.

It is against this backdrop that the innovation of the priestly legislation can be measured. Repentance is operative in sacrificial expiation, as indicated by the term "confess" (Lev 5:5; Num 5:7).

The priestly doctrine of repentance is pre-exilic. Though the power of repentance in Leviticus is such that it can reduce a deliberate sin to an unintentional one, it insists that for the complete annulment of sin sacrificial expiation is mandatory. It does not know the prophetic teaching that repentance suffices in itself to nullify sin.

The prophets differed among themselves on the function of repentance, especially in their eschatological prophecies. Isaiah, for example, withdrew the offer of repentance at an early point in his career (cf Is 1:16-20 with 6:9-13). He insisted that only the few survivors of God's purge will be allowed to engage in a program of repentance that will qualify them for the new Zion (e.g., Is 32:1-8, 15-17; 33:5-6).

In the teaching of Jeremiah, on the other hand, the call to repent was never abandoned. When Jeremiah despaired of men's capability of self-renewal, he postulated that God would provide a "new heart" which would overcome sin and merit eternal forgiveness (Deut 30:6; Jer 31:33).

In line with the Hebrew prophets John the Baptist is portrayed as proclaiming repentance (Mark 1:4) and Jesus did the same (Luke 13:3), in turn commissioning his disciples to act likewise (Mark 6:12). Repentance is seen as part of the proclamation of the early church as portrayed in Acts and is an important motif in the Apocalypse of John where it appears above all as a motive for the punishments visited upon the earth, in the sense that these tragedies of history give people an opportunity to repent and accept the sovereignty of God over their lives (Apocalypse of John 9:20-21; 16:9-11).

The Greek word for repentance (*metanoia*) denotes a change of mind, which is given external credence by a change of allegiance and of life-style in accordance with the new values adopted. It has little to do with feelings or emotions and has much to do with how one lives.

Paul, unlike the Synoptic Gospels, did not lay great stress on repentance. He used the verb once (II Cor 12:21), and this is important because it refers to Christians who should repent for sins committed even after conversion and presumably, baptism. Paul used the noun three times. In Romans 2:4, it is a general appeal to both unconverted Jews and to Gentiles, to repent; and in II Corinthians 7:9-10, it again refers to Christian repentance. Paul could describe the divided and guilty conscience with great depth of psychological insight (Rom 7:7-25), and, although interpretations differ here, this description most probably refers to the person before the grace of repentance and conversion. For Paul's comparative lack of emphasis on repentance was no doubt due to his strong belief in the great difference which faith in Christ makes (or should make) in the converted. He stressed the joy of the new life in Christ and in the Holy Spirit, not on submerging oneself in useless and free-floating, unfounded guilt. This enthusiastic, eschatological conviction that the believer was already living primarily in the new eon or new creation (II Cor 5:17; Gal 6:15) led the author of I John to go even further than Paul. He stated (I John 3:9): "Whoever has been born of God does not sin, for his seed remains in him; and he cannot sin, because he has been born of God". However, the author balanced this extreme, enthusiastic view by many appeals to avoid sin, e.g., I John 1:8-10; 5:21.

The Epistle to the Hebrews seems to rule out forgiveness for sins committed after initial repentance (Heb 6:1-8; 12:17), but this is often taken to mean that it rules out being baptized a second time. Nevertheless, the problem of post-baptismal sins remained a difficult one for early Christians and was not resolved until a pattern of penitential and confessional practice was worked out in the following centuries. Hebrews also stresses the role of the risen Christ as high priest interceding for sinners, as Moses and others did in the OT (Heb 7:23-27).

REPHAEL ("the Lord healed"). A Levite, second son of Shemaiah; a gatekeeper in the House of the Lord at the time of King David.

REPHAH A man of Ephraim, one of the ancestors of Joshua.

REPHAIAH

1. The son of Jeshaiah in the genealogy of the family of Jeconiah.

2. A man of Simeon, son of Ishi. He was one of the captains who defeated the Amalekites on Mount Seir and settled there.

3. Second son of Tola, the firstborn of Issachar, and one of the heads of the family of Issachar.

4. Son of Binea and father of Eleasah No.2; another name for Rapha.

5. Son of Hur; he was among those who repaired the wall of Jerusalem during the time of Nehemiah.

REPHAIM (probably originally meaning "heroes", "great ones").

1. An ancient people in pre-Israelite Canaan, legendarily giants. They were conquered by Amraphel (Gen 14:5). They are identified with the Zamzummim in the land of Ammon (Deut 2:20) and their land is also placed in Bashan (Deut 3:13). The Rephaim are not known from any other historical source.

2. A valley to the south of Jerusalem. One of the landmarks between the territories of Judah and Benjamin (Josh 15:8; 18:16) through which the Philistines invaded Judah (II Sam 5:18, 22), and where they were defeated by David (II Sam 5:25).

REPHIDIM One of the stations on the route of the Exodus where Moses smote the rock in order to provide the people with water (Ex 17:1-7) and Amalek fought Israel (Ex 17:8-16). According to Numbers (33:14-15) Rephidim was situated between Alush and the wilderness of Sinai. The identification of this site depends on the identification of Mount Sinai and the wilderness of Sinai. Those who believe that the Israelites took a northerly route on their way from Egypt to Canaan look for Rephidim closer to the Mediterranean coast, between el-Arish and Jebel Hillal, while others suggest that it lies in Wadi Firan, in the vicinity of Jebel Musa, more to the south.

RESEN One of the cities built by Nimrod the mighty hunter "between Nineveh and Calah". Its location is unknown.

RESHEPH ("flame").

1. A member of the tribe of Ephraim.

2. A Canaanite deity of plague or destruction. The name itself, as well as compound personal and place names containing the divine element "Resheph", is known from Ugaritic and Aramaic inscriptions. Some scholars believe that Habakkuk 3:5, in which *resheph* has been variously

translated as "plague", "burning coals", "pestilence", etc. in fact depicts this deity as one of the attendants of the Lord. Other possible images are found in Job 5:7 and Song of Solomon 8:6.

RESURRECTION The OT writings do not stress a belief in life after death. The ancient Israelites believed that life ended at death (Job 7:7-9; 14:10-12), although there still remained some form of shadowy existence in Sheol (Job 3:13-19). Some scholars, however, contend that there is a reference to immortality or some form of resurrection in Isaiah 26:19, but the only explicit reference to resurrection from the dead in the OT is found in Daniel 12:2-3 which dates to the time of the persecution of Antiochus IV, during the Maccabean period. Ezekiel chapter 37 represents a figurative image of national restoration and not a literal resurrection of the "dry bones".

Other Jewish writings, contemporaneous with or later than Daniel, develop the concept of a bodily resurrection from the dead. The earliest Jewish reference to this belief is found in the Book of Enoch, dating from the 3rd century B.C.

Of the many Jewish works written between 200 B.C. and A.D. 100,

The resurrection of Lazarus depicted on a marble carved plaque of the Crusader period, from the portals of the Church of the Holy Sepulcher. (Rockefeller Museum, Jerusalem)

both in Palestine and the Diaspora, some make no mention of life after death, others mention both resurrection of the body and immortality of the soul, others mention only immortality of the soul, and still others mention only resurrection of the body. Conservative elements, e.g., the Sadducees (Mark 12:18; Acts 23:8), rejected the novel concept of resurrection, whereas others were influenced in how they conceived the mode of individual survival after death by differing views of the person. Those who postulated immortality of the soul, adopted the dualistic Greek understanding of the person as a temporary composite of body and soul, whereas those who believed in resurrection of the body, retained the monistic Semitic conception of the person as a unified whole; the soul could not function without the body and vice versa.

The Pharisees believed that the spirit could not function without the body, and hence, its survival after death had to involve possession of a body. They debated the many questions resurrection raised. One school insisted that it would take the form of the resuscitation of corpses, while another thought that it would be the creation of a new body. It was only after the destruction of the Temple in A.D. 70, when the Pharisees assumed the dominant position within Judaism that they succeeded in imposing their view of the modality of survival after death on other Jewish groups. They then decreed that a Jew would be excluded from life in the world to come if he denied the resurrection.

Like the prophets Elijah (I Kgs 17:17-24) and Elisha (II Kgs 4:18-37), Jesus restored life to those who had died (Matt 9:18-26; Luke 7:11-17; John 11:1-44; cf Acts 9:36-41; 20:9-10), but these are not interpreted as instances of resurrection. Jesus spoke of his own survival in terms of resurrection (Matt 16:21; 17:22-23; 20:17-19). The fact of the empty tomb (Luke 24:12) brought Jesus' disciples to adopt the category of resurrection. The disciples proclaimed that he had risen from the dead (Acts 4:10) and a similar statement was attributed to the interpreting angel (Mark 16:6).

For the first Christians, Jesus' resurrection was the vindication of his ministry; through it he became "Son of God with power" (Rom 1:4) and a life-giving Spirit (I Cor 15:45). It is in this sense that the resurrection is a saving event for believers (Rom 4:25; 6:3-11). As the risen lord, Jesus communicates to them his new life. Through Jesus, resurrection also becomes a possibility for others. It was not longer merely a speculation for it had become concrete in his case.

In Jewish belief, resurrection would take place at the end of time, and this idea was taken over by Christians (I Cor 15:22-24), but while looking forward to their resurrection at a date that some thought would be very close (I Cor 15:51-52; I Thes 4:15). Christians could already say that they had risen with Christ (Col 2:12). See AFTERLIFE.

REU Firstborn son of Peleg, father of Serug and many other sons and daughters. He lived 239 years.

REUBEN, REUBENITES ("see a son!"). The firstborn of Jacob and Leah. His name always heads the list of the 12 sons of Jacob (Gen 29:32; 35:23; 46:8-9; 49:3-4; Ex 1:2; I Chr 2:1; 5:1). A twin popular etymology of his name is given in Genesis 29:32 by his mother "The Lord has surely looked on my affliction" and "now therefore, my husband will love me". After he brought his mother mandrakes in order to rekindle Jacob's affections, she bore Jacob Issachar (Gen 30:14-18).

According to Genesis 35:22, Reuben lay with Bilhah his father's concubine and thus by desecrating his father's bed lost his firstborn privileges, which accounts for the later decline in the numbers of the tribe. A more positive picture emerges from his intervention with his brothers to save Joseph's life (Gen 37:21-30) and his offer of his own sons as surety for the safety of Benjamin (Gen 42:37).

In the first census in Sinai, the Reubenites numbered 46,500 men, fit for military service (Num 1:21). By the time of the second census they numbered 43,730 men (Num 26:7). Members of the tribe of Reuben participated in Korah's revolt against Moses (Num 16:1-3). After the conquest, the Reubenites, along with the tribe of Gad and half of Manasseh, dwelt in the land east of the Jordan (Josh 13:8). In the song of Deborah the Reubenites are rebuked for not joining the battle against Sisera (Judg 5:15-16). By the period of the kings, the Reubenites had declined in importance, and their history became interwoven with that

REU
Gen 11:18-21.
I Chr 1:25.
Luke 3:35

REUBEN, REUBENITES
Gen 29:32; 30:14; 35:22-23; 37:21-22, 29; 42:22, 37; 46:8-9; 48:5; 49:3. Ex 1:2; 6:14. Num 1:5, 20-21; 2:10, 16; 7:30; 10:18; 13:4; 16:1; 26:5, 7; 32:1-2, 6, 25, 29, 31, 33, 37; 34:14. Deut 3:12, 16; 4:43; 11:6; 27:13; 29:8; 33:6. Josh 1:12; 4:12; 12:6; 13:8, 15, 23; 15:6; 18:7, 17; 20:8; 21:7, 36; 22:1, 9-11, 13, 15, 21, 25, 30-34. Judg 5:15-16. II Kgs 10:33. I Chr 2:1; 5:1, 3, 6, 18, 26; 6:63, 78; 11:42; 12:37; 26:32; 27:16. Ezek 48:6-7, 31. Rev 7:5

The territory of the tribe of Reuben.

Paul stayed at Rhodes on his final journey to Jerusalem (Acts 21:1) but by that time the port was more a leisure resort than an international trade center.

RIBAI A Benjamite from Gibeah, father of Ithai, one of David's thirty "mighty men".

RIBAI
II Sam 23:29
I Chr 11:31

RIBLAH

1. A place mentioned in conjunction with the description of the eastern limits of the land of Canaan (Num 34:11). Eusebius (*Onom.* 14:18-21) knew this place by the name of Arbela, which is apparently the correct form. Identification uncertain.

RIBLAH 1
Num 34:11

2. A city in Aram, near Hamath-on-the-Orontes. After the decline of the Assyrian empire Riblah became a political and military center for the armies that ruled Syria. It was there, in 609 B.C. that Pharaoh Necho II arrested Jehoahaz, king of Judah (II Kgs 23:33-34). After the conquest of Jerusalem by the Babylonians (586 B.C.) Zedekiah, king of Judah, his sons and his ministers were brought there to be judged before Nebuchadnezzar (II Kgs 25:6, 20-21, etc.). Identified with Ribleh, on the east bank of the Orontes, about 20 miles (32 km) south of Homs.

RIBLAH 2
II Kgs 23:33;
25:6, 20-21.
Jer 39:5-6;
52:9-10, 26-2?

RIGHTEOUSNESS The English word "righteousness" has no equivalent in Hebrew, and is used to translate various Bible concepts. The basic word *tzedek* refers to weights and balances (e.g. Lev 19:36) and things which are correct and precise (cf Deut 33:19; Ps 23:3). Applied to legal processes, it means "just" ("You shall follow what is altogether just" — Deut 16:20). The cognate *tzedakah* is also translated "righteousness" (Gen 15:6; Deut 6:25; 24:13) and its opposite is "wickedness". (Later, the word *tzedekah* came to mean "charity").

Righteousness consists in doing what is just and right. A primary application is in the legal process. The verdicts of judges and the edicts of rulers must be righteous. "Righteousness" means innocence of a charge (Gen 20:4; 44:16; I Kgs 2:32) and Job, for example, repeatedly affirms his righteousness (Job 9:2; 13:18, etc.). Righteousness is the first quality required of a ruler (I Kgs 3:6; 10:9) and it goes without saying that it is an attribute of the divine ruler (Ps 45:7; 72:1-3; Ezek 45:9) whose ordinances are the ultimate righteousness (cf Ps 119:7).

Beyond mere abstention from wrongdoing, righteousness requires positive action (Jer 22:3; Prov 16:17) which transcends the legal context to issues of ethics and morality. It therefore becomes the keynote both of the legal code and of the teaching of the prophets. God accepted Abraham as a covenant partner so that he and his descendants "keep the way of the Lord, to do righteousness and justice" (Gen 18:19) while Israel is told by Moses "You shall follow what is altogether just that you may live and inherit the land" (Deut 16:20).

Persons who have violated ordinary canons of morality can occasionally be considered righteous. For instance, Tamar is acknowledged to be more righteous than Judah although she has played the harlot, thus forcing her father-in-law to meet the demands of a relationship (Gen chap. 38). Similarly, King Saul conceded that David was more righteous than he, for David had remained a loyal subject by refusing to slay his sovereign (I Sam 24:17; cf I Sam 26:23 where David takes comfort in his own righteousness and in the assurance that the deity will reward him for sparing the king's life).

The covenant relationship between God and Israel is the primary context for understanding righteousness. Since the deity initiated this bond, it could only be abrogated by divine action. Of course, the claims within the relationship could be ignored; worse still, Israel could rebel against the very bond itself. The Law served as a guide within the relationship, for it stipulated the precise manner by which individuals could fulfill the demands imposed on the covenant people. The Law covered both positive and negative injunctions; it was therefore a valuable guide to life within a covenant relationship.

Another application of the word "righteous" designates a concrete reality in society. Victims of oppression were called righteous as early as the prophet Amos (Amos 2:6). The poor were apparently considered righteous, a tendency that becomes more noticeable within the Psalms. By NT times a community of the poor (Ebionites) was thought to occupy a special place in the divine plan. The Essene sect at Qumran called its leader the Teacher of Righteousness.

The OT concept of righteousness is taken up by the NT, where it can mean "innocent" (Matt 27:4) and "right" or "proper" (Matt 20:4; Luke 12:57). The Passion narrative uses righteousness in its forensic sense when Pilate's wife warns her husband about "that just man" (Matt 27:19) and the centurion declares Jesus' innocence (Luke 23:47). The range of use, is however broadened, particularly in the Pauline letters, where it is claimed that none but Christ can fulfill the demands of righteousness (Rom 3:10). Nevertheless God is acknowledged to be the true source of righteousness and the gift is an act of grace. Christians faithful to God will be considered righteous (Rom 4:22). God's righteousness is revealed through faith: "the just shall live by faith" (Rom 1:17) and apart from law (Rom 3:21). The Christian having been set free from sin becomes a slave of righteousness (Rom 6:18). See JUSTIFICATION.

RIMMON Name of a person, deity and of several places.

1. A Beerothite, the father of Baanah and Rechab, Saul's "captains of troops" (II Sam 4:2) who slew Ishbosheth.

2. Assyrian god whom Naaman, the Syrian army commander, worshiped at "the temple of Rimmon" (II Kgs 5:18). In Syria this deity was known as "Baal" ("the Lord" par excellence), in Assyria as "Ramanu" ("the Thunderer").

3. A city assigned to Judah "toward the border of Edom in the south" (Josh 15:20), later given to Simeon (Josh 19:1, 7). In Zechariah 14:10, Rimmon is the southernmost edge of the land which "shall be turned into a plain" on "the Day of the Lord" (Zech 14:1).

4. A town in the territory of Zebulun (Josh 19:13), it became a Levitical city (I Chr 6:77). Identified with er-Ruman, north of Nazareth.

5. The rock of Rimmon, to which 600 Benjamites fled after their battle with the Children of Israel. The cause of the fighting was the rape of a Levite's concubine by the men of Gibeah (Judg 20:4-9). Later, the Children of Israel made peace with the surviving Benjamites at the rock of Rimmon (Judg 21:13) and provided them with wives from the women of Jabesh Gilead and Shiloh (Judg 21:14, 21).

RIMMON-PEREZ (RIMMON-PAREZ) ("the breach, [or "pass"] of the pomegranate"). Between Rithmah and Libnah it was one of the stations of the Children of Israel on their way to the promised land.

RINNAH Second son of Shimon in the genealogy of the family of Judah.

RIPHATH Second son of Gomer the firstborn son of Japheth (youngest son of Noah); he was the brother of Ashkenaz and Togarmah. In Chronicles he is called Diphath (I Chr 1:6) but this is generally held to be a scribe's error. The reference is to a non-semitic people identified by Josephus with the Paphlagonians (*Antiq.* 1, 6, 1). They were most likely Anatolian, as was their father Gomer and their "brothers" Ashkenaz and Togarmah. Their name is perhaps preserved in the Riphean mountain range which was believed by the ancients to skirt the northern shore of the world.

RISSAH One of the stations where the Children of Israel halted on their way to the promised land, between Libnah and Kehelathah. Its location is unknown.

RITHMAH ("broom plant"). The 14th station of Israel on their journey from Egypt and the third after Mount Sinai. It is mentioned between Hazeroth and Rimmon-Perez. Its location is unknown.

RIVER, THE Term used mainly to describe the Euphrates. ("Then he sent messengers to Balaam the son of Beor at Pethor, which is near the River" [Num 22:5]). Occasionally the River Nile is called "the River (e.g., Is 19:7-8).

RIZIA A man of Asher, third son of Ulla, and a "mighty man of valor".

RIZPAH ("glowing coal"). Daughter of Aiah; she was the concubine of Saul and bore him two sons, Armoni and Mephibosheth (II Sam 21:8). After the death of the king, Abner, Saul's cousin and army commander, in a bid for the crown, tried to make her his concubine; Saul's son Ishbosheth reproved him, whereupon Abner left his camp to side with David. Later David handed over her two sons along with five other descendants of Saul as expiation for Saul's guilt in the slaying of the Gibeonites. The latter hanged the victims and left them unburied. Rizpah kept vigil by the corpses "from the beginning of harvest until late rains poured on them from heaven" (II Sam 21:8-10), when David brought them to burial.

ROCK OF ESCAPING A rock in the wilderness of Maon where David took refuge from King Saul.

ROCKS OF THE WILD GOATS The name of the location of a cave in the wilderness of En Gedi where David hid while he was being pursued by King Saul (I Sam 24:2).

RODANIM In the Table of Nations (Gen 10:4) Dodanim is listed among the sons of Javan, but in the parallel source in I Chronicles 1:7 they are called Rodanim, i.e. the inhabitants of the island of Rhodes, and this is the rendering in the Septuagint. Some scholars, however, believe that Dodanim is a corrupt form of Dananim, and they go so far as to identify the Dananim with Danan, who are mentioned in the inscriptions of Rameses III among the Sea Peoples who invaded Egypt. The land of Danuna is mentioned in the El Amarna Letters, a country by this name was situated to the north of the territory of King Abimilki of Tyre, and could thus be located at Cilicia, known from inscriptions of the 9th and 8th centuries B.C.

ROE, ROEBUCK See ANIMALS

ROGELIM A site in the region of Gilead, so far unidentified. The home of Barzillai who aided David and his army when they arrived at Mahanaim in their flight from Absalom.

ROHGAH Second son of Shemer in the genealogy of the family of Asher; he was head of a family or clan.

ROMAMTI-EZER A son of Heman, he was head of the 24th and last division of musicians officiating in the House of the Lord at the time of King David. The words, however, are most likely not a proper name but part of a prayer.

ROMANS, EPISTLE TO THE The sixth book of the NT.

The longest of St. Paul's epistles and the most systematic in its theology. The letter was dispatched from Corinth probably around A.D. 58, when Paul, at the close of his third missionary journey, was about to leave for Jerusalem, and subsequently, for Rome, which he had not previously visited. It is the only epistle addressed by Paul to a church which he did not himself found. He writes as one conscious of his apostolic commission from Christ, yet deferentially, as not wishing to "build on another man's foundation" (15:20).

RISSAH
Num 33:21-2?

RITHMAH
Num 33:18-1!

RIVER, THE
Ex 23:31.
Num 22:5.
Josh 24:2-3,
14-15. II Sam
10:16. I Kgs
4:21, 24;
14:15. I Chr
19:16. II Chr
9:26. Ezra
4:10-11, 16-1?
20; 5:3, 6; 6:6
8, 13; 7:21,
25; 8:36.
Neh 2:7, 9;
3:7. Ps 72:8;
80:11. Is 7:20:
8:7; 11:15;
19:7-8; 23:3,
10; 27:12. Jer
2:18. Ezek
29:3, 9. Amos
8:8; 9:5. Mic
7:12. Nah 3:8.
Zech 9:10;
10:11

RIZIA
I Chr 7:39

RIZPAH
II Sam 3:7;
21:8, 10-11

ROCK OF
ESCAPING
I Sam 23:28

ROCKS OF
THE WILD
GOATS
I Sam 24:2

RODANIM
I Chr 1:7

ROGELIM
II Sam 17:27;
19:31

ROHGAH
I Chr 7:34

ROMAMTI-
EZER
I Chr 25:4, 31

It is usually not doubted that Paul wrote the letter, but the integrity of the text has been questioned. One ancient manuscript ends at 14:23, another at 15:33, both followed by the doxology in 16:25-27. Scholars sometimes question whether the long list of personal greetings in chapter 16 belongs to this letter.

But these questions do not affect the letter's theological content, which has long been recognized as of great importance. Romans represents Paul's best attempt to set down his understanding of the Christian message in an orderly, dispassionate, balanced and complete way; it may have been his last will and testament. But it is not exhaustive; it omits or barely mentions the church, the eucharist, the resurrection of the body, or eschatology, important topics treated more fully in other letters.

From the biographical point of view, the epistle may be understood as a justification of Paul's bold, revolutionary and successful missionary policy (abolition of the requirement of circumcision for Gentile male converts), and a defense against the charge that he had thereby fallen away from the faith of Israel. This defense provides missionary lessons of permanent value to the church.

From the point of view of Paul's doctrinal development, The Epistle to the Romans has been regarded as a step beyond his letter to the Galatians where, writing in the heat of controversy, he had allowed himself to give vent to some intemperate expressions (Gal 3:10, 13, 19, 23ff; 5:2-4, 12). These, taken altogether, could give rise to suspicions that he had broken all connection with the message of the OT; that he regarded the Torah as an unmitigated evil, and the God who inspired it as either no God at all (so later Marcion) or as having made a mistake later corrected in Christ; that the gospel Paul was preaching led only to libertine excess and immorality (cf Rom 3:1-8; 6:1-23; and the reaction of James chap. 2); finally, that he rejected all observant Jews. In Romans, especially in chapters 3, 4, 9, 10, 11, 13, he seeks to allay these suspicions by emphasizing the continuity of God's saving plan and activity in history, by an abundance of OT quotations as support for his positions, and by sketching the outline of a whole new way of reading the OT.

As in his other letters, Paul's positive teaching takes as its starting point the preaching of the Hellenistic church which he had inherited, for example the message about Christ (1:3ff), the atoning value of Christ's death (3:24ff), forgiveness of sins through baptism (6:1-11) and the gift of the Spirit (chap. 8). But in every case he deepens and expands the interpretation of these concepts. Perhaps most noteworthy among his special contributions in this epistle is his understanding of Christ's death as having in some sense terminated the era of the Mosaic (ceremonial) law. It seems unlikely that he drew on any historical source for this understanding of the cross; rather, he derived it from the revelation accorded him at the time of his conversion (cf Gal 1:11ff; Acts 22:7ff). It is closely connected with his positive doctrine of the body of Christ, i.e., that by baptism men are incorporated into Christ (Rom 6:1-11), so that it is no longer the baptized who live but Christ who lives in them (Gal 2:20); since Christ has died, he (and the baptized with him) is beyond the pale of the law (Rom 7:1-6). This is a bold idea, though a radical application of the OT way of thinking in terms of "corporate personalities", e.g., Jacob-Israel is both an individual person and the name of a people in Genesis. The difficulty with this idea is that even the faithful are still in a measure leading their own lives, "in the flesh". Paul therefore breaks the continuity of his thought by restating the Ten Commandments for his readers (13:8-10), though emphasizing that they can all be reduced to love. Paul's basic message in this epistle is that "We are now in Christ, and he is in us; this is how we are saved, through faith."

There are many ways of analyzing the structure of the epistle. Paul's argument is close and complex, the central part of the letter being a pattern of three sets (diptychs) of facing panels, one side presenting sin in one of its forms, the other the remedy in Christ. The three sets may be considered successive approximations of the same message; they may also be deliberate restatements employing different theological imagery in order to incorporate as much OT material as possible or to reach several different audiences of Gentile and Jewish Christians. (See Outline).

Chapters 9-11 are the most difficult to fit into the plan of the letter but they form an important part of the argument, teaching that though Jewish (ceremonial) law is no longer binding on Gentile converts, there is still no ground for hatred of the Jewish people. Even without faith in Christ, the Jews remain part of salvation history, and of God's plan which is in the process of being worked out. It is not the Christian's task to judge them, but to wait upon God's designs.

OUTLINE

1:1-7	Greeting, containing Christological kerygma
1:8-15	Thanksgiving
1:16-17	Statement of theme
1:18-4:25	First diptych:
Panel A: 1:18-3:20	The sin of the Gentiles and Jews without Christ, idolatry and hypocrisy
Panel B: 3:21-4:25	Salvation (redemption, justification) through faith in Christ
5:1-6:23	Second diptych:
Panel A: 5:1-21	The sins of the first man
Panel B: 6:1-23	Deliverance from sin through dying and rising with Christ in baptism and incorporation into his body
7:1-8:39	Third diptych:
Panel A: 7:1-26	The sin of concupiscence provoked by the Law
Panel B: 8:1-39	Salvation as adopted sons and daughters, in whom the Spirit dwells as a new principle (*nomos*) of life
9:1-11:36	The destiny of Israel in God's providence
12:1-13:14	General moral exhortation
14:1-15:33	Specific moral exhortation
16:1-27	Conclusion

ROME, ROMANS A city located on the west bank of the Tiber River, about 18 miles (29 km) from its mouth. Although its origins are obscure, around 600 B.C. it was inhabited by Latins (one of the Italic tribes who migrated into the peninsula from the north) and Etruscans. For the next 200 years, the Latins struggled for control of the city, first with the Etruscans and then with the Gauls. In 390 B.C. the Romans succeeded

ROME,
ROMANS
**John 11:48.
Acts 2:10;
16:21, 37-38;
18:2; 19:21;
22:25-27, 29;**

Remains of the Forum at Rome. To the left is the Coloseum, the Arch of Constantine in the center.

23:11, 27; 25:16; 28:14, 16-17. Rom 1:7, 15. II Tim 1:17

in consolidating their rule and, by 265, had taken the entire Italian peninsula, assigning full Roman citizenship and rights to certain towns. The struggle for control of the Mediterranean followed immediately, beginning with a confrontation with Carthage for control of Sicily and the Carthaginian Wars; by 146 B.C., Rome had taken Carthage as well as substantial portions of the rest of the Mediterranean region.

As Roman influence grew in the eastern Mediterranean, the Hasmoneans allied themselves with Rome against the Seleucids and enjoyed peaceful relations for about 100 years. Following the death of Salome Alexandra in 67 B.C., her two sons, Hyrcanus the high priest and Aristobulus II, competed for power, ultimately appealing to Rome and Pompey to settle the issue. Pompey seized Jerusalem, making it a tributary to Rome and putting an end to the Hasmonean monarchy. In 47 B.C. Julius Caesar appointed the capable and ambitious Idumean Antipater as regent of Judea. Because of the support Caesar gained from Hyrcanus and Antipater in his war against Pompey and his party, the Jews in the Mediterranean world were granted special rights. Together with the privileges later bestowed by Caesar's successor, Augustus, these included exemption from emperor worship, from military service and from certain other taxes. Antipater's son Herod the Great succeeded him, though not without a struggle: he was appointed king by the Senate in 40 B.C. and ruled Judea for 33 years as a loyal Roman ally. Herod's kingdom was divided among his sons. Archelaus received Judea, but was deposed in A.D. 6 because of his oppressive rule. Rome replaced him with a procurator (or more properly, a prefect) thus establishing direct rule in Judea. It was under such a prefect, Pontius Pilate, that Jesus was crucified according to Roman law. Roman domination of Judea continued throughout the rest of the NT era and thereafter.

The origin of Rome's Christian community is unknown. Aquila and Priscilla, Christian Jews, left Rome in A.D. 50 because of Claudius' decree expelling the Jews (Acts 18:2). The Jews were permitted to return upon his death in 54.

Paul's desire and destiny was to go to Rome (Acts 19:21; 23:11; Rom 1:15). The Book of Acts closes with him in custody there (Acts 28:16). Onesiphorus (slave to Philemon) visited Paul in Rome according to II Timothy 1:17 (cf Philem). Paul, exercising his rights as a Roman citizen,

Burial niches in the catacombs at Rome.

appealed to Caesar (Acts 22:25-29; 23:27). His longest letter, bordering on a theological treatise, was addressed to the church at Rome (Rom 1:7). The Prison Epistles — Galatians, Ephesians, Philippians and Colossians — may have been written from Rome, as well as Philemon and possibly II Timothy.

The Romans initially regarded the Christians as a Jewish sect, but once Jewish rejection of Christianity led to recognition of the latter as a distinct religion, the refusal of Christians to participate in emperor worship induced the Roman authorities to institute severe anti-Christian measures, local at first but ultimately general. Nero's persecution (A.D. 64-65), under which, according to tradition, Peter was crucified and Paul beheaded, was local. Domitian was the first emperor to claim divinity for himself; his persecution of the Christians was centered in Asia Minor and is reflected in the Book of Revelation, where Rome is equated with Babylon "the great harlot" (Rev chap. 18; 19:2; cf I Pet 5:13). The universal persecutions reached their zenith under Diocletian (284-305) only a few years prior to the recognition of Christianity as a legitimate religion by the Edict of Milan (313) under Constantine the Great. Christianity became the Roman state religion c. 381.

ROOSTER See ANIMALS

ROSE See PLANTS

ROSH ("head"). Seventh of the ten sons of Benjamin. Some translations of Ezekiel 38:2-3 take Rosh as a place, but it is in fact a title.

RUE See PLANTS

RUFUS ("red haired").

1. One of the two sons of Simon of Cyrene.

2. An early Christian in Rome; Paul sent him greetings in his Epistle to the Romans. Some scholars believe he is identical with No. 1.

RUMAH A town mentioned as the birthplace of Pedaiah father of Zebuda (wife of Josiah and mother of Jehoiakim); perhaps Khirbet Rumeh in Galilee.

RUTH The central character in the Book of Ruth. A Moabitess, she married one of the sons of Elimelech and Naomi of Bethlehem in the course of that Judahite family's sojourn in Moab. When Naomi decided after the death of her husband and her sons to return to Bethlehem, Ruth

ROSH
Gen 46:21.
Ezek 38:2-3;
39:1

RUFUS 1
Mark 15:21

RUFUS 2
Rom 16:13

RUMAH
II Kgs 23:36

RUTH
Ruth 1:4, 14,
16, 22; 2:2, 8,
21-22; 3:9;
4:5, 10, 13.
Matt 1:5

insisted on accompanying her and adopting her God and her people as her own. Exercising the right of the poor to gather the grain which falls to the ground in the course of the harvest (Lev 19:9-10; 23:22), she met Boaz, the owner of the field in which she was gleaning. He married her, and she bore him a son named Obed, the father of Jesse, the father of King David (Ruth 4:17). Hence she appears also in the NT in Matthew 1:5 as an ancestress of Jesus.

RUTH, BOOK OF Biblical book telling the romance of Ruth, ancestress of King David. In Christian editions of the OT the Book of Ruth appears among the historical books immediately after the Book of Judges. This arrangement accords with the statement in Ruth 1:1 that the story "came to pass in the days when the judges ruled". In present-day Jewish editions of the Bible the Book of Ruth appears as the second of "the five scrolls", i.e., Song of Solomon, Ruth, Lamentations, Ecclesiastes and Esther, which are read in the synagogue on special occasions (The Book of Ruth on Pentecost). However, the sequence of books of the Bible prescribed in the Babylonian Talmud (Bava Batra 14b) — which was edited at the end of the 5th century A.D. — records no such subdivision as "the five scrolls"; instead the Book of Ruth precedes the Book of Psalms as the first of the 11 books of the Hagiographa. Thereby the genealogy found in Ruth 4:18-22 serves as a fitting introduction to the Psalter, which is often attributed in its entirety to David.

The Book of Ruth is a short story, whose three main characters are Ruth, her mother-in-law Naomi and Boaz, who becomes Ruth's second husband. The setting is Moab (Ruth 1:2-6) and Bethlehem in the period of the Judges (1200-1020 B.C.). The story may be summarized as follows: during a famine, Elimelech, his wife Naomi, and their two sons Mahlon and Chilion, move temporarily from Bethlehem to Moab. After the death of Elimelech, his sons marry the Moabite women Orpah and Ruth; ten years later, with the two women still childless, their husbands die. Naomi hears that the famine is over, and decides to return to Bethlehem, urging her daughters-in-law to go back to their Moabite extended families. Orpah agrees, but Ruth insists on accompanying Naomi to Bethlehem, proclaiming "...your people shall be my people, and your God my God" (Ruth 1:16). These words have made her the paradigmatic proselyte to Judaism.

While exercising the right reserved to the poor to pick up the grain which falls to the ground during the barley harvest (See Lev 19:9-10;

Women gleaning in a field near Bethlehem.

23:22), Ruth meets Boaz, who is a relative of her late father-in-law. Naomi encourages Ruth to seek protection from him as next of kin. Boaz agrees to purchase from Naomi and from Ruth the field, which had belonged to Elimelech, and at the same time to marry Ruth "to raise up the name of the dead on his inheritance" (Ruth 4:5). However, in order for Boaz to do so, a prior "right of redemption" must first be renounced by an unnamed closer relative of Elimelech. The latter does so by means of the symbolic act of removing his sandal in the presence of the elders at the city gate. Boaz marries Ruth, and she bears him a son named Obed, who is the paternal grandfather of King David. Most scholars interpret Boaz's marriage of his cousin's childless widow, and the unnamed relative's removal of his shoe, as referring respectively to a form of LEVIRATE marriage and release from the levir's obligation.

Fragments from the Book of Ruth found at Qumran. (Shrine of the Book, Jerusalem)

The assertion that King David was descended from a Moabitess has been interpreted as aimed against Ezra and Nehemiah, who insisted that the Jews of their time annul their marriages to women from Moab and the other nations listed in Deuteronomy 7:1; 23:3-8 (See Ezra chaps. 9-10; Neh 13:1-3).

The linguistic features of the Book of Ruth have been invoked in favor of a variety of dates from the period of the Judges to the period of Ezra and Nehemiah.

Ruth is mentioned in the NT as the ancestress of David and hence of Jesus (Matt 1:5).

OUTLINE

1:1-5	Elimelech's family go to Moab; his two sons marry Moabite women; the three men die
1:5-22	Ruth insists on returning with her mother-in-law, Naomi, to Bethlehem
2:1-23	Ruth gleans in the fields of Boaz
3:1-18	Following Naomi's advice, Ruth claims kinship with Boaz
4:1-12	Boaz gets the next-of-kin to renounce his duties
4:13-22	Boaz married Ruth and their descendant is King David

SABAOTH, LORD OF See HOSTS, LORD OF HOSTS

SABBATH The concept that the last of the seven days of the week is a day of rest is contained in the story of Creation at the very outset of the Bible. God rests from his work of Creation on this day and blesses it accordingly (Gen 2:1-3). In the Mosaic code, Sabbath observance is one of the basic Ten Commandments (Ex 20:8-11) and thereafter is regularly stressed. Throughout the biblical era, it remained one of the distinguishing signs of the Jewish people.

While all societies subdivided time into years, months and days, the seven-day week culminating in a holy day called Sabbath, which means "cessation", was unique to Israel among the peoples of the ancient Near East. The eventual universal adoption of the seven-day week as a unit of time came about as a result of the influence of the Hebrew Bible upon Christianity and Islam.

Some scholars believe that the biblical week may reflect the concept, frequently reflected in Mesopotamian and Ugaritic literature, that seven represents "the whole" or "the culmination". The hypothesis that the Hebrew Sabbath derived from an Assyrian "day of ill-luck" called *shapattu* is unacceptable for three reasons: (a) the Assyrian days of ill-luck varied from month to month, were dependent on the lunar cycle, and did not fall every seven days; (b) the Assyrian days of ill-luck were never called either *shapattu* or *shabattu*; (c) Assyro-Babylonian *shapattu* designates the 15th of the month.

The Sabbath appears at the head of the lists of holy days in Exodus 23:12; Leviticus 23:3; Numbers 28:9. According to all of the sources into which biblical criticism divides the Pentateuch, it is forbidden on the Sabbath to engage in work (Ex 23:12; 34:21; 35:2; Lev 23:3; Deut 5:14). The prohibition of work on the Sabbath, observed from sundown on Friday until nightfall on Saturday, applies not only to Israelites but also to resident aliens, slaves and farm animals (Ex 20:10; 23:12; Deut 5:14). Several biblical texts specify the kinds of work prohibited on the Sabbath. Baking, cooking, food-gathering and travel are forbidden on the Sabbath (Ex 16:23-30). Food for the Sabbath is to be prepared in advance. Plowing and reaping on the Sabbath are prohibited (Ex 34:21). Most likely the expression plowing and reaping denotes all work connected with agriculture. Kindling fire on the Sabbath is forbidden (Ex 35:3) and the carrying of burdens is forbidden on the Sabbath (Jer 17:21-27); moreover, Jeremiah 17:27 asserts that the violation of this prohibition may result in the destruction of Jerusalem. Nehemiah asserts that when he saw Jews pressing grapes into wine, carrying burdens and engaging in commerce on the Sabbath, he warned them that it was as punishment for these transgressions that God had exiled the Jews to Babylon (Neh 13:14-18). Nehemiah proudly reports that he was able to put a stop to the violation of the sanctity of the Sabbath by closing the gates of Jerusalem during the Sabbath and stationing guards atop the walls (Neh 13:19-21). Amos intimates that in his time (mid-8th century B.C.) even the most unscrupulous merchants refrained from engaging in commerce on Sabbath and the New Moon (Amos 8:5). The Sabbath was an occasion for visiting the Temple (Is 1:13) or a prophet (II Kgs 4:23).

Rabbinic exegesis sees in the juxtaposition of the prohibition of kindling fire on the Sabbath (Ex 35:3) with the description of the building of the tabernacle, its appurtenances, and the making of the priestly vestments (Ex 35:4-39:32) an intimation that none of this work may take place on the Sabbath. However, the 8th century B.C. prophet Isaiah takes this for granted (Is 1:13); and both Numbers 28:9-10 and Ezekiel 46:4 prescribe the offering of sacrifices on the Sabbath. This form of worship requires the use of fire, which is otherwise forbidden on the Sabbath. Hence in the NT Jesus reasons that since the priests in the Temple are permitted to perform labors otherwise forbidden on the Sabbath and since Jesus is greater than the Temple, it should be permitted for Jesus and his disciples to violate the Sabbath (Matt 12:5-8). The observance of the Sabbath is a basic requirement which is demanded of Gentiles who adopt the worship of the Lord and thereby attach themselves to Israel (Is 56:3-8). The reward for the observance of the Sabbath, which includes calling it "a delight" and refraining from any commercial activity, is Israel's possession of the land of Israel (Is 58:13-14). The Sabbath and the New Moon are occasions when people of all nations will come to Israel to pay homage to the Lord (Is 66:23). While according to Genesis 2:1-3 and Exodus 20:11 the Sabbath is part of the natural order established at Creation, Deuteronomy 5:14-15 states that God ordained the Sabbath as a reminder of his having liberated Israel from enslavement in Egypt. Jesus asserts, "The Sabbath was made for man, and not man for the Sabbath" (Mark 2:27).

In NT times the celebration of the Sabbath in the synagogue already included reading from the Pentateuch and the Prophets and a sermon based upon a biblical text (Matt 4:23; Mark 1:21-22; 6:2; Luke 4:16-21, 31-32; Acts 13:27; 15:21; 17:1-2; 18:4). The chanting of Psalm 92 by the Levites in the Second Temple on the Sabbath (Mishnah Tamid 7:4) is intimated already by the designation of that psalm as "A Psalm. A song for the Sabbath day" in Psalms 92:1. The Hebrew term "Sabbath" may also refer to the Day of Atonement (Lev 16:31; 23:32), the week (Lev 23:15-16), or "the year of rest" (Lev 25:5, 8). In Leviticus 23:11 "the Sabbath" may designate the first day of the festival of unleavened bread (see PASSOVER). Such usages of "Sabbath" are not included in the list of references of this entry.

SABBATICAL YEAR One year in seven is marked by cessation of all work in field, orchard and vineyard. Just as the weekly Sabbath, the seventh day of the week, is to be observed by a cessation of all work including agricultural activity (Ex 34:21), so the recurrent seventh year is observed in a similar manner (Ex 23:10-11). Farm produce growing without tillage in the seventh year is to be freely available as food, not only to the owner and his family, but to the poor; anything not consumed is to be left for animals, both domestic and wild (Lev 25:6-7). This fallow year is called a "Sabbath to the Lord" (Lev 25:1-7, 18-22). The Book of Deuteronomy (Deut 15:1-3:9) calls for the remission of all debts in the sabbatical year. The fact that the cancellation of debts appears only in this legislation may be attributed to the growth of commercial activity in the later biblical period. The linkage between the sabbatical year, the cancellation of debts and the suspension of all agricultural work, is clearly stated in Nehemiah 10:31.

The motif behind the legislation of the sabbatical year in both its aspects — permitting the land to lie fallow and the remission of debts — is explicitly social in nature: it provided free food for the poor, prevented the creation of a permanent debtor class and also permitted the land to rest undisturbed.

Seven such annual sabbatical cycles culminated with the year of the jubilee (Lev 27:16-25; Num 36:4). Like the sabbatical year, the jubilee year features elements known from the earlier Mesopotamian practice of periodic royal remission of debts and obligations, and the restoration of property to its lawful owner.

SABEANS See SHEBA No.7

SABTA, SABTAH Third son of Cush, the firstborn son of Ham, and the name of a clan or tribe.

SABEANS
Job 1:15. Is 45:14. Ezek 23:42. Joel 3:8

SABTA, SABTAH
Gen 10:7. I Chr 1:9

SABTECHA, SABTECHAH Fifth son of Cush the firstborn son of Ham, and the name of a clan or tribe.

SACAR

1. Sacar the Hararite, father of Ahiam one of David's thirty "mighty men".

2. A Levite, fourth son of Obed-Edom; he was one of the gatekeepers in the House of the Lord at the time of King David.

SACHIAH A man of Benjamin, sixth of the seven sons of Shaharaim by his wife Hodesh.

SACRIFICES AND OFFERINGS An act of worship expressing submission to the deity and seeking his favor; in the biblical context the sacrificer was also atoning for his sins. The Hebrew word for sacrifice comes from the root meaning "to approach" and signified that which is brought near, or offered, to God. The nations surrounding the Israelites made human sacrifices but the story of Isaac was to show God's displeasure with such practice. Sacrifice is first mentioned in the story of Cain and Abel while for Noah and the patriarchs, it was an accepted form of worship. In those times, every religious cult included sacrifice and until the time of the Deuteronomic code, the only animals slaughtered by the Israelites were for that purpose. Once in their own land, the Israelites concentrated sacrifice in the Jerusalem Temple.

The sacrificial laws were incorporated into the Pentateuch as "a heritage of the congregation of Jacob" (Deut 33:4). As the following verses indicate (Lev 1:2; 4:2; 7:38; 12:2; 15:2; 16:29-31; etc.), these laws were made available to the people at large. The person making the offering participated in the following rituals involving his animal: laying on of the hands (whose purpose has yet to be determined), elevation (raising his offering), slaughter, skinning, dissecting and washing; these acts were performed in the forecourt. The rituals reserved for the priests were: elevation (jointly with the offerer), blood manipulation, arrangement of the wood and sacrifice on the altar and incineration. The division followed the rule that anything to do with the altar was the exclusive domain of the priest. This rule is clearly evident in Leviticus chapter 1. In the case of the bird offering, however, the offerer was omitted from the procedure (Lev 1:14-17), because there was no lay participation. Even the "slaughter", performed by pinching off the head at the altar, was done by the priest. The centrality of the blood in the sacrificial ritual is evidenced by the rule that the priestly portions of the sacrifices were assigned to the one who manipulated the blood (Lev 6:26; 7:7).

The expiatory sacrifices were the sin offering and the guilt offering, at times the whole burnt offering and the cereal offering, and, in one case, the well-being offering. The purpose of the sin offering was not to purge

Fragment of a stone vessel inscribed "Sacrifice" (Corban in Hebrew), and two birds depicted upside down. Herodian period. (Israel Museum)

Two offering bowls found in the courtyard of a temple of the late 9th century B.C. at Arad. Both bowls bear a blurred inscription thought to be the word "holy". (Israel Dept. of Antiquities and Museums)

the offerer but the sanctuary. This took place in three stages: (a) when an individual committed an inadvertency or contracted a severe impurity, the blood of the offering was daubed on the horns of the outer altar (e.g., Lev 4:25; 9:9). (b) When the entire community (even through its anointed priest: Lev 4:3) committed an inadvertency, the blood was brought inside the shrine where it was sprinkled before the veil and daubed on the horns of the inner altar (Lev 4:5-7, 16-18). (c) For presumptuous sins, of the individual or the group, the blood was brought inside the adytum where it was sprinkled before and upon the ark, followed by the ritual of the previous two stages in reverse order. Only one postulate explains these data: the greater the offender and the graver the offense, the more the resultant impurity penetrated into the sanctuary. Inadvertences of the individual polluted the outer altar, inadvertences of the group polluted the shrine; but presumptuous sins penetrated into the adytum and only the rites of the Day of Atonement could purge them.

The main cases of the guilt offering are cited in Leviticus 5:14ff and its sacrificial procedure in Leviticus 7:1-7. The first case of such an offering (Lev 5:14-16) deals with inadvertent trespass upon sanctums. The trespasser had to restore the value of the desecrated sanctums, pay a one-fifth fine and bring a ram or its monetary equivalent as a reparation offering. Leviticus 5:17-19 deals with suspected trespass on sanctums. He who suffers in body or conscience without knowing the cause suspects that he is being punished by God for trespassing on his sanctums. This is thus a continuation of verses 14-16 — the first case dealing with known trespass, the second with suspected trespass. The third case, Leviticus 6:1-7, concerns the defrauding of a man, compounded by a false oath to God. It presumes that the false oath follows all the previously enumerated crimes, i.e., that the fraudulent act was followed by a lying oath. This case states that, if the offender repents of his deed before he is apprehended, he need only restore the value of the property to the owner, add a one-fifth fine and bring a reparation offering to God. That the "whole offering" expiates is expressly stated in its prescription (Lev 1:4), in certain rituals (Lev 9:7; 14:20) and in nonpriestly sources (Job 1:5; 42:8). Since it is entirely consumed on the altar (the skin excepted, Lev 7:8) it is called "burnt offering" (Deut 33:10; I Sam 7:9).

The cereal offering probably served as a cheap whole offering for those who could not afford an animal. The "well-being" offering is subject to much discussion. The motivations for bringing this offering as a special sacrifice are adduced in Leviticus 7:11-16 — thanksgiving, fulfillment of a vow or freewill offering. The common denominator to all these motivations is rejoicing: "You shall offer peace offerings, and shall eat there and rejoice before the Lord your God" (Deut 27:7).

The sacrifices filled a wide range of spiritual and emotional needs. True, the prophets jeered at their ineffectiveness in refining ethical behavior. But this cannot negate the fact that the masses participated in the sacrificial services with reverence and love.

The priestly gifts are listed or adumbrated in a single passage, Numbers 18:8-19. The most sacred offerings (v.9) are: the cereal offering, except for its token portion burnt on the altar (Lev 2:2-3, 9-10), the flesh of the purification and reparation offerings (Lev 8:29; 7:5-6), and the hide of the burnt offering (not included here: cf Lev 7:8). These gifts were assigned only to male priests (Lev 6:18, 29; 7:10) and had to be eaten in the sanctuary court (Lev 7:6).

The sacred gifts (in contrast to the most sacred, above) are: the first-processed of the wine and grain (Num 18:12); the first ripe produce (v.13); all proscriptions (v.14); the firstborn of animals and the redemption price of firstborn humans (vs. 15-17); the breast and right thigh of the well-being offering (v.18); and all sacred gifts to the sanctuary (v.19).

The NT takes for granted that the sacrifical system of Judaism is ordained of God. Jesus' parents took him to the Temple and made the prescribed sacrifice (Luke 2:24). When criticized for eating with unsavory people, Jesus replied: "Go and learn what this means: 'I desire mercy, and not sacrifice.'" (Matt 9:13, quoting Hos 6:6). In Matthew 12:7 the same statement is made in connection with a discussion of eating grain from a field on the Sabbath, in Mark 12:33 it appears in connection with the discussion of the greatest commandment. These three different contexts make it clear that the saying was important to the early Christian redactors of the traditions.

Most significantly, however, the early Christians saw the crucified Jesus as a sacrifice on their behalf. Paul for example states: "For indeed Christ, our Passover, was sacrificed for us" (I Cor 5:7). Along similar lines the author of Ephesians admonishes his readers to live in love "as Christ also has loved us and given himself for us, an offering and a sacrifice to God for a sweet-smelling aroma" (Eph 5:2). The writer to the Hebrews, eager to show that Christianity has a better way, stresses that Jesus is the high priest (Heb 2:17; 3:1) par excellence who has been designated like the high priest to offer gifts and sacrifices for sin (Heb 5:1), has learned obedience through suffering and was therefore named high priest (Heb 5:8-10). He describes the high priest as devout, guileless, undefiled, separated from sinners, raised high above the heavens (Heb 7:26). Above all he does not have to offer sacrifices daily, for this "he did once for all when he offered up himself" (Heb 7:28). In this the writer sees the superiority of the New Covenant (Heb 8:6). He is convinced that better sacrifices are needed (Heb 9:23) and that in fact Christ has offered them, by offering his body once and for all (Heb 10:10). Now there is no longer any offering for sin (Heb 10:18). The sprinkled blood of Jesus which calls for unbounded love even towards enemies "speaks better things than that of Abel" (Heb 12:24) which cries for vengeance.

In line with the sacrifice made by Christ, Paul calls upon Roman Christians to "present your bodies: a living sacrifice, holy, acceptable to

Abraham about to sacrifice Isaac, shown on a bas-relief from the panel of a 4th-century A.D. sarcophagus. (Grotto Vaticane, Rome)

God" (Rom 12:1) and expresses his joy should he be "poured out as a drink offering on the sacrifice and service of your faith" (Phil 2:17). In Romans 15:16 he describes his priestly service as the preaching of the Gospel of God, so that "the offering of the Gentiles might be acceptable, sanctified by the Holy Spirit" (cf also I Pet 2:5). Jesus, by renouncing violence, teaching the love of enemies, and accepting his death, is seen as breaking the link between sacred awe and the displaced aggression entailed in traditional blood sacrifice.

SADDUCEES (from Zadok, high priest in the days of Solomon [I Kgs 1:39] or from *Tzaddikim* righteous men). Members of one of three major parties in Judaism from the last centuries B.C. until the destruction of the Second Temple in A.D. 70. The Sadducees came from the affluent sections of society, their members mainly belonging to the priestly class (Acts 4:1; 5:17). Their doctrines were based exclusively upon the Written Law whose interpretation in the Oral Law, they, unlike the Pharisees, did not treat as binding. They denied the resurrection of the dead, immortality of the soul and the world to come (Acts 23:6-8). According to their belief, biblical Scriptures offered no basis for belief in the resurrection of the dead, a matter on which they approached Jesus — "Then some of the Sadducees, who deny that there is a resurrection, came to him and asked him..." (Luke 20:27 and parallels).

SADDUCEES
Matt 3:7;
16:1, 6, 11-12;
22:23, 34.
Mark 12:18.
Luke 20:27.
Acts 4:1; 5:17;
23:6-8

The Sadducees thus differed greatly from the Pharisees, in their way of thinking but equally in their attitude towards the common people. During the final Temple period the Sadducees, who included the chief priests and the elders supervising Temple worship, were identified with the aristocracy and sought to ingratiate themselves with the Roman rulers by collaborating with them in keeping the population quiescent and obedient. They were consequently less popular than the Pharisees with the ordinary people.

The NT records the frictions between the Sadducees and the Pharisees. Paul's imprisonment highlighted the divisions between the two groups: "'Men and brethren, I am a Pharisee, the son of a Pharisee: concerning the hope and resurrection of the dead I am being judged!' And when he had said this, a dissension arose between the Pharisees and the Sadducees, and the assembly was divided. For the Sadducees say there is no resurrection — and no angel or spirit; but the Pharisees confess both." (Acts 23:6-8). In spite of these differences, John the Baptist confronted both Sadducees and Pharisees by calling them "brood of vipers" and challenged them to "bear fruit", namely repentance among the people (Matt 3:7-11).

Unlike the Pharisees, who regularly debated important religious issues with Jesus, the latter's teachings hardly interested the Sadducees, probably because of his greater affinity with the Pharisees.

Only on one occasion did the Sadducees approach Jesus, together with the Pharisees, to demand a sign from heaven (Matt 16:1ff).

As the Sadducees were in charge of the Temple they must have been bewildered and alarmed when Jesus said: "not one stone shall be left here upon another, that shall not be thrown down" (Matt 24:2). (According to the Gospel of John, and to the false witnesses he said "I am able to destroy the temple of God and to build it in three days" [Matt 26:61]). These apparent threats to the Temple could have been among the reasons why the Sadducees, as defenders of public order, wished to have Jesus executed (Matt 26:3-4). After the destruction of the Temple in A.D. 70, the Sadducees disappeared, while the Pharisees continued to represent the main stream within Judaism.

SAFFRON See PLANTS

SALAH Firstborn son of Arphaxad the third son of Shem (Gen 10:22,

SALAH
Gen 10:24;
11:12-15

24). He lived 433 years (Gen 11:15) and begot Eber and other sons and daughters. In the genealogy of Jesus as given by Luke (Luke 3:35), he is listed as Shelah "the son of Cainan the son of Arphaxad" and the father of Eber.

SALAMIS
Acts 13:5

SALAMIS A large town on the southern coast of Cyprus, north of modern Famagusta. Paul, Barnabas and John preached in its synagogue during their first missionary expedition (Acts 13:5).

SALCAH
Deut 3:10.
Josh 12:5;
13:11. I Chr
5:11

SALCAH An important city on the eastern border of Bashan in the former kingdom of Og, which was conquered by Moses (Deut 3:10; Josh 12:5; 13:11) and given to half the tribe of Manasseh (Deut 3:13). It was on the border of the territory of Gad (I Chr 5:11). In the Hellenistic-Roman period a large village called Triakome flourished there. In surface surveys numerous Greek and Nabatean inscriptions were discovered, and also fragments of Nabatean architecture.

SALEM
Gen 14:18. Ps
76:2. Heb 7:1-2

SALEM The city of Melchizedek (Gen 14:18), identified by Jewish tradition with Jerusalem.

SALIM
John 3:23

SALIM A place in the Jordan Valley near Aenon, where John baptized people. Identified with Tell Abu Jus, about 5 miles (8 km) south of Beth Shean and with a large tell east of Shechem, where architectural remains of the Roman period were found. The latter is near the copious springs of Wadi Raria, to which some believe the "much water" of John 3:23 refers.

SALLAI

SALLAI 1
Neh 11:8

1. A man of Benjamin, among those who settled in Jerusalem after the return of the exiles from Babylon.

SALLAI 2
Neh 12:20

2. Head of a priestly family who lived in Jerusalem at the time of Joiakim the high priest; he is probably identical with Sallu No.2 (Neh 12:7).

SALLU

SALLU 1
I Chr 9:7. Neh
11:7

1. A man of Benjamin, son of Meshullam; he settled in Jerusalem after the return of the exiles from Babylon.

SALLU 2
Neh 12:7

2. Head of a priestly family who returned with Zerubbabel from the Exile in Babylon, settling in Jerusalem.

SALMA

SALMA 1
I Chr 2:11

1. Firstborn son of Nahshon and father of Boaz. Alternately spelled Salmon.

SALMA 2
I Chr 2:51-54

2. Second son of Hur (the son of Caleb), called the father, or founder, of Bethlehem. He is the ancestor of the Netophathites, of Atroth Beth Joab and half of the Manahethites.

SALMAI
Neh 7:48

SALMAI Head of a family of Nethinim (Temple servants) who returned from Exile with Zerubbabel. In Ezra 2:46 he is called Shalmai.

SALMON
Ruth 4:20-21.
Matt 1:4-5.
Luke 3:32

SALMON An alternate spelling for Salma No.1.

SALMONE
Acts 27:7

SALMONE Place near Crete where Paul sheltered from the wind on his voyage to Rome. It is generally identified with present-day Cape Sidero.

SALOME
Mark 15:40;
16:1

SALOME One of the women who witnessed the crucifixion; she went to the tomb to anoint Jesus' body (Mark 15:40; 16:1). She was the wife of Zebedee and mother of the apostles James and John.

SALT SEA
Gen 14:3.
Num 34:3, 12.
Deut 3:17.
Josh 3:16;
12:3; 15:2, 5;
18:19

SALT SEA See DEAD SEA

SALU
Num 25:14

SALU A man of Simeon and father of Zimri, the man who had taken a Midianite woman and was killed with her by Phinehas the son of Eleazar.

SALVATION In the OT salvation comes from acts through which God effects deliverance. This can be directed towards the individual or towards the nation. References, especially in the Books of Psalms and Proverbs, stress the power of God to deliver the individual. Promises in the Pentateuch often refer to the prosperity of the community rather than the individual. The context almost always relates to deliverance from specific sufferings, such as oppression or exile, and not to the removal of sin. Messianic hopes are directed largely towards national restoration. Later Jewish thinkers saw the Torah as the instrument by which both the individual and the nation would be saved. For Christians, salvation and redemption imply primarily, God's liberation of the individual.

Salvation is the most general term for the positive contribution of God in Christ to the condition of humankind. The NT vocabulary expressing the benefits of faith is rich and varied, its variations to some extent reflecting the different predicaments from which the believer needs to be saved. For people who have grown up in a religious-legal system (e.g. Jews, Romans) the oppression felt is that of a guilty sinner, and salvation comes as the good news of the forgiveness of sins. For others (e.g. pagan Greeks) the problem acutely felt is that of death. To them the answer comes: "I am the resurrection and the life: he who believes in me, though he may die, he shall live" (John 11:25ff). Yet others experience lack of direction and meaning in their life. To them biblical revelation offers a goal and a way of life (the Kingdom of God, the Kingdom of Heaven, the Sermon on the Mount, etc.). To some extent the biblical answer varies with the audience addressed and its needs. Some biblical concepts are more individualistic, others stress social aspects. The following treatment considers salvation in the NT. (a) Matthew and Mark. In the older Synoptic Gospels, which provide the earliest information about the teaching of Jesus himself, salvation is primarily given expression through Jesus' proclamation of the imminent arrival of the Kingdom of God. The poor are blessed because theirs is the Kingdom of God (Matt 5:3). Jesus' public ministry begins and ends with this message (Mark 1:14ff; 14:25) which is a socio-political term for a salvation consisting of justice and peace for all and freedom from oppression. Resurrection from the dead is also taught (Mark 12:18-27) and given concrete realization in the empty tomb (Mark 16:1-8). Eternal life is also mentioned (Mark 10:17, 30). (b) The fourth gospel, John, tends to replace the kingdom theme by that of more abundant life (John 10:10) in Jesus' name (John 20:31). Eternal life (John chap. 11) is begun on earth and continued in the resurrection. (c) Luke strongly emphasizes the gift of the Holy Spirit as the great blessing in the present (Acts 2:1-4), and this is connected with the forgiveness of sins (Luke 1:77; 3:3; 24:47; Acts 2:38; 5:31; 10:43; 13:38; 26:18). (d) Paul has the richest and most varied terminology for salvation or soteriology. Justification of the sinner (especially frequent in Galatians, Romans, e.g. Rom 1:17) refers to the acquittal of a guilty person in a courtroom. Redemption (Rom 3:24) refers to the ransom or sacral manumission of a slave who thus acquires freedom. Reconciliation (Rom 5:11) refers to the restoration to friendship of two people who have fallen out. Adoption as sons and daughters of God (Rom 8:15, 23) refers to the conferral of legitimacy on rootless orphans. Paul also uses the vocabulary of freedom (Gal 2:4; 5:1, 13; Rom 8:21; II Cor 3:17) and of new creation "If anyone is in Christ, he is a new creation" (II Cor 5:17; Gal 6:15).

Subjectively then, faith in Christ is experienced as freedom and more intensive life in the spirit. Objectively, it refers to a new relationship of friendly intimacy with God a future promise of the Kingdom of God on earth and eternal life in heaven.

SAMARIA

1. Region of the land of Israel, whose geographical limits are not clearly delineated in the Bible. Originally the name denoted the territory of the tribes of Ephraim and half of Manasseh, bounded by the Jordan

37-38, 51.
II Kgs 1:2-3;
2:25; 3:1, 6;
5:3; 6:19-20,
24-25; 7:1, 18;
10:1, 12, 17,
35-36; 13:1, 6,
9-10, 13; 14:14,
16, 23; 15:8,
13-14, 17, 23,
25, 27; 17:1,
5-6, 24, 26,
28; 18:9-10,
34; 21:13;
23:18-19.
II Chr 18:2, 9;
22:9; 25:13,
24; 28:8-9, 15.
Ezra 4:10, 17.
Neh 4:2. Is
7:9; 8:4; 9:9;
10:9-11; 36:19.
Jer 23:13;
31:5; 41:5.
Ezek 16:46,
51, 53, 55;
23:4, 33. Hos
7:1; 8:5-6;
10:5, 7; 13:16.
Amos 3:9, 12;
4:1; 6:1; 8:14.
Obad v.19.
Mic 1:1, 5-6.
Luke 17:11.
John 4:4-5, 7,
9. Acts 1:8;
8:1, 5, 9, 14;
9:31; 15:3

to the east and the coastal plain to the west. The southern border ran from north of Jericho to south of Bethel and westwards to Gezer. To the north it included the rich valleys of Beth Shan and Jezreel, touching the foothills of Lower Galilee to reach the Mediterranean north of Mount Carmel. After the division of the United Kingdom Samaria's domain extended to Galilee. Except for the exclusion of Gezer, the southern border did not basically change. After the Assyrian campaigns, the Kingdom of Israel shrunk to encompass only the geographical region of Samaria proper. Thus after the campaign of Tiglath-Pileser III in 732 B.C., Israel included the hill country north and south of its capital Samaria; of the fertile valleys, only the valley of Aijalon remained. Known by the name of Samarina, the Assyrian province of Samaria, founded by Sargon II in 712 B.C., included the hill country, as well as the western foothills and the coastal plain. It was in this area that the Assyrians settled deportees from other countries alongside the remnants of the Israelite population, who in time became known as the Samaritans. In the Persian period the province consisted only of the hill country.

Samaria's wealth stemmed from agriculture, the valleys yielding wheat and barley, while the gentle slopes of the hill country were planted with grapevines and olives. The kingdom was traversed by one of the major branches of the Via Maris (the coastal highway) important in international trade.

After the Jews' return from the Babylonian Exile, when they began to rebuild the Temple in Jerusalem, the Samaritans with their center at Shechem, offered to help. The rejection of their offer was the origin of the subsequent antagonism between Jews and Samaritans (Ezra chap. 4; Neh 2:10).

In the second half of the 5th century B.C. the governor of the province of Samaria was named Sanballat (Neh 2:10,19). This same governor and his sons are also known from the papyri of the Jewish community in Elephantine in Egypt.

The plains and hills of Samaria.

Samaria.

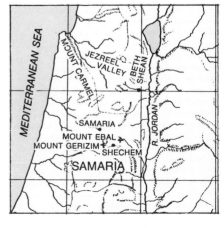

In 63 B.C. Pompey annexed Samaria to the Roman province of Syria. Augustus gave the capital of Samaria to Herod. Samaria is mentioned on various occasions in the NT. Jesus crossed it en route to Jerusalem (Luke 17:11); on his way back, he came to Sychar, a city of Samaria, where he spoke to the Samaritan woman at Jacob's Well (John 4:4ff). The apostles were to preach there (Acts 1:8).

2. Called Shomron in Hebrew; it was the capital of the ancient Kingdom of Israel. Built on a hill about 300 feet (90 m) above the surrounding fertile agricultural area, the city occupies a strategic point, that gives access in three directions: in the west to the coastal plain; in the east to Shechem (modern Nablus) and from there to the River Jordan or to Jerusalem; and in the north to Megiddo and the Jezreel Valley.

According to I Kings (16:24) the hill was purchased by King Omri of Israel, from a man named Shemer (hence Shomron) for two talents of silver. Omri made it his capital, moving to it from Tirzah. Omri's son Ahab, the next king, put up "an altar for Baal in the temple of Baal" in Samaria (I Kgs 16:32) under the influence of his Phoenician wife Jezebel. Phoenician influence is also indicated in Ahab's "ivory house" (I Kgs 22:39), his palace, where the furniture and perhaps the walls were embellished with ivory plaques. During this period the city was threatened by the Arameans of Damascus, who attacked it several times but failed to conquer it (I Kgs 20:1ff; II Kgs 6:24ff). Omri's dynasty ended with the revolution of Jehu, the founder of the new dynasty, who destroyed Ahab's shrine (II Kgs 10:18-28). In the next century another shrine contained the "calf of Samaria" (Hos 8:5-6). No remains of the two shrines have been discovered during excavations. In the time of Jeroboam II "houses of ivory" and "beds of ivory" are again mentioned (Amos 3:15; 6:4). His death brought to an end a period of

(right)
Ostracon from Samaria of the 8th century B.C. inscribed with what appears to be a letter giving instructions for the distribution of a certain quantity of barley. (Israel Dept. of Antiquities and Museums)

A coin of Sebaste (Samaria) with a sphinx. Struck in A.D. 201.

prosperity for the Kingdom of Israel. There were six kings within 15 years and the Assyrians began to pose a threat. Samaria withstood the Assyrian attack for three years (725-722 B.C.) until it was captured and many of its citizens were deported (II Kgs 17:6).

According to the Bible, the city fell in the last months of the reign of Shalmaneser V (II Kgs 18:9-10) who died in 722 B.C., but Assyrian records show that Sargon II claimed this victory. The city became the center of administration for the Assyrian province of Samerina, which was settled by newcomers of different origins (II Kgs 17:24), each worshiping his own god (II Kgs 17:29). Under Persian rule (6th-4th centuries B.C.) it remained a provincial capital.

During the 4th century B.C. the Samaritans built their center at Samaria. In 332 B.C. the city was captured by Alexander the Great, who settled Macedonian veterans there. Then in 108 B.C. it was conquered and utterly destroyed by John Hyrcanus and the Hasmoneans imposed Judaism on its Samaritan inhabitants. Herod renamed it Sebaste in honor of the emperor, and his building activities made it into one of the most magnificent cities in Palestine. During the First Jewish Revolt in A.D. 66 it was destroyed, but was soon rebuilt. Septimius Severus gave

Remains of the Roman basilica at Sebaste (Samaria).

A priest holding the Samaritan Pentateuch.

it the status of *colonia* in A.D. 200. In the late Roman period the city declined and it was no more than an unimportant village in the Byzantine period. A popular Christian tradition placed the tomb of St. John the Baptist at Samaria and several churches were constructed there for this reason, the latest by the Crusaders in the 12th century.

The site has been extensively excavated. The Israelite settlement consisted of an acropolis and the lower city, each with a separate system of fortifications. The acropolis contains a building identified as the palace of the Israelite kings. Ivory inlays were found there, some belonging to the time of Ahab but most to the reign of Jeroboam II. Ostraca from the reign of Jeroboam II or Menahem appear to be records of taxes, written in the ancient Hebrew script. Later remains throw light on the city in Hellenistic and Roman times.

SAMARITANS Inhabitants of the district of Samaria, following the exchange of population effected by the Assyrians after their conquest of the Northern Kingdom in 722/1 B.C. Pursuing their policy of transferring conquered peoples, the Assyrians deported many of the original inhabitants of the Northern Kingdom and replaced them with a mixture of people from the east: from Babylon, Avva, Hamath, Sepharvaim and Cuth (deriving from the latter, the Samaritans are often referred to in rabbinic literature as Cuthim). The name Samaritans appears only once in the OT, in II Kings 17:29 where it is used for these newcomers, who persisted in their pagan ways. However, the majority of the population was constituted by the Israelites who had not been deported and who continued in their Israelite faith. The beliefs brought by the newcomers did not survive and no paganism is found in later Samaritan theology.

SAMARITANS
II Kgs 17:29.
Matt 10:5.
Luke 9:52;
10:33; 17:16.
John 4:9,
39-40; 8:48.
Acts 8:25

The mixed population of Samaria was not accepted as Jewish by the Jews of the south. When the Jews returned from the Babylonian Exile and began to rebuild the Temple, the Samaritans offered to help but were rebuffed, whereupon they proceeded to attempt to prevent or delay the project (Ezra 4:1-6). When the returned exiles began to rebuild the walls of Jerusalem, the Samaritans protested to the authorities that this constituted an act of rebellion and the work was stopped until the arrival of Nehemiah as governor (Ezra 4:7-24). The Samaritans maintained their hostile attitudes and actions which were now directed against Nehemiah (Neh 6:1-13). Their opposition proved unsuccessful but the schism was now complete. Samaritans were forbidden to offer sacrifices at the Jerusalem Temple or to intermarry with Jews, while the Samaritans built their own temple on Mount Gerizim, near Shechem. Their Bible consisted of the Pentateuch alone; the text featured minor divergences from the accepted Hebrew text and contained an additional verse specifically mentioning Gerizim as the site of the temple.

In the following centuries, the Samaritans suffered when Shechem was destroyed by Alexander the Great, while in 128 B.C. John Hyrcanus captured Shechem and destroyed the Samaritan temple. It remained in ruins until the 2nd century A.D. when it was rebuilt by the Emperor Hadrian as a reward for Samaritan help against the Jews during the Bar Kokhba revolt (132-135).

The continuing hostility between Jews and Samaritans is reflected in the NT. One of the worst insults that hostile Jews could offer to Jesus was to call him a Samaritan (John 8:48). When Jesus was refused hospitality by a Samaritan village because he was en route to Jerusalem, his disciples were angered, for which Jesus rebuked them (Luke 9:51-56). The story of Jesus' conversation with a Samaritan woman in John chapter 4 also shows up the rift between Jews and Samaritans as the disciples are amazed that Jesus should talk to her (John 4:27). The

Samaritan sarcophagi of the Roman period from Shechem.

(top left)
Stone Mezuza *of the beginning of the Byzantine period, from Samaria. (Israel Museum)*

Remains of a Samaritan settlement of the 4th-5th centuries at Kadum.

parable of the "good Samaritan" (Luke 10:33-37) further illustrates the cleavage, as the Samaritan is obviously viewed by Jews as a person least likely to act charitably. In general, the NT relates favorably to the Samaritans (Luke 10:30-37; 17:11-16). Samaritans received Jesus' ministry (John 4:39-40) and were among the first to accept the message of the gospel (Acts 8:5-25).

SAMGAR-NEBO One of the princes of Babylon who took part in the final assault on Jerusalem by the army of Nebuchadnezzar. However, some scholars believe "Samgar-Nebo" is not a proper name but another title of prince Nergal-Sharezer.

SAMGAR-NEBO
Jer 39:3

SAMLAH Fifth king in Edom "before any king reigned over the Children of Israel" (Gen 36:31).

SAMLAH
Gen 36:36-3?
I Chr 1:47-4?

SAMOS A Greek island off the western coast of Asia Minor. It benefited in antiquity from its offshore position near the trade routes from the interior of Asia Minor and in the Mediterranean Sea, and by the 7th century B.C. it was one of the leading commercial centers of Greece. The island achieved its greatest prosperity in the 6th century B.C. During the Roman period Samos was part of the Roman province of Asia. Paul passed through it on his return journey to Palestine from Greece (Acts 20:15).

SAMOS
Acts 20:15

SAMOTHRACE A mountainous Greek island in the northeast Aegean Sea, off the coast of Thrace. Samothrace was famous in antiquity for its sanctuary of the great gods. The cult involved mystery rites centered around a mother goddess figure, her spouse and attendant demons. The sanctuary was active from the 7th century B.C. on, but most of the buildings are Hellenistic in date. The remains include the Rotunda dedicated by Queen Arsinoe II of Egypt in the 280's B.C., and the Nike Fountain, over which stood the winged "Victory", probably erected by the Rhodians c. 190 B.C. in commemoration of a naval victory.

SAMOTHRACE
Acts 16:11

Paul spent a night in Samothrace on his way from Alexandria to Philippi and Greece (Acts 16:11).

SAMSON ("little sun"). A member of the tribe of Dan, described in the Book of Judges as the last of Israel's judges. According to Judges 16:31, he judged Israel for 20 years. His heroic deeds are recorded in chapters 13-16 of the Book of Judges.

SAMSON
Judg 13:24;
14:1, 3, 5, 7,
10, 12, 15-16,
20; 15:1, 3-4,
6-7, 10-12, 16
16:1-3, 6-7, 9-
10, 12-14, 20,
23, 25-30. He?
11:32

The Samson saga consists of a birth and recognition story, followed by romantic encounters with three Philistine women and the complications associated with these unions. The story's moral could have been to warn against marriage with non-Israelites. Scattered throughout the stories are three prayers, the first by Manoah, Samson's father (Judg 13:8), and the other two placed in the son's mouth (Judg 15:18; 16:28). Manoah's request is couched in proper cultic language, whereas Samson's are appropriate expressions on the lips of an unconventional soldier. The request for water comes close to rebuking the Lord, and the final plea for death in the two-part prayer can be translated as grim determination: "Let me die with the Philistines." Two victory songs enliven the narrative, the first attributed to Samson after his slaughter of a thousand Philistines with the jawbone of an ass (Judg 15:16) and the second ascribed to victorious Philistines who had

Remains of the temple of Hera (Juno), goddess of marriage and childbirth, at Samos.

(bottom right)
Region between Zorah and Eshtaol where Samson was born.

Statue of Nike (Victory) from Samothrace. Early 2nd century B.C.

blinded their prisoner, the mighty Samson (Judg 16:23-24). The latter song is unusual because of its powerful use of rhyme, rare in Hebrew poetry. Equally rare in the Bible are the three riddles in the story about the lovely Timnite (Judg 14:14, 18). The bulk of the story is made up of heroic deeds. Samson slew a young lion with his bare hands; he killed 30 men from Ashkelon and took their clothes to pay a wager; he caught 300 foxes and set them on fire, turning them loose in the Philistines' grain fields; he broke a rope and then slew 1,000 men with the jawbone of an ass; he pulled up the gate of Gaza, together with its posts, and took it several miles from the city; he pulled down the temple of Dagon, killing about 3,000 people.

The religious dimension shines through these earthy tales from start to finish. Samson's mother received a visit from an angel, who told her that she would conceive and give birth to an unusual son, a Nazirite. Naturally, the prayers call attention to the religious dimension of the story, but it is even noted that in most instances Samson's strength derived from seizure by the spirit rather than from long hair. In the end the mighty warrior lifts his eyes in prayer toward the real hero of the story, God. The victorious Philistines will never again make sport of God's champion. Not every feature of the saga serves the purpose of entertainment and teaching. Occasionally, tribal jealousy creeps into the picture, for example when the inhabitants of Judah are portrayed as cowardly subjects who preferred bondage to the Philistines over fighting for freedom. Even Samson's lack of respect for his father is underscored; refusing to seek a wife among his own people, as his parents suggest, Samson orders his father to get the beautiful Timnite for him. The early church therefore had difficulty accepting Samson, despite the identification of him as a saint in Hebrews 11:32. His liaisons with women of dubious virtue and his suicide caused great difficulty at first, but eventually Samson came to represent a type of Christ. The emphasis therefore fell on his mighty deeds, some of which seemed to parallel Jesus' acts as reported in the gospels.

SAMUEL Prophet and last of the Israelite judges. He was the son of Elkanah of the tribe of Ephraim and his wife Hannah. Hannah had been barren for many years and Samuel was born after she vowed that her firstborn child would be dedicated to the service of God (I Sam chap. 1). He was brought to Eli, the chief priest, at Shiloh at a young age and grew up there as a Nazirite. While still a youth he experienced a theophany in which he was informed of the termination of the line of Eli (I Sam 3:10-14).

Samuel became the most outstanding personality in early Israelite history in Canaan, functioning in a variety of leadership roles: seer, priest, judge and military leader, and he was recognized "from Dan to Beersheba" (I Sam 3:20). His home was in Ramah where he headed groups of prophets devoted to the restoration of the traditional worship. He also acted as judge, regularly visiting the religious centers at Bethel, Gilgal and Mizpah.

Samuel was responsible for the establishment of the monarchy. Growing pressure for national unity, especially in view of the Philistine threat, led the people to demand the appointment of a king. Samuel was totally opposed to such a step which he interpreted as apostasy and rejection of the kingship of God. However, he had to accede to the pressure. His own sons proved unsuitable as they had been shown up as corrupt judges (I Sam 8:1-3) and so, after taking council with the notables of Israel at Mizpah, he selected and anointed Saul the son of Kish of the tribe of Benjamin, and his choice was accepted by the people (I Sam chap. 10).

The site of the tomb of Samuel has traditionally been associated with the shrine known as Nabi Samwil (the Prophet Samuel in Arabic), on the highest mountain overlooking Jerusalem.

Interior of the shrine at Nabi Samwil.

In the course of time, the relations between the king and the prophet deteriorated. The break came when Saul took over certain functions which Samuel felt belonged to the priest (I Sam 13:8-14) and also over Saul's leniency towards the Amalekites (I Sam 15:1-23). The king repented but relations between the two were not healed and Samuel, deciding to reject Saul's line, secretly anointed David as Saul's successor (I Sam 16:3-13). Subsequently, when David was fleeing Saul, he was given refuge by Samuel in his home in Ramah (I Sam 19:18-23), which was where the prophet was later buried. (Nebi Samwil, the highest mountain overlooking Jerusalem, is the traditional identification of his grave, at various times in history revered by Jews, Christians and Moslems). The death of Samuel is reported twice (I Sam 25:1; 28:3). In the second case, it is part of the story of Saul's request to the witch of En Dor to evoke the spirit of Samuel. This incident forms a powerful conclusion to the account of the fluctuating relationship between the two men.

15:1. Acts 3:24; 13:20. Heb 11:32

The NT mentions Samuel among the prophets (Acts 3:24; 13:20) and judges (Heb 11:32).

SAMUEL, BOOKS OF I Samuel and II Samuel were originally a single book. The division was first introduced in the printed Hebrew Bible of 1516-1517 which was based on the Septuagint and the Vulgate. The books derive their name from the Hebrew prophet Samuel, the last judge of Israel and the hero of the first half of the period described in the books. Samuel, moreover, is also central to the other major heroes of the book, Kings Saul and David, whom he selects and anoints. The two books can be divided into six parts, each dealing with a portion of the saga concerning the rise and succession of the monarchy in Israel. The narrative starts with the birth of Samuel and continues well into David's reign.

I Samuel begins with the events leading up to the birth of Samuel and his subsequent dedication to service in the sanctuary at Shiloh (chap. 1). As a child he was privy to the future downfall of the priestly family of Eli, his mentor (chaps. 2-3). Eli's sons, Hophni and Phinehas, died in the battle at Aphek against the Philistines who captured the ark. The news of this personal and national-religious disaster killed Eli (chap. 4). The ark was eventually returned after it was seen as the cause of various calamities in the Philistine cities and was kept first in Beth Shemesh and then in Kirjath Jearim (chaps. 5-6).

The seventh chapter, in which Samuel acts as the judge of Israel,

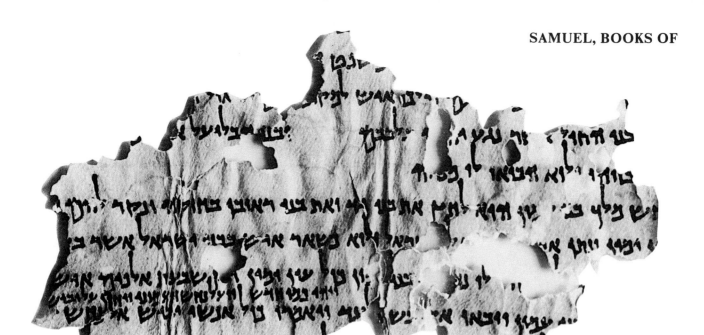

Fragment from the First Book of Samuel found at Qumran. (Shrine of the Book, Jerusalem)

describes his call to the nation to repent; and records God's intervention on the people's behalf in a battle against the Philistines.

Chapter 8 relates the people's demand for a king to lead them in place of the judge Samuel. Samuel gave his consent to their demand even though he regarded it as contrary to God's will. Saul is first introduced searching for his father's lost asses. In accordance with the divine directive given to Samuel, Saul was secretly anointed when he came to Ramah to seek Samuel's advice (chaps. 9-10). The public proclamation of Saul is described in 10:17-27. Saul's first exploit as king of Israel was the freeing of Jabesh Gilead from the Ammonite siege (chap. 11). Samuel then delivered his final oration in which he asserted the complete justness of his leadership, recounted how God had come to the aid of the people at various periods in their history and exhorted them to be faithful to him. This is followed by a description of Saul's campaigns against the Philistines (chaps. 13-14), prior to one of which he illicitly offered a sacrifice. This presumption raised the ire of Samuel who had commanded the king to wait for his arrival before making the sacrifice. Samuel told Saul that as a result of this action, his direct descendants would not inherit his kingdom (chap. 13). This section concludes with a summary of Saul's battles and family. Saul again gave Samuel cause for rejecting him when he disobeyed the command not to take any spoil from the battle against the Amalekites. Samuel did not accept Saul's reasons for sparing both the cattle and Agag, king of the Amalekites whom he subsequently "hacked in pieces" (chap. 15).

David was secretly anointed by Samuel during the reign of Saul and came to the court as Saul's harp player (chap. 16). Saul's jealousy of David was aroused by David's popularity both with the king's son Jonathan and with the people, following David's killing of the Philistine giant Goliath (chap. 17). In a fit of anger, Saul even tried to kill David. He nevertheless gave David his daughter Michal as wife (chap. 18). The friendship with Jonathan and his marriage to Michal served David in saving him from the anger of Saul; Michal, for example, helped him escape from Saul. David took refuge with a group of prophets led by Samuel (chap. 19). Jonathan and David met surreptitiously and pledged everlasting friendship, despite the animosity of Saul towards David (chap. 20). Chapters 21-22 describe David's flight from Saul. The priest of Nob, Ahimelech, who helped David, together with the other priests of Nob, were slaughtered by Saul in reprisal. Only the priest Abiathar escaped and he went to join David. David spent a short time in

Philistine territory, and then assembled a small army with whom he stayed in the hills of Judah. He continued to flee from Saul, and on two occasions refused the opportunity to kill him (chaps. 23-26). David took his army into service of the Philistines guarding Ziklag (chap. 27).

In an attempt to forestall disaster at the hands of the Philistines who were camping at Gilboa, Saul through the medium of the witch of En Dor called up the spirit of Samuel who told him that he would be defeated (chap. 28). In the battle at Gilboa, the Israelite army was defeated by the Philistines and Saul and his three sons were killed, Saul by his own hand (chap. 31).

With the death of Saul, David was anointed king by the elders of Judah. Saul's son Ishbosheth, however, became king in the North (II Sam chap. 2). Ishbosheth was murdered by two of his officers who informed David of their deed, expecting reward but David had both of them killed (chap. 4). Without a rival for the monarchy, David spread his rule over all Israel, establishing his capital at Jerusalem, and fought two successful battles against the Philistines (chap. 5). The ark was brought to Jerusalem (chap. 6), but David was refused the right to build a temple for it by the prophet Nathan. God nevertheless affirmed that the Davidic house would be established forever (chap. 7).

David invited Mephibosheth, son of Jonathan, to the court and returned Saul's estate to him (chap. 9). He then engaged in a protracted series of battles with the Ammonites and their Syrian allies (chap. 10). Bathsheba, wife of Uriah, one of David's officers, became his mistress. David used the war to arrange Uriah's death and subsequently married Bathsheba (chap. 11). When the prophet Nathan accused David both of adultery and murder, David repented his sin, but his child born illicitly to Bathsheba, died. Bathsheba gave birth to a second child, Solomon (chap. 12). David's eldest son, Amnon, raped his half-sister, Tamar, and was murdered in revenge by her brother, Absalom who fled the court (chap. 13) and only returned three years later (chap. 14).

Chapters 15-18 describe the rebellion of Absalom against his father David. After winning popular support, Absalom was able to force David to flee the city with his army. Misled by Hushai, a supporter of David, Absalom mistimed his attack on David's army, allowing it to retreat across the Jordan and regroup. In the subsequent battle the rebel troops were defeated by David, and Absalom was killed against David's orders. The concluding chapter of this section concerns the revolt of Sheba the Benjamite and the northern tribes which was successfully put down by Joab's army (chap. 20).

Chapter 22 is a poem identical to Psalm 18. Chapter 23 is also a poem and the final words of David. The final chapter describes God's punishment of David for the census he conducted, as atonement for which David built an altar on a threshing floor purchased from Araunah.

The Books of Samuel comprise narratives, oracles, poems and lists of names and military exploits. The books are not the work of a single author, and various inconsistencies and discrepancies, and even differences of religious outlook within them indicate that they are composed from different sources.

The books preserve important information for the understanding of the development of the monarchy in Israel. Kingship replaced the sporadic and charismatic rule of the judges, and was not accepted at first without serious difficulties. Both pre-monarchial and anti-monarchial sentiments are found in several chapters of I Samuel, voicing undoubtably the religious conflict which split the population into two divergent camps when this new political system was instituted in Israel.

Within the chapters of these books the reader gets multiple insights into the multi-dimensional and complex personalities of Samuel, Saul and David, as well as their mutual and contrasting conflicts with one another, eventually climaxing in the selection of David and his dynasty as the permanent rulers of Israel.

OUTLINE

I Samuel 1:1-7:17 Samuel
- 1:1-3:21 **Birth** and vocation of Samuel
- 4:1-6:21 The story of the ark; its capture by the Philistines and its return
- 7:1-17 Samuel as judge

8:1-15:35 Samuel and Saul
- 8:1-10:27 Selection of Saul as king
- 11:1-15 Saul's victory over the Ammonites
- 12:1-25 Samuel's farewell
- 13:1-15:35 Saul's campaigns against the Philistines and Amalekites

16:1-31:13 Saul and David
- 16:1-23 Anointing of David
- 17:1-58 David and Goliath
- 18:1-19:10 David at court
- 19:11-27:18 David the outlaw
- 28:1-25 The witch of En Dor
- 29:1-30:31 David with the Philistines and his campaign against Amalekites
- 31:1-II Samuel 1:27 Battle at Gilboa; death of Saul and Jonathan; David's lament

II Samuel 2:1-8:18 David becomes king
- 2:1-4:12 David king in Hebron
- 5:1-25 David king of Israel; capture of Jerusalem
- 6:1-23 Ark brought to Jerusalem
- 7:1-29 Prophecy by Nathan
- 8:1-18 David's war: lists of officials

9:1-20:26 David's court
- 9:1-13 David and Mephibosheth
- 10:1-19 Wars against the Ammonites and Arameans
- 11:1-12:31 David and Bathsheba
- 13:1-18:33 Rebellion of Absalom
- 19:1-44 David's Return
- 20:1-26 Rebellion of Sheba

21:1-24:25 Appendix
- 21:1-22 Burial of Saul and his sons; David's heroes
- 22:1-51 Psalm attributed to David
- 23:1-39 Last words of David; feats of his heroes
- 24:1-25 Census

SANBALLAT

SANBALLAT ("Sin [the moon-god] gave life [to him]"). Governor of the province of Samaria in the Persian period. He was known as the "Horonite"(Neh 2:10, 19; 13:28), probably designating his provenance Beth Horon in southern Ephraim (Josh 10:10; II Chr 8:5) which would make him the descendant of an Israelite family. However, some scholars hold that the name Horonite refers to the city of Haran in Mesopotamia — renowned as a center for the cult of the moon-god Sin, from which the name Sanballat is derived. According to this assumption Sanballat was a descendant of the officials sent to Samaria by the Assyrian kings. He accepted a syncretistic belief in the God of Israel (II Kgs 17:33) and gave his sons Delaiah and Shelemiah Yahwistic names (known from an extra-biblical papyrus).

SANBALLAT
Neh 2:10, 19;
4:1, 7; 6:1-2,
5, 12, 14;
13:28

Sanballat was the main adversary of Nehemiah. Together with Tobiah the Ammonite and Geshem the Arabian, he employed threats to discourage the Jews from restoring the walls of Jerusalem, accusing them of rebellion against the Persian king (Neh 2:10, 19; 4:1-2; 6:6-7). In spite of these harassments Nehemiah succeeded in building the wall, whereupon they proclaimed war against him (Neh 4:7-8). When Nehemiah discovered their plan they gave up the war (Neh 4:15), but continually sought ways to hamper his endeavors (Neh 6:2). Sanballat even hired the Judahite prophet Shemaiah the son of Delaiah to threaten Nehemiah (Neh 6:10-13). During Nehemiah's absence from Jerusalem, Sanballat married off his daughter to one of the sons of the high priest Joiada, but Nehemiah returned and banished them from the city (Neh 13:28).

Extra-biblical sources indicate that three governors of Samaria during the Persian period bore the identical name, probably being members of the same family.

SANCTIFICATION See HOLINESS

SANCTUARY See CITY OF REFUGE; TEMPLE

SANHEDRIN The supreme Jewish political, religious and judicial body in Judea during the Roman period. The name Sanhedrin is a Greek word, used only in the Roman period (from the 1st century B.C.), but the existence of such a council goes back to Persian times, when it was called "Gerusia" (council of elders).

One of the rock-hewn tombs of the Sanhedria complex in Jerusalem where it is thought that the members of the Sanhedrin were buried. The entrance is decorated with carved floral motifs in the Hellenistic style.

Tradition links 70 members of the Sanhedrin with the 70 elders who, with Moses, were the leaders of the people (Num 11:16). The structure of the Sanhedrin varied according to the internal situation of the Jewish communities and the external political conditions, but it functioned in the Second Temple period as the supreme Jewish judicial body.

The many disputes between the Pharisees, the teachers of Jewish learning to the masses, and the Sadducees, the aristocratic priestly leaders of the Temple worship, strongly influenced the composition and structure of the Sanhedrin. In many cases the Sanhedrin itself was the focus of clashes between the two groups. This is reflected in the NT, for example, in the Marcan account of the trial of Jesus (Mark 14:43) where it is the priests or high priests who are trying to seize Jesus while the Pharisees are not mentioned. In earlier times, the priestly element was dominant in the Sanhedrin, but the Torah-sages (the Pharisees) eventually got the upper hand. This, however, did not exclude the Sadducees from sometimes obtaining a majority, especially in the last period of the Temple's existence.

The Sanhedrin was situated in the Chamber of Hewn Stone in the Jerusalem Temple, meeting daily, only between the hours of the two daily sacrifices, and never at night, on Sabbaths or festivals or on their eves. In NT times it was composed of three elements — the priests, the scribes (some of whom were Pharisees) and representatives of cities in Palestine.

The gospels describe three trials before the Sanhedrin, all of them presided over by the high priest, but apparently in different locations. Jesus was tried on Passover night, or on the preceding night, in the palace of the high priest (Mark 14:53-65; John 18:13). His disciples, Peter and John were arrested in the evening, "at Jerusalem" (Acts 4:3-6). It is disputed whether the Sanhedrin itself tried Jesus or a certain group from within the Sanhedrin. The Sanhedrin could not execute capital sentences (John 18:31) which had to be referred to the Roman authorities. Peter, John and other apostles (Acts 4:5-21; 5:17-41), Stephen (Acts 6:12) and Paul (Acts 22:30; 23:15; 24:20) were later also brought before the Sanhedrin.

SANSANNAH A city or place in the south of the territory allotted to Judah when the land of Canaan was divided among the tribes; it was "towards the border of Edom" (Josh 14:1; 15:21) that is in the Negeb. The site has been identified with present-day Khirbet es Shamsaniat, some 10 miles (16km) northeast of Beersheba.

SAPH One of the giants fighting with the Philistines during the final days of the reign of King David; he was killed at Gob by Sibbechai the Hushathite, one of David's thirty "mighty men".

SAPPHIRA The wife of Ananias No.1, a Christian of Jerusalem. Her husband sold a property whose proceeds were to be distributed among the believers. But, with Sapphira's knowledge, he kept back a portion of the price. When Peter exposed the fraud, Ananias was struck dead. Three hours later, Sapphira appeared before Peter, likewise reaffirming that the whole amount received had been donated for distribution among the disciples, and she too fell down on the spot and died (Acts 5:1-10).

SARAH (SARAI) ("princess"). Abraham's wife and Isaac's mother: the first matriarch of the Hebrew people (Is 51:2). Her original name, Sarai, was changed by God's command, together with Abraham's name (from Abram, Gen 17:15), presumably a symbolic act which represented the change in the couple's fate after the formal covenant with God. Sarah was Abraham's sole and beloved wife. Her position was enhanced by her origin from Abraham's own family (Gen 11:29-31). Her beauty

SANSANNAH
Josh 15:31

SAPH
II Sam 21:18

SAPPHIRA
Acts 5:1

SARAH (SARAI)
Gen 11:29-31;
12:5, 11, 17;
16:1-3, 5-6, 8;
17:15, 17,
19, 21; 18:6,
9-15; 20:2, 14,
16, 18; 21:1-3,

(described in magnificent detail in an Aramaic text discovered among the Dead Sea Scrolls at Qumran) was legendary (Gen 12:11), giving rise to instances in which she was coveted by foreign rulers (Gen 12:10-20; chap. 20). While her status within her household was undisputed, her prolonged barrenness mentioned early on as a theme that governed her personal biography like that of other matriarchs (Gen 11:30) — endangered the continuity of the family and the fulfillment of the divine promise to Abraham's house.

Sarah accompanied Abraham on his trek to and across Canaan, and his subsequent journey to Egypt (chap. 12). Still childless she gave her slave-girl Hagar to her husband for the purpose of producing an heir, but when Hagar became pregnant, Sarah, unable to abide by her earlier decision, drove Hagar away. Hagar returned, however, and gave birth to Ishmael (Gen 16:15). When advanced age seemed to have dispelled all hope of Sarah bearing Abraham a son and heir, God's messengers informed Abraham of the imminent birth of a child. Sarah, eavesdropping, was incredulous and laughed — supplying a hidden etymology for her future son's name (from a Hebrew root that means "to laugh; have fun" Gen chap. 18). After a sojourn in Gerar, the couple returned to Canaan where Isaac was born. Sarah now took steps to remove Ishmael and his mother from the household and Abraham's inheritance; gaining her way on the occasion of Isaac's weaning (Gen chap. 21). Sarah lived to the age 127, died in Hebron, and was buried there in the Cave of Machpelah which Abraham had bought for that purpose (Gen 23:19).

The NT makes a number of references to Sarah. She is mentioned in Romans 4:19 in connection with Abraham's faith. Divine election is exemplified in Romans 9:9 by her giving birth to Isaac. Hebrews 11:11 cites her devout faith, while her submissiveness to Abraham is mentioned in I Peter 3:6.

SARAI See SARAH

SARAPH A man of Judah who "ruled in Moab".

SARDIS A town in the west of Asia Minor, 50 miles (80 km) east of Smyrna; one of the seven cities in Asia Minor to which a message is directed in the Revelation of John: "to Ephesus, to Smyrna, to Pergamos, to Thyatira, to Sardis, to Philadelphia and Laodicea" (Rev 1:11). Formerly a capital of the kingdom of Lydia, it became part of the Roman Empire from 129 B.C.

Mystery religions, like that of Cybile, flourished in Sardis. This is probably the meaning of Revelation 3:4 where John speaks of "a few names even in Sardis who have not defiled their garments; and they shall

6-7, 9, 12; 23:1-2, 19; 24:36, 67; 25:10, 12; 49:31. Is 51:2 Rom 4:19; 9:9 Heb 11:11. I Pet 3:6

SARAI Gen 11:29-31; 12:5, 11, 17; 16:1-3, 5-6, 8; 17:15

SARAPH I Chr 4:22

SARDIS Rev 1:11; 3:1, 4

(right)
Ruins of the temple of Artemis at Sardis.

Main prayer hall at the synagogue of Sardis.

On the left, the synagogue fore-court at Sardis, with a detail of its columns on the right.

walk with me in white: for they are worthy".

The Christian community in this town was small and weak and the majority of the population returned to their original religions. One of the earliest synagogues so far discovered outside Israel — dating from the 2nd century A.D. — has been excavated at Sardis.

SARDITES See SERED

SARGON Name of three Mesopotamian kings. Sargon is the Hebraized form of the Akkadian personal name šarru-kēn, which means "the king is legitimate". The semantic equivalent of Hebrew Melchizedek, this name is characteristically adopted by a usurper of the throne. The first of these was Sargon of Akkad (2334-2279 B.C.), Sargon the Great, the founder of the first Semitic empire, which is said to have extended from the island of Cyprus in the northwest to the island of Bahrain in the southeast. Like Moses, Sargon of Akkad was placed by his mother in a basket, which was set afloat on the river. Just as Moses was adopted by Pharaoh's daughter so Sargon of Akkad was adopted by Akki, the drawer of water. Almost nothing is known of Sargon I of Assyria (c. 1850 B.C.). King Sargon mentioned in the Bible is Sargon II, son of Tiglath-Pileser III, who ruled Assyria from 721 to 705 B.C. At the end of the reign of his predecessor Shalmaneser V, Sargon commanded the armies that conquered Samaria and exiled its inhabitants. The biblical account of this event contained in II Kings chapter 17 can be supplemented by Sargon's own record inscribed on the walls of his palace at Khorsabad, the site of the unfinished city Dur-Sharrukin near Nineveh which Sargon II began building in his own honor in 713 B.C. Sargon claims to have rebuilt Samaria more gloriously than before. It has been suggested that the reference in Isaiah 19:23-25 to a highway stretching from Assyria to Egypt via Israel may have been inspired by Sargon's opening Egypt to trade with Assyria in 716 B.C. Isaiah chapter 20 refers to Sargon's crushing the rebellion of the king of Ashdod in 711 B.C. In 709 B.C. Sargon ousted the Chaldean Merodach-Baladan from Babylon and made himself king of Babylon. In 705 B.C. he met his death on the field of battle in the course of a campaign in Asia Minor against the Cimmerians. His remains were not recovered. He was the only king in the entire history of Babylonia and Assyria to whom this happened, and his successor Sennacherib appointed a commission of enquiry to determine what sin Sargon committed that he was so humiliated. The Judean prophet Isaiah also refers to his humiliating

Head of Sargon II from Khorsabad. 8th century B.C.

Fragment of a stele of Sargon II found at Ashdod. It was erected after the city had been conquered by Sargon and relates his exploits. 8th century B.C.

death and declares in the name of the Lord that Sargon's sins were arrogance and brutality (see Is 14:20-21).

SARID A town in the northern part of the territory of Zebulun (Josh 19:10). It appears as Sereth in the list of Thutmosis III. The Septuagint has Sedoud instead of Sarid, and for this reason it is identified with Tell Sadud, in the northern part of the Jezreel Valley.

SARSECHIM One of the princes of Babylon who took part in the final assault on Jerusalem by the army of Nebuchadnezzar. Some scholars believe Sarsechim is not a proper name but the title of an official.

SATAN The noun Satan derives from the Hebrew word meaning "adversary". In three post-exilic books of the Bible, Satan appears as the accuser of man before God and as the inciter of man to evil. He remains, however, a member of the divine entourage and, as such, is subordinate to the will of God and is not an independent force of evil. This is clearly illustrated in the prologue to the Book of Job (chaps. 1-2) where Satan appears among the "sons of God" (Job 1:6), and insists that it is only because God has protected and shielded Job from all harm that Job has shown himself virtuous and God-fearing. God then agrees to put Job in Satan's power to test whether under adversity he would remain loyal and steadfast to God.

In a passage in Zechariah (3:1-2) Satan is also pictured as accusing an individual, this time the high priest Jeshua (Joshua) son of Jozadak. The third reference to Satan in the OT occurs in I Chronicles 21:1. The passage is to be compared with II Samuel 24:1 where God incites David to take a census of the people, a forbidden act entailing dire consequences. The Chronicler, however, casts Satan, not God, in the role of inciter. The change is due to the later view that it is Satan, not God, who provokes man to do evil.

Satan is frequently referred to in the NT both by his own name and by a variety of other names. As the "Devil", he subjects Jesus to a number of temptations (Matt 4:1-11). It is Satan who is ultimately responsible for Judas Iscariot's betrayal of Jesus and Simon Peter's denial of knowing Jesus (Luke 22:3, 31). He appears as the "Wicked One" (Matt 13:19; cf Mark 4:15) in Jesus' parable of "The Sower" who robs men of "the word that has been sown in their hearts" (Mark 4:15). As the "Father of Lies", he is responsible for the Jews' lack of belief in Jesus' divine mission (John 8:44). Physical afflictions and pain are caused by Satan (Luke 13:16) and as the "Lord of Death", he brought death into the world (Heb 2:14). Under the title of "The Great Dragon", he is hurled down from heaven to earth (Rev 12:9). In one passage, Satan is termed "the Ruler of Demons" (Matt 9:34). He is subject to God's will and eventually will be subdued. He will be "cast into the lake of fire and brimstone" (Rev 20:10).

SAUL

1. The first king of Israel, son of Kish of the tribe of Benjamin. Handsome and tall (I Sam 9:2), he proved a charismatic leader (I Sam 11:7). The account of his election as king is presented in parallel narratives, which differ in their viewpoints, being either favorable or hostile to the monarchy. The background to his election was the military successes of the Philistines and the growth of unrest among the tribes of Benjamin and Ephraim. The pro-monarchic account of his election narrates how Samuel found Saul searching for his father's lost asses and anointed him privately in Ramah (I Sam 9:1-10:16). Interwoven with this narrative, and possibly a separate account, is the story of his victory over the Ammonites who had attacked the city of Jabesh Gilead (I Sam chap. 11). An anti-monarchic version of his selection (I Sam chap. 8; 10:17-27; chap. 12) tells of Samuel's opposition

SARID
Josh 19:10,

SARSECHIM
Jer 39:3

SATAN
I Chr 21:1.
Job 1:6-9, 1
2:1-4, 6-7.
Zech 3:1-2.
Matt 4:10;
12:26; 16:23
Mark 1:13;
3:23, 26; 4:1
Luke 4:8;
10:18; 11:18
13:16; 22:3,
31. John 13:2
Acts 5:3; 26:
Rom 16:20.
I Cor 5:5; 7:
II Cor 2:11;
11:14; 12:7.
I Thes 2:18.
II Thes 2:9.
I Tim 1:20;
5:15. Rev 2:9
13, 24; 3:9;
12:9; 20:2, 7

SAUL 1
I Sam 9:2-3, 5
7-8, 10, 15,
17-19, 21-22,
24-27; 10:11-
12, 14-16, 21,
26; 11:4-7, 11
13, 15; 13:1-4,
7, 9-11, 13,
15-16, 22;
14:1-2, 16-21,
24, 33-38, 40-
47, 49-52;
15:1, 4-7, 9,
11-13, 15-16,

to the demand of the people for a king. However, he eventually relented and presided over Saul's formal election at Mizpah. Samuel's main argument against appointing a king (I Sam 8:6-8) was based on his interpretation of the people's demand as a rejection of the kingship of God. His solemn warning of the consequences of the behavior of the king (I Sam 8:11-18), became a famous denunciation of the institution of the monarchy.

Due to the varying accounts, it is difficult to reconstruct the sequence of events during Saul's reign. It seems that after a brief period of organization, Saul directed his attention towards the Philistines, who had overrun the southern tribes of Israel, destroyed Shiloh, and were so thoroughly the masters of Judah and the central hill country that they maintained an outpost in Benjamin (I Sam 13:3). Saul's son, Jonathan, slew the Philistine governor at Geba (I Sam chap. 13), and thus the signal was given for the uprising. The Philistines took up a position opposite Gibeah in the gorge of Michmash, and Jonathan, without the knowledge of his father scaled the cliff and slew 20 men of the Philistine outpost. The Philistine armies were routed and driven back to Philistia (I Sam chaps. 13-14). Thus their control of the mountain area was broken, although they continued to threaten Israel throughout Saul's reign.

The expulsion of the Philistines marked the beginning of Saul's kingship. In his attempts to assert his authority over the Israelite population of the central mountain area and unite the tribes under his rule, he uprooted the foreign enclaves in his tribe's territory. In this context, he killed an unknown number of Gibeonites in violation of the treaty made in Joshua's day (Josh chap. 9). After Saul's death, to rectify this, the Gibeonites demanded the lives of seven of Saul's sons; David handed over five of Saul's grandsons and two sons who were hanged at Gibeon (II Sam 21:1-9). The Ammonites, Moabites, Edomites and Arameans were driven off from the country east of the Jordan (I Sam 14:47). In order to deliver Judah from the raids of the Amalekites, Saul undertook an expedition against them; his army captured Agag, their king, and Samuel personally slew him, rebuking Saul for initially sparing his life (I Sam chap. 15). The breach between Saul and Samuel, a result of Saul's apparent usurpation of authority during the war against Amalek, was to cast a gloom on the remainder of the monarch's reign. An evil spirit seemed to possess the king; he was given to fits of terror and suspicious brooding; a profound melancholy crept over him, and only the sound of music gave him temporary relief. Perhaps it is in this context that David, a skilled musician, joined Saul's entourage; the narrative contrasts David's heroic personality, charm and popularity with the increasing nervous depression of Saul (I Sam 16:14-23).

Apparently after David's victory over Goliath (I Sam chap. 17), Saul grew increasingly jealous of David's popularity, even casting a spear at him (I Sam 18:10-11; 19:9-10). Later, in a fit of anger, Saul threw his spear at his own son Jonathan, who had become David's close friend and admirer (I Sam 20:33). David was forced to flee from Saul's wrath to the border regions of Judah and later as far as Gath in Philistia. Saul's rage against David extended beyond pursuing him and his followers, to attacking the priesthood which he felt had been siding with David (I Sam 22:17-19). This widened the gulf which had come to separate him from many of his people.

The end of his reign came when he engaged in one last forlorn struggle with his earliest enemy. The Philistines had invaded Israelite territory and gathered forces at Shunem; Saul established his headquarters on the slope of Mount Gilboa. Sad forebodings of his fate troubling him, he traveled to En Dor to consult a witch about the outcome of the battle (I Sam 28:7-8), since he could no longer use the official means of divination (I Sam 28:6). The result of the séance confirmed his worst fears and filled his soul with despair (I Sam 28:20ff). The Israelite army had no chariots and could not withstand the assault of the heavy Philistine weaponry. On Mount Gilboa, Saul and his three sons, including Jonathan, were killed. The biblical narrative describes how Saul, being seriously wounded, called upon his armor-bearer to "thrust me through", and when the young man refused, the king fell upon his sword and died (I Sam 31:4). (In a contrasting account, in II Samuel 1:6-10, a young Amalekite claimed that he had slain Saul). The Philistines next day found their enemy dead, and hung his decapitated body on the walls of their city Beth Shan (I Sam 31:8-10). The inhabitants of Jabesh, remembering how Saul had responded to their cry for help, removed his body during the night, and gave it an honorable burial in their own city, the site of his first victory. According to I Samuel 31:12 they burned the bodies of Saul and Jonathan to spare them from further Philistine indignities (but see I Chr 10:12).

The outcome of the battle meant a state of vassalage for Israel; the Philistines regained control of much of the country and kept it until well into David's reign. Saul left behind him a tribal alliance weakened and in disarray, and it was David who was to establish the national unity of the Israelite tribes.

2. Saul of Rehoboth-by-the River was the sixth king of Edom. His reign succeeded that of Samlah of Masrekah and was followed by that of Baal-Hanan the son of Achbor "before any king reigned over the Children of Israel" (I Chr 1:43).

3. Saul of Tarsus "who also is called Paul" (Acts 13:9). See PAUL.

SCAPEGOAT See AZAZEL

SCEVA A Jewish high priest in Ephesus at the time of Paul's visit there. He had seven sons who exorcized evil spirits in the name of Jesus.

SCORPION See ANIMALS

SCYTHIANS The inhabitants of a country lying between the Carpathians and the River Don. Due to its geographic position the country was frequently invaded by nomadic peoples. In the 7th century B.C. it was occupied by a people of unknown origin, speaking an Indo-

SAUL 2
Gen 36:37-38
I Chr 1:48-49

SAUL 3
**Acts 7:58; 8:1,
3; 9:1, 4, 8,
11, 17, 19, 22,
24, 26; 11:25,
30; 12:25;
13:1-2, 7, 9;
22:7, 13; 26:14**

SCAPEGOAT
**Lev 16:8, 10,
26**

SCEVA
Acts 19:14

SCYTHIANS
Col 3:11

Scythian horseman shown on a felt cloth from the frozen burial chambers in the Altai Mountains. 300 B.C. (Hermitage, Leningrad)

European language. In the second half of the 6th century B.C. these Scythians invaded Syria and Palestine and destroyed Ashkelon and Ashdod. The Scythians remained active until Roman times when the last traces of them were obliterated. In Palestine they were commemorated in the name of Scythopolis given to the city of Beth Shan (Beisan).

In Colossians 3:11 the Scythians are mentioned together with the barbarians.

SEA (THE) When the Bible mentions "the Sea" (II Chr 20:2), it is referrring to the Mediterranean, which laps the shores of three continents: Asia, Africa and Europe. It is referred to in various ways in the Bible, firstly as the "Western Sea" (Deut 11:24; 34:2); the "Great Sea" (Josh 23:4). Off Joppa it is called the "sea at Joppa" (Ezra 3:7), while the part bordering the land of the Philistines, from Joppa to the border of Egypt, is referred to as the "Sea of the Philistines" (Ex 23:31).

SEAGULL See ANIMALS

SEA, MOLTEN (BRONZE) A large vessel constructed of bronze which was cast by Hiram, king of Tyre and placed in Solomon's Temple; it is described in I Kings 7:23-26 and II Chronicles 4:2-5. I Chronicles 18:8 records that it was made from the bronze which David had taken as booty. It had a diameter of 10 cubits and stood 5 cubits; its circumference was 30 cubits. According to the thickness of a "handbreath" specified in the text (I Kgs 7:26), it may have weighed 33 tons or more. The brim of the molten sea was "like a lily blossom". Its basin stood upon 12 bronze oxen which faced in four directions. During the reign of King Ahaz it was removed from the bronze oxen and placed "on a pavement of stones" (II Kgs 16:17). Upon the conquest of Jerusalem in 586 B.C., the Babylonians destroyed the molten sea and carried off its bronze pieces to Babylon (II Kgs 25:13). The function of this vessel which is referred to in Hebrew simply as "sea" was the same as the laver of the tabernacle (Ex 30:17-21): to provide a place for the ritual washing of the priests prior to service (II Chr 4:6).

SEALS In ancient times seals were used to denote personal ownership of certain objects, and sealing a document with a personal or public seal confirmed the authenticity of the contents. The device was probably first used in Mesopotamia, where thousands of seals and seal impressions were found. The seal was also in common use in the Holy Land. A document written on a clay tablet would be placed in a clay envelope and sealed, while a document written on papyrus or parchment would be rolled and tied with string; a ball of soft clay would then be placed on the knot and sealed. Seals brought to Palestine from other countries were either made of steatite or of faience. The ancient Hebrew seals were normally made of semi-precious hard stones, carnelian (brought from Egypt or Arabia), rock-crystal, hematite, amethyst, lapis lazuli and local hard limestone.

From the 18th century B.C. and especially from the arrival of the Hyksos, the number of seals increases. These are of the scarab type, many of which originate in Egypt. They are elliptical in shape, and decorated on the back with a beetle (scarab) — an insect venerated by the Egyptians.

From the Iron Age, there are many seals inscribed with the owner's name, written in Hebrew, Phoenician or Aramaic. They date mainly to the 8th-6th centuries B.C. The Hebrew seals are also scaraboidal in shape, flat at the bottom and convex on top. Some, however, are conical. These are chiefly of the 7th-6th centuries, and are typical mainly of the Kingdom of Judah.

In the various sites where Iron Age strata have been excavated, numerous seals, and still more seal impressions, have been found. The more famous ones are of persons known from the Bible, such as the "servant of the king" (Asaiah, a servant of Josiah) in II Kings 22:12, and Gedaliah (II Kgs 25:22).

Large numbers of seal impressions have been found on jar-handles on many sites in Judea. These seals bear the inscription *lamelek* — "of the king" on the upper part of the seal. At the bottom comes one of four names: Hebron, Ziph, Socoh or *mmst*. Between the lines appears a two- or four-winged symbol of the sun.

Carnelian Phoenician seal inscribed "[Belonging] to Hanan". In the center is a figure with hands raised in prayer. 8th-7th centuries B.C. (Israel Dept. of Antiquities and Museums)

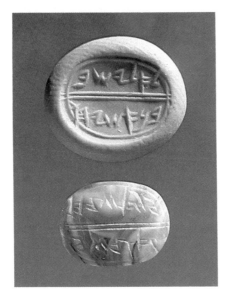 

At the beginning of the Persian period the seals resemble the ancient Hebrew ones in shape and script, but gradually the square Aramaic script replaces the older ones. The decoration consists of representations of priests. In some places in Judea, seals carrying the name *Yahud* were found. This was the official name of the province of Judea in the Persian period. Other seals have *ha'ir*, meaning "the City" — Jerusalem, and still others have the name of Jerusalem inscribed on them in full. It is believed that the jars thus stamped were used for the collection of taxes pertaining to the Temple.

From the Roman period there are two types of seals in Palestine, one found on pottery vessels, the other on documents. The seals of the first group are found on handles of jars, bases of bowls, lamps, etc. In the case of the jars the handles are stamped with official seals, bearing the names of Roman consuls. Seal impressions of the second type, those stamped on documents, are less common.

The significance of the seal and its usage is found on several occasions in the OT. It first appears in Genesis chapter 38 when Judah leaves his seal with Tamar as a pledge. The king's ring, which was the same as his seal, symbolized royal power (Gen 41:42; Est 3:10, 12; 8:2, 8, 10). Books, letters, prophecies and legal deeds of purchase were sealed (I Kgs 21:8; Job 38:14; Is 8:16; 29:11; Jer 32:10-11, 14, 44; Dan 9:24; 12:4, 9). The notables of Jerusalem set their seals to a written deed to keep the laws of the Torah (Neh 9:38; 10:1). A royal seal closed the lion's den into which Daniel was cast (Dan 6:17).

The seal also served in figures of speech, denoting that which was precious and dear (Jer 22:24; Hag 2:23); cf especially the simile in the Song of Solomon 8:6: "Set me as a seal upon your heart, as a seal upon your arm", which refers symbolically to the seals which were actually worn around the neck and on the hand.

Decorated Ammonite seal mounted on a ring. 8th-7th centuries B.C. (Archaeological Museum, Amman)

*(top right and center)
Hebrew seals inscribed "[Belonging] to Eliashib [son of Eshayahu]". Late 7th century B.C. (Israel Museum)*

In the NT nouns and verbs for seal and sealing are used both literally and figuratively. Literally a seal is set upon the stone in front of the tomb where Jesus is laid (Matt 27:66). In John, Jesus sets his seal on revelation from God (3:33) and God sets his seal on the Son of man (John 6:27). Abraham receives circumcision as a seal (Rom 4:11), Paul receives the seal of apostleship (I Cor 9:2), and God has sealed Christians with the Holy Spirit (II Cor 1:22; Eph 1:13; 4:30), probably in baptism. God's seal is a sign of truth in II Timothy 2:19. The most frequent reference to seals in the NT is to be found in the vision of the book sealed with seven seals and its opening by the Lamb of God in the Book of Revelation (Rev 5:1-2, 5, 9; 6:1, 3, 5, 7, 9, 12; 7:2-8). There the martyrs from the twelve tribes receive the seal on their forehead. In Revelation 20:3 Satan is sealed in a pit during the millennium.

Ancient Hebrew seals from the collections of the Israel Museum.

SEAT OF MOSES Pharisees and scribes were said by Jesus to sit in Moses' seat. Some scholars have suggested that the reference is to a place of honor in the synagogue (as have been discovered in excavations); others say it was the stand for the scroll of the Law.

SEBA Son of Cush. Seba is mentioned together with Sheba as a people that will bring gifts to the king (Ps 72:10) and together with Ethiopia in Isaiah 43:3. Some scholars suggest that it is identical with Sheba No.7, a land in southwest Arabia inhabited by the Sabeans. Others believe that it is located in Africa, close to Ethiopia. Various regions of Africa have been proposed.

SECACAH One of the cities allotted to Judah when the land of Canaan was divided among the tribes (Josh 14:1; 15:61). It was in the wilderness of Judah by the Dead Sea; its location is unknown.

SECHU While searching for Samuel and David, King Saul came to "the great well that is at Sechu". Nothing further is known about it.

SECUNDUS ("the second one"). One of the Thessalonians who accompanied Paul on his last journey to Jerusalem.

SEGUB

1. One of the two sons of Hiel of Bethel, who rebuilt Jericho during the reign of King Ahab, in defiance of the curse laid on the city by Joshua. Both Segub and his eldest brother, Abiram, died during the construction work and it has been suggested that they were offered up by their father as foundation sacrifices.

Seat carved out of a single basalt stone in the form of an armchair found at Chorazin. It may have been "Moses'seat" referred to in Matthew 23:2.

2. A son of Hezron (the grandson of Judah) by his wife the daughter of Machir. Segub begot Jair "who had 23 cities in the land of Gilead".

SEIR

1. The Horite. Eponymous ancestor of the inhabitants of Seir No.2.

2. A mountainous region southeast of the Dead Sea. In the El Amarna Letters, the prince of Jerusalem informs the king of Egypt that the war against the king ranges in the mountains of Seir. A papyrus of the time of Rameses III (12th century B.C.) refers to the destruction of Seir, possibly caused by nomadic tribes who sojourned there. It was attacked by Ashurbanipal in his ninth campaign against the Arabs. Seir was formerly inhabited by Horites (Gen 14:6). Later Esau, identified with Edom, lived there (Gen 36:8ff) and God gave the mountain to Esau (Josh 24:4). The Children of Israel "skirted Mount Seir for many days" on their way from Egypt to the land of Canaan (Deut 2:1, 5). The Lord revealed himself to Israel from Mount Seir (Deut 2:1). Ezekiel's oracle against Mount Seir (chap. 35) refers to the plundering of Judah by Edomites after the fall of Jerusalem in 586 B.C.

3. Name of a mountain on the borders of the territory of Judah (Josh 15:10), lying between Horeb and Kadesh Barnea (Deut 1:2). Its present location is not known. Five hundred Simeonites defeated the Amalekites at Mount Seir and settled there (I Chr 4:42-43).

Sela in the mountains of Edom.

SEIRAH (SEIRATH) ("wooded"?). A place to which Ehud managed to escape after having killed Eglon king of Moab. Its location is uncertain, beyond the fact that it was "in the mountains of Ephraim" (Judg 3:26-27).

SEIRAH
Judg 3:26

SELA ("rock"). A town in northern Edom. When Amaziah, king of Judah, conquered and slew 10,000 Edomites he changed its name to Joktheel (II Kgs 14:7; II Chr 25:12ff). The name Sela has been preserved in modern es-Sela, where a small Edomite-Nabatean fortress has been discovered 5 miles (8 km) southwest of Tafileh. The identification of Sela with Petra, ancient Rekem, has no foundation in fact.

SELA
Judg 1:36.
II Kgs 14:7.
Is 16:1; 42:11

SELED A man of the tribe of Judah, firstborn son of Nadab in the genealogy of the family of Jerahmeel; he died childless.

SELED
I Chr 2:30

The harbor wall of Seleucia, the port of Antioch.

SELEUCIA The port city of classical Antioch, located at the mouth of the Orontes River; now Suediah, in Turkey. Enjoying the dual advantages of a virtually impregnable acropolis and a superior natural harbor, the site was occupied continuously from at least 2000 B.C. In the 8th century B.C. it developed as a prosperous emporium, colonized largely by Greeks. In 301 B.C. it passed to Seleucus I Nicator, a general of Alexander the Great and the eponymous founder of the Seleucid dynasty. Seleucus refounded the site, its name reflecting his intention of establishing it as the capital of his newly enlarged empire. Upon his death in 281/0 B.C., however, this distinction was transferred to Antioch, some 16 miles (26 km) inland, and Seleucia reverted to the position of mercantile harbor and port-of-entry for the capital.

As such it served as the port from which Barnabas and Paul set out on the first missionary journey and, though not mentioned specifically, it was certainly via Seleucia that they returned to Antioch (Acts 14:26) and set out a second time (Acts 15:39-41). The city continued to serve the larger community of Antioch, until the latter's decline in the 6th century.

SEMACHIAH Levite from the family of Obed-Edom, perhaps son of Shemaiah; he was gatekeeper at the Temple in the time of King David.

SEMEI ("famous"). Son of Joseph and father of Mattathiah in the genealogy of Jesus according to Luke.

SENAAH A family which returned from Exile in Babylon with Zerubbabel; they numbered 3,630 persons according to Ezra and 3,930 according to Nehemiah. Members of the family aided the latter in the repair of the wall of Jerusalem.

SENEH The name of a cliff; "Between the passages, by which Jonathan sought to go over unto the Philistines' garrison, there was a sharp rock on one side and a sharp rock on the other side. And the name of one was Bozez, and the name of the other Seneh" (I Sam 14:4). This pass is located in the narrow Wadi Suweinit, in the vicinity of Michmash, where it was traversed by a strategically important road to Jerusalem.

SENIR One of the many names of Mount Hermon; this one was used by the Amorites.

SENNACHERIB King of Assyria, 705-681 B.C., Sennacherib is the Hebraized form of the Akkadian personal name *Sîn-ahhē-eriba,* which means "The moon-god Sin replaced for me the brothers", suggesting that Sennacherib was born after two or more older siblings had died. He became king upon the death of his father Sargon. His confrontation with Hezekiah, king of Judah is described in II Kings chapters 18-19; II Chronicles chapter 32; Isaiah chapters 36-37 and in his own account of the third campaign. The references to Sennacherib's conquest of Lachish and his receiving tribute there are supplemented by pictorial illustrations on reliefs recovered from Sennacherib's palace at Nineveh. Incited by the Egyptian ruler Shabaka and the Chaldean ruler of Babylon, Merodach-Baladan (see II Kgs chap. 20), Judah, together with the Phoenician and Philistine states, withheld tribute from Assyria. Having driven Merodach-Baladan from Babylon (702 B.C.), Sennacherib marched against the rebellious states in Lebanon and Palestine. The last of the rebel rulers to hold out against the Assyrians was Hezekiah. From Lachish, Sennacherib sent three high officials, the Tartan, the Rabsaris and the Rabshakeh — with a large army to persuade the Judeans to capitulate. However, according to all biblical versions, a plague broke out in Sennacherib's camp; he promptly fled for his life to Nineveh where he was murdered by his own sons while at prayer. According to II Kings chapter 19 and Isaiah chapter 37 this happened in the temple of the god Nisroch, and the names of the sons

(bottom of page)
The Prism of King Sennacherib on which is inscribed a record of his principal campaigns and victories. 689 B.C.

Mount Hermon also known as Senir in the Bible.

Part of a relief showing Senna-cherib seated on his throne. (British Museum)

were Adrammelech and Sarezer. Sennacherib's prism inscription, on the other hand, reports that the destruction of Jerusalem was averted, not by an act of God, but by Hezekiah's covenant to pay a heavy tribute.

SENUAH Father of Judah (No.6) who was one of the administrators of the tribe of Benjamin in the last days of Nehemiah.

SENUAH
Neh 11:9

SEORIM ("barley"). A Levite, head of the fourth division of priests in the Temple at the time of King David.

SEORIM
I Chr 24:8

SEPHAR The dwelling place of the sons of Joktan was "from Mesha as you go towards Sephar, the mountain of the east" (Gen 10:30). The exact location of Sephar is unknown and some scholars suggest that it should be translated as "border".

SEPHAR
Gen 10:30

SEPHARAD A place name occuring only once in the Bible, in Obadiah verse 20: "The captives of Jerusalem, who are in Sepharad, shall possess the cities of the South".

SEPHARAD
Obad v. 20

Sepharad was usually identified with Saparda, a country mentioned in the Assyrian annals of Sargon II as a district southwest of Media. However, the discovery of an Aramaic-Lydian inscription at Sardis in Asia Minor, showed that Sepharad was the Aramaic name for Sardis, which name applied first to the Lydian kingdom in Asia Minor, and later to the Persian satrapy and its capital.

This short reference in Obadiah is thus of great historical importance, because it attests the early settlement of Jews in this important commercial center. The mistaken identification of Sepharad with Hispania, Spain, originates in the Aramaic translation of the Bible.

SEPHARVAIM, SEPHARVITES City conquered by the Assyrians. Men deported from it were settled by the king of Assyria in Samaria, to take the place of the exiled Israelites (II Kgs 17:24, etc.). It should probably be identified with Sippar southwest of Baghdad.

SEPHARVAIM,
SEPHARVITES
II Kgs 17:24,
31; 18:34;
19:13. Is
36:19; 37:13

SEPTUAGINT See BIBLE TRANSLATIONS

SERAH A daughter of Asher, who accompanied Jacob and his family to Egypt.

SERAIAH

1. A scribe at the court of King David. He is called Sheva in II Samuel 20:25; Shisha in I Kings 4:3, and Shavsha in I Chronicles 18:16.

2. High priest in Jerusalem during the reign of Zedekiah, last king of Judah. When the city fell to the armies of Nebuchadnezzar, Seraiah was captured by Nebuzaradan, the captain of the guard, taken to Riblah in the land of Hamath and put to death by the king of Babylon (II Kgs 25:18, 20-21).

3. A captain of the armies of Judah, Seraiah son of Tanhumeth the Netophathite was among the officers who joined Gedaliah at Mizpah after the fall of Jerusalem to Nebuchadnezzar. After Gedaliah's assassination, Seraiah and his men fled to Egypt.

4. Second son of Kenaz and father of Joab from the family of Judah.

5. A prince of the tribe of Simeon, son of Asiel, father of Joshibiah and grandfather of Jehu.

6. One of the leaders who returned from the Babylonian Exile with Zerubbabel. He is called Azariah in Nehemiah 7:7.

7. Father of Ezra, the scribe.

8. One of the leaders of the people who sealed the covenant at the time of Nehemiah.

9. Son of Hilkiah; he was one of the "chief priests" of the Temple who returned from the Exile in Babylon with Zerubbabel. He is called Azariah in I Chronicles 9:11.

10. A priestly family at the time of Joiakim the high priest; headed by Meraiah, probably the same as No.9.

11. Son of Azriel, he was one of the officers sent by King Jehoiakim to arrest Baruch the scribe and Jeremiah the prophet.

12. Son of Neriah and grandson of Mahseiah, to whom Jeremiah entrusted his oracle foreseeing the doom of Babylon. Seraiah was instructed to read this oracle in Babylon and then sink it in the Euphrates, thereby symbolizing the end of Babylon.

SERAPHIM The word seraphim in the English and Latin Bible is a transliteration from the Hebrew, and appears to be the plural of the Hebrew noun *saraph*. The plural form *seraphim* occurs in the Bible only in Isaiah 6:2, 6 where it designates the winged creatures positioned above the throne of the Lord. According to Isaiah, each of the seraphim has six wings. One pair of wings is for covering the seraph's face so that he will not behold the Lord (the underlying assumption is that whoever does see the Lord will die; Ex 33:20); a second pair of wings is for covering the seraph's genitals for modesty's sake; the third pair of wings is for flying (Is 6:2). In Isaiah's description of his vision of the Lord enthroned in the Temple, the seraphim declaim to each other, "Holy, holy, holy is the Lord of hosts; the whole earth is full of his Glory" (Is 6:3), their voices making the doorposts of the Temple shake (Is 6:4). To Isaiah's exclamation, "I am a man of unclean lips, and I dwell in the midst of a people of unclean lips" (Is 6:5) one of the seraphim reacts by scorching the prophet's lips with a hot coal from the altar and proclaiming: "Your iniquity is taken away, and your sin purged." (Is 6:6-7).

Because the singular noun *saraph* designates the brazen serpent in Numbers 21:8 and because Isaiah 14:29 and 30:6 both designate a flying serpent as "flying saraph" it is generally surmised that the seraphim of Isaiah chapter 6 were winged serpents. Such mythological creatures are amply attested in the artistic legacy of the ancient Near East and in

Two winged genii on an ivory plaque from Arslan Tash, northern Syria. 8th century B.C. (Musée du Louvre, Paris)

Greek and Roman art. It is generally accepted that the noun *saraph* ("serpent") derives from the Hebrew verb *saraph* meaning "to burn", the derivation arising from the burning sensation caused by snake bites.

SERED, SARDITES Zebulun's firstborn son Sered was the founder of the family of the Sardites.

SERED, SARDITES
Gen 46:14.
Num 26:26

SERGIUS PAULUS The Roman proconsul in Cyprus, described as "an intelligent man", who "sought to hear the word of God" (Acts 13:7). He was converted to Christianity by Paul. An inscription found in Cyprus speaking of Sergius Paulus, the Roman proconsul, may refer to the same person.

SERGIUS
PAULUS
Acts 13:7

SERMON ON THE MOUNT, THE The major sermon of Jesus in Matthew chapters 5-7 containing the gospel ethic, beginning with a series of beatitudes (q.v.) and also containing the Lord's Prayer (q.v.). A shorter form of the same sermon is found in Luke 6:20-49. Scholars generally think that the version in Luke contains the more authentic form, unglossed by later interpretation, and centered on love. The sermon in Matthew has as its thematic words the Kingdom of God and justice or the higher righteousness (Matt 5:20; 6:33) and can be divided into three main sections. The introduction in Matthew 5:1-16 consists of the beatitudes, which were originally a messianic manifesto of good news and were gradually lengthened into a list of Christian virtues or desirable qualities, and a missionary thrust in Matthew 5:13-16. The conclusion in Matthew 7:13-29 contains a teaching on the two ways of life and death illustrated by the parable of the house built on sand and rock; this covenant pattern extends the Deuteronomic theology of history (Deut 28-30) into the NT.

The long central section (Matt 5:17-7:12) contains a new, centered commentary on the ethical commandments of the OT, the Decalogue and related material. It requires further subdivision. Matthew 5:17-20 contain the basic program, principles and theme; the law is not destroyed but fulfilled. Matthew 5:21-48 contain what are called the six antitheses, or hypertheses, a kind of commentary on and radicalization of the second table of the Ten Commandments, with the commandment to love one's neighbor being extended to the teaching to love one's enemies. Matthew 6:1-18 contains a reformation of three main acts of personal piety: alms, prayer and fasting. These are man's special duties toward God, or a commentary on the commandment to love God with heart, soul and strength, a way also of treating the first three commandments of the Decalogue. Inserted into them is a presentation of the Lord's Prayer, a revised form of the Jewish *Kaddish* prayer. Matthew 6:19-7:12 contains further instructions on how to love God with our whole being and possessions. The arrangement is looser in this section, which is grouped around the necessities of life: food, drink and clothing, culminating in the Golden Rule of Matthew 7:12.

The Sermon is fairly systematic, covering the main areas of ethical and religious life, so far as these were understood in the framework of the OT and early Judaism. It gives a new and important orientation to ethical and religious life but is not an exhaustive or complete code. It is a series of pointers illustrated by "focal instances" which suggest: now use your common sense to go and do likewise in your own circumstances. It would be a mistake to dismiss the Sermon on the Mount as a purely random, arbitrary collection of isolated sayings with no guiding principle or effort to touch the main bases of ethical life.

SERPENT See ANIMALS

SERPENT, COPPER (BRONZE) When the Israelites were stricken by serpents as a punishment during their wanderings in the desert (Num 21:6-7), God commanded Moses to set up a copper serpent (RKJV: "bronze") on a standard: the symbol had a therapeutic effect and anyone bitten by the venomous serpents could be healed by merely looking at it (Num 21:8-9). Later, when the serpent came to be worshiped by the people, King Hezekiah of Judah, as part of his multiple religious reforms, smashed it to pieces (II Kgs 18:4). The copper serpent is referred to in the latter passage as NEHUSHTAN, a word with the double meaning of "snake" and "copper".

Jesus drew a parallel between his own experience and the story of the copper serpent (John 3:14). Serpents which symbolize life and death are familiar from the literature and the excavations of the ancient Near East.

SERUG Son of Reu and father of Nahor in the genealogy of Shem. He lived 230 years and had many sons and daughters. The name is identified with the city Sarugi situated in Mesopotamia.

SERVANT OF THE LORD The designation of a personality, sometimes referred to as the Suffering Servant, mentioned explicitly or implicitly in the four so-called Servant songs found in Isaiah 42:1-4; 49:1-6; 50:4-9; 52:13-53:12. The identity of the "servant" has been the subject of debate throughout the centuries. There are two main categories of interpretation: individual and collective. Many candidates have been proposed for the individual interpretation, from Moses, by way of King Cyrus of Persia to the anonymous prophet Second Isaiah himself in whose book the oracles are found. The collective interpretations range from all of Israel, ideal Israel, the pious remnant of Israel, priests or prophets. Each proposal has its own set of difficulties, and it is still questionable whether all four prophecies relate to one and the same party or group. Many scholars now agree that the first two refer to the collective body of Israel. However, the third song and especially the fourth, with their intensive individualization and descriptive tones of the suffering of the Servant, are replete with unresolved enigmas, such as the actual mission of the Servant, and whether or not the Servant described in Isaiah chapter 53, died.

Jesus thought of himself and his sufferings as being related to the description of the Servant in Isaiah. Jesus is referred to as the Servant in Acts 3:13, 26; 4:27, 30. The Servant songs are cited in Matthew 8:17; 12:18-21; Luke 2:32; 22:37 (referring to the Passion); Romans 4:25; 15:21, and are probably implied elsewhere, especially with reference to the Passion.

SETH Third son of Adam and Eve, born after the murder of Abel by his brother Cain; he was the father of Enosh and lived 912 years. His name was given him by Eve who said, "For God has apointed (Hebrew *Seth*) another seed for me instead of Abel" (Gen 4:25).

SETH
Gen 4:25-26; 5:3-4, 6-8. I Chr 1:1. Luk 3:38

SETHUR ("concealed in the shadow [of the Lord]"). Son of Michael, of the tribe of Asher, Sethur was one of those sent by Moses from the wilderness of Paran to spy out the land of Canaan.

SETHUR
Num 13:13

SHAALBIM, SHAALABBIN A city in the territory of Dan (Josh 19:42); also occupied by the Amorites after the conquest (Judg 1:35). It was in the second district of Solomon (I Kgs 4:9) and within the territory of Emmaus in the Roman period. Identified with Salbit.

SHAALBIM, SHAALABBIN
Josh 19:42. Judg 1:30. I Kgs 4:9

SHAALBONITE A native of the city of Shaalabbin or Shaalbim; as was Eliahba, one of David's "mighty men".

SHAALBONITE
II Sam 23:32. I Chr 11:33

SHAALIM, LAND OF Land crossed by Saul on his way to look for his father's asses (I Sam 9:4). The correct reading of this name is land of Shual. This, and other regional names in the area derive from the names of families who owned these territories.

SHAALIM, LAND OF
I Sam 9:4

SHAAPH

1. The youngest son of Jahdai in the genealogy of the family of Caleb.

SHAAPH 1
I Chr 2:47

2. A son of Caleb and his concubine Maachah; he was the father of Madmannah.

SHAAPH 2
I Chr 2:49

SHAARAIM, SHARAIM

1. A town at the northern end of the Shephelah (coastal plain) district of the territory of Judah (Josh 15:36). The Israelites pursued the Philistines after their victory along the road to Shaaraim (I Sam 17:52). Following the Septuagint it has been suggested that rather than a place name, Shaaraim denotes its literal Hebrew meaning of two gates. Modern scholars seek to identify Shaaraim with Khirbet Saira 2½ miles (4 km) southeast of Beth Shemesh. This village is located on a lofty hill, with a spring at its foot, and thus suitable for an ancient town.

SHAARAIM, SHARAIM 1
Josh 15:36. I Sam 17:52

2. A town in the territory of Simeon (I Chr 4:31). Not identified.

SHAARAIM, SHARAIM 2
I Chr 4:31

SHAASHGAZ The eunuch in charge of the royal concubines in the court of the Persian king Ahasuerus.

SHAASHGAZ
Est 2:14

SHABBETHAI ("born on the Sabbath"). A Levite who supported Ezra in his campaign to ban marriage with pagan wives (Ezra 10:15). He was one of the men who helped to interpret the Law which Ezra read from the Book (Neh 8:7). According to Nehemiah 11:16, he was also one of the Levites in charge of "the business outside of the house of God".

SHABBETHAI
Ezra 10:15. Neh 8:7; 11:16

SHADRACH See ABED-NEGO

SHADRACH
Dan 1:7; 2:49; 3:12-14, 16, 19-20, 22-23, 26, 28-30

SHAGEH Shageh the Hararite was the father of Jonathan (No.6) one of David's "mighty men".

SHAGEH
I Chr 11:34

SHAHARAIM One of the ancestors of King Saul. He had three wives, Hushim, Baara and Hodesh. Hushim bore him Abitub and Elpaal but was later banished together with Baara. Hodesh bore him seven sons.

SHAHARAIM
I Chr 8:8

SHAHAZIMAH (SHAHAZUMAH) A city on the border of the territory allotted to Issachar when the land of Canaan was divided among the tribes (Josh 14:1; 19:22). It was "between Tabor and the Jordan River". Its location is unknown.

SHAHAZIMAH
Josh 19:22

SHALISHA (SHALISHAH) When young Saul set out in pursuit of his father's asses, he went "through the land of Shalisha" somewhere in the Mountains of Ephraim. The city of Baal Shalisha was probably in that area.

SHALLECHETH, GATE OF A gate on the western side of the Temple where Shuppim and Hosah kept watch in the time of King David.

SHALLUM

1. Son of Jabesh, Shallum conspired against Zechariah, the son of Jeroboam, king of Israel. In 748 B.C. he killed him and reigned in his stead for just one month before being assassinated in his turn by Menahem, the son of Gadi.

2. A son of Tikvah and grandson of Harhas, Shallum, "keeper of the wardrobe", was the husband of Huldah the prophetess.

3. Son of Sismai and father of Jekamiah in the genealogy of the family of Jerahmeel.

4. Fourth son of King Josiah of Judah, and his successor to the throne in 609 B.C. He is better known by his royal name, Jehoahaz.

5. Son of Shaul No.1, the youngest son of Simeon, and father of Mibsam No.2.

6. A high priest, son of Zadok, and father of Hilkiah; one of the ancestors of Ezra.

7. Fourth son of Naphtali by his wife Bilhah (called Shillem in Gen 46:24). He founded the family of the Shillemites.

The region of Shalisha in the mountains of Ephraim.

Chalcedony cylinder seal impression with a cult scene and the name of the owner "Shallum" incised on the side. Late 8th-7th centuries B.C. (Israel Museum)

8. A Levite, chief of the gatekeepers of the Temple after the return of the exiles from Babylon, perhaps the same as No.9. He is called Shelemiah in I Chronicles 26:14, Meshullam in Nehemiah 12:25 and Meshelemiah in I Chronicles 9:21. One of those forced by Ezra to repudiate his foreign wife (Ezra 10:24).

9. A Korahite Levi, son of Kore; he was gatekeeper of the tabernacle of the Temple after the return of the exiles from Babylon. His son Mattithiah was in charge of "the things that were baked in pans". Perhaps identical with No.8.

10. Father of Jehizkiah, a leader of Ephraim at the time of Pekah son of Remaliah, king of Israel.

11. Head of a family of gatekeepers who returned from the Exile of Babylon with Zerubbabel. Perhaps related to Nos.8 and 9.

12. One of the men who, having taken pagan wives, had to repudiate them upon the decree of Ezra. Perhaps related to Nos.8 and 9.

13. Another of the men who, having taken a pagan wife, had to repudiate her in observance with Ezra's decree.

14. Son of Hallohesh, leader of half the districts of Jerusalem in the time of Nehemiah; he and his daughters helped repair the walls of the city.

Limestone Hebrew seal from Jerusalem inscribed "[Belonging] to Shallum". 7th century B.C. (Israel Museum)

Store-jar found in a tomb at Azor, inscribed with the name of the owner "Shalmai". Late 7th-6th centuries B.C.

15. An uncle of Jeremiah the prophet. He sent his son, Hanameel to sell the prophet his field in Anathoth.

16. Father of Maaseiah, keeper of the door of the Temple at the time of Jehoiakim king of Judah.

SHALLUN (a variant of Shallum). Son of Col-Hozeh, leader of the district of Mizpah; he repaired the Fountain Gate as well as the wall of the Pool of Shelah in the time of Nehemiah.

SHALMAI A family of Nethinim (Temple servants) who returned from Exile in Babylon with Zerubbabel and settled in Jerusalem.

SHALMAN The prophet Hosea predicted a military defeat of Israel comparable to the destruction of Beth Arbel by Shalman (Hos 10:14). Most likely, Shalman is to be identified with Shalmaneser III, king of Assyria (859-825 B.C.). The latter recorded in his annals that, during his 18th regnal year (841 B.C.), in the course of his march from Hauran to Tyre he "destroyed, tore down, and burned innumerable towns" lying in his path. The first such Israelite town to suffer the atrocities typically inflicted by Assyrian kings could have been Beth Arbel.

SHALMANESER The name of five kings of Assyria, only two of whom seem to be connected with the OT.

Shalmaneser I, son of Adad-Nirari II, ruled 1274-1245 B.C. Shalmaneser II, successor to Tiglath-Pileser II, ruled 1031-1020 B.C.

Shalmaneser III, son of Ashurnasirpal, ruled 859-824 B.C. He continued his father's expansionist policies, extending Assyria's frontiers from Urartu to Persia, from Media to the Mediterranean coast including Asia Minor. He invaded Babylon and secured her complete

SHALLUM 15
Jer 32:7

SHALLUM 16
Jer 35:4

SHALLUN
Neh 3:15

SHALMAI
Ezra 2:46

SHALMAN
Hos 10:14

SHALMANESER
II Kgs 17:3; 18:9

The Black Obelisk of Shalmaneser III, a stone monument bearing an account of the king's wars and depicting various nations bringing tribute to him. (British Museum)

subjection. He consolidated Assyrian domination over his conquests by establishing a sophisticated imperial structure, vassals, annual tribute, autonomy, trade relations and alliances and military campaigns, thus laying the foundations for the neo-Assyrian empire. The first Assyrian king to come into contact with kings of Israel, in 853 B.C. he fought at Karkar on the Orontes River against a formidable anti-Assyrian coalition of 12 kings headed by Ben-Hadad of Aram-Damascus. While the Bible does not mention this incident, his "Monolith inscription" testifies to the prominence of Ahab, king of Israel, who fielded the largest armored force of chariots — 2,000, as well as 10,000 foot soldiers. Although Shalmaneser claims a great victory, the fact that he avoided Syria for several years afterwards, suggests that his victory was indecisive. The "Black Obelisk" found in Nimrud records his military achievements against the western kings, and depicts the payment of tribute by Jehu, king of Israel, humbly prostrating himself before him — an incident also passed over in silence in the Bible. Despite his boasts as "the mighty king, king of the universe", he died amid revolts which broke out throughout the empire and with which his brother and successor had to contend.

Shalmaneser IV, son of Adad-Nirari III. ruled 783-774 B.C. Shalmaneser V, successor of Tiglath-Pileser III, ruled 727-722 B.C.; he laid siege for three years against Samaria when Hoshea king of Israel backed by Egypt, rebelled against Assyria. At the end of the siege, Samaria capitulated and Hoshea was taken prisoner (II Kgs 17:1-6; 18:9-10). Apparently Shalmaneser V died or was murdered during the siege and his successor Sargon completed the conquest of the city.

SHAMA ("[the Lord] listens"). Shama and his brother Jeiel, sons of Hotham the Aroerite, were among David's thirty "mighty men".

SHAMA
I Chr 11:44

SHAMARIAH ("whom the Lord protects"). Second son of Rehoboam by his wife Mahalath the granddaughter of David; sometimes known as Shemariah.

SHAMARIAH
II Chr 11:19

SHAMER Son of Mahli, the grandson of Mushi, and father of Bani No.7 one of the ancestors of Ethan the son of Kishi, a Levitical singer in the Temple of Jerusalem. An alternate spelling for Shomer and Shemar.

SHAMER
I Chr 6:46

SHAMGAR The son of Anath; he succeeded Ehud, the son of Gera as Israel's deliverer. Using an ox goad, Shamgar killed 600 Philistines.

SHAMGAR
Judg 3:31; 5:6

SHAMHUTH An Izrahite, captain of the fifth division of David's army. He is probably identical with Shammoth the Harorite (I Chr 11:27) or Shammah the Harodite (II Sam 23:25) one of David's "mighty men".

SHAMHUTH
I Chr 27:8

SHAMIR

1. A Levite, son of Michah the son of Uzziel; he lived at the time of King David.

SHAMIR 1
I Chr 24:24

2. A city or place allotted to Judah when the land of Canaan was divided among the tribes (Josh 14:1; 15:48). It was "in the mountain country". Nothing is known about it beyond the fact that it probably lay in the southern part of the hills of Judah.

SHAMIR 2
Josh 15:48

3. A city in the hills of Ephraim. It was the home of Tola, who was judge in Israel for 23 years, and was buried there. Its location is unknown.

SHAMIR 3
Judg 10:1-2

SHAMMA Eighth of the sons of Zophah in the tribe of Asher.

SHAMMA
I Chr 7:37

SHAMMAH

1. Third son of Reuel the son of Esau by his wife Basemath.

SHAMMAH 1
Gen 36:13, 17.
I Chr 1:37

2. The third son of Jesse, and one of the elder brothers of David. When Samuel came to seek a king among the children of Jesse, Shammah was among those passed over. Shammah fought under Saul against the Philistines. (The name is sometimes spelled Shimeah).

SHAMMAH 2
I Sam 16:9;
17:13

3. Son of Agee the Hararite; he was one of David's thirty "mighty

SHAMMAH 3
II Sam 23:11,
33

men". He singlehandedly fought off a Philistine raid. His son, Jonathan, was among the thirty "mighty men".

4. Shammah the Harodite, one of David's thirty "mighty men". He was the commander of a unit of 24,000 soldiers of David's army (I Chr 27:8, where his name is given as Shamhuth the Izrahite).

SHAMMAH 4
II Sam 23:25

SHAMMAI

1. Firstborn son of Onam, father of Nadab and Abishur.

SHAMMAI 1
I Chr 2:28, 32

2. Son of Rekem and father of Maon in the genealogy of the family of Caleb.

SHAMMAI 2
I Chr 2:44-45

3. Son of Mered and his Egyptian wife Bithiah, in the genealogy of the family of Judah.

SHAMMAI 3
I Chr 4:17

SHAMMOTH Shammoth the Harorite, one of David's thirty "mighty men". In the parallel list in II Samuel 23:25, he is called Shammah the Harodite.

SHAMMOTH
I Chr 11:27

SHAMMUA

1. Son of Zaccur, from the tribe of Reuben. He was one of the 12 men sent by Moses from the wilderness of Paran to spy out the land of Canaan.

SHAMMUA 1
Num 13:4

2. The first of David's children born in Jerusalem, identical with Shimea in I Chronicles 3:5.

SHAMMUA 2
II Sam 5:14.
I Chr 14:4

3. A Levite, son of Galal and grandson of Jeduthun, who was the father of Abda, one of the Levites who dwelled in Jerusalem at the time of Nehemiah. He is called Shemaiah in I Chronicles 9:16.

SHAMMUA 3
Neh 11:17

4. Head of the priestly family of Bilgah at the time of Joiakim the high priest.

SHAMMUA 4
Neh 12:18

SHAMSHERAI Firstborn son of Jeroham in the genealogy of King Saul; he lived in Jerusalem.

SHAMSHERAI
I Chr 8:26

SHAPHAM One of the leaders of Gad who dwelt in the land of Bashan at the time of Jotham king of Judah and Jeroboam king of Israel (I Chr 5:12, 17).

SHAPHAM
I Chr 5:12

SHAPHAN ("rock badger"). The son of Azilia; secretary of King Josiah. The king dispatched him to the high priest Hilkiah to fetch money for the men who repaired the House of God. It was then that Hilkiah gave him the "Book of the Law" that had been discovered in the Temple. Shaphan read it before the king, who thereupon commanded him, together with his son Ahikam and Achbor, the son of Michaiah, to inquire of the Lord through the prophetess Huldah concerning the words of this book (II Kgs 22:3-14; II Chr 34:8-21).

SHAPHAN
II Kgs 22:3,
8-10, 12, 14;
25:22. II Chr
34:8, 15-16,
18, 20. Jer
26:24; 29:3;
36:10-12;
39:14; 40:5, 9,
11; 41:2; 43:6.
Ezek 8:11

Another son of Shaphan, Elasah, was the messenger who carried Jeremiah's letter from Jerusalem to the Jews in Babylonia (Jer 29:3). Yet another son, Gemariah, had a chamber in the upper court of the Temple, where Baruch son of Neriah read Jeremiah's scroll in the hearing of all the people (Jer 36:10-11). It is possible that Jaazaniah the son of Shaphan, accused by Ezekiel of an act of abomination in the Temple (Ezek 8:11), was another son of the same Shaphan.

Shaphan's grandson, Gedaliah, son of Ahikam, was appointed by Nebuchadnezzar to govern the people who remained in the land of Judah (II Kgs 25:22).

SHAPHAT ("[the Lord] judges").

SHAPHAT 1
Num 13:5

1. A man of the tribe of Simeon, Shaphat the son of Hori, was among the 12 men sent by Moses from the wilderness of Paran to spy out the land of Canaan.

SHAPHAT 2
I Kgs 19:16,
19. II Kgs
3:11; 6:31

2. A man of Abel Meholah who was the father of Elisha the prophet.

3. Sixth and last son of Shemaiah (No.2) and great-grandson of Zerubbabel in the genealogy of the family of David.

SHAPHAT 3
I Chr 3:22

4. One of the leaders of the tribe of Gad who lived in Bashan at the time of Jotham king of Judah and Jeroboam king of Israel.

SHAPHAT 4
I Chr 5:12

Amazonite Hebrew seal mounted on a gold ring inscribed with the name "Shaphat". 8th century B.C. (Israel Museum)

5. A son of Adlai; he was one of the officials at the court of King David and was in charge of "the herds that were in the valleys".

SHAPHIR (SAPHIR) A city in Judah mentioned by Micah the prophet. Its location is uncertain.

SHARAI One of the sons of Bani who had to repudiate his foreign wife at the decree of Ezra.

SHARAIM See SHAARAIM

SHARAR Sharar the Hararite, father of Ahiam, one of David's thirty "mighty men". An alternate name for Sacar (I Chr 11:35).

SHAREZER ("protect the king"). One of the two sons of Sennacherib king of Assyria (the other was Adrammelech) who murdered their father in the temple of Nisroch in Nineveh and then fled to the land of Ararat.

SHARON, SHARONITE The coastal plain between the River Yarkon on the south and Mount Carmel on the north, famous for its forests and luxuriant vegetation (Is 33:9; Song 2:1). It was rich in pasture and David appointed an overseer for the herds that grazed there (I Chr 27:29). The famous route called the Via Maris passed through the Plain of Sharon, connecting Egypt with Palestine and Syria. The lists of the Egyptian kings who took that road mention many of the cities along it. The name Sharon appears in the list of Amenophis II, who traveled through it on

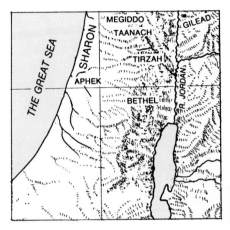

The Sharon

Tell el Farah (south) identified with Sharuhen.

his way to northern Syria. In the Persian and Hellenistic periods Phoenician colonies were built along the coastal strip. In the Roman period it was called *drymos* ("forest"), and some of the most important cities of Palestine were built along the coast at that time.

SHARUHEN A town in the territory of Simeon (Josh 19:6). It is not mentioned in the list of Simeonite towns within the territory of Judah which has Shilhim instead of Sharuhen (Josh 15:32), while in the list of Simeonite cities until the days of David it is replaced by Shaaraim (I Chr 4:28-31). Scholars are of the opinion that Shilhim and Shaaraim are both corrupt forms of the name Sharuhen, which occurs in the very same form in Egyptian sources. Others, however, suggest that there is no corruption in the three different place names which merely reflect changes in the territory of this tribe over different periods.

As confirmed by Egyptian sources, Sharuhen was a well fortified town throughout the Hyksos period and the Late Bronze Age, when it was apparently the seat of an Egyptian ruler. After the expulsion of the Hyksos it became the main Egyptian stronghold in the land of Canaan, and retained its importance as late as the time of Rameses II.

Most scholars tend to identify Sharuhen with Tell el-Fara (south) 15 miles (24 km) south of Gaza and 19 miles (30 km) west of Beersheba. It is located on an elevated mound; more than 16 acres (6.5 ha) in size; protected by Nahal Besor, it dominates the road leading from the Via Maris eastward.

The Philistine pottery found in its tombs indicates that only after the reign of David, apparently under Solomon, did the town become part of the territory of Simeon. Sharuhen was destroyed in the course of Shishak's campaign and was rebuilt by the Israelites in the 7th-6th centuries B.C.

SHASHAI One of the sons of Bani who, having taken a pagan wife, had to repudiate her at the decree of Ezra.

SHASHAK One of the sons of Beriah, and the father of Iphdeiah and Penuel, in the genealogy of King Saul.

SHAUL, SHAULITES ("asked for/dedicated"). The Hebrew spelling is identical to that of Saul.

1. The son of Simeon by a Canaanite woman; the founder of the Shaulite family; he is the father of Shallum No.5.

2. A Kohathite Levi.

SHAVEH Place where the king of Sodom went to meet Abraham after vanquishing Chedorlaomer (Gen 14:17-18); identified with the "King's Valley" (II Sam 18:18) where Absalom erected his monument. Josephus puts it at a distance of 2 stadia from Jerusalem.

SHAVEH KIRIATHAIM A place to the east of the Jordan where Chedorlaomer defeated the Emim (Gen 14:5). As Shaveh Kiriathaim is mentioned between Ham and Seir, it should apparently be sought in southern Gilead. The combination of Shaveh and Kiriathaim may be understood as a place by the name of Shaveh, which is near to, or in the district of, Kiriathaim.

SHAVSHA An alternate spelling for Seraiah No.1.

SHEAL One of the sons of Bani who, having taken a pagan wife, had to repudiate her at the decree of Ezra.

SHEALTIEL (SALATHIEL) A son of King Jeconiah (Jehoiachin). The father (in Chronicles, the grandfather) of Zerubbabel.

SHEARIAH Fourth son of Azel, a descendant of King Saul.

SHEAR-JASHUB ("a remnant shall return"). The symbolic name given to the firstborn son of Isaiah the prophet.

SHEBA The name of several biblical characters, of a city and a country.

1. Firstborn son of Raamah the son of Cush.

2. One of the many sons of Joktan the great-great- grandson of Shem.

3. Firstborn son of Jokshan, son of Abraham by Keturah.

These three characters are usually considered to be the ancestors of Semitic tribes of the Arabian Peninsula, perhaps from the kingdom of Sheba (see No. 7). The Hebrew spelling of their name is identical to that of the kingdom.

4. Son of Bichri, a Benjamite who led a revolt against King David. Joab, the commander of the king's army, besieged his stronghold Abel Beth Maachah. A "wise woman" persuaded the inhabitants of Abel to decapitate Sheba and throw his head over the wall to Joab.

5. A man of Gad who dwelled in Gilead at the time of Jotham king of Judah and Jeroboam king of Israel.

6. A town situated in the territory which was allotted to the tribe of Simeon.

7. A land in southwest Arabia identified with present-day Yemen. Inhabited by the Sabeans. According to biblical and external sources supported by archeological evidence, the kingdom of Sheba flourished for over 1,500 years — from the first millennium B.C. until c. A.D. 500. The people of Sheba were merchants and traders who made the most of

SHASHAI
Ezra 10:40

SHASHAK
I Chr 8:14, 25

SHAUL,
SHAULITES 1
Gen 46:10. Ex 6:15. Num 26:13. I Chr 4:24

SHAUL,
SHAULITES 2
I Chr 6:24

SHAVEH
Gen 14:17

SHAVEH
KIRIATHAIM
Gen 14:5

SHAVSHA
I Chr 18:16

SHEAL
Ezra 10:29

SHEALTIEL
I Chr 3:17. Ezra 3:2, 8; 5:2. Neh 12:1. Hag 1:1, 12, 14; 2:2, 23. Matt 1:12. Luke 3:27

SHEARIAH
I Chr 8:38; 9:44

SHEAR-JASHUB
Is 7:3

SHEBA 1
Gen 10:7, I Chr 1:9

SHEBA 2
Gen 10:28. I Chr 1:22

SHEBA 3
Gen 25:3. I Chr 1:32

SHEBA 4
II Sam 20:1-2, 6-7, 10, 13-14, 21-22

View of Shaare in North Yemen.

Gavra in Yemen.

SHEBA 5
I Chr 5:13

SHEBA 6
Josh 19:2

SHEBA 7
Job 6:19. Ps
72:10, 15. Is
60:6. Jer 6:20.
Ezek 27:22-23;
38:13

their country's strategic position between the Far and Near East. "The merchants of Sheba traded for your wares the choicest spices, all kinds of precious stone and gold" (Ezek 27:22). Myrrh and frankincense, two perfumes much valued in biblical times, originated from Sheba. The Sabeans also traded in slaves (Joel 3:8) and did not refrain from robbery (Job 1:15; 6:19). The history of the Sabean kingdom is still not well known. The names of some of their kings appear in the records of Sargon II and Sennacherib, kings of Assyria, while others are known from some of the thousands of pre-Islamic inscriptions found since the second half of the last century onwards. But it is only since about 1950 that more serious archeological research has been undertaken in the area. From the scanty literary evidence, we know that by the beginning of the Christian era most of the Arabian peninsula was ruled by the Sabeans. It was at about that time that the Romans attempted to lay their hands on the fabulous riches of Sheba, but without success.

Sheba in southwest Arabia.

SHEBA,
QUEEN OF

I Kgs 10:1, 4,
10, 13. II Chr
9:1, 3, 9, 12

SHEBA, QUEEN OF Sabean queen who went to Jerusalem laden with gifts of gold, precious stones and spices, to see Solomon's wealth and to test his wisdom (I Kgs 10:1-13).

The visit was probably the occasion of the establishment or expansion of trade relations between the wealthy South Arabian state of

Sheba and Israel, which controlled important trade routes. This is hinted at by the exchange of gifts between Solomon and the queen, and accords well with the heavy involvement of both parties in trade.

In the NT Jesus calls her the queen from "the south" (Matt 12:42; Luke 11:31).

SHEBAH (SHIBAH) ("oath"). The name of the well dug by Isaac which, according to Genesis 26:33, gave its name to the city Beersheba, the well of Shebah. (In Genesis 21:31, the origin of the name is attributed to an oath taken by Abraham).

SHEBAM, SHIBMAH, SIBMAH A city on the eastern bank of the Jordan River, in the territory of Sihon, king of the Amorites. After Sihon's defeat it was taken by the tribe of Reuben. It was famed for its wine and vines. Perhaps present-day Quran-el-Kibsh, 2 miles (3 km) west of Heshbon.

SHEBANIAH

1. One of the priests who "were to blow the trumpets before the ark of God" when David brought the ark into Jerusalem.

2. One of the Levites who stood on "the stair of the Levites" and repented loudly on the day of the great fast in the time of Nehemiah and later put his seal on the covenant.

3. Another leader who put his seal on the covenant.

4. Yet another leader, a Levite, who put his seal on the covenant.

5. Name of a priestly family at the time of Joiakim the high priest; it was headed by Joseph No.10. Probably the family of No.2.

SHEBARIM A place somewhere between Ai and Jericho where the men of Ai pursued the Israelites and killed 36 of them (Josh 7:5). It has been suggested that this is not a proper name and should be translated literally as "the quarries".

SHEBAT The 11th month of the Hebrew calendar, corresponding to January/February. Mentioned only once in the OT as the month in which Zechariah had a vision.

SHEBER A son of Caleb by his concubine Maachah, among the descendants of David.

SHEBNA A scribe of King Hezekiah of Judah during the siege of Jerusalem by the Assyrian king, Sennacherib (II Kgs 18:17-18).

After conquering Babylon, the Assyrian king turned to the west, and attacked Judah in 701 B.C. Having besieged Lachish, Sennacherib sent delegations to King Hezekiah, demanding negotiations for total surrender (II Kgs 18:17-25; Is 36:2-10). Hezekiah, for his part, was represented by three men: Eliakim, son of Hilkiah, who was in charge of the household, Shebna the scribe and Joah, son of Asaph the recorder (II Kgs 18:18; Is 36:3).

It is not clear whether King Hezekiah's scribe is identical with the Shebna mentioned in Isaiah 22:15 as the palace governor. The latter was denounced by the prophet for building his own tomb (Is 22:16), and it was prophesied that he would die in a foreign land (Is 22:17-19).

SHEBUEL, SHUBAEL

1. Eldest son of Gershon, a descendant of Moses; he was a Levite, overseer of the treasury at the court of King David, and assisted in the Temple service.

2. One of the sons of Heman, King David's seer; he was in charge of the fourth division of priests, and assisted with the Temple music.

SHECANIAH, SHECHANIAH

1. Head of the tenth division of priests in the Temple at the time of King David.

2. One of the descendants of David, King Jeconiah (Jehoiachin in II Kgs 23:31), and Zerubbabel, father of Shemaiah No.2.

Store-jar found in a tomb at Azor, inscribed with the name of the owner "Shalmai". Late 7th-6th centuries B.C. (Israel Dept of Antiquities and Museums)

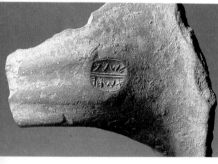

Seal impression on a pottery jar handle from Mizpah inscribed in Hebrew "[Belonging] to Shebna [son of] SHR". Late 8th-7th centuries B.C. (Israel Department of Antiquities and Museums)

SHEBAH
Gen 26:33

SHEBAM, SHIBMAH, SIBMAH
Num 32:3, 38. Josh 13:19. Is 16:8-9. Jer 48:32

SHEBANIAH 1
I Chr 15:24

SHEBANIAH 2
Neh 9:4-5; 10:10

SHEBANIAH 3
Neh 10:4

SHEBANIAH 4
Neh 10:12

SHEBANIAH 5
Neh 12:14

SHEBARIM
Josh 7:5

SHEBAT
Zech 1:7

SHEBER
I Chr 2:48

SHEBNA
II Kgs 18:18, 26, 37; 19:2. Is 22:15; 36:3, 11, 22; 37:2

SHEBUEL, SHUBAEL 1
I Chr 23:16; 24:20; 26:24

SHEBUEL, SHUBAEL 2
I Chr 25:4, 20

SHECANIAH, SHECHANIAH 1
I Chr 24:11

SHECANIAH, SHECHANIAH 2
I Chr 3:21-22

3. A family of exiles who returned from Babylon with Ezra; Ben Jahaziel belonged to this family.

4. One of the priests at the time of King Hezekiah, who aided in the distribution of Temple offerings.

5. Son of Jehiel and one of those who urged Ezra to have the exiles who returned from Babylon repudiate their foreign wives.

6. Father of Shemaiah No.18, among those who assisted in repairing the walls of Jerusalem during the time of Nehemiah.

7. Son of Arah; his daughter married Tobiah, the archenemy of Nehemiah, and his son Jehohanan married the daughter of Meshullam No.13 the son of Berechiah.

8. One of the priests and Levites who returned from the Exile in Babylon with Zerubbabel.

SHECHEM

1. Son of Hamor, a Hivite (Gen 34:2), but according to Genesis 48:22 he may have been an Amorite. Jacob bought a parcel of land from the children of Hamor (Gen 33:19; Josh 4:32; cf Judg 9:28). Shechem raped Dinah, Jacob's daughter (Gen 34:1-2) and in revenge, Simeon and Levi, Jacob's sons, killed Shechem along with all the men of the city (Gen 34:25ff). The personal name Shechem is common among certain northern Arabian tribes.

2. Town in the hill area of Ephraim, the capital of its region, and one of the capitals of the Kingdom of Israel. On his arrival in the land of Canaan Abraham built an altar at Shechem, where the Lord appeared to him (Gen 12:5-7). Jacob bought a field at Shechem (Gen 33:18).

Reconstructed façade of the Late Canaanite temple at Tell Balata.

Shechem seems to have been settled at an early stage, and for this reason it is not mentioned among the conquests of Joshua. However, Joshua made a covenant with the people at Shechem, "and took a large stone, and set it up there under the oak that was by the sanctuary of the Lord" (Josh 24:25-26). Gideon's family dwelt at Shechem. When Abimelech son of Jerubbaal (i.e. Gideon) came to Shechem (Judg chap. 9), he was accepted in a friendly manner by the Shechemites. After his family was slain, they made him king. But eventually they cursed Abimelech (Judg 9:27), and "Abimelech fought against that city all that day; he took the city, and killed the people who were in it, and he demolished the city, and sowed it with salt" (Judg 9:45). After the conquest of the tower of Shechem, "a certain woman dropped an upper millstone upon Abimelech's head, and crushed his skull" (Judg 9:53). Shechem was

Stone chair with a sculptured dolphin from the Roman theater at Shechem.

(top of the page)
The Roman theater at Shechem.

assigned to the Levites by David as a city of refuge (Josh 21:21; I Chr 6:67). In the tribal system Shechem assumed a central place and was of cultic importance, and for this reason Rehoboam chose Shechem as the place of his enthronement (I Kgs 12:1). Immediately after the division of the kingdom, Jeroboam made Shechem his capital for some time (I Kgs 12:25). It seems that numerous conquests and destructions of Shechem caused it to decline during the rest of the Israelite period, although the city was continuously settled (cf Jer 41:5). The town was abandoned until the 4th century B.C., when Alexander the Great made it into a rest camp for his soldiers. It was subsequently occupied by the Samaritans, and this town was probably the Sychar of John 4:5-7; ("Sychem" in the Syriac version), near which was Jacob's well, where Jesus met the woman of Samaria.

In external historical sources Shechem, by the name of Sekmem, is mentioned in an Egyptian inscription of the Middle Kingdom (1878-1843 B.C.). The ruler of Shechem, Labashi-Hadad is also cursed in the Egyptian Execration texts (19th-18th centuries B.C.). In the El Amarna Letters the city of Shechem (Sikmi) and its ruler Labayu and his sons are mentioned several times. At this time Shechem and its rulers were of great importance and their rule seems to have extended over the central part of Palestine.

Ancient Shechem is identified at Tell Balata, situated at the saddle between the mountains of Gerizim and Ebal, about 1 mile (1.6 km) northwest of modern Nablus. The ancient city extended over some 10-12 acres (4-5 ha), and herdsmen were camping on the mound by the Chalcolithic period (3700 B.C.). In the first phase of the Middle Bronze Age II (c. 1850-1750 B.C.) large areas were leveled for major building operations and public buildings were built in the otherwise unfortified Canaanite town. In the following phase (1750-1650 B.C.) this quarter was surrounded by a heavy wall, which served as fortification until at least the 16th century B.C. Within this area four temples were built. With the resumption of Egyptian rule over Palestine, the fortifications and the temple of Shechem were destroyed. The city was rebuilt in the second half of the 15th century B.C.; to this period belong a sumptuous

A coin of Neapolis (Shechem) depicting Asklepios and Hygieia with Mount Gerizim in the background.

(left)
Two details of an unfinished Greek monastery begun in the 19th century over Jacob's Well in Shechem (Sychar).

palace, where its 19 superimposed floors testify to its continuous use throughout the 13th and 12th centuries B.C., and a large altar, to the east of which is a high-place with a polished massebah pillar. This could have been the great stone which Joshua set up under the oak, "that was by the sanctuary of the Lord" (Josh 24:26). Shechem of the Late Bronze Age was destroyed in the mid-12th century B.C. and abandoned for about a century. The city was rebuilt in the time of King Solomon and was finally abandoned after its conquest by John Hyrcanus in 107 B.C.

3. A descendant of Joseph and Manasseh (Num 26:31) and progenitor of the Shechemites.

4. Son of Shemida, of the family of Manasseh (I Chr 7:19). May be identical with No. 3.

SHECHEMITES The family or clan founded by Shechem, a descendant of Joseph and Manasseh.

SHEDEUR ("Shaddai is light"). Father of Elizur who led the tribe of Reuben in the wilderness of Sinai.

SHEEP See ANIMALS

SHEEP GATE After the return from the Babylonian Exile, the reconstruction of Jerusalem began at the Sheep Gate: "Then Eliashib the high priest rose up with his brethren the priests and built the Sheep Gate; they consecrated it, and hung its doors" (Neh 3:1). The gate was apparently situated at the northeastern corner of the northern wall. Previously known as the Gate of Benjamin (Jer 37:13; 38:7), its new name apparently derived from a sheep market accessible through it. Close by was the Bethesda pool, where Jesus healed a sick man (John 5:2-9).

SHEERAH Daughter of Ephraim. She built "Lower and Upper Beth Horon and Uzzen Sheerah".

SHEHARIAH Second son of Jeroham and one of the leaders of Benjamin who dwelled in Jerusalem; he was one of the ancestors of King Saul.

SHELAH, SHELANITES

1. Second son of Judah by his Canaanite wife Shua; the founder of the Shelanite family or clan. He was the father of Er the father (or

SHECHEM 3
Num 26:31.
Josh 17:2

SHECHEM 4
I Chr 7:19

SHECHEMITES
Num 26:31

SHEDEUR
Num 1:5; 2:10;
7:30, 35; 10:18

SHEEP GATE
Neh 3:1, 32;
12:39. John
5:2

SHEERAH
I Chr 7:24

SHEHARIAH
I Chr 8:26

SHELAH,
SHELANITES 1
Gen 38:5, 11,
14, 26; 46:12.
Num 26:20.
I Chr 2:3; 4:21

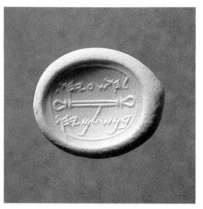

Hebrew seal impression from Jerusalem inscribed "[Belonging] to Hoshaiahu son of Shelemiahu". Late 8th-7th centuries B.C. (Israel Museum)

founder) of Lecah, Laadah and "of Mareshah, and the families of the house of the linen workers of the house of Ashbea" (I Chr 4:21).

2. Son of Arphaxad the son of Shem, and father of Eber. In the genealogy of Jesus according to Luke, he is called the son of Cainan the son of Arphaxad.

SHELAH, POOL OF See SHILOAH

SHELEMIAH ("the Lord gave a reward").

1. A Korahite Levi (called Meshelemiah in I Chr 26:1) who was a gatekeeper at the East Gate of the Temple in the time of King David. His son was in charge of the North Gate.

2. One of the sons of Bani who having taken a pagan wife, had to repudiate her at the decree of Ezra.

3. Another son of Bani who had taken a pagan wife and was made to repudiate her.

4. The father of Hananiah who repaired the wall of Jerusalem at the time of Nehemiah.

5. A priest appointed by Nehemiah to be the treasurer of the storeroom of the Temple, in charge of the distribution of the tithes of produce.

6. Son of Cushi, father of Nethaniah and grandfather of Jehudi.

7. Son of Abdeel. Jehoiakim king of Judah sent him and two others to arrest Baruch the scribe and Jeremiah the prophet after the reading of the first scroll of Jeremiah's prophecies.

8. Father of Jehucal or Jucal.

9. Son of Hananiah and father of Irijah who arrested Jeremiah the prophet.

SHELEPH One of the sons of Joktan who also represents the name of a tribe in southern Arabia.

SHELESH ("the third one"). One of the sons of Helem in the genealogy of the family of Asher.

SHELOMI Father of Ahihud, leader of the tribe of Asher appointed by the Lord to help Joshua divide the land of Canaan among the Children of Israel (Num 34:17, 27).

SHELOMITH ("peace"). The name of several biblical characters. Since it is a woman's name, it has been suggested that whenever borne by a man, it is a misspelt variant of Shelomoth.

1. Daughter of Dibri, of the tribe of Dan; she married an Egyptian. Her son blasphemed the name of the Lord and Moses had him put to death by stoning.

2. A daughter of Zerubbabel.

3. A Gershonite Levite son of Shimei and head of a family in Laadan in the final days of the reign of King David.

4. A Levite, son of Izhar. During the reign of King David, he was in charge of the spoils taken by the army and dedicated to the Temple.

5. A son or daughter of Rehoboam king of Judah by his second wife Maacah, granddaughter of Absalom.

6. A family of exiles who returned from Babylon with Ezra and numbered 160 males; it was headed by the son of Josiphiah.

SHELOMOTH ("peace"). A Levite, son of Izhar; an alternate name for Shelomith No.4.

SHELUMIEL ("the Lord is my peace"). A man of the tribe of Simeon, son of Zurishaddai, who was appointed by the Lord to help Moses take a census of the Children of Israel in the wilderness. Later he was appointed leader of his tribe (Num 2:12) on behalf of which he presented the ritual offering to the tabernacle set up by Moses (Num 7:36-41). He led the armies of his tribe when the Children of Israel set out on their march to the promised land.

SHEM ("name, renown"). One of the three sons of Noah. Their descendants, among whom were the Children of Israel, peopled the entire earth after the Flood (Gen 9:19). Shem was the "father of all the children of Eber" (Gen 10:21) and traditionally of the Semitic peoples. His sons were Elam, Asshur, Arphaxad, Lud and Aram (Gen 10:22). When Noah was drunk and slept naked in his tent, his son Ham summoned his two brothers, Shem and Japheth to see him in his stupor. The latter two covered their father with a garment, while their faces were turned away so that they would not see his nakedness. For this Noah blessed them and cursed Canaan son of Ham: "Blessed be the Lord, the God of Shem, and may Canaan be his servant. May God enlarge Japheth, and may he dwell in the tents of Shem and may Canaan be his servant" (Gen 9:18-28).

Seal impression inscribed "[Belonging] to Shema". 7th century B.C. (Israel Museum)

SHEMA

1. A city which fell to the lot of the children of Judah when Joshua divided the land of Canaan (Josh 14:1; 15:26). It was at the southern limit of the territory of Judah "towards the border of Edom in the South" (Josh 15:21). Generally considered to be the same as Sheba.

2. Last son of Hebron and father of Raham the father of Jorkeam in the genealogy of Caleb.

3. Son of Joel, father of Azaz and grandfather of Bela in the genealogy of the family of Reuben.

4. One of the sons of Elpaal who lived in Aijalon after having driven out the inhabitants of Gath; he is listed in the genealogy of King Saul.

5. One of the men who stood to the right of Ezra when he read the Law to the people after the return from the Exile.

SHEMAAH A Gibeathite who was the father of Joash and Ahiezer, two men of Benjamin who defected from the armies of Saul and joined David in Ziklag.

SHEMAIAH ("the Lord listened").

1. A prophet who lived at the time of Rehoboam king of Judah, the son of Solomon. He averted a war between Judah and the seceding Kingdom of Israel (I Kgs 12:22). He later warned the king that the Lord, angry because Judah had transgressed against him, would let the armies of Shishak triumph (II Chr 12:5). The leaders of Judah repented and "The wrath of the Lord" turned from the king (II Chr 12:7, 12).

2. Firstborn son of Shechaniah No.2 and father of Hattush, Igal, Bariah, Neariah and Shaphat in the genealogy of the family of David. The text is not clear and the five named sons of Shemaiah may in fact have been his brothers.

3. Father of Shimri and one of the ancestors of Ziza, a leader of the Simeonites.

4. A man of the tribe of Reuben, son of Joel and one of the ancestors of Beerah (who was carried into captivity by Tiglath-Pileser king of Assyria).

5. A Merarite Levite, son of Hasshub, who settled in Jerusalem after the return of the exiles from Babylon.

6. A Levite, son of Galal and grandson of Jeduthun, father of Obadiah who dwelled in Jerusalem after the return of the exiles.

7. A Levite, head of the family of the sons of Elizaphan, and one of the two hundred Levites who carried the ark of the covenant into Jerusalem at the time of King David.

8. A Levite son of Nethaneel; he was a scribe at the court of King David and recorded the divisions of priests in the Temple.

9. A Levite, firstborn son of Obed-Edom, and father of Othni, Rephael, Obed, Elzabad Elihu and Semachiah, gatekeepers of the Temple at the time of King David.

10. A Levite, one of the men sent by Jehoshaphat king of Judah to teach the word of the Lord throughout his kingdom. *SHEMAIAH 10* **II Chr 17:8**

11. A Levite, descendant of Jeduthun, among the 14 who helped cleanse the Temple in the time of King Hezekiah. *SHEMAIAH 11* **II Chr 29:14**

12. One of the assistants of Kore the son of Imnah who aided in the distribution of Temple offerings to the priests and Levites at the time of King Hezekiah. *SHEMAIAH 12* **II Chr 31:15**

13. One of the leaders of the Levites at the time of Josiah king of Judah; he donated many animals for the Passover holiday in Jerusalem. *SHEMAIAH 13* **II Chr 35:9**

14. One of the last sons of Adonikam and head of a family who returned from the Exile in Babylon with Ezra. *SHEMAIAH 14* **Ezra 8:13**

15. One of the leaders of the people who were with Ezra in exile; he was among those sent to Iddo in Casiphia to bring back Levites to Israel. *SHEMAIAH 15* **Ezra 8:16**

16. One of the priests, sons of Harim, who having taken a pagan wife, had to repudiate her at the decree of Ezra. *SHEMAIAH 16* **Ezra 10:21**

17. Another of the sons of Harim, though not a priest, he too repudiated his pagan wife. *SHEMAIAH 17* **Ezra 10:31**

18. Son of Shechaniah No.6 and keeper of the East Gate; he helped repair the walls of Jerusalem at the time of Nehemiah. *SHEMAIAH 18* **Neh 3:29**

19. Son of Delaiah and grandson of Mehetabeel. Sanballat and Tobiah, Nehemiah's archenemies hired him to try and frighten the prophet in order to discredit and weaken him. The plot failed. *SHEMAIAH 19* **Neh 6:10**

20. One of the priests, leaders of the people, who put his seal to the covenant at the time of Nehemiah, perhaps a descendant of No.21. *SHEMAIAH 20* **Neh 10:8**

21. One of the leaders of the priests who returned from Exile in Babylon with Zerubbabel. Perhaps father or ancestor of No.20. *SHEMAIAH 21* **Neh 12:6**

22. A priestly family in Jerusalem at the time of Joiakim the high priest. At its head was Jehonathan. Probably the family of Nos.20 and 21. *SHEMAIAH 22* **Neh 12:18**

23. One of the leaders of Judah who took part in one of the two thanksgiving choirs at the dedication by Nehemiah of the completed wall of Jerusalem. *SHEMAIAH 23* **Neh 12:34**

24. Grandfather of Zechariah who played the trumpet in the same choir as No.23, in the dedication ceremony. *SHEMAIAH 24* **Neh 12:35**

25. Another participant in the dedication ceremony, in the same choir, "with the musical instruments of David the man of God". *SHEMAIAH 25* **Neh 12:36**

26. Another Levite musician who was at the dedication ceremony. *SHEMAIAH 26* **Neh 12:42**

27. A man of Kirjath Jearim, father of Urijah who was a prophet in the days of Jeremiah. *SHEMAIAH 27* **Jer 26:20**

Kirjath Jearim, the native town of Shemaiah, Jeremiah's father.

28. Shemaiah the Nehelamite, a false prophet in Babylon in the days of Jeremiah. Shemaiah proclaimed a speedy return from Exile. He wrote a letter to Jerusalem opposing Jeremiah and demanding his imprisonment. The letter denounced him and foretold his eventual punishment.

29. Father of Delaiah, one of the leaders at the time of Jehoiakim.

SHEMARIAH ("may the Lord grant protection").

1. A man of the tribe of Benjamin, who defected from Saul's army and joined David in Ziklag; one of the "mighty men".

2. One of the sons of Harim who, having taken a pagan wife, had to repudiate her at the decree of Ezra.

3. One of the sons of Bani who, having taken a pagan wife, had to repudiate her.

SHEMEBER King of Zeboiim who joined the ill-fated coalition of five kings against Chedorlaomer king of Elam and was defeated in the Valley of Siddim.

SHEMED One of the sons of Elpaal. He built Ono and Lod after the return from the Babylonian Exile. The name is generally considered to be a misspelt form of Shemer.

SHEMER The person from whom Omri king of Israel purchased a hill on which the king built his capital, naming it Samaria after the former owner.

SHEMIDA, SHEMIDAITES A man of Gilead who founded the family or clan of the Shemidaites, one of the leading families of the tribe of Manasseh. Among his sons were Ahian, Shechem, Likhi and Aniam.

The name is found on an ostracon from Samaria dating from the 8th century.

SHEMIRAMOTH

1. One of the Levites who played the harp when the ark of the covenant was taken from the house of Obed-Edom to Jerusalem by King David; he later played in Jerusalem.

2. One of the Levites sent by Jehoshaphat king of Judah to teach the word of the Lord throughout his kingdom.

SHEMUEL (Note: the Hebrew spelling is identical to that of Samuel, the prophet).

1. Youngest son of Tola, firstborn of Issachar (son of Jacob and Leah).

2. A man of the tribe of Simeon, son of Ammihud, who was appointed by the Lord to help Joshua divide the land of Canaan among the Children of Israel (Num 34:17, 20, 29).

SHEN A place not far from Mizpah; midway between these two locations Samuel set up the stone which he called Ebenezer.

SHENAZZAR The fourth son of Jeconiah (or Jehoiachin) king of Judah. Generally considered to be an alternate form of Sheshbazzar.

SHEOL The domain of the dead, according to the OT; the region where the departed are laid to rest.

Sheol was located beneath the earth (Num 16:30), under the waters (Job 26:5). All the dead descended there never to return (Job 7:9, 16), although the OT records two exceptions who went straight to heaven: Enoch (Gen 5:24) and Elijah (II Kgs 2:11). All the dead were treated equally (Job 3:13-19; Ezek 32:18-32) and according to Ecclesiastes there was in Sheol "neither doing nor thinking, neither understanding nor wisdom" (Ecc 9:10). The belief that God ruled the universe from heaven to Sheol (Ps 139:7-8; Job 26:6), implied that death also belonged to God's domain (cf I Sam 2:6). But despite God's power over Sheol, the dead did not have any communication with him (Ps 88:6), nor could they praise him (Is 38:18; Ps 30:9). See ABADDON; GEHENNA; HADES.

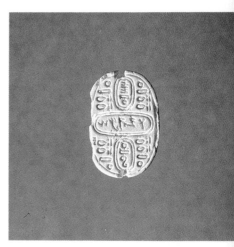

Steatite Hebrew seal from Samaria inscribed "Shemaria[hu]". 8th century B.C. (Israel Dept. of Antiquities and Museums)

Quartz Hebrew seal and impression from Lachish inscribed "[Belonging] to Shephatiah [son of] Asiah".

SHEPHAM A place on the northeastern border of the land of Canaan.

SHEPHATIAH ("the Lord is my judge").

1. The fifth of the sons of David born in Hebron. His mother was Abital.

2. Son of Reuel and father of Meshullam No.6.

3. Shephatiah the Haruphite, one of the men of Benjamin who defected from Saul's army and joined David in Ziklag; one of the "mighty men".

4. Son of Maachah and leader of the tribe of Simeon at the time of King David.

5. Youngest son of Jehoshaphat king of Judah; he was the brother of King Jehoram and thus uncle to the latter's son King Ahaziah.

6. A family or clan who returned from the Babylonian Exile with Zerubbabel and numbered 372 people.

7. A family, descended from Solomon's servants, who returned from the Babylonian Exile with Zerubbabel.

8. Another family who returned from Exile, this time with Ezra. It was headed by Zebadiah the son of Michael and numbered 80 males.

9. Son of Mahalaleel, of the children of Perez; one of the ancestors of Athaiah, a man of Judah who settled in Jerusalem after the return of the exiles.

10. Son of Mattan; one of the four ministers at the court of King Zedekiah who wanted Jeremiah put to death during the siege of Jerusalem by the armies of Nebuchadnezzar. They tried to kill the prophet by lowering him to the bottom of a cistern and leaving him to die.

SHEPHELAH See PLAIN

SHEPHER, MOUNT A station on the journey of the Children of Israel to the promised land.

SHEPHI, SHEPHO Fourth son of Shobal the second son of Seir the Horite.

SHEPHUPHAN (SHEPHAPHAN, SHEPHUPHAM) A descendant (perhaps a son) of Benjamin; one of the many variations of the name Shupham (Shuppim, Huppim, etc.).

SHEREBIAH

1. One of the priests and Levites who was brought back from Casiphia by Ezra. "A man of understanding" descended from Mahli, he was later among those entrusted with the keeping of the treasures of the Temple.

2. One of the Levites who helped the people understand the Law when Ezra read publicly from the Book of the Law in Jerusalem. He was among those who stood on "the stairs of the Levites" on the day of the great fast; he was also one of those who sealed the covenant.

3. One of the heads of the Levites who returned from Exile in Babylon with Zerubbabel and settled in Jerusalem.

SHERESH ("root"). A man of Manasseh, second son of Machir by his wife Maachah; father of Ulam and Rakem.

SHEREZER Bethel-Sherezer, a compound name of one who sent Regem Melech to seek the favor of the Lord during the fourth year of the reign of King Darius.

SHESHACH An alternate or code word (based on a reverse alphabet) used by Jeremiah to describe Babylon.

SHESHAI One of three giant brothers (the other two were Ahiman and Talmai) who lived in Hebron when the spies sent out by Moses came to reconnoiter the land of Canaan. The trio were driven out of the city by Caleb the son of Jephunneh (Josh 14:14) and later killed by the men of Judah (Judg 1:10).

SHESHAN Son of Ishi, one of the descendants of Jerahmeel, by his second wife Atarah. He had a child called Ahlai (I Chr 2:31). However, the text later says he had no sons, only daughters (2:34); he gave one of them in marriage to his Egyptian servant, Jahra, and she bore a son, Attai.

SHESHBAZZAR (Variant form of Shenazzar; "Sin [the moon-god] guard the father"). Bearing the title "prince of Judah" (Ezra 1:8), Sheshbazzar was appointed governor of the province of Judah by Cyrus (Ezra 5:14); he led the first group of exiles back from Babylon to Judah, bringing with him the vessels taken from the Temple (Ezra 1:8, 11; 5:14) by Nebuchadnezzar (II Kgs 24:13) and laid the foundations of rebuilding the Temple (Ezra 5:6).

Most scholars agree that Sheshbazzar was a descendant of the Davidic dynasty, being identified with Shenazzar the son of King Jehoiachin (I Chr 3:18) born just before his father went into exile. At the time of the return from Babylon he was about 60 years old and died shortly afterwards. He was succeeded as governor of the province of Judah by his nephew Zerubbabel (Ezra 5:1-2; Hag 1:1).

The nomination of Sheshbazzar as governor of Judah accords with the overall policy of the Persian kings who generally appointed members of the local ruling class as governors in order to gain the support of their subjects. However, the fact that the first two governors of Judah were of the Davidic dynasty and that they rebuilt the Temple, aroused in the people messianic expectations (Hag 2:20-23; Zech 4:6-10) which were dangerous for the Persians, and was probably the reason why the Persians later nominated governors who were not of that dynasty.

According to some scholars, Sheshbazzar and Zerubbabel were the same person. They reason that Sheshbazzar was his Akkado-Babylonian name, with Zerubbabel as the Hebrew equivalent; but this assumption is unfounded, as Zerubbabel is also an Akkadian name: *zer-babili* (see ZERUBBABEL). In addition, they cite Zechariah's prophecy (Zech 4:9) "The hands of Zerubbabel have laid the foundation of this temple; his hands shall also finish it…" implying that the reconstruction was the work of one person. Sheshbazzar was indeed the first to lay the foundation of the altar but his endeavors were checked and the building of the altar and Temple was completed by Zerubbabel. Moreover, as stated in the Books of Haggai and Zechariah, Zerubbabel was governor in the time of Darius, and not in the reign of Cyrus, when Sheshbazzar was governor.

Sheshbazzar's brief political career was marked by messianic hope but later, when the books of Ezra and Nehemiah were composed, he was overshadowed by Zerubbabel.

SHETHAR One of King Ahasuerus' seven counselors; princes of the provinces of Persia and Media "who ranked highest in the kingdom"; they were consulted by the king when Queen Vashti defied his command to appear before him.

SHETHAR-BAZNAI, SHETHAR BOZENAI, SHETHAR BOZNAI A Persian official who, along with Tattenai governor of the region "beyond the River", wrote to King Darius querying the Jews' authority to rebuild the Temple in Jerusalem.

SHEVA

1. One of the many variations of the name of one of David's officials, a scribe. (See also SERAIAH; SHAVSHA; SHISHA).

2. One of the sons of Caleb by his concubine Maachah; he was the father (or founder) of Machbenah and Gibea.

SHEWBREAD See SHOWBREAD

A view of the Siloam Tunnel which outskirts the village of Silwan.

(top of page)
The village of Silwan (Siloam).

SHIBMAH See SHEBAM

SHICRON A town on the northern border of Judah, one of several listed as running from east to west: "The border went out unto the side of Ekron northward. Then the border went around to Shicron, passed along to Mount Baalah, and extended to Jabneel; and the border ended at the sea" (Josh 15:11). The site of Shikron must thus be sought between Ekron and Jabneel, and has been identified with Tell el-Ful, on the northern bank of the Valley of Sorek, 5 miles (8 km) east-northeast of Gederah.

SHIHOR, SIHOR A stream in Egypt. Joshua 13:3 refers to Sihor "which is east of Egypt" as the southern border of the land of Canaan, and in I Chronicles 13:5 the extremities of David's kingdom run "from Shihor in Egypt to as far as the entrance of Hamath". In Isaiah 23:3 the Sihor is paralleled with "the River" (the Nile) and in Jeremiah 2:18 the waters of Sihor symbolize Egypt.

Egyptian monuments apply the name Shihor to lakes in the eastern Delta and also to Lake Fayum, while a topographical list of the Hellenistic period uses the term for the Pelusiac arm of the Nile. It thus seems that Shihor was a common Egyptian name for streams and bodies of water.

SHIHOR LIBNATH A stream in the vicinity of Mount Carmel, in the southwestern sector of the territory of Asher (Josh 19:26). Identified as the mouth of the River Kishon, near Tell Abu Hawam.

SHILHI Father of Azubah who married Asa king of Judah and was the mother of his son King Jehoshaphat.

SHILHIM A city in the territory of the tribe of Judah which appears to have been included in the inheritance of Simeon, or "within the inheritance of the children of Judah" (Josh 19:1,6). In its latter reference it is called Sharuhen and in I Chronicles 4:31, Shaaraim.

SHILLEM, SHILLEMITES An alternate name for Shallum No.7, the fourth son of Naphtali and the founder of the Shillemite family.

SHILOAH (SILOAH) Source of water for Jerusalem mentioned once in the Bible as "the waters of Shiloah" (Is 8:6) and later as "the Pool of Shelah" (Neh 3:15); it is referred to in the NT as "the Pool of Siloam" (John 9:7). Except for the indication in Nehemiah (3:15) that the wall of the pool was close to the king's garden, which is known to have been on the south of the city, no hint to its location is given. It seems that "the waters of Shiloah that flow softly" (Is 8:6) refers to part of the tunnel that brought the waters of the Gihon into the city. The reservoir built by Hezekiah (II Kgs 20:20) is identified with the Pool of Shiloah located at Birket el-Hamrah. In 1880, an inscription from the time of Hezekiah was discovered in the roof of the tunnel towards the center recording the meeting of the two groups of navvies who had been digging the tunnel from either side. Ancient traditions, still widely believed, have ascribed therapeutic properties to the waters of Siloam (John 9:1-7)

SHILOH A town in Mount Ephraim. Its location is described in the Bible as "a place which is on the north side of Bethel, on the east side of the highway that goes up from Bethel to Shechem, and on the south of Lebonah" (Judg 21:19). Shiloh was a religious center of the tribes and after the conquest of the country by Joshua the tabernacle of the congregation was set up there (Josh 18:1). It was there also that Joshua distributed territorial allotments to the tribes who had not previously received them (Josh 18:2-10). The House of God (Judg 18:31) in which Eli and his sons officiated was at Shiloh, and God appeared there before Samuel (I Sam 1:9; 3:1ff). When the Israelites were hard-pressed by the Philistines at Ebenezer the tabernacle was transported from Shiloh to the battlefield, but fell into the hands of the enemy (I Sam 4:1-5; 5:1). It

SHIBMAH
Num 32:38

SHICRON
Josh 15:11

SHIHOR,
SIHOR
Josh 13:3.
I Chr 13:5. Is
23:3. Jer 2:18

SHIHOR
LIBNATH
Josh 19:26

SHILHI
I Kgs 22:42. I
Chr 20:31

SHILHIM
Josh 15:32

SHILLEM,
SHILLEMITES
Gen 46:24.
Num 26:49

SHILOAH
Is 8:6

SHILOH
Gen 49:10.
Josh 18:1, 8-
10; 19:51;
21:2; 22:9, 12.
Judg 18:31;
21:12, 19, 21.
I Sam 1:3, 9,
24; 2:14; 3:21;
4:3-4, 12;
14:3. I Kgs
2:27; 14:2, 4.
Ps 78:60. Jer
7:12, 14; 26:6,
9; 41:5

seems that after this battle the city was set on fire and was only later rebuilt (Jer 4:5; 7:12; 26:6, 9). Ahijah, who prophesied to Jeroboam, son of Nebat, that he would rule over the ten tribes, came from Shiloh (I Kgs 11:29-31). Men of Shiloh were among those who returned from the Babylonian Exile (Neh 11:5). The town existed under the same name in the Roman and Byzantine periods.

The site of Shiloh was still known in the Middle Ages and in the 19th century it was correctly identified with Khirbet Seilun, about 20 miles (32km) north of Jerusalem. The mound is about 12 acres (5 ha) in area, and contains the remains of biblical Shiloh. Excavations have uncovered finds from various periods beginning with the Middle Bronze.

The translation of "until Shiloh comes" in Jacob's blessing of the tribe of Judah (Gen 49:10) has been traditionally understood as referring to the messiah. This, however, is extremely problematic because there is no reason to interpret Shiloh as an epithet of the messiah. Others assume that the city itself is intended: "until he [the king of Judah or the Judean empire] comes to Shiloh" (expansion of Judah over Israel). By a revocalization of the Hebrew, however, the phrase may be interpreted as "so that tribute will come to him" (to Judah).

Incense stand from Shiloh. 11th-10th centuries B.C.

(top left)
The site of ancient Shiloh.

(top right)
Bronze implements from Shiloh. Note the battle-axe (top left) made in the Hittite tradition.

(bottom left)
Ruins of biblical Shiloh.

SHILONI, SHILONITE

1. A native of Shiloh, such as Ahijah the prophet.

2. A family of exiles who returned from the Exile in Babylon and settled in Jerusalem; it was headed by Asaiah.

3. An ancestor of Maaseiah, one of the men of Judah who settled in Jerusalem after the return from Babylon; he probably belonged to the family of No.2.

SHILSHAH One of the sons of Zophah in the genealogy of the family of Asher.

SHIMEA ("[the Lord] listened").

1. First of the sons born to David in Jerusalem; his mother was Bathshua or Bathsheba.

2. A descendant of Merari the son of Levi; he was son of Uzzah and father of Haggiah.

3. A Levite, son of Michael and father of Berachiah.

4. An alternate name for Shimeah No.1, a brother of David.

SHIMEAH ("the Lord listened").

1. The third son of Jesse, brother of David and father of Jonadab (II Sam 13:3) and Jonathan (II Sam 21:21). Spelled Shimea in I Chronicles 20:7.

2. Son of Mikloth in the genealogy of King Saul.

SHIMEAM Alternative spelling for Shimeah No.2.

SHIMEATH A man of Ammon, father of Jozachar (II Kgs 12:21) or Zabad (II Chr 24:26) who conspired against Joash king of Judah and killed him.

SHIMEATHITES A family of scribes from the tribe of Caleb who dwelled in Jabez.

SHIMEI ("[God had] heard").

1. A Levite, son of Gershon (Num 3:18; I Chr 6:17), and founder of the Shimite family. He is given as Shimi in Exodus 6:17.

2. The son of Gera, a Benjamite of the house of King Saul, who dwelt at Bahurim (II Sam 16:5). When David was fleeing Jerusalem during the revolt of his son Absalom, Shimei cursed him and accused him of the destruction of Saul's family (II Sam 16:6-8). After David overcame the rebellion and returned to Jerusalem, he forgave Shimei when the latter came to greet him, along with 1,000 Benjamites (II Sam 19:17-23). Nevertheless, David ordered his heir Solomon to punish Shimei (I Kgs 2:8-9). Solomon accordingly ordered Shimei to take up residence in Jerusalem, forbidding him on pain of death to leave the city (I Kgs 2:36-38). Three years later, Shimei nevertheless journeyed to Gath to bring back two of his runaway slaves; on his return Solomon had him killed (I Kgs 2:39-46).

3. One of King David's officials, he withheld his support from Adonijah when the latter plotted to gain the throne.

4. The son of Ela, one of King Solomon's administrative officers in Benjamin.

5. The son of Pedaiah and brother of Zerubbabel.

6. A Simeonite, son of Zacchur, who had 16 sons and 6 daughters

7. A Reubenite son of Joel.

8. A Levite, descendant of Merari.

9. A Levite, descendant of Gershom.

10. One of the heads of the tribe of Benjamin who dwelt in Jerusalem.

11. A Levite, head of a family of singers appointed by King David to serve in the Temple.

12. A Ramathite, appointed by King David over the king's vineyards.

13. A Levite, descendant of Heman, who took part in the purification of the Temple during the reform of King Hezekiah of Judah.

SHILONI, SHILONITE 1
I Kgs 11:29; 12:15; 15:29. II Chr 9:29; 10:15

SHILONI, SHILONITE 2
I Chr 9:5

SHILONI, SHILONITE 3
Neh 11:5

SHILSHAH
I Chr 7:37

SHIMEA 1
I Chr 3:5

SHIMEA 2
I Chr 6:30

SHIMEA 3
I Chr 6:39

SHIMEA 4
I Chr 2:13; 20:7

SHIMEAH 1
II Sam 13:3, 32. II Sam 21:21

SHIMEAH 2
I Chr 8:32

SHIMEAM
I Chr 9:38

SHIMEATH
II Kgs 12:21. II Chr 24:26

SHIMEATHITES
I Chr 2:55

SHIMEI 1
Num 3:18. I Chr 6:17; 23:7, 9-10. Zech 12:13

SHIMEI 2
II Sam 16:5, 7, 13; 19:16, 18, 21, 23. I Kgs 2:8, 36, 38-42, 44

SHIMEI 3
I Kgs 1:8

SHIMEI 4
I Kgs 4:18

SHIMEI 5
I Chr 3:19

SHIMEI 6
I Chr 4:26-27

SHIMEI 7
I Chr 5:4

SHIMEI 8
I Chr 6:29

14. A Levite, brother and second official of Cononiah the overseer, who was appointed over the offerings to the Temple at the time of Hezekiah king of Judah.

15. One of the Levites who married an alien woman and was forced by Ezra to repudiate her.

16. One of the sons of Hashum who married an alien woman and was forced by Ezra to repudiate her.

17. One of the sons of Binnui who married an alien woman and was forced by Ezra to repudiate her.

18. Father of Jair and son of Kish, a Benjamite, ancestor of Mordecai.

SHIMEON ("[the Lord] listened"). One of the sons of Harim who, having taken a pagan wife, had to repudiate her at the decree of Ezra.

SHIMI, SHIMITE ("the Lord listened"). Second son of Gershon the son of Levi and founder of the Shimite family. An alternate form of SHIMEI.

SHIMON In the genealogy of the family of Judah, father of Amnon, Rinnah, Ben-Hanan and Tilon.

SHIMRATH ("watch over"). Son of Shimei in the genealogy of King Saul; head of a family who dwelled in Jerusalem.

SHIMRI ("the Lord protects me").

1. A man of the tribe of Simeon, son of Shemaiah No.3 and father of Jedaiah; one of the ancestors of Ziza.

2. Father of two of David's "mighty men", Jediael and Joha the Tizite.

3. A Merarite Levite son of Hosah, gatekeeper at the Temple.

4. A Levite of the sons of Elizaphan who helped cleanse the Temple at the time of King Hezekiah.

SHIMRITH An alternative name for Shomer, a person of Moab, father (or mother) of Jehozabad who conspired against Joash king of Judah and killed him.

SHIMRON

1. Son of Issachar and ancestor of the Shimronites.

2. One of the Canaanite city-states that took part in the battle by the waters of Merom, in the north of the country (Josh 11:1ff); subsequently a city in the territory of Zebulun (Josh 19:15). It is mentioned in the El Amarna Letters as Shiman and identified with Khirbet Sammuniyeh, where remains of the Late Bronze Age were discovered.

SHIMRONITES See SHIMRON No.1

SHIMRON MERON A town to the west of the Jordan River. Its king was among the many defeated by Joshua. Scholars do not agree as to the original form of the name (Shimron, Shimeon?) and the exact location of the town.

SHIMSHAI ("sun"). A scribe, one of the officials in the Persian government, who, along with Rehum, wrote the letter to Artaxerxes against the rebuilding of Jerusalem by the Jews. They succeeded in halting the building of the wall for a time.

SHINAB King of Admah who joined the ill-fated confederation of five rulers who rebelled against King Chedorlaomer.

SHINAR A place name designating Babylonia. It appears several times in the OT. According to Genesis 10:10, Nimrod ruled over Babel, Erech and Akkad, all in the land of Shinar. The tower of Babel was erected there (Gen 11:2). One of the kings with whom Abraham fought was Amraphel, king of Shinar (Gen 14:1, 9). The prophet Isaiah foresaw a time when God will gather together his dispersed people, some of whom will be residing in Shinar (Is 11:11). In one of the visions of Zechariah, Shinar is the site of a shrine to be built for the woman, Wickedness

Coin of Bar-Kochba with the name Shimon on one side and a vine leaf with the inscription "For the freedom of Jerusalem" on the other side. (A.D. 134-8).

(bottom of page)
Assyrian ship on bas-relief from Sargon II's palace at Khorsabad. 8th century B.C. (Musée du Louvre, Paris)

Hebrew seal impression with a ship and the name of the owner, Oniahu, *which also means "a ship". 8th century B.C. (According to N. Avigad in Qadmoniot, XVI, 4, 1983)*

(Zech 5:5-11). Finally, it is stated in the Book of Daniel (1:2) that after the destruction of Jerusalem by Nebuchadnezzar, king of Babylon, the Temple treasures were removed and brought to Shinar. The land of Shinar, which comprises ancient Mesopotamia, may somehow be related etymologically to the indigenous term "summer" in Sumerian.

SHION (SHIHON) A town on the border of the territory allotted to Issachar when the land of Canaan was divided among the tribes (Josh 14:1; 19:19). It was between Haphraim and Anaharath and its location is unknown.

SHIPHI A man of the tribe of Simeon, son of Allon and father of Ziza who was leader of the tribe at the time of King Hezekiah.

SHIPHMITE Belonging to the Shupham-Shephupham family. Such was Zabdi, an official at the court of King David.

SHIPHRAH ("beautiful"). One of the two Hebrew midwives (along with Puah) who defied Pharaoh's decree that all males born to Hebrew women should be killed (Ex 1:15-21).

SHIPHTAN ("[the Lord] has judged"). A man of the tribe of Ephraim, father of Kemuel, who was appointed by the Lord to help Joshua divide up the land of Canaan among the Children of Israel.

SHIPS AND NAVIGATION As early as the middle of the 4th millennium B.C. the use of the sail was already known in Mesopotamia, and from about the 3rd millennium B.C. boats were sailing on the Nile. Small ships also sailed from Egypt along the Mediterranean coast as far as Byblos. In the 1st millennium B.C. the Phoenicians began to develop their naval might. At first they did not dare to take their small oar-propelled ships into deep waters, but later, when sails were in use, they made voyages as far as the west coast of Spain, north Africa and even to the southernmost part of England. In the Persian period seafaring became still more common and from the time of Alexander the Great occasional voyages were made to the western coast of India via the Red Sea. The Romans greatly improved all aspects of shipping.

According to the Bible the tribe of Zebulun was connected with seafaring activities (Gen 49:13). In Deborah's song, Dan and Asher were also seafarers (Judg 5:17). The close commercial relations between Israel and Tyre, which developed in the time of David, led to advances in Israelite shipping, which increased under Solomon with the foundation of the merchant navy at Ezion Geber (I Kgs 9:26). These ships were jointly operated by Israelite and Tyrian sailors (II Chr 9:21). After that nothing further is said in the Bible about Israelite naval enterprises, but Ezekiel (27:5-9) has a wonderful and detailed description of a Tyrian ship. An Egyptian relief at Medinet Habu, of the 12th century B.C., depicts Philistine ships. These were very shallow vessels, with a raised prow and stern to give better protection from the waves. The Philistine ships had one mast but no rudder. No Phoenician drawings of ships have yet come to light but Assyrian reliefs show that their ships, which were built by the Phoenicians, were tall vessels, with one high mast and an upper and a lower deck, the latter being used by the sailors while the former was reserved for passengers.

The conquest of the whole of the inhabited world by Rome and the institution of the *Pax Romana*, which permitted travel throughout the provinces of the Roman Empire, both helped in the development of navigation. Roman colonies were established in many of the provinces, while Syrian colonies were set up in various Italian ports. Against this background it is easy to understand how St. Paul was able to voyage between the different provinces of the Roman Empire. The Jews themselves took an active part in Mediterranean seaborne trade, following the conquest of Joppa by Alexander Jannaeus.

11:2; 14:1, 9.
Is 11:11. Dar
1:2. Zech 5:1

SHION
Josh 19:19

SHIPHI
I Chr 4:37

SHIPHMITE
I Chr 27:27

SHIPHRAH
Ex 1:15

SHIPHTAN
Num 34:24

The absence of a sextant, or its equivalent, by which the course of a ship could be accurately fixed, was a great disadvantage to ancient navigators. Similarly, the comparatively small size of the earliest ships and the primitive sails and rudders prevented them undertaking long voyages. At first sea crossings were limited to the summer months (i.e., March to October), when the waters were calm and visibility good (cf Acts 27:9). The ships sailed mainly close to the shore from port to port and in emergencies could find shelter in the lee of small promontories. When larger ships were built in the Roman period, long voyages became safer and more frequent. Sea traffic was no longer limited to the summer months, and instead of following the coastline, ships could sail direct from Alexandria to Italy. The Romans also cleared the seas of pirates, thereby greatly contributing to safer voyages. The speed of ships of the Roman period was not great; a freighter making good headway did not exceed 3-4 knots, thus taking eight days between Alexandria and Puteoli in Italy. In the Hellenistic period, but mainly from the time of Augustus, the eastern shores of the Mediterranean had excellent ports, the best in Judea being Acre (Acco), Caesarea and Joppa.

There were two types of ships in the Roman period: long, narrow and very fast vessels used mainly in war; and heavy broad craft, used as freighters and passenger ships. The freighters were built mainly of wood, with simple prows, and were not provided with battering-rams. The aft was raised high, inclining towards the center of the vessel. They had fixed masts and travelled mainly under sail, though long oars were also used. The early ships had one square sail close to the prow, but in imperial times two or three triangular sails were used. The capacity of these vessels was about 3 tons (3 metric tons approx.). The length of a freighter was up to 140 feet (43 m), its breadth 36 feet (11 m) and its depth 33 feet (10.5 m). Sea travel was in difficult and crowded conditions. The boat in which St. Paul was wrecked carried 276 people (Acts 27:37).

(left)
A sailing ship in stormy weather shown on a Roman sarcophagus. 3rd century.

Remains of a boat found in the Sea of Galilee, 1st century B.C. - 1st century A.D. (Israel Dept. of Antiquities and Museums)

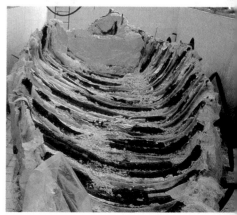

SHISHA Father of the scribes Elihoreph and Ahijah, officials at the court of King Solomon. An alternative form of Shavsha and Seraiah.

SHISHAK An Egyptian king (Sheshonk) the founder of the 22nd (Libyan) Dynasty that ruled over Egypt c. 945-924 B.C.

Shishak reigned at the time of King Solomon. Both kings shared an interest in developing trade with Byblos, and therefore soon became rivals for influence over the Phoenicians in general and the Byblites in particular. As no direct military action was feasible in the early days of

SHISHA
I Kgs 4:3

SHISHAK
I Kgs 11:40;
14:25. II Chr
12:2, 5, 7, 9

Fragment of an Egyptian stele found at Megiddo incised in hieroglyphs with the names and titles of Shishak (Sheshonk I). 10th century B.C.

(right)
Shishak (Sheshonk I) celebrates the conquest of Judah and Israel with raised hands before the god Amun. The captured cities are named in cartouches. From a relief of c.925 B.C. at Karnak.

Shishak's reign, he chose to support Solomon's opponent, offering asylum to Jeroboam II until the latter would return to Israel (I Kgs 11:40). Later, after Solomon's death, Shishak found the time ripe for a military move. He invaded Judah and Israel (II Chr chap. 12) destroying numerous towns (c. 925). Details of this expedition were discovered in a long and detailed inscription on the walls of Amon's temple in Karnak. Confirmation of details has been found in some of the sites mentioned in the inscription, where traces of severe destruction were identified in archeological excavations. A fragment of one of Shishak's triumphant inscriptions, uncovered at Megiddo, also illustrates this campaign.

SHITRAI A Sharonite official in the administration of King David.

SHITTIM

1. A town in the plains of Moab near the northeastern corner of the Dead Sea where the Israelites camped before crossing the Jordan (Num 25:1; Josh 2:1; 3:1). In this region Balaam attempted to curse the

SHITRAI
I Chr 27:29

SHITTIM 1
Num 25:1.
Josh 2:1; 3:1.
Mic 6:5

The lower course of the Kidron identified with the Valley of Shittim.

Israelite tribes (Num chaps. 22-23), and here they sinned with Moabite women and practised idolatry for which they were punished (Num 25:1-9).

2. The Valley of Shittim (Acacias in the NKJV) in Joel 3:18 may refer to a valley of acacia trees or to a valley in the lower course of the Kidron.

SHIZA A chief of the Reubenite tribe; father of Adina, one of David's "mighty men".

SHOA One of the Babylonian peoples, mentioned together with the Chaldeans, Pekod and Koa (Ezek 23:23). The identification of this people is unknown, as is the region where they lived. It may be a generic name for nomads.

SHOBAB

1. The second son of Caleb the son of Hezron by his wife Jerioth (though some, interpreting the text differently, explain that he was the son of Caleb's first wife Azubah).

2. One of the sons born to David in Jerusalem, probably by his wife Bathsheba.

SHOBACH, SHOPHACH The commander of the armies of the Aramean king Hadadezer; he was killed by David at the battle of Helam in Transjordania (II Sam 10:16, 18). In I Chronicles 19:16, 18 he is called Shophach.

SHOBAI A family of gatekeepers who returned from the Exile in Babylon with Zerubbabel.

SHOBAL The name of two or three biblical characters who are probably related.

1. Second son of Seir the Horite who lived in Edom; he had five sons.

2. Son of Hur and grandson of Caleb, father or founder of Kirjath Jearim; among his descendants were "Haroeh and half of the families of Manuhoth".

3. Fifth and youngest son of Judah; he was the father of Reaiah.

(Nos. 2 and 3 may very well be identical, with "Reaiah" an alternate form of Haroeh).

SHOBEK One of the leaders of the people who sealed the covenant of Ezra after the return of the exiles from Babylon.

SHOBI A son of Nahash, the king of the Ammonites deposed by David, and the brother of Hanun. When David fled from Absalom, Shobi, along with Ammiel from Lo Debar and Barzillai the Gileadite was among those men who welcomed the king at Mahanaim and saw to his needs and to those of his men.

SHOHAM ("precious stone"). A Merarite Levite, son of Jaaziah.

SHOMER ("[God is] a guardian").

1. The father of Jehozabad, who assassinated Joash king of Judah (II Kgs 12:21). The parallel passage in II Chronicles 24:26 gives the name of Jehozabad's mother as Shimrith.

2. An Asherite, descendant of Heber (I Chr 7:32). In Chronicles 7:34 he is called Shemer.

SHOPHACH See SHOBACH

SHOWBREAD (SHEWBREAD) A term used in the AV of the Bible for the twelve loaves displayed on the table that stood across from the lampstand in the tabernacle (Ex 40:24). They are referred to by different terms in different versions of the Bible: "bread of the presence", "the continual bread" and "bread of the arrangement". These twelve loaves, arranged in two rows of six (Lev 24:6) were probably symbolic of the twelve tribes of Israel (cf Ex 24:4; 28:9-10). The Kohathites were responsible for the preparation of the loaves (I Chr 9:32), but according to Leviticus 24:9 only the priests were allowed to eat them. Fresh loaves were brought into the sanctuary every Sabbath. The old ones were then consumed by the priests (Lev 24:5-9).

Frankincense accompanied the bread of the presence, but was offered separately as a "token offering" to the Lord (Lev 24:7; cf Lev 2:2).

In Solomon's Temple there were ten tables of the presence (II Chr 4:7-8). The bread of the presence is also mentioned in the account of David's request to Ahimelech, the priest of Nob, to give him the bread in order to feed his hungry men (I Sam 21:4-6).

The ritual bears resemblance to certain pagan "bread" offerings which were condemned by the prophets (Is 65:11; Jer 7:18). Parallels are also attested in Babylonian rituals. However, there is no indication that the showbread in the Israelite cult was either offered as "food" to God or used on the altar as a sacrifice.

SHUA
1. Daughter of Heber who was a grandson of Asher son of Jacob.
2. A Canaanite, father of the first wife of Judah, son of Jacob.

SHUAH Son of Abraham by Keturah. He is considered by some to be the forbear of the Shuhites, a tribe who may have lived in the region on the banks of the Euphrates.

SHUAL ("jackal"). Name of a biblical character and of a territory.
1. Third son of Zophah in the genealogy of the family of Asher.
2. During Saul's campaign against the Philistines, one of the three companies of the Philistines went "to the land of Shual", an area in the mountains of Ephraim with Ophrah in its center. Probably identical with the land of Shaalim mentioned in I Samuel 9:4.

SHUBAEL An alternate form of Shebuel.

SHUHAH Brother of Chelub of the tribe of Judah.

SHUHAM, SHUHAMITES Only son of Dan son of Jacob. He was the head of the Shuhamite family.

SHUHITE A native of Shuah; appellation of Bildad, one of the three friends of Job.

SHULAMITE A title appearing only once in the Bible (Song 6:13). It is usually interpreted as a variant form of "Shunammite" (q.v.) i.e., a woman from the town of Shunem. Some scholars, however, interpret it as the feminine form of Solomon (in Hebrew, *Shelomo*).

SHUMATHITE One of the family of Kirjath Jearim who were the forebears of "the Zorahites and Eshtaolites", probably connected with Shobal No.2.

SHUNAMMITE A native of Shunem, a border town in Issachar. Abishag, who ministered to David in his old age is called a Shunammite (I Kgs 1:3, 15; 2:17, 21-22). An unnamed woman who helped Elisha and was rewarded with a son is also referred to as Shunammite (II Kgs 4:12ff). When the son later died, Elisha prayed to God and the boy revived (II Kgs 4:33-35). See also SHUNEM.

SHUNEM A town in the territory of Issachar (Josh 19:18), near Mount Gilboa. It is mentioned in a list of Thutmosis III. A Philistine army

SHUA 1
I Chr 7:32

SHUA 2
Gen 38:2, 12.
I Chr 2:3

SHUAH
Gen 25:2. I
Chr 1:32

SHUAL 1
I Chr 7:36

SHUAL 2
I Sam 13:17

SHUBAEL
I Chr 24:20;
25:20

SHUHAH
I Chr 4:11

SHUHAM,
SHUHAMITES
Num 26:42-43

SHUHITE
Job 2:11; 8:1;
18:1; 25:1;
42:9

SHULAMITE
Song 6:13

SHUMATHITE
I Chr 2:53

SHUNAMMITE
I Kgs 1:3, 15;
2:17, 21-22.
II Kgs 4:12,
25, 36

SHUNEM
Josh 19:18.
I Sam 28:4.
II Kgs 4:8

Agate Ammonite seal and impression inscribed "[Belonging] to Shual [son of] Yeshayahu". 7th century B.C. (Israel Museum)

The village of Solem near the site of Shunem.

gathered at Shunem before the battle in which Saul was slain (I Sam 28:4). It was the birthplace of Abishag (I Kgs 1:3). Elisha lived for some time there and revived the son of the Shunammite woman (II Kgs 4:8-37). It was a small village in the Roman period. Identified with a small mound near the village of Solem.

SHUNI, SHUNITES Third son of Gad and father or founder of the Shunite family.

SHUPHAM, SHUPHAMITES Descendants of Benjamin; listed in the second census of Israel. Called Shephuphan in I Chronicles 8:5.

SHUPPIM

1. Descendant of Benjamin. Also written Shupham or Shephupham (Num 26:38).

2. Descendant of Merari, son of Levi, who was one of the guards of the western gates of the Temple.

SHUR The desert crossed by the Israelites on their way from the Red Sea. Hagar the Egyptian found refuge by a fountain on the way to Shur (Gen 16:7), and the sons of Ishmael dwelt between there and Havilah (Gen 25:18). Abraham lived for a time between Kadesh and Shur (Gen 20:1). Exodus (15:22) indicates that Shur was close to the Red Sea. Some scholars look for its location east of the Red Sea and the Bitter Lakes while others, who believe that the Israelites took a more northerly route, seek it closer to the Mediterranean.

SHUSHAN The capital of Elam; Shushu or Shushun in the Elamite kingdom, Susa in the Hellenistic period, today Shush in southwest

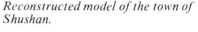

Reconstructed model of the town of Shushan.

Persia; on the River Karha. The city is mentioned in Babylonian documents of the 3rd millennium B.C. Its ruins extend over an area of about 400 acres (166.5ha), but it is estimated that the full extent of the city was about 1,800-2,300 acres (750-960ha). It was subdivided into four districts: a fortified mound which was the acropolis of the Achamaenids; a royal city with the palaces of Darius and his successors; and two quarters for artisans, merchants and others, the last occupying the right bank of the river. In the extensive excavations made at Shushan palaces and temples of the various periods have come to light.

Shushan is mentioned in the Bible in connection with various events such as the scene of the Book of Esther and of Daniel's imprisonment. Settlers from Shushan were transferred to northern Israel by Osnapper (Asshurbanipal) (Ezra 4:9-10).

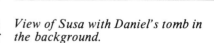

View of Susa with Daniel's tomb in the background.

*(left)
Aerial view of the ancient mound of Susa (Shushan) in the plain of modern Khuzistan.*

SHUTHELAH, SHUTHALHITE (SHUTHELAHITE)

1. Firstborn son of Ephraim, father of Bered, and founder of the family of the Shulthalhite; he was killed by the men of Gath (I Chr 7:20-21).

2. Son of Zabad, a descendant of Shuthelah No.1; he was also killed by the men of Gath. It has been suggested that he is identical with No.1.

SIA, SIAHA One of the Nethinim (Temple servants) who returned from Exile in Babylon during the time of Ezra and Nehemiah (Neh 7:47). In the Book of Ezra he is referred to as Siaha (Ezra 2:44).

SIBBECHAI One of David's thirty "mighty men", he slew Saph (or Sippai) the Philistine giant (I Chr 20:4). When David became king in Jerusalem, Sibbechai was made captain of the eighth monthly course of the king's servants (I Chr 27:11).

SIBMAH See SHEBAM

SIBRAIM A place on the border of the land of Canaan "between the border of Damascus and the border of Hamath".

SIDDIM, VALLEY OF The valley which was the scene of the battle between Chedorlaomer's coalition and the alliance headed by the kings of Sodom and Gomorrah (Gen 14:3, 8, 10). In verse 3 the Valley of Siddim is identified with the Salt Sea, and according to biblical tradition it was submerged when Sodom and Gomorrah were destroyed. The reference to "asphalt pits" in verse 10 hints at the location of the Valley of Siddim in the flat country to the south of the Dead Sea where bitumen was collected and shipped to Egypt, for use in embalming.

SHUTHELAH, SHUTHALHITE 1
Num 26:35-3
I Chr 7:20

SHUTHELAH, SHUTHALHITE 2
I Chr 7:21

SIA, SIAHA
Ezra 2:44.
Neh 7:47

SIBBECHAI
II Sam 21:18.
I Chr 11:29;
20:4; 27:11

SIBMAH
Josh 13:19. Is
16:8-9. Jer
48:32

SIBRAIM
Ezek 47:16

SIDDIM, VALLEY OF
Gen 14:3, 8,
10

(bottom of page)
A coin of Sidon struck under Abdastart in the 4th century B.C.

The Valley of Siddim, south of the Dead Sea.

SIDON, SIDONIANS

1. The firstborn son of Canaan, the progenitor of the Sidonians.

2. One of the most ancient Phoenician cities, situated in the narrow fertile plain between the mountains of Lebanon and the Mediterranean 25 miles (40km) north of Tyre with which it had a close relationship and a frequent rivalry. Lying at the northern end of the plain, it was fortified by a strong wall, and had two harbors defended by a few small islands and a breakwater. Sidon is mentioned in the Babylonian sources of the late 3rd millennium. In Genesis (10:19) Sidon is referred to as the border of Canaan, and in Joshua (11:8) it is described as Greater Sidon.

Sidon was the first Phoenician city to send ships on to the open seas, and its navigators could find their way at night by the stars. The Sidonians were the first people in their region to establish contacts with the Greeks; they are mentioned several times by Homer. Sidon was

SIDON, SIDONIANS 1
Gen 10:15

SIDON, SIDONIANS 2
Gen 10:1, 19;
49:13. Deut
3:9. Josh 11:8;
13:4, 6; 19:28.
Judg 1:31; 3:3;
10:6, 12; 18:7,
28. II Sam
24:6. I Kgs
5:6; 11:1, 5,
33; 16:31;
17:9. II Kgs

3:13. I Chr
:13; 22:4.
Ezra 3:7. Is
3:2, 4, 12.
er 25:22;
7:3; 47:4.
Ezek 27:8;
8:21-22;
2:30. Joel
:4. Zech 9:2.
Matt 11:21-22;
5:21. Mark
:8; 7:24, 31.
Luke 4:26;
6:17; 10:13-14.
Acts 12:20;
27:3

famous at an early period for its artisans, its gold and silver, its coppersmiths and its weavers, who also undertook embroidery and dyeing. In the Hellenistic period it became one of the largest centers of glass production.

Sidon, like other Phoenician cities, was ruled by kings, and their sovereignty soon extended over the cities to the south of it. The Sidonians built Laish (Dan), but the Danites set it on fire (Judg 18:7, 27). The Sidonians also founded many commercial colonies along the shores of the Mediterranean.

The independence of Sidon was curtailed when the kings of Egypt conquered Palestine and Syria (16th-13th centuries B.C.), but the kings of Sidon were left free to administer their realm as long as tribute was paid. In the middle of the 12th century B.C. the city was destroyed and its inhabitants fled to Tyre, where they helped in the development of that city. But Sidon soon recovered from this crisis and it seems that it was at that time that the Sidonians exerted pressure over the Israelites (Judg 10:12).

With the rise of Assyria Sidon was subdued along with the other Phoenician towns, and was also required to pay tribute. Ahab, king of Israel, married Jezebel, daughter of Ethbaal, king of the Sidonians, who introduced her native cults into Israel. The Assyrian rulers Shalmaneser VI, Sennacherib and Esarhaddon conducted numerous campaigns to subdue Sidon. Nebuchadnezzar conquered Sidon on his way to Judah: during his siege half of the inhabitants of the city died of plague. After the fall of Babylon Sidon revived, however, and under Persian protection its domain extended over the Plain of Sharon, from Mount Carmel to Joppa.

Sidon was destroyed when it rebelled during the reign of Artaxerxes III (352 B.C.). When Alexander the Great besieged and conquered Tyre Sidon willingly opened its gates and benefited greatly from the fall of its rival. After Alexander's death the town was held by the Ptolemies of Egypt, but in 198 B.C. it was conquered by the Seleucids of Syria. In 64 B.C. Sidon was taken by Pompey, who acknowledged its autonomy and granted it the right to mint coins.

A view of Sidon today.

Jesus traveled through the region of Sidon and cured the daughter of a Syro-Phoenician woman who showed faith in him (Matt 15:21-28; Mark 7:24-30). On his way to Rome as a prisoner Paul was allowed to visit his friends in the city (Acts 27:1, 3).

SIHON King of the Amorites who ruled east of the Jordan, from the Arnon River northwards (Num chap. 21). Israel, led by Moses, fought against him and seized all his land after he would neither let them pass through his country, nor sell them water and food (Deut 2:28-30). Later, the tribes of Reuben and Gad settled in his territory (Deut 3:12; Josh 13:8, 10).

SIHON
Num 21:21, 23, 26-29, 34. 32:33. Deut 1:4; 2:24, 26, 30-32; 3:2, 6; 4:46; 29:7; 31:4. Josh 2:10; 9:10; 12:2, 5; 13:10 21, 27. Judg 11:19-21. I Kgs 4:19. Neh 9:22. Ps 135:11; 136:19. Jer 48:45

Region of the Arnon River to which point Sihon, king of the Amorites at one time extended his kingdom.

Sihon's defeat is mentioned in order to strengthen the spirits of Israel (Josh 2:10), and also in prayers, in praising the might of God and thanking him (Ps 135:11; 136:19; Neh 9:22).

In the Book of Judges, Jephthah recalls Sihon's conquest of Moab in his argument with the king of Ammon (Judg chap. 11).

SIHOR See SHIHOR

SIKKUTH A pagan deity mentioned in Amos when the prophet chastises the Israelites for worshiping false gods.

SILAS A leading member of the first Christian community in Jerusalem and a colleague of Paul. In the epistles he is called by a Roman name, Silvanus (II Cor 1:19; I Thes 1:1); he may have been a Roman citizen (Acts 16:37). In Jerusalem he was a prophet who preached and admonished (Acts 15:32) and was sent to Antioch, together with Paul, Barnabas and Judas, to convey the resolutions adopted at the council of Jerusalem (Acts 15:22).

After a disagreement between Paul and Barnabas, Paul selected Silas to be his companion on his second missionary journey (Acts 15:40; 18:23) and Silas accompanied him through Galatia. In Philippi Paul and Silas were cast into prison because "they teach customs which are not lawful for us, being Romans, to receive or observe." (Acts 16:21).

Silas and Timothy stayed in Berea when Paul continued alone to Athens (Acts 17:14) but Silas rejoined him in Corinth (Acts 18:1-5).

Paul's Epistles to the Thessalonians were also sent in the name of Timothy (I Thes 1:1; II Thes 1:1). The last verses of the Epistle of Peter indicate that the letter was sent through Silas.

SIHOR
Josh 13:3. Jer 2:18

SIKKUTH
Amos 5:26

SILAS
Acts 15:22, 27, 32, 34, 40; 16:19, 25, 29; 17:4, 10, 14-15; 18:5

SILLA A place in Jerusalem by the Millo (where Joash king of Judah was killed). It is mentioned only once and nothing further is known about it.

SILOAM See SHILOAH

SILVANUS See SILVUS

SIMEON ("[God] has heard").

1. The second son of Jacob and Leah and the founder of the tribe of Simeon. The name comes from the Hebrew word *shema* "to hear", and was given to her son by Leah "because the Lord has heard that I am unloved" (Gen 29:33).

When the ten sons of Jacob went down to Egypt from Canaan to buy corn during the famine, Simeon was imprisoned by Joseph as a guarantee that Benjamin, Joseph's younger brother, would be brought to him (Gen 42:19, 24; 43:23).

Genesis chapter 34 relates how Simeon and Levi massacred the inhabitants of Shechem because their sister Dinah had been raped by Shechem the son of Hamor, a prince of that city. Jacob rebuked them for their murderous deed and sharply criticized them in his last words before his death (Gen 49:5-6).

The territory of the tribe of Simeon was in the south of Judah, with Beersheba listed among the principal cities of the area (Josh 19:1-9; I Chr 4:24-33).

In Deuteronomy 27:12 Simeon led those tribes which pronounced the blessing on Mount Gerizim. However, the tribe of Simeon is excluded from Moses' final blessing (Deut chap. 33), possibly because of its having been absorbed into the large territory of Judah. Nevertheless the tribe retained its own identity and genealogical ties, as well as embarking on independent expansions of tribal territory (I Chr 4:24-43).

In Revelation 7:7 Simeon is among the tribes who are promised a seal of God in order to protect them from the damage foreseen in the prophecy.

2. An ancestor of Jesus, mentioned in the genealogy given by Luke.

3. An ancestor or teacher, also called Niger, who was teaching in the community of Antioch when it was visited by Paul and Barnabas.

4. See PETER SIMON.

5. A just and devout man (Luke 2:25), who was in the Temple in Jerusalem when Joseph and Mary brought the infant Jesus. According to Jewish law, a father has to redeem his firstborn son, a ceremony performed by a priest. While they were presenting their son to the priest and bringing the sacrifice after Mary's period of purification (cf Lev 12:8), Simeon saw them and took Jesus in his arms, praising God.

The Holy Spirit had previously revealed to Simeon that he would see the messiah before his death (Luke 2:26). Simeon recognized in the child a light that would be a revelation to the Gentiles and a glory for his people, Israel (Luke 2:32). Praising God and blessing the parents with their child, Simeon knew that he could now die in peace. Simeon's words found their way into the Christian liturgy under the name "Nunc Dimittis".

SIMEONITES See SIMEON No.1

SIMON ("[God] has heard").

1. See PETER SIMON.

2. Simon the zealot. One of the twelve apostles of Jesus; he received the authority to cast out unclean spirits and to heal every kind of ailment and disease (Matt 10:1-4; Mark 3:14-18; Luke 6:15). Simon was a member of the Zealot party, Jewish nationalists willing to resort to violence against Roman rule rather than violate the Torah. Mark (3:18)

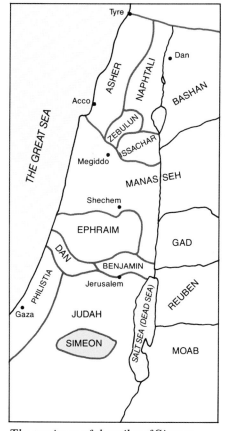

The territory of the tribe of Simeon.

The house traditionally said to be that of Simon the tanner in the old city of Jaffa (Joppa).

calls Simon "the Cananean", (sometime incorrectly translated as "Canaanite"), the Aramaic term for Zealot, but as Greek readers would not have associated Cananean with Zealot, the evangelist was avoiding any association between Jesus' disciples and the Zealots. Some Christians found it hard to accept that a Jewish nationalist and militant patriot could be among the disciples of Jesus, whose kingdom, they believed, was not of this world and would certainly not come through man's power or violence. | Luke 6:15. Acts 1:13.

3. One of the brothers (or kinsmen) of Jesus, according to the Gospels of Matthew and Mark. | SIMON 3 Matt 13:55. Mark 6:3

4. Simon the leper, Jesus' host in Bethany. It was in his home, a few days before Passover, that a woman washed Jesus' feet and anointed his head with oil (Matt 26:2-7; Mark 14:1-3). Some scholars suggest that Simon invited Jesus to his home after being healed by him. | SIMON 4 Matt 26:6. Mark 14:3

5. Simon of Cyrene. A Jew who was pressed by the Romans into helping Jesus to carry the cross to Calvary (Matt 27:32; Mark 15:21; Luke 23:26). According to the Gospel of Mark, Simon, a native of Cyrene in North Africa, was the father of Alexander and Rufus who became Christians. It was not uncommon for the Roman ruler to order pilgrims to carry out certain services, sometimes connected with keeping order among the people, especially during the festival seasons. | SIMON 5 Matt 27:32. Mark 15:21. Luke 23:26

6. A Pharisee who invited Jesus to eat with him. During the meal, a woman who had been living an immoral life entered the room and anointed Jesus' feet. Simon failed to understand how Jesus could permit her to act in this way and in response Jesus told a parable to show that one should be willing to forgive repentant sinners (Luke 7:36-50). | SIMON 6 Luke 7:40, 43-44

7. Father of Judas, the disciple who betrayed Jesus. | SIMON 7 John 6:71; 12:4; 13:2, 26

8. Simon the tanner. A Christian of Joppa (modern Jaffa) in whose house by the sea Peter lodged for some time (Acts 9:43). Here Peter received messengers from the Roman centurion Cornelius, who had been instructed in a vision to send for a man named Simon, lodging with Simon, the tanner in Joppa (10:1-8). | SIMON 8 Acts 9:43; 10:6, 17, 32

According to an ancient tradition, the house of Simon the tanner is located in Jaffa, close to the monastery of St. Peter.

9. Simon the magician (Simon Magus). A man who practiced magic, to the amazement of the natives of Samaria who came to regard him as "the great power" (Acts 8:10). Simon was converted to Christianity by the preaching of Philip, whom he joined in evangelistic activities (Acts 8:9-13). When Peter and John were sent from Jerusalem to Samaria, they prayed for the local people "that they might receive the Holy Spirit" (8:15). Observing that the Holy Spirit was conveyed through the laying on of the apostle's hands, Simon offered them money in order to acquire the same power (8:18-19) (hence the term "simony"). In response Peter castigated him so severely that Simon begged him to pray to God to avert the threatened punishment (8:20-24). | SIMON 9 Acts 8:9, 13, 18, 24

SIN A city in northern Egypt, mentioned in Ezekiel 30:15-16 (Sun in Egyptian, translated as Pelusium in some versions). Two demotic documents refer to it as the northern extremity of the land of Egypt. The city is identified with el-Farama, at northeastern edge of the Delta, close to the embouchure of the Pelusiac arm of the Nile, $1\frac{1}{2}$ miles (2.5 km) from the Mediterranean. As its name implies (Sun means fortress), it fulfilled an important strategic role from early times. | SIN Ezek 30:15-16

SIN The general concept of sin derives from the fact that the entire Law is from God, imposed upon his covenanted people, so that any infraction is automatically an offense against God.

The OT contains about 30 different words referring to sin, and they are frequently employed with different shades of meaning. The following are three of the main terms: (a) *Het*, the most common word for sin. In its various verbal and noun forms it is found almost 600 times in the OT. The strict translation of *het* is a "missing of the mark". While sin is a missing of the mark from the ideal of perfection, it also contains the idea of moral responsibility. The term often refers to sin in a general way, without specifying the particular nature of the wrong committed; but at times the word does relate to a particular offense such as idolatry. It is the term most used for ritual sins, and the only word which describes an unwitting sin. (b) The second main term is *avon*, usually translated "iniquity". In its verbal form the word means to make "perverse" or "crooked" and it frequently refers to wrongdoing against one's fellow man. (c) *Pesha*, meaning "to break away", "to rebel", implying a willful departure from God's authority.

Although there are many more terms to describe and condemn a large variety of wrongs, it is possible to view the whole range of sins in the OT under the above three key words. In the first place, every sin is "a missing of the mark" in its failure to keep to the right path (*het*). Secondly, it is an act inherently wrong in that it twists or deviates from the norm (*avon*). It is, further, an act of rebellion against the divine lawgiver (*pesha*). OT writers, however, were by no means consistent in their usage of these terms, which were frequently interchangeable.

An examination of the OT's theology of sin can provide a number of pointers as to its distinctive character. The first touches upon the difference in the doctrine of original sin, between normative biblical Judaism and classical Christianity. The OT neither mentions nor reflects the idea of original sin whereby Adam's sin in disobeying God makes all his descendants predestined to sin. Cain's sin is not traced back to his father. The generation of the Flood is decribed as wholly evil without reference to Adam. The prophets preach against the sins of their contemporaries with no relevant mention of Adam's sin to suggest any connection to his fall or to a belief in original sin.

Admittedly, the OT accepts as a fact that man has a tendency to sin (Gen 6:5; 8:21), and even acknowledges its universality (I Kgs 8:46 and especially Ecc 7:20). But this is very different from the doctrine which holds that man has a destiny to sin.

On the other hand, there is a very heavy emphasis on human freedom (Deut 11:26-28; 28:1, 15; 30:15, 19). With all the weaknesses inherent in human nature, the power of free will still makes it possible to overcome temptation and the sinful element within oneself (Gen 4:7). So central is this concept of the freedom to overcome sin, that in the apparently deterministic texts of the Exodus story (Ex chaps. 3-12) where God is initially depicted as hardening Pharaoh's heart, it is later recorded that Pharaoh himself hardened his own heart. Only after he had several opportunities to repent did God influence his behavior. In other words, Pharaoh's own continual obstinacy molded his hard character.

In brief, the origin of sin is in man himself. He has the freedom to choose, and he carries with him the responsibility of that choice.

Several lines of theological development can be seen in the OT. The non-prophetic concept of sin makes no apparent distinction between ritual sins, and offenses against the moral code. The prophets, however, emphasized transgressions of the moral law (see for example Is 1:10-17; 58:3-7; Hos 4:1; 6:6; Mic 6:6-8).

Another development is the shift from collective, to individual responsibility. Initially, a person, albeit innocent, could be swept away in the guilt of his community (Gen 19:15; Ex 20:5; 34:7; Num 14:18; Deut 5:9; Josh chap. 7). The doctrine finds clear expression in II Samuel

21:5ff and II Kings 5:27. In some cases the punishment was delayed to future generations, but that still left innocent people to carry the burden of punishment for the guilt of others. The old teaching that the sins of the fathers were visited on innocent successors was, however, repudiated by a different doctrine which placed the emphasis on individual responsibility (Deut 24:16; II Kgs 14:6; Jer 31:29-30; Ezek 18:2-9; 33:12).

A third line of development can be seen in the relationship between suffering and sin. The dominant theological concept interprets suffering as the necessary punishment of God for a previous sin (Num 11:33; 14:37; Josh 7:5; II Sam 21:1). This same belief was reiterated by Job's comforters to explain his suffering. The book, however, vindicates Job, and in declaring his innocence, breaks the nexus between suffering and sin.

Perhaps the most important line of development is found in the change from sin as a formal breach of the law to the more spiritual teaching which embraces the psychological dimensions of sin by showing it to be a subjective feeling of guilt experienced in man's sensitive conscience. This is the profound religious meaning of sin as an offense "against the soul" (cf Hab 2:10) where sin becomes that which disturbs man's spiritual equilibrium and causes his alienation from God (Job 5:6; 18:5-21; 20:4-29; Ps 38:3; Is 48:22; 57:21). Sin is the obverse of the holy which cuts man off from God.

In OT theology, sin's evil outcome is the sinner's alienation from God and the inner unhappiness which it brings. But sin can be remedied and the sinner can become whole again through an act of sincere repentance. This alone can bring about the sinner's atonement with God.

The various terms used in the Christian as well as the Hebrew Scriptures to describe sin, share a common element in that sin represents a rupture of a relationship of trust to God. Whether humans rebel against God by questioning his commandment or by consistently falling below their calling as creatures of the Divine Father, the net result is the same. The God, who led his people from chaos to order, or from captivity to freedom, finds them in rebellion against him and refusing to live in comformity with his will.

The Israelites stand out with the variegated vocabulary they developed regarding violation of a covenant with God. But their main interest was with cures, not with diagnoses. In this, early Christian literature followed the piety of Judaism. More effort was put into praising God for the release from sin than in lamenting the pitiful plight of humans. This is most clearly illustrated by the Qumran sect with its rich confessional literature and its highly developed ways of accountability, confession and of lamenting failures, and also of release. Unlike either Judaism or Christianity, Greco-Roman religions did not stress the forgiveness of sins. John the Baptist is described in NT literature as being concerned with such forgiveness (Mark 1:4; Luke 3:3), and even kings were not excluded from his judgment (Mark 6:18). The response of the common people, however, indicates the particular need they felt for the release from the weight of guilt, a release to be attained by a clear denunciation of wrongdoing. The Greek word meaning to miss the mark which — following the Hebrew — became central in the Christian definition of sin, was not used with any depth in Greco-Roman religions which rather assumed that ignorance, the human failure familiar at first hand to all, could be overcome by insight or learning.

Consistent with the Jewish approach, Jesus generally dealt with sin directly, on a one-to-one basis; perceiving sickness as a manifestation of sin, he healed and forgave simultaneously (Mark 2:5, 9-11). He dismissed people with the words, "your faith has made you well. Go in peace" (Mark 5:34), or proclaimed: "your sins are forgiven" (Mark 2:5). It was this direct declaration which created difficulties for him, even more so when he delegated this same authority to his disciples who had scarcely showed themselves as being equal to such responsibility (Matt 16:19; 18:18; Luke 17:4; John 20:23).

It is important to observe that Jesus did not try to intensify people's sense of failure and of sin. He presented God as a loving father who will accept the prodigal son even after he has lived a life of squalor (Luke 15:32); to a woman being tried for adultery, Jesus said, "Has no one condemned you?... Neither do I condemn you; go and sin no more" (John 8:10-11). Refusing to choose between the integrity of the law and the release of the sinner, Jesus used the law to assist the sinner in finding a new perspective and a new orientation in life.

Paul's writings are marked by the lack of any confession of sins. He does not appear familiar with the Lord's prayer; the petition: "forgive us our debts as we forgive our debtors" (Matt 6:12), seems to have played a very slight role in his life. As a devout Jew, Paul probably believed that God is merciful and that there are better things to do with one's life than wade in guilt or self-examination (I Cor 4:1-4; but compare I Cor 15:9; I Tim 1:15). That does not mean that Paul was not acutely aware of the power of sin over one's life. He wrote graphically about the power of sin to distort and twist human conduct, and the consequent wrath of God (Rom 1:18-32). It is also clear that before he became "in Christ" he had first-hand knowledge of the power of sin for it "killed me" (Rom 7:11) and he was in fact "sold under sin" (Rom 7:15). He experienced the power of sin so acutely that "the law of sin... is in my members" (Rom 7:23; cf 7:25; 8:2). Whatever that may refer to, it is clear that Paul sees the new normative element in Christ as a victory over the crippling effects of sin with its attendant guilt. Hence his vigorous rejection of the notion that one may sin in order that grace might abound (Rom 6:1-2) or that any justification or excuse can be offered to continue to live in sin (Rom 6:15); it is simply inconsistent with the confession that Jesus is Lord.

The Johannine writings also have a profound view of sin as the almost metaphysical power which invades human existence (I John 1:8-10). At the same time they agree with others in the early Christian community in seeing sin fundamentally as a defiance of God's commandments (I John chap. 2) and a refusal to love God and one's neighbor. More important than a definition of sin, however, is the release provided in Christ and the invitation to live in that freedom, like those who have been washed "white in the blood of the Lamb" (Rev 7:14) and can now afford to live under the sovereignty of the Lord of Lords and the King of Kings (Rev 1:5; 5:9).

Throughout the NT there is agreement that human responsibility and sin go hand in hand. One cannot speak of sin, unless one speaks of a basic covenantal relationship in which God has freed his people and given them a path to follow. Hebrew and Christian scriptures jointly affirm that sin is to be viewed as a power from which we are released — its threat to our existence has been greatly diminished for God's intervention in history delivers us from it.

SIN, WILDERNESS OF See ZIN

SINAI A large peninsula lying between Egypt and Palestine. Triangular in shape, bordered by the two arms of the Red Sea, the Gulf of Elath on the east and the Gulf of Suez on the west, it was the scene of some of the most important events in the history of the Israelites. The northern part

The Sinai Peninsula.

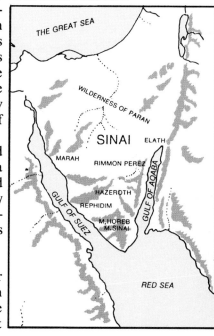

On the left, some three thousand steps leading up to the summit of Jebel Musa, "The Mount of Moses" in the heart of the ragged range in southern Sinai, on the right.

An hieroglyphic inscription in southern Sinai, where turquoise and copper mines were exploited, relates the story of a Semitic slave being beaten by an Egyptian official.

of the peninsula is a sandy plateau with low hills, while the southern part consists of granite mountains, reaching to a height of 8,660 feet (c. 2,650 m). The climate is that of a desert — dry, with an annual rainfall that does not exceed $2\frac{1}{2}$ inches (60 mm) in the north and $1\frac{1}{2}$ inches (40 mm) in the south. Springs are few, and the two larger ones produced the oasis of Kadesh Barnea (Num 20:1-14). Sinai was therefore the habitat of nomads, who found some pasture in the valleys, though agriculture was never practiced there.

In addition to the trade routes that crossed Sinai from very early times, the turquoise mines in the southern mountainous part of the peninsula were also of great importance. They were exploited as early as the 1st Dynasty of Egypt (early 3rd millennium B.C.). The ancient port through which the minerals were exported to Egypt was discovered 5 miles (8km) south of Abu Zneima. It seems that the laborers in the mines were captives brought from Palestine and Syria, against which Egypt directed many campaigns.

Sinai is the only land bridge connecting Egypt with Palestine, Syria and Mesopotamia. It was traversed by several important routes from east to west, most of which passed through the northern part of the peninsula. Another road went along the western coast, turning to the north, to reach Elath. There was also a short cut from the western coast through Wadi Feiran to Dahab, probably biblical Dizahab.

In the Bible the name Sinai refers to a specific mountain (Ps 68:8); to a range of mountains (Deut 33:2; Judg 5:5) and to a desert or wilderness (Ex 19:2). The same mountain is sometimes called Horeb (I Kgs 19:8), and Mount Horeb is also referred to as the "mountain of God" (Ex 3:1) and sometimes just "the mountain" (Ex 19:2-3).

Even in early times the patriarchs were crossing Sinai on their way to Egypt and back to the land of Canaan. It was in this wilderness that the Israelites sojourned 40 years, and that Moses gave them the Law. The stations on the route of the Exodus are listed in Numbers (chap. 33). Only a few of these stations can now be identified and these very hesitantly. Kadesh Barnea, however, can be identified with more certainty, because of its large spring, which is big enough to supply a great multitude (Deut 1:46). The identification of Mount Sinai is also doubtful. See EXODUS, ROUTE OF.

31:18; 34:2, 4, 29, 32. Lev 7:38; 25:1; 26:46; 27:34. Num 1:1, 19; 3:1, 4, 14; 9:1, 5; 10:12; 26:64; 28:6; 33:15-16. Deut 33:2. Judg 5:5. Neh 9:13. Ps 68:8, 17. Acts 7:30, 38. Gal 4:24-25

SINIM, LAND OF A city in Upper Egypt, on the eastern bank of the Nile, north of the first cataract, opposite the island of Elephantine. Its Egyptian name was Suner, but it is mentioned in Isaiah 49:12 as "land of Sinim" and in Ezekiel 29:10; 30:6 as Syene.

The importance of this city lies in its location on the southern border of Egypt, facing Nubia. The expression in Ezekiel "from the tower (*migdal* in Hebrew) to Syene as far as the border of Ethiopia" apparently means: from Migdol at Egypt's northeastern border to Syene at its southern extremity. Syene is hardly mentioned in Egyptian documents until the Persian period, when it became the site of a fortress whose garrison included Jewish soldiers.

View of Syene, identified with Aswan.

SINITE A family descended from Canaan, the youngest son of Ham, second son of Noah.

SION A name mentioned only once, in Deuteronomy 4:48, where it refers to Mount Hermon.

SIPHMOTH A city in the Negeb in the territory of Judah. Its population helped David before his ascent to the throne.

SIPPAI One of the sons of the giants killed by Sibbechai the Hushathite, one of David's thirty "mighty men". His name is also spelled Saph (II Sam 21:18).

SIRACH See ECCLESIASTICUS

SIRAH ("cistern"). The place where Abner rested having made his peace with David (II Sam 3:21). He was found there by the messengers of Joab who brought him back to Hebron where Joab killed him (II Sam 3:27). Perhaps Ain Sarah, 1 mile (1.6 km) to the north of Hebron.

SIRION The Sidonian name of Mount Hermon; maybe a name for the Anti-Lebanon mountain range.

SISERA

1. Commander of the Canaanite forces defeated at the Brook Kishon in the time of the Judges. Sisera subjugated Israel for 20 years, until an Israelite army under Barak and Deborah succeeded in putting the Canaanites to flight, aided perhaps by a sudden flood of the Kishon, "by the waters of Megiddo" (Judg 5:19, 21). Sisera, whose chariot force numbered 900, escaped on foot to the encampment of his Kenite ally Heber. The latter's wife Jael concealed Sisera in her tent and subsequently assassinated him. The events surrounding the story of Sisera are preserved in both a pure narrative, Judges chapter 4, and the poetic Song of Deborah, Judges chapter 5.

Two traditions of Sisera's death have been preserved in these chapters. In Judges chapter 4, Sisera falls asleep, and Jael drives a tent peg through his head and into the ground (4:18-21). In Judges 5:26-27, Sisera is in a more upright position when he is struck, and then sinks to the ground dead. Some scholars have suggested that the writer of the prose account (Judg chap. 4) misunderstood the poetic parallelism of Judges chapter 5, or that possible sexual allusions in Judges chapter 5 were eliminated to produce the account in Judges chapter 4.

The defeat of Sisera at the head of the last major Canaanite force marked an important milestone in the process of the Israelite occupation of Canaan.

Sisera's base was Harosheth Hagoyim. His name, which is not Semitic, may be related in origin to one of the Sea Peoples.

2. The head of a family of Nethinim (Temple servants) who returned from the Babylonian Exile with Zerubbabel.

SISMAI (SISAMAI) Son of Eleasah and father of Shallum in the genealogy of Jerahmeel.

SITNAH One of the wells dug by the slaves of Isaac while he lived in Gerar. The name denoting denunciation and hatred, was given to the well because of the constant clashes between the herdsmen of Gerar and those of Isaac.

SIVAN The third month of the Hebrew calendar; the name only occurs once, in the Book of Esther. See CALENDAR.

SLAVERY An accepted social institution in the ancient world when it did not necessarily mean servitude for life. A distinction was made in Israelite law between Hebrew and alien slaves. The Hebrew slave was not forced to serve for more than six years, but if his wife had been given to him by the master, she and the children born to him had to remain with the master if the slave chose to go free (Ex 21:2-4).

There were a number of ways by which a Hebrew could fall into bondage, the most frequent being his inability to pay a debt (Lev 25:39, 47). Selling children was also legal (Ex 21:7; II Kgs 4:1; etc.). If poverty was the reason for servitude the slave had to be treated not as a bondsman but as a hired servant, and was to serve until the year of the jubilee (Lev 25:39-40). But when a girl was sold as a maidservant she had to remain with her owner (Ex 21:7). A thief could be sold to make restitution for the damage he had caused (Ex 22:3). If a Hebrew were sold to a stranger his brethren had to redeem him (Lev 25:47-48), and the same applied to Hebrew prisoners of war (Neh 5:8). The servitude of a Hebrew slave did not bring about any change in his social and personal status: after completing his term he was free to go to his own house. Moreover, it was the duty of his master to furnish him liberally from his own flock, and with grain and wine and "you shall remember that you were a slave in the land of Egypt, and the Lord your God redeemed you" (Deut 15:14-15). In certain cases where a slave preferred to stay with his master and his wife and children, the servitude did not last longer than the coming jubilee, when he was able to return to his land, which would be released to him (Lev 25:54).

Some slaves reached positions of eminence, examples being Eliezer, Abraham's slave (Gen 24:21), and Joseph (Gen 39:4). In some cases the master's daughter could be given to a slave (I Chr 2:34-35). A slave was allowed to acquire possessions of his own, including other slaves (II Sam 9:8-9), and to use the income in order to redeem himself (Lev 25:49-51). A master was allowed to strike a slave, but cruelty was punished (Ex 21:20, but see v.21). According to Deuteronomy (23:15) a fugitive slave was not to be handed back to his owner. The provisions for manumission were different for non-Hebrew slaves, who were mainly prisoners of war or women taken as concubines for their masters or their sons (Gen 34:29; Num 31:9; Deut 21:10-14).

After the conquest of Canaan by the Israelites a different kind of servitude emerged. Some Israelite tribes paid tribute, in most cases in

Male and female slaves shown on an Egyptian wall painting.

the form of forced labor; thus Issachar became "a band of slaves" (Gen 49:14-15). However, the references are generally to slaves of other nations (Deut 20:10-15; Josh 16:10, etc.). This system of servitude developed still further in the time of Solomon, during whose reign the greatly increased building activities called for enormous numbers of laborers, so that all that was left of the non-Israelite population came under bondage (I Kgs 9:21-22); and the male Israelites had to serve three months a year as well (I Kgs 5:13-14). The term "servant of Solomon" for this kind of servitude was still in use at the time of the return from Babylon (Ezra 2:58; Neh 7:57, 60). Associated with these servants were the Nethinim, some kind of public slaves (Ezra 2:58; Neh 7:60; 11:3). Similar were the Gibeonites, who became "woodcutters and water carriers for the house of my God" (Josh 9:23).

From Persian to Byzantine times slavery was still legally recognized. The Mishnah and the Talmud refer to all foreign slaves as Canaanite bondsmen. Slaves who were circumcised enjoyed many of the privileges of Jewish society, but they were not allowed to acquire property. Nor could they intermarry with foreign slaves and maidservants. Many Jews were sold into slavery after the destruction of the Second Temple, but they were quickly freed. A synagogue of Freedmen is referred to in Acts 6:9.

Many figures in the NT were either slaves, like Onesimus (Philem vs. 8-16), or were of servile background. The presence of slaves in the world and in the church is generally taken for granted in the NT. The ethical teaching of the early church toward slaves echoes in large measure the growing egalitarianism voiced by the Stoics and gradually reflected in Roman imperial legislation, partly under Christian influence. The NT urges the acceptance of the slave as a brother (Philem v. 16), recognizing that in Christ slave and free are one, as a result of dying and rising with Christ in baptism unto newness of life (I Cor 12:13; Gal 3:28; Col 3:11). Slaves are not to be abused (Eph 6:9), but to be treated with equality and fairness (Col 4:1). Revelation 18:13 decries the inhumanity of the slave trade and I Timothy 1:9-10 classifies slave-kidnapers among the "unholy and profane".

Slaves were so much a part of ancient life (some estimates put them between a fifth and a third of the total population of the Roman Empire) that the NT frequently uses slave imagery. The slave is a stock figure in many parables of Jesus, and figures in three of his sayings: Matthew 6:24; 10:24; Mark 10:43. In the Epistles and Revelation, servile metaphors are used for the status of the sinner (Rom 6:6; Titus 3:3; Gal 4:3, 9; II Pet 2:19), the status of the Christian (Rom 6:18, 22; Eph 6:6), and the role of Christ (Phil 2:6-11; I Pet 2:18-25).

SMYRNA
Rev 1:11; 2:8

SMYRNA A city in the Roman senatorial province of Asia on the shore of the Aegean Sea. The natural outlet for the ancient trade route through the Hermus Valley, the city had two ports: a small inner one with a narrow entrance which became silted up through neglect, and a second mooring ground. The city was renowned for its beauty and magnificent buildings. Its immediate hinterland was very fertile. Due to its excellent climate, strategic location and good water source, it became one of the most prosperous cities in Asia Minor. Smyrna was an Ionian Greek colony from early times (pre-1st millennium B.C.). At the end of the 7th century B.C. it was captured and destroyed by the Lydians and remained uninhabited until its reconstruction on the present site by Lysimachus in the 3rd century B.C. Even before Rome became the supreme power in the eastern Mediterranean, Smyrna was its faithful ally.

The gospel presumably reached Smyrna from Ephesus. Its church

Prisoners of war depicted on the so-called Cosmetic Palette of the Does from Abydos, Egypt.

Smyrna in Asia Minor.

was the second of the seven mentioned in the Book of Revelation and received the most encouraging letter of the seven. The Smyrna church encountered opposition from the city's Jews who denounced it to the Roman officials (Rev 2:9-11). Smyrna is present-day Izmir, the second largest city in Asiatic Turkey.

SNAIL See ANIMALS

SNAKE See ANIMALS

SO A king of Egypt to whom Hoshea sent messengers, seeking help against the Assyrians (II Kgs 17:4). Several pharaohs have been suggested as possible identifications. However, all of these were rulers of the 25th Ethiopian Dynasty, which came to power more than ten years after Hoshea's imprisonment by Shalmaneser V of Assyria in 724 B.C. More recently it has been suggested to regard So, not as a personal name, but as an Egyptian title, transcribed "si" in Semitic languages, and meaning "vizir", the biblical phrase thus read "the vizir of the king of Egypt". Still another proposal is to identify So with the city of Sais (Seo, in Egyptian), the capital of Egypt in Hoshea's time.

SO
II Kgs 17:4

SOCOH, SOCHOH

1. City in the Plain (Josh 15:35) where the Philistines gathered to fight Israel (I Sam 17:1; AV: "Shochoh"); and one of the cities fortified by Rehoboam (II Chr 11:7). It was taken by Pharaoh Sheshonk (biblical Shishak) of Egypt and later restored to Judah. In the days of Ahaz it was conquered by the Philistines (II Chr 28:18) but was again in the hands of Judah in the days of Hezekiah. In his time it was an administrative center, as is indicated by the numerous stamped jar handles with the seal of Socoh. Identified with Khirbet Abbad on the western side of the Judean hills.

SOCOH,
SOCHOH 1
Josh 15:35.
I Sam 17:1.
II Chr 11:7;
28:18

2. A town in the mountains of Judah (Josh 15:48); the seat of a family of scribes (I Chr 2:55; AV: "Suchathites"). Identified with Khirbet Shuweikeh, south of Hebron.

SOCOH,
SOCHOH 2
Josh 15:48

3. A town under the administration of Ben-Hesed in the third district of Solomon (I Kgs 4:10). It is identified with Tell er-Ras, north of Tulkarem.

SOCOH,
SOCHOH 3
I Kgs 4:10

4. The name of an individual in the genealogy of "the sons of Judah" (I Chr 4:1, 18). It may, however, also indicate a place name and then it would be identical with No. 2 above.

SOCOH,
SOCHOH 4
I Chr 4:18

SODI A man of Zebulun; father of Gaddiel who was sent by Moses to spy out the land of Canaan.

SODI
Num 13:10

SODOM City near the Dead Sea on which the Lord "rained brimstone and fire" because of its people's wickedness. Abraham's effort to save the city if it contained only ten righteous men proved unsuccessful as

SODOM
Gen 10:19;
13:10, 12-13;
14:2, 8, 10-12,
17, 21-22;
18:16, 20, 22,
26; 19:1, 4,
24, 28. Deut
29:23; 32:32.
Is 1:9-10; 3:9;
13:19. Jer
23:14; 49:18;
50:40. Lam
4:6. Ezek
16:46, 48-49,
53, 55-56.
Amos 4:11.
Zeph 2:9.
Matt 10:15;
11:23-24.
Mark 6:11.
Luke 10:12;

Tell Sochoh in the Valley of Elah.

Mount Sodom.

they could not be found (Gen 18:20-33; 19:24-25). Sodom and the other cities of the Jordan Plain (the others being Gomorrah, Admah, Zeboiim and Zoar) were on the southern border of the land of Canaan (Gen 10:19. Lot, Abraham's nephew, chose to live in the plain of the Jordan and pitched his tent towards Sodom. All efforts to locate the site of Sodom have been fruitless. It has been sought at the southern and northern ends of the Dead Sea while other excavators have looked for it in the depths of the sea. The name Sodom, however, has been preserved in the Arabic Jebel Usdum, Mount Sodom, a hill of table salt near the southwestern shore of the Dead Sea.

The wickedness of Sodom became proverbial (e.g. Is 1:9; Jer 23:14; Luke 10:12).

SOLOMON (The name is related to *shalom* "peace/welfare"). The son of David and Bathsheba, and the third king of Israel, Solomon was renowned for his wisdom, wealth and building projects. Under Solomon Israel enjoyed an era of security, prosperity and international political and economic importance.

Solomon (also named Jedidiah "beloved of the Lord", II Sam 12:25) was anointed king when his older brother Adonijah, the first in line for the throne, rashly tried to proclaim himself as ruler in his father's lifetime (I Kgs 1:5ff). Solomon's mother, Bathsheba, and the prophet Nathan, with the backing of others, succeeded in convincing the aged and feeble King David that his younger son should wear the crown (I Kgs 1:11ff).

Solomon's 40-year reign began c. 967 B.C., while David was still alive but infirm, their coregency thus lasting only a short while. Apparently Solomon's first act as king was the pardon of Adonijah, who had fled for refuge to the altar. But soon thereafter Adonijah was executed for seeking to marry David's nurse Abishag, a request which could be seen as a prelude to insurrection (I Kgs 2:22; cf II Sam 16:20ff). Adonijah's supporters were also removed: Abiathar the priest was banished; Joab, the commander of the army, was slain as he clung to the horns of the altar; and Shimei was placed under house arrest and killed three years later (I Kgs 2:13-46).

With political opposition eliminated Solomon could turn to ruling his kingdom. Thanks to the conquests of David, Solomon's domain, including conquered territories and vassal kingdoms, stretched from Tipshah on the Euphrates to Gaza, the border of Egyptian territory. The weakness of both Assyria and Egypt enabled Solomon to maintain hegemony over most of this area without recourse to serious military action. Nevertheless, upon hearing of the deaths of David and Joab, Hadad of Edom proclaimed his country's independence of Israelite rule. Rezon of Damascus likewise defied Solomon's overlordship. Solomon apparently did not attempt to win these territories back, although the Chronicler records (II Chr 8:3-4) that he added the city of Hamath Zobah to his kingdom. For the most part, Solomon's foreign policy seems to have rested on diplomacy rather than arms. In particular, he entered into numerous political marriages (I Kgs 3:1; 11:1). The most important of these was his marriage to the daughter of Pharaoh (probably Siamun), a rare event which testifies to Solomon's power. Pharaoh may have tried to conquer Philistia from the young Israelite king; upon failing, he was forced to make peace, offering his daughter in marriage, with Gezer as her dowry (I Kgs 9:16).

Solomon also established economic ties with surrounding nations, a profitable move both politically and financially. He apparently reached a trade agreement with the wealthy South Arabian state of Sheba (I Kgs chap. 10) and conducted joint business ventures with Hiram of Tyre (I

Kgs 9:26-28). With Phoenician help, Solomon built and manned a fleet of ocean-going vessels at Ezion Geber which returned once every three years from Ophir laden with cargoes of gold and other valuables (I Kgs 10:11-12). Solomon's income also included tribute from vassal states (I Kgs 4:21). In addition, he controlled all the important trade routes in the region, including the Way of the Sea and the King's Highway, from which he could therefore draw revenue (I Kgs 10:15). Supervision of these routes permitted him to dominate the lucrative trade in Egyptian chariots and in horses from Keveh (Cilicia) (I Kgs 10:28-29).

Model of the First Temple according to the plans of Père Roland de Vaux. (Israel Museum, Jerusalem)

Much of Solomon's revenue from these enterprises was used in various building projects. The most significant of these was the Temple, constructed over a seven-year period with the help of materials and craftsmen which Solomon received from Phoenicia in exchange for annual shipments of wheat and oil. The Temple's splendor is described in I Kings, chapter 6; 7:15ff. The even larger palace complex (I Kgs 7:1-12) took 13 years to construct. In addition, Solomon built a palace for Pharaoh's daughter (I Kgs 7:8) and shrines for other foreign wives (I Kgs 11:7-8).

Solomon's building activities also included military construction. His imposing fortifications in the key cities of Hazor, Megiddo and Gezer, with their characteristic six-chambered gates and casemate walls, have now been partially excavated. Solomon also fortified Jerusalem, Lower Beth Horon (according to II Chr 8:5, Upper Beth Horon, too), Tamar (II Chr 8:4 Tadmor) and Baalath, as well as other towns not mentioned in the Bible. A series of fortresses and settlements discovered in the central Negeb highlands may well be Solomonic. Solomon also strengthened and modernized his army by the introduction of cavalry and chariotry. According to II Chronicles 9:25, he built 4,000 stalls, although the stable-like structures found at Megiddo have now been assigned to the period of Omri.

Solomon's extensive construction projects drained his kingdom's resources to such an extent that he was forced to defray his debt to Hiram of Phoenicia, by ceding 20 Galilean cities. Moreover, Solomon imposed heavy taxes (I Kgs 4:7-19, 27-28) and forced labor on his subjects. Laborers were taken from the remaining Canaanite population (I Kgs 9:20-22), but native Israelites were also required to spend one month in three in forced labor (I Kgs 5:13-14; 11:28). In order to administer the corvée and collect taxes efficiently, Solomon divided the country into 12 districts not identical with the traditional tribal territories. Many scholars believe this to have been a deliberate attempt to strengthen central government at the expense of the established tribal hierarchy.

Resentment of Solomon's policies built up during his reign and led, upon his death, to the dissolution of the kingdom into the independent states of Israel and Judah. Even during his lifetime an attempted rebellion was led by Jeroboam, then taskmaster over the house of Joseph. It failed, and Jeroboam fled to Egypt, where he remained until Solomon's death (I Kgs 11:26-40; 12:2ff).

Solomon's proverbial wisdom is his most celebrated characteristic. I Kings 3:4-15 tells how God appeared to Solomon in a dream while he was in Gibeon to offer sacrifices. God offered the king whatever he wished, and granted Solomon his request: wisdom to rule his people. But Solomon is also credited with other sorts of sagacity. He was a master of wise sayings. According to the writer of I Kings chapter 4, Solomon authored 3,000 proverbs (as well as 1,005 songs). He discoursed upon nature (I Kgs 4:33), and in general excelled in the oriental wisdom of his day (I Kgs 4:29-34). It was with the stated aim of putting the king's wisdom to the test with various conundrums, that the Queen of Sheba visited Jerusalem (I Kgs chap. 10).

In the spiritual realm, Solomon is said to have followed the Lord (I Kgs 3:3). He built the Temple, perhaps before constructing his own palace (cf I Kgs 9:10; but in any case he devoted more time to the latter). Solomon experienced revelations from God while he was at Gibeon and upon the completion of the Temple. His reputation for piety may be seen in the large number of sacrifices which he offered at Gibeon and at the dedication of the Temple.

Solomon passing judgment over the two women. Possibly from Troyes, France, c. 1280. (British Museum)

Nevertheless, Solomon took many foreign women as wives — 700 wives and 300 concubines — whom the Deuteronomistic editor blames for turning Solomon's heart away from God in his old age (I Kgs 11:49). Certainly, though, Solomon's marriages, and his concessions to his wives must be seen as at least partially politically motivated.

In spite of the enormity of his harem, only three children of Solomon are named: his successor Rehoboam, and the daughters Basemath and Taphath, mentioned because their husbands were district governors.

Some of Solomon's many sayings are doubtless contained in the Book of Proverbs (1:1; 10:1; 25:1). The Song of Songs (Song of Solomon) is ascribed to him (1:1), and Ecclesiastes 1:1 is often understood to refer to Solomon. However, the late language of these works makes most scholars view their Solomonic authorship with skepticism. Likewise, the headings of Psalms 72 and 127, which mention Solomon, are probably late additions. The apocryphal Wisdom of Solomon was composed in Greek long after Solomon's day.

Solomon is cited in Nehemiah 13:26 as an example of the dangers of foreign women, but in general the trend was rather to magnify his wisdom and accomplishments. In the NT he appears as an example of wealth (Matt 6:29) and wisdom (Matt 12:42). A portico in Herod's temple was named for Solomon (John 10:23).

SOLOMON'S
PORCH
John 10:23.
Acts 3:11; 5:12

SOLOMON'S PORCH Part of the colonnade built by Herod when he restored and embellished the Temple. It was on the east side, facing the "Beautiful Gate". New biblical translations have "porch" instead of the traditional "portico".

SON OF GOD The only verse in the OT containing this phrase is Daniel 3:25 where it refers to a "divine being" seen in the fiery furnace along with Shadrach, Meshach and Abed-Nego. The plural form "Sons of God" is found several other times (Gen 6:2, 4; Job 1:6; 2:1; 38:7). The term "son" *vis-a-vis* God may at times refer to David (II Sam 7:14) or the Davidic king (Ps 2:7; 89:26-27). (See ADOPTION).

In the NT the expression becomes a title for Jesus. Early Davidic usages which refer to the future work of the risen Jesus as Son of God are the angel's words to Mary in Luke 1:32ff and Jesus' words at his trial, Mark 14:61ff, where Psalms 110:1 and Daniel 7:13 are combined. I Thessalonians 1:9ff also fits in here, as well as the two stage Christology of Romans 1:3ff; whereas the earthly Jesus is Son of David, the risen Jesus is Son of God.

The next stage represents a Hellenistic influence. Greek paganism held to the idea that some special people, in particular miracle workers, were "divine men." Thus, in the gospels, the earthly Jesus, not only the risen Christ, came to be seen as a divinely endowed and led man, particularly in his healings and exorcisms (Mark 1:24; 5:7; Luke 11:20).

The next stage in understanding Jesus as Son of God reflects the influence of Hellenistic Gentile Christianity. In this stage Jesus is Son of God not merely in his risen state or as inspired and empowered by God, but in his physical nature and metaphysical being, not only on earth or in the future, but preexisting with God the Father from all eternity. This stage can be seen in the mysterious story of Jesus' transfiguration (Mark 9:2-8). Although resembling OT theophanies like Exodus chapter 24, this story is different: Jesus as a man was transformed into a being of light, as a voice from heaven declared "This is my beloved Son." Power radiates from Jesus in Mark 5:30 (cf Mark 6:56; Acts 5:15; 19:12). The virginal conception in Matthew 1:18-25 reenforces this understanding. The high point in texts regarding the preexistence of Jesus as the divine word comes in the prologue to John's gospel (John 1:1-18). The early Christian hymns (Phil 2:5-11; Col 1:13-20) are also sometimes regarded in this light.

One further aspect of the matter concerns the personal union of love and communication between God as Father, referred to in Jesus' intimate, familiar Aramaic *abba*, and Jesus as his Son in a unique and absolute sense. Synoptic texts included Matthew 11:25-30; 28:18-20; and Mark 13:32. This personal relationship is developed throughout the fourth gospel (cf John 5:19-30 and 17:1-26).

SON OF MAN This Semitic phrase is used in various ways in the OT. It is a variant expression for "man" in poetic parallelism, as in Psalms 8:4, "What is man that you are mindful of him. And the Son of man that you visit him?" (cf Num 23:19). In the Book of Ezekiel, the Lord often (93 times) addresses the prophet in this way, e.g., "Son of man, stand upon your feet, and I will speak to you" (Ezek 2:1). Here it probably has no special meaning different from the address "man" but could stress the prophet's creaturely state of dependence upon God. By far the most important occurence is in Daniel 7:13ff. This is a poetic passage in which the prophet in a night vision sees "one like the Son of man" to whom God (the Ancient of Days) gives a kingdom. The immediate context clearly points to an individual figure in human form. But this poetic context is followed by a prose interpretation or commentary in Daniel 7:15-18. Here, in verse 18, it is the saints of the Most High who receive the kingdom. It is disputed whether these saints are the Israelites on earth or heavenly angels (in which case the Son of man is sometimes identified with the archangel Michael, Daniel 10:13). It is clear that an individual figure in Daniel 7:13 is interpreted as a collectivity in Daniel

7:18, 27. In later times both rabbis and Christians continued to see the Son of man in Daniel 7:13 as an individual mediator of salvation, identified with the messiah.

The use of this phrase in the NT is problematical. For some interpreters the phrase Son of man has the highest christological significance; for others it has no christological significance whatsoever. The NT usage is special, not identical with its employment in colloquial Aramaic. Sometimes it serves as a title for Jesus. For the most part it is found on the lips of Jesus himself as a self-reference. (Two exceptions are in John 12:34 and Acts 7:56; cf Rev 1:13; 14:14). In the Synoptic Gospels Jesus uses the phrase to refer to (a) his present earthly, at times humble, life and activity (Matt 8:20; Mark 2:10, 28); (b) predictions of his suffering, death and resurrection (Mark 8:31; 9:31; 10:33-34); (c) his (or another's) coming as the future Son of man in glory (Mark 8:38; 13:26; 14:62). Sometimes these usages refer directly or indirectly to Daniel 7:13.

SONG OF SOLOMON (SONG OF SONGS) The Song of Solomon is one of the Five Scrolls in the third section of the OT, the Hagiographa. In the Hebrew Bible it is the first of the five; in the Protestant and Roman Catholic Bibles it is found after Ecclesiastes. The scroll is also known as Canticles after the Latin translation of its Hebrew title (*Canticum Canticorum*). The name Song of Songs, which is a direct translation of the first two Hebrew words of the scroll, designates a superlative: the most beautiful of all songs, the song *par excellence*.

The Song of Solomon is a comparatively brief work, consisting of eight chapters with 117 verses. Yet despite its brevity, it has been the subject of extensive discussion and investigation throughout the ages. The rabbis of the Talmud debated at length as to whether or not to include the book within the biblical canon. The problem was its blatant secular nature devoid of all religious motifs, not even the name of God being included. The book attained canonical status, due to the allegorical interpretation, primarily associated with the name of Rabbi Akiba (died A.D. 135), who explained the book as a love song between God and Israel. The several references to Solomon (1:1, 5; 3:7, 9, 11; 8:11-12) and to a king (1:4, 12; 7:5), understood to be Solomon, played a key role in saving the scroll from oblivion, since Solomon was known to have authored numerous songs (cf I Kgs 5:12), and tradition also credited him with writing Proverbs and Ecclesiastes.

Today, however, the ascription of authorship to Solomon is not accepted by most scholars. On linguistic grounds — the presence of a Persian word (*pardes*, "orchard", 4:13) and later Hebrew words, expressions and syntax along with Aramaisms — the work is dated somewhere within the late Persian or early Greek period.

Throughout the centuries the book has been interpreted in several entirely different ways. The earliest line of exegesis, the allegorical, was adopted from the rabbis of the Talmud by the Church Fathers; the latter interpreted the figures of Solomon and the Shunammite maiden as representing Christ and the Church. In medieval times a philosophical-allegorical approach also developed. Other lines of interpretation include the dramatic — with two- and three-character versions. The latter expounded the scroll as a love story triad between the king who desires a shepherdess who is herself in love with a shepherd. Despite the many seductions and blandishments of the court, the young girl remains faithful to her beloved to whom she eventually returns. A cultic approach viewed the book as a reflection of a supposed cult of Tammuz, highlighting a dying and rising god motif. These theories are seldom expounded today and, except for the allegorical which still claims a few adherents among some Roman Catholic scholars, are forgotten.

The common consensus today is that the Song of Solomon is an anthology of lyric love songs. (The exact number of these songs, which vary in length betweeen a simple line and an extended paragraph, is also highly debated since it is very difficult to determine when one song ends and the next begins). These works are characterized by great emotion, poetic finesse, and bold and vivid imagery. Several poems include descriptive praises of the physical features of both the male and female protagonists in the Songs; but the descriptions, though sensual, are never vulgar or coarse.

Fragment from the Song of Solomon found at Qumran. (Shrine of the Book, Jerusalem)

The literary genre of love poetry has its antecedents both in Mesopotamian and Egyptian literature and several literary traits and imagery are shared by all three. The book may actually contain several songs whose origins are rooted in wedding ceremonies, as has been shown by comparison with marriage customs prevalent among Arab peasants in Syria and Palestine.

The songs express the longing and yearning of the lovers for one another and joy in final consummation, conveyed by expressive monologues and dialogues. Dream songs are also part and parcel of this lyric collection (3:1ff; 5:2ff). The flora and fauna of Israel are vividly employed within the songs whose geographical background and similes encompass Gilead, Heshbon, Lebanon, Hermon, Carmel, Tirzah, Sharon, Jerusalem and En Gedi. These multiple songs from different places, times and authors all form one grand paean to nature and natural love.

The scroll is read in the synagogue during the holiday of Passover, reflecting the season of spring.

OUTLINE

Various interpretations — allegorical, dramatic, ritual and literal — have been suggested for the Song of Solomon. The following outline is only one of the possible scenarios.

1:1-8	Songs of the bride
1:9-2:7	Dialogue of the lovers
2:8-3:5	Reminiscences of the bride
3:6-11	The wedding parade
4:1-5:1	Songs of the youth
5:2-6:3	Search for the lost bridegroom
6:4-7:10	The bride's beauty
7:11-14	Love in the vineyard
8:1-4	Brother and sister
8:5-14	Various songs and fragments

SONG OF SONGS See SONG OF SOLOMON

SOPATER (short for "Sosipater"). A man of Berea who accompanied Paul on his last journey to Jerusalem. Perhaps identical with Sosipater.

SOPHERETH (HASSOPHERETH) ("scribe"). A family of the "sons of Solomon's servants" who returned from the Exile in Babylon with Zerubbabel. Probably a generic name for a group or family of scribes.

SOREK Valley in the territory of the tribe of Dan. It is mentioned in the Bible only as the home of Delilah (Judg 16:4). It is generally identified with the present-day Nahal Sorek along which the railroad runs from Tel Aviv to Jerusalem. It is one of the main approaches into the Judean hills.

The Valley of Sorek.

SOSIPATER ("who saved his father"). A kinsman of Paul mentioned in his Epistle to the Romans.

SOSTHENES ("the strong one").

1. The head of the synagogue in Corinth after Crispus; he was beaten up by the Greeks during the proconsulate of Gallio.

2. A colleague (perhaps literally brother) of the apostle Paul.

SOTAI Head of a family of "sons of Solomon's servants" whose descendants returned with Zerubbabel from the Babylonian Exile.

SOUTH, THE See NEGEB

SPAIN The far western area of the European peninsula. The only reference to Spain in the Bible occurs in the Epistle to the Romans where Paul writes of his plans to travel to Spain (Rom 15:24, 28). It is uncertain whether Paul actually accomplished this, although according to Clement of Rome, in a letter written 30 years after the apostle's death, Paul traveled to "the limits of the west".

SPARROW See ANIMALS

SPICES AND PERFUMES The use of scents and ointments was very necessary in the primitive hygienic conditions of the ancient world. In private life perfumes and spices were used as ingredients in perfumed oils, ointments and powders, for cosmetic purposes, to protect the skin from the heat of the sun and the dry air, and in medicine. No less important was the role they played in the religious rituals of the ancient Near East. Spices were also used in the preparation of bodies for burial (John 19:39). Cosmetics were applied with the finger, or more frequently with a spatula made of wood, bone or, in the Roman period, bronze. One of the oils mentioned in connection with cosmetics was the "precious oil/ointment" (Ps 133:2; Is 39:2 etc.). This was made from flowers, aromatic seeds and fruits mixed with olive oil. Others were oil

The production of perfume shown on an Egyptian relief. 17th century B.C. (Musée du Louvre, Paris)

Alabaster ointment jar. From the tomb of Tutankhamun. 14th century B.C. (Egyptian Museum, Cairo)

of myrrh (Est 2:12) and the perfumer's ointment (Ecc 10:1). Perfume was made from flowers, seed and fruits soaked in oil or water. The mixture was sometimes heated and the essence was then extracted and strained through a cloth (cf Ex 30:34ff). Many perfumes were produced from resins and used either in powdered form or dissolved in oils and mixed with other substances to form an ointment. The perfumes were prepared by apothecaries, who were either men (Neh 3:8) or women (I Sam 8:13), and who in the days of Nehemiah formed a guild.

Pigments for tinting the hair, face and fingernails were used everywhere in the East. Kohl, to give emphasis to the eyes and to protect them from the strong sun, was applied on the eyebrows and eyelashes (II Kgs 9:30; Jer 4:30 etc.).

Aromatic plants in various forms were much used in all the religious cults of the East. They were mixed according to complicated formulas and burnt on the altars (Ex 37:25 etc.) and in Canaanite temples, in censers and incense-bowls; they were also puffed through incense ladles, numbers of which have been found in excavations.

Spices and aromatics were important items in the international trade of the ancient world. The OT refers to this commerce and mentions the Midianites and the Ishmaelites in connection with it (Gen 37:25).

Caravans brought perfumes from Somaliland in East Africa and from the southern Arabian kingdoms along the desert routes to Palestine (cf Is 60:6). Similarly, certain spices that grew in Palestine were exported to Egypt and Syria (cf Gen 37:25; 43:11; Ezek 27:17). Some spices and aromatics must have come great distances from the Far East, but how they found their way to the Near East is still a mystery. From the Hellenistic period onwards this trade grew in importance.

Numerous aromatic plants and spices used in private life or in religious cults or both are referred to in the Bible. Some of the more important ones are mentioned below.

ALOES (Ps 45:8; Prov 7:17; Song 4:14). This perfume comes from the resin of a tree that grows in northern India and Malaya. It was one of the spices used in preparing Jesus' body for burial (John 19:39).

BALM (styrax). Among the "best fruits in the land" that Jacob's sons brought to Joseph in Egypt (Gen 43:11) and one of the products exported to Tyre (Ezek 27:17). It grew in Gilead (Gen 37:25) and was used by the local doctors (Jer 46:11; 51:8). Some scholars believe that it was a mixture of many spices.

BALSAM (Song 5:1) NKJV "spice"; AV "myrrh"; KJV "mulberry". The Hebrew name may signify any perfume, but Josephus and the early commentators say that the aromatic resin was extracted from the opobalsamum tree, which grows round Mecca. Large balsam plantations between Jericho and En Gedi in the time of the Second Temple were also well-known to the classical writers.

CALAMUS A type of reed, mentioned only once (Song 4:14), it was one of the spices of the fragrant garden to which the bride is likened.

CANE An aromatic substance, sweet to the taste, extracted from a reed imported from India and employed mainly as a sweet spice or drug. It is mentioned several times in the OT (e.g. Ex 30:23; Jer 6:20 etc.).

CASSIA Possibly the *cinnamomum cassia* but orrisroot has also been suggested as a possible identification. Cassia was an ingredient of the holy anointing oil (Ex 30:24) and was also used as a perfume (Ps 45:8).

CINNAMON The fragrant bark of a tree of the laurel family, native to Ceylon. The oil extracted from it was an important ingredient in the anointing oil (Ex 30:23), and was also valued as perfume (Prov 7:17; Song 4:14; Rev 18:13).

FRANKINCENSE One of the four ingredients of the incense that was burnt in the tabernacle (Ex 30:34-35); it was also added to other sacrifices (Lev 2:1; 24:7). Frankincense was very expensive (Is 43:23-24) because it had to be brought a great distance from Sheba (Jer 6:20). Because of its high price it was kept almost exclusively among the treasures of the Temple (I Chr 9:29), where there was a special storeroom for it (Neh 13:9). Those condemned to death were given it mixed with wine before their execution so that they might not feel pain. See INCENSE.

GALBANUM One of the four ingredients of the incense burnt in the tabernacle (Ex 30:34). In the ancient world galbanum was also used as a spice and in medicine.

HENNA (Song 1:14; 4:13). This is the scented plant *Lawsonia inermis L.* which was grown in Palestine. It is a small tree whose fragrant flowers grow in clusters. The roots and leaves, when ground and dissolved in water, produce a yellowish-red pigment. It was celebrated in the East for its scent and as a dye for hair, nails and teeth.

MYRRH One of the most important perfumes in biblical times, myrrh was used in the preparation of the oil with which kings were anointed (Ex 30:23-24). It was also a precious gift (Matt 2:11) and was much used by women (Prov 7:17; Est 2:12; Song 4:14). Together with aloes it was used in preparing Jesus' body for burial (John 19:39). Myrrh is extracted by

Glass pomegranate-shaped perfume bottle from Cyprus. 14th century B.C. (Israel Museum)

Pottery imitation of an alabastron *(alabaster vessel) for perfumes. 1st century B.C. (Israel Dept. of Antiquities and Museums)*

means of incisions in the bark of a small tree that grows in tropical Africa and in Arabia. It was sold in both a solid and a liquid state.

SPIKENARD A fragrant, aromatic and very costly plant originating from the Himalaya Mountains. It is listed among fragrant flowers and spices in the Song of Solomon (4:13-14).

A fragrant oil was extracted from the spikenard and it was this oil with which Jesus was anointed at Bethany (Mark 14:3; John 12:3). According to John (12:5), a flask of oil cost 300 denarii (or about a year's wage for a common worker).

See also PLANTS.

SPIDER See ANIMALS

SPIKENARD See SPICES AND PERFUMES.

STACHYS ("ear of corn"). One of the Romans to whom Paul sent greetings; calling him "my beloved".

STACHYS
Rom 16:9

STACTE See PLANTS

STARS AND CONSTELLATIONS The worship of the stars as divine beings or mythological figures was widespread in the ancient Middle East and such worship is explicitly and repeatedly forbidden in the Ten Commandments (Ex 20:3; Deut 5:8). The prophets (Jer 19:13; Amos 5:26) as well as the Book of Kings (II Kgs 23:5) also denounce such practices. However, from these latter passages, it may be inferred that the worship of stars was not unknown in ancient Israel. King Manasseh is reported to have introduced the worship of the host of heaven (i.e., the stars) into the Temple itself (II Kgs 21:3-5). It was finally repressed by King Josiah (II Kgs 23:4-14).

The Bible clearly tends to negate the notion that the stars are live and independent bodies. This is done by referring to the stars only in general terms and also through stressing the supremacy of God by declaring that God is the creator of the stars (Gen 1:16; Ps 136:9). He counts them, gives them names (Ps 147:4; Is 40:26) and can put out their light (Job 9:7). Like all God's creatures, the stars join in the praise of God (Ps 148:3) and bow down to him. In Psalm 8 the sight of the starry sky moves the Psalmist to proclaim the might of God as the creator of the host of heaven.

Nevertheless, some faint allusions to the concept that the stars are living bodies may have survived. Thus, in Joseph's dream (Gen 37:9), the sun, moon and 11 stars bow down to him. Deborah (Judg 5:20) speaks of the stars as joining in the battle against Sisera. This notion emerges most explicitly in Job who declares that at creation "the morning stars sang together and all the sons of God shouted for joy" (Job 38:7). Such passages, however, may be mere poetic hyperbole.

There are several references to constellations of stars but their identifications are not always certain. The identification of Pleiades and Orion (Job 9:9; 38:31; Amos 5:8) is fairly certain. The astral body mentioned in Job 9:9 is rendered by most translators both ancient and modern as "he made the Bear, Orion and the Pleiades", others translate the first of these as Hyades. "The chambers of the south" in the same verse remain obscure as does the term "Mazzaroth" in Job 38:32. Amos apparently refers once to the worship of Saturn (called Sikkuth and Chiun) carried in a religious procession (Amos 5:26).

The notion that the constellations if properly read are portents of the future was widespread in the ancient Middle East, most especially in Babylonia. Jeremiah (10:2) warns against this belief and practice. "Do not learn the way of the nations, do not be dismayed at the signs of heaven, for the nations are dismayed at them", and Deutero-Isaiah mocks it (Is 47:13).

Stars are a popular simile in the Bible. Abraham's progeny will be too numerous to be counted — like the stars in heaven (Gen 15:5). The righteous will shine like stars (Dan 12:3) while Paul compares the degrees of glory of the elect with the glory of the stars, "for one star differs from another star in glory" (I Cor 15:41). The wicked, however, are like stars who have wandered from their courses (Jude v. 13). The seven churches of the Book of Revelation are seven stars (Rev 1:16, 20; 2:1; 3:1) while the morning star is given to the righteous (Rev 2:28). Jesus is called "the bright and morning star" in Revelations 22:16. The "star in the East" which brought the Wise Men to the manger in Bethlehem (Matt 2:2, 7, 9-10) has been taken as a symbol, or as an interpretation of Numbers 24:17 ("a star shall come out of Jacob"). Astronomers have tried to identify the phenomenon but have been hampered by uncertainty concerning the exact date of the event.

STEPHANAS A Christian of Corinth who was baptized by Paul, together with his whole household (I Cor 1:16). He was the first person baptized in the region of Achaia (I Cor 16:15). Subsequently Stephanas' family dedicated themselves to "the ministry of the saints" (I Cor 16:15). When Paul was in Ephesus, Stephanas visited him there, in the company of Fortunatus and Achaicus (I Cor 16:17).

STEPHEN ("crown"). One of the first Christian martyrs. Stephen was a Jew from the Diaspora living in Jerusalem; he accepted Christianity and was one of the seven deacons chosen by the disciples to care for the widows and other needy people in the Jerusalem community (Acts 6:1-5). Stephen is called "a man full of faith and the Holy Spirit" (Acts 6:5), who did great wonders and miracles among the people (Acts 6:8). When he was teaching in the synagogue of the Diaspora Jews, opponents disputed with him but they could not stand up to his wisdom (Acts 6:9-10). He was accused of blasphemy and was brought to the Jewish council (Acts 6:11-12) where false witnesses charged him with preaching that "Jesus of Nazareth will destroy this place and change the customs which Moses delivered to us" (Acts 6:13-14).

The high priest gave Stephen the opportunity to defend himself, but his defense only increased the anger of his adversaries, especially when he saw "Jesus standing at the right hand of God...the heavens opened and the Son of man standing at the right hand of God" (Acts 7:55-56). For his heretical views he was taken out of the city and stoned to death.

According to some traditions, his place of execution is near the present St. Stephen's Gate in Jerusalem (also called the Lion's Gate). Before his death Stephen prayed for those about to stone him: "Lord, do not charge them with this sin" (Acts 7:60). He was buried by devout men, who made a great lamentation over him (Acts 8:2). The martyrdom of Stephen was watched with approval by the young Saul, later to be called Paul (Acts 7:58-8:1) and was the signal for the onset of anti-Christian persecutions which forced the Christians to flee Jerusalem.

STOICS Followers of a Greek school of pantheistic philosophy founded by Zeno (335-263 B.C.), which stressed human brotherhood, opposed slavery and required severe self-discipline. From the 1st century B.C., it was the leading philosophy of the Roman ruling class and was highly influential throughout the Roman Empire. Together with the Epicureans they disputed the preachings of Paul whom they called a "babbler" preaching "strange gods".

STORES Royal and communal buildings for storing grain were common to most cities. The four Hebrew names by which they were known are rendered as "storehouses" and "barns" (Deut 28:8; Jer 50:26; Joel 1:17). The usual granary was circular, with openings below the almost flat roof so that the air could circulate. Stairs on the outside

Storehouses of the 8th century B.C. at Hazor.

formed a kind of ramp upon which the grain was carried, before being poured in at the top. Granaries were either built as freestanding structures or hewn into the rock. Such granaries have been unearthed at Megiddo, Jericho, Gezer, Beth Shemesh, Beth Shean, etc. In many of them grains of corn were found. Dating from the Late Bronze Age, they were between 7 and 10 feet (2-3m) in diameter. In the opinion of some, the frequency of granaries in early Israelite settlements provides evidence of the conditions of great insecurity in which the inhabitants lived.

A large number of circular stores of the Persian period were found at Tell Jemmeh. According to one calculation they could have held provisions for 35,000 people for two months. In addition to the circular structures there were also rectangular storehouses. Examples have been found at Hazor, the "House of Pillars" and at Samaria, the "House of the Ostracons", both from the time of Ahab.

STORK See ANIMALS

SUAH Firstborn son of Zophah in the genealogy of the family of Asher.

SUAH
I Chr 7:36

SUCCOT See TABERNACLES, FEAST OF

SUCCOTH

1. The first station on the route of the Exodus, between Rameses and Etham (Ex 12:37; 13:20); tentatively identified with a place near Jebel Mariyam, on the west bank of Lake Timsah, 15 miles (24 km) from Tell el-Maskhute.

SUCCOTH 1
Ex 12:37;
13:20. Num
33:5, 6

Tell Dair Alla, identified with Succot.

(right)
Clay tablet of the 12th century B.C. found at Tell Dair Alla bearing an inscription which has not yet been deciphered.

2. A city in the territory of Gad, east of the River Jordan, but not far from it (Josh 13:27). There is a river-crossing which Jacob took on his way from Mesopotamia to Canaan (Gen 32:22-23; 33:17). Gideon took revenge on the princes and elders of the city for their refusal to forage his army (Judg 8:5-16). The copper vessels for Solomon's Temple were cast between Succoth and Zarethan (I Kgs 7:46).

The city has been identified with Tell Dair Alla 2 miles (3 km) north of the Jabbok.

SUCCOTH 2
Gen 33:17.
Josh 13:27.
Judg 8:5-6, 8,
14-16. I Kgs
7:46. II Chr
4:17. Ps 60:6;
108:7

SUCCOTH BENOTH A Babylonian deity. Referring to the Babylonians settled at Samaria, the Bible says "The men of Babylon made Succoth Benoth, the men of Cuth made Nergal, the men of Hamath made Ashima" (II Kgs 17:30). These are all names of deities, and Succoth Benoth seems to be a corrupted form of a deity, possibly the Babylonian deity Sikkuth (Amos 5:26). Marduk had a consort named Sarpanitum, and Benot may be the ending of her name. It has also been suggested that Benoth is identical with the deity Banitu "the builder", one of the epithets of Ishtar, identified with Sarpanitum.

SUCCOTH
BENOTH
II Kgs 17:30

HATHITES
hr 2:55

KKIIM
Chr 12:3

SUCHATHITES A family of Kenite scribes living in Jabez in Judah. Both the Kenites and Rechabites are traced back to Caleb in their ancestry.

SUKKIIM A group of soldiers in the Egyptian army during Shishak's campaign against Judah (II Chr 12:2-3). They are generally considered to have been mercenaries, perhaps of Libyan origin.

SUN Throughout the entire Near East the sun was conceived of as a supreme deity, whether masculine or feminine. In Israel, however, a demythologization took place and the sun was considered just one of the many objects created by God during the act of creation. It came into being on the fourth day, along with the moon and stars, in order to "rule the day" and regulate the seasons (Gen 1:14-19). Nevertheless, despite the prohibitions against sun worship found in Deuteronomy 4:19; 17:3, a cult of the sun did arise in Judah under King Manasseh (II Kgs 21:3, 5), which was eradicated by King Josiah in 621 B.C. as part of his extensive religious reforms (II Kgs 23:5). Josiah also destroyed the horses and chariots of the sun which were stationed at the entrance of the Temple (II Kgs 23:11). The popularity of an earlier sun cult is reflected in place names in Israel: Beth Shemesh, "house of the sun" (Josh 15:10; I Sam 6:9; I Kgs 4:9) and En Shemesh, "spring of the sun" (Josh 15:7; 18:17). Reference to the worship of the sun is also found in Ezekiel 8:16. According to Psalms 91:6 the midday sun is considered a demon.

A miniature stone sun-dial found in the excavations near the Temple Mount, Jerusalem.

(left)
Painted relief from Akhenaton temple at El Amarna showing Askhenaton and his wife Nefertiti making an offering to the sun. 14th century B.C.

The sun is connected with two miracles. According to the Book of Jashar as recounted in Joshua 10:12, Joshua commanded the sun to stand still until Israel defeated its enemies at Gibeon. II Kings 20:8-11 and Isaiah 38:7-8 relate how the sun recorded 10 degrees on the sundial as a sign that King Hezekiah would live 15 more years. The sun is also regarded as a symbol of permanence especially when expressing the long rule of a king (Ps 72:5; 89:3). The prophet Malachi (4:2) foretells that on the final day of judgment the "sun of righteousness shall rise with healing in his wings". In the days to come moreover, the sun will shine sevenfold as bright as the present (Is 30:26).

According to the gospels, the sun darkened at the crucifixion of Jesus: "there was darkness over all the land" (Matt 27:45-56; Mark 15:33; Luke 23:44-49).

SUPH
Deut 1:1

SUPH One of the places at which Moses expounded the Law to Israel (Deut 1:1). The place mentioned in this passage is in the Transjordanian wilderness. Some seek Suph in Moab, and suggest an identification with Khirbet Sufa, southeast of Medeba. Following the reading of the

Septuagint, the KJV translated "opposite the Red Sea (Hebrew: the Sea of Suph)".

SUPHAH A place in the vicinity of the Arnon River.

SUR, GATE OF One of the gates of Jerusalem (II Kgs 11:6), apparently part of the king's palace. Its location is unknown.

SUSA See SHUSHAN

SUSANNA ("lily"). One of the women who provided for Jesus when he was preaching in the cities and villages in Galilee.

SUSANNA AND THE ELDERS One of the apocryphal additions to the canonical text of the Book of Daniel. Found in the Greek translations, it is placed at the beginning of the book in order to explain how Daniel was so highly regarded by the people in Babylon (v. 64). The story tells of the righteous, God-fearing and beautiful Susanna, the wife of Joakim. Two elders lusted after her; when she rejected them, they falsely accused her of adultery, and she was condemned to death. Daniel refused to accept this verdict and interrogated the two elders separately; the discrepancies in their stories proving that they had given false witness, they were executed.

The date and place of writing of these additions is not certain. Scholars still dispute whether the original language was Hebrew or Greek. The story, told in a single chapter, is not included in the Protestant or Jewish Bible canon.

SUSI ("my horse"). A man of Manasseh; father of Gaddi who was sent by Moses to spy out the land of Canaan.

SWINE See ANIMALS

SYCAMORE See PLANTS

SYCHAR See SHECHEM No.2

SYENE See SINIM, LAND OF

SYNAGOGUES Synagogues are not mentioned in the OT and it is generally thought that the institution — houses of assembly and prayer of Jewish congregations — originated in Babylonia after the destruction of the First Temple and in the Persian period. By the Hellenistic period, synagogues were to be found wherever Jews lived. Even while the Temple was standing, synagogues were built in the Holy Land — as evidenced by the remains of two buildings identified as such by the excavators in the Herodian complexes at Masada and Herodium, near Bethlehem. Evidence exists of synagogues in Egypt and other

SUPHAH
Num 21:14

SUR,
GATE OF
II Kgs 11:6

SUSANNA
Luke 8:3

SUSI
Num 13:11

SYCHAR
John 4:5

SYENE
**Ezek 29:10;
30:6**

Greek inscription on the only remnant of a synagogue in Jerusalem built prior to the destruction of the Second Temple. The inscription refers to Theodotos of the family of Vettenos, priest and head of the synagogue. It gives the names of his ancestors who were also heads of the synagogue. (Rockefeller Museum, Jerusalem)

concentrations of Jewish population and over 50 references to synagogues in the NT convey important information. The synagogue was a meeting place and a place of prayer; unlike the Temple, it was not a place where sacrifices were offered. Jesus visited synagogues at Nazareth (Matt 13:54; Mark 6:2; Luke 4:16-17) and at Capernaum (Mark 1:21; Luke 4:33; 7:1, 5; John 6:59); the references to synagogues in Galilee show that they were widespread (Matt 4:23; 9:35; Mark 1:39; Luke 4:14-15). Jesus spoke often and openly to the assembly in various synagogues and this implies that congregations would regularly be addressed in this way. The custom of reading from the Scriptures as part of the synagogue service is also recorded by Luke 4:16-22. The management of the synagogue was in the hands of a synagogue ruler (Luke 8:41; Acts 18:8, 17ff) while various judicial powers were vested in the synagogue (Matt 10:17; Mark 13:9; Luke 21:12 etc.). Unique information on synagogues in the Diaspora is contained in the NT, especially in the accounts of the travels of Paul. He began his mission in the Damascus synagogue (Acts 9:20) and wherever he visited a Jewish community, he went first to the synagogue in order to preach, e.g. at Salamis in Cyprus (Acts 13:5), Thessalonica (Acts 17:1), Corinth (Acts 18:4) and Ephesus (Acts 19:8). The early Jewish Christians called their place of worship a synagogue (James 2:2) and this institution eventually influenced the development of the Christian church.

Remains of the synagogue at the fortress of Masada.

(top left)
Remains of a synagogue at Gamla in the Golan.

(top right)
Bar'am synagogue in the Galilee.

(bottom left)
Qasrin synagogue in the Golan.

SYNTYCHE ("coincidence, success"). A woman of Philippi among the early Christians. Paul urged her to settle her differences with Euodia, another member of the small Christian community.

SYRACUSE A city on the southeast coast of Sicily, the second of the Greek colonies established on the island (the first was Nexos). Syracuse became the residence of the governor when it was taken by the Romans in c. 21 B.C. Paul spent several days at Syracuse on his way to Rome.

A coin of Syracuse depicting Are-thusa, on one side, and dolphins and a quadriga on the other. 5th century B.C.

SYRIA, SYRIANS For the early history of the region see ARAM.

In the Persian period Syria formed the satrapy "Beyond the River". In order to distinguish it from "Syria between the rivers" (Aram-Naharaim; Mesopotamia), the Greeks named it Coele Syria, whose meaning is not clear. The area was conquered by Alexander the Great in 332 B.C. and thereafter formed part of the Hellenistic world. In 64/3, it became a Roman province, governed by an imperial legate resident in Antioch. The name found in the NT refers to this province; it was frequently visited by Paul whose conversion took place along the road to one of its main cities, Damascus (Acts chap. 9). Syria subsequently became a major center of the early Christian church.

SYRIA,
SYRIANS
**Matt 4:24.
Luke 2:2. Acts
15:23, 41;
18:18; 20:3;
21:3. Gal 1:21**

SYRO—PHOENICIAN Designation applied to a pagan woman, probably of Greek origin, from the region of Tyre-Sidon, who appealed to Jesus to cure her daughter who was possessed by demons; Jesus initially refused to listen to the woman's appeal but when she showed faith in him, he healed her daughter (Mark 7:24-30). Describing the same event, Matthew designates the woman as a Canaanite (Matt 15:21-28). The designation probably derived from Phoenicia forming part of the Roman province of Syria, and the Canaanites being the first inhabitants of Phoenica.

SYRTIS The Greek name of two shallow gulfs on the coast of North Africa. The larger was Syrtis Major, the modern Gulf of Sidris and the smaller Syrtis Minor, known today as the Gulf of Gabes in Tunisia. Ancient sailors dreaded those waters because of their sandbanks and rocks. When Paul was sailing to Rome and his ship was caught in a tempest, the crew feared that they would run aground on the Syrtis sands (Acts 27:13-18).

TAANACH, TANACH A fortified Canaanite town at the southern end of the Jezreel Valley, close to the Wadi Ara pass. The earliest mention of it comes in the account of the conquest of Megiddo in 1468 B.C. by Thutmosis III. It then appears in the El Amarna Letters. The king of Taanach appears in the list of 31 kings vanquished by Joshua (Josh 12:21), though other passages state that Taanach was not conquered by the Israelites (Josh 17:11-12; Judg 1:27). Even when Israel was strong

enough to impose tribute on the Canaanites the town was still not taken (Josh 17:13; Judg 1:28); it withstood conquest until the battle of Deborah which took place "in Taanach, by the waters of Megiddo" (Judg 5:19). It was designated a Levitical city (Josh 21:25). During the reign of Solomon, Taanach was in the same district as Megiddo and Beth Shean. It was destroyed by Pharaoh Shishak and is depicted in a relief in his temple at Karnak (Thebes).

Taanach is identified with Tell Taanak, about 5 miles (8 km) southeast of Megiddo. The mound covers an area of 16 acres (6.5ha) and rises about 160 feet (49m) above the valley. It occupies a strategic point at the intersection of important roads coming from Acco in the north, Jerusalem in the south and the Mediterranean coast in the west. The site has been extensively excavated and remains found from the Early Bronze Age down to the Arab period.

TAANATH SHILOH A place on the northeastern boundary of the territory allotted to Ephraim (Josh 16:6); 7 miles (11 km) southeast of the site of biblical Shechem.

TABBAOTH (the name is probably derived from *tabaat*, "ring"). The head of a family of Temple servants (Nethinim) who were among the exiles returning to Judah from Babylon with Zerubbabel.

TABBATH A place to which the Midianites fled after their first defeat by Gideon, in the valley of Jezreel. Its location is in Ras-Abu-Tabat on the western slopes of Mount Ajlun.

TABEEL (TABEAL) ("the goodness of God"). Father of a pretender to the throne of Judah who wanted to seize the crown from King Ahaz with the help of Rezin king of Damascus and Pekah king of Israel, in order to form an anti-Assyrian alliance (Is 7:6). The vocalization "Tabeal" instead of "Tabeel" is a deliberately derogatory alteration, denoting "no good" or "good for nothing". Tabeel was among those who sent a letter to Artaxerxes I king of Persia with the aim of blocking Jewish reconstruction plans (Ezra 4:7). Outside of the Bible this name appears in an Assyrian letter of the 7th century B.C.

TABERAH ("burning"). A station on the Israelites' route in the wilderness, after the Exodus from Egypt. It was here that their continual complaining angered God who sent a fire among them, destroying part of their camp.

Cultic stand from Taanach. 10th century B.C.

(top left)
Excavations at Taanach.

(top right)
Stone tablet of the Late Bronze Age found at Taanach written in the cuneiform Canaanite script.

Candelabrum depicted in an illuminated Bible. Spain c.1300. (Jewish National and University Library)

The consecration of the tabernacle. From one of the wall paintings at Dura-Europos synagogue. 3rd century.

TABERNACLE The portable shrine that the Israelites took with them into the desert, made by Moses according to God's command (Ex 25:8); also named the "Tent of Congregation". Its place was outside the camp, where all who sought the Lord could go (Ex 33:7); there God also spoke to Moses. The ark of the covenant was kept in the tabernacle even after the conquest of Canaan, its permanent place being at Shiloh (Josh 18:1). Eventually it was housed in Solomon's Temple (I Kgs 8:4).

The tabernacle was built by Bezalel, son of Uri (Ex 31:1-11), according to a design that was revealed to Moses on Mount Sinai (Ex 25:9; 26:30). It consisted of three walls made of boards of shittim wood (acacia), plated with gold (Ex 26:15-22). Colored curtains, embroidered with cherubim, were hung over the boards. Above the tabernacle were spread 12 plain goatskin curtains and these, in turn, were covered with rams' skins and badgers' skins painted red. The tabernacle was divided into the holy place and the Holy of Holies by a veil (Ex 26:31-33) suspended on four wooden posts. The tabernacle was 30 cubits long and 10 cubits wide and it stood within a courtyard measuring 100 cubits by 50 cubits (Ex 27:9-13). This courtyard was divided into two equal parts: in the eastern half stood the tabernacle, while in the western half the vessels used in services were kept. It was surrounded by a fence made of

posts from which hangings were suspended. The entrance to the court was on the east, and it was overhung with a veil (Ex 27:16), like the one at the entrance to the tabernacle. The most important ritual object was the altar of burnt offerings (Ex 27:1-2), which stood in the center of the eastern half of the court and measured 5 cubits by 5 cubits by 3 cubits. Like most of the furniture in the tabernacle it was made of acacia wood, a tree native to Sinai, and was plated with copper. The most important pieces of furniture in the tabernacle were the ark of the covenant, the golden cherubim, the incense altar and the table for the shrewbread, all of which stood in the holy place. At the southern end of the tabernacle stood the golden *menorah* (candelabrum).

In the NT, Jesus is the priest of the heavenly tabernacle, which is the true tabernacle (Heb 8:2, 5). The original tabernacle which is described in Hebrews 9:1-10, proceeds to state that Christ's tabernacle is more perfect, not made by man (Heb 9:11-14). The heavenly tabernacle is again mentioned in Revelation 15:5.

TABERNACLES, FEAST OF One of the three annual pilgrim festivals, it is celebrated during the fall. Commencing on the 15th day of the seventh month, Tishri, it is prescribed to last seven days with an extension of one day called the Eighth Day of Solemn Assembly.

TABERNACLES, FEAST OF
Lev 23:34.
Deut 16:13, 16; 31:10. II

The Festival of Tabernacles in Jerusalem. Fragrant branches of myrtle and branches of other trees are used to cover the booths which it is customary to erect on roofs, courtyards, gardens or even balconies during the festival.

Chr 8:13. Ezra
3:4. Zech
14:16, 18-19.
John 7:2

The Bible endows the festival with both historical and agricultural significance, giving it different names which reflect its place and purpose in Israelite life: "The Festival of Tabernacles", a reminder of Israel's sojourn in tabernacles during their wanderings in the wilderness (Lev 23:33-34); the "Festival of the Ingathering", the final harvest of the agricultural calendar (Ex 23:16; 34:22; Deut 16:13); and "The Feast", i.e., the festival *par excellence* (Lev 23:39-41; Deut 16:14; I Kgs 8:2, 65; 12:32; II Chr 5:3; 7:8; Neh 8:14; Ezek 45:25).

The Bible ordains several observances for the festival. First is the command to dwell for seven days in flimsy booths (Lev 23:42-43). Critical scholars are of the opinion that this is a late and rather forced connection with the period in the wilderness when, in any case, the Israelites dwelt in tents, not in booths.

The second biblical ordinance relates to the "four species" or plants which are to be used as symbols of rejoicing before God for the harvest which has just been completed. These are the fruit of "the goodly tree" (citrus fruit), the palm branch, boughs of a thick tree (the myrtle), and willows of the brook (Lev 23:40). According to Nehemiah 8:10-18 they were originally used in the construction of the booths.

Thirdly, according to Deuteronomy 31:10-11, every seventh year, on this feast, the Law was to be read publicly before a mass assembly of the entire people, men, women and children included.

In the Temple period, numerous sacrifices were offered each day of the festival. The individual brought a basket of harvest fruits (Deut 26:1-11) in addition to other animal sacrifices. Numbers 29:12ff prescribes as many as 70 bullocks, a symbolic number later associated by the rabbis with the "seventy nations of the world" thereby suggesting that the sacrifices were offered in pious concern for the welfare of all peoples. This universalist theme echoes the prophecy of Zechariah who predicted that all the nations of the world would join the People of Israel in Jerusalem to celebrate the Feast of Tabernacles (Zech 14:16). A further universalist dimension can be noted in the biblical account of the dedication of Solomon's Temple, which took place during this festival. In the king's long prayer at the ceremony, he urges God to hearken to the Gentile peoples who will come to pray to him (I Kgs 8:41-43). After the Babylonian Exile, celebration of the festival included the sojourn in the booths and recitation of the Law (Neh 8:14-18); the sacrificial observance was resumed (Ezra 3:4).

In the NT Jesus attended the feast secretly after declining to go openly (John chap.7).

TABITHA See DORCAS

TABOR (MOUNT) A mountain at the southern limit of lower Galilee 1,750 feet (563m) above sea level. Its inverted, bowl-like shape attracted attention in ancient times and it was therefore linked with Mount Hermon and Mount Carmel (Jer 46:18; Ps 89:12). It was a place of worship from the very ancient times (Hos 5:1) and it was the place where the boundaries of the territories of Zebulun, Issachar and Naphtali

The dome-shaped Mount Tabor rising from the Jezreel Valley.

met (Josh 19:23, 34). In the time of Deborah the tribes gathered there to give battle to the Canaanites (Judg 4:6, 12, 14). Early in the Hellenistic period the Ptolemies built a royal fortress here. Later it was conquered by the Hasmonean Alexander Jannaeus. Early Christian tradition placed the scene of the Transfiguration on the mountain, and churches to commemorate the event were erected there from an early period.

TABRIMMON ("the god Rimmon is good"). Son of Hezion, and father of Ben-Hadad I king of Damascus.

TACHMONITE An epithet affixed to the name of Josheb-Basshebeth, one of David's "mighty men". The name may be a scribal error for Jashobeam the son of a Hachmonite, as in I Chronicles 11:11.

TADMOR An oasis in the Syrian desert on the road from the Mediterranean to the Euphrates; a famous caravan city in classical

Remains at Palmyra (Tadmor).

times, it was called Palmyra. According to a biblical tradition it was founded by Solomon (I Kgs 9:18; II Chr 8:4). The actual text in Kings reads "Tamar" and many scholars feel that this reading should be retained, the reference being to Tamar (q.v.) in southern Palestine; they would then emend "Tadmar" in Chronicles to "Tamar". Others accept the traditional readings in Kings as "Tadmor" (followed by the AV), which is confirmed by Chronicles. These scholars feel that, despite the distance involved, it was quite plausible for Solomon to have constructed a fortress at Tadmor, possibly as a replacement after his loss of Damascus. Extensive excavations have uncovered a large quantity of inscribed material, with about 1,000 inscriptions in

Sacrifice ceremony at the temple of the Palmyrene gods. (Damascus Museum)

(left)
Relief showing the gods of Palmyra (Tadmor). (Musée du Louvre, Paris).

Palmyrene (some with a Greek translation) which have thrown much light on the social, civil and political life of the town and its trade and religion. Many buildings were found in an excellent state of preservation.

TAHAN, TAHANITES The third son of Ephraim and the ancestor of the family of Tahanites.

TAHATH

1. A Kohathite Levite, son of Assir and father of Uriel; one of the ancestors of Samuel. The name recurs in the same text as the son of Assir and the father of Zephaniah (I Chr 6:36-37) but it is generally agreed that this is the same man.

2. Mentioned twice in the genealogy of the sons of Ephraim, first as the grandson of Ephraim and the father of Eladah, then as the son of Eladah and the father of Zabad. Both were killed by the men of Gath together with the other children of Ephraim (I Chr 7:21).

3. One of the stations where the Children of Israel camped on their way through the wilderness to the promised land.

TAHPANHES, TEHAPHNEHES A city in lower Egypt, along the Pelusiac branch of the Nile Delta, on the caravan route leading to Palestine and Mesopotamia, known as Daphneh to the classical writers. In this city Baal-Zephon, the god of seafarers, was worshiped. In the days of Jeremiah it was a strong city (Jer 2:16). Ezekiel prophesied its destruction (Ezek 30:18).

In the excavations a small fort of the time of Rameses I and II was discovered, but the city itself was built during the reign of Psammetichus I (7th century B.C.). It was then an important commercial center, inhabited by Greeks and Jews, and it could offer refuge to Jeremiah and those with him (Jer 43:7, etc.). In the Hellenistic period it became an insignificant village. Identified with Tell Daphneh, about 20 miles (32km) south of Pelusium.

TAHPENES The wife of the pharaoh of Egypt at the time of David and perhaps Solomon. When the young prince of Edom, Hadad, fled to Egypt, Pharaoh gave him his wife's sister in marriage.

Scholars believe that Tahpenes is not a proper name and should be translated literally as "the wife of the king".

TAHREA, TAREA Third son of Micah (the grandson of Jonathan) in the genealogy of King Saul.

TAHTIM HODSHI One of the places visited by the men sent by King David to take a census.

TALITHA CUMI Aramaic for "girl, get up". The words were addressed by Jesus to the young daughter of the head of one of the synagogues near the Sea of Galilee (Mark 5:41). Although apparently dead, she immediately responded to the command by rising to her feet and walking.

TALMAI

1. One of the sons of Anak, along with Ahuman and Shishai, the trio lived in Hebron and were defeated by the Judahites in the time of Joshua.

2. Son of Ammihur king of Geshur, father of David's wife, Maacah who was the mother of Absalom. After murdering Amnon, Absalom escaped to Talmai's kingdom in Gesher and took refuge in his court.

TALMON Family of gatekeepers in the Temple at the time of Ezra and Nehemiah. Some members of this family were among those who returned to Judah after the Babylonian Exile.

TAMAH The name of an ancestor of a family of Temple servants (Nethinim) who returned to Judah after the Babylonian Exile.

TAMAR ("date palm"). Name of place and people.

1. The daughter-in-law of Judah, originally married to his eldest son, Er (Gen 38:6). When Er died childless, the second son Onan was told to impregnate his late brother's wife in order to raise issue for the departed. His evasion of the duty was punished by death. Tamar returned to her father's house but remained tied to her late husband's family and under the jurisdiction of its head, the patriarch Judah (Gen 38:7-11). When the third son, Shelah, reached maturity without marrying her, she took it into her own hands to secure an heir for her late husband. Masquerading as a prostitute, she offered her services to an unwitting Judah, taking his personal insignia — a seal, cord and staff — for a pledge against future payment. When she became pregnant as a result of their intercourse, Judah, unaware that he was the father, exercised his legal right by ordering her to be burnt for breaking the filial ties to which she was still subject. At that, she produced the insignia and he revoked his decision, conceding that justice was on her side rather than on his for she had remained attached to the family while he neither released her nor gave her to his remaining son. Tamar's reward was the birth of twins, Perez and Zerah (Gen 38:12-30). Perez, in his turn, became the head of a Judahite family which later produced Boaz, King David's paternal great-grandfather (Ruth 4:18-22; I Chr 2:4-5, 9-11).

The levirate customs described in Genesis chapter 38 are close if not identical to those prescribed in Deuteronomy, but differ from those in Ruth chapter 4 (which likewise reflect upon David's genealogy). Whatever the details, these customs all address the identical problems of land inheritance within the family and perpetuation of the dead person's line by means of a son the childless widow conceives through a brother or relative.

2. Daughter of King David and sister of Absalom (II Sam 13:1; I Chr

---

TAHPENES
I Kgs 11:19-2

TAHREA, TAREA
I Chr 8:35; 9:41

TAHTIM HODSHI
II Sam 24:6

TALITHA CUMI
Mark 5:41

TALMAI 1
Num 13:22. Josh 15:14. Judg 1:10

TALMAI 2
II Sam 3:3; 13:37. I Chr 3:2

TALMON
I Chr 9:17. Ezra 2:42. Neh 7:45; 11:19; 12:25

TAMAH
Ezra 2:53. Neh 7:55

TAMAR 1
Gen 38:6, 11, 13, 24. Ruth 4:12. I Chr 2:4. Matt 1:3

TAMAR 2
II Sam 13:1-2,

3:9). Her half-brother Amnon — then David's heir-apparent — fell in love with her. Employing trickery and coercion he achieved sexual intercourse with her, subsequently tiring of her and sending her away. Tamar appealed to her brother Absalom, who avenged her violated virginity by killing Amnon.

3. The daughter of Absalom and granddaughter of King David; she was reputed to be beautiful (II Sam 14:27) like her aunt and namesake, Tamar (II Sam chap. 13).

4. A place on the southern border of the Holy Land, mentioned in the description of Ezekiel (47:19): "The south side, toward the South, shall be from Tamar to the waters of Meribah by Kadesh, along the brook to the Great Sea". Tamar has been identified by some with Hazezon-Tamar and also with the city of palm trees (Judg 1:16). Various identifications have been suggested. The most likely identification of Tamar is Ein Husb (Mezad Hazevah) situated on an important crossroad in the Arabah, on the north-south road leading to the Gulf of Elath and on the east-west road coming from Mempsis.

5. See TADMOR

TAMARISK See PLANTS

TAMMUZ The object of abominable rites carried on at the entrance of the north gate of the Temple of the Lord, where "the women were seated weeping for Tammuz" (Ezek 8:14). According to Ezekiel, these rites were among the reasons for the Lord's decision to destroy the Temple and exile the Jews. Tammuz represents Sumerian/Babylonian Dumuzi, a fertility god and the mourning for Tammuz was an annual rite, observed in Mesopotamia in June or July. The death of Tammuz came to symbolize the death of nature in the heat of summer. The Church Fathers identified Tammuz with the Greek Adonis. Tammuz is also the post-exilic name of the fourth month of the Hebrew calendar. It does not, however, appear in the Bible.

TANACH See TAANACH

TANHUMETH ("consolation"). Tanhumeth the Netophathite was the father of Seraiah No.3, one of the army officers who joined Gedaliah at Mizpah after the fall of Jerusalem.

TAPHATH One of King Solomon's daughters, married to Ben-Abinadab who was one of the 12 district governors responsible for supplying food to the king and his household one month each year.

TAPPUAH

1. A descendant of Hebron, the ancestor of a Calebite family, and the eponym of the city of Beth Tappuah, in the vicinity of Hebron.

2. A city in the Judean hill country.

3. A Canaanite kingdom centered around the city of the same name that was conquered by Joshua. The city itself was assigned to the tribe of

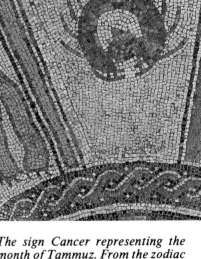

The sign Cancer representing the month of Tammuz. From the zodiac wheel on the mosaic floor of the 6th-century synagogue at Bet Alfa.

Sheik Abu Zarad, south of Shechem, identified with Tappuah.

Ephraim, while its lands were allotted to Manasseh. The location is probably modern Sheikh-Abu-Zarad, 8 miles (13 km) south of Shechem.

4. According to II Kings 15:16, Menahem, king of Israel attacked a city named Tiphsah and massacred its inhabitants because they refused to open the city gates and recognize him as king. According to Greek versions, however, the name of the city was Tappuah. This city would then be identical with No.3 above.

TARALAH A town in the territory of Benjamin, mentioned only once in the Bible (Josh 18:27), in the group of towns located between Mozah and Jerusalem. The proposed identifications have little base.

TARALAH
Josh 18:27

TAREA See TAHREA

TAREA
I Chr 8:35

TARPELITES One of the peoples settled in Samaria by Assyria after the fall of the Kingdom of Israel. Their representatives were among those who signed the letter to Artaxerxes protesting the rebuilding of Jerusalem.

TARPELITES
Ezra 4:9

TARSHISH

1. A grandson of Japheth, the third son of Noah. In I Chronicles 1:7, he is called Tarshishah.

TARSHISH 1
Gen 10:4

2. Country from which beaten silver (Jer 10:9), silver, iron, tin and lead were brought by the people of Tyre (Ezek 27:12). Tarshish is associated with an island (Is 23:6; 66:19) and Jonah went there by ship

TARSHISH 2
**II Chr 9:21;
20:36-37. Est
1:14. Ps 48:7;
72:10. Is 2:16;
23:1, 6, 10,
14; 60:9;
66:19. Jer
10:9. Ezek
27:12, 25;
38:13. Jonah
1:3; 4:2**

A Canaanite merchant ship, prototype of the Tarshish Ship. c. 1400 B.C., reconstructed according to a drawing on the tomb of Qenamon, governor of Thebes under Amenhotep III. (National Maritime Museum, Haifa)

(Jonah 1:3). Solomon also sent ships there (II Chr 9:21). The identification is not at all clear. Some scholars put forward Tartasus in southern Spain, to which, according to the classical authorities, the Phoenicians sailed with their ships to obtain silver, iron and tin. Josephus' identification with Tarsus in Cilicia (*Antiq.* I, 127; IX, 208) is accepted by many scholars today.

TARSHISHAH See TARSHISH No.1

TARSHISHAH
I Chr 1:7

TARSUS City in Asia Minor and the birthplace of Paul (Acts 9:11; 21:39; 22:3). The harbor city was built by the River Cydnus, 10 miles (16km) from the Mediterranean. Although not located on the coast, it had a harbor and enjoyed a prosperous overseas trade. As a junction of trade-routes under Roman rule (1st century B.C.), Tarsus became a government center. Mark Antony made it a free city and granted citizenship to its inhabitants. It was an intellectual and educational center, noted for its schools of stoic scholars.

TARSUS
**Acts 9:11, 30;
11:25; 21:39;
22:3**

Remains of the city gate, known as the Cleopatra Gate, at Tarsus.

Paul was born and raised in Tarsus and after his conversion spent many further years in this town (Acts 9:30; Gal 1:21; 2:1). He remained until he was visited by Barnabas who wished him to take part in the preaching to the Greeks (Acts 11:25). Probably he learned in Tarsus the craft of tentmaking (Acts 18:3) from which he earned his money during his travels (Acts 20:34; I Thes 2:9; II Thes 3:8). The cosmopolitan nature of the city doubtless greatly influenced his thought and personality.

Today Tarsus is the Turkish town of Tersoos.

TARTAK
II Kgs 17:31

TARTAK One of the gods of the Avites, who were resettled in Samaria by the king of Assyria after the destruction of the Kingdom of Israel (722 B.C.). The name may be a corruption of the Aramean goddess, Atargatis.

TARTAN
II Kgs 18:17.
Is 20:1

TARTAN The title (*turtanu*) of the commander of a division in the Assyrian army. The Assyrian officers bearing this title are mentioned in

Two fragments of an Assyrian stele found at Ashdod, supposed to have been set in 712 B.C. at the time that Sargon II sent his "tartan" to Ashdod.

the Bible. One served under Sargon II who besieged and captured the Philistine city of Ashdod (Is 20:1); the other was one of three high officials sent by Sennacherib to Jerusalem in order to convince King Hezekiah to surrender to the Assyrians (II Kgs 18:17).

TATTENAI
Ezra 5:3, 6;
6:6, 13

TATTENAI A high official of the Persian king Darius, he was in charge "of the region beyond the River" (Ezra 5:3) i.e. beyond the Euphrates, when Zerubbabel and Jeshua began to rebuild the Temple and the walls of Jerusalem.

Tattenai wrote to King Darius to query whether the work was authorized. After a search in the palace archives located a record of the authorization given by Cyrus, King Darius wrote back to Tattenai, enjoining him not only to let the Jews build their Temple, but to pay for the cost out of the taxes levied in the region. Tattenai "diligently did according to what King Darius had sent" (Ezra 6:1-13).

TAXES, TAXATION Both the Canaanite kings and the Egyptian authorities collected taxes from early times, as is well attested by the El Amarna Letters, and by some allusions in the Bible (e.g., I Sam 8:11-17). There was no taxation during the period of the conquest of Canaan by the Israelite tribes, nor during the days of the Judges; but with the establishment of the monarchy taxation became indispensable. At first, during the reign of Saul, it appears to have been limited to bringing gifts to the court (I Sam 10:27; II Chr 17:5). That some taxes were paid may be inferred also from the mention of "exemption" in the description of the reward for Goliath the Philistine's slayer (I Sam 17:25).

It seems that regular taxation was introduced by David in the later years of his reign. This necessitated taking a census of the population, a process not favored by the Israelites (II Sam 24:1ff). Censuses were also taken from time to time by other kings. In order to collect the tribute David appointed a special minister (II Sam 20:24). A more detailed list of officials dealing with tax collection is found in I Chronicles (27:25-31), where a minister "over the king's treasures" is mentioned. He was probably responsible for the taxes paid by the people for the upkeep of the court, the collection of booty taken in war and the tribute paid by conquered peoples. Ten other officials were appointed to supervise the revenues from the agricultural economy. This system of taxation was inherited by Solomon, and taxes were paid mainly in kind. To make the system more efficient Solomon subdivided the country into 12 provinces, each of which had to sustain the king's court for one month (I Kgs 4:7). Surplus produce was exchanged for foreign goods (I Kgs 10:15). In Solomon's time the gifts brought by vassal or visiting rulers were an important element in the kingdom's economy (II Sam 8:10-12; I Kgs 10:25; II Chr 17:11). Another form of taxation was forced labor, imposed on the conquered peoples as well as on the Israelites (I Kgs 9:20-21). Solomon recruited 30,000 of his subjects for the king's work. While one-third of the laborers were working in the Lebanon the remaining two-thirds worked at home, each shift lasting for one month.

In addition to these, 80,000 men hewed stone in the mountains, 70,000 hauled the stone and 3,300 supervised their work (I Kgs 5:13-17). The excessive burden of taxation and forced labor was one of the reasons for the division of the kingdom.

During the time of the return from Babylon the inhabitants of the country supplied the governor's table with the "governor's provisions". In addition to this the people paid 40 silver shekels each day (Neh 5:14-15). In Ezra (4:13) three additional taxes are mentioned: tribute, a tax paid by the king's subjects in the various provinces; custom, a tax on consumption; and toll, a road tax or tax on land.

There is also evidence in archeological finds of the payment of taxes in the biblical period. The numerous jar handles stamped with *lamelek* ("for the king") stamps, as well as the large number of ostraca found at Samaria, indicate that payment in kind was well established. It seems that this was the method used by villagers, while city-dwellers paid in silver. In addition to the taxes levied by the kings, half a shekel was paid by each Israelite into the Temple treasury.

In order to collect this tax, levied on all Jews of 20 years of age and over, tax collectors were sent throughout Israel (Matt 17:24). Such an

Jar handle bearing a stamp-seal impression with the Hebrew inscription "of the king". Lachish. Late 7th century B.C.

enrollment for taxation is found in Acts 5:37, where it is recorded that disturbances ensued. Matthew was one of the tax officials (Matt 9:9) and Jesus is said to have kept company with such officials (Matt 9:9-10; Mark 2:15-17; Luke 5:29-32). When asked by the Pharisees whether or not it was lawful to pay taxes to Caesar, Jesus replied "Render therefore unto Caesar the things that are Caesar's and unto God the things that are God's" i.e., the laws of the state are to be obeyed (Matt 22:17-21; Mark 12:13-17; Luke 20:22-25). Paul, too, said that taxes should be paid to the state (Rom 13:6-7). See PUBLICAN.

TEBAH The firstborn son of Nahor, the brother of Abraham, by his concubine Reumah.

TEBALIAH ("Yah purified"). Third son of Hosah, a Merarite Levite. He headed a division of Temple gatekeepers at the time of King David.

TEBETH Name of Hebrew month adopted in the Persian period from the Akkadian to replace the older Hebrew designation, "the tenth month," which corresponds to December-January. In the Bible the name appears only in Esther 2:16.

TEHAPHNEHES See TAHPANHES.

TEHINNAH ("supplication"). A man of Judah, father or founder of the town of Ir-Nahash.

TEKOA, TEKOITES A town in Judah, not mentioned in the lists of cities conquered by Joshua but supplemented to Joshua 15:59 in the Septuagint. In the genealogical lists of Judah, Ashhur was the father of Tekoa (I Chr 2:24; 4:5). It was the home of David's "mighty men" (II Sam 23:26) and a wise woman of Tekoa was sent to David by Joab, son of Zeruiah, to plead for Absalom's return to the court (II Sam chap. 14). It was one of the cities fortified by Rehoboam (II Chr 11:6). After the return from the Babylonian Exile the people of Tekoa participated in rebuilding the walls of Jerusalem (Neh 3:5), and even repaired another section (Neh 3:27); but "their nobles did not put their shoulders to the work of the Lord" (Neh 3:5). In that period Tekoa was the capital of a small district. Identified with Khirbet Tequa, about 5 miles (8 km) south of Bethlehem.

The sign Capricorn representing the month of Tebeth. From the zodiac wheel in the center of the mosaic floor of the 6th-century synagogue at Bet Alfa.

Khirbet Tequa, identified with Tekoa.

Part of the baptistery of the Byzantine period church found at Tekoa.

TEL ABIB Place name in southern Babylonia mentioned only in Ezekiel 3:15 as the location in the vicinity of the River Chebar to where the Jewish exiles had been brought in 597 B.C. Misunderstood as Hebrew, meaning "hill of spring", the words actually represent an Akkadian phrase meaning "hill of the storm flood".

TELAH Descendant of Beriah son of Ephraim and ancestor of Joshua.

TELAIM ("young lambs"). A town in Judah where Saul gathered his troops to number them prior to the battle with King Agag and the Amalekites. Maybe an alternate name for Telem No.1.

TELASSAR (THELASSAR) Place in Mesopotamia mentioned by Rabshakeh the Assyrian commander-in-chief in his warning to Hezekiah king of Judah. It was the home of the people of Eden.

TELEM

1. City towards the border of Edom in the south of the territory allotted to Judah when the land of Canaan was divided among the tribes. Generally considered to be identical with Telaim.

2. A gatekeeper who, having taken an alien wife, repudiated her following the decree of Ezra.

TEL HARSHA One of five places in Babylonia, from which persons who could not prove their Jewish ancestry, nevertheless followed Zerubbabel when he returned to Judah (Ezra 2:59; Neh 7:61) upon the proclamation of the Edict of Cyrus.

TEL MELAH ("hill of salt"). The Hebrew name of a Babylonian site. Although its inhabitants could not prove their Jewish origin, they responded to Cyrus' edict that all Israelites who so wished could go to Jerusalem to rebuild the Temple.

TEMA

1. One of the 12 sons of Ishmael.

2. An oasis identified with the famous oasis of Teima in northern Arabia, 250 miles (400 km) southeast of Elath. In ancient times, Tema was the main caravan halt on the route from south Arabia to the countries of the Fertile Crescent. From Tema one route led to Duma, and from there to Babylon, while a second route led by way of Tabuk or Bayir to the countries on the eastern shores of the Mediterranean. These routes were used for conveying precious Arabian commodities, such as spices, gold and precious stones. In the Bible these corteges are called "caravans from Tema", or "travelers of Sheba" (Job 6:19).

The ruins of Tema consist of a wall many miles long, surrounding the oasis. Tema itself has not yet been excavated, but inscriptions written in an Arabian script now identified as "Taymanite", have been discovered nearby. Dated to the 6th century B.C. they are the earliest inscriptions found in this region.

Tema surrendered to the Assyrian king Shalmaneser III and paid a very heavy tribute of gold, silver and spices. King Nabonidus of Babylon (556-539 B.C.) abandoned his country and lived in Tema for some ten years, rebuilding and repopulating it.

TEMAN

1. Son of Eliphaz, grandson of Esau and his Hittite wife, Adah (Gen 36:11; I Chr 1:36); a chief of Edom, named after his place of origin.

2. The name of a town and a district in Edom, in the territory of King Husham "of the land of the Temanites" (Gen 36:34; I Chr 1:45). Teman is paralleled in the Bible with Edom (Jer 49:20; Ezek 25:13), and with the Mount of Esau (Obad v. 9). The comparison between Teman and Bozrah, the capital of Edom (Amos 1:12), only enhances the importance of Teman. The place has not been identified.

TEMANITES Inhabitants of Tema or Teman No.2.

TEL ABIB
Ezek 3:15

TELAH
I Chr 7:25

TELAIM
I Sam 15:4

TELASSAR
II Kgs 19:12
Is 37:12

TELEM 1
Josh 15:24

TELEM 2
Ezra 10:24

TEL HARSHA
Ezra 2:59.
Neh 7:61

TEL MELAH
Ezra 2:59.
Neh 7:61

TEMA 1
Gen 25:15.
I Chr 1:30

TEMA 2
Job 6:19. Is
21:14. Jer
25:23

TEMAN 1
Gen 36:11, 15,
42. I Chr 1:36,
53

TEMAN 2
Jer 49:7, 20.
Ezek 25:13.
Amos 1:12.
Obad v.9. Hab
3:3

TEMANITES
Gen 36:34. I
Chr 1:45. Job
2:11; 4:1; 15:1;
22:1; 42:7, 9

TEMENI Third son of Ashhur (the founder of Tekoa) by his second wife Naarah.

TEMPLE In ancient Israel, as in other cultures of the ancient Near East, the primary function of a temple was to serve as the dwelling place for the deity. The Bible provides indications, explicit and implicit, that in ancient Israel there were more than a dozen such houses of the Lord. They were found in Bethlehem and Hebron in Judah, Nob, Mizpah and Gibeah of Saul in Benjamin, Shiloh, Bethel, Gilgal, Shechem and Micah's house in Ephraim, Ophrah in Manasseh, Mizpah in Gilead and Dan in Naphtali. These temples were closed structures which housed tokens of divine presence (the ark, sacred pillars, teraphim) as well as objects for performance of daily cult (altars, lampstands and bread tables) and divination (ephod, Urim and Thummim). They were tended by priestly families, and served as places for pilgrimage and worship, community celebration of annual festivals and performance of public ceremonies of various types. Activities performed within their precincts were said to have been conducted "in the presence of the Lord". Several of these temples were maintained by private families, while others fostered traditions linking their foundation with the lives and migrations of the patriarchs. The tabernacle, which accompanied the Israelites in the desert, is also portrayed as a temple, only structurally adapted so as to be portable. No archeological remains of the temples mentioned have been found. The only Israelite temple uncovered in excavations — the one in Arad — is not mentioned in the Bible. A temple of God Yhw is mentioned in the Persian period papyri from the Jewish community of Elephantine in Egypt.

Of all the temples, the one which achieved prominence in later Israelite history and in the history of civilization in general was one of the latest — that in Jerusalem. The plan to build this Temple was conceived by King David as part of his program to make a tribally neutral and strategically located city both the political capital and the spiritual center (II Sam chaps. 5-7). He selected and purchased the site for the Temple, and made certain material preparations for the building project (II Sam 24:18-25; I Chr 21:17-29:20). Opposition of an unclear nature from Nathan the prophet (II Sam 7:1-17) and David's constant involvement in war are said to be the reasons that implementation of the design was postponed until the time of David's son and successor, Solomon.

The detailed account of the building of the Jerusalem Temple (I Kgs chaps. 5-8) is meant to portray Solomon as an ideal king. It contains certain literary material contemporary with the events described, but in its overall design it is a typical ancient Near Eastern royal building report of the kind found in numerous Mesopotamian inscriptions from the early 2nd millennium until the mid-1st millennium B.C. The building of the Temple is reported to have been started in Solomon's fourth year (I Kgs 6:1, 37). The building project lasted seven years, a typological number lending heroic proportions to the endeavor. Despite the positive portrayal of the building project, building the Temple and other public works actually placed a heavy burden on the public treasury and the native populace. This led to a large national debt, the eventual secession of border land to the neighboring king, and ultimately to popular unrest and the dissolution of the United Monarchy.

The prestige of the Temple in Jerusalem overshadowed that of other Israelite temples by its proximity to the royal court and patronage of the crown. The fact that it housed the venerated ark of the covenant designated it as the successor of the temple in Shiloh. Following the

Ostracon from Arad, early 6th century B.C. inscribed with a letter addressed to Eliashib and mentioning "the House of God". This is the earliest extra-biblical reference to the Temple.

Drawing of a reconstruction of Solomon's Temple according to G. Wright and F. Albright.

Assyrian devastation of the Northern Kingdom (722 B.C.) and its numerous temples, and the religious reforms under Kings Hezekiah and Josiah, the Jerusalem Temple achieved the status of the sole recognized site of legitimate cult. It was destroyed by the Babylonian army in 586 B.C. During its history of four centuries, the Temple had been repaired several times and changes introduced in its structure and furnishings. Under Kings Manasseh and Amon, the cults of other gods were temporarily introduced.

With the agreement and material assistance of the new Persian empire, the Temple of Jerusalem was refounded during the time of Cyrus the Great by repatriated exiles, but completion of its reconstruction was delayed through the opposition of Judah's neighbors and economic crisis until the time of Darius (Ezra chaps. 1-6; Hag; Zech chaps. 1-8). The rebuilt (Second) Temple, which was more modest than the first, was defiled and rededicated during the Hasmonean period and was eventually demolished and totally rebuilt as a magnificent new structure by King Herod. Herod's Temple was destroyed by Roman legions in A.D. 70.

As was the case with the other Israelite temples, nothing remains of the Solomonic Temple. Nonetheless, there is sufficient biblical evidence for a reasonably clear reconstruction of the details of the Temple, its decorations and furnishings. A minute description is found in I Kings chapters 6-7. A parallel, even though somewhat variant, description is provided by II Chronicles chapters 3-4. The prescription for the future Temple in Ezekiel chapters 40-48 as well as the description of the tabernacle in Exodus chapters 25-31, 35-40 are both reflections of the Solomonic Temple. Additional details of temple architecture may be gleaned from various stories preserved in the Book of Kings as well as from the prophetic books, especially Jeremiah and Ezekiel.

The Temple was a hewn stone building standing within a royal compound which also contained the palace, a Hall of Judgment, the Hall of Cedars and a house for Solomon's wife, Pharaoh's daughter. It was 60 cubits long, 20 wide and 30 high. It was faced by a patio of the forecourt which added 10 cubits to the length. The main structure

Model of the Second Temple based on the reconstruction made by Prof. Avi-Yonah, and now in the Holy Land Hotel, Jerusalem.

(excluding the patio) was surrounded by a three-story building. It was divided into chambers and the stories were connected by trap doors. This probably served as store rooms for Temple treasures. The main building was divided into an inner room, "Holy of Holies", measuring 20x20 cubits and an outer room measuring 20x40 cubits. Around the Temple was a walled-in courtyard.

The inner walls of the Temple were paneled with cedar wood. The floor of the Holy of Holies was likewise of cedar wood while less expensive cypress wood was used for the floor of the outer room. The walls were decorated with carvings of gourds, cherubim, palm trees and flowers in bloom. They were also encrusted with gold. There were doors to both the outer room and the Holy of Holies. The ones to the inner sanctum were of olive wood and the door posts were pentagonal. The doors to the outer sanctum were of cypress and the doorposts rectangular. The walls of the Holy of Holies were decorated on both sides and its floor was plated with gold (I Kgs 6:29-30). There thus seems to have been a material and technological gradation, the more expensive and ornately made items in the areas of greater sanctity, with less valuable and simpler ornamentations in areas of lesser sanctity.

The most important Temple vessel was the ark which was installed in the Holy of Holies on the occasion of the Temple's dedication. This sacred object linked the new Temple historically to the prestigious Shiloh temple as well as to the heroic age of the wanderings in the desert, but its main function was as a symbol of the divine presence within the Temple, for it represented God's footstool or throne. It was placed under the outspread wings of the two olive wood cherubim which Solomon had manufactured, also symbols of divine presence. In the outer room stood the main implements of the Temple's daily cult: an incense altar, a bread table and ten lampstands. These implements were made of gold or were gilded and their fabrication was attributed to Solomon. The most visible and impressive, although far from the most important cultically, were the bronze monumental implements produced by the Phoenician artisan Hiram and placed in the forecourt and in the courtyard in front of the Temple. In the forecourt stood the

A coin struck by Bar Kochba, leader of the revolt against the Romans in A.D. 132, showing the façade of the Temple.
(right)
Façade of the Second Temple model at the Holy Land Hotel, Jerusalem.

two pillars Jachin and Boaz. In front of the Temple, stood a "Sea", an immense bronze water basin supported by twelve bronze cattle. Along the east front of the building stood ten smaller water basins, each on its own wheeled stand, five to the north of the entrance and five to the south. The wheeled stands were decorated with lions, cherubim and bovine forms. A bronze altar also stood in the courtyard.

The original concept of the Temple as a House of God, a divine dwelling place within the human society, seems to have fallen out of favor and the Deuteronomistic literature associated with the religious reforms of King Josiah tries to redefine the function and meaning of the Temple. These new ideas are expressed especially in the great dedication prayer attributed to Solomon (I Kgs 8:14-61). The Temple is no longer thought of as God's dwelling place but rather a building associated with his name. It is a place on earth towards which God's eyes and ears are constantly directed and prayers said in the Temple or directed towards it from anywhere outside will therefore be heard and accepted. Despite the new ideas, the old concept of the Temple as a place of tangible divine presence never died out. In Ezekiel's vision of the Temple of the future, the Divine Majesty is to enter the Temple, just as it left the Old Temple prior to its destruction.

The most important task that faced the people on their return from the Babylonian Exile was the building of the new House of God. Both Zerubbabel, the secular leader and Jeshua the priest, erected the altar from which the sacrificial offerings were made (Ezra 3:2, 6). One of the important changes introduced into this new building was the addition of an outer court, which surrounded the Temple and the inner court. This new court was the Court of Women, to which both men and women were admitted (the inner court, the Court of Israel, was for men only). In the Hellenistic period, some embellishments were added from time to time. The Temple was defiled in the days of Antiochus IV (Dan

9:27, etc.), and was then reconsecrated by the Maccabees. It was completely rebuilt by Herod the Great, who began to build the new Temple in the 15th or 18th year of his reign. Ten thousand skilled laborers (1,000 of them priests), half stone-dressers, half carpenters, were engaged in the operation.

By building huge retaining walls Herod doubled the area of the Temple Mount. On top of this huge podium, most of which is still preserved, he built the Temple proper. All round the Temple Mount beautiful marble porticos were constructed. Two large bridges connected the Temple with the city on the west. In front of the Temple was the inner court, the Court of Israel, in which were the large altar, the laver, the slaughterhouse and the tables on which the offerings were prepared. Around this court were storerooms for the materials necessary to the ritual. To the west of it was the huge Court of the Women, with large rooms at each corner for Nazirites (people who had taken certain vows of abstinence) and lepers, and also for wood and oil.

The Temple itself contained the same three elements as Solomon's Temple: porch, hall and Holy of Holies. The back wall of the porch was gold-plated and in it hung a golden lamp. In the center of the facade was the main entrance, over which was suspended a golden bunch of grapes. The only pieces of furniture in the porch were the two tables, one of gold, the other of marble, on which the shewbread was placed. This entrance was covered only by a veil. In the hall stood the golden altar, the golden table for the shewbread, on which were two frankincense goblets and the golden candelabrum. A double veil separated the hall from the Holy of Holies, to which only the high priest had access, and then only on the Day of Atonement. There was no furniture at all in this part of the Temple.

The whole complex of Temple and courts was surrounded by a rail and entry to the enclosure was forbidden to Gentiles. The approach to

Stone inscribed with the words "To the place of trumpeting", found when excavations were undertaken on the Temple Mount.

(left)
The southern part of the Temple with the stairway leading to the stoa. From the model based on Prof. Avi-Yonah's reconstruction.

the Temple Mount was by two gates on the south, the Double and the Triple Gates. The king and the priests used the bridges on the west.

As a child Jesus was presented in the Temple (Luke 2:22-39), and was brought there when he reached the age of legal responsibility (Luke 2:41-51). During his ministry he visited the Temple (John 2:13-14), and approved its ritual practices (Matt 5:23-24), but he was critical of the formalism that menaces every cult, and reacted violently against certain corrupt practices associated with the Temple (Matt 21:12-17). He is reported as having predicted the destruction of the Temple (Matt 24:1-2) and its replacement by his own body as the place of God's encounter with humanity (Mark 14:58; John 2:18-22). The symbol of the tearing of the veil of the Temple (Mark 15:38) implied the end of the Temple as the sign of God's presence.

Nonetheless, those of his early disciples who were Jews continued to frequent the Temple (Acts 2:46; 3:1-11). Even Paul, who had repudiated Jewish practices for his pagan converts, went there to present an offering (Acts 21:26). Stephen, however, was put to death because of his criticism of the Temple (Acts 7:47-48).

Paul developed the concept of the community as a spiritual temple (I Cor 3:16-17; 6:19; II Cor 6:16), a theme that appears elsewhere only in the Dead Sea Scrolls. Paul derived the idea from the presence of God in the community, whereas the Essenes derived it from the concept of prayer as a spiritual sacrifice. For the latter it was but a temporary substitute for the polluted Temple in Jerusalem, but for the former it had a much more profound significance. It was a Temple in which all humanity could approach God, the wall dividing Jews from pagans, which had characterized the Jewish Temple, having been abolished (Eph 2:14-22).

A very different use of the Temple theme appears in Hebrews and Revelation. The Temple of Jerusalem is transferred to the heavenly sphere, and becomes the celestial sanctuary in which Christ, the new and eternal high priest, offers not the flesh of animals but his own blood (Heb 9:11ff), and in which the holy ones perform a continuous liturgy of prayer and praise (Rev 5:6-14; 7:15).

TEN COMMANDMENTS The imperatives pronounced by the Lord to the Israelites on Mount Sinai (decalogue, literally, "ten words"). They are recorded twice in the Pentateuch (Ex 20:1-17; Deut 5:6-21) with some differences in the formulation. These commandments were engraved on two stone tablets (Ex 31:18; 34:28; Deut 4:13; 5:19) inscribed on both sides (Ex 32:15). The biblical text does not specify the division of the commandments or their arrangement on the tablets. According to one tradition each tablet contained five commandments.

There are several ways to count the commandments. The first cluster of injunctions concerns the sole worship of the Lord God: opening with God's self introduction.

1-2 (1) a. "I am the Lord your God" (Ex 20:2).

b. "You shall have no other gods before me" (Ex 20:3).

c. "You shall not make for yourself any carved image" (Ex 20:4).

Commentators variously take the prohibition of polytheism and worship of images as a single commandment, considering God's self introduction, the root of all imperatives, as the first commandment; others take this self introduction as a preamble and count the first prohibitions as two separate commandments; still others consider the whole cluster one single injunction. This paragraph is rounded off by the prohibition of perjury; 3(2) "You shall not take the name of the Lord your God in vain" (Ex 20:7), 4(3) and the commandment on the Sabbath "Remember the Sabbath day, to keep it holy" (Ex 20:8). This

The tablets of the Law carved in stone.

The Ten Commandments from the so-called Nash Papyrus, dating from the 2nd century B.C.

last commandment relates both to the worship of God as well as to the world of man. Accordingly, it marks the transition to the next imperatives which concern human conduct in general.

5(4) "Honor your father and your mother" (Ex 20:12).

6(5) "You shall not murder".

7(6) "You shall not commit adultery".

8(7) "You shall not steal".

9(8) "You shall not bear false witness against your neighbor" (Ex 20:13).

In this cluster, the first injunction, positive as it is, might be considered a parallel to the first commandment. The four ensuing prohibitions all belong to the realm of criminal law. By contrast, the last commandment relates to ethics and intent, and concerns the roots of human ill-behavior.

10(9) "You shall not covet your neighbor's house; you shall not covet your neighbor's wife, nor his manservant..." (Ex 20:14).

Those commentators who take the first cluster as one injunction, split the last commandment into two clauses, one concerning desire of one fellow's property, the other relating to desire of his wife. This view is made possible by the recast of this commandment in Deuteronomy 5:2; which distinguished between the two:

a. "You shall not covet your neighbor's wife"

b. "and you shall not desire your neighbor's house, his field...".

A further difference between the version of Deuteronomy and the text in Exodus occurs in the Sabbath commandment; here Exodus 20:8 reads "Remember the Sabbath day", whereas Deuteronomy 5:12 has "Observe the Sabbath day". Other divergences relate to the motivation of the adjacent commandments on the Sabbath and the honoring of one's parents (Ex 20:9-12; Deut 5:13-16).

These differences probably arise from the special rhetorical style of Moses' oration on Deuteronomy, and the emphasis on humanism found in this book. Thus the reason for the Sabbath is here stated to be the redemption from Egypt and the need to give rest to all and not, as in Exodus, a reminder of the custom of the world.

The decalogue stands out as God's proclamation of his will to all the people of Israel. This revelation thus forms the foundation for all ethical and religious obligations.

TERAH

1. Son of Nahor (See NAHOR No.1), father of Abraham (See ABRAHAM), Nahor (See NAHOR No.2) and Haran (See HARAN No.1). According to Joshua 24:2, Terah worshiped "other gods". According to Genesis chapter 12 the Lord summoned Abraham to leave his native land and his father's house, and set out for the land of Canaan, but Genesis chapter 11 claims that it was Terah who devised the move from Ur of the Chaldees via Haran (See HARAN No.2) to Canaan. However, Terah did not manage to complete the journey as he died in Haran. Modern scholars have associated the personal name Terah with the Akkadian place name *til sa Turahi*, i.e., "Terah's hill", which is located near Haran.

2. Twelfth of the 21 encampments of the Israelites between the wilderness of Sinai and Mount Hor (Num 33:16-37). Its location has not been identified.

TERAPHIM While the term teraphim probably originally referred to a very active protective spirit of the individual (according to a probable Hittite etymology), the biblical term teraphim, is used to designate the images of protective spirits and household idols. Thus the use of the teraphim as vehicles for augury and divination (Ezek 21:21) was

TERAH 1
Gen 11:24-28, 31-32. Josh 24:2. I Chr 1:26. Luke 3:34

TERAH 2
Num 33:27-28

TERAPHIM
Hos 3:4

considered idolatrous and rebellious (I Sam 14:23; II Kgs 23:24) and doomed to failure because it was untrue (Zech 10:2). The term teraphim was connected on the one hand with the vocabulary of fetishistic idolatry e.g., "carved image and molten image" (Judg 18:14, 17-18), and on the other hand with technical terms having to do with augury and divination, e.g., "ephod" (Judg 17:5; Hos 3:4) and even ghosts and familiar spirits. Two other narratives in which the teraphim play an important role are Genesis chapter 31 and I Samuel chapter 19. In the former, the teraphim are stolen by Rachel (Gen 31:19), placed in a camel cushion, sat upon (Gen 31:34) and sought to no avail (Gen 31:35); in the latter, the teraphim (here with a singular force despite the plural form) is laid upon a bed with a net of goat's hair at its head and covered with a cloth by Michal (I Sam 19:13, 16), in order to give the impression that David was lying sick in the bed. In the case of Rachel's theft of the teraphim, her motive is not specified. Some interpret Rachel's theft in accordance with the custom of taking along the household gods when traveling to a foreign land (probably to ensure good luck). Since Rachel was breaking up her family unit and leaving secretly, she could not ask her father for replicas of the household gods, and she therefore stole them. Others assume that she took these household gods in order to insure her future share in the family inheritance.

TEREBINTH See PLANTS

TERESH One of two eunuchs of King Ahasuerus who guarded the threshold and who sought to lay hands on the king. Mordecai foiled their plot and they were hanged (Est 6:2).

TERTIUS ("the third"). One of the scribes or secretaries to whom Paul dictated his epistles and the only one whose name is known — because he inserted a salutation of his own in the Epistle to the Romans.

TERTULLUS The spokesman of Paul's accusers before Felix the governor of Judea in Caesarea. Tertullus first praised Paul and then accused him of being a public nuisance, creating dissension among the Jews and belonging to the sect of the Nazarenes (Acts 24:1-9).

THADDAEUS A disciple of Jesus mentioned as one of the twelve disciples in Matthew 10:3 and Mark 3:18 but not in the Gospel of Luke nor in Acts 1:13 where "Judas the son of James" appears in his place. In some translations, his first name is given as Lebbeus.

THAHASH (TAHASH) ("badger"). Third son of Nahor (the brother of Abraham) by his concubine Reumah.

THARSHISH See TARSHISH

THEBES See NO AMON

THEBEZ A town in the vicinity of Shechem, where Abimelech was slain (Judg 9:50-54; II Sam 11:21). A place of this name also existed in the Roman period. This distance fits well the modern village of Tubas, north of Nablus, where remains from the Israelite and later periods were found.

THEODICY A defense of divine justice. Although the term was coined by the philosopher Leibniz, the concept itself is ancient. From Mesopotamia two literary works pertaining to the problem of theodicy have survived: *I Will Praise the Lord of Wisdom* and the *Babylonian Theodicy*. These were preceded by a Sumerian parallel to Job, *Man and his God*. The only extant Egyptian parallel occurs within the *Admonitions of Ipuwer*, but belief in an afterlife and in the divinity of the pharaohs probably explains the paucity of references to theodicy in Egyptian texts. In Israel the issue achieved significance because of the conviction that the Lord was moral, a view placed in the mouth of the patriarch Abraham: "Shall not the Judge of all the earth do right?" (Gen 18:25). The prevailing views of priests, prophets and sages took for granted a harmonious universe operating on the principle of reward for goodness and punishment for wickedness. The classic presentation of Israel's divine election, Deuteronomy, and the history based on that work, Joshua-Kings, applied this principle to the nations and thereby offered an explanation for defeat at the hands of Assyria and Babylonia. A later version of this history, Chronicles, took the principle of reward and retribution to an extreme, individualizing a concept that had been applied to the nation. Cracks in this world view, however, are highlighted in the Books of Job and Ecclesiastes. Various attempts to recognize inequities and to explain the deity's role in them occur within the OT: Gideon's audacious response to an angel's reassuring words (Judg 6:13), the prophet Habakkuk's attempt to understand injustice occasioned by divine inaction; Jonah's astonishing complaint because the Lord had compassion on wicked, but repentant, inhabitants of Nineveh; Jeremiah's immensely poignant laments, often labeled confessions, that God has raped and betrayed him; Ezekiel's insistence that people who reject divine justice are guilty of faulty logic; the psalmist's inner struggles to affirm the Lord's goodness (Ps 37, 49, 73). Within the apocryphal literature, one work stands out for the intensity with which it addresses the problem of theodicy (Second Esdras), but other books also reflect on the issue at length (Tobit, Ecclesiasticus, Wisdom of Solomon). No satisfactory answer to what humans perceived to be divine injustice were put forward, but several responses brought a measure of relief: humans are innately sinful, so that they have no claim on the deity; the suffering is temporary and will be removed in a future act by a long-suffering Lord; the presence of the Lord is the supreme good, not health, prosperity and happiness; injustice will be set right in another life. In NT times belief in a resurrection removed some of the sting from such inequities, although they persisted nonetheless. It is noteworthy that Jesus is said to have observed that God bestowed gifts (sunshine and rain) on the just and on the unjust, but the assumption of reward and retribution persisted in the NT as well.

THEOPHILUS ("friend of God"). The man to whom the Gospel of Luke (Luke 1:3) and the Acts of the Apostles (Acts 1:1) are dedicated. He is called "excellent" in the Gospel of Luke.

THEOPHILUS
Luke 1:3. Acts 1:1

THESSALONIANS, THE FIRST EPISTLE TO THE Thirteenth book of the NT.

In about 49 or 50, Paul's second missionary journey brought him to Thessalonica (Acts 17:1-9). Accompanied by Silas and Timothy, he went, as was his custom, to preach in the local synagogue. His message was simple and to the point: the Scriptures say that the messiah must suffer (i.e. die) and rise from the dead. Jesus, being the fulfillment of those Scriptures is, therefore, the messiah. Some Jews believed, as did many devout Greeks and influential women. But this success among the Gentiles aroused a jealous zeal in some of those Jews who did not believe, and they chased the apostles out of town. They went to Berea but were followed by the Thessalonian zealots. Paul proceeded to Athens and thence to Corinth (Acts 17:9-18:1). Here he was rejoined by Silas and Timothy, who came from Macedonia.

It was from Corinth that the three men wrote back to the young church in Thessalonica. The events of Acts 18:1-18 took place in Corinth in the time of the Achaian proconsul Gallio, who was in office in c.51. This gives an accurate chronological point of reference for the composition of both I and II Thessalonians, which were written a few weeks apart. They may be the earliest of Paul's writings, depending on the dating of Galatians (q.v.).

Acts 17:2 would seem to indicate that Paul and his companions were in Thessalonica only about three weeks, although it could have been somewhat longer. While the two letters show that Paul had been able to impart a great deal to them, his stay was nonetheless a short one. Some problems of the community had not been adequately dealt with, and some areas of teaching had not been fully clarified. Paul wanted to return to them but having been hindered from doing so (I Thes 2:18), the next best alternative was a letter.

Paul's letters are usually characterized by the close personal relationship between the writer and the recipients. His epistles to Thessalonica are exemplary of this. Again and again he recalls little details of his recent time with them, what he said to them, how they responded, how he acted, what affection they shared. This intimacy has its disadvantages for the third party, since much is hinted at but unspoken. Assuming they will remember what he had taught, Paul does not always repeat it, leaving the later reader guessing. The letter gives special insight into Paul's missionary methods, the kinds of things he emphasized in his teaching, and the way he conducted himself.

One doctrinal matter, the question of eschatology, is unique to Paul's letters to the church in Thessalonica. This subject must have occupied a significant portion of his teaching there, and Paul seeks to clarify it in both letters. In this first letter (4:13-5:5) he focuses on the questions of the future order of events when the Lord comes for his church, and specifically, what will happen to those believers who have already died. He emphasizes that the day of the Lord will come suddenly, without warning, that the "dead in Christ" will rise to meet the coming Lord, followed by those who are still alive. (See also the following entry).

OUTLINE

1:1-10	Greeting and Paul's praise of their good name
2:1-12	On the conduct of Paul and his friends while in Thessalonica
2:13-16	How they received the gospel amidst tribulation
2:17-3:13	Paul's longing to see them
4:1-12	Exhortation to holiness and right conduct
4:13-5:11	On the Lord's coming and the resurrection of the brethren who have died
5:12-28	More practical exhortation and closing words

THESSALONIANS, THE SECOND EPISTLE TO THE The fourteenth book of the NT. This letter of Paul to the Macedonian church at Thessalonica was written shortly after the letter known as I Thessalonians. For details of date, context and venue, see the previous entry.

During his sojourn with the Thessalonians and in his first letter to them, Paul had spoken extensively about the coming of the Lord. Certain statements in his first letter (or similar ones made while he was at Thessalonica), may have led them to expect Jesus to return in the immediate future (I Thes 2:19; 3:13; 5:23). Paul's intention in the first letter had been to show the suddenness of Jesus' coming (I Thes 4:16). In this second letter he clarifies this by pointing out (II Thes 2:2-12) that the "day of the Christ" could not have come yet because certain conditions had still to be met. There will first be a falling away from the faith by some and the appearance of a figure Paul calls "the man of sin,... the son of perdition". If these things are obscure to the modern reader, it is because Paul had explained them in detail to the Thessalonians while he was with them; now it was enough for him to say "you know what is restraining" (2:6) without further elaboration.

Because members of the congregation seem to have understood (as some were actually saying), that the end had already begun, there were those who decided it was not necessary to work and earn a living. Some may have been predisposed to this even before Paul's coming to them, because he had already spoken out against such laziness while he was there (I Thes 4:1ff; II Thes 3:10). In this second letter he goes to some length (3:6-15) to stress the need for honest industry. He recalls that he and his companions had worked even during the short time they were in Thessalonica, and he lays down disciplinary measures to be taken against any who persist in their voluntary unemployment.

OUTLINE

1:1-2	Greeting
1:3-5	Praise of the Thessalonians' good conduct in face of persecution
1:6-12	Their promised vindication
2:1-12	Events to precede the Lord's coming
2:13-3:5	Exhortation to steadfastness in light of God's faithfulness
3:6-15	On dealing with undisciplined church members
3:16-18	Closing

THESSALONICA, THESSALONIANS Now Saloniki (Salonica). Capital of Macedonia. Its direct overland and overseas connections made the city into a commercial and strategical center. Under the Roman Empire it was a free city and developed into the most important city of Macedonia.

During his second missionary journey Paul went to Thessalonica where he visited the synagogue and "for three Sabbaths reasoned with them from the Scriptures." (Acts 17:1-2). Paul founded a Christian community in the city, but he also aroused envy and anger among those of its Jews who did not accept his teachings (Acts 17:5-10): the uproar raised by the latter obliged Paul to leave Thessalonica, together with Silas.

THEUDAS A false prophet who led a rebellion in Judea. With a mass of followers (put at 400 in Acts 5:36), he went to the Jordan River which he said would part at his command. The Roman procurator sent troops who killed or captured the followers and took Theudas to Jerusalem where he was beheaded. Information on the uprising comes both in Acts and in Josephus (*Antiq.* XX, 97-99) although with a discrepancy concerning the date. Josephus says it took place during the procuratorship of Cuspius Fadus (A.D. 44-46) but Acts places it much earlier, even before the appearance of Judah the Galilean (who died A.D. 6). Historians consider Josephus' dating more accurate.

THISTLE, THORN See PLANTS

THOMAS One of the twelve disciples of Jesus. In Matthew 10:3; Mark 3:18; Luke 6:15 and Acts 1:13 he is called Thomas, but in John 11:16; 20:24 and 21:2 he is given a further name, Didymus ("twin"). In the Synoptic Gospels and Acts no special details are mentioned about him, but in the Gospel of John, he is more prominent, especially towards the end of Jesus' life. When Jesus decided to return to Jerusalem, Thomas encouraged the other disciples saying "Let us also go, that we may die with him" (John 11:16). Thomas also participated in the conversation after the Last Supper (John 14:5). On the evening of the day of the resurrection Thomas declined to believe that Jesus had appeared to the other disciples (John 20:24) — hence the term "doubting Thomas". When Jesus appeared again after eight days, Thomas was there also and on seeing him confessed: "My Lord and my God" (John 20:28). John 21:2 mentions Thomas among those who were at the Sea of Galilee when Jesus appeared to them. One of the apocryphal gospels bears his name.

THREE INNS, THREE TAVERNS A halt on the apostle Paul's journey to Rome, by the Appii Forum, 33 miles (50km) from Rome.

A tavern of the same name is mentioned several times in the works of Cicero.

Jesus shows his wounds to St. Thomas. Relief on the capital of a column of the Crusader period, found during excavations at the site of the Church of the Annunciation in Nazareth.

*(top of page)
Remains of Galerius' triumphal arch at Salonika, formerly called Thessalonica.*

The place said to be the site of the Three Inns or the Three Taverns, a few miles south of Rome where the Christians of the city came to meet Paul.

A coin struck in Tiberias with the name of the town in a wreath. A.D. 28.

A view of Tiberias.

A stone bust of the emperor Tiberius.

THUMMIM See URIM AND THUMMIM

THYATIRA A city in Lydia (Asia Minor) on the Lycus River with a thriving local industry, including purple dyeing. Lydia, the seller of purple at Philippi, was from Thyatira (Acts 16:14). Thyatira was one of the seven churches to which an epistle in the Book of Revelation is addressed (Rev 1:11, 2:18). Identified as present-day Akhisar.

TIBERIAS A city on the western shore of the Sea of Galilee, near hot springs, founded about A.D. 18 by Herod Antipas and named in honor of the Emperor Tiberius. The layout was that of a Hellenistic or Roman city, with streets intersecting at right angles, and Herod adorned it with public buildings, including a stadium on the seashore, a large synagogue and a place for himself on a high hill where he set up sculptures and thereby aroused the condemnation of orthodox religious circles.

Tiberias is mentioned only once in the NT (John 6:23). The Sea of Galilee is sometimes called Tiberias after the name of the city on its western shore (John 6:1; 21:1).

TIBERIUS Roman emperor A.D. 14-37, murdered by Caligula, who succeeded him. The ministry of John the Baptist began in the 15th year of Tiberius' reign.

TIBHATH A town in Aram Zobah which was conquered by David after he defeated Hadadezer. David took a great quantity of bronze from Tibhath (I Chr 18:8). In II Samuel 8:8, it is called Betah.

TIBNI The son of Ginath, Tibni tried unsuccessfully to wrest the Israelite throne from Omri, who had killed Zimri (the murderer of Elah son of Baasha, king of Israel). A three-year long civil war with Omri culminated in Tibni's death (I Kgs 16:10ff).

TIGLATH-PILESER (In Chronicles Tiglath-Pilneser). Name borne by three Assyrian kings, the last of whom was Tiglath-Pileser III, who ruled Assyria from 745 to 727 B.C. It is the Hebraized form of the Akkadian personal name Tukulti-apil-Ešarra, which means, "My hope is the son of the temple of Assur at Assur."

Tiglath-Pileser III defeated Azriyau king of Yadiya in 742 B.C. and the remaining independent rulers of Syria-Palestine, including Menahem of Israel and Azariah of Judah, acknowledged his overlordship by presenting tribute. Eight years later various Syro-Palestinian rulers led by Rezin of Damascus and including Pekah of Israel, again sought to assert their independence. Since King Ahaz of Judah was pro-Assyrian, Pekah and Rezin sought to depose him and to

Tiglath-Pileser III and attendants shown on a wall painting from his palace at Til Barsip (Tell Ahmar, Syria) 8th century B.C.

enthrone in his stead a certain "son of Tabeel" (Is 7:3-6). Ahaz acknowledged the suzerainty of Tiglath-Pileser, and received the latter's support. Tiglath-Pileser defeated the rebel kingdoms including Israel, most of whose territory was taken away. For the first time numerous Israelites were exiled to Assyria (II Kgs 15:29). Possibly with the help of Tiglath-Pileser, Hoshea son of Elah overthrew Pekah and became king of Israel. From 729 B.C. Tiglath-Pileser also ruled as king of Babylon. There, apparently, he was known as Pulu; hence he is referred to as Pul in II Kings 15:19 and I Chronicles 5:26.

TIGRIS See HIDDEKEL

TIKVAH ("hope"). Alternate form of Tokhath (II Chr 34:22).

1. The son of Harhas and father-in-law of the prophetess Huldah.

2. The father of Jahaziah who is mentioned as opposing the repudiation of alien women.

TILON Fourth son of Shimon in the genealogy of the family of Judah.

TIMAEUS Father of Bartimaeus the blind beggar cured by Jesus.

TIME For those who reckoned according to a lunar calendar, as did the ancient Hebrews, the 24-hour day lasted from evening to evening: "and God called the light Day and the darkness he called Night. And the evening and the morning were the first day" (Gen 1:5). For the Egyptians, on the other hand, the day began at dawn. The Babylonians divided day and night into three watches each, while the Egyptians divided the same periods into four watches each.

The ancient Hebrews did not have such a rigid system of divisions. Instead the following terms appear: "rising of the morning" (Neh 4:21), "dawning of the day" (Job 3:9), "light of the morning" (II Sam 23:4), "morning" (Ps 55:17), "noon" (Ps 55:17), "noonday" (Job 5:14), "twilight" (Prov 7:9), "evening" (Prov 7:9) and "dark night" (Gen 1:5; Prov 7:9). The time of day could also be fixed by reference to certain activities that normally took place at a certain time, one example being "the time of the evening, even the time that women go out to draw water" (Gen 24:11). Thus midday was the "heat of the day" (Gen 18:1). The later hours of the afternoon were defined by the long shadows (Jer 6:4) and the early morning by "until the day break, and the shadows flee away" (Song 2:17). But the system of dividing the night into watches is not completely missing among the ancient Hebrews, who probably borrowed the practice from the Babylonians. The first watch was named "the beginning of the watches" (Lam 2:19); the second, the "middle watch" (Judg 7:19) and the last, the "morning watch" (I Sam 11:11). The Babylonians divided the day into equal parts by using sundials. There is no indication in the Bible of such a division, although a time-measuring device, the sundial of Ahaz (Is 38:8; II Kgs 20:9), is mentioned. The basic difference between the Babylonian and biblical conception of time is that the first began the day in the morning, while it was the other way round with the Hebrews, whose festivals began in the evening of the day preceding the feast (Ex 12:18, etc.).

The week, a unit of time, consisting of seven days, is found for the first time in the Bible. It accords approximately with the moon's orbit; but as the week does not necessarily begin on the day of the new moon, it is not affected by inconsistencies in relation to the positions of the moon during the month. In contrast to this the Babylonian and Assyrian week began on the first day of the month. The week of seven days was thus completely independent of the month, a factor which became more important when the Sabbath took the place of the day of the New Moon as the sacred day.

At first the term "month" was applied only to the first day of the month, but later the whole period between the first and last days was so called. There are three systems of naming months in the Bible: by early Canaanite names; by consecutive numbers; and by Babylonian names. The Canaanite names were in use in Judah and Israel until the time of the Babylonian Exile. Of these only four are now known: Abib, the first month (Ex 13:4); Ziv, the second (I Kgs 6:37); Ethanim, the seventh (I Kgs 8:2); and Bul, the eighth (I Kgs 6:38). The last two are also known from Canaanite sources, in which five additional months are listed. There are notable preferences in the Bible for numerical names rather than Canaanite ones. The meaning of the name of the first month, Abib, is "ripening barley", but the meaning of the others remains obscure.

During the Babylonian Exile the Jews adopted the local Babylonian calendar. Of the Babylonian names of months seven are known from the Bible: Nissan (Neh 2:1); Sivan (Est 8:9); Elul (Neh 6:15); Kislev (Neh 1:1); Tebeth (Est 2:16); Shebat (Zech 1:7) and Adar (Est 3:7). In certain cases the Bible gives both the name of the month and its numerical order (Est 3:7; 8:9).

TIMNA

1. Sister of Lotan, the Horite chief in the land of Edom (Gen 36:22). She was the concubine of Eliphaz (the firstborn son of Esau) and the mother of his son Amalek (Gen 36:12).

2. A son of Eliphaz, the son of Esau; the name is sometimes spelt Teman though the Hebrew spelling is identical to that of Timna. May be identical with Timnah No.3.

3. An alternative spelling for Timnah No. 3 in some translations.

TIMNA 1
Gen 36:12
I Chr 1:39

TIMNA 2
I Chr 1:36

TIMNA 3
Gen 36:40
Chr 1:51

TIMNAH (TIMNATAH)

1. A town in the northern Judean plain. Timnah plays a prominent role in the Samson story, being the home town of his first wife, and the setting of the tale of the lion and the honey (Judg 14:1-2, 5-18). According to biblical record, the town had a checkered history, changing hands among the Danites, Judahites and the Philistines during the time of both the Judges and the kings of Judah (Josh 15:10; 19:43; Judg 14:1-5; II Chr 28:18). It is apparently this same Timnah which appears in the tale of Judah and Tamar (Gen chap. 38).

Timnah, identified with Tell Batashi, has been recently excavated. The excavations have shown a continuous occupation of the site from the Middle Bronze Age II through the Persian period, including severely burnt Late Bronze levels rich in finds, a prominent — and perhaps fortified — Philistine level and an Israelite level which gradually develops into a well-planned and fortified town, extremely well preserved.

2. A town in the southeast Judean hill country, on the fringes of the Judean desert.

3. One of the chiefdoms of Esau. The name is today applied to a valley near Elath where ancient copper mines and industrial settlements, chiefly of the Egyptian New Kingdom period, have been discovered.

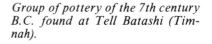

Group of pottery of the 7th century B.C. found at Tell Batashi (Timnah).

(above)
Mycenean pottery from the Late Bronze Age found at Tell Batashi (Timnah).

(above left)
Tell Batashi, the ancient site of Timnah.

(left)
The so-called Window at Timnah excavations near Elath. (Nature Reserves Authority)

(right)
Votive cup of the 13th century found at the Midianite temple, at Timnah. (Courtesy B. Rothenberg)

TIMNAT HERES, TIMNAT SERAH A place in the hill country of Ephraim. It was apportioned by the Israelites to Joshua after the conquest (Josh 19:50) and it was there that he was later buried (Josh 24:30). The site has been identified with Khirbet Tibna in the western hills of Ephraim, and has yet to be excavated.

TIMNITE Inhabitant of Timnah No.1. Samson's father-in-law is referred to as a Timnite.

TIMON ("honorable"). One of the seven "men of good reputation" (Acts 6:3) among the Hellenists chosen to help the apostles in Jerusalem in their lay work.

TIMOTHY Traveling companion and fellow worker of Paul. A native of Lystra in the province of Galatia, Timothy was the son of a heathen father and a Jewish mother, Eunice. Both his mother and his grandmother Lois were believers in Jesus, and Timothy seems to have received a good Bible education (II Tim 1:5; 3:14ff). His parents did not circumcise him (Acts 16:3), but when Paul returned to Lystra on his second missionary journey, he circumcised Timothy and took him along. In Philippi he must have been present when Paul and Silas were beaten with rods, if he was not in fact himself beaten with them. Timothy became a useful messenger for Paul, representing him at various times in Thessalonica (I Thes 3:2), Corinth (I Cor 4:17), Ephesus (I Tim 1:3) and Macedonia (Acts 19:22; cf Phil 2:19). He is named as co-author of no less than seven of Paul's 11 letters (excluding the two to Timothy himself). From the two pastoral letters addressed to Timothy, the impression is created that he may have been a reticent person. The laying on of hands by Paul and the elders endowed him with spiritual gifts (perhaps as evangelist and teacher [I Tim 4:16; II Tim 4:5]) and yet in both letters Paul has to exhort him to get out and use them (I Tim 4:14; II Tim 1:6). In these and the surrounding verses Timothy appears as timid, fearful of asserting himself, perhaps because of his relative youth. According to later traditions Timothy became the first bishop of Ephesus and was martyred there in the year 97.

TIMOTHY, FIRST EPISTLE TO Fifteenth book of the NT; with II Timothy and Titus, one of the "Pastoral Epistles", so called because they were written to individuals for the purpose of offering personal guidance and advice in the matter of administering a local church. The following section is valid for all three letters.

Until the early 19th century no one seriously called into question the veracity of the opening word of these letters, which identifies the author as the apostle Paul. Since Schleiermacher, however, an ever-increasing number of scholars have put forward reasons for doubting Paul's authorship. The objections, and the defense of the Pauline authorship, may be considered in five areas.

(a) The Pastoral Epistles contain numerous references to events in Paul's life which cannot be fitted into the chronological framework of the Acts of the Apostles. From linguistic and other considerations, it is evident that the three letters were composed around the same time. Free to move about in I Timothy and Titus, Paul is a prisoner at the writing of II Timothy (1:8; 2:9). He has evidently recently visited Ephesus, Macedonia (I Tim 1:3), Troas, Corinth, Miletus (II Tim 4:13, 20) and Crete (Titus 1:5), and is planning a trip to Nicopolis (probably in Epirus, Titus 3:12). A tradition is preserved by Eusebius that Paul, released after his first imprisonment in Rome, spent further time of travel and ministry before being again imprisoned in Rome and subsequently martyred. If true, this could adequately encompass the travels mentioned here and Paul's apparent presence in Rome at the time of writing II Timothy (1:17).

TIMNAT HERES
TIMNAT SERAH
**Josh 19:50;
24:30. Judg
2:9**

TIMNITE
Judg 15:6

TIMON
Acts 6:5

TIMOTHY
**Acts 16:1;
17:14-15; 18:
19:22; 20:4.
Rom 16:21. I
Cor 4:17;
16:10. II Cor
1:1, 19. Phil
1:1; 2:19. Col
1:1. I Thes
1:1; 3:2, 6. II
Thes 1:1. I
Tim 1:2, 18;
6:20. II Tim
1:2. Philem v.
Heb 13:23**

Page of the First Epistle to Timothy from the 18th-century illuminated Burgos Bible. (Jewish National and University Library)

(b) The false teaching mentioned in I Timothy 6:20 especially would seem to be Gnosticism, which is known to have flourished in the 2nd century. However, the heresies attacked in the epistles are far from developed Gnosticism, and more recent scholarship has suggested that this heresy had its beginnings much earlier than was previously thought.

(c) Some have negated Paul's authorship on the grounds that the letters lack any discussion of the doctrines which are known to have been so central to Paul. Those who affirm his authorship point to the unique nature of the letters, written to individual co-workers and disciples of Paul who were thoroughly acquainted with his doctrines. They feel that the absence of such standard Pauline material only tends to preclude the likelihood that they were consciously fathered on Paul by a later writer.

(d) It has been suggested that the organization discussed in I Timothy chapters 3 and 5 and in Titus chapter 1 reflects a later development of ecclesiastical structure. The counter-argument contends that the picture in these epistles is more primitive than that in the letters of Ignatius of Antioch, who would, on this view, be contemporary with the Pastorals; and that moreover, the Book of Acts can be shown to contain the same supposedly later developments (cf Acts 6:1; 14:23; 20:17, 28).

(e) The final objection to Paul's authorship has to do with the vocabulary of the Pastorals. Numerous words here appear nowhere else in the NT. Most significant are the smaller words, the particles, prepositions and pronouns which can so characterize a writer's style. Statistical analyses are important for this argument, though caution must be used in this respect because the numerical sample from all of Paul's letters is not large enough to make results certain. While the Pastorals differ considerably from Paul's acknowledged letters, even the latter display a wide variation of vocabulary. Defenders of the Pauline authorship explain the vocabulary differences here by the personal nature of the epistles, the age of the author and the possible use of a secretary who put Paul's basic ideas into letter form. If Paul's authorship be accepted, then the letter will have been written in the mid-60's, possibly from Macedonia (I Tim 1:3). Scholars who think otherwise date them somewhat later, in the 1st century.

The epistle depicts Paul as having recently left Timothy (see previous entry) at Ephesus for the purpose of countering certain strange and unhealthy doctrines which have cropped up there (1:3ff). Timothy was a younger man (4:12), and a letter from the apostle may have been of help in maintaining his authority. Included are a number of pointers on church administration, and even some personal advice on how to relate to different age groups (5:1-2). Of special significance is the treatment of certain ecclesiastical offices (overseer, or bishop elder or presbyter, deacon, widow) and the qualifications for membership in each.

OUTLINE

1:1-2	Salutation
1:3-10	Warning against strange doctrines
1:11-16	Paul's personal testimony
1:17	Doxology
1:18-20	Personal exhortation to Timothy
2:1-7	Strategy for the salvation of all people
2:8-15	Standards of conduct for men and women
3:1-13	Standards for church leaders
3:14-15	Paul's reason for writing
3:16	Hymn on the mystery of godliness
4:1-10	On the proper focus of good teaching
4:11-5:2	Personal advice to Timothy
5:3-16	Treatment of widows in the church
5:17-22	On relating to elders
5:23	Medicinal advice
5:24-25	The visibility of our good and bad deeds
6:1-2	Slaves
6:3-10	Godliness and material gain
6:11-16	Personal exhortation
6:17-19	Instructions for the rich
6:20-21	Final instruction

TIMOTHY, SECOND EPISTLE TO Sixteenth book of the NT, and one of the so-called "Pastoral Epistles". For a full discussion of questions of authenticity and authorship, see the previous entry.

Near the end of his life in the mid-60's Paul wrote this letter from prison in Rome (1:8, 17). Paul probably enjoyed an interlude of freedom after his first two-year imprisonment in Rome (Acts 28:30; cf II Tim 4:16ff). During this time, which could have lasted a couple of years, he wrote letters to Timothy in Ephesus (I Tim 1:2-3) and Titus in Crete (Titus 1:4-5). Then he was again imprisoned, and at the writing of this letter he seems to foresee his own imminent end (II Tim 4:6-8, 18). On this reconstruction, and on the assumption that Paul was indeed the author, II Timothy would be the last of his extant letters.

While properly classed together with I Timothy and Titus, II Timothy must be seen as "pastoral" in a sense different from the other two. The epistle still contains warnings against troublemakers and heretics (e.g. 2:14-18; 3:1-9; 4:3-4, 14ff), but almost entirely absent is the practical advice on running church affairs which so dominates the two earlier letters. There is a deeper personal sense here, with more information about Timothy himself than anywhere else in the NT (1:5-7; 3:14ff); concomitantly, it is Paul himself who is in focus as he shares his frustrations, fears and hopes for the future. The text tells of his heartbreaking experience of being deserted by erstwhile friends in his hour of need (1:15; 4:10, 14-16). While still expecting with full certainty the coming of his Lord (1:12; 4:1, 18), he reflects on his own difficult life of service (2:3-10; 3:10-12) and, with a sober realism born out of that experience, he foresees more hard times ahead for the church he has worked to establish (3:1-9). And yet here is no embittered pessimist but rather a man convinced that his life's greatest moment is not far away: "I have fought the good fight, I have finished the race, I have kept the faith. Finally, there is laid up for me the crown of righteousness, which the Lord, the righteous Judge, will give to me on that day" (4:7ff).

OUTLINE

1:1-2	Salutation
1:3-14	Timothy exhorted to show initiative in his ministry
1:15-18	Unfaithful and faithful brethren
2:1-13	Endurance enjoined and illustrated
3:1-9	The last days described
3:10-17	Timothy encouraged to remember Paul's example and his own Bible training
4:1-5	Fulfill your ministry
4:6-18	Paul describes his present situation and looks to the future
4:19-22	Greetings and closing words

TIPHSAH ("crossing place").

1. A city or place on the northern border of the kingdom of Solomon, by the Euphrates River.

2. A city attacked by Menahem king of Israel when it refused to surrender. The king destroyed the entire city and killed all its pregnant women. Many scholars believe that the name of the city should in fact read Tappuah, a city some 30 miles (50km) north of Jerusalem, near Tirzah.

TIRAS One of the sons of Japheth (I Chr 1:5), apparently of the nations of the Aegean Sea.

TIRATHITES A family of scribes, belonging to the Kenite tribe, who dwelled at Jabez.

TIRHAKAH Last pharaoh of Egypt's Ethiopian (25th) Dynasty, as well as king of Ethiopia, c. 690-664 B.C. Tirhakah the "king of Ethiopia" is mentioned in II Kings 19:9 and Isaiah 37:9 as opposing the Assyrian monarch Sennacherib, who at the time was besieging Hezekiah in Jerusalem. Sennacherib's records tell of a successful battle against Egyptian and Ethiopian forces at Eltekeh. These events, however, transpired in 701, before Tirhakah became king. A plausible solution is that Tirhakah was the commander of the Egyptian forces in 701, the term "king" being applied to him anachronistically. Other proposals are that the name "Tirhakah" was mistakenly added to the biblical account, which told of an earlier pharaoh, or that Sennacherib made a second (unattested) campaign to the west after Tirhakah's accession.

Tirhakah returned to Egypt but was forced to retreat south before the invading armies of Sennacherib's son Esarhaddon in 671. He regained control of Egypt upon Esarhaddon's death in 669, only to be defeated decisively by the latter's successor Ashurbanipal at Thebes in 664.

TIRHANAH The son of Caleb by his concubine Maachah.

TIRIA The son of Jehaleleel, apparently descended from Perez son of Judah.

TIRZAH One of the Canaanite cities conquered by Joshua (Josh 12:24), although it does not appear in the later lists of places inhabited by the Israelites. On the other hand, Tirzah is mentioned as the name of one of the daughters of Zelophehad (Num 26:33; 27:1). Scholars therefore assume that Tirzah, and the other "daughters" mentioned in these verses, were all towns inhabited by the families of Manasseh. In later times Tirzah was the capital of the kings of Israel until the days of Omri

Clay model of the Iron Age temple at Tell el-Farah (north).

(right)
Remains of the Middle Bronze Age II at Tell el-Farah (north) identified with Tirzah. (Israel Dept. of Antiquities and Museums)

(I Kgs 14:17; 15:21; 16:10-18). Omri reigned in Tirzah for six years before he built his new capital at Samaria (I Kgs 16:23-24). It seems that Tirzah was embellished by the kings of Israel who reigned there and so became a symbol of beauty (Song 6:4). Tirzah is identified with Tell el-Farah (north) which is located about 6 miles (10 km) to the north of Nablus. Excavations have uncovered layers ranging from the Neolithic period down to its occupation by an Assyrian garrison in the late 8th century B.C.

TISHBITE An epithet affixed to the name of Elijah the prophet; it is generally taken to indicate the place of his birth.

TITHES The verb "to tithe" denotes setting aside a tenth of one's property, the portion thus detached being called a "tithe".

The tithe is referred to twice in the patriarchal narratives. After defeating the coalition of eastern kings, Abraham tithed the booty to Melchizedek, king of Salem, "priest of God Most High". Two generations later, Jacob vowed at Bethel that upon his safe return from Haran, he would dedicate to God a tithe of his possessions (Gen 14:18-20; 28:16-22).

Tithing is legislated on several occasions in the last three books of the Pentateuch, the details, however, varying. (a) All produce, whether "seed from the ground" or "fruit from the tree", must be tithed, to become "holy to the Lord". Should the landowner subsequently wish to redeem his tithe, he must add a payment of 20 percent (Lev 27:30-31). (b) One tenth of a person's herd or flock, "whatever passes under the staff", is to be dedicated as "holy to the Lord". The expression "passes under the staff" probably means that as the animals walked in file, every tenth one would be set aside as the tithe (Lev 27:32). (c) The tithe is to be the property of the Levites, as reward for their participation in the divine service, and as compensation for being denied land grants (Num 18:21-24). (d) In turn, the Levites are required to set aside one tenth of their tithe as a gift "to the Lord", to be given to the priests. This was designated a "tenth of the tithe" (Num 18:25-30). (e) A different kind of tithe is prescribed in Deuteronomy, where each individual is to take one tenth of his grain, wine and oil to the sanctuary (together with firstborn animals and other sacrifices) to the "place which the Lord your God chooses", to be eaten "before the Lord your God". Should it be impractical to carry so much food to the sanctuary, a monetary equivalent may be brought to be used for purchasing food at the selected site. The entire family is to rejoice at the banquet and invite the Levites to participate (Deut 14:22-27; and cf 12:5-12). (f) Every third year, a tithe is given to the Levites and to other poor people, who will eat "and be filled" (Deut 26:12-15).

Although the concept and terminology of tithing is well known from the ancient Near East, the last two categories mentioned i.e. the tithe as a family experience and the tithe as support for the laity poor, are unique to the Bible. During First Temple times, at least some of the aforementioned tithes were observed. The prophet Amos, addressing the northern Israelites in the reign of King Jeroboam II mockingly contrasts the people's scrupulousness in tithing with their moral insensitivity (Amos 4:4). The Chronicler lauds Judean zeal in tithing, as part of Hezekiah's reforms (II Chr 31:5-12).

The tithe was an important feature of Second Temple times. Malachi, the last of the prophets, urges the people to "bring all the tithe into the storehouse, that there may be food in my house" (Mal 3:10). This passage implies that the tithe was no longer to be given to the Levites, but was for the priests and Temple. Yet one of the commitments made by the people with Nehemiah was that the tithe would be given to the Levites, who would, in turn, send their tithes to the Temple (Neh 10:37-38; 12:44; 13:5, 12).

The Bible mentions one other kind of tithe — a tax that might be levied by the king for the royal coffers. Samuel warned the people of this possible consequence of kingship (I Sam 8:15-17).

In the NT, Jesus condemns the Pharisees for tithing while yet neglecting justice and love of God. However, he stresses that the tithe also should not be neglected (Luke 11:42; Matt 23:23).

TITUS A traveling companion of Paul, one of the earliest-named non-Jewish leaders in the 1st century church, and the addressee of one of the "Pastoral Epistles". Titus is first mentioned in Paul's letter to the churches of Galatia (Gal 2:1, 3). Titus' parents were both Gentiles and for that reason Paul refused to circumcise him (cf the case of Timothy in Acts 16:1-3). The Galatians' reference indicates that Titus was one of Paul's earliest companions. Inasmuch as Paul calls him "my true son in our common faith" (Titus 1:4), it would seem that Paul was instrumental in leading Titus to faith in Jesus. In II Corinthians Paul calls him "my brother" (2:13), "my partner and fellow worker" (8:23). It is clear from other references in the same letter (e.g. 7:13ff) that Titus had developed a special relationship with the church at Corinth. In addition to an embassy to Corinth (II Cor 12:18), Titus also undertook a mission on Paul's behalf to Nicopolis (probably in Epirus, Titus 3:12) and to Dalmatia (II Tim 4:10). After a visit to Crete together with Paul, which must be dated after the latter's release from prison in Rome, Titus stayed on the island in order to oversee the organization and growth of the newly-founded churches there. It was advice on this matter which occasioned the writing of the Epistle to Titus. The church historian Eusebius indicates that Titus stayed on in Crete (or returned after his trip to Dalmatia) to be the island's first bishop.

TITUS, EPISTLE TO Seventeenth book of the NT, and one of the so-called "Pastoral Epistles". For a full discussion of the authenticity and authorship of the letter, see TIMOTHY; FIRST EPISTLE TO.

The setting probably follows Paul's release after his trial in Rome in 61 or 62, when he has undertaken another missionary journey towards the east. One stop on this trip had been the island of Crete, where he labored with his young friend Titus. As an aging man, Paul was no longer able to devote years to the thoroughgoing establishing of churches as he had in Corinth and Ephesus (Acts 18:11; 20:31). He soon

TITUS
1 Cor 2:13;
7:6, 13-14;
8:6, 16, 23;
12:18. Gal 2:1,
3. II Tim 4:10.
Titus 1:4

moved on from Crete, leaving behind Titus, who was well-acquainted with his ways and doctrines. This letter was then written as a sort of memorandum.

Several elements stand out. The bulk of the epistle is taken up with practical pointers on church administration, including the sorts of teaching which should be directed at the various components of the congregation. Hence, there is a list of characteristics expected of an elder or overseer (Titus 1:5-9); teaching instructions concerning men and women of all age groups and slaves (2:1-10) and general words for all on submissiveness (3:1ff). Secondly, Paul includes a concise outline of basic Christian doctrine (2:11-14; 3:3-7). The third element is a warning against certain false teachings (1:10-16; 3:9-11). Prominent among these may have been a Judaizing doctrine among the Gentile Cretans (1:4).

One peculiarity of this letter is its repeated emphasis on the importance of engaging in good works (1:16; 2:7, 14; 3:1, 8, 14); verse for verse, Paul mentions good works more often here than does James in his epistle. But that constitutes no contradiction of Paul's doctrine of salvation apart from works, as detailed in Romans or Galatians. In 3:5 he states clearly that "not by works of righteousness which we have done, but according to his mercy he saved us." As in James, the question is really a matter of emphasis, and his Epistle to Titus may be seen as forming a bridge between Paul's other writings and James' doctrine.

OUTLINE

1:1-4	Salutation
1:5-9	Appointment of elders
1:10-16	Warning against deceivers
2:1-10	Desired traits for various elements in the church
2:11-14	The grace of God
2:15-3:3	How to exhort the congregations
3:4-8	The salvation of God
3:9-11	Handling controversies and factions
3:12-15	Final instructions and greetings

TIZITE An epithet affixed to the name of Joha, one of David's "mighty men", and generally understood to refer to his city of origin.

TIZITE
I Chr 11:45

TOAH A Kohathite Levite listed among the ancestors of the prophet Samuel and of Heman the singer. Toah was the son of Zuph and the father of Eliel (I Chr 6:34); in Samuel he is called Tohu and his son Elihu (I Sam 1:1).

TOAH
I Chr 6:34

TOB (LAND OF) A region in the northeast of Transjordan, where Jephthah the Gileadite fled from his brothers (Judg 11:3). In the time of David the people of Tob, together with those of Beth Rehob and Zoba, went to the assistance of Ammon (II Sam 10:6-8; "Ish-Tob"). Its location is not certain, but it should perhaps be identified with the land of Tobiah, the Ammonite (Neh 2:19).

TOB
(LAND OF)
Judg 11:3, 5

TOBADONIJAH ("my Lord is good"). One of the Levites sent by King Jehoshaphat in the third year of his reign to teach the Law throughout the Kingdom of Judah. Some scholars believe that Tobadonijah may be merely a misspelt repetition of Adonijah and Tobijah, the two names preceding it.

TOBADONIJAH
II Chr 17:8

TOBIAH ("Yah is good"). An Ammonite; his designation "the servant" may be an official title granted him by the Persian government (Neh 2:10, 18). Together with Sanballat the Horonite, Tobiah bitterly opposed the rebuilding of the wall around Jerusalem by Nehemiah (Neh 2:10, 19; 4:1-7; 6:6, 16).

They mocked the Jews building the wall (Neh 4:1-3), and conspired actively with other hostile groups against the project (Neh 4:8) but to no avail (Neh 6:1).

They challenged Nehemiah to a meeting in the valley of Ono but Nehemiah, aware of their ruse, sent a letter saying he was unable to come (Neh 6:2-3). They then accused Nehemiah of plotting a rebellion against the king (6:6-7), and tried to ambush him (Neh 6:10-14). The wall was nevertheless completed in 52 days (6:15).

During Nehemiah's absence from Jerusalem, Tobiah, taking advantage of his connections with the priest Eliashib, received a chamber in the courts of the Temple for his residence (Neh 13:7). Upon Nehemiah's return he was ejected from this residence and commanded to cleanse the chamber.

TOBIJAH ("Yah is good").

1. A Levite, who was sent by King Jehoshaphat to teach the Book of the Law in the cities of Judah (II Chr 17:8).

2. One of the men who returned from Babylon, from whom silver and gold were taken in order to make the crown for the high priest Joshua (Zech 6:10-11).

TOBIT, BOOK OF A Jewish book of the Apocrypha preserved in two Greek versions. The original language was Hebrew or Aramaic, as in fragments of the book found at Qumran among the Dead Sea fragments. It was probably written in the 5th or 4th century B.C. perhaps in Media.

It tells the story of the pious Tobit, an Israelite of the tribe of Naphtali, taken in captivity to Nineveh in Assyria. His piety and righteous deeds bring him suffering. Having buried a dead man he becomes impure and goes blind (2:7-10). He accuses his wife Anna of

Araq el-Emir, west of Amman, where Tobiah the Ammonite lived.

(left)
Tomb of Tobiah with the name inscribed on the lintel at the entrance.

theft, they quarrel, and Tobit wishes to die. At the same time the righteous Sarah prays for death because each of her previous seven husbands has been killed by the demon Asmodeus on their wedding night (3:7-8). Tobit's son, Tobias, aided by the angel Raphael, drives away Asmodeus, marries Sarah and restores Tobit's wealth and eyesight. The idea that the righteous, even though they may be first scourged, are eventually rewarded by God, is reiterated several times (11:15; 13:2, 5). Tobit's pious and righteous behavior is rewarded by the recovery of his money, the healing of his blindness, the marriage of his son Tobias to Sarah and the grandsons subsequently born.

Through the personal tragedies and blessings of Tobit and Sarah, the author stresses God's concern for his people (3:2-5, 16-17). As Tobit was scourged and then enjoyed God's mercy, so "he will scourge us for our iniquities, and will have mercy again, and will gather us out of all nations, among whom he has scattered us" (13:5). God shall restore the people from their exile, rebuild the Temple and Jerusalem, and all nations will fear God (14:5-6).

The book was included in the Septuagint and in the Vulgate canon.

TOCHEN A village in the territory of Simeon, in the southern part of Judah.

TOCHEN
I Chr 4:32

TOGARMAH In the Table of Nations, Togarmah is a son of Gomer, and brother of Ashkenaz and Ripath (Gen 10:3; I Chr 1:6); the house of Togarmah is mentioned in Ezekiel (38:6). According to Ezekiel 27:14 Togarmah traded with Tyre in pack horses, riding horses and mules. In the prophecy of Gog king of Magog, Togarmah is mentioned alongside Meshech as allies in the war against Israel in the distant future.

TOGARMAH
Gen 10:3.
I Chr 1:6.
Ezek 27:14;
38:6

Togarmah is the name of a city and a region in Asia Minor. In documents of the 2nd millennium B.C. the name is spelled Tegarama. Assyrian documents called it Til Garimmu, and in the Classical period it was Gauraena, present-day Gurun, lying midway between Kayseri and Malatya.

TOHU Ancestor of Samuel. See TOAH.

TOHU
I Sam 1:1

TOI, TOU King of Hamath at the time of King David. He was the enemy of Hadadezer, king of Jobah, and when the latter was defeated by David, Toi sent his son Joram (II Sam 8:10) or Hadoram (I Chr 18:10) to David with numerous gifts.

TOI, TOU
II Sam 8:9-10.
I Chr 18:9-10

TOKHATH Alternative form of Tikvah.

TOKHATH
II Chr 34:22

TOLA, TOLAITES ("crimson").

1. The firstborn of the four sons of Issachar (Gen 46:13; Num 26:23; I Chr 7:1-2). The founder of the Tolaite family (Num 26:23).

TOLA,
TOLAITES 1
Gen 46:13.
Num 26:23.
I Chr 7:1-2

2. The son of Puah and grandson of Dodo, of the tribe of Issachar. Succeeding Abimelech, he judged Israel for 23 years and was buried in Shamir (Judg 10:1-2).

TOLA,
TOLAITES 2
Num 26:23.
Judg 10:1

TOLAD, ELTOLAD A town in the domain of the tribe of Simeon (Josh 19:4; I Chr 4:28), lying within the territory of the tribe of Judah. In Joshua 15:30, it is listed as belonging to Judah.

TOLAD, ELTOLAD
I Chr 4:29.
Josh 15:30;
19:4

TONGUES, GIFT OF Phenomenon attested at Caesarea (Acts 10:46) and Ephesus (Acts 19:6), but the closest description is in Paul's negative reaction in I Corinthians chapter 14, where he contrasts it unfavorably with the gift of prophecy. The gift of tongues does not benefit the community because, though the intention of the speaker is recognized as laudable (praise of God, thanksgiving, etc.), his language is unintelligible (I Cor 14:2). This latter aspect clearly distinguishes tongues from the gift of speaking foreign languages accorded to the apostles at Pentecost (Acts 2:4-11). It is to be presumed that the speaker began to praise God in ordinary language, and that as his emotional fervor intensified his speech became progressively less intelligible through the use of foreign words out of context or obscure dialectical expressions. Christians at Corinth would have come from very varied linguistic backgrounds and in ecstasy would have reverted to long dormant speech patterns. This interpretation of the phenomenon is recommended by two arguments. The Greek term *glossea* was applied to words used in an unusual way, to neologisms, archaic terms and to dialectical turns of phrase. Moreover, in I Corinthians 14:5, which should be translated, "He who prophesies is greater than he who speaks in tongues, unless the latter can put it into words," Paul implies that if the speaker were capable of controlling himself he could express himself clearly. This is why the apostle says, "let him who speaks in a tongue pray that he may interpret" (I Cor 14:13; cf I Cor 14:27-28). Paul was forced to react in this way because the status-conscious Corinthians tended to prize the gift of tongues above more useful charisms because it seemed to be indisputable evidence of the Spirit that possessed them.

TOPHEL The name of a place in the Arabah wilderness near Paran, Laban and Hazeroth, where Moses addressed the Israelites.

TOPHET, TOPHETH The place where sacrifices were made to the pagan cults of Molech and Baal (Jer 32:35). It was located in the Valley of Hinnom, outside the southeast corner of Jerusalem's walls (II Kgs 23:10; Jer 19:2), in the vicinity of the Brook of Kidron.

Burial urns from the Tophet at Carthage.

Child sacrifices were offered at Topheth to the Ammonite god, Molech (II Kgs 23:10; Jer 7:31). This practice is first mentioned during Ahaz's reign (II Kgs 16:3; II Chr 28:3) and continued through the reign of Manasseh (II Kgs 21:6; II Chr 33:6) until Josiah stopped it, and defiled the altar (II Kgs 23:10). It was at this spot that Jeremiah likened the inhabitants of Jerusalem and Judah to a broken flask, because of their sacrifices to foreign deities and shedding of innocent blood (Jer 19:1-13). The prophet cursed Topheth and gave it the name "the Valley of Slaughter", because God will slay all the apostates there and display their bodies as an open spectacle (Jer 7:32-8:3).

TORAH Hebrew word, meaning "instruction" or "guidance" which became used by Jews for the general guidance received through divine revelation and derived therefrom (often, but misleadingly, translated as "law"). It was also used to designate the Pentateuch, the first five books of the Bible, and later to the entire Hebrew Bible.

TOWER OF THE HUNDRED One of the towers in the wall of Jerusalem, mentioned together with the Sheep Gate and the tower of Hananel (Neh 3:1). It was apparently located in the northern wall, between the Sheep Gate and the tower of Hananeel, in the northeastern corner of the city.

Copper Torah scroll case from the Samaritan synagogue in Nablus.

TRACHONITIS A region that formed part of Herod Philip's tetrarchy (Luke 3:1); it lay northeast of the Sea of Galilee.

TRADE Despite the lack of good natural harbors Palestine played an important part in international trade. Some of the most important trade routes, leading to Egypt from Mesopotamia, Syria and Phoenicia, crossed Palestine which represented the only approach to Egypt from the north, except by sea. For this reason the trade routes of Palestine were always thronged with merchants from all parts of the world (Gen 37:25; I Kgs 10:15, etc.). The tolls collected from them were an important factor in the country's economy at all periods.

A reconstruction of "Hippos", a Phoenician long-distance trading ship, 700 B.C. (National Maritime Museum, Haifa)

Among the finds on the sites that were occupied as early as the Neolithic and Chalcolithic periods are objects and materials that certainly did not originate in Palestine, and must therefore have been brought from abroad.

The Phoenicians were intermediaries in the great maritime trade between western Asia and the cities on the Mediterranean coast, as well as in the trade between Syria, Egypt and the other countries along the shores of the Mediterranean.

In times of peace, merchants would make their way singly or in small groups, with a few beasts of burden. They would travel from village to village buying the local products (Prov 31:24). Larger companies of traders used camels (Gen 37:25), donkeys (Gen 42:46, etc.), mules (I Chr 12:40) and servants (II Kgs 5:23). During the Persian period armed guards accompanied the caravans (Ezra 8:22).

The chief exports from Palestine in the biblical period were grain, oil and wine. Tyre bought the products of Palestine in order to resell them in the Mediterranean ports (Ezek 27:17); oil was shipped to Egypt (Hos 12:1), along with balm, honey, spices, myrrh, nuts and almonds (Gen 43:11). Tyre bought fir trees and cedars for the masts of its ships and the oaks of the Bashan for its oars (Ezek 27:5-6), while the Israelites imported cedars and pines from the Lebanon (I Kgs 5:6, 9, etc.).

Few trade regulations are mentioned in the Bible, but certain laws were not calculated to encourage it. A self-contained economic system was the ideal, according to the Bible (Prov 31:10-27), and "the laying of usury" was prohibited (Ex 22:25, etc.). The precept of using a just stone (AV: "weight") and a just measure, was clearly laid down (Lev 19:35-36).

It was not until the time of Solomon that the Israelites began to engage in international trade on a large scale. After the return from the Babylonian Exile international trade was mostly in the hands of foreigners, including the men of Tyre, Sidon and Greece. Not much is known about the development of trade in the 4th century B.C. but the rise of the port of Alexandria and the granting of permission to Jews to settle there and in the newly founded Antioch-on-the-Orontes did much for its expansion under the Ptolemaic and Seleucid kingdoms. The conquest of Joppa by the Hasmoneans provided the Judean kingdom with access to the sea routes; and the opening of this port to Greek merchants, who took the place of the Phoenicians, turned it into an international center of commerce.

In the Roman period Judea became part of the huge Roman commercial complex, and its great prosperity in the first centuries A.D. is due to this connection. The flourishing Nabatean trade flowed through southern Palestine, its countless camel-trains bearing spices, perfumes, herbs, precious wood and gems from the Far East and southern Arabia. The long trade routes teminated at Gaza and the ports to the south of it. Other very important routes to Syria, Phoenicia and Egypt also passed through Judea, and the tolls collected in the ports and at its borders formed an important part of the country's revenue.

TRANSFIGURATION An event in the life of Jesus, recorded in all the Synoptic Gospels (Matt 17:1-9; Mark 9:2-10; Luke 9:28-36). Jesus with three disciples — Peter, James and John — ascended a high mountain where the disciples witnessed his appearance in glory, beside Moses and Elijah, and heard God say "This is my beloved Son; in whom I am well pleased. Hear him" (Matt 17:5).

It has been suggested that the transfiguration is not mentioned in the fourth gospel because Jesus is transfigured throughout that gospel in the sense that his divinity shines through from start to finish (cf John 8:2; and 12:28-30). The transfiguration is alluded to in II Peter 1:18 and

(left)
The façade of the Church of the Transfiguration at Mount Tabor.

The Transfiguration depicted on a mosaic at the church of Santa Caterina in the Sinai. 6th or 7th century.

Paul applies the experience to believers in his moral exhortations (Rom 12:2; II Cor 3:18).

The event is a complex cluster of several elements. There is the inner circle of disciples chosen as privileged witnesses. There is the unnamed high mountain, popularly identified with Mount Tabor in Galilee. Although the mountain is in a sense symbolic, a place of revelation, other candidates for its identification have been suggested, Mount Hermon for its height and snow cover, Carmel for its associations with Elijah and revelation. There are the two heavenly witnesses, Moses and Elijah, often said to represent the Law and the Prophets respectively; perhaps they are the two great OT seers of God. There is Peter's address to Jesus ("Lord" in Matthew; "Rabbi" in Mark, "Master" in Luke; Matthew may be translating the Hebrew correctly). There is Peter's strange suggestion to make three booths. Finally, there is the voice from the cloud, of mystic unknowing. The words from the cloud combine allusions to three parts of the OT: Deuteronomy 18:15; Psalms 2:7; Isaiah 42:1; 44:2, and suggest that Jesus was the suffering servant of God, the Son of God, and like Moses the prophet of the end-time. It is therefore, a passage of rare theological density.

The transfiguration contains, in the Marcan version, so many supernatural aspects that historical scholars are inclined to classify it as a religious legend or myth, beyond the grasp of history. Thus many recent studies of Jesus do not even discuss it.

In the last century the similarities between OT theophanies such as Exodus chapters 24 and 34 and the NT texts of the transfiguration were noted. Moses' face too shone as he descended from the mountain and it was suggested that the evangelists took these OT passages as their model. However, this argument does not explain enough elements in the gospel story, e.g. no figures appear alongside God in the OT. Alternatively, some scholars see the transfiguration as an appearance of the risen Christ (thus after Easter) retrojected into the life of the earthly Jesus. But this too is doubtful because it does not take sufficient account of the differences between this story and the appearance narratives.

TREE OF KNOWLEDGE Tree in the Garden of Eden (Gen 2:16-18; 3:1-24). God permitted Adam to eat from all the trees in the garden, excluding only the tree of knowledge of good and evil "for in the day that you eat of it you shall surely die" (Gen 2:17). In the story, Adam alone is the recipient of God's prohibition; but Eve appears well aware of its precise details: when the serpent tempts her and says "Has God indeed said, 'You shall not eat of every tree in the garden?' " Eve answers "We may eat the fruit of the trees of the garden; but of the fruit of the tree which is in the midst of the garden, God has said, 'You shall not eat of it...' " (Gen 3:1-3). Nevertheless, Eve was persuaded by the serpent to eat of the fruit, and she induced Adam to do likewise (Gen 3:6ff). Adam, Eve and the serpent were all punished by God for their disobedience (Gen 3:13-24).

The account does not specify the nature of the knowledge withheld from Adam and Eve, and obtainable only by eating the fruit. Commentators have suggested that the knowledge is of maturity, rationality or a mature appreciation of the outside world.

In classical Christianity, unlike the OT, the story is a central text for the doctrine of the Fall and Original Sin.

TREE OF LIFE The tree of life is the symbolic representation of immortality, for partaking of it is expected to bring eternal life. The Bible begins and ends with references to such a tree (Gen 2:9; 3:22, 24; Rev 2:7; 22:2, 14). Between these two extremities, scant references or allusions are found (cf Prov 11:30; 13:12; Ezek 31:3-9; 47:12). The tree of

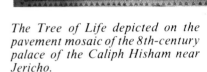

life is also mentioned in some of the apocryphal and pseudepigraphical writings (I Enoch 24:1-25:6; II Enoch 8:1-7; II Esdras [IV Ezra] 8:52).

In the ancient Near East the idea of a tree of life is quite common and is manifested in many forms. In the Gilgamesh epic, Utnapishtim tells Gilgamesh that the eating of a plant from the bottom of the sea will grant rejuvenation. In Egypt the pharaoh partakes of the tree of life in order to sustain himself in the "heavenly" realm of Re. In Sumer, a tree which may be similar to the tree of life was said to have existed in the land of Dilmun, which was duplicated in the temple of Apsu at Eridu.

Genesis chapters 2-3 tells the story of the Garden of Eden and its two trees: the tree of knowledge of good and evil; and the tree of life (Gen 2:9). Adam and Eve eat of the first tree (Gen 3:5-8) and then are sent out of the garden, "lest he put out his hand and take also of the tree of life, and eat, and live forever" (Gen 3:22). The tree of life represents the potential of eternal life for Adam and Eve, a potential which God does not want to see realized. In literary terms, this material should be viewed as a myth, that is a "story designed to convey a truth about God". However, this understanding can be refined further by realizing the etiological character of the entire story as well as of the tree. The account explains why snakes crawl, why women have pain in childbirth, and why work must be done to find food. In relation to the tree, the story provides an explanation to the ageless theological and human questions of "why humans are mortal" — because they were expelled from the garden before they could eat of the tree of life.

Ezekiel may have had the tree of life in mind in two of his descriptions. Ezekiel 31:3-9 mentions a cedar tree unparalleled in height and significance which is not rivaled by the trees in the garden of God (Ezek 31:8) and is envied by the trees of Eden (Ezek 31:9). In Ezekiel 47:1-12 a sacred river, the river of life, flows out of the temple (cf Joel 3:18; Zech 14:8) and on its banks grow all kinds of trees for eating and healing (Ezek 47:12). However, he does not mention it by name. In Proverbs, Wisdom is considered to be a tree of life to those who possess her (Prov 3:18). Proverbs 11:30; 13:12 and 15:4, also employ poetic parallelism when referring to the tree of life, in which the tree is antithetical to death and sickness. The sense of the life-sustaining qualities of the tree of life is maintained in these passages.

The future possibility of eating from the tree of life is the focus of the references in the Book of Revelation. The writer of this apocalyptic work holds out a hopeful future to his readers, to counter their current situation of persecution (probably under the Emperor Domitian). Part of that hope, for the true followers, is to "eat from the tree of life which is in the midst of the Paradise of God." That hope is offered early in the

The Tree of Life depicted on the pavement mosaic of the 8th-century palace of the Caliph Hisham near Jericho.

(center)
Kylix with decoration representing the tree of life. 8th-7th centuries B.C. (Israel Museum)

(left)
Detail from a Canaanite cult stand of the late 10th century B.C., showing two goats nibbling from a stylised tree of life. (Israel Dept. of Antiquities and Museums)

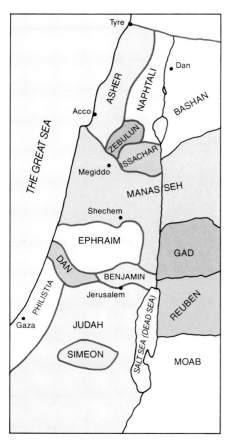

The territories of the tribes.

Apocalypse when the seven churches are addressed (Rev 2:7) and near the end when the river of life is described with the tree of life on its banks (Rev 22:2); and the possibility of denying access to the tree to those who are unfaithful is the threat at the close of the book (22:14).

TRIBES The first mention of the tribes in the Bible is in the patriarch Jacob's last words to his sons, ending with the statement "All these are the twelve tribes of Israel, and this is what their father spoke to them" (Gen 49:28). The word "tribe" occurs for the first time in the same text (Gen 49:16). The twelve tribes are thus shown as being derived from one single family. In the blessings given by Jacob to his sons, the tribes are listed in the following order: Reuben, Simeon, Levi, Judah, Zebulun and Issachar (the six sons of Leah); Dan (the son of Bilhah); Gad and Asher (the sons of Zilpah); Naphtali (the other son of Bilhah); and lastly, Joseph and Benjamin (the sons of Rachel). The twelve are listed in a different order in Genesis 35:23-26 which records the sons of Leah, Jacob's first wife; followed by those of Rachel, Rachel's maidservant Bilhah, and lastly, those of Zilpah, Leah's maidservant.

Very few details are given in the Bible about the structure and organization of the tribes. Their political role seems to have been minimal. It has been suggested that their main function was religious, and they have been compared to Greek and Roman religious institutions which were comprised of twelve groups or units called an amphictyony. The number twelve occurs regularly in family chronicles: to compare the twelve tribes of Ishmael (Gen 17:20; 25:13-16) and of Nahor (Gen 22:20-24).

The tribes played an important role during the wanderings of the Children of Israel in the wilderness. A representative of each tribe was designated to help Moses take the first census of the Children of Israel (Num 1:2, 4). He was appointed leader of the army of his tribe (Num 2:1-34) and was responsible for presenting the offerings to the tabernacle built by Moses (Num chap. 7). He later led his tribe out of the wilderness of Sinai (Num 10:12-27). Moses also selected one man from each tribe to spy out the land of Canaan (Num 3:2-15).

Wall painting from the synagogue of Dura-Europos showing a well which Moses is touching with his rod and twelve streams flowing out to twelve tents, in each of which stands a figure.

The order of the tribes in their tents, showing knights holding banners with the emblems of the four leading tribes of Israel. From the Duke of Sussex Pentateuch, *c. 1300.*

The tribes played a key role in the conquest and settlement of the land of Canaan. The designation of the territories attributed to each tribe, and its natural boundaries, is the first complete description of the country (Josh chaps. 13-21). Before his death Joshua convened all the tribes at Shechem and renewed with them the covenant of the Lord (Josh 24:25).

At the time of the division of the land the sons of Levi, who had been set apart "from among the Children of Israel" (Num 3:12) received no territory of their own, but were put in charge of the cities of refuge (Josh chaps. 20-21). Since, however, the tribe of Joseph was divided into two — Ephraim and Manasseh — there still remained twelve territories, attributed to twelve tribes. This division is already found in the blessing of Moses where the tribe of Simeon is omitted (Deut chap. 33). With the completion of the conquest and the settlement of the land, each tribe has its own history.

After Solomon's death the United Kingdom split in two: the Kingdom of Israel in the north encompassed ten of the twelve tribes while the Southern Kingdom included only Judah and Benjamin (I Kgs 12:16-17, 21). The ideal of twelve nevertheless still remained in later times (Ezek chap. 48).

In the NT Jesus promises his apostles that they would judge the twelve tribes (Matt 19:28), and James writes to the twelve tribes in the diaspora (James 1:1). Compare also Paul and John who mention the twelve tribes (Acts 26:7; Rev 7:1ff). See also entries on individual tribes.

TROAS An important port in the northwestern region of the Roman province of Asia. It was in Troas on his second missionary journey that Paul had a vision of a man of Macedonia who beseeched him, saying "Come over into Macedonia, and help us". Paul immediately left Troas and traveled to Macedonia (Acts 16:8-10).

On his way back from Greece, on his third missionary journey, Paul stayed for a week in Troas. During his teaching there, a young man named Eutychus dozed off, and fell from the third story; he was assumed dead but Paul revived him (Acts 20:9). From Troas Paul went by land to Assos, where he joined his companions sailing for Palestine (20:13).

Greco-Roman remains at Troas, on the northwestern coast of Asia Minor (in Turkey today).

TROGYLLIUM A promontory on the shore of Asia Minor, opposite the island of Samos. Paul halted there during his voyage to Jerusalem, after he had left Mitylene and before he stopped at Miletus.

TROPHIMUS ("foster child"). A man of Ephesus who joined Paul on his journey back to Jerusalem (Acts 20:4; 21:29) where he and several companions accompanied Paul to the Temple grounds. Suspecting Trophimus, a Gentile of going beyond the Court of the Gentiles, thereby defiling the Temple, the Jews mobbed Paul (Acts 21:26-30; 24:6). During his travels with Paul Trophimus fell sick and remained behind at Miletus (II Tim 4:20).

TRYPHENA A woman saluted by Paul in Romans 16:12. She "labored in the Lord", together with Tryphosa who may have been her sister (Rom 16:12).

TRYPHOSA A woman "laboring in the Lord", who is greeted by Paul in his Epistle to the Romans.

TUBAL A kingdom in Asia Minor, listed in the Table of Nations among the sons of Japheth (Gen 10:2; I Chr 1:5). It is also mentioned in Ezekiel (27:13; 32:26; 38:2-3; 39:1) and once in Isaiah (66:19), almost always with its neighbor Meshech. It has been identified with the Tabal of Assyrian sources, and, usually, with the Tybarenoi of classical sources.

Tabal is first mentioned in the description of the campaign of Shalmaneser III in 837 B.C. to the country of Melid, the northernmost of the neo-Hittite kingdoms, from where he continued his march on the caravan route leading to Tabal. In the following year Tabal paid tribute to Assyria, as it did on its reappearance in Assyrian sources in the time of Tiglath-Pileser III in the years 743-740. Tabal rebelled during the reign of Shalmaneser V, and its king Hullaku was deported to Assyria. Sargon II initially ruled Tabal by appointing vassal kings, but the ascendancy of Phrygia (biblical Meshech) under its king Mita (Midas of the classical sources) compelled Sargon to annex the kingdom to Assyria. Sargon died in a campaign against Tabal in 705 B.C. (cf Is 20:1). The rise of the Cimmerians (biblical Gomer) necessitated repeated forays into Asia Minor by Sennacherib, Esarhaddon and Ashurbanipal, the last being called "King of Tabal". The kingdom of Tabal was finally destroyed by the Cimmerians.

TUBAL-CAIN "Tubal the smith", the son of Lamech and Zillah, and brother of Naamah. He was the master of all coppersmiths and blacksmiths (Gen 4:22).

TURTLEDOVE See ANIMALS

TYCHICUS A man from Asia, who accompanied Paul into Asia together with Trophimus (Acts 20:4). Tychicus brought Paul's Epistle to the Ephesians. He was highly appreciated by Paul, who called him "a beloved brother and faithful minister in the Lord" (Eph 6:21; Col 4:7). Paul sent him to Colossae to encourage the Christian community there and considered sending him to Titus in Crete (Titus 3:12) but the latter moved to Ephesus (II Tim 4:12).

TYRANNUS The "hall" or the "school" of Tyrannus was the place where Paul preached at Ephesus. He began preaching in the synagogue, but growing opposition made he and his disciples move to a new meeting place whose name may refer to its owner.

TYRE (TYRIANS) An important Canaanite city in Phoenicia, its name meaning "rock"; called Zara or Zaru by the Assyrians and Tyros by the Greeks. The modern Arab town of the same name was constructed over the ancient site. The oldest part of Tyre was built on the narrow coastal strip (modern Lebanon). The city subsequently extended over an island separated from the mainland by straits about $\frac{1}{2}$ mile (0.8 km) wide.

Tyre is mentioned for the first time in the Execration Texts of the 19th-18th centuries B.C. By the end of the 13th century B.C. the Sea Peoples exerted pressure on the whole region and Tyre seems to have suffered destruction. It was refounded at the beginning of the 12th century B.C. It was only after the decline of Egypt that the great prosperity of Tyre set in. It eventually rose to the position of ruler of the sea and was a great commercial and cultural center. After its emancipation from Egyptian influence during the reign of Rameses III it became the most important city in Phoenicia, founding large commercial colonies along the shores of the Mediterranean. There was virtually no place in the known world with which Tyre did not have commercial relations.

During the period of the Israelite conquest of Canaan it was known as the "strong city of Tyre" and lay on the border of the lot of the tribe of Asher (Josh 19:29). David sent for cedar trees, carpenters and masons from Tyre in order to build his "house" (II Sam 5:11). Hiram king of Tyre (969-936 B.C.) enlarged the island by uniting it with a small island and rebuilt the old temples of Melkart and Astarte.

Solomon renewed his father's pact with Hiram (I Kgs 5:1-3), and enlisted his help in the building of his Temple in Jerusalem. In return for this help Solomon gave Hiram the land of Cabul and 20 cities in Galilee (I Kgs 9:11-13). Israel and Tyre had close relations during the reign of Ahab, who married Jezebel, daughter of Ethbaal, king of the Sidonians

Roman columns at Tyre.

(I Kgs 16:31). This marriage led to the introduction of idolatry into Israel. It was for this reason that Isaiah (chap. 23), Jeremiah (25:22), Ezekiel (chaps. 26-28), Joel (3:4), Amos (1:9-10) and Zechariah (9:2-4) foretold the destruction of the town and its colonies. After the return from Babylonian Exile, the people of Tyre were again selling on the Sabbath in the markets of Jerusalem (Neh 13:16).

Tyre reached its zenith in the 9th century B.C. after the foundation of Carthage, which was later to become Rome's bitter enemy. At that period the Assyrians were expanding westwards towards the shores of the Mediterranean. In 701 B.C. Sennacherib divided the Tyrian kingdom, which extended up to that time from Sidon on the north to Acco on the south into two kingdoms, Tyre and Sidon. When Esarhaddon crushed the revolt of Sidon in 677/76 B.C. the southern part of Sidon was annexed again to Tyre. This was followed by the strengthening of the power of Tyre, and the city felt secure in making an alliance with Turhakah the Egyptian. This alliance was defeated by Esarhaddon at Ashkelon. In later decades, at the instigation of the Egyptians, Tyre opposed Assyria, then at the end of its power, as well as the new rising Babylonian kingdom. Nebuchadnezzar besieged Tyre for 13 years (585-573 B.C.), but eventually concluded a pact with it. In the Persian period Tyre planted many colonies on the Palestinian coast, spreading as far south as Ascalon (Ashkelon). In 332 B.C. Alexander the Great besieged the town, but he succeeded in taking it only after constructing a causeway between the island and the coast.

The subsequent rise of Alexandria as a competing commercial power caused the decline of Tyre. It was freed from the Ptolemaic yoke in 273 B.C. but fell to the Seleucids in 198 B.C. It was freed again in 126 B.C., when Pompey conquered the city and proclaimed its autonomy. It was known again as an important and flourishing commercial center throughout the Roman period. In the gospels it is usually mentioned along with Sidon and even visited by Jesus (Mark 7:2ff). Paul arrived at its port en route to Jerusalem and already at this time the city had a Christian community (Acts 21:3-7). It was the seat of an early Christian bishopric.

UCAL One of the men, to whom Agur son of Jakeh addressed his proverbs (Prov 30:1).

UEL One of the sons of Bani. Having married an alien woman, he repudiated her following Ezra's reform (Ezra 10:34).

UGARIT An ancient town in northern Syria whose remains have been identified at Ras Shamra. It was a key point on the route leading from Mesopotamia to Crete and it was by this route that elements of the Mesopotamian culture reached the Mediterranean islands.

Ugarit is of the utmost importance to research into the development of the Canaanite script and literature, for in addition to the Akkadian documents and Horite dictionaries, documents written in a special script have been found there. This is an alphabetic, cuneiform and consonant script, belonging to the Canaanite family but closer to biblical Hebrew. The most important literature in it consists of epic songs in which the deeds of gods and heroes are praised. There is much in common, both in language and in content, between these epics and the biblical literature.

Ugaritic abecedary.

Tablet with the Epic of Akhat written in Ugaritic script. 13th century B.C.

ULAI A canal near Susa where Daniel had his vision of a ram and a goat.

ULAM

1. The son of Peresh, a descendant of Manasseh.
2. The firstborn son of Eshek of the tribe of Benjamin. His own sons won renown as archers (I Chr 8:39-40).

ULLA A descendant of Asher, and a prominent prince (I Chr 7:39).

UMMAH A town in the territory of Asher. Many scholars believe that the text should read Acco.

UNNI

1. One of the gatekeepers or singers appointed by David to accompany the ark of the covenant to Jerusalem (I Chr 15:18, 20).
2. One of the Levites who returned from the Babylonian Exile with Zerubbabel (Neh 12:9).

UPHAZ Jeremiah (10:9) and Daniel (10:5) both mention Uphaz as a place (otherwise unknown). Some scholars suggest the text should read Ophir, a place noted for its gold. Others think that it indicates the nature and purity of the gold (*paz* means pure gold) and not its provenance.

UPPER GATE One of the gates of the Temple of Solomon which led into the king's palace. It was through this door or gate that the young Joash, who had been hidden in the Temple for six years, left there to be crowned king of Judah after the death of Athaliah (II Chr 23:20). In the parallel account it is called "gate of the escorts" (II Kgs 11:19). Its exact location is not clear and there is no further mention of it in the Bible except for the fact that Jotham king of Judah built or rebuilt it (II Chr 27:3). Some translations, including KJV, call it the High Gate.

UR A very ancient city in southern Babylonia; identified with Tell Muqayyar, close to the right bank of the Euphrates, halfway between Baghdad and the Persian Gulf. Terah and his sons, including Abraham, were born there and set out from there for Haran (Gen 11:26-31).

At the center of the mound of Ur remains of a huge tower were discovered in the middle of the 19th century. This was the temple of the Moon God and excavations have brought to light Babylonian inscriptions which prove that this was Ur. In ancient times it occupied a great stretch of land along the Euphrates. The inscriptions record a populous city, inhabited by artisans and merchants and frequented by

ULAI
Dan 8:2, 16

ULAM 1
I Chr 7:16-17

ULAM 2
I Chr 8:39-40

ULLA
I Chr 7:39

UMMAH
Josh 19:30

UNNI 1
I Chr 15:18, 20

UNNI 2
Neh 12:9

UPHAZ
Jer 10:9. Dan 10:5

UPPER GATE
II Kgs 15:35. II Chr 23:20; 27:3

UR
Gen 11:28, 31; 15:7. I Chr 11:35. Neh 9:7

(bottom of page)
The so-called Standard of Ur, a mosaic made of lapis lazuli, shell colored stones and mother-of-pearl, depicting the Sumerian army in a battle scene and victory parade. c. 2500 B.C.

Bull's head forming part of a reconstructed lyre found in the royal tombs at Ur. c. 2500 B.C.

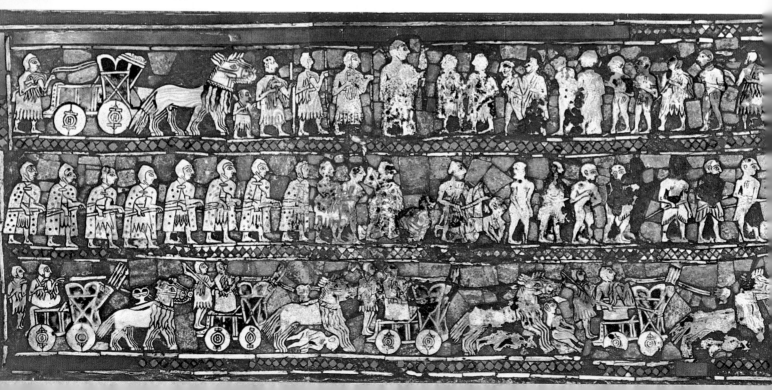

numerous strangers, since all the important trade routes of the ancient world, running from Elam, India and southern Arabia to the countries in the north and west, converged there.

Ur had a history of about 3,000 years. The Sumerians arrived there in about the 4th millennium B.C., driving out a more ancient culture and turning it into a center of their own. The remains of the 1st Dynasty of Ur belong to the 28th century B.C. The great richness of this culture is displayed in the royal tombs, where the king, his queen and their attendants and slaves lay amid numerous beautifully made objects fashioned in gold and precious stones. The heyday of Ur, however, came during the 3rd Dynasty (end of 3rd to early 2nd millennium B.C.), whose influence spread over Asshur and Haran.

URBANUS ("refined, courteous"). A Roman Christian to whom Paul sent greetings, calling him "our fellow worker in Christ".

URI

1. The son of Hur and father of Bezalel of the tribe of Judah. One of the builders of the tabernacle in the wilderness.

2. The father of Geber who was a regional governor in the land of Gilead under Solomon (I Kgs 4:19).

3. A Levitical gatekeeper. Having married an alien woman, he repudiated her in keeping with Ezra's reform (Ezra 10:24).

URIAH, URIJAH ("Yah is light").

1. A Hittite, one of the foreigners listed among David's thirty "mighty men" (II Sam 23:39; I Chr 11:41).

His permanent residence was in Jerusalem. After his wife, Bathsheba, conceived to David, the king summoned Uriah to Jerusalem from the battlefield, ostensibly to bring him news of the campaign, but in fact, in order to cover up his misdeed. However, Uriah, out of loyalty to his comrades who were camped in the open fields refused to go home and sleep with his wife. Instead he lay down by the palace gate with the king's slaves. David then dispatched Uriah back to the battlefield with a letter to his commander Joab, ordering Joab to station Uriah in the front line so that he would be killed. After Uriah's death, Bathsheba became David's wife and bore him a son (II Sam 11:3-27). The prophet Nathan in a parable denounced the sin of the king which the latter then admitted (II Sam 12:1-15).

2. The chief priest in the days of Ahaz, king of Judah. He replaced the former bronze Temple altar with a new one patterned on the altar of Damascus, according to detailed instructions sent to him from Damascus by King Ahaz who had gone there to meet the Assyrian king Tiglath-Pileser III (II Kgs 16:10-16). This Uriah is most probably identical with the priest whom Isaiah summoned as a witness when he wrote his oracle concerning Samaria on a tablet (Is 8:2).

3. The son of Shemaiah of Kirjath Jearim, a prophet at the time of Jeremiah. His prophecy against the city and the kingdom angered King Jehoiakim, who sought to put him to death. Uriah fled to Egypt, but Elnathan son of Akbor was sent to fetch him. Jehoiakim slew him and had his body flung into a common graveyard (Jer 26:20-23).

4. The father of Meremoth, a descendant of Hakkoz (Ezra 8:33; Neh 3:4-21).

5. One of the men who stood by Ezra during the public reading of the Law (Neh 8:4).

URIEL ("God is light").

1. The son of Tahath son of Assir, descended from Kohath son of Levi (I Chr 6:24). Probably identical with the Uriel who, with 120 sons of Kohath, helped convey the ark of the covenant from the house of Obed-Edom to Jerusalem (I Chr 15:5, 11).

Silver ring surmounted by a rein, from the royal tombs of Ur. c. 2500 B.C.

Limestone Hebrew seal and seal impression inscribed "[Belonging] to Uriah[u] [son of] Hananyahu." Late 8th-7th centuries B.C. (Israel Museum)

2. A resident of Gibeah; the father of Michaiah (Maachah in I Kgs 15:2 and II Chr 11:20-21), who was the mother of Abijah, king of Judah (II Chr 13:2).

URIEL 2
II Chr 13:2

URIM AND THUMMIM An oracle for discovering God's will, worn by the high priest inside the "breastplate of judgment" which contained 12 precious stones engraved with the names of the tribes (Ex 28:15-30; Lev 8:8). When Moses asked God to appoint a successor, he was told to choose Joshua, who in turn could seek the decision of the high priest Eleazar, with the instrument of the Urim (Thummim is not mentioned here).

URIM AND THUMMIM
Ex 28:30. Lev 8:8. Num 27:21. Deut 33:8. I Sam 28:6. Ezra 2:63. Neh 7:6

Aside from one allusion to their use in the context of the blessing of Levi (Deut 33:8), there are no further references to the Urim and Thummim in the Pentateuch.

After David's time (I Sam 28:6) they apparently fell into disuse, the divine will now being conveyed solely by the prophets. However, upon the return from the Babylonian Exile the priests were instructed not to eat of their most holy things until a priest with "Urim and Thummim" could attest to their genuine priestly genealogy (Ezra 2:63).

The etymology of the term Urim and Thummim is not clear.

UTHAI

1. Son of Ammihud, a descendant of Judah, who settled in Jerusalem with the exiles who returned from Babylon.

UTHAI 1
I Chr 9:4

2. A descendant of Bigvai who returned from Babylon with Ezra.

UTHAI 2
Ezra 8:14

UZ

1. Firstborn son of Aram (the youngest son of Shem) in the genealogy of the nations descended from Noah.

UZ 1
Gen 10:23. I Chr 1:17

2. Firstborn son of Dishan the Horite chief in the land of Edom.

UZ 2
Gen 36:28. I Chr 1:42

3. The land of Uz where Job lived (Job 1:1). It is also mentioned by Jeremiah in his "judgment on the nations" (Jer 25:20) and in Lamentations 4:21, which states that the daughter of Edom lived in Uz. Scholars are divided as to whether the land of Uz in Job refers to Aramean or Edomite territory.

UZ 3
Job 1:1. Jer 25:20. Lam 4:21

UZAI The father of Palal who was among those who repaired the wall of Jerusalem at the time of Nehemiah.

UZAI
Neh 3:25

UZAL The traditional punctuation of the Hebrew Bible distinguishes between the Uzal of Genesis 10:27 and I Chronicles 1:21; and the Uzal of Ezekiel 27:19 (RSV). In Genesis 10:27 and I Chronicles 1:21 Uzal is one of the 13 sons of Joktan, the great-grandson of Shem, Noah's son. Like the other 12 sons of Joktan, this Uzal designates a location in South Arabia which since the 3rd century A.D. has been identified with Sanaa, now capital of Yemen.

UZAL
Gen 10:27. I Chr 1:21

Uzal in Ezekiel 27:19 (RSV) is to be identified with the place name of Izallu which is located in Mesopotamia.

UZZA, UZZAH

1. A Levite descended from Merari. The son of Shimei and father of Shimea.

UZZA, UZZAH 1
I Chr 6:29

2. One of the sons of Benjamin.

UZZA, UZZAH 2
I Chr 8:7

3. The son of Abinadab of Kirjath Jearim in whose house the ark of God remained for 20 years (I Sam 6:19-7:2). Uzzah and his brother Ahio led the cart bearing the ark. When they came to the threshing floor of Nacon, the oxen stumbled and Uzzah, fearful the ark would fall, seized it whereupon God struck him down and he died there. David, displeased at his fate, called the place Perez Uzza, "the breaking forth upon Uzza" (II Sam 6:3-9; I Chr 13:6-12).

UZZA, UZZAH 3
II Sam 6:3, 6-8. I Chr 13:7, 9-11

4. Garden of Uzza. A burial place in the neighborhood of Jerusalem, for the last kings of Judah; Manasseh and Amon were interred there (II Kgs 21:28, 26).

UZZA, UZZAH 4
II Kgs 21:18, 26

5. One of the Temple servants who returned from the Babylonian Exile with Zerubbabel (Ezra 2:49; Neh 7:51).

UZZEN SHEERAH A village built by Sheerah, the daughter of Beriah and granddaughter of Ephraim; it probably lay in the vicinity of Beth Horon, which was also built by Sheerah. Mainly because of the similarity of names, it has been identified with present-day Beit Sira, 3 miles (5km) west of Beth Horon, but the identification has not as yet received archeological confirmation.

UZZI ("[God is] my strength").

1. A priest descended from Eleazar son of Aaron.

2. The son of Tola son of Issachar.

3. One of the five sons of Bela son of Benjamin.

4. A man of the tribe of Benjamin; the father of Elah who, as head of a household, settled in Jerusalem at the time of Nehemiah.

5. The son of Bani descended from Asaph the singer; the overseer of the Levites in Jerusalem in the days of Nehemiah.

6. A man of the family of Jedaiah; the head of a priestly household in the time of the high priest Joiakim.

7. A Levitical singer. He took part in the dedication of the wall of Jerusalem at the time of Nehemiah.

UZZIA An Ashterathite, one of David's "mighty men".

UZZIAH ("Yah is my strength") (alternately AZARIAH).

1. King of Judah (769-733 B.C.), enthroned at the age of 16 after the assassination of his father (II Kgs 14:21; II Chr 26:1). Much of the historical background to his reign is reflected in the Book of Amos. The only significant information on Uzziah in the Book of Kings is that during part of his reign, he was afflicted with leprosy (II Kgs 15:5). II Chronicles 26:16-21 explains Uzziah's affliction as arising out of the

Tablet recording the reburial of the remains of King Uzziah, between the 1st century B.C. and the 1st century A.D. The tablet, found on the Mount of Olives, reads: "Hither were brought the bones of Uzziah, King of Judah. Do not open".

Limestone Hebrew seal inscribed "[Belonging] to Uzziahu son of Neriahu". 7th century B.C. (Israel Museum)

struggle between the monarchy and the priesthood for supremacy over Temple ritual: the king had put on priestly garments and attempted to burn incense on the altar, hitherto a sole prerogative of the priests. Uzziah's grave was separated from those of the house of David (II Chr 26:23). Talmudic references report that because of his leprosy, Uzziah's remains were removed from their original grave at some unspecified date, and this is supported by an Aramaic burial inscription from the Second Temple Period found on the slopes of the Mount of Olives which reads "Hither were brought the bones of Uzziah, king of Judah — do not open!" As a result of his affliction, Uzziah resided in "a house set apart" and his son Jotham acted as regent. One of the most difficult problems in biblical chronology is determining the exact number of years of Jotham's co-regency. According to some scholars, the 52 years attributed to Uzziah's reign include the period of his joint reign with his father, all of Jotham's reign, and even some of the reign of Ahaz, Jotham's son. The reign of Uzziah-Jotham was the most notable following the division of the kingdom, and is referred to as one of the golden eras of the Kingdom of Judah.

II Chronicles gives much more information on Uzziah's reign, describing his successes in external and internal policies. Apparently, his first steps were directed towards reinforcing the economic and

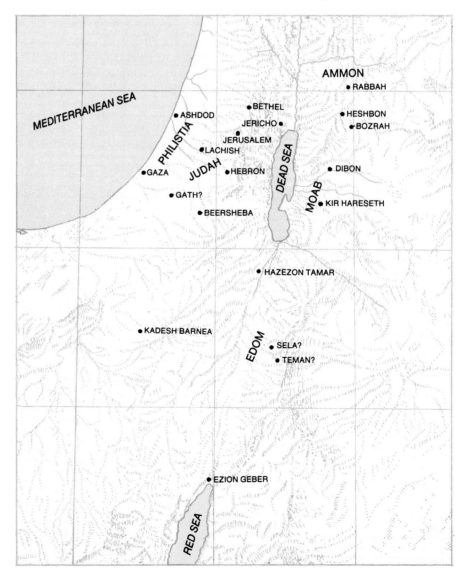

Expansion of Judah under Uzziah.

military power of the kingdom: reorganization of the army, with an increase in the number of soldiers and the production of more effective weapons (II Chr 26:11-15). He built numerous fortifications in and around Jerusalem, strengthening the city walls and adding towers (II Chr 26:9). Pursuing the policy of his father, Uzziah extended his domain southward to the Red Sea, restoring Elath to Judah and rebuilding it (II Kgs 14:22; II Chr 26:2). He constructed a line of fortifications and towers in the Arabah and Negeb in order to safeguard the transit routes to the Red Sea and to establish strong defenses against the desert tribes, such as the Meunites and the Arabians (II Chr 26:7). In the west he expanded his territory, penetrating deep into Philistia and breaching the walls of Ashdod, thus establishing control of the main trade route of Egypt (II Chr 26:6-8). To the north, he restored to Judah territory which had been lost by Amaziah in his war against King Jehoash of Israel. His expansions eastwards and his subjugation of the Ammonites (II Chr 26:8; 27:5, but in the Septuagint — Meunites) are of special interest, suggesting a shift of power from Israel to Judah, as the areas east of the Jordan had always lain within Israel's sphere of influence. After the death of Jeroboam II of Israel in 748 B.C., Uzziah seems to have gained control of the Northern Kingdom, and to some extent imposed his rule over its areas of influence. The defeat of Uzziah by Tiglath-Pileser III in 738 B.C. as recorded in the annals of the Assyrian king, marked the beginning of the decline of the Kingdom of Judah, which was compelled to withdraw altogether from Syria and Israel during the latter part of the reign of King Menahem of Israel.

2. See AZARIAH No.7

3. Father of Jehonathan who was responsible for King David's storehouses.

4. Son of Hurim; he was among those who repudiated their foreign wives at the decree of Ezra.

5. Father of Athaiah, a Judahite who lived in Jerusalem at the time of Nehemiah.

UZZIEL

1. A Levite, grandson of Levi, son of Kohath and father of Mishael, Elzaphan and Zithri, and the founder of the Uzzielites, a family of Levites.

2. One of the heads of the families in the Bela clan of the tribe of Benjamin. According to some scholars this name is a dittography of the name Uzi that precedes it.

3. Son of Heman, a member of a family of singers in the time of King David.

4. A Levite, member of the family of Jeduthun, he was among those who purified the Temple in the time of King Hezekiah.

5. A Simeonite; leader of 500 members of his tribe who defeated the Amalekites at Mount Seir during the reign of King Hezekiah.

6. Son of Harhaiah. He was among the builders of the wall of Jerusalem in the time of Nehemiah.

UZZIELITES See UZZIEL No.1

UZZIAH 2
I Chr 6:24

UZZIAH 3
I Chr 27:25

UZZIAH 4
Ezra 10:21

UZZIAH 5
Neh 11:4

UZZIEL 1
Ex 6:18; 22.
Lev 10:4.
Num 3:19, 30.
I Chr 6:2, 18;
15:10; 23:12,
20; 24:24

UZZIEL 2
I Chr 7:7

UZZIEL 3
I Chr 25:4

UZZIEL 4
II Chr 29:14

UZZIEL 5
I Chr 4:42

UZZIEL 6
Neh 3:8

UZZIELITES
Num 3:27.
I Chr 26:23

VAJEZATHA One of Haman's ten sons, killed in Shushan (Susa).

VALLEY GATE One of the gates of Jerusalem where King Uzziah of Judah erected a tower (II Chr 26:9) and through which Nehemiah, coming from Babylon, entered the city when he went to view the walls of Jerusalem. The gate was repaired by Hanun and the inhabitants of Zanoah. Its exact location is disputed.

VANIAH A man of Judah, one of the many sons of Bani who, having taken pagan wives, had to repudiate them following the decree of Ezra.

VASHTI The queen of Persia who refused to obey the command of her husband, King Ahasuerus at a feast he was holding (Est 1:12). Ahasuerus sought and followed the counsel of his advisers who told him to repudiate her in order to ensure that "all wives will honor their husbands, both great and small" (Est 1:20). Nothing is known about her subsequent fate. Her place as queen was later taken by Esther.

VINE, VINEYARD See PLANTS

VINEGAR A beverage made from wine or beer before the process of fermentation is complete. Like wine, it was forbidden to the Nazirite (Num 6:3). It was used as a flavoring in food (Ruth 2:14), was sour (Prov 10:26) and caused one to feel more thirsty (Ps 69:21). In the NT Roman soldiers drank vinegar ("sour wine") mixed with water, and offered some to Jesus before his crucifixion (Matt 27:48; Mark 15:36).

VIPER See ANIMALS

VIRGIN BIRTH A common designation for an aspect of faith professed by many Christians. While it can refer simply to the virginal conception of Jesus in the womb of Mary without a male progenitor, it also covers the more complex belief in the three-fold virginity attributed to Mary during the course of the Christian centuries: before, during and after the birth of Jesus. Here, the focus will be primarily on the scriptural foundations for the belief and therefore limited by the evidence itself to the aspect of virginal conception.

The first thing that strikes the inquirer into the question of virginal conception is the scantiness of the evidence. In only one verse of scripture is Mary specifically called a virgin (Luke 1:27). This is supplemented by four indirect references all of which occur in the infancy narratives of the Gospels of Matthew and Luke. Matthew's account of the birth of Jesus climaxes in the quotation of Isaiah 7:14 (cf Matt 1:23): "a virgin shall conceive and bear a son" (the Hebrew actually speaks of "a young woman" but was translated as "virgin" in the Septuagint); and the same evangelist makes a two-fold reference to the child conceived within Mary being "of the Holy Spirit" (Matt 1:18, 20). Luke, on the other hand, presents the child's conception as the result of the overshadowing of Mary by the Holy Spirit (Luke 1:35) and Mary acknowledges surprise at the angel's message because of the obstacle: "I do not know a man" (Luke 1:34).

When these references are examined in their context, it seems that they imply a tradition of virginal conception known to both Matthew and Luke prior to the composition of their gospels. This tradition is then employed by each evangelist in his own way to underline a developing Christological claim that Jesus was Son of God. The history of the early development of this belief indicates the relative tardiness of its emergence and provides some clue as to why it is confined to the Gospels of Matthew and Luke.

The earliest Christian preaching and faith acknowledged Jesus' sonship of God at the resurrection (cf Rom 1:3-4). In time, believers claimed this sonship was operative during the life of Jesus (cf Matt 16:16: Mark 15:39) being inaugurated at his baptism (Mark 1:11). But only with the Gospels of Matthew and Luke is there evidence of the belief

VAJEZATHA
Est 9:9

VALLEY GATE
**II Chr 26:9.
Neh 2:13, 15;
3:13**

VANIAH
Ezra 10:36

VASHTI
**Est 1:9, 11-12
15-17, 19; 2:1,
4, 17**

VINEGAR
**Num 6:3. Ruth
2:14. Ps 69:21.
Prov 10:26;
25:20**

that the divine sonship of Jesus extended back to his actual conception. A separate tradition developed regarding the preexistence of Jesus as professed in the Johannine gospel (cf John 1:1-18).

The claim to virginal conception within the Gospels of Matthew and Luke, while certainly very strongly underlining Jesus' divine sonship, also links this belief to his humanity as a man born of a woman (Gal 4:4). Only the moment of conception is said to be extraordinary, pointing to a unique intervention of God into human history, while the child's gestation in his mother's womb, and his birth, are both related in very ordinary terms (Matt 1:25; Luke 2:6-7), emphasizing his humanity.

VOPHSI A man of the tribe of Naphtali; the father of Nahbi, one of the spies sent by Moses to explore the land of Canaan.

VOW A vow is a sacred obligation voluntarily undertaken either to give something or someone to God or to refrain from a specific act. The inviolability of such an undertaking is reflected in the case of Saul who had put his soldiers in pursuit of the Philistines under a vow to refrain from eating until evening. When Jonathan unknowingly violated the vow, it was only the intervention of the people which prevented Saul from putting his son to death (I Sam 14:24, 45).

The most common vow was a pledge to bring a sacrifice (a votive offering). The Pentateuch prescribes in detail the procedure to be followed in bringing such a sacrifice (Lev 7:16-17); the type of animal to be offered in fulfillment of a vow (Lev 22:18-23) could be either a whole burnt offering or a peace offering (Lev 7:18; 22:18; Ps 66:13; Prov 7:14). These votive offerings were usually brought on the occasion of one of the three Pilgrimage Festivals. Vows would be made when one was in a situation of danger or distress (Ps 66:12-13).

The vow may be conditional upon God's granting some boon. Jacob pledged himself to erect a sanctuary at Beth El and devoted a tithe of his possessions to God, if God returned him home safely (Gen 28:20-22). Hannah vowed (I Sam 1:11) that, if blessed with a male child, she would give him to the service of God. It was evidently the practice of barren women to take a vow in the hope of bearing a male child. Proverbs (31:2) has such a mother speak of her son as "son of my vows".

A striking example of a human sacrifice in fulfillment of a vow is provided by Jephthah. Jephthah had vowed that, if he returned victorious from his battle against the Ammonites, he would offer up whatever came forth from his house. To his dismay, his daughter came out to greet him and it was she that he sacrificed (Judg 11:30-31). A vow once having been uttered may not be broken.

A distinct type of oath undertakes abstenance from something, e.g., the vow of the Nazirite (q.v.) "If a man vows a vow to the Lord...to bind himself by some agreement, he shall not break his word, he shall do according to all that proceeds out of his mouth" (Num 30:2). Deuteronomy (23:22-23) adds the injunction that one must not delay fulfilling a vow, but declares that a man incurs no guilt if he refrains from vowing. Ecclesiastes 5:4 echoes the latter notion when it advises: "Better not to vow than to vow and not pay". These verses indicate the tendency to limit the vows of abstention as well as those uttered rashly. "It is a snare for a man to devote rashly something as holy, and afterward to reconsider his vows" (Prov 20:25).

For a vow to be valid it cannot be taken under the authority of someone else. But silence on the part of the person in authority is taken as acquiescence. Thus, the vow of an unmarried woman can be annulled by her father. The vow of a married woman can be declared void by her husband (Num 30:14-16). See OATHS.

VULTURE See ANIMALS

WAHEB The name of a place, apparently in Moab near the Arnon.

WAR, WARFARE War was a constant feature in the history of Israel from its beginnings until the destruction of the Second Temple. The nature of the Israelite wars changed according to political and sociological conditions. This can be seen in the differences between the conquest and settlement, the defensive wars of the tribes against their aggressive neighbors in the period of the Judges, the wars of consolidation on the borders during the first days of the Monarchy, the constant struggle for the existence of the Kingdoms of Israel and Judah, and the last desperate stand against the great imperial forces. The days of the Second Temple were marked, too, with long periods of continuous warfare.

In the earlier wars mainly concerned with border disputes, and in the later wars of liberation from imperial control, first Seleucid and then Roman, the principal cause was religious; that is, they were struggles to preserve a national identity based on the Temple in Jerusalem and the Jewish religious laws.

Two types of wars from ancient times can be distinguished: (a) wars of defense and expansion, which were basically political, fought out of physical necessity and to which there were fixed legal limitations; and (b) holy wars, compulsory for the entire nation.

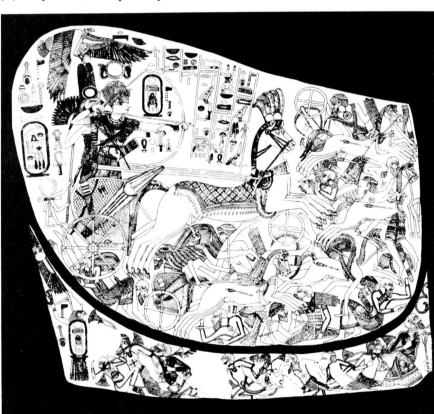

(right and facing page)
Panels on the exterior of the chariot of Pharaoh Thutmosis IV showing a battle between Egyptians and Canaanites. 15th century B.C.

Deuteronomy chapters 20 and 21 contain some of the laws of war which were upheld in the First Temple period, describing the encouragement of the troops by the priests, who assured them of the support of the Lord (Deut 20:1-4). Other sources indicate that the kings and military leaders often consulted oracles for signs of assurance. The priests and holy ark even accompanied the army on the battlefield in the earlier wars (1 Sam 4:4; 30:7; II Sam 11:11). Further, to secure God's aid, the troops would offer sacrifices prior to battle (Judg 6:20, 26; 20:26).

The laws concerning war in the Book of Deuteronomy deal, *inter alia*, with the instances in which persons could be exempt from military service, such as those who were seized with fear, were newly married, had recently built a house, planted a vineyard and so forth. Other laws deal with vanquished peoples, spoils, prisoners and the prohibition of cutting down fruit trees in conquered lands.

The customs and laws of war were fixed and had much in common throughout the ancient Near East. Troops were often drawn from the peasantry, fighting was generally limited to the agricultural off-seasons — from just after harvest till the first rains. Only by keeping a strong army could a nation keep potential enemies at bay, and the only satisfactory alternative to war was to accept all the enemy's demands.

Israelite military inferiority forced the tribes to rely on deception of the enemy; they usually found it too difficult to penetrate fortified cities by force and thus they resorted to other means, such as sending spies into the city to seek out hidden ways (Josh chap. 2). At Ai (Josh chap. 8), the Israelites succeeded in luring the enemy out of the city by a ruse. Later, David captured Jerusalem by secretly penetrating an underground water conduit (II Sam 5:7-8). Night or dawn attacks were also sprung (I Sam 11:11), as well as other forms of surprise attacks (Josh 10:9).

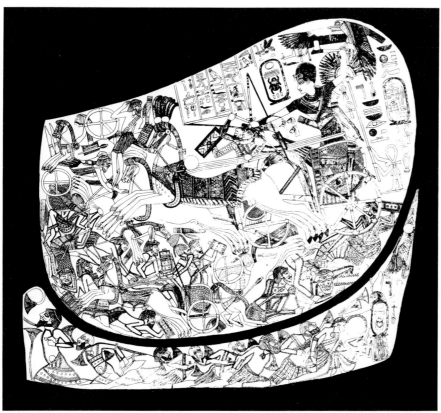

In the period of the settlement, the Israelites had to withstand the attacks of various nomadic tribes especially in the south (the Amalekites) and in the Jezreel Valley (the Midianites), who would raid villages and take prisoners. Warfare against these peoples was conducted by means of small and maneuverable units.

Using these tactics of combined small attacks and opposing the enemy in open array, the Israelites succeeded, at least at first, in standing up to their bitterest rivals, the Philistines.

Upon the death of Saul and his son Jonathan, it became obvious that new tactics were needed. The Philistine threat was the main impetus for the union of the Israelite tribes into a single kingdom since only political unity could bring about a standing well-trained and equipped army.

The army organized by David, under the skilled leadership of Joab, soon gave the Israelites military superiority over the small surrounding states but there was never a day of peace throughout David's reign.

The great victories of the Israelite army in the days of David, and the expansion into most of Syria, can be explained only by the fact that by this time the great empires were no longer able to control this region.

When Israel was divided into two kingdoms they were at first rivals, but later came to conduct combined operations against their common enemies, especially the Arameans who, with their soldiers and weapons, were as strong as the armies of Israel and Judah, and the struggle between them was long-lived. Ahab gathered his troops and ambushed the Arameans while they were still on the march, thoroughly routing them (I Kgs chap. 20). This method of ambushing in narrow mountain passes by large, well-equipped forces, took maximum advantage of the difficulties encountered by anyone attempting to penetrate the hills of Samaria or the Judean mountains; it became one of the standard methods of warfare among the Israelites until the fall of the kingdoms.

The wars fought against the mighty armies of Assyria and Babylonia were different from those waged previously. In the initial clash (in the mid-9th century B.C.), Ahab participated in a league of southern Syrian rulers against Assyria, which repulsed them in four successive campaigns. A hundred years later when the Assyrians attacked, the petty kingdoms were unable to unite, and the war degenerated into mere defensive actions, centered upon fortified cities with the Assyrians in complete control of the countryside.

This stone carving from the 7th century B.C. depicts a battle between Assyrian soldiers and desert warriors mounted on camels. Works of art such as this provide valuable information about the weapons used in ancient times.

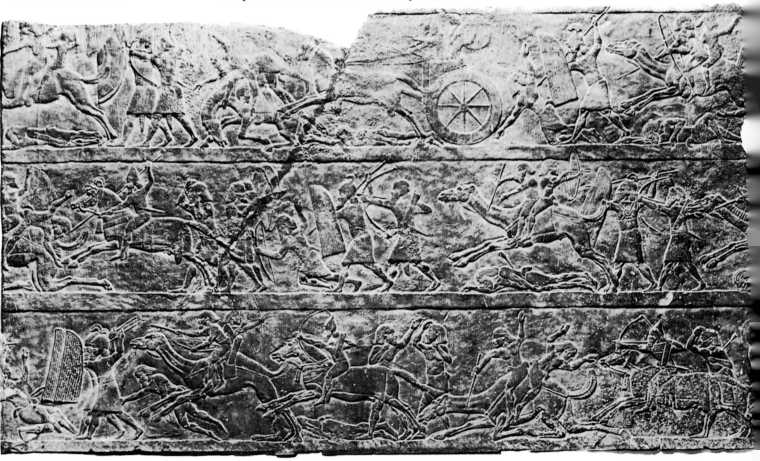

The main problem in preparing a city to withstand a siege, besides the construction of the fortifications, was to provide for an adequate source of water within the city walls. This was achieved either by digging vast cisterns for storing quantities of rain water, or by diverting water sources beneath the ground to within the fortified area, concealing any original opening outside.

The methods of pressing siege in the ancient Near East were many and varied. Egyptian and Assyrian reliefs show the scaling of walls by means of ladders; breaching walls with battering rams; breaking down gates with axes and fire; and mining beneath walls. Often several methods were employed simultaneously. The Assyrians were depicted as slaying prisoners beneath the very eyes of the besieged so as to weaken their morale.

If a city resisted all these measures, the attackers had to fall back upon the difficult pursuit of an extended siege, cutting off the inhabitants of the city from all supplies, and making continuous attacks upon the walls at various locations until a weak spot was found or the city gave in. After the appearance of the great imperial armies in Palestine, the Israelite kings concentrated their efforts on fortifying and preparing their cities to withstand prolonged sieges. They sometimes succeeded in stemming a siege of many months or even years. There is a depiction of a Judean city under siege by the Assyrian army, in a relief from Nineveh, showing Lachish as the Assyrian troops were storming its walls with many battering rams, light archery in the fore (mostly non-Assyrian troops from vassal kingdoms), then heavy Assyrian spearmen and archers, followed by slingers. The defenders, on their part, attempted to forestall the work of the siege machines by shooting arrows and throwing stones, oil and flaming torches down upon them.

The idea that God himself initiates war (Ex 15:3) and leads Israel in its military campaigns is prevalent throughout the OT (I Sam 18:17; 25:28). Israel cannot be successful in battle without the approval and participation of God. The deity declares war (Ex 17:16; Num 31:2), is consulted by various cultic means prior to battle (I Sam 28:6; 30:7-8; II Sam 5:19, 23; I Kgs 22:5-7), and selects a charismatic military leader to command his people in warfare (Judg 6:34). Any enemy of Israel is by definition the Lord's enemy. Since the Lord is the strength of Israel, any initiative on the part of secular rulers to participate in war, relying on their own strength and resources is doomed to failure (Is 30:1-5; 31:1, 3; Jer 9:23; Amos 2:13-16). Moreover, it is considered a flagrant violation of the covenant between Israel and God, and is punished by God's employing a foreign nation as his own instrument of war against Israel (Is 10:5-6).

The Lord of Israel also conducts warfare against foreign nations. They are punished for either oppressing Israel (Jer 46:10; Obad vs. 10-14), or for their own pride and major infractions of human conduct (Is 16:6-7; 18:1-5; Jer 49:16; Amos 1:3-2:3).

The prophets, however, foresaw the day when all warfare would cease and in its stead there would reign a universal peace (Is 2:2-4; 11:1-9; Mic 4:3-4).

The NT on the whole is inclined to peace rather than war (see PEACE). This attitude reflects Jesus' personal character as a non-violent sage both in his practice (Luke 9:54-56) and teaching (Matt 5:9; 26:52). On the other hand, he did not forbear to accept a zealot among his followers (Luke 6:15). Jesus' characteristic attitude remains the supremacy of love of God and neighbor (Matt 22:36-40) even to the point of loving enemies (Matt 5:43-48). These different attitudes can be reconciled; for the NT, war is not an ideal (as it was for example in Homeric society). It reflects a lower stage of morality in comparison with love of enemies. But it is sometimes a regrettable necessity until one's opponent has evolved to the same higher moral level (negotiations and compromise are better than war), or until the coming of the Kingdom of God in its fullness.

WEAPONS The warrior and his weapons play a central role in the historical books of the OT. There are hundreds of different words relating to weapons and in many cases their meaning is far from clear. Some terms occur only once; on the other hand a dozen words may relate to the same type of weapon and it is difficult to understand what differentiates them. The weapons used in biblical times in the Holy Land would not have differed from those in use in neighboring countries, especially Egypt to the south and Assyria to the north. In these countries weapons figure prominently on monuments, steles and sculptures and an impressive number of weapons have been found in archeological excavations.

The first weapon mentioned in the Bible is the knife: "And Abraham stretched out his hand and took the knife to slay his son" (Gen 22:10). Stone and staffs were the weapons of the shepherds. When David faced Goliath, he declined Saul's offer of a coat of mail and a sword because he was not used to them and found them cumbersome (I Sam 17:39-40). The sling, simple but effective, is mentioned in the fight of Israel with the Benjamites among whom were "seven hundred select men who were left-handed; every one could sling a stone at a hair's breadth and not miss" (Judg 20:16). By contrast Goliath is presented as wearing almost all the known weapons, offensive and defensive (I Sam 17:5-7).

The bow is first mentioned as a weapon used for hunting (Gen 27:3) but Jacob used it in fighting the Amorites (Gen 48:22). In his

Mold for casting weapons and tools from Tell el-Ajjul. Middle Bronze Age. (Israel Dept. of Antiquities and Museums)

Assyrian stone ballista-balls found at Lachish. (Dept. of Archaeology, Tel Aviv University)

"proclamation against Arabia" Isaiah mentions "archers" (Is 21:17). Bows were made of wood or horn, and arrows of wood with a metal tip.

Javelins, spears, lances and pikes could be used in close combat or be thrown; for instance Saul tried "to pin David to the wall with the spear"

Dagger and javelin-heads dating from the 2nd millennium B.C.

Battle-axe and mace-heads. Egypt, 2nd millennium B.C.

(I Sam 19:10). The exact difference between these weapons is not clear. They were all constructed in the manner of Goliath's spear: a wooden staff and an iron spearhead.

The dagger and sword were the most common weapons. They were sharpened regularly (Ps 7:12). The sword could be carried in a sheath (I Sam 17:51) which could be hung on a belt (II Sam 20:8). Swords and daggers were not usually double-edged; when they were, a special mention was made of the fact as in the case of the weapon used by Ehud the son of Gera to kill King Eglon (Judg 3:16).

Warriors wore a number of protective devices. There was the helmet,

Gold helmet from Ur. 25th century B.C. (British Museum)

which could be of bronze, but sometimes of wood or leather, or of wood covered with leather. The shield, as is learned from archeological excavations, came in many shapes. Like the helmet it was usually made of leather, or of wood covered in leather, and was oiled before the battle (II Sam 1:21).

For ceremonial purposes shields were made of gold: King Solomon had "three hundred shields of hammered gold" (I Kgs 10:17); when they were taken by the armies of Shishak (I Kgs 14:26) King Rehoboam replaced them with bronze replicas (I Kgs 14:27).

A smaller shield was carried on the arm (II Chr 23:9). There was also the coat of mail, as worn by Goliath. This was very popular and came in all shapes and lengths. Usually it was made of leather or of some woven fabric with metal scales sewn on, and was articulated. The joints seem to have been especially vulnerable: King Ahab was struck by an arrow "between the joints of his armor" (I Kgs 22:34) and died.

A warrior could also wear some kind of protective armor on his legs similar to the greaves worn by Goliath. With all this equipment Hebrew warriors often used the services of an armorbearer. David was Saul's armorbearer (I Sam 16:21); King Abimelech fatally wounded by a stone asked his armorbearer to kill him with his sword, that he might die a warrior's death (Judg 9:54). Deuteronomy 20:20 contains the earliest mention of the great variety of instruments used during a siege. See also WAR, WARFARE.

WEAVING The weaver's craft was known in the ancient Near East from early times. In Palestine it was mainly wool from sheep and goats that was used, as is known from the Bible and from a considerable number of garments of the Roman period that have come to light in the Judean Desert Caves. From the Bible we learn that the wool was spun (Ex 35:25-26) on a spindle with the help of a distaff (Prov 31:19). The spindle consisted of a rod about 3 feet (1m) long, at the end of which were one or two weights. These weights, hundreds of which have been found on sites inhabited from the Iron Age and later, were made of wood, bone or stone. The method of spinning was quite simple and does not differ essentially from the one used today by Bedouin women. The fibers of wool are placed in a ball on the distaff, which is held under the left arm, and the spindle is held in the left hand. The wool is plucked from the distaff with the right hand and drawn on to the spindle, which is turned at great speed, so producing the yarn. There are variations in the method of using the spindle, however.

Man at a weaving loom shown on a stone relief from Susa. 4th millennium B.C.

The yarn so spun (cf Ex 35:25) was washed and cleaned with niter and soap (cf Jer 2:22) and was then ready for dyeing (see DYES AND DYEING). The yarn was placed in a pot or basin containing a weak solution of the dyeing pigment and then transferred to another pot, in which the final stage of dyeing took place in a more concentrated solution. The dyed yarn was then rinsed in clean water and subsequently left to dry. It was now ready for weaving. Horizontal hand looms were used; they were placed on the ground and consisted of two parallel rows of pegs driven into the ground, to which the warp threads on which the actual weaving was done were attached. The process is referred to in Judges (16:14).

Another type of loom, much employed in Egypt and also used in Palestine, was vertical. Two long posts were driven into the ground and a third was placed horizontally on top of them. The warp threads were tied to the horizontal post, each thread being suspended by a weight. Loom weights made of stone have been found on almost every site in Palestine. The horizontal post of the vertical loom is the "weaver's beam" referred to in I Samuel 17:7.

On hand looms such as these either monochrome or polychrome fabrics were produced. Joseph's coat of many colors (Gen 37:31), or Aaron's "skillfully woven tunic" (Ex 28:4) may have been of the latter kind, as may the "plunder of garments embroidered and dyed" of Sisera (Judg 5:30). If multicolored cloth was to be made groups of fibers of different colors were tied to the horizontal beam. It was not until late in the Roman period that more advanced systems of weaving were introduced.

WEEKS, FEAST OF See PENTECOST

WEIGHTS AND MEASURES The most ancient standards of weights and measures are those of Egypt and Babylon. The Babylonian six-decimal system is based on a linear unit derived from astronomical calculations. The capacity unit is the basic linear unit cubed, and the weight of water that such a cube can contain gave the basic unit of weight. The Babylonian system of measures was accepted by all the peoples of the ancient Near East.

In Palestine both the Babylonian system and the Egyptian decimal system were in use. The Hebrews, who had used the Babylonian system, introduced changes into it, as a result of Egyptian influence. Further changes were introduced by the Phoenicians and the Persians, who added some units of their own to the Babylonian system and dropped others.

The units of weights and measures referred to in the Bible belong to both these systems, according to the degree of contact with the different cultures at the particular time in question.

LINEAR MEASURES Among primitive peoples the limbs of the human body served as units of length. Thus in the Bible the finger was the smallest unit (Jer 52:21); 4 fingers made 1 hand (I Kgs 7:26); 3 hands made 1 span (Ex 28:16) and 2 spans made 1 cubit. There were at least two kinds of cubit: the long cubit that was used for sacred matters (Ezek 40:5); and the ordinary cubit, which was 1 hand shorter than the sacred cubit.

MEASURES OF VOLUME Israelite measures of volume were based on the Babylonian six-decimal system. The smallest unit was the *log* (Lev 14:10, etc.) which was used both for dry goods and for liquids; 4 *logs* make 1 *kab* (II Kgs 6:25); 1⁴/₅ *kab* make 1 *omer* (Ex 16:16) etc.; 5 *ephah* make 1 *leteck*; 2 *leteck* make 1 *homer* (or *kor*) (Is 5:10; Ezek 45:10-14).

LIQUID MEASURES *Log* (Lev 14:10 etc.); *kab* (II Kgs 6:25); *hin* (Ex 29:4); *bath* (I Kgs 7:26, 38), equal in capacity to the *ephah; kor* (I Kgs 4:22; 5:11), equal to the *homer*. The *mesurah* is not a specific measure, but denotes a small quantity of liquid (Lev 19:35, etc.).

WEIGHTS The Israelite weight system was based on the Babylonian standard, although the values of some of the weights were not always identical. The Babylonian values were as follows:

60 shekels = 1 *maneh*

60 *manehs* = 3,600 shekels = 1 *kikar*

There were two weight systems, the values of one being double the other. This double standard of weights which included a light *maneh* (weighing about 15¾ oz [450 g]) spread over all the ancient Near East.

In addition to the Babylonian system the Phoenicians and the Greeks developed another system with a heavy shekel weighing 218-224 grains and a light one of 112 grains. In this system the *maneh* contained 50 instead of 60 shekels, and there were 3,000 instead of 3,600 shekels to the *kikar*. The division into 50's probably originated in the Egyptian decimal system. This system, which was used by the Phoenician merchants, was accepted by the Israelites, the Persians, the Greeks and later also by the Romans, who all made some modifications arising from their specific needs. Alongside these systems others were also used at different times and in different places.

Shekel stone weights found at En-Gedi. 7th century B.C. (Israel Dept. of Antiquities and Museums)

In the excavations in Palestine, especially in the strata of the 7th-6th centuries B.C., small stone weights with symbols on them have been found. Some of these symbols represent metrological values, while others are the actual names of the weights. Hundreds of weights have been measured and the results have shown that the same unit could vary considerably. It seems in fact that different values of the same basic units were used for different commodities, as is still done in some places today.

In the Hebrew Bible a weight is called a stone, indicating the material from which it was made. The Scriptures warn against cheating by using small weights for selling and heavy ones for buying (Deut 25:15; Amos 8:5, etc.). The merchant would carry the weights on his person (Deut 25:13, etc.). A weight that had been approved by the authorities was known as the "king's standard" (II Sam 14:26). Commodities were weighed on scales consisting of two bowls, equal in size and weight, suspended on three or four strings at the ends of a horizontal cane, which was held by a short rope. Another method involved placing the cane on a fixed base standing on the ground. Many such balances of all periods have been found in the excavations.

ISRAELITE WEIGHTS The smallest unit is the *gerah,* or $^1/_{20}$ shekel (Ex 30:13). There was also a $^1/_4$ shekel (I Sam 9:8: "fourth part"); a $^1/_3$ shekel and a *beka,* or $^1/_2$ shekel (Ex 38:26). These are all small units. The unit most frequently mentioned in the Bible is the shekel (Ex 30:23ff etc.) and it is not always easy to decide which standard it was related to in any particular passage. It is possible that the shekel referred to in the Books of Exodus, Leviticus and I Kings was equal to the shekel of Aegina, which weighed about 177 grains. The *maneh* ("mina") (Neh 7:71, etc.) belongs to the Phoenician standard and was therefore equal to 50 shekels. The *maneh* of the earlier books (I Kgs 10:17) was probably the Babylonian one of 50 heavy shekels. The *kikar* ("talent") is mentioned frequently in terms of a quantity of silver and sometimes as a weighing unit (Ex 37:24). The *kikar* of the later books of the Bible is the Phoenician *kikar* of 3,000 shekels, while in the early writings the Babylonian or Syrian unit is referred to.

Two groups of weights with scale pans. On the left of the pans are uninscribed weights from the Canaanite period. The inscribed shekel weights on the right of the scales are of the Judean period.

During the time of the Second Temple the Jews developed a system of weights based on a combination of the Phoenician with the Greek (Attic) and Roman systems. The values of the weights according to this system are:

      6 *maoth* (*maah* = obolos) = 1 *zuz*
      2 *zuzim* = 1 *shekel* (light)
      4 *zuzim* = 1 *shekel* (heavy)
     50 *zuzim* = $^1/_2$ *maneh*
    100 *zuzim* = 1 *maneh*
  6,000 *zuzim* = 1 *kikar*

WHEAT See PLANTS

WILLOW See PLANTS

WINE
Gen 9:21, 24;
14:18; 19:32-
35; 27:25, 28,

WINE According to biblical tradition Noah was the first man to plant a vineyard (Gen 9:20-22). From the Bible, Egyptian wall paintings and reliefs and the remains of installations found in Palestine, it is possible to reconstruct the methods by which wine was made. The grapes were

Wine press at the Garden Tomb, Jerusalem. 1st century A.D.

Wine merchant in his shop shown on a Gallo-Roman tombstone. 1st century A.D. (Musée Archéologique de Dijon)

brought in baskets from the vineyards to the winepress, which in the biblical period was either a natural flat rock or one flattened artificially (Is 5:2; 16:10; Jer 48:33). The grapes were spread out on the rock and trodden, so that the juice flowed through shallow channels to a vat hewn at the foot of the pressing ground. It was left to settle during the night and then collected into jars, which were closed with clay stoppers. The skins of the grapes, which had been left behind after the first pressing, would be pressed again in order to extract the remaining juice. The jars containing the juice were then taken to the wine cellar for fermentation. The cellar might be a natural cave or a hewn cistern, in which the correct temperature for the fermentation process could be maintained. Once the fermentation was completed the origin and quality of the wine, plus the name of its owner, would be marked on the seal.

The Bible records several names and types of wines, e.g., "blood of grapes" (Gen 49:11), "wines on the lees" (Is 25:6), "wine of Helbon" (Ezek 27:18), "wine of Lebanon" (Hos 14:7). Additional names have been found on inscribed jars from the biblical period in Palestine.

Wine was also made from dates, pomegranates, apples and other fruit, and from grain. From the NT we know that wine was sometimes mixed with other substances such as gall (Matt 27:34), myrrh (Mark 15:23) or oil for medicinal purposes (Luke 10:34).

Wine played an important role in the religious rituals of the ancient Near East. It was used in the daily (Ex 29:40) and monthly (Num 28:14) sacrifices and holy days (Num 15:5ff). The law of the Nazirites forbade the consumption of wine (Num 6:3; Judg 13:4) and the Rechabites willingly refrained from it (Jer 35:2 ff). The priests officiating in the tent of congregation also refrained from drinking wine (Lev 10:9; Ezek 44:21).

The vine was a symbol of prosperity and fertility (I Kgs 4:25; II Kgs 18:31) and grapes were one of the seven "fruits" of which the Holy Land boasted (Deut 7:13). Important personages would be greeted with bread and wine (Gen 14:18). The Bible does not favor intoxication (Prov 23:29-35; Is 22:12-14; 28:1, etc.), but abstention was a token of mourning (Dan 10:3). Wine was given to those who worked hard (II Chr 2:10). People on a journey would drink it (Josh 9:13; Judg 19:19), as would the weary, those who had lost their way and those who were embittered (II Sam 16:2; Prov 31:6-7). As well as being used in medicine it was an everyday beverage for kings and special ministers were appointed to supply it (Gen 40:2; Neh 2:1). The kings of Israel and Judah owned large vineyards and the wine was stored in the royal stores which were also used to house taxes paid in kind (I Chr 12:40; 27:27; II Chr 11:11).

The importance of viticulture in Palestine in biblical items, as well as in the Roman and Byzantine periods, is well attested by the archeological finds. Many hundreds of winepresses, some of which were most elaborate, have been discovered almost everywhere in the country.

Alongside the local wines foreign wines were imported into Palestine, as can be seen both in some of the biblical passages referred to above and in evidence from the Hellenistic and Roman periods. Thousands of stamped jar handles from Rhodes, Chios, Cos and other wine-producing islands, as well as from different parts of Italy, attest to this. Pagan cults, in which wine was an important ingredient, were also common in Palestine throughout these periods.

Jesus uses the metaphor of old and new wine skins to explain the newness of his own ministry in announcing the near arrival of the Kingdom of God (Matt 9:17 etc.). John the Baptist was destined to be a Nazirite and would therefore avoid strong drink (Luke 1:15). In

37; 49:11-1
Ex 29:40.
10:9; 23:13
Num 6:3, 2
15:5, 7, 10;
18:12; 28:1
Deut 7:13;
11:14; 12:1
14:23, 26; 1
28:39, 51; 2
32:14, 33, 3
33:28. Judg
9:13; 13:4,
14; 19:19.
I Sam 1:14-
24; 10:3; 16:
25:18, 37.
II Sam 13:2
16:1-2. II Kg
18:32. I Chr
9:29; 12:40;
27:27. II Chr
2:10, 15; 11:
31:5; 32:28.
Ezra 6:9; 7:2
Neh 2:1; 5:1
15, 18; 10:37
39; 13:5, 12,
15. Est 1:7,
10; 5:6; 7:2,
8. Job 1:13,
18; 32:19. Ps
4:7; 60:3; 75:
78:65; 104:15
Prov 3:10;
4:17; 9:2, 5;
20:1; 21:17;
23:30-31; 31:
6. Ecc 2:3;
9:7; 10:19.
Song 1:2, 4;
4:10; 5:1; 7:9;
8:2. Is 1:22;
5:11-12, 22;
16:10; 22:13;
24:7, 9, 11;
25:6; 27:2;
28:1, 7; 29:9;
36:17; 49:26;
51:21; 55:1;
56:12; 62:8;
65:8. Jer
13:12; 23:9;
25:15; 31:12;
35:2, 5-6, 8,
14; 40:10, 12;
48:33; 51:7.
Lam 2:12.
Ezek 27:18;
44:21. Dan
1:5, 8, 16; 5:1-
2, 4, 23; 23;
10:3. Hos 2:8-
9, 22; 4:11;
7:5, 14; 9:2, 4;
14:7. Joel 1:5,
10; 2:19, 24;
3:3, 18. Amos

Basket of fruit and grape-gathering scene depicted on a mosaic floor of the Byzantine period at Beth Shean.

Men treading grapes shown on a Byzantine mosaic floor at Beth Shean.

2:8, 12; 4:1;
5:11; 6:6;
9:13-14. Mic
2:11; 6:15.
Hab 2:5. Zeph
1:13. Hag
1:11; 2:12, 16.
Zech 9:15, 17;
10:7. Matt
9:17; 27:34,
48. Mark 2:22;
12:1; 15:23,
36. Luke 1:15;
5:37-39; 7:33;
10:34; 23:36.
John 2:3, 9-10;
4:46; 19:29-30.
Acts 2:13.
Rom 14:21.
Eph 5:18.
I Tim 3:3, 8;
5:23. Titus
1:7; 2:3. Rev
6:6; 14:8, 10;
16:19; 17:2;
18:3, 13

comparison with him Jesus was thought to be a "winebibber" (Matt 11:19; Luke 7:34). Jesus even turned water into wine at the wedding feast of Cana (John 2:2-10). Wine is recommended for medicinal purposes in I Timothy 5:23. The most exalted use of wine in the NT is at the Lord's supper, communion or eucharistic meal of thanksgiving (Matt 26:26-29; Mark 14:22-25; Luke 22:17-19; I Cor 11:23-26). At his last meal with his disciples, Jesus took a cup, presumably filled with Passover wine, though the texts do not mention wine explicitly, and interpreted it during the blessing as his blood which would be shed for the forgiveness of sins. He also announced that he would not drink of the "fruit of the vine" again until he would drink it new in the Kingdom of God. Thus when he was offered painkilling wine just before his crucifixion (Mark 15:23) and sour wine during it (Mark 15:36), he refused it.

WISDOM The Bible censured pagan wisdom as inferior (Gen chap. 41; Ex 7:8-9:12; Dan chaps. 2-4) and the prophets were especially critical (Is 19:3-4, 11-12; Jer 50:35-36; Ezek 28:1-19). Nevertheless the Bible is open to pagan wisdom (see WISDOM LITERATURE).

In the spirit of authentic biblical wisdom, the prophets criticized the false wisdom of royal counselors (Jer 8:8-9; 9:22-23 but see Prov 21:30; 26:12; 28:11). In the NT, part of Jesus' preaching is sapiential (Matt chaps. 5-7, John chap. 6); his parables also are related to wisdom and some of his sentences are true proverbs (Matt 16:25; 22:21; 26:52; Acts 20:35).

The Bible connected the growth of wisdom in Israel with Solomon (I Kgs chaps. 3-10). Seeking and gaining wisdom from God (I Kgs 5:12), he became a skillful judge, a great organizer and builder, and a truly international figure. Proverbs and the Song of Solomon are literally ascribed to him and he is traditionally regarded as the author of Ecclesiastes; in the NT, he is recalled as an ideal sage (Matt 12:42). Like Hezekiah subsequently, Solomon probably had wise men and scribes at his court (Prov 25:1). But, as elsewhere, Israel's wisdom stemmed principally from the common people; there are proverbs which come, not from the court, but from the villages and contryside (II Sam chap. 14; Prov 14:4; Jer 31:29). The wise men of the royal court would have collected this popular wisdom and reorganized it for publication.

Gifted individuals, exercising patient observation, noted the repetition of certain phenomena in nature, or in human existence, to uncover the principles which rule the apparent multiplicity of the same experience; moreover, they succeeded in expressing these principles in a pithy, well-balanced sentence, pleasant to the ear and provoking reflection with its enigmatic aspect; these sentences, accepted and repeated by generations, were finally included in an official collection which became part of the Bible.

The wise strove above all to comprehend the reality of the world, of things and of man; they were convinced that reality is subject to rules which can be recognized and expressed by man. The wise men studied reality in its entirety, without distinction beween religious and profane, being equally interested in both. Once put in writing, their wisdom became the standard in regulating the conduct of society.

The path of the wise differs from that of the king, the priest or the prophet. He remains a seeker, being aware of the limits of his knowledge. For people trying to observe and understand, reality often retains its mystery — hence, the reserve of the wise (Prov 16:1; 19:14; 20:24; 21:31; 26:12). Altogether true wisdom has to deny itself (Prov 21:30), for understanding is the preserve of the Lord, the creator and guide of history. Only in the 8th century B.C. is the wisdom of God mentioned explicitly (Job 12:13; Ps 104:24; Is 11:2; 31:2; Jer 10:12), even if divine wisdom was acknowledged in David (II Sam 14:20) and in Solomon (I Kgs 3:28) and in the special wisdom of a leader (Deut 34:9).

Proverbs proposes a religious synthesis of Israelite wisdom in the famous sentence: "The fear of the Lord is the beginning of wisdom" (Prov 9:10). But because it made too close a connection between virtuous life and happiness on earth, or between misfortune and sin (Prov 3:33; 10:3), OT didactic wisdom went into a crisis, which was expressed in the speculative Wisdom Books of Job and Ecclesiastes. Only in a late Greek book included in the Septuagint, Wisdom of Solomon chapters 1-6, does a new solution appear with the afterlife's retribution.

In certain texts of the Hebrew Bible, wisdom is personified. In Proverbs 1:20-33; 8:9 ff, she speaks publicly: firstborn of the Lord, she was with him when he put order and stability in the world (see also Job 28:23-27). She is also counselor of the rulers of society, and therefore she summons all to hear her and follow her advice. Later Wisdom works, translated into Greek in the Septuagint, Ben Sira chapter 24 and Baruch 3:9-4:4, perceive the OT as the best expression of divine wisdom granted to Israel (see Deut 4:6), whereas Wisdom of Solomon chapters 6-10 interprets wisdom as the presence of God in the world and in the just.

In the NT these various functions of wisdom are ascribed to Jesus. He also summons people to follow him (Matt 11:28-30), in him is a higher wisdom (Matt 7:29; 11:19; 12:42); through him all was created (John 1:2-4; Col 1:16); being created before all things they hold together in him (Col 1:15, 17); he came from above and he is true food, like wisdom (John 6:32-58). Paul adds that the cross which Jesus endured elucidated God's wisdom, which accepts what is against human pretensions (I Cor 1:17-3:23); the permanence of Israel, with its refusal to acknowledge the messiah in Jesus, is a part of the mysterious wisdom of God (Rom 11:33).

WISDOM LITERATURE The Books of Proverbs, Job and Ecclesiastes in the OT, Ecclesiasticus (Sirach) and Wisdom of Solomon in the Apocrypha. Israelite Wisdom literature belongs to an international tradition; therefore parallels to minor collections are well known. For example, within Proverbs, to the Sumerian *Proverbs of Suruppak*, various collections of Babylonian proverbs; the Egyptian Instruction literature (*Ptahhotep, Kagemni, Merikare, Amenemhet, Ani*), and sayings (*Papyrus Insinger* and *Onksheshongy*). The same goes for Job (the Sumerian *Man and His God*, the Babylonian *I Will Praise the Lord of Wisdom* and *The Babylonian Theodicy*) and Ecclesiastes (*The Dialogue between a Master and his Slave*; a brief excerpt in the Egyptian *Admonitions of Ipuwer*). Foreign authors for two brief collections in Proverbs are acknowledged (Agur, 30:1-7; Lemuel's mother, 31:1-9), and a number of instructions from the Egyptian King Amenemopet appear in Proverbs 22:17-24:22. The truths preserved in such succinct sayings are universal, and the problems examined in Job and Ecclesiastes were experienced throughout the ancient Near East. Hence this body of literature has nothing that applies specifically to Israel until Ecclesiasticus; instead of emphasizing saving history by a self-revealing Lord on behalf of an elect people, it focuses on the creator and on human efforts to cope with reality. The oldest teachings within the wisdom books were addressed to children in the home (of "my son" in Proverbs), but later ones functioned in the royal court as advice on how to advance, and in schools, which are first mentioned in Ecclesiasticus (about 190 B.C.). The figure of Dame Wisdom, deriving from the Egyptian goddess Ma'at, is associated with the act of creation in Proverbs chapter 8 and in Ecclesiasticus chapter 24, where she is equated with the Mosaic Torah (See WISDOM). Certain other texts within the Bible bear resemblances of one kind or another to these books: a few psalms and narratives, proverbial sayings attributed to Jesus, portions of the Epistle of James, the prologue to the Gospel of John, and a Pauline hymn about Jesus as the agent of creation (Col 1:15-20). Elsewhere Paul seeks to stand wisdom's claims on their head, exalting divine "foolishness" as superior to human wisdom (1 Cor 1:17-31).

WISDOM OF SOLOMON (called in the Latin tradition: Book of Wisdom). One of the apocryphal books, belonging to the Wisdom Literature, written in Greek by a Jewish religious sage and ascribed to Solomon. The place of origin may have been Hellenistic Alexandria and the date of writing, the 1st century B.C. or A.D. The survival of this

Jewish book is due to Christianity. Jewish writers of the first centuries do not refer to this work, and its first mention is by the Church Fathers at the end of the 2nd century.

The Wisdom of Solomon contains three different themes, interconnected by the recurring concept of wisdom. The first part (chaps. 1-6) on the rewards of wisdom, is addressed to "the rulers of the earth" (1:1), who should learn and honor wisdom and not go astray (6:9). The second part (chaps. 7-9) is the story of a wise man, with a poetic description of the advantages brought to him by wisdom, which was granted to him by God in response to his prayer. The final section (chaps. 10-19) is an interpretation of human history according to the biblical tradition. All the central personalities mentioned in the Books of Genesis and Exodus, from Adam to Moses, are extolled for their wisdom. The story of the Exodus from Egypt is retold and reinterpreted to contrast the plagues with the blessings granted to Israel (see e.g. chaps. 17-18). The Wisdom of Solomon ends with the comforting words that even the elements in nature were changed by a "kind of harmony", in order to exalt God's people (19:18-22).

WITCHCRAFT See MAGIC

WOLF See ANIMALS

WOMEN According to the law in biblical times, an unmarried woman was subordinate to her father or, in his absence, to her elder brother. Thus, her father could sell her as a maidservant in the hope of having her master take her as a wife or assign her as a wife to one of his sons (Ex 21:7-9). It was her father or elder brother who gave her in marriage (Gen 24:50-51; Deut 22:16). Though marriage at times required her consent (Gen 24:57-58; cf Num 36:6), her husband could divorce her freely (Deut 24:1).

Upon being divorced or widowed, she returned to the home and authority of her father (Lev 22:13). As long as she was unmarried, her father could annul her vows (Num 30:5); if married, her vows could be annulled by her husband (Num 30:8). Her inferior economic status is indicated by her paying 30 shekels for the purpose of vows whereas a man paid 50 shekels (Lev 15:19-24). After childbirth, if the child were female, the mother's period of impurity was doubled (Lev 12:1-5).

Her subordinate legal status did not preclude the Hebrew woman from taking an active part in religious life as well as in social, political and even military affairs. In the sphere of religion, she could fulfill the role of prophet, the highest spiritual order in ancient Hebrew society. At least four women prophets are known by name: Miriam (Ex 15:20-21), Deborah (Judg 4:4-9), Huldah (II Kgs 22:14-20) and Noadiah (Neh 6:14). But within the sanctuary, she held no official position. Priestesses, while common in the religious life of the ancient Near East, were unknown in Hebrew society. Their deliberate exclusion from this sphere was probably due to the role of sacred prostitute which women played in ancient Canaanite sanctuaries.

Women appear to have been particularly susceptible to idolatrous practices, soothsaying and witchcraft. King Saul, when troubled, sought the services of a woman in En Dor who called up the spirit of the prophet Samuel from the grave (I Sam chap. 28). Both Jeremiah and Ezekiel refer to women as involved in these practices (cf Jer 44:15-19; Ezek 8:14; 13:17-23).

An Israelite woman, together with her husband, could visit and pray at a sanctuary on stated occasions (I Sam 1:4-5). She was commanded together with all Israel to be present at the reading of the Torah at the end of every Sabbatical year (Deut 31:12; cf Josh 8:35), as she was at the rejoicing of the Festival of Tabernacles (Deut 16:14). Unmarried girls observed an annual vintage festival by dancing in the vineyards (Judg 21:19-21).

The woman as mother was to be honored and respected no less than one's father (Ex 20:12; Deut 5:16). Disobedience of one's mother was as severely punished as disrespect of one's father (Lev 20:9; Deut 21:18-21; 27:16). The middle passage assigns to the mother a role equal to that of the father in the punishment of a rebellious son. On the level of legal status and rights, biblical legislation granted the right of inheritance to daughters in cases where there were no surviving sons (Num 36:1-8). As mother, the woman was responsible for caring for her children and household. She made clothing (Prov 31:19), baked bread for visitors (Gen 18:6) and prepared food (Gen 27:9, 14). The mother's economic activity would take her well beyond the limits of her home. According to the Book of Proverbs, she "brings her food from afar" and engaged in the purchase of real estate (Prov 31:14, 16).

The two significant occasions in the social life of ancient Hebrew society were weddings and funerals. Women fulfilled leading roles on both occasions. At weddings, they would sing love songs. Women also served as professional mourners and chanted dirges (Jer 9:17). On learning of the death of Saul and Jonathan, David in his lament, called upon the daughters of Israel to weep for their fallen king (II Sam 1:24).

Another role occupied by certain women was that of the "wise woman". The town of Abel Beth Maacah was saved from destruction by such a woman (II Sam 20:14-22). A "wise woman" of Tekoa was also employed by Joab in order to persuade King David to lift the banishment imposed upon his son Absalom (II Sam chap. 14).

The title "mother in Israel" (Judg 5:7) bestowed upon Deborah, reflects the leadership role certain women played. The OT records a number of instances in which women turned the tide of battle by their exploits. The outstanding example is that of Deborah who roused Barak and the troops of Naphtali and Zebulun to march against Sisera (Judg 4:4, 6). In the end, Sisera met his death at the hands of a woman, Jael, the wife of Heber the Kenite (Judg 4:17-21). When Abimelech threatened to burn the tower in which the men and women of Thebez had taken refuge, a woman in the tower threw down an upper millstone that crushed his skull (Judg 9:53). Two powerful royal women were Jezebel (I Kgs chaps. 18-19) and Athaliah (II Kgs chap. 11).

Women traditionally greeted men when they returned victorious from battle; they would welcome the returning heroes with song and dance in praise of their exploits (I Sam 18:6-7). This role is reflected in David's lament over the death of Saul and Jonathan "Tell it not in Gath, proclaim it not in the streets of Ashkelon, lest the daughters of the Philistines" rejoice (II Sam 1:20). Songs of derision and scorn were also the province of women (Jer 38:22).

In its estimate and characterization of women, the OT is patently ambivalent. On the one hand, there is Ecclesiastes' misogynic "One (true) man among a thousand I have found but a (true) woman among all these I have not found" (Ecc 7:28), or the no less caustic "And I find more bitter than death the woman whose heart is snares and nets" (Ecc 7:26). A negative portrait of the woman emerges from Proverbs 9:13; 11:22, a portrait in which the woman is characterized as noisy, contentious and indiscreet. Against this is juxtaposed the saying in Proverbs, "He who finds a wife, finds a good thing and obtains favor from the Lord" (18:22). The final verses of Proverbs are a paean of praise for the "virtuous wife" (31:10-31) lauded both by her husband and her children for her industriousness, her kindness, her wisdom and her ability to manage the affairs of her household.

Fragment of a scroll from Qumran known as "The Evil of the Strange Woman". (Shrine of the Book, Jerusalem).

At the heart of the NT stands the event of the death and resurrection of Jesus to which the primary witnesses are women (Matt 27:55-56; 28:1-10; Mark 15:40-41; 16:1-11; Luke 23:49; 24:1-11; John 19:25-27; 20:1-18). The preservation of this memory together with that of the woman who anointed Jesus within each of the early church traditions represented by the evangelists (Matt 26:6-13; Mark 14:3-9; Luke 7:36-50; John 12:1-8) and in the face of the dominant patriarchal religious and social culture, points to a strong historical basis for the tradition. It also indicates the significant presence of women within early Christianity. The earliest traditions include women among the beneficiaries of the kingdom which Jesus proclaimed and effected (cf Matt 8:14-15; Mark 5:21-43; 7:24-30).

This equality of women with men in the kingdom of Jesus continued to be effective and to be proclaimed in the course of the Pauline mission. Philippians 4:2-3 and Romans 16:1-15 point to shared ministerial roles within the early communities and associate the language of ministry with both men and women. This suggests that women shared not only in the missionary activity of the early church but also in its leadership roles. Paul's theological basis for this activity finds expression in Galatians 3:28: "there is neither male nor female; for you are all one in Christ Jesus." In his First Epistle to the Corinthians, he tries to give the pastoral application of this principle in the face of difficulties arising in the Corinthian community. His response to the Corinthian belief that their new-found freedom allowed them to blur the natural distinction between the sexes is found in I Corinthians chapter 11. Paul argues from the contrast between male and female in the first creation (I Cor 11:3) and from the authority which woman shares with man in the new creation (I Cor 11:10-12) to the position that men should appear to be men and women appear to be women in order to preserve the natural distinction between the sexes (I Cor 11:14-16). Their new-found freedom is to lie in their shared authority within the Christian community. This was challenged by certain groups within the community, possibly the Judaizers (cf I Cor 14:34-35), and drew a strong reaction from Paul (I Cor 14:36). Thus, at the earliest stages of its development, the radical nature of the kingdom of Jesus, especially as regards women, came into conflict with established beliefs and practices.

The tension created by such conflicts is reflected in the Gospel of Matthew which opens with the patrilineage of Jesus (Matt 1:1-17) and closes with the commissioning of the 11 male disciples to a universal mission (Matt 28:16-20). Matthew introduces significant references to women at key positions within the narrative. Four OT women and Mary break the dominant patriarchal pattern of the genealogy (Matt 1:3, 5-6, 16) and two of the women who remained faithful to Jesus, even to the foot of the cross, witness the empty tomb, encounter the risen Jesus, and are given the mission of proclaiming the resurrection to the disciples (Matt 27:55-56; 28:1-10). In the body of the narrative, not only are women healed and restored to the religious community of Israel (Matt 8:14-15; 9:18-26), but a Canaanite woman enters into a dialogue with Jesus which results in his extending his mission beyond the confines of Israel in prophetic expectation of the mission which he will entrust to his disciples beyond the resurrection (Matt 15:21-28; cf Matt 28:16-20). Finally, the prophetic action of the woman who anoints Jesus as he enters his passion is interpreted by Jesus: her act of recognition of Jesus in his climactic hour will be told in her memory just as the actions of Jesus are to be told in his memory (cf Matt 26:6-13, especially v. 13).

Both Luke and John preserve unique traditions regarding women. In Luke's infancy narrative, Mary's faithful response to the invitation of the angel stands in contrast to Zechariah's hesitation in the face of the role offered to himself and Elizabeth (Luke 1:26-38; cf 1:5-20), while the prophetic voices of Mary, Elizabeth and Anna (Luke 1:39-56; 2:36-38) parallel those of Zechariah (Luke 1:67-79) and Simeon (Luke 2:25-35). Twice within the Gospel of Luke, Jesus reaches out in compassion to a woman in need beyond traditional religious and social boundaries, and without the usual request from the one in need (Luke 7:11-17; 13:10-17); and twice Luke specifically mentions women ministering to Jesus as well as listening to his words of teaching (Luke 8:1-3; 10:38-42).

The NT also preserves, however, evidence of the later tendency to domesticate and patriarchalize the initial vision. The household codes of Ephesians and Colossians call for the submission of women to their husbands according to the model of the ancient patriarchal household (cf Eph 5:22-24; Col 3:18); and I Timothy reflects the loss of the community model of shared authority which Paul presented in I Corinthians 11:10-12 — a result of the church's acceptance of the dominant social patriarchal model (cf I Tim 2:12). Women are now to be under the control of male leaders (cf I Tim 5:3-16).

Thus, within the NT, we see reflected the struggle which ensued when the vision of Jesus regarding women met powerful religious and cultural forces arrayed against it. It preserves both the roots of liberation and also the roots of patriarchal domination and submission of women.

WORMWOOD See PLANTS

WRITING MATERIALS Both the Bible and archeological finds indicate that many different materials were used for writing in the biblical period. The earliest documents were written on stone (Ex 24:12; Deut 4:13; Jer 17:1), the inscriptions being engraved on large rocks with a hammer and chisel, a stylus (a pointed metal engraving tool) or an iron pen. Many steles inscribed in this way have been found in Egypt, Mesopotamia and Syria (cf Job 19:23-24). Stones might also be plastered with lime and the writing applied with a brush or a pen dipped into ink (cf Deut 27:2-3). Stones could also be chiseled and smoothed, as with the tablets on which the Ten Commandments were written (Ex 31:18), or the famous stele of Mesha, king of Moab.

Tablets for writing on were in use throughout all periods. Very common in Mesopotamia, but also found frequently in the other

Scribe recording the harvest. Detail of a wall painting from the tomb of Mennah, Egypt. New Kingdom.

Inkwell found at Qumran. 1st century A.D.

(top right)
Statue of an Egyptian scribe.

(top left)
The first five letters of the alphabet in early Hebrew script carved on the steps of a palace at Lachish. 9th-8th centuries B.C.

countries of the ancient Near East, were clay tablets. Millions of such tablets have been found. Sherds of broken jars, called ostraca, with the writing mostly executed by means of ink and a fine brush, or sometimes a pointed tool, were also very common. In Egypt and in Palestine wooden tablets were also commonly used (Ezek 37:16), with writing in ink or stylus.

The commonest writing material in Egypt was papyrus. A large number of papyrus documents have also been found in Palestine, but these belong to the Roman and Byzantine periods.

Another material frequently used in the Near East, and especially in Palestine, was parchment. This was made from the skins of animals, mostly sheep. The skins would be tanned, cut into sheets and, when necessary, sewn into scrolls. The writing was again done with pen and ink.

Writing on hard materials such as stone, clay and wood, was done with a stylus (Is 8:1). On softer materials, such as papyrus and parchment, a pen was used. The main writing pigment was ink (Jer 36:18). This was a thick sticky substance, so that the scribe could safely carry it in an inkpot in his belt (Ezek 9:2). To make it ready for writing, water was added. The scribe kept his pens, penknife and inkpot in an inkhorn.

An educated man was one who could read a book (Is 29:11-12). Sometimes the word "scroll" supplants "book"; implying that it was written on a flexible material that could be conveniently rolled (Jer 36:17-29). Numerous such scrolls were discovered in the Judean Desert caves. The term "letter" is found in the Hebrew only in the later books of the Bible (Neh 2:7-9). The letter could be a written document or a moral message (II Chr 30:6). The NT epistles were presumably written on papyrus with ink (II Cor 3:3; II John vs. 5, 12).

YAH Short form of the divine name YHWH (Yahweh; see GOD: NAMES OF GOD). It occurs 25 times in the Hebrew Bible, both in relatively early texts (e.g. Ex 15:2; Ps 68:5, 19) and in later passages (e.g. Ps 115:17-18; 118:5, 14, 17-19). It features a further 23 times in the expression Hallelujah, which means "Praise Yah" (the spelling Jah instead of Yah comes from medieval Latin). The name Yah also appears as the final component in such biblical names as Micaiah, which means "Who is like Yah?"; Azariah, which means "Yah helped"; and Abijah, which means "Yah is my Father". Scholars are divided as to whether the name Yah is derived by shortening from YHWH or as to whether the forms Yahu and YHWH were expanded from the original Yah.

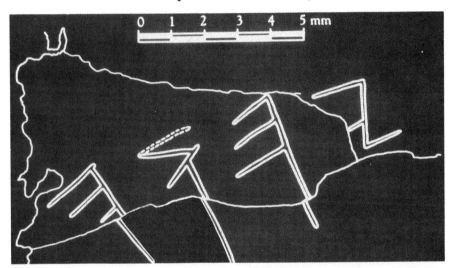

The Divine Name YHWH, top, which is included in the Priestly Benediction incised on the silver plaque, left, before it was unrolled. Dated to the 7th century B.C., this is the earliest known inscription bearing the Divine Name. The scroll was found in one of the burial caves in the Hinnom Valley.

Z

ZAANAIM, ZAANANNIM A place in the south of the territory of Naphtali, between Mount Tabor and the Jordan (Josh 19:33). Heber the Kenite "pitched his tent unto the Plain of Zaanaim, which is by Kedesh" (Naphtali) (Judg 4:11), and Jael killed Sisera there (Judg 4:21). Not identified.

ZAANAN An alternate form for Zenan used in Micah. See ZENAN.

ZAAVAN The son of Ezer, of the chiefs of the Horites, a descendant of Seir.

ZABAD ("gift").

1. The son of Nathan; a descendant of Sheshan the Jerahmeelite.

2. The son of Ephraim. According to some, he was among the children of Ephraim killed by native Gittites.

3. The son of Ahlai; one of David's "mighty men".

4. The son of Shimeath, an Ammonite woman. Together with another servant, he conspired against King Joash and killed him in order to avenge the death of the son of Jehoiada the priest (II Chr 24:26). In II Kings 12:21 he is called Jozachar.

5. One of the family of Zattu.

6. One of the family of Hashum.

7. One of the family of Nebo.

The above three, having married alien women, repudiated them, together with their children, according to Ezra's reform.

ZABBAI

1. One of the sons of Bebai; he is listed among those who married alien women.

2. The father of Baruch, mentioned among those who repaired the wall of Jerusalem in the days of Nehemiah (Neh 3:20). The name is also read as Zaccai (Ezra 2:9; Neh 7:14).

ZABBUD Son of Bigvai who returned with Ezra from the Babylonian Exile.

ZABDI

1. A man of the tribe of Judah. Father of Calmi, the son of Zerah and the grandson of Achan (Josh 7:1, 17-18). In I Chronicles 2:6 he is called Zimri.

2. One of the sons of Shimei, head of a family of the tribe of Benjamin.

3. The Shiphmite. An overseer at the court of David in charge of produce of the vineyards for the wine cellars.

4. A Levite descended from Asaph. In I Chronicles 9:15 he is called Zichri.

ZABDIEL ("present of God").

1. A descendant of Perez from the tribe of Judah; the father of Jashobeam who was an officer over a unit of 24,000 in King David's service.

2. A priest and overseer of 128 priests who settled in Jerusalem at the time of Nehemiah.

ZABUD The son of Nathan the prophet and an officer ("king's friend") of Solomon.

ZACCAI A family of 760 which returned from the Babylonian Exile with Zerubbabel.

ZACCHAEUS A Jewish inhabitant of Jericho and its chief tax collector, mentioned only in the Gospel of Luke (Luke 19:1-10). In his curiosity to see Jesus, Zacchaeus climbed up a tree (Luke 19:4). Later Jesus invited himself into Zacchaeus' house and accepted the repentance of his host who gave half of his goods to the poor, in compensation for all the money he had amassed from the people.

ZACCHUR The son of Mishma of the tribe of Simeon.

ZAANAIM, ZAANANNIM
Josh 19:33.
Judg 4:11

ZAANAN
Mic 1:11

ZAAVAN
Gen 36:27.
I Chr 1:42

ZABAD 1
I Chr 2:36-37

ZABAD 2
I Chr 7:21

ZABAD 3
I Chr 11:41

ZABAD 4
II Chr 24:26

ZABAD 5
Ezra 10:27

ZABAD 6
Ezra 10:33

ZABAD 7
Ezra 10:43

ZABBAI 1
Ezra 10:28

ZABBAI 2
Neh 3:20

ZABBUD
Ezra 8:14

ZABDI 1
Josh 7:1, 17-18

ZABDI 2
I Chr 8:19

ZABDI 3
I Chr 27:27

ZABDI 5
Neh 11:17

ZABDIEL 1
I Chr 27:2

ZABDIEL 2
Neh 11:14

ZABUD
I Kgs 4:5

ZACCAI
Ezra 2:9. Neh 7:14

ZACCHAEUS
Luke 19:2, 5, 8

ZACCHUR
I Chr 4:26

ZACCUR ("remembered").

1. A man of the tribe of Reuben, father of Shammua, one of the spies sent by Moses to explore the land of Canaan.

2. A Levite, son of Jaaziah, son of Merari.

3. The firstborn son of Asaph the singer, the head of the third division of singers (I Chr 25:2, 10). In I Chronicles 9:15 he is called Zichri, and in Nehemiah 11:17, Zabdi.

4. The son of Imri. He was among the priests who helped repair the wall of Jerusalem.

5. One of the Levites who witnessed the sealing of Nehemiah's covenant.

6. The father of Hanan, the assistant to the men in charge of the storehouses at the time of Nehemiah.

ZACHARIAS The father of John the Baptist. According to Luke 1:5, Zacharias was a priest of the division of Abijah (I Chr 24:10) which periodically served in the Temple. These divisions served in rotation and their duty was to conduct the sacrificial service on weekdays. (Those who did not live in or around Jerusalem went up to the holy city and stayed there during their service). Zacharias' wife, Elizabeth, was of priestly descent and the couple were noted for their devoutness.

Elizabeth was barren and the couple advanced in years. One day as Zacharias was serving in the Temple, the angel Gabriel appeared to him and announced that he and his wife would have a son, who would be called John. Because Zacharias doubted this message, he was struck with dumbness until the birth of his son (Luke 1:5-20).

At the circumcision, when the child was eight days old, the people wanted to name him after his father, Zacharias. As he could not yet speak, Zacharias wrote on a tablet that the name should be John. At that moment he regained the power of speech and praised God, uttering the prophecy which is known as the "Benedictus" in Christian liturgy.

Zacharias inscribing the name of his newborn son on a tablet. From the Pidzak Hymnal of 1335.

ZADOK ("righteous").

1. At the outset of David's kingship, Zadok, son of Ahitub, was appointed priest together with Abiathar (alternately Ahimelech) (II Sam 8:17). The two priests accompanied David out of Jerusalem during Absalom's rebellion and were responsible for the ark. At David's behest, they returned to the capital to keep him informed as to what was happening there (II Sam 15:24-35). After the rebellion, they were given the task of influencing the elders of Judah to rejoin David's cause (II Sam 19:11-14). Towards the end of the king's life, the two differed over the choice of David's successor — Abiathar following Adonijah, and Zadok favoring Solomon (I Kgs 1:7-8). Together with the prophet Nathan, Zadok anointed Solomon as king (I Kgs 1:32-40).

After Abiathar's exile, Zadok became head priest (I Kgs 2:26-27, 35; I Chr 29:22) followed by his son Azariah (I Kgs 4:2). Several hundred years later, under King Hezekiah, the high priesthood was still in the hands of the house of Zadok (II Chr 31:10). Ezekiel's vision of the future sees Zadok's descendants continuing as high priests, for they "have kept my charge... did not go astray" (Ezek 48:11).

The Chronicler stresses Zadok's descent from Aaron (I Chr 6:3-8; 24:3). Ezra is portrayed as a direct descendant of Aaron, through Ahitub and Zadok (Ezra 7:1-6).

2. Father of Jerusha (II Kgs 15:33; Jerushah in II Chr 27:1), and grandfather of King Jotham of Judah.

3. One of the leaders of troops who came to the aid of David in Hebron.

4. A descendant of Zadok the priest. He may, however, be identical with Zadok himself.

5. Descendant of Baana; he helped to rebuild the wall of Jerusalem in Nehemiah's time.

6. Descendant of Immer, he helped repair the wall of Jerusalem.

7. One of those who sealed the covenant in the time of Nehemiah.

8. A scribe, appointed as one of the treasurers of the storehouses in the time of Nehemiah.

9. Son of Azor and father of Achim in the genealogy of Jesus.

ZAHAM The son of King Rehoboam of Judah, and of Mahalath, the daughter of Jerimoth.

ZAIR A place along the route which King Joram of Judah took in his campaign against Edom. Being mentioned only once in the Bible, there is no way to identify Zair unless it is identical with Zoar to the south of the Dead Sea.

ZALAPH ("caperberry"). The father of Hanun, one of the priests who repaired the wall of Jerusalem at the time of Nehemiah.

ZALMON A high mountain range on which much snow falls in the winter; also called the "hill of God" and "the hill of the Bashan" (Ps 68:15). Should probably be identified with Hauran, or Jebel ed-Druz.

ZALMONAH A station on the Israelites' route in the wilderness, between Mount Hor and Punon.

ZALMUNNA One of the two Midianite kings (the other was Zebah) who were slain by Gideon, in retribution for the slaughter of his brothers (Judg 8:4-21; Ps 83:11).

ZAMZUMMIM According to Deuteronomy 2:20 Zamzummim is the Ammonite term for the race of giants who lived in Ammon before the arrival of the Ammonites; the Hebrew term is Rephaim while the Moabite term is Emim (Deut 2:11).

ZANOAH

1. A place in the north of the Plain (Josh 15:34). In the period of the return from Babylon its inhabitants built the Dung Gate of Jerusalem.

Khirbet Zanu northeast of Azekah, identified with Zanoah.

Identified with Khirbet Zanu, northeast of Azekah.

2. A place on the southern border of the territory of Judah, on the edge of the Negeb (Josh 15:56). Not identified.

ZAPHNATH-PAANEAH The name given to Joseph by Pharaoh (Gen 41:45). Scholars do not agree as to its meaning. Some read it as a Hebrew name and translate it as "he who reveals hidden secrets" — a reference to the unraveling of Pharaoh's dream by Joseph. Others take it as an Egyptian name, to be translated "God spoke and will grant life" or "God spoke and the bearer of the name lives on".

ZAPHON A town in the territory of Gad, east of the Jordan, in the Valley of Succoth, formerly a city of Og, king of Bashan (Josh 13:27). Here the men of Ephraim crossed the Jordan to meet Jephthah (Judg 12:1). In the Hellenistic-Roman period it was known as Asafon, in the northern part of the Perea, where the Hasmonean Alexander Jannaeus was defeated about 108-107 B.C. in a battle with Ptolemy, king of Cyprus. Identified with Tell es-Saidive.

ZAREPHATH An important Sidonian harbor, modern Ras Sarafand, about 6 miles (10km) south of Sidon. It is first mentioned as being situated along the Via Maris in a list of the time of Rameses II. Later it is mentioned among the Phoenician towns taken by Sennacherib in 701 B.C. It was at Zarephath that Elijah revived the widow's son (I Kgs chap. 17). Recent excavations at the site have uncovered the Phoenician and Roman towns. The name of the town was found inscribed on a glass stamp at the site.

ZARETAN See ZERERAH

ZARHITES (ZERAHITES) A family descended from Zerah, the son of Simeon (Num 26:13). According to Numbers 26:20, the family was of the tribe of Judah. Two officers, Sibbecai the Hushathite and Maharai the Netophathite, each heading divisions of 24,000, were members of this family (I Chr 27:11, 13).

ZATTU The head of a family who returned with Ezra from the Babylonian Exile; they numbered 945 men (Ezra 2:8), 845 according to Nehemiah 7:13. Zattu was among those who witnessed the sealing of Nehemiah's covenant (Neh 10:15).

ZAZA The son of Jonathan a descendant of Jerahmeel.

ANOAH 2
Josh 15:56.
Chr 4:18

ZAPHNATH-
PAANEAH
Gen 41:45

ZAPHON
Josh 13:27.
Judg 12:1

ZAREPHATH
I Kgs 17:9-10.
Obad v.20;
Luke 4:26

ZARETAN
Josh 3:16.
I Kgs 4:12;
7:46

ZARHITES
Num 26:13,
20. Josh 7:17.
I Chr 27:11,
13

ZATTU
Ezra 2:8;
10:27. Neh
7:13; 10:14

ZAZA
I Chr 2:33

ZEBADIAH ("Yah has given as a gift").

1. The son of Beriah; the head of a family of the tribe of Benjamin.

2. One of the sons of Elpaal of the tribe of Benjamin.

3. One of the two sons of Jeroham; he joined David at Ziklag.

4. The son of Meshelemiah, a Levite gatekeeper.

5. The son of Asahel, the brother of Joab. He succeeded his father as commander of a division of 24,000.

6. One of the Levites sent by Jehoshaphat to teach the Law throughout Judah (II Chr 17:8).

7. The son of Ishmael, from the tribe of Judah. He was the chief judicial officer at the time of Jehoshaphat.

8. The son of Michael, a head of an 80-strong family who returned from the Babylonian Exile with Ezra.

9. A priest of the family of Immer. Having married an alien woman, he repudiated her in keeping with Ezra's reform.

ZEBAH ("sacrifice"). One of the two Midianite kings (the other was Zalmunna), who were slain by Gideon, in retribution for the slaughter of his brothers at Tabor (Judg 8:19-21; Ps 83:11).

ZEBAIM Mentioned in the list of families of "Solomon's servants". It may be part of the name Pochereth which precedes it.

ZEBEDEE ("God has given"). The father of the two disciples James and John (Matt 4:21; 10:2; 26:37) and like them a fisherman (Mark 1:19). When Jesus called James and John from their father and the nets, they obeyed, leaving Zebedee behind in his boat. Nothing is related of him subsequently.

ZEBINA The son of Nebo; having married an alien woman, he repudiated her in keeping with Ezra's reform.

ZEBOIM, ZEBOIIM One of the "cities of the Plain" on the border of the land of Canaan (Gen 10:19; 14:2, 8; Deut 29:33; Hos 11:8); the other cities included Sodom and Gomorrah. King Chedorlaomer of Elam and his allies made war against King Shemeber of Zeboiim and the other cities of the Plain (Gen 14:2, 8, 10). Zeboiim was probably destroyed together with Sodom and Gomorrah, because Moses later referred to its destruction alongside the other cities (Deut 29:23) and Hosea cited it as an example of the judgment which befalls evil cities (Hos 11:8). Its location is unknown, but it may have been situated to the south of the Dead Sea.

ZEBUDAH ("gift"). The mother of Jehoiakim, daughter of Pedaiah of Rumah (II Kgs 23:36).

ZEBUL The governor of the city of Shechem. As lieutenant of Abimelech son of Jerubbaal, his advice helped Abimelech to frustrate a plot by Gaal son of Ebed (Judg 9:30-41).

ZEBULUN, ZEBULUNITES The sixth son born to Leah (Gen 30:20) and the tenth of Jacob's 13 children. Zebulun was the founder of one of the twelve tribes of Israel.

Zebulun had three sons: Sered, Elon and Jahleel (Gen 46:14). When the 12 scouts were sent to tour the land of Canaan, the tribe was represented by Gaddiel son of Sodi (Num 13:10). Zebulun appears among the six tribes assigned to stand upon Mount Ebal when the curse was spoken (Deut 27:13).

The tribe of Zebulun is closely connected with the tribe of Issachar, both geographically in southern Galilee (Josh 19:10-16, 17-23) and in the blessings of Jacob and Moses (Gen 49:13-15; Deut 33:18-19). The number of its males eligible for military service is given as 60,500 in Numbers 26:27.

The tribe played a prominent role in the victory over Sisera's army at the Brook of Kishon (Judg 4:6; 5:11, 18) and in Gideon's victory over

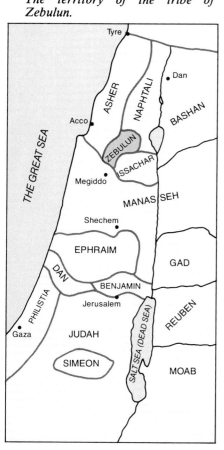

The territory of the tribe of Zebulun.

the Midianites (Judg 6:35). The judge Elon and possibly the judge Ibzan were of the tribe of Zebulun (Judg 12:8-12) as was the prophet, Jonah the son of Amittai, who came from Gath Hepher (I Kgs 14:15) in the territory of Zebulun (Josh 19:13). In the time of King David the leader of the tribe was Ishmaiah son of Obadiah (I Chr 27:19). The tribe won renown as seafarers (Gen 49:13; Deut 33:18) although its access to the sea may not have been direct but only by arrangement with friendly Canaanites.

ZECHARIAH ("Yah has remembered").

1. A king of Israel, son of Jeroboam II, and last ruler of the dynasty of Jehu (748-747 B.C.). He came to the throne of Samaria in the 38th year of Uzziah, king of Judah and reigned for only six months before he was assassinated by Shallum who succeeded him.

2. Maternal grandfather of King Hezekiah.

3. Head of a family of Reubenites.

4. A Levite gatekeeper; son of Meshelemiah.

5. Brother of Ner and great-uncle of Saul from the family of Benjamin (I Chr 9:37), also called Zecher (I Chr 8:31).

6. A Levite harpist who attended the bringing of the ark to Jerusalem.

7. One of the priests who blew the trumpet before the ark when David brought it to Jerusalem.

8. A Levite of the family of Kohath.

9. A Levite gatekeeper of the family of Merari.

10. Father of Iddo from the tribe of Manasseh.

11. One of the five princes of Judah who were sent by King Jehoshaphat to teach the Law in Judah.

Tombs in the Kidron Valley. The one on the left is the Hezir family tomb and that in the center, the tomb traditionally ascribed to Zechariah, although it is a Second Temple period structure.

12. A Levite, one of the sons of Asaph and father of Jahaziel.

13. Fourth son of King Jehoshaphat who was killed along with other sons of the king by Jehoram, the firstborn, when he became king.

14. Son of Jehoiada the priest (II Chr 24:20-21); stoned on command of King Joash for his anti-idolatrous opinions. His martyrdom was cited by Jesus (Matt 23:35; Luke 11:51).

15. A man of God who counseled Uzziah in the early years of his reign.

16. A Levite decended from Asaph. He took part in the cleansing of the Temple during the reign of Hezekiah.

17. A Kohathite Levite, overseer of the workmen employed to repair the Temple in Josiah's reign.

18. One of the three priests who donated sacrifices for the celebration of Passover during Josiah's reign.

19. A prophet, son of Berechiah, and grandson of Iddo (Zech 1:1). His first recorded prophecy was delivered in the second year of Darius I Hystaspis, 520 B.C. A contemporary of Zerubbabel the governor, Joshua the high priest and Haggai the prophet (Ezra 5:1-2; Zech 3:1; 4:6; 6:11).

Along with Haggai, he exhorted the people in Jerusalem to resume work on the rebuilding of the Temple. See ZECHARIAH, BOOK OF.

20. A descendant of Parosh who returned from Babylonia along with Ezra.

21. A son of Bebai who returned from the Babylonian Exile with Ezra.

22. One of those who were sent by Ezra to secure Levites to accompany the returning exiles.

23. A son of Elam, who put away his foreign wife following Ezra's decree.

24. One of the men who stood beside Ezra at the public reading of the Law.

25. A man of Judah of the family of Perez.

26. A man of Judah, son of the Shilonite.

27. A priest descended from Pashhur of the house of Malchijah.

28. A priest, head of the house of Iddo in the days of the high priest Joiakim. May be the same as the prophet Zechariah (No.19).

29. A Levite, son of Jonathan, and a descendant of Asaph. He led a division of Levitical musicians at the dedication of the rebuilt walls of Jerusalem.

30. A priest who blew a trumpet at the dedication of the rebuilt walls of Jerusalem.

31. Son of Jeberechiah. One of the two witnesses to an oracle of Isaiah.

ZECHARIAH, BOOK OF The 11th book of the twelve Minor Prophets. It belongs, together with Haggai and Malachi, to a group of prophecies delivered after the Babylonian Exile. Zechariah contains two distinctly different parts: the first eight chapters, having as their backdrop the return from Babylon, state the name of the prophet and give a clear account of the dates of the prophecies. The remaining six chapters, eschatological in concern, are written in an obscure style with allusions to a background that is unclear. Authorship and date of composition of this part are unknown. Although the entire work is attributed to one prophet, most modern scholars agree that the author of these chapters cannot be the same prophet and that the oracles stem from a later period. This conclusion is based on linguistic and stylistic grounds, as well as on the theological ideas and historical background inherent in the section.

The historical background to the first part of this book is largely the same as that of the prophet Haggai. After the return from the Babylonian Exile, the people of Jerusalem were a poor and dispirited community (8:10). Adding his voice to that of Haggai, Zechariah urged them to continue building the Temple as a necessary prelude to the messianic kingdom. The results of their combined efforts was the completion of the restoration in 516 B.C. (Ezra 6:15). Zechariah's focus of attention is the glories of the messianic kingdom with Zerubbabel (who was then functioning as the Persian governor of Judah) as its ruler (Zech 3:8; 6:12). It may even be inferred that Zechariah proposed to crown Zerubbabel king (6:9-14). However, Zerubbabel mysteriously disappeared from the scene and was probably replaced by Sherezer (7:1-2).

Fragment from the Book of Zechariah found at Qumran. (Shrine of the Book, Jerusalem)

The first six chapters contain eight visions which are recorded as having taken place in a single night sometime during February-March of 519. The connecting theme of these visions is the assurance that the messianic age is about to begin despite appearances to the contrary. In the first vision Zechariah sees an angel riding on a red horse and then standing among the myrtle trees. Behind him are three other horses of varying colors. In response to the prophet's questions, the angel explains that the horses have been sent to report on the state of the world (1:7-11). Their report that the world is tranquil disturbs the angel, and he prays for the rebuilding of Jerusalem to which God replies that he will return to the city (1:12-17). The reference is to the widespread revolts which broke out in the Persian Empire and were quelled in 512.

In the second vision (1:18-21), the prophet sees four horns, representing the four nations that participated in the destruction of Jerusalem. Zechariah is then shown four craftsmen who are going to cut off these horns and thus restore the city.

In the third vision (2:1-5) the prophet sees the man sent to measure Jerusalem being sent away by the angel. He is told that Jerusalem will not need man-made walls because God himself will form the wall about the people and be their protection.

The fourth vision (chap. 3) is that of a heavenly court in session. On trial is the high priest Joshua whose filthy clothing, the symbol of his human impurity, is replaced with festive garments and a miter. As the representative of the people, Joshua is declared cleansed and forgiven, the angel promising him access to God on terms of equality with the angels if he will only walk in the ways of God and keep his charge.

The fifth vision (4:1-6, 10-14) is full of difficult symbols which are only partially resolved in the second part of the vision. The "two anointed ones" who stand by the Lord (4:14) are most probably Zerubbabel and Joshua who are the civil and religious leaders of the community.

The sixth and seventh visions (chap. 5) are interrelated, both concerning the moral standards of the new community. In the first (5:1-4) the prophet sees a large scroll flying through the air, symbolizing the curse which will fall upon the thief and upon him who swears falsely. The seventh vision (5:5-11) consists of a seated woman who is being carried off to the land of Shinar by two winged women, symbolizing the expulsion of wickedness to a distant place.

The "candlestick all of gold" of Zechariah's vision. From the Cervera Bible, *Spain c. 1300. (Biblioteca Nacional de Lisboa)*

The final vision (6:1-8) is of four chariots, harnessed to horses of various colors appearing between "mountains of bronze." The import of this vision is the world at peace again, but this time under the control of God.

The remainder of the chapter, together with chapters 7 and 8, consist of a series of oracles whose central theme is the messianic age. The important lesson is that ethical conduct, not fasting, is the major requirement leading to redemption (7:9; 8:16). Chapter 8 ends with the claim that, at the end of days, "many peoples and strong nations" (8:22) will recognize the Lord through the example of the Jews. Together they will share the blessing of the golden age.

The first part of Chapter 9 (vs. 1-8) concerns the divine punishment of Israel's neighbors, who will either be destroyed or annexed to Israel. The second part (vs. 9-17) concerns the redemption of Israel through the savior king, who, appearing "lowly and riding on a donkey", will end war in Ephraim and Jerusalem with God taking the part of Israel and restoring the people from captivity.

Chapter 11 is one of the most enigmatic in the OT with everything about it, from the interpretation to the historical allusions, in doubt. Chapters 12 to 14 can be understood as two apocalyptic oracles (chaps. 12-13; chap. 14) dealing with the assault on Jerusalem and its deliverance by God who transforms the city into the spiritual center of the world. According to chapter 13, a general purification will take place throughout the land with idols and false prophecy being destroyed and the nation itself undergoing purification which only one third survive.

The final oracle, chapter 14, also consists of a description of the end event. Jerusalem is assaulted by the heathens and her people are in terrible straits. Half are carried off to exile, but the other half escape through a miraculous gorge which opens in the Mount of Olives. At the last moment, when all seems lost, God intervenes to reign over the whole world from Mount Zion. The enemies of Israel learn by their fate to acknowledge God. Year by year they come to Jerusalem on pilgrimage to attend his enthronement at the Feast of Tabernacles.

Both sections of the book contributed greatly to the later literary genre of apocalypticism.

OUTLINE

ZECHER Abbreviated form of Zechariah.

ZEDAD A place on the northern border of the land of Canaan. Many scholars identify it with present-day Sadad, northeast of the Anti-Lebanon chain, some 60 miles (100km) from Damascus; according to others it is Khirbet Tsrada, 1 mile (1.6km) north of Metullah, close to the present Lebanon-Israel border.

ZEDEKIAH ("Yah is [my] righteousness").

1. The son of Chenaanah (I Kgs 22:11, 24; II Chr 18:10, 23) and one of Ahab's 400 court prophets. At the request of King Jehoshaphat of Judah, Ahab summoned these prophets to consult them concerning the chances of success in the proposed military expedition against the Arameans at Ramoth Gilead. Zedekiah joined with other false prophets in predicting Ahab's victory. In order to impress his audience, he placed horns of iron on his head, a symbol of great power (cf Deut 33:17), signifying that Ahab would defeat the Arameans, and thus encouraging the king to attempt the ill-fated campaign. When Micaiah son of Imlah made a contrary prediction, Zedekiah insulted him by casting doubt on the source of his inspiration.

2. The son of Hananiah, one of the princes of Judah during the reign of King Jehoiakim, before whom Baruch the scribe read the scroll of Jeremiah's oracles.

3. The youngest son of King Josiah and Hamutal (II Kgs 24:18), brother of Jehoahaz, uncle and successor of Jehoiachin as king of Judah; (according to I Chronicles 3:15 he was the third son of Josiah). His original name was Mattaniah (II Kgs 24:17) and he reigned between 596-586 B.C. With Zedekiah's exile to Babylonia, the fate of Judah was sealed. The direct account of his reign is contained in II Kings 24:17-25:7; II Chronicles 36:10-21; and Jeremiah 39:1-7; 52:1-11; while supplementary records such as the Babylonian Chronicle, an important source for the history of the period between 605 and 594 B.C., makes available more contemporary material for Zedekiah's reign than exists for any other Hebrew monarch.

Following the revolt of King Jehoiakim, who was encouraged by Egypt, the Babylonian king, Nebuchadnezzar, moved on Jerusalem, which capitulated in 597 B.C. He then exiled King Jehoiachin and installed Zedekiah in his place (II Kgs 24:10-17). The idea of a king appointed by a foreign ruler was not accepted by the people who continued to regard Jehoiachin as their legitimate king (Jer 37:1; Ezek 1:2; 17:16). Indeed, Ezekiel, regarding Jehoiachin as *de jure* king, dates his prophecies not by the years of Zedekiah's reign, but by those of King Jehoiachin's captivity (Ezek 1:2; 8:1; 20:1; 24:1). Although bound by oath to serve the king of Babylon (II Chr 36:13; Ezek 17:14-18), Zedekiah was unable to withstand the nationalist currents which urged rebellion against Babylonia (Jer chaps. 37-38). It was not long before the entire nation became entangled in international intrigue as a result of Zedekiah's inexperience and weak character. He was forced to summon an anti-Babylonian conference of ambassadors from Edom, Moab, Ammon, Tyre and Sidon (Jer 27:3), which signaled a rebellion against the power which had enthroned him. The rebellion was condemned by Jeremiah who was regarded as a traitor by public opinion (Jer 37:11-16). Nevertheless, the king more than once turned to him for advice although he disregarded the prophet's warnings. Ultimately, the anti-Babylonian plot came to naught, and Zedekiah aimed to allay the suspicions of the Babylonian king by sending Elasah and Gemariah (Jer 29:3) to Babylon. Apparently, Zedekiah's personal attendance was required and he journeyed to Babylon (Jer 51:59) to clear himself of complicity in the treasonable plot and to assure

Entrance to the so-called Zedekiah's Cave in Jerusalem where the king is said to have hidden during his attempted escape from Jerusalem.

Nebuchadnezzar of his loyalty. However, when the Phoenician coastal cities yielded to the force of Egyptian arms, Zedekiah allied himself with Egypt. Nebuchadnezzar, determined to make an end of the Egyptian aggressions, dispatched his army to crush the rebellion. All the members of the coalition, except Tyre and Judah, recanted and joined the Babylonians. With Tyre besieged, Judah was left to face the Babylonian might alone and in a desperate attempt to alleviate Judah's plight, Zedekiah, in the spirit of the laws of the Book of Deuteronomy (chap. 15), entered into a covenant with the whole nation to let all Hebrew slaves go free (Jer 34:9). At this point, the Babylonians temporarily lifted Jerusalem's siege in order to drive back an approaching Egyptian relief force. No sooner had their army withdrawn than the people of Jerusaelm reduced their freed slaves to bondage again (Jer 34:11). The relief force failed and the siege was renewed.

Nebuchadnezzar depended mainly on starving the city into surrender but it withstood one and a half years of siege, until its walls were breached and Jerusalem destroyed. In the confusion, Zedekiah and his entourage stole away but were captured near Jericho (Jer 39:4-5; 52:7-8). Zedekiah was dragged to Riblah, where Nebuchadnezzar had stationed his headquarters. There he was tried for treason, his sons were killed before his eyes and he himself was blinded before being carried captive to Babylon and imprisoned until his death (Jer 52:9-11).

4. The son of Maaseiah, and a contemporary of Jeremiah the prophet. He and another false prohet, Ahab, were denounced by Jeremiah (Jer 29:21-23) for their adulterous and immoral lives, and for falsely prophesying an early return from captivity to the exiles in Babylon. Jeremiah predicted their cruel death at the hands of Nebuchadnezzar, king of Babylonia, who roasted them in a fire. **ZEDEKIAH 4** **Jer 29:21-22**

5. One of the officials who signed the covenant at the time of Nehemiah. **ZEDEKIAH 5** **Neh 10:1**

ZEEB ("wolf"). One of the two Midianite princes killed by the men of Ephraim in the course of Gideon's campaign against the Midianites. He met his death at "the winepress of Zeeb" and his head was brought to Gideon "on the other side of the Jordan". Nothing further is known about the winepress or its location. **ZEEB** **Judg 7:25; 8:3. Ps 83:11**

ZELAH ("rib?"). One of the cities which fell to the lot of Benjamin (Josh 18:28) when the land of Canaan was divided among the tribes. Saul and his son Jonathan were buried there, in the tomb of Kish, the father of the king. Nothing is known about the place though it must have been in the vicinity of Jerusalem. **ZELAH** **Josh 18:28. II Sam 21:14**

ZELEK An Ammonite, one of David's thirty "mighty men", he was an armorbearer to Joab. **ZELEK** **II Sam 23:37. I Chr 11:39**

ZELOPHEHAD Son of Hepher and grandson of Machir the son of Manasseh. Zelophehad owes his fame to having had five daughters but no sons. When he died in the wilderness, his daughters went to Moses and claimed their inheritance. It was then formulated for the first time that "if a man dies and has no son, then you shall cause his inheritance to pass to his daughter" (Num 27:8), provided that the daughter does not marry out of the tribe (Num 36:1-9). **ZELOPHEHAD** **Num 26:33; 27:1, 7; 36:2, 6, 10-11. Josh 17:3. I Chr 7:15**

ZELZAH The place where Rachel was buried according to Samuel's words to the young Saul (I Sam 10:2). This ties in with the tradition whereby Rachel was buried in Ramah (Jer 31:15) and not near Bethlehem (Gen 35:19). The site is not identified. **ZELZAH** **I Sam 10:2**

ZEMARAIM A town in the territory of Benjamin (Josh 18:22), which gave its name to Mount Zemaraim in the mountains of Ephraim. From there Abijah, king of Judah, spoke to the people before the war with **ZEMARAIM** **Josh 18:22. II Chr 13:4**

Jeroboam (II Chr 13:4). The Septuagint and Josephus refer to the mountain as Oros Somoron, possibly Mount Samaria (Shomron).

ZEMARITES A clan descended from Canaan.

ZEMIRAH The son of Becher, head of a family of the tribe of Benjamin.

ZENAN A city in the territory of Judah (Josh 15:37). It was in the district of Lachish, in the vicinity of Hadashah and Migdal Gad. Micah mentions it in his "Mourning for Israel and Judah" where it is spelled Zaanan. The exact location is unknown.

ZENAS A lawyer and a Christian, who traveled with Apollos in Crete. Paul asked Titus to assist them "that they may lack nothing".

ZEPHANIAH ("The Lord has hidden away").

1. Zephaniah son of Cushi, the son of Gedaliah, the son of Amariah, the son of Hezekiah (Zeph 1:1), the prophetic author of the Book of Zephaniah (q.v.). It is generally accepted that this Zephaniah's ancestor Hezekiah was none other than King Hezekiah of Judah. Hence Zephaniah was a third cousin once removed of King Josiah during whose reign he prophesied.

2. Zephaniah the son of Maaseiah the priest. According to Jeremiah 21:2 King Zedekiah sent him, along with Pashhur son of Malchiah to ask Jeremiah the prophet to pray to the Lord that Nebuchadnezzar's siege of Jerusalem be lifted. The parallel account in Jeremiah 37:3 names his fellow messenger not as Pashhur but as Jehucal son of Shelemiah. According to Jeremiah 29:25-29 it was to the same Zephaniah the priest that the false prophet Shemaiah sent a letter from Babylon complaining that Jeremiah had not been imprisoned for telling the exiles to build houses and plant gardens and patiently await deliverance from Exile (Jer 29:1-14). When Zephaniah read the letter to Jeremiah (Jer 29:29), Jeremiah immediately experienced a divine revelation (Jer 29:30), on the basis of which he announced that Shemaiah's false prophecy would be punished by the latter's not living to see the deliverance of Judah from Exile and by his being denied any descendants. According to II Kings 25:18 and Jeremiah 52:24, Zephaniah, who was deputy high priest, was among the leaders of Judah, whom Nebuzaradan brought to Riblah where Nebuchadnezzar put them to death.

3. Father of Josiah, one of those who returned from the Babylonian Exile (Zech 6:10).

4. Son of Tahath, great-great-grandson of Korah and ancestor of Heman the singer.

ZEPHANIAH, BOOK OF The Book of Zephaniah is the ninth book of the Minor Prophets. It contains three oracles delivered by a Judean prophet (See ZEPHANIAH No.1) during the early years of the reign of King Josiah (640-609 B.C.) before the reform carried out in 622 B.C. The first oracle (1:2-18), castigates the people of Judah for idol worship, for adopting the characteristically Philistine practice of skipping over the threshold (1:9; cf I Sam 5:5), and for their non-Israelite patterns of dress (1:8). Their punishment is to be a cataclysm, which Zephaniah, following Amos (Amos 5:18-20) and Isaiah (Is 2:9ff), calls "the Day of the Lord". His descriptions of this judgment day being the most detailed in all of the Bible, Zephaniah is often called "the prophet of the Day of the Lord" (his description inspired the medieval Latin hymn *Dies Irae*). The second oracle (2:1-15) is a call to repentance apparently addressed to Judah. The prophet says that the cataclysm described in great detail in 1:12-18 can be averted if the people of Judah devote themselves to justice (2:2-3). Moreover, in 2:4-15 the prophet asserts that if Judah indeed repented, all its oppressors, including Assyria, would be wiped off the map. In Zephaniah's final oracle (3:1-

Fragments from the Book of Zephaniah found at Qumran. (Shrine of the Book, Jerusalem)

20) the prophet denounces Judah's political and religious leaders. The Lord promises to bring against them an army of people from all over the world (cf Is 5:26), composed of devotees of the Lord. The surviving remnant of Judah (cf Is 11:11) will include ingathered exiles, and it will be characterized by justice and humility; it will be the pride of all humanity.

In both ideas and diction, Zephaniah was heavily influenced by the prophet Isaiah, whose last prophecies preceded him by 80 years. Examples of Isaian influence on Zephaniah include the following: Isaiah 11:14 on Zephaniah 2:4-11; Isaiah 13:19-20 on Zephaniah 2:9; Isaiah 16:6 on Zephaniah 2:8, 10; Isaiah 5:14-17 on Zephaniah 3:1-13. Zephaniah 3:1-8 in turn influenced Ezekiel 22:23-31. Unlike his younger contemporaries, Jeremiah and Ezekiel, Zephaniah was influenced neither by the diction nor by the characteristic ideas of Deuteronomy.

Zephaniah 1:10-11 is a primary source for knowledge of the geography of Jerusalem in the 7th century B.C.

The assertion in Zephaniah 1:12 that the Lord will search Jerusalem with candles is reflected both in the Jewish rite of searching for leaven by candlelight on the night before Passover eve and in the depiction of Zephaniah holding a lamp in medieval Christian iconography.

OUTLINE

1:1	Denunciation of idolatry in Judah and pronunciation of judgment
2:1-3:7	Nations called to repentance
3:8-13	After judgment of the wicked, the remnant will be redeemed
3:14-20	Deliverance of Israel

ZEPHATH ("observation point"). A Canaanite city in the Negeb destroyed by Judah and Simeon and thereafter called Hormah ("destruction"). It was probably in the vicinity of present-day Arad.

ZEPHATHAH A valley near Mareshah where King Asa of Judah defeated Zera the Ethiopian.

ZEPHI Alternately Zepho (Gen 36:11, 15). The third son of Eliphaz, the Edomite, one of the chiefs descended from Esau (I Chr 1:36).

ZEPHO See ZEPHI

ZEPHON, ZEPHONITES The first son of Gad (Gen 46:16); head of the Zephonite family (Num 26:15).

ZER One of the fortified cities of Naphtali; listed between Ziddim and Hammath. Its exact location is unknown.

ZERAH ("shining").

1. Second son of Reuel, the son of Esau by his wife Basemath, the daughter of Ishmael (Gen 36:3, 13) and a chief in Edom (Gen 36:17).

2. Zerah of Bozrah, an Edomite whose son Jobab was the second king of Edom.

3. One of the twin sons (along with Perez) born to Tamar and her father-in-law Judah (Gen 38:18, 30). He was the ancestor of a family of the tribe of Judah, called Zarhites (Num 26:20) also called the children of Zerah who dwelled in Jerusalem after the return from the Babylonian Exile (I Chr 9:6; Neh 11:24).

4. The fifth son of Simeon, an alternative name for Zohar (Gen 46:10; Ex 6:15), and the ancestor of a Simeonite family called Zarhites.

5. A Levite, son of Iddo and father of Jeatherai of the family of Gershom.

6. A Kohathite Levi, son of Adaiah and father of Ethni, it has been suggested that he is the same as No.5.

7. An Ethiopian who, "with an army of a million men and three hundred chariots" fought King Asa of Judah and was defeated at the valley of Zephathah at Mareshah (II Chr 14:8-13).

ZERAHIAH ("Yah has shone").

1. The son of Uzzi, a descendant of Eleazar, the son of Aaron the high priest.

2. The father of Elihoenai, one of those who returned from Babylon with Ezra.

ZERED (ZARED) Valley and brook crossed by the Children of Israel led by Moses after 38 years of wandering in the wilderness. The brook and the valley marked the boundary between Edom and Moab. The brook is generally identified with Wadi Hasa, a perennial river which flows into the Dead Sea from the southeast. The deep valley of the wadi is a natural border between the flat plains of Moab and the mountain ranges of Edom.

ZEREDA See ZERERAH

ZEREDAH See ZERERAH

ZERERAH Zererah (Judg 7:22), Zereda (I Kgs 11:26), Zeredah (II Chr 4:17) and Zaretan (Josh 3:16; I Kgs 4:12; 7:46) may denote an identical locality or two different ones. The difficulty in making the distinction stems from the confusion of the names as far back as early biblical tradition and in the early translations of the Bible, where the verses in which they occur are open to different, sometimes contradictory, interpretations; occasionally the order of the letters in the names change. Moreover, there is no positive identification for any of these places.

I Kings 11:26 reads: "Jeroboam the son of Nebat, an Ephraimite from Zereda". Two manuscripts of the Septuagint give Zarida and Zereira for the same place. Eusebius (*Onom* 16:21) reads Zerora, and Jerome (*Onom* 161:21) has Sarara. According to II Chronicles 4:17 Solomon cast the Temple vessels in the clay ground between Succoth and Zeredah, but the latter is given as Zaretan in the parallel source in I Kings 7:46. In the Septuagint the two versions have Zairam and Zeira respectively, both apparently a corruption of Zererah. In Judges 7:22 the name Zererah (also read Zererath) is mentioned in conjunction with a topographical description similar to that of I Kings 4:12, where the name is rendered Zaretan. Because of the different forms of these three names, some commentators have suggested that they denote one and the same place, which should be located to the west of the Jordan. The basis for this hypothesis is that Jeroboam was of the tribe of Ephraim, and that the fifth district in Solomon's kingdom was west of the Jordan. It has been proposed that this place be identified with Qarn Sartaba (ancient Sartaba, Alexandrion), more than 4 miles (7 km) west-southwest of the Jordan crossing near Adam (Josh 3:16 "the city of Adam, that is beside Zaretan"). However, archeological surveys there found no remains earlier than the Hellenistic and Roman periods. Countless other identifications have been proposed.

ZERESH The wife of Haman. She was among those who advised him to have a gallows erected for Mordecai (Est 5:10-14); later, she prophesied that Haman would fail because Mordecai was "of Jewish descent" (Est 6:13).

ZERETH A man of the tribe of Judah; the son of Helah and Ashur, the father of Tekoa (I Chr 4:70).

ZERETH SHAHAR A city or place in the territory given to the tribe of Reuben by Moses (Josh 13:15, 19). It was "on the mountain of the valley". Although generally accepted that it lay on the east bank of the Jordan River, its exact location is unkown.

ZERI ("balsam"). The son of Jeduthun who headed a group of singers in the Temple (I Chr 25:3).

ZEROR The grandfather of Kish, father of Saul (I Sam 9:1).

ZERUAH The wife of Nebat and the mother of Jeroboam who rebelled against Solomon. She was a widow at the time of the rebellion.

ZERUBBABEL ("scion of Babylon"). Grandson of King Jeconiah of Judah, exiled to Babylonia in 597 B.C., and governor of the province of Judah during the reign of Darius I (Hag 1:1; Ezra 6:15). According to I Chronicles 3:19 Zerubbabel's father was Pedaiah, but other references call him the son of Shealtiel (both were sons of Jeconiah).

Being of royal descent, Zerubbabel was a natural choice for governor of the province. In September 520 B.C., prompted by the prophecies of Haggai (Hag 1:2-11, 13-15; 2:2-9) he joined Joshua the high priest in initiating the resumption of the building of the Temple, badly neglected since its foundations had been laid in 537 B.C. (Ezra 3:8-13). Tattenai, the satrap of Syria (Ezra 5:3) tried to halt the work (Ezra 5:3-10) but the Judeans, citing the permission granted by Cyrus (Ezra 5:11-16), appealed to Darius to intervene (Ezra 5:17). The king upheld their request and the builders continued, inspired by the prophets Haggai and Zechariah, until the Temple was finally completed in 515 B.C. (Ezra 6:15).

From the prophecies of Haggai it appears that Zerubbabel was the focus of messianic hopes. Haggai expected the Lord to overthrow all kingdoms and to elect Zerubbabel as his "servant". He is called "God's chosen" and his "signet ring" (Hag 2:21-23). Zechariah's reference to "the Branch" (Zech 3:8) is likewise interpreted as referring to Zerubbabel.

It is not known when Zerubbabel's activity commenced nor when it came to an end. Some texts state that Zerubbabel was the leader of the first group which returned from the Exile (Ezra 2:2; Neh 7:7) and that he was involved in building the altar and laying the Temple foundations in the years 538-537 B.C. (Ezra 3:2, 8; 4:2). The first governor of Judah and the leader of the first group, however, was Sheshbazzar (Ezra 1:8-11; 5:14, 16). In order to account for the discrepancy, it has been suggested that Sheshbazzar was leader in name only, and that Zerubbabel bore responsibility for all practical activity. On the other hand, it has been pointed out that Zechariah credits Zerubbabel with laying the foundations for the Temple, while ignoring the role played by Sheshbazzar (Zech 4:9). Thus there may have been a tendency to credit Zerubbabel with all early constructive activity from the first period of the return from the Exile. (See SHESHBAZZAR).

Matthew 1:12 and Luke 3:27 mention Zerubbabel in the ancestral line of Jesus, since he was descended from the Davidic house.

ZERUIAH The mother of Joab, Abishai and Asahel (II Sam 2:18). According to the account in I Chronicles 2:16, she was the daughter of Jesse and the sister of David. In II Samuel 17:25, Zeruiah, like Abigail her sister, was the daughter of Nahash.

ZETHAM A Levite, a grandson of Gershom (I Chr 23:8). One of the men in charge of the stores of the House of God (I Chr 26:22).

ZETHAN ("olive-dealer"). The son of Bilhan. The head of a family of the tribe of Benjamin (I Chr 7:10).

ZETHAR The sixth of seven eunuchs commanded by King Ahasuerus to bring Queen Vashti before him (Est 1:10).

ZERETH SHA...
Josh 13:19

ZERI
I Chr 25:3

ZEROR
I Sam 9:1

ZERUAH
I Kgs 11:26

ZERUBBABEL
I Chr 3:19. Ezra 2:2; 3: 8; 4:2-3; 5:2 Neh 7:7; 12: 47. Hag 1:1 12, 14; 2:2, 21, 23. Zech 4:6-7, 9-10. Matt 1:12-1. Luke 3:27

ZERUIAH
I Sam 26:6. II Sam 2:13, 18; 3:39; 8:16; 14:1; 16:9-10; 17:25; 18:2; 19:21-22; 21:17; 23:18, 37. I Kgs 1:7; 2:5, 22. I Chr 2:16; 11:6, 39; 18:12, 15; 26:28; 27:24

ZETHAM
I Chr 23:8; 26:22

ZETHAN
I Chr 7:10

ZETHAR
Est 1:10

ZEUS An Indo-Germanic god, who was adopted by the Greeks and became the chief deity of their pantheon. As ruler over heaven and earth, Zeus was called father of both gods and men.

A temple dedicated to Zeus stood in Lystra in Galatia (Acts 14:13). The inhabitants of the town were so impressed by the two apostles Paul and Barnabas, that they "called Barnabas Zeus [or in Latin, Jupiter] and Paul they called Hermes [or in Latin, Mercury]" (Acts 14:12).

ZIA The head of a family of the tribe of Gad.

ZIBA One of the servants of Saul. He informed King David that the only survivor of Saul's family was Mephibosheth, the crippled son of Jonathan. David granted Mephibosheth the entire legacy of the house of Saul, including Ziba, his 15 sons and his 20 servants (II Sam 9:9-12).

During Absalom's revolt, Ziba took advantage of Mephibosheth's condition and falsely accused him of remaining in Jerusalem in order to regain the kingdom of his ancestors. David believed Ziba and transferred to him all of Mephibosheth's property. After the revolt, Mephibosheth told the king that he had made preparations to join the royal cause, but was foiled when Ziba abandoned him. David accepted Mephibosheth's version, but remaining grateful to Ziba for his actions during the revolt, he decided to divide the property between the two of them (II Sam 19:24-29).

ZIBEON ("hyena"). One of the Horite chiefs. The third son of Seir (Gen 36:20, 29). The father of Aiah and Anah and grandfather of Oholibamah, one of Esau's wives (Gen 36:2, 14).

ZIBIA ("gazelle"). Head of a family of the tribe of Benjamin, born to Shaharaim and Hodesh in the country of Moab.

ZIBIAH ("gazelle"). Mother of King Jehoash of Judah.

ZICHRI ("remembrance").

1. A Levite, the son of Izhar and grandson of Kohath.
2. The son of Shimei the head of a family of the tribe of Benjamin; inhabitant of Aijalon.
3. The son of Shashak of the tribe of Benjamin; an inhabitant of Aijalon.
4. The son of Jeroham of the tribe of Benjamin; an inhabitant of Aijalon.
5. A Levite, the son of Asaph. He is probably the same individual as Zaccur No.4 and Zabdi No.4.
6. A Levite, descendant of Eliezer son of Moses, father of Shelomith.
7. The father of Eliezer who served as chief officer of the tribe of Reuben at the time of David.
8. The father of Amasiah of the tribe of Judah. A commander of thousands at the time of Jehoshaphat.
9. The father of Elishaphat. A commander of hundreds who joined Jehoiada the priest in the plot against Athaliah.
10. A mighty man of Ephraim, probably an officer in the army of Pekah; he killed three notables in the court of Ahaz during the war waged by Syria and Israel against Judah.
11. The father of Joel, overseer of the clans of Benjamin who settled in Jerusalem at the time of Nehemiah.
12. The head of the post-exilic priestly family of Abijah.

ZIDDIM A fortified city in the territory allotted to Naphtali. Nothing is known about it and some scholars believe the reference to be a scribe's error and that there was no such city.

ZIHA

1. A family of Nethinim (Temple servants) who returned from the Babylonian Exile (Ezra 2:43; Neh 7:46)
2. An overseer of the Nethinim.

Air view of Tell Halif, tentatively identified with Ziklag. (Lahav Research Project)

ZIKLAG A town on the southern boundary of Judea, in the lot of Judah (Josh 15:31). It was given to Simeon (Josh 19:5), although it seems that it was not conquered by the Israelites, since in the days of Saul it was in the hands of the Philistines. When David escaped from the wrath of Saul to the land of the Philistines they gave him Ziklag at his request (I Sam 27:1-6). It was burnt down by the Amalekites, but David recovered the town and took his revenge (I Sam 30:1-31). It was there that he learned of the death of Saul (II Sam 1:1). The town was resettled after the return from the Babylonian Exile.

The identification of Ziklag is not certain.

ZILLAH ("shadow, protection"). One of the two wives of Lamech. The mother of Tubal-Cain and of Naamah (Gen 4:19-23).

ZILLETHAI

1. The son of Shimei, the head of a family of the tribe of Benjamin at the time of David (I Chr 8:20).

2. A Manassite who joined David at Ziklag.

ZILPAH The maid of Leah, Jacob's wife (Gen 29:24; 46:18). Leah gave her to Jacob to whom she bore Gad and Asher.

ZIMMAH

1. A Levite, the son of Jahath and grandson of Gershom (I Chr 6:20). According to I Chronicles 6:42, he was the son of Shimei.

2. The father of Joah, one of the Levites who, at King Hezekiah's command, cleansed the House of God (II Chr 29:12-15).

ZIMRAN A son of Abraham and Keturah and the name of a place somewhere in Arabia (Gen 25:2; I Chr 1:32). In Jeremiah 25:25 it is called Zimri.

ZIMRI

1. The eldest of the five sons of Zerah and grandson of Judah and Tamar (I Chr 2:5-6). He is probably identical with Zabdi (Josh 7:1; 17-18).

2. Son of Salu, prince of a chief house of the Simeonites. According to Numbers chapter 25, while the Israelites were in the wilderness of Shittim, they had intercourse with Moabite women and worshiped Baal-Peor. Incensed, the Lord brought a plague on Israel. He then ordered Moses to hold a public execution of all those who sinned against the Lord, resulting in a slaughter of 24,000 Israelites. This sinful episode

was further exacerbated by Zimri, who brought in a Midianite woman named Cozbi, daughter of Zur, in the sight of Moses and all the Israelite congregation, who were then weeping at the entrance of the tabernacle, probably calling for God's forgiveness. Thereupon, Phinehas, the grandson of Aaron the priest, seized a lance, followed Zimri into his tent and, in a moment of zeal for the Lord's honor, pierced him along with Cozbi. As a result, the Lord's wrath was turned away from Israel, and both the plague and the slaughter were checked.

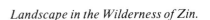

MRI 3
Kgs 16:9-10,
2, 15-16, 18,
0. II Kgs
:31. I Chr
:36; 9:42

3. King of Israel in 882 B.C. Having previously been the commander of half of King Elah's chariotry, Zimri conspired against his master while he was feasting, assassinated him, and seized the throne. He then exterminated the entire house of Baasha, Elah's father, not sparing a single male (I Kgs 16:8-12). However, when Elah's army, which was then besieging Gibbethon of the Philistines, heard of Zimri's coup and the assassination of the king, they proclaimed Omri, their commander-in-chief, king of Israel. Omri at once marched up from Gibbethon and captured the city of Tirzah, the royal residence of those days. In view of the hopeless situation, Zimri retreated to the royal palace and committed suicide by setting it on fire while he was within (I Kgs 16:16-18). Zimri reigned for only seven days. A generation later, Jezebel sarcastically addressed Jehu, the usurper of her son's throne, as "Zimri, murderer of your master" (II Kgs 9:31). Thus Zimri became a symbol of the slave who turns against his master.

Wadi Zimri, between Alemeth and Beth Azmaveth, called after Zimri No.4.

ZIMRI 4
I Chr 8:36;
9:42

ZIMRI 5
Jer 25:25

ZIN
Num 13:21;
20:1; 27:14;
33:36; 34:3-4.
Deut 32:51.
Josh 15:1, 3

4. Son of Jehoaddah (I Chr 8:36) or Jareh (I Chr 9:42) from the tribe of Benjamin.

5. See ZIMRAN.

ZIN Wilderness south of Canaan. The Israelites passed through it on their way from Egypt to Canaan. It lies between Kadesh Barnea and Akrabbim, and is referred to as the wilderness from which the spies went up to Canaan (Num 13:21). It was in this region that the incidents at Massah and Meribah took place (Ex 17:7; Num chap. 20). It was the southern limit of the territory of Judah (Josh 15:1-3). Identified as the wilderness lying south of Kadesh Barnea.

Landscape in the Wilderness of Zin.

ZINA An alternate form of Zizah.

ZION In the Bible, Zion is the eastern hill of Jerusalem which included the Temple Mount and the hill south of it, in the site of the ancient city of Jerusalem. The fortress on the hill south of the Temple Mount is named the stronghold of Zion (II Sam 5:7). The etymology of this name remains unexplained and may be of great antiquity. After David's conquest of the city, the stronghold of Zion was called the City of David (II Sam 5:7, 9; I Chr 11:7). Solomon brought up the ark of the covenant of the Lord "from the City of David, which is Zion" (I Kgs 8:1-2; II Chr 5:2). It then became the city of God, the city of the great king (Ps 46:4; 48:2); it is a holy hill (Ps 2:6; Joel 2:1; Zech 8:3); God dwells there (Ps 9:11; 132:13) and there is his sanctuary (Ps 20:2), which is a goal of pilgrimage (Ps 84:5, 7), a place of deliverance and salvation (Ps 20:1-2; 69:35), and of praise and worship (Ps 9:14; 65:1). When the ark was transferred to Mount Moriah, it came to be called Mount Zion (Ps 78:68-69).

The name Zion became synonymous with Jerusalem (Is chap. 40; Mic 3:12). The sons of Zion (Lam 4:2) and the daughters of Zion (Song 3:11; Is 10:32) denoted the inhabitants of Jerusalem (Jer 51:35). Zion is the whole city, which, like other fortified cities of Judah, was a place of safety; people of other cities will be brought to Zion (Jer 3:14; 4:5-6).

After the Exile the Israelite nation came to be called "Zion...who dwelt with the daughter of Babylon" (Zech 2:7). The "daughter of Zion" personifies the entire people (Jer 6:23; Zech 9:9), as do the "sons of Zion" (Zech 9:13). Divine protection makes the city — "the virgin (the) daughter of Zion" — pure (II Kgs 19:21; 37:22; cf Jer 14:17; 18:13; 31:4, 21; Lam 1:15; Amos 5:2). Since God himself founded Zion, the people may anticipate safety within its walls, because it is protected by God himself (Is 14:32; 31:8-9; 33:1-5). But should the people of Israel forsake God, he will smite the daughter of Zion (Is 3:17; 49:14; Jer 6:2ff; 9:19).

A view of Mount Zion.

The mere existence of the Temple on Mount Moriah is not a safeguard and reliance on it alone is equated with "lying words" (Jer 7:4, 8, 12); sin leads to the destruction of Zion (Jer 9:20).

There is little reference to Zion in the NT. It is named "the city of the living God, the heavenly Jerusalem" (Heb 12:22). The term refers to the people of Israel (Rom 9:33; I Pet 2:6), and of Jerusalem (Matt 21:5; John 12:15), and to the mountain upon which Jesus and his followers will stand in triumph on his Second Coming (Rev 14:1).

ZIOR A city in the region of Hebron (Josh 15:54). It is identified with the Arab village of Si'ir, less than 2 miles (3 km) east of Halhul.

ZIPH, ZIPHITES

1. A town in the mountains of Judah (Josh 15:55), whose inhabitants revealed David's hiding-place to Saul (I Sam 23:19ff); one of the cities built by Rehoboam for defense (II Chr 11:8). It was known in the Roman period as a village called Zif on the main road leading from Hebron southwards. Identified with Tell Zif, southeast of Hebron.

2. A place in the Negeb (Josh 15:24). Not identified.

ZIPHAH The son of Jahateleel, the head of a family of the tribe of Judah.

ZIPHION See ZEPHON

ZIPHRON A place on the northern boundary of Canaan.

ZIPPOR ("bird"). The father of Balak, king of Moab who dispatched Balaam to curse Israel (Num 22:2, 4, 10, 16; 23:18).

ZIPPORAH ("bird"). One of the seven daughters of Jethro, priest of Midian (Ex 2:16); she became the wife of Moses and the mother of his sons Gershom and Eliezer (Ex 2:16, 21-22).

When God was about to kill Moses, Zipporah saved him by circumcising her son (Ex 4:24-26). Later she and her sons returned to her father's home (Ex 18:2).

ZITHRI A Levite. The third son of Uzziel, cousin of Moses (Ex 6:22).

ZIV The Canaanite name for the second month of the year (later known as Iyyar) during which King Solomon began to build the House of God, in the fourth year of his reign (I Kgs 6:1, 37).

ZIZ The cliff of Ziz is a steep ascent on the way from En Gedi to Tekoa (II Chr 20:16). Its exact location is unknown.

ZIZA

1. The son of Rehoboam and Maachah (the latter was Absalom's granddaughter).

2. The son of Shiphi a descendant of Shemaiah; the head of a family in the tribe of Simeon. His family journeyed to Gedor to seek pasture for their flocks and settled there.

ZIZAH Alternate form of Zina (I Chr 23:10). Second son of Shimei, the son of Gershon (I Chr 23:11). The head of a Levite family.

ZOAN A city in Lower Egypt, called Saanat in Egyptian, and Saanu in Assyrian records of the time of Ashurbanipal. In the Septuagint and in classical sources it is named Tanis. The ancient name is preserved in San el-Hajjar in the northeastern Delta.

Numbers 13:22 states: "Now Hebron was built seven years before Zoan in Egypt." The accepted view is that this tradition connects the foundation of Hebron with Avaris, the Hyksos capital of Lower Egypt. Zoan, mentioned in Isaiah's prophecies as the seat of the counselors of Pharaoh, was thus a city of importance (Is 19:11, 13; 30:4). This fits well with its position in the period of the 21st-23rd Dynasties. As a place of importance it is also referred to in Ezekiel 30:14. Zoan is not mentioned in connection with the bondage in Egypt, but Psalm 78:12, 43 praises the Lord for the marvelous things he did in the field of Zoan, which again fits the Egyptian name Sakhat Saanat.

The region south of the Dead Sea where Zoar was located.

ZOAR The city to which Lot fled from Sodom and Gomorrah (Gen 19:20-23, 30). Its earliest biblical name was Bela (Gen 14:8). At Lot's request it was saved from the destruction that befell the other cities of the Plain (Gen 19:18-23). Zoar is frequently mentioned in the Bible together with the cities of the Valley of Siddim, and the identification of this valley also determines that of Zoar. Deuteronomy (34:1-3) relates that Moses saw from the top of Mount Nebo the whole of the country from the land of Naphtali in the north to Zoar south of Jericho, the city of palms. According to Isaiah (15:5) the town was situated at the edge of the land of Moab. It is therefore commonly accepted that it should be sought somewhere south of the Dead Sea.

ZOAR
Gen 13:10;
14:2, 8; 19:22-
23, 30. Deut
34:3. Is 15:5.
Jer 48:34

ZOBAH, ZOBA An Aramean kingdom from whose cities David "took a large amount of bronze" (II Sam 8:8). The exact boundaries of this kingdom are not known. It has been suggested that it lay in the valley between the mountain ranges of Lebanon. Others consider that it extended from the region of the Anti-Lebanon eastwards to Tadmor (Palmyra) and the Syrian desert. The kings of Zobah are mentioned among the enemies of Saul (I Sam 14:47). At the time of David, Zobah expanded into the Valley of Lebanon, up to Damascus on the south, and the Aramean kingdom to the east of the Jordan. Hadadezer king of Zobah extended his rule towards the Euphrates (II Sam 10:16). Zobah united all the Aramean kingdoms of Syria and Transjordan into a league (cf II Sam 10:19) which was defeated by the Israelites on three occasions. The first time was by Joab before Medeba (I Chr 19:7), when the army of Aram-Zobah came to assist the Ammonites in their war against Israel (II Sam 10:4-16; I Chr 19:6-15). A year later in a battle in northern Transjordan, "David killed seven hundred charioteers and forty thousand horsemen of the Syrians, and struck Shobach the commander of their army who died there" (II Sam 10:18; I Chr 19:16-19). In the third battle "David took from him a thousand chariots, seven hundred horsemen, and twenty thousand foot soldiers" (II Sam 8:4; I Chr 18:4). After these defeats Zobah is not mentioned again in the Bible, its place being taken by Aram Damascus. In the 8th century B.C. Zobah is mentioned among the Assyrian provinces.

ZOBAH, ZOBA
I Sam 14:47.
II Sam 8:3, 5,
12; 10:6, 8;
23:36. I Kgs
11:23-24.
I Chr 18:3, 5,
9; 19:6

ZOBEBAH The son of Koz of the tribe of Judah.

ZOBEBAH
I Chr 4:8

ZOHAR
1. The father of Ephron the Hittite.
2. The grandson of Jacob by his son Simeon (Gen 46:10; Ex 6:15); he is also called Zerah (Num 26:13; I Chr 4:24).
3. Son of Ashhur of the family of Judah, by his wife Helah.

ZOHELETH, STONE OF The place where Adonijah the son of David sacrificed cattle in the course of his ill-fated bid for the crown. Nothing is known about it beyond the fact that it was "by En Rogel". It is often translated as the Stone of the Serpent.

ZOHETH Son of Ishi of the tribe of Judah.

ZOPHAH Son of Helem of the tribe of Asher.

ZOPHAI See ZUPH No.1

ZOPHAR A Naamathite; he was one of the three friends who came to comfort Job.

ZOPHIM ("watchers"). When the Children of Israel camped in the plains of Moab, Balak the king of Moab brought Balaam the seer "to the field of Zophim, to the top of Pisgah" in his endeavors to get the seer to curse the Israelites. There he built seven altars and offered a bull and a ram on each. The location is unknown.

ZORAH A town in the Shephelah (lowland), on the border of the territory of Dan (Josh 19:41), always mentioned together with Eshtaol in this context (Josh 15:33); the birthplace and burial place of Samson. From Zorah five men went up to look for a new place for the Danites (Judg 13:2; 16:31). In the time of Rehoboam it was one of the fortified cities in Judah (II Chr 11:10), and it was resettled at the time of the return from Babylon (Neh 11:29). The ancient name of the site has been preserved in the Arabic Saraa, near Artuf, where the villagers point out a rock called the Altar of Manoah (cf Judg 13:19) and also Samson's tomb.

ZORATHITES Inhabitants of Zorah, descendants of Shobal, the founding father of Kirjath Jearim (I Chr 2:50).

ZORITES Descendants of Salma of Bethlehem (I Chr 2:54). Possibly identical with the Zorathites.

ZUAR The father of Nethaneel who led the tribe of Issachar in the wilderness.

ZUPH
1. Ancestor of ELKANAH No.2, an Ephraimite.
2. A place between Mount Ephraim and Gibeah, where Saul decided to give up the search for his father's asses (I Sam 9:5). Its exact location is not known, but it should be sought near Ramallah.

ZUR
1. The tribal head of an ancestral house in Midian. He was the father of Cozbi who, together with her Israelite husband Zimri, was slain by Phinehas the son of Aaron the high priest at Baal Peor (Num 25:15). Zur and four other Midianite kings were slain by the Israelites (Num 31:8). According to the account in Joshua 13:21 the five Midianite kings were vassals of Sihon, king of the Amorites.
2. A Benjamite; second son of Jeiel.

ZURIEL ("God is my rock"). The son of Abihail, a Levite who led the clan of Merari (Num 3:35).

ZURISHADDAI ("Shaddai [i.e. the Almighty] is my rock"). The father of Shelumiel who led the tribe of Simeon when the Children of Israel wandered through the wilderness.

ZUZIM People mentioned in connection with the war of the kings of Shinar against the kings of the region of the Dead Sea. According to the Bible Chedorlaomer conquered the Zuzim in Ham. On the other hand (Deut 2:10-11, 20-21) the Zuzim (i.e. Zamzummim) lived in the land of Ammon.

ANIMALS

ANT
Prov 6:6; 30:25

ANTELOPE
Deut 14:5. Is 51:20

APE
I Kgs 10:22. II Chr 9:21

ASP
Ps 140:3. Rom 3:13

BADGER
Ex 25:5; 26:14; 35:7, 23; 36:19; 39:34. Num 4:6, 8, 10-12, 14, 25. Ps 104:18. Prov 30:26. Ezek 16:10

BAT
Lev 11:19. Deut 14:18. Is 2:20

BEAR
I Sam 17:34, 36-37. II Sam 17:8. II Kgs 2:24. Prov 17:12. Is 11:7; 59:11. Lam 3:10. Dan 7:5. Hos 13:8. Amos 5:19. Rev 13:2

BEE
Deut 1:44. Judg 14:8. Ps 118:12. Is 7:18

BITTERN
Zeph 2:14

BOAR
Ps 80:13

BULL
Gen 32:15. Ex 29:1, 3, 10-12, 14, 36. Lev 1:5; 4:3-5, 7-8, 10-12, 14-16, 20-21; 8:2, 14, 17; 9:2, 4, 18-19; 16:3, 6, 11, 14-15, 18, 27; 22:23, 27; 23:18. Num 7:15, 21, 27, 33, 39, 45, 51, 57, 63, 69, 75, 81, 87-88; 8:8, 12; 15:8-9, 11,

24; 23:1-2, 4, 14, 29-30; 28:11-12, 14, 19-20, 27-28; 29:2-3, 8-9, 13-14, 17-18, 20-21, 23-24, 26-27, 29-30, 32-33, 36-37. Deut 17:1; 18:3; 33:17. Judg 6:25-26, 28. I Sam 1:24-25. I Kgs 8:63; 18:23, 25-26, 33. I Chr 15:26; 29:21. II Chr 7:5; 13:9; 15:11; 29:21-22, 32-33; 30:24. Ezra 6:9, 17; 7:17; 8:35. Job 21:10; 42:8. Ps 22:12; 50:9, 13; 51:19; 66:15; 68:30; 69:31. Is 1:11; 34:7; 66:3. Jer 31:18; 46:21; 50:11, 27; 52:20. Ezek 39:18; 43:19, 21-23, 25; 45:18, 22-24; 46:6-7, 11. Hos 12:11. Heb 9:13; 10:4

BUZZARD
Lev 11:13. Deut 14:12

CALF
Gen 18:7-8. Ex 32:4, 8, 19-20, 24, 35. Lev 9:3, 8. Deut 9:16, 21. I Sam 6:7, 10; 14:32; 28:24. I Kgs 12:28, 32. II Kgs 10:29; 17:16. II Chr 11:15; 13:8. Neh 9:18. Job 21:10. Ps 29:6; 68:30; 106:19. Prov 15:17. Is 11:6; 27:10. Jer 34:18-19. Ezek 1:7. Hos 4:16; 8:5-6; 10:5; 13:2. Amos 6:4. Mic 6:6. Mal 4:2. Luke 15:23,

27, 30. Acts 7:41. Heb 9:12, 19. Rev 4:7

CAMELS
Gen 12:16; 24:10-11, 14, 19-20, 22, 30-32, 35, 44, 46, 61, 63-64; 30:43; 31:17, 34; 32:7, 15, 25. Ex 9:3. Lev 11:4. Deut 14:7. Judg 6:5; 7:12; 8:21, 26. I Sam 15:3; 27:9; 30:17. I Kgs 10:2. II Kgs 8:9. I Chr 5:21; 12:40; 27:30. II Chr 9:1; 14:15. Ezra 2:67. Neh 7:69. Job 1:17; 42:12. Is 21:7; 30:6; 60:6; 66:20. Jer 49:29, 32. Ezek 25:5. Zech 14:15. Matt 3:4; 19:24; 23:24. Mark 1:6; 10:25. Luke 18:25

CATERPILLAR
Ps 78:46. Is 33:4

CHAMELEON
Lev 11:30

COBRA
Deut 32:33. Job 20:14, 16. Ps 58:4; 91:13. Is 11:8

COLT
Gen 32:15; 49:11. Job 11:12. Zech 9:9. Matt 21:2, 5, 7. Mark 11:2, 4-5, 7. Luke 19:30, 33, 35. John 12:15

COW, CALF, HEIFER
Gen 15:9; 18:7-8; 32:15; 41:2-4, 18-20, 26-27. Lev 9:3, 8; 22:28. Num 18:17;

19:2, 5-6, 9-10, 17. Deut 21:3-4, 6. Judg 14:18. I Sam 6:7, 10, 12, 14; 14:32; 16:2; 28:24. I Kgs 12:28, 32. II Kgs 10:29; 17:16. II Chr 11:15; 13:8. Neh 9:18. Job 21:10. Ps 29:6; 68:30; 106:19. Prov 15:17. Is 7:21; 11:6-7; 15:5; 27:10. Jer 34:18-19; 46:20; 48:34; 50:11. Ezek 1:7; 4:15. Hos 4:16; 8:5-6; 10:5, 11; 13:2. Amos 4:1; 6:4. Mic 6:6. Mal 4:2. Luke 15:23, 27, 30. Acts 7:41. Heb 9:12-13, 19. Rev 4:7

CRANE
Is 38:14

CRICKET
Lev 11:22

DEER, DOE, FAWN, ROE, ROEBUCK
Gen 49:21. Deut 12:15, 22; 14:5; 15:22. II Sam 22:34. I Kgs 4:23. Job 39:1. Ps 18:33; 29:9; 42:1. Prov 5:19. Song 4:5; 7:3. Is 35:6. Jer 14:5. Lam 1:6. Hab 3:19

DOE
Prov 5:19

DOG
Ex 11:7; 22:31. Deut 23:18. Judg 7:5. I Sam 17:43; 24:14. II Sam 3:8; 9:8; 16:9. I Kgs 14:11; 16:4; 21:19, 23-24; 22:38. II Kgs 8:13; 9:10, 36. Job 30:1. Ps 22:16,

20; 59:6, 14; 68:23. Prov 26:11, 17. Ecc 9:4. Is 56:10-11; 66:3. Jer 15:3. Matt 7:6; 15:26-27. Mark 7:27-28. Luke 16:21. Phil 3:2. II Pet 2:22. Rev 22:15

DONKEY, FOAL (ASS)
Gen 12:16; 22:3, 5; 24:35; 30:43; 32:5, 15; 34:28; 36:24; 42:26-27; 43:18, 24; 44:3, 13; 45:23; 47:17; 49:11, 14. Ex 4:20; 9:3; 13:13; 20:17; 21:33; 22:4, 9-10; 23:4-5, 12; 34:20. Num 16:15; 22:21-23, 25, 27-30, 32-33; 31:28, 30, 34, 39, 45. Deut 5:14, 21; 22:3-4, 10; 28:31. Josh 6:21; 7:24; 9:4; 15:18. Judg 1:14; 5:10; 6:4; 10:4; 12:14; 15:15-16; 19:3, 10, 19, 21, 28. I Sam 8:16; 9:3, 5, 20; 10:2, 14, 16; 12:3; 15:3; 16:20; 22:19, 22. Lam 4:19. Ezek 1:10; 10:14; 17:3, 7. Dan 4:33; 7:4. Hos 8:1. Obad v. 4. Mic 1:16. Hab 1:8. Matt 24:28. Luke 17:37. Rev 4:7; 12:14

FALCON
Lev 11:14. Deut 14:13. Job 28:7

FAWN
Song 4:5; 7:3

FLEA
I Sam 24:14; 26:20

FLY
Ex 8:21-22, 24, 29, 31. Ps

23:20. Dan 5:21. Hos 8:9. Zech 9:9; 14:15. Matt 21:2, 5, 7. Luke 13:15; 14:5. John 12:14-15. II Pet 2:16

DOVE
Gen 8:8-12. II Kgs 6:25. Ps 55:6; 68:13. Song 1:15; 2:14; 4:1; 5:2, 12; 6:9. Is 38:14; 59:11; 60:8. Jer 48:28. Ezek 7:16. Hos 7:11; 11:11. Nah 2:7. Matt 3:16; 10:16; 21:12. Mark 1:10; 11:15. Luke 3:22. John 1:32; 2:14-16

DROMEDARY
Is 60:6. Jer 2:23

EAGLE
Ex 19:4. Lev 11:13. Deut 14:12; 28:49; 32:11. II Sam 1:23. Job 9:26; 39:27. Ps 103:5. Prov 23:5; 30:17, 19. Is 40:31. Jer 4:13; 48:40; 49:16, 22. Lam 4:19. Ezek 1:10; 10:14; 17:3, 7. Dan 4:33; 7:4. Hos 8:1. Obad v. 4. Mic 1:16. Hab 1:8. Matt 24:28. Luke 17:37. Rev 4:7; 12:14

GECKO
Lev 11:30

GNAT
Matt 23:24

GOAT, KID
Gen 15:9; 27:9, 16; 30:32-33, 35; 31:38; 32:14; 37:31; 38:17, 20, 23. Ex 12:5; 23:19; 25:4; 26:7; 34:26; 35:6, 23, 26; 36:14. Lev 1:10; 3:12; 4:23-24, 28; 5:6; 7:23; 9:3, 15; 10:16; 16:5, 7-10, 15, 18, 20-22, 26-27; 17:3; 22:19, 27; 23:19. Num 7:16-17, 22-23, 28-29, 34-35, 40-41, 46-47,

78:45; 105:31. Ecc 10:1. Is 7:18

FOAL
Gen 32:15. Zech 9:9. Matt 21:5

FOWL, CHICKS, HEN
I Kgs 4:23. Neh 5:18. Ps 78:27; 148:10. Matt 23:37. Luke 13:34

FOX
Judg 15:4-5. Neh 4:3. Song 2:15. Lam 5:18. Ezek 13:4. Matt 8:20. Luke 9:58; 13:32

FROG
Ex 8:2-9, 11-13. Ps 78:45; 105:30. Rev 16:13

GAZELLE
Deut 12:15, 22; 14:5; 15:22. II Sam 2:18. I Kgs 4:23. I Chr 12:8. Prov 6:5. Song 2:7, 9, 17; 3:5; 4:5; 7:3; 8:14. Is 13:14

GECKO
Lev 11:30

GNAT
Matt 23:24

GOAT, KID
Gen 15:9; 27:9, 16; 30:32-33, 35; 31:38; 32:14; 37:31; 38:17, 20, 23. Ex 12:5; 23:19; 25:4; 26:7; 34:26; 35:6, 23, 26; 36:14. Lev 1:10; 3:12; 4:23-24, 28; 5:6; 7:23; 9:3, 15; 10:16; 16:5, 7-10, 15, 18, 20-22, 26-27; 17:3; 22:19, 27; 23:19. Num 7:16-17, 22-23, 28-29, 34-35, 40-41, 46-47,

52-53, 58-5 64-65, 70-7 76-77, 82-8 87-88; 15:1 24, 27; 18:1 28:15, 22, 3 29:5, 11, 16 19, 22, 25, 2 31, 34, 38; 31:20. Deut 14:4-5, 21; 32:14. Judg 6:19; 13:15, 19; 14:6; 15: I Sam 10:3; 16:20; 19:13, 16; 24:2; 25:2 I Kgs 20:27. II Chr 17:11; 29:21, 23; 35:7. Ezra 6:17; 8:35. Jo 39:1. Ps 50:9, 13; 66:15; 104:18. Prov 27:26-27; 30:31. Song 1:8; 4:1; 6:5. Is 1:11; 11:6; 13:21; 34:6, 14. Jer 51:40. Ezek 27:21; 34:17; 39:18; 43:22, 25; 45:23. Dan 8:5, 8, 21. Matt 25:32-33. Luke 15:29. Heb 9:12-13, 19; 10:4; 11:37

GRASSHOPPER
Lev 11:22. Num 13:33. I Kgs 8:37. II Chr 6:28. Ecc 12:5. Is 40:22. Jer 46:23. Nah 3:17

HARE
Lev 11:6. Deut 14:7

HAWK
Lev 11:16. Deut 14:15. Job 39:26. Is 34:15

HEIFER
Gen 15:9. Num 19:2, 5-6, 9-10, 17. Deut 21:3-4, 6. Judg 14:18. I Sam 16:2. Is 15:5. Jer 46:20; 48:34; 50:11.

os 10:11.
eb 9:13

N
att 23:37.
uke 13:34

ERON
ev 11:19.
eut 14:18

HOOPOE
ev 11:19.
eut 14:18

ORNET
x 23:28.
eut 7:20.
osh 24:12

HORSE
Gen 47:17; 49:17; 50:9. Ex 9:3; 14:9, 17-18, 23, 26, 28; 15:1, 19, 21. Deut 11:4; 17:16; 20:1. Josh 11:4, 6, 9; 24:6. Judg 5:22. I Sam 8:11; 13:5. II Sam 1:6; 8:4; 10:18; 15:1. I Kgs 1:5; 4:26, 28; 10:25-26, 28-29; 18:5; 20:1, 20-21, 25; 22:4. II Kgs 2:11-12; 3:7; 5:9; 6:14-15, 17; 7:6-7, 10, 13-14; 9:17-19, 33; 10:2; 11:16; 13:7, 14; 14:20; 18:23-24; 23:11. I Chr 18:4; 19:6. II Chr 1:14, 16-17; 9:24-25, 28; 12:3; 16:8; 23:15; 25:28. Ezra 2:66; 8:22. Neh 2:9; 7:68. Est 6:8-11; 8:10, 14. Job 39:18-19. Ps 20:7; 32:9; 33:17; 76:6; 147:10. Prov 21:31; 26:3. Ecc 10:7. Is 2:7; 5:28; 21:7, 9; 22:6-7; 28:28; 30:16; 31:1, 3; 36:8-9; 43:17; 66:20.

Jer 4:13, 29; 6:23; 8:6, 16; 12:5; 17:25; 22:4; 31:40; 46:4, 9; 47:3; 50:37, 42; 51:21, 27. Ezek 17:15; 23:6, 12, 20, 23; 26:7, 10-11; 27:14; 38:4, 15; 39:20. Dan 11:40. Hos 1:7; 14:3. Joel 2:4. Amos 2:15; 4:10; 6:12. Mic 5:10. Nah 3:2-3. Hab 1:8; 3:8, 15. Hag 2:22. Zech 1:8; 6:2-3, 6; 9:10; 10:3, 5; 12:4; 14:15, 20. Acts 23:32. James 3:3. Rev 6:2, 4-5, 8; 9:7, 9, 16-17; 14:20; 18:13; 19:11, 14, 18-19, 21

HYENA
Is 13:22

JACKAL
Job 30:29. Ps 44:19; 63:10. Is 13:22; 34:13-14; 35:7; 43:20. Jer 9:11; 10:22; 14:6; 49:33; 50:39; 51:37. Lam 4:3. Mic 1:8. Mal 1:3

JACKDAW
Lev 11:18. Deut 14:17

KID
Gen 27:9, 16; 37:31. Lev 4:23, 28; 5:6; 9:3; 16:5; 23:19. Num 7:16, 22, 28, 34, 40, 46, 52, 58, 64, 70, 76, 82, 87; 15:24; 28:15, 30; 29:5, 11, 16, 19, 25. Ezek 43:22; 45:23

KITE
Lev 11:14. Deut 14:13

LAMB
Gen 21:28-30; 22:7-8; 30:32-33, 35, 40. Ex 12:3-5, 21; 13:13; 29:38-41; 34:20. Lev 3:7; 4:32, 35; 5:6-7; 9:3; 12:6, 8; 14:10, 12-13, 21, 24-25; 17:3; 22:23; 23:12, 18-20. Num 6:12, 14; 7:15, 17, 21, 23, 27, 29, 33, 35, 39, 41, 45, 47, 51, 53, 57, 59, 63, 65, 69, 71, 75, 77, 81, 83, 87-88; 15:5, 11; 28:3-4, 7-9, 11, 13-14, 19, 21, 27, 29; 29:2, 4, 8, 10, 13, 15, 17-18, 20-21, 23-24, 26-27, 29-30, 32-33, 36-37. Deut 32:14. I Sam 7:9; 15:9; 17:34-35. II Sam 12:3-4, 6. II Kgs 3:4. I Chr 29:21-22, 32; 30:15, 17; 35:1, 7. Ezra 6:9, 17, 20; 7:17; 8:35. Ps 114:4, 6. Prov 27:26. Is 1:11; 5:17; 11:6; 16:1; 34:6; 40:11; 53:7; 65:25; 66:3. Jer 11:19; 51:40. Ezek 27:21; 39:18; 45:15; 46:4-7, 11, 13, 15. Hos 4:16. Amos 6:4. Mark 14:12. Luke 10:3. John 21:15. Acts 8:32. I Pet 1:19. Rev 13:11

LEECH
Prov 30:15

LEOPARD
Song 4:8. Is 11:6. Jer 5:6; 13:23. Dan 7:6. Hos 13:7.

Hab 1:8. Rev 13:2

LICE
Ex 8:16-18. Ps 105:31

LION
Gen 49:9. Num 23:24; 24:9. Deut 33:20, 22. Judg 14:5-6, 8-9, 18. I Sam 17:34, 36-37. II Sam 1:23; 17:10; 23:20. I Kgs 7:29, 36; 10:19-20; 13:24-26, 28; 20:36. II Kgs 17:25-26. I Chr 11:22; 12:8. II Chr 9:18-19. Job 4:10-11; 10:16; 28:8; 38:39. Ps 7:2; 10:9; 17:12; 22:13, 21; 34:10; 35:17; 57:4; 58:6; 91:13; 104:21. Prov 19:12; 20:2; 22:13; 26:13; 28:1, 15; 30:30. Ecc 9:4. Song 4:8. Is 5:29; 11:6-7; 15:9; 21:8; 30:6; 31:4; 35:9; 38:13; 65:25. Jer 2:15, 30; 4:7; 5:6; 12:8; 25:38; 49:19; 50:17, 44; 51:38. Lam 3:10. Ezek 1:10; 10:14; 19:2-3, 5-6; 22:25; 32:2; 38:13; 41:19. Dan 6:7, 12, 16, 19-20, 22, 24, 27; 7:4. Hos 5:14; 11:10; 13:7-8. Joel 1:6. Amos 3:4, 8, 12; 5:19. Mic 5:8. Nah 2:11-13. Zeph 3:3. Zech 11:3. II Tim 4:17. Heb 11:33. I Pet 5:8. Rev 4:7; 5:5; 9:8, 17; 10:3; 13:2

LIZARD
Lev 11:29-30

LOCUST
Ex 10:4, 12-14, 19. Lev 11:22. Deut 28:38, 42. Judg 6:5; 7:12. I Kgs 8:37. II Chr 6:28; 7:13. Job 39:20. Ps 78:46; 105:34; 109:23. Prov 30:27. Is 33:4. Jer 51:14, 27. Joel 1:4; 2:25. Amos 4:9; 7:1. Nah 3:15-17. Matt 3:4. Mark 1:6. Rev 9:3, 7

MAGGOT
Job 25:6. Is 14:11

MOLE
Lev 11:29. Is 2:20

MONKEY, APE
I Kgs 10:22. II Chr 9:21

MOTH
Job 4:19; 13:28; 27:18. Ps 39:11. Is 50:9; 51:8. Hos 5:12. Matt 6:19-20. Luke 12:33. James 5:2

MOUSE, RAT
Lev 11:29. I Sam 6:4-5, 11, 18. Is 66:17

MULE
II Sam 13:29; 18:9. I Kgs 1:33, 38, 44; 10:25; 18:5. II Kgs 5:17. I Chr 12:40. II Chr 9:24. Ezra 2:66. Neh 7:68. Ps 32:9. Is 66:20. Ezek 27:14. Zech 14:15

ONAGER
Job 39:5

OSTRICH
Lev 11:16. Deut 14:15.

Job 30:29; 39:13. Is 13:21; 34:13; 43:20. Jer 50:39. Lam 4:3. Mic 1:8

OWL
Lev 11:16-18. Deut 14:15-17. Ps 102:6. Is 13:21; 34:11

OX
Gen 12:16; 20:14; 21:27; 32:5; 34:28; 49:6. Ex 9:3; 20:17, 24; 21:28-29, 32-33, 35-36; 22:1, 4, 9-10, 30; 23:4, 12; 24:5; 34:19. Lev 7:23; 17:3; 27:26. Num 7:3, 6-8, 17, 23, 29, 35, 41, 47, 53, 59, 65, 71, 77, 83, 87-88; 22:4, 40; 23:22; 24:8. Deut 5:14, 21; 14:4, 26; 22:1, 4, 10; 25:4; 28:31; 33:17. Josh 6:21; 7:24. Judg 3:31; 6:4. I Sam 11:7; 12:3; 14:32, 34; 15:3, 9, 14-15, 21; 22:19; 27:9. II Sam 6:6, 13; 24:22, 24. I Kgs 1:9, 19, 25; 4:23; 7:25, 29, 44; 8:5; 19:19-21. II Kgs 5:26; 16:17. I Chr 12:40; 13:9; 21:23. II Chr 4:3-4, 15; 5:6; 18:2; 31:6. Neh 5:18. Job 1:14; 6:5; 24:3; 39:9-10; 40:15; 42:12. Ps 8:7; 22:21; 29:6; 69:31; 92:10; 106:20; 144:14. Prov 7:22; 14:4. Is 1:3; 7:25; 11:7; 22:13; 30:24; 32:20; 34:7; 65:25. Jer

51:23. Ezek 1:10. Dan 4:25, 32-33; 5:21. Amos 6:12. Matt 22:4. Luke 13:15; 14:5, 19. John 2:14-15. Acts 14:13. I Cor 9:9. I Tim 5:18

PARTRIDGE
I Sam 26:20. Jer 17:11

PELICAN
Ps 102:6. Is 34:11. Zeph 2:14

PIGEON
Gen 15:9. Lev 1:14; 5:7, 11; 12:6, 8; 14:22, 30; 15:14, 29. Num 6:10. Luke 2:24

PORCUPINE
Is 14:23; 34:11

QUAIL
Ex 16:13. Num 11:31-32. Ps 105:40

RAM
Gen 15:9; 22:13; 31:10, 12, 38; 32:14. Ex 25:5; 26:14; 29:1, 3, 15-20, 22, 26-27, 31-32; 35:7, 23; 36:19; 39:34. Lev 5:15-16, 18; 6:6; 8:2, 18, 20-22, 29; 9:2, 4, 18-19; 16:3, 5; 19:21-22; 23:18. Num 5:8; 6:14, 17, 19; 7:15, 17, 21, 23, 27, 29, 33, 35, 39, 41, 45, 47, 51, 53, 57, 59, 63, 65, 69, 71, 75, 77, 81, 83, 87-88; 15:6, 11; 23:1-2, 4, 14, 29-30; 28:11-12, 14, 19-20, 27-28; 29:2-3, 8-9, 13-14, 17-18, 20-21, 23-24, 26-27, 29-30, 32-33, 36-

37. Deut 32:14. Josh 6:4-6, 8, 13. I Sam 15:22. II Kgs 3:4. I Chr 15:26; 29:21. II Chr 13:9; 15:14; 17:11; 29:21-22, 32. Ezra 6:9, 17; 7:17; 8:35; 10:19. Job 42:8. Ps 66:15; 114:4, 6. Is 1:11; 34:6; 60:7. Jer 50:8; 51:40. Ezek 27:21; 34:17; 39:18; 43:23, 25; 45:23-24; 46:4-7, 11. Dan 8:3-4, 6-7, 20. Hos 5:8. Mic 6:7

RAT
I Sam 6:4-5, 11, 18

RAVEN
Gen 8:7. Lev 11:15. Deut 14:14. I Kgs 17:4, 6. Job 38:41. Ps 147:9. Prov 30:17. Song 5:11. Is 34:11. Luke 12:24

ROE
Deut 14:5

ROEBUCK
I Kgs 4:23

ROOSTER (COCK)
Matt 26:34, 74-75. Mark 13:35; 14:30, 68, 72. Luke 22:34, 60-61. John 13:38; 18:27

SCORPION
Deut 8:15. Ezek 2:6. Luke 10:19; 11:12. Rev 9:3, 5, 10

SEAGULL
Lev 11:16. Deut 14:15

SHEEP, LAMB, EWE
Gen 4:2; 12:16; 20:14;

21:27-30; 22:7-8; 29:2-3, 6-10, 38; 30:32-33, 35, 40; 31:19, 38; 32:14; 34:28; 38:13. Ex 9:3; 12:3-5, 21; 13:13; 20:24; 22:1, 4, 9-10, 30; 29:38-41; 34:19-20. Lev 1:10; 3:7; 4:32, 35; 5:6-7; 7:23; 9:3; 12:6, 8; 14:10, 12-13, 21, 24-25; 17:3; 22:19, 21, 23, 27-28; 23:12, 18-20; 27:26. Num 6:12, 14; 7:15, 17, 21, 23, 27, 29, 33, 35, 39, 41, 45, 47, 51, 53, 57, 59, 63, 65, 69, 71, 75, 77, 81, 83, 87-88; 15:5, 11; 18:17; 22:40; 27:17; 28:3-4, 7-9, 11, 13-14, 19, 21, 27, 29; 29:2, 4, 8, 10, 13, 15, 17-18, 20-21, 23-24, 26-27, 29-30, 32-33, 36-37; 31:28, 30, 32, 36-37, 43; 32:24, 36. Deut 14:4-5, 26; 17:1; 18:3-4; 22:1; 28:31; 32:14. Josh 6:21; 7:24. Judg 6:4. I Sam 7:9; 8:17; 14:32, 34; 15:3, 9, 14-15, 21; 16:11. 19; 17:15, 20, 28, 34-35; 22:19; 25:2, 4, 16, 18; 27:9. II Sam 6:13; 7:8; 12:3-4, 6; 17:29; 24:17. I Kgs 1:9, 19, 25; 4:23; 8:5, 63; 22:17. II Kgs 3:4; 5:26. I Chr 5:21; 12:40; 17:7; 21:17; 29:21. II Chr 5:6; 7:5; 14:15;

15:11; 18:2, 16; 29:21-22, 32-33; 30:15, 17, 24; 31:6; 35:1, 7. Ezra 6:9, 17, 20; 7:17; 8:35. Neh 3:1, 32; 5:18; 12:39. Job 1:16; 31:20; 42:12. Ps 8:7; 44:11, 22; 49:14; 74:1; 78:52, 71; 79:13; 95:7; 100:3; 114:4, 6; 119:176; 144:13. Prov 27:26. Song 4:2; 6:6. Is 1:11; 5:17; 7:21, 25; 11:6; 13:14; 16:1; 22:13; 34:6; 40:11; 43:23; 53:6-7; 65:25; 66:3. Jer 11:19; 12:3; 13:20; 23:1; 50:6, 17; 51:40. Ezek 27:21; 34:6, 10-12, 17, 20, 22; 39:18; 45:15; 46:4-7, 11, 13, 15. Hos 4:16; 12:12. Joel 1:18. Amos 6:4. Mic 2:12; 5:8. Zech 10:2; 13:7. Matt 7:15; 9:36; 10:6, 16; 12:11-12; 15:24; 18:12-13; 25:32-33; 26:31. Mark 6:34; 14:12, 27. Luke 10:3; 15:4, 6; 17:7. John 2:14-15; 10:2-4, 7-8, 11-16, 26-27; 21:15-17. Acts 8:32. Rom 8:36. Heb 13:20. I Pet 1:19; 2:25. Rev 13:11; 18:13

SNAIL
Ps 58:8

SNAKE
Is 34:15. Mic 7:17

SOW
II Pet 2:22

SPARROW
Ps 84:3; 102:7. Prov 26:2. Matt 10:29, 31. Luke 12:6-7

SPIDER
Job 8:14. Prov 30:28. Is 59:5

STORK
Lev 11:19. Deut 14:18. Job 39:13. Ps 104:17. Jer 8:7. Zech 5:9

SWALLOW
Ps 84:3. Prov 26:2. Is 38:14. Jer 8:7

SWINE, SOW
Lev 11:7. Deut 14:8. Prov 11:22. Is 65:4; 66:3, 17. Matt 7:6; 8:30-32. Mark 5:11-14, 16. Luke 8:32-33; 15:15-16. II Pet 2:22

TURTLEDOVE
Gen 8:8-12; 15:9. Lev 1:14; 5:7, 11; 12:6, 8; 14:22, 30; 15:14, 29. Num 6:10. Ps 55:6; 68:13; 74:19. Song 1:12, 15; 2:12, 14; 4:1; 5:2; 6:9. Is 38:14; 59:11; 60:8. Jer 8:7; 48:28. Ezek 7:16. Hos 7:11; 11:11. Nah 2:7. Matt 3:16; 10:16; 21:12. Mark 1:10; 11:15. Luke 2:24; 3:22. John 1:32; 2:14, 16

VIPER
Gen 49:17. Job 20:16. Prov 23:32. Is 11:8; 14:29; 30:6; 59:5. Jer 8:17. Matt 3:7; 12:34; 23:33. Luke

3:7. Acts 28:3

VULTURE
Gen 15:11. Lev 11:13, 18. Deut 14:12, 17. Jer 12:9

WOLF
Gen 49:27. Is 11:6; 65:25. Jer 5:6. Ezek 22:27. Hab 1:8. Zeph 3:3. Matt 7:15; 10:16. Luke 10:3. John 10:12. Acts 20:29

WORM, MAGGOT
Ex 16:20, 24. Deut 28:39. Job 7:5; 17:14; 21:26; 24:20; 25:6. Ps 22:6. Is 14:11; 41:14; 51:8; 66:24. Jonah 4:7. Mark 9:44, 46, 48. Acts 12:23

ISRAEL, KINGDOM OF ISRAEL
Gen 32:28, 32; 34:7; 35:10, 21-22; 36:31; 37:3, 13; 42:5; 43:6, 8, 11; 45:21, 28; 46:1-2, 5, 8, 29-30; 47:27, 29, 31: 48:2, 8, 10-11, 13-14, 20-21; 49:2, 7, 16, 24, 28; 50:2, 25. Ex 1:1, 7, 9, 12-13; 2:23, 25; 3:9-11, 13-16, 18; 4:22, 29, 31; 5:1-2, 14-15, 19; 6:5-6, 9, 11-14, 26-27; 7:2, 4-5; 9:4, 6, 26, 35; 10:20, 23; 11:7, 10; 12:3, 6, 15, 19, 21, 27-28, 31, 35, 37, 40, 42, 47, 50-51; 13:2, 18-19; 14:2-3, 5, 8, 10, 15-16, 19-20, 22, 25, 29-31; 15:1, 19, 22; 16:1-3, 6, 9-10, 12, 15, 17, 31, 35; 17:1, 5-8, 11; 18:1, 8-9, 12, 25; 19:1-3, 6; 20:22; 24:1, 4-5, 9-11, 17; 25:2, 22; 27:20-21; 28:1, 9, 11-12, 21, 29-30, 38; 29:28, 43, 45; 30:12, 16, 31; 31:13, 16-17; 32:4, 8, 13, 20, 27; 33:5-6; 34:23, 27, 30, 32, 34-35; 35:1, 4, 20, 29-30; 36:3; 39:6-7, 14, 32, 42; 40:36, 38. Lev 1:2; 4:2, 13; 7:23, 29, 34, 36, 38; 9:1, 3; 10:6, 11, 14; 11:2; 12:2; 15:2, 31; 16:5, 16-17, 19, 21, 34; 17:2-3, 5, 8, 10, 12-14;

18:2; 19:2; 20:2; 21:24; 22:2-3, 15, 18, 32; 23:2, 10, 24, 34, 43-44; 24:2, 8, 10, 15, 23; 25:2, 33, 46, 55; 26:46; 27:2, 34. Num 1:2-3, 16, 20, 44-45, 49, 52-54; 2:2, 32-34; 3:8-9, 12-13, 38, 40-42, 45-46, 50; 4:46; 5:2, 4, 6, 9, 12; 6:2, 23, 27; 7:2, 84; 8:6, 9-11, 14, 16-20; 9:2, 4-5, 7, 10, 17-19, 22; 10:4, 12, 28-29, 36; 11:4, 16, 30; 13:2-3, 24, 26, 32; 14:2, 5, 7, 10, 27, 39; 15:2, 18, 25-26, 29, 32, 38; 16:2, 9, 25, 34, 38, 40-41; 17:2, 5-6, 9, 12; 18:5-6, 8, 11, 14, 19-24, 26, 28, 32; 19:2, 9-10, 13; 20:1, 12-14, 19, 21-22, 24, 29; 21:1-3, 6, 10, 17, 21, 23-25, 31; 22:1-3, 7, 10, 21, 23; 24:1-2, 5, 17-18; 25:1, 3-6, 8, 11, 13; 26:2, 4-5, 51, 62-64; 27:8, 11-12, 20-21; 28:2; 29:40; 30:1; 31:2, 4-5, 9, 12, 16, 30, 42, 47, 54; 32:4, 7, 9, 13-14, 17-18, 22, 28; 33:1, 3, 5, 38, 40, 51; 34:2, 13, 29; 35:2, 8, 10, 15, 34; 36:1-5, 7-9, 13. Deut 1:1, 3, 38; 2:12; 3:18; 4:1, 44-46; 5:1; 6:3-4; 9:1; 10:6, 12; 11:6; 13:11; 17:4, 12, 20; 18:1, 6; 19:13; 20:3;

21:8, 21; 22:19, 21-22; 23:17; 24:7; 25:6-7, 10; 26:15; 27:1, 9, 14; 29:1-2, 10, 21; 31:1, 7, 9, 11, 19, 22-23, 30; 32:8, 45, 49, 51-52; 33:1, 5, 10, 21, 28-29; 34:8-10, 12. Josh 1:2; 2:2; 3:1, 7, 9, 12, 17; 4:4-5, 7-8, 12, 14, 21-22; 5:1-3, 6, 10, 12; 6:1, 18, 23, 25; 7:1, 6, 8, 11-13, 15-16, 19-20, 23-25; 8:10, 14-15, 17, 21-22, 24, 27, 30-33, 35; 9:2, 6-7, 14, 17-19, 26; 10:1, 4, 10-12, 14-15, 20-21, 24, 29-32, 34, 36, 38, 40, 42-43; 11:5-6, 8, 13-14, 16, 19-23; 12:1, 6-7; 12:7; 13:6, 13-14, 22, 33; 14:1, 5, 10, 14; 17:13; 18:1-3, 10; 19:49, 51; 20:2, 9; 21:1, 3, 8, 41, 43, 45; 22:9, 11-14, 16, 18, 20-22, 24, 30-33; 23:1-2; 24:1-2, 9, 23, 31-32. Judg 1:1, 28; 2:4, 6-7, 10-11, 14, 20, 22; 3:1-2, 4-5, 7-10, 12-15, 27, 30-31; 4:1, 3-6, 23-24; 5:2-3, 5, 7-9, 11; 6:1-4, 6-8, 14-15, 36-37; 7:2, 8, 14-15, 23; 8:22, 27-28, 33-35; 9:22, 55; 10:1-3, 6-11, 15-17; 11:4-5, 13, 15-17, 19-21, 23, 25-27, 33, 39-40; 12:7-9, 11, 13-14; 13:1, 5; 14:4; 15:20;

16:31; 17:6; 18:1, 19, 29; 19:1, 12, 29-30; 20:1-3, 6-7, 10-14, 17-20, 22-27, 29-36, 38-39, 41, 42, 48; 21:1, 3, 5-6, 8, 15, 17-18, 24-25. Ruth 2:12; 4:7, 11, 14. I Sam 1:17; 2:22, 28 30, 32; 3:11, 20; 4:1-3, 5, 10, 17-18, 21-22; 5:7-8, 10-11; 6:3, 5; 7:2-4, 11, 13-17; 8:1, 4, 22; 9:2, 9, 16, 20-21; 10:18, 20; 11:2-3, 7-8, 13, 15; 12:1; 13:1-2, 4-6, 13, 19; 14:12, 18, 22-24, 37, 39-41, 45, 47-48; 15:1-2, 6, 17, 26, 28-30, 35; 16:1; 17:2-3, 8, 10-11, 19, 21, 24-26, 45-46, 52-53; 18:6, 16, 18; 19:5; 20:12; 23:10-11, 17; 24:2, 14, 20; 25:30, 32, 34; 26:2, 15, 20; 27:1, 12; 28:1, 3-4, 19; 29:3; 30:25; 31:1, 7. II Sam 1:3, 12, 19, 24; 2:9-10, 17, 28; 3:10, 12, 17-19, 21, 37-38; 4:1; 5:1-3, 5, 12, 17; 6:1, 5, 15, 19-21; 7:6-8, 10-11, 23-24, 26-27; 8:15; 10:9, 15, 17-19; 11:1, 11; 12:7-8, 12; 13:12-13; 14:25; 15:2, 6, 10, 13; 16:3, 15, 18, 21-22; 17:4, 10-11, 13-15, 24, 26; 18:6-7, 16-17; 19:8-9, 11, 22, 40-43; 20:1-2, 14, 19, 23; 21:2, 4-5, 15, 17, 21; 23:1,

; 24:1-2, 4, 5, 25.
gs 1:3, 20, 34-35, 48;
-5, 11, 15, 3:28; 4:1, 20, 25;
3; 6:1, 13; -3, 5, 9, 14-, 20, 22-23, -26, 30, 33-, 36, 38, 41, , 52, 55-56, , 62-63, 65-; 9:5, 7, 20-; 10:9; 11:2, 16, 25, 31-, 37-38, 42; :1, 3, 16-21, , 28, 33; :7, 10, 13-, 18-19, 21, ; 15:9, 16-, 19-20, 25-, 30-34; :2, 5, 8, 13-; 16-17, 19-, 23, 26-27, 9, 33; 17:1, , 18:17-20, 1, 36; 19:10, 4, 16, 18; 20:2, 4, 7, 11, 13, 15, 20-22, 26-29, 31-32, 40-41, 43; 21:7, 18, 21-22, 26; 22:1-6, 8-10, 17-18, 26, 29-34, 39, 41, 44, 51-53. II Kgs 1:1, 3, 6, 16, 18; 2:12; 3:1, 3-6, 9-13, 24, 27; 5:2, 4-8, 12, 15; 6:8-12, 21, 23, 26; 7:6, 13; 8:12, 16, 18, 25-26; 9:3, 6, 8, 12, 14, 21; 10:21, 28-32, 34, 36; 13:1-6, 8, 10-14, 16, 18, 22, 25; 14:1, 8-9, 11-13, 15-17, 23-29; 15:1, 8-9, 11-12, 15, 17-18, 20-21, 23-24, 26-29, 31-32; 16:3, 5, 7; 17:1-2, 6-9, 13, 18-24, 34; 18:1, 4-5, 9-11; 19:15, 20, 22; 21:2-3, 7-9, 12, 15, 18;

23:13, 15, 19, 22, 27; 24:13. I Chr 1:34, 43; 2:1, 7; 4:10; 5:1, 3, 17, 26; 6:38, 49, 64; 7:29; 9:1; 10:1, 7; 11:1-4, 10; 12:32, 38, 40; 13:2, 5-6, 8; 14:2, 8; 15:3, 12, 14, 25, 28; 16:3-4, 13, 17, 36, 40; 17:5-7, 9-10, 21-22, 24; 18:14; 19:10, 16-19; 20:7; 21:1-5, 7, 12, 14; 22:1-2, 6, 9-10, 12-13, 17; 23:1-2, 25; 24:19; 26:29-30; 27:1, 16, 22-24; 28:1, 4-5, 8; 29:6, 10, 18, 21, 23 25-27, 30. II Chr 1:2, 13; 2:4, 12, 17; 5:2-4, 6, 10; 6:3-7, 10-14, 16-17, 21, 24-25, 27, 29, 32-33; 7:3, 6, 8, 10, 18; 8:2, 7-9, 11; 9:8, 30; 10:1, 3, 16-19; 11:1, 3, 13, 16; 12:1, 6, 13; 13:4-5, 12, 15-18; 15:3-4, 9, 13, 17; 16:1, 3-4, 11; 17:1, 4; 18:3-5, 7-9, 16-17, 19, 25, 28-34; 19:8; 20:7, 10, 19, 29, 34-35; 21:2, 4, 6, 13; 22:5; 23:2; 24:5-6, 9, 16; 25:6-7, 9, 17-18, 21-23, 25-26; 27:7; 28:2-3, 5, 8, 13, 19, 23, 26-27; 29:7, 10, 24, 27; 30:1, 5-6, 21, 25-26; 31:1, 5-6, 8; 32:17, 32; 33:2, 7-9, 16, 18; 34:7, 9, 21, 23, 26, 33; 35:3-4, 17-18, 25, 27; 36:8, 13. Ezra 1:3;

2:2, 59, 70; 3:1-2, 10-11; 4:1, 3; 5:1, 11; 6:14, 16-17, 21-22; 7:6-7, 10-11, 13, 15, 28; 8:18, 25, 29, 35; 9:1, 4, 15; 10:1-2, 5, 10, 25. Neh 1:6; 2:10; 7:7, 61, 73; 8:1, 14, 17; 9:1; 10:33, 39; 11:20; 12:47; 13:2-3, 18, 26. Ps 14:7; 22:3, 23; 25:22; 41:13; 50:7; 53:6; 59:5; 68:8, 26, 34-35; 69:6; 71:22; 72:18; 73:1; 76:1; 78:5, 21, 31, 41, 55, 59, 71; 80:1; 81:4, 8, 11, 13; 83:4; 89:18; 98:3; 103:7; 105:10, 23; 106:48; 114:1-2; 115:9, 12; 118:2; 121:4; 122:4; 124:1; 125:5; 128:6; 129:1; 130:7-8; 131:3; 135:4, 12, 19; 136:11, 14, 22; 147:2, 19; 148:14; 149:2. Prov 1:1. Ecc 1:12. Song 3:7. Is 1:3-4, 24; 4:2; 5:7, 19, 24; 7:1; 8:14, 18; 9:8, 12, 14; 10:17; 20, 22; 11:12, 16; 12:6; 14:1-2; 17:3, 6-7, 9; 19:24-25; 21:10, 17; 24:15; 27:6-7, 12; 29:19, 23; 30:11-12, 15, 29; 31:1, 6; 37:16, 21, 23; 40:27; 41:8, 14; 16-17, 20; 42:24; 43:1, 3, 14-15, 22, 28; 44:1, 5-6, 21, 23; 45:3-4, 11, 15, 17, 25; 46:3, 13; 47:4; 48:1-2, 12, 17;

49:3, 5-7; 52:12; 54:5; 55:5; 56:8; 60:9, 14; 63:7, 16; 66:20. Jer 2:3-4, 14, 26, 31; 3:6, 8, 11-12, 18, 20-21, 23; 4:1; 5:11, 15; 6:9; 7:3, 12, 21; 9:15, 26; 10:1, 16; 11:3, 10, 17; 12:14; 13:11-12; 14:8; 16:9, 14-15; 17:13; 18:6, 13; 19:3, 15; 21:4; 23:2, 6-8, 13; 24:5; 25:15, 27; 27:4, 21; 28:2, 14; 29:4, 8, 21, 23, 25; 30:2-4, 10; 31:1-2, 4, 7, 9-10, 21, 23, 27, 31, 33, 36-37; 32:14-15, 20-21, 30, 32, 36; 33:4, 7, 14, 17; 34:2, 13; 35:13, 17-19; 36:2; 37:7; 38:17; 39:16; 41:9; 42:9, 15, 18; 43:10; 44:2, 7, 11, 25; 45:2; 46:25, 27; 48:1, 13, 27; 49:1-2; 50:4, 17-20, 29, 33; 51:5, 19, 33, 49. Lam 2:1, 3, 5. Ezek 2:3; 3:1, 4-5, 7, 17; 4:3-5, 13; 5:4; 6:2-3, 5, 11; 7:2; 8:4, 6, 10-12; 9:3, 8-9; 10:19-20; 11:5, 10-11, 13, 15, 17, 22; 12:6, 9-10, 19, 22-24, 27; 13:2, 4-5, 9, 16; 14:1, 4-7, 9, 11; 17:2, 23; 18:2-3, 6, 15, 25, 29-31; 19:1, 9; 20:1, 3, 5, 13, 27; 21:2-3, 12, 25; 22:6, 18; 24:21; 25:3, 6, 14; 27:17; 28:24-

25; 29:6, 16, 21; 33:7, 10-11, 20, 24, 28; 34:2, 13-14, 30; 35:5, 12, 15; 36:1, 4, 6, 8, 10, 12, 17, 21-22, 32, 37; 37:11-12, 16, 19, 21-22, 28; 38:8, 14, 16-19; 39:2, 4, 7, 9, 11-12, 17, 22-23, 25, 29; 40:2, 4; 43:2, 7, 10; 44:2, 6, 9-10, 12, 15, 22, 28-29; 45:6, 8-9, 15-17; 47:13, 18, 21-22; 48:11, 19, 29, 31. Dan 1:3; 9:7, 11, 20. Hos 1:1, 4-6, 10-11; 3:1, 4-5; 4:1, 15-16; 5:1, 3, 5, 9; 6:10; 7:1, 10; 8:2-3, 6, 8, 14; 9:1, 7, 10; 10:1, 6, 8-9, 15; 11:1, 8, 12; 12:12-13; 13:1, 9; 14:1, 5. Joel 2:27; 3:2, 16. Amos 1:1; 2:6, 11; 3:1, 12, 14; 4:5, 12; 5:1-4, 25; 6:1, 14; 7:8-11, 15-17; 8:2; 9:7, 9, 14. Obad v.20. Mic 1:5, 13-15; 2:12; 3:1, 8-9; 5:1-3; 6:2. Nah 2:2. Zeph 2:9; 3:13-15. Zech 1:19; 8:13; 9:1; 11:14; 12:1. Mal 1:1, 5; 2:11, 16; 4:4. Matt 2:6, 20-21; 8:10; 9:33; 10:6, 23; 15:24, 31, 19:28; 27:9, 42. Mark 12:29; 15:32. Luke 1:16, 54, 68, 80; 2:25, 32, 34; 4:25, 27; 7:9; 22:30; 24:21. John 1:31, 49; 3:10; 12:13. Acts

1:6; 2:22, 36; 3:12; 4:8, 10, 27; 5:21, 31, 35; 7:23, 37, 42; 9:15; 10:36; 13:16-17, 23-24; 21:28; 28:20. Rom 9:6, 27, 31; 10:1, 19, 21; 11:2, 7, 25-26. I Cor 10:18. II Cor 3:7, 13. Gal 6:16. Eph 2:12. Phil 3:5. Heb 8:8, 10; 11:22. Rev 2:14; 7:4; 21:12.

JUDAH 1, KINGDOM OF JUDAH

Gen 29:35; 35:23; 37:26; 38:1-2, 6-8, 11-12, 15, 20, 22-24, 26; 43:3, 8; 44:14, 16, 18; 46:12, 28; 49:8-10. Ex 1:2; 31:2; 35:30; 38:22. Num 1:7, 26-27; 2:3, 9; 7:12; 10:14; 13:6; 26:19-20, 22; 34:19. Deut 27:12; 33:7; 34:2. Josh 7:1, 16-18; 11:21; 14:6; 15:1, 12-13, 20-21, 63; 18:5, 11, 14; 19:1, 9, 34; 20:7; 21:4, 9, 11. Judg 1:2-4, 8-10, 16-19; 10:9; 15:9-11; 17:7-9; 18:12; 19:1-2, 18; 20:18. Ruth 1:1-2, 7; 4:12. I Sam 11:8; 15:4; 17:1, 12, 52; 18:16; 22:5; 23:3, 23; 27:6, 10; 30:14, 16, 26. II Sam 1:18; 2:1, 4, 7, 10-11; 3:8, 10; 5:5; 11:11; 12:8; 19:11, 14-16, 40-43; 20:2, 4-5; 21:2; 24:1, 7, 9. I Kgs 1:9, 35; 2:32; 4:20, 25; 9:18; 12:17, 20-21, 23, 27, 32; 13:1, 12, 14, 21; 14:21-22, 29; 15:1, 7, 9, 17, 22-23, 25, 28, 33; 16:8, 10, 15, 23, 29; 19:3; 22:2, 10, 29, 41, 45, 51. II Kgs 1:17; 3:1, 7, 9, 14; 8:16, 19-20, 22-23, 25, 29; 9:16, 21, 27, 29; 10:13; 12:18-19; 13:1, 10, 12; 14:1,

9-13, 15, 17-18, 21-23, 28; 15:1, 6, 8, 13, 17, 23, 27, 32, 36-37; 16:1, 6, 19; 17:1, 13, 18-19; 18:1, 5, 13-14, 16, 22; 19:10, 30; 20:20; 21:11-12, 16-17, 25; 22:13, 16, 18; 23:1-2, 5, 8, 11-12, 17, 22, 24, 26-28; 24:2-3, 5, 12, 20; 25:21-22, 27. I Chr 2:1, 3-4, 10; 4:1, 21, 27, 41; 5:2, 17; 6:15, 55, 65; 9:1, 3-4; 12:16, 24; 13:6; 21:5; 27:18; 28:4. II Chr 2:7; 9:11; 10:17; 11:1, 3, 5, 10, 12, 14, 17, 23; 12:4-5, 12; 13:1, 13-16, 18; 14:4-8, 12; 15:2, 8-9, 15; 16:1, 6-7, 11; 17:2, 5-7, 9-10, 12-14, 19; 18:3, 9, 28; 19:1, 5, 11; 20:3-5, 13, 15, 17-18, 20, 22, 24, 27, 31, 35; 21:3, 8, 10-13, 17; 22:1, 6, 8, 10; 23:2, 8; 24:5-6, 9, 17-18, 23; 25:5, 10, 12-13, 17-19, 21-23, 25-26, 28; 26:1-2; 27:4, 7; 28:6, 9-10, 17-19, 25-26; 29:8, 21; 30:1, 6, 12, 24-25; 31:1, 6, 20; 32:1, 8-9, 12, 23, 25, 32-33; 33:9, 14, 16; 34:3, 5, 9, 11, 21, 24, 26, 29-30; 35:18, 21, 24, 27; 36:4, 8, 10, 23. Ezra 1:2-3, 5, 8; 2:1; 4:1, 4, 6; 5:1; 7:14; 9:9; 10:7, 9. Neh 1:2; 2:5, 7;

5:14; 6:7, 17-18; 7:6; 11:3-4, 20, 25; 12:44; 13:12, 15-17, 24. Est 2:6. Ps 48:11; 60:7; 68:27; 69:35; 76:1; 78:68; 97:8; 108:8; 114:2. Prov 25:1. Is 1:1; 2:1; 3:1, 8; 5:3, 7; 7:1, 6, 17; 8:8; 9:21; 11:12-13; 19:17; 22:8, 21; 26:1; 36:1, 7; 37:10, 31; 38:9; 40:9; 44:26; 48:1; 65:9. Jer 1:2-3, 15, 18; 2:28; 3:7-8, 10-11, 18; 4:3-5, 16; 5:11, 20; 7:2, 17, 30, 34; 8:1; 9:11, 26; 10:22; 11:2, 6, 9-10, 12-13, 17; 12:14; 13:9, 11, 19; 14:2, 19; 15(4; 17:1, 19-20, 25-26; 18:11; 19:3-4, 7, 13; 20:4-5, 7, 11; 22:1-2, 6, 11, 18, 24, 30; 23:6; 24:1, 5, 8; 25:1-3, 18; 26:1-2, 10, 18-19; 27:1, 3, 12, 18, 20-21; 28:1, 4; 29:2-3, 22; 30:3-4; 31:23-24, 27, 31; 32:1-4, 30, 32, 35, 44; 33:4, 7, 10, 13-14, 16; 34:2, 4, 6-7, 19, 21-22; 35:1, 13, 17; 36:1-3, 6, 9, 28-32; 37:1, 7; 38:22; 39:1, 4, 6, 10; 40:1, 5, 11-12, 15; 42:15, 19; 43:4-5, 9; 44:2, 6-7, 9, 11-12, 14, 17, 21, 24, 26-28, 30; 45:1; 46:2; 49:34; 50:4, 20, 33; 51:5, 59; 52:3, 10, 27, 31. Lam 1:3, 15; 2:2, 5; 5:11. Ezek 4:6; 8:1, 17; 9:9; 21:20; 25:3, 8, 12; 27:17; 37:16, 19; 48:7-8, 22, 31. Dan 1:1-2, 6; 2:25; 5:13; 6:13; 9:7. Hos 1:1, 7, 11; 4:15; 5:5, 10, 12-14; 6:4, 11; 8:14; 10:11; 11:12; 12:2. Joel 3:1, 6, 8, 18-20. Amos 1:1; 2:4-5; 7:12. Obad v.12. Mic 1:1, 5, 9; 5:2. Nah 1:15. Zeph 1:1, 4; 2:7. Hag 1:1, 14; 2:2, 21. Zech 1:12, 19, 21; 2:12; 8:13; 15, 19; 9:7, 13; 10:3, 6; 11:14; 12:2, 4-7; 14:5, 14, 21. Mal 2:11; 3:4. Matt 1:2-3; 2:6. Luke 1:39; 3:33. Heb 7:14; 8:8. Rev 5:5; 7:5

PLANTS

ACACIA
Ex 25:5, 10, 13, 23, 28; 26:15, 26, 32, 37; 27:1, 6; 30:1, 5, 7, 24; 36:20, 31, 36; 37:1, 4, 10, 15, 25, 28. Ex 38:1, 6. Num 25:1. Deut 10:3. Josh 2:1; 3:1. Is 41:19. Mic 6:5

ALMOND
Gen 30:37; 43:11. Ex 25:33-34; 37:19-20. Num 17:8. Ecc 12:5. Jer 1:11

ALMUG
I Kgs 10:11-12

ALOES
Num 24:6. Ps 45:8. Prov 7:17. Song 4:14. John 19:39

ANISE
Matt 23:23

APPLE
Deut 32:10. Ps 17:8. Prov 7:2; 25:11. Song 2:3, 5; 7:8; 8:5. Joel 1:12. Zech 2:8

BALM
Gen 37:25; 43:11. Jer 8:22; 46:11; 51:8. Ezek 27:17

BARLEY
Ex 9:31. Lev 27:16. Num 5:15. Deut 8:8. Judg 7:13. Ruth 1:22; 2:17, 23; 3:2, 15, 17. II Sam 14:30; 17:28; 21:9. I Kgs 4:28. II Kgs 4:42; 7:1, 16, 18. I Chr 11:13. II Chr 2:10, 15; 27:5. Job 31:40. Is 28:25. Jer 41:8. Ezek 4:9, 12; 13:19; 45:13. Hos 3:2. Joel 1:11. John 6:9, 13. Rev 6:6

BEANS
II Sam 17:18. Ezek 4:9

BITTER HERBS
Ex 12:8. Num 9:11

BRIAR, BRIER, BRAMBLE
Judg 8:7, 16; 9:14-15. Is 5:6; 7:23-25; 9:18; 10:17; 27:4; 32:13; 34:13; 55:13. Ezek 2:6; 28:24. Mic 7:4. Luke 6:44. Heb 6:8

BROOM
I Kgs 19:4-5. Job 30:4. Ps 120:4

BULRUSH
Is 9:14; 19:15; 58:5

CALAMUS
Song 4:14

CANE
Ex 30:23. Is 43:24. Jer 6:20. Ezek 27:19

CASSIA
Ex 30:24. Ps 45:8. Ezek 27:19

CEDAR
Lev 14:4, 6, 49, 51-52. Num 19:6; 24:6. Judg 9:15. II Sam 5:11; 7:2, 7. I Kgs 4:33; 5:6, 8, 10; 6:9-10, 15-16, 18, 20, 36; 7:2-3, 7, 11-12; 9:11; 10:27. II Kgs 14:9; 19:23. I Chr 14:1; 17:1, 6; 22:4. II Chr 1:15; 2:3, 8; 9:27; 25:18. Ezra 3:7. Job 40:17. Ps 29:5; 80:10; 92:12; 104:16; 148:9. Song 1:17; 5:15; 8:9. Is 2:13; 9:10; 14:8; 37:24; 41:19; 44:14. Jer 22:7, 14-15, 23. Ezek 17:3, 22-23; 27:5; 31:3, 8. Amos 2:9. Zeph 2:14. Zech 11:1-2

CHESTNUT
Gen 30:37. Ezek 31:8

CINNAMON
Ex 30:23. Prov 7:17. Song 4:14. Rev 18:13

CITRON WOOD
Rev 18:12

CORIANDER
Ex 16:31. Num 11:7

CUCUMBER
Num 11:5. Is 1:8

CUMIN
Is 28:25, 27. Matt 23:23

CYPRESS
I Kgs 5:8, 10; 6:15, 34; 9:11. II Kgs 19:23. II Chr 2:8; 3:5. Is 14:8; 37:24; 41:19; 44:14; 55:13; 60:13. Hos 14:8. Zech 11:2

FIG
Gen 3:7. Num 13:23; 20:5. Deut 8:8. Judg 9:10-11. I Sam 25:18; 30:12. I Kgs 4:25. II Kgs 18:31; 20:7. I Chr 12:40. Neh 13:15. Ps 105:33. Prov 27:18. Song 2:13. Is 34:4; 36:16; 38:21. Jer 5:17; 8:13; 24:1-3, 5, 8; 29:17. Hos 2:12; 9:10. Joel 1:7, 12; 2:22. Amos 4:9. Mic 4:4. Nah 3:12. Hab 3:17. Hag 2:19. Zech 3:10. Matt 7:16; 21:19-21; 24:32. Mark 11:13, 20-21; 13:28. Luke 6:44; 13:6-7; 21:29. John 1:48, 50. James 3:12. Rev 6:13

FLAX
Ex 9:31. Josh 2:6. Judg 15:14. Prov 31:13. Is 19:9; 42:3. Ezek 40:3. Matt 12:20

FRANKINCENSE
Ex 30:24. Lev 2:1-2, 15-16; 5:11; 6:15; 24:7. Num 5:15. Neh 13:5, 9. Song 3:6; 4:6, 14. Jer 6:20. Matt 2:11. Rev 18:13

GALBANUM
Ex 30:34

GALL
Deut 32:32. Ps 69:21. Jer 8:14; 9:15. Lam 3:19. Amos 6:12. Matt 27:34

GARLIC
Num 11:5

GOPHER WOOD
Gen 6:14

GRAPE, GRAPEVINE
Gen 40:10-11; 49:11. Lev 19:10; 25:5, 11. Num 6:3-4; 13:20, 23. Deut 23:24; 24:21; 28:30, 39; 32:14, 32. Judg 8:2; 9:27. Neh 13:15. Job 15:33. Song 2:13, 15; 7:12. Is 5:2, 4; 17:6; 18:5; 24:13. Jer 6:9; 8:13; 25:30; 31:29-30; 49:9. Ezek 18:2. Hos 9:10. Amos 9:13. Obad v.5. Mic 7:1. Matt 7:16. Luke 6:44. James 3:12. Rev 14:18

GOURDS
II Kgs 4:39

HEMLOCK
Hos 10:4

HENNA
Song 1:13; 4:13

HYSSOP
Ex 12:22. Lev 14:4, 6, 49, 51-52. Num 19:6, 18. I Kgs 4:33. Ps 51:7. John 19:29. Heb 9:19

JUNIPER
Jer 48:6

LEEKS
Num 11:5

LENTILS
Gen 25:34. II Sam 17:28; 23:11. Ezek 4:9

LILY
I Kgs 7:19, 22, 26. II Chr 4:5. Song 2:1-2, 16; 4:5; 5:13; 6:2-3; 7:2. Hos 14:5. Matt 6:28. Luke 12:27

LOTUS
Job 40:21-22

MALLOW
Job 30:4

MANDRAKE
Gen 30:14-16. Song 7:13

MANNA
Ex 16:31, 33, 35. Num 11:6-7, 9. Deut 8:3, 16. Josh 5:12. Neh 9:20. Ps 78:24. John 6:31, 49, 58. Heb 9:4. Rev 2:17

MELON
Num 11:5

MILLET
Ezek 4:9; 27:17

MINT
Matt 23:23. Luke 11:42

MULBERRY
II Sam 5:2 24. I Chr 14:14-15. L 17:6

MUSTARD
Matt 13:31; 17:20. Mark 4:31. Luke 13:19; 17:6

MYRRH
Gen 37:25; 43:11. Ex 30:23. Est 2:12. Ps 45:8 Prov 7:17. Song 1:13; 3:6; 4:6, 14; 5:1, 5, 13. Matt 2:11. Mark 15:23. John 19:39

MYRTLE
Neh 8:15. Is 41:19; 55:13. Zech 1:8, 10-11

NETTLE
Job 30:7. Prov 24:31. Is 34:13. Hos 9:6

NUT
Gen 43:11. Song 6:11

OAK
Josh 24:26. I Kgs 13:14. Is 2:13; 6:13; 44:14. Ezek 6:13; 27:6. Hos 4:13. Amos 2:9. Zech 11:2

ONIONS
Num 11:5

ONYCHA
Ex 30:34

PALM
Ex 15:27. Lev 14:15, 26; 23:40. Num 33:9. Deut 34:3. Judg 1:16; 3:13; 4:5. I Sam 5:4. I Kgs 6:29, 32, 35; 7:36. II Kgs 9:35. II Chr 3:5; 28:15. Neh

5. Ps 92:12.
ᵃg 7:7-8. Is
4; 19:15;
16. Jer
5. Ezek
16, 22, 26,
, 34, 37;
18-20, 25-
, Dan 10:10.
el 1:12.
att 26:67.
ark 14:65.
hn 12:13;
:22. Rev 7:9

PYRUS
ᵇb 8:11. Is
:7

STACHIO
en 43:11

NE
41:19;
4:14; 60:13

OD
uke 15:16

OMEGRANATE
x 28:33-34;
9:24-26. Num
3:23; 20:5.
Deut 8:8. I
Sam 14:2. I
Kgs 7:18, 20,
42. II Kgs
25:17. II Chr
3:16; 4:13.
Song 4:3, 13;
6:7, 11; 7:12;
8:2. Jer 52:22-
23. Joel 1:12.
Hag 2:19

POPLAR
Gen 30:37.
Hos 4:13

RAISIN
Num 6:3. I
Sam 15:18;
30:12. II Sam
6:19; 16:1. I
Chr 12:40;
16:3. Song
2:5. Hos 3:1

REED
Ex 2:3, 5. I
Kgs 14:15. II
Kgs 18:21. Job
8:11; 40:21. Ps
68:30. Is 18:2;
19:6-7; 35:7;
36:6; 42:3. Jer
51:32. Ezek
29:6. Matt
11:7; 12:20;
27:29-30, 48.
Mark 15:19,
36. Luke 7:24.

Rev 11:1;
21:15-16

ROSE
Song 2:1. Is
35:1

RUE
Luke 11:42

SAFFRON
Song 4:14

SPIKENARD
Song 1:12;
4:13-14. Mark
14:3. John
12:3

STACTE
Ex 30:34

SYCAMORE
(SYCOMORE)
I Kgs 10:27. I
Chr 27:28. II
Chr 1:15;
9:27. Ps 78:47.
Is 9:10. Amos
7:14. Luke
19:4

TAMARISK
Gen 21:33. I
Sam 22:6;
31:13. I Chr
10:12

TEREBINTH
Gen 12:6;
13:18; 14:13;
18:1; 35:4, 8.
Deut 11:30.
Josh 19:33.
Judg 4:11;
6:11, 19; 9:6,
37. I Sam
10:3. II Sam
18:9-10, 14. Is
1:29-30; 6:13.
Hos 4:13

THISTLE, THORN
Gen 3:18. Ex
22:6. Num
33:55. Josh
23:13. Judg
2:3; 8:7, 16. II
Sam 23:6. II
Kgs 14:9. II
Chr 25:18. Job
5:5; 31:40. Ps
58:9; 118:12.
Prov 15:9;
22:5; 24:31;
26:9. Ecc 7:6.
Song 2:2. Is
5:6; 7:19, 23-
25; 9:18;
10:17; 27:4;
32:13; 33:12;
34:13; 55:13.
Jer 4:3; 12:13.

Ezek 2:6;
28:24. Hos
2:6; 9:6; 10:8.
Mic 7:4. Nah
1:10. Matt
7:16; 13:7, 22;
27:29. Mark
4:7, 18; 7:16;
15:17. Luke
6:44; 8:7, 14.
John 19:2, 5.
II Cor 12:7.
Heb 6:8

VINE, VINEYARD
Gen 9:20;
40:9-11; 49:11.
Ex 22:5;
23:11. Lev
19:10; 25:3-5,
11. Num 6:3-4;
13:20, 23;
16:14; 20:5,
17; 21:22;
22:24. Deut
6:11; 8:8; 20:6;
22:9; 23:24;
24:21; 28:30,
39; 32:14, 32.
Josh 24:13.
Judg 8:2; 9:12-
13, 27; 13:14;
14:5; 15:5;
21:20-21. I
Sam 8:14;
22:7. I Kgs
4:25; 21:1-2,
6-7, 15-16, 18.
II Kgs 4:39;
5:26; 18:31-32;
19:29; 25:12. I
Chr 27:27. II
Chr 26:10.
Neh 5:3-5, 11;
9:25; 13:15.
Job 15:33;
24:5, 18. Ps
78:47; 80:8,
14-15; 105:33;
107:37; 128:3.
Prov 24:30;
31:16. Ecc 2:4.
Song 1:6, 14;
2:13, 15; 6:11;
7:8, 12; 8:11-
12. Is 1:8;
3:14; 5:1-5, 7,
10; 7:23; 16:8-
10; 17:6; 18:5;
24:7, 13; 27:2;
32:12; 34:4;
36:16-17;
37:30; 61:5;
65:21. Jer
2:21; 5:17; 6:9;
8:13; 12:10;
25:30; 31:5,
29-30; 32:15;

35:7, 9; 39:10;
48:32; 49:9;
52:16. Ezek
15:2, 6; 17:6-
8; 18:2; 19:10;
28:26. Hos
2:12, 15; 9:10;
10:1; 14:7.
Joel 1:7, 11-
12; 2:22. Amos
4:9; 5:11, 17;
9:13-14. Obad
v. 5. Mic 1:6;
4:4; 7:1. Nah
2:2. Hab 3:17.
Zeph 1:13.
Hag 2:19.
Zech 3:10;
8:12. Mal
3:11. Matt
7:16; 20:1-2,
4, 7-8; 21:28,
33-35, 38-41;
26:29. Mark
12:1-2, 7-9;
14:25. Luke
6:44; 13:6-7;
20:9-10, 13-16;
22:18. John
15:1, 4-5. I
Cor 9:7. James
3:12; 15:1. Rev
14:18-19

WHEAT
Gen 30:14. Ex
9:32; 29:2;
34:22. Deut
8:8; 32:14.
Judg 6:11;
15:1. Ruth
2:23. I Sam
6:13; 12:17. II
Sam 4:6;
17:28. I Kgs
5:11. I Chr
21:20, 23. II
Chr 2:10, 15;
27:5. Ezra 6:9;
7:22. Job
31:40. Ps
81:16; 147:14.
Song 7:2. Is
28:25. Jer
12:13; 23:28;
31:12; 41:8.
Ezek 4:9;
27:17; 45:13.
Joel 1:11;
2:24. Amos
8:5-6. Matt
3:12; 13:25,
29-30. Luke
3:17; 16:7;
22:31. John
12:24. Acts
27:38. I Cor
15:37. Rev 6:6;

18:13

WILLOW
Lev 23:40. Job
40:22. Ps
137:2. Is 15:7;
44:4. Ezek
17:5

WORMWOOD
Deut 29:18.
Prov 5:4. Jer
9:15; 23:15.
Lam 3:15, 19.
Amos 5:7;
6:12. Rev 8:11

ACKNOWLEDGMENTS

The Publishers wish to express their gratitude to Professor Ya'akov Meshorer for his help in the selection of the coins included in this work and for providing us with the transparencies from his collections;

to Dr Rivka Gonen for her advice on archeological matters;

to the following for their help: Irène Lewitt; Ayala Sussmann; Peretz Kidron; Jeff Black; Lori Glasshofer; Judy Rabinowitz; Judith Meissner-Assif; Tali Bieler.

to Margalit Bassan for paging;

to Haim Eytan for preparation of the maps;

to the following who provided photographs:
Azaria Alon/JPH: Animals (bees; boar; camel; caterpillar; chameleon; crane; dog; donkey; falcon; hare; heron; hoopoe; lion; moth; porcupine; viper; sheep; carpet viper); Plants (acacia; wild tulip; olives; pomegranate, grapes; wheat; barley; palm dates); Hermon; Galilee, Sea of; Ijon. *Dalia Amotz:* Ashtoreth; Bathing (Phoenician figurine). *Werner Braun:* Bethlehem; Hebron. *Baruch Brendl:* Achmetha; Alexandria (2); Amon; Ararat; Beth Pelet; Chephirah; Cilicia; Cyrus (tomb); Daniel (tomb; with the lions); Darius (wall painting; palace); Death; Debir; Elam; En Haddah; Esther (tomb); Euphrates (two views); Eve; Furniture (stone relief); Gibbethon; Hamath; Haran; Hittites (Hattushah); Jarmuth; Lydia (Sardis); Moab (inscript.); Mordecai (tomb); Naphtali (Adami Nekeb); No Amon (Thebes; statue); Palaces (Persepolis); Philistines (Egypt. relief); Phrygia; Sardis (2); Shushan; Sochoh; Tappuah; *Moshe Caine:* Acel Dama; Ten Commandments (stone tablets); all illustrations from Sarajevo Haggadah; all illustrations of Dura-Europos wall paintings. *Sidney Corcos:* Animals (partridge; stork). *David Darom:* Animals (locusts; scorpion); Manna (tamarisk); Plants (almond; algum; aloes; apple; anise; balm; barley; briar; broad beans; broom; calamus; cedar; citron; cumin; coriander; carob; flax; garlic; hemlock; hyssop; gourds; juniper; leeks; lentils; lily; mallow; mandrake; (water)melon; millet; mint; mulberry; mustard; myrrh; nettle; walnut; oak; olive tree; onion; pistachio nuts; plane tree; papyrus; poplar; reeds; rue; saffron; sycamore; tamarisk; terebinth; thistle; thorns; weeds); Shittim. *I. Ephron:* Dalmatia (coast). *N. Garo:* Abel Keramim; Absalom; Alamoth; Amaziah (Sela); Ammonites; Anathoth; Ar Moab; Arnon (2); Balaam (inscript.); Baptism (Medeba map); Beth Azmaveth; Beth Haccherem; Bethlehem (Nativity); Betonim; Bochim; Decapolis (Gerasa; Pella); Dibon; Dizahab; Elealeh; Ephron; Fortifications (Herodian); Gadara; Geba; Gethsemane; Gihon Spring; Golgotha (hill); Hauran; Herod (Herodion); Heshbon; Mt. Hor; Jabbok; Jabesh Gilead; Jehoshaphat Valley; Jephteh; Jerusalem (Medeba map; Western Wall; Temple Mount, general views and excavations); Jezreel; John the Baptist (Machareus); Kedar; Kir Haraseth; Last Supper (Coenaculum); Lot (Pillar); Luz; Maktesh; Medeba (excavations); Michmash; Miracles (Tabgha); Mesha (inscr.); Moab (landscape; Balu'a stone); Nabateans (Petra; jewelry); Nebo; Noah (mosaic); Ophel; Parah; Pilgrimage (ship); Plain (shephelah); Pottery (Nabatean); Rabbah (Rabbat Ammon excavations; theater at Philadelphia; seal); Seir; Siddim; Sihon; Sodom; Succot (Tell Deir Alla; stone tablet); Tiberias, Tobiah (tomb; inscr.); Wine press; Zimri; Zoar; Mt. Zion. *Shai Ginott / Nature Reserves Authority:*

Animals (addax; deer; fox; frog; geckoe; wild goat; horse; onager; ostrich; owl; rock badger; turtledove; vulture); Dead Sea; En Geddi (2); Jordan (Banias); oil press (Gamla); Phoenician coast; Timnah (the Window). *Abraham Hai:* Aphek (palace); Beersheba (egg); Ebenezer; Fortifications (Khirbet Uzzah); Lachish (gold sheet; assault ramp; excavations); Weapons (ballista stones). *David Harris:* Jacket. Acts (Ascension exter.); Adonijah (En Rogel); Ajalon; Altar; Anointing (horn); Annunciation (church); Antonia; Arad (tell); Ashdod; Bashan; Benjamin; Beth Horon; Bethlehem (Nativity); Bethphage; Bethsaida; Burial (Philistine); Caesarea (statue); Cana; Carmel (cave); Chinneroth; Cross (Monastery); Dabberath; Dead Sea Scrolls (Qumran); Dothan; Edom; Elath; En Rogel, Eshtaol; Esthemoa (Menorah); Esther (Scroll); Ezion Geber; Gath; Gibeah; Gihon; Gilboa; Golden Calf; Goshen; Harod; Hezekiah inscription; Hezir; Hinnom; Isaac (Foundation Rock); Jachin and Boaz; Jeremiah (Anata); Jericho (fortifications); Jesus (Holy Sepulcher); Judas (Grotto of Betrayal); Kadesh Barnea (reconstruct. fortress); Kirjat Jearim; Lachish (tell); Lebonah; Levirate shoe; Levites (Torah crown); Magdala; Mamre; Mizpah; Nabateans (Oboda); Nazareth; Negeb (Zin); Pisgah; Plants (willow); Priest (breastplate); Red Sea; Ruth (women gleaning); Samuel (Nebi Samwil); Shiloh; Sinai (steps to Mt Sinai); Synagogue (inscription); Temples; Weapons (javelin head). *Hirmer Fotoarchiv:* Hunting (bowl from Ugarit); Mesopotamia (Code of Hammurabi); Samothrace (Nike statue); Ur (silver ring). *Rolf Kneller:* Ammah; Amos (Tekoa); Arabah; Armageddon; Besor; Bethel; Beth Hoglah; Beth Zur; Mt Carmel; Chesalon; Job (Ill. MS); Jaffa (excavations); Megiddo; Psalms (Ill.MSS); Zedekiah (Cave). *Erich Lessing:* Accad; Adam; Admatha (Mede); Agriculture (Egypt. wall painting; seal); Anna; Antioch; Ark (on wheels); Army (Persian archer; Stele of the Vultures; Roman soldier); Assyrians (carrying wood); Bel and the Dragon; Building (Egypt. wall painting); Cain; Caphtor; Cherub; Carchemish; Coins ("banker"); Cornelius; Creation (Egypt papyrus; omphalos); Cush (head of Nubian; Nubian on shoe); Dress (Roman); Eden (Egypt. painting); Flood (Ill. MS); Hazael; Hierapolis; Hunting (Egypt. wall painting); Ivory (deer); Javan; Jeshua (inscription; John the Baptist (ivory carving); Jonah (bas-relief); Joseph of Arimathea (tomb); Jubilee (model of granary); Laodicea; Lebanon (Assyr. relief); Ludim; Malta (Paul's miracle); Matthew, Gospel of (Jesus' ancestry); Metals (Egypt. wall painting); Miletus; Music (Egypt. harpist); Neapolis; Onesimus; Paul (fleeing Damascus), Philip (miracle of the paralytics); Prayer (bone sculpture); Prayer of Azariah (wall painting); Puteoli; Resurrection (relief of women and angel); Rome (catacombs); Sacrifice of Isaac (14th cent. relief); Salamis; Scythian; Ships (Roman); Seraphim; Spices (Egypt. jar; alabastron); Three Taverns; Tribes; Troas; Weapons (Egypt); Weaving; Wine (merchant); Writing (Egypt. tomb painting). *Palphot:* Acts (Gamla); Nain; Praetorium. *Zev Radovan:* Acco (view; archaeol. finds); Achzib (view; figurine); Adar (mosaic); Adoraim; Adullam; Adummim; Ai (remains; incense stand); Akrabbim; Altar; Ammonites (2 figurines); Anakim (Gaza); Animals (goat; horse; lions; monkey; ram); Antipatris; Aroer; Asherah; Ataroth; Azekah; Baalath; Baruch (seal); Beeroth; Beersheba (tell; figurine); Beth Abarah; Beth Haccerem; Beth Shean (tell; theater); Bezek; Burning Bush; Caesarea (aqueduct; theater); Calendar (mosaic); Capernaum; Carmel in Judah; Canaanite (plaque from Megiddo); Caiaphas (model of house); Cherub (ivory); Chesulot; Chislev (mosaic); Chorazin; Circumcision; Coins (mold); Corban (inscription); Dead Sea; Decapolis (Hippos); Demons (inscr. on bowl); Dothan (tell; valley); Dress (fragment of cloth); Ebal; Elah; Elijah (Sartaba); En Dor; Elizabeth (Church of Visitation); En Eglaim; Ephraim (view of Samaria); Essenes (Qumran); Etam; Fortifications (Acco); Gates (Megiddo; Tell Dan; Shechem); Gaza; Gezer; Gibeon; Gilgal; Giloh; Halhul; Hammath (figurine); Hazor (excavations); Hebron (excavations); Hiram (1); Hormah; Hunting (Beth Shean, Kissufim mosaics); Incense burners; Isaac sacrifice (mosaic); Israel (mosaic from Jericho); Jaazaniah; Jattir; Jeremiah (Anata); Jericho (Herod's palace); Jezebel (seal); Joppa (tomb inscr.); Jotbah; Judah (landscape); Juttah; Kadesh Barnea; Lamps (4); Last Supper (relief); Lord's Prayer; Maccabees (Hanukkah lamp); Mourning (Phoenician figurine); Music (3); Nabateans (Mamshit jewelry); Negeb (Solomon's Pillars); Nile; Nisan (mosaic); Oil press; Ophir (ostracon); Palaces (Herodion); Pottery (Philistine); Proselytes

ACKNOWLEDGMENTS

(inscription); Rachel (tomb inter.); Rehob; Samaritans (sarcophagi); Sharuhen; Shemaiah (Kirjat Jearim); Shiloh (weapons); Sidon; Synagogues (Gamla; Bar Am; Qasrin); Tammuz (mosaic); Tebeth (mosaic); Timnah (Tell Batash); Tyre; Uzziah (inscript.); Wine (mosaic). *Seger House-P. O'Connor:* Ziklag. *Lawrence Stager:* Tophet. *Turkey Ministry of Tourism:* Colosse (Hierapolis); Ephesus; Patmos; Pergamum. *A.A.M. van der Heyden:* Abarim; Abel (tiller); Abel Beth Maachah; Achor; Acts (St Stephen's Gate); Ahab (Megiddo stables; Alpha; Amalekites (Rephidim); Anab; Annunciation (well in church); Anointing (Slab in Holy Sepulchre); Ascension (church); Baptism (Jordan); Bathing (Masada); Ashkelon coast; Beatitudes (church); Beer Lahai Roi; Berachah; Beth Acacia; Bethany; Bethesda; Bible (Jerome's cell); Caesarea (columns in the sea); Cabul, Cana; Capernaum; Cherith (Wadi Kelt); Corinth; Crete (Knossos); Cross (Golgotha); Damascus; Demons (Mt of Temptation); Eder Tower; Egypt (Abu Simbel); Elijah (Cave); Elisha spring; Elizabeth (grotto Ein Karem); En Shemesh; Ephrath; Fasting (Quarantal); Fortifications (Tell Balata; Sebastia); Gabatha; Galatians (Ill. MS); Galilee; Gamaliel (Beth Shearim); Gath Hepher; Gibeon (Pool); Golan; Golgotha (chapel); Greece (Delphi); Hades (Armenian Ill. MS); Hazor; High places (Megiddo; Gezer); Huldah (Gate); Israel (Shishak inscript.); Iturea (Banias); James (embroidery); Jarmuth (Belvoir); Jehoshaphat Valley; Jesus (icon; star at Nativity Church; Nazareth Primacy); Jethro (tomb); John the Baptist (tomb); Jokneam (Karnak inscript.); Jordan; Joseph (tomb); Judah (landscape); Kedesh; Kidron; Lazarus (tomb); Lebanon; Luke, Gospel of (MS); Maccabees (Modi'in); Machpelah; Mareshah; Mark (St Mark's church); Mary (well in Nazareth); Megiddo; Me Jarkon; Meron; Messiah (Golden Gate); Moab (landscape); Mourning (Egypt. wall painting); Naaran; Negeb; Nephtoah; Noph (Sphinx); Olives, Mt of; Palaces (Masada); Paran; Pentateuch (Samaritan); Peter; Pontius Pilate (inscript.); Prayer (Western Wall); Ramses; Rhodes (Lindus); Rome (Forum); Samaria (Sebastia); Sanhedrin; Shalisha; Sheba; Shechem (Jacob's Well); Shiloah Pool; Shiloh; Shishak; Simon the Tanner; Sinai; Sinnim; Tabernacles, Feast of; Tabor; Tadmor; Torah Scroll (Samaritan); Transfiguration (mosaic); Zechariah (tomb).

Additional credits not indicated on the page on which they appear in the book: *British Museum:* Calah; Ur. *City of David Excavations* (Jerusalem, City of David). *Israel Department of Antiquities and Museums:* Acco (lead slingshot); Achzib (Phoenician goddesses); Ahab (ivory horn); Arad (ostracon); Ashdod (clay goddess; harp player); Asherah; Babylon (Epic of Gilgamesh); Bathing (clay figurine); Beth Shean (stele); Bread (ostracon); Burial (coffin lid); Caesarea (column); Canaan (dagger; jewelry); Cherub; Chinnereth (gold disc); Coins (mold; hoards of ingots); Corban (stone jar); Dress (cloth; sandal); Edom (ostracon); Eshtemoa (hoards of silver); Food (bowl; figurine); Furniture (clay models); Gezer (Astarte); Glass (amphora); Golden Calf; Hoshea (jar handle); Incense (2 burners); Jabneh (ostracon); Jecamiah; Jericho (clay jar; sculpture); Jerusalem (grafitto); Jezebel, Kadesh (clay figurine); Last Supper; Metals (ingots); Moon; Mourning (mourner); Moza; Obadiah; Ornaments (Canaanite jewelry; Nabatean jewelry); Pekah (detail of jar); Philistia (vase; coffin lid); Phoenicia (pottery); Pontius Pilate (stone from Caesarea); Pottery (potter's wheel); Rehob (inscription); Sargon (stele); Seals (Hebrew seals); Seat of Moses; Shephatiah; Taanach (cultic stand); Tartan; Taxes; Temple (ostracon; stone); Tishbite (clay model). *Israel Museum:* Jerusalem (pottery), Sennacherib (model Prism); Uzziah (inscription). *Ketef Hinnom Excavations:* Jerusalem (silver plaque with Priestly Blessing. *Shrine of the Book:* Ecclesiasticus; Habakkuk; Phylacteries. *Arnold Spaer Collection:* Jeroboam (coin).